THE CONTROL AND MANIPULATION OF MONEY

Basic Economics
A Financial and Economic History of the United States

2nd Edition

EDWARD D. DUVALL

Fremont Valley Books LLC

Also by Edward D. Duvall

The Federalist Companion: A Guide to Understanding *The Federalist Papers*

This book contains a direct account of the historical events of the Revolutionary era from 1760 to 1788, emphasizing the causes of the war, its conduct, and the failures of the Articles of Confederation following the peace. It also shows the structure of the arguments presented by Jay, Hamilton, and Madison in their defense of the Constitution as contained in *The Federalist Papers*, and a cross-reference between the Federalist essays and provisions of the Constitution.

Can You Afford That Student Loan?
How To Avoid Excessive Student Loan Indebtedness

This book describes the basics of the student loan programs as well as the risks and benefits of student loan. It then provides a clear method by which the student can determine the affordability of a student loan. This is done using an extensive table of occupations and their starting salaries from the Bureau of Labor Statistics. Using some common rules for debt repayment, the book contains a unique nomographic method for determining what amount of loan is affordable when the payments come due, given starting salaries and repayment terms. It concludes with several examples that illustrate the most common issues regarding the affordability of student loans.

Real World Graduation
The Entrance Exam for Adulthood

This book contains 101 questions and answers that will help young people adjust from school to the real world. Warning: the real world does not function in the neat, organized fashion as represented in the school textbooks. The real world operates entirely differently.

A Solar Energy Estimator
A Simple Solar Panel Viability Model

The Solar Energy Estimator consists of a book showing the complete derivation of a model that calculates the energy savings and return-on-investment of a solar panel installation. An Excel® spreadsheet is provided that permits the user to make the actual calculations, using only a small number of inputs. It may be used for any non-commercial purpose.

https://fremontvalleybooks.com

The Control and Manipulation of Money
Basic Economics
A Financial and Economic History of the United States

Edward D. Duvall

Fremont Valley Books, LLC
Queen Creek, AZ

First Edition: 9 Jan 2022 (ISBN 978-0-9845773-3-0)
Second Edition: 9 Jun 2023

ISBN: 978-0-9845773-7-8

For further information, contact edward.d.duvall@gmail.com

Published by Fremont Valley Books, LLC
https://fremontvalleybooks.com

Edward Duvall's blog: http://edduvall.com

To my sons,
Edward Charles II and
Ryan Christopher

For all the joy that they have brought

CONTENTS

Preface to the Second Edition

This second edition corrects the usual assortment of minor errors in the original, corrected some formatting errors, and updated a few of the references. The important updates include:

a. A comment on central bank digital currency in chapter 2

b. A discussion of the "Federal Funds Rate" in chapter 17

c. Added interest rates (prime commercial and Federal Funds Rate) in chapters 15 through 23

d. Revised the methodology for calculating estimated family income for the years 1800 to 1952 as shown in the Introduction to Part 2, this also caused changes to the "Median Income, CPI, and Standard of Living Indices" in chapters 10 through 23.

e. Added a summary of the national debt situation compared to family income in chapter 23.

EDD
9 Jun 2023

Preface to the First Edition

Most decisions in this life are economic, and most economic decisions are personal. I have therefore decided to cast off the usual formalism of 'we' and 'us' and proceed to discuss economic and monetary issues directly with you, the reader. The main goal of this book is to explain how the U. S. monetary system has operated throughout its history. But to do so, it soon became evident to me that an explanation of basic economics was in order. I have chosen to refer back to the older writers because they discussed the issues at their most elementary level, which I believe aids in understanding. Once the basic economic trends are understood, it is easier to understand the workings of the banking system.

It turns out that reams of monetary data with its associated jargon mean little without a firm understanding of the banking system. The banking system and its workings cannot be appreciated without understanding its decision-making process, and that those decisions ultimately depend on general economic conditions. The economic situation depends in turn mostly on personal decisions made by individuals in the society, which brings me back to you, the reader. I hope this book will help you sort out fact vs. fiction when the prominent people of our society discuss economics and national finances. There is a great deal of bad economics out there, leading to even worse policies, and only an educated public can force the necessary changes.

The book is divided into two parts. Part 1 (chapters 1 through 6) present a summary of important economic principles, including wealth, money, prices, rent, labor, capital, business cycles, inequality, national debt, along with a discussion on money and banking.

Part 2 (chapters 7 through 24) is a financial and economic history of the United States from 1775 to 2020. The history itself, as contained in chapters 7, 9 through 13, 15, 16, and 18 through 23, is divided into 14 periods based on the characteristics of the monetary and banking system in effect. Chapter 8 is a review of debate on money during the Constitutional Convention of 1787; the other two chapters (14 and 17) are digressions on the new banking systems introduced in 1862 and 1913. Each chapter describes the important economic events and legal changes relative to money and banking, along with a relevant set of statistics that indicate the general trends of the period. The statistics include: a) condition statements of the banks; b) coinage; c) total money supply; d) the relative value of the U. S. dollar ("purchasing power"); e) U. S. government revenues and expenditures; f) U. S. national debt, and g) prevailing interest rates. The statistics are mostly derived from U. S. government publications.

Chapter 24 concludes Part 2 with a discussion of the operation of the current economic and financial situation in the U. S. Last I give my opinion on how and why the Federal Reserve System has failed the American people, and identifies where the true problems lie.

Where appropriate, I have added comments in square brackets in order define obscure terms, or otherwise clarify the context, especially when quoting some of the older writers.

Part 1: A Summary of Economics

Introduction

The first chapter describes basic economic concepts. These include the component parts of any economic system: capital, labor, rent, the utility of money, fluctuation, credit, commerce, and debt. All of these are present in any economic system, whether it is free or not. You will find that the ideas summarized here are not new, but they are important to understand because they explain economic behavior, not simply describe it, as is often the case in modern economic theories. Radio stations do not play Benny Goodman records anymore, and in a few years none will play Buddy Holly either, but that doesn't mean the music was inferior. It simply went out of style. (Maybe you've never heard of Goodman or Holly; see what I mean?) It is in the same way that the "classical" economics writers are now casually regarded as old-fashioned. But economics is not a matter of style, it is a matter of explaining how and why prosperity or depression occurs. It turns out that the work of the older writers is still valid for the same reason that Mozart's music is still performed: it rings true over the long term.

The second chapter takes a closer look at the attributes of money per se. It turns out that money has some unique features that are not evident until its true nature is examined. A survey is given of the types of money that have been used throughout history. Last, this chapter considers in detail the methods and effects of depreciation of the monetary unit (such as the U. S. dollar). Unfortunately, 'depreciation' is commonly called 'inflation', as if inflating something implies a benefit. It is this depreciation of the monetary unit that is most destructive to the poor and middle class in the long term, and can, if uncontrolled, destroy nations.

Chapter three recounts the historical examples of the engineered depreciation of the money in England and France from the medieval era to the 1700's. Nearly all of the depreciation involved changes to the coinage in circulation, or changes to the definition of the monetary unit in terms of gold and silver. This chapter also contains a detailed history of the depreciation and consequences thereof that occurred in France during the Revolution.

Chapter four is a digression on the history of the production of gold and silver from prehistoric times to the modern era. The reason for including it is that gold and silver have been used as money throughout history, although the last two centuries have seen a transition away from gold and silver as money. Their historical importance should not be ignored even though the metals do not circulate as money today.

Chapter five brings together the previous discussions on economics and money to explain the general nature of banking systems, how they arose historically, and why they are essential to civilization. The various types of banks and their operations are described. First considered are the simplest types that accept deposits and lend them out; these institutions do not create money but only allocate it based on their judgment. Next is the description of commercial banking based on the technique of fractional reserves. Last is described the features and operation of centrals banks (such as the Bank of England and the Federal Reserve). There is nothing mysterious about the banking industry; it is a profit-seeking business (as it should be), but one that has a unique feature that separates it from how other businesses operate. The methods by which the banking industry makes adjustments are also shown.

Chapter six presents a survey of modern non-commercial banking establishments in the U. S. These financial institutions are not part of the reserve system; thus they do not create or destroy money. These institutions are the closest to what was once the primitive banking industry: the matching of savers and borrowers by those who are skilled at evaluating risk.

Units

Various monetary units are called out in some of the chapters, and some of the legislation on money refers to weights that are not in common use. Here is a guide to those units and conversion factors.

Avoirdupois ounce (oz.) = 28.3495231 grams = 437.5 grains
Avoirdupois pound (lb.) = 16 oz. = 453.5924 grams = 7000 grains
Grain = the weight of a single grain of barley, by convention is 64.79891 mg (0.0647981 g)
Gram (g) = 15.43236 grains
Kilogram (kg) = 1000 grams = 2.204623 avoirdupois pounds = 15432.36 grains
Metric ton (Mt.) = 1000 kg = 2204.623 avoirdupois pounds = 2679.2293 troy pound
Pennyweight (dwt.) = 24 grains = 1/20th ozt.
Tower pound (obsolete), a.k.a. Mercian pound = 349.9144 grams = 5400 grains
Troy ounce (ozt.) = 480 grains = 31.10347 g
Troy pound = 12 ozt. = 5760 grains

English Money

Pound (£) = 240 pennies (d.) = 20 shillings (s.) at 12 pennies each
Farthing = 1/4 of a penny
English money was initially defined as weight of silver in a penny, with the pound and shilling as accounting units.

French Money

Livre = 240 denier = 20 sou (a.k.a. solidi) at 12 denier each
Franc (new definition) = 81 livres
French money was initially defined as weight of silver in a denier, with the livre and sou as accounting units.

Spanish Money

Spanish Milled Dollar: formally defined as 394.46 grains of silver, but commonly reckoned in the 1700's as 386.7 grains of pure silver

Dutch Money

Florin (a.k.a. guilder): defined as 148.38 grains of pure silver or 9.345 grains of pure gold in the 1700's

Basic Economic Concepts

1.1 The Nature of Wealth

The wealth of a society is nothing more than the degree to which a population can maintain itself above bare subsistence. Accumulation of wealth, that is to say, the ability to obtain necessities and all the other desirable things beyond necessities is the objective of any economic system. You may object that the aborigines of the Brazilian rain forest and the native people of North America survived many centuries before the Europeans arrived, and had established societies suitable to their needs. That is true: each society maintained what their leaders advised or tradition demanded. All it proves is that from a purely economic standpoint, those "Stone Age" people were content with what we would consider a minimal standard of living. The two continents had vast resources available to them, which they chose not to utilize. It wasn't always that way. Archeologists have shown that the Mayan and Aztec peoples in South America had previously built advanced economies (at least for the upper classes), and it is possible that the North American Iroquois, Cahokia, and other native peoples people had done likewise. These native tribes were certainly capable of building wealth. They were not pathologically lazy or ignorant; they simply chose not to do so, but the archeologists have thus far not explained why. All groups of people have an economic system, whether they are conscious of it or not. Economic systems determine how far above a minimal existence the people shall live.

Personal wealth is the evaluation by each individual as to their place in the economy. Human nature dictates that the desire for comfort and leisure motivates most people most of the time. But there are many people who are perfectly happy to live in a tent and eat bacon cooked over an open fire as the sun comes up, and spend the rest of the day hunting or fishing for their next meal. Such a person regards themselves as wealthy because they have everything they desire. They have little care for material goods; they are content to live as our distant ancestors did, and it is easy to see that they are in fact wealthy by their standards. But the vast majority of people now living would regard themselves as desperately poor if they found themselves in that economic situation. It seems that various cultures have developed different notions of personal wealth. The Arab tradition states that wealth is the amount of time one can survive if the rest of society collapses. In this tradition, the possession of sheep, goats, camels, and a water supply in the desert environment is considered the pinnacle of wealth. Western societies tend to regard wealth as the degree of economic independence and insulation from other people's mistakes, to be accomplished by obtaining a good education, saving, and investing in real estate and earning securities.

A more common concept defines wealth as the amount of material goods that can be accumulated to impress others or to procure their services. (Some Americans embrace this idea.) Historically it is prevalent in Asia and Africa; it was common in the medieval feudal system, the plutocratic system, and the mercantile system. In the European medieval period it became a quest by the ruling class for more land and more peasants. Everything above what was necessary to maintain the peasants (who did the agricultural work) was devoted to employing knights to pillage and rob other manors for land and peasants, or to build castles and pay for luxuries for the nobility, or to pay tribute to the king. Personal wealth was unknown to the vast majority of the population, and national wealth, to the extent it was recognized, lay in the personal resources of the king and his vassals.

The numerous poor serve the tiny enclave of the rich in a plutocratic system. The fabulously rich and their followers acquire enough military and economic power to force everyone else into slavery or serfdom. The common people are allowed just enough to deter a revolt; wealth above that minimum went to the ruling elite. It was the foundation of the warlord system in the Middle East, India, and China; in modern times it is the end state of socialism (or as the advocates now call it, "progressivism"). Once again, personal wealth is virtually unknown, and the national wealth is vested in the ruling class.

The mercantile system was a refined concept of national wealth based on foreign trade as an improvement over the feudal system. The idea is that the wealth of a nation depends on how much money it can accumulate. Money is acquired by exporting more to foreign nations than is imported; thus more money is in the hands of the nation's people. Therefore (the logic went), people have a greater ability to buy things, which in turn promotes employment, production, and economic expansion. But a greater amount of money naturally would mean higher prices and higher wages. This system can work only if workers' wages can be suppressed and prices controlled by government power. Meanwhile, the leaders exempt themselves from all controls. Personal wealth could and did accumulate, standards of living among the working people improved, and the national wealth was regarded as the sum of the resources of both the people and the government.

Economics (once called 'political economy') is the science that reveals the sources and uses of wealth. Wealth concerns everything of value, and economics is the method by which value is measured. Value is the assessment, in the mind of the individual, as to the balance between desire for something and the amount of effort necessary to obtain it. "Amount of effort" in modern societies refers to the amount of labor. Suppose you desire a diamond ring. If labor is compensated by money, and the means of acquiring the ring is measured in money, the value of the ring is actually indicated (albeit indirectly) by the amount of labor required to obtain it. Money is only the intermediary between the amount of labor and the ring.

Economic value is not the same as utility. The diamond ring has economic value as measured by the amount of labor to acquire it. But what is the utility of the ring? It has 'value' for ornamentation, or as a sign of affection, but in truth it does not have much economic utility. It is the relative assessment of value that determines its money price, but the price does not determine utility. A quantity of 2x4's always has the same utility, but will have differing money value based on location or rarity. The 2x4's may be fairly cheap when bought at a sawmill located next to a large forest where the raw material is readily available. Those same 2x4's may be very expensive in a desert a thousand miles away. The difference lies in the cost of transportation between the forest and the desert. If the wood can frame identical houses, the necessary 2x4's will be priced higher in the desert. Thus the economic value is higher in the desert than at the sawmill, even though the utility is identical. At the other extreme is air: no one puts an economic value on air since neither labor nor money is required to obtain it, even though it is of great value and utility.

The earth has been blessed with a very large amount of natural capacity for man's use: the growth of plants, the procreation of animals, sunlight, etc. These exist whether man uses them or not, and if not used, simply remain as latent wealth. Economic wealth can be created only by three means: a) labor expended to promote agriculture and animal husbandry; b) labor expended to extract raw materials from the earth; and c) the combination of labor and materials to create tools that do the work for us, which we call "technology". Most labor expended throughout human history was devoted to agriculture. There has always been some mining for gold, silver, copper, and some rare minerals. But it was not until 300 years ago or so, with the advent of the industrial revolution, that large-scale mining was undertaken.

Man's application of labor to materials to produce technology has been in progress for a long time, including advances in agriculture and mining. It continued to progress even through the medieval 'dark ages'. A brief survey [1.1-1] is sufficient:

a) Development of the heavy plow by the Germanic tribes, probably before the invasion of Rome

b) Wheeled plow with mould-boards in Europe in the 11th century

c) Spinning wheels with flyer in Europe in the 14th century

d) Water wheels for draining copper mines was developed by the Romans about 200 AD

e) Separation of copper from sulfide ore by the Moors in Spain

f) Suction pumps for draining mines was developed about 1540

Other innovations were created as the product of materials and man's ingenuity: windmills, metalworking, hand tools, glassmaking, printing, canals, dikes, surveying, timekeeping, boatbuilding, chemistry, and many others. In all these cases labor was available because agriculture had advanced far enough for some people to have the spare time to investigate and experiment. In other words, agricultural technology had advanced to the point where a surplus permitted some people to engage in activities other than farming. Those people used their heads, not their hands, to make a living. They slowly developed other technologies that led to a general improvement in the standard of living, and thus an increase in personal wealth. So long as the rulers did not steal the additional wealth, each new inquiry or research built upon discoveries made beforehand, and the pace of innovation accelerated. It was the growth of wealth in one area that permitted the growth of wealth in another, since advances in one area cross-fertilized advances elsewhere. The pace of technology has accelerated since the industrial revolution: the steam engine, electric power, optics, sanitation systems, railroad, photography, telegraph, telephone, electric light, industrialized agriculture, oil and gas refining, internal combustion engine, aircraft, spacecraft, and the computer.

The history of the computer illustrates the principle of cross-fertilization and acceleration of technology. A computer consists of software (instructions) that directs the hardware (arithmetic processors and memory) what to do. Without hardware, there would be no need for software. The hardware necessary to perform large scale arithmetic consists of a large number of switches that must be integrated and linked together. Where did the switching hardware come from? At first this was done with vacuum tubes in the 1940's, and these were so expensive and required such high air conditioning loads that only governments and large corporations could afford them. Their capabilities were less than is found now on the pocket calculators that are given away as trinkets. But the modern computer industry truly began with the invention of the "transistor", which permitted computers to become practical.

Where did the transistor come from? A transistor is a small piece of silicon (the metallic component of beach sand) into which is embedded trace amounts of poisons like arsenic, gallium, and antimony. All of these are elements found in nature. How did they come to be combined into a transistor configuration? That happened because some engineers at Bell Laboratories in the 1940's were searching for a way to "transfer resistance" in electronic circuits, and in the course of their experimentation, discovered the switching and amplification properties of germanium and silicon "semiconductors". Why were they trying to "transfer resistance"? Because doing so would allow them to reduce the size and cooling requirements of the large above-mentioned relay and vacuum-tube computers of the 1940's. The quest for smaller heat loads led to the discovery of low-power switching capability.

The researchers discovered that the transistors used as switches could perform all the required mathematical operations if they could be arranged into various "gates" (called AND, OR, NOR, NAND, EXCLUSIVE OR, and NOT). Mathematicians discovered that all the gates could be constructed from various configurations of NAND gates. The electronics designers established that these NAND gates could all be integrated on a large scale by a common transistor design and circuit configuration. So the race was on to pack as many NAND gates into as small a package as possible, while consuming the minimum amount of electrical power. This drive toward commonality led to a great reduction in overall cost, weight, and cooling requirements. Ultimately the process of miniaturization (the reduction of components to reduce power consumption) led to the microprocessor chip. The microprocessor chip led to the widespread availability of computers and the overall reduction in their cost. They are all based on the microprocessor chip, which is based on "transistors", which are the electronic switches that are able to keep track of voltage levels in memory locations, upon which capability all software depends.

On the software side, engineers created common "instruction sets" called computer languages (such as Assembler, FORTRAN, c, c++, PL/1, COBOL, Pascal, Ada, Java, and many others) so that other people could write programs (applications) to instruct the computer to perform math operations. (FORTRAN is the only divinely-inspired language, just so you know.) Thanks to the efforts of scientists and engineers who created all the refinements and improvements in silicon processing technologies, logic, and software, you can play a large number of video games on the internet, not to mention all the productive work that can be done now that could not be done with the old computers. More work that can be done means more work will be done, which means more people will be able to earn a living and save a little. So, in this computer example, wealth was created from the work of nature (refined beach sand and some naturally-occurring poisons), the ingenuity of scientists and engineers, and the labor of all those who use and maintain the many computers now in existence.

All of these technological improvements represent the creation of wealth that permits the expansion of production and ultimately improves the standard of living (to the extent that computers, when used appropriately, actually improve things).

Wouldn't the world be a better place if all of us had everything we needed and wanted to live well? That's a trick question: needs and wants are unlimited but the capability to meet them is not. Economic theory is the science that examines exactly that issue. Given that resources are limited, but needs and wants are unlimited, the search is on for the best way to utilize the available resources. Once again, the things that are free do not have any place in economic theory because they cannot be assigned a value based on scarcity. The atmosphere is an example: no one pays to breathe on earth. The issue of relative scarcity of resources and how best to utilize them becomes more difficult as population increases. There was once a time in the U. S. when water was uneconomic because it was so readily available that it was free for the taking. But in modern times, with the growth of densely populated cities, water commands economic value because of its relative scarcity. Therefore water is metered and the customer pays so much per month for it. There once was a time in history when land was mostly vacant; it also had no value then since it was available simply by occupying it. But there are very few places left on earth where land may be obtained just for showing up (nearly all are places where few want to live). Everywhere else it commands an economic value, and can be obtained only by buying it from the current owner.

Technological improvements (generally) allow available resources to be used more efficiently. Burning coal for heating each home was common in the U. S. up until the 1930's, but it is clearly more efficient overall to burn coal in centralized power plants and to then distribute electricity to homes to power electric furnaces. Central water supplies and treatment plants are more efficient than individual wells. Sewage treatment plants are both more efficient and more sanitary than individual "outhouses". The printing press made book copying by hand obsolete, and allowed common people to have access to knowledge. The same general principle applies to transportation, agriculture, and energy distribution (such as gas stations).

Economic decisions and the growth of economies in general are partly determined by the political environment. With no political system, such as might occur among a few shipwrecked people on a remote island with plenty of land and water, allocation of resources is accomplished informally by first-use. In a free political system it is characterized by a common set of rules that the population generally agrees to, but which provides the maximum individual discretion. In that system, economic choices are made by individual thought and action, subject only to the small number of agreed-to restraints. A political system dominated by warlords and tyrants represents the opposite non-free case: here economic decisions are made by commands from the top, as was the case with feudal lords allocating land to his serfs. Socialism is the most recent innovation in economic non-freedom, in which the government spends a great deal of energy coercing the people into economic decisions that the dictator prefers. In tribal systems, which are somewhere between the two extremes, most economic decisions are by custom and tradition. Only the ruling class can achieve wealth in the tribal and non-free systems.

The common working people can achieve an increase of wealth only within a free political system that in turn recognizes the value of free enterprise by the individual. But economic freedom means both the freedom to succeed and the freedom to fail; which is to say, the increase or decrease of one's wealth by taking risks. This level of economic freedom only became common after the Protestant Reformation in the early 16th century, and then only in Europe and some parts of the Middle East. The underlying guiding philosophy is based on a combination of the Judeo-Christian heritage and a revival of the Roman-Greek legal system (having been brought into the Anglo-Saxon legal system). The tyranny of the caste system still prevails in India; the tyranny of the religious ruling class still prevails in places where Islam dominates.

Economic choices are ultimately personal choices in a free political system. They are not centrally planned or controlled, and the government does not coerce decisions one way or the other. A consequence is that there will always be differences in the standard of living among the population. They are due to different abilities, good or bad fortune, or good or bad priorities. This is not to imply that such a freedom has always existed in the U. S. The U. S. had a dual system until the 1960's. Many Americans of African descent in the Southern States experienced economic non-freedom either by direct hereditary slavery or the imposition of "Jim Crow laws", whereas all the other racial and ethnic groups generally experienced economic freedom.

"Equality of opportunity" prevails in a free political and economic system. "Economic Equality", or its new code-name "Equity", is the non-natural economic state of a population when force or coercion is used by the rulers. If the ruling class has sufficient power, it can limit economic choices to whatever pleases or benefits the ruling class. The long-term result is that nearly everyone is equally poor except for the ruling class, which (surprise, surprise, surprise) ends up possessing all the wealth. For example, the Roman Empire was a purely kleptocratic nation. In order to maintain security from other nations, it devised a 'colony' system in which everything that could be stolen was stolen. The historian Charles Marivale described it [1.1-2]:

> "But the Romans planted their colonies with a settled purpose, and that purpose was the acquisition of political strength. With that view they selected the most appropriate sites in a newly conquered territory, some city strong in its position or its defenses, or important from its geographical relations; they expelled from it the whole or a portion of its inhabitants, and replaced them with a band of Roman citizens, armed and equipped for military possession, to be encamped as it were in a fixed military station. They assigned to these colonists a sufficient portion of the conquered lands, allowed or required them to transplant with them their wives and children, their slaves and dependents, and to establish a local government after the Roman model, with all the social and religious appliances of the metropolis."

The decline of the Roman Empire began when it ran out of places to invade, people to enslave, and property to steal. Once it exacted everything it could from other nations, it turned inward and started stealing from its own citizens, which resulted in the fatal weakness that led to its final collapse. Both the Eastern and Western Empires collapsed for the same reason, although 1000 years apart (1453 vs. 476).

Other nations have exerted abnormal economic control to finance the operations necessary for the ruling class to remain in power. Lord Kinross discussed the taxation approach adopted by Suleiman I (ruled 1520-1566), recognized as the greatest ruler of the Ottoman Turkish Empire [1.1-3]: a) regulation of markets; b) price controls; c) taxes on profits and trade; and d) taxes on the means of production.

David Morgan described the example of the Mongol Empire of the early 13th century [1.1-4]: a) the conquered subjects were little more than animals to be exploited; b) they existed only to produce revenue for the Mongol rulers; and c) they were allowed to live only for the purpose of being further taxed.

Many other examples of policies enacted by ancient empires that served to retard economic growth could be cited. These were characteristic of all the landed aristocratic systems prior to the medieval European Middle Ages. There the manorial system prevailed, in which a lord controlled the activities of his tenant serfs [1.1-5]: a) the serfs were allowed to use enough land to support a family; b) all had to render services and pay dues as benefits to the lord, generally two or three days per week; and c) they were generally regarded as belonging to the lord, although were not technically slaves. This variation of feudalism was different than the previous cases: since there was no market for excess production, there was no profit motive. Each lord was content to produce what was necessary for him and his serfs. In other words, it was not based on a desire for growth, but rather a stable system founded on tradition and custom, and included mutual duties and obligations between a lord and his serfs. It was the gradual growth of population in the towns, the freedom of those living in the towns, the slow expansion of commerce, and the growth of money and credit that eventually ended the feudal system [1.1-6]. One of the main problems of the medieval era was the poor state of the roads, and the fact that nearly every merchant had to finance his own travels, usually by hiring armed guards. Eventually merchants learned how to use bills of credit to avoid carrying large amounts of money [1.1-7], and trade was carried on via the fairs held in the larger towns. The medieval towns became the center of the trade guilds which imposed their own set of restrictions on the economy, such as apprenticeships, protection from competition, fixed work hours, wage controls, price controls, prescription of allowable tooling, and inspections to verify compliance [1.1-8]. Usually they were granted local monopolies by the local officials. It was certainly an improvement over the feudal system in the sense that each member of the guild was an individual entrepreneur, but it still restrained economic growth.

Eventually the restrictions of the medieval system gave way under the principle of true economic freedom, meaning that individuals are the best judge of their own interests, and will act accordingly. In the course of each pursuing their own interests, the entire society benefited because each created their own opportunity to acquire wealth.

The characteristics of the 'social' economic systems are well known. What is commonly called 'socialism' is really nothing more than the philosophy that a population all thinking the same way and obeying the same orders will generate more prosperity than a society in which individual thought and initiative is permitted. This philosophy is actually very old, but was written down under the guise of "economic research" by Karl Marx. 'Socialism' is based on a mindset of collectivism, but, since it so contrary to human nature, must be imposed either by intimidation, propaganda, or force. Marx's writings have been modified into various forms: Fascist, Communist, Fabian, and "progressive". They are different variants of the same collectivist Marxian religious system, and all end up with less wealth and greater poverty for the general population.

The Fascist system permits private ownership, but the government actually controls the businesses and regulates the profits. The people who "own" the businesses become little more than managers working for a salary. Consider the description of fascist economic policy summarized by Sternhell [1.1-9]. He states that the main attributes of fascism are: a) a gradual replacement of private enterprise by central economic organization; b) elimination of capitalism on the grounds that it is no longer socially useful; and c) the control of productive enterprises not by outright confiscation, but by a transfer of authority in which the State essentially manages all production, even if technically is privately owned.

Communist political systems actually take outright possession of all productive businesses and hand them over to political appointees (usually the most successful parasites). Here is a quote from the patron saint of all "progressives", Mr. V. I. Lenin (real name: Vladimir Ilych Ulyanov), leader of the 1917 Bolshevik Revolution in Russia that produced the Soviet Union [1.1-10]:

> "We accomplished instantly, at one revolutionary blow, all that can, in general, be accomplished instantly; on the first day of the dictatorship of the proletariat, for instance, on November 8, 1917, the private ownership of land was abolished without compensation for the big landowners -- the big landowners were expropriated. Within the space of a few months practically all the big capitalists, owners of factories, joint-stock companies, banks, railways, and so forth, were also expropriated without compensation. The state organization of large-scale production in industry and the transition from "workers control" to "workers management" of factories and railways -- this has, by and large, already been accomplished; but in relation to agriculture it has only just begun ("state farms", i.e., large farms organized by the workers state on state-owned land)."

The word "proletariat" refers to the working people in Russia, whom he turned into slaves. But that was not enough for Vladimir, the Marxist Messiah. He then goes on to reveal how he planned to take over all the small peasant-owned farms and turn them into the inefficient "collectives". Lenin and Stalin succeeded, and the well-known result of their economic policy was the near-total destruction of the economy (except for military hardware) in which people were forced to wait in line for hours for necessities in the large cities, or suffered actual starvation in the rural areas. Over five million people were deliberately starved to death in the Ukraine in the 1920's, just to demonstrate who was in charge. It eventually became necessary to murder over 25 million Russians. People living under Fascist or Communist systems are little more than serfs to the state with very little economic prospects unless they agree to become part of the mass-murdering ruling class.

In modern times, socialist governments use the term 'nationalization' to give the illusion that the government is allocating resources for the benefit of the people. But 'nationalization' is simply a code word for large-scale theft of privately-owned enterprises by the government, to be handed over to cronies, hacks, and regime loyalists. Those industries are then destroyed by incompetence, and the only thing left is to blame the public for the government's failures.

The Fabian method (adopted in England in the 1920's) tried to split the difference: some industries were to be owned and controlled by the government, and other industries were permitted to operate independently. All that happened was a decline in the quality and production quantity of the government-operated enterprises, and the growth and prosperity of the independent ones, thus proving the failure of the collective government-run approach.

"Socialism" used to be an economic philosophy but has now become a contagious religion based solely on emotion. America is now going through a Marx-inspired revolution under the name of the "progressive" religion; its goals are to destroy the small businessman and herd all Americans into a rigid centrally-controlled economy under the guise of "environmental salvation" or "compensation for racism". The intimidation tactic is simple: anyone who believes in freedom is called a racist, which shuts down all opposing debate on the subject.

The colonial system as practiced by the European powers in the 16th through 19th centuries was mostly mercantile; the colony existed to benefit the mother country. Normally this amounted to extraction of natural resources for the profit of companies chartered in the mother country (such as Spain's treatment of Peru). But the people in most of the colonies were allowed some latitude in their economic choices. As their experience and population grew, many of the colonies were able to obtain political independence.

Last, religious cults are very much like closed communist or socialist societies, and the inmates thereof usually have very little independent economic choices. They are therefore generally stagnant and can maintain themselves only by winning new converts or convincing existing and new inmates to donate their wealth to the cult in return for a promise of some advantage in the afterlife.

The history of the past century is sufficient to prove that a free economic system can quickly degenerate into a non-free one. Usually the tactic is to adopt economic policies that transfer power to the government or corporations that either are owned by or intimidated by the government. Socialism ruined Russia, North Korea, Vietnam, Spain, France, Germany, Poland, Hungary, Romania, Albania, Italy, and a few other nations in Europe; more recently it has ruined Zimbabwe and South Africa, not to mention many nations in South America and the Caribbean, most notably Cuba and Venezuela. China has always been under the warlord system, and since 1948 has been ruled by its Communist party. The Chinese Communist Party is simply the most successful of the warlords. It permits just enough prosperity to avoid mass starvation or a revolt, much like the Mongols mentioned above.

The historical evidence is clear that economic freedom by individuals is the most successful system for increasing wealth and improving the living standard for everyone in a nation. But the socialist movement is not interested in what benefits everyone. Socialists seek to maximize the power of the ruling elite (i.e., the socialists) so they can create a utopian paradise on earth of their own design. Their propaganda is devoted to claiming that socialism is the superior way to maximize equality, wealth, and happiness. The problem is always the same: its guiding principles and methods are so contrary to human nature, not to mention common sense and basic morality, that socialism must be imposed by force. Everyone with a teaspoon of common sense knows that those methods cannot achieve the advertised results, regardless of what techniques are used to implement and sustain it. That is why socialism, if imposed on America, will fail the same as it has failed everywhere else.

Free enterprise cannot solve all the problems of poverty and inequality, but it is the best system available. Socialism on the other hand guarantees that both are maximized. In the long run, a nation that starts off mildly socialist will eventually drift toward complete government domination simply because socialism as an economic system is fundamentally flawed. When the industries first taken over by the socialists begin to fail, socialists will claim it is due to sabotage, obstruction, or some other nefarious activities by unseen enemies. In the Soviet Union, anyone who did not fully support becoming a slave was called a 'wrecker'. Socialists are always self-righteous, and never take responsibility for the failure of socialism itself. Refusing to admit defeat, an ideological civil war erupts among the socialist faction, arguing over which sector of the economy to take next. It is always a quest for more power to control economic choices. When they continue to fail, there is no choice but to adopt the confiscatory policies of communism, which imitates the ancient kleptocratic empires. It can end only with total collapse or revolution and all the chaos and poverty that go with it.

1.2 Wealth vs. Money

Money is to wealth as a diamond ring is to love. The former does not equal the latter; at best it is a representation or sign of it. The analogy ends there, since a shiny rock can never actually be converted into love. But money can be converted into wealth by using it to procure the things that do constitute wealth.

Economics as the science of wealth is intimately connected with the science of money. It is true that (Ecclesiastes 5:10):

> "Whoever loves money never has money enough; whoever loves wealth is never satisfied with his income..."

and that (1 Tim 6:10):

> "For the love of money is the root of all kinds of evil..."

Notice that neither passage claims that money itself is evil. Money was in fact a great advance of civilization, because it enabled people to conduct trades more easily. The system in place prior to the advent of money is called barter. In that system, commodities traded directly for commodities. If you had three dozen eggs that your family farm did not require, but you desired a few pounds of pork, it was necessary in that instance to find someone who had the pork and was willing to trade it for the eggs. A trade of that nature may be fairly simple among a small agricultural community, since your farm may specialize in chickens and thus have a surplus of eggs, and your neighbor may specialize in hogs with a surplus of pork. So the trade of your three dozen eggs would be made for as much pork as both you and your neighbor thought reasonable.

But what happens if your farm has all the food products it needs, but with a surplus of eggs? Suppose you needed shoes more than anything. Now it gets complicated. You could go out and find a shoemaker who has the size shoes you want and needs eggs. Even so, he is not likely to part with a pair of shoes that took him many hours to manufacture for three dozen eggs; more eggs would be required, perhaps thirty dozen. You may have the thirty dozen to give him, but why would a shoemaker want thirty dozen eggs? He is not in the egg business, and if he accepted the thirty dozen, he then has the task of finding others who do want eggs in return for whatever it is that he wants. It is easy to see that unless a great number of coincidences occur, the likelihood of you being able to unload thirty dozen eggs for a pair of shoes is slim indeed. The most likely outcome is that you could provide the shoemaker with eggs over a period of time, three dozen at each occasion, in return for the shoes. At best, it would be a primitive form of "layaway", and you would have to do without the shoes until the full thirty dozen eggs were delivered over time. It is equally likely that no such trade would ever occur because of the amount of labor that has to be expended just to arrange the trade in addition to the work you did raising the chickens and harvesting the eggs, and the shoemaker's labor to make the shoes. Most likely you would end up trying to make your own shoes, and the shoemaker might have to find a way to procure a few chickens. The key insight here is that both your labor and the shoemaker's labor is valuable for producing the respective commodities, eggs and shoes, and yet in a barter system both have to expend additional labor to obtain other items. That is a built-in inefficiency of a barter system that tends to keep a society economically stagnant since surpluses cannot be easily disposed of. That systemic inefficiency is cured by the use of money.

Money replaced barter once people recognized that not only are exchanges more efficient, but more exchanges are possible. The use of money changed the commodity-for-commodity barter system into one that involved the indirect use of a third intermediate commodity. The necessary attribute of this third commodity, which we call money, is that it be widely accepted by everyone who is interested in making economic exchanges. Barter was an exchange of commodity 1 for commodity 2; a money system is an exchange of commodity 1 for money, and exchange of money for commodity 2. In other words, a single trade became two sales, both sales involving the use of money as a commonly-accepted commodity [1.2-1]. It is evident that money is nothing more than the most marketable of commodities: everyone who possesses it can obtain what they really want in exchange for it, and those who have goods for sale will accept it because they in turn can exchange the money for other items they want. Money is therefore both a commodity and a common metric for making exchanges between real goods. Referring back to the previous example of the eggs and shoes, money allows you, the egg producer, to sell eggs to a grocer for money, and then use the money to buy the shoes. What about the grocer? He was not part of the former example. His job is to buy eggs and many other things in large quantities that no one wants to handle, and sell them in smaller quantities that people do want. But he expends labor in doing so, and his labor must be accounted for in the exchanges. Whereas before thirty dozen eggs would exchange for the pair of shoes, the pair of shoes might command from you indirectly thirty-five dozen eggs. The revenue from thirty dozen goes to the shoemaker, and the other five goes to the grocer for his labor. Does money then not increase the amount of labor you have to expend for the shoes? No: remember that the existence of the money, and the willingness of the grocer to take the risk of preserving and reselling your eggs, is simply a replacement cost for the labor you would have otherwise expended trying to find a buyer for the thirty dozen eggs in a barter system. The value of your labor expended doing barter coordination and negotiation is always greater than the grocer's take; you come out ahead once the value of your time is accounted for. Money thus is not only a more efficient exchange system but it is also a labor-saving device. Also, don't forget that the money system allows you to dispose of the eggs and get the shoes on the same day. Thus it shortens the time necessary to satisfy wants.

Money is just another commodity, and the amount of it required to complete an exchange is called the money-price, or more commonly, simply the price. Value, as observed earlier, is the relation of two commodities to each other. In the barter example, there is some amount of eggs that will trade for an amount of pork and a different quantity of eggs for a pair of shoes. There is in all three cases of production an amount of labor expended in obtaining the eggs, pork, and making the shoes. The price of each in terms of money depends on the value of the money with respect to the eggs, pork, and shoes, which in turn depends on the relative scarcity of all four (three real commodities plus the common one, money). The relative value of any two commodities (not counting money) becomes evident by the intermediate prices. A dozen eggs retailed on 10 Nov 2020 for $2.80, and pound of pork retailed for $3.80. Therefore, if we translated this back to a barter system, ignoring the effect of the intermediate grocer, your three dozen eggs would equate to about 2.2 pounds of pork. But it is not clear how the prices I just quoted came about. In other words, how is money valued? It will be shown later that the "value" of money depends on one of two things: a) either by the production cost of the money itself; or b) the scarcity of the money unit. But first a little more insight into the nature of money is required before an inquiry into the value of money can be undertaken.

Money is a commodity, but is different than other commodities like eggs, pork, and shoes [1.2-2]. Money per se does not satisfy a tangible want or a need. A great deal of money lying around may be a psychological comfort to a miser, but no actual physical needs are satisfied by that money. Money's primary use is to trade it for things that do satisfy wants and needs. It is fundamentally different from other commodities because it is not consumed. Real needs are ultimately consumed or wear out like the eggs, pork, and shoes. Money is simply the most marketable of commodities so long as it is readily accepted by those who trade real goods.

If the value of a money unit is stable and prices are stable, an increase in your money income will lead to an increase in your standard of living, since more can be purchased with the additional money. What applies to an individual does not in this case apply to the economy in general. A greater quantity of money in the overall economy does not necessarily improve the overall standard of living. There is a common fallacy that a greater amount of money by itself leads to prosperity. Since money is a commodity, it is subject to supply and demand, and therefore a larger supply of it means each unit has less value. If the value of each money unit is diminished, which is to say, its purchasing power is reduced from what it was at some previous time, the worker is not better off. This is a very common illusion about money. It is the belief that a person's standard of living is increasing if his money income is increasing even as the value of the money is declining. His income may increase by 20%, but he fails to notice that the prices of things he buys have increased 25%. This phenomenon is actually due to depreciation of the value of the money, usually called by the confusing term "inflation". The word inflation implies that something is increasing, but here it refers to the value of money decreasing. The "inflation" is actually the amount of money that exists, not the value of each unit of it. Increasing the amount of money is a favorite trick of governments and banks, done to give the illusion of prosperity. But in fact, any amount of money will work so long as the unit can be subdivided into small enough portions that are sufficient for purchases.

Money as a commodity is subject to supply and demand the same as any other. When a person's demand for money increases, he will hold onto it as a cash balance; when his demand for money decreases, he will spend it. Once again, when considering a purchase of some items (or as the economists say, "goods"), each individual must weigh in his own mind rather he wishes to part with the money and obtain the goods, or if he prefers to keep the money in hand. It depends on his evaluation of the relative merits of having money or the goods. If he is confident that he will have a sufficient supply of money coming in (because he has stable employment), his immediate demand for money decreases, and he may decide possessing the good is preferable to holding onto the money. If he has very little money or few prospects of obtaining more of it, it is precious to him and is less likely to part with it. These are subjective evaluations, and clearly every person considers each situation based on their economic condition and priorities. An alcoholic values booze more than money, and he will readily part with any money he has, no matter how little, in order to get that next drink. His demand for money is low compared to his demand for alcohol. On the other hand, a person who refuses to do yard work and is content to pay someone else to do it has a far higher demand for money as against lawnmowers and rakes, and therefore he doesn't buy them. At the same time, he has a higher demand for lawn care workers than for money, and so he spends his money hiring the lawn workers.

It is easy to see that as a society advances, it produces more goods above subsistence; it develops greater levels of technology; its population increases; and thus the number of transactions to be made with money increases. What sufficed for money among a primitive population (certain rocks or beads) will not serve the same function when the necessity of an increased number of transactions presents itself. That need was met through the use of more valuable items as money: items that were fairly rare, commonly recognized as desirable, and met certain other requirements.

Money should not be confused with wealth; money at best represents one means to obtain wealth, as is evident by the fact that money in and of itself does not satisfy wants or needs, nor does it produce anything directly. It has instead several other advantages. First, it permits expansion of an economy because it facilitates specialization and division of labor, which in turn increases overall productivity [1.2-3]. Specialization and division of labor simply means that nearly everyone in a money economy is both a producer and consumer. Each person produces more than he can consume, and the rest is sold to others. Likewise, no one consumes everything that any other person produces; each buys from several different producers to obtain what they want. A baker who produces 500 loaves of bread and 50 dozen cupcakes is not in a position to consume them all. They are sold, and the money is used to buy what the baker wants after he pays his costs of production. The baker specializes in bread and cupcakes; in doing so, he can produce them much more efficiently than an individual making their own. If you decided to bake your own bread it would be a simple matter to acquire all the ingredients and bake it at home. But you are likely to find that some of your ingredients go to waste because you can't buy in the exact quantities required. The total cost of the ingredients that you use will exceed the cost of the bread purchased from the baker; the reason is that the baker buys in large quantities and thus gets each unit cheaper (since there is less packaging involved). The baker has the equipment to turn out many loaves of bread that are all identical; you baking at home will notice some variation on each occasion. You may get a better product baking it yourself because you add more eggs or more sugar or a different kind of oil, but your bread will cost more. The family will enjoy it, but the family would not like the price if they had to buy it every day.

A second advantage is that the use of money allows small quantities to be bought and sold. Very few people can use 20 lb. of sugar at a time, and because money can be subdivided into small amounts, commodities like sugar can be divided into amounts as small as a few ounces. This ability to subdivide large bulk quantities into smaller portions tends to minimize waste; it also minimizes the need to store or hold larger quantities that either are not needed or not needed for some period of time. If you only need 2 cups of sugar for a recipe, and you only make that recipe once per week, a 20 lb. bag lies in your pantry for a long time, or in what amounts to the same thing, means the money you spent for it lies idle for a long time. It is also likely that some of it will go to waste.

The third advantage of money is that it permits accurate calculation of gains and losses. Once all items are tabulated in terms of the common commodity (money), it is possible to add up the costs of production (being labor, rent, equipment, and utilities) to determine if the sales of the product covers the costs. "Price" is the tabulation of all commodities in terms of the one common commodity, money. Prices and costs are two sides of the same coin. The selling price of wheat to the farmer is a cost to the miller; the selling price of flour to the miller is a cost to the baker and so on. Accurate calculation of gains and losses makes it possible to determine if an undertaking is productive or not. If not, the resources are being wasted in comparison to some other use. In a society with economic freedom, the general trend is to maximize the utility of available resources because cost accounting is the metric by which efficiency is measured. But as will be shown later, the most accurate accounting, and thus the most accurate evaluation of efficiency, depends on the use of money with a stable value per unit. It is not so in a non-free society where economic decisions are made from the top down. In that case it is not important if resources are utilized efficiently; the priorities of the ruling class are important. Whatever suits the ruling class is acceptable no matter how wasteful.

The fourth advantage of money is that more areas of production can be pursued than would otherwise be undertaken [1.2-4]. The reason is that the common acceptability of money and accurate assessment of gains and losses tempts people to take a risk on some new product. Since the component parts of the new product can be bought with money, and the buying public pays with money, the entrepreneur may have a reasonable expectation that at least some members of the buying public will try it out. The entrepreneur is able, through the use of money, to attract a large number of people interested in selling the necessary components to him, even in small quantities. The money revenue derived from the sale of the final product, whether it is an electronic device or a new type of chocolate, allows the entrepreneur to pay himself and his suppliers, and to fund additional expansion if the demand is present. This can happen only if the money in use is widely accepted among both buyers and sellers.

There is a list of attributes money should have if it is to confer the advantages just named. First, it must function as a "measure of value". That is nothing more than a means for a person to estimate the value of some item relative to the amount of money in hand, or to their income. It establishes the relative value of the two commodities, money and the thing desired. If a car costs $15,000 and your annual take-home income is $45,000, the car represents 4 months work. Either it is worth it to you or not: the use of money makes such a calculation possible. Second, money must function as an efficient medium of exchange, meaning it must be widely recognized and accepted by the people in a society as already explained. Third, it must function as a suitable standard for lending. In economics this is called a standard for deferred obligations. That means the lender must have reasonable confidence that the value of the money he receives when the loan is repaid is the same as when he lent it out. Fourth, it is preferable, although not essential, that the money unit function as a store of value. Money consisting of gold and silver coins are said to be a store of value because those metals have always had uses other than money. Paper money may function as an indirect store of value under certain specific conditions. Maintaining a stable value is the core problem of paper money, as will be shown more directly in chapter 2.

1.3 Money and Prices

A money system regulates economic decisions based on price. If we were to compare two commodities, as in the eggs vs. pork example, price is how those two relate to each other. The relative values are simply expressed in the common denominator, which is money. Prices and costs are the same thing, just viewed from different perspective. To the seller, price is revenue; to a buyer, price is cost. Wages therefore are the price of labor and its revenue for the worker; to the employer, wages are a cost. But they are still the same thing in economic terms: the value expressed in a common exchange medium. There are some who falsely claim that the selling price of a good is the result of its production cost. That notion is easily disproven by the fact that a large number of buggy whips can't be sold in 21st century America. No matter how well they are made, or how finely engraved, or how well its spurs a horse to its work, the market for buggy whips is very small and therefore hardly any will be sold regardless of how high the production costs are or how low the selling price. That is a clear case of technology driving price: no one wants buggy whips because they are obsolete, and their selling price (if any are sold at all) is unrelated to production costs. However, a more important factor in selling cost vs. production cost is the opinion of buyers, good or bad. When I was young, I worked with my father in the wholesale grocery business. I believe it was in 1976 that a certain bakery produced what they called "Monster Cookies" for the Halloween season. They were magnificently packaged: in rigid boxes, with colorful cartoon monsters on the box, clever names for the monster shapes, each monster had a different color and flavor, and the price was actually a little lower than other commercial cookies of the era. (They were flavored shortbread, nothing fancy.) Everyone agreed that the packaging was the best we had ever seen. But -- the stores couldn't sell them even when displayed in the highest traffic locations. The stores practically couldn't give them away. I don't know why they didn't sell; maybe the packaging was too slick, maybe the public would rather have stale candy than fresh cookies at Halloween. Maybe the problem was that the box was solid and did not have a cellophane window that would permit the cookies themselves to be seen. People do like to see what they are buying, especially with baked goods. Maybe money was tighter than usual; maybe a hundred other things. In any case, "Monster Cookies" was a giant failure, at least that year. The public simply didn't want them. The selling price ended up being zero, as they were all eventually donated to a local orphanage. Clearly the final "selling price" was less than the cost of production. And so it is with any product: the final selling price is not necessarily related to production cost, although the initial asking price nearly always is.

It is fairly easy for an individual to assess prices. The best assessment of price for an individual economic decision is the amount of hours you have to work to afford an item. That is a simple direct connection between effort on your part and the satisfaction that comes from owning that item. Suppose you earn $10.00 per hour and a can of soda costs $2.00. Your net wage is actually about $9.25 because you have to pay 7.4% Social Security and Medicare payroll taxes. So the cost of the can of soda in terms of labor is 0.216 hours, or about 13 minutes. It is easy to evaluate whether the soda is worth it or not. But a businessman has a more complicated task: he must be able to calculate the prices of all his inputs. First he has to calculate labor, materials, equipment, transportation, rent, and utilities. Secondly, he has other expenses to account for, such as taxes, legal fees, and government licenses. Once he knows his total costs, he has to compare that sum to the revenue he expects to generate from the sale of his product. A business person has to estimate, based on costs, how much product to supply, and balance that against revenue, which depends on his estimate of the demand for his product. The goal is to earn a profit, which is the compensation to the business operator. There are some mental midgets who claim that profit is evil or is oppressive to the poor. An opinion that stupid is simply a failure to realize that the prospect of profit is what makes it worth the businessman's time and effort to go into business in the first place. Profit, being defined as the difference between revenues and costs, is the underlying motive for economic activity in a free society. Without a profit motive, less is done because there is no incentive to bother. Even a "non-profit" organization has to earn enough above costs (or obtain sufficient donations) to pay their expenses; otherwise it could not afford to exist at all.

It turned out that there was no "demand" for "Monster Cookies" that year in that location, which is why they had to be given away. Demand in economic terms has two components: a) a desire for the product; and b) the ability to pay. I'd like to have a Rolls Royce in my driveway, but I can't afford one. So while I may have the desire, I don't have the ability to pay for it, thus my demand in economic terms is zero. On the other hand I can easily afford one of those fancy new mobile phones, but I don't want one. I have the money, but I refuse to be chained with an electronic tether, even if I got it for free. Again, my demand for the high-class phone in economic terms is zero.

I may well be an anti-technology old coot, so my attitude about certain electronic devices is not necessarily in tune with the rest of the population. The general demand for a product is nothing more than the aggregate of the population's opinion. Suppose a certain group of people is aware of a certain product (such as the new mobile phone), and they recognize the value in possessing such a product. The value as determined by each individual depends on his tastes and attitudes and their willingness to part with their money. Mankind lived a very long time without mobile phones, but they now are commonly considered essential. At a very high price, very few fancy phones will be sold because most people value other things more highly, or the phone is affordable only to the wealthy. At first, most people don't want them in economic terms (since they can't pay), and the demand is thus very low, and few are sold. But as the asking price is lowered, more people will be willing to buy them because it becomes more affordable relative to their income. This assumes they still want it. Each person regulates his demand for money in his pocket vs. the desire for the phone and what he is willing to pay for it. "Demand" at the individual level is actually the tension between price of an item and how much money resources a person is willing to spend on it, which varies from person to person. Or, in what amounts to the same thing, how much work they have to do to get the money. Each individual makes their evaluation based on what they regard as essential, convenient, or stylish, and those categories of evaluation also vary from person to person. The demand is therefore an indirect measure of how much a person values their labor and their priorities. I technically could afford the Rolls Royce, but only if I am willing to give up a lot of other things over a long period of time. I would also have to find someone dumb enough give me a car loan for 25 years. The amount of money I can get for my labor, balanced with the other bills I have to pay, dictates that the Rolls is not a practical expense for me. At the commercial trade level, demand is the average tension between the general population's desire and their average ability and willingness to pay. Demand is ultimately proven by the quantity that actually is sold. The number actually sold is a consequence of how much the individual buyers indirectly value their labor against the selling price of the item. As the price comes down, more and more people value the item favorably as against a certain amount of their labor, and more are sold. There will come a point when the demand is saturated, meaning only a certain amount can be sold, and it doesn't matter how much lower the price goes. For example, the number of non-business mobile phones that can be sold is probably limited to the number of people in the population above age 8. The number that can be sold in a given year is less than that owing to the number currently in existence, especially since very few people would want more than one of them.

There is no guarantee that demand will remain constant once a certain level is established. Demand changes because people's priorities and tastes change, new items supersede the older ones, or more necessary items become more expensive for some reason. It is possible that someday, people then living will look back at our mobile phones and laugh them off as a passing fad or an antique curiosity, much as we view the dance marathons and silent movies of a century ago. (Maybe they'll have learned the value of privacy.)

Even when demand for a product exists, it is obvious that none can actually be sold unless they are somehow supplied. The mirror image of demand is the available supply. Suppose a group of investors or entrepreneurs contemplates supplying a certain item. If they estimate that the selling price that would be attractive to buyers is lower than their unit costs, none will be produced. No one in their right mind goes into business with the intention of losing money. But if the prospective selling price is at a point where profits are possible, more people will become interested in participating in the supply chain. There must be some incentive to take the risk, which is the prospect of profit. Since profit is the difference between revenues and costs, there is naturally a point at which the amount to be supplied at some particular selling point represents a suitable profit. Thus there is a tension between price to be obtained (or believed to be obtained) and quantity to be supplied. It is based on the evaluation by the supplier of how much capital he is willing to invest on producing that item. Production occurs by the use of capital, and capital is acquired using money. Therefore the viability of entering into production is indirectly an evaluation of how much money is to be risked. Each producer regulates his demand for money in his pocket (or capital) vs. the prospect of profit in producing the item, and what he is willing to risk for it. Once again, the prospective producer conducts an indirect measure of how much of his labor and capital is worth expending. So long as the profit seems likely, production will begin and continue. But production does not progress along a linear path. As production expands, each additional injection of capital leads to a smaller profit margin due to the principle of diminishing returns. This occurs because the producers' fixed costs (usually of equipment, maintenance, and utilities) have increased. Although such an expansion allows a large quantity to be made, recall that the demand (generally) expands only if selling price prices are falling. The producer now is faced with slightly higher costs per unit with a slightly lower profit per unit sold. There is usually some optimum point at which the selling price and quantity produced leads to the highest overall profit to the producer, at least on paper. Does that mean that every producer limits his production in order to get the most profit, thus depriving some part of the population of the benefit of his wares? If there is only one supplier, yes, and that supplier is in a monopoly situation. He has the ability (if he has sufficient data) to manipulate his output in order to maximize his overall profit. But in a free economic system that includes competition among suppliers, none of them has any such advantage. Each will produce as much as is practical according to their costs (which is different for each of them), and the total amount supplied either leads to profits or not. The buying public ultimately decides. There could come a point when the profit is so low, either from competition, increase of costs, taxation, or regulation, that none are produced no matter how high the prospective selling price.

It turns out that the amount actually supplied depends partly on the type of demand. If the demand is highly correlated with price (meaning that more is demanded as price declines), then the demand is said to be elastic. The supplier may find that he actually generates a greater overall profit by selling at a low price, which is to say, less profit per unit, because his costs of production per unit are low enough that he earns more by selling a greater amount. This situation prevails so long as there is suitable profit at the lower price. Typically an elastic demand applies to items that are not considered necessities and is almost always the case with luxuries. For example, many people need a car to get to work, but custom floor mats and tinted windows are not essential. Those items are a matter of opinion; the demand for them is likely to vary significantly with the asking price. A person can certainly do without them, but if a person's demand for money is low enough (he has extra money to spend), they may decide to buy the floor mats and get the windows tinted not because they are necessary but because they are a nice additional feature to have. At the other end of the scale is an inelastic demand. In this case, demand is invariant or nearly invariant with price. The general public tends to buy the same amount more or less regardless of how high the price goes. If necessary, most people will cut back on something else in order to maintain the ability to purchase this type of item. This characteristic applies to necessities: bread, milk, meat, shoes, electricity, soap, hygienic items, and so on. Inelastic demand also applies to items that are minor incidental expenses, such as the price of chewing gum. Such small amounts are consumed and represent such a small fraction of weekly expenses that most people do not care too much about the price, even if it doubles. Thus the economic demand is about constant over the long run.

That was a lot of economic jargon, don't you think? Here is a concrete example which I hope will clarify the concepts. Suppose you noticed when you were a kid that all the aunts and uncles liked your grandmother's fruit-flavored tarts. Even crabby old Uncle Lenny became quite the comedian after three or four. Later on you found out why: Grandma used heavy whipping cream with pure raw brown sugar, except she marinated the sugar and cream in flavored brandy overnight. No wonder the relatives even liked the apricot ones. Suppose now it occurs to you that Grandma's recipes may be a good starting point for a bakery business, and you intend to offer ten delicious brandy flavors: peach, apple, apricot, chocolate, honey, grape, plum, pear, blackberry, and Uncle Lenny's favorite, vanilla. Suppose you decide to call your venture "Granny's Sublime Tarts". Like any smart entrepreneur, you do your homework first and try to estimate your costs. So, after talking to landlords and looking at retail spaces, and investigating the prices of ingredients, you came up with the following parameters. First, a landlord with a suitable space is willing to be flexible on how much space he rents. You estimate that the initial space at $2000/month will permit workers to make 300 tarts per day; an additional space, at $2500/month, will allow up to 700 per day to be made; and a space expansion permitting up to 1100 per day will cost $3000 per month. You estimate that each helper can make about 300 per day, and command a wage of $12 per hour. You are reasonably certain that the ingredients will run about $0.85 per unit, owing partly to the specialized sugar. Utilities (gas and electric, water and sewer) are invariant with the amount of space rented and come in at $350 per month. Then there are miscellaneous costs: a little advertising, minor maintenance, insurance, and accounting services. Also included here are the Social Security and Medicare taxes for the workers at about 8% of their wages. The total start-up costs come to around $55,000, and you have $15,000 that you can contribute from your savings. You must take out a loan for $40,000 to pay for the equipment you require (mixing, refrigeration, display cases, and upgrading the space for retail bakery); the loan is $40,000 at 6% for 2 years. If all these are broken down to a per-unit cost, and evaluated by the number of tart units that could be produced daily, the result is a table as shown on Figure 1.3-1. Notice I have not included other costs, such as health care.

1	2	3	4	5	6	7	8	9	10	11	12	13	14
Quantity Per Day	Rent Per Day	Rent Per Unit	Labor Per Day	Labor Per Unit	Ingredients Per Unit	Utilities Per Month	Utilities Per Unit	Misc. Per Month	Misc. Per Unit	Loan Per Unit	Production Cost Per Unit	Owner's Share Per Unit	Desired Sale Price
100	66.66	0.67	96.00	0.96	0.85	350	0.12	430.40	0.14	0.59	3.33	1.60	4.93
200	66.66	0.33	96.00	0.48	0.85	350	0.06	430.40	0.07	0.30	2.09	0.80	2.89
300	66.66	0.22	96.00	0.32	0.85	350	0.04	430.40	0.05	0.20	1.68	0.53	2.21
400	83.33	0.21	208.00	0.52	0.85	350	0.03	699.20	0.06	0.15	1.81	0.40	2.21
500	83.33	0.17	208.00	0.42	0.85	350	0.02	699.20	0.05	0.12	1.62	0.32	1.94
600	83.33	0.14	208.00	0.35	0.85	350	0.02	699.20	0.04	0.10	1.49	0.27	1.76
700	83.33	0.12	336.00	0.48	0.85	350	0.02	1006.40	0.05	0.08	1.60	0.23	1.83
800	100.00	0.13	336.00	0.42	0.85	350	0.01	1006.40	0.04	0.07	1.53	0.20	1.73
900	100.00	0.11	336.00	0.37	0.85	350	0.01	1006.40	0.04	0.07	1.45	0.18	1.63
1000	100.00	0.10	480.00	0.48	0.85	350	0.01	1352.00	0.05	0.06	1.55	0.16	1.71

Figure 1.3-1: Component Costs for Granny's Sublime Tarts, and Associated Unit Costs ($)

Column 1 shows the prospective number made per day. Column 2 shows the rent per day, assuming 30 day months; for making up to 300 per day, have $2000/month = $66.66 per day, and for 100 units actually produced, the cost of rent per tart is $0.67. The rent per month increases slightly as the number of tarts produced increases, but the rent cost per unit declines since more are being produced. In other words, each additional unit of space permits a greater amount of production. The marginal unit cost of rent is decreasing because the additional number that can be produced more than offsets the increase in the rent that allows it. By the time 1000 per day are produced, the unit cost allocated to rent is down to a dime, even though the rent for space necessary to produce 1000 has increased to $3000 per month ($100 per day). Column 4 shows the labor cost per day. Although each worker can produce 300 per 8-hour day at $12 per hour, something seems wrong when the unit cost of labor jumps at each 300 unit increment. The workers are still only getting $12 per hour. But actually their efficiency does decrease slightly because as the business grows: more of their time will be taken up with answering the phone from customer inquiries, taking deliveries, working the counter, cleaning the equipment and other things. (You, the entrepreneur, will be cleaning the bathrooms and taking out the trash.) So the two workers are actually slightly less efficient, and the effective wage on a per hour basis can be assumed to be $13 per hour. Likewise, the three workers (starting at 700 tarts produced) are essentially at $14 per hour, and four workers (starting at 1000 tarts produced) actually operate at an efficiency corresponding to $15 per hour.

Column 5 shows the unit cost of labor per tart; it is the total labor cost per day divided by the number produced per day. Gradually the unit cost of labor is declining, but notice that it is not monotonic. That is because the additional unit of labor may not be fully utilized for every increase of production. (The third worker, starting at 700 produced, actually only produces 100, since the first two bake the first 600.) The ingredients are expected to remain constant on a per-unit basis at $0.85 per tart as shown on column 6. Column 7 indicates that the utilities are constant at $350 per month, which is $11.66 per day on average. For 100 tarts the utilities portion of the cost is then about $0.12 as shown in column 8. The miscellaneous costs as indicated in column 9 includes the other minor expenses of insurance and maintenance, but also includes the FICA and Medicare payroll taxes for each worker. Keep in mind that Social Security and Medicare taxes come to about 14.7%, half paid by the worker as a payroll tax, and half paid by the business as an overhead cost. You also have to pay unemployment insurance taxes. Notice that these costs increase slightly on a per-unit basis as the number of workers increases per column 10. Next is the loan repayment; for $40,000 at 6% for two years, the repayment is $1772.83 per month, which is $59.09 per day. The portion of production costs for 100 tarts is then $0.59 and so on as indicated in column 11. The total unit production cost is the sum of columns 3, 5, 6, 8, 10, and 11; the result for each quantity produced is shown in column 12. Well, that about covers it, right? No -- it does not cover your compensation. Remember you, the person who took all the risks, who quit your steady job and invested your savings, who borrowed heavily, who has to do all the paperwork for the government, who has to deal with the OSHA and health inspectors, who has to deal with the liquor board, deal with the bank, make deliveries, take orders, resolve complaints, who found out Granny's secrets, who takes out the garbage, who pays off the local politicians and their mafia friends, who covers for the workers that call in sick, and does all the other jobs no one else will do? Certainly you deserve some compensation. Suppose a reasonable compensation is $20 per hour at 8 hours, although everyone knows you will be working far more hours than that. Your compensation is shown in column 13. The total desired asking price is the sum of column 12, the raw production cost per unit, and your compensation in column 13, and is shown in column 14. This is the desired selling price because it covers all your expenses as well as your compensation, and any price above this is profit that goes back into the company. (Technically, your compensation is out of profit, but is shown here as an example of how the desired selling price is calculated as distinct from the surplus profit accruing to the company itself.) One thing is very important in this layout of costs, which is: for this case, as production approaches 1000 units per day, the per-unit cost is always dominated by labor and materials costs, as seen by comparing the per-unit costs in columns 5 and 6 with the other components in columns 3, 8, 10, and 11. There is one last thing to discuss regarding column 13, your compensation. You, the person whose life will become the business, and the business will become your life, gets paid last. The politicians get paid first (withholding taxes), then your employees, then your suppliers, then the bank, and then you. When bad times roll around, it is you who will take the pay cut in order to keep your workers employed. Running a small business is the hardest job in the world.

Figure 1.3-2 shows the exact same unit cost data as a set of curves. The lines have been smoothed a little for clarity. The raw production cost (corresponding to column 12) is shown as the thick black dashed line and the thick solid black line is the desired asking price including your compensation as entrepreneur. If you only produced 100 per day, a selling price of about $4.75 each would cover everything, but $3.33 would cover at least the production cost if you worked for free (which you often will). It is easy to see that as production expands it becomes more efficient, and the unit cost of production declines from $3.33 at 100 per day down to around $1.53 at 800 per day.

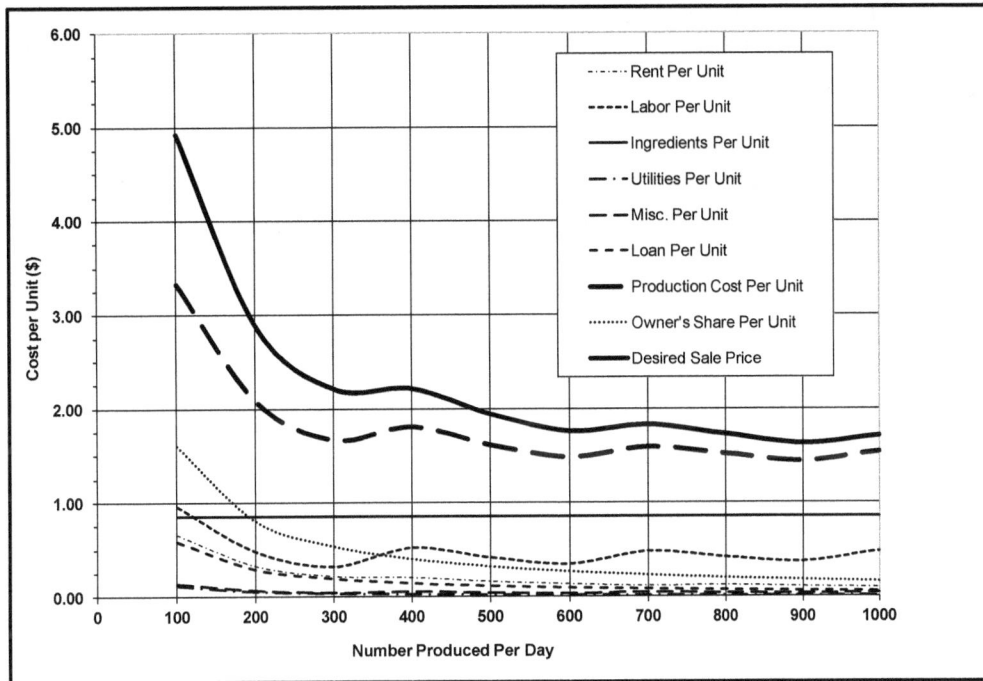

Figure 1.3-2: Unit Costs of Granny's Sublime Tarts

A common complaint made by economists of the "social good" persuasion is that the dotted line (your per-unit compensation) is sometimes larger than, and for production up to about 600 per day, comparable to the sum of all the other labor. Even at 1000 tarts per day, your per-unit compensation (16 cents) is one-third the per-unit total for all other labor (48 cents). You can hear the screeching a mile away:

"This is oppression by the owners, exploitation of the workers; why should the owner's compensation be anywhere close to what the workers get? It is an outrage that a single person is getting one-third as much as all the other labor combined."

Figure 1.3-1 fully explains it, but facts do not matter to "progressive" economic crusaders. The per-unit relative compensation does not indicate how much you earn above the workers. In this example, you are only making a little less than twice your employees on an hourly basis ($20 per hour vs. $12), actually much less because you will probably be working seven days a week. That complaint is a feature of the Marxist economists: they actually are dumb enough to demand that entrepreneurs, who take all the risks, should work for free. Not only that, but pay taxes besides in the interest of 'equity'. When their type of economics takes hold, the first casualties will be people like you, small outfits that seek to earn enough to qualify as an honest living. You are the enemy of the "social good" economists, no matter what fancy slogans they may employ to convince the public otherwise. The real reason you have earned their hatred is that since you can do for yourself in business, you don't need the government. That is their real problem with you and your snotty independent "capitalist" attitude.

It is all well and good that you have a good sense of your costs. But that is only one part of the problem, the other one being, how much will people pay and how many will they buy? In other words, what is the real economic demand for Granny's Sublime Tarts? Suppose by trial and error, by giving out samples at the local festivals, and just asking around, you are able to estimate the relation between the number that can be sold and the selling price. This would be the economic demand curve: the local buying public has claimed, truthfully or not, that so many would be sold at various prices. Suppose the demand curve looks like the dotted curve in Figure 1.3-3. It shows that if you could price them at $1.40 each, the public would buy about 1000 of them; priced at $2.80 each, only 100 could be sold. Also shown are the two thick curves from Figure 1.3-2 (raw production costs and desired selling prices). The maximum per-unit profit occurs when the vertical distance between the dotted and solid line is maximum; this occurs at production levels between 300 and 600 per day. For example, at 300 per day, the per-unit profit is about 30 cents, creating a profit of $90.00. At 600 per day, the per-unit profit is 25 cents, for a total profit of $150.00. The raw cost of production is covered for every level of production greater than about 150 units (i.e., where the dotted line lies above the dashed line). Overall profitability (including your compensation) occurs for production levels above 225 (the dotted line is above the solid line). It is clear that if you can get more than $2.50 for them you would produce as many as possible. That would continue until some master chef comes in and tries one, uses his expertise to reverse-engineer Granny's recipe, and then proceeds to make them on an industrial scale cheaper than you can.

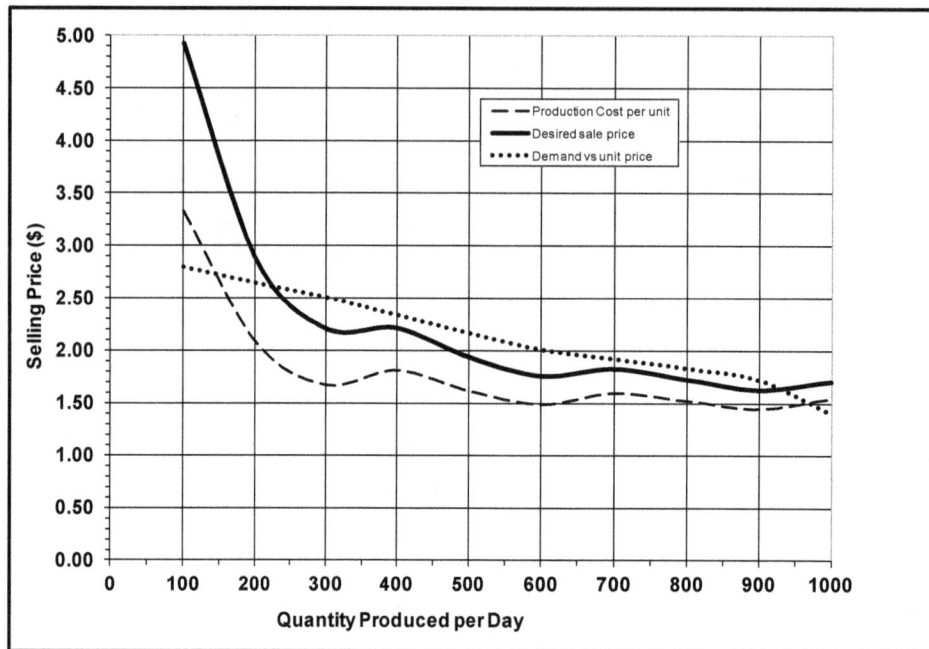

Figure 1.3-3: Demand Price vs. Supply Price for Granny's Sublime Tarts

At the other end of the scale, it is easy to see that profits fail to pay your compensation for production levels above 950 per day or so. If the dotted demand curve remains unchanged, the only way to deal with that is to be content with less profit or to lower production costs. Perhaps instead of using first-rate brandy, you could switch to the ones made by the Lighter-O Fluid-O Distillery. Good advertising may improve demand. In any case, given the situation as here, would you bother to produce quantities less than 200? That depends: if you haven't invested much yet, maybe not; maybe you would try to improve demand first. If you are already set up and operating, you probably would produce them and sell at a loss on the grounds that at least some revenue is being generated. The objective then is to once again cut costs or increase demand by whatever means are available. Maybe Granny's Sublime Tarts are never going to go over that well; maybe there is a problem with keeping them fresh long enough that limits the geographical distribution; maybe there are too many Mormons in the neighborhood. Maybe you would then decide to produce some other baked good with better margins. That is an additional job for entrepreneurs like you.

This example shows that supply and demand are linked; they represent the equilibrium point between the amount supplied vs. the amount desired, as expressed in the common medium of the money price. The demand for money among both buyers and sellers determines the price indirectly. The buyer decides how much money to part with to obtain the offered product, and the supplier determines how much money is worth investing in supplying the same product as expressed by the costs vs. the potential selling price. Supply and demand is normally shown as a pair of lines on a chart with the amount provided lying on the horizontal axis and price on the vertical axis. Supply is typically shown as low quantities provided at low selling prices, with increasing amount willing to be supplied as price increases. (The slope of price vs. quantity is positive). Demand is shown as low quantities demanded at high prices, and drifting downward; more are demanded as price is lowered. These are called respectively the "supply and demand schedules". The crossing point of the lines is supposed to indicate the current market state. Such a set of schedules is a more conventional way of looking at it, and the result is the same as described in the example. There is some price point at which the amount supplied is sold to the buying public; i.e., the "equilibrium" point.

Going back to the data for Granny's Tarts, it may well be that the actual equilibrium occurs at 600 units per day. The public has as much as they desire at the price they are willing to pay, and you, the baker, are willing to provide that many. But that intersection may not be valid in the long term. Tastes and preferences change as they always do. There is likely to be a natural fluctuation in the amount of tarts demanded, more during the holiday seasons, and less in the summer. There is also likely to be fluctuations in the amount that can be supplied: there may be a brandy shortage because of a failure of fruit crops, or an increase in the price of one or more ingredients. Over the long run, these fluctuations are met on both sides by educated guesses tempered by experience. Typically some will still be sold even at higher prices, other times that regular customer with her three bratty kids may decide the tarts are an extravagance that can wait until her economic condition improves. Ultimately a free economic environment will cause supply to approximately meet demand at a price that is just above the cost of production plus a reasonable profit to the supplier for his efforts. Small profit margins are the result of competition among suppliers and shopping around for the best price on the part of buyers. Thus the overall economy continues to nominally regulate itself without any special interest by the government. That is the essential definition of economic freedom: the government sets the bare minimum number of rules (usually in the form of enforcing contracts) but otherwise stays out of the way.

Suppose there is a sudden increase in the demand for Granny's Sublime Tarts. It may well be that a small supplier like yourself could make reasonably quick adjustments to satisfy it; start a second shift at the bakery, and making sure adequate ingredients are on order. The same is true in reverse to address a sudden decline in demand. But there are a great many products, especially in this modern technological age, where rapid changes in demand cannot be accommodated so easily. The reason is that complex products are fabricated in a large number of stages, and each of those stages of production has their own limitations. For example, there was a large increase in the demand for bathroom tissue in the early stages of the 2020 Wuhan virus pandemic. The increase in demand did not occur because anyone expected to use more of it; it was caused by public concern that the supply would be interrupted. The panic became self-fulfilling. In any case, there were a few weeks in some parts of the U. S. where bathroom tissue had to be rationed by the retail stores until the suppliers could ramp up production to meet the new demand level. Bathroom tissue is much more complicated than Granny's Tarts. The tissue itself has to be manufactured from wood, which requires chemicals in large vats; those have to be transported from their source of manufacture. The tissue has to be cut and put on rolls, and those cardboard rolls have to be manufactured by a different process. The finished tissue rolls have to be bundled together with plastic packaging, and then are packed into large boxes (both of which are specialty items from a different manufacturer), then have to be transported from the factory to the distribution centers to the stores. All the packaging has to be marked with number of sheets and contents, and the additional ink has to be procured. All this the bathroom tissue supplier has to coordinate; and his first-tier suppliers have to coordinate with their lower-level suppliers, and so on. The production process is done in a "roundabout" way [1.3-1], and sudden changes in demand cannot be easily accommodated. Advanced economies are characterized by a great many products being manufactured in this roundabout method. The reason is that large-scale production is necessary in order to reduce the overall fixed costs; and the larger the enterprise, the more difficult it is to make radical changes to the supply due to inertia.

A sudden large increase in the supply of a product operates differently. Generally a great expansion of supply does not lead to a corresponding increase in demand unless the expansion is accomplished with economies of scale such that the selling price can be reduced to attract new customers. It is unlikely that putting on three shifts at the bakery that serves to triple supply will generate a corresponding demand for Granny's Tarts unless the selling price now becomes so low that the caterers decide to add them to their standard menus. An increase in supply due to the entry of many producers tends to lower the price and also the profit margin; but at the same time, production can expand such that more people can afford it.

The same principle applies to application of technology. Items that were considered luxuries in the 1950's (such as air conditioning in cars) have become common now through the advent of technological improvements by many suppliers. It is difficult in the U. S. to buy a car without air conditioning. The same is true of those lousy electric windows and door locks. Once again, equilibrium is reached wherein producers earn reasonable profit at a certain supply rate, and the public demand is satisfied at a price they are willing to pay. No one in these modern times in the U. S. inquires about the extra cost of air conditioning in their car; it is now pretty much "standard". There was a time, as recently as the 1960's, when radios and heaters in cars were "options", which indicates how far costs have come down in the automotive industry. So why are cars so much more expensive now? That subject is one of the topics in chapter 2.

History shows that prices should be left to seek their natural level. First, the natural price is the one regulated by supply and demand; supply and demand are regulated by the desires of the public and the opportunities presented to suppliers. This natural price level is the method that minimizes waste and maximizes the use of resources because production is optimized. Optimized, that is, in the sense of the educated guesswork or intuition of suppliers. Over the long run, supply approximates demand most of the time based on experience of what the public wants and is willing to pay. Of course, there will always be the occasional "Monster Cookies" events. The entrepreneurs' job is to make estimates of demand and price prior to production. If the estimates are incorrect, losses accrue; if correct, profits accrue. Secondly, all prices are local. Even with the internet offering products worldwide, demand depends on income, and income varies by region. An item that is easily affordable to workers in Manhattan may be well out of reach for the people in Appalachia, or even in Brooklyn. Therefore, affordability varies by region and consequently demand varies by region. The price that can be obtained is therefore local, even if advertised nationwide or worldwide.

What happens when the general public values money more highly than products? It means that their cash balances increase (since they have decided to save more rather than spend). That in turn results in a decrease in demand, and thus prices fall. Consider your position as proprietor of Granny's Sublime Tarts. Your customers were in the habit of buying a certain number of tarts at a certain price as shown by the demand curve above. But now, they desire to spend less, not just on your tarts, but on many other products. You, and other people in business, are probably going to do one of two things: a) either cut prices and still generate some revenue; or b) keep the same prices, and reduce output. In both cases, the profits of business may be reduced. The particular choice will vary with the type of business. Suppose businesses believe that the publics' new sentiment is temporary. For a small operation like Granny's, it is probably better to cut prices, maintain staff, and endure temporary losses until the public changes its mind again, on the grounds that it may be difficult to ramp up production once it has been cut back. For an operation that can cut back and ramp up quickly, it may be better to maintain prices and reduce output. Typically most businesses, especially the larger ones making complex products, will choose to cut prices since the complicated supply chain is difficult to reconstruct after large disruptions in the supply chain or access to qualified labor. Fortunately, these kind of changes in public attitude are usually temporary, and the net effect is (usually) a fall in prices. On the other hand, if businesses believe the publics' sentiment about reducing consumption is permanent, then most businesses, including Granny's, will probably try to reduce costs, cut back production, and maintain the former price levels as a way to maintain (or regain) profitability. Once again, the tension between how the individual demands for money vs. products determines the state of the overall economy.

Price controls are detrimental to the operation of any economy. The price of some things cannot be controlled, or are easy to evade. If interest rates are limited, the issuer can make up the difference by adding "loan origination fees". If fees that can be charged for legal work are limited, it can be made up by inflating expenses. (Did you get the joke? No politician or bureaucrat has ever proposed limiting lawyer's fees, since most politicians and policy-making bureaucrats are lawyers themselves, and so are most of their friends. Limiting the fees charged by other professions is not a problem.) Likewise, limits on school tuition can be made up by a host of additional individual charges: library, laboratory, parking, etc. Price controls on industrial production will lead to obvious workarounds. Prices may conform to the dictates, but may be augmented by new additional items such as "documentation", "compliance", and "marketing"; these are simply ways to regain the selling price while pretending to conform to the price controls. Some production could be carried on in secret, and the product sold on the hidden market for whatever the true price is per supply and demand. Items can also be smuggled in and sold under the same principle.

Price controls always lead to bad consequences and usually hurt the ones they were intended to help. A price set below production costs only leads to shortages, since no supplier is going to volunteer to lose money. A classic example is the price of bread in the Soviet Union. In 1935, the price of one kilogram of bread in the Soviet Union was approximately 1.1 ruble [1.3-2]. A ruble in 1935 was equal in value to about $0.87 U. S. [1.3-3]. The price of bread in the U.S. at the time was about 9 cents per pound. A kilogram is 2.2 lbs, so the Soviet price of one pound of bread was 96 cents/2.2 = 43 cents, or a little less than five times the price of bread in the U. S. at the time. The problem was, even with the command/slave labor system that prevailed in the Soviet Union, a kilogram of bread could not be produced for 1.1 rubles. Regardless of their fine rhetoric, Lenin, Stalin, Malenkov, Khrushchev, and all the other Bolshevik gangsters kept in power by the criminal KGB were still subject to the basic laws of economics. Since it could not be produced economically at that price, very little was produced, and bread was generally available only during the main political holidays (1 May and 7 Nov), but at higher prices. What happens when price controls below production costs produce the same condition in a nominally free economic system? The government will be tempted to take over production in order to "save" the industry. In other words, more government to be applied in order to save the industry that is failing because of the current amount of government. That will lead to a greater shortage, and in order to provide the product at all, the government will be forced to violate its own price controls, same as the Soviet government did. The other alternative is that the government will make special exceptions (usually to its political favorites): either exemptions from the price controls, or subsidies to give the illusion of effectiveness [1.3-4]. But doing so leads to other problems: it creates a new class of rent-seekers (payment-demanders) who will insist that the subsidies continue forever, and it also creates a system of inequality whereby the governments' close political allies benefit over and above the rest of the potential suppliers. A price that is set too high under a control regime will lead to wasted surpluses from overproduction. That occurs because too many suppliers get in on the game, expecting large profits, only to be surprised that the demand does not justify it. Once again, those suppliers will find a sympathetic ear among the politicians. All they have to do is threaten large layoffs, and the politicians will typically lower the price control while supplying a subsidy to the new suppliers. So the public gets the (correct) lower price, but now has to pay taxes to finance the subsidies.

Rationing is the extreme form of price controls. Rather than try to control prices (difficult at best), a government may decide to limit quantities that can be purchased. If production of many items can be restricted, such a rationing scheme may well be successful at first, except it creates a secondary problem. The public is forced to save because it is unable to buy what it desires; meanwhile, the public becomes concerned that the money saved is being depreciated [1.3-5].

Why are government enterprises so inefficient? To understand that, it is necessary only to observe that the Motor Vehicle Bureau is the highest form of efficiency possible within a government. You have to take time off from work to stand in line, you get to fill out all the forms, you get shuffled from one line to another; all the Motor Vehicle Bureau does is collect the taxes from you and rubber-stamp a form. See how efficient?

There are several other negative effects of price controls. First, if a producer cannot earn a living by producing normal commodities for regular people because the profit margin is too low, he will change his operation and manufacture luxuries for the wealthy [1.3-6]. The wealthy do not have a money problem, and they are not likely to complain about the high cost of luxuries (in fact, they may brag about them). If luxuries are more profitable than necessities, then luxuries will be produced instead of necessities. If the price of regular vegetable oil is set low on the grounds that it should be more affordable to the poor, but is set too low for production, very little will be produced. Instead the vegetable oil will be replaced by extra-extra-virgin olive oil, which is far less affordable to the poor than vegetable oil at the old price.

A second problem with price controls, more insidious in its operation because it is better hidden, is that they serve to lower the overall standard of living. If a landlord has imposed upon him limits on the amount of rent he can charge, what is his incentive to maintain the property? He will do the bare minimum to avoid being harassed by the health and building inspectors. Meanwhile the tenants may be enjoying a lower rent payment, but pay for it indirectly through worse living conditions. If the landlord cannot make a profit on his rental, he also cannot pay the local property taxes. It is those taxes that fund most public schools. It is hard to see how inferior public schools are a benefit to a community.

A third problem occurs when price controls reduce the profitability of items currently produced such the ability of a company to engage in research and development declines. If costs of current production cannot be recovered, naturally there will be less incentive for new developments and fewer opportunities for investments.

A fourth problem is the increased risks borne by businessmen. If price controls indirectly require large economies of scale, then the cost of entering into a market (as competition) becomes too high, and the result is less competition. There will be at the same time a perception that the system is rigged on behalf of political favorites or large corporations that can afford the smaller margins. Controls of this type can lead to economic stagnation; workers with low skill levels will be hurt the most by the reduced opportunities; and part-time work will replace full-time work. The small businessman is injured the most: they have to take the greatest individual risk, as they do not have the backing of a large number of shareholders. Generally the small businesses work on small profit margins as it is, without the additional burden of price controls. Suppose your local government decides to impose price controls on cupcakes (which would include Granny's Tarts), setting the maximum price at $0.10 per ounce. If Granny's Tarts weigh 5 oz., clearly you would be out of business, since your raw unit production costs, even if you maximized production, are never below $1.45.

A fifth problem is produced by price controls on interest rates [1.3-7], or what used to be known as the 'usury laws'. A limit on the interest rate causes lenders to send their money elsewhere, thus depriving some of an opportunity for borrowing. A price control on interest demonstrates that the regulator lacks the basic understanding that interest is simply the fee for acquisition of capital. Control of interest rates tempts lenders and borrowers to engage in other measures to evade the law (i.e., the 'fees' mentioned above); and it deprives lenders of an opportunity to take greater risks in return for a greater reward.

Nothing of true economic value is free. Ultimately everything must be paid for in some manner. Every personal debt must be paid, either by services rendered in-kind, or by running up debt that must be paid out of future earnings or through a lower standard of living if one goes bankrupt. The same is true at the national level. A nation could ultimately pay its creditors by rendering services in some fashion or producing in-kind for exportation to another nation. It could pay its debt by taxation or theft. It can appear to reduce the amount of the debt by depreciating the money unit; but that will serve only to damage its future creditworthiness. Or a nation can simply refuse to pay its debts, and the entire society suffers a reduced standard of living because those who invested in the government bonds (such as pension plans and the banking system) take the loss.

There is one economic philosophy, adopted by several political parties, that claims that college education, health care, and housing can be provided for free. All that is required (they falsely claim) is good scientific management. But how will higher education be provided for free? If it were possible, wouldn't the public schools be free now? But they are not free: they are paid for by taxation, mostly in the form of property and sales taxes. How then will college education be free? Shall the professors be turned into slaves and forced to teach for bread and water? Will the electric company be forced to provide energy at no charge? Will the buildings be maintained by volunteers? Of course not; all those costs have to be paid for either by taxation or increased debt. If debt is chosen, then it means increased taxation either now or at some future time. The increased taxation may be grossly unfair for those who must pay the taxes but do not pursue a college degree. How will they be compensated, if at all? It may well be that the educational standards have to be lowered because taxes cannot be raised high enough to maintain the former standards. Those students will then get a watered-down college degree, much like the high school graduates in the Baltimore public schools that cannot read, write, or do arithmetic. This will give the illusion of success, but not the highly educated workforce that was advertised.

How can the illusion of free health care be engineered? Make no mistake; it will be an illusion. Shall doctors and nurse work for free? If doctors, among our most intelligent and highly educated citizens, can make just as much and live just as well selling insurance, and not have the long hours and liabilities that come with practicing medicine, what doctor would bother to practice? If prices are controlled such that doctors make the same as car salesmen, we will have a lot of car salesmen but few doctors, exactly the opposite of the stated objective. The government that imposes price controls on the practice of medicine will ultimately have to resort to rationing since the shortages of medical talent will be real. (Notice that "rationing" is the claim made against health insurance companies at present by the "progressive" activists.)

Private medical insurance is the most cost effective way to control costs in the long run. That is especially true since they are motivated by profit and thus have a vested interest in reducing fraud. The profit motive requires efficiency of administration. Keep in mind that your local Motor Vehicle Bureau is the pinnacle of governmental efficiency. It is worse than that. If health care is to be rationed, only the most routine procedures will be covered since there will be little incentive (due to price controls) for research and innovation. The public is likely to end up with veterinary care for people: simple things only, such as the flu and broken bones. Complex procedures will be rationed based either on political connections or how much you are worth as a taxpayer.

The same principles apply to housing; materials for construction and maintenance are not free and neither is labor. Rent control below costs leads to the well-known failed government-run facilities. They are invariably plagued with shabby standards and high crime rates because no one has a private incentive (i.e., profit motive) in maintaining the property or ensuring that only responsible people are allowed to live there.

There is an additional societal cost of this "progressive" propaganda about obtaining valuable things for "free". The people who have to pay (the working people, the ones the politicians and philosophers never talk about), will over time become resentful because someone else is getting benefits on their dime. But the recipients also have a detrimental attitude: since they did not expend any effort to obtain the benefits ("free" education, for example), they tend regard it as having no value. They join the philosophers and politicians in disrespecting the working people who paid for it. The things of value received for "free" are now regarded as "entitlements". There will be a general lack of interest in preserving what was given (free housing is the best example). The society is then in danger of adopting the "demand syndrome": those with the most political power will continue to demand more benefits at greater expense, which will ultimately cause the system to collapse.

1.4 Money and Individual Decisions

Overall economic activity in a free society is determined by individual decisions about money. A person possessing money has three options [1.4-1]: consuming, saving, and hoarding. A person buys for consumption both necessities and non-essential items, and may even choose to spend money on extravagances and luxuries. Everyone has their own definition of necessities; what is necessary to some may be regarded as irrelevant to others. In any case, those choices are their own, since it is their money. Saving is a reduction in consumption as a means of preparing for a future decline in income (the proverbial 'rainy day'), especially the loss of a job. A slightly different form of planning for contingencies is to pay for insurance, in which the premium is spent for that purpose instead of for consumption. A person may choose to use savings to prepare for a future retirement, either by investing in stocks or bonds, or by financing some business venture. If not set aside for retirement, savings and investment amounts to risking money already in hand, bypassing consumption, and using it to obtain an additional income. Last, a person may decide to hoard money as cash, neither spending nor saving. They may do so because they believe one of three possibilities [1.4-2]: a) the money in hand will become more valuable; b) that prices will fall and thus be able to buy more; or c) as a hedge against some future problem in the general economy.

Most individuals are better judges of how their money should be spent than a government or institution [1.4-3]. Most people desire to save for contingencies or retirement. Those who do not save for retirement either do not earn enough to afford it above their immediate consumption needs, or have knowingly decided to rely on future "entitlement" payments (such as "Social Security" in the U. S.). People generally understand that economic advances can occur only with additional investment, and they will invest if they can afford it. One economic theory that has taken hold in America claims that saving and investing are evil, and that spending everything one earns on immediate consumption leads to a stronger economy. But history shows the true virtues of individual economics: frugality and saving, the work ethic, and the preservation of the family. The false economic philosophy favors a system in which all personal income should either be consumed or taxed away, presumably for everyone's benefit. Of course, that is not how it works in practice. A person whose after-tax income is entirely consumed soon becomes dependent on the government when any unanticipated problem arises. After all, they do not have the means to set aside something for contingencies. If the contingency is not covered by some government program, that person will suffer accordingly. A long-term consequence of this false philosophy is the decline of self-reliance among the general population. It is no secret that those who rely on the government make reliable serfs indeed. Last, such a false system promotes and in fact requires the growth of governmental power over individual choices. If you, the citizen, fall into the trap of spending all your after-tax income, you have few individual economic choices left. You will become in fact little more than an animal to be herded about as someone in power decides. Now that I've mentioned taxes, what are they and who pays them?

All money that a government receives is a tax, no matter what other euphemism is used. Some taxes are honestly called taxes, such as income, value-added, consumption, use, sales, property, excise, capital gains, inventory, profits, and estate taxes. But there are also a great many hidden taxes, usually called fees, duties, or royalties. All taxes are payments to the government, and all of them have one thing in common: ultimately, all are paid by individuals. This fact is the one thing that neither the government nor the "progressive" parasites want you to realize. Politicians are skilled at devising a host of taxation schemes, naming them in such a way as to disguise this fact. The idea is that individuals will not object to tax increases if some other entity, such as a corporation, has to pay, so long as the individual is technically exempt. The fact is, which few in political circles want to discuss, is that individuals ultimately pay all the taxes, no matter who writes the physical check to the tax collector. They are either paid directly or indirectly.

The U. S. has a system of direct taxes paid by individuals regardless of how they are framed or collected. Direct taxes on individuals consist of the following categories:

a. Payroll taxes are paid out of current income, and are used to fund certain "social benefits", namely Social Security and Medicare. The tax rate is a fixed percentage of income (about 7.5% for the worker, and another 7.5% imposed on the company he works for). Individual business owners pay the entire 15%. It is known as a "payroll" tax, since there are no deductions, exclusions, or exemptions, except the portion of income liable for the Social Security tax is limited to a certain income level. The reason is that benefits are calculated only up to that income level, as a way to restrain excessive payments to upper income earners.

b. A personal income tax is levied on current income. Although the taxes are technically due in April, nearly all workers are subject to "withholding", meaning the taxes actually are paid every paycheck, and the April date is only for settling the account. The U. S. uses a graduated system in which lower income levels are subject to lower tax rates, and the tax rate increases as the income level increases. Certain deductions are allowed in order to reduce the income on which the tax is to be paid. These progressively higher rates applicable to higher incomes are referred to as the "marginal rates".

c. Most Americans are subject to "use" taxes. This cleverly named tax is commonly called a sales tax, although it is actually a tax on consumption. In most States it is paid at the retail level on nearly everything that an individual purchases, with some exceptions for food and medicine. Some people claim falsely that the retailer somehow benefits from this tax. Not so: the retailer is simply collecting it for the government. Not only does he collect it, he also has to do all the administrative record-keeping for the government's benefit. Use taxes are levied by States and localities (there is as yet no federal sales tax), and are mostly used to fund the State and local government agencies. This tax is paid directly at the point of sale; the retailer collects the tax from the consumer and passes it on to the appropriate government entity.

d. Most States and localities levy taxes on property. Usually they apply only to residential homes, but some States also levy taxes on "personal property" such as recreational vehicles, cars, and motorcycles. In most States and localities, property taxes are mostly used to fund the local public schools.

e. An excise tax is a form of consumption tax, usually levied on three categories of items: a) things that were once called "sins"; b) on necessities; and c) on luxuries. "Sin" taxes are those placed on tobacco and alcohol in the form of a "stamp". The excise taxes on necessities include those levied on gasoline and fuels. "Luxury" taxes include special taxes on tanning salons, and certain high-value items such as yachts and private jets. They are paid to the government by the manufacturer, and added to either the wholesale or retail cost of the item. All of these excise taxes are simply passed on to the individual consumer by adding them to the wholesale or retail prices.

f. Estate and inheritance taxes are paid on the value of a deceased person's estate. It is actually a tax on the transfer of assets from the deceased person to their heirs. For purposes of the tax, nearly all assets and property are counted toward the estate's value, including real estate, anything transferred to an heir in the three years prior to death, some annuities, and some types of life insurance. The federal government and most States have set a high threshold before the tax applies (for federal purposes, is about $11,000,000 as of 2018). The taxes are technically paid by the estate, but in truth are paid by the individual heirs, since the tax reduces the amount inherited.

g. Gift taxes are levied on personal transfers above a certain threshold. These taxes are paid in conjunction with the regular personal income tax payments.

h. "Fees" are taxes that are levied as either entrance costs to a line of work (such as professional and business licenses), or for supporting the maintenance of a public park, or for legal registration of property ownership (cars, homes, etc.).

i. The U. S. also has a system of taxation on profits. Certain businesses (proprietorships, Limited Liability Companies (LLC), and S-corporations) are chartered in such a way that profits are passed directly to the owner, and the owner pays the tax on profits as part of their personal income tax. Profits are revenue less expenses, and revenue comes from the sale of products. The sales price paid by the business' customers must indirectly include the taxes, thus are paid by individuals.

The other taxes are levied on individuals indirectly. A corporation pays taxes on its net income, which is revenue less its operating expenses. The corporation may write the check to the tax authorities, but who pays? Recall that the profit is the difference between revenue and expenses, and where does the revenue come from? It comes from the corporation's customers. If the customers are individuals, those individuals pay it directly as above. If another business is the customer of the first corporation, no intermediate tax on that transaction is imposed. But recall that the profits of the first corporation comes from the sales price to the second one, and so on down the line until the last business sells to the individual consumer. The accumulation of profits at every step is financed by all the intermediate sales; and ultimately the customers of the last business in the chain are paying the corporate income taxes. Businesses also are liable for property taxes, fuel taxes, road use taxes, and in some States, an "inventory tax" or a "gross receipts tax"; all of which must be added to the selling prices, and all are ultimately paid by individuals.

Businesses also pay royalties to the government if they conduct mining operations on public lands (usually oil and gas, but also gold and silver). The company pays the royalty, but the cost thereof goes into the cost calculations of the company when determining the selling price of its product.

Corporations may also distribute part of their earnings to their shareholders as dividends. An individual receiving the dividends is liable for payment of a tax as part of their regular personal income tax. If the dividend is paid to a pension fund or another corporation, it is counted as income to that entity. A tax must then be paid on that income, after deduction for expenses. If a pension fund pays taxes on its income, who actually pays? The tax payment reduces the value of the fund, since taxes are paid out of the profits of the fund. Therefore, the people who are invested in the pension fund are paying the tax, although it is completely hidden from view. A corporation receiving dividends from another will pay the tax on that income as described above, and ultimately those taxes are passed on in the form of higher selling costs of its products.

A person who owns shares in a corporation and receives a profit on the sale of the shares is liable for the "capital gains" tax, which is a tax on the increase in the price of the stock during the time it was held. The tax is paid as part of the personal income tax. If a corporation receives capital gains (such as an investment bank), it is counted as income, and taxes are paid on it after expenses. The taxes then are paid by other corporations or by individuals because they will be built into the fees and commissions charged by the investment bank for its services. Once again, tracing the money, these taxes are ultimately paid by individuals somewhere in the economy.

A "value-added tax" (not currently part of the U. S. system) is a tax levied on the gradually increasing value of products as they pass through the stages of production.

It is not my place here to argue whether these tax categories are good, bad, or indifferent; or whether the current rates or exemptions should be higher or lower. My point is: no matter what the tax is called, no matter who writes the check, no matter what claims of "equality" or "fairness" are made, or who the advocates claim will pay, all of them are ultimately paid by individuals. Most of the total tax revenue ultimately comes from the pockets of working people. It is true that that the very wealthy pay a higher percentage on their personal income taxes, but that does not mean that everyone else pays a lower rate in percentage overall. The total tax percentage levied on individuals, hidden as they are, may exceed their personal income taxes, and may exceed the income tax rates paid by the wealthy. Our politicians like to debate tax policy by focusing on who the immediate payer is, whether an individual or a business entity. What the politicians are careful not to discuss is that businesses only collect the tax. It is worse than that: it is not only the cost of the tax that is passed on, but also the cost of administering the tax on behalf of the government. Don't be fooled by the "progressive" politician who says he will "make the rich and corporations pay their fair share"; it is you who will pay. Those "progressive" politicians are always careful to avoid stating who is 'rich', or what the 'fair share' amounts to in concrete terms. The greater the ambiguity, the easier it is to fool the voters.

That explains the case of businesses that produce products for use by individuals. What if the ultimate customer is the government? It's the same answer: where does the government get the ability to pay? It gets it from taxes, paid either by individuals directly, or paid indirectly through the corporate profit tax. But as just noted, ultimately individuals pay the cost of business taxes as part of the sales price; the corporations only collect them, albeit indirectly.

Why do corporations pass the taxes onto their customers? The socialist demands to know: why can't those "lying, cheating oppressors of the working class" (i.e., businesses) simply pay the tax and keep the prices the same? The answer is: because they can't. Every business entity, except the few that are set up as "non-profits" in order to obtain some government privilege, is a profit-seeking entity. But why, asks the enlightened collectivist, are profits necessary? Why can't those "lousy rich exploiters" (i.e., people in business) do what is right by the workers? The answer is: they are doing what is right. Without the prospect of a profit, there would be no point in establishing the business. There would be no incentive to do so, because there would be no reward for the risk. Without businesses (as the American labor unions learned in the 1980's), there is no work. Without work, what exactly will the workers do? But why, whimpers the "progressive" earth-saver, why can't the workers form their own outfit in the interest of "fairness", and adjust prices such that they just break even, and sell at lower prices than those greedy capitalists? The answer is: they can, so what are they waiting for? If the new "Worker's Fairness Enterprise" doesn't make a profit, no corporate taxes are due, and that will reduce the government's revenue. (Of course, the socialists will then complain about that.) But if the "Worker's Fairness Enterprise" does make money, it will pay the taxes. Once again, it will be the customers of the "Worker's Fairness Enterprise" that will actually pay. The "Worker's Fairness Enterprise" will require managers, and those managers will have to make sure to price their products accordingly. There is a hidden fallacy in the entire "progressive" argument that businesses should forego profits. It is based on a false premise that profits can be reduced without any other consequences. The truth is that any business that produces something, even at no profit, still requires "capital" for its formation and continuing function. One can reduce profits to zero, but not capital. Capital is not free. The great failure of "progressive economics" (i.e., socialism) is the inability to account for the workings of capital, which is considered next.

1.5   The Principles of Capital

The word 'capital' is sometimes used as a pejorative in an effort to demean the function of a free economy. Those who engage in that type of rhetoric find it most convenient to ignore what capital actually is and how it works. Capital, in the economic sense, is existing wealth put to productive use [1.5-1]. It is any property that is capable of being used to generate an income [1.5-2]. It includes all the tangible items needed for production: land, equipment, and infrastructure [1.5-3]. 'Capital goods' are all the raw materials, fuel, equipment, equipment for manufacturing machines, and the equipment for maintaining machines. As Sumner [1.5-4] put it:

> "Capital is that portion of all the previous product of a nation which at any given time is available for new production. This will be a certain amount of tilled land, houses, buildings, stock, tools, food, clothing, roads, bridges, etc., which have been made and are ready for producing, transporting, and exchanging new products. These things are all the product of labor, and require time for their production."

Capital is partly the means by which labor is financed until production can begin, and to improve the productivity of labor, as described by the British economist W. Stanley Jevons in 1871 [1.5-5]:

> "The single and all-important purpose of capital is to enable the laborer to await the result of any long-lasting work, to put an interval between the beginning and the end of an enterprise. Not only can we, by the aid of capital, erect large works which would otherwise have been impossible, but the production of articles which would have been very costly in labor may be rendered far more easy. Capital enables us to make a great outlay in providing tools, machines, or other preliminary works, which have for their sole object the production of some other commodity, but which will greatly facilitate production when we enter upon it."

Since capital includes the required infrastructure, it implicitly includes all the results of labor already expended, but does not include labor to be supplied in current production. The great advantage of capital is that it allows expenditures in advance of production [1.5-6], including living expenses for workers, the acquisition of materials, fabrication of tools (including in modern times, software), paying rent, acquiring equipment; all the things that must occur before production actually commences. Consider the process of starting production of Granny's Sublime Tarts. Labor and materials were expended to build the building, install the plumbing, electric, and ventilation systems. That is the consequence of past labor and materials, and is included as part of the rent. But your current capital (the $40,000 you borrowed) goes to paying the rent while the building is modified for your production. You have to buy and install the refrigeration units, the display cases, ovens, mixing equipment, storage shelves, and paint and decorate the place. You will have to pay for those items and the labor to put them in. You will have to acquire the ingredients and get them transported to your location. You will require some sort of legal and accounting help to establish the business. All those represent capital items necessary before the first tart rolls out into the display case to be sold.

Starting up Granny's Sublime Tarts is like nearly every other business, in that a great majority of work is done by intermediaries, or "middlemen". In fact, the entire free enterprise system depends on these middlemen. Obviously, you would not personally modify the plumbing or the electric lines in the course of renovating the space. You are not going to waste your time building display cases, and so on. Your talent is in organizing the workers to make the tarts, and tending to all the other things have to be done in order to bring them to market. The same principle applies to the ingredients: surely you are not going to travel to the Dominican Republic for the raw sugar; you don't milk your own cows for the cream; you don't distill your own liquor; you don't make the baking trays or the paper packaging. A long series of middlemen handle the milk from the dairy farm, to the processing plant, to the packager, to the wholesaler to you. Likewise, a long string of middlemen handled the fruit from the farm to the processor to the wholesaler to the distillery that mixed the fruit with all the other ingredients to make the brandy. The middlemen handle large quantities that are not practical for each buyer; they allow you, the baker, to bypass the inconvenience of having to go directly to the producers of the raw materials. Middlemen are neither the wheel nor the road; they are the grease and ball-bearings between the axle and the wheel that makes the wheel and road work efficiently. Some "progressive" economists dismiss the middlemen as unnecessary, claiming that they are nothing more than parasites. They claim that items can be purchased cheaper from the large manufacturers. Technically that is true, but two important points are overlooked. It may be cheaper on paper to buy sugar from the grower, but why would the grower, with 100 million pounds to sell, bother with selling 1000 pounds to you? That is an enormous expenditure of his time (and money) to deal with small quantities, and since he must recover his costs (by building it into the price), it will not be as cheap as the faulty theory suggests. Secondly, even if you could buy sugar from the foreign grower, how does it get to you? It has to be transported, and that means you will have to do all the work of getting your 1000 pounds of sugar from the Dominican Republic to your bakery. Now you could in fact buy enough at one time to last for several years, but then you have tied up money in a large amount of sugar you don't need for near-term production. It then has to be stored somewhere without spoiling, and those expenditures represent money that could be more efficiently spent on advertising or something else that advances your business. Don't be fooled by the grand theorists who claim that central planning and distribution is the most efficient method of production. The most efficient system is the one in which middlemen acting in their own interest reduce the overall price of commodities for you, the local baker. They have already assumed the risk of transportation, they have paid for insurance, they know how to clear customs, and they are prepared to break down the initial large quantities to small amounts that maximize your efficiency. The commissions charged by the middlemen (i.e., their profits) are far less than the cost you would incur if you had to deal with the original producers.

It is important at this point to make an important distinction between money and capital [1.5-7]. To a business, money is not capital because it is not the thing that actually causes production. Granny's Tarts are made using the true capital items: refrigerators, freezers, mixers, and ovens. Those items are the means to earn a profit. Money is only the means to obtain the capital items, and therefore to a normal business, money is involved in a transaction that acquires capital; it is a means to an end. I used the phrase "normal business" to distinguish them from the banking business. To a bank, money is capital, since money is the bankers' means of earning a profit. The banking business is distinct from all other businesses and will be discussed in detail in Chapter 5. For now the important point is that a greater amount of money does not in and of itself produce more wealth (i.e., capital for productive purposes). Only an increased amount of capital leads to greater production. Money is at most the intermediate means of acquiring the capital [1.5-8].

There are two classes of capital, so-called 'fixed' and 'circulating'. They may be distinguished by defining 'fixed' capital as that which is designed and operated for a specialized purpose, and cannot be easily modified or diverted to other uses. Examples would include the large scaffolding and cranes used in building commercial aircraft, or closer to home, the machines that are used to build commercial ovens. Once in place, they are useful for those tasks, but not much else. 'Circulating' capital is the type that keeps the fixed capital in operation, such as spare parts, lubricants, and software updates. Circulating capital is necessary to replace what is destroyed in the process of production [1.5-9]. These distinctions are conceptual, as there is no hard-and-fast rule about duration or component category that separates them. You may classify your refrigerator and ovens as fixed capital because they will be in use for ten or twenty years, but the mixing bowls and flatware are circulating because they have to be replaced annually. A bridge in use for a hundred years is fixed capital. On the other hand, the vehicles used to maintain the bridge are be regarded as circulating capital, even though they are used for five or ten years (much longer than the flatware at Granny's).

"Progressive" economists are quick to demonize "Wall Street" as the home of those who cheat or gain some secret advantage over the working people through buying and selling of stocks and bonds. They do not regard it as a market for efficient investing; they regard it as a gambling casino for the evil rich with their sinister intentions [1.5-10]. Is there corruption on Wall Street? Of course, there will always be some corruption in any place where money is involved. Does that make the system illegitimate, and therefore a target for abolition? Of course not: no rational person proposed abolishing major league baseball because a few players used steroids to boost their home run count. Despite the insider trading and other types of incompetence and corruption, stock exchanges perform a valuable service for those who wish to invest. A unit of stock in a company is a title to the materials, knowledge, technology, and processes used by that company to develop and market a product [1.5-11]. In other words, stock is a title to a portion of capital that produces a profit and earns a profit. Of course there are some investors who spend a lot of time doing short-term trades, betting as it were on a change in the stock price. Those people do regard shares of stock as gambling chips. But don't be led astray by the claim that they constitute the majority of traders or the majority of total investment. Those gambling types are a fairly small number, and the volume of their trades is small compared to the overall activity of the exchanges. The stock exchange, especially in these modern times (since the Reagan administration), is the only means by which regular people (like you and me), with small amounts to invest, can gradually build up wealth by investing, thus permitting the money you don't spend to work on your behalf. When we invest, are placing our money with people who are probably smarter than us; they now work on our behalf. Investing in a stock is nothing more than lending to the company, except there is no guarantee of repayment. (The stock could go to zero, and you would then lose your investment.) That's why they are called investments, and not savings: you have trusted your money (via buying shares) to the company with reasonable confidence that they will use it wisely to produce a viable product and earn a profit, some of which is passed on to you, the investor. Now here is the test: do you, or anyone you know, own any shares in mutual funds, or are members of a pension plan, or participate in a 401K, IRA, or Roth IRA? If so, then you and your acquaintances are the "evil rich" that the socialists hate. You are the "oppressor" the Marxists are always demonizing. The simple reason for their animosity is that all of those retirement plans pay out of earnings that were made by investing in the stock and bond market. You can safely disregard all those adherents of the "progressive" religion who ridicule the stock market as the symbol of reprobate capitalists feeding at the trough of economic debauchery.

Likewise, a bond (corporate or government) is simply a promissory note (an IOU) in which you, the buyer, are promised repayment with interest over a certain time period. Buying a bond is lending money directly, since the repayment is due on a regular basis (unlike a stock).

A discussion on stocks and bonds belongs here in this section on capital because the proceeds of the sales of stocks and bonds are usually devoted to buying fixed capital items (i.e., equipment for improving production or processes), or to provide circulating capital (materials, spare parts, new software) to maintain and expand the business. Suppose Granny's Sublime Tarts becomes a big success, and you decide to expand. That takes capital, to be purchased with money, and you may decide to take on a partner, or you may decide to issue stock in the company. If you sold shares of stock, what would you do with the money? If the goal is expansion, you would invest that money in additional storefronts, or in a warehouse, new refrigerators, and other equipment, vehicles to make deliveries, etc.; all the same capital items you needed to start the original location, but on a larger scale. In other words, you would do exactly what the large corporations do with stock proceeds: improve the product, reduce costs, expand, and employ more people. In return, if Granny's expansion is profitable, you would pay out dividends to the shareholders, just like Exxon-Mobil and Lockheed Martin.

The capital stock of a nation is accumulated over centuries [1.5-12, 1.5-13]. It represents the labor of the past that has been preserved for present use. It is not just the physical roads, buildings, ships, and canals; it is also the knowledge passed down. Because the total stock of capital rests on efforts of the past, wars and riots are actually more destructive than they appear to be at first sight, because current wealth has to be used to replace what had been previously accumulated. The other alternative is to not replace it (which is accepting an increase in inefficiency), or to replace it by incurring debt, which is nothing more than a burden to be placed on future wealth. The production of Granny's Tarts benefits from the efforts of the past: existing streets, sewer system, and electric grid. The steel for the tables and display cases and even for the mixing bowls was developed many years ago, and the same is true of the glass, plastic, furniture, floor tiles, ventilation fans, and air conditioning and heating. You, the new baker, now have access to the equipment you need, which are the results of past capital created, used, destroyed, and replaced with new investments along the way.

Obviously both fixed and circulating capital is subject to destruction. Both types of capital must be replaced either because it wears out or becomes obsolete with the advance of technology. Fixed capital is most susceptible to being made obsolete by advances in technology, and the circulating portion consisting of spare parts will tend to wear out first. Both types of capital are also subject to obsolescence owing to a change in the tastes of the consumers. Technological improvements represent the replacement of past capital. For example, steel is no longer made using the original Bessemer furnaces; it was gradually replaced by the open hearth furnace, which in turn was replaced by the basic oxygen process, and that method is now being replaced by the electric arc furnace [1.5-14]. The Bessemer process sometimes caused the steel to be too brittle, and it did not permit scrap metal to be used as the source material. The open-hearth process allowed scrap metal to be used, and because it is a slower process, better quality steel could be made due to reduction of impurities. The basic oxygen process was a more efficient version of the open hearth system. The advantage of the electric arc system is that it requires lower start-up capital costs, and permits finer tailoring of the final product. Now many different grades and types of steel can be specified and manufactured, and those specifications can be engineered to be optimal for some purpose. The old capital infrastructure is cast aside as better techniques are developed; hence the recurring destruction and creation of capital. There is hardly anyone in the U. S. who uses a typewriter; they have been mostly replaced by the personal computer. Horses were once the mainstay for agriculture and transportation in the U. S., but their use has gradually decreased in the last 100 years. There are about 9 million horses in the U. S.; a small number are still used by the Amish in their traditional farming techniques, but most are used in recreation and tourism applications. Gasoline was once a cast-off by-product of kerosene production until the internal combustion engine was invented that could make use of the gasoline. It was the internal combustion engine and the by-product gasoline fuel that caused the horse to become economically obsolete in the U. S. That has also caused changes in employment: no one enrolls in school in modern times to learn how to make a buggy whip or a carriage wheel.

Central economic planning as advocated by some usually contains a particularly bad assumption: that the production infrastructure (i.e., the necessary capital) is permanent once it is established. Such theories tend to ignore the fact that capital has to be constantly replaced. The all-seeing, all-knowing central planners in the Soviet Union saw no need to produce spare parts for their grain trucks and tractors. Nor did they see the utility of paving roads in the rural areas. Naturally the result was that the tractors and trucks could not be repaired when parts wore out. The ones that were still operating routinely got stuck in the muddy dirt roads. Thus the Soviet Union, which prided itself as a modern industrial giant, had to put its Army to use every year harvesting crops by hand and transporting it by horse-drawn cart. The tractors and trucks, which represented a considerable capital investment, went to waste because the circulating capital necessary to keep them running did not exist. Surprise, surprise, surprise: the U. S. S. R. experienced perennial food shortages. Here we see the triumph of central planning: hunger for all (except the ruling elite). There again is the fallacy of centralized government operation: no one was permitted to fix the problem because the planners were afraid to give up control, or admit a mistake, or permit someone to benefit by earning a profit for doing so. There is no incentive without a potential for profit.

A free enterprise system utilizes capital as a means to increase production over the long run, but at the same time, recognize that there is a time delay in doing so. With all the modern access to workmen and materials, Granny's Sublime Tarts bakery could be designed and set up in a few months, but a bridge or a steel mill may take ten years to design and build. New capital assets cannot be created instantaneously, but the incremental costs of building it have to be incurred immediately. Capital permits the intermediate expenses to be paid in the course of preparing for the production of Granny's Tarts, a more efficient means of crossing the river, and a larger production of steel. Once again in all three cases, the expansion of production tends to lower the selling costs via economy of scale. It would be easy to make the tarts in your kitchen, but not as many can be produced, and the per-unit cost of doing so will be higher than in a bakery-style production process. (That is why few housewives bake their own bread, even though they may have the time.) A bridge is cheaper to use than a ferry, and large scale steel mills are more efficient than backyard furnaces. Technological improvements arising from the use and replacement of capital over a long period leads to an improved standard of living.

Jevons provided one of the clearest analyses of the use of capital [1.5-15]. His conclusion was that a continuous application of capital over a period of time will continue until such time as the added production compared to the total production, expressed as a ratio, is approximately equal to the rate of interest. It turns out that there are several reasons why the continuous application of capital results only in a finite payoff. First, as time progresses, some of the capital employed early on is consumed, whether by payment of wages or from machines wearing out. Thus the succeeding applications of capital are partly used to compensate for the losses built into the process itself. Machines wear out because of friction, a basic fact of physics. Machines become obsolete because some newer machine works better. Labor must be paid, otherwise it is not performed. Regarding labor, there is one thing the socialists and the Democratic Party slaveholders in the Old South never understood: slave labor is not actually free, since the slave has to be fed, housed, and clothed. Every slave (if he has any common sense) will do as little work as possible, and every inmate in a socialist economy does the same. Returning back to Jevons' conclusion, the second reason for a finite return on continuous capital investment is that, while production efficiency increases, costs decline, but in a competitive environment, selling prices and profits also decrease. The additional capital infusion ends when the per-unit costs descend to a per-unit stable point. The third reason for the finite return is that as efficiency increases, workers will be able to claim a share of it in the form of higher wages, thus reducing the overall return to the entrepreneur. Over the long run the continuous application of capital through borrowing continues until the profitability of the last increment of the investment approximates the interest paid on the money borrowed to obtain the capital. This type of continuous capital investment is not applicable to the example of Granny's Tarts because in that example, a single capital investment was made.

Expenditure of capital enhances efficiency and permits more commodities to be produced. Even though the capital is expended and has to be replaced, the selling prices of commodities produced this way is lower than before, partly due to increased efficiency and partly due to competition between producers. Competition is the reason that selling prices decrease, and so the profit margin decreases. Referring back to Figure 1.3-3, it is seen that if the demand curve shown there is accurate, the profit margin, even in the absence of competition, is decreasing. (The per-unit profit margin is the vertical distance between the solid and dotted curves.) Thus in a free enterprise system, use of capital leads to lower prices and lower profit margins for commodities, but a higher standard of living, since more is being produced. There are some cases where competition is not a factor: a) government-granted monopolies, b) products produced under patent; and c) certain luxury items such as yachts and so-called 'supercars'. An example of a government granted monopoly in the U. S. is the game of baseball. No one can start a revenue-generating baseball league without paying a concession or tribute to the Major League Baseball organization. A patent permits the inventor an exclusive right to production for a period of years. In those cases, the selling price is whatever the buyers and sellers agree to, usually the cost of production plus the amount necessary to cover profits plus research and design expenses.

The increase in productivity due to capital expenditure does not necessarily mean an increase in employment. Increased productivity means that the nature of the industry has changed; carriages made by hand gave way to the automotive assembly line. Higher productivity can lead to an increase in employment if the decline in selling price brings in enough new customers to justify hiring more workers. This will prevail until production is at capacity, at which case the entrepreneurs must decide whether further expansion is justified on the basis of profit potential. In any case, the wage rates of the workers must be such that the enterprise is still profitable. Over the long run, the underlying cause of increased employment was the use of capital: it made products more affordable to the public, which motivated the public to part with money to obtain it (the item being unaffordable before), which justified expansion of production and increased employment. It was the capital that permitted production to expand in the first place, because it paid for the expenses (wages and tools) incurred during the construction period.

If capital is so beneficial, why do poor nations remain poor, and why is it that some wealthy nations become poor? Poor nations do not need money; they need capital, which is the means of production. Money to a poor nation serves no purpose but to acquire capital. Many poor nations are poor because of corruption among the political class, and so long as the corrupt system remains intact, the existing capital, or means to procure it, will flee the country or stay hidden. A poor nation that has any intention of improving economically must recognize the importance of private property, that is, capital privately owned and utilized. There is no sense in a population saving their money to make investments and thus obtain capital if the politically well-connected or professional criminals can steal it. Societies where property rights are non-existent, weak, or poorly enforced have low savings rates and low amounts of capital. They tend to be societies that consume what little that is produced, and sometimes they remain economically stagnant with a standard of living little above subsistence. There is no particular incentive to succeed because it will all be swept away by criminals or the ruling elite. This is another reason why the 'socialist' economic systems fail: the socialist makes the fatal assumption that incentive is not necessary for economic progress. A socialist assumes without proof, in fact, with proof to the contrary, that people will work just as hard to fulfill some absurd ideology as they would for themselves and their family. A "progressive" theoretician believes that individuals will be content to stand by and watch others do less work and receive the same rewards. We have proof of the reduction of incentive as illustrated by the maxim common among Russian workers trapped in the U. S. S. R.: "they pretend to pay us and we pretend to work". The principles of capital are not defective; socialist political systems prevent capital from operating and the standard of living declines. Here is some evidence: Cuba has to ration eggs, 5 eggs per person per month.

A nation may remain poor or become poor if it has an inferior money system, by which I mean, a money unit subject to depreciation. A depreciating money unit, as observed before, prevents the accurate calculation of profit and loss; and without accurate calculations of this type, entrepreneurs will be reluctant to take the risk with the money or capital that they have. A wealthy nation may become poor in several ways. It can export its capital by transferring its industrial base to other countries. Capital will go where it is most profitably employed; if wages are lower elsewhere, it will remove to that place, other things being equal. (But here's the fallacy of exporting capital to obtain access to lower wage labor: the other things are never equal.) It is possible that a nation may decide to ignore research and development, may decide to educate more political scientists and lawyers than engineers or real scientists and gradually lose the technological edge that made it wealthy in the first place. The productive people may be evicted for some religious or ideological reason; high taxes may drive them to other places. Here are a few historical examples. The first example is the tax policy of the Roman Empire, in which it imposed such high taxes on farmers that it drove farmers off the land. The consequence was that the Western Roman Empire, headquartered in Italy, with the best farmland in Europe, had to import food from Egypt. The historian de Sismondi describes the destruction of capital that had occurred by the time of the co-Emperors Valentinian (ruled 364-375) and Valens [1.5-16]:

> "The finances of the empire demanded a reform, which neither of the emperors was in a condition to undertake. They wanted money, and they were ignorant where to seek the long exhausted sources of public wealth. Three direct taxes, equally ruinous, pressed upon the citizens; the indictions [imperial edict], or territorial impost, calculated on the third of the income, and often doubled or tripled on superindictions [amendments to imperial edicts], which the necessities of the provinces compelled the government to exact; the capitation or poll tax, which sometimes amounted to a sum equivalent to twelve pounds sterling per head, and the heavy gratuitous labors imposed for the service of the land, and the transport of commodities belonging to the revenue. These taxes had so utterly ruined the landholders, that in all parts of the country they abandoned estates, which no longer produced enough to pay the charges upon them. Vast provinces in the interior were deserted; enlistments daily became more scanty and difficult; the magistrates of the curia or municipalities, who were responsible both for the contributions and the levies of the respective towns, sought by a thousand subterfuges to escape the perilous honor of the magistrature."

Here de Sismondi (writing in 1834) refers to an annual poll tax on agricultural workers amounting to the equivalent of twelve pounds English sterling. A pound sterling (£) consisted of 20 shillings (s.), and each shilling 12 pence (d.). Clark [1.5-17] reports that the daily wage of a farm worker in England in the 1830's was 19.6 d. per day, which is 1.63 s. If we allow Sunday rest and work 312 days per year, his annual wage was about 510 s., equal to about £25.50. Thus the £12 cited by de Sismondi correlates to about a 47% tax on income, or in the context of the Roman agricultural system, a 47% tax on the workers' productivity. Keep in mind that this was only one of the taxes.

The level of Roman taxation at the time of Constantine (ruled 306-337) eventually eliminated all incentive, even to have children, as the historian Edward Gibbon [1.5-18] describes:

> "The horrid practice, so familiar to the ancients, of exposing or murdering their new-born infants, was becoming every day more frequent in the provinces, and especially in Italy. It was the effect of distress; and the distress was principally occasioned by the intolerable burden of taxes, and by the vexatious as well as cruel prosecutions of the officers of the revenue against their insolvent debtors. The less opulent or less industrious part of mankind, instead of rejoicing in an increase of family, deemed it an act of paternal tenderness to release their children from the impending miseries of a life which they themselves were unable to support."

Louis XIV was one of France's worst kings, and one of his worst decisions was to revoke the Edict of Nantes. This edict had been issued in 1598 by France's best king, Henry IV; it recognized religious toleration for Protestants (known as Huguenots) in the traditionally Catholic France. But Louis XIV decided, in his usual colossal arrogance, that France should be a wholly Catholic nation, and revoked the Edict in Oct 1685. There had been some persecution the previous few years, but this was the one that allowed people to be sentenced to slavery just for refusing to become Catholic. The historian A. J. Grant [1.5-19] relates what happened then: a) Protestants were prohibited from worshiping or operating schools; b) Protestants were prohibited from leaving the kingdom under penalty of lifetime sentence to the galleys; and c) French soldiers were quartered in Protestant homes. Many fled the kingdom despite the threats, ultimately leading to a general depopulation of France's industrial and commercial centers, especially Normandy and Pays de Gex. Thus France lost the entrepreneurial and industrious class to Germany by emigration.

Guizot, the French historian provides a similar view [1.5-20]:

"He [Louis XIV] set at naught all the rights consecrated by the edicts, and the long patience of those Protestants whom Mazarin called 'the faithful flock;' in vain has persecution been tried for several years past; tyranny interfered, and the edict of Nantes was revoked on the 13th of October, 1685. Some years later, the reformers [Protestants], by hundreds of thousands, carried into foreign lands their industries, their wealth, and their bitter resentments."

The same effect was achieved on a lesser scale by many American politicians (especially Presidents Bill Clinton, George W. Bush, and Barack Obama), who allowed Communist China into the World Trade Organization and then granted them most-favored nation status. We can chalk this up to the work of naive gullible dreamers who put their faith in the integrity of people (Chinese Communists) morally reprobate enough to admire Marx, Lenin, and Mao.

Not much more needs to be said about the lowlifes like V. I. Lenin as described above. He managed to gain power and steal the productive capital in order to hand it over to his minions for abuse and decay. Exactly the same pattern was repeated by Mao in China, Hitler in Germany, Mussolini in Italy, Castro in Cuba, Kim in North Korea, Amin in Uganda, Mugabe in Zimbabwe, Ho Chi Minh [Nguyen Sinh Cung] in North Vietnam, Pol Pot [Saloth Sar] in Cambodia, Chavez in Venezuela, and many others. Those nations suffered greatly because the capital they confiscated "for the common good" was destroyed by misuse and corruption. Those nations ended up with universal poverty.

A socialist or "progressive" system will fail because the allocation of existing capital is based on politics and not economics. Typically capital is wasted in a socialist nation because it is employed to meet some political or ideological objective rather than an increase in production and improvement in the standard of living for the population. But it just not the socialist nations that waste capital; it can occur in free enterprise nations as well. Capital can be wasted in many ways: a) on projects that are never completed (such as railroads, bridges, and tunnels); b) on projects that never turn a profit (high-speed rail); and c) on projects that are not necessary (some stadiums, convention centers, and airports in small towns). Another type of wasted capital is in the form of projects that are done too early before they are needed. For example, a 6-lane limited access highway through a town of 10,000 is not necessary to support the businesses there (in fact it may destroy those businesses). Even if there is no effect on the local businesses, the unnecessary highway represents money that could have been better spent elsewhere.

Some may argue that the destruction of capital and reduction of production occurred in the Soviet Union only because it was the first practical test of socialism, and of course, "mistakes were made". They now claim to have corrected those errors, and are ready to usher in utopia. Such an assertion ignores the history of later socialist regimes. The socialists took over in Cuba 42 years after the Bolshevik Revolution in Russia, and capital was destroyed in Cuba just as quickly. The socialists came to power in Venezuela in 1998, 81 years after the Bolsheviks, and capital was destroyed there in a few years. What about China -- doesn't the prosperity of China prove that socialism can work? No, China is giving the illusion of prosperity. China appears to be prospering only because it is being given capital and technology through the idiotic policies of the Western nations. What isn't given on a silver platter is stolen by the Chinese. The destruction of capital in socialist nations is not the result of mistakes, or accidents, or by some magic sabotage by unseen and unheard enemies: the destruction of capital, the decline in production, and the lowering of living standards are all "features" of socialism. It is worse than that: it also demoralizes labor.

One other question remains: what are the prospects for a small outfit like Granny's Tarts under a socialist regime? If Granny's is in business when the socialists take over, it will gradually be run into the ground either by taxation, regulation, or outright confiscation. If you, the entrepreneur, try to establish Granny's Tarts with a socialist regime already in place, it is unlikely to happen at all. The reason is that a top-down regimented economic system does not permit (or is afraid of) independence. No capital will be forthcoming to start the business because all the owners of capital are running scared; capital will either be hidden or taken out of the country. Government bureaucrats won't let you begin because socialist paper-shufflers are trained to be suspicious of any initiative and envious of someone else's potential success.

1.6   The Principles of Rent of Land

Rent is money paid for the use of land. It is a unique category of expense, and is due solely to the fact that the total amount of land is limited. It can have economic value without people expending any effort on it. The rent to be paid for farmland arises from three different causes: a) the relative fertility of land; b) the marginal utility of each portion; and c) the proximity to transportation that serves to reduce the overall cost of cultivation.

To illustrate the first cause, consider two adjacent parcels of farmland of the same size, but of different fertility, set aside for growing the same crop. With the same amount of capital and labor applied to each, the more fertile one will permit a larger produce to be grown, and thus higher revenue returned per acre. Both fields are devoted to raising the same crop, and although the two fields yield different amounts, there is only one price in the market for the produce of both. The portion produced on the more productive land does not sell for more or less per bushel than that grown on the inferior land [1.6-1]. An adequate return must be obtained for the inferior land or else it will not be cultivated at all. Therefore it is clear that there must be a greater profit per acre realized on the superior land. If the revenue of the inferior land just covers costs plus profit, then no rent can be paid for it. This relative profit per acre, due to the relative fertility of two parcels, justifies the rent that should be paid for the use of the superior land [1.6-2].

The second cause is known as "marginal utility" of land also leads to a varying rent. Suppose once again two parcels of land equal in size but if different fertility. If equal amounts of additional labor and capital are applied to the two parcels, the increase in the crop will likely be higher with the inferior land. The reason is that a certain amount of fertilizer per acre will aid the inferior land proportionally more than land that is already more fertile. Marginal utility is the phenomenon under which each additional increase in labor or capital results in a gradually declining increase in production [1.6-3]. The fifth increment of additional labor is not nearly as productive as the fourth, which was less than the addition produced by the third, etc. A similar behavior will occur in the Granny's Tarts bakery. If the space is set up to produce 1200 tarts using four workers, each is producing 300 per day as observed in the previous example. But adding a fifth or sixth worker in the same space without increasing the amount of equipment will not cause the production to increase by 300 for each additional worker. The reason is that the fifth and sixth worker will be getting in the way of the first four. The six of them will have to coordinate the use of the equipment. Both of these effects will tend to reduce the productivity of the fifth and sixth worker; perhaps they will only add 250 and 200 tarts respectively per shift. So it is with farmland: the increase in the crop is not linear with additional labor or fertilizer. Additional amounts of effort and fertilizer produce a proportionally smaller increase until the land has reached it productive limit. At that point no amount of additional labor or fertilizer will cause an increase in the crop. Since each parcel of land has a different degree of marginal utility, the rent of land varies according to the returns from the additional capital applied to it.

Third, farmland commands a higher rent if it is located closer to transportation facilities than if remote [1.6-4]. The reason is that better transportation leads to lower overall costs of production since the cost of transportation to the market must be included in the selling price. Once again the selling price of like commodities in the same locale is the same for all parcels, and the advantage gained by the lower transportation costs justifies a higher rent to be paid for the land that is closer to the transportation facilities.

In summary, agricultural rent is the difference between the highest and lowest overall cost of production [1.6-5]. Capital improvements to the land, such as fences, buildings, and irrigation systems also justify a higher rent since those improvements increase the value of the land by increasing the yield (i.e., lowering overall production costs). These improvements are subject to the same limits of capital replacement; if not maintained, they will lose their effectiveness. History shows that technological improvements in planting, use of better seeds, and harvesting by machines have greatly increased the productivity of land. The result is a general reduction of selling prices because, as shown earlier, profit margins decrease with increasing production, especially in the presence of competition. With better transportation facilities, it is now possible to raise a larger variety of crops and to transport them where desired. It is only by these improvements that people in the northern cities can have tropical fruits in the winter.

The concept of marginal utility of agricultural land is not appropriate for residential or industrial land. Rent paid for land that is used for building of factories, houses, and bridges does not come from any property of the soil itself. The rent of industrial, residential, and infrastructure land arises mostly from the benefits conferred by the capital and labor employed in raising those structures. The factory has economic value because of the profits that can be obtained by the production that is carried on, but the rent for the land is paid only as a fee for the placement of the factory. (An exception arises for land used for mining; rent may be paid for it, but in fact the money paid is in the form of royalties for the minerals taken from the soil, not for the soil itself). Industrial land located close to transportation facilities, that serve to reduce the overall costs of production will generally command a higher rent than a factory located in a remote area in the same way as agricultural land. Rent paid for residential land is based on the fact that a place to live is of great utility and value, and the degree of rent paid is likewise dependent on, as the realtors inform us, "location, location, location". It is true that the overall rents derived from a high-rise apartment building is higher than that derived from single-family homes or townhouses, but that overall increase of rent is due to the capital invested in the more expensive high-rise building than the land itself.

1.7   The Principles of Labor

Wages as income and wages as costs are two sides of the same coin. Wages, being the price of labor, is revenue to the worker and are a cost to the employer. The only difference is the point of view. But even for the worker, money wages are not his true compensation. Recall that money is a medium of exchange, so the workers' money wages are merely an intermediate step to what the worker actually needs and wants in order to live. He works for the things that the money can buy, not for the money per se [1.7-1]. But since wages, viewed from the employer's standpoint, are a money cost, it is evident that the selling price of everything produced must necessarily include the cost of labor. Even in societies based on slavery or serfdom or some other form of labor coercion, the workers must be clothed, housed, and fed, which will cost something. These costs, small as they may be, are part of the cost of production.

Wages as a cost is an important element in a productive economy. The only labor that gets employed is the labor that is profitable to employ [1.7-2]. This was a problem in the U. S. when the trade unions became powerful in the northern States and took an antagonistic attitude toward management. Those State governments generally had adopted "closed shop" laws that strengthened the unions such that if a majority of workers voted for a union, all workers at that company were required to join (or at least pay dues). The union leaders then took over negotiation of wages on behalf of the workers. They could intimidate management into granting large wage increases, and the unions were aided by the government's definition of "prevailing wage" in government contracts. However, productivity did not always increase at the same rate as the additional labor costs, and the increased costs led to prices above what the public was willing to pay. Management then sought alternative locations, sometimes relocating to the southern States that did not permit "closed shops", sometimes relocating to other nations where labor was cheaper. Gradually American industries began to export the manufacturing base to other nations. But not all of it was the fault of unions. Local governments did their fair share of damage with regulation and taxes; management did their fair share with failure to re-invest in the companies. It is easy to see the result: there is chronic high unemployment in the northern U. S. States because the industrial base was chased out.

I mentioned earlier that only profitable labor is employed. I was referring then to the productive economy, which mostly excludes the government. It is true that some government employees do important things, but they are not generally devoted to production. Every rational person agrees that police and firemen are important occupations; the police serve notice that crimes will be investigated, and firemen prevent a fire in one building from spreading to the entire neighborhood. Those occupations are essential to a modern economy, but support it only indirectly. NASA promotes scientific investigations and its objectives led indirectly to the development of many new and useful products; the Department of Defense provides essential research, development, and deployment for national defense; the FDA researches and verifies claims by medical companies. Some of these are essential and some are not, but none of them are production per se. Government employment operates on a different set of rules: there is little concern about profitability or productivity; there is no penalty for inefficiency; a government can cover its financial failures by additional taxes or debt; and can paper over its operational failures by blaming the people. A great many government bureaucracies of questionable merit exist, but no one has ever successfully reduced their size or power based on their productivity.

An important distinction should be made between wage rates and total wages. Some economists erroneously assume that a reduction in wage rates is identical to a reduction in overall wages [1.7-3]. Clearly this assumption is based on the notion that a worker is willing to work only a certain number of hours per week. With the decline of the industrial base in the U. S., many people now are working more than one job and total hours worked exceeds the traditional forty hours per week. The working people do not sit back and whimper about what the government has failed to deliver; they do what is necessary for their families.

The U. S. federal government has established a "minimum wage" on the grounds that workers deserve a living wage. Every State has likewise adopted a minimum wage, some of which are higher than the federal minimum. There are at present many activists demanding that the minimum wage be increased on the grounds that the minimums now existing do not permit a reasonable standard of living. The real problem is the lack of higher-paying industrial work, not the minimum wage itself. Increasing the minimum wage does not actually solve anything. Suppose a certain State has set the minimum wage at $10 per hour. Some workers are earning the $10/hour minimum, some at $12/hour, some at $15/hour, and some at $18/hour. Why are the last three categories getting more than the minimum? They have higher wage rates than the minimum worker because their employers value their labor more highly: they may have more experience, or are more efficient, have taken on more responsibility, or are able to resolve problems. Consider what happens when the government decrees a new minimum wage of $15/hour. The minimum wage worker, formerly getting $10/hour, receives a 50% increase in his wage rate.

What about the person who was making $12/hour before the increase in the minimum wage? Her wage rate now goes to $15/hour, but in fact she has taken a pay cut because her work has just been devalued to the same level as the minimum-ability worker. The workers who were formerly making $15/hour and $18/hour would see no immediate change in their wages. But all three of the latter categories have taken a pay cut, not in money terms, but as a moral issue. The person formerly making $18/hour before received that level because her labor was valued at 80% more than the minimum capacity worker. But with the new minimum wage, she finds that her labor is valued at only 20% more than the minimum worker. Either those higher-capability workers will accept the same wage and the reduction in incentive that goes with it, or they will try to obtain more, either from the current employer or another. If the employer is smart, he will increase the wages proportionally for his best workers. He will likely ensure that they can at least obtain the same total wage even if they work fewer hours. But not so fast: on paper, the higher paid workers would now be receiving the same pay as before and have fewer hours to work. No assumption can be made that said workers will value that free time; maybe they would rather be working full-time as before, earning more, and increasing their standard of living. The increase in the minimum wage that led to a higher wage rate but the same take-home pay has not benefitted the higher-paid workers at all unless they desire the free time. They were left out of the minimum-wage debate. Their best option is to find employment elsewhere and try to obtain wages commensurate with their performance above the minimum-capacity worker.

Those dynamics indicate that increasing the minimum wage will tend, if possible, to increase everyone's wages back to the proportions that prevailed previously. But the change will not be uniform. There will in fact be many workers who must continue to accept the implicit cut in pay because they will be happy to still have a job. Why is that? An increase in labor costs means that the selling price has to be increased, which in many cases may lead to a reduction in demand for the product being produced, if demand is sensitive to price as is normally the case. If the higher price cannot be obtained, the result of the minimum wage increase may be a reduction in overall employment or a reduction in hours worked. Naturally, the employer will try to keep his best workers, and will increase their wages if he can retain them. At the same time, he is likely to release his lowest-performing workers. The lowest capacity worker, who had his hourly wages increased the most by the new minimum rate, is likely to suffer the most by a reduction in hours worked, contrary to the intention of the government that decreed the increase. A worker making $10/hour at 40 hours takes home more than 25 hours worked at $15/hour; he is worse off at the higher wage rate. It is important to remember that a workers' total wage is what matters, not the wage rate.

If the prices of necessary items begin to increase, it is said that the "cost of living" is increasing. Sometimes these increases are due to natural disasters that affect crops, sometimes due to other natural causes. Sometimes a permanent increase in costs occurs because of some new difficulty somewhere in the production process, or a new grant of monopoly. Mostly they are due to depreciation of the value of the money, which will be considered in detail in Chapter 2. A depreciating money unit will cause wages to rise to accommodate the average price increase, although there will be a time delay. The poor are injured the most, since they have to pay the higher prices until wages catch up. The poor would benefit the most if the average price level were to fall because wages would fall, but with the same time delay. There would be a period in which prices were falling, but wages were at their previous level. In modern societies, wages are not permitted to fall, partly due to contracts or union action, but partly due to the fear of a loss of "purchasing power".

There is the other side of the coin. Modern economies go through cycles, a fast expansion followed by a recession. When producers are pressed for customers during a recession, they will usually lower prices. But as seen above, lowering prices reduces profitability unless wages can also fall. The classical economists pointed out that during a recession, prices and wages both tend to fall, but prices tend to fall faster. That means that the real wage may actually increase slightly, at least for those still employed. But what if wages cannot fall, due to contracts or minimum wage laws? It means that the producer is at a disadvantage: he can't lower his primary costs (wages, the price of labor), and cannot raise his prices (since he still must generate some revenue). If the economy does not recover, the producers that cannot restore their profitability will either get out of business or change to some other area. What happens if the producers of necessities, especially food products and basic materials, cannot become profitable? That is when a power-grabbing "progressive" government will step in to "save the industry" and preserve employment. To do so, the government may propose to take over production and finance it with government spending [1.7-4]. It may also try to stabilize employment by implementing wage fixing, price fixing, and additional taxes on businesses. Along with it comes the prioritization of politics over economics along with the usual government inefficiencies. When private firms cannot be profitable, then governments are tempted to adopt fascist or communist tactics: either retaining private enterprise on paper but regulating as if government owned, or government owned directly. History shows that both lead to a general decline in economic output and the standard of living.

In lesser developed economies, it may be said that there is a sharp dividing line between "labor" and "capitalist". A person who works for wages and spends all he earns to live is rightly classified as "labor only". Likewise, a person who can live purely on income from investments may be said to be purely "capitalist". But the vast majority of people in modern societies are both laborers and capitalists. Most workers can earn more than they spend, and the difference can be invested in other productive enterprises through the purchase of securities or bonds. So, if you are a welder and you have a 401k that invests in the stock market, or if you are a participant in a pension plan that invests, or if you deposit the money in a bank and the bank subsequently invests it, the "social" economists agree that you are a greedy capitalist oppressor. Investing money from the portion of income that is not spent and not hoarded makes you a capitalist, whether you like the term or not. A second reason why most people are capitalist and labor combined is that very few people consume everything they produce, especially those who run a small business; most of what they produce is sold to others. Most people are part and parcel of an economy that is based on the use of capital to improve production, and therefore cannot be considered pure laborers. The true economic problem is that even in modern societies there are always some who cannot afford to participate in the investment opportunities because they must spend everything they earn just to get by. The problem is made worse if they do not have access to a pension plan to cover them in old age.

The social problem regarding labor is that many people in modern societies have been adequately trained to consume, but not adequately trained to work. Professional economists would say that "the propensity to consume exceeds the propensity to work". It is easy to consume until the bill comes due. It is hard to work to pay the bills. History shows that work is the foundation not only of healthy economies, but also healthy societies. People willing to work are the ones who are willing to do for themselves and their families, and not become dependent on handouts or the government. That independence breeds confidence in the future. Constant work means that married couples and even single parents can provide for their families, and preserve the family structure. Working people are less likely to fall into the trap of drug addiction or crime, since they are neither depressed enough to seek escape or desperate enough to break the law. The availability of work is the foundation of a strong society, and when work becomes scarce, the society begins to degenerate, both economically and morally. Historically the most prosperous and free societies are built and maintained by a population with a work ethic, rejecting the latest popular high-sounding theories, such as socialism; as it says in Proverbs 12:11:

> "He who works his land will have abundant food, but he who chases fantasies lacks judgment."

"Full employment", defined as a condition in which everyone who can work is working, is not the natural state in a free society [1.7-5]. Some are voluntarily unemployed because they have accumulated enough wealth that they do not have to work. There are many reasons for involuntary unemployment: some have skills that are obsolete; some are in the midst of transitioning between jobs; and some have health problems which preclude work. Involuntary unemployment frequently occurs as noted above because labor has been priced too high to be attractive to employers. Such a condition may occur either by the workers' own demands or by government regulation. Wage rates that are high enough to preclude a profit only leads to unemployment [1.7-6]. Last, many may be unemployed even though able because the economy has entered in to a recession or depression. A later section will show that periodic recessions are a normal part of modern economies a part of the "business cycle". For now, it is important to remember that true "full employment" can exist only in a non-free command economy, in which all labor is compensated according to the bare minimum necessary. This bare minimum is calculated as the smallest amount that will keep the creaky inefficient economy going well enough to maintain the ruling class in power, and just large enough to prevent a general revolt.

Entrepreneurs are sometimes said to be the ones who step up and begin production to satisfy a demand. That is not exactly true. The actual role of the entrepreneur is to achieve profitability for himself and his investors. Satisfaction of some demand may be the means to obtain the profit, but satisfying demand per se is not his principal motivation [1.7-7]. Surely you did not establish Granny's Sublime Tarts to save the world or because you thought they would improve everyone's life. You did it to make a living selling a product at a profit, not for the "good of mankind". It is this profit motivation that spurs investment for production, and since wages of labor, (being the price of labor) is a cost, the wages of labor play an important part in assessing the viability of a venture. The entrepreneur must be able to accurately calculate both the expected revenues from selling and the costs of production in the course of evaluating profitability. He can do so only if the money unit has a reasonably stable value, since he has to evaluate both labor and materials. The assessment of viability of a new venture is made easier by accurate estimates, and accurate estimates are made easier with stable money values.

Value is not conferred on a product simply due to the amount of labor expended on it. Value is in the eyes of the buyer, and once again it comes back to her valuation of money vs. her valuation of the product [1.7-8]. The selling price cannot be assigned simply by the amount of labor expended: 100 hours expended making a hand-made fur hat will be sold based on a comparison that the buyer makes as against other hats, not 100 times the prevailing wage. In other words, the price at which it is actually sold is a result of supply and demand for that category of hat. This is one of the fallacies of Marx's theory, namely, that all labor is of equal value. People are of equal value, not their labor. It is easy to see the modern "progressive" symptom of this error: the labor of a political hack sitting in his Mama's basement in his pajamas typing Marxist slogans on social media is more highly valued than a cancer researcher.

1.8 The Principles of Credit

If you enter a bank or institution to obtain a business loan, you are asking for credit. Credit is normally extended by lending of money and it will be described that way here, but capital (goods used for production directly) can also be lent and is also a credit transaction. Credit is the transfer of money or capital goods that is provided to you in return for a promise on your part to repay. It is a present good (the existing money or capital) that is lent for a time in return for a promise to return a future good (money or capital). A credit transaction depends on the good faith of both parties [1.8-1]. On the lender's part, he is providing the borrower with money that will be readily accepted by those that the borrower wishes to buy from. The lender must have confidence that the borrower will use the money to create value, control costs, and generate a profit in order to repay. The lender therefore requires confidence in the prospects for the borrower's economic success. Good faith on the borrower's part is their intent to repay the money at some future date. The borrower must also have confidence that the lender's money will be widely accepted. Credit is an essential part of starting up a new business. Recall the example above in which $40,000 was borrowed to start up Granny's Sublime Tarts. Having the idea to make Granny's Tarts commercially is obviously not the same as having the money to do it. The owners of the money trusted the lending institution to risk it by lending it to you; the lending institution provides it you based on your promise and obligation to repay it on time. Credit is also an important part of establishing new farms, and in settling unused land, since capital is scarce and money must be borrowed to obtain it [1.8-2].

Credit works best when the value of the money unit that was loaned remains stable for the life of the loan. After all, the lender has a reasonable expectation, since he has deferred the use of the money for other purposes, to receive money back equal in value to what he lent. To illustrate, suppose you decided to lend your car to Uncle Vito for a week. Your expectation should be that Uncle Vito will return the car in good condition, complete with a fresh oil change and a full tank of gas. You should not be content to have it returned with bloodstains on the seat and the smell of death emanating from the trunk; that would lower the value of the car. It is exactly the same with money. The money returned should ideally have the same value as what was lent. To make that happen, and thus to promote confidence in the economy in general, one contributing factor at the national level is for the money unit to be uniform throughout the nation. Part 2 of the book will demonstrate how such a lack of uniformity was sometimes a problem in the U. S. until the mid-1800's.

The medieval Catholic Church prohibited the payment of interest on loans, supposedly to restrain the greed of the rich. Of course, there were just as many ways then as there are now to get around such a prohibition. The important point is that there are two reasons why the charging of interest is perfectly legitimate. First, money lent is money risked, and the lender deserves some compensation for taking the risk. Secondly, money in the lender's hand is more valuable to him than money later; he therefore deserves some compensation for holding off on his natural inclination to use the money for consumption. Or as the professional economists put it [1.8-3], "present goods are valued more highly than future goods". The money in hand, which the lender volunteers to lend out, came from his savings. The best credit system is one in which the money to be lent comes from voluntary savings. Unfortunately, modern credit is not generally based on the amount available from savings, and this is one of our main economic problems. The effects will be described more fully in section 1.9.

The loan to start Granny's Tarts is a commercial loan; the lender has concluded that you are a good commercial risk. Commercial loans are an advance of money or capital to finance a business venture during the time it takes to get the business up and running. Commercial loans normally fall into four categories [1.8-4]. First are long-term loans for large scale equipment, land, or buildings that will be in use for many years. These are repaid by the future earnings generated by those capital assets. The second type is long-term permanent working capital, usually tools and equipment that must be maintained or replaced in the course of production, or upgrades to the facilities. This type is also repaid out of earnings, whether current or future as the case may be. The third type is short-term working capital, normally used to pay wages and rent until production begins, or to pay those expenses during a reconfiguration of a factory, also repaid by current or future earnings. Fourth are the short-term "self-liquidating" working capital loans. In this case the money is lent not against some future profit, but against an existing or soon-to-be existing tangible asset. The most common examples are crops to be harvested and sold at some known time, or the inventory of a merchant that deals mostly in seasonal merchandise such as wedding dresses, Easter candy, Christmas trees, and summer tourist services.

Extension of credit is not limited to the banking system [1.8-5]. Businesses also lend credit directly. For example, automobile companies routinely lend credit to car buyers, and many companies exist that will lend money on certain mortgages or major appliances. These types of loans are called consumer credit. They require the same degree of confidence in the borrower's willingness and intent to repay, but the loan is secured by the property in question, and is subject to repossession or foreclosure if not repaid. The difference between a commercial loan and a consumer loan is that ability to repay comes about in different ways: for a commercial venture like the bakery, it is the lenders' confidence that you will make a profit; in the consumer credit case, it is the lenders' confidence that the borrowers' employment will provide sufficient wages such that repayment can be made.

There are many independent businesses that will install flooring, a roof, or windows in a home without requiring immediate payment. These are examples of "unsecured personal credit", since the lender is relying on the ability of the borrower to repay, even though the lender cannot typically claim the roof or windows as security; nor can he repossess them in the event of a failure to repay. The most the lender can do is put a lien against the house, but the prospect of collecting is small since such a lien cannot be enforced until the property is sold. The same is true of a purely personal loan and the use of credit cards for an unspecified purpose: the lender is relying solely on the borrower's income and willingness to repay. The lender does so based on his knowledge of the borrowers' reliability, i.e., the "credit score".

The principles of credit are the same in commercial, consumer, and personal cases. Mutual trust and confidence are necessary on both sides in order for a successful transfer of a present good for the promise of a future good via repayment.

The use of credit has historically demonstrated three important characteristics that advanced the growth of wealth. First, the available amount of money does more work because it can be used more times. Without credit, all sales must be made immediately in cash [1.8-6]; with credit, sales can be made and capital transferred based on confidence and good faith of both parties. Secondly, those who have a surplus of money do not keep it idle but lend it out; this enhances economic growth because it makes money more efficient [1.8-7]. Credit permits many transactions to be performed with a smaller amount of money, which is accomplished by balancing accounts within the banking system. Third, the use of credit accommodates fluctuations in the demand for capital. Fourth, an efficient credit system allows faster economic growth than would otherwise occur, even with the same amount of total money. It stimulates the creation of wealth, but at the same time, it also is an indirect cause of trade cycles as will be discussed in section 1.9.

Nothing is free, including credit. Since present goods are valued more highly than future, the interest rate is therefore related to the relative valuation of present vs. future goods. Reward for the risk on the part of the lender is reflected in the interest rate. The interest rate is the price of credit [1.8-8]; and in the case of commercial loans, it is actually the price of acquiring capital [1.8-9], since that is the purpose of most commercial loans. Nominal interest rates are affected by three factors. First, interest rates are high where there is a small amount of capital to be had, and low where capital is plentiful [1.8-10]. The interest rate is paid for the use of the capital that the money acquires, not on the money per se. Secondly, rates are determined by the rate of return on the capital acquired. This rate of return is the margin between the cost of production and the selling price of the products, in other words, profitability affects the amount of interest that can be paid [1.8-11]. As a simple example, a high interest rate can be tolerated if the purpose of the loan is to secure a few soft ice cream machines or a tie-dyeing machine that can be utilized immediately to generate revenue and profit. But if the loan is to be used to build a factory that produces the ice cream machines, the time delay between borrowing and generation of profit through the sale of the machines is much longer, and the interest rate tolerance may be low. The "natural rate" of profit thus indirectly determines the "natural rate of interest", which is to say, the rate at which borrowers will believe it is worth their while to borrow and lenders believe it is worth the risk. In practice, the "natural rate" has been traditionally defined as the rate on long term first-class loans [1.8-12]. Third, the interest rate is affected by the source of the money to be lent. The "normal rate of interest" based on the normal rate of profit defined above may continue for long periods if the supply of credit comes from the supply of savings [1.8-13]. But interest rates may be low if the source of the money is based on an expansion of the money supply.

Several other secondary factors partly determine interest rates [1.8-14]. First are the particular aspects of the loan: a) reliability of the borrower; b) duration of the loan; c) the relative size of the loan; and d) the general demand for credit. Reliability of the borrower is self-evident. People and businesses have poor credit reputations if they do not pay their bills on time. They end up being charged a higher interest rate due purely to the perceived risk and difficulty to be experienced by the lender in obtaining repayment. That additional cost and risk is built into the interest rate as compensation for the lenders' expected costs of administering the loan; it is an assessment by the lender as to the safety of the loan. Generally a long term loan commands a higher interest rate because of the ambiguity of future events, and the willingness of the lender to wait for a return. The longer he has to wait, the more risk he incurs in making the loan and that risk justifies a higher interest rate as compensation. Loans for large amounts of money normally will command a higher interest rate simply due to the size of the overall risk.

Demand for credit causes variations in interest rates in a variety of ways. If the opportunities for investment are low, or perceived to be low, the demand for capital is low and therefore the demand for credit is low. The interest rate would then also be low, since supply of available credit may outstrip the demand. If a commercial loan is to be used for acquiring capital equipment to manufacture durable items such as cars or washing machines, the demand for credit is related directly to the perceived demand for those durable items. Last, the interest rate may reflect the general economic conditions. If profitability is low, or expected to become lower due to a shortage of materials or high taxation, demand for credit and the interest rate worth paying will both be low.

How does the rate of interest affect costs of production? Consider the small-scale case of Granny's Tarts. The example assumed a loan of $40,000 at 6% interest for two years, and that repayment contributed to the cost of production as shown in Column 11 of Figure 1.3-1. Consider now Figure 1.8-1, which compares that per-unit cost using other assumptions about the term of the loan and the interest rate. Column 2 of Figure 1.8-1 is the same as Column 11 of Figure 1.3-1 for easy reference. It is easy to see that the interest rate has a minor effect on the per-unit cost of production. If 500 units per day are produced, the per-unit cost from borrowing the $40,000 at 6% for two years was $0.12 as shown in column 2. If the term of the loan was extended to 5 years at 9%, the per-unit cost of the loan when producing 500 units per day per column 6 is $0.06, which amounts to a reduction of $0.06 per unit. Referring back to Figure 1.3-1, the total per-unit production cost of 500 tarts with the loan at 6% for two years was $1.62; at 9% over 5 years, would be $1.56 (i.e., the reduction of 6 cents). In the grand scheme of things, this is not a big deal, and there are probably greater errors in the other estimates that have more important consequences than any difference in the cost of money.

Chapter 1: Basic Economic Concepts | 45

		Two Year Term			Five Year Term			Ten Year Term		
		1	2	3	4	5	6	7	8	9
Loan	Interest Rate	3%	6%	9%	3%	6%	9%	3%	6%	9%
	Per Month	1719.25	1772.83	1827.39	718.75	773.32	830.34	386.25	444.09	506.71
	Per Day	57.31	59.09	60.91	23.96	25.78	27.68	12.88	14.80	16.89
Quantity Per Day	100	0.57	0.59	0.61	0.24	0.26	0.28	0.13	0.15	0.17
	200	0.29	0.30	0.30	0.12	0.13	0.14	0.06	0.07	0.08
	300	0.19	0.20	0.20	0.08	0.09	0.09	0.04	0.05	0.06
	400	0.14	0.15	0.15	0.06	0.06	0.07	0.03	0.04	0.04
	500	0.11	0.12	0.12	0.05	0.05	0.06	0.03	0.03	0.03
	600	0.10	0.10	0.10	0.04	0.04	0.05	0.02	0.02	0.03
	700	0.08	0.08	0.09	0.03	0.04	0.04	0.02	0.02	0.02
	800	0.07	0.07	0.08	0.03	0.03	0.03	0.02	0.02	0.02
	900	0.06	0.07	0.07	0.03	0.03	0.03	0.01	0.02	0.02
	1000	0.06	0.06	0.06	0.02	0.03	0.03	0.01	0.01	0.02

Figure 1.8-1: Cost of Money as Part of Cost of Production of Granny's Tarts ($)

If the source of credit is the supply of voluntary savings, then credit is actually a transfer of labor: it is the accumulated labor of the past that is now in the form of money or capital goods that is provided to the borrower in return for a promise to repay. It results in the "normal rate of interest" as described above.

But an artificial expansion of expansion of the money supply by a bank or government can cause the interest rates to be lower (since the expansion of the money supply makes money cheaper and gives the illusion of greater savings). A bank or government that creates money in excess of the supply of savings creates a distortion in the market, since the interest rate is no longer tied to natural market forces. In other words, it appears that money is more plentiful, thus gives the appearance that less risk is incurred by lending it. An artificial expansion may be desirable from the government viewpoint since it permits the government to borrow at low rates and also induces greater borrowing to stimulate the economy. Governments always desire low interest rates when they run deficits that must be covered by borrowing, as low interest rates exact a lower toll on the overall debt and interest payments. However, the unintended consequence is nearly always an intensification of the business cycle; instead of relatively mild recessions and expansions, it may lead to booms and depressions. A secondary consequence of an artificial expansion of credit is normally accompanied by depreciating the value of the money unit. It does so by creating an excess of money above what is needed by the public. The initial expansion of money is accompanied by low interest rates. But when the effect of depreciated money comes into view, interest rates must rise because the lender must be compensated for the fact that the money he receives back has less value than the money he lent. The higher interest rate, necessary due to the depreciating value of the money unit is an important instability in the credit system that leads to more drastic booms and busts [1.8-15]. The process by which this occurs is discussed in section 1.9.

Interest as the fee for the use of money is a sufficient justification from the lenders' standpoint. Considered from the borrowers standpoint, it is not "free money paid to exploiters" as the collectivists would have you believe. In fact, from the borrowers' standpoint, paying interest is an insurance premium against risk. Consider your foray into Granny's Tarts: would it be higher risk or lower risk for you to completely capitalize the business at start-up (assuming you had sufficient savings)? Obviously it would be higher risk: if the business fails, you would lose all of your investment. On the other hand, putting up some of the money up front, borrowing the rest, and paying interest on the loan indirectly reduces your risk: if the business fails, the other investors take part of the loss. So, paying interest is an insurance against risk, same as paying life and health insurance premiums.

1.9 Economic Expansions and Contractions

This section presents a summary of the economic conditions and actions that leads to unwarranted expansions of the economy followed by depressions. Such wide variations in economic activity are not due to normal business fluctuations. Normal fluctuations occur for a variety of reasons: people's tastes change, fads come and go, intermittent crop failures, labor strikes in a major industry, technological advances causing disruptions in certain industries, and many others. These types of business cycles are a normal feature of an economic system based on free private enterprise. Military veterans are sometimes warned when discharged back to civilian life into a free economy: "be careful out there, no one is in charge". In a free economic system, the public is in charge; the public indirectly sets priorities based on its whims and desires, and its' optimism or pessimism (some of which are completely arbitrary). Contrast that system with a command economy, in which there is always "someone in charge" who sets policies that are subsequently forced upon the general public. Command economies try to determine what should be produced and then control production from the top down. A free economy functions from the bottom up: producers respond to wants and desires by the public (or what they believe are the wants and desires). The leaders of a command economy never make a mistake (just ask them). Producers in a free economy make plenty of mistakes, but their freedom allows them to make the changes necessary to successfully provide what the public demands while earning adequate compensation for doing so.

An economic depression is characterized by a large disconnect between supply and demand: it appears that demand is far less than supply. It clearly is not conforming to Say's Law [1.9-1], commonly known as the Law of the Market. The economist Jean-Baptiste Say in 1803 argued that the income received by all workers, including the entrepreneurs, those who held landed estates, and middlemen was used to buy all the products that were produced; in other words, production would indirectly create its own demand because everyone has to eat, live somewhere, send their children to school, etc. The basic idea is that everything finds a market. This law is true if is recognized that losses do occur because some things produced are not wanted or are priced too high. In general it is fairly descriptive of an economy under normal circumstances [1.9-2], but not during a depression. The problem is not that Say was incorrect, but that he did not account for the large disturbances that can occur in modern banking and monetary systems. One thing is certain: if the economy finds itself in a state of depression where Say's Law is not operating, the solution is not to promote depreciation of the money, as is often claimed by Keynesian economists. Depreciation of the money is often the cause of depressions, not their cure.

One of the great proven fallacies of John Maynard Keynes' [1.9-3] theory is known as "maintaining purchasing power". He claimed, as a general rule, that the way to recover from a recession (regardless of cause) and even to avoid recessions was to improve the purchasing power of individuals by creating money. For normal business cycles, the approach is sometimes correct, but it does not work when the economy has slowed down due to a cost problem within the production process. The cost problem is usually caused by wages that are too high relative to productivity. The fallacy lies in the claim that increasing wage rates to maintain "purchasing power" will stimulate demand [1.9-4]. It is accomplished by expanding the money supply. Expanding the money supply sounds good on paper since people now have more money to spend. But it contains the seed of its own destruction because the additional money injected into the economy causes the value of money in general to decline; thus wages must increased to compensate, which only makes the original problem worse. Some people will come out ahead in the depreciation scheme, but most working people will lose. Only those who can remain employed benefit, not the public in general.

If a depression is defined as a condition in which supply is greater than demand, what is the cause? It is the growth of production that expands capacity assuming a demand magnitude that does not actually exist. Keep in mind that expansion of production in large industries cannot happen overnight because as shown in section 1.5, a great many intermediate steps must be taken and all those intermediate steps are paid for with money. For example, an expansion of production of Granny's Tarts within moderate limits could be done fairly easily by adding a few more workers and expanding the work space. But if the production of those tarts were to go nationwide, clearly considerable time and investment and intermediate steps would be required to do so. You would have to find all the commercial bakeries with capacity, they would have to be close enough to the retail stores keep them fresh, the transportation system has to be coordinated and possibly customized, formal contracts have to be executed, and advertising must be done on a larger scale. The packaging would have to be adapted for commercial sale to avoid the "Monster Cookies" fiasco. The tarts would have to be tested for calories and carbohydrates to establish their nutritional value, and all the ingredients would have to be listed along with warnings about peanut content.

That may be a problem: Grandma's recipes were about enjoyment, not nutrition. All that takes time and money, most of which has to be borrowed on credit. Your expansion of Granny's Tarts would of course be based on expectations of nationwide demand. But remember that demand is a "guesstimate"; it is actually a prospective, not certain demand. Expansion of larger industries making complex items involving more intermediate production steps and greater amounts of money is also based on prospective demand. An economy-wide depression would not occur if Granny's Tarts failed to sell nationwide (although you might be depressed), and likewise a nationwide failure of a handful of items would not cause a general depression. A general depression results from supply exceeding demand in many industries, including all their intermediate steps. That can occur if production has been expanded throughout beyond what would be justified by the true existing demand.

The disproportion between supply and demand that occurs in a depression is directly observable, but does not explain the cause or the remedy. Isaac Newton developed a formula for the force of gravity between two objects in terms of the product of the two masses and a numerical "gravitational constant" divided by the square of the mean distance. His formula gives the correct observable (the force), but does not explain how gravitation actually comes about. (Your bathroom scale indicates the gravitational force between your keister and the earth, which is called "weight".) One of Hayek's great insights [1.9-5] is that economic theory is plagued by the same problem as Newton's gravity formula, namely that an assessment of poor economic conditions based on observations does not explain the cause. The great number of transactions throughout the production process consists of too many moving parts for a general theory of economy-wide expansions and contractions to explain. All the observations compiled together are insufficient to explain why the economy behaves as it does in any particular instance. Even if such a theory did exist, a model thereof it would be too complicated to use because it would require enormous amounts of accurate data as inputs. The best that can be hoped for is to state the general behavior of free economies to show some general trends and their likely consequences. The theories of Hayek [1.9-6] and Ludwig von Mises [1.9-7] appear to offer the best self-contained explanations; these involve the behavior of interest rates and credit underlying a large-scale free economy.

It is necessary to digress here and explain the general historical trend of economic progress before discussing the behavior of business cycles. The startup of Granny's Tarts required procurement of a large number of various items. It is evident that the outlay for a single bakery is small compared to the total produced among those items. For example, if the display cases are made of steel and plastic, the amount necessary for the bakery is small compared to the total production of steel and plastic. Those two commodities are intermediate goods as far as the bakery is concerned, since they are not the end product to be sold to your customers. They are only conveniences necessary to help you make the sale. If we were to trace backwards the history of the steel you need, we would have the following chain of events. The first step prior to delivery to you is a sheet of steel fastened to the plastic part of the case along with the other sections. Prior to that a section of rolled steel was cut and trimmed to the proper size, and coated with a rust inhibitor. Prior to that, the sheet steel was rolled to the correct thickness. Prior to that, the large steel ingots were produced; prior to that, the raw materials were mined and transported to manufacture the steel ingots. All of these processes are done on a massive scale, since the overall quantity of steel produced is used to satisfy the requirements of many industries. The same is true of the plastic, glass, floor tiles, paint, the pipes in the refrigeration units and the Freon that makes them work, all the way down to the connectors on the wires that complete the power connections. These are all intermediate capital goods because they are not purchased by end consumers; they are purchased and used as capital items by producers like you. All these end products are manufactured in a series of intermediate steps (which the economists call "roundabout production"). The fact that all of these are done on a large scale allows them to be done more cheaply than a small production. But it also means there is a great deal of economic inertia if the levels of production are to be increased; that inertia is in the form of a time delay between the start of an expansion and the point at which the new facilities are producing for a profit. The thing to notice here is that all the intermediate steps are continuously in progress, and the product of each step is paid for by the business or person who uses it. For example, the company that manufactures the display cases buys the sheet steel in specific lengths with a specific coating on it; different than the characteristics of steel supplied to automobile manufacturers. It is obvious then that a great deal more money changes hands continuously in the course of producing the intermediate capital items (i.e., producers' goods) than is spent on end consumer products. It is a simple consequence of the fact that the production of capital items necessarily must occur on a larger scale than the consumer items it supports [1.9-8]. Most of those intermediate steps represent the production of producers' goods.

How then is production capacity increased over time? It is done gradually as the demand for consumers' goods prompts the production of capital goods necessary to satisfy the end consumer. Clearly all those intermediate steps do not appear by magic; they are the result of investments. There are two sources of investment. The first source is savings, which is the portion of income not consumed or hoarded, as described previously. A bank or other lending institution collects the savings of many people and issues a loan to the borrowers in order to start the building of the necessary capital projects. If the rate of savings is constant, the economy will simply adapt to the new conditions afforded by the expansion of production facilities. As explained in sections 1.3 and 1.5, more will be produced, and in the long run, producers' profits and selling prices will slowly decrease, partly due to increased efficiency and partly due to competition. The second source is an increase of money available to producers through the banking system that is not based on savings, which is to say, it is money created on the bank's credit. If the expansion of production is financed by credit money, there is always a risk that depreciation of the money unit will occur, which will raise both wages and prices, but even worse, may trigger a decline in overall production because of the hidden decline of profitability in the intermediate stages in the production of capital items. Stable progress can occur only if end consumption increases at about the same rate as production, and if the increase in production is financed by voluntary savings [1.9-9]. If the rate of increase in consumption rises above the rate of increase of production, and production is financed by credit money, there will be a temporary illusion of prosperity followed by a recession or depression.

The "business cycle" (the irregular fluctuations in economic activity) is a normal feature of all economies in which money is used as a common medium, especially in monetary systems based on credit money. A great deal of statistical research has been conducted in studying fluctuations, but unfortunately has not produced much useful guidance. The reason is that there are so many parallel activities in play in an advanced economy that the volume of statistics necessary to characterize the entire economy becomes impractical. Statistics can show that business cycles have occurred or are in progress, but do not explain why. Hayek has pointed out that statistical research can partly verify a theory but not establish one [1.9-10]. A monetary system that includes provision for an elastic currency founded on bank credit tends to permit more rapid expansions than a system in which productive expansion is based only on credit supplied by voluntary savings. If the rapid expansion is desired, then the bad part comes with it, namely fairly deep recessions that serve to correct the distortion of supply and demand that inevitably results. No matter what banking system is used, and no matter how well regulated, it is unlikely that business fluctuations can be eliminated [1.9-11]. The best that can be hoped for is that the banking system suppresses the rate of expansion in order to ensure that the recession is not too severe.

Haberler [1.9-12] makes a distinction between two types of recessions and depressions. One he calls the "secondary or accidental"; these are caused by war, crop failures, poor judgment on the part of bankers, bankruptcies caused by technological changes, and other events not related to the basic behavior of an advanced economy. These "secondary" ones occur intermittently and sometimes many years pass without any occurring at all. They are usually characterized as a financial panic, in which the stream of payments due comes into question or when the public loses faith in the stability of the banking system, whether real or imagined. Generally those occur because the banking system experiences a disruption from one of the above-stated causes. On the other hand he describes as "primary and fundamental" those depressions that are a result of an actual general decline in production. Overall production in an advanced economy tends to experience oscillations around an average rate of increase, not a continuous linear growth. These are natural variations in economic activity regardless of the monetary system, but the oscillations can become dangerously large if the monetary system is misused. The underlying cause of the large downward industrial trend is hidden in the expansion that preceded it.

A survey of the observables of expansions and contractions will provide common ground for explaining the underlying causes thereof. The following behavior is generally observed during an economic expansion: a) an increase in the prices of both production goods and end-use goods; and b) an increase in the overall number of transactions which, combined with the increase in prices, results in an increase in the volume of payments. A general increase in prices, aside from increases that would occur due to supply and demand, can occur only if there is more money in the economy. If the money within the economy is based solely on gold, silver, or some other metal, then the increase in money would have to be due to an increase in the amount of physical metal, either by discovery of new mines or by importation. If the money in the economy is based on the printing of notes issued by banks, the increase in money is caused by more active printing presses. If the money used is primarily checks drawn against bank deposits, then the increase in money is caused by an expansion of deposits. These last two are in turn caused by an expansion of credit granted by banks to their customers. Since the money supply is thus expanded, money is more common (i.e., in greater supply), and the interest rate, being the fee paid for the use of the money, is lower. Regardless of the exact mechanism of money expansion, the result is an increase in overall production because there is a greater capacity to finance it. Not only is more money available, it is cheaper to borrow.

Likewise an economic downturn has several direct observables: a) a decrease in prices or at least a slowdown in the rate of price increases; b) a decrease or at least a decrease in the rate of increase of production; c) a decrease or at least a reduction in the rate of increase in the total volume of transactions. If total production and total transactions are decreasing, the economy is in a depression. If the rate of increase of production and the rate of increase in transactions is slowing, then the economy is in a recession.

The price observables are somewhat ambiguous. A general decline in prices indicates one of three things: a) more efficient production plus competition has forced profits and prices lower; b) overproduction has forced producers to cut prices in order to generate some revenue, even at a loss; or c) the value of the money unit is increasing (i.e., becoming more valuable). The first is actually the desired outcome; the second is the characteristic of an initial over-expansion of the money supply followed by declining profits in capital industries. The third is a consequence of an outright reduction in the money supply.

The fact that prices are falling does not necessarily mean that businesses are incurring outright losses [1.9-13]. Businesses can be profitable in the face of falling selling prices if their costs are falling faster. Suppose a recession occurs and you find you have to reduce prices on Granny's Tarts in order to continue to generate revenue. If the landlord is having trouble keeping his properties rented, he may cut you a deal to keep you there, a cost reduction for you. If the prices of your ingredients decline, your costs decline. You can afford to reduce selling prices a little if these fall. The most important factor is still wages; if the wage rate cannot fall and you have to cut your selling prices, there is no choice but to reduce the amount of labor you employ. You, as the entrepreneur, will have to take up the slack to maintain production.

Initially an expansion of bank credit causes an expansion of production. That is not to say that unlimited expansion of bank credit or money would result in unlimited production and prosperity. A monetary expansion above what is justified by demand contains the seeds of its own destruction, namely: a) the depreciation of the money unit (which increases prices); b) a distortion of the interest rate that causes a change in the structure of the stages of production, and c) a problem with profitability within the stages of the production of capital goods. Referring back to Figure 1.8-1, it was evident that the interest rate was a fairly small factor in the cost of production for Granny's Tarts. The other part of low interest rates is that it is always accompanied by an increase in the money supply. The increase in the money supply above what is required by demand causes the value of the money unit to depreciate (referred to as 'inflation'), which causes prices to rise. Wages are the price of labor; if the monetary expansion causes prices to rise, then wages must rise also. As noted earlier, the greatest per-unit cost components for Granny's Tarts are labor and ingredients at production levels exceeding 600 per day. If the price of labor increases, so too does the cost of production. If the customers are willing to pay more, you could raise your prices. But if labor costs get too high, the cost of production will lie above what the consumers are willing to pay for the tarts (see Figure 1.3-3). Now the tarts are unprofitable, and a decision must be made to end production, reduce production, or find new ways to eliminate labor costs. If there is a general downturn in the economy, most of the businesses throughout the economy will experience the same pressure and will tend to increase unemployment. Keep in mind also, in the presence of monetary inflation, the demand curve for the tarts cannot be assumed to remain as it was before: because the prices of all products are going up, the tarts may come to be regarded as an unaffordable luxury, and you may see demand fall off precipitously. Even if demand remains adequate, the effects of the inflation are an increase in your selling price along with the price of everything else. The bad news here, if we are interested in the overall state of the economy, is that an unhealthy economy poised for depression does not always exhibit an increase of prices beforehand. Economists have traditionally only examined the increase in prices as a metric to determine if the economy is stable, but that alone is a poor indicator of the risk to prosperity.

Effects of interest rates upon costs for a small retail establishment are simple enough, and it is easy to see that an industry dominated by labor costs would end up having to raise retail prices accordingly if monetary depreciation persists. The reason that an examination of retail prices is not adequate to predict overall economic health and stability is that the change in interest rates affects the profitability of capital industries, which is not indicated directly by retail prices. Capital industries are those in which the costs and thus the profitability is affected by land, equipment, research and development, tooling, and creation of large fixed capital projects, which is very different situation from retail. Suppose you decided to end production of Granny's Tarts, and switch production to cupcakes or pies or broccoli-flavored ice cream. You would simply re-use the existing equipment to produce those products and try to make the same profit as before. Those capital goods have the flexibility to make other consumer goods. What would happen if instead you decided to liquidate the bakery business altogether? All the durable equipment (refrigerators, freezers, display cases, furniture) could all be sold off and re-used in some other business, and the proceeds could be used to partly repay the borrowed sum. But capital industries that produce capital goods are generally devoted to one purpose; a rolling mill cannot easily be adapted to any other purpose, nor can facilities for casting glass or plastic, or those devoted to the production of raw steel or plastic or refining of petroleum upon which plastic is based. Should those become unprofitable, they amount to uncompensated losses; they are abandoned or sold off for scrap.

Hayek, building on the work of von Mises and Wicksell, gave a cryptic description of the underlying cause of unhealthy economies not indicated by a rise in the general price level [1.9-14]. He pointed out that if an economy is expanding because new money is being injected into the economy, the interest rate that would maintain price stability is less than the interest rate that would prevail if the amount of money available for loans came only from public savings; and so, although prices may be stable, the lower interest rates may be camouflaging trends that will disturb the economic equilibrium.

The equilibrium position is a condition in which the economy is stable with production approximating demand, more or less, and the rate of personal voluntary savings vs. consumption is the same over the long term, more or less. In other words, under equilibrium conditions a certain amount of income is saved and is subsequently lent out to entrepreneurs at the "normal rate of interest" defined above. That particular interest rate reflects the supply of money available for lending (via savings) and the demand for loans, which is as seen above, actually the demand for capital that the money can procure. The application of Hayek's observation is that when an economy is expanding because of an expansion of the money supply, the interest rate is lower than the normal case; the general price level may remain stable, but this situation may initiate a hidden movement of declining profitability (in capital industries) that disturbs the equilibrium.

There are two different monetary causes by which production may be expanding. The first case is an increase in the rate of voluntary savings [1.9-15]. When that happens, more money is obviously available for investment, and as a result, supply and demand being what it is, there is a greater demand for loans for capital projects, and the rate of interest is lower than it was at the old savings rate. Because the public and industries have shifted toward greater savings, less is spent on consumers' goods, and their prices tend to fall. But, the prices of capital goods (which Hayek is referring to here) increases due to competition among the producers of capital goods. It is the lower rate of interest that permits the profitability to be maintained even though the prices of establishing capital plant have increased. As the projects are completed, resulting in more "roundabout", or "capitalistic" production, per-unit costs decline owing to economy of scale, and the selling prices of the consumers' goods is lower. That is not a problem and does not indicate or produce a recession. The consumers can afford to buy the products of increased production even though they have a smaller fraction of their income available (since they increased their savings rate previously that got the expansion going in the first place). This situation (a smaller fraction of income devoted to consumption combined with lower prices from more efficient production) can be maintained so long as the increased rate of savings continues long enough for the capital projects to be completed. The conclusion is, if an increase in voluntary savings occurs long enough for new capital projects to be completed, production increases, prices decline, the economy remains stable, and the public can afford to maintain or increase their standard of living even though they spend a smaller portion of their income.

The second case (which Hayek addresses directly) is where there is no increase in the voluntary savings rate, and a new supply of money is created via bank credit [1.9-16]. Again, since more money is available, the interest rate is lower than it would be if only money from savings was available to be loaned. The increased demand for capital goods causes those prices to rise. Over the long run, the trend should be that more capitalistic production processes are created, production expands with more efficient processes, and prices of consumers' goods would fall. But that is not what actually happens. When the expansion is fueled by an increase in bank credit, it is an increase in the total money supply. As seen before, if the total amount of money is increased, the value (purchasing power) of each unit is depreciated, thus prices rise. But, prices rise faster in producers' goods than consumer goods because of competition among the producers of capital goods. If so, then wages in those industries also must rise in order for the new industrial expansion to attract and retain workers. But that same increase in wages in the capital goods sector causes the profitability of the intermediate stages of production to decrease because wages are an important cost factor. At some point the expansion of the planned capital projects, especially the marginal ones, either must be aborted or additional injections of credit are required. If additional money is created, the process of increased production of producers' goods continues until the depreciation created thereby creates a situation in which the profits do not cover for principal and interest, even if the interest rate is low. Therefore there will be a decline in the demand for producers' goods. Then there must be a contraction or stagnation in those intermediate stages in the production of capital goods, some of which are completed and some not, and the result is a contraction of production. But notice that this can occur without much effect on the prices of consumers' goods.

Hayek's main point is that the lower interest rate induced by the expansion of the money supply creates a problem not easily detected by the behavior of prices. The lower interest rate appears on the surface to be a good thing, but it comes with the additional burden of a depreciation of the money unit. The depreciation causes prices to rise and may lead to instability in the economy of capital goods. The consumer's general price level may be stable, and if this is the only metric by which the health of the economy is gauged, such an analysis may miss the falling profitability of producers goods that would pose a danger to the economy.

A few examples of how recessions and depressions occur can be given, now that the general trend is clear. Six cases will be considered: a) large, non-productive projects; b) "forced savings"; c) a change in the structure of production; d) large-scale speculation; e) transfer of capital; and f) an error in ascertaining the duration of trends.

The first example is large investments in non-productive enterprises financed by bank credit that eventually lead to a decline in capital goods production. The money supply being expanded, and banks competing for business tends to reduce the interest rate. Expansion of the money supply thus leads indirectly to increases in the prices of capital goods, as the entrepreneurs, armed with the proceeds of the loans compete for resources. The intermediate costs are paid out in the course of setting up the new capital projects in the form of rent and material acquisition. At the same time, workers are employed in those new capital projects, and the entrepreneurs likewise compete for those workers, bidding up wages. The workers then spend the additional income mostly on consumption, and the reason that they do so is that their pattern of consumption vs. saving has not changed: the additional money available for investment occurred not from savings, but from bank credit. This does not go on indefinitely; eventually there is a decline in the demand for capital goods on the part of entrepreneurs. There are two possible reasons. First, is when entrepreneurs realize the planned production, if implemented, will saturate the consumer market, and prices, hence profits, have to fall. Second, is when the continuing application of capital tends to reach a point of diminishing returns such that the additional production cannot cover the costs of the borrowed money, even if the interest rate is low [1.9-17]. It is the same behavior as observed before with Granny's Tarts: if you try to squeeze five workers into a space designed for three, with the expectation that all five will produce 300 per day, you will find that the last two are not able to be as productive as the first three workers. The same "marginal utility" applies to capital: there is a point at which additional capital fails to pay for itself. In either case, as the demand for producers' goods falls off, capital projects that provided those producers' goods begin to lose money (their sales to other producers cannot meet their expenses, due mostly from labor, materials, and loan repayment). Now that some of these projects are losing money, the value of those capital items falls, and they may have to be sold off at a loss. The result is that workers also lose their jobs. At the same time, interest rates now begin to rise. There are two reasons for it. First, because of the inflation generated by the influx of monetary expansion, a lender has to charge more for a loan in order to have reasonable assurance he will be repaid an amount that compensates for the depreciated money. The second reason is that prices in the producers' goods market are falling, and thus there is higher risk of lending in those industries. At this point, since the prices and values of capital goods are falling, the prices of real estate and stocks will also fall. All of this can occur without a noticeable increase in the prices of commodities, especially if the expansion of production is geared to products that are not normally considered traditional commodities. Commodities may continue to be produced in the old way and the end prices do not change. Meanwhile, the investments in the new products or improvements to some old ones are becoming unprofitable, which poses a risk to the economy. Stable commodity prices are not the best way to judge whether poor investments have been made in capital goods.

The second example of the causes of recessions and depressions is what economists refer to as 'forced savings'. It is a disproportion between the production of consumer goods and capital goods in favor of the latter, ending with a greater portion of wealth in the hands of producers. It was first described in part by the English economist Henry Thornton [1.9-18], but the best exposition was given by Thomas Malthus [1.9-19]. Here is part of his essay describing 'forced saving'. He had at this point in the essay just concluded a discussion on trade in gold and silver (explanatory notes in square brackets):

"There is yet another point, still more important [than the trade in bullion], where the experience of the merchant will be apt to lead him to a conclusion quite different than that which generally maintained by the writers in question [David Ricardo, William Blake, Charles Bosanquet]. A merchant, or manufacturer, obtains a loan in paper from a bank; and, with the loan, he is able to command materials to work upon, tools to work with, and wherewithal to pay the wages of labor; and yet, he is told that this transaction does not tend, in the slightest degree, to increase the capital of the country.

The question of how far, and in what manner, an increase of currency tends to increase capital, appears to us so very important, as fully to warrant our attempt to explain it. No writer that we are acquainted with has ever seemed sufficiently aware of the influence which a different distribution of the circulating medium of a country must have on those accumulations which are destined to facilitate future productions; although it follows, as a direct consequence, from the most correct and legitimate view of capital that can be taken.

Dr. A. Smith [Adam Smith, author of *The Wealth of Nations*] justly observes, that 'though the whole annual produce of the land and labor of every country is, no doubt, ultimately destined for supplying the consumption of its inhabitants, and for procuring a revenue to them; yet, when it first comes, either from the ground, or from the hands of the productive laborers, it naturally divides itself into two parts. One of them is, in the first place, destined for replacing a capital, and for renewing the materials, provisions and finished work [circulating capital] which had been withdrawn from a capital; the other for constituting a revenue; which of course is destined to be spent without any view to reproduction [money to be spent in consumption].

Now, it is quite certain, that anything like an equal distribution of the circulating medium among all the members of the society would almost destroy the power of collecting any considerable quantity of materials, of constructing proper machinery, warehouses, shipping, etc., and of maintaining a sufficient quantity of hands to introduce an effective division of labor. The proportion between capital and revenue [investment and consumption] would evidently, by this distribution, be altered greatly to the disadvantage of capital; and in a few years, the produce of the country would experience a rapid diminution [because an equal distribution of the currency would not support replacement of capital]. On the other hand, if such a distribution of the circulating medium were to take place [by forced confiscation and redistribution], as to throw the command of the country chiefly into the hands of the productive classes, that is, if a considerable portions of the currency were taken from the idle, and those who lived upon fixed incomes, and transferred to farmers, manufacturers, and merchants, the proportion between capital and revenue [investment and consumption] would be greatly altered to the advantage of capital; and in a short time, the produce of the country would be greatly augmented [although the people were robbed to pay for it].

Whenever, in the actual state of things [normal lending practice in a free economy], a fresh issue of notes [bank credit] comes into the hands of those who mean to employ them in the prosecution and extension of a profitable business, a difference in the distribution of the circulating medium takes place, similar in kind to that which has been supposed, and produces similar, though of course comparatively inconsiderable effects, in altering the proportion between capital and revenue in favor of the former [producers of capital goods and their employees]. The new notes go into the market, as so much additional capital, to purchase what is necessary for the conduct of the concern. But before the produce of the country has been increased [capital projects completed], it is impossible for one person to have more of it, without diminishing the shares of some others. This diminution is effected by the rise of prices, occasioned by the competition of the new notes, which puts it out of the power of those who are only buyers, and not sellers, to purchase as much of the annual produce as before [the effect of monetary depreciation that raises prices occurs before the ultimate lowering of prices due to more efficient production]. While all the industrious classes, all those that sell as well as buy, are, during the progressive rise of prices, making unusual profits; and even when the progression stops, are left with the command of a greater portion of the annual produce [wealth accumulates faster among business owners than workers] than they possessed previous to the new issues [of credit].

It must always be recollected, that it is not the quantity of the circulating medium which produced the effect here described, but the different distribution of it. If a thousand million of notes were added to the circulation, and distributed to the various classes of society in the same proportion as before, neither the capital of the country, nor the facility of borrowing, would be in the slightest degree increased [wages and prices would both increase at about the same rate]. But, on the fresh issue of notes, not only is the quantity of the circulating medium increased, but the distribution of the whole mass is altered. A larger proportion falls into the hands of those who consume and produce [owners and workers in capital industries], and a smaller proportion into the hands of those who only consume [other workers]. And as we have always considered capital as that portion of the national accumulations and annual produce, which is at the command of those who mean to employ it with a view to reproduction, we are bound to acknowledge, that an increased issue of notes tends to increase the national capital, and by an almost, though not strictly necessary consequence, to lower the rate of interest."

Note he explains in the first part of the fourth paragraph above, why the utopian "flower-power" communes did not work, and also why "equal distribution of wealth" as advised by the "equality of outcome" advocates will not work. But his main point is that an increase in bank credit tends to be lent to those who engage in business or industries that produce capital goods, for this is the only way that production increases over the long term. That is accomplished by increasing the number of steps in the chain of production, each of them capitalizing on the division of labor, so as to ultimately increase production while reducing the unit production costs thereof. He points out correctly that those who accomplish this goal end up with a larger share, or in what is the same thing, greater control of production. But recall that this was written in 1811, before regular working people had the means to invest in stocks and bonds. In modern times, those who have a little extra to invest can do so and thereby acquire for themselves a share in the increased means of production. Screeching "progressives" may point to the fifth and sixth paragraphs above, and claim that evil sinister capitalists are always preying on workers, and therefore "equity" is the appropriate solution. But they are making a false assertion, since they are 210 years behind the times. There is no harm in reward for risk, either by those already wealthy or the small investor in his IRA or 401K or pension fund. But an important problem arises when low-income consumers cannot invest, having to deal with the depreciated currency, cannot buy as much as they did before simply because their wage increases do not match the increase in prices. If the new production is successful, the prices may come down enough to offset the price increase from depreciation. But what if the new production facilities fail, say if they are done to excess? Then they become unprofitable, and have to be abandoned. Losses add up and there is a collapse in the capital portion of the nation's economy: a depression. As a result, the less efficient ways of production must resume. Meanwhile, the consumer then has lower purchasing power both because of the depreciation (which led to higher prices) and the fact that the intended more-efficient production did not prevail (therefore did not compensate for the price increase due to depreciation). It is a curious phenomenon that socialists are constantly advocating for greater monetary expansion, thus injuring the very people they claim to be helping.

The origin of the problem is the expansion of credit at interest rates set below what they would be if only voluntary savings were available to fund the investments [1.9-20]. If investment was based entirely on savings, then the increase in production would proceed more slowly, but would be more stable and less susceptible to this type of disruption in the capital industries. Once this kind of depreciation has occurred, it cannot be cured by additional depreciation. Unfortunately, that is what the banking system tends to do: it tends to continue funding the expansion by issuing more bank credit and creating additional monetary depreciation. But that only postpones the day of reckoning, and makes the resulting depression worse.

The third cause of recessions and depression is similar to the first two; it is a change in the structure of production caused by a change in interest rates as described by Hayek [1.9-21, 1.9-22]. Hayek's insight (based partly on earlier work by Wicksell and von Mises) is that changes in the volume of money, especially bank credit money, cause fluctuations in the interest rate, and those interest rate fluctuations may cause the intermediate stages in the production of capital goods to become unprofitable. The key observable is the change in prices in specific intermediate capital goods industries. For example, there may be a large change in prices and profitability in the steel industry, but relatively stable conditions in the glass, plastics, or timber industry. As the steel industry expands, the intermediate prices increase. The general trend is that continued expansion into more stages requires a decline in the interest rates due to the greater time lag between the beginning of production and the end product. Greater production means greater efficiency, which means lower prices and profit margins and a rise in the interest rate cannot be accommodated. It is this delay time that is the critical factor: if there should be a decline in the demand for steel while new production facilities are being set up, those new facilities become unprofitable to maintain or continue, the prices fall, and there will be some decline in the steel-related industries. Typically some portions of the expansion will be completed before the demand falls off; if so, they are likely to remain profitable. At the other end, consumers who buy products that use steel as a component have not reduced their consumption expenditures; they simply get less for it because of the depreciated value of the money unit. There may be a second effect in play, namely that some companies may find that they are better off to divert part of their resources to aiding in the production of other capital goods, taking away resources from the current production geared toward consumer's goods. That will result in less being produced toward consumers' goods, causing prices to rise by simple supply and demand. Meanwhile, wages have increased owing to depreciation (although with a time lag). Many people will realize that the higher prices combined with lagging wages is a reduction in their real wages, and will have no choice but to shift more of their income to consumption. When that occurs, the demand for consumer goods increases, and higher prices result. Production of consumers' goods is now more likely to be profitable, and there is a shift away from the intermediate capital productions back to production of consumers' goods, leaving any intermediate stages that have not been completed unprofitable or a total loss. In this case there may remain production facilities are either incomplete or unused even though complete, owing to the shift in demand toward consumers' goods. Once again, these effects are produced by an extension of credit for investment beyond voluntary savings.

This type of behavior cannot be detected by examining a general price level until it becomes obvious near the end of the expansion. As described, the general price level may be stable for long periods, but prices at higher stages of production are fluctuating. The indicator is the profit margin at each stage, which in turn is affected by the interest rate. Each industry is different, which different relative proportions between labor and materials, and the number of stages required to produce the end product.

Hayek [1.9-23] has shown that when the depression occurs, the proper monetary policy is to avoid stimulating demand for consumers' goods by a further expansion of credit. Expanding consumer demand will only make the existing imbalance between producers and consumers' goods worse, the reason being that the increased demand will increase prices for those goods, and tend to draw investment away from producers' goods. What is required is to restore the proportion between consumers' goods and producers' goods, which can be accomplished only permitting interest rates to be determined by the demand for credit and the supply of voluntary savings. But so often it is the policy of central banks to lower interest rates and expand credit at the first signs of a recession; all this does is extend the unhealthy conditions (hopefully until after the next election).

Now the question is: how is the undue of money expansion be detected so that it can be corrected? Conventional wisdom states that it should be easy to observe the changes in the consumer price index (CPI); if they are increasing too rapidly, then it is time to restrain the growth of the money supply. It should be inferred from Hayek [1.9-24] that such an approach is incorrect. First, the CPI is an amalgamation of goods assembled according to a "nominal household", segregated by rural or urban, and typically includes retail prices of items used by households. In itself, it has four problems. First, the makeup of the weighting of the CPI may not reflect any recent changes to households buying habits. Second, CPI is generally based on retail prices, which are a lagging indicator (since the problem is with producers' goods). Third, a CPI cannot, by design, uncover profitability problems and the price variations among producers' goods, which is in fact the prime indicator of an unhealthy monetary expansion. The expansion of money (setting or causing interest rates to be below the natural rate) is the indirect cause of overexpansion and losses in producers' goods industries. Fourth, a CPI cannot account for the profitability fluctuations that are different for every industry. Each has a different production schedule, number of stages, and the ratio of the amount of work done by labor directly as opposed to machines. As production becomes more capital-intensive, the profit margins tend to decrease (as shown before, profits approach costs), and profitability is then very sensitive to changes in the interest rate or in disruptions in the supply chain.

A fourth cause of recessions and depressions is speculation in stocks that are purchased with "margin" loans. A margin loan on stocks is the fraction that has to be put up by the individual investor; for example, an 80% margin loan means the investor has to put up 80% and can borrow the other 20%. The earlier economics writers called this phenomenon "overtrading". A large degree of stock speculation on borrowed money tends to drive up the price of stocks above safe levels of price-to-earnings ratio (which preferably should be less than 20). The depression sets in under two conditions. The first case is when the banks experience a liquidity problem from some other cause, and these margin loans have to be called in. That results in a sell-off of the stocks to get the cash to repay the loans, and that sell-off may generate large losses for the investors. The second case is a decline in consumer demand from some other cause that results in a decline in stock prices, which in turn affects the ability of borrowers to repay the bank for the margin loan. In both cases this situation causes a financial panic, in the sense that the industrial base may be intact, but the economy is experiencing a problem with payment obligations. In other words, it is caused by an extension of credit for the purpose of large-scale speculation. The Federal Reserve has the authority to limit margins on stock loans, although the control is weak because there is not much actual control over what borrowers do with the proceeds of the loan. This is a financial recession caused by bank credit expansion.

A fifth cause of recessions and depressions is the transfer of circulating capital into fixed capital items that are found to be unnecessary or extravagant [1.9-25]. An example occurred in the 1870's in the U. S. when it was discovered too late that a great deal of circulating capital in the form of steel, iron, and wood had been invested in the building of a railroad network that was not justified by the traffic needs. All of that material, not to mention the labor and land, could have been put to more practical use. Overestimates of the freight and passenger demands led to an explosion of railroad construction, which later became worthless when the revenues failed to materialize. Modern examples, on a lesser scale, are the building of large sports stadiums that are only used a few times during specific sports seasons. Suppose every town of 100,000 or greater population decided that a sports stadium was the path to revenue and wealth. The result would be a large glut of stadium space with only a fraction of the capacity in actual use. Only then would the realization come that a great deal of capital had been lost, with the debt still remaining. A similar principle applies to the building of convention centers in small towns, or those same small towns building airports with runways designed to accommodate large jets and terminals designed for fifty flights a day, when only ten flights with small commuter planes is justified. A common feature of these types of projects is that they are devoted to building large capital facilities that have only one use. When there is not enough demand for that one purpose, the project becomes a total loss. If funded privately (hardly ever the case) the debt has to be written off and the investors take the loss. If funded publicly, the taxpayers continue to pay off the bonds through higher taxes. That explains why sports stadiums are very seldom financed privately. The smart people (who who own the sports teams) can con the public into supporting the projects, knowing full well that the revenue never justifies the cost. This is a financial recession, but not necessarily caused by monetary expansion.

If a convention center is such a great idea, why don't the local restaurants, hotels, retail stores, car rental companies, taxi services, construction companies, and local tourist attraction operators all get together, form a corporation, buy some land, build a convention center, and reap all the profits? It's pretty simple: all those are smart business people, and they know full well that the convention center investment will never pay off, and that not even the increase in their current businesses will justify it. The convention center benefits them only if someone else (i.e., the taxpayers) can be convinced to pay for it. Enter the politicians and community promoters, full of high-sounding rhetoric and fantastic claims about growth and prestige, but never willing or able to prove it.

A sixth cause of recessions and depressions is the inability or unwillingness to determine the duration of an economic trend. They are financial recessions, sometimes caused by expansion of bank credit. It is characterized by a widespread sentiment that some new type of investment is sure to remain profitable indefinitely, as if no future events could alter it. One historical example is the "Tulip Craze" in 1636 and 1637 in Holland in which the public actually came to believe that common tulip bulbs constituted real wealth. Another case was the "South Sea Bubble", in which a British outfit called the South Sea Company sold stock on the premise that it would achieve large profits from its government-granted monopoly on trade with between Great Britain and South America. The Company was a failure and never achieved any profitability; as a result its stock price collapsed in 1720 and many investors were ruined.

A third historical example was the "Company of the Indies", controlled by Scottish financier John Law. He had developed a novel method of finance ("printing money"), and had proposed it to many of the leaders in Europe. All of them rejected it until he gained the confidence Philippe, duke of Orleans, Regent for the minor king Louis XV of France. The Regent granted Law a 25-year monopoly on trade between the Louisiana Territory in North America and France in 1717. The French historian Guizot [1.9-26] describes the events that led to the collapse of the Company of the Indies (also known as the Mississippi Company):

> "The Regent ... authorized the Scot [John Law] to found a circulating and discount bank which at once had very great success and did real service. Encouraged by this first step, Law reiterated to the Regent that the credit of bankers and merchants decoupled their capital; if the State became the universal banker and centralized all the values in circulation, the public fortune would naturally be decoupled. A radically false system, fated to plunge the State and consequently the whole nation into the risks of speculation and trading

without the guarantee of that activity, zeal, and prompt resolution which able men of business can import into their private enterprises. The system was not as yet applied; the discreet routine of the French financiers was scared at such risky chances, the pride of the great lords sitting at the council was shocked at the idea of seeing the State turning banker, perhaps even trader. ... Law went on, however; to his bank he had just added a great company. The king ceded to him Louisiana, which was said to be rich in gold and silver mines superior to those of Mexico and Peru. ... He [M. d'Argenson, keeper of the seals] however, like his predecessors, attempted before long to hamper the march of the audacious foreigner [Law]; but the die had been cast and the duke of Orleans outstripped Law himself in the application of his theories. A company, formed secretly and protected by the new keeper of the seals, had bought up the general farmings, that is to say, all the indirect taxes, for the sum of 48,052,000 livres [a livre at this time was 84.72 grains of pure silver, so the 48,052,000 livres came to 8,481,178 ozt. of silver]; the Company of the Indies re-purchased them for 52,000,000 [in paper money issued by his bank]; the general receipts were likewise conceded to it, and Law's bank was proclaimed a Royal Bank; the Company's shares already amounted to the supposed value of all the coin circulating in the kingdom, estimated at 7 or 8 hundred millions [of livres; 700 M livres corresponds to 123,550,000 ozt. of silver; the population of France at this time was about 21,000,000]. Law thought he might risk everything in the intoxication which had seized all of France, capital and province. He created some 15 hundred millions of new shares, promising his shareholders a dividend of 12 per cent. From all parts gold and silver flowed into his hands; everywhere the paper of the bank was substituted for coin. The delirium had mastered all minds. The street called *Quincampoix*, for a long time past devoted to the operations of the bankers, had become the usual meeting place of the greatest lords as well as of discreet burgesses. It had been found necessary to close the two ends of the street with gates, open from six AM to nine PM; every house harbored business agents by the hundred; the smallest room was let for its weight in gold. The workmen who made the paper for the banknotes could not keep up with the consumption. The most modest fortunes suddenly became colossal; lackeys of yesterday were millionaires tomorrow; extravagance followed the progress of this outburst of riches, and the price of provisions [i.e., the necessities of the common people] followed the progress of extravagance. Enthusiasm was at its height in favor of the able author of so many benefits. At the pinnacle of his power and success the new comptroller-general fell into no illusion as to the danger of the position. 'He had been forced to raise seven stories on foundations which had been laid for only three,' said a contemporary as clear-sighted as impartial. Some large shareholders were already beginning to quietly realize their profits [i.e., losses]. The warrants of the Company of the Indies had been assimilated to the banknotes; and the enormous quantity of paper tended to lower its value."

The avalanche of paper and unwarranted speculative optimism soon took its toll. The Company of the Indies never panned out as a commercial enterprise. The stock price collapsed in 1720, and again many investors all over France were left with nothing. Notice also that the excessive paper bank notes caused the prices of food and housing to rise, and those who could not benefit from the intermediate profits lost even more by the depreciation.

We Americans should not be too quick to laugh at the Dutch, English, and French examples. American investors did largely the same thing, although on a smaller scale, during the "dot-com boom" of the 1990's, which collapsed in 2000. It was caused at least partially by an assumption that the growth and importance of technology stocks would continue indefinitely. It continued for a short time until the investors realized all the "innovative tech companies" were writing computer code to do the same things; i.e., a redundancy in the market. So the price of tech stocks collapsed, and many companies went out of business or were absorbed by others, leaving investors out of luck.

A disaster of worse magnitude was the American "housing boom" of the early 2000's, which collapsed in 2007 [1.9-27]. It was also caused partly by an assumption that there was no limit to the number of new houses that could be built and sold, or existing ones that could be refinanced. But another factor was the willful acceptance of this assumption by those who should know better; the go-along-while-it-lasts attitude unfiltered by any critical thought about overall risk; the lack of any desire to understand the new credit instruments (credit default swaps, collateralized debt obligations, and synthetic collateralized debt obligations) that funded the buying frenzy; in other words, fundamental financial incompetence by those who claimed to be the best and brightest in the industry. The U. S. government greatly assisted in creating the conditions that led to the financial collapse: political pressure to get more people to buy homes even when they couldn't afford it; lowering of requirements to obtain loans on residential homes; expansion of the power and influence of "government-sponsored enterprises" (GSE) to manipulate the financial system; and lack of supervision or regulation of those new entities that implemented the political objectives. There were also a certain number of professional criminals who got into the act by conning unwary or unsophisticated borrowers into taking out loans with confusing terms and conditions, at the same time not bothering to verify adequate ability to make repayment.

As soon as the first cracks in the edifice appeared, fear took over, and the rush was on by investors to unload the mortgage "securities". Because the credit instruments were new and poorly understood, it was not clear at the time what fraction of the securities actually represented mortgages in default. But it didn't matter: the prices fell, and enormous losses were absorbed. But the losses were not limited to the investors: banks held a great many of these, and insurance companies had extended insurance in the form of credit default swaps against losses on the collateralized debt obligations; now they were on the hook also. The "housing crisis" was a financial panic. The houses were still valuable as dwellings; they were not inherently unusable, nor had they become obsolete, nor was there a decline in demand by the public. The problem was the inability of borrowers to repay or confusion in the industry over exactly which mortgages were unhealthy. Some houses did become unusable when the banks demonstrated further inability to adjust to reality by not selling them promptly after foreclosure. In those cases, the houses fell into disrepair or were looted for the copper, and those houses did amount to a total loss. But don't worry: the banking and insurance incompetents, the crusading politicians, the bureaucratic regulators, and the financial crooks all got raises and promotions. Meanwhile the taxpayers got the privilege of bailing out the banking system and the insurance companies that had made guarantees they could not fulfill.

There are a host of other causes of depression within certain industries. These are cases where an isolated depression may occur, but not due to the expansion of bank credit. First among these is a loss of an important material. The American Civil War interrupted the export of cotton, with the result of a depression in the weaving and clothing manufacturing industry in England. Regulators in California have decided to deprive the fertile fields of the southern part of the State with adequate water in the interest in preserving a fish known as the 'snail darter'; and there is now a permanent depression in the once-active farming industry. Some regulators in Oregon and Washington State have likewise decided that a spotted owl must be preserved at all costs, and there is now a permanent depression in the lumber industry in those States. A second cause is excessive tax increases or the threat of them such as to provoke uncertainty in the minds of businessmen as to whether it is worthwhile to expand or even to continue in business. Exactly the same prevails among the investing class: who will risk their money by investing if all the profits from the risk are taxed away? A third type is a general loss of confidence in the business environment, especially regarding trust in the banking system. A number of events can cause a loss of general confidence: a) if banks fail to pay on deposits (as they did in the 1930's depression); b) a fast decline in stock market (as it did in 1929); c) fear that there will be a default on the payment of bonds which present a risk to pension funds; and d) fear of government activism or the rise of radical elements unrestrained by the government, or induced by a political revolution. A fourth type is natural disasters, such as the Dust Bowl of the 1930's. A fifth type is widespread epidemics of disease such as the Spanish flu of 1918-1920, or the (probably) man-made pandemic known as the Wuhan virus of 2019-2020.

The economics experts have developed a set of three notional trends that show the progression of expansions and recessions due to monetary over-expansions by bank credit. This list is a combination of Hayek [1.9-28] and Fairchild et al [1.9-29].

1. The expansion of credit at interest rates below that which would result from matching of voluntary savings and the demand for capital will lead to projects that are not completed either because it is discovered too late that they are not needed, or are unprofitable to complete. These lead directly to losses.

2. The extension of credit at interest rates below that which would result from matching of voluntary savings increases the demand for loans (since money is plentiful and cheap to obtain).

2a. The initial expansion of bank credit leads to higher employment and wages, especially in the production of producers' goods. Profits tend to increase as prices rise.

2b. The initial increase in profitability causes the prices of stocks to increase.

2c. The increase in profits, accompanied by the depreciation of the money unit, means the public seeks to demand higher wages to compensate. The wage increases tend to reduce the profitability of businesses in general.

2d. Declining profitability leads to a depression those industries accompanied by layoffs and unemployment.

3. An expansion of credit does not have much effect on the ratio of savings to consumption of the general public. The increase in credit leads initially to an increase in the demand for producers' goods, and an increase in those prices. Production of producers' goods continues until the monetary depreciation filters down to the public, who now have more money in their pockets, albeit with lower purchasing power per unit. At that point the public begins to increase its demand for consumer goods (saving only the same proportion as before), which draws investment away from the producers' goods. With the increased demand for consumers' goods, the continued expansion of producers' goods begins to slow down, and losses begin to accumulate among producers, starting with the basic industries (mining, steel, rubber, etc.).

3a. As profits in producers' goods decline, the banking system becomes more circumspect in its lending operations, not renewing loans or increasing interest rates. This puts additional pressure on the profitability of manufacturing producer's goods.

3b. Changes in either interest rates or demand leads to a decrease in the profitability of producers' goods, and a reduction in output.

3c. The decline in profits causes the prices of stocks to decline.

3d. The pressure on manufacturer's profits causes them to decrease prices, cut back production, and lay off workers. The fall in wholesale and intermediate prices ripples though the production stages, and the increase in unemployment causes a reduction in the demand for consumers' goods, which causes prices and profits to become even lower.

The same economists have provided some important lessons:

1. Additional credit provided directly to consumers only serves to increase the demand for consumers goods and increase their prices.

2. An increase in taxation is likely to cause a reduction in savings, which puts pressure on the banks to retrain the growth of credit, which is accomplished by raising interest rates. The increase in interest rates has its first negative effect on the profitability of long-term capital projects, which leads to cutbacks in construction and the basic industries.

3. The amount of bank credit should not be made in response to "demand" by entrepreneurs; the amount of bank credit should be based on voluntary savings. Expansion of credit beyond what would occur through the natural matching of savings and demand for loans leads to an unwarranted expansion of the money supply, an increase in prices by depreciation of the money unit, and a loss of confidence in the money unit and the economy in general. It will tend to accelerate the demand for consumers goods since the public desires to spend what they have before it depreciates further. One remedy is to increase interest rates on savings in order to encourage it, which necessarily leads to an increase in the interest rate on loans.

The comedian W. C. Fields once observed that "there comes a time when one has to take the bull by the tail and face the situation". There are several options for recovery when the "situation" is a recession or depression, depending partly on political and social considerations. Before reviewing those, there are some fundamental rules that are important.

First, if the depression was caused by an undue extension of bank credit that in turn led to depreciation of the money unit (inflation), then the policy should be based on accepting the depreciation as permanent. Therefore it is not helpful to decrease the volume of money in order to create an artificial increase in the value of the money unit (called deflation) [1.9-30]. The reason is that the deflation will injure the same people who have already been injured by the inflation, mostly in the form of unemployment.

Secondly, it is important to recall that a depression starts when the industrial expansion ends; industrial expansion ends when the intermediate stages become unprofitable; they become unprofitable when costs (mostly in the form of wages) begin to approach selling prices; costs approach selling prices when the cost of labor (wages) goes up; wages must go up to compensate for the increased cost of living caused by higher retail prices; higher retail prices are caused by depreciation of the monetary unit; the depreciation was caused by the bank credit extension in the first place. Meanwhile, there are losses in the intermediate capital industries; those losses are caused by the fact that additional increments of capital improve production, but less so than the cost of interest on the borrowed money; those losses cause bankruptcies which generates losses for the banks; and the expansion of bank credit slows down or ends [1.9-31].

An alternate scenario is: industrial expansion ends when the intermediate stages become unprofitable; they become unprofitable when costs (mostly in the form of wages) begin to approach selling prices; the depreciation of the money causes businesses to add a little onto prices to compensate for increased labor costs; meanwhile businesses must borrow more in order to do the same amount of business (to maintain some level of profitability); borrowing more means higher interest rates; the increased demand for loans overwhelms the banking system due to liquidity considerations; the banking system then must increase interest rates; the higher interest rates means businesses costs have increased again and they increase prices a little to compensate for it; the cycle of increasing costs, decreasing profitability, and risks to the financial position of the banks causes the expansion of bank credit to slow down or end. This cycle ends when the banks are facing insolvency because they have extended all the credit they can but are not being repaid for the loans due to losses in the capital industries.

Both of these scenarios include depreciation of the money, which increases prices. This inflationary cycle can persist only as long as labor can be fooled into thinking they are prosperous when wages are increasing but with retail prices rising faster [1.9-32]. This is one of the fallacies of John Maynard Keynes' theory. He believed that workers will continue to work for a declining real wage (i.e., slowly rising money wages with prices that rise faster) for an indefinite period. But in fact, there will come a time when labor will recognize that the slowly rising wages are only an illusion of prosperity, and will demand a better share. This is true especially if the output of labor has actually resulted in increased productivity.

Third, banks should be allowed to fail. Otherwise, the banking system as a whole will continue to take unwarranted risks because, having achieved the status of a protected class, there is no penalty for incompetence or corruption. If the current generation of bankers experiences the same negative economic consequences as everyone else, the next generation will be more careful about taking risks.

The most efficient means for an economy to recover from a depression caused by an undue expansion of bank credit are: a) allow prices and wages to fall (wages generally will fall slower than prices) [1.9-33]; b) accept that losses in the industrial sector are real and write them off [1.9-34]; c) banks should continue lend to solvent businesses but at the natural rate (i.e., higher than the case during the expansion) [1.9-35, 1.9-36]; d) banks should end the expansion of credit and the depreciation of the money that goes with it [1.9-37]; and e) permit the natural re-adjustment of the demand for consumer vs. capital goods to occur, as determined by the voluntary savings rate. This last one simply means that the structure of production, having been distorted by the influence of interest rates and credit, will revert to some other pattern, usually a refocus on production for consumers rather than capital projects. At the same time, the government must stay out of the way [1.9-38]: a) do not promote policies that require another expansion of credit and depreciation; b) do not support insolvent banks or other non-viable businesses (except those critical for national defense); c) minimize the subsidizing of unemployment (i.e., promote the inclination to work); d) do not try to support high wage rates that are unprofitable to business (under the guise of supporting "purchasing power"); e) do not impose price controls in order to keep prices high (under the guise that high prices imply better profits); f) do not adopt policies that promote consumption (i.e., with welfare payments); g) do not raise taxes; lower them if possible; and h) balance the government's budget by reducing government spending (thus to free up savings for investment). Unfortunately, bankers tend to prefer a continued expansion of the money supply and credit, since their profits depend mostly on interest from loans.

The preceding all sounds correct in theory. But some of these are a problem in modern times because minimum wages and certain contracts prevent wages from falling. If so, an additional requirement is for the government and banking system to ensure that the money supply does not decrease. That means, contrary to the politicians' and bankers' claims, the inflation they created is permanent. There is in fact too much political interference in the economy because there is always a desire to support certain industries and maintain employment, even if it is not the best overall approach.

The classical economists recognized that the short-term cure for a depression is to lower interest rates and utilize government deficit spending. It should only be done as a temporary measure until the economy is able to complete the recovery on its own. This is the one case in which Keynes' theory is correct: the recovery phase after the liquidation of the previous expansion. This tactic has been known for a very long time, and it works to recover from a depression [1.9-39, 1.9-40] if used judiciously. But it has the secondary effect that the previous monetary depreciation is permanent. It is generally bad policy to use inflation to counteract a depression [1.9-41].

Once the liquidation is complete at the depth of the depression, the classical economists advocated a reduction in interest rates and government intervention in the form of public works projects. It nearly always involves deficit spending and creation of a national debt. It is very important that such a scheme be done only for short periods, just enough to get the economy stabilized; after which the government must run a surplus and pay off any debt incurred. If kept in place too long, this plan will cause another round of inflation and will also make the national debt permanent. This is exactly the problem the U. S. has had since it adopted the policies of John Maynard Keynes as if his theory was applicable in general. Keynes' theory only applies at the depth of a depression, not in normal periods. But many governments, including the U. S., have adopted it as normal economic policy, which has contributed in part to the enormous U. S. national debt.

Prevention is always better than a cure. The best prevention for depressions (given that there will always be minor up and down cycles in any money-based economy) is not to permit inflation caused by unwarranted expansion of bank credit money [1.9-42]. Money should be scarce in prosperous times; the interest rate should be the market rate, being the intersection of the supply of voluntary savings and the demand for investment, known as the normal, or going, rate of interest. That rate of interest suppresses the tendency for over-expansion in the production of capital goods; it tends to encourage slower but steadier growth of production; it allows reasonable profits in the long run; promotes the gradual lowering of retail prices as production expands. It is the artificially low interest rates accompanied by expansion of bank credit that tends to spur the excessive expansion of capital industries that subsequently cause the depression when they become unprofitable.

1.10 Economic Inequality

Modern American atheists are fond of quoting a certain passage in the Christian New Testament to justify correcting what they call "economic inequality" or "income inequality". They do so as a means to demonize anyone who has accumulated wealth; who has worked hard and set aside a little for retirement; to accuse large corporations of robbing the poor; to ridicule and hold in contempt anyone who is not in favor of confiscation and redistribution. The first passage in question is Matthew 25:34-36:

> "Then the King will say to those on his right, "Come you who are blessed by my Father; take your inheritance, the kingdom prepared for you since the creation of the world. For I was hungry and you gave me

something to eat, I was thirsty and you gave me something to drink; I was a stranger and you invited me in; I needed clothes and you clothed me; I was sick and you looked after me; I was in prison and you came to visit me."

Sometimes they quote Acts 2:44, 45:

"All the believers were together and had everything in common. Selling their possessions and goods, they gave to anyone as he had need."

It turns out, naturally, that the atheist crusaders always quote them out of context. The first is a prophecy to be fulfilled in the distant future [1.10-1]. They conveniently ignore the fact that in the quote from Acts the believers did the common pooling of assets and charity of their own initiative, without instruction by Jesus Christ or the apostles, or coercion by the Pharisees or the Roman government. But the "progressives" use these to falsely imply that free enterprise is evil and that it is based on exploitation. Therefore (they claim) forced "economic equality" and "equity" are legitimate functions of government through taxation and distribution. For that I would remind them of 1 Peter 2:1:

"Therefore, rid yourselves of all malice and all deceit, hypocrisy, envy, and slander of every kind."

The issue of income inequality has been an important topic for several centuries. It is important first to distinguish between "income" and "economic" inequality. I suspect that the average "rich" person in Chad or Bolivia would be happy to exchange his position for the advantage of being "poor" in the U. S. or Switzerland. It is useless therefore to compare the relative economic status of people among different nations, as nations have widely differing levels of general economic development. In considering the relative status of people of a single nation, say the U. S., it is important to stress that "economic" inequality refers to the relative amount of wealth owned or controlled by one person vs. another. "Wealth" in this context means the having resources to affect production and investment. "Income" inequality refers only to the money income in a certain period, usually a year. A person of great wealth may decide to take only a small annual income on the grounds that most common expenses, such as a homes, cars, insurance, etc. are all paid for already, and therefore he can live well with a fairly low annual income. With these definitions it is easy to see that "economic inequality" is the result of many years of "income inequality".

Many of the socialist arguments favoring the destruction of free enterprise are based on the fallacy that somehow the total output and created wealth has to be "distributed". Therefore they focus on the "distribution of wealth" and point out that in a free enterprise economy a few people become very wealthy while some remain very poor. Some of the rhetoric can be discarded as good old-fashioned jealousy of the rich. The more devoted socialists demonize freedom because the end result is inequality of wealth, failing to recognize, or failing to admit, that freedom guarantees inequality simply because ingenuity, intelligence, inheritance, ambition, and luck are not equally distributed. That said, we should always try to ensure people have equal opportunity, which is very different from equality of outcome. If Granny's Tarts becomes successful and you enjoy a solid middle-class life, these same "progressive" activists will demand that you reduce your standard of living down to the same as some person who has never worked a day in their life. But our charming socialist wimpizoids would be mighty offended and run home crying to their Mommies if you demanded in return that each of them settle for straight D's in their Post-Modern Semi-Binary Poly-Heterophobic Cultural Studies program. Wealth in a free society is not "distributed" in the sense that poker dealers hand out aces, eights, and deuces. Wealth accumulates in the people who possess the attributes just listed. "Progressives" desire a system in which they can satisfy their jealousy and assuage their guilt by establishing and operating an all-seeing, all-knowing, government-sponsored economic poker dealer. Then they get to hand out wealth to themselves and their favorites while robbing the middle class, eliminating economic freedom, and enslaving the poor.

It is true that there are a number of very wealthy people and corporations in the U. S. Some individuals acquired it by inheritance or won a lottery. Some leading corporations became wealthy by exploiting poor workers in poor countries. Both individuals and corporations can get rich by theft. Even the corrupt ones are not the important issue. The vast majority of wealthy individuals and successful businesses acquired it honestly by hard work, a good idea, and good management and fortunate timing. A wealthy person does not spend her time counting Federal Reserve Notes in her basement, nor does she convert everything to gold coins and fill her swimming pool with them. Normally a wealthy person will provide themselves and their families with a big house, a summer home or two, maybe a yacht, and a few Rolls Royce's. Do they live any better? How many rooms in a 40-room mansion become museums to display Elvis memorabilia or bottles of olive oil or whatever the latest collectible fad is? If she watches a prime-time TV show on her 300-inch screen, is the dialogue or plot any better? Do the Seattle Mariners win more games because a rich guy follows the team? Is the wealthy person's favorite chair any more comfortable than yours? A rich man finds that the social pressure of the upper-crust crowd forces him to entertain many people he doesn't like on his yacht. But you can allow only your best friends on your bass boat. A rich guy may be coerced into attending some boring caviar-tasting party and has to pretend to care about the local queen matron's custom china pattern. You and your friends have much more fun over pizza and beer. Would you rather ride to work in the back of a limousine, stuck in traffic on Manhattan's 3rd Avenue, or a casual ride to work in the fresh air in your good old Dodge pickup?

The "lifestyle of the rich and famous" may be no better than yours, and could be much worse. They may spend a fraction of their money on things you cannot afford, but the rest of it does not lie idle. It is invested to make a profit, and it should be pointed out, the vast majority of corporate revenue is returned to the workers in the form of wages. Just because a person is on the Board of Directors of IBM does not mean he owns IBM. He owns a tiny fraction, just like everyone else. That is the thing that the casual thinkers are unable to understand: they see the big houses and large assets, but assume (mostly out of envy) that all of it is used only for consumption by the idle rich. The rich lady may personally be idle, but her money isn't. It is at work every day, usually providing opportunities for working people.

The rich have another problem which is a symptom of human nature: they tend to be deathly afraid of losing any money, even if the amount is small. Consider the following two examples. Suppose a young lady has worked a year or two and has managed to save $1,000. Then one day she goes over to the soda machine and starts putting money in, but she drops a nickel, it rolls under the machine, and she is unable to retrieve it. Our lady with a net worth of $1,000 has just lost five cents. Should that ruin her whole day, or her year, or her life? Of course not -- who in their right mind cares about a lousy nickel? Sure she'll swear at her crappy luck, but it doesn't affect her economic situation. She will simply get another nickel and puts it in the machine. Suppose however (just after losing the nickel), she receives a text message from a friend who has a hot stock tip. Unfortunately, it involves insider information. The friend tells our young lady, "Look, I can get that nickel back for you in a half hour. I have inside information on stock SDF#$%: it's going to go up by 10% in the next 30 minutes; all you have to do is buy one share at $0.50 now and sell it in an hour. The profit will be $0.05, and you can recover your loss from that lousy pop machine. I'll even forgo my commission on the trade because I'm looking out for you." Only if our young lady is a complete moron will she buy and sell based on this illegal insider trading tip (recall that all text messages are eternal). Put that in perspective: five cents divided by $1,000 is 0.00005 of her net worth; why would she bother doing the stock transaction? But consider the second example, concerning the famous Martha Stewart (Martha H. Kostyra). She was convicted of a felony on a securities fraud charge because she made a trade based on inside information received in a phone call that allowed her to avoid losing $45,000. To regular people, $45,000 sounds like a lot of money. But Martha Stewart was worth $1,000,000,000 at the time; and $45,000 divided by $1,000,000,000 is 0.000045 of her net worth, about same ratio as the lost nickel is to our young lady. Makes you wonder why a smart experienced person like Stewart, worth a billion dollars, would take a phone call and concern herself with a lousy forty-five grand; it was less than pocket change to her. Many rich people tend lose sight of this fact. This is the human-nature problem that rich people have to deal with: they are afraid to lose what to them is actually insignificant; always concerned that someone will do a little better than they; that someone else can get some secret advantage; that they will miss out on some attractive deal; even if the amount in relative terms is small. Don't envy the rich: they have plenty of problems.

My father was a friend of a guy who ran the fanciest restaurant/banquet hall in our city. He once told my father that he would much rather rent out the hall to a poor or middle-class guy because the bill will always be paid. He had great difficulty collecting from the local rich people. Maybe that's how they stay rich...

The important thing to focus on is the situation of the working people, not the rich. The rich can take care of themselves: they can buy political power; they can buy immunity from the law; they can pay for the lawyers who can find all the appropriate tax loopholes; they can avoid paying their bills. A successful economy is characterized by a rising standard of living among the working people, including both the poor and the middle class. A rising standard of living can occur in one of three ways: a) rising money income with stable prices; b) stable money income with falling prices; or c) falling income, but with prices falling faster than income. All of these arise from improved productivity: in the first case, wages increase because the workers are more efficient; and in the second two cases, the improved productivity permits business to sell at lower prices and still remain profitable. Economies in this position are generally stable. At the other end of the spectrum are inherently unstable economies, marked by a falling standard of living, which can also occur in three ways: a) declining money income with stable prices; b) stable money income with rising prices; or c) rising income with prices rising faster than income. Money income can fall if the value of the money unit is increasing (not the usual case) or if work becomes scarce resulting in lower wage rates and/or fewer hours that can be worked. Work can become scarce if there is a lack of capital to employ it, or if the available capital cannot be employed efficiently. Wages can decrease if there is a surplus of available labor due to immigration. Rising prices always occur when the value of the money unit is depreciating as described earlier (in addition to the normal fluctuations from supply and demand).

A society can advance beyond bare subsistence only through the advance of technology; from the stick to the plow to the automated planter and harvester; from candles to kerosene to the electric light; from the campfire to coal to the oil and electric furnaces; from walking to horse-drawn cart to the train to the automobile to the aircraft; from the kayak to the sailing ship to the steamship to the ocean-going freighters and so on. Each of these improvements served to increase the general standard of living: more could be produced with less labor. Not only is more produced, but items that were once rare or believed impossible come into development and production for common use and common benefit. There are exceptions, of course. Most "social media" applications are optimized for college students studying basket weaving, widows whose children have married and moved away, and people languishing on welfare. It doesn't just fill up idle time; it is known to be addictive. It is also a surveillance tool for corporations and possibly the government; if abused, it will lead to control over our lives. But unlike those applications, most technological advances benefit society as a whole in the long run.

Technological innovations are provided in modern times by free enterprise based on the accumulation of capital, and the costs come down enough for the average worker to afford them only by competition among producers. Selling prices fall toward the cost of production when competition exists, since the competitors are willing earn smaller profit margins as the costs of production come down through efficiency, and the total production increases. The total profitability is preserved by producing in quantities, even though the margin on each unit may be small. Without competition, which is a called monopoly, or in what is worse, government run production, prices do not generally come down because there is neither incentive for improvement nor penalty for shoddiness. Under monopoly conditions, you get what the monopolist decides to produce, at the highest price the public will tolerate.

No serious person believes that technology per se can lead to an equal standard of living for everyone. Each person has different priorities; some choose to have the latest gadgets and appliances, some choose to live as people did in the 14th century. The best that can be hoped for is a situation in which most modern people are able to obtain the basic necessities: a) a place to live; b) enough to eat; c) access to basic utilities; d) an education for their children; and e) a reasonable expectation that living standards will gradually improve. Those five can occur only if there is enough work for people to earn a respectable living and have confidence in the future. The American dream was always to see our children prosper more than ourselves. Unfortunately the U. S. has, in the past few decades, adopted policies contrary to the interests of many people who desire work but cannot find it. The true problem to be addressed is not how to decimate the rich or elevate the poor as the crusaders advise; the true problem is how to obtain a situation in which all those who are able to work can find steady employment.

Gross economic inequality is the natural outcome when force can be used by the ruling class against everyone else, as was discussed in section 1.1. The social theorists want you to believe that the core problem is that the poor are poor because the rich are rich; the rich have money and the poor do not. The "progressives" fail to realize that widespread poverty is not caused by a lack of money; poverty is caused by a lack of work and the lack of money is merely a symptom. Some poor people, usually the long-term residents of Baltimore and other Eastern cities, have given up confidence in the economic system because they have seen the mismanagement and corruption up close. They are not representative of the majority of the poor. The vast majority of the poor in the U. S. who are not working would much rather be working than not. A different group of economic analysts takes the simplistic view. It is easy to point out the relatively small fraction of the population who will never work because they actually are lazy, or another small fraction who think that somehow the world owes them something, and conclude that those types constitute the majority of the poor. The conclusion then is that nothing needs to be or can be done since the poor are derelicts. The chronically lazy welfare-demanders are actually a fairly small portion of the poor.

There will always be some who are unemployed due to illness or disability. Otherwise the majority of the poor are poor involuntarily, either because of a general recession or depression; or are unemployed or under-employed because legal wage rates that are unprofitable, or because the banking system, aided sometimes by the government, have caused a collapse in the capital portion of the industrial base. One of the worst-case scenarios, often observed in socialist nations, is when the local wealthy people bid up prices so high for necessities that the poor are priced out of the market altogether. A variant of the same condition occurs when price controls on common items cause shortages because they cannot be produced at that price; consequently production is shifted to luxuries that only the rich can afford. Then the poor cannot get lettuce, peaches, hamburger, or tuna; but the rich can get arugula, dragonfruit, foie gras, and caviar.

A free society is characterized by economic inequality, but not for the reason the social theorists claim. A free economic system rewards the productive people for taking risks, developing useful new ideas, and accurately predicting what the public wants and is willing to pay for. It rewards those who engage in enterprises that add value, which is to say, to earn a profit on labor and capital. Here is another issue that the high-minded planners fail to see: initiative varies inversely with nearness of family. A person works harder for themselves and their family than for some paper-shuffling tyrant a hundred miles away. Coercive economic systems fail because the planners remove both the initiative and the rewards and replace them with devotion to some obscure ideology that only Ivy League graduates can pretend to understand. The net result, predictable as ever, is that people will do the bare minimum to get by (as in North Korea and Cuba) out of lack of confidence in the future. The important thing to get correct is to promote equality of opportunity, not outcome or income. Natural incentive must be allowed to act in its own best interest.

It is perfectly normal for the rich to get richer in an advanced society. A great amount of production requires great outlays of capital, or the credit to obtain loans. If the rate of profit is 2% for both the large and the small producer, the one who does a billion dollars in business is naturally, just by basic arithmetic, going to earn ten times the profits of a producer who does one hundred million in business. Once again, the larger profits are not the main point: those profits come after paying wages to workers, and the profits will either be re-invested in the business, distributed to investors as dividends (which is income to them), or taxed. No rational person despises honest profits; it is the built-in dishonesty or collusion between business and government that people reject. As Bolles pointed out [1.10-2]:

"Those who are industrious and sagacious, and who do more through natural or properly acquired endowments than others to create wealth, ought to be permitted to retain it. Society does not rebel at this proposition. Society rebels over the enormous fortunes, the great landed estates, the using of government for individual gain by the loss of a larger number."

The rich getting richer is not a real problem so long as everyone else is also increasing their standard of living. Shall we tax away the income or assets of the rich in the cause of 'equity', as the socialists demand? How simplistic is their plan; they forget that if the rich become poor, everyone else gets poorer faster. If a tax cut allows for greater investment by the rich, workers employed thereby generally will benefit (so long as the work remains in the U. S.). If the profits are taxed away, the lack of incentive kicks in, and the economy will begin to decline. An axiom should be kept in mind when evaluating economic policy: inequality of income is a feature of freedom; equality of income is the promise of tyranny.

There is a common complaint that "the rich get richer and the poor get poorer". As far as I know, the phrase comes from an 1869 report by U. S. Special Commissioner of Revenue David A. Wells. He conducted a study of prices and the cost of living in the U. S. between 1860 and 1867; he found that generally, the working people lost ground; they had a lower standard of living because prices increased faster than wages. Here is his conclusion (explanatory comments in square brackets) [1.10-3]:

"The aggregate wealth of the country is increasing, probably, as rapidly as at any former period; yet it does not follow that there is the same increase in general prosperity. The laborer, especially he who has a large family to support, is not as prosperous as he was in 1860. His wages have not increased in proportion to the increase in the cost of his living. There is, therefore, an inequality in the distribution of our annual product, which we must, in no small degree, refer to artificial causes. This inequality exists even among the working classes themselves. The single man or woman, working for his or her support alone, is in receipt of a rate of wages from which savings may be made equal, or greater than ever before, especially in the manufacturing towns, where the price of board is, to a certain extent, regulated artificially by the employer [referring to 'company towns', where the company provided subsidized housing for its employees]. Unmarried operatives, therefore, gain; while those who are obliged to support their own families in hired tenements lose. Hence, deposits in savings banks increase, while marriage is discouraged; and the forced employment of young children is made almost a necessity in order that the family may live.

Now whence comes this inequality, and this unnatural distribution of the results of labor? The student of political economy [the old word for economics] would predict *a priori* that such must be the result of the enforced use of a fluctuating measure of value, viz.: inconvertible paper money [i.e., fiat money, like the Federal Reserve Notes]. It would be predicted *a priori* that the use of such money involves a most oppressive tax, which falls heaviest on the laborer and lightest upon the owner of capital [i.e., similar to the 'forced saving' of section 1.9]. Antagonism is produced where none ought to exist; the capitalist is forced to charge an additional profit for the increased risk involved in the use of a false measure of value [fiat paper money], and the consumer is forced to pay for such risk [since it has to be included in selling prices]. There is no dishonesty to be inferred, and no injustice which the honest capitalist can avoid, so long as the law is as it is; he must either cover all risks, or withdraw his capital entirely from industrious enterprise.

It has been well said that there can be no true theoretic conclusion which will not be proved by the facts whenever the theory can be applied. We have given the theory of the effects of inconvertible paper money, and we find that the facts prove it. *The rich become richer and the poor poorer.*"

Mr. Wells' conclusion was correct for America and Europe at that time, and is correct for Mexico, Central America, most of South America, and most of Asia and Africa even now. It is correct whenever the money supply grows to excess, depreciating the value of the money unit as we have in the U. S. at the present time. You will notice that those who complain the loudest about the disparity between rich and poor are also the strongest advocates for expansion of the fiat money supply which contributes to it as Wells pointed out. That proves, if it proves anything, the so-called advocates for the poor fail to understand one of the basic causes.

Bolles cites the common causes of the increase of wealth among the various industries and individuals [1.10-4]:

> "It will suffice for our purpose to divide wealthy persons into the following classes: 1) those who possess inherited wealth; 2) or have gained it principally by accident like miners and the owners of land that has risen in value; 3) or have acquired fortunes in trade; 4) or have acquired it through the assistance afforded by tax or patent laws; 5) or have acquired illegal fortunes through unlawful speculation, stock watering, abuse of trusts, the perversion of corporate interest for private gain, and the like. Of the enormous fortunes, many of them belong to the fifth class; while those of the third class are very numerous. Those of the fourth class, which include the manufacturers, are doubtless neither so numerous nor so large as others."

It is the manufacturers that have been instrumental in promoting an increase in the standard of living. "Living conditions", so to speak, were about the same in 1860 and 1867. But here we are in 2023, reaping the benefits of the enormous improvements in the quality of life due to the advances of the past 135 years. It is true that the American working poor of today have little money, savings, or accumulated wealth, but at the same time, most of them can afford indoor plumbing, air conditioning, and cable TV. While their monetary position as against the Martha Stewart class has declined, the working poor enjoy a living standard unimaginable to those of 1867. As John F. Kennedy put it, "a rising tide lifts all boats". There are in fact relatively few in the U. S. so desperately poor that they have to beg on the streets. Most of the people you see in the "homeless camps" are mentally ill or have some drug addiction; most of them are not forced to live there solely from economic conditions.

There is an intermediate stage between a free economy and a controlled economy, in which those at the upper income levels use their political and economic influence to ensure that they are the beneficiaries of any economic policy enacted by the government. This situation is known best by the term 'crony capitalism'. That phrase is unfortunate, because implies that there is something wrong with capitalism per se. The problem is not free enterprise or capitalism; the problem is control and influence by those with large establishments to the detriment of smaller establishments. Typically that control comes about by government-sanctioned monopolies, government granted subsidies, or tax incentives and the like. Those are usually granted only to large operations that can increase their market share or possibly undercut their smaller competitors. We now have multi-national corporations that regard themselves as 'global citizens' and adopt policies detrimental to the people of their original country. That is not free enterprise at all: it is a trend toward an oligarch system or a monopolistic system. It tends, if left unchecked, to increase the wealth and power of the upper class (which may be bad, but may be neutral) while suppressing opportunity for the small independent operators (which is always bad). I would prefer that the phrase 'crony capitalism' be replaced by its true description, 'crony oligarchy'.

The best economic situation that can be hoped for in the long run is the presence of a growing middle class, both in numbers and prosperity. A large middle class is proof that the system is promoting and protecting the best combination of economic opportunity and stability: steady work, stable families, a generally stable political system, and equal opportunity for prosperity and advancement. It is the middle class that can afford to try new innovations in sufficient numbers that will justify the creation of an industrial base, from which costs decline in such a way that eventually even the poor can afford them. Historically the members of the middle class have a common set of goals and aspirations, with only minor variations in degree. They have the ability to choose where they live and where to send their children to school. They generally have a similar standard of living, even with large differences in income. The result of a decline in the middle class is described by de Sismondi; here he describes conditions in the Roman Empire during the fourth century (300-399 AD) [1.10-5]:

> "It is, in fact, in the middle classes that the domestic virtues - economy, forethought, and the spirit of association - mainly reside. It is in them that a certain degree of energy is incessantly called into operation, either as a means of rising, or of keeping the position already acquired. It is in them alone that the sentiment of social equality, on which all justice is based, can be kept alive. We must see our equals, live with them, meet them daily and hourly, encounter their interests and their passions, before we can get the habit of seeking our own advantage in the common weal alone. Grandeur isolates a man; vast opulence accustoms each individual to look upon himself as a distinct power. He feels he can exist independently of his country; that his elevation, or his fall, may be distinct; and ere long, the servile dependants, by whom a man spends as much as a petty state is sure to be surrounded, succeed in persuading him that his pleasures, his

pains, nay, his slightest caprices, are more important than the welfare of thousands of families whose means of subsistence he engrosses. ... In the Roman Empire, at the time of the great Theodosius [Theodosius the Great, emperor of the Western Roman Empire 379-395 and sole emperor 392-395], the only two remaining classes of society [rich and poor] were equally ashamed of the past, equally afraid of the future, equally driven to drown all reflection in the present. At the bottom of the social scale, the populace, recently emerged from slavery, or ready to sink into it again, lived on the public distribution of provisions, or on a daily largess, beyond which they saw nothing. Without hope for the future, these men had nothing to lose but their lives; and even these they were not permitted to ensure to themselves the power of defending [deprived of arms for self-defense]. ... At the other extreme of the scale, the senators were nurtured with the same indifference. Their possessions were almost invariably situated in remote provinces: he who learned that his harvests in Gaul had been burned, could still reckon on his granaries in Spain or Africa; he who could not protect his Thracian fields from the ravages of the Goth, calculated that his Syrian olive grounds, at least, were safe from the incursions of the Persian. ... Improvidence, and an unbridled appetite for pleasure, equally characterizing the highest and lowest class, are visible in every page of the Roman history of this period."

Eventually the policies of the Roman government led to a complete elimination of the middle class. Here is de Sismondi again [1.10-6]:

"The higher classes of a nation may impress upon the government a character of wisdom and virtue, if themselves are wise and virtuous; but they cannot give it strength, for strength must always come from the mass. But in imperial Rome this mass, so varied in its language, its manners, its religion, its habits; so savage in the midst of civilization; so oppressed and brutified, was scarcely perceived by those who lived on its toils; it is hardly mentioned by historians; it pined in wretchedness, it perished and disappeared in some provinces, while no one condescended to notice extinction; and it is only by a series of comparisons that we can discover its fate. In the present state of Europe [1834], the class of husbandmen - those who live by the manual labor of agriculture - forms four fifths of the whole population, England alone excepted. We may conclude that, in the Roman Empire, the agricultural population was proportionally larger, since manufactures and commerce were in a less advanced state than with us. But, whatever their numbers, they formed no part of the nation. They were regarded as scarcely superior to the domestic animals whose labors they shared. The higher classes would have dreaded to hear them pronounce the name of country; dreaded to call forth their moral or intellectual faculties; above all, that courage which they might have turned against their oppressors. The peasantry were rigorously deprived of arms, and were incapacitated from contributing to the defense of their country, or from opposing resistance to any enemy, foreign or domestic."

Long-term stability of an economy requires that the middle class have confidence in the workings of the system; that they will not be taxed out of their earnings; that they will not be regulated out of their businesses, and that they will be able to buy and sell without interference. That means there should be a bare minimum of licensing and permitting. The middle class is the foundation of the economy in advanced societies. When the middle class is pillaged, or if it loses confidence, there won't be a middle class nor much of an economy left. That is because everyone will then be either rich or poor; the rich will not have the incentive and the poor will not have the means to improve the overall conditions.

Who are the "oppressors" the "progressives" are always screeching about? If you belong to a union with a pension fund, or work for a corporation that has a pension fund; or have an IRA, Roth IRA, 401K, or 403B plan, or own your own business, here's the good news: the "oppressor" is you. A Marxist ("progressive") believes that profit is evil (much like the medieval Catholic Church) unless they get it all (much like the medieval Catholic Church). The profit motive is what ignites industriousness and ability in an economy such that individuals can do for themselves - that is what the Marxists truly hate. Marxism is nothing more than a method to turn society back to the feudal serfdom system; a small wealthy powerful ruling elite dominating and controlling the other 98% in poverty. Don't allow those thirty-five year olds still living in Mommy's basement to intimidate you into believing that socialism will level the playing field and make everyone equal. It will do no such thing. First it will scare off the wealthy; they will pack up everything they can and send it out of the country before it gets confiscated. (They have the means to evade the revolutionaries, at least initially.) Afterwards the race is on to see how fast the nation can degenerate into a pathetic shell of its former prosperity once the mighty planners, aided by their pink leprechauns, rainbow unicorns, and the collected slogans of Chairman Mao, proceed to implement the daydreams of Karl Marx. When they are finished it will be evident that the poor continue to suffer the most; the one thing the socialists claimed they would alleviate.

1.11 International Commerce

Engineering is the art of taking a big problem that you don't know how to solve and breaking it down into a large number of small problems that you do know how to solve. Then the race is on to make the appropriate tradeoffs among those smaller portions so as to arrive at the desired solution of the large problem. It is nothing more than the principle of "division of labor" as outlined many centuries ago by the economists as applied to complex problems. The main idea is that productive enterprises become efficient in proportion as the "division of labor" is applied: a long complex string of tasks leading up to a product is broken down to many smaller ones, and each worker is assigned to perform one or a few of the smaller tasks. Each worker then becomes highly skilled at those few tasks, and he can perform them much faster and more accurately than if he had to be trained to do all the tasks, but was only called upon to do each one sporadically. The downside is, as observed in many factories, the boredom resulting from such repetition, and the smart manager devises plans to alleviate it as much as practical. The number of steps involved in making Granny's Sublime Tarts may be small enough that each worker can perform all of them equally well. But that is not the case when manufacturing machine tools from raw steel or electric guitars from wood and metal; too many processes requiring high skill are involved, and the tasks must be specialized and segregated. The same principle applies to nations as to companies. A nation such as the U. S. may have distinct advantages in growing wheat and corn, but can grow sugar and coffee only at high expense. On the other hand, Columbia and the Dominican Republic have exactly the right climate and expertise for coffee and sugar. Naturally each nation should concentrate on what it does best, export it, and import what is best done by other nations. In other words, the people of each nation logically should recognize their comparative advantages and disadvantages in production, capitalize on what it does best, and trade for what it lacks. In this way each nation optimizes production of items it is naturally suited for, which is nothing more than the principle of the division of labor at the national level.

Trade between nations, or "international commerce", is the division of labor applied to its advantages as against other nations. A merchant goes into the export business because he can get a higher price by exporting than selling domestically [1.11-1]. No one incurs the costs of transportation unless he can recover those costs in the higher selling price in the other nation. But why can he buy cheap at home, and sell higher abroad? The answer is: there is a surplus of a product at home above what the local population can use, and there are a group of people in some other nation who have both the desire for the product and the means to pay. Supply and demand show up the same way in international commerce as it does domestically. If a merchant cannot obtain a suitably higher price to afford a profit by exporting, then he will sell domestically for what he can get.

Most nations are willing to engage in trade except for some that desire to remain self-sufficient. Generally the motive for "self-sufficiency" is political, as is the presently case with North Korea. Certainly there are shortages of desired goods in that nation which could be alleviated by trade, except of course, the communist government there steals everything that isn't nailed down. International commerce in North Korea, to the extent is exists, is owned and controlled by the government. The people of North Korea have access only to what that nation, ground into universal poverty by politics, can produce itself.

There are two valid exceptions to trading among nations. The first is that a nation may decide to import what it could do for itself on the grounds that it has other things that it does even better [1.11-2]. For example, the U. S. is a net importer of cut flowers. Clearly the U. S. has the ability to produce its own flowers, but American businessmen and farmers realize that the resources that would be used in doing so are put to better use growing something more valuable. The second exception is that a nation must preserve a minimal industrial base for defense needs. An example is that the U. S. cannot allow itself to be completely dependent on foreign nations for raw steel, oil, machine tools, pharmaceuticals, or the ability to make large castings. Even if other nations do them more efficiently, there is every reason to maintain the capability domestically on the grounds that a shortage of critical materials and processes could render the U. S. too weak to respond to a national emergency. The net result is that those items will be more expensive domestically than they would be if imported, but it is a reasonable price to pay for independence from foreign obstruction or interference. It should be noted in general that a nation, if it chooses to engage in trade with other nations, must be both a buyer and seller. The reason is that a nation that exports only will accumulate a large amount of foreign money for which has no domestic use. The only way to get rid of it, so to speak, is to buy from other nations that may have a use for the foreign money, or to buy directly from that foreign nation. Over the long run international trade ultimately comes down to trading in commodities and/or services, with money as only the intermediary, the same as money is used in transactions between persons.

Imbalances in the amount of mutual trade are resolved by the exchange rates between the money used by the two nations. Some definitions are required before showing the effect of money per se.

a. The exchange rate between two money units is the price to be paid in the domestic nation for a unit of the money unit in the foreign nation. The exchange rate in the U. S. on Britain denotes the number of dollars that must be paid into a U. S. bank or money dealer in the U. S. for a British pound sterling payable in Britain.

b. A bill of exchange is defined as [11.1-3] a note signed by the first person or company (drawer) that directs some second person or company (drawee) to make payment of a certain amount to a third one (payee) at some other place. A bill of exchange is issued by an exporter as a claim against his foreign debtor, so the bill of exchange can be clarified by reading it as: an unconditional note signed by the exporter directing his foreign customer (the foreign importer) to pay the foreign customer's local bank an amount equal to the exported amount at some future time and place. The procedure is that the domestic exporter draws the bill of exchange on the foreign importer; then, because the exporter is only interested in obtaining payment in his domestic money, sells the bill of exchange along with other documents proving ownership to a domestic bank, and is paid directly in his domestic money. The domestic bank, now in possession of the bill of exchange, transmits it to a foreign bank in which the domestic bank has an account denominated in the foreign money unit. The foreign bank receives the bill, collects the amount in question from the importer in the foreign unit, then credits the domestic bank with the deposit. Both the importer and exporter are thus relieved of converting the currencies or handling the transaction; the banks and money dealers can do it far more efficiently since that is one of their businesses, and they collect a small commission for buying and collecting the bill.

c. A demand or sight draft is the same thing, except now the payee is a foreign creditor, the second entity is a foreign bank, and the first entity is an importer. The procedure is that a domestic importer, in order to pay his foreign creditor, buys a demand draft or sight draft, which operates as a bill of exchange, from his domestic bank for the amount of the import. The domestic importer pays the domestic bank or money dealer in domestic money for a draft denominated in the foreign money. Then the importer transmits the bank sight draft to his foreign creditor (or the domestic bank sends it to the foreign bank). In either case the foreign creditor (exporter) is paid by the foreign bank in the foreign money, and the foreign bank debits the domestic (importer) bank's account accordingly. If the transaction between importer and exporter is on credit, meaning payment is delayed for some time the bank will discount the bill to account for the interest charge accruing before payment is received. Again, both exporter and importer can make the transactions entirely in their own money units through the intermediary of the foreign exchange dealer or banks. A second benefit is that a bank's credit is more widely accepted and recognized than is the credit of either the importing or exporting commercial companies.

It is evident that a bank cannot specialize in only one of these transaction types or else the bank would end up with a great surplus of one money type in one place and a shortage of the other in the foreign account. So the banks perform both the buying of bills and the selling of drafts in approximately equal amounts in order to maintain adequate balances of both and collect a commission for each. The role of the banks is to provide a middleman market for handling foreign transactions, the same as a check clearinghouse [1.11-4]. On one side, the banks buy claims against foreign companies owed to domestic exporting companies and on the other side sell bills of exchange to domestic importing companies that have obligations to pay to a foreign exporting company. The demand for bills of exchange comes from domestic importers who have to make foreign payments; the supply of bills comes from domestic exporters to whom foreigners owe money. If the demand for exchange (by importers) exceeds the supply, then the exchange rate (the amount of domestic money units required to buy a foreign money unit) is higher; if the demand is lower than supply, the rate of exchange is lower. So, considering the overall status of imports and exports between two nations, it is seen that if imports are greater than exports, the foreign exchange rate is high; if exports exceed imports, the foreign exchange rate is low.

The exchange rate between the two money units depends only marginally on the difference between the total annual values of imports and exports; mainly it depends on the supply and demand for the respective currencies as the trade is being conducted. The relative supply and demand for the currencies is indirectly related to the overall difference in the trade volume. If the dollar value of U. S. imports from Great Britain exceeds the dollar value of what the U. S. exports to Great Britain, it is said that the U. S. has a "balance of trade deficit" with Great Britain. But there are in fact a great many other categories of transactions that exist besides just trade in commodities: tourism, interest and dividend payments to foreigners who own U. S. securities, costs of shipping and insurance, gifts from government to government, capital investments by Americans in foreign nations, and a few others. All of these, together with the trade situation, determine the balance of payments surplus or deficit. The following example illustrates the process for imports and exports of goods only.

Consider the following recent partial data [1.11-5]: a) Britain exported £7.4 billion in cars and £2.7 billion in works of art to the U. S.; b) the U. S. exported £4.0 billion in aircraft, £1.5 billion in scientific instruments, £1.7 billion in medicine, and £1.9 B in electrical power equipment to Britain. Assume for the sake of brevity that the nominal relation between the U. S. dollar and British pound sterling (as of 12 Dec 2020) is $1.33 = £1.00, and that approximately the same ratio applied throughout the year (which is not usually the case). Translating these to dollar values, we have:

a. Britain imported $5.32 B in aircraft, $1.995 B in instruments, $2.261 B in medicines, and $2.527 B in electrical equipment, for a total of $12.103 B from the U. S.

b. Britain exported $9.842 B in cars and $3.591 B in art for a total of $13.433 B to the U. S.

Britain thus has a trade surplus of $1.33 B with the U. S., or stated another way the U. S. has a balance of payments deficit of $1.33 B with Britain. The U. S. aircraft manufacturers are probably Cessna, Boeing, Lockheed Martin, and Beechcraft among others; the U. S. instrument makers are likely to be Raytheon, Westech, and Ametek among others; the U. S. medical suppliers may be Pfizer, Johnson & Johnson, and McKesson among others; and the electrical equipment suppliers may be General Electric, Whirlpool and Rockwell among others. On the other side, the British car makers in question may be Jaguar, Land Rover, Rolls Royce, and Aston Martin among others; the British art dealers may be Philip Mould & Co., Haynes Fine Art, and Academy Fine Paintings and others. Now it is pretty clear that the U. S. aircraft manufacturers and their agents are not the ones importing paintings, nor are the pharmaceutical companies importing British cars. Likewise the British car companies and their agents are not importing vaccines or spectrometers, nor are the art dealers importing power generators or aircraft. Even if they did know each other, the likelihood of the total amounts exactly canceling out is slim and none. Each set of agents, manufacturers and agents buy and sell in their business, and banks or money dealers handle the international payment transactions using bills of exchange as described above. None of the importers and exporters know each other or what the others are doing, and no coordination among them is required.

Suppose the Cessna Co. sells several aircraft to a flying club in Britain, say $5 M, which is £3.759 M. Although the sale was made on credit, Cessna would prefer to have its money now. It therefore issues a bill of exchange for the £3.759 M against the flying club, and the flying club accepts it (agrees to payment at a future date). That bill denominated in pounds sterling can now be sold at a discount to a bank or money dealer in the U. S. and Cessna receives its payment in dollars directly from the U. S. dealer. Meanwhile the U. S. dealer sends the bill of exchange to its counterpart in Britain; the British dealer collects the debt from the flying club in British pounds. The same thing works in reverse for British sales to U. S. companies. If Aston Martin Ltd. sells a certain number of cars to a U. S. dealership, it can sell a bill of exchange denominated in dollars to a bank in Britain at a discount and receive payment in pounds sterling immediately. The British bank or exchange handler transmits the bill to a U. S. bank, and the U. S. bank collects the debt from the American Aston Martin dealership. The use of bills of foreign exchange for the total amount of trade prevents a large amount of currency from being transmitted directly; it economizes on the use of money (making it more efficient) by offsetting debts. But it is not just transactions between two nations in play. Each nation trades with many others, and it is rare that the balances cancel for any pair of them. The banks or foreign exchange dealers handle this the same way: through buying and selling bills for or against all nations eventually canceling out as many as can be done. Once again, this minimizes the cost of doing business with foreign nations, and indirectly compensates for the fact that each nation may use money units of differing values.

The foreign exchange rate between two money units is the ratio of their values; for example, as indicated above, it is the price of a pound sterling expressed in dollars ($1.33 = £1.00). But the exchange rate in practice is not a constant as in the simple example above. It tends to fluctuate depending on the relative abundance or scarcity of bills in the correct denominations. For example, there may be a surplus of bills on the U. S. in Germany (thus a lower price) and a shortage in France (justifying a higher price). The money dealer in Europe can arbitrate these two prices by buying cheap in Berlin and reselling them in Paris, and by doing so acquire a profit on the difference in prices. When all the nations involved were on the gold standard in which the value of each money unit in terms of gold was fixed, the exchange rate could never deviate from the cost of shipping gold and insurance (about 1 to 2%). In other words, if the U. S. dollar and British pound sterling were fixed as weights of gold, the exchange rate would always lie within the range $1.303 to $1.356 per £1.00. The account could be balanced by shipping the required weight of gold. The reason is that if there was an imbalance in the available foreign exchange, it would be better to settle the account by shipping gold than to pay the difference in the exchange rate.

When the money units are not fixed to gold or some other commodity (i.e., fiat currencies), the exchange rate fluctuates or floats based on the relative depreciation of each money unit, the supply and demand for each, and not on the balance of trade [1.11-6]. In the present example the U. S. imports more from Britain than it exports (the U. S. has a balance of payments deficit). Exporters on the U. S. side are drawing less from U. S. banks than the U. S. importers are paying in. The U. S. importers are buying bills of exchange from U. S. money dealers in order to pay off the debts incurred in Britain, and are paying into the money dealers more than the U. S. exporters are drawing out. (The U. S. exporters are drawing out in the course of receiving payments from British importers.) When British exports exceed imports from the U. S., the amount of U. S. exchange for sale in Britain, payable in the U. S. in dollars, has increased but there is little demand for them by the British importers. Then the price is low due to supply being greater than demand. So the British exporter can buy New York exchange in London at less than par (he receives more than $1.33 per pound sterling) and the U. S. importer, wanting to buy London exchange in New York has to pay more than par (he must pay more than $1.33 for each 1 pound sterling).

The U. S. dollar is not accepted by most British merchants, and the British pound sterling is not accepted by U. S. merchants. Each currency is readily accepted as money only in the own nation. Therefore the relative value of the two money units ultimately depends on what a U. S. dollar will buy in the U. S. and what a British pound sterling will buy in Britain. Supply and demand plays into the exchange rate because in order to be useful, the money units must be returned to their home nations. As always, a supply of a money unit above what is demanded will tend to drive the price of that money unit down compared to those for which demand exceeds supply. But once again, the fact that Britain has a trade surplus with the U. S. does not means that the supply of U. S. dollars is depressed by that ratio in foreign exchange; it simply means that the British bankers and money dealers can export the bills denominated in dollars to some other nation that requires them owing to a trade deficit with the U. S. Variations in the rate of exchange will, in the long run, tend to bring about an equilibrium point in overall trade [1.11-7].

The rates of foreign exchange are subject to arbitrage (making a small profit on exchange rates in various places) and speculation (taking a risk that an exchange rate will go up or down). Both activities tend to level out the prices of exchange among all the various money units.

Fluctuations in the exchange rate will occur through natural forces, i.e., the relative supply and demand for articles of foreign nations, as arbitrated around some narrow limits by the local surpluses and shortages. When the money units are both stable, either consisting of a commodity like gold or silver, or being readily converted to same, the ultimate limits on the variations in foreign exchange is the cost of shipping coin or bullion instead of paying a premium on bills [1.11-8]. But here is also a non-natural source of exchange rate fluctuations, which can occur only with a fiat money system, namely, that the banks in each nation are in competition to depreciate the values of their monetary units. If more money is issued than is required, the value of each unit declines, and domestic prices increase. But the ratio of the relative value of a depreciating currency compared to the non-depreciating one will increase, meaning domestic products are cheaper to a foreign trader with the non-depreciating currency; that will tend to expand exports from the nation with the depreciating currency, decrease imports to it, or increase the volume of bills of exchange. If the U. S. depreciates its currency compared to Britain, the exchange rate of $1.33 to £1.00 will increase above $1.33, and those possessing pounds sterling will be able to buy more goods priced in dollars. The exchange rate of the depreciating currency will then fall, compounded by the fact that the foreign trader is less desirous of trading in the depreciating currency. Raguet [1828] gives a summary [1.11-9]:

> "Upon every view of the subject which we have been able to take, we consider all profits made by the bank upon its foreign exchange transactions, beyond the amount of a fair share of guarantee, and brokerage for bringing buyers and sellers together, as a tax upon the consumption of the country, for which no equivalent service is rendered. We also consider that its dealings in Europe, which can only be done, we apprehend, by extra issues of paper, prejudicial to the currency, and consequently to the nation, is destructive of the only imaginable check upon over-trading and over-banking, inasmuch as it conceals for long periods altogether, the real state of the competition of the market, the only guide by which the merchants and banks can regulate their transactions, with advantage to the country. If it should be asked, whether there is any difference in the effect produced by the operations of the bank, from that which would be produced by the operations of private speculators, we would reply, that there is a most essential one. Independent of the powerful force of a huge capital, which gives a weight in the market, that no moderate number of citizens could bring to bear, the bank after it buys bills, has power to make an addition to the currency, the immediate effect of which is to raise the price of those bills [i.e., the ones denominated in the non-depreciating foreign currency], and thus afford a profit by their sale. Individual speculators, on the contrary, add nothing to the mass of the currency, and their operations must, in the nature of things, have but a very slight effect upon the market price of exchange."

The exchange rate has an effect on profitability [11.1-10]. Suppose a U. S. exporter to Britain finds that the exchange in the U. S. for pounds sterling in Britain is selling at a premium (£1.0 commands more than $1.33). The prices in Britain are in pounds sterling, and when they are ultimately traded back into dollars in the U. S., the U. S exporter obtains a higher profit than before. There is then a tendency to increase U. S. exports due to the higher profitability. Competition among U. S. exporters will result in lower prices for their British customers and likely an expansion of exports. The opposite is true of the American importing from Britain; he pays for the British products by buying exchange in the U. S. in dollars; since he has to pay more than the usual $1.33 or pound sterling, his profit is reduced. But keep in mind that the premium on exchange in the U. S. on pounds sterling in Britain was caused by an imbalance of greater imports than exports. The example above shows a type of corrective action built into the exchange rates that will tend to equalize imports and exports in the long run, which is to say, the overall balance of payments, of which the balance of trade in merchandise is only a portion. The exceptions are when a nations' currency can be exported, or if a nation is willing to finance imports with debt.

Is it better to import more or to export more? When nations were on the gold standard, and trade imbalances were offset by shipments of gold, the "mercantile" theorists claimed that a large trade surplus was beneficial because it led to large importations of gold that the foreigners had to pay. It is now recognized that a large influx of gold, being the money of the time, is not necessarily desirable. First of all, since gold was money, the result was a large increase in the volume of money, which depreciated its value. This is the problem that Spain ran into when it began to import large amounts of silver from South America in the 1500's. More monetary silver in circulation in Spain meant higher domestic prices. Secondly, gold and silver are not necessarily the most valuable things: a starving man does not want gold and silver, he only wants the bread it can buy. Commodities add to the true wealth of a nation, not the amount of metal; the metal is useful only for what it can be traded for. A focus on gold and silver under the mercantile approach meant that gold and silver were considered to be the most useful thing to possess. That may have seemed like a rational concept to the medieval rulers who wanted gold to finance their wars, but there is no evidence that those wars benefited anyone except the ruling elite.

It is a mistake to look only at the balance of trade between two nations and make a conclusion as to whether the balance is favorable or unfavorable. The U. S. trades with a great many nations; it may have trade surpluses with some and very large deficits with others. The most important thing to look for is the overall balance of payments between the U. S. and all its trading partners taken together, including capital transfers, loans, and foreign aid [1.11-11]. On a gold money system, the general trend is that a deficit in the balance of payments (importing more than exporting) would lead to a net shipping of gold. But a nation cannot afford to ship all its gold if gold is the monetary unit. Even with a fiat currency, it is important in order for accurate pricing to have a reasonably stable exchange rate against other currencies. The central problem as usual is an excess of credit currency, and the typical cure for a negative balance of payments is for the government to use some combination of these methods to intervene [1.11-12]:

a. Increase interest rates: the effect is to make foreign investment in the domestic economy more attractive; the foreigners must convert to the domestic currency in order to make the investments, which will serve to increase demand for the domestic currency and cause the exchange rate to drift back close to par. On the other hand, increasing interest rates will reduce the amount borrowed by foreign companies.

b. Reduce the amount of foreign aid provided by the U. S., or require the recipient nation to buy from the U. S. as a condition of the loan or grant.

c. Impose credit restrictions. These are measures designed to prevent the domestic population from investing in foreign nations. It can be is done in three ways: restrictions or limits on the amounts domestic banks can lend to foreign industries; restrictions on how much Americans can invest in foreign stocks or securities; and restrictions on the amount of expansion by domestic companies into plants in foreign nations.

d. Impose tariffs on imports. An import tariff increases the price of imports, and indirectly influences the public to buy from domestic producers

e. Impose direct limits on imports. This has the same effect as tariffs; it makes imports scarce and thus their price rises domestically.

f. Increase taxes; with less money to spend, the population will demand fewer imports.

g. Reduce government spending; if the government can reduce spending, it would free up capital in the U. S., which would allow the public to borrow to begin new domestic businesses, reducing the need for imports.

h. Impose limitations on the amount of currency that can be exchanged, thus setting the exchange rate indirectly.

i. Use political power to induce other nations to inflate their currency at the same or higher rate (what Britain did to the U. S. in the 1920's).

I mentioned earlier that sometimes a nation can export its fiat currency [1.11-13]. The U. S. currently has this ability. During the Bretton Woods regime (1945 to 1971), the U. S. dollar was defined as a unit of gold, and many other nations linked the value of their currencies, not to an amount of gold, but to the U. S. dollar directly. U. S. dollars became highly valued because they were always useful for trade.

Secondly, since the dollar was linked to gold, the foreign nation under the Bretton Woods system could trade dollars for gold (although Americans were prohibited from possessing gold). Third, because the U. S. has never defaulted on its Treasury bonds, the U. S. dollar was considered reliable enough that it was used as reserve currencies in the central banking systems of foreign nations. Since they are held in reserve, the dollars did not return to the U. S. If they did, Americans would see the full force of price increases due to the abundance of dollars in circulation. Thus it is correctly said that the U. S. exported its inflationary addiction to foreign nations by using this advantage.

There is a second way the U. S. exports dollars. In the early 1970's, President Richard Nixon convinced Saudi Arabia, at that time one of the largest oil producers and de facto head of the OPEC oil cartel, to price of their oil exports in dollars. In return, the U. S. promised to guarantee the security of the regime of the House of Saud (the ruling family). Every modern nation needs oil, and if the major producers only sell for dollars, then every nation must somehow secure dollars to pay for the oil. The advantage to the U. S. is that it can depreciate the U. S. dollar, import products from foreign countries and pay for them in dollars. But the dollars spent never return to the U. S., since they are used either to buy oil or to retain as reserves in the foreign banking systems. The oil-producing nations then use those same dollars to buy products from both the U. S. and from other foreign nations (since many of those nations use the U. S. dollar as a reserve currency).

1.12 National Debt

There are some good reasons for a national debt: those incurred to fight necessary and justifiable wars; debts incurred to finance a response to national emergencies such as the 1918 Spanish flu epidemic or the 2020 Wuhan virus epidemic; and in rare cases, debts incurred to restore an economy after a depression. Other than those emergencies, national debt is usually the result of two forces that come together: a) a government that cannot control its spending; and b) a banking system that is influenced by politics more than economics. Politicians have no trouble spending money the taxpayers don't have in order to increase their personal popularity and retain their offices.

One of the lessons of history is that national debt tends to benefit the wealthy to the detriment of the common working people. The reason is that the wealthy can afford to invest in government debt and receive the annual interest payments, and are in no hurry to have the debt paid off. Meanwhile, those investments can still be sold on the open market for their current value. In other words, government debt becomes an asset if the holder thereof can find someone to buy it. It is instructive to examine the details by which the first great national debt with regular financing was developed, namely the example of England beginning with the reign of William III (a.k.a. William of Orange, Holland) and Mary II (Stuart) as related by Walker [1.12-1]:

> "When William of Orange succeeded to the throne of England [1689], Louis XIV [of France], then at the zenith of his power, refused to acknowledge him as a legitimate monarch, and espoused the cause of the exiled Stuart [James II of England]. War, of course, followed. But fighting, in consequence of the invention of gunpowder, and the changes it gradually introduced into warfare, had become an expensive luxury; a game which kings, with their limited and uncertain revenues, could ill afford to play at, particularly for a great length of time. War with one so powerful as the *Grand Monarque* [Louis XIV] could not be safely commenced or successfully prosecuted, while every penny must be extorted from a reluctant and now independent Commons [Parliament], and the taxes immediately assessed on the large land or other property holders of the realm.

> Such was the difficulty which King William encountered; but, fortunately for his fame, he was a shrewd financier, as well as an able soldier. Up to this time, England had never had a permanent organized national debt, a national bank, or any regular and reliable system of revenue. Grants and subsidies had been voted from time to time; duties and special taxes had been imposed, but these were not to be counted upon.

> The monarch might and did borrow money from time to time, in great emergencies, but on the most disadvantageous terms. The credit of the government was always low, because there was no regularity or system in the public finances. Men had no confidence in the responsibility or punctuality of the government. Wil-

liam changed all this. He borrowed for a specified period, and promised the punctual payment of the interest semi-annually, and the principal when due; and pledged "the public funds" for the fulfillment of his promises. Hence the public securities [government bonds] were called "the funds".

He negotiated loans and issued stocks [government debt obligations]. He granted annuities upon the payment of specific sums. Interest and principal were secured by a pledge of the public funds, or revenues derived from various sources.

This put a new face upon the financial affairs of England: but something further was desirable; viz., an agency by which the national debt could be readily managed, and its semi-annual interest promptly paid.

This was accomplished by the incorporation of a national bank [Bank of England, 1697], consisting of the holders of the public stocks [government debt], to the amount of £1,200,000.

One thing more was wanting; viz., a permanent and sufficient income, to meet not only the interest on the accumulated debt, but the current expenses of the government, already large, and constantly increasing. To effect this, a land-tax was established; small, indeed, in amount, and upon a fixed valuation, so that it could not be increased with the increasing value of the land.

A system of duties on all imports was also enacted, and an excise upon all home manufactures and products. In short, a system of indirect taxation was adopted, far more general and effective than any which had before existed.

Thus was completed the grand triad of the system of finance, inaugurated by the English Revolution [1688]; viz. -- funding, banking, and indirect taxation. The immediate as well as ultimate, results of the new system are alike remarkable and worthy of our attention.

First, the credit of the government was firmly established. It could borrow more money, and at a lower rate of interest than ever before. Men of small means could now loan money to the government, and with entire confidence. The whole community could be laid under contribution [i.e., payment of taxes].

Second, government was enabled to carry on war by borrowing, instead of imposing taxes. War could be waged with credit, instead of cash. Parliament had only to vote a loan. No expenditure need be stopped for want of funds, while the national credit was unimpaired. This was a great change. Many a war had been abruptly closed for want of funds. There was no such necessity hereafter.

Third, this course removed the fear of immediate and pressing taxation from the rich, because the greater part was now to fall upon the masses of the people, who pay taxes, not in proportion to property, but to consumption [in the form of tariffs and excise taxes]. This was an agreeable consideration to the wealthy classes; and the more so, because, as the public stocks [debt] were multiplied, better opportunities were afforded for investments [in government debt].

Fourth, especially was the new policy acceptable to the aristocracy, who, at that time, even more perhaps than now [1867], monopolized the public offices, and whose revenues and patronage were increased by governmental expenditures."

The American patriot Thomas Paine [1.12-2] of *Common Sense* fame and some additional details by Walker [1.12-3] give an accounting of how the national debt in Great Britain grew with each war from 1688 (under William III and Mary II) to 1867 (under Victoria), starting with the initial debt (investors in the £1.2 M of government debt administered by the newly formed Bank of England):

a. War vs. France from 1688 to 1697: cost = £20.3 M; total debt in 1697 = £21.5 M

b. War of Spanish Succession, 1702 to 1713: cost = £32.25 M; total debt = £53.75 M

c. Approximately £7.5 M paid off between 1727 and 1739; total debt in 1739 = £46.25 M

d. War of Austrian Succession, 1739 to 1748: cost = £31.75 M; total debt in 1748 = £78.0 M

e. Then came eight years of peace, during which £3.0 M of the debt was repaid; the debt in 1756 was £75.0 M

f. Seven Years War, known in America as the French and Indian War, 1756 to 1763: cost = £72.5 M, total debt in 1763 = £147.5 M

g. Then came peace for twelve years, and in that time £11.5 M was paid off; the debt in 1775 was about £136.0 M

h. The American War [American Revolution], 1775 to 1783: cost = £103 M; total debt in 1783 was £239 M

i. Ten years of peace, and the debt was reduced by £5.0 M; total debt in 1793 was £234 M

j. The Jacobin War, 1793 up to 1796, when Paine wrote: additional debt to that time was £44.0 M; total debt in 1796 was about £278 M

k. The total cost of the Jacobin War that ended in 1802 turned out to be £248 M; and the debt in 1803 was £526 M.

l. Then came the final Napoleonic War, from 1803 to 1815, which cost £339 M; the debt in 1815 was £865 M

m. From 1815 to 1835 a total of £87 M was paid off; and the debt in 1835 was £778 M

n. Then 800,000 slaves were emancipated in the West Indies at a cost of about £22 M; and the debt as of 1867 was about £800 M or so

Paine's great contribution was to notice that each war cost about 50% more than the preceding one. He was correct except for the War of Austrian Succession (£31.75 M vs. his projection of £48 M) and the Jacobin War (£248 M vs. his estimate of £162 M). Walker [1.12-4] informs us why repayments were so slow during time of peace:

> "Because it was no object with the ruling class to pay off the debt, since the national stocks [national debt] had become the most eligible investments [interest paid to the holders of the debt by the government but actually paid by the people]; so the resources of the nation were squandered upon the court [aristocratic class]."

Walker informs us that this convergence of debt and taxation in England resulted in the impoverishment of the working class [1.12-5]:

> "This is especially apparent in England. What has become of the yeomanry [small independent landowners], once the pride of the country? Their little estates have disappeared; have been swallowed up by the terrible system of taxation to which they have been subjected. The pleasant hedges which still surround the small enclosures, once constituting the freeholds of her yeomanry, may yet be seen in all parts of the country. They are the monuments of an industrious, brave, and independent class of men, now extinct. These lands are indeed tilled by the hands of their descendants, no longer yeomanry, but peasants, almost the paupers of the nation. ...
>
> The economy of a national debt, under the modern financial system, must always impoverish the productive classes. Its entire influence on them is oppressive. It deprives them of their honest reward, by a false currency [i.e., a fiat money], which robs them of a large share of their nominal wages; it imposes upon them, through indirect taxation, an undue proportion of the public burdens, and is in fact, a stupendous enginery for depressing them, though perhaps not so intended. Hitherto we have known little of its effects in the United States. Until the present time we have felt little pressure from public indebtedness and consequent taxation; but the case is now [1866] altered. We have an immense debt, and a larger amount of annual interest than any other people on the face of the earth."

Here we are in 2023, and the same is true again of the U. S. Every debt ultimately gets paid in some fashion, and the debts incurred by nations are no different. A nation in debt will eventually run out of places to borrow. It may try to repay the debt by exporting goods to its creditor nations. It may try increased taxation, and endure the decline in the standard of living among the people. It may simply rob its creditors (mostly its own people) by refusing to pay or paying pennies on the dollar. But increasing taxes and repudiating the debt will make the politicians look bad, and that is the least likely option. What is more likely is that the debtor nation will simply become the servant of its creditors; fighting wars as proxies for the creditor nation, compensating for the creditor nations' agricultural or industrial failures by exporting goods, or performing other services to the creditor nation. The important thing is that the debtor nations' politicians don't suffer.

The problem isn't whether or not the debt will be paid; it will certainly be paid, either in money, commodities, or a reduced standard of living. The problem is who will pay. Consider first three reasons why the wealthy are not going to pay much of it: 1) there aren't enough rich people compared to the population; 2) the total wealth of the upper classes is not enough to pay the debt, even if all their wealth were confiscated; and 3) the wealthy have good political connections and thus ability to avoid paying. Consider the poor: they cannot pay; they are struggling enough just to get by. It is always the middle class that pays (if it exists). The reason is simple: if the middle class exists, it is likely a majority of the population and has the ability to pay moderate amounts. What happens if there is no middle class? Then the government has only two choices: either sell off the nation's natural resources (possibly including its best people), or repudiate the debt, default, and destroy the nation's credit. If the latter is chosen, the politicians inherit another problem: since they won't able to borrow a wooden nickel, they will have to balance the national budget and will no longer be able to buy votes with promised government handouts paid for by the middle class. That will hurt the politicians the most. But of course you (selling Granny's Tarts for a living) and all the millions of other middle class people will get the blame.

Depreciation of the monetary unit tends to promote a large national debt on the grounds that that depreciation of the currency implicitly reduces the debt. The logic is: the nation can run up a debt, expand the money supply, and repay the debt with depreciated currency. Then the amount repaid has less purchasing power than the original debt, so therefore the nation comes out ahead and the public gets part of it for free. It is true that debtors benefit from depreciation because they are repaying the debt denominated in a money unit, each of which has less purchasing power than when the debt was contracted. Also, since the depreciation is a result of an increased money supply, the money is actually easier for the debtor to come by. Therefore, the claim goes, not only does the debtor have an easier time acquiring the required number of money units, each of them has less buying power than before. Figure 1.12-1 illustrates the situation. Here a person has borrowed $10,000 at 5% annual interest for a term of ten years. The monthly payment is $106.07 and thus the annual payment is $1272.84. The solid line near the top shows the $1272.84 paid annually, and on the far right side, have $12728.40 total repayment over ten years. If there is no depreciation of the money, the lender will receive $1272.84 each year over the ten years, and the purchasing power of each of those dollars will equal that of the dollars he lent.

Consider now what happens when the annual depreciation rate is 3, 5, and 10%, as indicated by the various dashed lines. The upper set curves are read on the left side and the lower set are read on the right side. The upper line in the lower set shows the value of the repaid dollars at 3% annual depreciation referred back to the purchasing power of the initial loan (read on the right side). In the first year, the dollars are still the same, 1.0; but in year two they are worth only $0.97; in year three they are worth $0.97 squared, which is $0.94, relative to the initial purchasing power. At year ten, the dollars are worth $0.76 compared to the initial dollars due to depreciation at 3% annual. The long dashed line in the lower set shows the 5% depreciation case, and the dollars at the end of ten years have a purchasing power of $0.63 compared to initial; the dot-dash line in the lower set shows the 10% annual depreciation rate, and the purchasing power at year ten is $0.389 compared to year one. Keep in mind that the borrower is continuing to pay $1272.84 each year, but the value of each dollar is declining. The upper set dotted line shows the repayment for each year scaled to initial-year dollars per the 3% annual depreciation, and at year ten, the borrower's effective repayment is $11140.57 in initial dollars. Likewise, the short-dashed line shows the 5% depreciation rate, and the total repayment is only $10214.87 in initial dollars; the longer-dashed line in the upper set shows the effective repayment value at 10% annual depreciation, and the effective repayment is only $8290.28 in initial dollars. It is said then that depreciation of the money unit benefits debtors, since they can pay back less than what they borrowed in terms of purchasing power. What about the lender? He is being robbed because he receives less than was contracted for. In the 10% depreciation case, he actually receives less in buying power than the total loan; the effective interest rate is negative. But, since he received $12728.40, he may be obligated to pay a tax on the "profit"; in other words he could end up paying taxes on a loss if he waits to account for the profit all at one time. Actually it is worse than that. Who will lend money at 5% if the annual depreciation rate is 10% or even 5%? The lender has no choice, unless he is interested in losing money, but to raise the interest rate he charges.

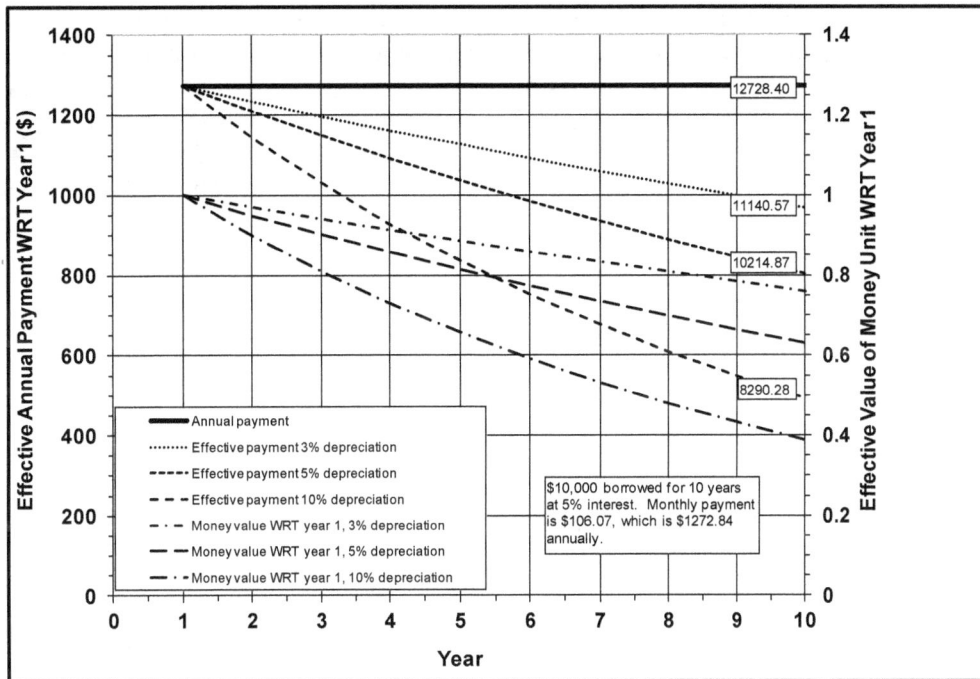

Figure 1.12-1: Example of Borrowing and Repayment with Depreciating Money Unit

All of that is correct, but the principle can only be stretched so far. In this example, the borrower only took out one loan, and proceeded to pay it back over the ten years; with depreciation, the borrower gives back less in purchasing power while the lender is under the illusion that he is receiving back more than he lent [1.12-6]. But that is not how nations operate. Normally a nation will continue to borrow annually over a long period of time, analogous to the person in the example borrowing $10,000 every year. Any nation who does so will obviously continue to build up debt; will never reduce the amount owed; and will never become debt free, no matter how much the money unit depreciates. It can stop only when the borrowing stops. It is true that the nation continues to repay in depreciating money units. So what? If the nation cannot control its spending, and is adding to the debt in current money units, obviously it won't be able pay the current debt in depreciated units any more than it can pay the debt if it were tabulated in original units; it is all the same. The debt cannot be paid in depreciating units because the people cannot afford the necessary taxation to do so and still maintain their standard of living. That is a consequence of the fact that depreciation is caused by the injection of more money into the system, which means that prices must rise. Ultimately the pressure builds because the ruling class cannot bring themselves to reduce spending, especially on social programs that bring in the votes. Under these conditions, the claim that depreciation reduces the national debt is akin to saying that a newborn infant should be at home with Mom instead of out in the bars drinking with his buddies: it is true but is never relevant. Depreciation can reduce the debt only when the accumulation of new debt stops. But it is a crooked way to manage the nation's finances, since depreciation of the money unit has other far-reaching negative side effects, as will be shown in Chapter 2.

If a government stops borrowing and decides to pay its national debt, it is best done by organizing it into long-term bonds at the prevailing interest rate. Then comes the hard part: maintaining the discipline necessary to run an annual surplus and pay it off over several decades. The other thing to keep in mind is that a government bond is both an asset and a liability. If you have U. S. bonds in your 401k, and the interest and principal is being paid, it is then a working asset. It continues to be an asset so long as it can be bought and sold, and the payments are being made. But as a taxpayer, that same bond is a liability.

There is a limit to the amount of debt a government can issue, and that limit depends on the buyer's confidence that the note can be repaid without too much depreciation [1.12-7]. A large enough debt will cause doubts to arise among the buying public, whether they are the people of a nation or foreign investors. Foreign investors are partly influenced by whether the risk is lower here or in their own nations; they may decide to invest in U. S. bonds only if they are regarded as less risky than the ones issued by other countries. In other words, they may choose the least of a host of evils. Corporate buyers also gauge their risk based on confidence in repayment. When there is sufficient doubt about the principal, new debt can be issued only to cover interest payments; in essence, not being able to increase the principal liability. Then the government has two choices: it can either balance the budget by some means, or forced to ruin the money unit by a rapid depreciation (known as hyperinflation).

Every national debt will be "paid" somehow. The debt cannot be deleted by depreciation unless the policy of destroying of the money unit is an acceptable economic outcome. Not only will it destroy the nation's credit, it will first ruin the current investors. Who will trust the government again, except at very high interest rates? There is one thing we can be sure of: if the destruction of the money is the adopted policy for eliminating the debt, the government will make sure to segregate investors into two groups: a) the ruling elite and their enablers, who will be notified in time to divest themselves of the bonds and evade losses; and b) the chumps who are left holding the bonds and actually take the loss (i.e., you and me).

If the U. S. does ever get to the point where it can no longer issue government debt because no one will buy it, the politicians and bureaucrats will have no choice but to take steps to restore the nation's credit. The first one, the only honest one, mentioned above, is to consolidate the entire debt into a set of long-term bonds at a reasonable interest rate, then: 1) run annual surpluses in the government budget, 2) devote those surpluses for the next 20 or 30 years to paying off the bonds, and 3) restrain the banking system from depreciating the money unit. This is what the U. S. government did from 1789 to 1836, when the national debt was finally paid off. But that option is probably politically impossible under the current system: it would require the politicians to stop buying votes, stop lying, stop spending money the taxpayers don't have, reduce the welfare state, and end the money-expanding alliance with the banking system.

1.13 Economic Analysis

Modern economists use their expertise with charts, graphs, and equations to explain how an economy works. They are useful only in a limited way because it is easy to show the immediate observable effects of a policy. For example, if a demand curve "shifts" in a certain direction, the selling price will change. But there is an implicit assumption that the shape of the supply curve will remain static even if demand changes. In other words, the models ignore or cannot show the secondary and tertiary effects. Hazlitt pointed out in his classic 1946 book [1.13-1] that it is those other effects, which are not usually subject to accurate forecasting, that determine the overall net effects of policies. What we call "economics" in a free country is actually the result of millions of decisions made by the entire population, and it must be remembered that many of those decisions are not rational or logical. People get caught up in fads; make decisions based on assumptions (good or bad); are subject to moods of pessimism or optimism; react to opinions based on both fact and fiction; and may fail to account for the element risk in their decision-making. None of these can be modeled by professional economists; the best that can be hoped for is to recognize them in hindsight. Modern economic models often produce incorrect predictions because they either contain incorrect assumptions about human behavior, or because they contain embedded assumptions regarding the interrelations between economic forces [1.13-2]. Experience, as always is the best guide for forecasting, and even then it should be remembered that there is potential for wide variations in outcome.

Economics cannot be rigorously modeled as a set of equations. If an economy could be modeled with a system of equations at all, the complexity of the algorithms and requirements for accurate input data would be so large as to make the system practically unworkable. There is a saying in the engineering business:

"Cheap, fast, and good: pick any two."

If something can be designed and built quickly and sold cheaply, it won't be any good; a good product can be developed and marketed quickly, but it won't be cheap; a good product can be designed and sold at a cheap price, but it will take some time. There is a corresponding rule in economics:

"Growth, price stability, and low unemployment: pick any two".

Economic growth can be achieved with stable prices, but only if unemployment can be tolerated; or can have high employment with price stability but sacrifice growth; or can have growth and high employment, but accompanied with higher prices. Most nations have chosen growth and high employment; the mechanism for doing so is to increase the money supply, which depreciates the value of the money unit, which increases prices, which we call "inflation". Unfortunately, even this strategy only works temporarily, after which, as described in section 1.9, wages must increase to compensate for higher prices. At that point there are two options. The first option is to continue more inflation followed by more price increases until such time as the system is saturated and a depression occurs, with negative growth and high unemployment. The second option is to stop the inflation and a recession occurs with slower growth and moderate unemployment. Normally the temptation is to continue the inflation as long as it can be tolerated.

There are no complete economic theories that show us the way to a stable equilibrium between price stability, growth and full employment. Modern economies contain too many moving parts; operate under varying conditions of profitability; and are subject to differing forces that influence people's decisions. It is probably impossible even to define what an equilibrium state looks like. Even if that could be defined, there is not enough data available in time to make whatever corrections or policy changes necessary to maintain the so-called "equilibrium". You can just visualize row after row of servers and computers at the Census Bureau and the Bureau of Labor Statistics, munching and crunching away, analyzing mountains of data and statistics, slicing and dicing us into race, ethnicity, age, marital status, height, birth weight, current weight, eye color, urban vs. rural, families vs. individuals, number of cousins, affinity for wine, Zodiac sign, and who knows what else. The only result is a different mountain of statistics, useful only for fine-tuning preferences and benefits for certain segments of the population, claiming to only be acting in the general interest, especially those of the poor; but at the same time, missing the big picture, which is that depreciation of money is the core problem of poverty because it hurts the poor the most.

That does not mean that economics is the "dismal science" as it is often called; it means that there are a few simple, well-known rules as outlined in preceding sections that will in the long run provide the best economy achievable. Most policy changes are recommended based on an examination of the general price level: if it begins to accelerate, it is evident that there is too much credit money in place. But a stable price level is not necessarily a reliable indicator as discussed in section 1.9: it is possible to have underlying risk to the economy in the presence of general price stability because the decline in profitability is hidden. Therefore, an increase in production efficiency may mask what would ordinarily be observed as an increase in prices. On the other hand, a decrease in production due to declining profitability, which means a decline in employment, can occur with an increase in prices. The price increases may be caused by the increase in credit, but could be caused by a reversion to less efficient methods of production.

Many modern economic theories are based on variations of John Maynard Keynes' theory, published in 1936 [1.13-3]. The later economists (Hahn, Friedman, Hazlitt, and Rothbard, among others), armed with the proven principles of classical economics (Smith, Ricardo, Hume, Thornton, Jevons, Raguet, A. Walker, F. Walker, Menger, Marshall, Wicksell, von Mises, Fisher, Pigou, Hayek, and others), have concluded that Keynes' theory is not generally applicable because is founded on assumptions that are not usually valid. Several excellent books have been written on this subject [1.13-4, 1.13-5, 1.13-6, 1.13-7].

It applies only in the narrow case of a recovery from a depression, and even then must be used carefully. Here is a short list of the shortcomings of Keynes' "general" theory:

1. Keynes' book was first published in English in 1936, and was translated to other languages the next year. In the Preface to the German Edition, dated 7 Sep 1936, Keynes admitted that his theory is more suitable for economic tyranny than economic freedom [1.13-8] because it is more readily adaptable to a top-down command economy than one that is inconvenienced by people making their own decisions under a free-market system.

2. Keynes ignored the influence of individual economic choices and instead assumed that the general trends in an economy can be inferred from aggregate data [1.13-9]. Much of his analysis is based on predicting trends in "national income", which says nothing about prices, wages, or profitability in the very large number of businesses and activities that comprise national income. In other words, Keynes' assumption is that an aggregate, which is the integral (or sum) of all the components, is a suitable representation of the conditions in general [1.13-10]; he ignores the obvious outliers which may be a source of instability in the economy.

3. Keynes assumed that economics is deterministic and that a set of equations with a few constants and a few variables can be used to describe the workings of an economy [1.13-11]. By making this claim, he had to first assume all the elements are independent, and then choose which elements in the model are "static" and which are "variable". He also made assumptions about the behavior of the variable ones. The truth is that there are no "static" factors in an economy: they are all variable (at least in a free economy where individual choice matters). It is worse than that: they are not all "independent". The fact that they are not independent means that the behavior of some variables depends on the behavior of other variables, and all those cross-terms would have to be accounted for in the model. Therefore a "complete" theory would be recursive at minimum, or to put it simply: impossible to use because one could never establish the correct starting point or ever acquire enough data to feed the model. Keynes spends a great deal of time in his chapters 20 and 21 showing a mathematical model. In chapter 21, section 6 he recognized correctly that the variables are not independent, and yet the operation of his theory demands that economists pretend that they are [1.13-12].

4. Keynes assumed that the public generally will be content with declining real wages for an indefinite length of time, and will not object or hold out for a restoration of their purchasing power [1.13-13]. Recall that declining real wages is either a static money income with rising prices or a falling money income with stable prices; in each case the workers; standard of living is decreasing. It may be true that people will tolerate a declining real wage during the depths of a depression when work is scarce, but it is not true in general. Sooner or later they will demand some compensation for the depreciation of the money unit, which is normally the cause of a declining standard of living [1.13-14, 1.13-15]. He also made a false assumption that wage rates are a direct indication of total wages, as if individuals were unable or unwilling to work more hours than before. Keynes actually had a correct model of how prices, wages, and production behave in a depression; the problem is that he assumed that the policies appropriate for that condition are applicable at all times. But they are not applicable at all times or in all places. If the workers can, they will demand higher wages to compensate for the depreciation of the money. Sometimes the workers have no choice but to tolerate a declining standard of living due to a surplus of labor from immigration or the exportation of industry to a foreign country. But give Keynes his due: there are a great many workers who will in fact succumb to the grand illusion that their standard of living is increasing if they receive more dollars in their paycheck. That is the core of the deception brought about by a depreciating currency.

5. Keynes assumed that savings permanently reduces or replaces consumption [1.13-16]. By this error, his theory led to the absurd conclusion that savings are inherently evil, and consumption is inherently good, therefore his advice was to create more money and expand purchasing power [1.13-17, 1.13-18]. It was shown above (section 1.9) that in healthy economies, proper levels of investment cannot exceed savings (which oddly, Keynes admitted at one point [1.13-19, 1.13-20]). Since investment leads to greater

production at lower prices, consumption increases gradually, albeit with a time lag. Savings, being the source of investment, delays and expands consumption; it does not replace it [1.13-21].

6. Keynes assumed that governments are always more efficient in utilizing capital and should spend on public works when private investors or entrepreneurs become reluctant to invest during a recession or depression [1.13-22]. History shows that this is a very tenuous proposition [1.13-23]. Governments are competent only in matters of national defense and perhaps a few large-scale public works like the Hoover Dam, the Rural Electrification Administration, and the Interstate Highway System. Otherwise, history is pretty clear that private initiative, coupled with the competition and the profit motive are the most efficient uses of capital over the long run, although no doubt many mistakes are made along the way. Governments tend to make mistakes since the priorities are politically driven.

7. Keynes assumed that public works "investments" automatically improve an economy, including employment, by some mysterious "multiplier effect" [1.13-24], and that the multiplier is based on increased consumption. He also assumed indirectly that an additional increment of government investment will always lead to an increase in consumption according to some factor that he called the "investment multiplier". He had another concept called the "acceleration principle", which predicts that consumption spending will increase at some rate faster than the rate at which investment increases. Keynes never offered any proof of their actual existence. It is illogical: the "multiplier" as described by Keynes is too good to be true because it implies that economic growth will be infinite if the public agrees to spend all of their income [1.13-25]. That lack of proof hasn't stopped the politicians from claiming that the expense of some new stadium or convention center "will generate X times more growth than the cost of the project". Often these white elephant projects are sold to the public exactly on the basis of such a claim, supported by the usual quackery of public spending advocates.

1.14 General Concepts Summarized

This section contains a brief summary of the important points discussed so far.

1. Money is superior to barter because it permits exchanges to be made at a lower overall cost in labor.

2. Money is a commodity with four differences from other commodities: a) it does not satisfy wants or needs directly; b) it is not consumed; c) it is the most marketable of commodities when widely accepted; and d) a supply of money above what is needed depreciates the value of it.

3. Individual economic freedom is the best path to general prosperity.

4. Economic demand is the desire plus the ability to pay. Supply is based on the estimate of economic demand and prospects for profit.

5. Profit is the difference between revenue and costs, which is the incentive to bother taking the risk of production.

6. Production only occurs if there is an expectation of profit, true or not.

7. Nothing of value is free; the politicians can hand out goods as if they were free, but ultimately the bill must be paid. Meanwhile, the productive people, who paid for the "free goods", become resentful, and the freeloaders demand more.

8. Individuals generally (in aggregate) make better economic decisions than the government. The government has legitimate control of national defense, certain types of research and development, and some large-scale infrastructure that can only be paid by the general taxpayers.

9. All taxes are ultimately paid by individuals, regardless of who writes the check to the government.

10. Capital is the means of production and is largely the result of the labor of the past (tools, knowledge, and infrastructure); it is the things produced in the past now available to contribute to current production.

11. Money is not capital; money is only the means to acquire capital.

12. Rent paid on farmland depends on relative fertility, the returns on employed capital, and proximity. Rent paid for industrial and residential property is mostly based on proximity.

13. Entrepreneurs seek profit, not to 'satisfy a demand'.

14. Accurate profitability estimates require a stable money value.

15. Only the labor that is profitable to employ gets employed in the long run.

16. Minimum wage increases can hurt the people it was designed to help.

17. Credit is the lending of a present good (usually money) in return for a promise to repay a future good; interest being the fee for the time the present good is employed by the borrower.

18. Credit depends on the good faith of the borrower and lender; it is a system that relies on trust and confidence.

19. Credit permits economic expansion because it makes money more efficient: there is less idle surplus, and it reduces the need for cash.

20. Business fluctuations are a normal part of any economy, and are usually caused by crop failures, labor strikes, and other temporary events.

21. Recessions and depressions are a large disparity between supply and demand (supply greater than demand), and are usually caused by a monetary expansion that led to an over-supply of producers' goods and a decline in the profitability of those industries.

22. A recession or depression cannot be cured by a further expansion of the money supply at the first sign of an economic decline; it will only put off the inevitable and make the crash worse. At the same time, it is important not to permit a decline in the money supply unless wages are allowed to fall along with prices.

23. Previous depreciation of the money unit is permanent unless wages and prices can both fall in a recession or depression.

24. Income and economic inequality are the natural result of a free economic system. Only a controlled economy can achieve near-equality: 2% of the ruling elite with all the wealth and power dominating the other desperately poor 98%.

25. National debt usually benefits the wealthiest people, since they receive revenue in the form of interest paid mostly by the middle class. That said, it is not always true that it leads to large incomes if the interest rate on the debt is low.

26. There are a variety of corrupt means to "pay off" a national debt, but the best policy is long-term national fiscal discipline.

27. Any complete model of an advanced economy would be too complex to use. Even if one existed, it would still give incorrect predictions because too many of the required inputs would have to be done by assumption, intuition, or guesswork.

1.15 Detecting Socialism

The philosophy of socialism makes the following claims against free enterprise: a) that freedom is inefficient, or is less efficient than it actually is; b) that free enterprise is neither resilient nor adaptive and is inherently unfair; c) that an overall directed system of economics will bring equality and prosperity to all workers; and d) that a socialist system will protect and improve the means of production. Fairchild et al [1.15-1], writing in 1927, provided a good criticism of these claims: a) capitalism has in fact become more efficient with time; b) it does adapt to changing situations because it does accommodate collective bargaining and liability for fraud; c) that unity, brotherhood and altruism are not sufficient substitutes for individual initiative and reward; d) that a top-down command system would require a level of knowledge and control that is impractical; and e) that a socialist system would reward people based on loyalty to the government instead of actual ability. All of these criticisms have been shown to be valid whenever socialism has actually been adopted.

"Progressivism", or as it should be called, "Marxist socialism", is often advertised these days as the "cure" for "capitalism", or as it should be called, "free enterprise". It seems that the advocates of socialism are unaware that Karl Marx's theory was never intended to promote equality or prosperity or to lift up the poor. So what was the intent? Recall in section 1.1 the description of the medieval agricultural feudal system, wherein the aristocracy, numbering about 2% of the population, owned all the wealth (land) and kept the other 98% of the population in subjection. The Church was the intermediary between the two groups. In its religious capacity it tried to impress upon all the importance of faith, family, and salvation. In its moral capacity it tried to restrain the worst impulses of the aristocracy. In its economic capacity it had a large stash of gold and silver in the form of artifacts donated by the congregations, it owned a great deal of land granted under feudal tenure, and was a prominent moneylender [1.15-2]. The aristocracy spent most of its time using up the surplus created by the peasants to fight each other in a quest for more land, more peasants, and more power. Marx wanted a return to that system with two changes. First, he desired to eliminate Christianity and replace it by a secular government ruling an atheist population because morality could then be defined as whatever the ruling class said it was. Second, he desired to establish an industrial rather than an agricultural economy. Marx was dumb enough to reject the morality of Christianity in favor of "human nature", but smart enough to realize there was no going back once the industrial revolution started. Only a power-demanding hypocrite like Marx could have devised a political system in which every economic actor, from the captains of industry down to the little kid with the lemonade stand, buys and sells according to the arbitrary dictates of some government bureaucrat. That's all socialism was intended to do, and that's about all it has accomplished wherever it has been implemented: a fabulously wealthy, arbitrarily powerful ruling elite in control of industry, government, and the other 98%. Once the 98% realize what has happened, they reject it altogether. But it is too late; they are trapped until the system collapses of its own weight. Once free people realize what socialism leads to, they also reject it. That is why socialism usually had to be implemented by force in the past. But in modern times, it is possible through the influence of social media propaganda to intimidate the public into passively accepting it. That is why the advocates of socialism resort to the tried-and-true tactics of all non-thinking revolutionaries: screeching slogans in the streets about the defects or shortcomings of free enterprise, and announcing various "initiatives" to create paradise on earth using disproven theory. The latest tactic in the U. S. is the widespread accusation of "systemic racism". Meanwhile, the revolutionaries maneuver secretly to intimidate the existing institutions into either adopting their governing philosophy or handing power over to the revolutionaries directly.

Socialists are pretty adept at re-naming their movements in order to breed confusion. When one movement fails, they simply call it something else. That is why we appear to have so many competing ideological systems: communism, fascism, neo-liberalism, humanism, Fabianism, progressivism, "third way", "new way", "futurism", "building better communities", "equity", and so on. ("Fabian" is an old-fashioned euphemism for guerilla warfare.) But they are all the same thing: a dictatorship of bureaucrats based on the fundamentals of socialism as laid out by Karl Marx; a system of absolute control. But here is the subtle thing: a socialist is happy to criticize other socialists, and then advocate an economic system that leads to the very same thing. Adolf Hitler gave a correct denunciation of communism on 22 Sep 1933 [1.15-3]: that communism demands the people give up their wants; abandon freedom; acquiesce to central control; to regress economically according to an ideology; that communism is backward-looking; that it is founded on jealousy; and leads to the destruction of the economy.

But on 6 Oct 1935, Hitler gave a speech in which he outlined the economic philosophy of the German National Socialists (a.k.a. NAZI) [1.15-4], stating that it was essential that the German economy be completely controlled per a central plan; that the system cannot function if people pursue their own interests; that individual liberty leads to starvation; and that the only way to ensure economic stability and progress is by the fixing of wages and prices.

What we have here is typical socialist hypocrisy: Hitler correctly demonized communism as a means of control so as to lower the standard of living, but then imposed economic controls in Germany that accomplished the same thing. He claimed that Germans would starve if not for central economic planning, when in fact it was the same central economic planning that caused the Russian people to starve. He claimed (as the communists did) that economic freedom is bad for the entire nation. Yet he has the audacity to criticize the communists for imposing the same polices that he pursued. He correctly points out that communism is based on jealousy and envy. But notice that that "economic planning", with the goal of economic "equality" has its roots in the same fallacies. My point here is that the NAZI (fascist) system and the communist system are slightly different variants of the same disease/religion: the socialist philosophy codified by Karl Marx. I need only point out that modern American "progressives" make exactly the same hypocritical arguments to support their policies, which will fail here the same as Communists and fascists failed everywhere they came to power.

But allow me to be more direct than Fairchild et al., now that we have 100 years of historical data on the "virtues" of Marxist socialism as advocated by the Ivy League economics departments, by whatever new buzzwords they call it. Now that we know what socialism leads to after a century of tyranny and 200 million murdered in its name, everyone has to ask themselves: "Am I enough of a moron to want it?" Caution: there will always be some morons, and they will want socialism, and it will necessary that they learn to think like a professional moron, that is, a robotic drone. If they can't think like a robot, believing every claim and obeying every order, they will start to question the socialist system, and they will inadvertently slow its progression (even though they embrace it). Your job, as a person who believes in freedom, is to be able to identify these mental midgets wherever they may appear.

A person who thinks like a robot will blindly follow any dictate issued by anyone with a government ID card. For example, a person who is on mental auto-pilot fails to see any evil in the following official order:

"Tote that barge, lift that bale, march those kindergarten kids into that gas chamber."

When Hitler's Third Reich issued that order, the suitably trained robotic German people elbowed each other to be granted the privilege of being the first to implement it. All moral standards were abandoned because a most sacred highness (i.e., any government employee) told them to: a socialist regards the government as the highest moral authority. Never mind right and wrong; just obey orders. Once a society has been trained to be zombies and robots, any tyrannical order can be issued. If the government of such a society announced that all girls shall be turned over for service in the official harem on their fourteenth birthday, the obedient android-father/male reproductive contributor will stand in line at the police station for a week beforehand, just to make sure his daughter is the first one in the neighborhood to be taken.

The socialism-embracing mechanical mind must ignore any inconsistencies in any official order, and must be prepared to believe two opposite things at the same time. For example:

"July and August are the warmest months in the Northern hemisphere, whereas the month following June and the month preceding September are the two coldest."

No qualified progressive will question the veracity of that statement, nor will he doubt the legitimacy of any order that uses that statement as a rationale. Here is an applicable official order:

"We [i.e., you] must make sacrifices to conserve energy to reduce pollution and climate change by restricting the heating of our [i.e., your] homes only during the two months where it is most needed. Therefore: oil, gas, and electric energy may be consumed for heating homes only in the month after June and the month preceding September."

A robot-thinker will obey without looking at a calendar, and gladly freeze from November to March. It is worse than that: a robot-thinker will not consider any ancillary effects of a policy. If a government official proclaims that cows should all be killed because they emit too much methane, no mechanical mental marvel will question how such an action will affect the availability of beef or leather. The robot-thinking businesswoman will permit a government official to set her prices and rate of "reasonable" profit; a knee-jerk reacting doctor will spend two-thirds of his time filling out government-mandated forms in the interest of "equal access to healthcare"; the average robot/serf will gladly convert to an all-electronic currency in the interest of "transaction security". "Reasonable" is the socialist code word for "just above minimum wage"; "equal access to healthcare" is the code phrase for "health care based on political connections", and "transaction security" is the code phrase for "tracking and spying on everything you buy and sell".

Here is one way to detect a "progressive". The "progressives" must always make sure they fit in. They can never question any official order; never question the rationale, logic, or objectives of any screaming mob; believe everything they see and hear on the American mainstream media; take pride in becoming a brainwashed retard; trust implicitly the "words of wisdom" coming from the Ivy League universities; and last but not least, accept the fact that their real job on earth is to only think sanctioned thoughts, blindly obedient to the god of government, owned and operated by uncaring bureaucratic drones.

Here is another method to identify them. Once a "progressive" has stopped thinking for himself, he can only advance socialist activism by becoming an emotional slogan-chanter. Then the race is on to see how well they can spontaneously direct hatred toward anyone (you) who is in favor of individual liberty. They will use their emotions to screech and scream arbitrary invectives (per the daily talking points) at anyone (you) who talks about freedom. They demand that normal people (like you) be punished for any opinions that are contrary to socialism, demand that those who oppose socialism (like you) be fired from their jobs. The socialist is willing to ruin the reputations of normal people (like you) by publicizing outright fabrications, and to march normal kindergarten children (yours) into re-education camps. You will come to recognize them easily enough, hopefully before it is too late.

Frederic Bastiat was a French economist writing in 1850, just after the 1848 Revolution, when France was stumbling toward a centralized economy. His most famous work is *The Law*, a short treatise that describes everything that is wrong with socialism. Bastiat's concluding advice was to "try liberty" [1.15-5]:

> "Away, then, with quacks and organizers! Away with their rings, chains, hooks, and pincers! Away with their artificial systems! Away with the whims of governmental administrators, their socialized projects, their centralization, their tariffs, their government schools, their state religions, their free credit, their bank monopolies, their regulations, their restrictions, their equalization by taxation, and their pious moralizations."

If you are one of those dummies that desire socialism, make sure you decide in advance whether you will feed your children out of other people's garbage cans, or send them to bed hungry. It will be the only parental decision you will be at liberty to make once your dream of "progressive utopia" comes true.

References

[1.1-1]   C. Singer, E. J. Holmyard, A. R. Hall, T. I. Williams, A History of Technology, Vol. II, NY: Oxford University Press, 1956. Heavy plow: pp. 87, 88; Wheeled plow: pp. 88, 89; Spinning wheels: pp. 202-204; Waterwheel: pp. 9 and 637; copper from sulfide ore, p. 11; suction pumps, pp. 13-17 and 39.
[1.1-2]   Charles Marivale, *A General History of Rome From the Foundation of the City to the Fall of Augustulus*, NY: Harper & Brothers, 1879, p. 125
[1.1-3]   Lord Kinross [John Patrick Douglas Balfour], *The Ottoman Centuries: The Rise and Fall of the Turkish Empire*, NY: Morrow Quill, 1977, p. 210
[1.1-4]   David Morgan, *The Mongols*, Cambridge, MA: Basil Blackwell, Inc., 1986, p. 102
[1.1-5]   Henri Pirenne, *Economic and Social History of Medieval Europe*, London: Routledge & Kegan Paul Ltd., 1936, pp. 61-65
[1.1-6]   op. cit., Pirenne, pp. 87-128
[1.1-7]   N. J. G. Pounds, *An Economic History of Medieval Europe*, London: Longman Group Limited, 1974, pp. 404-409
[1.1-8]   op. cit., Pirenne, pp. 180-187

[1.1-9]   Zeev Sternhell, "Fascist Ideology", an essay in Walter Laqueur, ed., *Fascism: A Reader's Guide*, Berkeley, CA: University of California Press, 1976, pp. 354, 355

[1.1-10] V. I. Lenin, *Selected Works*, NY: International Publishers, 1971, pp. 498, 499. The quote is from Lenin's essay of 30 Oct 1919 called "Economics and Politics in the Era of the Dictatorship of the Proletariat".

[1.2-1]   Carl Menger, *Principles of Economics*, Grove City, PA: Libertarian Press, 1994, pp. 259-261, translated by James Dingwall and Bert F. Hoselitz (originally published in Vienna in 1871, as *Grundesatze der Volkwirthschaftslehre*)

[1.2-2]   Murray N. Rothbard, *What Has Government Done to Our Money?*, Auburn, AL: Ludwig von Mises Institute, 1991, pp. 27, 28 (first published in 1963)

[1.2-3]   John E. Cairnes, *Essays in Political Economy*, NY: Augustus M. Kelley, p. 259 (originally published London: Macmillan & Co., 1873)

[1.2-4]   Francis Walker, *Money*, New York: Henry Holt and Company, 1891, p. 19

[1.3-1]   Friedrich A. von Hayek, *Prices and Production and Other Works*, Auburn, AL: Ludwig von Mises Institute, 2008, p. 257 (This volume is a collection of essays written in the 1930's.)

[1.3-2]   https://www.marxists.org/history/etol/newspape/ni/vol03/no03/wollenberg.htm

[1.3-3]   https://en.wikipedia.org/wiki/Soviet_ruble

[1.3-4]   Henry Hazlitt, *What You Should Know About Inflation*, NY: Funk & Wagnalls, 1968, pp. 13, 14 (originally published 1968 by D. von Nostrand)

[1.3-5]   L. Albert Hahn, *The Economics of Illusion*, Burlington, VT: Fraser Publishing Company, 1949, p. 179

[1.3-6]   op. cit., Hahn, *The Economics of Illusion*, p. 179

[1.3-7]   Condy Raguet, *A Treatise on Currency and Banking*, Philadelphia, PA: Grigg & Elliot, 1840, pp. 55-57 (Reprinted by Forgotten Books, FB&c Ltd., London)

[1.4-1]   Murray N. Rothbard, *America's Great Depression*, Auburn, AL: Ludwig von Mises Institute, 2000, p. 38 (originally published 1963)

[1.4-2]   op. cit., Rothbard, *What Has Government Done to Our Money?*, p. 43

[1.4-3]   Amasa Walker, *The Science of Wealth: A Manual of Political Economy*, Boston, MA: Little, Brown & Co., 1867, p. 446

[1.5-1]   op. cit., Amasa Walker, p. 55

[1.5-2]   William Brough, *The Natural Law of Money*, NY: Greenwood Press, (1969), p. 116 (originally published 1896 by G. P. Putnam's Sons)

[1.5-3]   op. cit., Raguet, p. 95

[1.5-4]   William Graham Sumner, *A History of American Currency*, NY: Augustus M. Kelley, (1968), p. 171 (original published 1874 by Henry Holt & Co., NY)

[1.5-5]   W. Stanley Jevons, *The Theory of Political Economy*, NY: Macmillan & Co., (1871), pp. 214, 215

[1.5-6]   op. cit., Jevons, *The Theory of Political Economy*, NY: Macmillan & Co., (1871), pp. 217, 218

[1.5-7]   op. cit., Brough, p. 116

[1.5-8]   op. cit., Amasa Walker, p. 207.

[1.5-9]   op. cit., Jevons, pp. 232, 233

[1.5-10] op. cit., Hazlitt, *What You Should Know About Inflation*, pp. 115, 116

[1.5-11] op. cit., Rothbard, *America's Great Depression*, p. 79

[1.5-12] Gottfried Haberler, "Money and the Business Cycle", essay in *Gold and Monetary Stabilization*, Lectures on the Harris Foundation, NY: Garland Publishing, (1983), p. 59 (originally published by the University of Chicago Press, 1932)

[1.5-13] op. cit., Brough, p. 118

[1.5-14] Daniel Schaeffler, "A Brief History of Steelmaking", 31 Aug 2020 at: https://www.metalformingmagazine.com/article/?/materials/mild-steel/a-brief-history-of-steelmaking-gu; see also https://www.britannica.com/technology/steel/History

[1.5-15] op. cit., Jevons, pp. 236-248

[1.5-16] J. C. L. de Sismondi, *History of the Fall of the Roman Empire*, London: Longman, Rees, Orme, Brown, Green, and Longman and John Taylor (1834), Vol. 1, pp. 96, 97

[1.5-17]   Gregory Clark, "The Long March of History: Farm Laborer's Wages in England 1208-1850", University of California at Davis, Table 4, p. 26
[1.5-18]   Edward Gibbon, *The Decline and Fall of the Roman Empire*, (1776), Vol. 1, chapter 14
[1.5-19]   A. J. Grant, "The Government of Louis XIV", *The Cambridge Modern History*, Vol. V, Chapter 1, (1934), pp. 24, 25
[1.5-20]   Francois P. G. Guizot, *The History of France*, NY: John B. Alden, (1885), Vol. IV, p. 253

[1.6-1]   John E. Cairnes, *The Character and Logical Method of Political Economy*, London: Frank Cass & Co. Ltd., 1965, pp. 194-201 (originally published London: Macmillan & Co., 1875)
[1.6-2]   op. cit., Amasa Walker, pp. 297, 298
[1.6-3]   op. cit., Cairnes, *Essays in Political Economy*, pp. 196, 197
[1.6-4]   op. cit., Cairnes, *Essays in Political Economy*, pp. 214-216
[1.6-5]   op. cit., Cairnes, *The Character and Logical Method of Political Economy*, p. 116

[1.7-1]   op. cit., Hahn, *The Economics of Illusion*, p. 114
[1.7-2]   op. cit., Hahn, *The Economics of Illusion*, p. 212
[1.7-3]   op. cit., Rothbard, *America's Great Depression*, pp. 45, 46
[1.7-4]   op. cit., Hahn, *The Economics of Illusion*, p. 241
[1.7-5]   op. cit., Hahn, *The Economics of Illusion*, p. 176
[1.7-6]   op. cit., Hahn, *The Economics of Illusion*, pp. 102, 110
[1.7-7]   op. cit., von Hayek, pp. 32-34
[1.7-8]   op. cit., Francis A. Walker, p. 286

[1.8-1]   Fred Rogers Fairchild, Edgar Stevenson Furniss, Norman Sydney Buck, *Elementary Economics*, NY: The Macmillan Company, 1926, Vol. 1, pp. 413, 414
[1.8-2]   op. cit., Raguet, pp. 49-53
[1.8-3]   op. cit., Rothbard, *What Has Government Done to Our Money?*, p. 60
[1.8-4]   Clifton H. Kreps, Jr., *Money, Banking and Monetary Policy*, NY: The Ronald Press Co., 1962, pp. 299, 300
[1.8-5]   op. cit., Fairchild et al, Vol. 1, p. 443
[1.8-6]   op. cit., Raguet, pp. 5, 6
[1.8-7]   op. cit., Fairchild et al, Vol. 1, pp. 444, 445
[1.8-8]   op. cit., von Hayek, p. 43
[1.8-9]   op. cit., Raguet, pp. 53, 54
[1.8-10]   op. cit., Jevons, pp. 240, 241
[1.8-11]   op. cit., von Hayek, pp. 37, 115
[1.8-12]   op. cit., Brough, p. 119
[1.8-13]   op. cit., von Hayek, pp. 113-116
[1.8-14]   op. cit., Brough, pp. 118-122
[1.8-15]   op. cit., von Hayek, pp. 93, 94

[1.9-1]   Jean-Baptiste Say, *Treatise on Political Economy*, 1803
[1.9-2]   op. cit., Hahn, *The Economics of Illusion*, p. 212
[1.9-3]   Lord John Maynard Keynes, *The General Theory of Employment, Interest, and Money*, NY: Harcourt, Brace & Company, 1936
[1.9-4]   op. cit., Hahn, *The Economics of Illusion*, pp. 140-143
[1.9-5]   op. cit., von Hayek, pp. 21, 25, 26
[1.9-6]   op. cit., von Hayek, pp. 189-403
[1.9-7]   Ludwig von Mises, *The Theory of Money and Credit*, Indianapolis, IN: Liberty Classics, 1981, pp. 377-445. It was originally published in 1934 as *Theorie des Geldes und der Umlaufsmittel*.
[1.9-8]   op. cit., von Hayek, pp. 235-240
[1.9-9]   op. cit., Raguet, pp. 13-137
[1.9-10]   op. cit., von Hayek, pp. 12, 13
[1.9-11]   op. cit., von Hayek, p. 102

[1.9-12]   Gottfried Haberler, "Money and the Business Cycle", an essay in *Gold and Monetary Stabilization*, Lectures on the Harris Foundation, NY: Garland Publishing, (1983), pp. 44, 45, 70. It was originally published: Chicago, IL: University of Chicago Press, 1932.

[1.9-13]   op. cit., Rothbard, *America's Great Depression,* p. 51

[1.9-14]   op. cit., von Hayek, p. 59

[1.9-15]   op. cit., von Hayek, pp. 115-117

[1.9-16]   op. cit., von Hayek, pp. 117, 120, 121

[1.9-17]   op. cit., Hahn, *The Economics of Illusion*, pp. 52, 53

[1.9-18]   Henry Thornton, "An Enquiry into the Nature and Effects of the Paper Credit of Great Britain", London: J. Hatchard, F & C. Rivington, 1802; reprinted in J. R. McCulloch, *A Select Collection of Scarce and Valuable Tracts on Paper Currency and Banking*, London: Privately printed for Lord Overstone, 1857, pp. 137-339

[1.9-19]   Thomas Malthus, "Publications on the Depreciation of Paper Currency", *The Edinburgh Review*, Vol. 17, No. 34 (Feb 1811), pp. 363, 364

[1.9-20]   Gottfried Haberler, "Money and the Business Cycle", Quincy Wright, ed., *Gold and Monetary Stabilization,* Harris Foundation Lectures, NY: Garland Publishing Inc. 1983, pp. 60-65 (The original set of lectures was published in 1932 by the University of Chicago.)

[1.9-21]   op. cit., von Hayek, pp. 73-95

[1.9-22]   op. cit., von Hayek, pp. 254-278

[1.9-23]   op. cit., von Hayek, p. 275

[1.9-24]   op. cit., von Hayek, pp. 254-266

[1.9-25]   op. cit., Francis A. Walker, p. 474

[1.9-26]   op. cit., Guizot, Vol. V, pp. 12-16

[1.9-27]   P. Angelides, B. Thomas, B. Born, B. Georgiou, B. Graham, K. Hennessey, D. Holtz-Eakin, H. H. Murren, J. W. Thompson, and P. J. Wallison (members of the Financial Crisis Inquiry Commission), *The Financial Crisis Inquiry Report*, NY: PublicAffairs, 2011. I am inclined mostly to the "dissenting views" of Hennessey, Holtz-Eakin, and Thomas on pp. 411-439; and that of P. J. Wallison on pp. 441-450.

[1.9-28]   op. cit., von Hayek, pp. 306-308

[1.9-29]   op. cit., Fairchild et al, Vol. 1, pp. 505-514

[1.9-30]   op. cit., Rothbard, *America's Great Depression,* pp. 14, 15

[1.9-31]   op. cit., Rothbard, *America's Great Depression,* pp. 15, 16

[1.9-32]   op. cit., Hahn, *The Economics of Illusion*, pp. 50-52.

[1.9-33]   op. cit., Rothbard, *America's Great Depression,* p. 72

[1.9-34]   op. cit., Francis A. Walker, p. 474

[1.9-35]   op. cit., Sumner, pp. 249, 303

[1.9-36]   op. cit., Francis A. Walker, pp. 475, 476

[1.9-37]   op. cit., von Hayek, p. 275

[1.9-38]   op. cit., Rothbard, *America's Great Depression,* pp. 19-24

[1.9-39]   op. cit., Hahn, *The Economics of Illusion*, pp. 59, 60

[1.9-40]   op. cit., von Hayek, p. 308

[1.9-41]   op. cit., von Hayek, p. 298

[1.9-42]   op. cit., Hahn, *The Economics of Illusion*, pp. 72, 73

[1.10-1]   Matthew 25:31-46 is a prophesy by Christ of an event that is to take place after His Second Advent, just prior to the commencement of the Millennial Kingdom. 'You who are blessed' refers to Gentile believers in the Tribulation; those who were hungry etc. are Jewish believers under persecution by the government in the Tribulation. The kindnesses described are only indications of the faith that makes them eligible for entry into the Kingdom. It says nothing about economics in the present day. The important part point for this discussion is the fact that all these acts of help and generosity were performed by individuals, not a government, contrary to the claims of the "socially conscious" crusaders.

[1.10-2]   Albert S. Bolles, *The Financial History of the United States*, NY: Augustus M. Kelley, Publishers, (1969), Vol. 3, p. 458. The original was published in 1894 by D. Appleton & Company.

[1.10-3]   David A. Wells, Report of the Special Commissioner of the Revenue for the Year 1868, Washington, DC: Government Printing Office, 5 Jan 1869, pp. 20, 21

[1.10-4]   op. cit., Bolles, Vol. 3, pp. 456, 457 (originally published NY: D. Appleton & Company, 1894)

[1.10-5]   op. cit., de Sismondi, Vol. 1, pp. 119-121
[1.10-6]   op. cit., de Sismondi, Vol. 1, pp. 21, 22

[1.11-1]   op. cit., Raguet, pp. 12, 22
[1.11-2]   op. cit., Cairnes, *The Character and Logical Method of Political Economy*, pp. 94, 114
[11.1-3]   op. cit., Fairchild et al, Vol. 1, pp. 535-539
[1.11-4]   op. cit., Raguet, p. 25
[1.11-5]   https://www.bbc.com/news/business-44802666
[11.1-6]   Paul F. Gemmill, *Fundamentals of Economics*, NY: Harper & Brothers Publishers, 3rd Edition, 1939, pp. 496, 497
[1.11-7]   op. cit., Gemmill, pp. 505, 506
[1.11-8]   op. cit., Raguet, pp. 27, 36
[1.11-9]   op. cit., Raguet, p. 123. The passage in question was first published in the Philadelphia Gazette, 17 Apr 1828 as part of an essay called "On Exchange".
[1.11-10] op. cit., Fairchild et al, Vol. 1, pp. 558, 559
[1.11-11] Lloyd G. Reynolds, *Economics A General Introduction*, Homewood, IL: Richard D. Irwin, Inc. 1966, p. 739
[1.11-12] op. cit., Reynolds, pp. 743, 744, 748, 749
[1.11-13] Murray N. Rothbard, "The Case for a 100 Percent Gold Dollar", in *What Has Government Done to Our Money?*, Auburn, AL Ludwig von Miss Institute, 1991, pp. 126-131 (originally published 1963.)

[1.12-1]   op. cit., Amasa Walker, pp. 363-365
[1.12-2]   Thomas Paine, *The Decline and Fall of the English System of Finance*, an essay dated 6 Apr 1797. It was banned in England for over 20 years, so that should tell you something.
[1.12-3]   op. cit., Amasa Walker, pp. 366, 367
[1.12-4]   op. cit., Amasa Walker, p. 366
[1.12-5]   op. cit., Amasa Walker, pp. 369-371
[1.12-6]   op. cit., Hahn, *The Economics of Illusion*, p. 55
[1.12-7]   op. cit., Hahn, *The Economics of Illusion*, pp. 15, 24, 55, 176

[1.13-1]   Henry Hazlitt, *Economics in One Lesson*, NY: Harper & Brothers, 1946. The lesson, presented in the first five pages, is that a policy must be examined not only for its immediate effects, but all the effects upon all affected groups of people. The other 189 pages are examples of the application of the lesson. If you only have time to read one economics book, this is it. It will dispel all the common economic fallacies that are so popular today, as it did when first published.
[1.13-2]   op. cit., Hahn, *The Economics of Illusion*, pp. 235, 236.
[1.13-3]   Lord John Maynard Keynes, *The General Theory of Employment, Interest, and Money*, NY: Harcourt, Brace & Company, 1936
[1.13-4]   op. cit., Hahn, *The Economics of Illusion*, pp. 50, 51, 97
[1.13-5]   Henry Hazlitt, *The Failure of the New Economics: An Analysis of the Keynesian Fallacies*, Irvington-on-Hudson, NY: The Foundation for Economic Education, 1994 (originally published by D. Van Nostrand Co., 1959)
[1.13-6]   L. Albert Hahn, *Common Sense Economics*, Auburn AL: The Ludwig von Mises Institute, 2010 (originally published in Great Britain by Jarrold and Sons Ltd, Norwich, 1956). In the preface he writes: "My conclusion was, briefly, that what is new in Keynes' work is not good, and what is good is not new."
[1.13-7]   op. cit., Hazlitt, *What You Should Know About Inflation*, p. 77, 111, 113
[1.13-8]   Lord John Maynard Keynes, *The General Theory of Employment, Interest, and Money*, NY: Harcourt, Brace & Company, 1936, Preface to the German Edition, p. 6; cf. International Relations and Security Network, https://www.files.ethz.ch/isn/125515/1366_KeynesTheoryofEmployment.pdf
[1.13-9]   op. cit., Keynes, Chapter 18 (pp. 245 ff)
[1.13-10] op. cit., Hazlitt, *What You Should Know About Inflation*, p. 66
[1.13-11] op. cit., Keynes, chapters 4, 20, 21
[1.13-12] op. cit., Hazlitt, *The Failure of the "New Economics": An Analysis of the Keynesian Fallacies*, pp. 304-307
[1.13-13] op. cit., Keynes, p. 9
[1.13-14] op. cit., Rothbard, *What Has Government Done to Our Money?*, p. 68

[1.13-15]   op. cit., Hahn, *The Economics of Illusion,* pp. 50-52

[1.13-16]   op. cit., Keynes, pp. 210-212, 248

[1.13-17]   op. cit., Hahn, *The Economics of Illusion,* p. 93

[1.13-18]   op. cit., Hazlitt, *The Failure of the "New Economics": An Analysis of the Keynesian Fallacies,* p. 127

[1.13-19]   op. cit., Keynes, pp. 62, 74

[1.13-20]   op. cit., Hazlitt, *The Failure of the "New Economics": An Analysis of the Keynesian Fallacies,* pp. 88-93

[1.13-21]   op. cit., Hahn, *The Economics of Illusion,* pp. 97, 98

[1.13-22]   op. cit., Keynes, pp. 315-320

[1.13-23]   op. cit., Hazlitt, *The Failure of the "New Economics": An Analysis of the Keynesian Fallacies,* pp. 322-326

[1.13-24]   op. cit., Keynes, pp. 115-117, 248, 249, 273

[1.13-25]   op. cit., Hazlitt, *The Failure of the "New Economics": An Analysis of the Keynesian Fallacies,* pp. 135-138

[1.15-1]   op. cit., Fairchild et al, Vol. 2, pp. 644-648

[1.15-2]   op. cit., Pirenne, pp. 120, 121

[1.15-3]   Norman H. Baynes, editor, *The Speeches of Adolf Hitler April 1922 - August 1939,* London: Oxford University Press, 1942, Vol. 1, p. 870

[1.15-4]   op. cit., Baynes, Vol. 1, pp. 914, 915

[1.15-5]   Frederic Bastiat, *The Law* (1850), translated and published by: Irvington-on-Hudson, NY: Foundation for Economic Education, 1950, p. 75

2

Money

The subject of money per se can now be examined in view of the basic principles of economics. This chapter is divided into four parts. First is a brief review of what was said earlier about the fundamental aspects of money. Section 2.2 contains a summary of the various types of monetary systems in use both historically and in modern times. Section 2.3 is an explanation of the oft-quoted but misunderstood "Gresham's Law". Last, sections 2.4 through 2.8 describe the effects, consequences, implementation, measurement, and the final end of one of the core issues facing working people: the depreciation of the monetary unit, known popularly as "inflation".

2.1 A Review

It is important to recall that there is nothing special about money per se. Money does not directly satisfy any need of real value such as food, clothing, rent, etc. It is only the means to procure the satisfaction of needs by exchanging it for tangible commodities, the items mentioned. Money is not the most valuable commodity by weight or volume, but it is the most marketable commodity because it is the one that everyone will accept for actual commodities. Money as a commodity is subject to the same principle of supply and demand as any other commodity.

If the public demand for money increases, that is, if people decide to retain cash balances instead of spending or saving it, then less is available for exchanges and prices will generally fall. But they can only fall so far since products whose selling price cannot clear the cost of production will soon cease to be produced. The reason is: money in circulation has become scarcer. If people demand less money to be held as cash balances, then more is available for exchanges and prices can increase. The amount held as cash balances depends on the flow of income. If people are paid daily, cash balances tend to be low as it is likely spent daily. If paid monthly, the average cash balances will be higher.

The demand for money depends on the amount needed for exchanges, and its relative "value" in the course of an exchange for commodities is expressed in the money-price [2.1-1]. If the supply of money is high and supply of a commodity is low, then it is said that money is more common than such a commodity, and thus the exchange value, or price, of the commodity is high. If the opposite prevails, where a commodity is more readily available than money, then the money-price of the commodity is low. The demand for money also depends on the demand for exchanges. The overall demand for exchanges depends on the organization of the society and the extent to which the division of labor has progressed. In modern industrial nations, division of labor is at a high level. Most people produce more than they require and the surplus is sold others; at the same time they buy with money the surplus of others people's production. Therefore the demand for exchanges is said to be at a high level in advanced economies. The demand for the exchange of these mutual surpluses is unrelated to the total wealth possessed by the society, since only a small fraction of total wealth is actually exchanged in any given year. Only the fraction of total wealth being used for current production is actually exchanged with money [2.1-2].

If money cannot be obtained, then the economy reverts back to a barter system in which commodities are traded directly without the intermediate use of money. It is a much less efficient method of conducting trade. The efficiency introduced through the use of money makes its study and understanding important.

The metric by which prices are established is the relative value of money, which is regulated by four factors [2.1-3]. The first is the quantity of transactions to be made; that in turn depends on a) population, b) the degree of division of labor, and c) the variety of products produced, consumed, imported, and exported. The second factor is the amount of money that is available for making those transactions, for the amount of money compared to the volume of commodities will determine the relative value of the money unit. Third, money varies in efficiency. If the money is absolutely recognized as having a standard value, it has a high efficiency in making transactions because little time or effort is wasted in debating the quality of the money itself. "Standard value" in this sense refers to the confidence that the money will be accepted in another transaction as readily tomorrow, next week, next year, and in ten years as it is today. When the monetary system permits exchanges to be made over long distances, or at very cheap rates, money is more efficient due to the reduction in the cost of transferring the money in exchange for the commodities. The fourth regulating factor is the amount of any additions to the current stock of money, and whether such additions are consistent with the amount and quantity of transactions to be made. The second and fourth are related: the value of money in exchange is regulated both by the current amount in circulation and also by its rate of increase or decrease.

Money has up to four functions. Paper money and commodity money both perform the first function, which is a measure of value. A weight of wheat may be exchanged for so many pieces of copper or so many pieces of paper; in that instance, both of the money units are a standard by which the value of the wheat is evaluated. The second is the function as a medium of exchange in which the inefficiency of barter is superseded by the intermediate action of money. The conceptual process is akin to two sales: the first commodity sells for money and the money is sold for the second commodity. Third, money has the function of a "standard for deferred payments", which is the measure of value at a future date as compared to the present. It comes into play when money is lent: the future measure of value depends on any change in the value of the money unit over the duration of the loan, and just as importantly, the current estimate of the change of value in the future. If the value of money unit does not change with time, then it is said that it is a stable standard for deferred payments (meaning the lender will get back money-units of the same value). The fourth function of money is as a store of value. This store of value applies only when the money unit itself consists of a commodity such as gold or silver or some other tangible physical item. Commodity money is said in this case to "store value" because it is made of something that has value independent of its use as money. If the money consists of gold, silver, copper, platinum, or palladium, that money is said to store value because each of those metals are valued for their use as part of an industrial process, or in art, or in ornamentation. Money made of paper clearly does not store value in this way.

It is easy to see, given the functions of money and the volume of exchanges made in advanced economies, that public confidence in the money is an important consideration [2.1-4]. Each person must be confident above all that the money he receives in exchange for his labor will be received with the same readiness at the next transaction, wherein he seeks to use that money buy a product. If the worker finds that the money is refused, the worker has been robbed: he now has money, but it is of lesser use to him than it was to his employer. His employer got his "money's worth", but how does the worker get his "money's worth" if the money is not accepted in trade? That is the crucial aspect of all monetary systems. An efficient and stable monetary system is one in which the public has confidence, based on experience, that the money will be readily accepted now and in the future. A money unit with a stable value leads to stable prices, stable interest rates, confidence in the future, and confidence in saving and investing. Stable money promotes overall confidence and trust in the economic system.

2.2   Types of Monetary Systems

This section contains a summary of the types of monetary systems and their characteristics. The types to be examined are: a) commodity money, in which the money itself is made from material recognized as having inherent value; b) paper money that is convertible to such a commodity (a.k.a. "mercantile", "representative" or "convertible"); c) token money; and d) fiat money. It also addresses demand deposits as money, which can exist within any of the four basic types.

A commodity monetary system is one in which the money itself is made of some material regarded as having value outside of its use as money. The "standard" money was that commodity in the hands of the public, passing from hand to hand in the course of exchanging it for goods. In principle, any commodity could be used. Over time societies came to agreement that certain metals in the form of coins were the most convenient commodities, although there were occasions in which other items were used. For example, beads were used as money among the North American aboriginal tribes, tobacco was used in the Virginia colony in the 17th century, and sea shells were once used by certain people in the islands of the South Pacific.

Metals such as silver, copper, and gold have certain properties that make them most attractive for use as money [2.2-1, 2.2-2, 2.2-3]. First, they are always perceived to have value whether used as money or not. Each of them has industrial uses and each of them is desired for their beauty or utility in decoration. Secondly, the amount in existence is stable over long periods of time, say fifty or a hundred years, and usually the amounts that could be added annually by mining is small compared to the existing amount. I say "usually" because there have been some important exceptions: the discovery of silver in South America in the 1500's, and the gold discoveries in California, Australia, and Alaska in the 1800's certainly caused a large influx of those metals into circulation. Those three metals rose to the top of the utility list because they were rare enough to be regarded as valuable, but not so rare as to require very small amounts to be tracked. For example, iron was always too common and platinum was always too rare. Aluminum is a peculiar case. It one of the most common elements on earth, but in practice it was the rarest of all because it could not be separated from the ore, and thus was too rare to be used as money. But Carl Joseph Bayer developed the process bearing his name in 1889 that allowed pure aluminum to be separated from bauxite; now aluminum is too common to be used as money.

Third, the metals, being rare enough to represent value while only occupying small volumes, were portable enough to use as money. It would be a great inconvenience to transport enough iron of sufficient value for transactions. Fourth, metals can be easily divided into large or small amounts as necessary, which overcomes one of the great hurdles in barter. The more common one (copper) could be used for very small transactions and the rarest one (gold) for large ones, again without too much inconvenience. Fifth, each of these metals can be refined to a high degree of purity and measured out by weight so as to establish an exact standard of value. They can also be mixed as an alloy if necessary to promote durability while retaining the property of accurate assessment by weight. Sixth, their durability and resistance to degradation by natural and man-made forces made them useful as money. It was estimated in the 1800's that a gold coin was reduced in weight by only 4% through wear and tear over a period of 100 years. That meant it was an excellent standard of value for deferred payments. Seventh, each of the metals was consistent; a weight of copper was the same as any other equal weight of copper so long as the purity was the same.

How then is the value of metal money established? The answer is: the same way as any other commodity, which is the total of the demand for it both as money as for industrial purposes as against the supply. A given supply combined with the recognized advantages of money regulated how much metal traded for an amount of some other commodity. Recall that money per se, regardless of its nature, does not satisfy any wants directly; its relative "value" is what it can be exchanged for. So, the value of the metal money as an intermediate commodity was regulated by supply and demand of money compared to the supply and demand of the other commodities.

Metal money has some other advantages. First, if every nation recognizes the same metal as money, then the metal can be shipped back and forth between them in trade of necessary; in other words, it can compensate for an imbalance in international trade. The secondary effect is that it indirectly regulates imports and exports. An export of metal money due to a large amount of imports causes the value of money domestically to rise (since the supply of money is reduced), so domestic money prices may fall. If domestic prices fall, domestic production is more attractive, greater domestic production is sold, imports decline, exports increase, and the metal money flows back. Thus a rough equilibrium is reached, at least over the long term. (This was the basis of the gold standard that prevailed prior to World War I.) Second, the metal commodity in the form of bullion can be converted into coined money as needed, and the coins can be converted back to some other industrial or bulk form as needed.

Certain advantages accrue to the case where all the trading nations use a metallic coinage standard, even if they use different metals. Each nation's coin is based on a standard weight of one of the metals, and the conversion between them is fairly simple. If two trading nations, say the U. S. and Britain, use the same coined metal as its money, then the conversion between dollars and pounds sterling is a direct conversion of weight. If one were to use gold and the other silver, then the conversion involves two straightforward calculations, one being the relative value of the metals and the other being the two weights of the coins. So long as the two metallic money units were of known standard weights, (either pure metal or some known alloy), there would be little depreciation in the money (except wear and tear). The result is a stabilized system of international payments. In other words, the exchange ratio between the two nations is more or less fixed, fluctuating only with the cost of shipping the coin or bullion. As described before, the use of standard metallic money served to indirectly regulate imports and exports, because domestic prices would fluctuate in response and cause an automatic correction.

A special problem arises when two different metals are in circulation concurrently, which is called the "bimetallic problem". It will be discussed in detail in section 2.3.

Depreciation of the money under a pure coinage system required direct action: either the coins had to be clipped or shaved to remove some of the metal, or coins had to be deliberately coined as underweight. Both actions are easily observed by the general public. Under the coinage standard, an underweight coin was not received at full value by the foreign trader; ultimately foreign trade had to be paid per the full weights per the recognized standard. But the same is not true of purely domestic trade. Walker [2.2-4] explains David Ricardo's point that underweight coins bearing the same name would be exchanged at par in purely domestic trade since the same number of monetary units performed the same number of transactions in goods:

> "There can exist no depreciation of money, but from excess; however, as debased coinage may become, it will preserve its mint value; that is to say; it will pass in circulation for the intrinsic value of the bullion which it ought to contain, provided it be not in too great abundance."

So, if the coins were given names, and dissociated from a weight of metal, it is a simple thing for a government issuing the coins to devalue them by using underweight coins and retaining the unused portion in bullion. Notice that the name is kept the same, but the weight is changed (known as coinage by 'tale'). In that case there would not be any increase in prices within the domestic economy. The reason is: if a quantity of wheat sold for a shilling of full weight, the same quantity of wheat can be bought for an underweight shilling so long as the total number of shillings in circulation hasn't changed. Thus there is no change in domestic prices; only the prices of foreign goods would change because foreign trade had to be conducted in weights. So governments issuing coin had three choices, given a total weight of metal available for use as coined money: a) keep the coins at full weight; b) issue coins at underweight and keep the remaining fraction in bullion uncoined; or c) use the full amount of metal available to issue underweight coins. In the first case, suppose a million pounds of silver were available for coinage and the standard monetary unit was defined to be a half-ounce troy of silver. There are twelve troy ounces in a pound, so if all the available metal were coined at full weight, the result is two million coins in the economy to be used as money. As full weight coins, they would circulate domestically and be convertible directly into any other metal-based foreign coinage also of full weight. In the second case, the coin could be redefined as a quarter-ounce of silver. The government then uses only a half million pounds of the available metal and issues two million of the revised (underweight) coins. The other half million pounds of silver is retained in the treasury. The result is that the coins, being just as common as before (i.e., two million in circulation) to conduct domestic trade, will not affect domestic prices. What was previously purchased with ten coins will buy domestically just as much even if the coins are half-weight. But an import that previously cost ten coins (5 ozt.) will now cost twenty since the international exchange is indirectly related to total weight, not by name. In the third case, all one million pounds will be coined into four million quarter-ounce coins (again retaining the name but not the weight). Since there are now twice as many coins available, underweight but with the same name, money prices of domestic products and imports will both double.

A metal-standard coinage system is not immune to depreciation, since new metal is always being mined and added to the existing stock of metal. The advantage is that the additional amounts are usually small compared to the existing amount and the depreciation occurs slowly. But that has not always been the case. Long-term contracts with the repayment specified in coin have sometimes resulted in losses to one party or the other due to fluctuations in the mining output of the metals, and this sometimes caused the metal money to fail as a standard of deferred payments. Walker points out several cases [2.2-5]:

> "Not to speak of the great changes produced between 1570 and 1640 by the influx of silver from the mines in [South] America, Professor Jevons estimates that the value of gold fell, between 1780 and 1809, 46 per cent; from 1809 to 1849 it rose 145 per cent; while between 1849 and 1874 it fell again at least 20 percent. Even if we allow for the insufficiency and inaccuracy of the data used in such computations, there would remain an unquestionable variation, of wide reach, within each of the periods indicated."

These were unusual but valid cases; normally the annual increase in production is small compared to the total existing amount. Normally it is the creditor who loses because of increases in metal production. It is true that those who mine the metal appear to benefit since they are essentially "creating money" out of the ground. But it should be remembered that nature does not give up its riches easily; miners normally have to expend a great deal of money in their operations and many of them are lucky to break even. If mining was so profitable, surely a great many more companies would begin operations.

One thing is certain: governments hate commodity money. Money consisting of metal coins of known weight prevents the government from excessive deficit spending; it prevents the government from getting involved in foreign wars of convenience or purely out of power lust. The money is in fact mostly in the hands of the people, and a government that wishes to abuse its power must find a way to pay for it: it must find a way to extract the money out of the people's hands. If the people retain the metal, the government will have a difficult time of it, and must resort to trickery to do so. The coinage can be debased as shown above only by an obvious fraud that the government cannot hide.

Even when the monetary fraud became known, it was accepted by the public. The public had either been convinced, or accepted by tradition, that management of money and coinage can only be done by governments. That is patently false. A money unit defined as an exact weight and fineness of a metal surely can be done by private industry. A government cannot redefine the unit of a kilogram of mass any more than it can redefine the length of a meter. Since those definitions are constant, coinage can be done as easily by private concerns as by a government mint. As Rothbard [2.2-6] has pointed out, stainless steel 1/4-20 bolts are manufactured to a specific standard; all the ones conforming to that standard are identical, and no government has found it necessary to get involved directly in the production of stainless steel 1/4-20 bolts. The same is true of coinage: once weights and measures, types of alloy, and degrees of fineness are established, coins can be produced privately as necessary for the consuming public.

Money consisted of gold and silver coins during the medieval era, and certain businesses were created to store that money for safekeeping. These were normally goldsmiths or silversmiths, who had strong safes constructed for safeguarding valuables. The money was deposited with them and returned on demand, and a small price was paid for the service. Those who engaged in this sort of business at first operated much like a warehouse; the specific coins were deposited in specific boxes, and the exact coins deposited were returned to the owner when he wanted them. Primitive banking operations were also created about the same time, mostly handling bills of exchange for merchants who bought and sold at the fairs located in the larger towns. Exchange of credit between merchants via bills of exchange issued by moneylenders was widely used in the medieval era, although often ignored or downplayed in importance. Pirenne [2.2-7] describes the coinage invented by the Carolingians (Charlemagne and successors), and how it became scarce as Europe descended into the feudal manorial system, in which little trade was conducted. The fairs gradually revived trade, especially as goods and money were gradually imported from the Far East. By the thirteenth century, European monarchs began to coin their own money, usually in silver but sometimes in gold. "Cash" was defined as the coins, not the bills of exchange or any other paper. Use of credit via bills of exchange was necessary because there was still relatively little coinage in existence. As commerce expanded in the 1500's, a more sophisticated system emerged: moneylenders borrowed from depositors and lent at interest. The moneylender issued a paper note citing the amount of the deposit, and because those moneylenders had a good reputation, the paper notes themselves were transferred hand-to-hand, functioning as money [2.2-8]. In the course of taking deposits, it was always understood that the depositor could demand his deposit back at any time. Local moneylenders mostly received deposits from individuals and made loans to other individuals or businesses.

Since carrying money in gold and silver was risky during the medieval era, merchants found it much more convenient to carry paper containing promissory notes from the moneylender to the fairs or remote towns, and this practice was gradually extended to the local public. The banking firms of Genoa in the 14th century gave receipts for deposits of coins; these paper receipts passed hand to hand, and came to be used as money directly. This system was imitated in other banks in Europe, most notably Amsterdam and Hamburg [2.2-9]. What we now call the banking business developed slowly because the Roman Catholic Church had developed a doctrine that usury was evil. Usury is what we now call charging interest on a loan. But the prohibitions against usury were easily evaded by the terms of an agreement, disguising the payment of interest as some other expense.

Most of the time, a moneylender could be reasonably sure that only a fraction of the total on deposit would actually be called for at any time. This observation was the beginning of what is known as "reserve banking", a situation in which paper money is issued by a moneylender or bank, but a sufficient "reserve" was kept on hand to redeem the paper in metal coin on demand. At first "reserves" meant that 100% of the face value of the paper was held as coin; gradually moneylenders only kept enough on hand to meet expected immediate needs and the rest was lent at interest. During a crop failure or war, the moneylenders sometimes found themselves unable to pay, and were subject to severe penalties [2.2-10].

Reserve banking developed in England during the time of the English Civil War (1642-1651) [2.2-11]. Paper is certainly more convenient than lugging metal, and makes money more efficient in the sense that the money itself was cheaper to produce. The amount of metal money compared to the face value of the paper, or what is actually the ratio of convertibility, is called the "reserve ratio", and is nothing more than the banker's estimate, based on experience or intuition, of what fraction of the paper is likely to be redeemed by the holders thereof from day to day [2.2-12]. The problem, as always, is that the total face value of the paper issues exceeded the bank's reserves of coin and bullion. So long as the reserves can meet the occasional demand for redemption in coin, the public was not concerned with the overall amount of paper in circulation. The fact that the money supply, having been increased, caused prices to rise, was camouflaged by natural price fluctuations due to weather, war, or labor shortages. When money circulates in the form of paper notes, but is redeemable in metal coin upon presentation of the paper notes at the bank, the system is known as "convertible on demand". The fact that the paper notes are not backed 100% by coin means that the bank is actually issuing paper on its own credit. As in any credit system, its stability depends on confidence.

Paper that is convertible into coin on demand is mercantile money; it has the reliability and stability of coinage but the convenience and cheapness of paper. "Cash" in a mixed system is defined as either the coin or the paper convertible into the coin since both are always accepted as money. The advantage is that the real commodity money, the metal, can be kept in reserve. As expected, the temptation to issue more paper than can be covered by the reserves has always led to abuse of the system, and as will be shown later, a great deal of paper money has been issued that eventually became worthless. The real reserves should be partly held by the public in the form of coins of small denomination. In an emergency, a large amount of metal could be obtained; meanwhile, in normal times, the public will continue to have confidence in the monetary system because most transactions are done with real money, and the paper is convertible to same [2.2-13]. At first banks only issued notes in large denominations for business transactions, leaving the coinage to circulate for day-to-day use by the public. Eventually banks issued small-denomination paper notes, and it tended to drive the coins out of circulation altogether.

There is one other question to be answered: if paper money is "convertible", is it necessary that it be convertible in metal? Couldn't some other commodity be used instead? In principle, yes, but it is difficult to devise any other commodity with the conveniences of the metals, as described above. It is worth noting, however, that there two experiments using paper money backed by land; the first was colonial paper in Pennsylvania, and the other is the 'assignats' of the French Revolution. Walker [2.2-14] gives an account of how the real-estate paper money in Pennsylvania operated between 1723 and 1763:

> "The paper-money loan-system of Pennsylvania was as follows: The trustees of the loan-office were to lend out the bills of the colony upon real security of at least double the value, for a term of sixteen years, to be repaid in yearly installments, with interest. Thus, one-sixteenth of the principal was to be yearly paid back. The interest was applied to the public services. The principal was, for the first ten years, to be let out again to fresh borrowers. The new borrowers, from year to year, were to have the money for only the remaining part of the term of sixteen years, repaying by fewer and proportionally larger installments. During the last six years of the sixteen, the sums paid in were not to be re-loaned, but the notes burned, so that the whole might be called in, and the accounts completely settled at the end of the term."

Incidentally, they were printed by Benjamin Franklin, who described them as "coined land". Apparently a farmer could borrow paper notes from the colonial government at twice the assessed value of his farm, and then use those notes as circulating money to pay for improvements, or join together with other farmers to build a bridge, road, house, hotel, or a canal. The notes were repaid over sixteen years, and presumably were received for taxes. Subsidiary borrowers were allowed to borrow on the first ten years worth, but at the end of sixteen years, the notes were all disposed of, and all that was left was the improvements that were paid for with the notes. It sounds like a practical system since the notes did not remain in circulation permanently. But their value depreciated over time such that by 1748 they had fallen to about half their face value; and the experiment ended when Parliament passed a law prohibiting the colonies from printing money.

Referring back to the other 'backed by land' experiment, the sordid history of the French 'assignats' will be recounted fully in section 3.2. They eventually depreciated to zero and went out of circulation.

The "Continentals" issued by Congress during the American Revolution were backed only by a promise to pay in gold and silver at some future time, but Congress could not pay since it had no ability to raise a tax. Those also depreciated greatly and went out of circulation, and their history will be described fully in chapter 7.

To review, consider what is actually happening under a system of paper money convertible on demand under a reserve banking system. The banks hold a certain amount of coin for redemption to maintain confidence in the paper. The paper constitutes the bank's credit, and is accepted by the public and merchants alike since it functions as a measure of value and a medium of exchange. The bank has credit because it always pays in coin on demand. At the same time, if the paper is lent at interest, the bank is earning interest on its credit; i.e., collects interest on some multiple of its paid-in capital. That multiple is the related to the inverse of the reserve ratio [2.2-15].

A convertible paper money system is beneficial only if it is stable. Stability requires two objectives to be fulfilled: a) it must actually be convertible on demand; and b) there must be real consequences for banks that fail to redeem on demand. Unfortunately, history shows that neither prevails in the long run, since the banks are always able to convince the government that they should be treated with special care, and thus avoid the consequences of their corruption or incompetence. The problem with paper money is not that it is paper per se; the problem is the degree of convertibility. A properly controlled convertible system has several advantages.

First, the purchasing power of the money unit is maintained if the total of paper and coin together is equal to the amount of coin that would circulate in the absence of paper; this means that there must be a means of exporting the coin as Raguet pointed out [2.2-16]:

> "... that paper is only beneficial when its quantity does not exceed the quantity of coin which has been removed from the currency by exportation. The actual extent to which this substitution may take place with safety to a banking system is a matter which cannot be determined by any fixed proportions. ... The channels of circulation will only hold, without depreciation, a certain quantity of paper in addition to the quantity of coin that must need exist as the basis of the mixed currency, and this is equally the case whether the paper be issued by one bank or by one thousand. All attempts to increase that quantity permanently beyond the quantity requisite to preserve an equivalency with the general level, must, in the nature of things, be futile."

But there is a limit to how much coin can be exported, since the banking system, if it is to remain stable, must have a sufficient amount on hand for redemption and for extraordinary expenses such as war [2.2-17].

Secondly, a convertible cheaper money can be used in place of an expensive coinage one, and if it is stable (not depreciating), will furthermore lead to an expansion of credit instruments in trade [2.2-18]. If confidence in the bank system is maintained, the greater will be the use of bank credit, exchange, and the offsetting clearinghouse system, thus the less use of coin per se. It permits transactions to occur without resorting to cash. But once again, the system is in danger if too much paper is issued, and is not able to be converted on demand; as this will cause a collapse of confidence.

"Representative money" consists of paper certificates that are redeemable in coin or bullion, not because a bank has a reserve that can redeem a fraction of them, but because a government or bank has the full amount of coin or bullion to redeem all of them. They are in fact warehouse receipts for the coin or bullion [2.2-19].

"Token" money consists of coins used for small change; they have less metal in them than their face value, but are redeemable in full weight money in limited amounts. In this case, these lightweight coins are limited legal tender. For example, the penny was defined per the 1792 Coinage Act as 264 grains of copper, and passed for a hundredth of a dollar, which was defined as 371.25 grains of silver. It is easy to see why copper was used instead: a silver coin representing one hundredth of a dollar would consist of 3.71 grains of silver, or (at 5760 grains to a troy pound), 0.000644 troy pounds = 0.00772 ozt. = 0.240 grams. The density of silver is 10.49 g/cubic cm, and therefore a penny silver coin would occupy a volume of 0.0229 cubic centimeters. If the thickness was a millimeter, the diameter would be 0.538 cm = 0.21 inches, a very small coin indeed. So a cheaper metal was used, copper being a convenient choice. The Coinage Act of 1792 specified a penny as 11 pennyweights of copper = 264 grains, which is 17.1 grams. The 1792 penny was 100% copper, and its diameter was much greater than the modern penny. The original was almost the diameter of a modern half-dollar, which is about 1.18 inches. The price of copper today (2 Jan 2021) is $3.59 per pound at 7000 grains (or $0.246 per ozt.), and the price of silver is $26.47 per ozt. Thus the ratio of the value of silver to copper is 107.6 or so. If those same ratios applied in 1792 (it appears as though the ratio has not changed too much in the last several hundred years [2.2-20]), then the value of the copper penny to the value of the silver dollar defined as 371.25 grains of pure silver was (264×$0.246)/(371.25×$26.47) = $0.0066, less than the $0.01 face value. Thus, although 100 pennies could be cashed in for a dollar, only small debts could actually be cleared. The same principle applied to the use of silver coinage as limited legal tender for gold coins.

Next is considered "demand deposits". There are two types: a) when a worker deposits the proceeds of his labor into a bank account; and b) when the bank creates deposits in the course of making loans against its own credit. There may be two sources of money held as deposits, but they are actually the same thing. The question is: when an employer pays into the workers account (or the worker deposits cash received from the employer), whose money is it? You may be surprised to find that bank owns it in both cases; the reason is that the money on deposit, whether by deposit or by creation, is a promise by the bank to pay money on demand, either by withdrawal in coin or by writing a check or by debit. That "promise to pay" is based on the bank's credit. The monetary system may be such that the deposits are redeemable in paper that is in turn payable on demand in coin, or checks may be redeemable in coin directly. But the main benefit of the bank's credit is that a great many transactions can be accomplished with the use of only a small amount of money changing hands, mostly by offsetting credits and debits among the various banks. This is called the "clearinghouse" function: it is the offsetting of the transfers of commodities and business credit using the reliable bank credit as the medium. A clearinghouse system permits efficient mutual cancellation of debts among banks, reconciling the credits and debits between banks based on the checks written to their customers' accounts or against their customers' accounts. The result is that a great volume of monetary transactions can be performed (since checks, although not money per se, function as money), by making fairly small balancing transactions. It increases the efficiency of credit-money, permitting transactions in checks against demand deposits instead of in bank notes or coin. That does not relieve the bank from paying in coin on demand under a convertible system for the simple reason that redemption on demand is what maintains the publics' confidence in the banking system, a necessary condition for the efficient transfers by the banks.

There was once a great debate among economists as to whether bank deposits were money or not. It turns out that they are for the simple reason that they perform the salient function of money, which it to pay debts and make transactions. Suppose you owe your friend $100. Payment of that debt is accomplished by writing a check against your checking account deposit, or in modern times, by arranging an electronic transfer between your account and your friend's account. The demand deposit functions the same as coins and notes, even though there may be no physical transfer of anything that appears to be money (the check itself is not money, it is the device used to make the transfer). There is one thing to keep in mind, though: a demand deposit, like a paper bank note, is actually the bank's credit. It has been said by some economists that writing a check only transfers a debt, but does not cancel it. There is a grain of truth in that: the debt you owed to the other person is canceled, but now the other person holds a book entry that represents the bank's credit liability, just as it did when the checking account book entry was in your name. The bank's credit has been transferred and the bank is still liable for redemption, although the debt between the two of you has been fulfilled. If the demand deposit is fully convertible into commodity money, and your friend, upon receiving the $100 transfer, could convert it into gold or silver, then the check or electronic transfer is a money substitute, since it could ultimately be redeemed in commodity money. The check or electronic transfer is then "credit money", defined as a situation in which the banks or the government regards the "credit money" as a promise to pay, and redeems it in standard money [2.2-21].

The accounts and the transfers thereof, if convertible, function as promissory notes of the bank and are on par with the commodity money standard [2.2-22]. But if not, then the check, the electronic transfer, and the deposits in both of your accounts consist of fiat money, to be described more fully below.

A credit-money system eventually drives coinage out of circulation, even if the paper or credit money is redeemable. The reason is, in accordance with human nature, it is worth the risk of depreciation by creating too much money if the prospect of near-term profit is sufficiently high. In a purely coinage money system, "cash" is the gold and silver coin; in a convertible money system, cash is the same; bank credit being redeemable on demand the same as paper bank notes. The difference is that the paper or credit tends to reduce the demand for coin, since it is fair to admit, paper is much more convenient to handle and carry than coin. The important thing to remember is that the main problem is not the paper bank note or the credit money per se. The main problem is when the bank refuses to redeem, meaning it has overextended itself, but the government gives it license to renege on its obligations. Credit, and the paper money used to extend it, is not inherently inflationary if the bank is forced to redeem on demand. In a commodity money system (convertible or purely coin), credit is the amount of metal money that has been saved. The bank may well operate on a reserve basis, in which the amount of metal being held for redemption is less than the amount of notes or deposits granted or issued, but so long as the paper or deposits are redeemable, the public will have confidence in the banking system. Under those conditions, possessing the paper is about the same thing as possessing the coin, and if that is true (or believed to be true), little coin will be demanded. If metal is required to ensure an adequate supply for redemption of the notes or credit money, then the burden falls on the bank to obtain it. If they do not obtain it, then, reserves being fixed, the supply of money must fall, and prices must fall with it. It is this combination of forces (the risk of high demands, fairly low reserves, and the fact that the bank must protect its capital) that generally limits the banks to loaning on short terms [2.2-23]. It is the possibility of a large sudden demand that restrains the banks from issuing in excess; when the public demands the metal in their hands, the bank has a real problem, and that is the one thing that will cause the bankers to limit the money supply. Now it is easy to understand why banks prefer fiat money.

History shows that governments allow the banking system to employ a simple trick. At first, "representative money" is issued as receipts for the "standard money", which is coin (i.e., 100% reserve). Then comes the advent of "credit money", which is paper issued by a bank, but redeemable in coin on demand based on a reserve of less than 100%, the ratio of which is based on the banker's experience and judgment. Now for the trick: the government redefines the "standard money" to exclude coin, and declare by law that the paper itself is the "standard money". When the paper itself is the standard, and cannot be redeemed for any commodity, it is then a fiat currency. The paper is money because the government says it is money (in other words, the circulation thereof is forced upon the public), and is known as making the fiat paper money a 'legal tender' for all payments and debts.

The legal tender laws are usually implemented as a way for a government to cover up its inability to control spending. Section 1.12 described the process that occurred in Great Britain from 1697 on. The government needed money to pay for the war, but could not raise enough in taxes. So, it created a bank to borrow money from the public, and pay at interest, thus creating a national debt. The largest investors in the debt were the upper classes, which benefited from them because the interest payments came in regularly, and the bonds could be sold on the open market as desired. Meanwhile, taxes on commodities and imports were imposed, essentially taxes on consumption, to raise the money necessary to pay the interest. Since the interest was always being paid, and the bonds were paid when due, both the Bank of England and the government were able to maintain a high credit standing. The government could always borrow more money, and the bank could even create paper money for which there was no coin in reserve. Eventually the people of lesser means became "invested" in the bonds, and everything, the new investments, the interest, and the taxes all were paid in paper. Meanwhile some people began to lose confidence in the quality of the paper, and they began to demand that it be redeemed in coin. This was essentially a run on the Bank of England. When the Bank of England could no longer redeem its notes, the government allowed it to "suspend payment" via the Bank Restriction Act of 1797, and Britain had a fiat system from 1797 to 1821. The "Restriction Act" was the means by which the British government "restricted" the Bank from redeeming in coin, although the Bank falsely claimed that it could. The Bank desired Parliament to "force its hand" in order to cover for its bankruptcy, and Parliament, always friendly with the Bank, went along. The remaining metal was either exported or held as a small reserve against the paper. But Britain did not nationalize all the metal in the country; in fact it did eventually resume payments in coin in 1821. Cobbett [2.2-24] summarized the process of the expanding debt, commenting on the 6 Jul 1811 debate in Parliament as to whether the Restriction should be continued:

> "With these matters [whether the Restriction is to be continued] we have nothing to do. The affair is all their own [those in Parliament who passed the Restriction Act]. They made the war that produced the loans that produced the paper that produced the run that produced the stoppage of cash payments [redemption in coin] that produced the depreciation that produced the sale of guineas [coins worth 21 shillings] and the hoarding and exportation of them. Their work the whole of it is, and which set of them were first at it, or which last, is of no consequence to us. They have it all amongst them. They chose the grounds of war, and

the time for beginning; they put down all those who opposed them; they have been, for twenty-six years [Prime Ministers: William Pitt the Younger, 1784-1801; Henry Addington, 1801-1804; William Pitt the Younger again, 1804-1806; William Grenville, 1806-1807; William Cavendish-Bentinck, 1807-1809; and Spencer Perceval, 1809-1812] the rulers of the country and the masters of all its resources. One set, therefore, is and ought to be, just the same as the other in the eyes of the people. Let them settle the matter of precedence between them; let them bait one another as long as they please; but let not us be, by such baiting, amused and drawn away from the great points at issue."

The "great point at issue" is whether the paper would become the standard money, or would England revert back to a commodity standard. As it turned out, England did return to redemption of notes in specie in 1821; it was not until the end of World War I that Britain abandoned it and made the paper standard money. The United States followed suit in 1933, and the standard money of both, and of all nations now, is a fiat "standard".

The example of the Bank of England is typical: governments, when dependent on the banking system to fund their excesses, will always permit the banks to violate the regulations, the laws, the spirit of the laws, and even the Constitution. The important thing to the government is to maintain its power; the important thing to the bank is to preserve its capital. If the bank finds it desirable or convenient to suspend redemption in a convertible money system, so be it. What happens when the suspension becomes permanent? It is what we have now; a fiat money system.

Paper money that is convertible into metal on demand is now a thing of the past. The redefinition trick has always followed the same pattern. First, the government runs up a large debt that it cannot pay except by exporting gold, so it then authorizes a bank to issue paper in its place. At first the paper is convertible on demand, but as the government's debt increases, it finds it necessary to issue bonds to borrow the money to pay its debts. The metal money is then slowly accumulated in the banks and is held as a reserve to pay out the convertible notes. But the power of propaganda is brought to bear, "educating" the public that only hayseeds and hillbillies want metal money; it is old-fashioned and obsolete. At the same time, the banks continue to issue bank notes of smaller and smaller denominations until practically all the money in use is paper, except for token coins used as small change. But then how are taxes paid? They are paid in paper, since that is the common money. The interest on the government debt is also paid in paper, since the coin is mostly tied up as reserves. Eventually, as the debt increases, the government finds that the paper money received in taxes is not enough to cover the interest payments on the debt, and more debt is issued, or in what is the same thing, more paper money is issued to pay the interest. Eventually the banking system does not have enough coin to maintain an adequate reserve against the constantly increasing amount of paper money, and the government releases the banks from its obligation to pay in metal coin on demand. This constitutes a fundamental change in the money: it goes from a convertible system, in which the paper is redeemable for metal that has value in and of itself, to a paper system that cannot be converted into anything of value; the paper becomes the only money. The government invariably forces circulation by making it a "legal tender" as mentioned above, meaning everyone is required to accept it in payment of debts, and the government agrees to accept it in payment of taxes. The money has no intrinsic value, it cannot be redeemed for anything of intrinsic value, and "cash" is the paper alone.

The face-value amount of paper money constantly increases, which naturally depreciates its value; because it is depreciated, the metal held by the banking system is more valuable, which increases the reserve ratio; the large reserve ratio is used as a justification for increasing the amount of paper money. But the "reserve ratio" has by now become a fiction: since the paper is not redeemable, the "reserves" consist of more paper, and the metal is held in some central bank as a "reserve" for all the paper. Usually the government finds it necessary to "nationalize" all the metal money and bullion, as happened in the U. S. in 1933 (all the gold was confiscated). That was actually a fairly simple process: since the public had been convinced over the previous twenty years that advanced nations use paper money, and gold is for the primitives, there was not then much gold coin in circulation anyway. Americans were once again allowed to possess gold only in 1976, and that was only because the experts believed that the price of gold would sink below the mint value of $42/ozt. Much to their surprise, it has never been below $42/ozt., and is now (due to the depreciation of the U. S. dollar), always above $1,200/ozt.

A "fiat" money system usually occurs when a government delegates the creation of paper money to private institutions under a government charter, for example the U. S. Federal Reserve, but is sometimes accomplished by governments directly. The Bank of France started out as a private institution, but was nationalized in 1945, and returned again in 1993 to a private institution. Likewise the Bank of England started as a private institution in 1694 and was nationalized in 1946. Fiat money cannot perform the function of a store of value, but it does nominally perform three of the other functions of money: a) a means of exchange; b) a relative measure of value; and c) a standard for deferred obligations. Whether a fiat money performs these adequately depends on the rate of depreciation, and it is a common theme of history that all fiat money depreciates; the question is: at what rate. The rate of depreciation depends, as shown above on the rate at which new money is created. Given that it always depreciates, a fiat money is a forced loan: something of lesser value is returned to a lender unless it is compensated by a higher interest rate. A fiat money system is stable so long as the members of the public have confidence that the fiat money can be passed to others in return for actual goods [2.2-25]. The system can last for a long time under certain conditions: a) it is not issued to excess, or in what is the same thing, so long as the depreciation is slow enough that the public does not notice it; b) there is no national debt; or c) a national debt that is being paid off using annual government surpluses. Fiat money is always made a legal tender; as it says on the Federal Reserve Notes: "This note is legal tender for all debts, public and private". That is the legal means of stating that the notes cannot be refused if offered; it is in fact the means by which the government forces them to circulate and be used as money.

Fiat money works as a measure of value, but recall that fiat money is also accompanied by debt. Gold and silver is "backed" by the labor of the past because it was produced by the labor of the past; it is already paid for. Fiat money, compounded by debt, is "backed" by the labor of the future (i.e., taxes and your assets).

Fiat money induces certain risks into the economy. First, since the money is depreciating because of the expansion of issues, the public can easily be misled into confusing the rise in prices with a rise in values. Rising prices can give the false sense that profits are increasing. That in turn promotes speculation, investment in unwanted products due to unwarranted optimism, industrial expansions before they are justified, and an increase in expenditures for luxuries [2.2-26]. Second, a depreciating money causes confusion in business, as costs, profits, and losses cannot be accurately calculated, and in the end it tends to diminish the desire for credit, as no one borrows if he cannot determine if it is worthwhile to him or not. The public will lose confidence in it entirely if the depreciation is rapid enough [2.2-27].

The behavior of fiat money can be summarized in a few points [2.2-28]. First, its value (i.e., "purchasing power") varies inversely with its amount; the more of it that is issued, the less each unit will buy. Second, if the government or banking system attempts to circulate a metal money alongside fiat currency, the metal money will disappear from circulation and either be hoarded or exported, since people naturally understand that it is more valuable than paper. If some guy comes into Granny's Tarts, and pays his $7.00 bill with five dollars in Federal Reserve Notes and two silver dollars, what will you do (if you're smart)? You'll put the two silver dollars in one pocket and replace them in the cash register with two dollars worth of Federal Reserve Notes out of your other pocket. Third, the main "benefit" of a fiat currency is that it is much easier for a government to control domestic wages and prices. Domestic prices become independent of foreign trade since the natural regulating process of the commodity money standard is eliminated [2.2-29]. The net result is of course, more power for the government and the banking system. The fiat currencies of two trading nations fluctuate against each other, not against some common standard such as gold or silver, and the balance of payments is restored by dynamic pricing of each fiat currency vs. the others, thus creating the new industry of currency speculation.

The long-term trends of a fiat currency can be summarized under four categories. First, its value cannot be maintained because the temptation for over-issue, either by the government or by the banking system, is too great [2.2-30]. The problem is that the depreciation does not affect everyone in the economy equally or at the same time. Some will come out ahead, and some will lose, as will be discussed in section 2.4. Governments always want more money to spend but don't want to raise taxes, and therefore the inclination is to spend on credit. The banking system is the means by which those plans are put into effect. Second, as a consequence of the first, the fiat money becomes political money: the quantity in existence is determined not by the needs of commerce, but by what the government needs for its purposes. Its supply is not regulated by any economic forces, but rather for political ends [2.2-31]. The amount of paper can be increased even when the demands for trade are decreasing. The illusion of prosperity caused by an expansion of money makes the economy appear to be prosperous; and of course the debtor class always benefits from repaying in depreciating money. Third, control over the amount of fiat money is partly determined by the desire for the government to please its political supporters and allies [2.2-32]. Fourth, since nations operating on fiat currencies must use floating exchange rates for trade between them, the government is able to exact control over the economy by controlling exchange rates directly [2.2-33].

A fiat money system is workable under certain conditions because it performs three of the four general functions of money, as noted above [2.2-34]. First, in order to function as a medium exchange, it is necessary that the government give it legitimacy as money by agreeing to receive it in payment of taxes. Otherwise the government would be in a position of demanding to receive money with value by forcing the public to obtain it using money of no value. The public will not be fooled: the government cannot mandate a fiat paper money as the medium of exchange between businesses and people, but then demand that taxes to be paid in gold and silver. The fundamental unfairness of such a proposition will undo the legitimacy of the fiat paper. Second, in order to perform the function of canceling of debts, it is necessary that the government instigate and maintain a demand for the fiat money by requiring that it be accepted in all transactions, in other words, making it a legal tender. In order for a fiat money to operate as a relative measure of value, the government must make the claim, true or not, that the fiat money is ultimately "backed" by some commodity that does have value. Usually the claim is made that the fiat money is really a substitute for gold and silver; even if not convertible. That is of course a patent falsehood: either the money is convertible or it isn't. If it's convertible, then it isn't fiat. If it is fiat, then it doesn't matter what claims are made since neither the banks nor the government will give metal in return for it. Third, in order for it to function as a standard for deferred payments, the fluctuations in the amount of fiat money in circulation must be controlled so as to keep the rate of depreciation reasonably small so as not to attract too much attention. This is necessary to attain two objectives: to maintain the quantity necessary for commerce, and to maintain parity between the currencies among trading nations. If these conditions can be met, then a fiat money system is sustainable over the long run [2.2-35].

But there is a problem: some of these conditions cannot be maintained. First of all, it is always subject to depreciation by over-issue; and we have seen that over-issue is the natural order of things. As Alexander Hamilton pointed out [2.2-36]:

> "The emitting of paper money by authority of Government is wisely prohibited to the individual States by the national constitution; and the spirit of that prohibition ought not to be disregarded by the Government of the United States. Though paper emissions, under a general authority, might have some advantages not applicable, and be free from some disadvantages which are applicable, to the like emissions of the States, separately, yet they are of a nature to be liable to abuse - and it may even be affirmed, so certain of being abused - that the wisdom of the Government will be shown in never trusting itself with the use of so seducing and dangerous an expedient. In times of tranquility, it might have no ill consequence; it might even perhaps be managed in a way to productive of good: but in great and trying emergencies, there is almost a moral certainty of its becoming mischievous. The stamping of paper is an operation so much easier than the laying of taxes, that a Government, in the practice of paper emissions, would rarely fail, in any such emergency, to indulge itself too far in the employment of that resource, to avoid as much as possible one less auspicious to present popularity. If it should not even be carried so far as to be rendered an absolute bubble, it would at least be likely to be extended to a degree which would occasion an inflated and artificial state of things, incompatible with the regular and prosperous course of the political economy.

Among other material differences between a paper currency, issued by the mere authority of a Government, and one issued by a bank, payable in coin, is this: that, in the first case, there is no standard to which an appeal can be made, as to the quantity which will not only satisfy, or which will surcharge, the circulation; in the last, that standard results from the demand. If more should be issued than is necessary, it will return upon the bank. Its emissions, as elsewhere intimated, must always be in a compound ratio to the fund and the demand: whence it is evident, that there is a limitation in the nature of the thing; while the discretion of the Government is the only measure of the extent of the emission by its own authority."

Hamilton is referring here, when he discusses "paper emission by the Government", to the paper issued by the States during colonial times, and by Congress when it issued the Continentals. But his objection is equally valid when the fiat paper is issued by a central bank: as he says, the difference lies in whether the paper is convertible or not. If not, it will at least "occasion an inflated and artificial state of things", meaning an increase in prices and ambiguity in calculating costs and profits, risky to business. It is easier to print paper than to raise taxes: and that is the core problem, with a bank or without. What patriotic citizen, willing to pay taxes, is willing to continue to pay them when he knows or suspects that the revenue is wasted? When governments begin to throw away the taxpayers money on useless programs or benefits to those who do not need or deserve them, it is no wonder that the taxpayers begin to doubt the integrity of the government; when that happens, it is always easier for the government to rely on fiat paper than to restrain it's spending impulses.

The method by which fiat paper distorts the economy is easy to trace. Since the early issues cause prices to rise, wages must rise, and before long there is a claim that there is not enough currency; then more is issued, and the cycle repeats. Secondly, a fiat currency does not behave in foreign trade the way a convertible system does. If the money consists of metal, or is convertible to metal, an increase in the metal, which will permit an increase in the convertible paper, prices will rise, but the rise in prices will be counteracted by an increased demand for foreign imports. Money consisting of coin and of convertible paper can be safely exported, since the recipients know it can ultimately be redeemed; the metal can then be exported to the foreign nation via redemption, and doing so will tend to drive the amount of domestic money in circulation back to equilibrium.

A fiat currency is actually a necessity of the government. It may perform well as the medium of exchange, and may do so for an extended time, but its true nature is political money issued for political purposes, and when the political actions lead to a financial failure, the paper will fail with it. Even small degrees of depreciation become a problem because decreasing values lead to additional charges for consumers. Businesses, operating mainly on a credit basis, must defend themselves against the prices they must pay for materials and labor, and do so by raising their prices. It is even worse when currencies must be traded between nations [2.2-37].

Walker [2.2-38] made the observation that a fiat paper money is only useful for domestic exchanges since it cannot be exported. That was true when he wrote that, since the world was mostly on a gold standard. But it is not true now for the United States. The U. S. dollar has become a de facto reserve currency (in other words, has come to be regarded as the most stable). As a result, many foreign governments are content to use dollars as a reserve against their own currencies, which means that U. S. dollars (Federal Reserve Notes), even though fiat, can be exported. Thus the U. S. is able to export the inflation of the Federal Reserve Notes. That will work until it stops working, and it will stop when foreign nations begin to realize that the U. S. dollar is not as stable as it appears because it is "backed" by a national debt that cannot be repaid in the same units. The U. S. taxpayers will never generate enough output to pay off the debt.

Sumner [2.2-39] has cited three options once a fiat money system is established: a) continue; b) "turn back"; or c) "stand still". Continuing means the constant increase of the fiat money. This is the case in which the fiat money is issued as deemed necessary by the government or the banking system, each time giving the illusion of prosperity, when it is actually depreciating; it will eventually become worthless, as did the Continentals. It is characteristic of a system in which there is no means of redemption, either because there is no authority to tax for their redemption (as was the case with the Continentals), or because the people cannot pay any more in taxes, or the government seeks to float a system long enough to meet some emergency. "Turning back" means going from a fiat system back to a convertible system; that requires budget surpluses, either by reducing government spending and/or raising taxes, and the acquisition of metal to be used as reserves as well as circulating coinage. It is the most difficult one to implement because it relies on both the integrity of politicians and the willingness of the public to do what is necessary to attain sound money. It can be done: England did it in 1821, and the U. S. did it in 1879. "Standing still" refers to the slow steady inflation in which the money supply is managed in such as way as to respond to fluctuating demand for currency. Over the long run, slowly increasing the amount of currency in circulation will lead to the same place: depreciation of the value in exchange. It will simply take longer to reach the point where the paper becomes worthless. This has been the policy of the U. S. since 1933.

A monetary system intermediate between a convertible-on-demand and a purely fiat system, is known as the "bullion standard". Here the domestic circulating medium is inconvertible paper, the same as the fiat money, but there is a limited convertibility open only to foreigners and importers with large imbalances that must be paid in metal. Because of the large threshold amount, the metal is transferred in bullion form, not in coin. A foreign person or government, holding the fiat paper, can in fact claim that it be redeemed in metal, usually by providing it to their government, who will pay, and that government in turn acquires payment from the nation that issued the fiat paper. But, it only applies to very large amounts of paper, the foreign holder with only a few hundred dollars is out of luck; he will have to cash it in to his government and receive in return whatever their money is. But, for large enough amounts, the domestic issuer of fiat currency will pay foreigners, and it will also allow importers with sufficiently large imbalances to remit bullion. All transactions in metal are actually outside the average person's abilities, since only very large amounts qualify; even then it is only foreigners who are ultimately allowed to take possession of the metal. Note what is going on here: the citizen of the nation issuing the fiat currency cannot get metal, but a foreigner can. A domestic businessman cannot trade in metal, unless he incurs large debts to foreigners.

Since the domestic money is fiat, no coins circulate, other than the token types used for small change. The fiat-issuing nation is thus biased against its own citizens, and a considerable amount of lies and propaganda is necessary to convince the citizens of the justice of it. Except: there is no justice in it. The U. S. was on the bullion system from 1933 to 1971, just so you know, after which the U. S. went entirely fiat, where we remain today.

Thus far we have spoken of money as that medium which can be used to make immediate transactions. There is a type of "near money", which is tabulated as part of the money supply, but requires an intermediate transaction before it is turned into money useful directly. The distinction between near money and money per se is that money per se is completely liquid, in the sense that it is accepted in payments without ambiguity as to the actual worth, or without any other intermediate transaction. This "near money" technically includes deposits in savings accounts and certificates of deposit, which require notice to withdraw. I say technically, because the rule for notification is hardly ever enforced in modern times (although it was sometimes enforced up to the 1970's).

It may seem like an odd thing to say, but it is true: no government can dictate that any type of money has value. A government can specify a standard for coinage, so many grains of metal to a money-unit, such as a franc or a shilling or a dollar, but it cannot dictate the value thereof. It cannot claim that a shilling shall buy so much wheat, or a dollar can buy so much sugar; the value of the money depends on the amount in circulation compared to the amount and type of transactions to be made; it depends on the opinion of the public. Sometimes governments attempt to dictate values by issuing decrees specifying that so much money shall be useful for obtaining so much in commodities, but those kinds of dictates are called price-fixing, which is an admission that government finds it necessary to supersede the opinion of the public. Price-fixing proves that the government has failed in some way or another; either it has issued too much money on its own account, or it has failed to properly regulate a banking system. Either way, price-fixing obtains exactly the opposite of the intended results. The value of a money unit depends on the confidence reposed in it by the public in the course of buying and selling: the people have high confidence in metal coins and paper redeemable on demand. Confidence in a fiat money system depends on the credit of the issuer: since a fiat money system arises because of national debt, and the national debt arises because the government spends beyond its means, and the national debt is in the form of bonds held by individuals, corporations, and other governments, the fiat money will be accepted in payment of the interest on the bonds so long as the holders thereof are confident they will be paid; and secondly that they can sell the bonds to others, and the prospective buyers of the bonds are confident they will receive payment of the principal when due. Since national debt is the basis for all of it, confidence ultimately depends on people's opinion as to whether the government can extract enough in taxes to meet the interest payments; i.e., does the government have access to enough real wealth to pay off the bonds. In other words, the value of a fiat currency depends on the government's ability to confiscate if it finds it necessary. That is the real danger of a fiat currency.

Somehow people got the idea, or maybe it was just by tradition, that governments should issue money as a matter of national pride, or as a function of sovereignty. So, throughout the centuries, people relied on the government to "supply" them with money. That was not entirely bad when in primitive times, when only a government had the means to make accurate dies for coinage and to make accurate measures of metal and alloy. Technology in modern times would allow for private manufacturing of money based on metal or alloys. Once the government gained a monopoly on manufacturing the money, it was open for abuse. In the U. S., the government has in the past taxed banknotes issued by State banks out of existence, it altered the laws on free coinage; it incorporated excess silver into the monetary system, and enacted legal tender laws, all of which constitute unwarranted interference by the government onto a monetary system.

There is no perfect monetary system. A coinage system is susceptible to depreciation when more metal is injected into the economy if new mines are discovered or more efficient methods of working existing mines are employed. The foreign exchange rate is fixed (assuming all the trading nations are on a coinage system), but imbalances in foreign trade can cause fluctuations in domestic prices. The other problem with a pure coin system is that there is not enough metal in existence to handle all the transactions if all of them have to be made with coin, unless we are prepared to tolerate either exceedingly small coins or coins that are mostly alloy. A pure coin system is probably obsolete. A convertible system has the virtue of enabling widespread credit; the bank can issue its notes and use the borrower's assets as commodities; the paper is more convenient than coinage at least for large transactions. But the convertibility on demand at the same time restrains the banking system from issuing too much credit over and above what is safe to lend to quality borrowers. The possibility of a large number of people demanding the coin, risking the bank's capital, will tend to force the banks to limit the amount of credit. A fiat system has the advantage of a fluctuating foreign exchange rate that allows the domestic economy to stabilize prices, but is also most susceptible to depreciation.

It is particularly dangerous for a government to issue currency, or to allow a bank to issue currency against government debt. It is easy to claim that a currency is backed by the debt instruments, and count the debt instruments as 'assets' on the ground that the government itself is the ultimate guarantor of the value of the currency. If the government actually had the means to guarantee the value of the currency, it would not have to issue debt to prove it. Governments generally cannot resist issuing more currency against ever increasing amounts of debt because it gives the illusion just mentioned: the debt is counted as if it were an asset. From the government standpoint, why not? It's all free (in the short term).

The politicians will make sure none of them are affected directly, nor their family, nor their cronies when the system collapses. The entire system of currency against debt is based on willful and deliberate ignorance of the fact that someone somewhere (meaning you, your children, your grandchildren etc.) are on the hook to pay off the debt. When the bill finally comes due, those left holding the bag may not be called upon to pay in money; most likely they will pay indirectly with a declining standard of living.

It seems the best practical system is: a) a large amount of coin in the hands of the public, mostly for small transactions; b) larger bills in paper, but backed 100% by metal; and c) a credit system in which the banks can issue notes or demand deposits secured by the borrower's assets or high-quality promissory notes. The government should stay out of the money business altogether, other than setting a standard for fineness and alloy ratios, and let private industry issue the coinage. If the public should lose confidence in the monetary system, it will be necessary to restore it by releasing all the coinage held as backing for the paper notes; this requires that all of the metal be in the form of coin, and not left as bullion. The public will likely be happy to return to the use of paper money once they are satisfied that it is fully backed by a store of value. It is important, however, to issue the coin and the paper money denominated as units of weight of metal, not in the names of currency such as the "dollar" or the "euro". It is this very habit of naming currencies that has tempted governments and banks throughout history to depreciate the money without the public noticing it. As depreciation begins, people will once again get into the habit of thinking that the cost of living is going up when in fact it is the quality of the money that is decreasing. The coins should contain a fixed amount of precious metal, and mixed with alloy to make them more durable, and the name of the coin should be the weight, as in "100 grains, .999 silver". Do not give such a coin a nickname because that name will once again be adopted as tale, and the depreciation plot will set in again.

2.3 Gresham's Law

One of the most famous "economic laws" is attributed to Thomas Gresham, a 16th century English economist, which is commonly stated as "bad money drives out good". That is a shorthand euphemism for what is really going on: Gresham's Law actually means that when two competing forms of money are employed, one that that is undervalued compared to the other will tend to be hoarded, and the overvalued one will circulate. This is also known the "bimetallic" problem.

Suppose two types of metal are in use within a nation as was the case in the U. S. from 1792 to 1900. The market will establish the value of the two metals against each other automatically. The problem is how to establish the relative values when both are used as money. A viable solution may appear at first to formally establish the relative values by law, say silver is decreed to be 15:1 against gold by weight. Thus the official "mint price" of an ounce of gold is fifteen ounces of silver. But history shows that such a scheme only makes things worse. The reason is that supply and demand of the metals, since they have other uses, is constantly fluctuating, and while 15:1 may be the correct ratio today, it will certainly be incorrect at some future time (in fact, at best it can only be an approximation). Fluctuating supply and demand for the two metals means that one of them is actually more common than the official ratio; say silver is actually 16:1 vs. gold in the market. The "official" rate of 15:1 is then seen to overvalue silver: officially an ounce of gold will buy only 15 ounces of silver, but on the market it will buy 16. Then the officially undervalued one (gold in this case) will disappear from circulation either by hoarding or exportation. A person in possession of 16 ounces of silver can trade 15 of them in for an ounce of gold, and still have an ounce of silver left over. The official mint ratio does exactly the opposite of what it was intended to do. It was intended to stabilize the values of two sources of money such that both could circulate side-by-side and perform the functions of money. But the market is always the determinant of value through the process of supply and demand, and will cause the mint ratio to be inconsistent with the true relative values. This imbalance drives the undervalued one out of circulation, contrary to the original goal. Gresham's Law goes into operation whenever there is a disparity between the official ratio and the market ratio.

The U. S. dollar was initially defined as both 371.25 grains of pure silver and as 24.75 grains of pure gold, thus the official mint ratio of silver to gold was 371.25/24.75, or 15:1 [2.3-1]. Between 1795 and 1805, the silver to gold mint ratio in Great Britain was 15.2:1, which was not enough of a difference, considering loss of interest at the mint while coining, insurance, and shipping, to cause Gresham's Law to come into operation [2.3-2]. Thus the two metals circulated in the U. S. at about parity.

But by 1820 the ratio was 16:1 in Great Britain, and despite the U. S. coinage of $1,504,355 in gold coins, none of them were in circulation. Gold obtained more silver in Great Britain; in fact the gold coins were worth more than 16:1 at the Philadelphia market. Thus, since the mint ratio pretended to fix the relative values, silver circulated and gold disappeared. The difference in the mint ratio 16:1 vs. 15:1 was enough to cover the cost of shipping and insurance. Congress decided to revise the mint ratio in 1834, redefining the dollar as 23.20 grains of gold, down from 24.75 grains with the dollar still defined as 371.25 grains of silver as before. This made the mint ratio of silver to gold as 371.25/23.2 equaling 16:1 [2.3-3]. But that did not solve the problem either, since the market ratio continued to fluctuate.

Congress chose to devalue the gold dollar in 1834. The other option was to define the dollar as either one or the other, i.e., demonetizing one of them. Silver was gradually demonetized in stages in the last decades of the 1800's, and the dollar was formally defined only in gold in 1900. There were other proposals to ensure that the mint ratio fluctuated with the market ratio; the most popular, but never enacted, was to require varying fluctuations in the charges for coinage so as to cause the completed coins to end up at the desired ratio [2.3-4].

Two metals functioning as money side-by side is not the problem; the problem arises when the government decrees that the ratio of value between them is some fixed value (called the mint ratio), and the mint ratio differs from the market ratio. A bimetallic system with fixed exchange rates has proven to be a failure since any formal exchange rate will overvalue one and undervalue the other, with the consequence that it will drive the undervalued one out of circulation. A bimetallic coinage system is workable, but only if there are two prices for every product. This may seem like a great inconvenience, but in practice, is probably a minor one since the two prices would not vary too much or very often. The important thing is that the market prices of the two metals dominate the exchange rate between them.

2.4 The Effects of Depreciation

The value of a money unit depends inversely on the quantity of it in circulation. It behaves this way because money, like any other commodity, is subject to the laws of supply and demand: a large supply means a lower price. "Price" is subtle thing when discussing money since prices are expressed in terms of money. One cannot describe the price of something in terms of itself. No one would say that the price of wheat could be expressed in terms of so many bushels of wheat. The value of what is expressed in terms of something else, so much money per bushel, or in the case of barter so many chickens per bushel. Therefore, the "price" of money can only be expressed in terms of something else; that "something else" being any other commodity for which it is traded. A low "price" of money means it has low value against other commodities, or in what is the same thing, a large amount of money of low value is required to obtain the other commodity. Money is said to then have a low "purchasing power".

"Depreciation" of the purchasing power of money means that each unit of it will buy less than it did before. When I was young, most stores sold "penny candy". Surprising as it may seem to younger people, yes, it's true: you could get a handful of real sugary candy for a penny. My mother used to give me a nickel every day when I was in kindergarten. Every day, on walking home from P.S. 9, I used to stop into Mike's Delicatessen on Doat St. between Brinkman and Sumner, and I spent the nickel on a Three Musketeers candy bar (which was about the same size as the current "regular" size). The current (2023) retail price of the same Three Musketeers bar is about $1.15. Keep in mind that the Three Musketeers that I bought in the 1960's is the same as it is now; the candy hasn't improved or gotten larger. What happened is that the money has "gotten smaller" through depreciation: it buys less candy than it once did.

So how did that happen? The reason is: the expansion of the money supply over the years exceeded the rate of growth of the population and the rate of growth at which new transactions were to be made due to improvements and expansion of industrial productivity. As in anything else, when the supply of money exceeds the need for it, the value must go down. If money is more plentiful, each buyer has more to spend. The competition among buyers for the same supply of products to buy tends to bid up the money-prices of those products (recall that the candy bar remained the same). If the supply of money is increased 5%, money is said to be easier to come by, and each buyer is willing to part with more of it when competing with other buyers; thus prices rise about 5%.

David Hume wrote an essay in the 1740's (published posthumously in 1777) in which he showed the general trend of an increase of money [2.4-1]:

"It is indeed evident, that money is nothing but the representation of labor and commodities, and serves only as a method of rating or estimating them. Where coin is in greater plenty, as a greater quantity of it is required to represent the same quantity of goods; it can have no effect, either good or bad, taking a nation within itself; any more than it would make an alteration on a merchant's books, if, instead of the Arabian method of notation, which requires few characters, he should make use of the Roman, which requires a great many. Nay, the greater quantity of money, like the Roman characters, is rather inconvenient, and requires greater trouble both to keep and transport. But not withstanding this conclusion, which must be allowed just, it is certain, that, since the discovery the mines in America, industry has increased in all the nations in Europe, except in the possession of those mines; and this may justly be ascribed, among other reasons, to the increase in gold and silver. Accordingly we find, that, in every kingdom, into which money begins to flow in greater abundance than formerly, everything takes a new face: labor and industry gain life; the merchant becomes more enterprising, the manufacturer more diligent and skillful, and even the farmer follows his plow with greater alacrity and attention. This is not easily to be accounted for, if we consider only the influence which a greater abundance of coin has in the kingdom itself, by heightening the price of commodities, and obliging everyone to pay a greater number of little yellow or white pieces for everything he purchases. And as to foreign trade, it appears, that great plenty of money is rather disadvantageous, by raising the price of every kind of labor.

To account, then, for this phenomenon, we must consider, that though the high price of commodities be a necessary consequence of the increase of gold and silver, yet it follows not immediately upon that increase; but some time is required before the money circulates through the whole state, and makes it effect be felt on all ranks of people. At first, no alteration is perceived; by degree the price rises, first of one commodity, then of another; till the whole at last reaches a just proportion with the new quantity of specie which is in the kingdom. In my opinion, it is only in this interval or immediate situation, between the acquisition of money and the rise of prices, that the increasing quantity of gold and silver is favorable to industry. When any quantity of money is imported into a nation, it is not at first dispersed into many hands; but is confined to the coffers of a few persons, who immediately seek to employ it to advantage."

He recognized that the additional infusion of money (in his time, was gold and silver imported from colonies) works only in the short term. It does so only because the new money goes into the hands of a few large merchants, manufacturers, and landlords. They can expand their businesses, employ more workers, and put to work labor and land that was formerly not worth doing. This is possible because they can pay their expenses at the prices prevailing at the time the new money arrived. But the benefits end when the additional money diffuses its way through the economy through the payment of wages, and prices begin to rise. Typically an increase in wages occurs only as a reaction to the increases in prices. The rate of change in prices is nearly always greater in magnitude than the rate of change in wages. Now the large industrialists find themselves back where they were: paying prevailing prices for their materials, and paying prevailing wages. The increased profits which they obtained during the transition period have vanished, and now, in order to return to those profit levels, would require an additional infusion of new money. Large additions of new silver and gold were not readily obtainable, given that the amounts are limited and distributed worldwide. But there is no such impediment when the currency consists of the product of a printing press or electronic entries in a computer. The infusions of new money are easy to obtain, which is why depreciation, once started (especially with central banks) tends to continue over the long term.

That is not to imply that prices and wages increase uniformly. Certainly wages will increase faster in occupations that are in current demand; prices will increase faster for popular items for which there is competition among buyers. The approximate total spent by a family to maintain its standard of living will tend to increase when the money supply is expanding. Average prices will rise more slowly than the inflation rate at first, then will match the inflation rate, and then will tend to exceed the inflation rate [2.4-2]. Prices rise slowly at first because the public initially holds back on spending, believing the price increases are temporary and will fall later [2.4-3]. Since the official estimates of price increases seem reasonable, the government and banking system will then be tempted to increase the money supply on the grounds that it seems to be expanding the economy. As more money is inserted into the economy, the price increases will begin to accelerate, and the public begins to understand that the price increases may be permanent; then they begin to demand higher wages while trying to cut back on non-essential items. Monetary depreciation can get bad enough that the public begins unloading their currency, buying tangible items instead of holding onto the money. Meanwhile business costs will tend to increase, and profits decrease, because wages (a business cost) must increase in order for the workers to maintain their standard of living. Businesses also have to pay increased prices for their materials and other capital items, again leading to a reduction in profitability; thus the "benefits" of inflation are only temporary and the tactic of increasing the money supply beyond the need for it must be used only as a temporary measure.

An increase in the money supply that causes depreciation will show up as an increase in prices, but only after a delay. A time delay occurs because the money is injected at some particular point in the economy. For example, if the monetary system is gold, and new sources are found, the increase in the amount of gold will have a depreciating effect, and the new money is injected into the economy when the miners and refiners use it to buy their supplies. Or, they may sell the raw bullion to a bank and have it coined; the new money is then injected into the economy through the banks' lending operations. The bank generally will lend to large corporations with substantial financial backing and good credit. In either case, the industries that first receive the "new money" have a distinct advantage: they can spend it at the current prices. As the new money is suffused through the economy, it will eventually reach those industries far removed from the initial injection point. Then retail prices will rise because the prices of all the intermediate production steps have increased. The prices increased because there is a greater amount of money competing for the same quantity of goods and services. The time delay arises because it takes time for all the intermediate transactions to take place.

If the "new money" is inserted directly into people's pockets or bank accounts, the time delay is very short and the effects on prices will be observed immediately. That can happen when a government issues "new money" as a "consumer stimulus" program.

This depreciation is actually a cleverly disguised tax on the poor. It is the poor who do not have the collateral to borrow from the bank and thus obtain the new money at old prices. It is the poor who work in low-end industries far removed from the center of money injection; they have to pay the gradually increasing prices while their wages lag. It also robs those who are on fixed incomes, since the value of what they receive has less purchasing power. It has a negative effect on long-term creditors who loan at fixed interest; even with the interest payments, they end up receiving back less in buying power than they lent, even though they receive an apparent large profit in terms of the number of money units received. Any person or corporation that lends over a long term at a fixed interest rate is injured by depreciation (bondholders, mortgage holders, people on fixed incomes, buyers of fixed annuities). These can only be partly alleviated by providing "cost of living increases" to people on fixed incomes, or adjusting interest rates on loans. But that not a solution because it amounts to applying a corrective while maintaining the core problem in place.

In practice, there will not be a uniform increase in all prices from a certain percentage increase in the money supply. Two effects are in play. First, the fact that productivity may be increasing in some industries, which will tend to lower prices that will compensate for the increase in prices due to depreciation. The mechanism was discussed in section 1.9; as money is employed to obtain capital to increase the efficiency of production, both prices and profits tend to decline. The second effect is that some industries lie outside the main channel through which the new money initially flows. To illustrate, suppose the new money is mostly lent to defense contractors. Those companies and their employees will receive the first benefits, and the new money will flow to those from whom they buy (exotic materials, plastics, electronics, highly-developed processes suited only for military equipment, etc.). The prices of those items will increase, and so will the wages of workers in those industries. Those workers have more to spend, and if they spend the same ratio of their total income as is their custom, those expenditures will tend to increase prices due to increased demand. The trend will eventually spread throughout the entire economy. So, although in the end most prices will rise (except for increased productivity), they will not all rise at the same rate.

Be careful not to conclude that every price increase is due to depreciation of the money. Prices of all items are still subject to supply and demand. The supply of oranges decreases after a frost in the orchards; the supply of corn increases if the summer weather is good; the supply of steel is decreased if there is a strike by the iron ore miners. Demand may increase because the public suddenly sees the benefit in some commodity they overlooked in the past, some new electronic fad may arise that leads to an increased demand for electronic equipment, and so on. Likewise, demand may decrease because some fad has passed, or some new technology has appeared. These are usually temporary since they are mostly due to natural fluctuations. On the other hand, a monetary depreciation is usually permanent since the supply of money cannot usually be withdrawn sufficiently after an expansion.

So the core of the problem is to separate the price changes due to natural fluctuations from the changes due to an alteration of the money supply. This is an inherently difficult problem because the price of an end product, say fresh peaches, depends not only on the weather, the relative efficiency of the competing orchards, and the financial health of the grower; but also on the cost of transportation, the efficiency of the wholesale distribution system, and the wages of the grocer. The problem is inherently ambiguous, and the political class can use that ambiguity to make any number of conflicting and inconsistent claims in order to advance their economic agenda. It is especially true in modern times that an increase in productivity, which would naturally lower prices, can mask a great deal of the natural price increases arising from an excess of money [2.4-4]. This is of great utility to those who demonize free enterprise. They demand to know why workers aren't being paid more when both prices and productivity are increasing. The real answer is: workers should get paid more, but only proportional to the gain in worker productivity. Because the money is depreciating, costs are increasing, and it is not clear as to how much the increase in productivity is offsetting the increases induced by monetary depreciation. But the know-it-all pampered political parasites will say: if productivity is increasing, all of it should go to the worker, conveniently ignoring two facts: a) some of the increase in productivity is from the workings of capital through the use of machines; and b) a depreciating money negatively affects profitability.

A decrease in prices is sometimes called a "relative deflation", a most confusing term since it implies that a decline in prices is necessarily a bad thing. If your rent went down, you would probably not complain too much. "Relative deflations" are mostly temporary fluctuations, same as the temporary fluctuations that cause prices to increase now and then. A reduction in the supply of money (which admittedly is rare) increases the value of each unit of money, and as a result causes a reduction in the general price level. Such a reduction is called an "absolute deflation". So now we have a situation in which prices are constantly changing. Normal temporary fluctuations can cause prices to increase or decrease depending on supply and demand. Then there are the more permanent ones that nearly always tend to increase prices: an increase in the money supply or an increase in costs due to taxes or regulation, and sometimes a reduction in the money supply that serves to reduce prices. Any attempt to gauge the rate of monetary depreciation runs into the difficulty of sorting out which factors are at play and to what extent. That is why the publication of the "general price levels" or other metrics such as the "consumer price index" are not as useful as they claim to be, unless (a tenuous assumption) there is no change in productivity and no change in either supply or demand of the items included in the index. The economy is complicated enough such that assessment of the true causes of price fluctuations is at best an approximation. It is worse than that: the errors are compounded when bad data is used as a guide to enact economic policy.

Given that it is difficult to separate out the effects of money depreciation vs. natural fluctuations vs. increasing productivity, the best that can be hoped for is to have a money unit that is as stable as practical. Stable in this sense means a stable quantity of some commodity, and the best choice of commodity is a precious metal because the natural fluctuations are fairly minor most of the time.

There is another factor to consider when comparing a "price index" over long intervals, namely, the fact that the general standard of living changes over time. It may be true that the "cost of living" has increased from the 1960's, but it is also true that the standard of living has changed with it. The poor of the 1960's lived a different life than the modern poor: in the 1960's, few of the poor had air conditioning, few owned a car, few had color TV. Sometimes people had to skip meals. But most people in America in

2020 who are listed among the poor have most of these material items and rarely miss a meal. Not everything has improved: most people in poor neighborhoods in the 1960's did not hear gunshots all night, and parents did not have to concern themselves with the safety of their children on the way to school. In some ways, the irrelevant details of life have seen significant improvement, but have seen a decline in the important things (quality of education, job opportunities, and public safety). Our high-class economic calculations do not take these standard-of-living issues into account, at least not when the subject is the depreciation of the money. I only mention it here because it is the depreciation of the money that has partly contributed to the decline in the important parts of the "standard of living". "Cost of living" comparisons are not of much value unless the standard of living between the two periods in question is the same. Today's working poor may have four times the money income of the working poor of the 1960's, but living in neighborhoods that were once fairly safe but are now dangerous is little comfort.

Here is an example of two workers, both are married with two children, filing taxes jointly, and taking the standard deduction in 1965 and 2019, and we will investigate how many months each has to work to buy a mid-size 4-door sedan. One worker earns the median, and one is just at the official poverty threshold for a married couple with two children. Granted this is a simplified example but it gives a sense of the general picture.

Row		1965	2019
	Cost of mid-size car, note 1	$2,082	$27,989
1	Poverty threshold income	$3,200	$25,926
2	Standard deduction	$2,400	$24,400
3	Income subject to tax	$800	$1,526
4	Federal tax rate (%)	14	10
5	Federal tax on net income	$112	$152
6	Net income	$3,088	$25,774
7	Months of work to buy the car	8.1	13.0
8	Median Income	$6,882	$65,712
9	Standard deduction	$2,400	$24,400
10	Income subject to tax	$4,482	$41,312
11	Federal tax rate (%)	19	$4,593 + 22% above $39,476
12	Federal tax on net income	$852	$4,996
13	Net income	$6,030	$60,716
14	Months of work to buy the car	4.1	5.5
	Note 1: 1965: 4-door Ford Falcon sedan; 2019: 4-door Ford Focus sedan		

Figure 2.4-1: Incomes, Federal Taxes, and Car Prices for 1965 and 2019

Figure 2.4-1 shows the relevant data. Just below the year is shown the price of mid-size cars, the 1965 Ford Falcon 4-door sedan and the 2019 Ford Focus 4-door sedan. The upper half (rows 1 through 7) addresses the economic situation of the worker whose income is at the official poverty threshold, and the bottom half (rows 8 through 14) shows the same for the worker at the median income level. Income values [2.4-5] and poverty thresholds [2.4-6] are taken from Census statistics and the federal tax rates are from the IRS [2.4-7]. The prices of the cars were obtained from car buyers guides [2.4-8]. Incomes, standard deductions, incomes subject to tax, federal tax rate (%) and federal taxes are calculated as shown. Row 6 and row 13 show the net incomes after federal taxes for both cases. Knowing the net income and the price of the cars, it is easy to calculate how long each worker had to work to obtain the cars. The formula is: the price of the car divided by the net annual income, multiplied by twelve gives the number of months worth of after-tax wages required to buy the car. Those results are shown on rows 7 and 14. In 1965, the car sold for about 8 months worth of the labor of the worker who wages were at the threshold of poverty, and in 2019 he has to work 13 months. Likewise, the median worker had to work 4.1 months in 1965 and 5.5 in 2019. In relative terms, cars cost more for both categories of workers, but the poverty-level worker is much worse off insofar as buying family cars. He is worse off because 13/8.1 = 1.6X, whereas 5.5/4.1 = 1.34X; the poverty-threshold worker has seen his labor expenditures to buy the car increase by 60%; but for the median worker, is only 34%. How did this happen? We don't know all of them, but we can say generally that since wages lag prices during a period of monetary depreciation, and the U. S. has been depreciating the dollar since the 1950's, it is not too surprising that the poverty-threshold person ends up worse off in relative terms. On the other hand, consider the cars: the 2019 Focus has more horsepower, will last longer, uses fuel injection requiring fewer tune-ups, and has conveniences either considered luxuries or were unheard of in the '63 Falcon (air conditioning, AM/FM radio, CD player, Bluetooth, and navigation). That is not to mention better gas mileage, safer seat belts, and air bags, all of which came about by regulation, which increases costs. There is no data on the life-cycle costs of the two cars, so the total cost of ownership is subject to speculation. Consider also the income levels. Recall that there was a much greater disparity between wages earned by white and black workers in the 1960's than there is now (but the data in Figure 2.4-1 uses a composite of all workers). There is probably a labor surplus in the U. S. now, driving down wages especially on the lower end, partly because the U. S. exported its industrial base to China, and partly because there are so many illegal aliens running around working for cash "under the table" (and not paying federal taxes either). (U. S. citizens do not have as many economic rights as illegal aliens, but only a small minority in Congress would vote to do anything about it.)

If cars are more expensive in relative terms for both income earners (although worse for the poorer person), does that mean the overall standard of living has decreased? Not necessarily: the fact that both may be worse off buying cars tells is nothing about everything else they buy. Remember also that we don't have data on the life cycle cost of the cars, so we don't even have the whole story about them. My Aunt Bunnie had a '63 Ford Falcon; it was a nice little car, much better than the '77 Chevy "cream of the crap" Nova I bought. But my Aunt Nancy had a '76 Chevy "rust while you wait" Vega; she got the worst deal of all. This small example should demonstrate the difficulty of assessing price increases when the standard of living is also fluctuating. But one thing should be clear even from this study: the working poor tend to be injured most from a depreciating currency over the long run.

Section 1.9 showed that a depreciation of the currency is often accompanied by a lowering of interest rates. The idea on the part of the banking system is to induce the public to borrow the new money to finance businesses so as to either revive or continue expansion of the economy. Usually this is applauded by the political elite, who claim that high interest rates are a drag on the economy. See the bait-and-switch? The depreciation of the currency, which is a hidden tax, especially on the working poor, is papered over by a claim that things are improving because interest rates are lower than they otherwise would be. But do not forget that business loans are generally for short periods; and as was seen before (section 1.8) a change in short-term interest rates did not materially affect the profitability of Granny's Tarts. In other words, a high interest rate did not have much effect on the price you would have to get for the tarts in order to remain profitable. High interest rates do have a large effect on the monthly repayment on long-term loans, such as mortgages, but those do not have a direct effect on commodity prices.

The maximum rate at which the money supply can be expanded by the banking system as a whole is related to the inverse of the reserve ratio. If the reserves consist of metal, the rate of increase in reserves is slow, if based on debt, depends on the amount of new debt that can be absorbed. The details will be shown in section 5.6.

2.5 The Consequences of Depreciation

The previous sections have alluded to problems generally induced by the depreciation of money. Now they are summarized: these are the general consequences of an economic policy that promotes "prosperity by providing more money".

First, a depreciating money unit gradually increases the real cost of living [2.5-1]. Naturally, when more money is injected into the economy, wages do increase over time, but they increase more slowly than prices increase, except for the offsetting factor of productivity improvements. Consumer prices for staples, where the production processes are already highly developed, will tend to increase with the rate of new money injection; meanwhile wages increase but with a time lag. Built up over decades, there is a serious risk of an overall decline in the standard of living for all workers, but especially for agricultural workers and industrial workers at the lower end of the income scale. The prices of luxuries tend to rise more slowly than the rate of money injection because the demand for them is always small.

Second, a depreciating currency reduces the incentive to save out of earnings, and encourages the tendency to spend on consumption or to speculate. It is a perfectly logical reaction [2.5-2]: why put money into a savings account when it will be worth less when drawn out? It works the same way with investing: if the money is known or suspected of being depreciated, there is greater temptation to take greater risks in the course of investing. Speculation on stock prices becomes a defense mechanism, more akin to gambling than investing to promote improved production [2.5-3]. This is most evident in the activities and philosophy of the day-trader: trying to predict what a stock price will do in the every short term, rather than investing based on solid business prospects. That is also perfectly rational when the money is depreciating: money is becoming cheaper (in terms of its buying power), and therefore there is an incentive to focus on short-term gains to outbid the depreciation. Because the supply of money is increasing, it gives the illusion of wealth without the reality of increasing wealth [2.5-4].

Third, depreciation of the money unit makes it more difficult for businesses to calculate gains and losses accurately. It becomes necessary, in order to set prices, to estimate the future value of money instead of simple costs vs. selling prices at the current values. The problem of course, is that the average person in business, especially a small business, does not have the time and probably does not have access to the necessary data. The merchant must therefore add in some hedge against the depreciation, but can only guess as to what the proper factor should be; thus the introduction of ambiguity in business transactions. Obviously no one wants to risk taking a loss just because the money is unstable, so the natural tendency is to add enough to prices "just to make sure"; an insurance policy against being robbed unaware. If this is done at every stage of production from the raw materials to the retailer, it is easy to see that the general trend is an acceleration of price increases, possibly more than the relative increase in the money supply. Thus the price increases inadvertently exceed the true monetary depreciation, but it is a natural result of ambiguity about the money stability.

This effect may not be too pronounced in the production of Granny's Tarts since most of the materials and expenditures are short-term. You will not likely buy sugar and flour two years in advance. The opposite is true in a dry goods business, such as selling yarn, cloth, ribbon, and embroidery materials. Those items are typically bought in fairly large quantities since the customers demand a variety of cloth and materials to choose from, and at long periods since the turnover in dry goods is much less than groceries. It is for that reason, low turnover, that high raw profit margins are justified. Suppose such a businesswoman bought cloth a year ago, and has been selling it off over the past year while the money was depreciating at 10% per year. She will of course raise her prices slowly, and will appear to make a large profit on what she bought last year, but what gets lost is the fact that those profits do not have the buying power it had the year before. On paper, profits are up. But when she goes to re-stock, she finds that wholesale prices have increased (because all the intermediate suppliers have added their small portion) and her new costs exceed her profits.

The conflation of profits with losses appears in other ways: the prices of stocks of profitable companies will tend to keep pace with the depreciation. Once again, the increase in the money supply hides the fact that each unit of apparent profit has less buying power than before. It gives the illusion that investing is more profitable than it really is; and now it is more difficult to distinguish real growth from an illusory growth. A favorite trick of socialists is to criticize the oil companies for making large profits, conveniently ignoring two facts: a) some of the profit is due to depreciation of the money [2.5-5]; and b) the capital employed to improve production was paid for in money that was worth more when it was employed (i.e., the return on capital is artificially increased). They also focus on total profits, conveniently ignoring the fact that an oil company may earn 11 cents per gallon of gasoline while the federal government gets 18 cents per gallon as an excise tax, and some States get even more than that. Who's greedy now?

Anyone who holds a mortgage over a long period of years, even if he is collecting a fairly large interest rate, is likely to gain on paper but lose in reality. Suppose you sell a house for $200,000 at 6% interest and agree to hold the mortgage for twenty years. The monthly payment received from the buyer comes to $1,432.87 or $17,194.44 per year and after 20 years of payments he will have paid you $343,888.80. On paper, you will have earned 143,888.80, which is the reward you earned for holding the mortgage. But suppose the money the buyer is paying you depreciates each year. Figure 2.5-1 shows the situation.

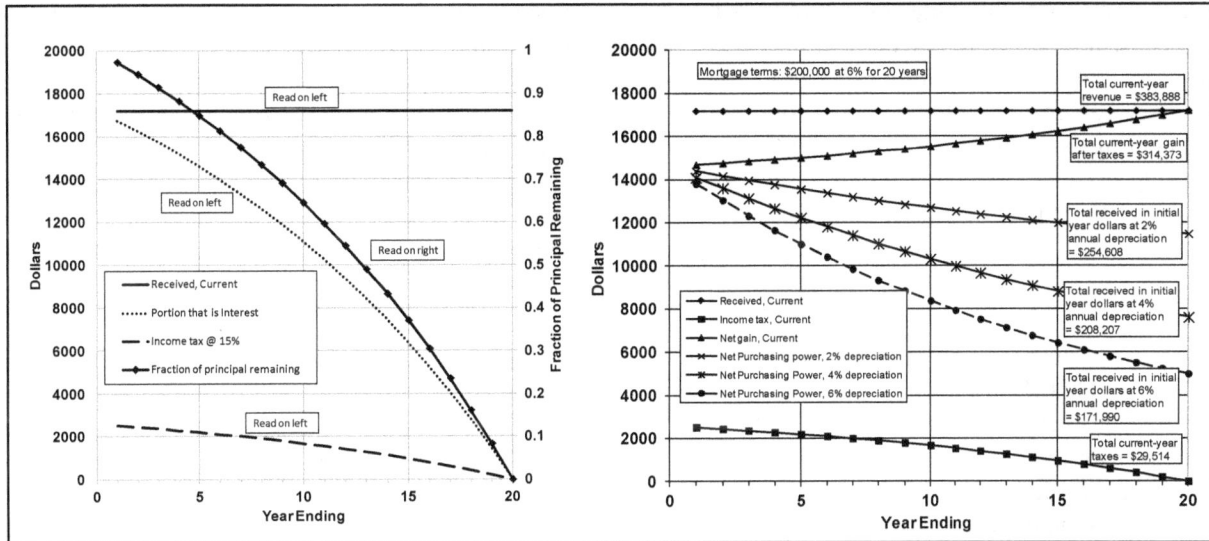

Figure 2.5-1: Illustration of Depreciating Returns from Mortgage

The left chart shows the amortization schedule (diamond marker line read on the right); here it is seen that most of the payments in the first ten years or so are interest. The upper solid line shows the annual payments; the dotted line shows the portion that is interest. Suppose you are in the 15% tax bracket; the dashed line shows how much in taxes you will have to pay on that interest earned. The right chart shows the net effect of both taxes and depreciation. The diamond line at the top shows the revenue received from the buyer each year in current-year dollars; after 20 years, you will receive $383,888. That looks like a pretty good reward for taking a 20-year risk on a $200,000 house: $143,888 in profit. The square-marker line shows the taxes to be paid in current year dollars (note it is the same as the dashed line on the left chart), assuming a 15% tax rate on the interest (your "profit"). The total taxes paid in current-year dollars over the 20 years comes to $29,514. The triangle-marker line shows the net gain after taxes in current-year dollars, which comes to a total of $314,373. Not as rosy as before taxes, but still represents $114,373 profit on paper. But the crossed and circle marker lines show what happens when the current-year revenue after taxes is referred back to the purchasing power of initial dollars (i.e., the dollars used to establish the value of the house). You are receiving the same number of dollars, but they have less purchasing power during each year that passes. When the purchasing power values are added up, you will receive only $254,608 in initial-year purchasing power if the money depreciates at 2% annually; $208,207 if it depreciates at 4% annually; and $171,990 if it depreciates at 6% annually. In other words, at 2% depreciation, you will earn only $54,608, at 4%, you will net $8,207, and at 6% depreciation you actually will lose $28,100 on your 20-year risk. This is how creditors get robbed: by holding long-term bonds or mortgages at a fixed interest rate. A creditor will approximately come out even on a 20-year note when the annual depreciation rate is about half the interest rate. A 14% loss occurs after taxes when the depreciation rate is comparable to the interest rate. But it is even worse than that. The total taxes paid in current-year dollars is $29,514. It is a simple matter to calculate the taxes in terms of the purchasing power of the initial year dollars. At 4% annual depreciation, total taxes referred to the initial year comes to $22,059. Well, there you go: at 4% depreciation, you earned $8,207 for taking the risk; the government, who did nothing and risked nothing, got $22,059, about 2.7 times more than you. Who is the loser now? But the "progressives" want your taxes to go up because you are an evil sinister capitalist preying on the borrower by making him pay interest. It is easy to see from this example why banks always benefit from a rapid turnover of homes: they come out ahead in the first few years and they avoid the losses that accumulate by holding notes over long terms.

An increase in a fiat currency above what is needed creates a demand for further increases of the currency for two reasons [2.5-6]: a) the fact the prices have increased means that more money is now required to perform the same transactions as before; and b) since the fiat currency is issued on the basis of government debt, more currency is needed to pay the interest and principal on the debt. If the currency were not fiat, the expansion of it would eventually be ended by demands for payment in metal; but fiat currency can in principle be issued to any arbitrary extent. The one thing that prevents the government and central banks from doing so is the recognition by the public that it is being robbed, that taxes are increasing because the higher dollar values push people into high tax brackets; because they see the buying power of their paycheck and savings dwindle; and begin to cast suspicion upon the banking system in general and the government in particular. Then either the government or the central bank acts to restore confidence. The restraint against arbitrary issues of fiat currency is thus limited by political considerations.

Fourth, depreciating money causes the public to lose confidence in the economic system [2.5-7, 2.5-8, 2.5-9]. This shows itself in various ways. If the public knows or suspects that the money is declining in value, it occurs to them sooner or later that they are working the same hours for a declining real income, a true fear of depreciation, unless they can obtain commensurate wage increases. Only a fraction of the workforce has this advantage. But suppose every worker was able to obtain a wage increase corresponding to the depreciation: then there would be no incentive for the banks or the government to do it. It is only because changes in wages always lag changes in the money supply that depreciation benefits the government and those who first receive the additional money. Low confidence in the money leads naturally to a low demand to hold money, and tends to stimulate spending on luxuries or other items that a worker ordinarily would not buy, instead of saving a portion of his income. The worse-case scenario, when the depreciation proceeds rapidly, is the loss of confidence on the part of the worker that he will be able to exchange it for what he needs.

Fifth, a depreciating currency tends to redistribute the wealth of a nation toward large industries and those who are already wealthy [2.5-10]. But don't be fooled by the false claim that "the rich get richer, and the poor get poorer". The rich may well get richer, but the poor do not necessarily get poorer; they mostly experience a slower growth in the standard of living. The wealth distribution mechanism and the exact effect depend on where in the economy the new money is injected. Those who obtain the new money, whether it is the rich or the poor, or the large corporation, or small businesses, are able to buy at current prices, before the expansion of the money supply creeps through the economy and raises prices generally. Those who receive the money last, (as it filters through the economy) lose the most. Prices will certainly rise faster than wages and those workers in industries that are not the immediate recipients or beneficiaries of the new money will end up paying higher prices before their wages increase. The price increases are mitigated only by the trend toward falling prices due to increased productivity. It does not matter what monetary system is in force. A paper system with an undue expansion of credit operates in the same way as a coin system that has received new metal by the opening of new mines.

Sixth, a depreciating currency, when it is known, motivates people to get into debt. Why not: as seen in the above mortgage example, he repays with money that has depreciated because it is easier to come by. Over the twenty years in the mortgage case, the buyer is likely to experience increasing wages, even if he keeps the same occupation simply due to the increase in the money supply. Who has the problem? Not the debtor, he repays with money that is easier for him to obtain than when he first contracted to mortgage debt. In fact, knowing the money is depreciating encourages the accumulation of debt on the grounds that repayment will be easier than it appeared on paper when it was contracted. Meanwhile, you, the dummy, that held the mortgage on the house you sold, may end up taking a loss. Speaking of encouraging the accumulation of debt, there is an old saying:

"If you owe the bank $10,000 and can't pay, then you have a problem. But if you owe the bank $100,000,000,000 and can't pay, the bank has a problem."

All that means is that a large enough accumulation of debt under a depreciating money system won't matter to the debtor: either he can pay in money of lower purchasing power, or he can run up such a large debt that someone else has to deal with it.

There is one mitigating factor in the apparent benefit to the debtor: even though he can repay in depreciating money, he still has to come up with them. If the expansion of the money supply causes a contraction later, and he loses his income, or his business, he will not be able to make the payments. He may have thought running up debt was ideal, but he many find himself worse off.

Seventh, when the depreciation rate is high, every individual will do their best to turn the money they have into property of some kind. The goal is to apply whatever amount would normally go to savings toward buying anything that appears to have tangible value, sometimes even things that are known to be bad investments. For example, when money is depreciating rapidly, people may decide to buy a car now to avoid the price increase next year, even though they may already have a perfectly serviceable car. Rather than saving at the old rate, it is now expended for consumption, and in this case, for redundant consumption (if the family only needs one car). Or, they may decide to sell the old car, and will get a higher price for it than if the money had been stable; that simply means that the used car buyer is paying more than they otherwise would. Consider what is happening here: the demand for new cars has increased, so naturally their prices increase. The rate at which prices increase often tends to outrun even the rate of depreciation (especially if, as noted above, each part of the productive stages adds a "little inflation insurance") until the correction sets in. These constant price increases generally lead to demands for additional expansion of the money supply. Continued long enough, a nation will experience a monetary death spiral: continuous expansion of the money supply causing new depreciation and continuously increasing prices, with wages lagging the price increases, until the public loses confidence in the monetary system.

Eighth, the depreciation of money, once it has occurred, is permanent [2.5-11]. The alternative is to forcibly reduce the amount of money in circulation, known as a monetary deflation. That sounds good on paper, but does not work in practice. The reason is the same as already been discussed, except in reverse. Less money in circulation means smaller amounts are available for transactions, thus prices will fall; unfortunately, wages always lag prices, and when prices are falling and wages are still high, the businesses begin to incur heavy losses, and must reduce employment. The first to lose employment are the working poor at the low end of the income scale, because their labor is the least flexible and has the lowest marginal profitability. The effect is even more pronounced when wages cannot fall due to minimum wage laws or labor union contracts, or when wholesale prices cannot fall because of long-term materials contracts. A contraction of the money supply is practical only if all prices and wages are allowed to fall, which is not politically possible in modern societies. So, a deflation (appreciation of the money) to correct an inflation (depreciation of the money) will further injure those who were already injured by the initial depreciation. Once depreciation has occurred, there is no practical means to go back to the original value of the money. Penny candy is gone forever, same as the nickel *Three Musketeers*. The best that can be hoped for is to end the depreciation, and stabilize at the current level [2.5-12]. The increase in fiat currency is only stopped or slowed down for political reasons; as Sumner [2.5-13] put it: "a paper currency never contracts itself".

A ninth negative effect of the depreciation of money is that a worker may find himself in a higher tax bracket because his wages have increased. He now has to pay a higher tax rate, even though prices have increased faster than his wages. The faster the depreciation, the worse off the worker is.

A tenth negative effect depreciating money is that the average consumer (like your customer with the three bratty kids) sees higher prices and comes to regard Granny's Tarts as a luxury, but she is also thinking that the old Chrysler has a year or two left in it, as well as the washing machine, dryer, and vacuum cleaner. If many people adopt the same attitude, the retailers have a problem; then the manufacturers have a problem; the companies that manufacture the components of those items have a problem; those who manufacture producers' goods become unprofitable; and the overall economy begins to decline as recounted in section 1.9.

The losers from depreciation of the money are [2.5-14]: a) lenders on fixed interest rates; b) workers with fixed wages or salaries; c) holders of mortgages and leases; and d) the liberty of the people (mostly due to increased regulation). The winners are: a) businesses who obtain first use of the created money (but only temporarily), b) the banks (but only temporarily); c) the government (mostly in the form of increased power); d) those in possession of commodities prior to the increase in prices; and e) currency speculators.

2.6   The Implementation of Depreciation

Depreciation of the money unit is caused by an increase in the amount of money in excess of what is required to conduct commerce. The exact mechanism by which it occurs varies with the type of monetary system in place: commodity money, a convertible paper money, or fiat money. Each of those is considered in turn. The results of depreciation are always the same, regardless of what system is used.

Four mechanisms tend to depreciate commodity money [2.6-1]. The first method is the discovery of new mines, or an improvement in mining efficiency such that new metal is brought into the system, or an importation of metal. The new mines in South America brought a great deal of silver into Spain in the 1500's, and the gold discoveries in California and Australia are examples where a large amount of metal was introduced in a fairly short time. Normally, the amount of new metal is small compared to the amount in existence, and the depreciation then occurs fairly slowly. What is held back in the arts or in industry, or as a reserve not used as money does not cause the money unit to depreciate in value. But these large increases were brought into the economy as money, and caused a rapid increase in prices in a short period. More efficient mining techniques may allow existing mines to increase production. Increased importation of coin can occur due either to an increase of exports, or because foreign persons wish to seek a safe haven for it out of fear it will be stolen by their own governments. In this case, more metal is brought in, which tends to raise domestic prices; the increase in domestic prices tends to make imports appear cheap, and thus imports increase with the commensurate exportation of the metal. So long as the trading nations are on metal or commodity standards, and those are kept in place, the money tends to depreciate uniformly as it is spread among nations by trade.

The second method with a commodity system is a revaluation of the coin by the government usually by either reducing weight or adding alloy in the coin while still calling it by the same name. So long as the number of coins remains the same, the coin itself is depreciated but has no effect on prices because the same amount of coins do the same amount of work in transactions. But once again, the reduced coin will not pass in foreign trade unless the trading nation has likewise depreciated its coin by the same amount. If the coin is increasingly lighter by government decree, people may begin to suspect that coin is not true, and will seek other means of making exchanges, or increase prices. Here the price increases occur because of suspicion about the coin, not because the coins are actually under the official weight -- the government has gone too far, and has excited the suspicion of the public [2.6-2]. Section 3.1 will show the history of commodity money depreciation in England and France.

A third method is the gradual wear and tear of the coinage over time that lead to variations in the weight; the underweight ones may still circulate domestically at par, but they have less value in foreign trade, since full weight is required for full shipment of commodities.

A fourth method of depreciation in a commodity system is the clipping of the coin (thus reducing its weight) or loss of weight by wear and tear. Historically, people tend to accept slightly clipped or worn coins by habit, with the caveat that they will do so as long as those coins will be received by others. Then such a coin is underweight and technically depreciated, still passes at the mint by tale instead of its true value. It is only when such coins become so light that they begin to be rejected; then prices will rise.

The method of depreciation in a convertible paper system is done by issuing more paper notes than can be redeemed on demand. In other words, paper has been issued that is redundant with the coin that would have served the same purposes. Banks issuing paper money tend to over-issue because it is profitable to do so, even if their notes in principle are redeemable on demand in coin [2.6-3]. Consider first the situation in which that banking system consists of independent banks, each issuing their own notes. There is no restraining force, and the nation's paper currency is not uniform. This system prevailed in the U. S. until the 1860's. Typically the government will specify the reserve ratio in coin, but there is no guarantee that the banks will limit their issues to what is legally permitted. Each bank, or consortium of banks, issues it own notes. The ones that circulate locally are likely to be re-deposited, and there may be some that are redeemed in coin. But as the economy expands, it is likely that many of the notes will circulate beyond the local area, and will be received by businesses in distant locations, to be deposited in their local banks. If the remote bank sends the notes back to the issuing bank for redemption, then the coin must either be shipped or a credit must be added onto the remote banks' account. But, if the remote bank does not redeem it, but instead circulates it because it is accepted in that locality, the note is likely to never be redeemed. Many banks in the U. S. in the 1800's made such a bet: that they could issue notes with small chance of being called upon to redeem them. As usual, as prices rose due to the increase in the money supply, more currency was demanded in order to make the same number and amount of transactions. The bank is of course anxious to lend all the paper it can, since it earns a profit from the interest. Typically the largest restraint on the over-issue was an imbalance of foreign trade. The notes of domestic banks are not accepted by foreign businesses or banks, and the trade imbalance has to be paid in metal. That caused a great domestic demand for coin and bullion, and the notes were redeemed in order for the importers to obtain the coin. Thus the amount of paper money contracts, usually in the form of banks calling in loans or failing to renew them. A bank that is weak, having little reserves to pay the redemption, must be bailed out by the stronger banks, otherwise the public will begin to lose confidence in the banking system, which is to say, in the paper notes themselves, even though they are technically redeemable in coin. Now the strong banks have a problem: they must now risk their capital to bail out the irresponsible banks. There is an alternative: the strong banks can convince the government to permit the banks to suspend redemption in coin, and thus revert to a fiat system. The strong bank's argument is simple: only by suspension can the banking system, and the credit system that supports the economy, be preserved. This saves the capital of the strong banks, and bails out the weak banks, or at least gives them time to obtain the necessary metal. In other words, no bank shall incur a penalty for failure, corruption, or incompetence.

A fiat system has already been defined as a system in which paper issued by a government or a bank performs all the functions of money except as a store of value. An independent bank issuing its own notes without any guarantee of redemption or of acceptability will soon be rejected; one counterfeit is as good as any other. Therefore, a fiat system usually requires the government to set up a central bank to control the amount issued, to regulate the reserve ratios, and to force circulation by decreeing that the fiat money must be accepted for all transactions. The method of depreciation with a central bank fiat system is only slightly different than the convertible system. In this case the notes are expanded for the same reason but the central bank ensures that reserve ratios are observed. The main way to induce depreciations is simply to change the reserve ratio. That will have the same effect as in the convertible system, except it will eventually lead to a fiat reserve standard (i.e., even the reserves are paper). The fiat system only became practical when the banking system became reliable enough, and the clearinghouse function secure and efficient enough to permit banks to create money by issuing "demand deposits", commonly known as commercial checking accounts. The demand deposit is a record of the amount of fiat currency created and allocated to a business concern on account, and the transfer of values via money is accomplished by sending checks instead of notes or coin. The transfer of values actually occurs on the bank's credit, secured by the customer's promissory note or by collateral. The degree to which banks can create demand deposits is regulated by the fractional reserve ratio, which in turn is regulated by a central bank employing powers given to it by a government.

The money supply tends to increase more rapidly in a fiat system than any other, because there really is no penalty for issuing too much money [2.6-4]. The central bank is chartered by the government and therefore it cannot be allowed to fail. If it cannot fail, then it must preserve the confidence in the banking system, and to do that it must have the power to rescue any bank that would normally fail (or to at least compensate depositors). A second, natural reason why fiat currency increases quickly is that commercial banks are profit-seeking institutions (which they should be). More money issued increases profits, which is perfectly legitimate because banks perform a very useful and valuable function, that of assessing the best risks for investments, and promoting the use of credit. The problem is not a profit-seeking banking system. The problem is the natural tendency for a central bank to attempt to increase the nation's economic growth by increasing the amount of money [2.6-5]. A central bank is a creation of a government and is therefore subject to political pressure. At the same time, central banks are tasked with maintaining some semblance of stable prices, and to regulate the commercial banking system so as to reduce the magnitude of expansions and recessions. An increase in the money supply is often used as central bank policy to offset a decrease in industrial output, or to directly increase employment or income.

No matter how the money is depreciated, it is devalued, and is a sign of bankruptcy on the part of the government [2.6-6]. It can't pay its debts in full money, so in a commodity system it issues money with less metal, but calling it by the same name. In a convertible or fiat system, it issues or allows banks to issue money that is of lower value than before.

Labor unions are sometimes (falsely) blamed for higher prices caused by depreciation. Since depreciation is caused only by the actions of money-creating institutions, and since unions cannot issue money, unions by definition are not responsible for depreciation. It is true that unions can force wages up beyond the market level, and it is true that this can sometimes increase the prices of products made by union labor, but the price increases only affect those products, and does not result in a general rise in prices throughout the economy. The worst that a union can do is demand wage increases that are unaffordable that result in layoffs because the company has to curtail production, move elsewhere to obtain lower labor costs, or in extreme cases, shut down entirely. None of these are due to depreciation of the money directly. But these kinds of actions on the part of unions can cause a political demand for a greater money supply, which does depreciate the money, which does increase prices. Demand for a greater money supply comes in the form of an argument that a greater supply of money is necessary to keep people employed; the government has a vested interest in "full employment". But keep in mind, the unions are only applying pressure on the central bank and government; that pressure can and should be resisted. Although the unions may be aiding and abetting depreciation, they are not the direct cause [2.6-7]. Only the government and the banking system can depreciate the money and thus cause price "inflation" through influence on the monetary system.

If depreciation of the money is so destructive, especially to the poor, why is it so common? Funding of wars has been a significant cause of depreciation throughout most of history, as described above with the example of Great Britain. Recall that the government debt was sold to the public for coin, and paper was issued by a government-chartered bank as circulating medium in its place. But obviously it couldn't stop there: after a while, the taxes were paid in paper, and the interest on the debt was paid in paper. Most of the metal had migrated out of the nation, or was retained only as reserves against the paper. The result was a large national debt contracted for in coin, but paid in paper, and a replacement of the coin with paper. The paper thus depreciated but the source of the depreciation was still the war debt, not the banks per se.

The government could have raised taxes to pay for the war, but the temptation to pay for wars with debt is too big to be resisted. Modern wars, even when fought remotely, tend to destroy the existing capital because it cannot be replaced; they are financed by what was produced at a previous time [2.6-8]. Thus the debt incurred by the government to fight the war merely compensates for the destruction of capital; the closer the war is to a nation's border, the worse it is. The debt leads to a greater issue of money than existed beforehand (in whatever form), depreciates due to supply and demand, and the result is a general increase in domestic prices.

The second, entirely modern reason for depreciation in the last hundred years is due to the growth of the power-demanding administrative state. It is a direct result of the expansion of tasks that the government has appointed itself to do: mainly the social welfare state, and a great deal of regulatory activities. All of them cost money, and keep in mind that the cost of regulation is not limited to the compensation of the regulators. Every regulation pervades the entire economy in some form or another. Those are additional costs, and can only be paid for by issuing more money. It is easy for politicians to buy votes: make a promise to give the people something of value, claim that it will come out of someone else's pocket, and presto: a whole new class of loyal voters. But politicians always promise more than they can deliver, and of course the voting public is infused with greed and envy to some extent; therefore the promises can only be implemented by issuing government debt. What the public fails to understand (and the political class hopes it never finds out) is that the growth of debt leads to depreciation of the money, and everyone ends up paying; usually more than the promise was worth. Not only that: all the future generations get to pay too if the government contents itself with merely paying interest on the debt without taking necessary actions to liquidate it. Meanwhile the banks likely hold a significant amount of the debt and can then collect interest on it. That same debt, counted as assets, are part of the banking system reserves, which permits the expansion of the money supply in the form of loans extended by creation of demand deposits, for which the banks also earn interest. All of it is based on debt and depreciation of the money.

A fiat money system sometimes leads to continuous wars and nearly always leads to increasing domestic spending in order to achieve political goals designed to keep the ruling elite in power. It does not seem to matter if the domestic spending programs actually achieve their goals or not. The U. S. has not seen a decline in poverty since the "War on Poverty" began in 1965 any more than we've seen a decline in drug use due to the "War on Drugs" since 1919.

2.7   The Measurement of Depreciation

Prices rise once the money starts depreciating. Since wages tend to lag prices (both upward and downward), governments attempt to keep track of how much prices are changing, usually as a guide to regulate the money supply. To do so, economists have developed a "price index" system. There are two types of indexes: a) a wholesale price index of common commodities, weighted by the volume of units sold nationwide; and b) a consumer price index. The wholesale price index tracks the wholesale prices of a large number of individual common items, including industrial metals, energy, building supplies, farm products, and many others. It main purpose is to determine trends in the production and supply of these items for use in forecasting supply and demand, to be used as a guide for investors. It is not all that useful as an indicator of inflation since these prices are so heavily dependent on industrial conditions.

The Consumer Price Index (CPI) consists of a "set of commodities" in "approximate" proportions that a "typical" family buys each week, obtains the "median" prices, and "averages" those together to be compared month-by-month or year-by year to "estimate" the degree to which prices are increasing or decreasing. The words in quotation marks are there for a reason: they indicate the variability that may be obtained using different assumptions about what components should be included in the index, how they are weighted, and how the indexes are calculated. The CPI is designed to show how retail prices of common household items vary from month to month or quarter to quarter. The idea is to develop an index that is representative of most households, and is intended to be used as an indicator of price variations, or the "inflation" experienced by the average household. The index itself is a single number, referenced to some baseline number (usually a particular year). This single number represents the composite prices of the component items in the index. The person designing the index has to consider what commodities should be included, how those are to be weighted within the composite. In other words, the index designer has to decide the relative importance of eggs, cheese, gasoline, children's toys, clothes, rent, etc. to the average household. He has to decide what prices are to be used (a survey of retail prices, calls to consumers, grocery ads, published reports, etc.), and in what locality should they be taken (Nashville, San Diego, Helena etc.). Ultimately the designer comes up with an estimated average of the overall allocation of resources such as housing vs. groceries vs. transportation by families. The items to be included in the index is a composite, weighting factors are averages, the makeup of families is an assumption, and the data is assembled ad hoc from wherever they can obtain it. A CPI may disguise secondary impacts. For example, if the cost of energy is increasing, it is not only the price of gasoline and heating oil that should be included, recall that the cost of energy affects all products because they all have to be transported. The price change of chemicals affects the costs of food production (fertilizers) and many industrial processes. It is worse than that: the definition of the CPI has changed slightly over time, so that it is impossible to make direct comparisons over long time periods. The definitions change for two reasons. The first is a legitimate alteration due to the fact that what people spend money on changes over time as new products come into the market and old ones die out. Average household consumption of bread, milk, and aspirin may be constant, but very little is spent in modern times on baking powder, lard, or castor oil. The second cause for changes in the CPI is an illegitimate one, in which the index is manipulated to make the monetary inflation appear to be less than it really is. So CPI's may well be an approximation to an average to a composite with inconsistent assumptions and ad hoc data, but despite its defects, is about as good as can be done.

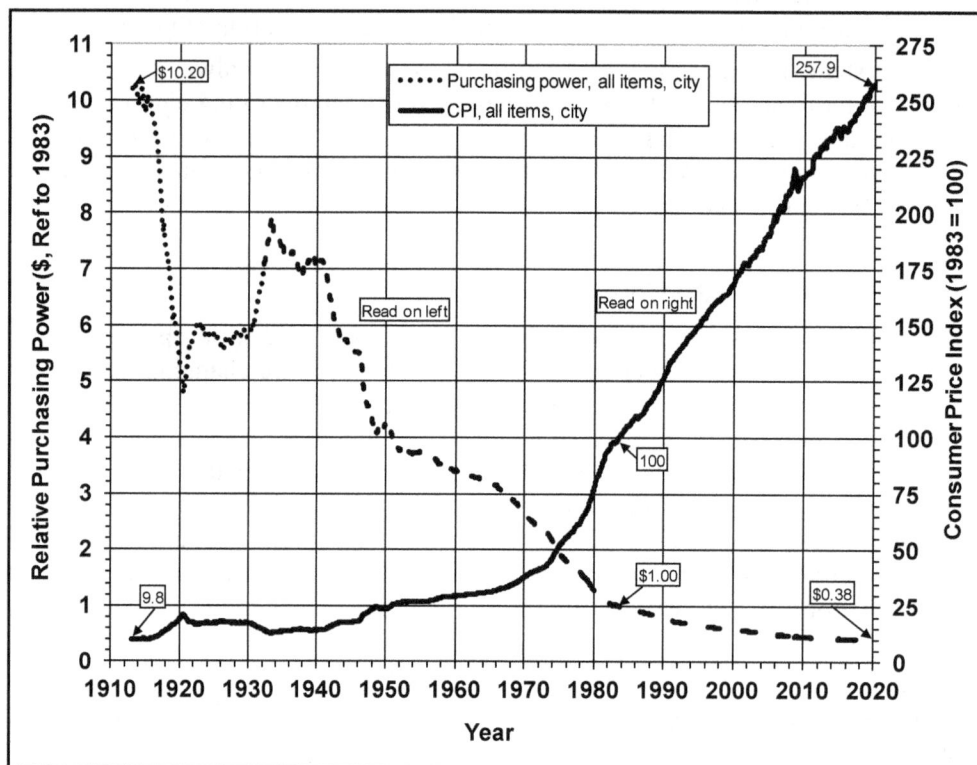

Figure 2.7-1: CPI and Purchasing Power of U. S. Dollar, 1913-2020, Referenced to 1983 [2.7-2]

Figure 2.7-1 shows the CPI [2.7-1] and relative purchasing power of the U. S. dollar from 1913 to 2020. It is the average across the U. S. for all city residents, including "all items". According to the Bureau of Labor Statistics, the CPI reflects "thousands of prices for commodities and services purchased by consumers are collected in a sample of 75 urban places" [2.7-2]. This CPI is referenced to 1983 (and thus has a normalized value of 100). The purchasing power of the dollar is simply the reciprocal of the CPI multiplied by 100, and is expressed in dollars. The solid line on the Figure is the CPI, and is read on the vertical scale at right; purchasing power is the dashed line, read on the left. The dashed purchasing power curve is more instructive (although both curves actually say the same thing). Looking at the endpoints compared to the reference point (1983), the purchasing power is currently down to 38 cents compared to what it was in 1983, and at the other extreme, a dollar in 1913 would buy what $10.20 would buy in 1983 dollars, meaning it would buy what $26.84 buys in 2020 dollars (the last figure calculated from 10.20 divided by 0.38). Keep in mind that one of the Federal Reserve's main tasks is "price stability", and it is clear that it has failed in that regard. But why has it failed? Looking at the trends, there is a large decrease in purchasing power from 1914 to 1920; that is the depreciation during World War I. There was a steep appreciation from 1920 to 1921; that was the industrial decline due to the end of wartime production; the dollar appreciated in purchasing power due to a decline in the money supply [2.7-3] and quickly restored after a year of liquidation. Purchasing power and CPI were fairly stable during the 1920's (the combined effect of two countering forces, as will be shown in chapter 18). Then there was a severe deflation and increase in purchasing power at the start of the Great Depression (a speculative stock market crash followed by a run on the banks followed by a decline in the money supply) from 1930 to 1933 [2.7-4]. But this increase in purchasing power was accompanied by 25 to 30% unemployment. A moderate depreciation in purchasing power occurred from 1933 to 1941 as the government attempted to stimulate the economy and spend its way out of the Depression. That did not work; the Depression ended in 1941 due to the increased industrial output necessary to supply World War II, with an accelerated depreciation of the dollar during the war and afterwards, extending from 1941 to about 1951. Since then, the U. S. has experienced a steady depreciation of the dollar until the present day. There have been no large deviations from the pattern despite the wars in Korea, Vietnam, Yugoslavia, Panama, Afghanistan, Iraq, or Syria. CPI only shows part of the story: surely incomes increase over time. That data will be shown as appropriate in Part 2.

2.8   The Final End of Depreciation

History shows that depreciation of the money ends in one of three ways. The first way is when an institution issues so much fiat money that people lose confidence in it, and it goes out of circulation because it is no longer received in trade. The amount is so plentiful that each unit becomes worthless. Recent examples include Germany in 1922, Hungary in 1945, Turkey in 1988 and 1994, Bolivia in 1985, Zimbabwe in 2008 and 2009, and Venezuela between 2014 and 2018. When the money unit is destroyed by over issue, the conventional action is to issue a new currency with a promise of scarcity, and to revalue all existing contracts in the new currency. But the lack of confidence persists, and the government has to make sure that the new currency is stable by restricting is quantity.

Secondly, depreciation ends when the people and institutions that benefit from it no longer do. The main beneficiaries of depreciation, as seen above, are those who obtain the new money issues first, when they can buy at existing prices. Those generally are the banks, the large government contractors, and foreign governments that invest in other nation's debt. They stop benefiting when the prospect of repayment starts to erode, or they have difficulty selling their bonds, or they learn that the interest will not be paid.

The third way depreciation can stop is if a central bank stops buying government debt. It is unlikely to ever occur, since most central banks exist for this very purpose. It could happen only if the customers of a central bank, the privately-owned commercial banks, recognize the dangers of a high rate of depreciation and convince the central bank to reject the new government debt. But that would also require that the commercial banks stop buying government debt.

The fourth method applies only to a convertible paper money: when it becomes evident that the public is getting nervous, and starts to demand redemption in coin. That requires the banking system to call in loans, and contract the money supply in order to obtain the metal necessary for redemption. That may have negative economic consequences, but at least it stops the depreciation.

A summary of the monetary depreciation death spiral was described by Hahn [2.8-1]. First, an excess of money is created, and is accompanied by low interest rates, which attracts the entrepreneurial and industrial groups to expand investments. Those with first access to the new money achieve some important benefits because their selling prices rise faster than costs, and profits are high. The expansion continues so long as the businesses expect to obtain higher prices, and so long as the injection of more money continues. The higher profit margins continue until wages must increase when the higher prices filter down to the consuming workers and others in the economy. That is when the costs of doing business increase, and profits start to fade. At the same time, interest rates begin to rise because the generally higher prices require a greater amount of credit to finance it. But there is a limit to the amount of credit that can be extended without causing a collapse of the currency, and the higher interest rates along with higher labor costs make the new ventures unprofitable. This cycle continues as long as the banking system can keep creating money, or as long as the government can continue to issue more debt without loss of confidence. Over the long run, even if the rate of depreciation is kept fairly low, the money eventually is seen to depreciate faster than can be compensated by rising wages; as always, it is the worker who pays the hidden tax. Taken too far at too high rate, the depreciation will destroy the currency altogether. Section 3.2 and chapter 7 will each show historical examples.

2.9   Determining the Correct Amount of Money

If constantly increasing the amount of money in circulation has so many negative effects, how is the correct amount of money to be determined? That depends on the monetary system in use. In a pure commodity system (coin), or a system of paper redeemable on demand, it does not need to be "determined"; it is controlled indirectly by the economic forces outside of any top-down control. The money necessary to make the necessary transactions at the prevailing prices is supplied by natural means. Every nation and community will obtain the amount required to make the exchanges the people thereof need to make. If the money is purely coin, the amount of metal that can be added depends on what price can be obtained for it, since, being a commodity itself, costs something to produce [2.9-1]. If the need for metal exists, it will be obtained by an exchange of other commodities. Whatever metal is required to assure redemption and thus promote confidence in the banking system will be obtained by the banking system; it is in their interest to do so. The risk is, of course, that the government will allow the banks to suspend payment. But without government interference, and allowing banks to fail if they do not meet their commitments, the necessary metal will be obtained. The amount of money necessary will increase in proportion to population, amount of trade, and the degree to which credit transactions improve the efficiency of money. If the money is coin or redeemable paper, the amount necessary will be obtained; we will have what we need. We will then know the answer but it won't matter [2.9-2].

The amount of money in circulation should be regulated such that it is better to export commodities than money. Walker quotes Lord Overstone (here he refers to both commodity money and convertible paper money) [2.9-3]:

> "When the exchanges are in an unfavorable state, I apprehend that is evidence that the relation of the money of the country to the commodities of the country is such that it is more profitable to export money than to export commodities; and the action on the part of the managers of the circulation ought to be directed to restoring such a relative state between money and commodities as shall render it in the interest of the community at large to export such a quantity of commodities as shall prevent a further export of money."

He means that if the money is depreciated, it will naturally lead to a large of importation of goods to be paid in commodity money (metal). Why does depreciated money lead to imports of commodities and export of money? Because depreciation raises the prices of domestic production; it is therefore economically viable for the public to import foreign goods, and export the money. Only by making the money scarcer, thus maintaining its value, domestic prices fall, and domestic suppliers are able to profitably supply domestic needs. Then the exportation of money be prevented and the economy stabilized.

Taken together, the amount necessary in a convertible system depends on the magnitude and quantity of the transactions to be made, the extent of trade with other regions and nations, and the efficiency at which money and credit can transmitted. A credit system reduces the amount of hand-to-hand money that is required. An efficient clearing house system for offsetting payments by check also reduces the need for money transfers, which in turn depends on the efficiency and integrity of the banking system. All this is based on the assumption that the money is fully redeemable in metal on demand.

If the economy utilizes fiat money, then keeping a money supply constant would require that wages fall along with prices. That is consistent with the economic behavior, but unfortunately is not politically possible. Because of the known ambiguities that are evident everyday in the present fiat money system, no one is willing to take a wage reduction even if prices are falling. It is tantamount to trusting in a paper promise without an enforcement mechanism - a recipe for disaster. On the other hand any injection of fiat money into the economy will affect the structure of production somewhere along the line. The key problem, as Hayek has pointed out [2.9-4], is to determine the magnitude and point of injection of new money into the economy in such as way that the demand for consumer's goods and producer's goods remains unaltered. Given that wages usually cannot fall as productivity increases, it means that even if the solution were known and practical (it is not), it would not have the desired effect. Increased investment would lead to more efficient production and lower prices, but wages would not fall, and thus costs would not fall. But the bigger problem is that there is probably no way to predict when and where any negative consequences will occur. It is a matter of observation and correction assuming accurate data can be collected in a suitably timely manner. But this is the best that can be hoped for in a fiat system. There will always be fluctuations in the need for money in advanced economies [2.9-5], and the main objective is not to try and develop some unworkable model that attempts to allocate money in exact proportions, but rather to ensure that the overall risk of depreciation and depressions is minimized.

As mentioned in section 2.3, there is a simpler system that bypasses these difficulties: a dual commodity system (gold and silver), with paper allowed at 100% reserve, but with the coinage denominated only in weight, not by name [2.9-6]. There should be no fixed proportion between the value of gold and silver be so they are free to float in the market like any other commodity. That means there will be two prices, one in gold and one in silver. That is to be expected, since the metals tend to fluctuate against each other slightly. It seems evident that "two prices" is not too inconvenient, especially with modern methods of tabulating. The main benefit is that a weight of a certain metal cannot be counterfeited, and it cannot be arbitrarily changed by government edict.

So far this discussion has addressed the items that we commonly regard as money: coin, credit, bank notes of various kinds. There is now a new type of "currency", called "crypto currency", which allegedly is "manufactured" by an algorithm, and is available only on the internet. The most-often claimed benefit of this "crypto currency" is privacy. The most common one in existence now is called "bitcoin". It seems to me that there are several reasons why bitcoin is neither money nor a money substitute. First, it is bought and sold, and the price is denominated in dollars; if it were money, other things like commodities would be priced in bitcoin, not bitcoin in dollars. Therefore, it fails the first test: it is not a widely recognized medium of exchange. Second, since it has to be bought and sold, and profits therefore are treated as "capital gains", and taxed accordingly, bitcoin is no different than a bond; it is an investment like gold and silver, but one that can sometimes be used to make purchases over the internet. Third, no one knows where it comes from or how it is made, or how much of it is in existence. It suffers from the same defect as the bank notes issued by the "wild cat" banks of the 1800's. The valuation of bitcoin may well be 100% propaganda, having no recognized standard of value; the makers thereof creating just enough of it in the short term to earn great profits on the sale, after which it may be issued in such abundance that it ends up being worth nothing. It is after all, the product of nothing more than an algorithm; algorithms can be broken or tainted. At least we have an accounting of how and where and how much money is created in the form of Federal Reserve Notes and demand deposits. There is no such corresponding insight into the origin of bitcoin. Fourth, I doubt it is all that private: since it has to be transferred electronically, there is no reason why those transactions are not already being tracked. These defects will continue until the ruling elite finds a way to use bitcoin for their benefit or changes the law for their benefit.

But bitcoin is not the worst of it. There is another movement to convert U. S. money into "central bank digital currency" (CBDC). The Federal Reserve has issued a research and analysis paper on the subject [2.9-7]. The CBDC is intended to function as a "digital form of paper money", that is, to replace the Federal Reserve Notes in electronic form. Several claims are made in favor of the CBDC. First, it would permit the present 5% of the public without banking services to obtain them. Secondly, the CBDC will be a direct obligation of the central bank, not obligations of a commercial bank, as is the case with checking and savings accounts at present. Therefore, there would be no credit risk and no deposit insurance would be necessary. Third, international payments would be simpler and cheaper. Fourth, it would reduce the risk inherent in crypto-currencies by regulation.

Despite the lofty words, there are three significant problems for you, the citizen. First, if it replaces the Federal Reserve Notes, it must be a legal tender. If it is legal tender, than you must accept it in payments; therefore you must have a CBDC account whether you want one or not. Likewise, all businesses will be required to have a CBDC account whether they want one or not. To promote uniformity, all savings and checking accounts will be converted to CBDC accounts "for your convenience". Secondly, if CBDC is a liability of the central bank, the central bank will have unlimited ability to create as much CBDC as it desires, which means the central bank can create as much monetary inflation as it desires. Third, CBDC constitutes a concentration of both economic and political power: all transactions can be monitored by any federal employee or government-approved activist. Your transactions will determine your conformity to the prevailing political environment. Should you fail to conform, your CBDC transaction history will be used as justification to limit your freedom.

References

[2.1-1]   Francis A. Walker, *Political Economy*, NY: Henry Holt & Company, 1892, p. 108
[2.1-2]   op. cit., Francis A, Walker, *Political Economy*, p. 106
[2.1-3]   John E. Cairnes, *The Character and Logical Method of Political Economy*, London: Frank Cass & Co. Ltd., 1965, p. 90 (originally published in 1875 by Macmillan & Co.)
[2.1-4]   op. cit., Francis A Walker, *Political Economy*, p. 105

[2.2-1]   Amasa Walker, *The Science of Wealth*, Boston, MA: Little, Brown & Co., 1867, p. 127
[2.2-2]   Francis A. Walker, *Money*, NY: Henry Holt and Company, 1891, pp. 24-43
[2.2-3]   Condy Raguet, *A Treatise on Currency and Banking*, Philadelphia, PA: Grigg & Elliot, 1840, pp. 3, 4
[2.2-4]   op. cit., Francis A. Walker, *Money*, p. 191. Walker is quoting Ricardo's "Reply to Bosanquet", pp. 94, 95, an essay issued in 1811 during the debate on *The Bullion Report*. (Reprinted by Forgotten Books, FB&c Ltd., London)
[2.2-5]   op. cit., Francis A. Walker, *Money*, p. 158
[2.2-6]   Murray N. Rothbard, *What Has Government Done to Our Money?*, Auburn, AL: Ludwig von Mises Institute, 2005, p. 35
[2.2-7]   Henri Pirenne, *Economic and Social History of Medieval Europe*, London: Routledge & Kegan Paul Ltd., 1936, pp. 97-141
[2.2-8]   Murray N. Rothbard, *The Mystery of Banking*, Auburn, AL: Ludwig von Mises Institute, 2008, pp. 85-90 (originally published 1983)
[2.2-9]   op. cit., Amasa Walker, pp. 224-226
[2.2-10]   N. J. G. Pounds, *An Economic History of Medieval Europe*, London: Longman Group, Ltd.,1974, pp. 403-434. Pounds reviews the early types of money, the growth of the fairs, and the means of issuing and redeeming bills of exchange.
[2.2-11]   op. cit., Rothbard, *The Mystery of Banking*, pp. 90-94
[2.2-12]   Fred Rogers Fairchild, Edgar Stevenson Furniss, Norman Sydney Buck, *Elementary Economics*, NY: The Macmillan Company, 1926, Vol. 1, pp. 429ff
[2.2-13]   op. cit., Raguet, pp. 128-131
[2.2-14]   op. cit., Francis A. Walker, *Money*, pp. 323, 324; quoting Benjamin Franklin, "A Modest Inquiry into the Nature and Necessity of a Paper Currency", 1729
[2.2-15]   op. cit., Raguet, pp. 76, 81
[2.2-16]   op. cit., Raguet, pp. 78, 79
[2.2-17]   op. cit., Raguet, pp. 77, 78
[2.2-18]   John E. Cairnes, *Essays in Political Economy*, NY: Augustus M. Kelley, 1965, pp. 125-127 (originally published London: Macmillan & Co., 1873)
[2.2-19]   op. cit., Fairchild et al, Vol. 1, p. 383
[2.2-20]   https://seekingalpha.com/article/4181917-copper-silver-ratio-range-for-thousands-of-years

[2.2-21]   op. cit., Fairchild et al, Vol. 1, pp. 383, 405, 406
[2.2-22]   William Graham Sumner, *A History of American Currency*, NY: Augustus M. Kelley, 1968, p. 186 (originally published 1874 by NY: Henry Holt & Co.)
[2.2-23]   William Brough, *The Natural Law of Money*, NY: Greenwood Press, 1969, p. 66 (originally published by G.P. Putman's Sons, 1896)
[2.2-24]   William Cobbett, *Paper Against Gold, or The History and Mystery of the Bank of England*, NY: John Doyle, 1846, p. 362 (Reprinted by Forgotten Books, FB&c Ltd., London)
[2.2-25]   op. cit., Fairchild et al, Vol. 1, pp. 407, 408
[2.2-26]   op. cit., Raguet, p. 135
[2.2-27]   op. cit., Cobbett, p. 226
[2.2-28]   op. cit., Sumner, pp. 249, 250
[2.2-29]   Clifton H. Kreps, Jr., *Money, Banking and Monetary Policy*, NY: The Ronald Press Co., 1962, pp. 68-70
[2.2-30]   op. cit., Amasa Walker, pp. 132, 133
[2.2-31]   op. cit., Francis A. Walker, *Political Economy*, pp. 340-342
[2.2-32]   Murray N. Rothbard, *What Has Government Done to Our Money?*, Auburn, AL Ludwig von Miss Institute, 1991, pp. 138, 139 (originally published 1963)
[2.2-33]   op. cit., Kreps, pp. 60, 69-71
[2.2-34]   op. cit., Francis Walker, *Money*, pp. 288ff, 376-383, 522, 523
[2.2-35]   op. cit., Rothbard, *What Has Government Done to Our Money?*, p. 149
[2.2-36]   Secretary of the Treasury, *Reports of the Secretary of the Treasury*, Washington: Blair & Rives, 1837, Vol. 1. It contains Alexander Hamilton's, "Report on a National Bank", 14 Dec 1790. It is available at https://fraser.stlouisfed.org/files/docs/publications/treasar/AR_TREASURY_1790.pdf.   The passage from Hamilton's report as quoted is on pp. 64, 65
[2.2-37]   op. cit., Francis A. Walker, *Money*, pp. 382, 383
[2.2-38]   op. cit., Francis A. Walker, *Money*, pp. 288, 298
[2.2-39]   op. cit., Sumner, pp. 326-330

[2.3-1]   op. cit., Raguet, pp. 45, 46, 207, 208, 217, 234
[2.3-2]   op. cit., Sumner, pp. 103-106
[2.3-3]   op. cit., Sumner, pp. 108, 109
[2.3-4]   op. cit., Raguet, pp. 213-217

[2.4-1]   David Hume, *Essays, Literary, Moral, and Political*, London: Ward, Lock, & Co., Essay 25: Money (pp. 169, 170)
[2.4-2]   Henry Hazlitt, *What You Should Know About Inflation*, NY: Funk & Wagnalls, 1968, pp. 85-87 (originally published by D. von Nostrand)
[2.4-3]   op. cit., Rothbard, *The Mystery of Banking*, pp. 68-73
[2.4-4]   Murray N. Rothbard, *America's Great Depression*, Auburn, AL: Ludwig von Mises Institute, 2000, pp. 85, 86 (originally published 1963)
[2.4-5]   1965: https://www2.census.gov/prod2/popscan/p60-049.pdf
           2019: https://www.census.gov/content/dam/Census/library/publications/2020/acs/acsbr20-03.pdf
[2.4-6]   For 1965: https://www.census.gov/data/tables/time-series/demo/income-poverty/historical-poverty-thresholds.html, 1965, filename = thresh65.csv
           For 2019: https://www.census.gov/data/tables/2020/demo/income-poverty/p60-270.html, poverty thresholds, filename = thresh_19.xls.
[2.4-7]   For 1965: https://files.taxfoundation.org/legacy/docs/fed_individual_rate_history_nominal&adjusted-20110909.pdf
           For 2019: https://files.taxfoundation.org/20190416151624/Tax-Foundation-FF6241.pdf
[2.4-8]   1965 Ford Falcon: http://www.theclassicford.com/1965_Ford_prices.htm
           2019 Ford Focus: https://www.carsguide.com.au/ford/focus/price/2019

[2.5-1]   op. cit., Sumner, p. 254

[2.5-2]   op. cit., Hazlitt, p. 76
[2.5-3]   op. cit., Kreps, p. 518
[2.5-4]   op. cit., Raguet, p. 155
[2.5-5]   op. cit., Hazlitt, p. 151
[2.5-6]   op. cit., Amasa Walker, pp. 156, 157
[2.5-7]   op. cit., Henry Hazlitt, p. 18
[2.5-8]   op. cit., Rothbard, *The Mystery of Banking,* pp. 65, 66
[2.5-9]   op. cit., Francis A. Walker, *Political Economy*, p. 107
[2.5-10] op. cit., Hazlitt, p. 21
[2.5-11] op. cit., Hazlitt, p. 50
[2.5-12] op. cit., Hazlitt, pp. 15, 47-51
[2.5-13] op. cit., Sumner, p. 220
[2.5-14] op. cit., Amasa Walker, pp. 182, 223, 304-308

[2.6-1]   op. cit., Raguet, pp. 42-44
[2.6-2]   op. cit., Francis A. Walker, pp.126-128
[2.6-3]   op. cit., Amasa Walker, pp. 156-159
[2.6-4]   op. cit., Rothbard, *What Has Government Done to Our Money?*, pp. 154, 155
[2.6-5]   op. cit., Kreps, pp. 452, 453
[2.6-6]   op. cit., Hazlitt, p. 24
[2.6-7]   op. cit., Hazlitt, pp. 128, 142
[2.6-8]   L. Albert Hahn, *The Economics of Illusion*, NY: Fraser Publishing Co., 1949, pp. 12, 13

[2.7-1]   Bureau of Labor Statistics, see https://data.bls.gov/cgi-bin/srgate; The CPI is from series called CUUR0000AA0, "All items in U.S. city average, all urban consumers, not seasonally adjusted". The Purchasing power is the reciprocal of the CPI, divided by 100 (also called series CUUR0000SA0).
[2.7-2]   Bureau of Labor Statistics, https://download.bls.gov/pub/time.series/cu/, file = cu.txt.
[2.7-3]   Milton Friedman, Anna Jacobson Schwartz, *A Monetary History of the United States, 1867 - 1960*, A Study by the National Bureau of Economic Research, NY, Princeton, NJ: Princeton University Press, 1963, p. 232
[2.7-4]   op. cit., Friedman and Schwartz, pp. 330-338

[2.8-5]   op. cit., Hahn, *The Economics of Illusion*, pp. 166 - 168

[2.9-1]   op. cit., Amasa Walker, pp. 180, 214
[2.9-2]   op. cit., Sumner, p. 222
[2.9-3]   op. cit., Francis A. Walker, *Money*, pp. 464, 465; here Walker is quoting from Overstone's "Evidence on Banks of Issue", 1840.
[2.9-4]   Friedrich A. Hayek, *Prices and Production and Other Works*, Auburn, AL: Ludwig von Mises Institute, 2008, p. 284. (This is a collection of essays Hayek published in the1930's.)
[2.9-5]   op. cit., Hayek, p. 287
[2.9-6]   op. cit., Raguet, pp. 211, 212
[2.9-7]   Board of Governors of the Federal Reserve System, *Money and Payments: The U. S. Dollar in the Age of Digital Transformation*, Jan 2022, available at:
https://www.federalreserve.gov/publications/files/money-and-payments-20220120.pdf

3

Historical Examples of Monetary Depreciation

Having summarized the basic economics and the general characteristics of the various types of money, this chapter now addresses some historical examples of depreciation. As mentioned in section 2.4, the main causes are: new mines, imports, wear and tear, clipping, or revaluation by the government. Section 3.1 recounts the cases of revaluation (mostly devaluation) that occurred in England, France, Scotland, and the Arab nations. Section 3.2 describes the depreciation of paper money during the French Revolution.

3.1 Depreciation in a Commodity Monetary System

The one great attribute of metallic money, if constrained to always operate on the basis of weight, is that it cannot be directly faked. An ounce of silver is an ounce of silver. People knew that trading tangible items of value for gold and silver entailed minimal risk because everyone else would be willing to trade that gold and silver for other items of tangible value. So, metallic coins were invented, and it may be said that this is the type of money in which the medium itself was inherently valuable. This type of coinage worked because those materials were recognized as being of value in their own right. Metallic coins can be counterfeited by altering the weights, but only if a series of clever ruses are employed [3.1-1]. The first of these tricks is that a government assumes a monopoly power of coinage, or appoints certain organizations to have that monopoly power. That way, only the authorized mint can decide what units of coinage will be created. The second trick is to define a unit of measure by a name unrelated to the weight of the metal, such as a *denier* or a *shilling*. The names and weights are dissociated and the name dominates in transactions. The third trick is to reduce the weight of metal in the coins while calling it the same name. Thus the person with the monopoly over the minting of the coins keeps the difference between the defined weight and the weight actually put into the coins. The fourth trick is to issue an edict that all the coins bearing the name of the unit are to be regarded as equal in value; the full-weight ones and the light-weight ones alike. Edicts and laws of this type are known as legal tender laws. It requires the people to pretend that the amount of metal in every coin is the same, since each coin is called by the same name. Ultimately the smart people (like the governments and their monopoly minters) keep part of the actual money for themselves, while the dumb people (like you and me) must accept the debased coin as if it possessed the full weight as originally defined. Over time, it took more of the light weight coins to buy the same tangible object, and we say that the light weight coins were "inflated" through debasement compared to their original definition. A few historical examples of debasement of metallic coinage will serve to illustrate the concept.

England to 1816

The most recognizable silver unit was the English pound sterling. The pound sterling (£) was defined by King Offa of Mercia in 757 AD as a physical Mercian pound of pure silver that came to be known as the "tower pound". It weighed 349.9144 grams, which is equivalent to 5400 grains. There were 20 shillings (s.) to a pound, 12 pennies (d.) to a shilling, and 4 farthings (d. 1/4) to a penny. Thus a penny was defined as 1/240th of a "tower pound" and was equivalent to 22.5 grains of pure silver. The pound and shilling were accounting units used to keep track of large amounts of pennies. Since coins were only needed for small local transactions at that period in history, only pennies were actually minted. Here is the history of the debasement of the English silver coinage [3.1-2, 3.1-3, 3.1-4] from 757 to 1816:

757: The penny was defined as 22.5 grains pure silver

1158: Henry II introduced "sterling" silver at 0.925 pure, which improved the durability of the coin. There were still 240 pennies to the tower pound (5400 grains); at 0.925 pure, thus the penny contained 20.812 grains pure silver.

1257: The penny was redefined as 242 pennies per tower pound at 0.925 pure; penny = 20.640 grains pure silver.

1300: The penny was redefined as 243 pennies per tower pound at 0.925 pure; penny = 20.555 grains pure silver.

1411: The penny was redefined as 360 pennies per tower pound at 0.925 pure; penny = 13.875 grains pure silver.

1464: The penny was redefined as 450 pennies per tower pound at 0.925 pure; penny = 11.100 grains pure silver.

1526: The tower pound at 349.9144 grams (equal to 5400 grains) was replaced by the troy pound at 373.2431 grams, consisting of 5760 grains. The penny was redefined as 540 pennies per troy pound at 0.925 pure (i.e., 540 pennies from 5328 grains pure silver); the penny was then 9.866 grains pure silver.

1543: The standard metal was redefined as 0.833 pure; and the penny redefined as 540 pennies per troy pound at 0.833 pure; penny = 8.885 grains pure silver.

1544: The penny was redefined as 540 pennies per tower pound at 0.500 pure; penny = 5.333 grains pure silver.

1551: The penny was redefined as 540 pennies per tower pound at 0.250 pure; penny = 2.666 grains pure silver.

1552: The coinage was reformed in response to the debasement of the past decade. The shilling became the normal coinage since the penny was now a small unit. The shilling was redefined as 1/60th of a physical troy pound of pure silver. The shilling thus consisted of 96 grains of pure silver and a penny was therefore 8 grains of pure silver. The physical coin was heavier, since copper and other metals were added for durability. But notice what happened here. The shilling was defined as 96 grains of silver, but the pound (as an accounting unit) was still tabulated as 20 shillings; hence the pound was implicitly debased, now having only 1920 grains of pure silver.

1601: The penny was defined as 7 and 23/31 (7.7419) grains of sterling silver (0.925 pure); thus the shilling became 92.9028 grains of 0.925 silver, and the pound sterling was 1858.056 grains at 0.925. The weights in pure silver are: penny at 7.1612 grains; shilling at 85.9350 grains; and pound at 1718.7018 grains. This is the pound sterling that was in use during the American War for Independence. The coins in circulation in America mostly consisted of the Spanish milled dollar ($SM); it was defined as 394.46 grains of pure silver, but in practice was commonly reckoned as 386.7 grains. Thus the official exchange rate between the English pound and the Spanish Milled Dollar was 1718.7018/386.7 = 4.44; thus 1 £ = SM $4.44.

1816: The penny was reduced to 7 and 3/11 (7.2727) grains of 0.925 silver; thus the shilling was 87.2724 grains at 0.925 and the pound sterling was 1745.488 grains at 0.925. The weights in pure silver are: penny at 6.7272 grains; shilling at 80.7272 grains; and pound at 1614.5454. A troy pound of sterling silver at 0.925 pure (5328 grains pure) was struck into 66 shillings; hence the physical shilling weighed 87.2727 grains and contained 80.7272 grains of pure silver.

There were three periods of debasement and one period of appreciation of the English penny:

a) From 757 to 1526 (769 years), the penny was debased by a factor of 22.5/9.866 = 2.28;

b) From 1526 to 1551 (25 years), the penny debased further by a factor of 9.866/2.666 = 3.700; and the total debasement since 757 was 8.439.

c) 1552: A reform upward to a penny = 8 grains of pure silver (and thus a shilling was 96 grains) constituted an improvement by a factor of 3; and then:

d) From 1552 to 1816 (264 years), the penny was debased further by a factor of 8/6.7272 = 1.189.

Up until 1552 the pound was merely an accounting unit, starting off at the 5400 grain tower pound and then revised to the troy pound at 5760 grains. The shilling replaced the penny as the common unit of exchange at 96 grains pure silver in 1552. But the pound was still defined in trade as 20 shillings, so the pound as an accounting unit was de facto debased from 5760 to 1920 grains pure silver by an accounting trick in 1552. All total, the English penny was debased a factor of 3.3446 from its original definition in 757 to 1816.

France to 1789

The coinage of France has some parallel to that of England, but the debasement thereof was much more rapid [3.1-2, 3.1-3, 3.1-4, 3.1-6]. King Charles I (Charlemagne) (about 800 AD) defined a Carolingian pound (*livre tournois*) to be 489.506 grams, which is equal to 7554.2 grains. The *livre* was divided into 20 *sou* or *solidi*, and each *sou* was divided into 12 *denier*. Thus a *denier* is the analog of an English *penny* in the sense that it is 1/240th of a pound, although it has a different weight (being 31.476 grains of pure silver). Similar to the case in England, and for the same reason, the French only coined *deniers*, and relegated *sou* and *livre tournois* to mere accounting units until the late medieval era. It is believed that the French coinage was reasonably stable until the reign of Philip I (1060 - 1108). The record of the debasement of the French *denier* from the reign of Philip II Augustus (1180 - 1223) is shown on Figure 3.1-1, given by year, grains of pure silver, and accumulated depreciation since the year 800.

Year	Grains pure silver in French denier	Accumulated Depreciation	Year	Grains pure silver in French denier	Accumulated Depreciation
800	31.476	0.000	1541	0.964	32.651
1200	6.301	4.995	1561	0.900	34.973
1226	5.787	5.439	1573	0.835	37.696
1291	4.629	6.800	1580	0.739	42.593
1301	3.858	8.159	1602	0.681	46.220
1321	3.536	8.902	1615	0.601	52.373
1351	2.121	14.840	1636	0.532	59.165
1361	2.572	12.238	1643	0.526	59.840
1390	2.186	14.399	1651	0.484	65.033
1411	1.993	15.793	1676	0.429	73.371
1426	1.864	16.886	1701	0.353	89.167
1446	1.671	18.837	1726	0.313	100.562
1456	1.543	20.399	1759	0.260	121.062
1488	1.350	23.316	1795	0.285	110.442
1512	1.157	27.205			

Figure 3.1-1: Depreciation of the French Silver Denier, 800 to 1795

The coinage was revamped in 1726, in which 8 troy ounces of silver (3840 grains) was worth 51 livres, 2 sou, and 3 deniers, or 51.1125 livres; thus a livre was 75.128 grains of silver, and a denier (1/240th of a livre), was 0.313 grains pure silver. This was the ratio that prevailed during the American War for Independence. The Spanish Milled Dollar was reckoned at 386.7 grains pure silver, so 1 livre = SM $0.194.

After the French Revolution (1795), the *livre* (i.e., 240 *denier*) was converted to *francs*; 80 *francs* to 81 *livre*. The franc was defined as 5 grams of silver at 0.9 pure, which is 4.5 grams pure = 69.445 grains pure. Since the franc was 81 livre, it contained 243 deniers; thus the denier was 0.2857 grains of pure silver.

In the first 400 years of its existence (800 to 1200), the French *denier* was debased a factor of 4.995; for the next 559 years to 1759, was further debased by a factor of 24.23; all total, debased by a factor of 121.051 from its original definition. The weight of the denier was indirectly increased slightly to 0.285 grains in 1795, making the total depreciation a factor of about 110.44 in the 995 years between 800 and 1795.

Scotland and the Arab Nations

The Scottish penny started off about the same as the French *denier*, but it was debased at a very rapid rate. By 1600, the Scottish penny was about 0.645 grains, that is, about 1/12th the weight of the English penny (in 1601, was 7.7419 grains pure silver).

The silver coinage was debased by nearly every nation in Europe, except for the Arabs in Spain, who were very careful to maintain the value of their coins. Also, the gold coins minted throughout the medieval era generally retained their full weight. The reason is simple: the gold coins, being of much greater value than silver, were used generally in transactions between great lords or important merchants in international dealings. Meanwhile, the silver coins were used for local trade. It was easy for the minters to debase the local coinage used by the dumb local people, since it did not have to be readily converted to any other standard, and the king could simply issue an edict requiring that it be accepted at full face value. But the gold coin had to maintain its value because the issuing king could not force another nation's merchants to accept it; it would be accepted only at full weight. Thus the large traders and their associates avoided any losses that would have occurred due to a reduction in the value of the coin.

3.2   Depreciation of the Assignats of the French Revolution

The history of the assignats, issued during the French Revolution, was documented by White [3.2-1], Dillaye [3.2-2], and von Sybel [3.2-3]. Before describing the details of the monetary fiasco of the French Revolution, it is important to have a cast of characters. They are:

Bergasse: Nicholas Bergasse, a member of the Estates-General as representing the nobility; member of the National Assembly.

Bonaparte: Napoleon Bonaparte, an army officer who became dictator of France after he seized power at the end of the Revolution. His reign consisted of twenty years of war and starvation for the French people.

Brillat-Savarin: Jean Anthelme Brillat-Savarin, a member of the Estates-General and member of the National Assembly.

de Cazales: Jacques Antoine Marie de Cazales, a member of the Constituent Assembly.

Du Pont: Pierre Samuel du Pont de Nemours, initially supported the French Revolution, President of the National Assembly; personally defended Louis XVI and was scheduled for execution but was spared by the death of Robespierre; his son founded the E. I. du Pont de Nemours Company in the U. S.

Jacobins: a political club founded by Robespierre (Society of the Jacobins, Friends of Freedom and equality), the group that instigated the Revolution and presided over the Reign of Terror.

Louis XVI: King of France (Bourbon dynasty).

Marie Antoinette: Wife of King Louis XVI, sister of Austrian Emperor Joseph II.

Marat: Jean-Paul Marat, journalist and primary propagandist for the Jacobins.

Maury: Jean-Sifrein Maury, a member of the Estates-General 1789 representing the clergy; member of the National Assembly until he fled France in Oct 1791, appointed cardinal in 1794.

Mirabeau: Honore Gabriel Riqueti, Count of Mirabeau: a member of the French aristocracy who was a leader of the Revolution in its early stages; member of the Estates-General (representing the nobility) from 5 May 1789 to 9 Jul 1789; member of the Constituent Assembly from 9 Jul 1789 to 2 Apr 1791.

Montesquieu: Charles-Louis de Secondat, Baron de la Brede et de Montesquieu, historian and political philosopher; author of *The Spirit of the Laws*.

Necker: Jacques Necker, a Swiss banker, served as Director-General of the Treasury from 29 Jun 1777 to 19 May 1781, Controller-General of the Finances from 25 Aug 1788 to 11 Jul 1789, and Chief Minister to the king from 29 Jul 1789 to 3 Sep 1790.

Robespierre: Maximilien Francois Marie Isidore de Robespierre, a leader of the Jacobin conspiracy to overthrow the French monarchy; member of the Estates-General from 6 May 1789 to 16 Jun 1789; member of the National Assembly from 17 Jun 1789 to 9 Jul 1789; member of the National Constituent Assembly from 9 Jul 1789 to 30 Sep 1791; President of the National Constituent Assembly from 22 Aug 1793 to 7 Sep 1793 and 4 Jun 1794 to 19 Jun 1794; President of the Jacobin Club from 31 Mar 1790 to 3 Jun 1790 and 7 Aug 1793 to 28 Aug 1793; member of the Committee of Public Safety from 25 Mar 1793 to 27 Jul 1794; led the Reign of Terror; guillotined 28 Jul 1794.

Talleyrand: Charles-Maurice de Talleyrand-Perigord, a member of the Estates-General (representing the clergy) from 12 Apr 1789 to 9 Jul 1789; member of the Constituent Assembly from 9 Jul 1789 to 30 Sep 1791; fled France in Sep 1792, was later Foreign Minister under Napoleon.

France had been both poor and bankrupt for some years by the late 1780's due to the irresponsibility of the government. For example, in 1787, the revenues were 351 M livres, but the expenses were 555 M; leaving a one-year deficit of 198 M livres [3.2-4]. The immediate problem was that France was in desperate financial condition early in 1789; it had a large national debt and little ability to raise taxes to cover the current budget deficit. The Catholic Church at this time was held in low regard by the leaders of the government. It owned between 25% and 35% of the land in France; the value of the lands was estimated at 2,000,000,000 livres. The Church's annual income was about 160,000,000 livres (100,000,000 in tithes, and 60,000,000 from income on the land); and paid a tax of 3,000,000 or 4,000,000 livres [3.2-5]. They were also derelict in providing for the poor, as was their alleged purpose. Necker had proposed an income tax at a 25% rate, but the measure failed.

Another cause of the Revolution was the inherent unfairness of the tax system [3.2-6]. The poor paid a large fraction of the taxes in the form of a poll tax and excise taxes on necessities. Worse than that, tyrannical means were used by the government to collect the taxes, and it was well known among the people that much of the money went to pay for frivolous expenses at the King's court.

King Louis XVI called a special session of the Estates-General (later called the National Assembly) on 5 May 1789 to discuss the nation's finances. The idea came to some of the members of the National Assembly that they could create prosperity by creating money. Since the nation was so deep in debt that it had no credit, borrowing or stealing from the Church seemed to be the only way to keep the government in operation. Talleyrand was the first to propose confiscation of the property of the Church (cf. 10 Oct 1789) and issue paper money against it in order to pay off the enormous debts that had been run up by the government [3.2-7]. Necker, the Minister of Finance, and others (such as Bergasse) who understood money opposed it. But the notion of prosperity through paper money became popular, aided by the propaganda of Marat. The National Assembly then entered into debate on how to issue paper money, to be secured by confiscating the property of the Catholic Church.

French money was denominated in *livre tournois*, commonly called a *livre*, which was defined as 75.1283 grains of silver, and thus were reckoned to be 0.194 Spanish milled dollars (using the actual amount of silver in the typical Spanish coin). No 1-livre coins were in use at this time; the actual coins were a gold coin called a *Louis d'or*, equal to 24 livres, a gold coin of 48 livres called a double Louis d'or, and a half Louis d'or worth 12 livres, and a silver coin called an *ecu*, worth 6 livres. There were also fractional ecu's at valued at 3.0, 1.5, and 0.75 livres. In the following "1.0 livre = A xxx" is used to denote the number of assignats equaling the value of a livre. At this time, the livre was also called a franc, although technically the franc had not been used since 1641. I have retained the units in the references, even when francs are called out prior to 1795. The franc was formally redefined in 1795; 1 franc = 1.0125 livre.

Herewith is the sad story of the depreciation of money during the French Revolution. Keep in mind as you read this, those who led the Revolution were the "enlightened" people, the ones who had read Voltaire (Francois-Marie Arouet) and Rousseau, who knew everything there was to know about how to create a "just" society. These were the "progressives" of their era. I would encourage you to pay close attention to what they did once they gained power.

5 May 1789: Louis XVI called the Estates-General into session to discuss the terrible financial condition of France. It consisted of 1145 members: 270 of the nobility, 291 representing the clergy, and 584 representing the people (also called the Third Estate) [3.2-8]. In the months that followed, the Third Estate argued against the privileges of the nobility, that the remainder of the feudal system in France should be abolished, and established a National Constituent Assembly. Eventually the nobility and clergy joined with them.

9 Jul 1789: The National Constituent Assembly convened.

14 Jul 1789: Riots in Paris and storming of the Bastille that began the French Revolution. It was a civil war begun by socialist revolutionaries who sought to destroy the old order and bring "justice and equality" to France. This was the beginning of the immigration of the nobility and wealthy people out of France [3.2-9].

27 Aug 1789: The National Assembly adopted The Declaration of the Rights of Man [3.2-10], having been debated since 4 Aug 1790.

12 Oct 1789: Talleyrand proposed issuing a new paper currency to be secured by a mortgage on lands owned by the Catholic Church [3.2-11]. Issuing a new paper currency was the only means available for the National Assembly to fund the Revolution. The idea was that they would be issued to those who had loaned the government money, and they would use them to buy the Church land if they desired and if not, to use them as bonds, to pay taxes, and to use as circulating money [3.2-12, 3.2-13].

2 Nov 1789: The lands of the Catholic Church were confiscated [3.2-14]. The Church had accumulated the land over the previous 1500 years; it consisted of between 25 and 33% of all the land in France, and was valued at about 2,000,000,000 livres. The goal was to issue paper money (assignats) so that middle-class people could buy the land; thus gaining their support for the Revolution. White [3.2-15] described the objectives:

> "It was urged, then, that the issue of four hundred millions of paper, (not in the shape of interest-bearing bonds, as had at first been proposed, but in notes small as well as large), would give the treasury something to pay out immediately, and relieve the national necessity; that, having been put into circulation, this paper money would stimulate business; that it would give to all capitalists, large or small, the means for buying from the nation the ecclesiastical real estate; and that from the proceeds of this real estate the nation would pay its debts and also obtain new funds for new necessities. Never was theory more seductive both to financiers and statesmen."

19 Dec 1789: The National Assembly finalized the plan for issuing the paper money, called assignats, and authorized 400,000,000 to be issued [3.2-16].

17 Apr 1790: The National Assembly issued 400,000,000 livres in assignats. They were to be used to purchase the church lands, but also to be used as circulating currency [3.2-17, 3.2-18], and the portion received for the land was to pay the current expenses of the government. The circulating portion was secured by the confiscated land formerly owned by the Catholic Church, and bore interest at 3%. The basic claim was that the assignats had the same virtue as metal money, in that it represented something tangible, namely the land, and therefore, the paper assignats would not suffer the same fate as the paper issues of John Law in the 1720's. The assignats thus were proclaimed to have true value, competitive with gold and silver. Louis XVI encouraged the public to begin using it. A few of the clergy opposed it, mostly on the basis of the theft of the Church lands, and some in the National Assembly opposed it, especially Necker, Maury, Cazales, and Bergasse.

27 Aug 1790: By this time, the assignats received by the government had already been spent, and the national finances were as bad as ever [3.2-19]. A report by Montesquieu recommended an additional issue of assignats. He recognized the risks, but thought it was necessary to save France.

Early Sep 1790: The government now needed money again. Mirabeau knew the dangers of paper money, but went along with it, believing it was the best way to get the people to buy the Church lands, and noting that the first issue had served to improve credit [3.2-20]. He advocated in the National Assembly for one additional issue of assignats, enough to cover the entire national debt (at that time was 2,400,000,000 livres). Brillat-Savarin and du Pont de Nemours correctly noted the inconsistencies in Mirabeau's argument, but they were disregarded. Necker opposed it, but was unsuccessful; he resigned and left France. Talleyrand gave a speech opposing the new issue; it ended with [3.2-21]:

> "You can, indeed, arrange it so that the people shall be forced to take a thousand livres in paper for a thousand livres in specie [i.e., specie he had lent to the government]; but you can never arrange it so that a man shall be obliged to give a thousand livres in specie [i.e., in his possession] for a thousand livres in paper -- in that fact is embedded the entire question; and on account of that fact the whole system fails."

29 Sep 1790: The National Assembly issued 800,000,000 livres in assignats; total = 1,200,000,000 livres. The law also specified that no more than 1,200,000,000 should ever be issued, and when assignats were paid into the treasury for purchase of land, they were to be burned [3.2-22]. But when 160,000,000 livres were received in payment for the former Church lands, they were not burned; they were re-issued. Also, this limitation was ignored when the government found it convenient (cf. 19 Jun 1791). At the same time the National Assembly started funding various "public works projects" that increased the national debt.

~15 Nov 1790: The National Assembly passed a law specifying a coinage standard; the standard money was silver, and the ratio of silver to gold was changed from 15.5:1 to 14.5:1 [3.2-23]. But the public decided to keep the silver coins, and it became necessary to issue another 100,000,000 assignats in small denominations that could be used for small transactions or change.

27 Nov 1790: The National Assembly passed a law requiring every member of the clergy to swear an oath to the Revolution; failure to do so would result in a loss of their position and their income. Most of them refused on the date called for, 4 Jan 1791 [3.2-24].

Jan 1791: Coin became very scarce, as people begin to recognize the depreciation of the assignats [3.2-25]. The propaganda of the day was to claim that the value of metal coins was rising, instead of the true cause, which was that the assignats were declining in value. This was nothing more than Gresham's Law in action: an inferior currency, when accepted, drives the superior one out of circulation.

~Feb 1791: The beginning of the decline in industry and manufacturing, since the businessmen could not calculate accurately with the depreciating assignats; this led to a general decline in the prospects for labor, and businessmen added to their prices to compensate for ambiguity about the value of the assignat. Also the markets were now saturated because the initial issue had over-stimulated business.

Meanwhile, many wealthy and powerful people were making large profits from speculation, betting on the value of assignats, instead of investing. At this point 1.0 livre was between A 1.06 and A 1.11 [3.2-26, 3.2-27], but the discount on foreign exchange was closer to 1.0 livre = A 1.30. High tariffs on imports did not affect the state of industry in France; it continued to decline. White explains [3.2-28]:

> "But what the bigotry of Louis XIV [in revoking the Edict of Nantes] and the shiftlessness of Louis XV could not do in nearly a century, was accomplished by this tampering with the currency in a few months."

Early Jun 1791: The 1,200,000,000 of assignats had been spent by the government: 108,000,000 to pay down the debt, 416,000,000 to pay overdue interest, and 476,000,000 to pay the current expenses [3.2-29].

19 Jun 1791: The National Assembly issued 600,000,000 livres in assignats, total = 1,800,000,000 livres [3.2-30, 3.2-31]. There was virtually no opposition to it in the National Assembly, as France had now adopted a scheme of permanent inflation by paper money; it was widely believed among the government leadership that officially-issued fiat money led automatically to prosperity.

~ Aug 1791: Growth of corruption among the legislators, being influenced and bribed by speculators in the national debt instruments [3.2-32] and debtors who had a vested interest in seeing the assignats depreciate. The speculators could sell at a profit in nominal terms, and the debtors could repay in amounts far less than they had borrowed.

3 Sep 1791: The New Constitution was adopted.

30 Sep 1791: The Constituent Assembly was abolished and replaced by the National Legislative Assembly.

~ Oct 1791: The assignat had depreciated about 20%: 1.0 livre ~ A 1.2 [3.2-33].

17 Dec 1791: The 800,000,000 assignats issued in Jun 1791 were all spent: 472,000,000 toward the pre-existing debt, and 128,000,000 for administration, but the Constituent Assembly had also run up another 800,000,000 in new debt [3.2-34]. The Legislative Assembly issued 300,000,000 in assignats, total = 2,100,000,000 livres.

1 Jan 1792: The assignat had depreciated about 32%: 1.0 livre ~ A 1.32 [3.2-35, 3.2-36].

1 Feb 1792: 1.0 livre ~ A 1.66 [3.2-37].

1 Mar 1792: 1.0 livre ~ A 1.88 [3.2-38].

~1 Apr - 1 Sep 1792: The other nations of Europe begin preparations to invade France, to prevent the spread of the Revolution.

20 Apr 1792: France declared war on Prussia and Austria.

30 Apr 1792: The Legislative Assembly issued 300,000,000 in assignats, total = 2,400,000,000 livres [3.2-39]. White explains the economic condition of the working people at this point [3.2-40]:

> "This [the new issue of assignats] was hailed by many as a measure in the interests of the poorer classes of people, but the result was that it injured them most of all. Henceforward, until the end of this history, capital was quietly taken from labor and locked up in all the ways that financial ingenuity could devise. All that saved thousands of laborers in France from starvation was that they were drafted off into the army and sent to be killed on foreign battlefields."

Jun-Aug 1792: There were food riots in Paris; the king and royal family were imprisoned; and the Revolutionary Commune took power.

31 Jul 1792: A finance report from the Assembly stated that 2,400,000,000 assignats had been issued, and that the worth of the national lands exceeded that value. The government then decided to issue another 300,000,000; total = 2,700,000,000 livres [3.2-41].

20 Sep 1792: The French were defeated at Valmy.

21 Sep 1792: The National Convention replaced the Legislative Assembly; the monarchy is abolished.

Oct 1792: Beginning of forgeries of the assignats by other nations in Europe, especially, Belgium, Switzerland, and England [3.2-42], then exported to France. Some of them were so good that only an expert could tell the real ones from the fake ones.

~ 1 Nov 1792: 1.0 livre ~ A 1.75 [3.2-43].

7 Nov 1792: The National Convention recommended that Louis XVI be tried before the Convention for treason.

14 Dec 1792: By this time, 600,000,000 assignats had been destroyed, but 700,000,000 replaced them; total = 2,800,000,000 livres [3.2-44].

21 Jan 1793: Louis XVI was executed.

31 Jan 1793: The National Convention issued 200,000,000 assignats; total = 3,000,000,000 livres [3.2-47].

9 Feb 1793: The National Assembly issued a decree that the estates of those who had fled France were to be confiscated [3.2-45, 3.2-46]. This was used, in the same way as the Church lands, to justify further issues of assignats. New issues of assignats were subsequently made in most months of 1792.

28 Feb 1793: Prices had become so high that even people who could find employment could not afford to live. Marat suggested that the problem could be solved by robbing the stores [3.2-48, 3.2-49]. So, a large number of people in Paris began rioting and looting about 200 shops on 28 Feb 1793. The mob was paid off with a bribe of 7,000,000 francs.

Feb 1793: The Reign of Terror began, led by the Committee on Public Safety. There were riots in Paris over high prices, and many executions, including those who refused to accept the assignats.

11 Apr 1793: The National Convention passed a law prohibiting the purchase of silver or gold under penalty of six years imprisonment [3.2-50].

3 May 1793: The Assembly enacted price controls on grains; but the prices set were too low, and the farmers could not afford to sell. So they held back their crops, producing a food shortage [3.2-51].

22 Jun 1793: The National Convention passed the Forced Loan decree [3.2-52], which amounted to a progressive income tax. It was levied on all married men with incomes above 10,000 francs, and all unmarried men with incomes above 6,000 francs. It was estimated to bring in 1,000,000,000 francs, but only brought in 200,000,000 francs; so later the National Convention extended it down to people with incomes of 1,000 francs. It was fixed at 10% for incomes of 1,000 francs, and at 50% for those with incomes above 9,000 francs.

31 Jul 1793: The National Convention authorized another issue of 2,000,000,000 assignats [3.2-53].

1 Aug 1793: Legislation was passed prohibiting trading in coin. Those caught selling silver or gold, or pricing in assignats and specie differently, received six years in prison; for refusing to accept assignats as legal tender, was fined 3,000 francs for a first offense and for a second offense to pay 6,000 francs and be imprisoned for 20 years [3.2-54].

10 Aug - 7 Sep 1793: General robbery of the people by the government [3.2-55]. On 29 Aug alone, about 3,000 wealthy people's homes were searched and robbed by the Committee of Surveillance (the Revolutionary secret police), and about 2,000 of these were subsequently arrested and executed. The government, led by Robespierre, organized a conspiracy to murder a large number of people who were in prison on political charges; about 15,000 were murdered. 1 livre = A 1.66 [3.2-56].

8 Sep 1793: The penalties for violating the 1 Aug 1793 currency law were increased to death and confiscation of property. Also, informers were given rewards for turning in violators, thus France became a nation of spies and informers [3.2-57].

~15 Sep 1793: 1.0 livre ~ A 3.35 [3.2-58].

29 Sep 1793: The National Convention passed the Law of the Maximum, which imposed price controls on all food. The price was calculated as the sum of four components [3.2-59]: a) the basic price to

be set at 1.33 of its price in 1790; b) an allowance for transportation; c) wholesale profit fixed at 5%; and d) retail profit fixed at 10%. This amounted to less than the cost of production, so naturally they were either evaded, or farmers didn't bother to bring items to markets, which led to severe shortages. The government found it necessary to issue ration papers that would allow people to buy at the official price, if there was any to be had. Farmers could not afford to sell at the official prices, and to relieve the food shortages, the government sent out the military to confiscate entire crops. The law proved to be difficult to enforce. Nonetheless, many businesses were ruined by losses, and the ones that stayed in business charged high prices for risking their lives: the penalty for violating the Law of the Maximum was death. The enforcement mechanism depended on a network of spies. Sometimes violators were let off with the destruction of their homes.

16 Oct 1793: Marie Antoinette was executed; by this time, another 3,000,000,000 assignats had been issued, although only 1,200,000,000 entered into circulation; total = 4,200,000,000 livres [3.2-60].

13 Nov 1793: All transactions in silver and gold were prohibited under penalty of death [3.2-61].

~15 Dec 1793: 1.0 livre ~ A 2.0 [3.2-62]. This temporary increase in value was promoted by optimism due to French victories.

1 Jan 1794: The number of assignats in circulation was 5,536,000,000 livres; the value of lands confiscated from the nobility and the church, held as security for them, was estimated at 15,000,000,000 livres [3.2-63].

15 May 1794: The National Convention passed a law specifying the death penalty upon anyone who inquired before a transaction was to be made as to what form of money was to be used [3.2-64].

4 Jun 1794: Robespierre was elected a President of the National Convention, and afterwards thousands were executed by the decree of the Revolutionary Tribunal.

28 Jul 1794: Robespierre was executed, which ended the Reign of Terror

8 Dec 1794: The law that had expelled the nobility and clergy was repealed, and their lands were to be restored [3.2-65]. They returned to France in the early part of 1795, hoping to restore a limited monarchy.

23 Dec 1794: The Law of the Maximum was repealed [3.2-66].

31 Dec 1794: The total number of assignats in circulation = 7,000,000,000 livres [3.2-67].

1 Apr 1795: 1.0 livre = A 9.9 [3.2-68].

1 May 1795: Approximately 12,000,000,000 counterfeit assignats were in circulation [3.2-69]; 1.0 livre = A 12.4 [3.2-70].

31 May 1795: An additional 3,000,000,000 assignats were issued, total = 10,000,000,000 livres [3.2-71]; 1.0 livre ~ A 14.2 [3.2-72]; see 1 May 1795 for amount of counterfeits.

~ 1 Jun 1795: 1.0 livre ~ A 18.29 to A 20.85 [3.2-73, 3.2-74].

1 Jul 1795: 1.0 livre = A 33.66 [3.2-75].

31 Jul 1795: An additional 4,000,000,000 assignats were issued, total = 14,000,000,000 [3.2-76]. Throughout the next 18 months, prices went up at the same rate as the depreciation, but wages remained stagnant. Wages actually had fallen since so many businesses had closed up due to the difficulty of dealing in paper money, and the laws necessary to enforce them. There was now a large labor surplus available to be drafted into the army [3.2-77].

1 Aug 1795: 1.0 livre ~ A 33.33 to A 36.8 [3.2-78, 3.2-79, 3.2-80].

15 Aug 1795: The franc was defined as a coin of 5 grams of silver at 90% pure, which is 4.5 grams = 69.44 grains pure silver.

22 Aug 1795: A Constitutional Convention adopted a constitution for a new government, to be run by a body called The Directory. By this time another 21,000,000,000 assignats had been issued; the total is now 35,000,000,000 in circulation [3.2-81].

1 Sep 1795: 1.0 livre ~ A 40.0 to A 48.0 [3.2-82, 3.2-83].

13 Sep 1795: Napoleon massacred the royalists in a street battle in Paris, and took power as dictator [3.2-84].

1 Oct 1795: 1.0 livre = A 50.2 [3.2-85].

1 Nov 1795: 1.0 livre = A 104.0 to A 107.8 [3.2-86, 3.2-87].

2 Nov 1795: Beginning of the Directory. The first item of business was to print more assignats. The problem was that the printers could only make 60 to 70 million per day, while the government was spending 80 to 90 million per day [3.2-88]. The second item of business was to exact a forced loan from the remaining wealthy citizens; it didn't work, since the assignat was now valued at less than 1/100th of a livre [3.2-89].

1 Dec 1795: 1.0 livre = A 122.0 to A 149.0 [3.2-90, 3.2-91].

1 Feb 1796: 1.0 livre = A 222.4 to A 288.0 [3.2-92, 3.2-93]. At this point, the assignat was virtually worthless, but most of it was in the hands of the working people. Those who could afford to had previously invested their money in real estate and other objects of tangible lasting value. Von Sybel [3.2-94] tells us:

> "Commerce had sunk to mere usurious gambling, since everyone had before his eyes the daily fall in the value of the assignats, and thus the consequent rise in the price of wares; even those, therefore, who had no thought of gain, but only wished to avoid loss, bought up as large stores of every kind of goods as they could in any way obtain. As ready money had been rendered very rare by the Emigration, the requisitions, and the unfavorable balance of trade ever since 1789; and as the rate of interest had risen in the wealthiest Departments to 12 per cent and in Paris to 30 percent -- there was virtually no banking business at all. The dealers in old stores had taken the place of money dealers, and advanced, not ready money, as formerly, upon pledges, but vice versa, exchanged the falling assignats for furniture, clothes, watches, rings, books, and provisions, at, of course, their own usurious prices. It is easy to understand the difficulty under such circumstances of providing for the people, in the midst of scarcity, when every possessor of property was endeavoring to invest his capital in stores of goods, and thereby withdrawing the latter for a long time from circulation. Before the end of the year [1796] the paper money was in the hands of the proletaries [workers], the officials, and the small rentiers [small farmers], whose property was not large enough to invest in stores of goods or national lands."

18 Feb 1796: The assignats were now valued at 1.0 livre = A 600 [3.2-95]. They were exchanged for a new paper currency called the mandat, claimed to be "as good as gold", at 30 assignats for one mandat. The plates and paper for printing the assignats were destroyed. White [3.2-96] cites 40,000,000,000 in assignats had been in circulation; now exchanged for 1,333,000,000 mandats.

~ Mar 1796: 1 livre = M 2.85 = A 85.5 [3.2-97].

~ May 1796: 1 livre ~ M 6.66 = A 199.8 [3.2-98].

16 Jul 1796: The Directory issued a decree stating that all the paper money, assignats and mandats, should be accepted at their real value compared to silver or gold, and that trade could commence in whatever currency the parties agreed to [3.2-99]. This was the practical end of the legal tender status of both paper issues; the mandats depreciated further to 1 livre = M 50.0 = A 1500.0

~ Aug 1796: 1 livre ~ M 50.0 = A 1500.0; about 2,500,000,000 mandats were in circulation [3.2-100].

14 Feb 1797: The Directory formally decreed that assignats and mandats were no longer legal tender, the plates and paper for printing mandats were to be destroyed as were the assignat machines previously, and that taxes could be temporarily paid to the government in both paper currencies at 100:1 [3.2-101].

May 1797: The assignats and mandats still in circulation are both are worthless; the Directory formally proclaimed that the 21,000,000,000 of assignats are of no value and should be discarded [3.2-102].

30 Sep 1797: The Directory ordered that two-thirds of the national debt was to be paid in bonds that could be used to buy the confiscated Church lands, and the remaining third was to remain on the books to

be paid in some future unknown way. These bonds soon depreciated to 3% of their face value, same as the assignats and mandats had [3.2-103]. This was the end of the paper money experiment, and it took forty years to recover from it. Metal money came out of the hoards, and came in from foreign nations in the course of trade as it was required.

1798: Arbitrary government by the Directory, etc.

10 Nov 1799: Napoleon assumed power "to save the Republic". Of course, that is patently false. There was no working "republic" to save; all Napoleon did impose a personal dictatorship to replace the dictatorship run by socialist crusaders that had replaced an irresponsible aristocratic oligarchy. Whereupon France pursued the same moronic policies as Louis XIV had done: useless wars, poverty, and the ruin of France.

So ends the story of the assignats and mandats, paper money supposedly "secured" by the real estate confiscated from the Church. The 'assignats' were doomed at the start. Such a system of "backing" by land, or redemption, was a pure fantasy: if one was in possession of a certain amount of assignats, how exactly would he cash them in for land? The paper notes did not each describe a section of land, nor was any of the land marked out as being assigned to a particular note. There was no practical way for a person to actually obtain the land that supposedly backed the paper, and the entire system was sold to the public with propaganda. It turned out to be a particularly vicious fiction; the assignats depreciated greatly, and the promises of rainbows and unicorns soon turned into the reality of prisons and the guillotine as the government attempted to maintain the value of the assignats by force.

We should not relegate this episode to obscurity as the work of fanatics. It is instructive to us because it indicates what happens when governments get desperate. It is easy to see the tyrannical acts perpetuated under the guise of "liberty, equality, and fraternity" (the slogan of the French Revolution). First was the outright confiscation of the property of the Church that had been accumulated over the previous 1500 years. It is true that the Church had become corrupt and had deviated from its true mission, but if the Church lands were to be secularized, surely a more equitable method could have been used. Second was the persecution of the old aristocracy and the Church officials simply because they did not agree with the Revolution. But the persecutions did not stop with the nobility; how can it, if the goal is power? The paper assignats were issued as a means to gain public support for the Revolution; the claim that they were issued against and secured by the confiscated Church lands was some combination of fantasy, ignorance, or knowing and deliberate lying. There was no way to redeem them; they were no better than the paper issued by John Law only 70 years earlier. Once the assignats began to fail, the lies and persecutions began: a) wage and price controls that led to shortages; b) false claim that gold and silver were becoming more valuable, when in fact it was the paper that was depreciating; c) collapse of business since the depreciation had destroyed the principle of accurate accounting; d) prohibitions on trading in gold and silver, or even asking what form of money was to be used in a transactions; e) riots out of desperation due to shortages, high prices, and stagnant wages; f) open robbery of the people by the government; g) capital punishment for minor (but necessary) offenses; h) confiscation of property owned even by the poor and middle class; and finally, i) collapse of the system followed by 20 years of starvation and warfare under a new dictator. France has still not fully recovered from this fiasco.

It is worse than that. This entire episode was led by the foremost modern thinkers of their time. Our modern "progressives" have adapted the Jacobin slogan of "liberty, equality, and fraternity" to "liberal, equity, and united"; but make no mistake, they will pursue the same basic tactics. It won't be necessary to break out the guillotine because the progressives will pursue a gentler, kinder brand of tyranny: they will be content with "mandatory re-education" and bankrupting their opponents with legal bills.

The continuing issue of the assignats violated a basic principle of paper money, as pointed out by von Sybel [3.2-104]:

> "Wherever a great quantity of paper money is suddenly issued, we invariably see a rapid increase of trade. The great quantity of the circulating medium sets in motion all the energies of commerce and manufac-

tures; capital for investment is more easily found than usual, and trade perpetually receives fresh nutriment. If this paper represents real credit, founded upon order and legal security, from which it can derive a firm and lasting value, such a moment may be the starting point of a great and widely extended prosperity; as for instance, the most splendid improvements in English agriculture were undoubtedly owing to the emancipation of the country banks. If, on the contrary, the new paper is of precarious value, as was clearly seen to be the case with the French assignats as early as February 1791, it can have no lastingly beneficial fruits. For the moment, perhaps, business receives an impulse all; the more violent, because everyone endeavors to invest his doubtful paper in buildings, machines and goods— which under all circumstances retain some intrinsic value. Such a movement was witnessed in France in 1791, and from every quarter there came satisfactory reports of the activity of manufactures. The commercial excitement, and, in an equal degree, the commercial danger, were enhanced by one particular circumstance. The exchange with foreign countries had been for some years unfavorable to France. Since the year 1783 the country imported more than it exported; then came Necker's wholesale purchases of corn, and lastly the utter derangement of commercial relations by the Revolution, which every where prostrated the home production, and rendered it necessary to give orders in foreign countries. France had, therefore, to make more payments than it received, and consequently to bear the expenses of those payments, and to lose in the exchange. The loss in the spring of 1791 was from 9 to 11 percent. Here too the assignats exercised an influence; for as, at this period, they stood at 4 to 6 percent discount, and the foreign merchant had to be paid in silver, the total loss to the French exchange was 15 percent."

Dillaye gave several false reasons as to why the assignats depreciated so quickly (opposition by the clergy and counterfeiting), but he was correct on two points, first, the excessive amount, and secondly [3.2-105]:

"Want of title to the land dedicated as security for the redemption of the assignat; it having been confiscated from clergy and nobility, without any forms of law, by a government purely revolutionary, and before that government had acquired any single element of that stability and permanence essential to sovereignty."

Or, to put it simply, illegitimate is as illegitimate does, which is the collectivist way.

References

[3.1-1]   Murray N. Rothbard, *What Has Government Done to Our Money?,* Auburn, AL: Ludwig von Mises Institute, 1991, pp. 69-77
[3.1-2]   Encyclopedia Britannica, Vol. 16, pp. 483, 726, 727 (1904)
[3.1-3]   www.economics.utoronto.ca/munro5/MONEYLEC.htm
[3.1-4]   W. A. Shaw, *The History of Currency, 1252 to 1894,* London: Wilson & Milne, (1895), p. 44 has slightly different values for the silver content of the English penny: 1300 = 22 grains; 1344 = 20.25 grains, 1346 = 20 grains; 1351 = 18 grains; 1412 = 15 grains; and 1464 = 12 grains.
[3.1-5]   www.histoirepassion.eu/spip.php?article36
[3.1-6]   Henri Pirenne, *Economic and Social History of Medieval Europe,* London: Routledge & Kegan Paul Ltd., 1936, pp. 108 - 114

[3.2-1]   Andrew Dickson White, *Fiat Money Inflation in France,* NY: Irvington-on-Hudson, The Foundation for Economic Education, 1959. It was originally given as lectures to members of Congress on 12 Apr 1876, and later revised by the author and published in 1912.
[3.2-2]   Stephen D. Dillaye, *Assignats and Mandats: A True History,* Philadelphia, Henry Carey Baird & Co., 1877
[3.2-3]   Heinrich von Sybel, *History of the French Revolution,* London: John Murray, 1867
[3.2-4]   op. cit., von Sybel, Vol. 1, p. 47
[3.2-5]   op. cit., von Sybel, Vol. 1, pp. 142-145; he also states in Vol. 1, pp. 510, 511 that sales of the Church lands had brought in 1,800,000,000 livres as of Feb 1792 (but recall that the assignat was depreciated to 1.6 at this time), and the value of the remaining part was less than 350,000,000. The 2,000,000,000 livre valuation is given by op. cit., White, p. 28.
[3.2-6]   op. cit., von Sybel, Vol. 1, pp. 43-45, 255-257
[3.2-7]   op. cit., von Sybel, Vol. 1, pp. 141-146
[3.2-8]   op. cit., Dillaye, p. 10

[3.2-9]   op. cit., Dillaye, p. 14
[3.2-10]   op. cit., von Sybel, Vol. 1, pp. 87-95
[3.2-11]   op. cit., von Sybel, Vol. 1, p. 144
[3.2-12]   op. cit., von Sybel, Vol. 1, p. 167
[3.2-13]   op. cit., White, p. 28
[3.2-14]   op. cit., von Sybel, Vol. 1, pp. 146, 147, 169
[3.2-15]   op. cit., White, p. 28. See also op. cit., von Sybel, Vol. 1, pp. 146, 147
[3.2-16]   op. cit., Dillaye, pp. 15, 16
[3.2-17]   op. cit., von Sybel, Vol. 1, p. 167
[3.2-18]   op. cit., White, pp. 31, 32
[3.2-19]   op. cit., von Sybel, Vol. 1, p. 252
[3.2-20]   op. cit., White, pp. 37-40
[3.2-21]   op. cit., White, p. 43; quoting an appendix in Thiers' *History of the French Revolution*
[3.2-22]   op. cit., White, pp. 46, 47, 113
[3.2-23]   op. cit., White, pp. 49, 50
[3.2-24]   op. cit., Dillaye, p. 20
[3.2-25]   op. cit., White, p. 56
[3.2-26]   op. cit., von Sybel, Vol. 1, pp. 281, 282
[3.2-27]   op. cit., White, pp. 55-62
[3.2-28]   op. cit., White, p. 55
[3.2-29]   op. cit., von Sybel, Vol. 1, p. 264
[3.2-30]   op. cit., von Sybel, Vol. 1, pp. 265, 266; see also op. cit., Dillaye, p. 19
[3.2-31]   op. cit., White, p. 113
[3.2-32]   op. cit., Dillaye, p. 35
[3.2-33]   op. cit., White, p. 66
[3.2-34]   op. cit., von Sybel, Vol. 1, p. 393
[3.2-35]   op. cit., White, pp. 68, 69; see also op. cit., von Sybel, Vol. 1, pp. 510, 511
[3.2-36]   op. cit., von Sybel, Vol. 1, pp. 510, 511
[3.2-37]   op. cit., White, p. 68
[3.2-38]   op. cit., White, p. 68
[3.2-39]   op. cit., White, p. 114
[3.2-40]   op. cit., White, p. 68
[3.2-41]   op. cit., White, 68, 69
[3.2-42]   op. cit., Dillaye, pp. 32, 33
[3.2-43]   op. cit., White, p. 71
[3.2-44]   op. cit., White, pp. 69, 114
[3.2-45]   op. cit., von Sybel, Vol. 1, pp. 417, 418
[3.2-46]   op. cit., White, p. 69
[3.2-47]   op. cit., White, p. 114
[3.2-48]   op. cit., White, pp. 72, 73
[3.2-49]   op. cit., von Sybel, Vol. 1, pp. 418-421
[3.2-50]   Francis A. Walker, *Money*, NY: Henry Holt and Company, 1891, p. 344
[3.2-51]   op. cit., White, pp. 75, 76, 114
[3.2-52]   op. cit., White, pp. 73, 74
[3.2-53]   op. cit., White, p. 75
[3.2-54]   op. cit., White, pp. 78, 79, 114
[3.2-55]   op. cit., von Sybel, Vol. 2, pp. 47-91
[3.2-56]   op. cit., von Sybel, Vol. 2, p. 89
[3.2-57]   op. cit., White, p. 79
[3.2-58]   op. cit., White, p. 71
[3.2-59]   op. cit., White, pp. 76-79
[3.2-60]   op. cit., White, pp. 83, 84, 115
[3.2-61]   op. cit., White, p. 79
[3.2-62]   op. cit., White, p. 71
[3.2-63]   op. cit., Dillaye, p. 29
[3.2-64]   op. cit., White, p. 79

[3.2-65]   op. cit., Dillaye, pp. 38, 39
[3.2-66]   op. cit., Dillaye, pp. 38, 39
[3.2-67]   op. cit., White, p. 115
[3.2-68]   op. cit., Walker, p. 345, quoting M. Bresson's *History Financiere de la France*, Vol. 2, p. 225
[3.2-69]   op. cit., Dillaye, p. 69
[3.2-70]   op. cit., Walker, p. 345
[3.2-71]   op. cit., White, p. 87
[3.2-72]   op. cit., von Sybel, Vol. 4, p. 330
[3.2-73]   op. cit., von Sybel, Vol. 4, p. 333
[3.2-74]   op. cit., Walker, p. 345
[3.2-75]   op. cit., Walker, p. 345
[3.2-76]   op. cit., White, p. 115
[3.2-77]   op. cit., White, p. 89
[3.2-78]   op. cit., von Sybel, Vol. 4, p. 336
[3.2-79]   op. cit., Walker, p. 345
[3.2-80]   op. cit., White, p. 88
[3.2-81]   op. cit., White, p. 115
[3.2-82]   op. cit., White, p. 88
[3.2-83]   op. cit., Walker, p. 345
[3.2-84]   op. cit., Dillaye, pp. 41-43
[3.2-85]   op. cit., Walker, p. 345
[3.2-86]   op. cit., White, p. 88
[3.2-87]   op. cit., Walker, p. 345
[3.2-88]   op. cit., White, pp. 91, 92
[3.2-89]   op. cit., White, pp. 95, 96
[3.2-90]   op. cit., White, p. 88
[3.2-91]   op. cit., Walker, p. 345
[3.2-92]   op. cit., White, p. 88, 89
[3.2-93]   op. cit., Walker, p. 345
[3.2-94]   op. cit., von Sybel, Vol. 4, pp. 334, 335
[3.2-95]   op. cit., White, p. 93
[3.2-96]   op. cit., White, pp. 92, 93, 116
[3.2-97]   op. cit., White, p. 96
[3.2-98]   op. cit., White, p. 96
[3.2-99]   op. cit., White, pp. 98, 99, 104
[3.2-100]   op. cit., White, p. 116
[3.2-101]   op. cit., White, p. 99
[3.2-102]   op. cit., White, p. 99
[3.2-103]   op. cit., White, p. 99
[3.2-104]   op. cit., von Sybel, Vol. 1, pp. 281, 282
[3.2-105]   op. cit., Dillaye, p. 43

4

A Digression on the Historical Production of Gold and Silver

A great deal has been said about the use of metal as money, and to complete the story, this chapter will describe how much gold and silver has been produced throughout history, starting with estimates made by William Jacob (1831). Clearly not all of what is produced can be used for monetary purposes, since both have important industrial uses, especially in the past 75 years or so. Jacob [4-1] claims that very little mining was done in Europe between 800 and 1500 AD. He cites the amount of silver mined in Europe and Russia between 1780 and 1800 as equal in value to £600,000, which in the coinage of 1831 (1 £ = 3.363 ozt. silver), amounts to about 2,017,000 ozt. He then states that about one-seventh of this figure was mined during the entire period from, 800 to 1500, thus about 288,200 ozt. This was just enough to compensate for losses by wear and tear. Figure 4-1 shows the total amount in English pounds sterling [4-2, 4-3]. Jacob does not state gold vs. silver directly; so the second and third columns show the number of troy ounces of gold and silver if the total amount were one or the other [4-4, 4-5]. Jacob assesses prices between the Norman Conquest and the discovery of America, noting that there was little change in prices. He concludes that there was therefore little change in the amount of circulating money [4-6]:

> "An inference from hence [small change in prices] may perhaps be fairly drawn that no very great increase or decrease in the stock of the precious metals occurred during those centuries [1190 to 1492]; or it may be presumed that the supply from the mines was nearly equal to the consumption by friction on the circulation, and to that portion which either had been lost from being buried in the ground and not again found, or that had been lost by shipwrecks."

He concluded that the amount of metal in 1492 was about the same as had existed in the ninth century, accounting for what had been lost or destroyed.

Year (AD)	Combined gold and silver, £	If all gold, ozt.	If all silver, ozt.	Year (AD)	Combined gold and silver, £	If all gold, ozt.	If all silver, ozt.
14	358,000,000	84,279,167	1,203,954,000	446	96,692,332	22,762,986	325,176,313
50	322,200,000	75,851,250	1,083,558,600	482	87,033,099	20,489,042	292,692,312
86	287,980,000	67,795,292	968,476,740	518	78,229,700	18,416,575	263,086,481
122	259,182,000	61,015,763	871,629,066	554	70,406,730	16,574,918	236,777,833
158	233,263,800	54,914,186	784,466,159	590	63,364,057	14,916,955	213,093,324
194	209,937,420	49,422,768	706,019,543	626	57,027,652	13,425,260	191,783,994
230	181,943,678	42,832,574	611,876,589	662	51,324,887	12,082,734	172,605,595
266	163,749,311	38,549,317	550,688,933	698	46,192,399	10,874,461	155,345,038
302	147,374,380	34,694,385	495,620,040	734	41,573,160	9,787,015	139,810,537
338	132,636,942	31,224,947	446,058,036	770	37,415,840	8,808,312	125,829,470
374	119,373,248	28,102,452	401,452,233	806	33,674,256	7,927,481	113,246,523
410	107,435,924	25,292,207	361,307,012				

Figure 4-1: Total Amount of Precious Metals, 14 AD to 806 AD (= 1492 AD) [4-2, 4-3]

The split between gold vs. silver is not shown directly in Jacob's figures, but he estimated [4-7, 4-8] that the amount of silver to gold in use prior to 1700 was about 5:1. If we assume the split was measured in pounds sterling, then we would have, in 1492, £33,674,256 total, thus £5,612,376 in gold, and £28,061,880 in silver. These values equate to 1,321,153 ozt. of gold, and 94,372,102 ozt. of silver.

This value for silver is very far off from an estimate made by the United States Geological Service. Its values for silver as of 1492, 1900, and 1939 are [4-9]:

> "Total world silver mine production from prehistory through 2001 is estimated by the U. S. Geological Survey (USGS) to have been about 1.26 million metric tons (Mt), one-half of which was mined in the last 62 years of the period. About 8 percent of the silver was mined before the discovery of America, 22 percent from 1492 through 1900, 69 percent in the 20th century, and 1 percent in 2001."

If so, the total amount of silver in the above-named years is:

By 1492: 0.08*(1,260,000 Mt)*(1000 kg/Mt)*(1000 g/kg)*(1 ozt./31.10348 g) = 3.24 billion ozt.

By 1900: 0.30*(1,260,000 Mt)*(1000 kg/Mt)*(1000 g/kg)*(1 ozt./31.10348 g) = 12.15 billion ozt.

By 1939: 0.50*(1,260,000 Mt)*(1000 kg/Mt)*(1000 g/kg)*(1 ozt./31.10348 g) = 20.25 billion ozt.

By 2001: 1.00*(1,260,000 Mt)*(1000 kg/Mt)*(1000 g/kg)*(1 ozt./31.10348 g) = 40.50 billion ozt.

I have chosen to perform this analysis from the bottom up: starting with Jacob's estimate as of 1492, then added the amounts mined from 1493 to 1914 using data from the Annual Reports of the Comptroller of the Currency; and from 1914 on per the U. S. Geological Survey data. The results are shown in the following Figures. It has been estimated that about 12% of all the silver produced has been lost or consumed, but the values in the tables reflect only the production estimates. The USGS data referenced above indicated that about 40.5 billion ozt of silver had been produced as of 2001; Figure 4.4 below indicates, using the method described, as 37.387 billion ozt., which is the difference between Jacob's 1492 estimate and the USGS data. Overall, for 2001, the error in the estimate is 8%, assuming the true 2001 data is halfway between the USGS value and the accumulated value as described.

Approximate Silver Production, 14 AD to 1899							
Period	Average for Period (ozt.)	Total for Period (ozt.)	Accumulated (ozt.)	Period	Average for Period (ozt.)	Total for Period (ozt.)	Accumulated (ozt.)
14 AD to 1492	See text for Jacob's view		94,392,102	1851 to 1855	28,488,597	142,442,986	5,044,764,700
1493 to 1520	1,511,050	42,309,000	136,701,102	1856 to 1860	29,095,428	145,477,142	5,190,241,842
1521 to 1544	2,899,030	69,598,320	206,299,422	1861 to 1865	35,401,972	177,000,862	5,367,242,704
1545 to 1560	10,017,940	160,287,040	366,586,462	1866 to 1870	43,051,583	215,257,914	5,582,500,618
1561 to 1580	9,628,925	192,578,500	559,164,962	1871 to 1875	63,317,014	316,585,069	5,899,085,687
1581 to 1600	13,407,035	269,352,700	828,517,662	1876 to 1880	78,775,602	393,878,009	6,292,963,696
1601 to 1620	13,596,235	271,924,700	1,100,442,362	1881 to 1885	92,003,944	460,019,722	6,752,983,418
1621 to 1640	12,654,240	253,084,800	1,353,527,162	1886	93,297,200	93,297,290	6,846,280,708
1641 to 1660	11,776,545	235,530,900	1,589,058,062	1887	96,123,586	96,123,586	6,942,404,294
1661 to 1680	10,834,550	216,691,000	1,805,749,062	1888	108,827,606	108,827,606	7,051,231,900
1681 to 1700	10,992,085	219,841,700	2,025,590,762	1889	120,213,611	120,213,611	7,171,445,511
1701 to 1720	11,432,540	228,650,800	2,254,241,562	1890	126,095,062	126,095,062	7,297,540,573
1721 to 1740	13,863,080	277,261,600	2,531,503,162	1891	137,170,919	137,170,919	7,434,711,492
1741 to 1760	17,140,612	342,812,235	2,874,315,397	1891	153,151,762	158,151,762	7,592,863,254
1761 to 1780	20,985,501	410,711,820	3,285,027,217	1893	166,092,047	166,092,047	7,758,955,301
1781 to 1800	28,261,779	565,235,580	3,850,262,797	1894	167,752,561	167,752,561	7,926,707,862
1801 to 1810	28,746,922	287,469,225	4,137,732,022	1895	167,500,960	167,500,960	8,094,208,822
1811 to 1820	17,385,755	173,857,555	4,311,589,577	1896	157,061,370	157,061,370	8,251,270,192
1821 to 1830	14,807,004	148,070,040	4,459,659,617	1897	160,421,082	160,421,082	8,411,691,274
1831 to 1840	19,175,867	191,758,675	4,651,418,292	1898	169,055,253	169,055,253	8,580,746,527
1841 to 1850	25,090,342	250,903,422	4,902,321,714	1899	168,337,452	168,337,452	8,749,083,979

Figure 4-2: Accumulated World Silver Production, 14 AD to 1899 [4-10, 4-11]

				Approximate Production of Silver to 1959				
Year	Production (ozt.)	Accumulated (ozt.)	Year	Production (ozt.)	Accumulated (ozt.)	Year	Production (ozt.)	Accumulated (ozt.)
to 1899	from previous	8,749,083,979	to 1919	from previous	12,494,885,256	to 1939	from previous	17,069,193,089
1900	173,610,221	8,922,694,200	1920	173,288,721	12,668,173,977	1940	275,525,851	17,344,718,941
1901	172,967,221	9,095,661,421	1921	171,359,719	12,839,533,695	1941	261,701,334	17,606,420,275
1902	162,679,207	9,258,340,628	1922	209,939,768	13,049,473,463	1942	250,127,319	17,856,547,593
1903	167,823,214	9,426,163,842	1923	245,947,814	13,295,421,277	1943	205,117,262	18,061,664,855
1904	164,286,710	9,590,450,552	1924	239,517,805	13,534,939,082	1944	184,541,235	18,246,206,090
1905	172,324,220	9,762,774,772	1925	245,947,814	13,780,886,896	1945	162,036,207	18,408,242,297
1906	164,929,710	9,927,704,482	1926	253,663,823	14,034,550,719	1946	127,635,663	18,535,877,960
1907	184,219,735	10,111,924,217	1927	253,985,324	14,288,536,043	1947	167,823,214	18,703,701,174
1908	203,188,259	10,315,112,476	1928	257,843,329	14,546,379,372	1948	174,896,223	18,878,597,397
1909	212,190,271	10,527,302,747	1929	261,058,333	14,807,437,705	1949	179,075,728	19,057,673,125
1910	221,835,283	10,749,138,030	1930	248,841,317	15,056,279,022	1950	203,188,259	19,260,861,384
1911	226,336,289	10,975,474,318	1931	195,472,249	15,251,751,272	1951	199,651,755	19,460,513,139
1912	224,407,286	11,199,881,604	1932	164,929,710	15,416,680,982	1952	215,405,275	19,675,918,414
1913	225,371,787	11,425,253,392	1933	171,681,219	15,588,362,201	1953	221,835,283	19,897,753,697
1914	168,466,215	11,593,719,607	1934	192,578,746	15,780,940,947	1954	214,440,773	20,112,194,470
1915	184,219,735	11,777,939,342	1935	221,513,782	16,002,454,729	1955	225,050,287	20,337,244,757
1916	168,787,715	11,946,727,057	1936	254,628,325	16,257,083,054	1956	225,693,288	20,562,938,045
1917	174,253,222	12,120,980,279	1937	277,776,354	16,534,859,408	1957	231,158,795	20,794,096,840
1918	197,401,252	12,318,381,531	1938	267,488,341	16,802,347,749	1958	238,874,805	21,032,971,644
1919	176,503,725	12,494,885,256	1939	266,845,340	17,069,193,089	1959	222,156,783	21,255,128,428

Figure 4-3: Accumulated World Silver Production, 1899 to 1959 [4-12]

				Approximate Production of Silver to 2019				
Year	Production (ozt.)	Accumulated (ozt.)	Year	Production (ozt.)	Accumulated (ozt.)	Year	Production (ozt.)	Accumulated (ozt.)
to 1959	from previous	21,255,128,428	to 1979	from previous	26,974,299,221	to 1999	from previous	36,204,575,992
1960	235,338,300	21,490,466,728	1980	344,005,439	27,318,304,660	2000	581,915,742	36,786,491,734
1961	236,945,802	21,727,412,530	1981	360,080,459	27,678,385,119	2001	601,205,767	37,387,697,501
1962	245,947,814	21,973,360,344	1982	369,725,472	28,048,110,590	2002	604,420,771	37,992,118,272
1963	250,127,319	22,223,487,663	1983	389,015,496	28,437,126,087	2003	604,420,771	38,596,539,043
1964	248,519,817	22,472,007,479	1984	421,165,537	28,858,291,624	2004	643,000,820	39,239,539,863
1965	257,521,828	22,729,529,308	1985	421,165,537	29,279,457,161	2005	668,720,853	39,908,260,715
1966	266,845,340	22,996,374,648	1986	417,950,533	29,697,407,694	2006	646,215,824	40,554,476,539
1967	258,164,829	23,254,539,477	1987	450,100,574	30,147,508,268	2007	668,720,853	41,223,197,392
1968	275,204,351	23,529,743,828	1988	498,325,636	30,645,833,903	2008	684,795,873	41,907,993,266
1969	295,780,377	23,825,524,206	1989	527,260,672	31,173,094,576	2009	716,945,914	42,624,939,180
1970	300,924,384	24,126,448,589	1990	533,690,681	31,706,785,256	2010	749,095,955	43,374,035,135
1971	294,815,876	24,421,264,465	1991	501,540,640	32,208,325,896	2011	749,095,955	44,123,131,090
1972	301,567,385	24,722,831,850	1992	479,035,611	32,687,361,507	2012	781,245,996	44,904,377,087
1973	311,855,398	25,034,687,248	1993	453,315,578	33,140,677,085	2013	826,256,054	45,730,633,140
1974	297,709,380	25,332,396,627	1994	450,100,574	33,590,777,659	2014	861,621,099	46,592,254,239
1975	303,174,887	25,635,571,514	1995	479,035,611	34,069,813,270	2015	806,966,029	47,399,220,268
1976	316,356,403	25,951,927,917	1996	485,465,619	34,555,278,889	2016	826,256,054	48,225,476,322
1977	331,145,422	26,283,073,340	1997	530,475,677	35,085,754,565	2017	803,751,025	49,029,227,347
1978	344,005,439	26,627,078,778	1998	552,980,705	35,638,735,271	2018	864,836,103	49,894,063,450
1979	347,220,443	26,974,299,221	1999	565,840,722	36,204,575,992	2019	868,051,107	50,762,114,557

Figure 4-4: Accumulated World Silver Production, 1959 to 2019 [4-12, 4-13, 4-14]

Figures 4-5 through 4-7 show the world's production of gold from 14 AD to 2019, again starting with Jacob's data for 14 AD to 1492. It has been estimated that about 12% of all the gold produced has been lost or consumed, but the values in the tables reflect only the production estimates. The USGS estimate for 2004 [4-15] is 4.66 billion ozt., comparable to the 4.45 billion ozt. as shown on Figure 4-7. The error in 2004, assuming the true value is halfway between, is 4.57%.

Approximate Gold Production, 14 AD to 1899							
Period	Average for Period (ozt.)	Total for Period (ozt.)	Accumulated (ozt.)	Period	Average for Period (ozt.)	Total for Period (ozt.)	Accumulated (ozt.)
14 AD to 1492	See text for Jacob's view		1,321,153	1851 to 1855	6,410,324	32,051,621	186,151,824
1493 to 1520	186,470	5,221,160	6,542,313	1856 to 1860	6,486,262	32,431,312	218,583,136
1521 to 1544	230,194	5,524,656	12,066,969	1861 to 1865	5,949,582	29,747,913	248,331,049
1545 to 1560	273,596	4,377,544	16,444,513	1866 to 1870	6,270,086	31,350,430	279,681,479
1561 to 1580	219,906	4,398,120	20,842,633	1871 to 1875	5,591,014	27,955,068	307,636,547
1581 to 1600	237,267	4,745,340	25,587,973	1876 to 1880	5,573,110	27,715,550	335,352,097
1601 to 1620	273,918	5,478,360	31,066,333	1881 to 1885	4,794,755	23,973,773	359,325,870
1621 to 1640	266,845	5,336,900	36,403,233	1886	5,135,679	5,135,679	364,461,549
1641 to 1660	281,955	5,639,110	42,042,343	1887	5,116,861	5,116,861	369,578,410
1661 to 1680	297,709	5,954,180	47,996,523	1888	5,330,775	5,330,775	374,909,185
1681 to 1700	346,095	6,921,895	54,918,418	1889	5,973,790	5,973,790	380,882,975
1701 to 1720	412,163	8,243,260	63,161,678	1890	5,749,306	5,749,306	386,632,281
1721 to 1740	613,422	12,268,440	75,430,118	1891	6,320,194	6,320,194	392,952,475
1741 to 1760	791,211	15,824,230	91,254,348	1891	7,102,180	7,102,180	400,054,655
1761 to 1780	665,666	13,313,315	104,567,663	1893	7,608,787	7,608,787	407,663,442
1781 to 1800	571,948	11,438,970	116,006,633	1894	8,737,788	8,737,788	416,401,230
1801 to 1810	571,563	5,715,627	121,722,260	1895	9,615,190	9,615,190	426,016,420
1811 to 1820	367,957	3,679,568	125,401,828	1896	9,783,914	9,783,914	435,800,334
1821 to 1830	457,044	4,570,444	129,972,272	1897	11,420,068	11,420,068	447,220,402
1831 to 1840	652,291	6,522,913	136,495,185	1898	13,877,806	13,877,806	461,098,208
1841 to 1850	1,760,502	17,605,018	154,100,203	1899	14,837,775	14,837,775	475,935,983

Figure 4-5: Accumulated World Gold Production, 14 AD to 1899 [4-10, 4-11]

Approximate Production of Gold to 1959								
Year	Production (ozt.)	Accumulated (ozt.)	Year	Production (ozt.)	Accumulated (ozt.)	Year	Production (ozt.)	Accumulated (ozt.)
to 1899	from previous	475,935,983	to 1919	from previous	862,154,426	to 1939	from previous	1,338,585,883
1900	12,409,916	488,345,899	1920	16,300,071	878,454,496	1940	42,116,554	1,380,702,437
1901	12,699,266	501,045,165	1921	16,010,720	894,465,217	1941	34,722,044	1,415,424,481
1902	14,499,668	515,544,834	1922	15,464,170	909,929,386	1942	36,008,046	1,451,432,527
1903	15,946,420	531,491,254	1923	17,811,123	927,740,509	1943	28,806,437	1,480,238,964
1904	16,910,922	548,402,175	1924	19,032,824	946,773,333	1944	26,137,983	1,506,376,947
1905	18,486,274	566,888,449	1925	19,000,674	965,774,008	1945	24,498,331	1,530,875,278
1906	19,547,225	586,435,674	1926	19,354,325	985,128,332	1946	27,649,035	1,558,524,314
1907	20,029,476	606,465,149	1927	19,193,574	1,004,321,907	1947	28,935,037	1,587,459,350
1908	21,476,227	627,941,377	1928	19,386,475	1,023,708,382	1948	29,963,838	1,617,423,189
1909	22,087,078	650,028,455	1929	19,579,375	1,043,287,757	1949	30,992,640	1,648,415,828
1910	22,151,378	672,179,833	1930	20,833,227	1,064,120,983	1950	28,259,886	1,676,675,714
1911	22,472,879	694,652,712	1931	22,344,278	1,086,465,262	1951	28,388,486	1,705,064,200
1912	22,665,779	717,318,491	1932	24,241,131	1,110,706,393	1952	27,906,236	1,732,970,436
1913	22,312,128	739,630,619	1933	25,494,983	1,136,201,375	1953	27,777,635	1,760,748,071
1914	21,315,477	760,946,096	1934	27,038,184	1,163,239,559	1954	31,024,790	1,791,772,861
1915	22,633,629	783,579,725	1935	29,706,638	1,192,946,197	1955	30,446,089	1,822,218,950
1916	22,022,778	805,602,503	1936	33,114,542	1,226,060,740	1956	31,442,740	1,853,661,690
1917	20,286,676	825,889,179	1937	35,365,045	1,261,425,785	1957	32,793,042	1,886,454,732
1918	18,582,724	844,471,903	1938	37,615,548	1,299,041,333	1958	33,757,543	1,920,212,275
1919	17,682,523	862,154,426	1939	39,544,550	1,338,585,883	1959	36,329,546	1,956,541,821

Figure 4-6: Accumulated World Gold Production, 1899 to 1959 [4-12]

Approximate Production of Gold to 2019								
Year	Production (ozt.)	Accumulated (ozt.)	Year	Production (ozt.)	Accumulated (ozt.)	Year	Production (ozt.)	Accumulated (ozt.)
to 1959	from previous	1,956,541,821	to 1979	from previous	2,811,732,912	to 1999	from previous	4,051,438,493
1960	38,258,549	1,994,800,370	1980	39,223,050	2,850,955,962	2000	83,268,606	4,134,707,099
1961	39,544,550	2,034,344,920	1981	41,152,052	2,892,108,014	2001	83,590,107	4,218,297,206
1962	41,473,553	2,075,818,473	1982	43,081,055	2,935,189,069	2002	81,982,605	4,300,279,810
1963	43,081,055	2,118,899,528	1983	45,010,057	2,980,199,127	2003	81,661,104	4,381,940,914
1964	44,688,557	2,163,588,085	1984	46,939,060	3,027,138,186	2004	77,803,099	4,459,744,013
1965	46,296,059	2,209,884,144	1985	49,189,563	3,076,327,749	2005	79,410,601	4,539,154,615
1966	46,617,559	2,256,501,704	1986	51,761,566	3,128,089,315	2006	76,195,597	4,615,350,212
1967	45,653,058	2,302,154,762	1987	53,369,068	3,181,458,383	2007	75,552,596	4,690,902,808
1968	46,296,059	2,348,450,821	1988	60,120,577	3,241,578,960	2008	73,945,094	4,764,847,903
1969	46,617,559	2,395,068,380	1989	64,621,582	3,306,200,542	2009	80,053,602	4,844,901,505
1970	47,582,061	2,442,650,441	1990	70,087,089	3,376,287,632	2010	83,268,606	4,928,170,111
1971	46,617,559	2,489,268,001	1991	69,444,089	3,445,731,720	2011	86,162,110	5,014,332,221
1972	44,688,557	2,533,956,558	1992	72,659,093	3,518,390,813	2012	88,412,613	5,102,744,833
1973	43,402,555	2,577,359,113	1993	73,302,093	3,591,692,906	2013	93,878,120	5,196,622,953
1974	40,187,551	2,617,546,664	1994	72,659,093	3,664,351,999	2014	97,093,124	5,293,716,077
1975	38,580,049	2,656,126,713	1995	71,694,591	3,736,046,591	2015	99,665,127	5,393,381,204
1976	38,901,550	2,695,028,263	1996	73,623,594	3,809,670,184	2016	99,986,628	5,493,367,832
1977	38,901,550	2,733,929,813	1997	78,767,600	3,888,437,785	2017	101,272,629	5,594,640,461
1978	38,901,550	2,772,831,362	1998	80,375,103	3,968,812,887	2018	106,095,135	5,700,735,596
1979	38,901,550	2,811,732,912	1999	82,625,605	4,051,438,493	2019	106,095,135	5,806,830,731

Figure 4-7: Accumulated World Gold Production, 1959 to 2019 [4-12, 4-13, 4-14]

References

[4-1]   William Jacob, *An Historical Inquiry into the Production and Consumption of the Precious Metals*, London: John Murray, 1831, Vol. 1, pp. 360-362.

[4-2]   op. cit., Jacob, Vol. 1, p. 225. He begins with amount at the end of Augustus, and assumes 10% is lost every 36 years, with no additions made by mining.

[4-3]   op. cit., Jacob, Vol. 1, p. 237.

[4-4]   Jacob wrote in 1831, and calls out his values in pounds sterling. The silver coin in use was the shilling; per the re-coinage of 1816, 5760 grains (one troy pound) at 0.925 pure was made into 66 shillings. Then have 5760*0.925 = 5328 grains pure per pound sterling = 80.7272 grains pure per shilling. At 20 shillings per monetary pound (£) in order to match to Jacob's tally, have 1 £ = 1614.545 grains, which is 3.363 ozt. (480 grains ozt.). The U. S. dollar was 371.25 grains pure silver, which is 0.77342 ozt., so the conversion ratio between the UK pound sterling in silver and the U. S. silver dollar was 3.363/0.77342 = 4.348.

[4-5]   Jacob wrote in 1831, and calls out his values in pounds sterling. The gold sovereign was defined per the 1816 Coinage Act as one troy pound (5760 grains) of gold at 22 carat (0.91666 fine) as £46 14 s. 6 d., which comes to £46.725. The 5760 grains at 0.916666 pure is 5279.9616 grains, so the gold pound was 5279.9616/46.725 = 113 grains pure gold. At 480 grains per ozt., the gold pound £ was thus 113/480 = 0.2354 ozt. The U. S. dollar was defined at this time as 24.75 grains of gold (devalued in 1834 to 23.22 grains). The ratio of the gold British £ sterling to the U. S. gold dollar was thus 113/24.75 = 4.565.

[4-6]   op. cit., Jacob, Vol. 1, pp. 348.

[4-7]   op. cit., Jacob, Vol. 2, pp. 187, 188 He states: "If, then, the rate of loss by wear on gold money was at the rate of one part in six hundred, and that money was one sixth of the circulating medium, and if the rate of loss on the silver money was at the rate of one part in one hundred and fifty, the mean rate of depreciation would be as near to one part in three hundred and sixty as can be calculated. ... Although the amount of silver in circulation as money at all times must have been greater than that of gold, yet, as the gold has six times the durability of silver, the relative values of the two metals to each other could not be maintained unless the mines produced the two metals in proportion to the loss on them be wear respectively. It seems probable that he due proportion was kept up during the existence of the Roman power, and through the dark ages which succeeded, till the discovery of America, and till the dispersion over the world of the excessive surplus produce of silver above that of gold."

[4-8]   Francis A. Walker, *Money*, NY: Henry Holt and Company, 1891, p. 137

[4-9]   W. C. Butterman, H. E. Hilliard, *Mineral Commodity Profiles*, Open File Report 2004-1251, Reston, VA: United States Geological Survey, 2004, p. 4

[4-10]   R. E. Preston, *Twenty-Third Annual Report of the Director of the Mint to the Secretary of the Treasury for the Fiscal Year ending 30 Jun 1895*, Washington, DC: U. S. Government Printing Office, 1895, pp. 248, 249. I have added Jacob's assessment of the silver remaining in 1493.

[4-11]   For 1493 to 1894: R. E. Preston, *Twenty-Third Annual Report of the Director of the Mint to the Secretary of the Treasury for the Fiscal Year ending 30 Jun 1895*, Washington, DC: U. S. Government Printing Office, 1895, pp. 248, 249. For 1895 to 1899: *Annual Report of the Director of the Mint to the Secretary of the Treasury for the Fiscal Year ending 30 Jun 1914*, Washington, DC: U. S. Government Printing Office, 1914, p. 267

[4-12]   United States Geological Survey, https://www.usgs.gov/centers/nmic/historical-statistics-mineral-and-material-commodities-united-states

[4-13]   United States Geological Survey, *Mineral Commodity Summaries, 2018*, 31 Jan 2018, https://doi.org/10.3133/70192932

[4-14]   United States Geological Survey, *Mineral Commodity Summaries, 2020*, 31 Jan 2020, https://doi.org/10.3133/mcs2020

[4-15]   United States Geological Survey, Mineral Commodity Summaries, January 2004. It cites 145,200 Mt total to 2004, which comes to 4.668 billion ozt. at 32,150.7 ozt./Mt. https://www.usgs.gov/publications/mineral-commodity-summaries-2004

5

Banks and Banking

There is a famous American filmmaker who derides bankers as 'banksters', implying that bankers are part and parcel of some underhanded scheme to deprive people of their wealth. He declines to address the pervasive corruption in the movie industry. It is true that some bankers have been and may well be crooks. The incidence of corruption among bankers is probably no more common than among other trades, but it does have more severe consequences. Banking is in fact a necessary and important function for advanced societies. This chapter discusses the origin of banking, the various types of banks, their utility in advancing civilization, and some general observations on the banking business.

5.1   The Benefits of Banks

One thing should be mentioned up front regarding the fundamental operations of banks. You, as the proprietor of Granny's Sublime Tarts, are ultimately a dealer in sugar, flour, cream, booze, and eggs; and the local junk man is a dealer in scrap metal, plastic, and paper. Likewise, a banker is nothing more than a dealer in money. A bakery's capital is the ingredients and the machines necessary to make the product; the junk man's capital is his equipment and the stock of cast-off materials he can buy and sell; and a bank's capital is the money that it handles.

Banks save a great deal of labor and expense because they are able to efficiently match lenders to borrowers; that in turn makes money more efficient in its operation [5.1-1]. A bank performs this function as a common institution in which the public can deposit money, and borrowers, mostly businessmen, can borrow the money necessary to finance their ventures. As seen before, it is only by the expansion of production through business that the general standard of living can increase.

A bank matches lenders and borrowers by accepting deposits from those who have money they desire to save or invest, and lend to those who need to borrow. Here is where the banks demonstrate their utility: as dealers in money, a banker relies on his experience in evaluating the ability of the borrowers to repay the loan [5.1-2]. If the borrower desires money to start or maintain a business, the banker evaluates the probability of successful repayment and the risk in financing it. Typically a loan to a business will require some evidence that the borrowers themselves have risked their own money, and will require some sort of security for the loan. Often the inventory or equipment to be procured is pledged as collateral for the loan. If the borrower desires money to buy a house or a car, the banker evaluates the borrower's income, other liabilities, and the borrower's overall ability to repay. Likewise, the house or car is pledged as collateral for the loan, which would revert to the banker if the borrower fails to pay. Evaluation of risk is an essential part of the banking business, the same as any other profit-seeking enterprise. Accurate assessment of risk is ultimately the long-term source of the banker's stability and profitability.

An efficient banking system reduces the amount of money lying idle by amassing large amounts from small lenders (depositors) and lending it to profitable concerns. Aside from borrowing and lending, banks pay interest to depositors (in certain cases) and collect interest from borrowers. The difference in the interest rates is the fee the bank charges for the management of money. Some would claim that the interest paid to the bank is an illegitimate payment for the use of other people's money (i.e., the depositors'). That is not the case: the deposits no longer belong to the depositor; they belong to the bank in return for which the bank takes on the liability to repay any deposits on demand. Banks may also pay interest to their depositors for the use of their money. Banks also perform many no-cost services for their depositors (checking accounts, ATM's) and thus incur expenses in the course of keeping records of transactions, balancing accounts, and clearing checks. These last three functions also aid in making money more efficient. Only the residual balance from the large number of offsetting checks and transfers issued by account holders in many banks has to be settled, and can be done with a small number of transactions between the banks.

An efficient banking system is a concentration of money and credit in the hands of professional dealers in money on the grounds that by experience and knowledge, they are the best qualified to evaluate the creditworthiness of borrowers. This relieves lenders from having to take on the burden of finding borrowers. Done properly, banks make money much more useful than it otherwise would be. It is also true that the entire banking system depends on trust and confidence because trust is required in order to carry on trade without the use of money that has intrinsic value, such as coin [5.1-3]. Depositors must trust the bank to permit a withdrawal when desired; the borrower must have confidence that the banks' credit is good (i.e., that the money received will be accepted in trade); and the banks must have confidence that the borrowers will repay. One of the core problems for the banking system is maintaining that required level of trust.

Banks that match lenders and borrowers perform an essential service in the advance of civilization. There are two categories of banks. First is the category that performs a banking function without creating money, and permits businesses to take calculated risks. Second is the category that creates money, lends to business, but also injects risk into the economy. When a bank creates money, it is actually extending its credit, but such a bank does not generally have the capital to back up its credit. In other words, the money that is created by a bank does not always rest on sufficient collateral. Creation of money within the banking system amounts to a bank issuing unsecured liabilities. That process will be described further in section 5.6.

5.2 The Origin of Banking

Section 2.2 mentioned the activities of the goldsmiths and moneylenders in the medieval era, and how the safekeeping of valuables such as gold and silver began what we now call deposit banking. They recognized early on that the likelihood of all the depositors requiring their money at one time was very small. Thus they began to lend out the depositors' money, charging the borrower interest, and paying interest to the depositor for the use of the money. Gradually the use of bills exchange as a means to transmit money was developed in order to avoid the risks of traveling with large sums.

It is important to distinguish modern banking from the original meaning used in colonial America. Early American writers often use the term "bank" in its colonial meaning, which can be a source of considerable confusion if unaware. Walker describes the difference [5.2-1]; he is discussing the issues of paper money by the separate colonies prior to the American Revolution:

> "The use of the word Bank in the colonial days was peculiar. With us the word signifies an institution for conducting the functions of deposit, of exchange, and of discount, with generally a building of its own, and with permanent officials. A Bank in Rhode Island or Massachusetts was simply a batch of paper money."

That explains why some early American writers disparage "banking"; it is because they are actually disparaging the printing and distribution of paper money issued by a local government, not the business of banking as we know it.

Next is considered the five general types of banks: a) of deposit, b) of discount, c) of circulation; d) fractional reserve commercial; and e) central banks.

5.3 The Bank of Deposit

A bank of deposit [5.3-1] only performs three basic functions: it receives deposits from the public, it processes and pays checks drawn against those deposits, and it corresponds with other banks to collect checks deposited. This type of bank only transfers deposited money on the order of its depositors to individuals, businesses, or other banks. Its "reserves" consist of the entirety of deposits, always available to be withdrawn by depositors or sent as the depositors may so order. In other words, it does not create money or credit; it only handles incoming and outgoing transfers of the money that has been entrusted to it.

5.4 The Bank of Discount

A bank of discount [5.4-1] (normally a private institution) operates much the same as a bank of deposit, except it primarily lends to businesses for short terms, and only upon good collateral. The loans may consist of discounting promissory notes and acceptances, but again only on secured collateral. Discounting refers to the practice of charging interest on a promissory note indirectly. For example, if a merchant borrows $10,000 for six months at 6% and gives the bank a promissory note or bill of exchange, the bank deducts 3% and provides only $9,700 to the borrower. Such an institution can only lend what has been received either as capital by the owners or by deposits (if it accepts them). It is the first instance of a 'commercial bank' catering specifically to businesses. Normally the collateral consists of mortgages, inventory, or other securities. It does not create money or credit, and is not part of any overall reserve system. A small amount of cash may be kept on hand to satisfy withdrawals by its depositors (if any). A bank of discount cannot pay on demand to a depositor what it has lent to someone else with the same money; if it is in this condition, it has no choice but to call in a loan and pay the depositor. Therefore it is important that the management of this type of bank monitor the demands for withdrawals compared to what is loaned out.

5.5 The Bank of Circulation (Commercial)

A bank of circulation performs all of the functions of the first two types of banks: a) accepts deposits, b) keeps cash accounts, c) maintains checking accounts for the convenience of its depositors; d) makes loans to individuals and businesses; and e) performs recordkeeping, clearing and balancing checks. "Demand deposits" were originally defined as checking accounts upon which checks could be written; in recent times, demand deposits also include savings deposits. But this type of bank also did something that the others cannot: it issued bank notes on its own credit over and above what had been deposited by its customers. It lent "money" in the form of these notes. The bank is actually lending its own credit on the grounds that a bank's credit is more widely known, and thus more widely accepted, than the credit of an individual, or that of a promissory note from a business [5.5-1]. To do so, it gave its notes in return for the promissory notes and acceptances. Or, in what amounts to the same thing, and is more common in modern times, the bank creates demand deposits in lieu of physical bank notes. The borrower can then draw against the demand deposits by writing checks or transfers when making payments to others. The loan thus takes the form of bank notes and/or demand deposits against a checking account, and constitutes the creation of money. At the same time, this type of bank keeps an amount of cash on hand in coin or bullion or other money, calculated to ensure that the bank will be able to pay out if people demand their deposits or cash a check. These "demand deposits" and bank notes, although established solely on the bank's credit, are counted as part of the money supply. The reason is straightforward: they are money because they are accepted as money, the same as a check is accepted when drawn against an account. A check against a demand deposit has three of the four attributes of money per sections 1.2 and 2.1 (excluding 'store of value'). The distinction between a check (which is not money itself, only a substitute) and money is that the checks do not pass hand-to-hand; they are first "cashed" into notes, coin, or transferred to other deposit accounts. In the case of a check, it is the deposit that constitutes the actual money, not the physical check. But with bank notes, the note itself is considered money because no intermediate transaction is required before it can be used to buy on the market. By what means does a bank have the credit that allows it to issue notes upon its name? It can do so because it has established reputation of paying its obligations; in other words, it has over time built up a reservoir of trust such that the public has confidence in the quality of the notes, and thus has confidence that they will be accepted or redeemed upon presentation. But these types of banks do not issue bank notes or demand deposits on a whim: they must also seek some form of collateral or security when making a loan or creating deposits. If money can be created in this way, it can also be destroyed: the money supply can be reduced when notes are redeemed for coin and the bank declines to re-issue them. Likewise, a loan may be paid off and the associated checking account is closed without issuing a replacement loan. The important distinction between this type of bank and a formal reserve system is that in this case each banker decides what amount of cash on hand is suitable for its local business. In this manner these banks could respond to the needs for money by local businessmen, using its credit over and above deposits as a means of facilitating payments.

Because a bank of circulation can both create and destroy money, it injects some risk into the economy [5.5-2]. First, the issue of bank notes gives the illusion that capital can be created out of thin air. But the only thing created is the credit-money; which as shown in section 1.5, is very different than capital. Second, the creation of credit money gives the illusion that money can be made plentiful whenever it is desired, and that the value thereof can be made permanent and stable. It can be made plentiful, but it cannot be made stable in value because, as shown in sections 1.9 and 2.4, an expansion of the money supply tends to increase prices, since money has in fact become more common and of less value per unit. Third, credit money promotes the notion that an increase in the circulation of money equals an increase in wealth. It does no such thing: wealth comes from capital, and money at most can be the instrument of procuring capital. Fourth, if the bank notes are redeemable in coin, the money supply can be increased above the amount of metal upon which it is based. The risk is that an over-issue of the notes or demand deposits, or perception thereof, will lead to distrust of the bank, and possibly of the banking system in general. Fifth, is the inconvenience and suspicion that every borrower must have as to whether a loan obtained this year will be obtainable or renewable next year, owing to bankers' decisions whether to expand or contract the money supply. This is a risk imputed directly to all the businesses, based on assessments by one business. If the money supply is unstable, then business will be unstable to the same extent. An enterprise left unfinished because completion cannot be financed represents a total loss of the amount so far invested. Sixth is the obvious probability that the bank notes will be forged or counterfeited. Seventh is the temptation to use bank notes as a means of speculating and manipulating prices on the stock exchanges. After all, if money can be obtained easily, why not try to make more of it through gambling?

5.6   Fractional Reserve Commercial Banks

The next type is the commercial bank regulated such that they maintain a required "reserve". The "reserve" is some fraction of the total of notes and demand deposits held by the bank to meet immediate demands for withdrawal or redemption (which may be 100%). When the money is convertible on demand, the reserve takes the form of coin. The use of credit money with coin held in reserve against demands makes the coin more efficient: less of it is required to support a given volume of transactions. When coin is not used as reserve, the reserve is in the form of more credit money. In either case, the bank maintains enough on hand to pay depositors should they choose to withdraw their deposits. The total amount of money in the economy (including notes and demand deposits) is a multiple of the "reserve", and the fraction of total circulating money to the amount held in reserve is called the "reserve ratio". It is easy to see then that lowering the reserve ratio or acquiring more reserves permits an expansion of the money supply; and a loss of reserves or an increase in the reserve ratio decreases the money supply. The main benefit claimed for a credit money system based on reserves is that the money supply can fluctuate based on the demands from the business community. But there are some associated risks and advantages [5.6-1]: use of paper for hand-to-hand money is far more convenient than coin; paper is cheaper to issue; and the reserves can be altered rapidly to respond to changes in the demand for money. As always, the banker has to evaluate how much he must keep in reserve in order to pay any immediate demands. The reserve ratio has been prescribed by law in the U. S. at either the State or federal level since the 1850's. (It was abolished at the federal level in 2020.)

The question in the early 1800's, when banking theory was in its infancy, was how to properly regulate the amount of money, which is to say, how to indirectly manage the money supply by managing the reserve ratio directly. Two approaches to this problem were more or less formalized by the British economists and banking proponents, called the "Banking School" and the "Currency School". The British took the lead in outlining the issues because Britain was at the time the leading financial center of the world, a role it held until the 1920's. Before discussing their differences, it is helpful first to notice what both schools agreed upon. Keep in mind that these theories were developed when the money of the day was a combination of coin and paper bank notes convertible into coin on demand.

Walker [5.6-2] summarized the unified position of both schools. Both agreed that a coin system was the best that could be had if there was sufficient coin available. But, in the interest of convenience, a convertible paper system with coin in reserve was acceptable, with the caveat that the total amount of coin plus paper in circulation should not exceed the total amount of coin and bullion held throughout the economy, including the reserves in the banking system. In other words, the money supply was to be determined by the total amount of metal, but some of it could be in the form of paper so long as it was fully redeemable on demand. The second caveat was that if the total amount of money is to fluctuate, it should do so only on the basis of how the metals fluctuated. They agreed on the objectives, but disagreed on the likelihood and mechanism by which regulation of the banks would lead to a deviation from this baseline.

The Banking School claimed [5.6-3] that, so long as the paper was convertible into coin on demand with no delay or restriction, the issue of paper credit money would regulate itself, even in the presence of multiple banks issuing competing paper notes. Their assumption was that each bank, receiving the notes of another, would immediately return them for payment in coin. If so, then the amount of paper plus coin could never exceed the amount of coin alone, and the entire banking system was self-regulating with regard to the total amount of money in existence in the country. The total volume was indirectly suppressed to conform to the total amount of metal because an over-issue was returned immediately for payment, or the bearer of the notes could demand the coin. Since it is self-regulating, it could not lead to depreciation of its value, and the consequent increase in prices. The Banking School idea was later modified by emphasizing "credit quality". The claim was that depreciation was not caused by the volume of currency per se, but rather by using currency to invest in the wrong things. In this view, credit money expansion did not cause depreciation or an increase in prices so long as the investments were made entirely in short-term self-liquidating assets upon solid collateral. The problem, as Rothbard pointed out [5.6-4], is that the additional currency still spreads through the economy and tends to increase prices. The Banking School did recognize correctly that deposit balances were credit money, the same as circulating bank notes; as Hayek [5.6-5] puts it, was the only worthwhile contribution made by the Banking School.

The American Currency School [5.6-6] as advocated by Raguet and others had already concluded that deposits constituted money. But the Currency School [5.6-7] rejected the Banking School's claim that paper currency was self-regulating. This group of economists recognized (correctly) that paper always tends to be issued in greater amount than justified. There were three reasons put forward to show it. First, there is no compelling reason to assume that banks will limit their issues, since they obtain a profit by doing so (i.e., extending loans at interest). Second, experience shows that not every note, in the course of passing hand-to-hand, is eventually returned for payment in coin. This is especially true if the note travels far from the issuing bank; it simply becomes an additional amount of currency in circulation, which, as described before, will tend to depreciate its value. Third, a large number of issuing banks, all in competition with each other for business, will issue notes without knowing or caring what the other banks are doing. Usually the banks will create more money than is required.

History has shown that the Currency School, with the added insight from the Americans, was more accurate than the Banking School: a) that there is a natural tendency to over-issue paper; b) the over-issue of notes must be controlled directly; and c) that deposits created by banks are credit money, and must be subject to the same restrictions.

The use of demand deposits and checks started in the mid-1800's, but most transfers between businesses and individuals were made using bank notes of various types. Since the external notes served as a brake on the expansion of demand deposits, the supply of money per se was limited to the amount of notes the banks could safely issue. Demand deposits and payment by checks came into widespread use after World War I. It had always been commonly accepted that bank notes were money since they were (supposedly) redeemable on demand in coin. Technically, checks are not money, but because they are received in payment, and "redemption" occurs by simple deposit into one's own account or by cashing it at the bank, checks came to be received as money substitutes. Further, since the check is merely a claim against a demand deposit, and the demand deposit is the bank's credit, checks against demand deposits and bank notes are both credit-money, and there is no practical difference between a check and a bank note as far as transfers are concerned. Fairchild et al [5.6-8] explained this similarity in the context of a convertible bank note: a) a deposit in a bank is a right to receive money from the bank; b) deposits and the banks' circulating notes are two different forms of bank credit; and c) both are payable on demand (except for certain time deposits requiring notice of withdrawal).

The U. S. is now on a fiat money system, and the bank notes are called 'Federal Reserve Notes', which are technically liabilities of the Federal Reserve central bank (but in truth are liabilities of the taxpayers). The principle as stated by Fairchild is the same, except there is no payment on demand in "money", which, when Fairchild wrote, was coin. "Payment on demand" now is merely an exchange of one Federal Reserve Note for another, or receipt of Federal Reserve Notes when "cashing" a check.

A commercial bank under a formal reserve system can obtain the necessary reserves in a variety of ways. First, it can use its own capital as the reserve. Second, it can use its capital to procure coin or bullion and hold it as reserves. Third, if it operates within a central bank system, it can obtain reserves by issuing a promissory note, which is credited as a deposit at the central bank. The regulations of the central bank determine what underlying assets can back the promissory note thus deposited for use as reserves. Fourth, it can sell its loans to other banks (called re-discounting); the proceeds from which are used to maintain the reserve account. Last, it can sell any other assets or investments that it holds. In any case, reserves are held either as cash in the vault or as deposits in another bank, or at the central bank.

It is important to keep in mind that the total money supply under a formal fractional reserve system must be evaluated only in the context of the banking system as a whole [5.6-9, 5.6-10]. The activities of a single bank, issuing its own notes, and holding reserves it thinks appropriate, is a totally different case as discussed above. A formal reserve system causes fluctuations in the money supply through the process of issuing credit against new deposits. Consider first the situation of a single commercial bank; call it Bank #1, within the system. Suppose this Bank #1 has existing demand deposits outstanding of $1,000,000, and that the reserve ratio is 25%. It thus has $250,000 in primary reserves backing the $1,000,000 in demand deposit liabilities. Then one of its existing customers, having a demand deposit account at the bank, makes a $10,000 cash deposit. The additional $10,000 has now changed the banks' primary reserve position. If Bank #1 adds the $10,000 to its reserves, its primary reserve ratio is $260,000 to back the existing $1,000,000 in deposits, equal to 26%. But a bank doesn't make any money by holding reserves; it only makes money by lending or investing. At the opposite end, if it lends out the entire $10,000, its primary reserves are now below the required ratio: $250,000 against $1,010,000, which is 24.75%. It doesn't make sense to do the first action, and it cannot legally do the second. Bank #1 thus could use the $10,000 deposit to extend credit in the form of another demand deposit issued to either a new borrower or as an addition to an existing customers' account to the amount of $7,500, and hold the other $2,500 as a primary reserve against it. The $7,500 is called "excess primary reserves": it is the amount of additional money available to the banker after allocating the correct amount from the deposit to maintain the reserve ratio. In this case Bank #1 would receive a promissory note or collateral pledge from the new borrower and credit his demand deposit account. The position is now $252,500 in primary reserves as backing for $1,007,500 in total demand deposits, thus it maintains the 25% reserve ratio (actually slightly greater).

That is what our individual banker in Bank #1 could do, but not necessarily what he will do. If the depositor immediately writes a check for the $10,000 to local Merchant #1, and Merchant #1 happens to also have an account at Bank #1, he will deposit the check in his account in Bank #1. Then Bank #1 has merely transferred the $10,000 from one account to another; but notice that Bank #1 still has the potential to lend an additional $7,500, since the transfer of deposit from one customer to another does not affect his overall primary reserve to demand deposit ratio. But suppose Merchant #1 is not a customer of Bank #1, but is instead a customer of Bank #2; he deposits the $10,000 in Bank #2, and Bank #2 will collect the full amount from Bank #1. Bank #1 is now back where it started: the original $250,000 in reserves backing the original $1,000,000 in demand deposits, whereas Bank #2 now is able to re-lend 75% of the $10,000 to its customers. Here is the most important insight into this process: although Bank #1 eventually returned back to where it started, it did so in the course of creating deposits, that is, it created money although only temporarily. Bank #2 ended up with the deposits initially placed into Bank #1, and it could then create, based on the initial deposit, additional credit that it can lend out in the form of new demand deposits. This is the creation of purchasing power through the creation of demand deposits.

Next, consider the process of money creation looking at the entire banking system within a nation as a whole. For simplicity in understanding (since the exact distribution of subsequent check deposits come to the same end), allow the entire new demand deposit be placed only in Bank #1. Upon the new $10,000 deposit in Bank #1, it can issue $7,500 in new demand deposits to a borrower after holding $2,500 in reserve. Bank #2 received the $7,500 check from Bank #1's borrower; it could then create new demand deposits of 75% ($5,625) and hold 25% ($1,885) in reserves. The $5,625 from Banks #2's borrower is deposited in Bank #3; it re-lends 75% ($4218.75) and keeps ($1,406.25) in reserve. This process could continue as shown in Figure 5.6-1. The net effect of the money creation, as to its theoretical limit (i.e., when n is large), given by the equation:

$$M = \sum_{k=1}^{n} (1-r)^n = \left(\frac{1}{r}\right) - 1$$

where M is the multiple of new deposits created against a new initial deposit, r is the reserve ratio as a decimal (0.25 ~ 25%), and n designates the sequence of banks from first to last. So, if the reserve ratio is 0.25, then the total amount of new demand deposits that can be created is (1/0.25) - 1 = 3. If the reserve ratio had been 10%, the multiple would be (1/0.1) - 1 = 9.

1	2	3	4	5	6	7	8	9	10
Bank	Primary Deposits	Required Reserves	Possible New Demand Deposits	Cumulative Required Reserves	Bank	Primary Deposits	Required Reserves	Possible New Demand Deposits	Cumulative Required Reserves
#1	10,000.00	2,500.00	7,500.00	2,500.00	#14	237.57	59.39	178.18	9,821.82
#2	7,500.00	1,875.00	5,625.00	4,375.00	#15	178.18	44.54	133.63	9,866.37
#3	5,625.00	1,406.25	4,218.75	5,781.25	#16	133.63	33.41	100.23	9,899.77
#4	4,218.75	1,054.69	3,164.06	6,835.94	#17	100.23	25.06	75.17	9,924.83
#5	3,164.06	791.02	2,373.05	7,626.95	#18	75.17	18.79	56.38	9,943.62
#6	2,373.05	593.26	1,779.79	8,220.21	#19	56.38	14.09	42.28	9,957.72
#7	1,779.79	444.95	1,334.84	8,665.16	#20	42.28	10.57	31.71	9,968.29
#8	1,334.84	333.71	1,001.13	8,998.87	#21	31.71	7.93	23.78	9,976.22
#9	1,001.13	250.28	750.85	9,249.15	#22	23.78	5.95	17.84	9,982.16
#10	750.85	187.71	563.14	9,436.86	#23	17.84	4.46	13.38	9,986.62
#11	563.14	140.78	422.35	9,577.65	#24	13.38	3.34	10.03	9,989.97
#12	422.35	105.59	316.76	9,683.24	#25	10.03	2.51	7.53	9,992.47
#13	316.76	79.19	237.57	9,762.43	& following	30.10	7.53	22.58	10,000.00
Notes:					Totals	40,000.00	10,000.00	30,000.00	
1. Initial New Deposit in Bank #1 = $10,000									
2. Reserve Ratio = 25%									

Figure 5.6-1: The Theoretical Amount of Monetary Expansion Based on a New Deposit

Columns 1 through 5 in Figure 5.6-1 show the process in the first 13 banks, columns 6 through 10 are continuations of columns 1 through 5 for banks 14 through 25. The notation "& following" at the end of column 6 refers to all the succeeding banks after #25. Succeeding possible new demand deposits (columns 4 and 9) filter through the banking system, each of which is the amount that can be created at each bank allowing for the 25% reserve (columns 3 and 8). At lower right is shown the total primary deposits, required reserves, and possible created demand deposits as $40,000, $10,000, and $30,000 respectively. Columns 5 and 10 show the cumulative required reserves; it indicates that the allowable creation of new deposits stops when the cumulative primary reserves equal the amount of the new initial deposit ($10,000). The total new demand deposits comes to $30,000, conforming to the formula above: $10,000 times [1.0/0.25)-1] = $30,000.

What if the banking system was entirely on a 100% metal system, permitting the use of bank notes and checks only to the extent that the banking system has coin to back them up? Then the paper notes, checks, and demand deposits are actually warehouse receipts for the metal, and the "reserve ratio" is 1.0. Referring back to the equation above, it is easy to see that since r = 1, the multiple M by which the expansion of money can occur on a new deposit is zero. The money supply then depends only on the amount of metal available for monetary use that is added to the banking system.

There are three very important caveats to this analysis. First, notice that it is based upon the "entire banking system within a nation as a whole". If Bank #1 receives a new deposit of $10,000 as above as a result of a withdrawal from Bank #2, the growth of the money supply per that deposit occurs as described; but at the same time, there is a corresponding decline in the money supply because Bank #2 experienced a withdrawal. In other words, within the "banking system as a whole", nothing has changed; the overall money supply remains unchanged since a transfer within the banking system does not affect the total money supply. The growth of the money supply occurs only when money is injected from outside the banking system. That is a complicated topic to be discussed in section 5.7.

Second, it is important to keep in mind that Figure 5.6-1 shows only the maximum potential amount of new created money under these conditions. In other words, it assumes that every bank in the chain fully utilizes the amount of new loans (demand deposits) it can create, referred to as "being fully loaned up". It is desirable from a profitability standpoint for the banks to maximize their loans, subject to whether or not there are a sufficient number of good loan opportunities available. Normally the banks are not fully loaned up. Usually not all excess is used to make loans; some is used for investments or working cash.

Figure 5.6-2 shows the situation at a bank upon receiving a new deposit. (In the example described above, the portion allocated to additional working reserves was assumed to be zero for clarity.) After subtracting out the required reserve, the bank now has excess primary reserves, which it can use for three purposes: a) to keep as additional working reserves (F1); b) investments (F2), either in the form of secondary reserves which it anticipates it may lose in the short-term, as well as long-term investments for income; and c) secondary deposits (F3), which it can use to make loans. As an example of how this allocation of excess primary reserves affects the creation of money, suppose each bank decides to retain 2% of the total new deposits in working reserves, and allocates 8% of the total new deposit to overall investments.

Suppose further that the economic conditions are such that the average demand for loans throughout the banking system is only 90% of the new deposit; thus F3 is 0.10. Then the factor d as shown at the bottom of Figure 5.6-2 is d = 1.0 - 0.02 - 0.08 - 0.10 = 0.80. If this situation is typical overall, the banking system as a whole would function per an effective reserve ratio:

$$r_E = 1 - d(1 - r)$$

where d is the decimal accounting for working reserves, investments, and reduction of loan potential as above, and r is the statutory (legal) reserve ratio. The potential for money creation is found using the formula given previously, but substituting r_E for r. It is easy to see that the case where d =1 (no additional working reserves, none for new investments, and 100% potential for new loans) corresponds to the "fully loaned up" (maximum money creation) condition, and $r_E = r$. If the statutory reserve ratio is 0.25, and the factor d is 0.80, then r_E is 0.4, and the money creation multiple M is 1.5 per the previous formula (substituting r_E for r). Figure 5.6-3 illustrates how it filters through the banking system in the same manner as Figure 5.6-1.

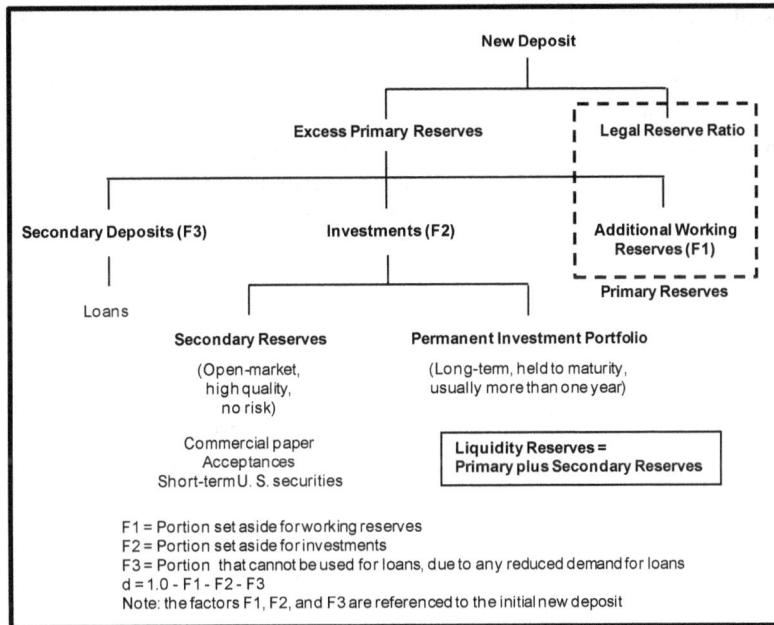

Figure 5.6-2: Segregation of New Deposits

1	2	3	4	5	6	7	8	9	10
Bank	Primary Deposit	Required Reserves	Possible New Demand Deposits	Cumulative Required Reserves	Bank	Primary Deposit	Required Reserves	Possible New Demand Deposits	Cumulative Required Reserves
#1	10,000.00	4,000.00	6,000.00	4,000.00	#14	13.06	5.22	7.84	9,992.16
#2	6,000.00	2,400.00	3,600.00	6,400.00	#15	7.84	3.13	4.70	9,995.30
#3	3,600.00	1,440.00	2,160.00	7,840.00	#16	4.70	1.88	2.82	9,997.18
#4	2,160.00	864.00	1,296.00	8,704.00	#17	2.82	1.13	1.69	9,998.31
#5	1,296.00	518.40	777.60	9,222.40	#18	1.69	0.68	1.02	9,998.98
#6	777.60	311.04	466.56	9,533.44	#19	1.02	0.41	0.61	9,999.39
#7	466.56	186.62	279.94	9,720.06	#20	0.61	0.24	0.37	9,999.63
#8	279.94	111.97	167.96	9,832.04	#21	0.37	0.15	0.22	9,999.78
#9	167.96	67.18	100.78	9,899.22	#22	0.22	0.09	0.13	9,999.87
#10	100.78	40.31	60.47	9,939.53	#23	0.13	0.05	0.08	9,999.92
#11	60.47	24.19	36.28	9,963.72	#24	0.08	0.03	0.05	9,999.95
#12	36.28	14.51	21.77	9,978.23	#25	0.05	0.02	0.03	9,999.97
#13	21.77	8.71	13.06	9,986.94	& following	0.07	0.03	0.04	10,000.00
Notes:					Totals	25,000.00	10,000.00	15,000.00	
1. Initial New Deposit in Bank #1 = $10,000									
2. Reserve Ratio = 25%, proportional demand for loans = 0.8; effective reserve ratio = 0.4									

Figure 5.6-3: The Scaled Amount of Monetary Expansion Based on a New Deposit

Some writers claim or at least imply that a certain reserve ratio always leads to an increase in the money supply by some fixed fraction assuming the banks are able to find adequate lending opportunities to maximize their loan portfolio. But that is clearly not the case in general, as the banks are subject to the opinions of the public, whether optimistic or pessimistic, and to the economic circumstances in general. The multiplier to which an initial new deposit may expand the money supply itself fluctuates, and may be different at the same time in different areas of the country. The best that can be hoped for is an estimate of the average, and it important to remember that the banking system as a whole has to be considered, not the actions of a single bank or sub-group within the system.

These examples show what happens when demand deposits are created based on a new deposit in one of the commercial banks. But a restraint on the creation of demand deposits comes about from a demand for cash (bank notes in either a convertible paper or fiat paper system). The reason is: the notes are liabilities of the bank (and are denominated as such even if inconvertible) because they are backed by the reserves. So, if any of the demand deposits are withdrawn in cash, the subsequent capability for money creation through demand deposits is reduced commensurately. For example, referring back to Figure 5.6-1, consider that Bank #15, receiving a primary deposit of $178.15, experiences a withdrawal of $100. Its reserves are reduced by that amount, and the values are changed: from $178.18 in primary reserves, $44.54 in required reserves, and $133.63 in possible new demand deposits becomes $78.18, $19.45, and $58.63 respectively. Those new values will filter through the system in the same manner as before. Therefore, cash in circulation reduces the money supply that can be created through reserve-backed demand deposits [5.6-11].

Third, suppose there is an initial deposit of $10,000 upon which $2,000 is immediately withdrawn in cash, which leaves only $8,000 for the banks to apply through the reserve system. If the reserve ratio is 25%, then the multiplier for all banks fully loaned up is still 3, but now the total money supply increase is only $24,000 vs. the $30,000 that would have occurred if the entire $10,000 initial deposit remained in the banking system. This process illustrates how money is expanded; and it is contracted in a reserve system by the exact opposite process.

A contraction of the money supply by a reduction in a primary demand deposit is illustrated using Figures 5.6-1 and 5.6-2 by simply placing a minus sign in front of each figure. If Bank #1 experiences a withdrawal of $10,000 from its current $1,000,000 demand deposits, and the withdrawal goes outside the banking system, the money supply cascade applies as before, but all the values are negative.

The profitability of a bank depends on the difference between the interest rate charged to borrowers and interest paid to depositors. Clearly the total revenue depends on the volume of good loan opportunities that are available. Kreps [5.6-12] states that banks must operate on a fractional reserve system in order to be profitable. But there is no reason why banks cannot be profitable if they charge for their services and if the interest received on loans is the rate based on the supply of savings, i.e., the "natural rate". Fees will depend on how much the public and businesses value the services of the banks [5.6-13], same as any other business. Since banking is an essential function in modern economies, the necessary service charges will be paid in one form or another.

5.7 Central Banks

Central banks are designed to perform four essential functions within a national economy. The first is to act as the fiscal agent for the government, handling sales and procurement of government securities, and keeping accounts for the Treasury and other major divisions of the government's administration. Secondly, a central bank typically oversees the check clearinghouse system, although it does not usually handle every check.

The third function of a central bank is to regulate the money supply so as to indirectly influence the general economy, meaning, to adjust the money supply to achieve some desired combination of increasing economic growth, maximize the employment level, and maintain a stable general price level. As discussed in section 1.13, these are not independent factors, and influencing the money supply to achieve all three is probably impossible. A central bank attempts to accomplish these by expanding or contracting the money supply, with four powers granted by the government: a) issue or contract the bank notes; b) create or destroy demand deposits by adjusting the reserve ratios; c) adjust certain rules for credit, such as restricting consumer credit or adjusting the rate on margin loans; and d) adjusting the interest rate it charges to the top-tier commercial banks.

Most economists generally agree that maximizing employment and maintaining price stability are incompatible if the only tool at hand is adjustment of the money supply. The central bank is thus given the difficult task of deciding, based on incomplete, late, or misleading data, how to set interest rates, discount rates, and credit availability in order to adjust the money supply that will hopefully achieve the best trade-off between employment, growth, and price stability.

Central banks perform a great deal of analysis in an effort to tailor their policies in order to maximize growth and employment and minimize depreciation (unless there is some larger benefit to be attained otherwise). The problem is, as described in section 1.9, no central bank can have enough accurate data, nor a model complex enough to be accurate while still being workable, and it certainly cannot predict changes in the public mood. The central bank becomes the single point of failure in the economy once the control and manipulation of money becomes concentrated in one institution. There is no practical way to "control" the rate of depreciation in such a way that the working poor do not suffer; the best that can be done is to stop depreciating the money. In other words, the only way to control depreciation is to stop doing it. What has been done until now is done, and the consequences are what they are as described in section 2.4.

The fourth function of a central bank is to instill public confidence in the banking system in general by holding the stock of monetary reserves and allocating it as necessary to stabilize the banking system. A central bank accomplishes this mostly by "preserving liquidity", that is, making sure adequate cash exists within the banking system to satisfy any unusual demands made by the public. It preserves liquidity by providing either notes or demand deposits to commercial bankers in return for whatever assets the bankers hold that are not liquid enough to be turned into immediate cash to satisfy an immediate need [5.7-1]. When it buys an asset from a commercial bank, it credits that banks' account with the central bank; that account represents primary reserves for the commercial banks, and thus allows it to create either notes or demand deposits to meet the need for cash. It therefore provides ultimate liquidity to the entire banking system, ensuring that the system can always meet its demand liabilities. If the monetary system is based on a convertible paper system or coin system, the central bank can release coin or bullion out of the reserves and provide them to the commercial banking institutions when needed [5.7-2]. Confidence in the banking system is also aided by "deposit insurance"; in fact it has been a more effective measure to instill confidence than the actions of the central bank. Chapters 18 and 19 will show proof of this in the U. S.

Central banks also perform another function, albeit an illegitimate one [5.7-3]. That function consists of bailing bankers out of their bad decisions, making excuses for corruption, and covering up incompetence of other members of the banking system. In other words, if necessary, the central bank will buy whatever assets a commercial bank needs to get rid of, even if they are known to be of questionable quality. In banking parlance, this function of a central bank is described in two common phrases: "the banker's bank", or "the lender of last resort". That is to say, it bypasses the normal market and risk assessment by guaranteeing (or nearly so) that commercial banks continue to operate even if they cannot meet their obligations. A central bank is the ultimate sanctuary for any commercial bank that is at risk of failure due to inadequate oversight or risk assessment.

Central banks operate generally under three assumptions [5.7-4]. First, it is assumed that the interest rate will fall to some extent if the money supply is increased. This is typically a valid assumption, given that an increase in money reduces its unit value, and therefore the cost to obtain it by borrowing is less. Often the central bank lowers the interest rate directly. The second assumption is that investment will be stimulated if the interest rate falls. A third assumption is that the overall income in the economy will generally increase if there is greater investment. So, the implied claim is that a generally rising income level is caused by increased investment, which is caused by lower interest rates, which is caused by an increase in the money supply. But section 1.9 showed that there are unintended consequences to such a policy. First, there is no reason to assume that all the new investments will pay off; some are not needed and represent a loss of capital. Secondly, a lowering of the interest rate below what is called for by the saving rate will tend to distort the pricing within the stages of production, with the risk of a boom followed by a recession. If the expansion is done when a future recession is anticipated, but not yet occurring, the expansion will prolong the prosperity, with the negative consequence that the ultimate recession will be worse. Third, an increase in the money supply tends to increase prices, and in turn will usually increase wages, but at a rate slower than the increase in prices. Thus the profitability of businesses decline as wage rates increase, while the workers' increased pay does not quite keep up with the increase in prices.

There are two problems with this implied claim based on the three assumptions. First, it will be easy to claim an increase in the national gross domestic product (GDP), but it may be an illusion simply because GDP is a linear function of the general price level. Politicians will gladly point to the increasing GDP, conveniently ignoring that it is partly a consequence of the depreciation of the money unit. Likewise, large gains in stock prices can be a result of depreciation, so long as those companies can remain profitable; but it is not necessarily a true indicator of increased value. Secondly, increasing prices will not increase wages if there is an oversupply of labor in the economy. In that case, prices rise but wages are stagnant, and the expected economic growth never materializes; in fact some people, especially the working poor, are worse off.

Central banks are usually chartered as not-for-profit institutions. It is true that they earn profits on the interest charged to commercial banks for borrowing reserves, interest on bonds it holds, and certain fees it can charge associated banks, but all the profits are given to the Treasury. Therefore, it is true that central banks can be considered as a "public service".

Section 1.12 described the origin of the Bank of England and how it contributed to a permanent national debt. To review briefly, King William III needed money to pay for a war against France; he permitted a private corporation to be established for the purpose of buying government bonds payable with interest and issued redeemable bank notes against the security of the bonds. The war was funded with money (coin) paid for the government securities. The bank expanded the issue of notes against the government securities, and these circulated as money, which caused the gold and silver coin to be exported (since the paper could not be traded internationally). Taxes were levied to pay off the bonds, and the taxes were paid with the notes instead of the actual money of that day (coin). The British government continued to borrow, which created the permanent national debt, upon which the holders thereof (the upper class) earned interest, the bank continued to issue more notes, which caused a decrease in coin, and a general increase in the amount of money in circulation. Thus the debt increased, taxes were increased to pay the interest on the debt, while the increase in the money supply increased prices for the working people.

A central bank virtually guarantees the perpetuation of a large national debt, and what is just as bad, a perpetuation of all the fallacies of a large national debt. The first fallacy is that national debt equates to wealth. This claim is made by pointing out that a government bond can be bought and sold readily, are not (usually) subject to default, and the buyer collects interest on it. Those aspects of a government bond are all true, but they are not characteristics of wealth. The bond draws interest, but it had to first be purchased; it did not appear out of thin air. Trading in a government bond is trading on a future debt, the principal of which has to be paid sooner or later. Sales of government debt are nothing more than transfers of credit [5.7-5], which will ultimately result in a drain by taxation. It is an apparent gain to the holder but potentially a partial real loss by depreciation, or an outright loss by repudiation.

The second fallacy is that a national debt promotes unity on the grounds that all the members of the society have benefitted from it and are liable for it. Therefore, the logic goes, a national debt will cause the public to support the government that incurs it because many members of the public are owners of the debt [5.7-6]. A foreign debt holder does so because there is some tangible benefit to him, not out of patriotism. Foreigners usually invest in U. S. debt because it is less risky than investing in his government's bonds. Americans who hold the debt are a minority of voters; the majority of the voters have to pay taxes in order to pay the interest on bonds held by a minority. There is nothing unjust about it; but it is not a particularly unifying principle. Those who hold the debt do not gain all the benefits: they have to pay taxes on their proceeds, which can only attenuate the benefit of holding the debt, especially if the money received has depreciated compared to the money used to buy the bond.

The third fallacy is that a national debt constitutes getting something for nothing because the expenses are transferred to the next generation. Given that the interest on the debt has to be paid, a tax has to be levied that would otherwise not be necessary. But there is no guarantee that the political class will do so; the result will be an increase in both the debt and the interest. Thus in an extreme case, the interest payment burden alone at the national level will justify more debt. The working of the fractional reserve system managed by a central bank causes the currency volume to be supported by the debt. But it is political money: the currency should be supported by capital and savings, not by debt. A large national debt may well benefit the current generation that incurs it, but it is hard to see how it benefits the succeeding generation. If the debt is not used to positive purposes, but only to finance day-to-day expenses, whether public or private, the succeeding generations will have the debt but no benefit from it. The politicians like to call increased debt an "investment", but if it is used for unwise expenses, it is only a burden imposed on the future generations. It is similar in concept to paying $250,000 for a college diploma qualifying one for a job that does not exist. It is not true that large national debts are always necessary in order to have a prosperous economy. The truth is that national debts are sometimes (rarely) necessary, only to fight legitimate wars or to maintain the society through a natural disaster. Accumulation of debt should to be avoided for day-to-day expenses. After an emergency is over, a wise government would seek to pay off the debt as soon as possible.

Central banks impose an inherent risk to a nation's economy because it accommodates the growth of the national debt. The analysis in section 5.6 showed that the expansion of the money supply depended on injection of money into the banking system as a whole. How exactly does "new money" get into the system? It occurs because the central bank is always ready to "buy" government debt, which it "pays for" by creating a demand deposit on its own account. See the trick? Once that is done, the process shown in section 5.6 takes its natural course. Central control of the money supply constitutes the primary means of depreciating the currency, since a central bank is always ready to buy as much government debt as necessary to satisfy the political establishment. This tendency exists throughout the banking system, since commercial banks earn profits on the loans, the total volume of which depends on the actions of the central bank. The government benefits (politically) so long as the banking system absorbs the new debt obligations. A political benefit arises because the government can claim to be doing more to "help people" by spending more on "programs" designed to aid individuals in some fashion. These expenditures are in addition to the usual (beneficial) spending on infrastructure and the military; the political benefit accrues mostly to politicians who are enabled to buy votes with debt. Since both the banking system and the government benefit (albeit for different reasons), there is a consistent tendency to expand the amount of money and credit above what is necessary for economic progress, which is in fact the main mechanism by which the currency depreciates.

Central banks usually have negative effects on the basic morality of a society. First, it does not operate solely on economic objectives; central banks tend to become political operations. A central bank serves the political purposes of politicians because, as a ready customer for government debt, it can create money that the politicians can spend without raising taxes. Politicians find out early in their careers that raising taxes for expenditures causes the public to question the merits of each expense, and indirectly restrains their frivolous spending habits. But with the central bank buying government debt, the politicians no longer are inconvenienced by having to justify to the public both the expense and the taxes to pay for them. This is in addition to the false concept of government debt being counted as an asset [5.7-7]. Thus the economy becomes politicized.

Second, the new injections of money using debt as a reserve is a distortion of the natural rate of saving; it gives the illusion that the public is saving more than it actually is. Since money is a commodity, more of it makes it cheaper, and the injection of additional money generally causes a reduction of the interest rate. But an interest rate that is lower than the natural rate tends to promote riskier or unprofitable ventures [5.7-8], as discussed in section 1.9.

Third, central banks tend to create two classes of economic citizens. Originally the phrase "banker to the bankers" was a shorthand phrase that meant the central bank could provide sufficient liquidity to commercial bankers to cover short-term losses or demands for cash. (That function can be performed without recourse to a central bank.) But in modern times, the "banker's banker" euphemism has come to mean that the central bank bails commercial banks out of long-term problems usually caused by excessive risk-taking, but occasionally caused by inefficiency or corruption. This second motivation makes bankers immune to their bad decisions. Think about that: is the U. S. central bank (the Federal Reserve) going to bail you out and rescue Granny's Sublime Tarts if you get into financial trouble? Of course not: you are not important enough. But under the expanded definition, bankers are now regarded as a special privileged class, not just regular businessmen. That is a distortion of a free economy.

Fourth, a central bank indirectly controls the entire banking system as a cartel [5.7-9] and serves to weaken local governments. The central bank controls the monetary reserves; and in some nations the central bank takes actual possession of all the gold and silver. Usually the central bank imposes the same rules and regulations on all the banks in the nation, ignoring the fact that those banks may serve areas with different requirements. Since central banks are political institutions and are either government-controlled or government owned, they obviously cannot be allowed to fail for political reasons, and the nation is pretty much stuck with any bad decisions made by the central bank. As a political institution, it also has the capability to blame someone else for its failures: the investing public, corporations, foreign banks, speculators; any institution will do so long as the failures of the central bank are camouflaged and papered over.

A central bank with sufficient power can control the amount of credit available to businesses, which means it can indirectly extend too much credit to businesses that are not profitable, or deny credit to those that are. I am not saying that a central bank does this deliberately: it is a consequence of a one-size-fits-all approach to controlling the banking industry. The central bank has enormous control over interest rates; and deviations from the natural rate will cause some distortion in the economy. As a reliable customer for government debt, it allows the existence of programs that the general public would never authorize: a welfare state that denigrates work or the family; it funds unnecessary wars; it permits the politicians to fund initiatives that get the central government involved in local education, local zoning, and local water districts. It can fund foreign aid; it can provide assistance to persons in the country illegally because it is politically convenient to do so. In other words, the central bank, through its function as a buyer of government debt, serves as an enabler for the central government to exert control down to the lowest levels of government. The public thus loses control of its own local government because the central government can use the central bank to fund things the public does not want.

But the level of control is not limited to governmental functions; it can be extended to individuals. The general trend among central banks is to eliminate the existence of cash on the grounds that a) electronic payments are more convenient; and b) represents a money supply cheaper to manage. Both are false: the reason for eliminating cash is because the government does not trust the people to make economic transactions without the governments' knowledge. Cash is not accounted for in the banking system records, other than the fact that it is a liability of the banks. This lack of control and knowledge is what disturbs the government, and the government will eventually impose upon the central bank to eliminate cash. It is tantamount to an implicit control over all consumers, using propaganda and intimidation as necessary. The U. S. government did not trust the people with gold and confiscated it in 1933; it did not trust the people with silver and fully demonetized it in 1965; and soon we will not even be trusted with fiat paper.

Fifth, governments historically have permitted central banks to change the rules whenever it suits either the bank or the government. When central banks were required to pay in metal coin on demand, but found it inconvenient, government typically allowed it to suspend payment. When central banks found it convenient to adopt a fiat currency, governments allowed it [5.7-10]. When central banks desire to decrease reserve ratios and expand the money supply, governments allow it to violate the legal reserve ratios or reduce them by legislation to aid the central bank. When the central banks find it convenient to buy assets not legally permitted in order to bail out commercial banks, governments permit it. Central banks generally can do whatever they can convince the politicians is best for the bankers, so long as it can be justified on some economic grounds, true or not. The central bank, already a protected institution, thus spreads the favoritism around, making all the banks members of a protected class immune to their errors and even their corruption (although outright corruption is rare).

Sixth, central banks enable the government to run continuous deficits since the central bank is always available to buy the new debt. That in turn, owing to the increase in the money supply, leads to depreciation of the money unit. But government deficits do not lead to depreciation if they are financed by the sale of bonds that are paid for with savings or taxes. Deficits lead to depreciation only if financed by the creation of money within the banking system [5.7-11]. Likewise, a budget surplus does not mean that there will be no depreciation of the money. Depreciation of the money is caused by the central bank and the banking system in general, not directly by government deficits. Although the deficits get the attention, and may be a contributing political force, only the monetary authorities can create depreciation of the money unit.

Central banking, with its inflationary tendencies, always leads to economic problems, but free enterprise always gets the blame [5.7-12]. Those who criticize free enterprise are quick to demonize anyone who tries to open a business and make a profit. The progressives are fond of telling people who run small businesses: "it is your fault that we have recessions; it is your fault that prices must be increased; it is your fault that prices go up faster than wages." The Marxists want you to believe that the proprietor of Granny's Sublime Tarts and all the other small outfits are the problem, not the central bank. Whether said "progressives" know better but are deliberately lying, or are merely chanting a bumper sticker remains to be seen.

The only true risk to a central bank is a general loss of confidence in it on the part of the public. The central banks and the banking system cannot go bankrupt because the government will not permit it: it is too big to fail; a failure of the banking system would take the entire economy with it, at least temporarily; and the ruling elite would take the biggest losses (unless they were notified in advance). There are two ways that such a loss of confidence on the part of the public could occur. The first is that the money will become valueless by depreciation. In that case, the public will gradually become aware that the money is depreciating quickly, and will proceed to buy assets to rid itself of any money in its possession. The public will unload the money on whoever will accept it. That will cause a further scarcity of money and will prompt the banking system to create more, which will cause more depreciation until it requires a dump truck full of notes to buy a loaf of bread. Then it stops, mostly because the suppliers of paper and ink will demand to be paid in gold. The only solution then is to re-issue a new type of notes, in which one unit of the new one is traded for a thousand or a billion of the old ones, and then the new notes are kept scarce. That is exactly what Germany did in 1923 when the German mark depreciated to about one-trillionth of its original value [5.7-13], and was replaced by the rentenmark. A second possible cause of a general failure of confidence is if the public realizes that the national debt that supports the money supply must be repudiated because the annual interest is too large to be obtained by taxation.

Back when the metallic standard was in use, the only two things banks had to fear was the demand for redemption in specie and the exportation of specie due to foreign exchange imbalance [5.7-14]. But with a fiat currency and deposit insurance, the banking system in general fears nothing, the reason being, that since the bank credit is underwritten by the purchase of government debt, it is the government (i.e., the taxpayers) who end up with ensuring that the banks do not suffer a loss of their capital. Banks pay a premium to insure their depositors, but it is those same depositors, along with the rest of the public, that insures the banks.

Governments have taken on the task of protecting the public from misconduct by bankers and the banking system in general. Their efforts fall into three categories. First is the use of audits to ensure that the bank is sufficiently capitalized, that it has adequate reserves, requiring regular financial statements of condition, and conducting on-site audits of the books. Usually bank examinations are conducted annually, and most banks are subject to examination by more than one agency. In the U. S., audits are conducted by a State, FDIC, Federal Reserve, or the Comptroller of the Currency, depending on how the bank is chartered. The main goal of such audits is to minimize the likelihood that depositors will lose their money [5.7-15]. The second category of protection is to a) revoke the charters of banks that do not comply with the law; and b) liquidate banks that are insolvent while compensating depositors for any loss via insurance. The third category of protection is to prosecute bank officers who engage in fraud or embezzlement.

5.8 General Observations on Banks and Banking

Some general observations on the banking system as a whole are warranted before proceeding to the details of how they conduct their operations. The banking system performs an essential function by matching savers and borrowers; the job of the banker is to use the savers' money wisely and accurately assess the viability of borrowers' abilities. A banking system makes money more efficient because it can use the accumulated savings of a large number of individuals to finance large scale projects that could not be accomplished otherwise. Those large-scale enterprises in turn capitalize on the division of labor, which makes labor more efficient, and increases production while reducing costs in the long run. A decline in costs and expansion of production tends to increase the standard of living among the general population. Banks also perform some other functions, such as security against loss by maintaining a safe deposit box system for its customers. Banks are beneficial to an economy when they loan out savings and pay interest to depositors, then loan out those savings and collect interest for the book-keeping and other miscellaneous services. Banks thus loan out money representing actual value that has been entrusted to their care based on savings from the labor of the past; which fundamentally different than loaning out on its own credit. Banks also perform a useful function when they lend money on good collateral; good collateral is a result of the labor and profits of the past. If the collateral consists of viable tangible items that can be sold, then the bank incurs little risk by lending against it. The operation of loans and deposits depends on confidence in the banking system; without confidence by the public, an economy will have to do without banks and their great contributions.

Traditional banking came down to a transfer of savings to borrowers who, in the bankers' estimation, could make good use of it. The increased efficiency through division of labor as described above brought with it a new problem. If the money was to build a new factory that would increase production of some article, making them more available to more people, wouldn't a larger amount of money be required to accommodate the additional transactions as more people were able to afford to buy the new production? Consider the example put forth by Adam Smith, when he discusses the production of pins [5.8-1]; in fact extend it to the production of nails to illustrate secondary effects. At one time nails were all made by hand. If an entrepreneur invented a set of machines that would perform each step, and trained workers to operate those machines, the net result would be a very large increase in the production of nails. Nails are more desirable in the building trades since they are easier to install than the older wood-fitting techniques; the availability of nails then has a secondary benefit: it requires less labor to build a house, and therefore the houses can be sold cheaper. So the result is a large supply of nails, each of which is much cheaper than the old hand-made ones, and the increased production of nails made house construction more efficient. The banking question then is: if more nails are to be bought and sold, even though each is cheaper than before, is more money required to make those transactions? Likewise, if single-family houses are cheaper, making them more affordable to more people, wouldn't more money be required to finance those purchases and conduct those transactions? The traditional answer given was 'yes'. This type of logic was used as the justification for banks to issue notes redeemable on demand based on a fraction held in reserve, and later to issue fiat notes: the claim that as an economy expands, a greater quantity of money is required to conduct all the additional transactions. But the real answer is 'no' because money is only an intermediary commodity; any number of transactions can be made with any amount of money: the only thing that will change is the prices. But price is nothing more than the matching of supply and demand, which is done with or without money. It makes no difference how much money is in existence; the amount of money will regulate prices. Suppose the money supply was regulated only by the amount of new gold and silver being injected; and furthermore, the absence of a central bank caused interest rates to fluctuate based on savings and demand for loans. The main difference for the average citizen will be: instead of increasing prices followed by increasing wages, there will be decreasing prices followed by decreasing wages. There is the psychological problem: people are reluctant to see a decrease in the number of dollars in their paycheck, even if the standard of living is increasing. That explains why there is probably no going back to a pure commodity monetary standard.

There is another argument, equally false, regarding the wages of the workers. The logic is: given that the workers formerly made so many nails per day, but now can make a great many more, they deserve much higher wages on the grounds that they are more productive. There are two reasons why this is false. First, it is not the workers alone that caused the greater output of nails; it was the combination of workers and machines. Those machines had to be built with labor and capital, both being the results of past labor. If the worker works the same hours, and makes more nails using the machines, it is true that his production has increased, but not necessarily his skills. (In fact, by the division of labor, the average worker now becomes focused on only a few steps in a now partially automated process, and actually requires less skill.) The fact that his per-day production is higher does not prove that he alone is responsible for it. (If he was the sole reason for increased production, certainly higher wages would be justified.) The second reason is that the worker is also a consumer, and he benefits from the lower prices of the nails he produces, as well as the lower costs of housing. More than that: he benefits to an even greater extent in general because many things are getting cheaper due to better production methods, not just nails. The same principle applies to better farming and lower grocery costs, new energy sources that replaced candles with kerosene and finally with electricity. Once again the general improvement in production in the industrial era led to a reduction in overall per-unit costs, which made each money unit more efficient. It was not the amount of money that mattered: it is the decline in prices due to more efficient production. But the fallacy of more money being required led to the expansion of banking away from simple savings and lending and into the creation of money on the bank's credit and a fractional reserve system.

There is one significant difference between the banking business and any other. When Granny's Sublime Tarts went into operation, you were able to buy from your suppliers on credit, so you got 30 or 60 days after delivery to pay for your flour, display cases, eggs, and the secret magic ingredients that go into the tarts. Those debts are liabilities, but they are not all due on demand. The sugar supplier, once he has extended credit, cannot call up and demand either the money or the sugar be returned to him. Your obligations are known in advance: each bill has to be paid be a certain date, but not before. It is not so in the banking industry: all the liabilities of a bank, which is to say, all the money that has been deposited and is on account, is due and payable by those depositors on demand. If a banker receives $10,000 in deposits, and lends out $8,000 of it to you, he is still liable on demand for the $10,000 from the depositors; meanwhile, although he could call in the loan to you, it is unlikely you could return it in money form, since you've already spent it on items to get Granny's Tarts up and running. That is the banker's dilemma: his assets (being the loan he extended to you in return for your promise to repay) is not "liquid"; whereas he is on the hook to have sufficient liquidity at all times in order to pay back upon demand the $10,000 that the depositors entrusted to him. The banker has to mitigate his risk by keeping a certain amount on hand to satisfy any deposits demanded back from him, with the knowledge that only a small minority will demand it at any given time. The money he holds in his vault to meet immediate demands earns him nothing. Therefore, the most profitable banks are the ones that increase their loans (their liabilities), which they do by creating deposits for their borrowers (like you), since those are the primary source of profits [5.8-2].

5.9   A Bank Balance Sheet

Since a bank is a profit-seeking enterprise like any other business, its financial status may be summarized in a balance sheet, or statement. A balance sheet simply shows the combined liabilities as against the combined assets, and of course, since they must be in balance, assets equal liabilities. From the bankers' standpoint, an asset is anything that either: a) can be used to reduce a liability; or b) anything that can produce earnings. A liability is anything that: a) requires the bank to make a payment; b) represents an extension of the bank's credit; or c) the bank's paid-in capital as a risk to the shareholders. Figure 5.9-1 shows the format of balance sheets for commercial banks (that can create money) under two different banking systems: on the left side is shown the case for "free banking" in which the banks issue their own bank notes; and the right side shows the case where the commercial banks operate under the auspices of a central bank.

Commercial Bank under "Free Banking"		Commercial Bank under Central Bank	
ASSETS	**Note**	**ASSETS**	**Note**
Cash in vault	1	Cash in vault	8
Cash due from other banks		Cash due from other banks	
		Reserve balance at central bank	9
Loans and discounts	2	Loans and discounts	2
Investments		Investments	
Government securities		Government securities	10
Other securities	3	Other securities	3
Other assets	4	Other assets	4
LIABILITIES	**Note**	**LIABILITIES**	**Note**
Demand deposits	5	Demand deposits	5
Time deposits		Time deposits	
Due to other banks		Due to other banks	
Notes in circulation	6		11
Capital	7	Capital	7

1. Consists of metal held for redemption of the bank's notes, if payable on demand. Otherwise it consists of whatever the standard paper money is.
2. Loan is the amount due from a borrower, discount is a borrowers promissory note or collateral.
3. This is the "investment portfoilo" to create earnings after all good loans have been made.
4. Consists of the bank's real estate, furniture, supplies, etc.
5. These are the deposits made by the public or checking accounts created upon receipt of a borrowers promissory note or collateral
6. These are bank notes issued by the bank on it's own credit.
7. Consists of capital stock, unallocated profits, surplus, etc. Undivided profit is the discount on a promissory note: the difference between the amount of a loan and the note.
8. This is a reserve of central bank or government notes for issue to the public if demanded.
9. This is the "primary reserve account" upon which demand deposits can be created.
10. These are the "secondary reserves" held in case of short-term demands for cash.
11. Notes in circulation under a central bank system are usually liabilities of the central bank, not the commercial banks. The issue of notes to a commercial bank is done by reducing the reserve account by the face value of the notes. It is then a transfer of reserves to notes, an asset of a different kind (i.e., becomes cash-in-vault until issued to the public per note 8).

Figure 5.9-1: Balance Sheet of Commercial Banks Under Two Banking Systems [5.9-1 to 5.9-3]

"Cash in vault" means very different things in the two banking systems. In "free banking", the bank was required to hold cash in its vault to pay any of its notes presented. If the notes were legally payable on demand in metal, then the "cash in vault" meant coin or bullion. The degree to which the amount of coin matched the amount of notes issued determined the reserve ratio; if 100%, then the notes were the same as the coin, since they were interchangeable, and the paper was only for convenience. The "cash in vault" was the means of liquidity for this commercial bank; it was the means to pay one category of its liabilities, namely, the "notes in circulation". Under a central bank system, commercial banks do not issue their own notes, which is why there is no "notes in circulation" under the liabilities. For example, the U. S. Federal Reserve Notes are not liabilities of the commercial banks; they are liabilities of the Federal Reserve (the central bank). "Cash in vault" in the U. S. central bank system means a certain amount of central bank or government notes that are held if the banks customers should prefer to have those instead of a demand deposit. This is the most important distinction between the two systems: in free banking, the bank that issues it own notes is liable for their redemption; in a central bank system, the commercial bank is not liable because the "cash" consists of bank notes that are obligations of either the central bank or the government. The commercial bank obtains the central bank notes by paying for them via a reduction in its reserve account at the central bank. However, the ultimate redemption (if any) falls upon the central bank. Commercial banks under the central bank system have an additional asset not present in the free banking system, which is the reserve balance at the central bank. This is a demand deposit owned by the commercial bank at the central bank, and it provides both the liquidity for redemption of the demand deposits and the basis for expansion of demand deposits made when issuing loans. Also, a commercial bank under a central bank system maintains short-term government securities that can be sold on the open market; these are the secondary reserves that back any new demand deposits created whenever a new cash deposit is made at the bank (cf. Figure 5.6-2). "Demand deposits" are the same in both systems: they are actually the loans in the form of checking accounts issued to borrowers; i.e., the bank's credit issued to borrowers. "Loans" under assets represents the amounts due from the borrower as he repays the loan.

References

[5.1-1]   Amasa Walker, *The Science of Wealth*, Boston, MA: Little, Brown & Co., 1867, p. 218

[5.1-2]   William Brough, *The Natural Law of Money*, NY: Greenwood Press, 1969, pp. 67, 68 (originally published by G. P. Putnam's Sons, 1896)

[5.1-3]   op. cit., Brough, pp. 68, 69

[5.2-1]   Francis A. Walker, *Money*, NY: Henry Holt and Company, 1891, p. 317

[5.3-1]   Condy Raguet, *Treatise on Currency and Banking*, Philadelphia, PA: Grigg & Elliot, 1840, pp. 68, 69 (Reprinted by Forgotten Books, FB&c Ltd., London)

[5.4-1]   op. cit., Raguet, pp. 69, 70

[5.5-1]   op. cit., Raguet, pp. 70-72, 90, 99

[5.5-2]   op. cit., Raguet, pp. 76, 77, 158-168

[5.6-1]   op. cit., Francis A. Walker, pp. 412-416

[5.6-2]   op. cit., Francis A. Walker, pp. 419-421

[5.6-3]   op. cit., Francis A. Walker, pp. 422-423, 427, 429

[5.6-7]   op. cit., Francis A. Walker, pp. 429-439

[5.6-4]   Murray N. Rothbard, *America's Great Depression*, Auburn, AL: Ludwig von Mises Institute, 2000, pp. 76-78 (originally published 1963)

[5.6-5]   Friedrich A. von Hayek, "Monetary Theory and the Trade Cycle", in *Prices and Production and Other Works*, Auburn, AL: Ludwig von Mises Institute, 2008, pp. 80, 81 (The essay was first published in 1933)

[5.6-6]   Murray N. Rothbard, *What Has Government Done to Our Money?*, Auburn, AL Ludwig von Miss Institute, 1991, pp. 178, 179 (originally published 1963)

[5.6-8]   Fred Rogers Fairchild, Edgar Stevenson Furniss, Norman Sydney Buck, *Elementary Economics*, NY: The Macmillan Company, 1926, Vol. 1, p. 434

[5.6-9]   op. cit., von Hayek, "Monetary Theory and the Trade Cycle", pp. 85-93

[5.6-10]   op. cit., Kreps, pp. 352-358

[5.6-11]   Murray N. Rothbard, *The Mystery of Banking*, Auburn, AL: Ludwig von Mises Institute, 2008, pp. 125-130 (originally published 1983)

[5.6-12]   op. cit., Kreps, p. 248

[5.6-13]   op. cit., Rothbard, *What Has Government Done to Our Money?*, pp. 54, 55

[5.7-1]   op. cit., Kreps, pp. 295, 296

[5.7-2]   H. Parker Willis, "Federal Reserve Policy in Depression", in Quincy Wright, ed., *Gold and Monetary Stabilization*, Harris Foundation Lectures 1932, NY: Garland Publishing Inc. 1983, p. 80 (The original set of lectures was published in 1932 by the University of Chicago.)

[5.7-3]   op. cit., Willis, "Federal Reserve Policy in Depression", p. 79

[5.7-4]   op. cit., Kreps, pp. 452, 453

[5.7-5]   op. cit., Amasa Walker, pp. 353-355

[5.7-6]   op. cit., Amasa Walker, pp. 356-358

[5.7-7]   Ron Paul, *End the Fed*, NY: Grand Central Publishing, 2009, pp. 29, 30

[5.7-8]   op. cit., Murray N. Rothbard, *America's Great Depression,* pp. 11, 12

[5.7-9]   op. cit., Murray N. Rothbard, *The Mystery of Banking,* p. 132

[5.7-10]   William Cobbett, M. P., *Paper Against Gold*, NY: John Doyle, 1846, p. 145 (Reprinted by Forgotten Books, FB&c Ltd., London)

[5.7-11]   Henry Hazlitt, *What You Should Know About Inflation*, NY: Funk & Wagnalls, 1968, p. 10 (originally published 1960 by D. Von Nostrand)

[5.7-12]   op. cit., Henry Hazlitt, pp. 17, 18

[5.7-13]   op. cit., Murray N. Rothbard, *The Mystery of Banking,* pp. 73, 74

[5.7-14]   op. cit., Amasa Walker, p. 349

[5.7-15]   op. cit., Kreps, p. 150

[5.8-1]   Adam Smith, *An Inquiry Into the Wealth of Nations*, 1776, Book 1, Chapter 1.

[5.8-2]   op. cit., Amasa Walker, pp. 145, 146

[5.9-1]   op. cit., Kreps, pp. 220-222

[5.9-2]   op. cit., Fairchild, et al, Vol. 1, pp. 418-420

[5.9-3]   op. cit., Amasa Walker, pp. 141-147

6

Modern Non-Commercial Banks and Financial Institutions in the U. S.

This chapter provides a brief summary of the various banking institutions in the U. S. that are not part of the commercial banking system. These institutions are segregated from the commercial banks because they do not have the ability to create demand deposits as money. The five categories of institutions reviewed are: a) Savings and Loans; b) Mutual Savings Banks; c) Credit Unions; d) Insurance Companies; and e) Consumer Finance Companies.

6.1   Savings and Loan Institutions

A Savings and Loan (S&L) institution [6.2-1] is a banking type that accepts deposits from individuals and makes loans from those deposits. They can be operated either as mutual institutions (owned by the depositors) or as stock institutions (owned by shareholders), and are chartered either by a State or the federal government. The U. S. government passed a series of laws in the 1930's and 1940's designed to help people obtain financing for residential homes, and these institutions performed that function. Deposits were initially insured by the Federal Savings and Loan Insurance Corporation (FSLIC). They initially offered only savings accounts, but were allowed to offer checking accounts to their customers starting in the 1970's. There were approximately 3,234 such institutions in 1986, 1,645 in 1995 [6.2-2], 936 in 2013, and 645 in 2019. The largest decline in numbers occurred in the late 1980's when many S&Ls went bankrupt owing mostly to bad commercial real estate investments and investments with higher risks than residential real estate. These were undertaken mostly as a means to improve their capital position. The FSLIC did not have the resources to indemnify the depositors, so the industry had to be bailed out by the federal government (i.e., the taxpayers) in 1989 under the Financial Institutions Reform, Recovery and Enforcement Act of 1989.

S&Ls are required to have 65% of their assets in residential mortgages [6.2-3], and are permitted to have up to 20% of assets in commercial ventures. Their deposits are now insured by the Federal Deposit Insurance Corporation (FDIC) since the FSLIC was abolished in the 1989 law. Interest rates on home mortgages are determined by market rates. S&L's are not concerned with "liquidity" since they can only lend what has been deposited with them, allowing for cash on hand for savings and checking account withdrawals. The income from residential mortgage payments provides sufficient liquidity. S&L's have no effect on the overall money supply.

6.2 Mutual Savings Banks

A Mutual Savings Bank is a financial institution that receives deposits and makes loans based on them. They are chartered only by States, and in fact are chartered only in six States in the Northeast. They are owned by their depositors (no stockholders). There were 514 such institutions in 1960 [6.3-1]; there are 374 as of Oct 2020 [6.3-2]:

Connecticut: Liberty Bank (55 locations); Newtown Savings Bank (15 locations); Savings Bank of Danbury (22 locations); Union Savings Bank (26 locations); Fairfield County Bank (17 locations); Connecticut Community Bank (9 locations)

Massachusetts: Middlesex Savings Bank (30 locations)

New York: Ridgewood Savings Bank (35 locations);

Pennsylvania, Virginia, and Ohio: Dollar Bank (70 locations)

New Hampshire and Massachusetts: Eastern Bank (95 locations), but began de-mutualizing in Oct 2020

The main objective of a mutual savings bank is safety of the deposits. They are managed to provide depositors with the highest interest rate available, and offer saving and checking accounts as well as certificates of deposit. Their lending operations are mostly focused on residential mortgages. A mutual institution cannot issue demand deposits, and thus has no effect on the overall money supply.

6.3 Credit Unions

Credit unions are financial institutions designed to serve a specific group or geographical area. For example, the Navy Credit Union serves active duty military and their families; the Suncoast Credit Union serves Tampa, Florida and adjacent counties. A credit union may be established under a federal charter, or by a State. All States except Wyoming, South Dakota, and Delaware permit credit union charters. They operate much like a mutual savings bank in that they are owned entirely by their depositors. The shares thereof are considered near-money, since conversion on demand to money requires a sale [6.4-1]. They receive deposits, maintain savings and checking accounts, and sell certificates of deposit. Their main loan business is for residential mortgages and consumer loans to their depositors. Credit unions operate as tax-exempt not-for-profit institutions. If federally chartered, they are covered under Section 501(c) of the tax code; if State chartered, are covered under Section 501(c)(14)(A) [6.4-2]. Credit unions that have a federal charter are supervised and deposits are insured by the National Credit Union Administration. Those with a State charter are supervised by the State administration, and the laws regarding deposits insurance vary from State to State. Credit unions cannot create demand deposits, and cannot affect the money supply.

6.4 Insurance Companies

Insurance companies are for-profit entities that receive insurance premiums (similar to a deposit) from their clients and use those funds to make investments in order to accumulate assets required to pay out any insurance claims. All insurance companies operate under a State charter. The company manages the assets in order to maintain its position against the liabilities, which is the face value of the insurance policies held by their clients. Certain types of life insurance policies ("whole life") are convertible on demand to their cash value, and thus are near-money. Insurance companies do not create demand deposits, and do not affect the money supply.

6.5 Consumer Finance Companies

Consumer finance companies are for-profit institutions that make loans to businesses and consumers entirely out of its capital. They do not accept deposits nor do they provide savings or checking account services. Some consumer finance companies provide insurance services for their customers, but are not chartered as insurance companies. Generally a consumer finance company charges higher interest rates than a bank, because they tend to serve higher-risk clients. They do not create demand deposits, and have no effect on the money supply.

References

[6.1-1]   Clifton H. Kreps, Jr., *Money, Banking and Monetary Policy*, NY: The Ronald Press Co., 1962, pp. 203, 204

[6.1-2]   https://en.wikipedia.org/wiki/Savings_and_loan_association

[6.1-3]   Office of the Comptroller of the Currency, *Key Differences Among National Bank, Federal Savings Association, and Covered Savings Association Requirements*, 2019, p. 6.

[6.2-1]   op. cit., Kreps, p. 202

[6.2-2]   https://en.wikipedia.org/wiki/Mutual_savings_bank

[6.3-1]   op. cit., Kreps, p. 205

[6.3-2]   https://en.wikipedia.org/wiki/Credit_union

Part 2: A Financial and Economic History of the United States, 1775-2020

Introduction

Part 2 contains a financial and economic history of the United States from 1775 to 2020. It has been divided into fourteen periods. The chapter limits were chosen as the start and end points of changes in the banking system, monetary base, or significant economic events. Part of the reason also lies in making each chapter self-contained and short enough to get a sense of the experiences of each generation. The division by years and categories is as follows:

Chapter 7: The War for Independence and the Articles of Confederation, 1775-1788
Chapter 8: The Debate on Money in the Constitutional Convention
Chapter 9: The Congress/Treasury System, 1789, 1790
Chapter 10: The First Bank of the United States, 1791-1811
Chapter 11: State Banks Only, 1812-1816
Chapter 12: The Second Bank of the United States, 1817-1836
Chapter 13: The State Bank/Sub-Treasury System, 1837-1862
Chapter 14: A Digression on the National Bank System
Chapter 15: The National Bank System Under Fiat Currency 1863-1878
Chapter 16: The National Bank System Under the Gold Standard, 1879-1914
Chapter 17: A Digression on the Federal Reserve System and Commercial Banks
Chapter 18: Federal Reserve Under the Gold Standard, 1915-1932
Chapter 19: Federal Reserve Under the Gold Bullion Standard, Part 1, 1933-1950
Chapter 20: Federal Reserve Under the Gold Bullion Standard, Part 2, 1951-1971
Chapter 21: Federal Reserve, Fiat System, Part 1, 1972-1986
Chapter 22: Federal Reserve, Fiat System, Part 2, 1987-2003
Chapter 23: Federal Reserve, Fiat System, Part 3, 2004-2020

For each of these periods, a series of tables and charts will show: a) U. S. Government revenue; b) U. S. government expenditures; c) the national debt; d) banking system condition statements; e) total money supply; f) types of money in circulation, and g) consumer price index. For the later periods, these will be supplemented by: a) Federal Reserve regulations; b) commercial bank reserve ratios; and c) prime interest and Federal Funds rates.

The U. S. attempted a bimetal system with silver the dominant coinage from 1792 to 1833, with the ratio of silver to gold changed by legislation from time to time. In 1834 the dollar was redefined in gold, and the U. S. had a competing bimetal system that prevailed until 1862. From 1863 to 1878 the U. S. monetary system consisted of fiat money competing with both gold and silver coin although silver was demonetized in 1873. From 1879 to 1932 the U. S. was on a gold standard, although there was brief attempt in the 1890's to return to a bimetal system. In 1933 the U. S. went to a fiat standard domestically with a gold standard for international payments (known as the Bretton Woods System). In 1971, the U. S. abandoned gold altogether, and the U. S. dollar has been entirely fiat since then. It will become evident in the history below that although technically the U. S. was on a bimetal standard from 1792 to 1862, in practice the circulating money consisted mostly of foreign coins and paper.

This history is presented in chronological order, including legislative dates. Under the U. S. Constitution (1789 ff), the actions of Congress must be signed into law by the President, unless the Congress overrides a Presidential veto. In the following history, the phrase "Congress passed" is used as shorthand for the latest relevant date (signed by the President, or override of a veto), in other words, the day it went into effect. In our early history, the President often signed legislation on the same day.

Under the Continental Congress (1775-1781) and Articles of Confederation (1781-1789), only the resolution of Congress was required, as there was no Executive function.

Notes on Calculation of the Money Supply, 1789-1833

The period from 1789 to 1914 may be summarized by a few of its characteristics. First, Congress defined a coinage system in 1792, but in fact the federal government did not coin much money. Foreign coins circulated freely from 1789 to the early 1830's, when it became important for the U. S. politically to get serious about making its own coins. Secondly, the U. S. always operated on a paper money system, whether the paper was issued by the U. S. Treasury, State banks, or the national banks. Since the U. S. was a large country with poor communications, bank notes issued by various banks circulated locally, and when they did travel far from their origin, were not generally redeemed by other banks. Third, there was widespread public opinion, promoted by the banks themselves, that demanding redemption in coin was non-patriotic or evidence of a hillbilly mentality. Walker described the general sentiment [I2-1]:

> "... in the paper money system of the United States during the period of which we speak [to 1836], was a public sentiment always unfavorable, and at times actively hostile, to the presentation of notes for redemption."

But that sentiment was not limited to this period: it continued to exist into the 1930's. Fourth, although the paper money was technically convertible on demand to coin from 1792 to 1862, in fact was loosely enforced, and in some States, the regulatory scheme was so poor that the redemption of paper notes could not be enforced at all. Walker again [I2-2]:

> "So completely without regulation, or even inspection, was the so-called Convertible Paper Money of the United States in this period [to 1836], that it is scarcely possible to recover any of the facts of banking capital, circulation, deposits, or specie reserve. Hardly a statistical fragment survives as an indication to the student of money. It is impossible to tell accurately what was the total circulation of the country at any time. There is only too much reason to suppose that the officers of many banks did not themselves know of the liabilities of the institutions whose affairs they were conducting."

Fifth, the U. S. was initially on a silver standard per the coinage act of 1792, but was converted to a gold standard in 1834. During the Civil War (1861-1865), the U. S. adopted a partial fiat system in which the U. S. Treasury issued 'Greenbacks', which were legal tender. Full convertibility on demand was not restored until 1879, which persisted, at least technically, until 1933.

There is no consistent reliable data for the money supply or condition of the banks between 1789 and 1833. This section will show how I derived estimates, based on the limited available data that is available. The best available data [I2-3] regarding overall number of banks, capital, circulation, and deposits is as shown on Figure I2-1. As seen here, there is little data on loans and deposits until 1806, and even then most of the data applies only to a few Northeastern States. Columns 1 through 8 are from the original, columns 9 through 11 are ratios of some of the values.

								Ratio, Deposits to Circulation	Ratio, Circulation to Capital	Ratio, Loans to Capital
Colonial and State Banks, 1784-1833, per 1918 Comptroller of the Currency, Vol. 2, Table 86, p. 835 (USD)										
1	2	3	4	5	6	7	8	9	10	11
Year	No. of Banks	Capital	Circulation	Deposits	Specie	Loans	Note	Ratio, Deposits to Circulation	Ratio, Circulation to Capital	Ratio, Loans to Capital
1784	3	2,100,000	2,000,000		10,000,000				0.952	
1790	4	2,500,000	2,500,000		9,000,000				1.000	
1791	6	12,900,000	9,000,000		16,000,000				0.698	
1792	16	17,100,000	11,500,000		18,000,000				0.673	
1793	17	18,000,000	11,000,000		20,000,000				0.611	
1794	17	18,000,000	11,600,000		21,500,000				0.644	
1795	23	19,000,000	11,000,000		19,000,000				0.579	
1796	24	19,200,000	10,500,000		16,500,000				0.547	
1797	25	19,200,000	10,000,000		16,000,000				0.521	
1798	25	19,200,000	9,000,000		14,000,000				0.469	
1799	26	21,200,000	10,000,000		17,000,000				0.472	
1800	28	21,300,000	10,500,000		17,500,000				0.493	
1801	31	22,400,000	11,000,000		17,000,000				0.491	
1802	32	22,600,000	10,000,000		16,500,000				0.442	
1803	36	26,000,000	11,000,000		16,000,000				0.423	
1804	59	39,500,000	14,000,000		17,500,000				0.354	
1805	75	40,400,000								
1806	15	5,400,000	1,600,000	2,000,000	900,000	7,000,000	1	1.250	0.296	1.296
1807	16	5,500,000	1,400,000	1,700,000	700,000	6,800,000	1	1.214	0.255	1.236
1808	16	5,900,000	1,000,000	2,500,000	1,000,000	7,400,000	1	2.500	0.169	1.254
1809	29	7,200,000	1,700,000	2,700,000	1,200,000	9,700,000	2	1.588	0.236	1.347
1810	28	6,600,000	2,500,000	2,900,000	1,600,000	11,100,000	2	1.160	0.379	1.682
1811	88	42,600,000	22,700,000		9,600,000				0.533	
1812	29	7,900,000	2,600,000	5,300,000	4,000,000	12,800,000	2	2.038	0.329	1.620
1813		65,000,000	66,000,000		28,000,000	117,000,000			1.015	1.800
1814		80,300,000								
1815	208	82,200,000	45,500,000		17,000,000	150,000,000			0.554	1.825
1816	246	89,800,000	68,000,000		19,000,000				0.757	
1817		90,600,000								
1818	27	9,700,000	2,600,000	2,900,000	1,100,000	12,500,000	1	1.115	0.268	1.289
1819		72,300,000	35,700,000	11,100,000	9,800,000	73,000,000		0.311	0.494	1.010
1820	307	102,100,000	40,600,000	31,200,000	16,700,000			0.768	0.398	
1821	28	9,800,000	3,000,000	5,400,000	3,000,000	13,000,000	1	1.800	0.306	1.327
1822	33	10,800,000	3,100,000	3,200,000	900,000	14,500,000	1	1.032	0.287	1.343
1823	34	11,600,000	3,100,000	3,100,000	1,000,000	15,600,000	1	1.000	0.267	1.345
1824	37	12,800,000	3,800,000	5,200,000	1,900,000	17,400,000	1	1.368	0.297	1.359
1825	41	14,500,000	4,000,000	2,700,000	1,000,000	21,900,000	1	0.675	0.276	1.510
1826	55	16,600,000	4,500,000	2,600,000	1,300,000	23,600,000	1	0.578	0.271	1.422
1827	60	18,200,000	4,900,000	2,900,000	1,400,000	24,200,000	1	0.592	0.269	1.330
1828	108	25,400,000	5,600,000	3,000,000	1,400,000	34,500,000	2	0.536	0.220	1.358
1829	329	110,100,000	48,200,000	40,700,000	14,900,000			0.844	0.438	
1830	329	110,100,000	48,400,000	39,500,000	14,500,000	159,800,000		0.816	0.440	1.451
1831	91	23,400,000	8,800,000	4,600,000	1,300,000	38,900,000	1	0.523	0.376	1.662
1832	172	35,500,000	10,200,000	4,700,000	1,600,000	53,200,000	3	0.461	0.287	1.499
1833	175	37,800,000	10,200,000	5,400,000	1,700,000	57,600,000	3	0.529	0.270	1.524

Notes:
1. Massachusetts only.
2. Massachusetts and Rhode Island only.
3. Massachusetts, Rhode Island, and Maine only.

Figure I2-1: Summary of Bank Data [I2-3]

Treasury Secretary Morrill noted [I2-4], regarding bank statements:

"The statements of the Massachusetts banks from 1803 to 1863 are the only ones which are complete as to all principal items, and tables showing their condition for the years named will be found in the appendix. The returns of the banks of the New England States, and those of the State of New York since 1834 are generally reliable."

I take this to mean that the New York banks are reliable after 1834, but the other New England ones are reliable throughout. Referring to his appendix, only data for the Massachusetts banks are provided [I2-5] for this period; the loans, circulation, and deposits of which are as shown on Figure I2-2. The data in his appendix for Rhode Island and New Hampshire does not begin until 1834.

Column 9 of Figure I2-2 shows that the difference in the ratios of deposits to circulation between the reporting State banks and Massachusetts State banks varies within a narrow range except for 1819, 1820, 1828, 1829, and 1830. Overall the fit is not too bad.

The next step is to use these ratios to estimate the total circulation and deposits for all banks from 1791 to 1833. There are two other sets of estimates that must be made: first, an estimate (or guess) as to the ratio of deposits to circulation for 1791 to 1802, and secondly, a scaling method for the first Bank of the United States, since data was provided only for 1809 and 1811 [I2-6]. The first was done using an average of the ratio of deposits to circulation for the Massachusetts banks from 1803 to 1807; the second was done by scaling for population as indicated in Figure I2-3. The notes and deposits of the second Bank of the United States are not shown in Figures I2-3, although it was in operation from 1817 to 1840 because the full data is available and will be shown in its appropriate place in Chapters 12 and 13.

Data Extracted from 1876 Treasury Report, p. 208, regarding Massachusetts banks (USD)							All Banks [1, 2]	
1	2	3	4	5	6	7	8	9
Year	No. of Banks	Capital	Circulation	Specie	Deposits	Ratio, Deposits to Circulation	Ratio, Deposits to Circulation	Normalized Difference in Ratios (%)
1803	7	2,225,262	1,565,189	1,079,928	1,522,271	0.973		
1804	13	5,012,817	1,695,301	977,902	1,122,119	0.662		
1805	16	5,460,000	1,553,824	847,998	1,021,229	0.657		
1806	15	5,485,000	1,613,684	950,394	2,036,490	1.262	1.250	0.952
1807	16	5,560,000	1,481,777	714,783	1,713,968	1.157	1.214	-4.979
1808	16	5,960,000	1,038,042	1,015,843	2,548,717	2.455	2.500	-1.820
1809	16	5,960,000	1,334,948	821,942	2,314,788	1.734	1.588	8.406
1810	16	6,685,000	2,098,491	1,347,722	2,461,877	1.173	1.160	1.122
1811	15	6,685,000	2,355,571	1,513,000	3,385,721	1.437		
1812	15	7,960,000	2,162,558	3,681,696	4,734,526	2.189	2.038	6.891
1813	16	8,895,000	2,186,137	5,780,798	6,903,593	3.158		
1814	16	11,050,000	2,922,611	6,946,542	9,201,718	3.148		
1815	21	11,462,000	2,740,511	3,464,241	4,057,394	1.481		
1816	25	11,475,000	2,134,690	1,260,210	2,133,278	0.999		
1817	25	9,298,050	2,495,260	1,577,453	3,520,793	1.411		
1818	26	9,749,275	2,680,477	1,129,598	2,905,797	1.084	1.115	-2.890
1819	27	10,374,750	2,464,057	1,198,889	2,574,346	1.045	0.311	70.240
1820	28	10,600,000	2,614,734	1,280,852	3,176,003	1.215	0.768	36.733
1821	28	9,800,000	3,010,762	3,048,829	5,448,608	1.810	1.800	0.537
1822	33	10,821,125	3,132,552	946,266	3,235,828	1.033	1.032	0.069
1823	34	11,650,000	3,128,986	1,033,375	3,122,058	0.998	1.000	-0.222
1824	37	12,857,350	3,842,641	1,939,842	5,238,644	1.363	1.368	-0.376
1825	41	14,535,000	4,091,411	1,038,986	2,715,375	0.664	0.675	-1.706
1826	53	16,649,996	4,549,814	1,323,820	2,636,735	0.580	0.578	0.302
1827	60	18,269,750	4,936,442	1,466,261	2,991,883	0.606	0.592	2.350
1828	61	19,337,800	4,884,538	1,144,645	2,063,072	0.422	0.536	-26.836
1829	66	20,420,000	4,747,784	987,210	2,545,233	0.536	0.844	-57.511
1830	63	19,295,000	5,124,090	1,258,444	3,574,947	0.698	0.816	-16.977
1831	70	21,439,800	7,739,317	919,959	4,401,965	0.569	0.523	8.097
1832	83	24,520,200	7,122,850	902,205	2,938,970	0.413	0.461	-11.675
1833	102	28,236,250	7,889,110	922,309	3,716,182	0.471	0.529	-12.389

1. Column 8 is from column 9 of Figure I2-1.
2. Column 9 is the difference in the ratios of deposits to circulation divided by the ratio from Massachusetts banks.

Figure I2-2: Massachusetts Bank Data and Relative Population [I2-5]

The other part of the money supply is metallic money in circulation, less what is held in the Treasury. Each chapter will show the overall money supply, and will use the results of deposits and note circulation shown on Figure I2-3 for all State banks and first bank of the United States. The bank data and other components of the money supply are more readily available for 1834 to 2020, and will be shown in their proper place.

	Scaling of Source Data to Estimate Total State Bank Deposits and Circulation								First Bank of U. S.	
	Circulation				Deposits				Circulation	Deposits
1	2	3	4	5	6	7	8	9	10	11
Year	All State Banks [2]	MA State Banks	All State banks to MA ratio [2,3]	Estimated Circulation, All State Banks [2,4]	All State Banks	Ratio, Deposits to Circulation, MA Banks [1]	Estimated Deposits, All State Banks [2,5,7]	U. S. Population	First Bank of U. S. Circulation [2,6]	First Bank of U. S. Deposits [2,6]
1791	9,000,000			9,000,000		0.942	8,478,766	4,059,956	2,595,306	4,902,244
1792	11,500,000			11,500,000		0.942	10,833,979	4,190,697	2,678,882	5,060,110
1793	11,000,000			11,000,000		0.942	10,362,937	4,321,439	2,762,458	5,217,976
1794	11,600,000			11,600,000		0.942	10,928,188	4,452,181	2,846,034	5,375,841
1795	11,000,000			11,000,000		0.942	10,362,937	4,582,923	2,929,610	5,533,707
1796	10,500,000			10,500,000		0.942	9,891,894	4,713,664	3,013,186	5,691,573
1797	10,000,000			10,000,000		0.942	9,420,851	4,844,406	3,096,762	5,849,439
1798	9,000,000			9,000,000		0.942	8,478,766	4,975,148	3,180,338	6,007,304
1799	10,000,000			10,000,000		0.942	9,420,851	5,105,889	3,263,913	6,165,170
1800	10,500,000			10,500,000		0.942	9,891,894	5,236,631	3,347,489	6,323,036
1801	11,000,000			11,000,000		0.942	10,362,937	5,436,956	3,475,546	6,564,921
1802	10,000,000			10,000,000		0.942	9,420,851	5,637,281	3,603,603	6,806,806
1803	11,000,000	1,565,189	7.028	11,000,000		0.973	10,698,376	5,837,606	3,731,660	7,048,690
1804	14,000,000	1,695,301	8.258	14,000,000		0.662	9,266,594	6,037,931	3,859,716	7,290,575
1805		1,553,824	8.455	13,137,682		0.657	8,634,557	6,238,256	3,987,773	7,532,460
1806		1,613,684	8.652	13,961,608		1.262	17,619,729	6,438,581	4,115,830	7,774,345
1807		1,481,777	8.849	13,112,175		1.157	15,166,822	6,638,906	4,243,887	8,016,230
1808		1,038,042	9.046	9,390,021		2.455	23,055,431	6,839,231	4,371,943	8,258,115
1809		1,334,948	9.243	12,338,712		1.734	21,395,218	7,039,556	4,500,000	8,500,000
1810		2,098,491	9.440	19,809,304		1.173	23,239,590	7,239,881	4,750,000	7,200,000
1811	22,700,000	2,355,571	9.637	22,700,000		1.437	32,627,277	7,479,738	5,037,125	5,900,423
1812		2,162,558	19.913	43,063,017		2.189	*94,278,616*			
1813	66,000,000	2,186,137	30.190	66,000,000		3.158	*208,421,127*			
1814		2,922,611	23.396	68,377,407		3.148	*215,283,394*			
1815	45,500,000	2,740,511	16.603	45,500,000		1.481	67,363,870			
1816	68,000,000	2,134,690	31.855	68,000,000		0.999	67,955,021			
1817		2,495,260	26.066	65,041,269		1.411	*91,772,739*			
1818		2,680,477	20.277	54,352,340		1.084	58,921,180			
1819	35,700,000	2,464,057	14.488	35,700,000	11,100,000	1.045	11,100,000			
1820	40,600,000	2,614,734	15.527	40,600,000	31,200,000	1.215	31,200,000			
1821		3,010,762	14.930	44,951,092		1.810	81,348,469			
1822		3,132,552	14.333	44,898,504		1.033	46,378,747			
1823		3,128,986	13.736	42,978,593		0.998	42,883,432			
1824		3,842,641	13.138	50,486,060		1.363	68,827,272			
1825		4,091,411	12.541	51,310,882		0.664	34,053,847			
1826		4,549,814	11.944	54,342,374		0.580	31,492,812			
1827		4,936,442	11.347	56,011,897		0.606	33,947,738			
1828		4,884,538	10.749	52,505,652		0.422	22,176,701			
1829	48,200,000	4,747,784	10.152	48,200,000	40,700,000	0.536	40,700,000			
1830	61,000,000	5,124,090	11.905	48,400,000	39,500,000	0.698	39,500,000			
1831	77,000,000	7,739,317	9.446	73,105,588		0.569	41,580,961			
1832	91,500,000	7,122,850	9.446	67,282,441		0.413	27,761,511			
1833	91,500,000	7,889,110	9.446	74,520,533		0.471	35,103,055			

1. The ratio of deposits to circulation for 1791 to 1802 is the average of the ratios from the MA banks for 1803 to 1807.
2. Values in **bold** to 1829 are from are from Annual Report of the Comptroller of the Currency, 1918, Vol. 2, p. 835. Data for 1830 to 1833 from Annual Report of the Comptroller of the Currency, 1896, Vol. 1, p. 544 (same as 1918, Vol. 2, p. 31). Items in normal are interpolated or calculated.
3. Items in normal font are linearly interolated from adjacent values in **bold**.
4. Values in column 5 are either copied from column 2 (original data) or are the product of columns 3 and 4.
5. Values in column 8 are the product of columns 5 and 7.
6. Values for Circulation and Deposits of First Bank of U. S. are scaled per U. S. population in 1809. 1810 values are linearly interpolated from 1809 and 1811.
7. Values for 1812, 1813, 1814, and 1817 shown in italics seem to be unreasonably large.

Figure I2-3: Overall Estimates of Circulation and Deposits, 1791 to 1833

Notes on Income Calculations

Beginning in Chapter 10, the consumer price index and income index will be shown for comparison. All of the data is normalized to 1913 for convenience. The goal is to develop family income data for the entire period from 1800 to 2020 because the Bureau of Labor Statistics has published family income data for the years 1953 to 2020 (series MEFAINUSA646N) [I2-7]. The difficulty lies in establishing like estimates for all the years prior to 1953.

Income data from 1800 to 1908 is very scarce, and is based on a scattered set of surveys. The first step is to establish wage data (not family income) per the 1929 Bureau of Labor Statistics data for 1800 to 1840 [I2-8]. It is shown on Figure I2-4, and applies only to wages in Massachusetts. Figures in bold type in columns 1, 2, 3 and 5 show the daily wage data directly from the 1929 document; normal type shows a linear interpolation. Column 4 shows the overall average for the skilled workers and column 6 shows a weighted overall average for skilled (10%) and laborers (90%). Columns 7, 8 and 9 show indices relative to 1838 for skilled, laborers, and the weighted average respectively.

Average Wages and Indices in Massachusetts, 1800-1838									
	Daily Wages (USD)						Indices		
	1	2	3	4	5	6	7	8	9
Year	Carpenters	Masons	Painters	Average, Skilled	Laborers	Overall Average [5]	Index, Skilled	Index, Laborers	Overall Index
1800	**1.23**			1.23	**0.68**	0.74	0.88	0.93	0.92
1801	**1.15**		**0.91**	1.03	**1.05**	1.05	0.73	1.44	1.31
1802	**1.11**		1.05	1.08	**1.11**	1.11	0.77	1.52	1.39
1803	**1.08**	**1.66**	1.19	1.31	**0.42**	0.51	0.93	0.58	0.64
1804	**1.16**	1.64	**1.33**	1.38	**0.89**	0.94	0.98	1.22	1.18
1805	**1.46**	1.62	1.39	1.49	**0.84**	0.91	1.06	1.15	1.14
1806	**1.46**	1.60	1.44	1.50	**1.00**	1.05	1.07	1.37	1.32
1807	**1.50**	1.58	**1.50**	1.53	**1.00**	1.05	1.09	1.37	1.32
1808	**1.00**	1.56	1.50	1.35	**0.85**	0.90	0.96	1.16	1.13
1809	**1.20**	**1.54**	1.50	1.41	**1.23**	1.25	1.01	1.68	1.57
1810	**1.06**	**1.17**	1.50	1.24	**0.84**	0.88	0.89	1.15	1.10
1811	**1.00**	**1.50**	1.50	1.33	**1.00**	1.03	0.95	1.37	1.30
1812	**1.40**	**3.25**	**1.50**	2.05	**1.07**	1.17	1.46	1.47	1.46
1813	**1.26**	**1.67**	1.38	1.44	**1.00**	1.04	1.02	1.37	1.31
1814	**1.04**	1.44	1.25	1.24	**1.00**	1.02	0.89	1.37	1.28
1815	**0.88**	**1.21**	**1.13**	1.07	**0.99**	1.00	0.76	1.36	1.25
1816	**1.00**	1.21	1.13	1.11	**1.07**	1.07	0.79	1.47	1.35
1817	**1.21**	1.22	1.13	1.19	**1.00**	1.02	0.85	1.37	1.28
1818	1.17	1.22	1.13	1.17	0.9	0.93	0.84	1.23	1.16
1819	**1.14**	1.23	1.13	1.17	**0.80**	0.84	0.83	1.10	1.05
1820	**1.00**	1.23	1.13	1.12	**0.68**	0.72	0.80	0.93	0.91
1821	0.94	1.23	1.13	1.10	**0.75**	0.79	0.78	1.03	0.98
1822	**0.89**	1.23	1.13	1.08	**0.74**	0.77	0.77	1.01	0.97
1823	**1.00**	1.24	1.13	1.12	**0.87**	0.90	0.80	1.19	1.12
1824	**0.83**	1.24	1.13	1.07	**0.84**	0.86	0.76	1.15	1.08
1825	**1.16**	**1.25**	**1.13**	1.18	**0.71**	0.76	0.84	0.97	0.95
1826	1.11	1.25	1.13	1.16	**0.79**	0.83	0.83	1.08	1.04
1827	1.06	1.26	1.13	1.15	**1.00**	1.02	0.82	1.37	1.27
1828	1.02	**1.26**	1.13	1.14	**0.69**	0.73	0.81	0.95	0.92
1829	0.97	1.28	1.13	1.13	**0.76**	0.80	0.80	1.04	1.00
1830	0.93	1.29	1.13	1.12	**0.74**	0.78	0.80	1.01	0.98
1831	0.88	1.31	1.13	1.11	0.81	0.84	0.79	1.11	1.05
1832	0.83	1.32	1.13	1.09	0.87	0.89	0.78	1.19	1.12
1833	0.78	1.34	1.13	1.08	**0.94**	0.95	0.77	1.29	1.20
1834	0.74	1.35	1.13	1.07	**1.00**	1.01	0.76	1.37	1.26
1835	**0.69**	**1.37**	**1.13**	1.06	**0.73**	0.76	0.76	1.00	0.96
1836	1.18	1.39	1.13	1.23	0.73	0.78	0.88	1.00	0.98
1837	**1.66**	1.40	1.13	1.40	0.73	0.80	1.00	1.00	1.00
1838	**1.66**	1.42	1.13	1.40	0.73	0.80	1.00	1.00	1.00

1. Some of the data was given in shillings and pence; these were converted to dollars (20 shillings per pound sterling, 12 pence per shilling; pound sterling = $4.44).
2. Values in bold in columns 1 to 5 are from original data; others in columns 1 to 5 are interpolated. In cases where only high and low rates were given the medium is assumed to be the average of the two. Columns 6 to 9 are calculated from columns 1 to 5.
3. All indexes are relative to 1838 (1838 = 100).
4. Source (data in bold): Bureau of Labor Statistics, History of Wages in the United States from Colonial Times to 1928, Bureau of Labor Statistics Bulletin No. 499, Oct 1929, Table 4, (p. 58)
5. The overall average is a weighted average assuming 90% laborers, 10% skilled workers.

Figure I2-4: Average Wage Data for Massachusetts, 1800-1840 [I2-8]

Wage rate data alone doesn't tell the entire story, since it does not account for unemployment due to weather, recessions, illness, the fraction of people in skilled professions vs. laborers vs. agricultural worker (who were sometimes partly paid in-kind). The best to be hoped for is to use per-capita data from later years, and try to estimate backwards using the wage rates as a guide. The next step was to compile per-capita income from 1897 to 1970 per U. S. Census Bureau data [I2-9] as shown on Figure I2-5. The total personal income data for 1897 to 1911 are based on 5-year averages. The Census Bureau reference gives only the total personal income; the population figures are interpolated from the 10-year Census figures. The results shown on Figure I2-5 for the years 1909 to 1921 matches closely with results reported by Mitchell et al [I2-10] and Fairchild at al [I2-11]; the error between Fairchild and Figure I2-5 (assuming Fairchild is correct) for 1909 to 1921 is -3.1% average with a standard deviation of 11.06%. The only years with significant errors (above 10%) were 1912 and 1916 to 1918.

Estimates of Annual Median Per-Capita Income, 1897-1970 [1]						
Year	Total Personal Income ($)	Population	Per-Capita Income ($)	Year	Total Personal Income ($)	Population	Per-Capita Income ($)
1897	14,300,000,000	72,242,447	197.94	1934	54,000,000,000	126,787,648	425.91
1898	14,300,000,000	73,565,688	194.38	1935	60,400,000,000	127,683,895	473.04
1899	14,300,000,000	74,888,928	190.95	1936	68,600,000,000	128,580,141	533.52
1900	14,300,000,000	76,212,168	187.63	1937	74,100,000,000	129,476,388	572.31
1901	14,300,000,000	77,813,804	183.77	1938	68,300,000,000	130,372,635	523.88
1902	20,200,000,000	79,415,441	254.36	1939	72,800,000,000	131,268,882	554.59
1903	20,200,000,000	81,017,077	249.33	1940	78,300,000,000	132,165,129	592.44
1904	20,200,000,000	82,618,713	244.50	1941	96,000,000,000	134,081,196	715.98
1905	20,200,000,000	84,220,350	239.85	1942	122,900,000,000	135,997,263	903.69
1906	20,200,000,000	85,821,986	235.37	1943	151,300,000,000	137,913,330	1,097.07
1907	26,700,000,000	87,423,622	305.41	1944	165,300,000,000	139,829,397	1,182.15
1908	26,700,000,000	89,025,258	299.91	1945	171,100,000,000	141,745,464	1,207.09
1909	26,700,000,000	90,626,895	294.61	1946	178,700,000,000	143,661,530	1,243.90
1910	26,700,000,000	92,228,531	289.50	1947	191,200,000,000	145,577,597	1,313.39
1911	26,700,000,000	93,607,835	285.23	1948	210,200,000,000	147,493,664	1,425.15
1912	33,700,000,000	94,987,138	354.78	1949	207,200,000,000	149,409,731	1,386.79
1913	33,700,000,000	96,366,442	349.71	1950	227,500,000,000	151,325,798	1,503.38
1914	33,700,000,000	97,745,746	344.77	1951	255,600,000,000	154,125,536	1,658.39
1915	33,700,000,000	99,125,050	339.97	1952	272,500,000,000	156,925,273	1,736.50
1916	33,700,000,000	100,504,353	335.31	1953	288,200,000,000	159,725,011	1,804.35
1917	62,500,000,000	101,883,657	613.44	1954	290,100,000,000	162,524,749	1,784.96
1918	62,500,000,000	103,262,961	605.25	1955	310,900,000,000	165,324,487	1,880.54
1919	65,000,000,000	104,642,264	621.16	1956	333,000,000,000	168,124,224	1,980.68
1920	73,400,000,000	106,021,568	692.31	1957	351,100,000,000	170,923,962	2,054.13
1921	62,100,000,000	107,739,677	576.39	1958	361,200,000,000	173,723,700	2,079.16
1922	62,000,000,000	109,457,786	566.43	1959	383,500,000,000	176,523,437	2,172.52
1923	71,500,000,000	111,175,896	643.13	1960	401,000,000,000	179,323,175	2,236.19
1924	73,200,000,000	112,894,005	648.40	1961	416,800,000,000	181,712,050	2,293.74
1925	75,000,000,000	114,612,114	654.38	1962	442,600,000,000	184,100,925	2,404.12
1926	79,500,000,000	116,330,223	683.40	1963	465,500,000,000	186,489,800	2,496.12
1927	79,600,000,000	118,048,332	674.30	1964	497,500,000,000	188,878,675	2,633.97
1928	79,800,000,000	119,766,442	666.30	1965	538,900,000,000	191,267,551	2,817.52
1929	85,900,000,000	121,484,551	707.09	1966	587,200,000,000	193,656,426	3,032.17
1930	77,000,000,000	123,202,660	624.99	1967	629,300,000,000	196,045,301	3,209.97
1931	65,900,000,000	124,098,907	531.03	1968	688,900,000,000	198,434,176	3,471.68
1932	50,200,000,000	124,995,154	401.62	1969	750,900,000,000	200,823,051	3,739.11
1933	47,000,000,000	125,891,401	373.34	1970	808,300,000,000	203,211,926	3,977.62

1. Source: U. S. Bureau of the Census, Historical Statistics of the United States, Colonial Times to 1970, Bicentennial Edition, Part 1, Chapter F, Table F-8 (Sep 1975)

Figure I2-5: Approximate Per-Capita Income Data, 1897-1970 [I2-9]

Comparing the family income data from the MEFAINUSA646N dataset to the per-capita dataset in Figure I2-5 for the years 1953 to 1970, it is easy to see that the median family size for 1953 to 1970 varies between 2.35 in 1953 to 2.48 in 1970. Furthermore, the 1983 Department of Commerce data for 1947 to 1983 [I2-12] shows reasonable agreement with the family results in MEFAINUSA646N for the years 1947 to 1953. If so, then the family sizes must be in the range of about 2.4 for these years.

To establish the family income for years 1897 to 1952, it was assumed that the effective family size for income estimates varied linearly from 2.35 in 1953 to 3.83 in 1800. The rationale is:

a. The Historical Statistics of the United States dataset [I2-13] calls out the following "family sizes": a) 1970, 3.58; b) 1965, 3.70; c) 1960, 3.67; d) 1955, 3.59; e) 1950, 3.54; and f) 1940, 3.76.

b. The same table calls out the following "household" sizes: a) 1970, 3.14; b) 1965, 3.29; c) 1960, 3.33; d) 1955, 3.33; d) 1950, 3.37; e) 1940, 3.67; f) 1930, 4.11; g) 1920, 4.34; h) 1910, 4.54; i) 1900, 4.76; j) 1890, 4.93; k) 1880, 5.04; l) 1870, 5.09; m) 1860, 5.28; n) 1850, 5.55; and o) 1790, 5.79.

c. Taking the ratio of family to household size for 1970 back to 1940, have: a) 1970, 1.14; b) 1965, 1.12; c) 1960, 1.10; d) 1955, 1.08; and e) 1940, 1.02. In other words, the ratio is converging to unity for years prior to 1940, and it is reasonable to assume household size and family size were about the same for years prior to 1940 or so.

d. The comparison of per-capita income and family income from the previous datasets showed that the family size (for income tracking purposes) was about 2.35 in 1953, 66% of the tabulated "family size" as above.

e. Using the 66% factor and the household/family sizes tabulated above, the "family earning size" values for income purposes are: a) 1800, 3.83; b) 1810, 3.80; c) 1820, 3.77; d) 1830, 3.75; e) 1840, 3.72; f) 1850, 3.69; g) 1860, 3.51; h) 1870, 3.38; i) 1880, 3.35; j) 1890, 3.28; k) 1900, 3.17; l) 1910, 3.02; m) 1920, 2.89; n) 1930, 2.73; and o) 1940, 2.56.

Figure I2-6 shows a wage index for manufacturing for the years 1840 to 1919 [I2-14].

Index of Wages per Hour, Manufacturing (1913 = 100)							
Year	Index	Year	Index	Year	Index	Year	Index
1840	33	1860	39	1880	60	1900	73
1841	34	1861	40	1881	62	1901	74
1842	33	1862	41	1882	63	1902	77
1843	33	1863	44	1883	64	1903	80
1844	32	1864	50	1884	64	1904	80
1845	33	1865	58	1885	64	1905	82
1846	34	1866	61	1886	64	1906	85
1847	34	1867	63	1887	67	1907	89
1848	35	1868	65	1888	67	1908	89
1849	36	1869	66	1889	68	1909	90
1850	35	1870	67	1890	69	1910	93
1851	34	1871	68	1891	69	1911	95
1852	35	1872	69	1892	69	1912	97
1853	35	1873	69	1893	69	1913	100
1854	37	1874	67	1894	67	1914	102
1855	38	1875	67	1895	68	1915	103
1856	39	1876	64	1896	69	1916	111
1857	40	1877	61	1897	69	1917	123
1858	39	1878	60	1898	69	1918	162
1859	39	1879	59	1899	70	1919	184

1. Source: United States Department of Labor, Bureau of Labor Statsictics, Handbook of Labor Statistics, 1936 Edition, Department of Labor Bulletin No. 616, Washington, DC: U. S. Government Printing Office, 1936, p. 1057

Figure I2-6: Wage Index for Manufacturing, 1840 to 1919

The approximate median family income for 1800 to 1952 can now be derived based on one tenuous assumption and two corrections. First, it is assumed that the manufacturing index in Figure I2-6 is reasonably accurate for all labor between 1840 and 1918, which admittedly is only weakly supported by column 9 of Figure I2-4. Secondly, since the per-capita income for 1897 to 1918 in Figure I2-5 is based on 5-year averages of overall income, the wage index in Figure I2-6 is used to correct it for those years, assuming the 1913 value is correct. (The result shown on Figure I2-5 for 1913 is 6% lower than the value per Fairchild [I2-11].) Third, the family income is calculated by multiplying the per-capita income by the average earning family size as discussed above. Figures I2-7 and I2-8 show the results for 1800 to 1952.

	Approximate Annual Per-Capita, Family Earning Scale, and Family Income, 1800-1875 (USD)										
Year	Per-Capita Income	Family Scaling	Family Income	Year	Per-Capita Income	Family Scaling	Family Income	Year	Per-Capita Income	Family Scaling	Family Income
1800	106.38	3.83	407.43	1826	119.74	3.76	450.23	1851	118.90	3.67	436.37
1801	151.68	3.83	580.93	1827	146.90	3.76	552.36	1852	122.40	3.65	446.75
1802	160.22	3.82	612.04	1828	106.33	3.75	398.74	1853	122.40	3.64	445.53
1803	73.67	3.82	281.41	1829	115.30	3.75	432.39	1854	129.39	3.62	468.40
1804	135.86	3.82	518.97	1830	112.55	3.75	422.08	1855	132.89	3.60	478.40
1805	130.98	3.82	500.35	1831	121.53	3.75	455.73	1856	136.39	3.58	488.27
1806	151.97	3.81	579.00	1832	129.15	3.74	483.02	1857	139.88	3.56	497.99
1807	152.36	3.81	580.47	1833	138.12	3.74	516.58	1858	136.39	3.54	482.81
1808	130.31	3.81	496.47	1834	145.79	3.74	545.27	1859	136.39	3.53	481.45
1809	180.67	3.80	686.56	1835	110.48	3.73	412.09	1860	136.39	3.51	478.72
1810	127.41	3.80	484.17	1836	112.94	3.73	421.26	1861	139.88	3.50	489.59
1811	149.56	3.80	568.32	1837	115.30	3.73	430.08	1862	143.38	3.48	498.97
1812	169.05	3.79	640.69	1838	115.40	3.73	430.44	1863	153.87	3.47	533.94
1813	151.05	3.79	572.49	1839	115.40	3.72	429.29	1864	174.86	3.46	605.00
1814	148.25	3.79	561.88	1840	115.40	3.72	429.30	1865	202.83	3.44	697.74
1815	144.49	3.79	547.62	1841	118.90	3.72	441.96	1866	213.32	3.43	731.70
1816	155.49	3.78	587.76	1842	115.40	3.71	428.15	1867	220.32	3.42	753.49
1817	147.43	3.78	557.30	1843	115.40	3.71	428.15	1868	227.31	3.41	775.13
1818	134.22	3.78	507.33	1844	111.91	3.71	415.18	1869	230.81	3.39	782.44
1819	121.09	3.77	456.52	1845	115.40	3.70	427.00	1870	234.31	3.38	791.95
1820	104.79	3.77	395.04	1846	118.90	3.70	439.94	1871	237.80	3.37	801.40
1821	113.61	3.77	428.33	1847	118.90	3.70	439.94	1872	241.30	3.77	909.70
1822	112.07	3.77	422.51	1848	122.40	3.70	452.87	1873	241.30	3.37	813.18
1823	129.58	3.76	487.24	1849	125.90	3.69	464.55	1874	234.31	3.37	789.61
1824	124.86	3.76	469.46	1850	122.40	3.69	451.65	1875	234.31	3.36	787.27
1825	109.56	3.76	411.95								

Figure I2-7: Approximate Family Income, 1800-1875

	Approximate Annual Per-Capita, Family Earning Scale, and Family Income, 1876-1952 (USD)										
Year	Per-Capita Income	Family Scaling	Family Income	Year	Per-Capita Income	Family Scaling	Family Income	Year	Per-Capita Income	Family Scaling	Family Income
1876	223.81	3.36	752.02	1901	258.79	3.16	817.76	1927	674.30	2.78	1,874.55
1877	213.32	3.36	716.77	1902	269.28	3.14	845.53	1928	666.30	2.76	1,838.98
1878	209.83	3.36	705.02	1903	279.77	3.13	875.67	1929	707.09	2.75	1,944.49
1879	206.33	3.35	691.20	1904	279.77	3.11	870.08	1930	624.99	2.73	1,706.21
1880	209.83	3.35	702.92	1905	286.76	3.10	888.96	1931	531.03	2.71	1,439.09
1881	216.82	3.34	724.18	1906	297.25	3.08	915.54	1932	401.62	2.70	1,084.36
1882	220.32	3.34	735.86	1907	311.24	3.07	955.51	1933	373.34	2.68	1,000.54
1883	223.81	3.33	745.30	1908	311.24	3.05	949.29	1934	425.91	2.66	1,132.92
1884	223.81	3.32	743.06	1909	314.74	3.04	956.81	1935	473.04	2.65	1,253.56
1885	223.81	3.32	743.06	1910	325.23	3.02	982.20	1936	533.52	2.63	1,403.16
1886	223.81	3.31	740.83	1911	332.22	3.01	1,000.00	1937	572.31	2.61	1,493.72
1887	234.31	3.30	773.21	1912	339.22	2.99	1,014.26	1938	523.88	2.59	1,356.86
1888	234.31	3.29	770.87	1913	349.71	2.98	1,042.14	1939	554.59	2.58	1,430.83
1889	237.80	3.29	782.37	1914	356.70	2.97	1,059.41	1940	592.44	2.56	1,516.65
1890	241.30	3.28	791.46	1915	360.20	2.96	1,066.20	1941	715.98	2.55	1,828.51
1891	241.30	3.27	789.05	1916	388.18	2.94	1,141.24	1942	903.69	2.54	2,292.56
1892	241.30	3.26	786.64	1917	430.14	2.93	1,260.32	1943	1,097.07	2.52	2,764.52
1893	241.30	3.25	784.22	1918	566.53	2.92	1,654.27	1944	1,182.15	2.50	2,958.89
1894	234.31	3.24	759.15	1919	621.16	2.90	1,801.38	1945	1,207.09	2.49	3,000.83
1895	237.80	3.23	768.10	1920	692.31	2.89	2,000.78	1946	1,243.90	2.47	3,071.23
1896	241.30	3.22	776.99	1921	576.39	2.87	1,654.24	1947	1,313.39	2.45	3,220.53
1897	241.30	3.20	772.16	1922	566.43	2.86	1,619.99	1948	1,425.15	2.44	3,470.40
1898	241.30	3.19	769.75	1923	643.13	2.84	1,826.48	1949	1,386.79	2.42	3,353.48
1899	244.80	3.18	778.45	1924	648.40	2.83	1,834.96	1950	1,503.38	2.40	3,609.91
1900	255.29	3.17	809.26	1925	654.38	2.81	1,838.81	1951	1,658.39	2.38	3,954.00
				1926	683.40	2.79	1,906.68	1952	1,736.50	2.37	4,110.77

Figure I2-8: Approximate Family Income, 1876-1952

Figure I2-9 shows the median family income in the United States from 1953 to 2020 per U. S. Census data [I2-7].

Median Family Income In the United States 1953-2020 (USD)									
Year	Family Income	Year	Family Income	Year	Family Income	Year	Family Income	Year	Family Income
1953	4,242	1967	7,933	1981	22,388	1995	40,611	2008	61,521
1954	4,167	1968	8,632	1982	23,433	1996	42,300	2009	60,088
1955	4,418	1969	9,433	1983	24,580	1997	44,568	2010	60,236
1956	4,780	1970	9,867	1984	26,433	1998	46,737	2011	60,974
1957	4,966	1971	10,285	1985	27,735	1999	48,831	2012	62,241
1958	5,087	1972	11,116	1986	29,458	2000	50,732	2013	65,471
1959	5,417	1973	12,051	1987	30,970	2001	51,407	2014	66,632
1960	5,620	1974	12,902	1988	32,191	2002	51,680	2015	70,697
1961	5,735	1975	13,719	1989	34,213	2003	52,680	2016	72,707
1962	5,956	1976	14,958	1990	35,353	2004	54,061	2017	76,135
1963	6,249	1977	16,009	1991	35,939	2005	56,194	2018	78,646
1964	6,569	1978	17,640	1992	36,573	2006	58,407	2019	86,011
1965	6,957	1979	19,587	1993	36,959	2007	61,355	2020	84,008
1966	7,532	1980	21,023	1994	38,782				

Source: U. S. Census Bureau, Median Family Income in the United States, Series MEFAINUSA646N. Available from: https://fred.stlouisfed.org/series/MEFAINUSA646N.

Figure I2-9: Median Family Income, 1953-2020 [I2-7]

Figure I2-10 shows the overall median family income index calculated based on the estimates above (1800-1952) and on the reported data (1953-2020) [I2-7], with 1913 as the reference year (1913 = 100).

Normalized Median Income Index (1913 = 100)													
Year	Index	Year	Index	Year	Index	Year	Index	Year	Index	Year	Index	Year	Index
1800	39.10	1832	46.35	1864	58.05	1896	74.56	1928	176.46	1960	539.28	1992	3,509.43
1801	55.74	1833	49.57	1865	66.95	1897	74.09	1929	186.59	1961	550.31	1993	3,546.47
1802	58.73	1834	52.32	1866	70.21	1898	73.86	1930	163.72	1962	571.52	1994	3,721.40
1803	27.00	1835	39.54	1867	72.30	1899	74.70	1931	138.09	1963	599.63	1995	3,896.90
1804	49.80	1836	40.42	1868	74.38	1900	77.65	1932	104.05	1964	630.34	1996	4,058.97
1805	48.01	1837	41.27	1869	75.08	1901	78.47	1933	96.01	1965	667.57	1997	4,276.60
1806	55.56	1838	41.30	1870	75.99	1902	81.13	1934	108.71	1966	722.75	1998	4,484.73
1807	55.70	1839	41.19	1871	76.90	1903	84.03	1935	120.29	1967	761.23	1999	4,685.67
1808	47.64	1840	41.19	1872	87.29	1904	83.49	1936	134.64	1968	828.30	2000	4,868.08
1809	65.88	1841	42.41	1873	78.03	1905	85.30	1937	143.33	1969	905.16	2001	4,932.85
1810	46.46	1842	41.08	1874	75.77	1906	87.85	1938	130.20	1970	946.81	2002	4,959.05
1811	54.53	1843	41.08	1875	75.54	1907	91.69	1939	137.30	1971	986.92	2003	5,055.00
1812	61.48	1844	39.84	1876	72.16	1908	91.09	1940	145.53	1972	1,066.66	2004	5,187.52
1813	54.93	1845	40.97	1877	68.78	1909	91.81	1941	175.46	1973	1,156.38	2005	5,392.20
1814	53.92	1846	42.21	1878	67.65	1910	94.25	1942	219.99	1974	1,238.03	2006	5,604.55
1815	52.55	1847	42.21	1879	66.33	1911	95.96	1943	265.27	1975	1,316.43	2007	5,887.43
1816	56.40	1848	43.46	1880	67.45	1912	97.33	1944	283.93	1976	1,435.32	2008	5,903.36
1817	53.48	1849	44.58	1881	69.49	1913	100.00	1945	287.95	1977	1,536.17	2009	5,765.85
1818	48.68	1850	43.34	1882	70.61	1914	101.66	1946	294.71	1978	1,692.68	2010	5,780.05
1819	43.81	1851	41.87	1883	71.52	1915	102.31	1947	309.03	1979	1,879.51	2011	5,850.87
1820	37.91	1852	42.87	1884	71.30	1916	109.51	1948	333.01	1980	2,017.30	2012	5,972.45
1821	41.10	1853	42.75	1885	71.30	1917	120.94	1949	321.79	1981	2,148.28	2013	6,282.39
1822	40.54	1854	44.95	1886	71.09	1918	158.74	1950	346.40	1982	2,248.56	2014	6,393.79
1823	46.75	1855	45.91	1887	74.19	1919	172.85	1951	379.41	1983	2,358.62	2015	6,783.86
1824	45.05	1856	46.85	1888	73.97	1920	191.99	1952	394.46	1984	2,536.43	2016	6,976.73
1825	39.53	1857	47.79	1889	75.07	1921	158.74	1953	407.05	1985	2,661.36	2017	7,305.67
1826	43.20	1858	46.33	1890	75.95	1922	155.45	1954	399.85	1986	2,826.69	2018	7,546.62
1827	53.00	1859	46.20	1891	75.71	1923	175.26	1955	423.94	1987	2,971.78	2019	8,253.34
1828	38.26	1860	45.94	1892	75.48	1924	176.08	1956	458.67	1988	3,088.94	2020	8,061.14
1829	41.49	1861	46.98	1893	75.25	1925	176.45	1957	476.52	1989	3,282.97		
1830	40.50	1862	47.88	1894	72.85	1926	182.96	1958	488.13	1990	3,392.36		
1831	43.73	1863	51.23	1895	73.70	1927	179.88	1959	519.80	1991	3,448.59		

Figure I2-10: Median Family Income Index, 1800-2020 (1913 = 100)

It must be admitted that this "median family income" and its index dataset is a workaround to a patch to a kludge based on approximations derived from averages of guesses, intuition, incomplete surveys, and not-fully-justified assumptions. If the data is so scarce and requires so much manipulation, why bother showing it? First, the ratio of income/CPI gives a crude (not definitive) estimate of the relative change in the standard of living. I have normalized this ratio to 1913 and called it the "standard of living index". We must be content with an approximation. For years prior to 1913 it shows approximately the improvement leading up to 1913; after 1913 it shows how much it has improved since then. It is at best a first-order estimate. The second reason for including median income is to see whether median wages keep up with CPI during any given period.

I would encourage you to keep in mind these warnings. First, the "standard of living index" is based on gross median family income before taxes (remember the income tax did not begin until 1916, and did not apply widely to most workers until the early 1950's). Second, CPI refers to retail prices and says nothing about the impact of sales taxes. Third, the median family income for later years is heavily weighted toward urban areas. The median urban worker generally has higher incomes than in rural areas. Fourth, when the standard of living index declines for the urban median wage earner, it declines much faster for the working poor, the reason being that the wages of the working poor decline faster and increase slower than the median wages. Meanwhile, the poor still have to buy the same commodities as the median wage earner in order to live. Fifth, the standard of living index says nothing about the unemployment rate; you will see that generally the standard of living index for the median wage earner declines slightly during recessions, but it does not account for the large number people for whom the standard of living declines greatly due to unemployment during a recession. So, this standard of living index as a simple ratio of income index to price index is useful only as a general rule of thumb and then only for certain narrow conditions; be careful not to make too much of it or apply it too broadly.

It is important to expand upon the third point above, which involves the meaning of a "median". Suppose family income data exists for 1001 families. The median is not actually calculated; it is simply all the data lined up in numerical order, and the value in the center represents the median (i.e., in this case, the 501st entry when put in strictly ascending or descending order). Normally we think of incomes as being smoothly distributed without large discontinuities, but that may not be the case, and the median will not reveal it. For example, if the first 300 incomes are $3,000, the 301st to 500th are $3,500, the 501st is $10,000, and the 502nd to 1001st are all $10,002, the median is $10,000 even though half the family incomes were significantly below it and the half above it were only slightly larger. The risk of medians is that it says nothing about any large gaps in income between the median and the half below it; likewise it says nothing about any gaps between the median and the half above it (say if the 502nd to 1001st were all $1,000,000).

The "standard of living index", crude as it may be, will show that there were two unusual periods in U. S. history in which the standard of living increased dramatically in a short period. The first occurred from 1866 to 1895 (see chapters 15 and 16), and was the result of the intensification of the industrial revolution after the Civil War. The second occurred from 1948 to 1968 (see chapters 19 and 20), it was mostly due to the fact that the U. S. had the only fully intact industrial base after World War II.

Later chapters will show (e.g. Figure 10.3-9) annual rates of changes in CPI and per-capita money supply, and also change rates over a period of years. In all cases, the formula used (with CPI as an example) is:

$$\% \ change = 100[ln(CPI_n) - ln(CPI_1)]/n$$

where CPI_n is the nth year and CPI_1 is the first year. This is the most practical formula for n > 2; but some error arises when n = 2 and the change is large (~ 10%).

The history that follows is devoted to a description of general economic conditions and monetary characteristics under the various banking systems. It is limited to a description of the evolution of the economy and finances as influenced by legislative events, but otherwise mostly ignores politics. It is important however, to keep in mind the politics of the Democratic Party throughout our history. It made four great economic attacks against black people. First was the institution of slavery under the assumption that black people are either too lazy to do for themselves or unfit for normal society, and in any case must be subject to and regulated by overlords (black or white). The second attack came after slavery was abolished, namely, the Jim Crow laws, enacted under the assumption that black people must be prevented from voting in their own interests. But Jim Crow ended up on his deathbed as soon as black people started shooting back; there were plenty of KKK members who still hated black people, but not enough to take a bullet over it. The Civil Rights movement of the 1960's merely pulled the plug on Jim Crow's life-support. The third attack was the Great Society programs, the objective of which was to destroy the black family and make black people wards of the government. The fourth attack is the federal Department of Education, the objective of which is to ensure that the quality of education in the schools attended by black students is worse than other schools. All of these attacks were engineered and enforced by the members of the Democratic Party: they owned the slaves; they staffed the KKK; they enforced the Jim Crow system; they ran the Great Society; and they maintain control of the Department of Education.

Chapter 24 concludes Part 2 with an assessment of the current situation in the U. S.

References

[I2-1]   Francis A. Walker, *Money*, NY: Henry Holt and Company, 1891, p. 482

[I2-2]   Francis A. Walker, *Money*, NY: Henry Holt and Company, 1891, pp. 498, 499

[I2-3]   1918 Annual Report of the Comptroller of the Currency, Vol. 2, 2 Dec 1918, Table 86 (p. 835)

[I2-4]   Lot M. Morrill, Annual Report of the Secretary of the Treasury for the Year 1876, 4 Dec 1876, p. 157

[I2-5]   Lot M. Morrill, Annual Report of the Secretary of the Treasury for the Year 1876, 4 Dec 1876, p. 208

[I2-6]   Lot M. Morrill, Annual Report of the Secretary of the Treasury for the Year 1876, 4 Dec 1876, p. 123

[I2-7]   Family income data estimates for 1953 to 2020 was tabulated by the U.S. Census Bureau, and published as Median Family Income in the United States, all races, data series MEFAINUSA646N. The data shown for this period matches the data in P-60, No. 146 for 1953 to 1983 as referenced below (cf. I2-12). It is available from: https://fred.stlouisfed.org/series/MEFAINUSA646N

[I2-8]   United States Department of Labor, Bureau of Labor Statistics, Bulletin No. 499, *History of Wages in the United States from Colonial Times to 1928*, Oct 1929, Table 4 (p. 58)

[I2-9]   U. S. Bureau of the Census, *Historical Statistics of the United States, Colonial Times to 1970, Bicentennial Edition, Part 1*, Chapter F, Table F-8, Washington DC, Sep 1975

[I2-10]   W. C. Mitchell, W. I. King, F. R. Macauley, O. W. Knauth (Staff of the National Bureau of Economic Research, Incorporated), *Income in the United States, Its Amount and Distribution, 1909-1918*, NY: Harcourt, Brace & Company, 1921, p. 76, Table 14

[I2-11]   Fred Rogers Fairchild, Edgar Stevenson Furniss, Norman Sydney Buck, *Elementary Economics*, NY: The Macmillan Company, 1926, Vol. 2, p. 274. They have the same data as Mitchell et al. for 1909-1918, and cite another of Mitchell's publications for income between 1919 and 1921.

[I2-12]   U. S. Bureau of the Census, *Current Population Reports*, Series P-60, No. 146, *Income of Households, Families, and Persons in the United States: 1983*, Washington DC: U. S. Government Printing Office (1985), Table 14 (p. 37). It matched MEFAINUSA646N exactly for the years 1953 to 1983.

[I2-13]   U. S. Bureau of the Census, *Historical Statistics of the United States, Colonial Times to 1970, Bicentennial Edition, Part 1*, Chapter A, Tables A-288, A-291, and A-304, Washington DC: U. S. Government Printing Office, Sep 1975

[I2-14]   United States Department of Labor, Bureau of Labor Statistics, *Handbook of Labor Statistics, 1936 Edition*, Department of Labor Bulletin No. 616, Washington, DC: U. S. Government Printing Office, 1936, p. 1057

7

The War for Independence and the Articles of Confederation, 1775-1788

7.1 Preview, 1775-1788

This chapter contains a record of the "Continental dollars", issued by Congress to finance the American Revolution. They were denominated in Spanish Milled dollars (nominally 386.7 grains silver), at 6% interest. They were actually bills of credit (bearer bonds) since they bore interest, but they circulated as money. John Adams described them [7.1-1]:

> "The American paper money is nothing but bills of credit, by which the public, the community, promises to pay the possessor a certain sum in a certain limited time. In a country where there is no coin or not enough in circulation, these bills may be emitted to a certain amount, and they will pass at par; but as soon as the quantity exceeds the value of ordinary business of the people, it will depreciate, and continue to fall in its value, in proportion to the augmentation of its quantity."

There was in the 13 colonies in 1775 a total of about $12,000,000 in circulation; about $7,000,000 of it was in the form of paper money previously issued by the colonies and about $5,000,000 in gold and silver (mostly in silver Spanish Milled Dollars). The colonial paper money was denominated in pounds sterling; each pound contained 20 shillings and each shilling contained 12 pence, same as in England, except the definitions of the colonial pounds differed from the English definition. The English pound sterling was at that time 1858.062 grains at 0.925 pure, which is 1718.7018 grains pure. The colonial pound in Georgia and South Carolina was 1547 grains; in Virginia, Massachusetts, Rhode Island, Connecticut, and New Hampshire as 1289 grains; in New Jersey, Delaware, Pennsylvania, and Maryland as 1031.25 grains; in New York and North Carolina as 966 grains of silver. The total of these colonial paper issues came to an equivalent of SM $7,000,000.

The core problem in fighting the war was that Congress had no authority to collect taxes; it could only requisition the States. Only South Carolina came close to meeting its obligations throughout the war. The issuance of Continentals was the only means Congress had to finance the war; but of course it was a paper mill built on a promise of future redemption. It is important to remember that between one-third and one-half of the population was loyal to the Crown, about 20,000 joined the British army, and other loyalists did the best they could to discredit the use of the Continentals as a way to disrupt the patriotic cause [7.1-2].

The amount issued by date is based on Schuckers [7.1-3], the depreciation schedule per Elliot [7.1-4], and the alternate claims of over-issue are per Schuckers [7.1-5] and Gouge [7.1-6], both of whom quote Philadelphia merchant Pelatiah Webster. Webster's original depreciation data only indicates the month, and they are recorded here as at the end of the month. Major events of the Revolution are shown for historical context. A more complete chronology is given elsewhere [7.1-7].

It is important to remember that although Congress issued 'Continentals', each State also issued its own paper money throughout the war until 1783. Jefferson estimated the total amount of paper issued by the States was about $200,000,000 [7.1-8]. The total emissions for the States are shown on 31 Dec for each year, as there are no records of the exact dates of emissions.

The nomenclature SM $1.0 ~ C $1.25 means that one Spanish milled dollar traded for $1.25 in Continentals. It turns out that more was issued than was authorized by Congress, according to both Schuckers and Gouge.

7.2 History, 1775-1788

5 Mar 1770: The Boston Massacre.

16 Dec 1773: The Boston Tea Party.

1 Jun 1774: Port of Boston closed by the British.

6 Aug 1774: The Quartering and Regulating Acts are enforced in Boston.

14 Oct 1774: The First Continental Congress issued a Declaration of Rights opposing various acts of Parliament dating back to 1767.

1 Jan 1775: The population of the States at this time was estimated [7.2-1] as: MA, 352,000; NH: 200,000 (discovered in 1782 to be only 82,000); RI: 58,000; CT: 202,000; NY: 238,000; NJ: 138,000; PA: 341,000; DE: 37,000; MD: 174,000; VA: 300,000; NC: 181,000; SC: 93,000; GA: 27,000; slaves in the Southern States, 500,000; for a total of 2,743,000 It was on this basis that the requisitions were allocated to the States.

1 Feb 1775: The 'Minutemen' was established in Massachusetts, they were people who formed themselves into a militia to defend the colony.

19 Apr 1775: Battles of Lexington and Concord, MA.

10 May 1775: First session of the Second Continental Congress (hereafter called Congress).

17 Jun 1775: Battles of Bunker Hill and Breed's Hill, Boston, MA.

22 Jun 1775: Congress authorized $2,000,000 in Continentals to be issued. They contained the inscription [7.2-2]:

CONTINENTAL CURRENCY

No. _____ Dollars
This Bill entitles the bearer to receive _____ Spanish milled dollars, or the value thereof in gold or silver, according to the resolution of Congress, held at Philadelphia, on the 10th of May, A.D. 1775.

3 Jul 1775: George Washington took command of the Continental Army at Boston.

25 Jul 1775: Congress authorized $1,000,000 in Continentals to be issued; total = $3,000,000.

~15 Aug 1775: Rhode Island is the first to make the Continental legal tender. The other colonies followed suit shortly thereafter [7.2-3]. The long-term consequences were, as the currency depreciated (after 1777), that people began to buy property rather than hold onto the currency. Some wealthy people sold off property at what they believed to be good prices, only to find later that the money they received was worthless. Others ran up large debts, knowing they would be able to pay off the debts easily with a small amount of real money as the Continentals depreciated.

12 Nov 1775: Surrender of Montreal to American General Montgomery.

29 Nov 1775: Congress authorized $3,000,000 in Continentals to be issued; total = $6,000,000.

31 Dec 1775: Battle of Quebec. During 1775, the States had issued paper money [7.2-4]: Massachusetts ($483,500 estimated), Rhode Island ($200,000), Connecticut ($500,000), New York ($112,500),

Pennsylvania ($420,000), Delaware ($80,000), Maryland ($535,111), Virginia ($875,000), and South Carolina ($4,182,365 estimated).

8 Jan 1776: Thomas Paine published 'Common Sense'.

11 Jan 1776: Congress passed a resolution against anyone who refused to accept the Continentals as a legal tender, or accepted them at less than face value [7.2-5]:

> "Whereas, it appears to this Congress that several evil disposed persons, in order to obstruct and defeat the efforts of the United Colonies, in defense of their just rights, have attempted to depreciate the bills of credit emitted by the authority of this Congress. Resolved, therefore, that any person who shall hereafter be so lost to all virtue and regard for his country, as to refuse to receive said bills in payment, or obstruct and discourage the currency or circulation thereof, and shall be duly convicted by the committee of the city, county, or district, or in case of appeal from their decision, by the assembly, convention, council, or committee of safety of the colony where he shall reside, such person shall be deemed, published, and treated as an enemy of his country and precluded from all trade or intercourse with the inhabitants of these Colonies."

17 Feb 1776: Congress authorized $4,000,000 in Continentals to be issued; total = $10,000,000.

27 Feb 1776: Battle of Moore's Creek, NC.

4-17 Mar 1776: Battle of Boston; British evacuate Boston for the remainder of the war.

27 May 1776: Congress authorized $5,000,000 in Continentals to be issued; total = $15,000,000.

5-14 Jun 1776: The Americans retreated from Canada, abandoning any further efforts to bring Canada into the war.

12 Jun 1776: The 'Declaration of the Rights of Man' (George Mason and James Madison) was passed as a resolution in the Virginia Legislature.

28 Jun 1776: Battle of Sullivan's Island, SC.

4 Jul 1776: Declaration of Independence was formally adopted by Congress (having been read and approved 2 Jul 1776).

12 Jul 1776: Congress proposed the Articles of Confederation.

13 Aug 1776: Congress authorized $5,000,000 in Continentals to be issued; total = $20,000,000.

27-29 Aug 1776: Battle of Long Island, NY.

15, 16 Sep 1776: Battle of Manhattan, NY.

3 Oct 1776: Congress established a loan office, seeking a loan of $5,000,000 at 4%, and paying 0.125% commission to those who sold the loan certificates [7.2-6]. The loan certificates were payable to the bearer, and passed as money. They added to the general depreciation of the money.

11-13 Oct 1776: Battle of Valcour Island (Lake Champlain, NY).

28 Oct 1776: Battle of White Plains, NY.

20 Nov 1776: Evacuation of Fort Lee, NY.

28 Nov - 12 Dec 1776: The Continental Army was defeated and retreated through New Jersey to Pennsylvania.

23 Dec 1776: Congress authorized a loan from France for up to £2,000,000; a net loan was subsequently obtained for 935,570 l. (SM $181,500) (Farmers-General of France) [7.2-7]

26-29 Dec 1776: Battle of Trenton, NJ.

28 Dec 1776: Congress authorized $5,000,000 in Continentals to be issued; total = $25,000,000.

31 Dec 1776: During 1776, the States had issued paper money [7.2-8]: Massachusetts ($483,500 est.), Rhode Island ($300,000), Connecticut ($366,300), New York ($637,500), New Jersey ($133,000), Pennsylvania ($227,000), Maryland ($415,111), Virginia ($1,500,000), and South Carolina ($4,182,365 estimated).

3 Jan 1777: Battle of Princeton, NJ.

7 Jan 1777: Battles of Elizabethtown, NJ and Newark, NJ.

14 Jan 1777: Congress imitated a prior resolution adopted in Rhode Island, making the Continentals a legal tender. It also adopted a resolution asking the States to stop issuing State currency in favor of Congress alone. The resolution reads, in part [7.2-9]:

> "Resolved, That all bills of credit, emitted by authority of Congress, ought to pass current in all payments, trade, and dealings, in these states, and be deemed in value equal to the same nominal sums in Spanish milled dollars; and that whoever shall offer, ask, or receive more in the said bills for any gold or silver coins, bullion, or any other species of money whatsoever, than the nominal sum or amount thereof in Spanish milled dollars, or more, in the said bills, for any lands, houses, goods, or commodities whatsoever, than the same could be purchased at of the same person or persons in gold, silver, or any other species of money whatsoever; or shall offer to sell any goods or commodities for gold or silver coins, or any other species of money whatsoever, and refuse to sell the same for the said continental bills; every such a person ought to be deemed an enemy to the liberties of these United States, and to forfeit the value of the money so exchanged, or house, land, or commodity so sold or offered for sale. And it is recommended to the legislatures of the respective states, to enact laws inflicting such forfeitures and other penalties on offenders as aforesaid, as will prevent such pernicious practices."

31 Jan 1777: SM $1.0 ~ C $1.25.

26 Feb 1777: Congress authorized $5,000,000 in Continentals to be issued; total = $30,000,000.

28 Feb 1777: SM $1.0 ~ C $1.50.

31 Mar 1777: SM $1.0 ~ C $2.00.

27 Apr 1777: Battle of Ridgefield, CT.

30 Apr 1777: SM $1.0 ~ C $2.25.

20 May 1777: Congress authorized $5,000,000 in Continentals to be issued; total = $35,000,000.

31 May 1777: SM $1.0 ~ C $2.25.

30 Jun 1777: SM $1.0 ~ C $2.25.

31 Jul 1777: SM $1.0 ~ C $3.00.

4-7 Jul 1777: Battle of Hubbardton, NY.

6 Aug 1777: Battle of Oriskany, NY.

15 Aug 1777: Congress authorized $1,000,000 in Continentals to be issued; total = $36,000,000.

16 Aug 1777: Battle of Bennington, NY.

31 Aug 1777: SM $1.0 ~ C $3.00.

11 Sep 1777: Battle of Brandywine Creek, PA.

19 Sep 1777: First Battle of Freeman's Farm, NY.

30 Sep 1777: SM $1.0 ~ C $3.00.

4 Oct 1777: Battle of Germantown, PA.

7 Oct 1777: Second Battle of Freemen's Farm (commonly known as the Battle of Saratoga). This defeat marked the end of the British attempt to split the colonies in two by controlling the Hudson River.

31 Oct 1777: SM $1.0 ~ C $3.00

7 Nov 1777: Congress authorized $1,000,000 in Continentals to be issued; total = $37,000,000.

22 Nov 1777: Congress urged the states to impose wage and price controls in an effort to support or stabilize the purchasing power of the Continentals. Schuckers [7.2-10] relates:

> "The second of the system of laws for supporting the value, or more properly the purchasing power of the bills [Continentals], were those for the limitation of prices. ... If prices could be kept down, the trouble would be prevented, anybody could see that. Why not limit prices, then? This idea seems to have originated in New England; and Congress, impressed with a belief that limitations would be effective in sustaining

the bills, seized upon the New England idea, and recommended it to the states (November 22nd, 1777) for their immediate adoption, and renewed it in respect of various details during the ensuing two years. Apply the regulations, said Congress in substance, to the prices of labor, to manufactures, internal produce and imported commodities, to the charges of innkeepers and to land and water carriage: limit the number of retailers in the counties, and make them take out licenses to observe laws made for their regulation; let such persons as have no licenses be restrained from purchasing greater quantities of clothing and provisions than are necessary for family use and upon offenders against these laws let such penalties be inflicted as will brand them with indelible infamy!"

But price limits had the opposite effect. Prices increased because of the depreciation as a matter of economics, regardless of the admonitions and threats from Congress [7.2-11].

30 Nov 1777: SM $1.0 ~ C $3.00.

3 Dec 1777: Congress authorized $1,000,000 in Continentals to be issued; total = $38,000,000. Congress also authorized a loan from France for £2,000,000; a net loan was subsequently obtained for SM $3,267,000 (18,000,000 livres) [7.2-12]

19 Dec 1777: Beginning of the winter at Valley Forge.

31 Dec 1777: SM $1.0 ~ C $4.00. During 1777, the States had issued paper money [7.2-13]: Massachusetts ($483,500 estimated), Rhode Island ($15,000), Connecticut ($17,500), Pennsylvania ($532,000), Delaware ($66,500), Virginia ($2,700,000), and South Carolina ($4,182,365 estimated).

8 Jan 1778: Congress authorized $1,000,000 in Continentals to be issued; total = $39,000,000.

22 Jan 1778: Congress authorized $2,000,000 in Continentals to be issued; total = $41,000,000.

31 Jan 1778: SM $1.0 ~ C $4.00.

6 Feb 1778: The Americans negotiated an alliance with France. Louis XVI agreed to loan Congress 18,000,000 l. (SM $3,492,000) to be paid in various installments. France agreed to recognize American independence, and to provide military support. The Americans agreed to conclude peace with Great Britain only if independence was recognized, and if France was a party to the treaty.

16 Feb 1778: Congress authorized $2,000,000 in Continentals to be issued; total = $43,000,000.

28 Feb 1778: France loaned Congress 750,000 l. (SM $145,000) (cf. 6 Feb 1778); SM $1.0 ~ C $5.00.

5 Mar 1778: Congress authorized $2,000,000 in Continentals to be issued; total = $45,000,000.

31 Mar 1778: SM $1.0 ~ C $5.00.

4 Apr 1778: Congress authorized $1,000,000 in Continentals to be issued; total = $46,000,000.

11 Apr 1778: Congress authorized $5,000,000 in Continentals to be issued; total = $51,000,000.

18 Apr 1778: Congress authorized $500,000 in Continentals to be issued; total = $51,500,000.

30 Apr 1778: SM $1.0 ~ C $6.00.

15 May 1778: Congress was unable to pay the army regularly, and when it did was in depreciated money. To compensate, Congress authorized half-pay for seven years to all army officers, and $80 for enlisted men, to be paid at the end of the war [7.2-14].

19 May 1778: France loaned Congress 750,000 l. (SM $145,000) (cf. 6 Feb 1778).

22 May 1778: Congress authorized $5,000,000 in Continentals to be issued; total = $56,500,000.

31 May 1778: SM $1.0 ~ C $5.00.

8 Jun 1778: Congress imposed an export embargo on livestock, corn, wheat, beef, and pork, and asked the States to enforce it until 15 Nov 1778. The purpose was to ensure adequate supplies would be available for the army [7.2-15].

20 Jun 1778: Congress authorized $5,000,000 in Continentals to be issued; total = $61,500,000.

28 Jun 1778: Battle of Monmouth, NJ.

30 Jun 1778: SM $1.0 ~ C $4.00.

4-7 Jul 1778: Massacre at Wyoming Valley, PA by the British and their Indian allies.

9 Jul 1778: Eight States (NH, MA, RI, CT, NY, PA, VA, and SC) ratified the Articles of Confederation.

20 Jul 1778: The American army was in place at White Plains, NY while the British Northern army occupied New York City. The war in the North was a stalemate until the end.

21 Jul 1778: North Carolina ratified the Articles of Confederation.

24 Jul 1778: Georgia ratified the Articles of Confederation

30 Jul 1778: Congress authorized $5,000,000 in Continentals to be issued; total = $66,500,000.

31 Jul 1778: SM $1.0 ~ C $4.00.

3 Aug 1778: France loaned Congress 750,000 l. (SM $145,000) (cf. 6 Feb 1778).

29 Aug 1778: Battle of Butts Hill, RI.

31 Aug 1778: SM $1.0 ~ C $5.00.

5 Sep 1778: Congress authorized $5,000,000 in Continentals to be issued; total = $71,500,000.

6 Sep 1778: The British burned New Bedford and Fair Haven, CT

26 Sep 1778: Congress authorized $10,000,000 in Continentals to be issued; total = $81,500,000.

30 Sep 1778: SM $1.0 ~ C $5.00.

8 Oct 1778: Congress passed a resolution encouraging that all price limitations be removed, seeing that it had not worked as intended. But the States continued the practice for another three years [7.2-16].

31 Oct 1778: SM $1.0 ~ C $5.00.

1 Nov 1778: France loaned Congress 750,000 l. (SM $145,000) (cf. 6 Feb 1778).

4 Nov 1778: Congress authorized $10,000,000 in Continentals to be issued; total = $91,500,000.

10 Nov 1778: Massacre at Cherry Valley, NY by the British and their Indian allies.

26 Nov 1778: New Jersey ratified the Articles of Confederation.

30 Nov 1778: SM $1.0 ~ C $6.00.

14 Dec 1778: Congress authorized $10,000,000 in Continentals to be issued; total = $101,500,000.

31 Dec 1778: SM $1.0 ~ C $6.00. During 1778, the States had issued paper money [7.2-17]: Massachusetts ($483,500 estimated), Virginia ($2,700,000), North Carolina ($2,125,000), and South Carolina ($4,182,365 estimated). The total amount of coin received and disbursed by the Treasury in 1779 came to $78,666 [7.2-18].

1 Jan 1779: The issues of Continentals from 20 May 1777 and 11 Apr 1778 had become so thoroughly counterfeited by the British that Congress called them in to be burned, but were still legal for payment of taxes until 1 Jun 1779 (later extended to 1 Jan 1780) [7.2-19]. The total amount of Continentals issued so far was $101,500,000 [7.2-20].

5 Jan 1779: Congress asked the States for $15,000,000 for 1779 to be used as a sinking fund for the loans and Continentals. None would be paid [7.2-21].

9 Jan 1779 ff: The British invaded Georgia from Florida and pillaged the countryside.

31 Jan 1779: SM $1.0 ~ C $8.00 (average).

3 Feb 1779: Congress authorized $5,000,160 in Continentals to be issued; total = $106,500,160.

12 Feb 1779: Delaware ratified the Articles of Confederation.

14 Feb 1779: Battle of Kettle Creek, GA.

19 Feb 1779: Congress authorized $5,000,160 in Continentals to be issued; total = $111,500,320.

24 Feb 1779: The Americans captured the British army at Vincennes and Detroit. This ended the British attempt to take the Northwest Territories (now the States of Wisconsin, Michigan, Indiana, and Illinois).

28 Feb 1779: SM $1.0 ~ C $10.00.

31 Mar 1779: SM $1.0 ~ C $10.50 (average)

1 Apr 1779: Congress authorized $5,000,160 in Continentals to be issued; total = $116,500,480.

28 Apr 1779 ff: A war of total destruction was waged by the British throughout Georgia and South Carolina, except Charleston (since there were many loyalists there).

30 Apr 1779: SM $1.0 ~ C $16.10 (average).

5 May 1779: Congress authorized $10,000,100 in Continentals to be issued; total = $126,500,580. Delaware ratified the Articles of Confederation, making twelve of the thirteen. Only Maryland held out.

7 May 1779: Congress authorized $50,000,100 in Continentals to be issued; total = $176,500,680.

21 May 1779: Congress requisitioned $45,000,000 from the States, owing to the depreciation. None would be paid [7.2-22].

30 May 1779: SM $1.0 ~ C $23.50 (average).

31 May - 2 Jun 1779: The British captured Stony Point, NY and Verplanck's Point, NY. The Americans now had to go around the mountains to get between New York and New Jersey.

4 Jun 1779: Congress authorized $10,000,100 in Continentals to be issued; total = $186,500,780.

10 Jun 1779: France loaned Congress 250,000 l. (SM $48,500) (cf. 6 Feb 1778).

30 Jun 1779: SM $1.0 ~ C $20.00 (average).

5 - 11 Jul 1779: The British burned New Haven, Fairfield, and Green Farms, CT.

17 Jul 1779: Congress authorized $15,000,280 in Continentals to be issued; total = $201,501,060.

31 Jul 1779: SM $1.0 ~ C $19.00 (average).

17 Aug 1779: George Washington wrote to a distant cousin, Lund Washington, who was managing Mount Vernon during the war, to give advice on accepting the depreciating Continentals in payment of debts owed to him. He will accept the Continentals on recent debts since they were contracted when they were already depreciated, but will not accept them for old debts contracted before they were emitted, or when they traded at par. He wrote [7.2-23]:

> "Some time ago (but how long I cannot remember) you applied to me to know if you should receive payment of General Mercer's bonds; and after this, of the bond due from the deceased Mr. Mercer's estate to me; and was, after animadverting a little upon the subject; authorized to do so; of course I presume the money has been received. I have since considered the matter in every point of view my judgment enables me to place it, and am resolved to receive no more old debts; such I mean as were contracted and ought to have been paid before the War at the present nominal value of the money, unless compelled to it, or it is the practice of others to do it. Neither justice, reason, nor policy requires it. The law, undoubtedly, was well designed; it was intended to stamp a value and give a free circulation to the paper bills of credit; but it never was nor could be intended to make a man take a shilling or sixpence in the pound for a just debt, which he is well able to pay, thereby involving himself in ruin. I am as willing now as I ever was to take paper money for every kind of debt, and at its present depreciated value for those debts which have been contracted since the money became so; but I will not in future receive the nominal sum for such old debts as come under the above description, except as before excepted."

29 Aug 1779: Battle of Newtown, NY (now Elmira).

31 Aug 1779: SM $1.0 ~ C $20.00.

1 Sep 1779: Congress passed a resolution that no more than $200,000,000 in Continentals should be in circulation at any time [7.2-24]. It is unlikely that this restraint was observed.

13 Sep 1779: Congress issued an address to the public explaining the current state of the finances [7.2-25]. A total of $159,948,880 in Continentals had been issued and in circulation, $7,545,196 had been borrowed from France before Mar 1778 with interest payable in France, $26,188,909 had been borrowed since then, with interest payable in America; and other amounts borrowed abroad were es-

timated at 4,000,000. But only $3,027,560 had been received in taxes. Thus the sum of loans received and interest due, less taxes paid came to $36,761,665. Part of the long address to the States reads [7.2-26, 7.2-27]:

> "Exclusive of the great and ordinary expenses incident to the war the depreciation of the currency has so swelled the price of every necessary article, and of consequence made such additions to the usual amount of expenditures, that very considerable supplies must be immediately provided by loans and taxes; and we unanimously declare it to be essential to the welfare of these States, that the taxes already called for be paid into the continental treasury by the time recommended for that purpose.
>
> The ability of the United States must depend on two things; first the success of the present revolution; and secondly, on the sufficiency of the natural wealth, value, and resources of the country.
>
> That the time has been when honest men might, without being chargeable with timidity, have doubted the success of the present revolution, we admit; but that period has passed. The independence of America is now fixed as fate, and the petulant efforts of Britain to break it down are as vain and fruitless as the raging of the waves which beat against their cliffs.
>
> Let it be remembered that paper money is the only kind of money which cannot 'make itself wings and fly away'. It remains with us, it will not forsake us, it is always ready and at hand for the purpose of commerce or taxes, and every industrious man can find it.
>
> Whether, admitting the ability and political capacity of the United States to redeem their bills, there is any reason to apprehend a wanton violation of the public faith?
>
> It is with great regret and reluctance that we can prevail upon ourselves to take the least notice of a question which involves in it a doubt so injurious to the honor and dignity of America. The enemy, aware that the strength of America lay in the union of her citizens, and the wisdom and integrity of those whom they committed the direction of their affairs, have taken unwearied pains to disunite and alarm the people, to depreciate the abilities and virtues of their rulers, and to impair the confidence reposed in them by their constituents.
>
> Hence has proceeded the notable discovery that as the congress made the money they also can destroy it; and that it will exist no longer than they find it convenient to permit it.
>
> You surely are convinced that it is no more in their power to annihilate your money than your independence, and that any act of theirs for either of those purposes would be null and void. We should pay an ill compliment to the understanding and honor of every true American, were we to adduce many arguments to show the baseness or bad policy of violating our national faith, or omitting to pursue the measures necessary to preserve it. A bankrupt, faithless republic, would be a novelty in the political world, and appear among respectable nations like a common prostitute among chaste and respectable matrons."

16 Sep 1779: France loaned Congress 250,000 l. (SM $48,500) (cf. 6 Feb 1778).

17 Sep 1779: Congress authorized $15,000,360 in Continentals to be issued; total = $216,501,420.

28 Sep 1779: Congress authorized a loan from Spain for SM $5,000,000; a net loan was subsequently obtained for SM $174,017 [7.2-28].

30 Sep 1779: SM $1.0 ~ C $24.00 (average).

4 Oct 1779: France loaned Congress 250,000 l. (SM $48,500) (cf. 6 Feb 1778).

9 Oct 1779: Battle of Savannah, GA.

14 Oct 1779: Congress authorized $5,000,180 in Continentals to be issued; total = $221,501,600.

26 Oct 1779: Congress authorized a loan from France for SM $10,000,000; a loan was obtained for SM $1,815,000 (10,000,000 livres). Congress also authorized a loan from Holland for SM $10,000,000, and loans were eventually obtained: SM $2,000,000 on 14 Sep 1782; SM $800,000 on 1 Feb 1785; SM $ 400,000 on 11 Oct 1787; and SM $400,000 on 2 Jul 1788 [7.2-29].

31 Oct 1779: SM $1.0 ~ C $30.00.

17 Nov 1779: Congress authorized $10,050,540 in Continentals to be issued; total = $231,552,140.

19 Nov 1779: Congress asked the States to limit prices based on 1774 prices [7.2-30]: a) wages of common labor, tradesmen, and mechanics to be limited to 20 times the rate in 1774; b) domestically produced items limited in price to 20 times the 1774 price; c) but items of military use to be exempt from price controls.

29 Nov 1779: Congress authorized $10,000,140 in Continentals to be issued; total = $241,552,280. (Schuckers has $241,552,780; it is not clear where the $500 discrepancy is.) However, Alexander Hamilton, in his report of 1790, says that a total of $357,476,541 of "old emission" had been made from 1776 to 1781, and an additional $2,070,486 in 'new emission' (1780 and 1781) [7.2-31]. The 'new emission' of Continentals was authorized 18 Mar 1780. It is not clear how this discrepancy arose unless Hamilton's figures include the "indents" (loan certificates).

30 Nov 1779: SM $1.0 ~ C $38.50 (average).

~15 Dec 1779: Congress was unable to obtain any money. The Continentals had depreciated so much that no one would loan metal money against them for a promise to pay in paper. Although Congress used legal tender laws and price controls, the over-issue of Continentals destroyed the nation's credit and commerce. The people simply lost confidence in the Continentals and they began to go out of circulation.

21 Dec 1779: France loaned Congress 250,000 l. (SM $48,500) (cf. 6 Feb 1778).

31 Dec 1779: SM $1.0 ~ C $41.50 (average). During 1779, the States had issued paper money [7.2-32]: Massachusetts ($483,500 estimated), Rhode Island ($133,000), Virginia ($2,500,000), North Carolina ($1,125,000), and South Carolina ($4,182,365 estimated). The amount of coin received and disbursed by the Treasury came to $73,000 for all of 1779 [7.2-33].

~15 Jan 1780: This marked the beginning of a large influx of hard money: a) English procurements for its army; b) French assistance and payments to its soldiers in the States; and c) loans from foreign nations.

31 Jan 1780: SM $1.0 ~ C $42.50 (average).

25 Feb 1779: Congress, instead of making requisitions for money, asked that the States make in-kind contributions to be delivered as requested by the military [7.2-34]: a) 330,000,000 pounds of beef; b) 455,000 gallons of rum; c) 123,000 barrels of flour; d) 695,000 bushels of corn; e) 53,000 bushels of salt; f) 9,000 tons of hay; g) 7,000 hogsheads of tobacco; and h) 52,000 bushels of rice. The costs were to be tabulated in Spanish Milled Dollars and Congress would settle accounts with the States later.

29 Feb 1780: France loaned Congress 750,000 l. (SM $145,000) (cf. 6 Feb 1778); SM $1.0 ~ C $50.00 (average).

29 Feb 1779: General Greene wrote to Joseph Reed, President of the Supreme Executive Council of Pennsylvania [7.2-35]:

"Our provisions are in a manner gone. We have not a ton of hay at command, nor magazines to draw from. Money is extremely scarce, and worth little when we get it. We have been so poor for a fortnight that we could not forward the public dispatches for want of cash to support the expresses."

~ 1 Mar 1780: Now that the Continentals had become so depreciated that they no longer circulated because no one would accept them, gold and silver replaced them. As Schuckers relates [7.2-36]:

"And it is a curious illustration of the laws which govern paper money, that as excessive issues had exiled the cash of the country from its accustomed place in the business of the people, it began to flow back as the paper money approached the period of its mortality. As this daily less capably performed the office of the instrument of exchange, gold and silver more certainly and amply flowed in to supply its place."

18 Mar 1780: Congress issued a report recognizing the depreciation of the Continentals, and proposing a method to redeem them. The idea was that the separate States may have better credit than did Congress. The resolution announced a plan for redemption and the issuing of new bills [7.2-37]:

"These United States having been driven into this just and necessary war at the time when no regular civil governments were established of sufficient energy to enforce the collection of taxes or to provide funds for the redemption of such bills of credit as their necessities obliged them to issue; and before the powers of Europe were sufficiently convinced of the justice of their cause or of the probable event of the controversy to afford them aid or credit, in consequence of which their bills increasing in quantity beyond the sum necessary for the purpose of a circulating medium and wanting at the same time specific funds to rest on for their redemption they have seen them daily sink in value notwithstanding every effort that has been made to support the same: insomuch that they are now passed by common consent in most parts of these United States at least thirty-nine fortieths below their nominal value and still remain in a state of depreciation whereby the community suffers great injustice, the public finances are deranged, and the necessary dispositions for defense of the country are much impeded and perplexed; and whereas, effectually to remedy these evils for which purpose the United States are now becoming competent, their independence being well assured, their civil governments established and vigorous, and the spirit of their citizens ardent for exertion, it is necessary speedily to reduce the quantity in circulation, and to establish and appropriate such funds that shall ensure the punctual redemption of the bills."

It then directs the States to send in taxes already levied on 7 Oct 1779 and 23 Feb 1780 but not paid. It continues:

"That silver and gold be receivable in payment of the said quotas at the rate of one Spanish milled dollar in lieu of forty dollars of the bills now in circulation.

That the said bills as paid in except for the months of January and February past, which may be necessary for the discharge of past contracts, be not reissued but destroyed.

That as fast as the said bills shall be brought in and be destroyed, and funds shall be established as hereafter mentioned for other bills, other bills not to exceed on any account one twentieth part of the nominal sum of the bills brought in to be destroyed."

That the bills which shall be issued be redeemable in specie within six years after the present, and bear an interest at the rate of five per centum per annum to be paid also in specie at the redemption of the bills or at the election of the holder annually."

Congress thus announced that the Continentals were to be discounted as 40:1 and destroyed; to be replaced when funding permitted by new bills (the "new issue") at the rate of 20:1; and the new bills would bear interest at 5%. The 40:1 provision signaled the end of the relevance of the Continental.

31 Mar 1780: SM $1.0 ~ C $62.50 (average).

18 Apr 1780: Congress passed a resolution calling for the redemption of the Continentals at the value they had in Spanish milled dollars at the time of issue [7.2-38]:

"That Congress will as soon as may be, make such provision for discharging or continuing the loans that have been made to these United States, or loan office certificates, as that the holders of them shall sustain no loss thereon by any depreciation of the bills loaned subsequent to the respective dates of the said certificates."

30 Apr 1780: SM $1.0 ~ C $60.00.

12 May 1780: The Americans surrendered Charleston, SC to the British.

23 May 1780: France loaned Congress 750,000 l. (SM $145,000) (cf. 6 Feb 1778).

29 May 1780: Battle of Waxhaws, SC.

31 May 1780: SM $1.0 ~ C $60.00.

Jun - Oct 1780: A guerilla war was conducted by the Americans under Williams, Sumter, Pickens, and Marion in the South. At the same time, the British under Tarleton waged a reign of terror throughout the Carolinas, which lasted until Jun 1782.

6 Jun 1780: Battle of Elizabethtown, NJ.

21 Jun 1780: France loaned Congress 750,000 l. (SM $145,000) (cf. 6 Feb 1778).

28 Jun 1780: Congress published the schedule of redemption of the Continentals [7.2-39]:

"Resolved, that the principal of all loans which have been made to these United States shall finally be discharged by paying the full current value of the bills when loaned; which payment shall be made in Spanish milled dollars, or the current exchange thereof in other money at the time of payment.

That the value of the bills, when loaned, shall be ascertained for the purposes above mentioned (cf. 18 Apr 1780) by computing thereon a progressive rate of depreciation, commencing with the first day of September, 1777, and continuing to the 18th of March, 1780, in geometrical progression and proportion of the time, from period to period, as hereafter stated, assuming the depreciation at the several periods to be as follows: On the first day of March, 1778, one dollar and three quarters of a dollar of the said bills for one Spanish milled dollar; on the first of September 1778, as four of the former for one of the latter; on the 1st day of March 1779, as eighteen of the former for one of the latter; and on the 18th day of March, 1780, as forty of the former for one of the latter." Thus the latter Continental issues were redeemed for 2.5 cents on the dollar.

30 Jun 1780: SM $1.0 ~ C $60.00.

10 Jul 1780: The first contingent of French troops landed in Newport, RI to aid the American cause.

11 Jul 1780: Congress fixed the redemption schedule of Continental currency and bills of credit at 40 to 1. Its reckoned value was about 65 to 1 at this time.

12 Jul 1780: Battle of Cross Roads, SC.

17 Jul 1780: The Bank of Pennsylvania was established by Robert Morris and other Philadelphia merchants, to aid in supplying provisions to the army [7.2-40]. Its initial capital was PA £315,000 and British sterling £150,000 in bills of exchange provided by the Treasury.

29 Jul 1780: The Treasury, pursuant to the directive of 28 Jun 1780, published a day-by-day depreciation schedule [7.2-41] for the Continentals from 1 Sep 1777 (at par) to 18 Mar 1780 (SM $1.0 ~ C $40.00)

31 Jul 1780: SM $1.0 ~ C $62.50 (average).

16 Aug 1780: Battle of Camden, SC.

18 Aug 1780: Battle of Fishing Creek, SC.

20 Aug 1780: Battle of Musgrave's Mills, SC.

26 Aug 1780: Congress again appealed to the States to pay the requisitions.

31 Aug 1780: SM $1.0 ~ C $70.00 (average).

15 Sep 1780: Congress asked MA, NH, CT, NJ, PA, and DE to supply 3,000 head of cattle to support the army [7.2-42].

22-25 Sep 1780: American General Benedict Arnold attempted to hand West Point over to the British; the plot is detected and he escaped to the British lines.

28 Sep 1780: Battle of Black Mingo, SC.

30 Sep 1780: SM $1.0 ~ C $75.00.

5 Oct 1780: France loaned Congress 750,000 l. (SM $145,000) (cf. 6 Feb 1778).

7 Oct 1780: Battle of King's Mountain, SC.

31 Oct 1780: SM $1.0 ~ C $77.50 (average).

20 Nov 1780: Battle of Blackstock Hill, SC.

27 Nov 1780: France loaned Congress 1,000,000 l. (SM $194,000) (cf. 6 Feb 1778).

30 Nov 1780: SM $1.0 ~ C $90.00 (average)

31 Dec 1780: SM $1.0 ~ C $100.00; Elliot [7.2-43] states that $891,326 of new emission was issued in 1780. During 1780, the States had issued paper money [7.2-44]: Massachusetts ($483,500 estimated), Rhode Island ($66,600), Connecticut ($632,700), New Jersey ($600,000), Pennsylvania ($1,516,000), Virginia ($30,666,000), North Carolina ($3,600,000), and South Carolina ($4,182,365 estimated).

1 Jan 1781: A mutiny was staged by most of the army in PA, complaining about not being paid, shortages of provisions, and not being released after three years per their original enlistments. It was resolved peacefully although British spies tried to instigate a full revolt. The British spies were caught and hanged [7.2-45].

15 Jan 1781: Congress requisitioned $879,342 in coin from the States [7.2-46], to be paid immediately for current expenses. None was ever paid.

17 Jan 1781: Battle of The Cowpens, SC.

31 Jan 1781: SM $1.0 ~ C $100.00.

15 Feb 1781: France loaned Congress 750,000 l. (SM $145,000) (cf. 6 Feb 1778).

21 Feb 1781: Robert Morris was appointed Superintendent of the Finances. He reformed the entire system, and organized the Treasury. Not only did he eliminate the corruption and incompetence, but went directly to military commanders to find out what was needed; and even issued his own promissory notes against his credit when necessary to supply the army. Schuckers writes [7.2-47]:

> "But in a word, arms and ammunition, pay of troops and subsistence stores, were supplied upon the private resources of Robert Morris. He bore upon his broad and ample shoulders, to the close of the war, almost the whole pecuniary burdens it entailed, and through its most critical and important period he was its vital stay and support. It is no figure of speech to aver that in his field of public duty he rendered services not less valuable than and splendid than those even of Washington; though it is necessary to state that he was reimbursed for all his advances."

28 Feb 1781: SM $1.0 ~ C $110.00 (average).

1 Mar 1781: Maryland finally ratified the Articles of Confederation; it then went into effect.

31 Mar 1781: SM $1.0 ~ C $127.50 (average).

18 Apr 1781: A Committee in Congress reported that the debt was SM $24,057,577 in specie, and that SM $19,507,457 would be needed for 1782. But in fact the details of the national domestic debt were so confused that no accurate figure has ever been devised. The foreign debt was about SM $6,000,000 with annual interest due of SM $360,000 [7.2-48].

23 Apr 1781: The British surrendered Fort Watson, SC to the Americans.

25 Apr 1781: Battle of Hobkirk's Hill, SC.

30 Apr 1781: SM $1.0 ~ C $167.50 (average).

10-15 May 1781: The British gradually evacuated Camden, Orangeburg, Fort Motte, Nelson's Ferry and Fort Granby (all in SC).

15 May 1781: France loaned Congress 750,000 l. (SM $145,000) (cf. 6 Feb 1778).

26 May 1781: The Bank of North America was established. It issued bank notes, which were payable on demand, and were accepted by Congress in payment of taxes. The initial capital was SM $400,000, but the actual amount of specie held was SM $40,000 [7.2-49].

31 May 1781: SM $1.0 ~ C $350.00 (average, 200:1 to 500:1). The Continental currency was abolished as circulating money.

5 Jun 1781: The British surrendered Augusta GA to Americans.

29 Jun 1781: The British abandoned Ninety-Six, SC.

6 Jul 1781: Battle of Green Springs, VA. General Greene and Lafayette pressured British General Cornwallis to evacuate to Yorktown, VA.

1 Aug 1781: France loaned Congress 1,000,000 l. (SM $194,000) (cf. 6 Feb 1778).

15 Aug 1781: France loaned Congress 750,000 l. (SM $145,000) (cf. 6 Feb 1778).

29 Aug - 21 Sep 1781: General George Washington secretly moved the Continental Army from White Plains, NY to Yorktown, VA.

8 Sep 1781: Battle of Eutaw Springs, SC.

20 Sep 1781: The Board of Treasury was abolished due to the inefficiency of its operation [7.2-50].

6-19 Oct 1781: Battle of Yorktown, VA; Lord Cornwallis surrendered, and this ended the war for practical purposes, except for some battles in Georgia lasting until Jun 1782.

30 Oct 1781: Congress requisitioned SM $8,000,000 from the States, payable in quarterly payments. But only SM $420,031 had been received by Aug 1782 [7.2-51].

5 Nov 1781: France guaranteed a 10,000,000 l. (SM $1,940,000) loan to Congress from Holland (cf. 6 Feb 1778).

15 Nov 1781: France loaned Congress 750,000 l. (SM $145,000) (cf. 6 Feb 1778).

31 Dec 1781: During 1781, the States had issued paper money [7.2-52]: Massachusetts ($483,500 estimated), New York ($411,250), New Jersey ($800,000), Pennsylvania ($1,330,000), Virginia ($87,500,000), North Carolina ($26,250,000), and South Carolina ($4,182,365 estimated). Meanwhile, $1,179,249 of new emission had been issued in 1781 by Congress, and the total of "new emission" was $2,070,485 [7.2-53].

7 Jan 1782: The Bank of North America began operations in Philadelphia. The capital consisted of SM $70,000 in hard money from individuals and SM $254,000 from Congress, using proceeds from one of the foreign loans. Robert Morris, head of the Bank, used some employees to deter people from redeeming the notes issued by the Bank, and they soon traded at par with the Spanish dollar.

27 Feb 1782: The Parliament of Great Britain passed a resolution declaring that the war in America was over.

1 Apr 1782: France loaned Congress 1,500,000 l. (SM $291,000) (cf. 6 Feb 1778).

4 Apr 1782: Trade in hard money was common among the people by this time (probably since early 1780) since a great deal had been brought in by the British but hoarded until the Continentals were withdrawn. Thomas Paine wrote in the Pennsylvania Packet of 4 Apr 1782 [7.2-54]:

> "The progress and revolution of our domestic circumstances are as extraordinary as the Revolution itself. We began with paper, and we end with gold and silver."

17 May 1782: Robert Morris, superintendent of finances, wrote to Congress explaining the financial situation [7.2-55]:

> "The habitual inattention of the States has reduced us to the brink of ruin, and I cannot see a probability of relief from any of them. I rather perceive a disposition to take money from the public treasury, than to place any in it. A variety of causes prevents the collection of taxes, and delays the payment of them, even after they are collected. In many States they are not laid. … The public departments are now absolutely at a stand, for the want of money, and many things already commenced I must desist from. This cannot be wondered at, when it is considered, that near five months of the present year have elapsed without my having received anything on account of its expenditures, except the trifling sum of five thousand, five hundred dollars, and that sum, calculating on the expenses of eight millions annually, is about one-fourth of what is necessary to support us for a single day."

1 Jul 1782: France loaned Congress 1,500,000 l. (SM $291,000) (cf. 6 Feb 1778).

5 Jul 1782: France loaned Congress 3,000,000 l. (SM $582,000) (cf. 6 Feb 1778).

11 Jul 1782: The British surrendered Savannah, GA; this ended the war militarily.

16 Jul 1782: Benjamin Franklin negotiated a contract with France, documenting the loans that France had made or guaranteed, along with a repayment schedule [7.2-56]. Per the 1778 treaty, the Louis XVI of France loaned Congress 18,000,000 livres (SM $3,492,000) at 5% interest, although interest was waived until the peace treaty with Britain. The loans and guarantees were as follows:

a. 1778: 750,000 l. (SM $145,500) on 4 occasions: 28 Feb, 19 May, 3 Aug, and 1 Nov 1778.

b. 1779: 250,000 l. (SM $48,500) on 4 occasions: 10 Jun, 15 Sep, 4 Oct, and 21 Dec 1779, plus 1,000,000 l. (SM $194,000) on 27 Nov 1779.

c. 1780: 750,000 l. (SM $145,000) on 4 occasions: 29 Feb, 23 May, 21 Jun, and 5 Oct 1780.

d. 1781: 750,000 l. (SM $145,000) on 4 occasions: 15 Feb, 15 May, 15 Aug, and 15 Nov 1780; plus 1,000,000 l. (SM $194,000) on 1 Aug 1780.

e. 1781: France guaranteed a loan of 10,000,000 l. (SM $1,940,000) from Holland on 5 Nov 1781.

f. 1782: 1,500,000 l. (SM $291,000) on 2 occasions: 10 Apr and 1 Jul 1782, plus 3,000,000 l. (SM $582,000) on 5 Jul 1782.

4 Sep 1782: Congress requisitioned SM $1,200,000 from the States [7.2-57], but did not require it be paid directly to Congress. The States were to use the revenue to pay down loan office certificates and other U. S. debt payable in their own States.

14 Sep 1782: Congress authorized a loan from France for SM $4,000,000; a net loan was obtained for SM $1,089,000 (6,000,000 livres) [7.2-58].

16 Oct 1782: Congress requisitioned another SM $2,000,000 from the States [7.2-59].

31 Dec 1782: The States did not issue any of their own paper money in 1782 [7.2-60].

1 Jan 1783: The financial condition was as follows [7.2-61, 7.2-62]: Total foreign debt = SM $7,885,085; domestic debt = SM $34,115,290; arrears due on both foreign and domestic debt = SM $2,415,956, excluding approximately SM $20,000,000 in debts contracted by the several States during the war. The State debts were later absorbed by the United States under the Constitution at SM $21,500,000.

20 Jan 1783: Britain, France, Spain, and the U. S. signed the preliminary articles of the Treaty of Paris that would end the Revolutionary War.

23 Jan 1783: Congress ratified the agreement with France made on 16 Jul 1782.

5 Feb 1783: Congress passed a resolution in which officers received one month's pay in notes [7.2-63]; private soldiers received one month's pay which was delivered in weekly installments of 50 cents each. The total for this one month's pay was SM $256,232.86.

21 Feb 1783: France loaned 600,000 l. (SM $116,400) to Congress, but Louis XVI made it clear that he was unwilling to loan any more since America's credit was so bad (but see 15 Apr 1783).

18 Mar 1783: General Washington wrote an appeal to the President of Congress and its members on behalf of the "Patriot Army." In it he recounted the Newburgh circular, his address on it, and the favorable response he received from the officers; he reiterated the army's long sufferings; he noted the obligation of Congress to treat the army justly; he reminded them of previous assurances given by Congress; and finally he urged Congress not to leave the army in want and destitution, as it would always be remembered as a sign of Congress' ingratitude for services rendered by the army [7.2-64]. He also recommended that men who had been promised half pay for life would be better served by full pay for a fixed number of years.

22 Mar 1783: Congress agreed to a resolution per General Washington's suggestion on payment to the army [7.2-65]. It modified the pay provision for soldiers from half-pay for life to full pay for five years at once, known as the commutation. The lump sum was to be paid by issuing certificates bearing 6% interest. This was a good bargain for the government, as it would reduce the total outlay, since most soldiers would likely live more than ten years. It would also benefit the soldiers, who, having left their farms and occupations, would find a lump sum handy in getting back on their feet. But the public was opposed to it, angry that such a large amount was to be paid at once, since their wages were small in comparison. The public had forgotten the sacrifices made by the army, and became occupied with their own problems.

15 Apr 1783: Congress ratified the peace treaty with Great Britain, formally ending the war. France loaned 6,000,000 l. (SM $1,164,000) to Congress [7.2-66]. This was the last Louis XVI could do.

18 Apr 1783: Congress passed a resolution [7.2-67] to recommend to the States that Congress be given a power to levy duties for a period of 25 years on certain imported items in order to raise revenues to pay the debts of the war. The items on which duties were to be paid amounted to between 1.1% to 26.6% on rum and other liquors, wines, tea, pepper, sugar, molasses, cocoa, and coffee; in addition to a 5% duty on all other items. It was estimated at this time that the import duties would bring about SM $1,000,000 annually to Congress. The resolution also recommended that a standing annual requisition of SM $1,500,000 be apportioned to the various States according to population (New Hampshire: SM $52,708; Massachusetts: SM $224,427; Delaware: SM $22,443; Maryland: SM $141,517; Rhode Island: SM$ 32,318; Virginia: SM $256,487; Connecticut: SM $132,091; North Carolina: SM $109,006; New York: SM $128,243; South Carolina: SM $96,183; New Jersey: SM $83,358; Georgia: SM $16,030; and Pennsylvania: SM $205,189). It was sent to the States on 26 Apr 1783 with an address by James Madison, Alexander Hamilton, and Oliver Ellsworth in which they outlined the need for revenue, as the current debt amounted to SM $42,000,325 (including SM $5,000,000 for the commutation) with an annual interest due of SM $2,415,956. Congress remained helpless in the meantime, since all thirteen States would have to ratify this amendment to the Articles before the revenue could be collected.

2 Jun 1783: The Continental Army received immediate discharge furloughs [7.2-68]. But Congress was unable to pay the three months salary that had been promised in Apr 1783. Instead, the soldiers received paper notes bearing 6% interest; the cash value was estimated at 10% of face value. The soldiers of the Continental Army, who had defeated the British Empire, dispersed peacefully and went home with no money in their pockets.

3 Sep 1783: British negotiators signed the Treaty of Paris, ending the Revolutionary War. The terms of the treaty included the following provisions: a) loyalists were to be compensated for loss of property suffered during the war; b) British creditors holding private debt were to be paid in full; c) there would be no persecution of loyalists; d) opportunity would be provided for loyalists to recover estates lost during the war; e) private debts owed to loyalists would be paid in sterling; and f) Britain would give up forts in the western New York and the Ohio Valley. But Congress had no power to force any of the States to observe any of these provisions.

At the return of peace, trade between the States and England resumed, as there was still considerable demand for English products. However, since the Continental currency had collapsed, the Americans had to pay for imports in hard money. The war had left many areas ruined. In the south, the farms had not recovered enough to resume trading in indigo, rice or tobacco. The same problem prevailed in the middle States, and they were unable to pay as they normally would, by exporting wheat and furs. The New England States fell on hard times because shipping had become unprofitable owing to the Navigation Acts. Many in the States were living off the land, and resorted to barter to obtain what they needed. Many demagogues claimed that the remedy was cheap paper money, and some States began to issue worthless paper in order to give the illusion of prosperity.

Although not perceived as such at the time, the treaty ending the war began the most crucial period in the history of America [7.2-69]. The American States were surrounded on the south and west by Spanish lands, and on the north by Canada, which was still a British colony. The big risk was that the States now had no common enemy, and without some sort of unifying force, would degenerate into thirteen petty republics bickering among themselves. They were also vulnerable to encroachment by the larger and more organized European powers.

3 Nov 1783: The Continental Army was formally disbanded [7.2-70], even though the British still occupied New York City. The main problem was that Congress could no longer afford to maintain the army; in fact, it owed considerable back pay to the soldiers. Many soldiers begin to think they would never get paid, and there was widespread dissension and distrust of Congress. Many members of the army from Pennsylvania, Maryland, Delaware, and Virginia had been previously furloughed on 26 May, 11 Jun, 9 Aug, and 26 Sep 1783.

31 Dec 1783: Of the SM $8,000,000 that had been requisitioned 30 Oct 1781, only SM $1,486,155 had been paid [7.2-71]. During 1781, the States had issued paper money [7.2-72]: Massachusetts ($483,500 est.), New Jersey ($85,000), Pennsylvania ($300,000), North Carolina ($100,000), and South Carolina ($4,182,365 estimated).

1 Jan 1784: Thomas Jefferson estimated the national debt to be about SM $68,000,000; about SM $8,000,000 was due from foreign loans; SM $36,500,000 represented the debts of the several States incurred during the war, and the rest was due to individuals or to States. Congress had made many requisitions to the States during the war, and the current status was [7.2-73, 7.2-74]:

a. Of the 19 May 1779 requisition for SM $45,000,000, none had been paid.

b. Of the 30 Oct 1781 requisition for SM $8,000,000, States had paid as follows: New Hampshire: $3,000 of $373,598; Massachusetts: $247,677 of $1,307,596; Rhode Island: $67,848 of $216,684; Connecticut: $131,578 of $747,196; New York: $39,064 of $373,598; Pennsylvania: $346,633 of $1,120,794; Delaware: zero of $112,085; Maryland: $89,302 of $933,996; Virginia: $115,104 of $1,307,594; North Carolina: zero of $622,677; South Carolina: $344,302 of $373,598; Georgia: zero of $24,905.

c. States were credited with having paid the SM $1,200,000 requisition of 4 Sep 1782.

d. Of the 16 Oct 1782 requisition for SM $2,000,000, none had been paid.

5 Feb 1784: John Adams was able to get a loan from moneylenders in Holland [7.2-75] for 2,000,000 guilders (SM $1,176,000) at 6% interest.

5 Apr 1784: Thomas Jefferson, as head of a finance committee in Congress, delivered a report [7.2-76] on the finances of the Confederacy. The expenses for 1784 were estimated as: a) SM $457,525 for public services; b) SM $442,648 for interest on foreign debt; c) SM $3,580,030 for interest on domestic debt; and d) SM $1,000,000 debts contracted but still unpaid from 1782 and 1783, which totaled to about SM $5,480,203. This figure was not practical as a revenue target. Jefferson proposed that the States be given credit for the SM $1,200,000 that had been requisitioned on 4 Sep 1782 (included in the SM$3,580,030 number), since it had given the States leeway to use it to pay interest due on certificates issued by the States and other liquidated debts. He then recommended that a new requisition be ordered that would get the States up to three-fourths of the original SM $8,000,000 that had been requisitioned on 30 Oct 1781. He calculated the apportionment, deducting for some receipts that had been made, and requested a requisition for 1784 of SM $4,577,591. This would be enough to meet the current needs. It was voted down by Congress, probably realizing the demands on the States were too great.

28 May 1784: Congress established a Board of Treasury to manage the finances, although it did not go into operation until 25 Jan 1785 [7.2-77].

3 Jun 1784: Congress passed an act specifying how accounts were to be settled with the States: a) Supplies that the States had furnished were to be assessed at their value in specie, plus 6% interest from the date they were provided; b) depreciation of the Continentals was accounted for; c) creditors of the U. S. were given certificates bearing 6% interest; d) old certificates issued by the Army officers could be exchanged for new ones [7.2-78].

17 Aug 1784: Robert Morris, superintendent of finances, informed French officials that the U. S. would default on its interest payment on the 10,000,000 livre loan from Holland that France had guaranteed (cf. 5 Nov 1781) [7.2-79]. He also informed the French officials that no interest could be paid on the direct loans from France. These defaults ruined American credit.

25 Jan 1785: The Board of Treasury went into operation, with John Lewis Gervais, Samuel Osgood, and Walter Livingston appointed to manage the finances.

6 Jul 1785: Congress defined the U. S. dollar as 375.64 grains of fine silver [7.2-80], and adopted a decimal system for smaller amounts (mills, pennies, nickels, dimes, quarters, and half-dollars). A mill is a tenth of a penny.

13-14 Jul 1785: A committee in Congress led by James Monroe introduced a motion [7.2-81] to amend the Articles of Confederation to grant Congress the power to regulate foreign commerce, levy import duties, send and receive ambassadors, enter treaties and alliances, and establish courts for trial of piracy, if eleven States were agreeable. Monroe's committee had concluded that granting such a power was desirable: a) a tax on foreign goods would aid domestic manufacturers; b) Congress would be able to deal reciprocally with foreign powers, such that America would not always be at a disadvantage; c) it would allow uniform commercial rules among the States; and d) it would prepare the way for the establishment of a navy to protect commerce. Richard Henry Lee of Virginia led the opposition to it, noting that granting powers to Congress would: a) endanger liberty; b) may tempt Congress to expands its powers even further; and c) increase the risk of undue foreign influence upon Congress if powers affecting foreign nations were concentrated in Congress. He also argued that the interests of the northern and southern States were different. Lee feared that the northern States would use their numerical advantage to vote themselves benefits in the carrying trade that would serve to impoverish the southern States (since it had no shipping industry). Congress took no action on it, preferring to leave propositions for amending the Articles to the several State legislatures.

13 Sep 1785: The charter of the Bank of North America was revoked by the State of Pennsylvania. This was revenge for the bank's opposition to issuing additional paper money, as many in Pennsylvania continued to believe that paper was the source of wealth. The Bank continued operations, since it had a second charter issued by Congress [7.2-82].

27 Sep 1785: Congress requisitioned SM $3,000,000 from the States; none of it would ever be paid. Estimated expenses for 1785 totaled SM $404,553 for military and civil department; SM $440,252 for interest on the foreign debt, and SM $743,054 for interest on the domestic debt. Also, interest on certificates issued to the soldiers was SM $289,423, and the actual expenses for 1784 had exceeded that years' estimate by SM $1,141,551; tax evasion was the common default position [7.2-83]:

> "Were States ever so able to bear taxation more disinclined to do their duty in this regard? Everywhere did individuals seek to evade the payment of taxes; not because they were too poor to pay, for the sums asked were small compared with the resources of the people, but rather from habit, and because evasion of the duty was so general."

1 Feb 1786: Of the four requisitions upon the States since 30 Oct 1781, totaling SM $15,670,987, only a total of SM $2,450,803 had been paid by the States [7.2-84]. Congress decided to allow holders of the unpaid certificates issued by Congress should present them to the loan offices in the States where they were issued, to be turned in for new ones after being assessed as to their current value in specie [7.2-85].

15 Feb 1786: The minimum anticipated expenses for 1787 associated with payment of interest on foreign loans and other foreign obligations was SM $577,307, including: a) interest on loans from France, SM $240,741; b) interest on certificates to foreign officers payable in France, SM $22,370; c) interest on a loan from Spain (to Mar 1787), SM $48,596; and d) interest on a loan from Holland (to Jun 1787), SM $265,600. The total receipts since 1781 amounted to SM $2,457,987: a) from requisitions made between 1 Nov 1781 and 1 Nov 1784, SM $2,025,089; b) from requisitions made between 1 Nov 1784 and 1 Jan 1786, SM $432,898 [7.2-86].

8 Aug 1786: Congress established a coinage standard, per the decimal system organized in Jul 1785 [7.2-87]. A dollar was defined as 375.64 grains of pure silver, or 24.6268 grains of pure gold. The fineness of the coinage was to be 11/12 (0.91666 fine). The ratio of gold to silver was thus 15.253 to one. It also specified two gold coins, one of ten dollars (Eagle) containing 246.268 grains of fine gold, and the other of five dollars (Half Eagle) containing 123.34 grains of fine gold. However, only the copper coins were actually minted.

23 Aug 1786: Congress authorized the issue of certificates, called 'indents', for payment of accrued interest on loan-office certificates and other debts. But these did not pay the debt or help the creditors, since there was very little coming in from the requisitions made on the States [7.2-88].

18 Sep 1786: Congress ordered the States to pay the requisitions in specie, declining to accept any type of paper money, including the Continentals. Meanwhile, the notes issued by the Bank of North America circulated at par; the bank had good credit because it had demonstrated its ability to redeem on demand. Its cash account was $5,957,000 Mexican dollars [7.2-89].

19 Sep 1986 to 1 Mar 1787: Shays' Rebellion began, which was a revolt led by Daniel Shays in Vermont, Massachusetts, New York, and New Hampshire, over the decline in value of the paper money, high taxes, and foreclosures. This rebellion and the continuing inability of Congress to raise money led to the calling of the Constitutional Convention.

20 Sep 1786: Congress refused to accept the Continentals in payment of taxes or even postage stamps. This marked the formal end of the Continental paper money [7.2-90].

17 Oct 1786: Congress asked the States for a requisition of SM $3,777,062, of which SM $1,606.632 to be in 'indents', and SM $2,170,430 in specie. Congress was now allowing people to pay part of their taxes in 'indents' instead of money. The annual interest on the domestic debt was at this time SM $1,606,560 [7.2-91].

31 Dec 1786: Congress had received approximately only SM $500,000 requisitioned from the States in the past two years [7.2-92]; Congress was delinquent on its interest payments.

1 Mar 1787: End of Shays' rebellion (cf. 19 Sep 1786).

25 May 1787: The Constitutional Convention began in Philadelphia.

17 Sep 1787: Proposed Constitution sent to the States for ratification.

22 May 1788: A committee of Congress reported that there had been a great deal of negligence and fraud in the handling of the government's accounts during the war, and in resolving accounts between Congress and the States. Some time was allowed to straighten out the accounts, but was never satisfactorily accomplished [7.2-93].

21 Jun 1788: New Hampshire became the ninth State to ratify the Constitution, and it went into effect (excluding Virginia, New York, North Carolina, and Rhode Island, since they had not yet ratified it).

30 Sep 1788: A committee in Congress issued a report on the finances concerning revenues remitted to Congress from the tax receivers between Nov 1784 and 21 Apr 1788. Between Nov 1784 and 21 Apr 1785, only SM $143,648 had been remitted, and from 21 Apr 1785 to 21 Apr 1788, only SM $996,448 was remitted. The rest that was obtained by Congress [7.2-94] for this period consisted of SM $1,881,139 in 'indents' (certificates of interest) and a fairly small amount from sale of public land.

24, 25 Nov 1788: South Carolina held elections for members of Congress.

26 Nov 1788: Pennsylvania held elections for members of Congress.

15 Dec 1788: Voting for the office of President began in the States (cf. 10 Jan 1789). Also, New Hampshire held elections for members of Congress.

18 Dec 1788: Massachusetts held elections for members of Congress.

22 Dec 1788: Connecticut held elections for members of Congress.

Note (cf. 13 Sep 1779): Elliot [7.2-95] cites Jefferson's claim that the C $50,000,000 authorized on 14 Jan 1779 was C $24,447,620 for new emission, the rest to replace mutilated bills. Schuckers [7.2-96] shows this as C $25,552,780, but as an addition to the C $50,000,000. Schuckers also cites an additional C $10,000,000 to replace counterfeit bills, but he does not cite the date. Admittedly, none of these are consistent; Schuckers gives the total of issued Continentals as C $359,547,126.

7.3 Data, 1775-1788

Figures 7.3-1 and 7.3-2 show the accumulated amount of Continentals issued along with the value of the Continental with respect to the Spanish Milled Dollar. The solid curve on Figure 7.3-2 (accumulated emissions) is read on the left scale and the dashed curve (relative value) is read on the right. At the end, in May 1781, the Continental dollar had depreciated to the point where it traded for two-tenths of a penny as seen at lower right.

Date	Amount Authorized	Total Authorized	Value WRT Spanish Milled Dollar (SMS)	Date	Amount Authorized	Total Authorized	Value WRT Spanish Milled Dollar (SMS)
22 Jun 1775	2,000,000	2,000,000	1.00	22 May 1778	5,000,000	56,500,000	0.25
25 Jul 1775	1,000,000	3,000,000	1.00	20 Jun 1778	5,000,000	61,500,000	0.25
29 Nov 1775	3,000,000	6,000,000	0.80	30 Jul 1778	5,000,000	66,500,000	0.20
17 Feb 1776	4,000,000	10,000,000	0.67	5 Sep 1778	5,000,000	71,500,000	0.20
27 May 1776	5,000,000	15,000,000	0.50	26 Sep 1778	10,000,000	81,500,000	0.20
13 Aug 1776	5,000,000	20,000,000	0.40	4 Nov 1778	10,000,000	91,500,000	0.17
28 Dec 1776	5,000,000	25,000,000	0.40	14 Dec 1778	10,000,000	101,500,000	0.14
26 Feb 1777	5,000,000	30,000,000	0.40	3 Feb 1779	5,000,160	106,500,160	0.13
20 May 1777	5,000,000	35,000,000	0.33	19 Feb 1779	5,000,160	111,500,320	0.10
15 Aug 1777	1,000,000	36,000,000	0.33	1 Apr 1779	5,000,160	116,500,480	0.10
7 Nov 1777	1,000,000	37,000,000	0.33	5 May 1779	10,000,100	126,500,580	0.06
3 Dec 1777	1,000,000	38,000,000	0.33	7 May 1779	50,000,100	176,500,680	0.04
8 Jan 1778	1,000,000	39,000,000	0.33	4 Jun 1779	10,000,100	186,500,780	0.05
22 Jan 1778	2,000,000	41,000,000	0.25	17 Jul 1779	15,000,280	201,501,060	0.05
16 Feb 1778	2,000,000	43,000,000	0.25	17 Sep 1779	15,000,360	216,501,420	0.05
5 Mar 1778	2,000,000	45,000,000	0.20	14 Oct 1779	5,000,180	221,501,600	0.04
4 Apr 1778	1,000,000	46,000,000	0.20	17 Nov 1779	10,050,540	231,552,140	0.03
11 Apr 1778	5,000,000	51,000,000	0.17	29 Nov 1779	10,000,140	241,552,280	0.03
18 Apr 1778	500,000	51,500,000					

1. Source: Joseph Nourse, Register of the Treasury, in a letter 30 Jan 1828 to the House of Representatives, cited by Schuckers, "Finances and Paper Money of the Revolutionary War", NY: Sanford J. Durst,1978, p. 125
2. Of the $50,000,100 authorized 7 May 1779, $25,552,780 was to replace old bills (cf. Schuckers, p. 126). It is not clear if the amount authorized was $50,000,100 or $50,000, 400.

Figure 7.3-1: Continental Currency Issued by Congress

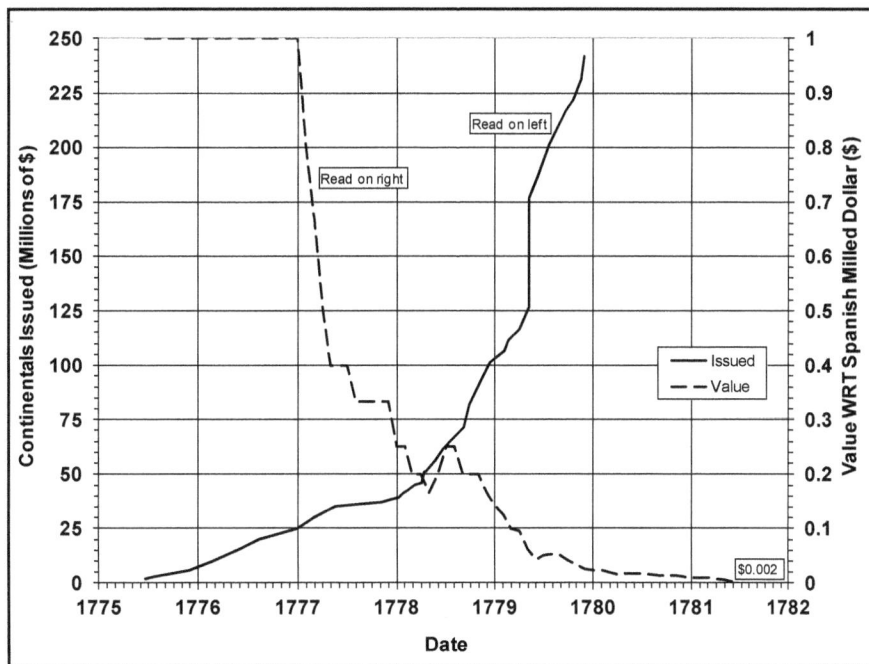

Figure 7.3-2: Continentals Issued and Value With Respect to the Spanish Milled Dollar

7.4   Summary, 1775-1788

So ends the history of the Continental paper money. There are some important lessons to be learned from this history. First, the Continentals were essentially fiat paper money, backed only by a promise of future redemption at interest. The history showed that such a promise could not be kept for the same reason the Continentals were issued in the first place: Congress, which claimed to have the power to direct the Revolution, did not have the power to raise a single penny in taxes. Without a reliable revenue stream, Congress had no choice but to risk depreciation, continue borrowing, and default; confident that the slack would be eventually be taken up by patriotism. They were correct in that estimation as it turned out, but a great many people lost everything they had worked for, and many took great losses by accepting the depreciating Continentals at face value. In fairness to Congress, there probably was no other way to finance the Revolution, and the Continentals succeeded long enough to get the Americans through the early parts of the war in the North.

Secondly, the British engaged in a great deal of counterfeiting of the Continentals, hoping it would drive the Americans into despair and end the revolt. As Bolles [7.4-1] put it:

> "Many in Great Britain and elsewhere believed, that, if Continental paper money could be destroyed, the Americans would be obliged to submit, from lack of funds to maintain their cause. This is why the British Government promoted so extensively the business of counterfeiting. But General Clinton wrote truthfully, in January 1780, "Every day teaches me the futility of calculations founded on its failure." Great Britain had not yet fathomed that depth of American patriotism, what the people were willing to suffer to acquire independence; nor had the mother-country reckoned accurately the aid which France was to bestow."

Third, price controls do not work, as no one will sell for money that is declining in value unless he can elevate the price. If an official price is below the price of production, or below the price that commands a reasonable profit, that item will not be produced at all. In that case, one of two things will happen. Either there will exist shortages (which is what governments claim they are trying to prevent), or the government itself will have to take up production.

Fourth, a fiat paper money must be made a legal tender because that is the only way to ensure that it will be accepted at all if there is competing money of better quality (cf. 14 Jan 1777). The fines and forfeitures had little effect as once again economic reality superseded the desires of Congress.

Fifth, as soon as the public realized the money was depreciating, they began to buy real property and increase their debts, knowing that it can be paid off easily in depreciated money later [7.4-2]. They also are tempted to engage in speculation.

Sixth, the depreciated Continentals were eventually withdrawn from circulation, starting in 1782. They were still accepted in payment of taxes, and were exchanged for bills of the new emission, and were exchanged for other money [7.4-3]. They were eventually redeemed for a small fraction of their face value (cf. 28 Jun 1780) and became obsolete; they were collected up and burned.

Seventh, Gresham's law was in full force. The paper circulated while the people hoarded the good money of gold and silver; when the paper depreciated to virtually nothing, the gold and silver went back into circulation (cf. 4 Apr 1782).

Eighth, the persecutions of those who refused the depreciating money failed to restore its value; they depreciated anyway because people realized the true declining value [7.4-4].

Ninth, there was a considerable amount of corruption and incompetence in handling the public finances; Bolles writes, summarizing the report of 30 Sep 1788 [7.4-5]:

> "The remainder of the report is, for the most part, a continuation of the dismal story. Extraordinary negligence, wastefulness, disorder, and corruption marked the early years of the government; even in the darkest periods through which the country has since passed, it may be questioned whether a greater lack of system or moral rectitude has prevailed."

Last, despite the inconveniences and moral hazard of the Continentals, it did serve to finance the revolution; there was no other way. Schuckers notes [7.4-6]:

"When, therefore, the Second Continental Congress - an immortal body! - addressed itself to a consideration of the finances, almost immediately upon its meeting, May 10th, 1775, nothing was more natural and probable than a prompt resort to paper money. First, it provided for the creation of an army. Having done this, and entirely conscious that a supply of cash [specie or coin] ... the members of the Congress being entirely aware, then that the supply of cash was inadequate even for the current and ordinary business of the colonists, immediately betook themselves to bills of credit..."

Brough summarizes its utility in retrospect [7.4-7]:

"Notwithstanding all the difficulties attending the use of this money [i.e., Continentals], it rendered considerable service to the colonists, and was generally admitted, even by its opponents, to have done excellent service during the revolutionary war. Thomas Paine said of it [in a letter to Abbe Raynal], 'Every stone in the bridge that has carried us over seems to have a claim on our esteem. But this was the cornerstone, and its usefulness cannot be forgotten.'".

Former Treasury Secretary Gallatin commented in 1831 on paper money and the necessity thereof during the Revolution [7.4-8]:

"The general objections to a paper issued by government, have already been stated at large. Yet it must be admitted, that there may be times when every other consideration must yield to the superior necessity of saving or defending a country. If there ever was a time, or a cause which justified a resort to that measure, it was the war for independence. It would be doing gross injustice to the authors of the revolution and founder of that independence, to confound them with those governments, which from ambitious view have, without necessity, inflicted that calamity on their subjects. The old Congress, as the name purports, were only an assembly of plenipotentiaries, delegated by the several colonies or states. They could only recommend, and had not the power to lay taxes; the country was comparatively poor; extraordinary exertions were necessary to resist the formidable power of Great Britain; those exertions were made, and absorbed all the local resources; the paper money carried the United States through the most arduous and perilous stages of the war; and, though operating as a most unequal tax, it cannot be denied that it saved the country. ... It is to be hoped that a similar state of things will not again occur; but at all events, the issue of a government paper ought to be kept in reserve for extraordinary exigencies."

References

[7.1-1]   Henry Phillips, Elisha Reynolds Potter, *Historical Sketches of the Paper Currency of the American Colonies: Pt. D Ser. Continental Paper Money*, Roxbury, MA: W. Elliot Woodward, (1866), p. 16, quoting *Adams' Works*, Vol. 7, p. 296

[7.1-2]   J. W. Schuckers, *A Brief Account of the Finances and Paper Money of the Revolutionary War*, NY: Sanford J. Durst Numismatic Publications, 1978, pp. 103, 104 (originally published 1874 by John Campbell & Son, Philadelphia)

[7.1-3]   op. cit., Schuckers, p. 125. Schuckers here is quoting a report issued by Joseph Nourse, Register of the Treasury to the House of Representatives, 30 Jan 1828.

[7.1-4]   Jonathan Elliot, *The Funding System of the United States and Great Britain*, Washington, DC: Blair & Rives, 1845, p. 9. Elliot reproduces here a set of statistics published by Pelatiah Webster of Philadelphia, who tracked the depreciation through the existence of the Continentals.

[7.1-5]   op. cit., Schuckers, pp. 110, 111

[7.1-6]   William Gouge, *A Short History of Paper Money and Banking In the United States*, Philadelphia: T. W. Ustick, 1833, Part 2, p. 25. Gouge quotes an "estimate by the Register of the Treasury in 1790".

[7.1-7]   Edward D. Duvall, *The Federalist Companion*, Gilbert, AZ: Fremont Valley Books, 2011, pp. 10-93; also *Historical Essays*, 2023, pp. 2-80

[7.1-8]   op. cit., Schuckers, pp. 20, 21

[7.2-1]   op. cit., Schuckers, p. 13
[7.2-2]   op. cit., Phillips and Potter, p. 25

[7.2-3]   op. cit., Schuckers, pp. 28, 29

[7.2-4]   op. cit., Schuckers, p. 127

[7.2-5]   op. cit., Phillips and Potter, p. 41

[7.2-6]   op. cit., Schuckers, pp. 18, 19

[7.2-7]   Annual Report of the Secretary of the Treasury on the State of the Finances for the Year 1876, Washington, DC: Government Printing Office, 1876, Table M, pp. 24, 25. This section of this report recounts the loans and debts incurred during the Revolution. Schuckers, p. 107 has the 23 Dec 1776 loan from the Farmers-General at 1,000,000 l. (SM $194,000), and has the 28 Sep 1779 loan from Spain at SM $150,000.

[7.2-8]   op. cit., Schuckers, p. 127

[7.2-9]   Albert S. Bolles, *A Financial History of the United States*, NY: Augustus M. Kelley (1969), Vol. 1, pp. 175, 176 (originally published 1884 by D. Appleton & Co., NY)

[7.2-10]   op. cit., Schuckers, pp. 32-34

[7.2-11]   op. cit., Bolles, Vol. 1, pp. 165-173

[7.2-12]   Annual Report of the Secretary of the Treasury on the State of the Finances for the Year 1876, Washington, DC: Government Printing Office, 1876, Table M, pp. 24, 25. This section of this report recounts the loans and debts incurred during the Revolution. Schuckers, p. 107 has the 23 Dec 1776 loan from the Farmers-General at 1,000,000 l. (SM $194,000), and has the 28 Sep 1779 loan from Spain at SM $150,000.

[7.2-13]   op. cit., Schuckers, p. 127

[7.2-14]   op. cit., Schuckers, pp. 74, 75

[7.2-15]   op. cit., Schuckers, p. 37

[7.2-16]   op. cit., Bolles, Vol. 1, p. 169

[7.2-17]   op. cit., Schuckers, p. 127

[7.2-18]   op. cit., J. W. Schuckers, p. 48

[7.2-19]   op. cit., Phillips and Potter, pp. 100-102

[7.2-20]   op. cit., Schuckers, p. 48

[7.2-21]   op. cit., Schuckers, pp. 52, 56

[7.2-22]   op. cit., J. W. Schuckers, pp. 52, 56

[7.2-23]   John C. Fitzpatrick, editor, *The Writings of Washington from the Original Manuscript Sources*, Washington, DC: United States Printing Office, 1937, Vol. 16, pp. 123, 124

[7.2-24]   Jonathan Elliot, *The Funding System of the United States and Great Britain*, Washington, DC: Blair and Rives, (1845), p. 11

[7.2-25]   op. cit., Schuckers, p. 57, 58

[7.2-26]   op. cit., Phillips and Potter, pp. 137-143

[7.2-27]   op. cit., Bolles, Vol. 1, p. 83

[7.2-28]   Annual Report of the Secretary of the Treasury on the State of the Finances for the Year 1876, Washington, DC: Government Printing Office, 1876, Table M, pp. 24, 25. This section of this report recounts the loans and debts incurred during the Revolution. Schuckers, p. 107 has the 23 Dec 1776 loan from the Farmers-General at 1,000,000 l. (SM $194,000), and has the 28 Sep 1779 loan from Spain at SM $150,000.

[7.2-29]   Annual Report of the Secretary of the Treasury on the State of the Finances for the Year 1876, Washington, DC: Government Printing Office, 1876, Table M, pp. 24, 25. This section of this report recounts the loans and debts incurred during the Revolution. Schuckers, p. 107 has the 23 Dec 1776 loan from the Farmers-General at 1,000,000 l. (SM $194,000), and has the 28 Sep 1779 loan from Spain at SM $150,000.

[7.2-30]   op. cit., Phillips and Potter, pp. 149-151

[7.2-31]   op. cit., Elliot, p. 11. There is a note on the same page calling out Senate Document 229, 25 Feb 1843 (27th Congress) as citing these same figures. However, the Senate document only cites the total amount of Continentals issued ($242,100,176) and the amount redeemed ($168,280,219.12).

[7.2-32]   op. cit., Schuckers, p. 127

[7.2-33]   op. cit., Schuckers, p. 48

[7.2-34]   op. cit., Schuckers, p. 62

[7.2-35]   op. cit., Schuckers, p. 62

[7.2-36]   op. cit., Schuckers, p. 84

[7.2-37]   op. cit., Phillips and Potter, pp. 151-153, 160

[7.2-38]   op. cit., Phillips and Potter, p. 210

[7.2-39]   op. cit., Phillips and Potter, pp. 210, 211

[7.2-40]   op. cit., Schuckers, p. 78

[7.2-41]   op. cit., Phillips and Potter, pp. 211-217

[7.2-42]   op. cit., Schuckers, p. 63

[7.2-43]   op. cit., Elliot, p. 11.

[7.2-44]   op. cit., Schuckers, p. 127

[7.2-45]   op. cit., Schuckers, pp. 81, 82

[7.2-46]   op. cit., Schuckers, p. 86

[7.2-47]   op. cit., Schuckers, pp. 92, 96, 97

[7.2-48]   op. cit., Bolles, Vol. 1, p. 272

[7.2-49]   op. cit., Bolles, Vol. 1, pp. 273, 274

[7.2-50]   op. cit., Bolles, Vol. 1, p. 306

[7.2-51]   op. cit., Bolles, Vol. 1, pp. 307, 320

[7.2-52]   op. cit., Schuckers, p. 127

[7.2-53]   op. cit., Elliot, p. 11

[7.2-54]   op. cit., Bolles, Vol. 1, p. 326

[7.2-55]   op. cit., Bolles, Vol. 1, p. 310

[7.2-56]   *The Secret Journal of the Acts and Proceedings of Congress*, Boston, MA: Thomas B. Wait, 1821, Vol. 3, pp. 281-289

[7.2-57]   op. cit., Bolles, Vol. 1, p. 313

[7.2-58]   Annual Report of the Secretary of the Treasury on the State of the Finances for the Year 1876, Washington, DC: Government Printing Office, 1876, Table M, pp. 24, 25. This section of this report recounts the loans and debts incurred during the Revolution. Schuckers, p. 107 has the 23 Dec 1776 loan from the Farmers-General at 1,000,000 l. (SM $194,000), and has the 28 Sep 1779 loan from Spain at SM $150,000.

[7.2-59]   op. cit., Bolles, Vol. 1, p. 314

[7.2-60]   op. cit., Schuckers, p. 127

[7.2-61]   op. cit., Schuckers, pp. 107-109

[7.2-62]   op. cit., Bolles, Vol. 1, p. 317

[7.2-63]   George Bancroft, *History of the United States of America from the Discovery of the Continent*, NY: D. Appleton & Company, 1888, Vol. 6, p. 62

[7.2-64]   op. cit., Fitzpatrick, Vol. 26, pp. 229-232

[7.2-65]   Gaillard Hunt, ed., *Journals of the Continental Congress*, Washington, DC: U. S. Government Printing Office, 1922, Vol. 24, pp. 206-210

[7.2-66]   op. cit., Bolles, Vol. 1, p. 244

[7.2-67]   op. cit., Hunt, ed., Vol. 24, pp. 256-261

[7.2-68]   op. cit., Bancroft, Vol. 6, pp. 82, 83

[7.2-69]   John Fiske, *John Fiske's Historical Writings*, NY: Houghton, Mifflin and Company, 1901, Vol. 12, pp. 65-69, 194-198

[7.2-70]   op. cit., Bancroft, Vol. 6, p. 105

[7.2-71]   op. cit., Albert S. Bolles, Vol. 1, p. 322

[7.2-72]   op. cit., Schuckers, p. 127

[7.2-73]   op. cit., Hunt, ed., Vol. 26, pp. 297-310

[7.2-74]   op. cit., Bolles, Vol. 1, p. 322

[7.2-75]   op. cit., Bolles, Vol. 1, p. 257

[7.2-76]   op. cit., Hunt, Vol. 26, pp. 185-198. See also Bolles, Vol. 1, p. 321

[7.2-77]   op. cit., Bolles, Vol. 1, p. 333

[7.2-78]   op. cit., Bolles, Vol. 1, p. 327

[7.2-79]   op. cit., Bancroft, Vol. 6, pp. 123, 124

[7.2-80]   op. cit., Bolles, Vol. 1, pp. 341, 342

[7.2-81]   op. cit., Bancroft, Vol. 6, pp. 140-147

[7.2-82]   op. cit., Bolles, Vol. 1, pp. 345, 346

[7.2-83]   op. cit., Bolles, Vol. 1, pp. 348, 349

[7.2-84]   op. cit., Bolles, Vol. 1, p. 348

[7.2-85]   op. cit., Bolles, Vol. 1, pp. 338, 339

[7.2-86]   op. cit., Hunt, Vol. 30, pp. 70-76
[7.2-87]   op. cit., Bolles, Vol. 1, pp. 341, 342
[7.2-88]   op. cit., Bolles, Vol. 1, pp. 346, 347
[7.2-89]   op. cit., Bolles, Vol. 1, pp. 344, 345
[7.2-90]   op. cit., Bolles, Vol. 1, pp. 344, 345
[7.2-91]   op. cit., Bolles, Vol. 1, p. 350
[7.2-92]   op. cit., Bancroft, Vol. 6, pp. 140-147
[7.2-93]   op. cit., Bolles, Vol. 1, pp. 338, 339
[7.2-94]   op. cit., Bolles, Vol. 1, p. 357
[7.2-95]   op. cit., Elliot, pp. 6, 7 Elliot reproduces here a set of statistics published by Pelatiah Webster of Phila-delphia, who tracked the depreciation through the existence of the Continentals.
[7.2-96]   op. cit., Schuckers, p. 110

[7.4-1]   op. cit., Bolles, Vol. 1, pp. 151, 152
[7.4-2]   op. cit., Schuckers, pp. 29, 30
[7.4-3]   op. cit., Bolles, Vol. 1, p. 287
[7.4-4]   op. cit., Schuckers, pp. 26-28
[7.4-5]   op. cit., Bolles, Vol. 1, p. 358
[7.4-6]   op. cit., Schuckers, p. 11
[7.4-7]   William Brough, *The Natural Law of Money*, NY: Greenwood Press, 1969, p. 87 (originally published by G. P. Putnam's Sons, 1896)
[7.4-8]   Albert Gallatin, *Considerations on the Currency and Banking System of the United States*, Philadelphia, PA: Carey & Lea, 1831, p. 86

8

The Debate on Money in the Constitutional Convention

8.1 The Provisions in the U. S. Constitution

Those who deposit money in a bank should be aware of what is actually transpiring legally. The money deposited technically no longer belongs to the depositor; it belongs to the bank. The bank, by keeping a record of the deposits, has only subscribed to an obligation to return it on demand. So, the depositor gives money to the bank in return for a right to receive it back at a later date. The money deposited is not considered as a pawn ticket or a warehouse receipt: it is a release of a title in return for a legal right to receive it back when desired [8.1-1]. How did the U. S. monetary system, in which money was defined as coin, change to a system of fiat bank notes, and banks obligated to recognize a right of payment on demand? In Great Britain, it was accomplished by a series of judicial rulings [8.1-2]. To answer that for the U. S., it is necessary to review two provisions in the federal Constitution. The first is Article 1, Section 8:

> Congress shall have the power ... to coin money, regulate the value thereof, and of foreign coin, and fix the standard of weights and measures.

The second is from Article 1, Section 10:

> "No State shall ... coin money; emit bills of credit; make anything but gold and silver coin a tender in payment of debts...

Congress was granted the power to coin money and regulate its value. A bill of credit is a note bearing interest designed to circulate as money backed by the credit of the government (such as the Continentals); it is most like a bearer-bond. The Constitution is silent as to whether the federal government could issue bills of credit (although the early writers and commentators on the Constitution generally recognized that it could do so under certain circumstances). For example, St. George Tucker [8.1-3] notes, discussing the prohibition of bills of credit issued by a State:

> "But why was not the prohibition extended to the federal, as well as to the state governments? The federal government, during the revolutionary war, was not more exempt from just cause of censure upon these grounds [issuing the depreciating Continentals], than the states respectively. Many of the laws passed by the states to support the credit of the continental money, by making it a legal tender in payment of debts, were passed on the recommendation of congress. The forty for one scheme originated there; why not prohibit some future congress from renewing the same breach of faith?"

Von Holst in 1887 [8.1-4] discusses the same issue; note he says 'right' when he should have said 'power':

> "But on the other hand the states are forbidden to issue "bills of credit," and the right of the federal government to do so is unquestioned, although this right was not expressly granted to it, but is merely deduced from the authority to borrow money [1]. Yet the debates of the Philadelphia convention leave it very doubtful whether the intention was to give the federal government the right to issue paper money. An express grant of this power was in the draft of the constitution, and was stricken out by a vote of nine states to

two. The views of the delegates differed, however, as to what rights congress would have in this respect, if nothing were said about it. The prevailing, if not quite unanimous view, was that congress would not be able to make the federal notes a legal tender.

[1] "Bills of credit" are simply direct obligations of the state intended to circulate as money. Bank notes do not fall under this description, even if the state is the sole holder of the bank stock. Craig vs. Missouri, Peters, IV, 410; Briscoe vs. Bank of the Commonwealth of Kentucky, ibid., XI, 257; Darrington vs. Bank of Alabama, Howard, XIII, 12

8.2 Debate at the Constitutional Convention

The power to issue notes on the government's credit was debated at the Convention, and the power to emit notes on the government's credit was explicitly eliminated as von Holst pointed out above. The version being debated was from 6 Aug 1787, and the provision in question read:

"Congress shall have the power to borrow money and emit bills, on the credit of the United States."

James Madison's notes taken during the debates on the Federal Constitution in Philadelphia on 16 Aug 1787 indicate the founder's change of opinion regarding bills of credit [8.2-1, 8.2-6], italics in the original:

The several clauses - for coining money - for regulating foreign coin -- for fixing the standard of weights and measures - were agreed to, *nem. con.*

On the clause, "to establish post-offices," -

Mr. GERRY moved to add, "and post-roads."

Mr. MERCER seconded; and on the question --

Massachusetts, Delaware, Maryland, Virginia, South Carolina, Georgia, aye, 6; New Hampshire, Connecticut, New Jersey, Pennsylvania, North Carolina, no, 5.

Mr. GOUVERNEUR MORRIS moved to strike out "and emit bills on the credit of the United States." If the United States had credit, such bills would be unnecessary; if they had not, unjust and useless.

Mr. BUTLER seconds the motion.

Mr. MADISON. Will it not be sufficient to prohibit the making of them a *tender*? This will remove the temptation to emit them with unjust views; and promissory notes, in that shape, may in some emergencies be best.

Mr. GOUVERNEUR MORRIS. Striking out the words will leave room still for notes of a *responsible* minister, which will do all the good without the mischief. The moneyed interest will oppose the plan of government, if paper emission be not prohibited.

Mr. GORHAM was for striking out without inserting any prohibition. If the words stand, they may suggest and lead to the measure.

Mr. MASON had doubts on the subject. Congress, he thought, would not have the power, unless it were expressed. Though he had a mortal hatred of paper money, yet, as he could not foresee all emergencies, he was unwilling to tie the hands of the legislature. He observed that the late war could not have been carried on, had such a prohibition existed.

Mr. GORHAM. The power, as far as it will be necessary or safe, is involved in that of borrowing.

Mr. MERCER was a friend to paper money, though, in the present state and temper of America, he should neither propose nor approve of such a measure. He was consequently opposed to a prohibition of it altogether. It will stamp suspicion on the government, to deny it a discretion on this point. It was impolitic, also, to excite the opposition of all those who were friends of paper money. The people of property would be sure to be on the side of the plan, and it was impolitic to purchase their further attachment with the loss of the opposite class of citizens.

Mr. ELLSWORTH thought this a favorable moment to shut and bar the door against paper money. The mischief's of the various experiments which had been made were now fresh in the public minds, and had excited the disgust of all the respectable part of America. By withholding the power from the new government, more friends of influence would be gained to it than by almost anything else. Paper money can in no case be necessary. Give the government credit, and other resources will offer. The power may do harm, never good.

Mr. RANDOLPH, notwithstanding his antipathy to paper money, could not agree to strike out the words, as he could not foresee all the occasions that might arise.

Mr. WILSON. It will have a most salutary influence on the credit of the United States, to remove the possibility of paper money. This expedient can never succeed whilst its mischief's are remembered; and, so long as it can be resorted to, it will be a bar to other resources.

Mr. BUTLER remarked that paper was a legal tender in no country in Europe. He was urgent for disarming the government of such a power.

Mr. MASON was still averse to tying the hands of the legislature *altogether*. If there was no example in Europe, as just remarked, it might be observed, on the other side, that there was none in which the government was restrained on this head.

Mr. READ thought the words, if not struck out, would be as alarming as the mark of the beast in Revelation.

Mr. LANGDON had rather reject the whole plan, than retain the three words, "and emit bills."

On the motion for striking out, --

New Hampshire, Massachusetts, Connecticut, Pennsylvania, Delaware, Virginia*, North Carolina, South Carolina, Georgia, aye, 9; New Jersey, Maryland, no, 2.

The clause for borrowing money was agreed to *nem. con.*

* This vote in the affirmative by Virginia was occasioned by the acquiescence of Mr. Madison, who became satisfied that striking out the words would not disable the government from the use of public notes, as far as they could be safe and proper; and would only cut off the pretext for a *paper currency*, and particularly for making the bills a *tender*, either for public or private debts.

The federal government, having the power to "coin money" did so through the Treasury. It is fair to conclude that the Constitution implicitly permits the U. S. government alone to issue paper money, but not as legal tender. Although the power to issue notes backed by the credit of the United States is not specifically called out in the Constitution, there was little dispute that the government did in fact have the ability to do so, especially since it was the only means to finance a war or other emergency. There was another complication here not mentioned by Madison, which is: Congress, under the current Articles of Confederation, had already chartered a private bank that was allowed to issue bank notes, although not on the credit of the United States. It seems then, that the founders did not consider "bills of credit" to be the same as bank notes [8.2-3]; thus Mr. Madison's disclaimer.

8.3 How the Original Consensus Was Modified

But notice what happened eventually: Federal Reserve Notes are not only fiat paper currency, but are legal tender for all debts, public and private, contrary to the powers of the government as envisioned by Madison and Morris. But Federal Reserve Notes were preceded during the Civil War by United States Notes (greenbacks), with the same provisions. Thus Congress eventually acquired by a series of court rulings, or merely assumed the power to authorize another institution to do indirectly what Congress lacked the authority to do directly. It was aided by the examples set by the States.

A State was prohibited from coining money or making anything other than gold and silver a legal tender. But the States got around this prohibition, as validated in a series of court cases [8.3-1]:

BILLS OF CREDIT

Within the sense of the Constitution, bills of credit signify a paper medium of exchanges, intended to circulate between individuals; and between the government and individuals, for ordinary purposes of society. It is immaterial whether the quality of legal tender is imparted to such paper. Interest bearing certificates, in denominations not exceeding ten dollars, which were issued by loan offices established by the State of Missouri, and made receivable in payment of taxes or other moneys due to the State, and in payment of the fees and salaries of State officers, were held to be bills of credit whose issuance was banned by this section [1]. The States are not forbidden, however, to issue coupons receivable for taxes [2], nor to execute instruments binding themselves to pay money at a future day for services rendered or money borrowed [3]. Bills issued by State banks are not bills of credit [4]; it is immaterial that the State is the sole stockholder of the bank [5], that the officers of the bank were elected by the State legislature [6], or that the capital of the bank was raised by the sale of State bonds [7].

[1] Craig v. Missouri, 4 Pet. 410, 425 (1830); Byrne v. Missouri, 8 Pet. 40 (1834)

[2] Poindexter v. Greenhow, 114 U. S. 270 (1885); Chaffin v. Taylor, 116 U. S. 507 (1886)

[3] Houston & T. C. R. Co. v. Texas, 177 U. S. 66 (1900)

[4] Briscoe v. Bank of Kentucky, 11 Pet. 257 (1837)

[5] Darrington v. Bank of Alabama, 13 How. 12, 15 (1851); Curran v. Arkansas, 15 How. 304, 317 (1853)

[6] Briscoe v. Bank of Kentucky, 11 Pet. 257 (1837)

[7] Woodruff v. Trapnall, 10 How. 190, 205 (1851)

So the States avoided the prohibition against issuing paper money by chartering and funding a bank, and giving it the power to do what the State could not do directly itself. (See the trick?) Banks then could issue money in the form of bank notes so long as they did not directly claim to be relying on the credit of the State. Never mind that the State created the bank, it's capital was paid for by the State taxpayers, the officers of the bank were installed by the State, and the credit of the State (i.e., the taxpayers) was called upon indirectly to bail out the banks when they got into trouble.

The prohibition on issuing legal tender notes was ruled to apply only to the States in 1884 [8.3-2]:

LEGAL TENDER

Relying on this clause, which applies only to the States and not the Federal Government [1], the Supreme Court has held that where the marshal of a State court received State bank notes in payment and discharge of an execution, the creditor was entitled to demand payment in gold or silver [2]. Since, however, there is nothing in the Constitution which prohibits a bank depositor from consenting when he draws a check, that payment may be made by draft, a State law which provided that checks drawn on local banks should, at the option of the bank, be payable in exchange drafts was held valid [3].

[1] Legal Tender Cases, 110 U. S. 421, 446 (1884)

[2] Gwin v. Breedlove, 2 How. 29, 38 (1884). See also Griffin v. Thompson, 2 How. 244 (1844)

[3] Farmers and Merchants Bank v. Federal Reserve Bank, 262 U. S. 649, 659 (1923)

Here is the story regarding 110 U. S. 421, 446, which is Juilliard v. Greenman (3 Mar 1884). At issue was payment for 100 bales of cotton totaling $5,122.90 due to Juilliard, in which Greenman offered to pay $22.50 in gold coin, $0.40 in silver coin, and two United States Notes (greenbacks), one for $5,000 and one for $100. The court concluded in the majority opinion (Justice Gray):

"The power of making the notes of the United States a legal tender in payment of private debts, being included in the power to borrow money and to provide a national currency, is not defeated or restricted by the fact that its exercise may affect the value of private contracts. If, upon a just and fair interpretation of the whole Constitution, a particular power or authority appears to be vested in Congress, it is no constitutional objection to its existence, or to its exercise, that the property or the contracts of individuals may be incidentally affected. The decisions of this court, already cited, afford several examples of this.

Upon the issue of stock, bonds, bills or notes of the United States, the States are deprived of their power of taxation to the extent of the property invested by individuals in such obligations, and the burden of State taxation upon other private property is correspondingly increased. The ten per cent tax, imposed by Congress on notes of State banks and of private bankers, not only lessens the value of such notes, but tends to drive them, and all State banks of issue, out of existence. The priority given to debts due to the United States over the private debts of an insolvent debtor diminishes the value of these debts, and the amount which their holders may receive out of the debtor's estate.

So, under the power to coin money and to regulate its value, Congress may (as it did with regard to gold by the act of June 28th, 1834, ch. 95, and with regard to silver by the act of February 28th, 1878, ch. 20) issue coins of the same denominations as those already current by law, but of less intrinsic value than those, by reason of containing a less weight of the precious metals, and thereby enable debtors to discharge their debts by the payment of coins of the less real value. A contract to pay a certain sum in money, without any stipulation as to the kind of money in which it shall be paid, may always be satisfied by payment of that sum in any currency which is lawful money at the place and time at which payment is to be made.

It follows that the act of May 31st, 1878, ch. 146, is constitutional and valid; and that the Circuit Court rightly held that the tender in treasury notes, reissued and kept in circulation under that act, was a tender of lawful money in payment of the defendant's debt to the plaintiff."

Justice Field concluded his dissenting opinion as follows:

"From the decision of the court I see only evil likely to follow. There have been times within the memory of all of us when the legal tender notes of the United States were not exchangeable for more than one-half of their nominal value. The possibility of such depreciation will always attend paper money. This inborn infirmity no mere legislative declaration can cure. If Congress has the power to make the notes a legal tender and to pass as money or its equivalent, why should not a sufficient amount be issued to pay the bonds of the United States as they mature? Why pay interest on the millions of dollars of bonds now due, when Congress can in one day make the money to pay the principal? And why should there be any restraint upon unlimited appropriations by the government for all imaginary schemes of public improvement, if the printing press can furnish the money that is needed for them?"

Keep in mind that Juilliard v. Greenman was decided in 1884, 22 years after Congress had already issued legal tender 'greenbacks'. Notice the first sentence in the majority opinion contradicts the understanding achieved at the debate on the Constitution. Thus the federal government was recognized as having a power to issue legal tender notes, presumably on its credit, which is indirectly based on the power of the government to borrow money, levy taxes, and define 'lawful money'. See the trick?

References

[8.1-1]   Fred Rogers Fairchild, Edgar Stevenson Furniss, Norman Sydney Buck, *Elementary Economics*, NY: The Macmillan Company, 1926, Vol. 1, p. 420

[8.1-2]   Murray N. Rothbard, *The Mystery of Banking,* Auburn, AL: Ludwig von Mises Institute, 2008, pp. 91-93 (originally published 1983)

[8.1-3]   St. George Tucker, *View of the Constitution of the United States With Selected Writings*, Indianapolis, IN: Liberty Fund, 1999, p. 250. Tucker's original commentary was published in 1803.

[8.1-4]   H. von Holst, *The Constitutional Law of the United States of America*, Chicago, IL: Callaghan & Co., 1887, pp. 124, 125

[8.2-1]   Jonathan Elliot, *Debates on the Adoption of the Federal Constitution in the Convention Held at Philadelphia in 1787*, Supplement to *Elliot's Debates*, Vol. 5, pp. 378, 434, 435

[8.2-2]   James Madison, *Notes of the Debates in the Federal Convention of 1787*, Athens, OH: Ohio University Press, 1966, pp. 469-471

[8.2-3]   William Graham Sumner, *History of American Currency*, 1874, p. 57. He writes, "As the Confederation had already chartered the Bank of North America, it does not seem that the "bills of credit" were understood to cover bank notes."

[8.3-1]   Edward S. Corwin, ed., *The Constitution of the United States of America, Analysis and Interpretation, Annotations of Cases Decided by the Supreme Court of the United States to Jun 30, 1952*, 82nd Congress, Senate Document No. 170, Washington, DC: U. S. Government Printing Office, 1953, p. 326: Legal Tender Cases, 110 U. S. 421, 446 (1884)

[8.3-2]   op. cit., Corwin, ed., p. 326

9

The Congress/Treasury System, 1789, 1790

9.1   Preview, 1789, 1790

One of the first orders of business of the new government was to correct one great defect of the Articles of Confederation, namely to establish some means of generating revenue, not only to pay the current expenses for defense, but also to pay the debts incurred during the war. The revenue was based mostly on import duties. Treasury Secretary Hamilton worked out the finances and presented a report to Congress, recommending that the revenues from import duties and internal taxes be devoted to a "sinking fund", to be used to pay off the debt. It was a novel concept at the time: pledging future revenues to pay off old debts, but as will be shown in the next few chapters it worked because Congress made it a high priority.

Meanwhile, the import duties were not yet sufficient to pay current expenses, and the U. S. continued to borrow from foreign nations. Treasury Secretary Hamilton issued a report recommending a bank be set up to act as fiscal agent for the government, and to stabilize the monetary system.

9.2   History, 1789, 1790

7 Jan 1789: Delaware held elections for members of Congress.

7 Jan - 11 Jan 1789: Maryland held elections for members of Congress.

10 Jan 1789: Voting for the President ended (cf. 15 Dec 1788).

2 Feb 1789: Virginia held elections for members of Congress.

9 Feb 1789: Georgia held elections for members of Congress.

11 Feb 1789: New Jersey held elections for members of Congress.

3 Mar - 5 Mar 1789: New York held elections for members of Congress.

4 Mar 1789: Congress assembled, but only 13 members were present (did not have a quorum).

1 Apr 1789: Thirty of 59 members of Congress assembled, it now had a quorum.

30 Apr 1789: George Washington was sworn in as first President of the United States.

4 Jul 1789: Congress established a system of import duties [9.2-1] to provide revenue via *ad valorem* duties, with drawbacks (refunds) for goods exported within a year, and a 10% discount on goods imported by ships owned by Americans [9.2-2]. Provision included: **a)** (S. 1) Congress' rationale: "whereas it was necessary for the support of the government, for the discharge of the debts of the United States, and the encouragement and protection of manufactures, that duties be laid on goods, wares, and merchandises imported"; **b)** (S. 1) a long list of items to which duties were to be imposed, so many cents per unit, and on others and *ad valorem* duty ranging from 5% to 15%; **c)** (S. 3) specific duties on hemp and cotton; **d)** (S. 4) drawbacks allowed on certain items, mostly fish products; and **e)** (S. 5) 10% discounts on duties permitted if imported on vessels owned by U. S. citizens.

20 Jul 1789: Congress established tonnage duties: ships owned by Americans to pay 6 cents per ton on imports, whereas foreign ships were to pay 50 cents per ton. For ships owned partly by Americans and foreigners, the tonnage duty was 30 cents per ton [9.2-3].

2 Sep 1789: Congress established the Treasury department, to be headed by Alexander Hamilton. The department was charged with collecting revenues and establishing an accounting system for their disbursement [9.2-4].

21 Sep 1789: Congress passed a resolution ordering Hamilton to assess the state of the finances.

9 Jan 1790: Alexander Hamilton sent his Report on the Finances to Congress. Figure 9.2-1 shows his calculation of the national debt of the U. S. as $54,124,464 [9.2-5]. The dollar here is assumed to be Spanish Milled Dollars, although Hamilton did not specify it. Note that it did not include the $25,000,000 estimated debts of the States, which was to be assumed by the federal government. He also estimated that the interest due on both foreign and domestic debt to the end of 1790 that should be included in the funding plan to be $2,239,163. Hamilton recommended a series of import duties on tea, wine, and other spirits, as well as excise taxes on alcohol distilled in the U. S. in order to pay off the debt.

Foreign Debt as of 31 Dec 1789	($)	Liquidated Domestic Debt as of 3 Mar 1789	($)	Note
Royal French Treasury	4,444,444	Registered debt	4,598,463	
in Holland, guaranteed by the French court	1,851,852	Credits per special acts of Congress	187,579	
Royal Spanish Treasury	174,011	Certificates issued by army commissioner	7,967,110	
Lenders in Holland	3,600,000	Net certificates issued by 5 departments	903,575	
Subtotal	10,070,307	Certificates issued by State commissioners	3,291,156	
Arrears on Foreign Debt		Loan-office certificates from 1781	112,704	
To France, 6 years on 6 million livres, 1 Jan 1789	277,778	Loan office certificates, old emission, after 1777	11,106,818	
To France, 6 years on 18 million livres, 3 Sep 1789	1,000,000	Credit to foreign officers during the war	186,427	
To France, 4 years on 10 million livres, 5 Nov 1789	296,296	Deduct, received into Treasury	-960,915	
To Spain, as of 21 Mar 1782	5,093	Subtotal, principal of liquidated domestic debt	27,383,917	1, 2
To Spain, 7 years interest 21 Mar 1782 to 1790	60,905	Arrears of Interest on Liquidated Domestic Debt	13,030,168	
Subtotal	1,640,072	Unliquidated Domestic Debt	2,000,000	3
Total foreign debt obligations	11,710,379	Total domestic debt obligations	42,414,085	4
Notes				
1. If the sub categories are correct, Hamilton's total is incorrect; should be 27,392,917 vice his 27,383,917.				
2. "Liquidated" in this context means that the face values of the original debts have been reduced to specie value according to a schedule published by Congress.				
3. The "unliquidated" debt is mostly Continental notes still outstanding. The 2,000,000 estimate is the specie value estimate.				
4. Hamilton also mentions the debt of the States, estimated at $25,000,000 that is not included in this statement of the finances.				

Figure 9.2-1: Total National Debt per Hamilton's Report, Jan 1790

1 Feb 1790: The U. S. obtained a loan of 3,000,000 florins (approximately $1,140,000) from Holland at 5% interest with 4.5% charges, payable in six equal installments between 1800 and 1804 [9.2-6]. The proceeds from this loan (and five others) were used to finance the U. S. government's capital stock in the Bank of the United States.

4 Aug 1790: Congress and the President approved a plan for funding the public debt [9.2-7, 9.2-8, 9.2-9]. The plan is solicit subscribers (i.e., creditors of the government) for a loan of the entire amount. This was not a loan in the conventional sense: it was a re-issue of debt notes to existing creditors of the government, to be paid by future revenues. Certificates (called "stocks") were to be issued to each subscriber specifying the terms of the repayment. Those subscribing to the loan prior to 30 Sep 1791 to be repaid at 6% interest payable quarterly on two-thirds of the principal, and that the government may choose to pay up to 8% of the principal annually before maturity. The remaining one-third of the principal was to be paid 6% interest starting in 1800. Those subscribing to a loan for the payment of interest on the loans made of the debt (called indents) were to be paid quarterly at 3% interest, subject to the same 8% early redemption at the government's discretion. (The date for subscribing to the loan was later revised in a series of resolutions, extending to 31 Dec 1799.) An additional loan for $21,500,000 was proposed to pay the debts of the States. The terms were slightly different:

four-ninths of the principal received 6% interest after 1792, payable quarterly; the next thee-ninths to bear interest at 3% starting in 1792, payable quarterly; and the remaining two-ninths to bear interest at 6% after 1800, payable quarterly. All were subject to the same pre-payment of the principal at 8% annually at the government's discretion. Public revenues, mostly from excise taxes and tonnage duties, and all the revenues from sale of western lands, were pledged to make the payments, except a total of $600,000 was first reserved for the operation of the federal government. Creditors were not required to subscribe to the loan, and their claims were not disregarded if they chose not to; they were to be paid on the same terms as those that did subscribe. The only requirement for those that did not subscribe was that the existing debt obligations be examined for counterfeits, and re-issued. This plan became known as the "sinking fund", in which subscribers to these obligations were paid off from current revenues. Thus the national debt was paid by "purchasing the debt" (i.e., buying back the debt obligations after paying interest). This process continued until 1836, when the debts incurred by the Revolution, the Louisiana Purchase, and the War of 1812 were fully paid off.

10 Aug 1790: Congress raised the import *ad valorem* duties [9.2-10], modifying the law of 4 Jul 1789. It increased the *ad valorem* duties on a large number of specified items (S. 1), mostly defined in so many cents per unit; others were specified in percent of value ranging between 5% and 15.5%. An additional 10% was imposed on goods imported on foreign vessels (S. 2). The lowest rate was 5%, but the free list was expanded, so long as duty-free was helpful to domestic manufacturers. The public was supportive of duties because they were opposed to direct taxation, and also because it was prudent to protect domestic manufacturers. Bolles [9.2-11] explains:

"Thus the duties grew heavier annually; yet, when the government was six years old, the burden of taxation did not cause any dissatisfaction, unless, perhaps, the duty on salt was regarded as too great. Even that was not very keenly felt, and might have been deemed moderate, compared with the tax imposed by some governments. ... Between 1789 and 1812, thirteen tariff laws were enacted, the general scope of which was to increase the duties as well as the number of dutiable articles. The increase was for the purpose of meeting the expenditures of the government, and the payment of the national indebtedness. But the protection of American industries was not ignored, as the history of the proceedings of Congress clearly shows. The subject, however, did not assume such importance in the debates of that body as it has subsequently acquired. One reason was, because public sentiment was so strongly united. The reports of the committees of Congress, and the subsequent debates thereon, show very clearly that the protection of American industries from foreign competition was a principle very widely accepted."

13 Dec 1790: The Treasury Department provided an estimate of the debts of the States, amounting to $21,500,000; and the annual interest on the loan to pay off the current debt at $788,333 [9.2-12]. Hamilton recommended a duty on foreign spirits and an excise tax on domestic spirits to provide the revenue for the annual interest.

14 Dec 1790: Hamilton presented his plan for a National Bank [9.2-13]. His main points were:

a. A national bank will be helpful for paying off the debt, as it will have sufficient capital to allow a large circulation of notes.

b. The notes to be issued are to be payable in metal on demand, and will allow faster payments on debt than selling lands in the west.

c. The bank should be funded using the debt certificates; this will permit the 6% interest payments from the government to enlarge the capital and produce a profit.

d. He reviewed the history of the Bank of England, the stock of which began as a loan to the government.

e. The bank should be restricted to the amount of debt it can contract for.

f. Loans made by the bank should require interest between 5 and 6% on loans in order to encourage the growth of business, but not below the market interest rate.

g. The federal government should own 20% of the bank stock.

9.3 Data, 1789, 1790

Figures 9.3-1 and 9.3-2 show the U. S. government revenues and expenditures for 1789 and 1790. It should be noted that these are somewhat conjectural, since the referenced source documents indicate expectations and estimates; I am not aware of any data that provides the actual revenue and expenditures.

U. S. Government Revenue, 1789, 1790 (USD)										
			Internal Revenue		Miscellaneous					
Day	Year	Customs [3]	Tonnage	Misc.	Sales of Public Lands	Direct Tax [4]	Other Misc.	Postal	Public Debt Sales	Total
31 Dec	1789	1,364,512	102,574	0	0	0	0	0	0	1,467,086
31 Dec	1790	1,140,000	0	0	0	1,703,400	0	0	0	2,843,400

1. Data for 1789 from W. Lowrie, Matthew St. Claire Clark, American State Papers, *Documents, Legislative and Executive of the Congress of the United States*, Washington, DC: Gales and Seaton, 1832, Vol. 5, p 14. These are estimates provided to Congress on 9 Jul, 27 Aug, and 24 Sep 1789.
2. Data from 1790 from *Reports of the Secretary of the Treasury of the United States*, Washington DC: Blair & Rives, 1837 (contains the Annual Report of the Secretary of the Treasury, 1790), p. 53. These are estimated projections.
3. Customs and Tonnage are combined in the 1790 source data.
4. In 1790, Direct Tax included duties on both imported and excise taxes on domestic spirits.

Figure 9.3-1: U. S. Government Revenue, 1789, 1790

U. S. Government Expenditures, 1789, 1790 (USD)										
		Ordinary Disbursements								
Day	Year	Civil & Misc.	War Dep't	Navy Dep't	Indians	Pensions	Interest on Public Debt	Postal	Public Debt Retired	Total
31 Dec	1789	334,000	163,079	0	41,000	92,022	2,610,994	0	0	3,242,884
31 Dec	1790	254,893	155,538	0	0	96,980	2,239,163	0	0	2,748,364

1. Data for 1789 from W. Lowrie, Matthew St. Claire Clark, American State Papers, *Documents, Legislative and Executive of the Congress of the United States*, Washington, DC: Gales and Seaton, 1832, Vol. 5, pp. 11, 12. These are estimates provided to Congress by Eldridge Gerry on 9 Jul, 27 Aug, and 24 Sep 1789. "Interest on the Public Debt" includes, for 1789 alone: a) $476,997 interest on foreign debt, b) $462,962 due on principal of foreign debt, c) $28,000 premium due on the Dutch loan of 9 Mar 1784, and d) $1,643,035 interest on the domestic debt. He also notes that there are other debts due: a) $1,840,071 interest due on foreign debt; b) $1,562,899 due on principal of foreign debt; c) $3,286,070 interest on the domestic debt; and d) $966,460 in arrearages due from previous requistions.
2. Data from 1790 from *Reports of the Secretary of the Treasury of the United States*, Washington DC: Blair & Rives, 1837 (contains the Annual Report of the Secretary of the Treasury, 1790), pp. 22, 45. There is no mention of payments to the Indians.

Figure 9.3-2: U. S. Government Expenditures, 1789, 1790

Figure 9.3-3 shows the national debt and per-capita debt for 1789 and 1790; this data is taken from tabulated data in the Annual Treasury Report of 1980. I am not aware of any figures published in the 1790 time period.

U. S. National Debt, 1789, 1790 (USD)				
Day	Year	Principal ($) [1, 3]	Population [2]	Debt per Capita ($) [2]
31 Dec	1789	71,060,509	3,798,472	18.71
31 Dec	1790	75,463,476	3,929,214	19.21

1. Public debt data for 1790 from the Annual Report of the Secretary of the Treasury, 1980, p. 61.
2. Population values are based on the dicennial census from the Census Bureau, and linearly interpolated. Per capita based on these values.
3. The total debt data for 1789 is from: https://fiscaldata.treasury.gov/datasets/historical-debt-outstanding/historical-debt-outstanding

Figure 9.3-3: National Debt and Per-Capita Share Thereof, 1789, 1790

There is very little data on the condition of banks during this period. The Annual Report of the Comptroller of the Currency in 1876 [9.3-1] refers to p. 216 of a report by Treasury Secretary Crawford of 3 Jan 1836, in which Crawford refers to a statement from *Blodgett's Economica*, estimating the condition of banks for various years. Crawford admits that some of these numbers are conjecture, but it was the best he had, as shown on Figure 9.3-4. Notice that these are for 1784 and 1790; there is no data for the intervening years. There is no reliable data on the money supply in these years, nor was any money coined by the U. S. Treasury. There are no reliable estimates of CPI or income.

Estimate of Banks in U. S., 1784, 1790				
		USD		
Year	Number of Banks	Metallic Medium	Notes in Circulation	Capital
1784	3	10,000,000	2,000,000	2,100,000
1790	4	9,000,000	2,500,000	2,500,000
Source: John Jay Knox, Annual Report of the Comptroller of the Currency, 1876, p. XXXIX, quoting a report by Secretary Crawford from 3 Jan 1836, p. 216.				

Figure 9.3-4: Condition of Banks, 1784, 1790

9.4 Summary, 1789, 1790

The U. S. government ran deficits in these years, still borrowing money from foreign nations, and still struggling to get its finances in order. Secretary Hamilton sorted out what was owed to the States and what was owed by the States, although eventually all the debts owed by the States were forgiven. Congress relied on import duties and excise taxes on domestic spirits as its main source of income.

References

[9.2-1]   Text of "An Act for laying a Duty on goods, Wares, and Merchandise imported into the United States", First Congress, Session 1, Chapter 2, 4 Jul 1789

[9.2-2]   Albert S. Bolles, *A Financial History of the United States*, NY: Augustus M. Kelley (1969), Vol. 2, pp. 75, 76 (originally published 1884 by D. Appleton & Co., NY)

[9.2-3]   op. cit., Bolles, Vol. 2, p. 76

[9.2-4]   op. cit., Bolles, Vol. 2, pp. 6, 7

[9.2-5]   Alexander Hamilton, *General view of the origin and the terms upon which the public debt has been contracted, with plans submitted for the restoration of the public credit*, 9 Jan 1790; submitted to Congress 14 Jan 1790. It is reproduced in Jonathan Elliot, *The Funding System of the United States and Great Britain*, Washington, DC: Blair & Rives, 1845, pp. 23, 34, 35, 42, 53, 54. The debt numbers quoted in the text are on pp. 34, 35.

[9.2-6]   Jonathan Elliot, *The Funding System of the United States and Great Britain*, Washington, DC: Blair and Rives, 1845, pp. 96, 160

[9.2-7]   op. cit., Elliot, pp. 83-90.

[9.2-8]   op. cit., Bolles, Vol. 2, pp. 24-29 (originally published 1884 by D. Appleton & Co., NY)

[9.2-9]   Text of "An Act making provision for the payment of the Debt of the United States", First Congress, Session 2, Chapter 34, 4 Aug 1790

[9.2-10]   Text of "An Act making further provision for the payment of the debts of the United States", First Congress, Session 2, Chapter 39, 10 Aug 1790

[9.2-11]   op. cit., Bolles, Vol. 2, pp. 76-78 (originally published 1884 by D. Appleton & Co., NY)

[9.2-12]   op. cit., Elliot, pp. 90, 91

[9.2-13]   op. cit., Elliot, pp. 91-95

[9.3-1]   Lot M. Morrill, *Annual Report of the Secretary of the Treasury on the State of the Finances for Year 1876*, Appendix containing the Report of the Comptroller of Currency (John Jay Knox), Washington, DC: Government Printing Office, 1876, p. 153

10

The First Bank of the United States, 1791-1811

10.1 Preview, 1791-1811

This period covers the operation of the first Bank of the United States, as proposed by Hamilton and authorized by Congress in 1791. It was opposed on Constitutional grounds by Jefferson and Madison, but in the end, President Washington was convinced that authorizing such a corporation was permitted. The Bank was not a "central bank"; it had no power or ability to enact any monetary policy, it did not hold reserves for other banks, it did not lend to other banks, it did not purchase or deal in government bonds. The main objectives were: a) to handle the government's finances by transferring deposits to branches and making payments; b) making loans to the government; and c) operating as a regular commercial bank. It had the power to issue currency on its own credit, and its notes were widely accepted and could be used to pay federal taxes. It did pay its notes in coin on demand, and it required payment of bank notes issued by State banks, which served to restrain the issue of those notes. Another purpose as conceived by Hamilton was that a bank would help establish the credit of the U. S.

There were some lingering questions about whether such an institution was authorized under the Constitution, and the renewal of its charter failed in 1811.

The U. S. continued to borrow from foreign nations early in this period, although by 1805 it was able to begin making payments on the national debt. Congress authorized a mint, and it began to manufacture coins, although most of the money in circulation consisted of either bank notes or foreign coin.

10.2 History, 1791-1811

25 Feb 1791: The Bank of the United States was established, to have a 20-year charter, expiring on 4 Mar 1811 [10.2-1, 10.2-2]. The capital stock was set at $400 per share, 25,000 shares, for a total capital of $10,000,000. One-fifth of the stock was to be owned by the federal government, paid for out of money borrowed from Holland per two Acts of Congress (4 Mar 1790 and 12 Aug 1790). (The Holland loans came to $8,200,000 total [10.2-3]). The U. S. government subscription was to be paid in ten equal annual installments; subscriptions by individuals or other entities were to be paid in six equal installments, semi-annually. Payments for shares by individuals or other entities had to be paid 25% in gold or silver, and the rest in the public certificates carrying 6% interest issued under the 4 Aug 1790 loan. A total of $8,000,000 was paid in by individuals, $2,000,000 in gold and $6,000,000 in "stock" certificates per the 4 Aug 1790 loan provision. The Bank was permitted to issue notes, payable on demand in gold or silver, and were received for all taxes due to the federal government. No other bank was to be chartered by the federal government during the Bank's existence.

1 Mar 1791: The U. S. obtained a loan of 2,500,000 florins (approximately $950,000) from Holland at 5% interest with 4% charges, payable in six equal installments between 1800 and 1804 [10.2-4].

3 Mar 1791: Congress enacted a system of internal revenue based on excise taxes on spirits: 11 cents per gallon from that distilled from foreign ingredients, and 9 cents per gallon on that made with domestic ingredients [10.2-5]. This type of tax was unpopular in the Southern States, since more alcohol was consumed per capita in that part of the country.

4 Mar 1791: The Bank of the United States began operations [10.2-6]. It was managed by 25 directors, elected by the shareholders, and the directors elected one of them to be president. All directors had to be U. S. citizens, and all served without pay except for the president. Transactions could only be made by a board, consisting of seven of the directors. The Bank was permitted to incur debts or liabilities only up to $10,000,000 above the amount of its deposits. It was permitted to sell any of the public debt certificates held as capital, but could not purchase any public debt of any kind. The Bank was headquartered in Philadelphia (with a capital of $4,700,000) and was permitted to open eight branches for granting discounts and taking deposits. The branches were in Boston, MA (capital = $700,000); New York, NY (capital = $1,800,000); Baltimore, MD (capital = $600,000); Washington DC (capital = $200,000); Norfolk VA (capital = $600,000); Charleston, SC (capital = $600,000); Savannah, GA (capital = $500,000); and New Orleans, LA (capital = $300,000). At the end of the Bank's charter in 1811, the annual dividends paid turned out to average between 8.38 and 8.66%.

1 Sep 1791: The U. S. obtained a loan of 6,000,000 florins (approximately $2,280,000) from Holland at 5% interest with 4% charges, payable in six equal installments between 1800 and 1804 [10.2-7].

11 Sep 1791: A tax revolt called the "Whiskey Rebellion" began against the excise taxes imposed in distilled liquor. On this day a tax collector named Robert Johnson was tarred and feathered in Washington County, PA. Because of threats, the tax became difficult to collect.

1 Dec 1791: The U. S. obtained a loan of 2,050,000 florins (approximately $779,000) from Holland at 4.5% interest with 4% charges, payable in six equal installments between 1800 and 1804 [10.2-8].

1 Jan 1792: The U. S. obtained a loan of 3,000,000 florins (approximately $1,140,000) from Holland at 4% interest with 5.5% charges, payable in six equal installments between 1800 and 1804 [10.2-9].

7 Feb 1792: Hamilton provided a report dated 23 Jan 1792 on the status of the debt funding per the 4 Aug 1790 legislation [10.2-10]:

a. Debt converted into "stock" (U. S. government debt obligations) totaled $31,797,491, consisting of:

    1. $14,177,450 bearing 6% interest, payable currently
    2. $7,088,728 bearing 6% interest, payable starting 1 Jan 1801
    3. $10,531,303 bearing 3% interest payable currently

b. Credit to the trustees owing to purchase of the public debt, $1,131,364

c. Unsubscribed residue or overall debt, $10,616,604, consisting of:

    1. $6,795,815 registered debt, principal and interest
    2. $15,675 unsubscribed in NJ, MD, and PA, principal and interest
    3. $107,649 credits on Treasury books for which no certificates have been issued
    4. $3,697,466 outstanding or floating evidences of debt (estimated)

2 Apr 1792: Congress passed the Coinage Act of 1792 [10.2-11, 10.2-12]. Sections 1 through 8 established a mint and the duties of employees. Section 9 specified the coinage for the U. S. The largest coin was called an Eagle, valued at ten dollars, and to contain 247.5 grains of pure gold (270 grains standard gold). Half-Eagles ($5) and Quarter Eagles ($2.50) at proportional weights were authorized. The dollar was defined as 371.25 grains of pure silver (416 grains of standard silver). Half-dollars, quarter-dollars, dimes, and half dimes were to contain the proportionate amount of silver. The one-cent coin was defined to contain 11 pennyweights of copper, and half-cents to contain proportional copper. Section 11 established the mint ratio of gold to silver as 1:15. Section 12 defined standard gold as 11 parts fine and 1 part alloy. Section 13 defined standard silver as 1,485 parts fine to 179 parts copper. The law allowed for free coinage at no cost to those who brought bullion to the

mint per sections 14 and 15. Section 16 specified that the gold and silver coins were legal tender at full weight, and were legal tender proportionally for underweight ones. Section 19 prescribed the death penalty for any mint employees who created underweight coins and diverted the metal for their benefit.

2 May 1792: Congress authorized Treasury Secretary Hamilton to borrow $400,000 from the Bank of the United States, the proceeds of which to be used to partly finance a war with the Indians [10.2-13]. The remainder of the financing came from a $150,000 surplus in 1791 and $523,000 in import duties.

8 May 1792: Congress passed a law imposing duties on domestic spirits [10.2-14]. Among its provisions: **a)** (S. 1): duties of so many cents per gallon on liquor, and on stills; **b)** (S. 1) requiring owners of stills to obtain a license; **c)** (S. 2 through 9) established a system of inspection of stills and verification of duties; and **d)** (S. 11) drawbacks permitted only on quantities exported in excess of 100 gallons.

8 May 1792: Congress authorized [10.2-15] the coinage of minor copper coins of cents and half-cents: **a)** (S. 1) authorized the director of the mint to procure up to 150 tons of copper for coinage; **b)** (S. 2) $50,000 of copper coins to be minted; and **c)** (S. 2) after six months, only the U. S. copper coins shall be received in commerce, with penalties up to $10 for offering foreign copper coins.

1 Jun 1792: The U. S. obtained a loan of 3,000,000 florins (approximately $1,140,000) from Holland at 4% interest with 5% charges, payable in six equal installments between 1800 and 1804 [10.2-16].

15 Sep 1792: President Washington issued a proclamation denouncing the Whiskey Rebellion.

14 Jan 1793: Congress redefined [10.2-17] the copper coinage: a) cents to contain 208 grains of pure copper; b) half cents to contain 104 grains of pure copper.

16 Jan 1793: Hamilton issued a report showing a federal government surplus of $277,305 for the calendar year 1792 [10.2-18].

9 Feb 1793: Congress enacted a law permitting foreign coins to circulate as legal tender at specified conversion rates, to expire in three years (when the mint was up and running), except Spanish Milled Dollars could continue to circulate indefinitely [10.2-19].

~15 Dec 1793: A final determination of the credits owed to the States and debts of States owed to the federal government was completed. The federal government paid what they owed, but the States never did. The federal government did not have the means to force payment, credits were given to the States for building defensive works, and eventually the remaining debt of those States was forgiven [10.2-20].

Creditor States: New Hampshire, $75,055; Massachusetts, $1,248,801; Rhode Island, $299,611; Connecticut, $619,121; New Jersey, $49,030; South Carolina, $1,205,978; and Georgia, $19,988; total = $3,517,584.

Debtor States: New York, $2,074,846; Pennsylvania, $76,709; Delaware, $612,428; Maryland, $151,640; Virginia, $100,879; and North Carolina, $501,082; total = $3,517,584.

1 Jan 1794: The U. S. obtained a loan of 3,000,000 florins (approximately $1,140,000) from Holland at 5% interest with 5% charges, payable in five equal installments between 1805 and 1809 [10.2-21].

28 Feb 1794: Congress authorized the Secretary of the Treasury to borrow from the Bank of the United States up to $1,000,000 (later increased to $2,000,000) [10.2-22].

20 Mar 1794: Congress authorized a loan of $1,000,000 at 5% interest or less [10.2-23], permitting the Bank of the United States to make the loan. It was to be used to pay the ransom to Algerian pirates who had been interfering in American commerce in the Mediterranean, and had kidnapped and were holding for ransom several American prisoners [10.2-24]. But only $200,000 could be borrowed (from the Bank of New York at 5% interest). Congress believed it was better to pay the ransom than to build a navy and fight the pirates. A second loan for $1,000,000 was authorized in anticipation of

a war with either Great Britain or France. Both sums were to be borrowed from the Bank of the United States.

25 Apr 1794: The U. S. government reached an agreement with the Bank of the United States: a) that the government would subscribe to 5,000 shares of the Bank stock at $400 each (a total of $2,000,000, which was 20% of the bank's capital), to be remitted from loans made by foreign nations; b) the Bank would pay the U. S. 6% interest on the capital stock; c) the U. S. government would, at the same time, borrow $2,000,000 from the bank at 6% interest, payable over ten years, but could be paid in advance [10.2-25].

22 May 1794: President Washington issued a report to Congress stating the total of the national debt and foreign loans, based on records provided by the Secretary of the Treasury. It included a long list of transactions between the U. S. and foreign governments as well as between the government and individuals from whom the government had borrowed [10.2-26]. It concludes with a summary of the debt situation:

a. The total debt as of 1 Jan 1794 was $76,322,842.38, consisting of $61,987,215.69 domestic, and $14,335,626.69 foreign.

b. The funded domestic debt (i.e., creditors having subscribed to the debt obligations issued by the government) came to:

      1. $18,169,213.15 at present 6% interest
      2. $9,084,608.46 at deferred 6% interest
      3. $12,432,649.64 at present 3% interest

c. Assumed funded domestic debt at:

      1. $8,120,924.11 at present 6% interest
      2. $4,060,311.78 at deferred 6% interest
      3. $6,090,551.57 at present 3% interest

d. Registered domestic debt of $606,600.42

e. A remaining balance of $3,422,356.56 of domestic debt was based on the estimate of 9 Jan 1790, composed of indents, settlement certificates, unreimbursed payments for supplies made by the States during the war, amounts due to creditor States, and arrearages on military pensions, less payments made by the U. S government.

f. Foreign: $2,611,587.88 owed to France, $136,938.81 was due to foreign officers who had aided the revolution, and $11,587.000 owed to Holland.

31 May 1794: Congress passed a law [10.2-27] specifying the manner in which the interest on debts of the U. S. to the States would be paid (cf. ~15 Dec 1793): a) (S. 1) The U. S. to pay 4% interest on balances due to the States from 31 Dec 1789; b) (S. 2) interest to be paid to the States quarterly starting in Mar 1795, to be paid out of import duties.

15 - 17 Jul 1794: Battle of Bower Hill, PA; a standoff in the Whiskey Rebellion between tax collectors and opponents to the excise tax on spirits.

4 Aug 1794: Supreme Court Justice James Wilson issued a ruling that several counties in western Pennsylvania were engaged in an insurrection (Whiskey Rebellion). This gave President Washington the authority he needed to call out the militia to suppress it.

2 - 10 Oct 1794: A federal army of about 13,000 men, led by Washington, Henry "Lighthorse Harry" Lee, and Daniel Morgan arrived in western Pennsylvania to end the Whiskey Rebellion. The rebels dispersed with no shots fired. Later two men were convicted of treason, but were pardoned by President Washington.

18 Dec 1794: Congress authorized a loan of $2,000,000 from the Bank of the United States at interest not exceeding 5% as a preparation for war with either France or Great Britain [10.2-28, 10.2-29].

25 Jan 1795: Treasury Secretary Hamilton forwarded to Congress a letter dated 26 Sep 1794 from U. S. commissioners in Amsterdam, explaining that they will not be able to obtain a loan in Holland, probably due to low credit of the U. S. and financial difficulties within Holland [10.2-30].

21 Feb 1795: Congress authorized a loan of $800,000 to partly reimburse the Bank of the United States for a loan taken out in 1794 [10.2-31, 10.2-32].

3 Mar 1795: Congress authorized a loan of $1,000,000 to improve the army and navy [10.2-33].

3 Mar 1795: Congress passed legislation with provisions for converting foreign debt to domestic debt by issuing "stock" (U. S. government debt certificates) against the debt owed to foreign nations [10.2-34]. Loans were solicited from Americans in return for certificates to pay the foreign debt, and the certificates were to be redeemed from revenue gained from import duties. The maximum interest rate was set at 6%. A total of $1,848,900 at 5.5% and $3,176,000 at 4.5% interest of the debt owed to France was converted [10.2-35].

7 Mar 1796: The U. S. Senate ratified a treaty [10.2-36] with the Dey and Regency of Algiers, ending the piracy of American vessels, and the U. S. agreeing to pay an annual tribute of $21,600.

28 Apr 1796: Congress passed legislation [10.2-37] authorizing the commissioners of the "sinking fund", which was to pay off public debt, to make dividend payments quarterly on the 6% portion of the funded debt for which payments were currently due. Payments were staggered as follows: a) 1.5% quarterly payments upon the original capital from 1797 to 1818; b) annual 3.5% payments upon the original capital on 31 Dec of each year from 1797 to 1817; and a final payment on 31 Dec 1818 as necessary to pay off the debt. For debt that was to commence repayment in 1801, the pattern of payments were to be made in the same manner, except the corresponding years are 1801 to 1823, with the final payment on 31 Dec 1824.

6 May 1796: Congress passed legislation [10.2-38] authorizing the annual tribute of $24,000 to be paid to the Dey and Regency of Algiers (cf. 7 Mar 1796).

31 May 1796: Congress passed legislation [10.2-39] authorizing a loan of $5,000,000 to be used for paying current debts owed to the Bank of the United States, the bank of New York, or foreign debt, at 6% interest, to be paid quarterly. Import and tonnage duties were pledged for repayment. The principal was not to be paid until 1819.

~ Aug 1796: The U. S. government was forced to sell 2160 of its 5000 shares in the Bank of the United States at $500 per share in order to make payments on a loan to the Bank. This was necessary due to Congress' incompetence in raising the necessary revenues to meet expenses [10.2-40].

~ Oct 1796: The U. S. government was forced to sell 620 of its shares in the Bank of the United States at $490.75 per share in order to make payments on a loan to the Bank [10.2-41]. The U. S. government sold its remaining shares in the stock of the Bank of the United States in 1802 [10.2-42].

28 Dec 1796: Treasury Secretary Wolcott provided a report to Congress showing that $2,710,168.89 of the funded debt had been redeemed in 1795, and that the total national debt as of 1 Jan 1796 was $85,065,423.22 [10.2-43].

3 Mar 1797: Congress passed legislation [10.2-44] imposing import duties on sugar, molasses, tea, velvet, and cotton goods as a means to increase revenues.

3 Mar 1797: Congress authorized a payment [10.2-45] of $96,246.63 for the first two years of annuity payments to the Dey and Regency of Algiers, and $280,259.03 toward the expenses of the negotiations, pursuant to the treaty of 7 Mar 1796.

6 Jul 1797: Congress passed legislation [10.2-46] imposing stamp duties on parchment and vellum for use in official or legal documents, including wills, bonds, promissory notes, insurance policies, and any documents requiring a notary. It was later postponed to begin collection starting 30 Jun 1798 (per legislation 15 Dec 1797).

8 Jul 1797: Congress passed legislation [10.2-47] increasing the import duties on salt (repealed 3 Mar 1807).

8 Jul 1797: Congress authorized [10.2-48] a loan for $800,000 payable in five years at interest not to exceed 6%.

22 Jul 1797: President Adams issued a proclamation stating that foreign coins, except Spanish Milled dollars, would no longer pass as legal tender as of 15 Oct 1797. After that, foreign coins received were melted and re-coined [10.2-49]. But the directors of the Bank of the United States concluded that it would be prudent to continue to use them, and the Treasury department allowed them to be received as before for import duty payments.

30 Nov 1797: Treasury Secretary Wolcott reported that $2,001,674.76 of national debt had been redeemed in 1797 [10.2-50].

1 Feb 1798: Congress enacted a law extending the legal tender status of foreign coin to 3 May 1802 [10.2-51, 10.2-52].

14 Jul 1798: Congress enacted a means to provide a steady revenue, rather than depending on import duties [10.2-53, 10.2-54]. It passed three types of taxes, to be levied as direct taxes to be collected by the States, apportioned according to the 1790 census: a) on houses, specifying nine classes thereof, and the rates for each; b) on slaves; and c) an *ad valorem* assessment on land. (Note that this was not a federal property tax levied on individuals; it was assessed proportionally to the States as a direct tax.) The federal government sent revenue agents to each State to assist with assessing the taxes based on the rates specified in the law. The total to be levied was $2,000,000, apportioned as follows: a) NH: $67,705.36; b) MA: $260,435.31; c) RI: $37,502.08; d) CT: $129,767.00; e) VT: $46,864.18; f) NY: $181,680.70; g) NJ: $98,387.25; h) PA: $237,177.72; i) DE: $30,430.79; j) MD: $152,599.95; k) VA: $345,488.66; l) KY: $37,643.99; m) NC: $193,697.96; n) TN: $18,806.38; o) SC: $112,997.73; and p) GA: $38,814.87.

16 Jul 1798: Congress authorized [10.2-55] the President to borrow $5,000,000 from the Bank of the United States or any other qualified individual or institution, with the proviso that the U. S. may make full repayment after 15 years at discretion.

12 Dec 1798: Treasury Secretary Wolcott reported that $1,118,016.03 of national debt had been redeemed in 1798 [10.2-56].

Feb - Mar 1799: There was a minor tax revolt in Pennsylvania in opposition to over the excise tax on liquor and a direct tax, to be paid on land, raised as a contingency against a war with France [10.2-57]. It was suppressed without casualties, and President Adams later pardoned those who had been convicted of treason. It is generally conceded that the Federalist Party over-reacted to a minor incident.

10 Dec 1799: Treasury Secretary Wolcott provided a report to Congress stating that $1,034,938.62 had been spent in redeeming the debt obligations of the U. S. in 1799 [10.2-58].

31 Dec 1799: At this point, the U. S. Mint had produced coinage of $696,530 in gold, $1,216,158.75 in silver, and $50,111.42 in copper coins; the expenses of running the Mint was $213,336, offset by a reimbursement on the copper coins totaling $48,041.42 [10.2-59].

7 May 1800: Congress authorized [10.2-60] the President to borrow $3,500,000 from the Bank of the United States or any other qualified individual or institution, with the proviso that the U. S. may make full repayment after 15 years at discretion.

13 May 1800: Congress passed legislation [10.2-61] increasing the import duties on sugar, candy, wine, and molasses, and increased the *ad valorem* duties from 10% to 12.5%; and an additional 10% was added to articles imported in foreign vessels.

6 Apr 1802: Congress passed legislation [10.2-62, 10.2-63]: **a)** (S. 1) repealing all internal duties on stills and domestic distilled spirit, sugar, licenses for retailers, sales at auctions, carriages, stamped vellum, parchment, and paper as of 30 Jun 1802; **b)** (S. 2) revenue offices to be closed after collection of duties due; **c)** (S. 3) banks that had agreed to pay 1% annual tax on their dividends in lieu of a stamp

duty on their notes to continue same until 30 Jun 1802; **d)** (S. 9) duties already paid on vellum etc. to be refunded. This was probably a mistake, since they had to be re-imposed during the War of 1812.

29 Apr 1802: Congress passed legislation [10.2-64] committing the import and tonnage duties, as well as other revenue, to payment of the public debt through the "sinking fund", at a minimum of $7,300,000 per year. Section 1 states:

> "Be it enacted by the Senate and House of Representatives of the United States of America in Congress assembled, That so much of the duties on merchandise and tonnage as, together with the monies, other than surpluses of revenue, which now constitute the sinking fund, or shall accrue to it by virtue of any provisions heretofore made, and together with the sums annually required to discharge the annual interest and charges accruing on the present debt of the United States, including temporary loans heretofore obtained, and also future loans which may be made for reimbursing, or redeeming, any installments, or parts of the principal of the said debt, will amount to an annual sum of seven millions three hundred thousand dollars, be, and the same hereby is yearly to be vested in the commissioners of the sinking fund, in the same manner as the monies heretofore appropriated to the said fund, to be applied by the said commissioners to the payment of interest and charges, and to the reimbursement or redemption of the principal of the public debt, and shall be and continue appropriated until the whole of the present debt of the United States, and the loans which may be made for reimbursing or redeeming any parts or installments of the principal of the said debt shall be reimbursed and redeemed: Provided, that after the whole of the said debt, the old six per cent stock, the deferred stock, the 1796 six per cent stock and three per cent stock excepted, shall have been reimbursed or redeemed, any balance of the sums annually appropriated by this act, which may remain unexpended at the end of six months next succeeding the end of the calendar year to which such annual appropriation refers, shall be carried to the surplus fund, and cease to be vested by virtue of this act in the commissioners of the sinking fund, and the appropriation, so far as relates to such unexpended balance, shall cease and determine."

30 Apr 1803: The Louisiana Territory was purchased from France for $15,000,000. France had only possessed it for three weeks, having received it from Spain as part of the Third Treaty of Ildefonso. In fact, France did not "own" it, as it was still occupied mostly by the American Indian tribes. But this agreement ensured that neither France nor Spain would attempt to settle it. The $15,000,000 was to be financed by issuing debt notes for $11,250,000 at 6%, with interest payable in France, and the principal to be paid in four installments in Washington starting in 1818, and $3,750,000 payable in the U. S. to U. S. citizens having claims against France [10.2-65].

30 Apr 1802: Congress passed legislation [10.2-66] recognizing foreign coin as legal tender, to expire after three years.

10 Nov 1803: Congress passed legislation [10.2-67] authorizing the issue of "stock" (U. S. debt) to France for $11,250,000 at 6% as payment to France for the Territory of Louisiana. The Treasury was to treat these debt certificates as part of the public debt, to be repaid the same way, with an additional appropriation to the sinking fund of $700,000.

23 Mar 1804: Congress passed legislation [10.2-68] permitting the Bank of the United States to open branches ("offices of discount and deposit") in territories and dependencies of the U. S.

27 Mar 1804: Congress revised the import duties [10.2-69], adding a few items to the free list, but increasing duties on many other items, with an additional 10% imposed on items imported in foreign vessels. It also imposed an additional tonnage duty (called "light money") on foreign vessels at 50 cents per ton.

10 Apr 1806: Congress passed legislation [10.2-70] permitting foreign coins to pass as current money within the United States, to expire on 10 Apr 1809. It specified the exchange rates for British, Portuguese, Spanish, and French coins, and directed the Treasury Secretary to assay foreign coins annually and report their value against the dollar to Congress. The large exportation of foreign coins, especially the Spanish Milled Dollar, and the inability of the U. S. mint to produce enough U. S. coins caused Congress to enact this law [10.2-71].

18 Apr 1806: Congress passed an embargo act [10.2-72] against Great Britain, Ireland, and their dependencies and colonies, effective 15 Nov 1806. It called out the specific items that were prohibited: anything made primarily from leather, silk, hemp, flax, tin, brass, wool, glass, silverware, paper, nails and spikes, clothing, machinery, playing cards, beer, ale, and pictures. It also prohibited imports from ports beyond the Cape of Good Hope.

11 Feb 1807: Congress passed legislation [10.2-73] designed to encourage holders of existing public debt roll it over into new debt, to be paid quarterly at 6% interest. The preamble reads:

> "WHEREAS it is desirable to adapt the nature of the provision for the redemption of the public debt to the present circumstances of the United States, which can only be done by a voluntary subscription on the part of the creditors."

27 Feb 1807: Treasury Secretary Gallatin issued a report detailing the national debt and payments made to redeem it from 1801 to 1806 [10.2-74]:

1 Jan 1801: national debt = $81,996,268.49; redemptions in 1801 = $2,325,418.55
1 Jan 1802: national debt = $78,750,669.83; redemptions in 1802 = $3,657,945.95
1 Jan 1803: national debt = $74,728,023.98; redemptions in 1803 = $5,627,565.42
1 Jan 1804: national debt = $85,349,744.35; redemptions in 1804 = $4,114,970.38
1 Jan 1805: national debt = $80,530,159.78; redemptions in 1805 = $6,588,879.84
1 Jan 1806: national debt = $74,539,058.75; redemptions in 1806 = $6,505,292.19
1 Jan 1807: national debt (estimated) = $67,727,756.76

3 Mar 1807: Congress repealed [10.2-75] the import duties on salt (cf. 8 Jul 1797).

22 Dec 1807: Congress passed the Embargo Act [10.2-76], prohibiting vessels destined for foreign ports to depart U. S. ports except as cleared by the President; and vessels going from one U. S. port to another to provide bonds equal to double the value of the cargo; was modified 9 Jan 1808 and 12 Mar 1808 to account for river trade and lakes within the U. S.

1 Mar 1809: Congress passed legislation [10.2-77] repealing the previous Embargo Acts, but imposing an absolute prohibition of trade with both Great Britain and France; their vessels were prohibited from U. S. ports except in cases of distress. This law was to expire after the end of the next session of Congress.

31 Dec 1809: To this point, the U. S. Mint had produced coins with a face value of $8,346,146.21, at a net expense of $350,082.77 [10.2-78]. (This value differs slightly from the 1895 Annual Report of the Director of the Mint, where it claims $8,349,421.21)

1 May 1810: Congress extended [10.2-79] the interdiction act against Great Britain and France (cf. 1 Mar 1809) until such time as they stopped interfering with the neutral commerce of the United States, and verified by Proclamation of the President.

1 May 1810: Congress authorized [10.2-80] the President to obtain a loan equal to the outstanding public debt: a) to be repaid in 1810; b) the maximum interest to be paid 6%; c) the maximum term is six years; and d) is to be repaid out of the annual appropriation of $8,000,000 for the sinking fund.

20 Feb 1811: The vote in the Senate to renew the charter for the Bank of the United States was tied at 17-17, and Vice President George Clinton cast the deciding vote against renewing the charter [10.2-81].

2 Mar 1811: Congress authorized [10.2-82] a loan for $5,000,000, to be repaid via the annual $8,000,000 appropriation for the sinking fund.

4 Mar 1811: The charter for the Bank of the United States expired [10.2-83]. The banks chartered by the States now took over as fiscal agents of the U. S. government. Treasury Secretary Gallatin worked out the change by directing the collectors of import duties at the ports to stop depositing customs bonds for collection at the Bank of the United States, and instead deposit them with State chartered banks [10.2-84]. Those coming due after 3 Mar 1811 were to be withdrawn from the Bank of the United States and re-deposited with the State banks. The U. S. government did keep a small balance

in its account at the branch in New Orleans (after the Bank of the United States was re-chartered by Pennsylvania). The revenue was collected normally, and no inconvenience arose from the closing of the Bank. The problem became obvious only when the State banks began to over-issue their notes.

~1 Apr 1811: Many new State banks were chartered by the States as limited-liability companies, and began issuing notes at a rapid rate [10.2-85].

30 Jun 1811: Approximately $1,700,000 of specie was exported to Great Britain after the Bank of the United States was closed, mostly to pay for imports purchased by residents of the New England States [10.2-86].

2 Sep 1811: The U. S. government closed its account at the former United States Bank except for a small account at the branch in New Orleans [10.2-87].

22 Nov 1811: Treasury Secretary Gallatin issued a report detailing the payment of the national debt during the past ten years. He observes that the national debt came to $79,926,999 as of 1 Apr 1801; from then until 31 Dec 1811, a total of $46,022,810 had been paid; and that the old debt as of 31 Dec 1811 was $33,904,189, with the total current debt as $45,154,189, due to $11,250,000 for the Louisiana Purchase. He explains how this was done (budget surpluses) and recognizes that the impending war (War of 1812) would cause new debt to be created [10.2-88]:

"The disposable national revenue, or that portion which alone is applicable to defray the annual national expenses, consists only of the surplus of the gross amounts of revenue collected, beyond the amount necessary for paying interest in the public debt. A diminution of that interest is, with respect to the ability of defraying the other annual expenses, a positive increase of revenue, to the same amount. With an equal amount of gross revenue, the revenue applicable to defray the national expenses is now, by the effect of the reduction of the debt, two million six hundred thousand dollars greater than on the 1st day of April, 1801. Or, if another view of the subject be thought more correct: the laws for the reduction of the debt have, in ten years and nine months, enabled the United States to pay in full the purchase money of Louisiana, and increased their revenue near two millions of dollars."

"If the amount of annual payments, on account of both the principal and interest of the public debt, during the last eight years, be contrasted with the payments hereafter necessary for the same purpose, the difference will be still more striking. Eight millions of dollars have been annually paid, on that account, during those eight years. The whole amount payable after the year 1812, including the annual reimbursement on the six per cent, and deferred stocks, is 3,792,382 dollars; making an annual difference of more than four million two hundred thousand dollars, which will be liberated from that appropriation. And this annual payment of about three million eight hundred thousand dollars would have been sufficient, with some small variations, to discharge, in ten years, the whole of the residue of the existing debt, with the exception of the three per cent stock, the annual interest on which amounts only to four hundred and eighty-five thousand dollars. The aspect of the foreign relations of the United States forbids, however, the hope of seeing the work completed within that short period. The redemption of principal has been effected without the aid of any internal taxes, either direct or indirect, without any addition during the last seven years to the rate of duties on importations, (which, on the contrary, have been impaired by the repeal of that on salt) and notwithstanding the great diminution of commerce during the last four years. It therefore proves, decisively, the ability of the United States, with their ordinary revenue, to discharge, in ten years of peace, a debt of forty-two millions of dollars; a fact which considerably lessens the weight of the most formidable objection to which that revenue, depending almost solely on commerce, appears to be liable. In time of peace, it is almost sufficient to defray the expenses of a war; in time of war, it is hardly competent to support the expenses of a peace establishment. Sinking, at once, under adverse circumstances, from fifteen to six or eight millions of dollars, it is only by a persevering application of the surplus, which it affords in years of prosperity to the discharge of the debt, that a total change in the system of taxation, or a perpetual accumulation of debt, can be avoided. But, if a similar application of such surplus be hereafter strictly adhered to, forty millions of debt, contracted during five or six years of war, may always, without any extraordinary exertions, be reimbursed in ten years of peace."

16 Dec 1811: There were two earthquakes on the New Madrid fault in eastern Missouri, estimated magnitude of 7.2 to 8.2.

10.3 Data, 1791-1811

Figures 10.3-1 and 10.3-2 show the U. S. government revenue and expenditures for 1791 to 1811.

			U. S. Government Revenue, 1791 - 1811 (USD)							
			Internal Revenue		Miscellaneous					
Day	Year	Customs	Income and Profits taxes	Misc.	Sales of Public Lands	Direct Tax	Other Misc.	Postal	Public Debt Sales	Total
31 Dec	1791	4,399,473	0	0	0	0	10,478	71,295	361,391	4,842,638
31 Dec	1792	3,443,070	0	208,942	0	0	17,946	92,988	5,102,498	8,865,447
31 Dec	1793	4,255,306	0	337,705	0	0	59,910	103,883	1,797,272	6,554,078
31 Dec	1794	4,801,065	0	274,089	0	0	356,749	129,185	4,007,950	9,569,041
31 Dec	1795	5,588,461	0	337,755	0	0	193,117	163,794	3,396,424	9,679,553
31 Dec	1796	6,567,987	0	475,289	4,836	0	1,372,215	195,043	320,000	8,935,373
31 Dec	1797	7,549,649	0	575,491	83,540	0	480,099	213,992	70,000	8,972,773
31 Dec	1798	7,106,061	0	644,357	11,963	0	216,787	233,144	200,000	8,412,315
31 Dec	1799	6,610,449	0	779,136	0	0	157,227	264,850	5,000,000	12,811,663
31 Dec	1800	9,080,932	0	809,396	443	734,223	223,752	280,806	1,565,229	12,694,784
31 Dec	1801	10,750,778	0	1,048,033	167,726	534,343	444,574	320,444	0	13,265,900
31 Dec	1802	12,438,235	0	621,898	188,628	206,565	1,540,465	326,831	0	15,322,625
31 Dec	1803	10,479,417	0	215,179	165,675	71,879	131,945	359,952	0	11,424,050
31 Dec	1804	11,098,565	0	50,941	487,526	50,198	139,075	389,711	0	12,216,018
31 Dec	1805	12,936,487	0	21,747	540,193	21,882	40,382	422,129	0	13,982,822
31 Dec	1806	14,667,698	0	20,101	765,245	55,763	51,121	446,520	0	16,006,451
31 Dec	1807	15,845,521	0	13,051	466,163	34,732	38,550	484,134	0	16,882,153
31 Dec	1808	16,363,550	0	8,190	647,939	19,159	21,822	460,717	0	17,521,379
31 Dec	1809	7,257,506	0	4,034	442,252	7,517	62,162	506,633	0	8,280,107
31 Dec	1810	8,583,309	0	7,430	696,548	12,448	84,476	551,754	2,750,000	12,685,969
31 Dec	1811	13,313,222	0	2,295	1,040,237	7,666	59,211	587,266	0	15,009,900

The data for the revenue for 1791 to 1811 is from W. G. McAdoo, "Annual Report of the Secretary of the Treasury on the State of the Finances for the Fiscal Year Ended June 30, 1914", Washington: U. S. Government Printing Office, 1915, pp. 230-241; Treasury Document 2721. This data was modified per Henry Morgenthau, "Annual Report of the Secretary of the Treasury on the State of the Finances for the Fiscal Year Ended June 30, 1940", Treasury Document 3111, pp. 642-649, which shows "internal revenue" broken out as income taxes and miscellaneous. It is the same data as reported previously (cf. 1914), but shows income taxes and miscellaneous taxes as separate categories.

Figure 10.3-1: U. S. Government Revenue, 1791-1811

			U. S. Government Expenditures, 1791 - 1811 (USD)							
		Ordinary Disbursements								
Day	Year	Civil & Misc.	War Dep't	Navy Dep't	Indians	Pensions	Interest on Public Debt	Postal	Public Debt Retired	Total
31 Dec	1791	1,083,971	632,804	0	27,000	175,813	1,177,863	67,113	699,984	3,864,550
31 Dec	1792	4,672,664	1,100,702	0	13,648	109,243	2,373,611	76,586	693,050	9,039,506
31 Dec	1793	511,451	1,130,249	0	27,282	80,087	2,097,859	74,161	2,633,048	6,554,139
31 Dec	1794	750,350	2,639,097	61,408	13,042	81,399	2,752,523	95,397	2,743,771	9,136,990
31 Dec	1795	1,378,920	2,480,910	410,562	23,475	68,673	2,947,059	125,038	2,841,639	10,276,278
31 Dec	1796	801,847	1,260,263	274,784	113,563	100,843	3,239,347	136,639	2,577,126	8,504,415
31 Dec	1797	1,259,422	1,039,402	382,631	62,396	92,256	3,172,516	156,588	2,617,250	8,782,465
31 Dec	1798	1,139,524	2,009,522	1,381,347	16,470	104,845	2,955,875	185,308	976,032	8,768,926
31 Dec	1799	1,039,391	2,466,946	2,858,081	20,302	95,444	2,815,651	184,835	1,706,578	11,187,232
31 Dec	1800	1,337,613	2,560,878	3,448,716	31	64,130	3,402,601	207,135	1,138,563	12,159,670
31 Dec	1801	1,114,768	1,672,944	2,111,424	9,000	73,533	4,411,830	248,141	2,879,876	12,521,518
31 Dec	1802	1,462,929	1,179,148	915,561	94,000	85,440	4,239,172	275,856	5,294,235	13,546,344
31 Dec	1803	1,842,635	822,055	1,215,230	60,000	62,902	3,949,462	316,312	3,306,697	11,575,296
31 Dec	1804	2,191,009	875,423	1,189,832	116,500	80,092	4,185,048	333,977	3,977,206	12,949,090
31 Dec	1805	3,768,598	712,781	1,597,500	196,500	81,854	2,657,114	386,115	4,583,960	13,984,424
31 Dec	1806	2,890,137	1,224,355	1,649,641	234,200	81,875	3,368,968	413,814	5,572,018	15,435,010
31 Dec	1807	1,697,897	1,288,685	1,722,064	205,425	70,500	3,369,578	418,916	2,938,141	11,711,209
31 Dec	1808	1,423,285	2,900,834	1,884,067	213,575	82,576	2,557,074	446,914	7,701,288	17,209,616
31 Dec	1809	1,215,803	3,345,772	2,427,758	337,503	87,833	2,866,074	505,115	3,586,479	14,372,342
31 Dec	1810	1,101,144	2,294,323	1,654,244	177,625	83,744	3,163,671	550,991	4,835,241	13,860,985
31 Dec	1811	1,367,291	2,032,828	1,965,566	151,875	75,043	2,585,435	517,920	5,414,564	14,110,525

The data for the expenditures for 1789 to 1914 is from W. G. McAdoo, "Annual Report of the Secretary of the Treasury on the State of the Finances for the Fiscal Year Ended June 30, 1914", Washington: U. S. Government Printing Office, 1915, pp. 230-241; Treasury Document 2721. The total expenditure numbers do not agree with the 1940 report because the 1940 values do not include "Public Debt Retired" as chargeable against ordinary revenues. Expenditure data for 1789 to 1914 is from the 1914 Treasury Report.

Figure 10.3-2: U. S. Government Expenditures, 1791-1811

Figure 10.3-3 shows the total national debt and per-capita debt for 1791 to 1811. Refer to the Introduction to Part 2 for a sense of the per-capita debt vs. income.

		U. S. National Debt, 1791-1811 (USD)								
Day	Year	Principal ($) [1]	Population [2]	Debt per Capita ($) [2]	Day	Year	Principal ($) [1]	Population [2]	Debt per Capita ($) [2]
31 Dec	1791	77,227,924	4,059,956	19.02	31 Dec	1802	77,654,686	5,637,281	13.78
31 Dec	1792	80,352,634	4,190,697	19.17	31 Dec	1803	86,427,120	5,837,606	14.81
31 Dec	1793	78,427,404	4,321,439	18.15	31 Dec	1804	82,312,150	6,037,931	13.63
31 Dec	1794	80,747,587	4,452,181	18.14	31 Dec	1805	75,723,270	6,238,256	12.14
31 Dec	1795	83,762,172	4,582,923	18.28	31 Dec	1806	69,218,398	6,438,581	10.75
31 Dec	1796	82,064,479	4,713,664	17.41	31 Dec	1807	65,196,317	6,638,906	9.82
31 Dec	1797	79,228,529	4,844,406	16.35	31 Dec	1808	57,623,192	6,839,231	8.43
31 Dec	1798	78,408,669	4,975,148	15.76	31 Dec	1809	53,173,217	7,039,556	7.55
31 Dec	1799	82,976,294	5,105,889	16.25	31 Dec	1810	48,005,587	7,239,881	6.63
31 Dec	1800	83,038,050	5,236,631	15.86	31 Dec	1811	45,209,737	7,479,738	6.04
31 Dec	1801	89,712,632	5,436,956	16.50					

1. Public debt data from 1790 to 1811 is from the Annual Report of the Secretary of the Treasury, 1980, pp. 61, 62.
2. Population values are based on the dicennial census from the Census Bureau, and linearly interpolated. Per-capita is based on these values.

Figure 10.3-3: National Debt and Per-Capita Share Thereof, 1791-1811

There is very little data on the condition of banks during this period. The Annual Report of the Comptroller of the Currency in 1876 [10.3-1] refers to p. 216 of report by Treasury Secretary Crawford of 3 Jan 1836, in which Crawford refers to a statement from *Blodgett's Economica*, estimating the condition of banks for various years. A note in the *Economica* states that some of these numbers are conjecture, and Figure 10.3-4 shows the data.

		Estimate of Banks in U. S., 1791-1804		
Year	Number of Banks	Metallic Medium	Notes in Circulation	Capital
1791	6	16,000,000	9,000,000	12,900,000
1792	16	18,000,000	11,500,000	17,100,000
1793	17	20,000,000	11,000,000	18,000,000
1794	17	21,500,000	11,600,000	18,000,000
1795	23	19,000,000	11,000,000	19,000,000
1796	24	16,500,000	10,500,000	19,200,000
1797	25	16,000,000	10,000,000	19,200,000
1798	25	14,000,000	9,000,000	19,200,000
1799	26	17,000,000	10,000,000	21,200,000
1800	28	17,500,000	10,500,000	21,300,000
1801	31	17,000,000	11,000,000	22,400,000
1802	32	16,500,000	10,000,000	22,600,000
1803	36	16,000,000	11,000,000	26,000,000
1804	59	17,500,000	14,000,000	39,500,000

Source: John Jay Knox, Annual Report of the Comptroller of the Currency, 1876, p. XXXIX

Figure 10.3-4: Summary of Condition of Banks in the U. S. 1791 to 1804 [10.3-1]

Although the Bank of the United States was required to provide regular financial statements to Congress, it only provided two, dated 2 Mar 1809 and 24 Jan 1811 showing the condition in January of those two years. They are shown in Figure 10.3-5.

Bank of the United States	USD	
Assets	**2 Mar 1809**	**24 Jan 1811**
Loans and Discounts	15,000,000	14,578,294
United States six per cent stock	2,230,000	2,750,000
Other United States indebtedness		57,046
Due from other banks	800,000	894,145
Real estate	480,000	500,653
Notes of other banks on hand		393,341
Specie	5,000,000	5,009,567
Totals	23,510,000	24,183,046
Liabilities		
Capital stock	10,000,000	10,000,000
Undivided surplus	510,000	509,678
Circulating notes outstanding	4,500,000	5,037,125
Individual deposits	8,500,000	5,900,423
United States deposits		1,929,999
Due to other banks		634,348
Unpaid drafts outstanding		171,473
Totals	23,510,000	24,183,046
Source: John Jay Knox, Annual Report of the Comptroller of the Currency, 1876, p. IX		

Figure 10.3-5: Financial Statement of the Bank of United States, 1809 and 1811 [10.3-2]

There were also in 1811 a total of 88 State-chartered banks in operation, and Crawford provided an estimate of their condition [10.3-3, 10.3-4]: capital = $42,610,000; notes in circulation = $22,700,000, with specie amounting to $9,600,000.

As indicated in the Introduction to Part 2, some estimates (and guesses) were necessary to establish the approximate money supply in this period. The estimated money supply is shown on Figure 10.3-6.

Estimated U. S. Money Supply, 1791-1811 [1] (millions USD)																
1	2	3	4	5	6	7	8	9	10	11	12	13	14	15	16	17
Year (~30 Jun)	Number of Banks [2]	Estimated State Bank Notes [3]	Estimated Notes of First Bank of U. S. [3]	Total Notes in Circulation	Total Specie in US [4]	Specie in Treasury [5]	Specie Outside Treasury	Total Notes & Specie Outside Treasury	Cash Held in All Banks [6]	Notes & Specie Outside Banks	Estimated State Bank Deposits [3]	Estimated Deposits of First Bank of U. S. [3]	Total Estimated Deposits	Estimated Interbank Transactions [7]	Estimated Deposits Adjusted	Estimated Total Money Supply
1791	6	9.000	2.595	11.595	16.000	1.500	14.500	26.095	8.090	18.006	8.479	4.902	13.381	1.311	12.070	30.075
1792	16	11.500	2.679	14.179	18.000	1.500	16.500	30.679	9.510	21.168	10.834	5.060	15.894	1.558	14.336	35.505
1793	17	11.000	2.762	13.762	20.000	1.500	18.500	32.262	10.001	22.261	10.363	5.218	15.581	1.527	14.054	36.315
1794	17	11.600	2.846	14.446	21.500	1.500	20.000	34.446	10.678	23.768	10.928	5.376	16.304	1.598	14.706	38.474
1795	23	11.000	2.930	13.930	19.000	1.500	17.500	31.430	9.743	21.686	10.363	5.534	15.897	1.558	14.339	36.025
1796	24	10.500	3.013	13.513	16.500	1.500	15.000	28.513	8.839	19.674	9.892	5.692	15.583	1.527	14.056	33.730
1797	25	10.000	3.097	13.097	16.000	1.500	14.500	27.597	8.555	19.042	9.421	5.849	15.270	1.496	13.774	32.816
1798	25	9.000	3.180	12.180	14.000	1.500	12.500	24.680	7.651	17.029	8.479	6.007	14.486	1.420	13.066	30.096
1799	26	10.000	3.264	13.264	17.000	1.500	15.500	28.764	8.917	19.847	9.421	6.165	15.586	1.527	14.059	33.906
1800	28	10.500	3.347	13.847	17.500	1.500	16.000	26.500	8.215	18.285	9.892	6.323	16.215	1.589	14.626	32.911
1801	31	11.000	3.476	14.476	17.000	1.650	15.350	29.826	9.246	20.580	10.363	6.565	16.928	1.659	15.269	35.849
1802	32	10.000	3.604	13.604	16.500	1.800	14.700	28.304	8.774	19.529	9.421	6.807	16.228	1.590	14.637	34.167
1803	36	11.000	3.732	14.732	16.000	1.950	14.050	28.782	8.922	19.859	10.698	7.049	17.747	1.739	16.008	35.867
1804	59	14.000	3.860	17.860	17.500	2.100	15.400	33.260	10.311	22.949	9.267	7.291	16.557	1.623	14.935	37.884
1805	75	13.138	3.988	17.125	19.585	2.250	17.335	34.460	10.683	23.778	8.635	7.532	16.167	1.584	14.583	38.360
1806		13.962	4.116	18.077	21.600	2.400	19.200	37.277	11.556	25.721	17.620	7.774	25.394	2.489	22.905	48.627
1807		13.112	4.244	17.356	23.750	2.550	21.200	38.556	11.952	26.604	15.167	8.016	23.183	2.272	20.911	47.515
1808		9.390	4.372	13.762	25.800	2.700	23.100	36.862	11.427	25.435	23.055	8.258	31.314	3.069	28.245	53.680
1809		12.339	4.500	16.839	28.000	2.850	25.150	41.989	13.017	28.972	21.395	8.500	29.895	2.930	26.965	55.938
1810		19.809	4.750	24.559	30.000	3.000	27.000	46.809	14.511	32.298	23.240	7.200	30.440	2.983	27.457	59.755
1811	88	22.700	5.037	27.737	29.400	2.900	26.500	54.237	16.814	37.424	32.627	5.900	38.528	3.776	34.752	72.176

1. Values in **bold** are from original sources; all others interpolated or estimated as described.
2. Number of banks from the Annual Report of the Comptroller of the Currency, 1918, 2 Dec 1918, Vol. 2, p. 835, Table 86.
3. See Introduction to Part 2 for derivation of items in normal font
4. **Bold** values from Annual Report of the Secretary of the Treasury, 1876, p. 153; items in normal font are linearly interpolated.
5. **Bold** values from Annual Report of the Comptroller of the Currency, 1896, Vol. 1, p. 544; normal font values are interpolated.
6 Cash held in banks for 1791 to 1811 estimated based on the average ratio of cash to outstanding currency from 1834 to 1914 (0.31)
7. Interbank from 1791 to 1811 based on average of interbank to total deposits from 1914 to 1940 (0.098).

Figure 10.3-6: Estimated Money Supply, 1791-1811

Figure 10.3-7 shows the gold coins minted by the U. S. during this period.

	Gold Coinage of the U. S., 1791-1811 ($)						
Year	$20 Double Eagles ($)	$10 Eagles ($)	$5 Half Eagles ($)	Three Dollar ($)	$2.50 Quarter Eagles ($)	Gold Dollars ($)	Total ($)
1793 to 1795		27,950.00	43,535.00				71,485.00
1796		60,800.00	16,995.00		165.00		77,960.00
1797		91,770.00	32,030.00		4,390.00		128,190.00
1798		79,740.00	124,335.00		1,535.00		205,610.00
1799		174,830.00	37,255.00		1,200.00		213,285.00
1800		259,650.00	58,110.00				317,760.00
1801		292,540.00	130,030.00				422,570.00
1802		150,900.00	265,880.00		6,530.00		423,310.00
1803		89,790.00	167,530.00		1,057.50		258,377.50
1804		97,950.00	152,375.00		8,317.50		258,642.50
1805			165,915.00		4,452.50		170,367.50
1806			320,465.00		4,040.00		324,505.00
1807			420,465.00		17,030.00		437,495.00
1808			277,890.00		6,775.00		284,665.00
1809			169,375.00				169,375.00
1810			501,435.00				501,435.00
1811			497,905.00				497,905.00
Totals	0.00	1,325,920.00	3,381,525.00	0.00	55,492.50	0.00	4,762,937.50

Source: Annual Report of the Director of the Mint, 1895, 28 Nov 1895, Treasury Document No. 1829, pp. 286-293 (Table XLIV).

Figure 10.3-7: Gold Coins Minted by the U. S., 1791-1811

Figure 10.3-8 shows the silver and copper coins minted by the U. S. during this period.

	Silver and Copper Coinage of the U. S., 1791-1811 ($)									
	Silver ($)								Minor ($)	
Year	Trade Dollars	Dollars	Half Dollars	Quarters	Twenty-cents	Dimes	Half-dimes	Three-cents	Cents & Half-Cents	Total ($)
1793 to 1795		204,791.00	161,572.00				4,320.80		11,373.00	382,056.80
1796		72,920.00		1,473.50		2,213.50	511.50		10,324.40	87,442.90
1797		7,776.00	1,959.00	63.00		2,526.10	2,226.35		9,510.34	24,060.79
1798		327,536.00				2,755.00			9,797.00	340,088.00
1799		423,515.00							9,106.68	432,621.68
1800		220,920.00				2,176.00	1,200.00		29,279.40	253,575.40
1801		54,454.00	15,144.50			3,464.00	1,695.50		13,628.37	88,386.37
1802		41,650.00	14,945.00			1,097.50	650.50		34,422.83	92,765.83
1803		66,064.00	15,857.50			3,304.00	1,892.50		25,203.03	112,321.03
1804		19,570.00	78,259.50			826.50			12,844.94	113,185.44
1805		321.00	105,861.00	30,348.50		12,078.00	780.00		13,483.48	162,871.98
1806			419,788.00	51,531.00					5,260.00	476,579.00
1807			525,788.00	55,160.75		16,500.00			9,652.21	607,100.96
1808			684,300.00						13,090.00	697,390.00
1809			702,905.00			4,471.00			8,001.53	715,377.53
1810			638,138.00			635.50			15,660.00	654,433.50
1811			601,822.00			6,518.00			2,495.95	610,835.95
Totals	0.00	1,439,517.00	3,966,339.50	140,261.25	0.00	58,565.10	13,277.15	0.00	233,133.16	5,851,093.16

Source: Annual Report of the Director of the Mint, 1895, 28 Nov 1895, Treasury Document No. 1829, pp. 286-293 (Table XLIV).

Figure 10.3-8: Silver and Minor (Copper) Coins Minted by the U. S., 1791-1811

Figure 10.3-9 shows the growth of the money supply, per-capita money supply, and the effect on prices per the CPI. The CPI is normalized to 1913.

Year	CPI [1] (1913 = 100)	Total Money Supply [5] (USD)	Population [6]	Per Capita Money Supply (USD)	Annual Rate of Change in CPI (%)	Annual Rate of Change in Per-Capita Money Supply (%)
1791	85.699	30,075,433	4,059,956	7.41		
1792	90.146	35,504,897	4,190,697	8.47	5.059	13.427
1793	112.110	36,315,079	4,321,439	8.40	21.805	-0.816
1794	126.123	38,473,998	4,452,181	8.64	11.778	2.794
1795	119.386	36,025,203	4,582,923	7.86	-5.490	-9.471
1796	126.123	33,730,385	4,713,664	7.16	5.490	-9.395
1797	116.691	32,815,567	4,844,406	6.77	-7.773	-5.486
1798	113.322	30,095,869	4,975,148	6.05	-2.929	-11.315
1799	115.209	33,905,692	5,105,889	6.64	1.651	9.326
1800	117.904	32,910,867	5,236,631	6.28	2.312	-5.506
1801	127.336	35,848,554	5,436,956	6.59	7.696	4.796
1802	105.809	34,166,833	5,637,281	6.06	-18.519	-8.423
1803	108.064	35,867,199	5,837,606	6.14	2.108	1.365
1804	117.258	37,883,771	6,037,931	6.27	8.165	2.096
1805	122.942	38,360,364	6,238,256	6.15	4.734	-2.014
1806	120.109	48,626,887	6,438,581	7.55	-2.331	20.554
1807	113.718	47,514,795	6,638,906	7.16	-5.468	-5.377
1808	109.964	53,679,574	6,839,231	7.85	-3.357	9.226
1809	118.802	55,937,698	7,039,556	7.95	7.731	1.234
1810	124.399	59,754,930	7,239,881	8.25	4.604	3.795
1811	120.443	72,175,601	7,479,738	9.65	-3.232	15.626

1. CPI is the average of L-1 and L-15 data, both re-aligned to 1913 as a reference.
2. L-1 data 1791 to 1938 (Snyder-Tucker) is a general price index (wholesale prices, wages, cost of living and rents).
3. L-15 data 1801 to 1945 includes wholesale prices, all commodities.
4. L1 and L-15 from Historical Statistics of the United States, 1789-1945, A Supplement to the Statistical Abstract of the United States, Bureau of the Census, US Department of Commerce, Washington, DC, 1949.
5. See notes in money supply data for sources.
6. Population is linearly interpolated from Census results.

Figure 10.3-9: Money Supply and CPI, 1791-1811

Figure 10.3-10 shows the CPI and per-capita data graphically. There are a great number of oscillations in both, with clear trends only for 1791 to 1794 and 1794 to 1811. For 1791 to 1794, the average annual growth in the CPI and money supply are 11.1% and 5.1% respectively; for 1794 to 1811, the average annual change in CPI and money supply are -0.3% and +0.65% respectively. It appears then, if this data is correct, that the change in money supply and CPI are weakly correlated; and that reasonably stable per-capita money supply leads to reasonably stable prices, as indicated by the 1794 to 1811 trend.

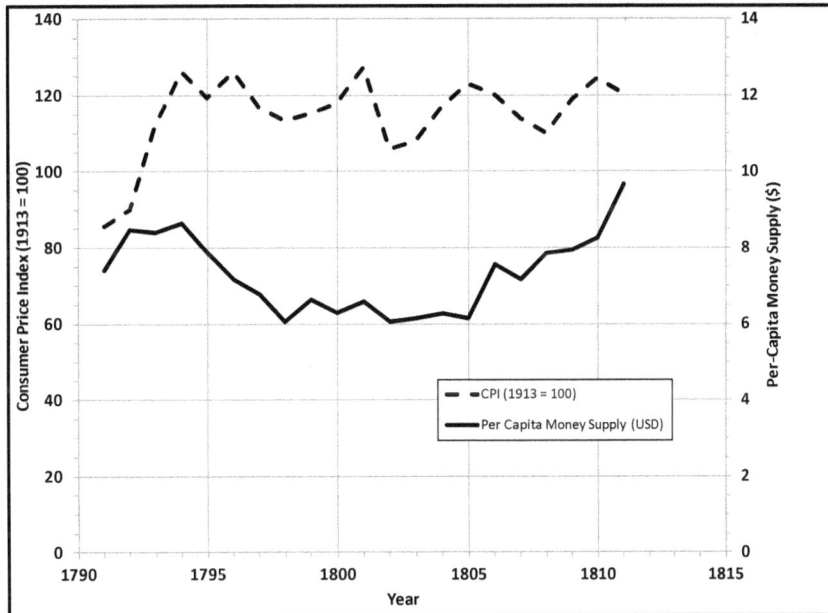

Figure 10.3-10: CPI and Per-Capita Summary

Figure 10.3-11 shows the approximate median income index, consumer price index, and standard of living index for this period. See the Introduction to Part 2 for cautions regarding these curves. There is insufficient data to show the income and standard of living results prior to 1800.

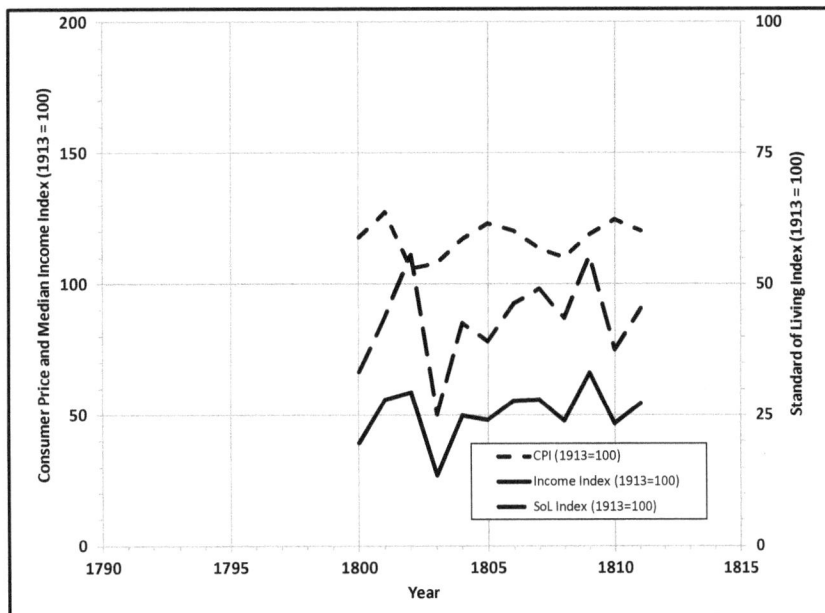

Figure 10.3-11: Median Income, Consumer Price, and Standard of Living Indices, 1800-1811

10.4 Summary, 1791-1811

The Bank of the United States was supposed to have been regularly audited, and to provide regular statements of its condition. As near as can be ascertained, it was never audited, and only two statements were provided as noted above. However, it did issue notes well within its capital position, and was able to pay in coin on demand. It also made loans to the government, for which it was not always promptly repaid [10.4-1]. It was only natural that the Bank would accommodate the government; the government initially owned 20% of the stock (although it sold all of it by 1802). The Bank was only moderately successful in restraining the growth of the money supply, issued mostly in the form of bank notes by State-chartered banks.

There was great opposition to the renewal of the charter [10.4-2]: a) that stock in the bank was owned by foreigners (although they could not vote as shareholders); b) members of the Democrat-Republican Party claimed that it benefitted the members of the Federalist Party; c) that the bank would become too powerful in political matters; and d) the lingering question as to whether chartering of banks was left only to the States under the Constitution. Those who opposed the renewal of the bank's charter got their wish, as will be shown in the next chapter. The result was an explosion of bank notes issued by State banks and a reduction of credit. At the same time, a decline in revenue caused by the repeal of some taxes led to a financial problem as the War of 1812 began.

References

[10.2-1]   Jonathan Elliot, *The Funding System of the United States and Great Britain*, Washington, DC: Blair and Rives, 1845, pp. 95, 96

[10.2-2]   Text of "An Act to incorporate the subscribers to the Bank of the United States", First Congress, Session 3, Chapter 10, 25 Feb 1791

[10.2-3]   Albert S. Bolles, *A Financial History of the United States*, NY: Augustus M. Kelley (1969), Vol. 2, p. 59 (originally published 1884 by D. Appleton & Co., NY)

[10.2-4]   op. cit., Elliot, pp. 96, 160

[10.2-5]   op. cit., Bolles, Vol. 2, pp. 103, 104 (originally published 1884 by D. Appleton & Co., NY)

[10.2-6]   op. cit., Elliot, pp. 95, 96

[10.2-7]   op. cit., Elliot, pp. 96, 160

[10.2-8]   op. cit., Elliot, pp. 96, 160

[10.2-9]   op. cit., Elliot, pp. 96, 160

[10.2-10] op. cit., Elliot, p. 120

[10.2-11] op. cit., Bolles, Vol. 2, pp. 160, 161

[10.2-12] Text of "An Act establishing a Mint, and regulating the coins of the United States", Second Congress, Session 1, Chapter 16, 2 Apr 1792

[10.2-13] op. cit., Bolles, Vol. 2, pp. 132, 133

[10.2-14] Text of "An Act concerning the Duties on Spirits distilled within the United States", Second Congress, Session 1, Chapter 32, 8 May 1792

[10.2-15] Text of "An Act to provide for a copper coinage", Second Congress, Session 1, Chapter 34, 8 May 1792

[10.2-16] op. cit., Elliot, pp. 96, 160

[10.2-17] Text of "An Act to amend an act entitled "An Act establishing a mint, and regulating the coins of the United States", so far as respects the coinage of copper", Second Congress, Session 2, Chapter 2, 14 Jan 1793

[10.2-18] op. cit., Elliot, p. 178

[10.2-19] op. cit., Bolles, Vol. 2, p. 169

[10.2-20] op. cit., Bolles, Vol. 2, pp. 39-41

[10.2-21] op. cit., Elliot, p. 325

[10.2-22] op. cit., Elliot, pp. 295, 296

[10.2-23] Text of "An Act authorizing a loan of one million of dollars", Third Congress, Session 1, Chapter 8, 20 Mar 1794

[10.2-24] op. cit., Bolles, Vol. 2, pp. 133, 134

[10.2-25]	op. cit., Elliot, pp. 297-300
[10.2-26]	op. cit., Elliot, pp. 300-324
[10.2-27]	Text of "An Act making provision for the payment of the interest on the balances due to certain States, upon a final settlement of the accounts between the United States and the individual States", Third Congress, Session 1, Chapter 37, 31 May 1794
[10.2-28]	op. cit., Bolles, Vol. 2, p. 134
[10.2-29]	Text of "An Act authorizing a loan of two millions of dollars", Third Congress, Session 2, Chapter 4, 18 Dec 1794
[10.2-30]	op. cit., Elliot, pp. 404, 405
[10.2-31]	op. cit., Bolles, Vol. 2, pp. 134, 135
[10.2-32]	Text of "An Act for the reimbursement of a loan authorized by an act of the last session of Congress", Third Congress, Session 2, Chapter 25, 21 Feb 1795
[10.2-33]	op. cit., Bolles, Vol. 2, p. 135
[10.2-34]	Text of "An Act making further provision for the support of Public Credit, and for the redemption of the Public Debt", Third Congress, Session 2, Chapter 45, 3 Mar 1795
[10.2-35]	op. cit., Bolles, Vol. 2, p. 60
[10.2-36]	William M. Malloy, *Treaties, Conventions, International Acts, Protocols, and Agreements Between the United States of America and Other Powers, 1776-1909*, Vol. 1, pp. 1-6, Washington, DC: U. S. Government Printing Office, 1910; 61st Congress, Session 2, Senate Document 357 (Republished by Scholarly Press, Grosse Point, MI)
[10.2-37]	Text of "An Act in addition to an act entitled 'An Act making further provision for the support of Public Credit, and for the redemption of the Public Debt'", 4th Congress, Session 1, Chapter 16, 28 Apr 1796
[10.2-38]	Text of "An Act making an appropriation for defraying the expenses which may arise in carrying into effect the Treaty made between the United States and the Dey and Regency of Algiers", 4th Congress, Session 1, Chapter 19, 6 May 1796
[10.2-39]	Text of "An Act making provision for the payment of certain Debts of the United States", 4th Congress, Session 1, Chapter 44, 31 May 1796
[10.2-40]	op. cit., Bolles, Vol. 2, pp. 137-139
[10.2-41]	op. cit., Bolles, Vol. 2, pp. 138, 139
[10.2-42]	op. cit., Bolles, Vol. 2, p. 143
[10.2-43]	op. cit., Elliot, pp. 440, 441
[10.2-44]	Text of "An Act for raising a further sum of money, by additional duties on certain articles imported, and for other purposes", 4th Congress, Session 2, Chapter 10, 3 Mar 1797
[10.2-45]	Text of "An Act authorizing the President of the United States to apply a further sum to the expense of Negotiations with the Dey and Regency of Algiers", 4th Congress, Session 2, Chapter 12, 3 Mar 1797
[10.2-46]	Text of "An Act laying duties on stamped Vellum, Parchment, and Paper", 5th Congress, Session 1, Chapter 11, 6 Jul 1797
[10.2-47]	Text of "An Act laying an additional Duty on Salt imported into the United States, and for other purposes", 5th Congress, Session 1, Chapter 15, 8 Jul 1797
[10.2-48]	Text of "An Act authorizing a loan of money", 5th Congress, Session 1, Chapter 16, 8 Jul 1797
[10.2-49]	op. cit., Bolles, Vol. 2, p. 169
[10.2-50]	op. cit., Elliot, pp. 441, 442
[10.2-51]	op. cit., Bolles, Vol. 2, p. 170
[10.2-52]	Text of "An Act supplementary to the act entitled 'An act regulating Foreign Coins, and for other purposes'", 5th Congress, Session 2, Chapter 11, 1 Feb 1798
[10.2-53]	op. cit., Bolles, Vol. 2, pp. 120-122
[10.2-54]	Text of "An Act to lay and collect a direct tax within the United States", 5th Congress, Session 2, Chapter 75, 14 Jul 1798
[10.2-55]	Text of "An Act to enable the President of the United States to borrow money for the public service", 5th Congress, Session 2, Chapter 79, 16 Jul 1798
[10.2-56]	op. cit., Elliot, pp. 443, 444
[10.2-57]	op. cit., Bolles, Vol. 2, pp. 107, 108
[10.2-58]	op. cit., Elliot, pp. 444, 445
[10.2-59]	op. cit., Bolles, Vol. 2, p. 166
[10.2-60]	Text of "An Act to enable the President of the United States to borrow money for public service", 6th Congress, Session 1, Chapter 42, 7 May 1800

[10.2-61]   Text of "An Act to lay additional duties on certain articles imported", 6th Congress, Session 1, Chapter 66, 13 May 1800

[10.2-62]   op. cit., Bolles, Vol. 2, pp. 110, 126

[10.2-63]   Text of "An Act to repeal the Internal Taxes", 7th Congress, Session 1, Chapter 19, 6 Apr 1802

[10.2-64]   Text of "An Act making provision for the redemption of the whole of the Public Debt of the United States", 7th Congress, Session 1, Chapter 32, 29 Apr 1802

[10.2-65]   op. cit., Elliot, pp. 475-478

[10.2-66]   Text of "An Act to suspend, in part, the act entitled 'An act regulating foreign coins, and for other purposes'", 7th Congress, Session 1, Chapter 38, 30 Apr 1802

[10.2-67]   Text of "An Act authorizing the creation of a stock, to the amount of eleven millions two hundred and fifty thousand dollars, for the purpose of carrying into effect the convention of the thirtieth of April, one thousand eight hundred and three, between the United States of America and the French Republic; and making provision for the payment of the same", 8th Congress, Session 1, Chapter 2, 10 Nov 1803

[10.2-68]   Text of "An Act supplementary to the act entitled 'An act to incorporate the subscribers to the Bank of the United States'"; 8th Congress, Session 1, Chapter 32, 23 Mar 1804

[10.2-69]   Text of "An Act for imposing more specific duties on the importation of certain articles; and also, for levying and collecting light money on foreign ships and vessels, and for other purposes", 8th Congress, Session 1, Chapter 57, 27 Mar 1804

[10.2-70]   Text of "An Act regulating the currency of foreign coins in the United States", 9th Congress, Session 1, Chapter 22, 10 Apr 1806

[10.2-71]   op. cit., Bolles, Vol. 2, pp. 170, 171

[10.2-72]   Text of "An Act to prohibit the importation of certain goods, wares, and merchandise", 8th Congress, Session 1, Chapter 29, 18 Apr 1806

[10.2-73]   Text of "An Act supplementary to the act entitled 'An act making provision for the redemption of the whole of the public debt of the United States'"; 9th Congress, Session 2, Chapter 12, 11 Feb 1807

[10.2-74]   op. cit., Elliot, p. 501

[10.2-75]   Text of "An Act repealing the acts laying duties on salt, and continuing of force, for a further time, the first section of the act entitled 'An Act further to protect the commerce and seamen of the United States against the Barbary powers'", 9th Congress, Session 2, 3 Mar 1807

[10.2-76]   Text of "An Act laying an Embargo on all ships and vessels in the ports and harbors of the United States", 10th Congress, Session 1, Chapter 5, 22 Dec 1807

[10.2-77]   Text of "An Act to interdict the commercial intercourse between the United States and Great Britain and France, and their dependencies, and for other purposes", 10th Congress, Session 2, Chapter 24, 1 Mar 1809

[10.2-78]   op. cit., Bolles, Vol. 2, p. 169; citing Gallatin's Annual Report on the U. S. Mint, 11 Jan 1811, p. 464

[10.2-79]   Text of "An Act concerning the commercial intercourse between the United States and Great Britain and France, and their dependencies, and for other purposes", 11th Congress, Session 2, Chapter 39, 1 May 1810

[10.2-80]   Text of "An Act authorizing a loan of money, for a sum not exceeding the amount of the principal of the public debt, reimbursable during the year one thousand eight hundred and ten", 11th Congress, Session 2, Chapter 45, 1 May 1810

[10.2-81]   Lot M. Morrill, *Annual Report of the Secretary of the Treasury on the State of the Finances for Year 1876*, Appendix containing the Report of the Comptroller of Currency (John Jay Knox), Washington, DC: Government Printing Office, 1876, p. 123

[10.2-82]   Text of "An Act authorizing a loan of money, for a sum of five millions of dollars", 11th Congress, Session 3, Chapter 32, 2 Mar 1811

[10.2-83]   op. cit., Morrill, p. 123

[10.2-84]   op. cit., Bolles, Vol. 2, pp. 151-153

[10.2-85]   Francis Walker, *Money*, NY: Henry Holt and Company, 1891, p. 492

[10.2-86]   op. cit., Bolles, Vol. 2, pp. 154, 155

[10.2-87]   op. cit., Bolles, Vol. 2, pp. 151-153

[10.2-88]   Albert Gallatin, *Annual Report of the Secretary of the Treasury for the Year 1811*, 22 Nov 1811, Washington, DC: U. S. Government Printing Office, 1811, pp. 446, 447

[10.3-1]   op. cit., Morrill, p. 153

[10.3-2]   op. cit., Morrill, p. 123

[10.3-3]   op. cit., Morrill, p. 154
[10.3-4]   Albert Gallatin, *Considerations on the Currency and Banking System of the United States*, Philadelphia, PA: Carey & Lea, 1831, pp. 101, 102. Gallatin reports on 50 banks for which returns had been received as of 1 Jan 1811 (15 in Massachusetts, 6 in Maine, 13 in Rhode Island, 1 in New York, 4 in Pennsylvania, 6 in Maryland, 4 in the District of Columbia, and 1 in Virginia); their total capital was $24,618,551, note circulation was $13,170,401, and specie was $5,673,442. He also notes 38 banks for which returns had not been received (8 in New Hampshire, 5 in Connecticut, 7 in New York, 3 in New Jersey, 3 in North Carolina, 4 in South Carolina, 1 in Louisiana, 1 in Tennessee, 1 in Kentucky, and 4 in Ohio); their total capital was $17,992,050. Apparently Treasury Secretary Crawford extrapolated circulation and specie based on capital from these figures to arrive at an estimate of circulation and specie for all 88 banks.

[10.4-1]   op. cit., Bolles, Vol. 2, p. 135
[10.4-2]   op. cit., Bolles, Vol. 2, pp. 146-151

11

State Banks Only, 1812-1816

11.1 Preview, 1812-1816

The closing of the Bank of the United States proved be a mistake, since the State-chartered banks did not correctly limit the amount paper notes they issued. The Bank of the U. S. had managed its note issue, and restrained the impulses of the State banks by demanding redemption of the State bank notes in specie. When this restraint was removed, the nation was soon flooded with paper money, and a serious depreciation resulted. After the charter of the Bank of the United States expired, a large number of State-chartered banks began business as limited-liability companies. They greatly expanded the issue of their notes, and when the War of 1812 broke out, many of them failed, except for the ones in New England, which had restrained their note issues, and continued to redeem in specie. Eventually the State banks had issued so much paper that they had to suspend redemption in 1814. It was Gallatin's opinion [11.1-1] in 1831 that the suspension would not have occurred if the charter of the Bank of the United States had not expired. This problem was compounded by the demands of the War of 1812.

Approximately $9,000,000 of the U. S. government's funds was lost, having been deposited in failed State banks [11.1-2].

11.2 History, 1812-1816

14 Mar 1812: Congress authorized [11.2-1] a loan of $11,000,000 at 6% interest payable quarterly, and principal payable within twelve years after 1813, in preparation for the war with Britain. A loan of this size became necessary because Congress had repealed all the internal taxes in 1802, had lost tariff and tonnage revenue due to the previous embargo, and spent the last three years authorizing loans but not raising taxes to pay for them. Congress now had no choice but to borrow, due to the necessity of financing the war [11.2-2].

23 Jan 1812: Approximate magnitude 7.3 earthquake on the New Madrid fault in eastern Missouri.

7 Feb 1812: Approximate magnitude 7.5 earthquake on the New Madrid fault in eastern Missouri.

19 Mar 1812: Congress repealed [11.2-3] section 10 of the law that incorporated the Bank of the United States (cf. 25 Feb 1791). The notes of the Bank of the United States were no longer valid as payments for taxes [11.2-4].

4 Apr 1812: Congress passed an Embargo Act [11.2-5]. Among its provisions: **a)** (S. 2) laid an embargo for 90 days upon all vessels in U. S. ports, and clearance to leave to be authorized by the President; and **b)** (S. 2) required ships leaving to provide a bond double the value of the cargo if passing between ports in the U. S.

14 Apr 1812: Congress passed a modification to the Embargo Act [11.2-6]: **a)** (S. 1) the 4 Apr 1812 Act now included specie and goods of foreign manufacture; and **b)** (S. 2) the President may call in the navy, army or militia to enforce the embargo.

1 Jun 1812: An additional $2,200,000 of specie had been exported to Great Britain in the past year, bringing to $3,900,000 the total amount exported after the Bank of the United States was closed in Mar 1811 [11.2-7].

18 Jun 1812: Congress declared war against Great Britain [11.2-8] in response to Britain's provocations (especially the impressments of American seamen). One of Great Britain's goals in the War of 1812 was to ruin American shipping. They were successful, but at the same time the loss of foreign trade promoted domestic manufacturing, which injured British manufacturers in the long run [11.2-9]. The blockades of the ports made Americans realize how vulnerable they were to foreign interference.

30 Jun 1812: Congress enacted [11.2-10] a new borrowing method: **a)** (S. 1) the President could authorize the Treasury to issue $5,000,000 in Treasury Notes; **b)** (S. 2) bearing 5.4% annual interest, to be repaid within one year; **c)** (S. 4) Treasury Secretary was authorized to borrow on the credit of the notes; **d)** (S. 6) be receivable for taxes; and **e)** (S. 9) the notes are to be repaid out of the sinking fund. The commissioners of the sinking fund were also authorized to buy them back if possible. These Treasury Notes were necessary because the Treasury was having difficulty obtaining subscriptions to previously authorized loans [11.2-11]. Treasury Secretary Gallatin recognized the risk of these, being similar to the Continentals, but believed it was a workable scheme so long as the quantity was restricted appropriately. The Treasury Notes were not technically a legal tender, and they were not paid as required at maturity; this led to "general distrust and commercial distress" [11.2-12].

1 Jul 1812: Congress passed a law [11.2-13, 11.2-14] increasing import duties. Among its provisions: **a)** (S. 1) doubled import duties on goods imported from any foreign place or port; **b)** (S. 2) an additional 10% on goods imported on foreign ships; **c)** (S. 3) an additional tonnage duty of $1.50 per ton on ships partly or entirely foreign-owned; and **d)** (S. 5) these provisions to continue until peace with Great Britain (cf. 17 Feb 1815).

~1 Aug 1812 ff: Many State-chartered banks began to fail, having over-issued their notes since 1811, when the Bank of the United States ceased operations [11.2-15]. Only the banks in New England, having restrained their note issues, continued in operations and to redeem their notes in specie.

8-16 Aug 1812: Battle of Detroit (now MI).

8 Feb 1813: Congress authorized a loan of $16,000,000 to finance the war [11.2-16, 11.2-17]. The Treasury had difficulty finding subscribers (only $5,838,200 would be subscribed by 31 Mar 1813). The government had to loosen the terms, and was able to obtain the full amount. The final negotiated terms were that the lenders paid in at par, receiving 6% interest payable quarterly, plus a 13-year annuity from 1 Jan 1813 of 1.5%, payable quarterly. The principal could be paid at the discretion of the government any time after 1825. These bad terms resulted from Congress not being willing to provide adequate internal revenue during peacetime (revenue from import duties had declined).

22 Feb 1813: Battle of Ogdensburg, NY.

25 Feb 1813: Congress authorized another $5,000,000 in Treasury Notes to be issued [11.2-18, 11.2-19] to finance the war.

25 Feb 1813: Congress passed a law [11.2-20] laying a duty on imported iron wire, with an additional 10% for wire imported on foreign vessels.

27 Apr - 1 May 1813: Battle of York (now Toronto, Ontario, Canada).

24 Jul 1813: Congress passed several revenue laws: a) imposing a 4 cents per pound duty on sugar refined in the U. S. [11.2-21]; b) a $2 to $17 annual tax on carriages not used for farming or business, depending on type [11.2-22]; c) licensing for distillers and retailers of alcohol ($0.09 to $1.08 per gallon of capacity depending on duration of license (2 weeks to one year)) [11.2-23]; and d) a 1% duty on sales at auctions and a 0.25% duty on sales of ships [11.2-24].

29 Jul 1813: Congress passed a law laying a duty of 20 cents per bushel (56 pounds) on imported salt [11.2-25].

2 Aug 1813: Congress passed a revenue bill [11.2-26] laying a $3,000,000 direct tax, apportioned among the States. The $3,000,000 was apportioned as follows: a) NH: $96,793.37; b) MA: $316,270.98; c) RI: $34,702.18; d) CT: $118,167.72; e) VT: $98,343.71; f) NY: $430,141.62; g) NJ: $108,871.63; h) PA: $365,479.16; i) DE: $32,046.25; j) MD: $151,623.94; k) VA: $369,018.44; l) KY: $168,928.76; m) Ohio: $104,150.14; n) NC: $220,238.14; o) TN: $110,086.55; p) SC: $151,905.48; q) GA: $94,936.49; and r) and LA: $28,295.11.

2 Aug 1813: Congress authorized [11.2-27] a loan for $7,500,000, containing a provision such that the certificates could not be sold at a discount greater than 12% [11.2-28].

2 Aug 1813: Congress passed a law [11.2-29] imposing: **a)** (S. 1) stamp duties on: 1) promissory notes issued by banks or bond-trading companies, ranging from 1% on $1 notes to 5% if above $1,000; and 2) discounts and bills of exchange on a declining scale, ranging from 0.5% on $1 to 0.05% if above $7,000; **b)** (S. 2) a 1.5% tax on dividends in lieu of the stamp duties per S. 1; and **c)** (S. 3 to S. 13) provisions for design of various types of stamps by the Commissioner of Revenue and penalties; and **d)** (S. 14) to continue until one year after peace with Great Britain (17 Feb 1816).

10 Sep 1813: Battle of Lake Erie (near what is now Put-in-Bay, OH).

17 Dec 1813: Congress renewed the embargo (cf. 4 Apr 1812) [11.2-30].

19 Dec 1813: Battle of Fort Niagara, NY.

30 Dec 1813: Battle of Buffalo, NY.

4 Mar 1814: Congress authorized [11.2-31] another $5,000,000 in Treasury Notes to be issued, at 5.4%, to be repaid in one year out of the sinking fund.

24 Mar 1814: Congress authorized a loan of $25,000,000 [11.2-32]. Initially only $10,000,000 was sought [11.2-33], since Treasury Secretary Gallatin believed the entire amount could not be obtained. A total of $9,795,056 was secured. Some of the offers came in at less than the required 88% of par.

14 Apr 1814: Congress repealed [11.2-34] the Embargo Act (cf. 17 Dec 1813), including the prohibition on importation of British goods.

1 Jun 1814: An additional $3,400,000 of specie was exported to Great Britain in the past two years, bringing to $7,300,000 the total amount exported after the Bank of the United States was closed in Mar 1811 [11.2-35].

3 Jul 1814: Battle of Fort Erie (Ontario, Canada).

25 Jul 1814: Battle of Lundy's Lane (a.k.a. Battle of Niagara Falls, NY).

1 Aug 1814: Another $6,000,000 of the $25,000,000 loan was sought, but only $2,520,300 at 20% discount could be obtained, since the government's credit standing was so low [11.2-36]. Those who had subscribed to the original $10,000,000 demanded an additional 8% discount, and additional bonds were issued accordingly.

24 Aug 1814: Washington D. C. was captured and burned by the British. As a result, all the banks except in the New England States began to suspend payment of notes in coin. These banks were already insolvent, since there had been a large drain of specie to Britain to pay for large imports, and also a large trade in British bills of exchange. The banks that were captured by the British contained very little worth taking [11.2-37]. By September, all the banks except in the New England States had suspended [11.2-38]. This "suspension" resulted in a large depreciation in the value of the notes as well as a loss of about $9,000,000 of U. S. government funds due to failures of the State banks [11.2-39].

Treasury Secretary Morrill [11.2-40] observed in 1876:

"Great distress resulted to the country from the depreciation of the currency [referring to 1813-1816], and from failures of banks in 1818, 1819, and 1820. The root of the evil lay in the attempt of the Government to carry on an expensive war by means of bank loans, and the notes of State corporations over which it had no control, thereby converting and irredeemable paper, issued by irresponsible institutions, into a national currency, assisting in its circulation and encouraging its expansion."

Gallatin [11.2-41] writing in 1831 gave three primary reasons for the suspension of payments in specie. First, most of the circulating capital that provided the loans was concentrated in the Eastern States, and the war was unpopular there. At the end of 1814, the Eastern States had lent $2,900,000; New York, Pennsylvania, Maryland, and Washington DC had lent $35,790,000, and the Southern and Western States lent $2,320,000. The Eastern Sates thus contributed less than they could and the Middle States had to compensate; they did so by expanding discounts and increasing the issue of bank notes. Second, the demise of the first Bank of the United States represented a loss of $7,000,000 in capital, the portion owned by foreigners, and this was exported when the Bank closed. Third, the new State-chartered banks were under-capitalized, and issued notes beyond their abilities that could not be redeemed in specie.

11 Sep 1814: Battle of Lake Champlain (NY).

14 Sep 1814: Battle of Fort McHenry, MD.

26 Sep 1814: Treasury Secretary George Campbell reported to Congress that the tax measures imposed in 1813 did not bring in enough money to continue the war. He recommended that import duties be increased, and suggested that Congress consider new tax methods in order to ensure a reliable revenue source [11.2-42].

15 Nov 1814: Congress authorized [11.2-43]: **a)** (S. 1) a loan for $3,000,000, principal to be paid any time after 15 years; **b)** (S. 4) previously issued Treasury Notes acceptable for subscribing to the loan; and **c)** (S. 6) to be repaid out of the sinking fund.

2 Dec 1814: Treasury Secretary Dallas wrote a letter to the House Ways and Means Committee regarding the precarious situation with the currency [11.2-44]: a) the Treasury Notes were suitable for use as money; b) most of the gold and silver had been exported; c) notes of the State banks were not being redeemed per the suspension; d) notes from the State banks were being discounted due to depreciation; and e) unlikely to be successful in obtaining a new loan with subscribers paying in coin. There was little option for the government to do but to accept the State bank notes in payment for taxes at par (should have discounted them as businesses were doing). A secondary problem was that the New England banks had not suspended, and banks tended to hoard their notes. Some banks were planning to resume payment, and so they restricted their notes, which caused a shortage of currency for normal trade. Eventually Secretary Dallas found it necessary to issue more Treasury Notes to offset the decline in the bank notes, at least in some areas; the result was an increase in the national debt above what it should have been.

10 Dec 1814: Congress passed a law [11.2-45] modifying the means by which the stamp duty on bank notes (cf. 2 Aug 1813) could be paid: **a)** (S. 1) in lieu of the stamp duty, the banker and Treasury Secretary could to agree to a tax of 1.5% of the bank's profit upon their capital; and **b)** (S.2) required banks who agree to this alternative to submit a monthly report.

21 Dec 1814: Congress passed legislation [11.2-46] as an extension of the 24 Jul 1813 law. Among its provisions: **a)** (S. 1) imposed duties on spirits and liquor distilled domestically, 20 cents per gallon produced; **b)** (S. 18) imposed taxes on stills based on their capacity; and **c)** (S. 25) permitted the Treasury Secretary to obtain a loan up to $6,000,000 at interest not exceeding 6% pledging these revenues for repayment.

24 Dec 1814: Agreement was reached on the Treaty of Ghent to end the War of 1812, but is not known in America.

26 Dec 1814: Congress authorized [11.2-47] the Treasury Secretary to issue up to $7,500,000 in Treasury Notes to make up any shortfalls in the loan authorizations of $25 M (24 Mar 1814) and $3 M (15 Nov 1814).

8 Jan 1815: Battle of New Orleans, LA.

9 Jan 1815: Congress passed a revenue bill [11.2-48] laying a $6,000,000 direct tax, apportioned among the States. The $6,000,000 was apportioned as follows: a) NH: $193,586.74; b) MA: $632,541.96; c) RI: $69,404.36; d) CT: $236,335.42; e) VT: $196,687.42; f) NY: $860,283.24; g) NJ: $217,743.66; h) PA: $730,958.32; i) DE: $64,092.50; j) MD: $303,247.88; k) VA: $738,036.88; l) KY: $337,857.52; m) OH: $208,300.28; n) NC: $440,476.56; o) TN: $220,173.10; p) SC: $303,810.96; q) GA: $189,872.98; r) and LA: $56,590.22.

18 Jan 1815: Congress passed an excise tax law [11.2-49]. Among the provisions: **a)** (S. 1) laying duties on a large variety of manufactures and raw materials in the U. S.; including iron, nails, candles, hats, umbrellas, paper, saddles and bridles, beer, ale, tobacco, and leather; **b)** (S. 2) also required licensing of manufacturers, and required them to give bonds for the payment of the duties; **c)** (S. 4) required oaths to be taken as to the accuracy of reporting; **d)** (S. 5) imposed a 10% penalty for late payments; and **e)** (S. 6) provided for forfeiture of goods for which the excise has not been paid.

18 Jan 1815: Congress passed a tax [11.2-50] on household furniture (excluding bedding, kitchen furniture, family pictures, and homemade articles) and gold and silver watches. Among the provisions: **a)** (S. 1) an annual graduated tax on household items based on valuation, ranging from $1 for valuations less than $400 to $100 for valuation exceeding $9000; **b)** (S. 1) an annual duty of $2 for every gold watch and $1 for every silver watch; **c)** (S. 2) property lists to be taken the same as specified in the law of 22 Jul 1813; **d)** (S. 4) $100 penalty for a fraudulent listing; and **e)** (S. 13) exemptions for books and maps.

20 Jan 1815: Congress passed a resolution re-authorizing the charter of the Bank of the United States [11.2-51]. But there were two powerful factions opposed to it [11.2-52]. First was the State banks who had three reasons: a) would cause them to stop expanding their note issues; b) they believed the capital requirements for national bank could not be obtained; and c) believed that even if the national bank notes were payable in coin, it would not last for long given current conditions. The second faction was the currency speculators, who earned a profit on the difference in depreciation in different areas of the country.

30 Jan 1815: President Madison vetoed the re-authorization of the Bank of the United States on the grounds that: a) capital could be subscribed in Treasury Notes [11.2-53]; and b) aside from the constitutional question (which he believed had been resolved), stating [11.2-54]:
"The proposed bank does not appear to be calculated to answer the purposes of reviving the public credit, of providing a national medium of circulation, of aiding the Treasury by facilitating the indispensable anticipations of the revenues, and by affording to the public more durable loans."

17 Feb 1815: The War of 1812 formally ended with the ratification of the Treaty of Ghent by the U. S. and Great Britain.

24 Feb 1815: Congress authorized the emission of $25,000,000 in Treasury Notes [11.2-55]. Among the provisions: **a)** (S. 3) those of denominations of $100 or more bore interest at 5.4%, and those of lesser denomination were payable to the bearer but at no interest; **b)** (S. 4) any combination totaling $100 or more could be converted to certificates bearing 7%, redeemable after 12 years; **c)** (S. 5, 6) the notes to be received for taxes, but could be re-issued; **d)** (S. 8) notes to be issued at par value to those willing to accept them; **e)** (S. 8) the Treasury allowed to borrow against the notes; and **f)** (S. 9) holders of Treasury Notes may convert them to the funded debt at 5.4% interest. Only $8,856,960 could be obtained, ultimately at 7%, running for nine years [11.2-56]. The plan was to either pay them off, or destroy those received for duties and taxes [11.2-57].

27 Feb 1815: Congress passed [11.2-58] an additional duty on gold, silver, plated ware, and jewelry, except clocks, at 6% *ad valorem* for all future manufactures of same, to be paid by the manufacturer. It was to be assessed in the same manner as called out in the law of 18 Jan 1815.

3 Mar 1815: Congress passed a law [11.2-59] repealing the additional import duties imposed previously (cf. 1 Jul 1812, 25 Feb 1813), so long as the foreign nation reciprocated.

3 Mar 1815: Congress authorized a loan [11.2-60] of $18,452,800 to cover the repayment of the Treasury Notes; and allowing previously issued Treasury Notes to be received in payment for the bonds. But only $9,284,044 at 5% discount was ultimately received [11.2-61, 11.2-62]. This was the last loan for the War of 1812. In 1830, the Ways and Means Committee calculated that of the $80,000,000 borrowed during this period, only $34,000,000 had been received after deducting discounts and depreciation [11.2-63].

31 Dec 1815: By the end of 1815, American production of iron, cotton, wool, lead, glass, and pottery made America nearly independent of British manufacturers [11.2-64].

5 Feb 1816: Congress passed a law [11.2-65]: **a)** (S. 2) imposed an additional 42% duty on foreign goods; and **b)** (S. 3) excluding cases where treaties are in effect to the contrary and excluding the provisions of the previous revision to the tariffs (cf. 3 Mar 1815).

22 Feb 1816: Congress repealed [11.2-66] the duties on manufactures (cf. 18 Jan 1815) and the duties on gold, silver, and plated ware (cf. 27 Feb 1815).

5 Mar 1816: Congress passed a modification [11.2-67] of the direct tax of 9 Jan 1815, reducing it to $3,000,000 with the apportionment corresponding reduced for each State. It also reduced the direct tax upon the District of Columbia (per a law passed 27 Feb 1815) from $19,998.40 to $9,999.00.

9 Apr 1816: Congress repealed [11.2-68] the duties on household furniture, etc. (cf. 18 Jan 1815).

10 Apr 1816: Congress [11.2-69] and President Madison concurred to re-establish the Bank of the United States, to correct the obvious problems with the over-issue of bank notes by the State-chartered banks [11.2-70]. Among the provisions: **a)** (S. 1 - 4) its capital was fixed at $35,000,000, and the U. S. Government was to subscribe to $7,000,000 payable in coin or in U. S. securities (funded debt) paying 5% interest, and the rest of the capital stock could be subscribed by corporations or individuals, 25% payable in coin, and the other 75% in either coin or U. S. securities representing the funded debt of the U. S., but the face value of the funded debt instruments discounted or improved (6% debt at par, 3% debt at $65 per $100 face value, 7% debt at $106.51 per $100 face value); **b)** (S. 5) the U. S. may redeem any funded debt and the bank may sell for gold and silver, and indebtedness aside from deposits was limited to the bank's capital; **c)** (S. 7) the Bank was chartered for 20 years, to expire 3 Mar 1836; **d)** (S. 8) the bank to have 25 directors, five of them being stockholders to be appointed by the President, and only the President can remove his appointees; **e)** (S. 9) the Bank may commence operations when 8,400,000 of capital has been paid in, either in gold and silver coin or public debt; **f)** (S. 11) notes issued by the Bank to have a minimum denomination $5; **g)** (S. 11) directors must be U. S. citizens and stockholders; **h)** (S. 11) the Bank was permitted to deal only in bills of exchange, gold and silver bullion, goods pledged for loans, and goods sales thereof; **i)** (S. 11) the maximum indebtedness of the Bank shall be limited to $35,000,000; **j)** (S. 11) loans made by the Bank are limited to 6% interest; **k)** (S. 11) "not at liberty to purchase any public debt whatsoever"; **l)** (S. 11) required to provide condition statements; **m)** (S. 11) loans to the U. S. or to any State limited to $500,000; **n)** (S. 14) the Banks' notes to be receivable for all taxes; **o)** (S. 15) the Bank was to act as the fiscal agent for the Government, and to negotiated loans on behalf of the Government; **p)** (S. 15, 16) the Bank to provide adequate facilities for transfer of U. S. funds; **q)** (S. 17) the Banks' notes are payable on demand in gold and silver coin; **r)** (S. 17) the Bank was to be taxed 12% annually for any failure to pay in coin on demand; **s)** (S. 20) for granting the charter, the Bank is to pay to the United States $1,500,000 (3 annual $500,000 payments starting in the second year after commencement of operations); **t)** (S. 21) Congress was not to charter any other bank during the 20-year period, except in the District of Columbia; and **u)** (S. 23) Committees of either House of Congress may inspect the Banks' books.

19 Apr 1816: Congress repealed [11.2-71] the specific duties on distilled spirits (cf. 21 Dec 1814), but retained and modified the provisions relating to licensing of stills and distillers.

27 Apr 1816: Congress passed a general revision of the tariff law [11.2-72], superseding the ones passed since 1812. Section 1 specified *ad valorem* duties: **a)** 1.5% on dyes, jewelry, gold, silver, precious

stones, lace, and silk; **b)** 15% on gold leaf; **c)** 20% on hemp and sail cloth, all items manufactured from brass, copper, iron, steel, pewter, lead, or tin, earthen ware, porcelain, and glass except window glass; **d)** 25% on all woolen manufactures for three years, afterwards reduced to 20%; **e)** 20% on cotton cloth if imported from or beyond the Cape of Good Hope; **f)** 30% on umbrellas and parts thereof, hats, artificial flowers, perfumes, all manufactures of wood, all manufactures of leather, parchment, vellum, canes, and walking sticks, among others; and **g)** duties per volume or weight on beer, ale, wine, bottles, playing cards, spices, nails, fruit, shoes, tea, gunpowder, tobacco, among others. Section 2 contained a free list, mostly books, maps, painting, drawings, educational materials, and tools of trades, among others. Section 3 specified an additional 10% duty on imports if brought in on certain foreign vessels not otherwise exempted. Section 8 made the provisions of the Act of 3 Mar 1815 permanent.

29 Apr 1816: Congress re-authorized [11.2-73] the use of foreign coins (of Great Britain, France, Portugal, and Spain) as legal tender, specifying the value of certain foreign coins in dollars, to expire in 1819, owing to the inability to mint sufficient U. S. coin [11.2-74].

30 Apr 1816: In order to counteract the depreciation of the notes issued by State banks, Congress resolved that duties, taxes, and other debts payable to the U. S. Government after 20 Feb 1817 could be paid only in coin, Treasury Notes, or in the notes of banks that paid specie on demand at face value [11.2-75]. The text reads [11.2-76]:

> "That the Secretary of the Treasury be, and he hereby is, required and directed to adopt such measures as he may deem necessary to cause, as soon as may be, all duties, taxes, debts, or sums of money, accruing or becoming payable to the United States, to be collected and paid in the legal currency of the United States, or treasury notes, or notes of the bank of the United States as by law provided and declared, or in notes of banks which are payable and paid on demand in the said legal currency of the United States, and that from and after the twentieth day of February next, no such duties, taxes, debts, or sums of money accruing or becoming payable to the United States as aforesaid, ought to be collected or received otherwise than in the legal currency of the United States, or treasury notes, or notes of the bank of the United States, or in notes of banks which are payable and paid on demand in the said legal currency of the United States."

30 Apr 1816: Congress passed a tariff measure designed to provide protection of American industries from foreign competition [11.2-77, 11.2-78]. On those items which could mostly be produced domestically, the tariff was very large; it was 20% on those that could not be entirely provided domestically, and the remaining ones were designed to produce revenue as large as practical. It was virtually prohibitory on cheaper grades of cotton cloth, being 25% duty on the minimum valuation (it assumed sale price here was the same as production cost in India).

11.3 Data, 1812-1816

Figures 11.3-1 and 11.3-2 show the U. S. government revenue and expenditures for this period.

			Internal Revenue		Miscellaneous					
			Income and Profits		Sales of Public		Other		Public Debt	
Day	Year	Customs	taxes	Misc.	Lands	Direct Tax	Misc.	Postal	Sales	Total
31 Dec	1812	8,958,777	0	4,903	710,427	859	126,165	649,151	12,837,900	23,288,183
31 Dec	1813	13,224,623	0	4,755	835,655	3,805	271,871	703,220	26,184,135	41,228,065
31 Dec	1814	5,998,772	0	1,662,984	1,135,971	2,219,497	164,485	730,953	23,377,826	35,290,490
31 Dec	1815	7,282,942	0	4,678,059	1,287,959	2,162,673	296,824	1,043,021	35,252,779	52,004,259
31 Dec	1816	36,306,874	0	5,124,708	1,717,985	4,253,635	342,447	961,718	9,425,771	58,133,139

U. S. Government Revenue, 1812 - 1816 (USD)

The data for the revenue for 1812 to 1816 is from W. G. McAdoo, "Annual Report of the Secretary of the Treasury on the State of the Finances for the Fiscal Year Ended June 30, 1914", Washington: U. S. Government Printing Office, 1915, pp. 230-241; Treasury Document 2721. This data was modified from 1791 to 1914 per Henry Morgenthau, "Annual Report of the Secretary of the Treasury on the State of the Finances for the Fiscal Year Ended June 30, 1940", Treasury Document 3111, pp. 642-649, which shows "internal revenue" broken out as income taxes and miscellaneous. It is the same data as reported previously (cf. 1914), but shows income taxes and miscellaneous taxes as separate categories.

Figure 11.3-1: U. S. Government Revenue, 1812-1816

U. S. Government Expenditures, 1812 - 1816 (USD)									
		Ordinary Disbursements							
Day	Year	Civil & Misc.	War Dep't	Navy Dep't	Indians	Pensions	Interest on Public Debt	Postal	Public Debt Retired	Total
31 Dec	1812	1,683,088	11,817,798	3,959,365	277,845	91,402	2,451,272	552,472	1,998,349	22,831,593
31 Dec	1813	1,729,435	19,652,013	6,446,600	167,358	86,989	3,599,455	635,411	7,508,668	39,825,932
31 Dec	1814	2,208,029	20,350,806	7,311,290	167,394	90,164	4,593,239	726,374	3,307,304	38,754,605
31 Dec	1815	2,898,870	14,794,294	8,660,000	530,750	69,656	5,990,090	743,755	6,638,832	40,326,248
31 Dec	1816	2,989,741	16,012,096	3,908,278	274,512	188,804	7,822,923	807,875	17,048,139	49,052,370

The data for the expenditures for 1812 to 1816 is from W. G. McAdoo, "Annual Report of the Secretary of the Treasury on the State of the Finances for the Fiscal Year Ended June 30, 1914", Washington: U. S. Government Printing Office, 1915, pp. 230-241; Treasury Document 2721. The total expenditure numbers do not agree with the 1940 report because the 1940 values do not include "Public Debt Retired" as chargeable against ordinary revenues. Expenditure data for 1789 to 1914 is from the 1914 Treasury Report.

Figure 11.3-2: U. S. Government Expenditures, 1812-1816

Figure 11.3-3 shows the growth of the national debt in this period, due to the War of 1812. Refer to the Introduction to Part 2 for a sense of wages vs. the per-capita national debt.

U. S. National Debt, 1812-1816 (USD)				
Day	Year	Principal ($) [1]	Population [2]	Debt per Capita ($) [2]
31 Dec	1812	55,962,827	7,719,595	7.25
31 Dec	1813	81,467,846	7,959,453	10.24
31 Dec	1814	99,833,660	8,199,310	12.18
31 Dec	1815	127,334,933	8,439,167	15.09
31 Dec	1816	123,491,965	8,679,024	14.23

1. Public debt data from 1812 to 1816 is from the Annual Report of the Secretary of the Treasury, 1980, pp. 61, 62.
2. Population values are based on the dicennial census from the Census Bureau, and linearly interpolated. Per-capita is based on these values.

Figure 11.3-3: National Debt and Per-Capita Share Thereof, 1812-1816

Figure 11.3-4 shows the conditions of the banking system during this period. But the Annual Report of the Comptroller of the Currency of 1876 [11.3-1] cites Secretary Crawford, who claims that the notes issued by the State banks came to between $62,000,000 and $70,000,000; in 1815, between $99,000,000 and $110,000,000. The figures from later in the 1876 Report are used in Figure 11.3-4 since they correspond reasonably close to Gallatin's estimate [11.3-2] and as cited by Elliot [11.3-3] for those two years.

Banking System in U. S., 1812-1816 (USD)				
Year	Number of Banks	Capital	Notes in Circulation	Specie
1815	208	82,259,590	45,500,000	17,000,000
1816	246	89,822,422	68,000,000	19,000,000

Source: Albert Gallatin in "Considerations on the Currency and Banking System of the United States", Philadelphia, PA: Carey & Lea, 1831, pp. 101, 103. Gallatin actually shows two tables, one for which returns had been received, and one for which only capital is shown. The total notes and specie includes an extrapolation of those reporting only capital, based on the complete returns of the first table.

Figure 11.3-4: Summary Condition of Banks in the U. S., 1812-1816

Figure 11.3-5 shows the estimated money supply in the U. S. for 1812 to 1816. Notice the large increase in the amount of bank notes issued by the State-chartered banks. The values in italics in column 12 seem unreasonably large, for reasons mentioned in the Introduction to Part 2.

	1	2	3	4	5	6	7	8	9	10	11	12	13	14	15	16	17

Estimated U. S. Money Supply, 1812-1816 [1] (millions USD)

Year (~30 Jun)	Number of Banks [2]	Estimated State Bank Notes	Estimated Notes of First Bank of U. S.	Total Notes in Circulation	Total Specie in US [3]	Specie in Treasury [4]	Specie Outside Treasury	Total Notes & Specie Outside Treasury	Cash Held in All Banks [5]	Notes & Specie Outside Banks	Estimated State Bank Deposits [6]	Estimated Deposits of First Bank of U. S.	Total Estimated Deposits	Estimated Interbank Trans-actions [7]	Estimated Deposits Adjusted	Estimated Total Money Supply
1812		43.063	0.000	43.063	28.800	2.800	26.000	69.063	21.410	47.653	*94.279*	0.000	94.279	9.239	85.039	132.693
1813		**66.000**	0.000	66.000	**28.000**	2.700	25.300	91.300	28.303	62.997	*208.421*	0.000	208.421	20.425	187.996	250.993
1814		68.377	0.000	68.377	22.250	2.600	19.650	88.027	27.288	60.739	*215.283*	0.000	215.283	21.098	194.186	254.925
1815	208	**45.500**	0.000	45.500	**16.500**	2.500	14.000	59.500	18.445	41.055	67.364	0.000	67.364	6.602	60.762	101.817
1816	246	**68.000**	0.000	68.000	17.700	2.400	15.300	83.300	25.823	57.477	67.955	0.000	67.955	6.660	61.295	118.772

1. Values in **bold** are from original sources; all others interpolated or estimated as described.
2. Number of banks from the Annual Report of the Comptroller of the Currency, 1918, 2 Dec 1918, Vol. 2, p. 835, Table 86.
3. **Bold** values from Annual Report of the Secretary of the Treasury, 1876, p. 153; items in normal font are linearly interpolated.
4. Linearly interpolated from values for 1810 and 1820 from the Annual Report of the Comptroller of the Currency, 1896, Vol. 1, p. 544
5. Cash held in banks for 1812 to 1816 estimated based on the average ratio of cash to outstanding currency from 1834 to 1914 (0.31)
6. Values for 1812, 1813, and 1814 shown in italics seem to be unreasonably large.
7. Interbank from 1812 to 1816 based on average of interbank to total deposits from 1914 to 1940 (0.098).

Figure 11.3-5: Estimated Money Supply, 1812-1816

Figure 11.3-6 shows the depreciation of the paper currency due to over-issue by the State-chartered banks between the suspension of redemption in Sep 1814 and the start of operations of the second Bank of the United States in 1817.

Depreciation of Bank Notes Due to Suspension of Redemption, 1814-1817 (%)

Date	New York	Philadelphia	Baltimore	Date	New York	Philadelphia	Baltimore
Sep 1814	10.0	0.0	20.0	Jan 1816	12.5	14.0	15.0
Oct 1814	10.0	0.0	15.0	Feb 1816	9.0	14.0	13.0
Nov 1814	11.0	0.0	10.0	Mar 1816	12.5	12.5	18.0
Dec 1814	11.0	0.0	14.0	Apr 1816	10.0	14.5	23.0
Jan 1815	15.0	0.0	20.0	May 1816	12.5	14.0	20.0
Feb 1815	2.0	0.0	5.0	Jun 1816	12.5	17.0	20.0
Mar 1815	5.0	0.0	5.0	Jul 1816	6.0	15.0	15.0
Apr 1815	5.5	0.0	10.0	Aug 1816	5.0	10.0	12.0
May 1815	5.0	5.0	14.0	Sep 1816	3.0	7.5	10.0
Jun 1815	11.5	9.0	16.0	Oct 1816	2.0	9.5	8.0
Jul 1815	14.0	11.0	20.0	Nov 1816	1.3	7.0	9.0
Aug 1815	12.5	11.0	19.0	Dec 1816	2.3	7.0	9.0
Sep 1815	13.0	15.0	20.0	Jan 1817	2.5	4.5	3.0
Oct 1815	16.0	15.0	21.5	Feb 1817	2.5	4.0	2.5
Nov 1815	12.5	16.0	15.0	Source: J. J. Knox, Annual Report of the Comptroller			
Dec 1815	12.5	14.0	18.0	of the Currency, 1876, Appendix, p. LXXXIX			

Figure 11.3-6: Depreciation of Bank Notes, During Suspension of Redemption 1814-1817

Figures 11.3-7 and 11.3-8 show the gold and silver coinage by the U. S. Mint during this period.

Gold Coinage of the U. S., 1812-1816 ($)

Year	$20 Double Eagles ($)	$10 Eagles ($)	$5 Half Eagles ($)	Three Dollar ($)	$2.50 Quarter Eagles ($)	Gold Dollars ($)	Total ($)
1812			290,435.00				290,435.00
1813			477,140.00				477,140.00
1814			77,270.00				77,270.00
1815			3,175.00				3,175.00
1816							0.00
Totals	0.00	0.00	848,020.00	0.00	0.00	0.00	848,020.00

Source: Annual Report of the Director of the Mint, 1895, 28 Nov 1895, Treasury Document No. 1829, pp. 286-293 (Table XLIV).

Figure 11.3-7: Gold Coins Minted by the U. S., 1812-1816

Silver and Copper Coinage of the U. S., 1812-1816 ($)

Year	Trade Dollars	Dollars	Half Dollars	Quarters	Twenty-cents	Dimes	Half-dimes	Three-cents	Cents & Half-Cents	Total ($)
		Silver ($)							Minor ($)	
1812			814,020.50						10,755.00	824,775.50
1813			620,951.50						4,180.00	625,131.50
1814			519,537.50			42,150.00			3,578.30	565,265.80
1815				17,308.00						17,308.00
1816			23,575.00	5,000.75					28,209.82	56,785.57
Totals	0.00	0.00	1,978,084.50	22,308.75	0.00	42,150.00	0.00	0.00	46,723.12	2,089,266.37

Source: Annual Report of the Director of the Mint, 1895, 28 Nov 1895, Treasury Document No. 1829, pp. 286-293 (Table XLIV).

Figure 11.3-8: Silver and Minor Coins Minted by the U. S., 1812-1816

Figure 11.3-9 shows the estimated CPI and per-capita money supply for this period.

Year	CPI [1] (1913 = 100)	Total Money Supply [5] (USD)	Population [6]	Per Capita Money Supply (USD)	Annual Rate of Change in CPI (%)	Annual Rate of Change in Per-Capita Money Supply (%)
1812	124.446	132,692,794	7,719,595	17.19	3.269	57.737
1813	144.489	250,992,857	7,959,453	31.53	14.933	60.679
1814	174.345	254,924,532	8,199,310	31.09	18.783	-1.415
1815	142.234	101,817,211	8,439,167	12.06	-20.356	-94.662
1816	122.590	118,772,429	8,679,024	13.68	-14.863	12.600

1. CPI is the average of L-1 and L-15 data, both re-aligned to 1913 as a reference.
2. L-1 data 1791 to 1938 (Snyder-Tucker) is a general price index (wholesale prices, wages, cost of living and rents).
3. L-15 data 1801 to 1945 includes wholesale prices, all commodities.
4. L1 and L-15 from Historical Statistics of the United States, 1789-1945, A Supplement to the Statistical Abstract of the United States, Bureau of the Census, US Department of Commerce, Washington, DC, 1949.
5. See notes in money supply data for sources.
6. Population is linearly interpolated from Census results.

Figure 11.3-9: Money Supply and CPI, 1812-1816

Figure 11.3-10 shows the CPI and per-capita money supply graphically. For the interval 1812 to 1814, the money average annual increases in CPI and money supply are 16.8% and 29.6% respectively; for the interval 1814 to 1816, the average annual changes in CPI and money supply are -17.6% and -41.0% respectively. Overall, from 1812 to 1816, the average annual changes in CPI and money supply are -0.3% and -5.7% respectively.

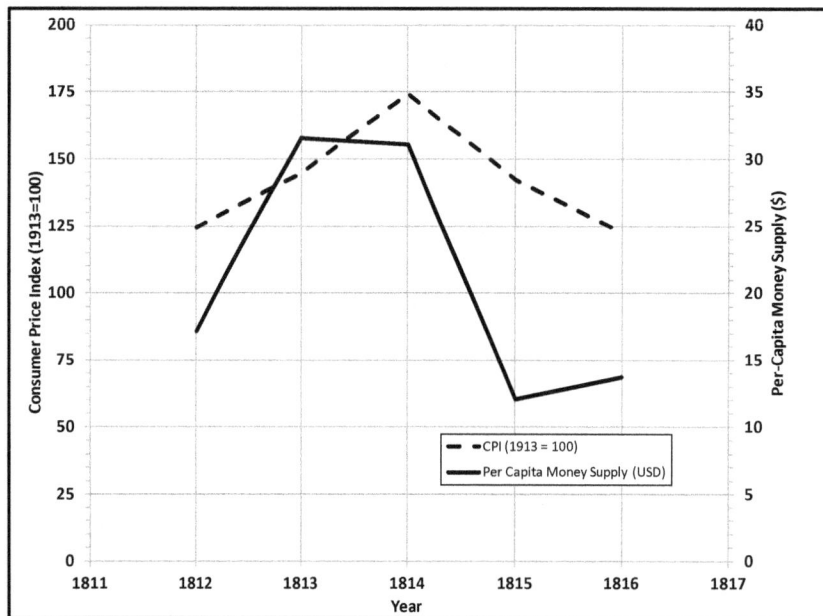

Figure 11.3-10: CPI and Per-Capita Summary, 1812-1816

Figure 11.3-11 shows the approximate median income index, consumer price index, and standard of living index for this period. See the Introduction to Part 2 for cautions regarding these curves.

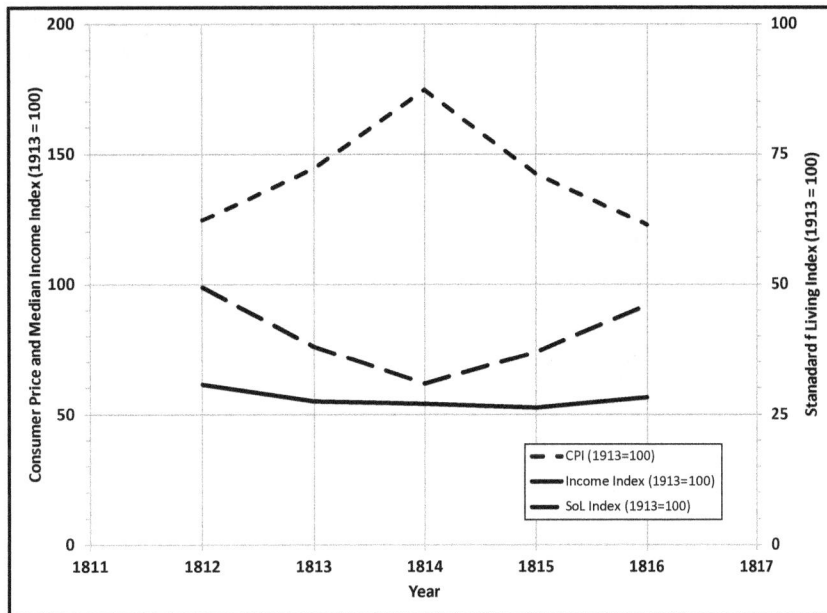

Figure 11.3-11: Median Income, Consumer Price, and Standard of Living Indices, 1812-1816

11.4 Summary, 1812-1816

There was an enormous increase in bank notes issued by State banks between 1812 and 1814. Treasury Secretary Dallas commented in 1814 [11.4-1]:

> "The multiplication of State banks in the several States has so increased the quantity of paper currency that it would be difficult to calculate its amount, and still more difficult to ascertain its value... There exists at this time no adequate circulating medium common the citizens of the United States."

Albert Gallatin, Treasury Secretary until the end of 1813, gave a summary review in 1831 on the monetary events of this period [11.4-2]:

> "The dissolution of the Bank of the United States deprived the country of a foreign capital of more than seven millions of dollars, vested in the stock of that institution, and which was accordingly remitted abroad during the year that preceded the war. At the same time, the state banks had taken up a considerable part of the paper formerly discounted by that of the United States. As the amount of this exceeded fifteen millions, their aid in that respect was absolutely necessary, in order to prevent the great distress, which must have otherwise attended such diminution of the usual accommodations.
>
> The creation of new state banks, in order to fill the chasm, was a natural consequence of the dissolution of the Bank of the United States. And, as usual, under such circumstances, the expectation of great profits gave birth to a much greater number than was wanted. They were extended through the interior parts of the country, created no new capital, and withdrew that which might have been otherwise lent to the government, or as profitably employed. From the 1st of January 1811, to the 1st of January 1815, not less than one hundred and twenty new banks were chartered and went into operation, with a capital of about 40, and making an addition of near thirty millions of dollars to the banking capital of the country. That increase took place on the eve of, and during a war which did nearly annihilate the exports, and both the foreign and coasting trade. And, as the salutary regulating power of the Bank of the United States no longer existed, the issues were accordingly increased much beyond what other circumstances already mentioned rendered necessary."

When the first Bank of the United States was abolished, State-chartered banks stepped in and did a good job of continuing the banking function of discounting bills and lending to businesses. Unfortunately, many new banks were established with State charters and began to issue paper currency over and above what was necessary. The excess of paper currency caused a great amount of depreciation in the value of the money; also the banks had to suspend redemption in coin in September of 1814. It was not until the second Bank of the U. S. was chartered that sound money began again. But, the second Bank had its own problems of mismanagement and corruption, as will be shown in chapter 12.

References

[11.1-1]   Cited in Albert S. Bolles, *A Financial History of the United States*, NY: Augustus M. Kelley (1969), Vol. 2, p. 155 (originally published 1884 by D. Appleton & Co., NY).
[11.1-2]   Francis A. Walker, *Money*, NY: Henry Holt and Company, 1891, p. 492

[11.2-1]   Text of "An Act authorizing a loan for a sum not exceeding eleven millions of dollars"; 12th Congress, Session 1, Chapter 41, 14 Mar 1812
[11.2-2]   op. cit. Bolles, Vol. 2, pp. 214, 221
[11.2-3]   Text of "An Act repealing the tenth section of the act to incorporate the subscribers to the Bank of the United States", 12th Congress, Session 1, Chapter 43, 19 Mar 1812
[11.2-4]   op. cit., Bolles, Vol. 2, p. 152
[11.2-5]   Text of "An Act laying an embargo on all ships and vessels in the ports and harbors of the United States, for a limited time", 12th Congress, Session 1, Chapter 49, 4 Apr 1812
[11.2-6]   Text of "An Act to prohibit exportation of specie, goods, wares, and merchandise for a limited time", 12th Congress, Session 1, Chapter 56, 14 Apr 1812
[11.2-7]   op. cit., Bolles, Vol. 2, p. 154
[11.2-8]   Text of "An Act declaring War between the United Kingdom of Great Britain and Ireland and the dependencies thereof, and the United States of America and their territories", 12th Congress, Session 1, Chapter 102, 18 Jun 1812
[11.2-9]   op. cit., Bolles, Vol. 2, pp. 284, 285
[11.2-10] Text of "An Act to authorize the issuing of Treasury Notes", 12th Congress, Session 1, Chapter 111, 30 Jun 1812
[11.2-11] op. cit., Bolles, Vol. 2, pp. 223, 224
[11.2-12] op. cit., Walker, p. 495
[11.2-13] op. cit., Bolles, Vol. 2, pp. 250, 251
[11.2-14] Text of "An Act for imposing additional duties upon all goods, wares, and merchandise imported from an foreign port or place, and for other purposes", 12th Congress, Session 1, Chapter 112, 1 Jul 1812
[11.2-15] op. cit., Walker, p. 492
[11.2-16] op. cit., Bolles, Vol. 2, pp. 225-226
[11.2-17] Text of "An Act authorizing a Loan for a sum not to exceed sixteen millions of dollars", 12th Congress, Session 2, Chapter 21, 8 Feb 1813
[11.2-18] Text of "An Act authorizing the issuing of Treasury notes for the services of the year one thousand eight hundred and thirteen", 12th Congress, Session 2, Chapter 27, 15 Feb 1813
[11.2-19] op. cit., Bolles, Vol. 2, pp. 228, 229
[11.2-20] Text of "An Act to impose a duty on the importation of iron wire", 12th Congress, Session 2, Chapter 30, 25 Feb 1813
[11.2-21] Text of "An Act laying duties on sugar refined in the United States", 13th Congress, Session 1, Chapter 21, 24 Jul 1813
[11.2-22] Text of "An Act laying duties on carriages for the conveyance of persons", 13th Congress, Session 1 Chapter 24, 24 Jul 1813
[11.2-23] Text of "An Act laying duties on licenses to distillers of spirituous liquors", 13th Congress, Session 1, Chapter 25, 24 Jul 1813
[11.2-24] Text of "An Act laying duties on sales of auction of merchandise and of ships and vessels"; 13th Congress, Session 1, Chapter 26, 24 Jul 1813
[11.2-25] Text of "An Act laying a duty on imported salt, granting a bounty on pickled fish exported, and allowance to certain vessels employed in the fisheries", 13th Congress, Session 1, Chapter 35, 29 Jul 1813
[11.2-26] Text of "An Act to lay and collect a direct tax within the United States", 13th Congress, Session 1, Chapter 37, 2 Aug 1813
[11.2-27] Text of "An Act authorizing a loan for a sum not exceeding seven millions five hundred thousand dollars", 13th Congress, Session 1, Chapter 51, 2 Aug 1813

[11.2-28] op. cit., Bolles, Vol. 2, p. 229

[11.2-29] Text of "An Act laying duties on notes of banks, bankers, and certain companies; on notes, bonds, and obligations discounted by banks, bankers, and certain companies, and on bills of exchange of certain description"; 13th Congress, Session 1, Chapter 53, 2 Aug 1813

[11.2-30] Text of "An Act laying an embargo on all ships and vessels in the ports and harbors of the United States", 13th Congress, Session 2, Chapter 1, 17 Dec 1813

[11.2-31] Text of "An Act to authorize the issuing of treasury notes for the service of the year one thousand eight hundred and fourteen", 13th Congress, Session 2, Chapter 18, 4 Mar 1814

[11.2-32] Text of "An Act to authorize a loan for a sum not exceeding twenty-five millions of dollars", 13th Congress, Session 2, Chapter 29, 24 Mar 1814

[11.2-33] op. cit., Bolles, Vol. 2, p. 229, 230

[11.2-34] Text of "An Act to repeal an act entitled 'An act laying an embargo on all ships and vessels in the ports and harbors of the United States', and so much of any act or acts as prohibit the importation of goods, wares, and merchandise of the growth, produce, or manufacture of Great Britain or Ireland, or of any of the colonies or dependencies thereof, or of any place in the actual possession of Great Britain", 13th Congress, Session 2, Chapter 56, 14 Apr 1814

[11.2-35] op. cit., Bolles, Vol. 2, p. 154

[11.2-36] op. cit., Bolles, Vol. 2, pp. 231-233

[11.2-37] op. cit., Bolles, Vol. 2, pp. 263-266

[11.2-38] Lot M. Morrill, *Annual Report of the Secretary of the Treasury on the State of the Finances for Year 1876*, Appendix containing the Report of the Comptroller of Currency (John Jay Knox), Washington, DC: Government Printing Office, 1876, p. 123

[11.2-39] op. cit., Morrill, p. 124

[11.2-40] op. cit., Morrill, pp. 123, 124

[11.2-41] Albert Gallatin, *Considerations on the Currency and Banking System of the United States*, Philadelphia: Carey & Lea, 1831, pp. 43-45

[11.2-42] op. cit., Bolles, Vol. 2, p. 255

[11.2-43] Text of "An Act to authorize a loan for a sum not exceeding three millions of dollars", 13th Congress, Session 3, Chapter 4, 15 Nov 1815

[11.2-44] op. cit., Bolles, Vol. 2, pp. 271-273

[11.2-45] Text of "An Act supplementary to an act, laying duties on notes of banks, bankers, and certain companies, on notes, bonds, and obligations, discounted by banks, bankers, and certain companies, and on bills of exchange of certain descriptions", 13th Congress, Session 3, Chapter 11, 10 Dec 1814.

[11.2-46] Text of "An Act to provide additional revenues for defraying the expenses of government and maintaining the public credit, by laying duties on spirits distilled within the United States, and territories, thereof, and by amending the act laying duties on licenses to distillers of spirituous liquors", 13th Congress, Session 3, Chapter 15, 21 Dec 1814

[11.2-47] Text of "An Act supplementary to the acts authorizing a loan for the several sums of twenty-five millions of dollars and three millions of dollars", 13th Congress, Session 3, Chapter 17, 26 Dec 1814

[11.2-48] Text of "An Act to provide additional revenues for defraying the expenses of government, and maintaining the public credit, by laying a direct tax upon the United States, and to provide for assessing and collecting the tax", 13th Congress, Session 3, Chapter 21, 9 Jan 1815

[11.2-49] Text of "An Act to provide additional revenues for defraying the expenses of government, and maintaining the public credit, by laying duties an various goods, wares, and merchandise, manufactured within the United States", 13th Congress, Session 3, Chapter 22, 18 Jan 1815

[11.2-50] Text of "An Act to provide additional revenues for defraying the expenses of government, and maintaining the public credit, by laying duties on household furniture, and on gold and silver watches", 13th Congress, Session 3, Chapter 23, 18 Jan 1815

[11.2-51] op. cit., Morrill, pp. 124, 125

[11.2-52] op. cit., Bolles, Vol. 2, pp. 279, 280

[11.2-53] op. cit., Bolles, Vol. 2, p. 281

[11.2-54] op. cit., Morrill, p. 125

[11.2-55] Text of "An Act to authorize the issuing of treasury notes for the service of the year one thousand eight hundred and fifteen", 13th Congress, Session 3, Chapter 56, 24 Feb 1815

[11.2-56] op. cit., Morrill, p. 124

[11.2-57] op. cit., Bolles, Vol. 2, p. 238

[11.2-58]   Text of "An Act to provide additional revenues for defraying the expenses of government, and maintaining the public credit, by laying a duty on gold, silver, and plated ware, and jewelry and pastework, manufactured within the United States", 13th Congress, Session 3, Chapter 61, 27 Feb 1815

[11.2-59]   Text of "An Act to repeal so much of the several acts imposing duties on the tonnage of foreign ships and vessels, an on goods, wares, and merchandise, imported into the United States, as imposes a discriminating duty on tonnage between foreign vessels and vessels of the United States, and between goods imported into the United States in foreign vessels and vessels of the United States", 13th Congress, Session 3, Chapter 77, 3 Mar 1815

[11.2-60]   Text of "An Act to authorize a loan for a sum not exceeding eighteen millions four hundred and fifty-two thousand eight hundred dollars", 13th Congress, Session 3, Chapter 87, 3 Mar 1815

[11.2-61]   op. cit., Bolles, Vol. 2, pp. 240, 241

[11.2-62]   op. cit., Morrill, p. 124

[11.2-63]   Report of the Committee of Ways and Means, 13 Apr 1830, cited by op. cit., Bolles, Vol. 2, p. 241

[11.2-64]   op. cit., Bolles, Vol. 2, pp. 288, 289

[11.2-65]   Text of "An Act to continue in force the act, entitled "An Act for imposing additional duties upon all goods, wares, and merchandise, imported from any foreign port, or place, and for other purposes"", 14th Congress, Session 1, Chapter 10, 5 Feb 1816

[11.2-66]   Text of "An Act to repeal duties on certain articles manufactured within the United States", 14th Congress, Session 1, Chapter 18, 22 Feb 1816

[11.2-67]   Text of "An Act to reduce the amount of direct tax upon the United States and the District of Columbia, for the year one thousand eight hundred and sixteen; and to repeal in part the act entitled 'An act to provide additional revenue for defraying the expenses of government, and maintaining the public credit, by laying a direct tax upon the United States, and to provide for assessing and collecting the same', and also the act entitled 'An act to provide additional revenue for defraying the expenses of government, and maintaining the public credit by laying a direct tax upon the District of Columbia'", 14th Congress Session 1, Chapter 24, 5 Mar 1816

[11.2-68]   Text of "An Act to repeal the act entitled 'An act to provide additional revenues for defraying the expenses of government and maintaining the public credit, by laying duties on household furniture and on gold and silver watches'", 14th Congress, Session 1, Chapter 41, 9 Apr 1816

[11.2-69]   Text of "An Act to incorporate the subscribers to the Bank of the United States", 14th Congress, Session 1, Chapter 44, 10 Apr 1816

[11.2-70]   op. cit., Morrill, pp. 125, 126

[11.2-71]   Text of "An Act to abolish the existing duties and spirits distilled within the United States, and to lay other duties, in lieu of those at present imposed, on licenses to distillers of spirituous liquors", 14th Congress, Session 1, 19 Apr 1816

[11.2-72]   Text of "An Act to regulate the duties on imports and tonnage"; 14th Congress, Session 1, Chapter 107, 27 Apr 1816

[11.2-73]   Text of "An Act regulating the currency within the United States, of the gold coins of Great Britain, France, Portugal, and Spain, and the crown of France, and five-franc pieces", 14th Congress, Session 1, Chapter 134, 29 Apr 1816

[11.2-74]   op. cit., Bolles, Vol. 2, p. 283

[11.2-75]   op. cit., Bolles, Vol. 2, p. 320

[11.2-76]   Text of "A Resolution relative to the more effectual collection of the public revenue", 14th Congress, Session 1, Resolution 8, 30 Apr 1816

[11.2-77]   op. cit., Bolles, Vol. 2, pp. 364, 365

[11.2-78]   Text of "An Act to regulate the duties on imports and tonnage", 14th Congress, Session 1, Chapter 107, 30 Apr 1816

[11.3-1]   op. cit., Morrill, pp. 123, 155

[11.3-2]   op. cit., Gallatin, pp. 101, 102; op. cit. Bolles, Vol. 2, p. 265 regards Gallatin's estimate (which corresponds to Knox and Elliot) as more accurate than Crawford's.

[11.3-3]   op. cit., Elliot, p. 984

[11.4-1]   op. cit., Walker, *Money*, NY: Henry Holt and Company, 1891, p. 494

[11.4-2]   op. cit., Gallatin, p. 44

12

The Second Bank of the United States, 1817-1836

12.1 Preview, 1817-1836

The nation's financial condition was very bad at this point; the depreciation of the currency in the previous five years had caused lands and agricultural prices to fall by half compared to 1808 and to one-third compared to 1814 [12.1-1]. There were many bank failures (owing to a contraction of their notes) and corporate bankruptcies between 1818 and 1820, as the nation entered into a general recession, having not fully recovered from the War of 1812. The second Bank of the United States attempted to import money from Europe to restore the currency, but mismanagement at the branch in Baltimore nearly caused the entire system to fail. A fundamental change occurred when the Bank was led by Nicholas Biddle: the second Bank of the United States began to behave like a central bank, which the first Bank did not attempt [12.1-2]. But the economy recovered between 1820 and 1835, and the national debt was paid off in 1836.

Walker [12.1-3] gives a summary of the banking system during this period, citing lax management, incompetence, and corruption:

> "Practical inconvertibility characterized the issues of the joint-stock banks of the United States down to 1834. Looseness of management, the want of legal regulation, the absence of any authoritative and effective business traditions and maxims, with, in not a few cases, purposed swindling of the most outrageous character, committed always with entire impunity, make the early history of paper-money banking in the United States exceedingly discreditable. The popular term, "Wildcat Banking," not inaptly described much, the greater part, indeed of the operations of American banking of a period reaching even down to 1837."

Walker then proceeds to give four general causes: haste to become rich, arrogance and ignorance of finances, rapidity of national growth, and an incorrect concept of money. Of this last one he writes:

> "4. ... a false view of money which regards coin as the proper subject of governmental regulation, but considers the manufacture of paper money, which will drive coin out of circulation and take its place, as a branch of ordinary business with which the state has no right to interfere." He quoted Alexander Hamilton from his Report on the Bank: "If the paper of a bank is to be permitted to insinuate itself into all the revenues and receipts of a country; if it is even to be tolerated as the substitute for gold and silver in all the transactions of business, it becomes, in either view, a national concern of the first magnitude."

The term "wildcat" refers to the situation wherein a State bank office was located in such a remote areas that only a wild cat could find it. The purpose was to deter people from redeeming the bank notes in coin.

But the banks in New England were the exception: their notes were always convertible because they were taxed by those States for failure to do so, and were required to keep a specie reserve in the Suffolk Bank in order ensure redemption could be made. There were three main causes for the relatively low incidence of real convertibility in the United States banking system [12.1-4]. First, was a popular notion that only an immoral individual would demand to be paid in specie. Second, the banks held a great deal of each other's notes, for which they did not demand payment, but simply re-circulated them. Since they never returned for payment, the banks assumed they could issue more than was wise. Third, the banks issued notes of very small face value; these were mostly used by people of little means, who likely did not have the opportunity to demand redemption. Also the widespread use of small notes tended to release to the banks the specie that should be kept as a reserve against them.

12.2 History, 1817-1836

7 Jan 1817: The second Bank of the United States began operations. At this time nearly all bank notes were depreciated, except for those issued by the banks in the New England States. The New England State banks had to pay a heavy fine for failing to pay, so they restrained their note issue. Depreciation of bank notes was 22% in Washington and Baltimore, 17% in Philadelphia, 7 to 10% in New York and Charleston, and was upwards of 22% in the interior States [12.2-1]. The State banks were earning large profits on their depreciated notes, and although bank stockholders received less in buying power than stable money, the profits made up for it. Also, debtors favored a continuation of State bank issues since they could repay their loans in depreciated money. A total of $7,000,000 in specie was imported as reserve against the notes of the Bank of the United States. The Bank of the United States was to have [12.2-2], by charter, $7,000,000 subscribed by the U. S. Government, $7,000,000 in specie, $14,000,000 in "stocks" (U. S. Government securities), and the remainder ($8,000,000) in "stock notes" (probably unfunded debt of the U. S).

1 Feb 1817: Since the Bank of the United States began taking bonds from importers for duties, and since only redeemable bank notes would be accepted for taxes on 20 Feb 1817 (cf. 30 Apr 1816), the Bank of the United States and State-chartered banks in New York, Philadelphia, and Richmond agreed to begin redeeming their notes in specie starting 20 Feb 1817. U. S. Government balances held in the State-chartered banks were to be transferred to the Bank of the United States and held until 1 Jul 1817, at which time they would be paid, with interest [12.2-3]. But there were many places in the West and South where the local circulation consisted only of inconvertible bank notes. Instead of discounting them, the Bank of the United States accepted them at par, holding them in anticipation that they would eventually be redeemed in specie by the State-chartered banks. Trade with other locations requiring a discount was made in the local notes; this caused an expansion of the local non-redeemable notes. But those banks had no intention of redeeming them in coin; so the Bank of the United States issued its notes (payable on demand) in exchange for those that were not redeemable throughout 1817 and 1818. The State banks got into debt to the Bank of the United States and caused considerable distress when it came time to redeem the notes. Meanwhile, the main office and northern branches of the Bank of the United States were being drained of specie because they were redeeming notes issued at branches in the South and West (those that were accepting State-chartered bank notes at par). This led to the problem of 20 Jul 1818. This policy was mostly due to the incompetence of William Jones, president of the Bank of the United States.

20 Feb 1817: The banks agreed to resume payment on demand in specie [12.2-4, 12.2-5].

3 Mar 1817: By this time, only $635,963 of the $36,133,794 of Treasury Notes remained; the rest had been liquidated by being accepted for taxes and duties, and by conversion into the funded debt. Congress repealed the measures for funding the Treasury Notes, and enacted that $10,000,000 from the proceeds of tonnage duties, internal taxes, and sales of land in the West was to be devoted to the "sinking fund", i.e., to pay down the national debt [12.2-6]. Revenues were large in 1817, and about $19,000,000 was used to reduce the debt.

3 Mar 1817: Congress passed a modification to the import duties [12.2-7], imposing an additional 20% *ad valorem* on items imported from places beyond the Cape of Good Hope, and an additional 10% on all others.

3 Mar 1817: Congress passed monetary legislation [12.2-8]: **a)** (S. 1) repealed the previous acts authorizing the President to obtain loans and issue stock on the credit of the U. S.; **b)** (S. 2) repealed the au-

thority of the Treasury Secretary to issue Treasury Notes; **c)** (S. 3) prohibited the Treasury Secretary from re-issuing Treasury Notes that had been received in taxes; and **d)** (S. 4) required the Treasury Secretary to destroy all redeemed Treasury Notes that come into possession of the United States.

3 Mar 1817: Congress passed legislation [12.2-9] addressing the payment of the public debt through the sinking fund: **a)** (S. 1) repealed the previous laws regarding payment of principal and interest on the debt; **b)** (S. 2) appropriated an annual sum of $10,000,000 to the sinking fund from revenues derived from import and tonnage duties, internal duties, and sales of western lands to be used toward paying the debt; **c)** (S. 3) appropriated an additional $9,000,000 to the sinking fund for 1817 for redemption of the debt; **d)** (S. 4) after 1817, any surplus in the Treasury was to be devoted to the sinking fund, except to maintain a balance in the Treasury of $2,000,000; **e)** (S. 5) any surpluses in the sinking fund are to be used to purchase outstanding debt as available; and **f)** (S. 6) certificates of debt that are paid to be cancelled and destroyed.

1 Apr 1817: The second capital installment for the Bank of the United States ($2,800,000) was mostly paid by notes and discounts of the Bank; only $32,400 was paid in specie [12.2-10] (which should have been 25%).

1 Aug 1817: The Bank of the United States discounted its own notes at par in order to make the third capital installment [12.2-11]; it also refused to accept the notes of State banks. The branches of the Bank of the United States refused each other notes. There was a general mutual demand for payment in specie (which the banks did not have) [12.2-12]. This caused many banks, especially in the South and West, to call in their loans, and many of those defaulted.

23 Dec 1817: Congress passed legislation on internal duties [12.2-13]: **a)** (S. 1) the internal duties on licenses to distillers, sugar, licenses to retailers, sales at auction, carriages, and stamped vellum, parchment, and paper were abolished (repealing most of the law passed 24 Jul 1813); **b)** (S. 2) the offices of collector and assessors to be gradually phased out after collection of taxes currently due; and **c)** (S. 3) pro-rata refunds for those who have paid duties in advance.

20 Apr 1818: Congress revised [12.2-14] the import duties on certain items: **a)** (S. 1) imposing *ad valorem* duties of 25% on items made of copper or silver plated; 30% on cut glass; tacks and brads, 5 cents per thousand; and **b)** (S. 2) an additional 10% *ad valorem* on items imported on foreign vessels;

20 Apr 1818: Congress enacted a duty [12.2-15] of $10 to $15 per ton on iron imports (pig, castings, nails, bars, and anchors) to permit the struggling domestic iron producers to stay in business. But the end of the war in Europe led to an expansion of the European iron industry, which undersold the Americans beginning in 1819. By 1824 the American producers demanded more protection [12.2-16].

20 Jul 1818: The second Bank of the United States had to restrict its business, since it had been drained of specie by its branches in the south and west [12.2-17].

~15 Feb 1819: A depression began that lasted until 1821 [12.2-18, 12.2-19]. It was caused by a series of problems: a) great expansion of State bank notes since 1816, and of the Bank of the United States since 1817; b) the expanded volume of bank notes used to buy up land in the West, and investments in agriculture in 1815 and 1816, owing to optimism about future agricultural prices, since there had been crop failures in Europe in 1814 to 1816; c) subsequent falling off of agricultural prices and land values because the European agriculture recovered 1817 ff; d) collapse of the cotton market in Jan 1819 and decline of land values; e) the Bank of the United States made a mistake in pretending that the State bank notes were at par and did not demand redemption, which induced the State banks to increase the amount of paper; f) the notes of State banks were only nominally convertible; and g) contraction of the notes of State banks and the Bank of the United States starting in Mar 1819 continuing to early 1821.

22 Feb 1819: The U. S. concluded a treaty with Spain [12.2-20], in which Spain ceded Florida to the U. S. and the U. S. agreed to pay certain claims made by Spain, up to $5,000,000.

3 Mar 1819: Congress extended the use of foreign coins (Great Britain, France, Portugal, and Spain) as legal tender until 1821 [12.2-21] owing to the fact that the banks had a large amount of them, and would incur losses of they did not maintain their legal tender status [12.2-22].

3 Mar 1819: Congress reduced the import duties on wine [12.2-23, 12.2-24] (later modified 24 May 1828)

6 Mar 1819: Curtailment of U. S. Bank activities was ordered for all of its branches [12.2-25]. The Bank of the United States had imported a great deal of specie ($7,000,000) since 1817 [12.2-26], but it was mostly gone; the Bank was nearly insolvent. It had failed thus far to provide a stable circulating medium.

9 Apr 1819: Langdon Cheves had replaced William Jones as the president of the Bank of the United States in March. He and the board of directors proposed the following measures to preserve the Bank [12.2-27]: a) continue curtailments; b) prohibit offices in south and west to issue notes when exchanges were made against them; c) collection of balances owed by State chartered banks; d) request that the government provide adequate time for the bank to transfer money between branches when needed; e) pay debentures in the same manner as the duties on them had been paid; and f) obtain a loan from Europe for $2,500,000 for three years. With these simple measures the Bank's financial difficulties were resolved by 17 May 1819. The second Bank of the U. S. succeeded in restoring specie payments, although it incurred large costs. State-chartered banks began to redeem their notes in specie (in order that their notes could be received in duties and taxes); this required the State banks to contract the volume of their notes throughout 1819. This was a case of a deflation of the money when it should have remained stable. Sumner states [12.2-28]:

"The bank [Bank of the United States] now took the most energetic measures to save itself; and in seventy days was once more solvent, but it had ruined the community. The golden age was now far in the past, and was seen to be only a gilt-paper age after all. The ruin was almost universal."

21 Apr 1819: Although a large amount of specie had been imported as reserve against the notes of the Bank of the United States, only $126,745.28 remained, and the bank owed $79,125.99 to city banks in Philadelphia [12.2-29].

29 Jan 1820: Condy Raguet, head of a committee appointed by the Senate of Pennsylvania to examine the effects of the contraction of currency in 1819, issued a report outlining the problems that had occurred, stating in part [12.2-30]:

"This distress exhibits itself under the varied forms of:
1. Ruinous sacrifices of landed property at sheriff's sales, whereby in many cases lands and houses have been sold at less than a half, a third, or a fourth of their former value, thereby depriving of their homes and of the fruits of laborious years, a vast number of our industrious farmers, some of whom have been driven to seek in the uncultivated forests of the west, that shelter of which they have been deprived in their native state.
2. Forced sales of merchandise, household goods, farming stock and utensils, at prices far below the cost of production, by which numerous families have been deprived of the common necessaries of life, and of the implements of their trade.
3. Numerous bankruptcies and pecuniary embarrassments of every description, as well among the agricultural and manufacturing, as the mercantile classes.
4. A general scarcity of money throughout the country, which renders it almost impossible for the husbandman or other owner of real estate to borrow even at usurious interest, and where landed security of the most indubitable character is offered as a pledge. A similar difficulty of procuring on loan had existed in the metropolis previous to October last, but has since then been partially removed.
5. A general suspension of labor, the only legitimate source of wealth, in our cities and towns, by which thousands of our most useful citizens are rendered destitute of the means of support, and are reduced to the extremity of poverty and despair.

6. An almost entire cessation of the usual circulation of commodities, and a consequent stagnation of business, which is limited to the mere purchase and sale of the necessaries of life, and of such articles of consumption as are absolutely required by the season.

7. A universal suspension of all large manufacturing operations, by which in addition to the dismissal of the numerous productive laborers heretofore engaged therein, who could find no other employment, the public loses the revenue of the capital invested in machinery and buildings.

8. Usurious extortions, whereby corporations instituted for banking, insurance and other purposes, in violation of the law, possess themselves of the products of industry without granting an equivalent.

9. The overflowing of our prisons with insolvent debtors, most of whom are confined for trifling sums, whereby the community loses a portion of its effective labor, and is compelled to support families by charity, who have thus been deprived of their protectors.

10. Numerous lawsuits upon the dockets of our courts and of our justices of the peace, which lead to extravagant costs and the loss of a great portion of valuable time.

11. Vexatious losses arising from the depreciation and fluctuations in the value of bank notes, the impositions of brokers and the frauds of counterfeiters.

12. A general inability in the community to meet with punctuality, the payment of their debts even for family expenses, which is experienced as well by those who are wealthy in property, as by those who have hitherto relied upon their current receipts to discharge their current engagements.

Having thus enumerated the most prominent features of the general distress, your committee will proceed to point out the cause which in their opinion has occasioned it. That cause is to be found chiefly in the abuses of the banking system, which abuses consist, first, in the extensive number of banks, and secondly, in their universal bad administration. For the first of these abuses the people have to reproach themselves, for having urged the legislature to depart from that truly republican doctrine, which influenced the deliberations of our early assemblies, and which taught that the incorporation of the monied interest already sufficiently powerful of itself, was but the creation of odious aristocracies, hostile to the spirit of free government, and subversive of the rights and liberties of the people. The second abuse, the mismanagement of banks, is to be ascribed to a general ignorance of the true theory of currency and banking, and to the avarice of speculators, desirous of acquiring the property of others, by an artificial rise in the nominal value of stock, and by the sharing of usurious dividends."

Raguet went on to offer basic rules and trends of money and banking:

a. "Without liability to prompt payment [redemption in specie], uninfluenced by any considerations of fear, forbearance, or delicacy, on the part of the public, the community has no guarantee against a depreciated and fluctuating currency"

b. "The depreciation of money enhancing the prices of every species of property and commodity, appeared like a real rise in value, and led to all the consequences which are ever attendant upon a gradual advance of prices. The false delusions of artificial wealth increased the demand of the farmer of foreign productions, and led him to consume in anticipation of his crops. The country trader seduced by a demand for more than his ordinary supply of merchandise, was tempted to the extension of his credit, and filled his store at the most extravagant prices with goods vastly beyond what the actual resources of his customers could pay for, whilst the importing merchant having no guide to ascertain the real wants of the community but the eagerness of retailers to purchase his commodities, sent orders abroad for a supply of manufactures wholly disproportioned to the effective demand of the country. Individuals of every profession were tempted to embark in speculation, and the whole community was literally plunged into debt."

c. "The plenty of money, as it was called, was so profuse, that the managers of the banks were fearful they could not find a demand for all they could fabricate, and it was no infrequent occurrence to hear solicitations used to individuals to become borrowers, under promises as to indulgence, the most tempting."

d. "Real property has been raised in nominal value, and thousands of individuals have been led into speculations, who without the facility of bank loans would never have been thus seduced. The gradual nominal rise in the price of land, has produced an artificial appearance of increasing wealth which has led to the indulging of extravagance and luxury, and to the neglect of productive industry. Foreign importation and domestic consumption have been carried on to an extent, far beyond what the actual resources of the country and people would justify, and in pursuing a shadow the community has lost sight of the substance."

15 May 1820: Congress authorized [12.2-31] the President to borrow $3,000,000 on the credit of the U. S., and issue debt certificates at interest not exceeding 6%, redeemable at discretion of the Treasury Secretary.

2 Mar 1821: Congress passed a law [12.2-32] to provide debt relief to people who had purchased public lands, and were unable to pay per the original contract. Among its provisions: **a)** (S. 1, 7, 9) purchasers may relinquish any part of the land previously contracted for if application is made prior to 30 Sep 1821, and said parcel shall be considered as forfeited back to the U. S.; **b)** (S. 2) interest paid for any public land is remitted back to the purchaser; **c)** (S. 3) current debtors divided into three classes, and payment schedule arranged as follows: 1) class 1, who have paid 25% due, shall pay the rest in eight equal annual installments beginning 31 Mar 1822; 2) class 2, who have paid 50%, shall pay the rest in six equal annual installments beginning 31 Dec 1821; 3) class 3, who have paid 75% shall pay the rest in four equal annual installments beginning 30 Sep 1821; **d)** (S. 4) any land paid in full before 30 Sep 1822 to be entitled to a 37.5% discount on the amount remaining as of 2 Mar 1821; and **e)** (S. 6) lands not paid in full within three months of the last scheduled installment shall be forfeited back to the U. S.

3 Mar 1821: Congress authorized [12.2-33] the President to borrow $5,000,000 on the credit of the U. S., and issue debt certificates at interest not exceeding 5%, redeemable at any time after 1835, and permitting the Bank of the United States to extend the loan.

3 Mar 1821: Congress extended the use of foreign coins (Great Britain, France, Portugal, and Spain) as legal tender until 29 Apr 1823 [12.2-34, 12.2-35].

~15 Jun 1821: Approximate end of the depression (cf. 15 Feb 1819) [12.2-36].

3 May 1822: Congress passed legislation [12.2-37] taking the Treasury Notes out of circulation, and permitting them to be accepted for payments or redeemed only at the U. S. Treasury.

3 Mar 1823: Congress extended the use of foreign coins (Great Britain, France, Portugal, and Spain) as legal tender until 4 Mar 1827 [12.2-38, 12.2-39].

22 Jan 1824: Congress authorized Secretary Crawford to use the surplus balance at the Treasury to pay off most of the 7% bonds that had been issued during the War of 1812 [12.2-40]. Nearly all of the $8,606,490 of 7% bonds outstanding were paid off in 1824.

22 May 1824: Congress passed a new tariff law [12.2-41] amounting to a complete revision of the import duty system. Provisions included: **a)** (S. 1) *ad valorem* duties between 25% and 35% on sail-duck, burlap, woolen goods, cotton and cotton goods, 50% on hats, 25% on metalware (anything made with brass, iron, steel, tin, pewter, lead), 15% on bolting cloths, 30% on hair cloth, 30% on marble items and 12.5% on lace; **b)** (S. 1) per-unit duties on a wide variety of items, including lead, carpets, hemp, cables, iron, nails, wire, blacksmith tools, rifles, muskets, candles, soap, all types of crops and other foods, boots, spices; **c)** (S. 1) on glass depending on pane size; 30 cents per pound on books; and on paper; **d)** (S. 2) an additional 10% was due if imported on foreign vessels; and **e)** (S. 3, 4) drawbacks permitted if re-exported in a certain time. Duties on linen, silk, spices, and cutlery were designed as a revenue source, and the ones on iron, wool, glass, lead, and hemp were designed to protect American producers [12.2-42].

24 May 1824: Congress authorized a loan [12.2-43] and creation of debt certificates of $5,000,000 to pay off claims per the Florida treaty. It was borrowed from the Bank of the United States at 4.5% without discount [12.2-44].

~1 Jun 1824ff: The State banks expanded the issue of their bank notes [12.2-45].

3 Mar 1825: Congress authorized [12.2-46] the President to borrow and create loan certificates: **a)** (S. 1) up to $12,000,000 at a maximum interest rate of 4.5%, half of which to be redeemable at any time, and half redeemable after 31 Dec 1829, to be used to pay off and discharge part of the outstanding debt from 1813 (which was at 6%); **b)** (S. 2) permitted the Treasury Secretary to borrow from the

Bank of the United States, and the certificates to be sold only at par; and **c)** (S. 6) debt incurred to be repaid by the sinking fund.

~15 Jul 1825: A recession began in the U. S. [12.2-47] caused by: a) large expansion of bank notes in 1824 with the usual expansion of non-productive enterprises, especially speculation in cotton; and b) a decline in prices in the U. S. as a result of price collapses in England during May. Many banks failed in the U. S., fifty of them in New York alone between Jul and Dec 1825.

~1 Dec 1826: Approximate end of the recession (cf. 15 Jul 1825) [12.2-48].

19 May 1828: Congress revised the tariffs on imports [12.2-49]: **a)** (S. 1) increased the duties on iron, cutlery, steel, and lead; **b)** (S. 2) *ad valorem* duties: 50% on raw wool, 40% on woolen goods; **c)**, S. 2) 40 to 70 cents per square yard on carpets and cotton cloth; **d)** (S. 3) per-ton duties on hemp ($5), on flax ($60); and **e)** (S. 4 to 7) other duties on sail duck, molasses, silk, indigo, window glass, roofing slates, and cotton cloth. This law imposed duties of up to 62% on the vast majority of imported products, to the highest level to that time [12.2-50]. There was concern that the duties would force prices upwards, but instead the high values caused losses as the people found alternatives. It was greatly opposed in the Southern States because it applied to many goods the South did not produce, and the higher duties paid by the British reduced the amount the British could pay for exports from the Southern States.

8 Dec 1829: President Jackson delivered his first annual address, commenting on the Bank of the United States [12.2-51]:

> "The charter of the Bank of the United States expires in 1836, and its stockholders will most probably apply for a renewal of their privileges. In order to avoid the evils resulting from precipitancy in a measure involving such important principles and such deep pecuniary interests, I feel that I cannot, in justice to the parties interested, too soon present it to the deliberate consideration of the Legislature and the people. Both the constitutionality and expediency of the law creating this bank are well questioned by a large portion of our fellow-citizens, and it must be admitted by all that it has failed in the great end of establishing a uniform and sound currency.
>
> Under these circumstances, if such an institution is deemed essential to the fiscal operations of the Government, I submit to the wisdom of the Legislature whether a national one, founded upon the credit of the Government and its revenues, might not be devised which would avoid all constitutional difficulties and at the same time secure all the advantages to the Government and country that were expected to result from the present bank."

24 Apr 1830: Congress passed a modification [12.2-52] to the law regarding the payment of the public debt: **a)** (S. 1) the commissioners of the sinking fund were authorized to appropriate more than the usual $10,000,000 annually to paying off the debt; **b)** (S. 2) any surplus in the sinking fund above what is due and payable in that year may be used to pay down additional public debt; and **c)** (S. 3) sections 4 and 5 of the 3 Mar 1817 law were repealed.

20 May 1830: Congress reduced [12.2-53] the import duties on tea, coffee, and cocoa.

29 May 1830: Congress reduced the duty on molasses (to 5 cents per gallon) and drawbacks certain spirits (4 cents per gallon) [12.2-54] and on salt (from 15 cents per bushel to 10 cents) [12.2-55].

31 May 1830: Congress abolished [12.2-56] all tonnage duties on U. S. vessels, and on foreign vessels, if the foreign nation has reciprocal provisions.

6 Dec 1830: President Jackson again commented on the Bank of the United States in his second annual address [12.2-57]:

> "The importance of the principles involved in the inquiry whether it will be proper to re-charter the Bank of the United States requires that I should again call the attention of Congress to the subject. Nothing has occurred to lessen in any degree the dangers which many of our citizens apprehend from that institution as at present organized. In the spirit of improvement and compromise which distinguishes our country and its institutions it becomes us to inquire whether it be not possible to secure the advantages afforded by the pre-

sent bank through the agency of a Bank of the United States so modified in its principles and structure as to obviate constitutional and other objections.

It is thought practicable to organize such a bank with the necessary offices as a branch of the Treasury Department, based on the public and individual deposits, without power to make loans or purchase property, which shall remit the funds of the Government, and the expense of which may be paid, if thought advisable, by allowing its officers to sell bills of exchange to private individuals at a moderate premium. Not being a corporate body, having no stockholders, debtors, or property, and but few officers, it would not be obnoxious to the constitutional objections which are urged against the present bank; and having no means to operate on the hopes, fears, or interests of large masses of the community, it would be shorn of the influence which makes that bank formidable. The States would be strengthened by having in their hands the means of furnishing the local paper currency through their own banks, while the Bank of the United States, though issuing no paper, would check the issues of the State banks by taking their notes in deposit and for exchange only so long as they continue to be redeemed with specie. In times of public emergency the capacities of such an institution might be enlarged by legislative provisions.

These suggestions are made not so much as a recommendation as with a view of calling the attention of Congress to the possible modifications of a system which cannot continue to exist in its present form without occasional collisions with the local authorities and perpetual apprehensions and discontent on the part of the States and the people."

6 Dec 1831: President Jackson again commented on the Bank of the United States in his third annual address [12.2-58]:

"Entertaining the opinions heretofore expressed in relation to the Bank of the United States as at present organized, I felt it my duty in my former messages to frankly disclose them, in order that the attention of the Legislature and the people should be seasonably directed to that important subject, and that it might be considered and finally disposed of in a manner best calculated to promote the ends of the Constitution and subserve the public interests. Having thus conscientiously discharged a constitutional duty, I deem it proper on this occasion, without a more particular reference to the views on the subject then expressed, to leave it for the present to the investigations of an enlightened people and their representatives."

4 Jul 1832: Congress passed a bill to renew the charter of the Bank of the United States.

10 Jul 1832: President Jackson vetoed the bill to renew the charter of the Bank [12.2-59]. His reasons were: a) the Bank had an unfair monopoly as fiscal agent of the U. S. Government; b) the privileges granted by the existing charter caused the value of its stock to rise above par, at the expense of the public; c) renewing the charter would continue the benefits enjoyed by the wealthy shareholders; d) the new act continues advantages of payment in specie enjoyed by State banks but denied to private persons; e) dividends paid to foreign shareholders deprives Americans of specie that could be better used in America; f) there is a national security risk if a majority of the stock were to be held by foreigners; g) the Supreme Court has not agreed that all the provisions in the charter are consistent with the Constitution; h) Congress does not have a constitutional power to grant a monopoly to a bank; i) Congress seeks to make the Bank an agent of the Executive branch, but the Executive does not want it, on the grounds that it is neither necessary or proper; and j) would prohibit the States from taxing the Bank of the United States in the same manner as their State-chartered banks. Near the end, he stated:

"Nor is our Government to be maintained or our Union preserved by invasions of the rights and powers of the several States. In thus attempting to make our General Government strong we make it weak. Its true strength consists in leaving individuals and States as much as possible to themselves -- in making itself felt, not in its power, but in its beneficence; not in its control, but in its protection; not in binding the States more closely to one another, but leaving each to move unobstructed in its proper orbit.

Experience should teach us wisdom. Most of the difficulties our Government now encounters and most of the dangers which impend over our Union have sprung from an abandonment of the legitimate objects of Government by our national legislation, and the adoption of such principles as are embodied in this act. Many of our rich men have not been content with equal protection and equal benefits, but have besought us to make them richer by act of Congress. By attempting to gratify their desires we have in the results of our legislation arrays section against section, interest against interest, and man against man, in a fearful commotion which threatens to shake the foundations of the Union."

14 Jul 1832: Congress revised the tariff laws [12.2-60]: **a)** (S. 1) the 19 May 1828 law was repealed; **b)** (S. 2) duties on raw wool eliminated, *ad valorem* on woolen goods reduced; **c)** (S. 2) duties on cotton good unchanged; **d)** (S. 2) reduction of duties on iron, steel, cutlery, metal ware, blacksmith tools, firearms, hemp, sail duck, silk, tea, salt, roofing slate, glass; and **e)** added *ad valorem* duties on a wide variety of other items. The reductions of import duties were designed such that they were sufficient to pay the cost of operating the Government (since the national debt would soon be paid off), but not as protections for domestic manufacturers [12.2-61]. Duties on tea and coffee were eliminated when imported on American owned ships, and *ad valorem* duties were reduced from 30 to 25% on most items.

4 Dec 1832: President Jackson again commented on the Bank of the United States in his fourth annual address [12.2-62]:

"It is my duty to acquaint you with an arrangement made by the Bank of the United States with a portion of the holders of the 3 per cent stock, by which the Government will be deprived of the use of the public funds longer than anticipated. By this arrangement, which will be particularly explained by the Secretary of the Treasury, a surrender of the certificates of this stock may be postponed until October, 1833, and thus the liability of the Government, after its ability to discharge the debt, may be continued by the failure of the bank to perform its duties.

Such measures as are within the reach of the Secretary of the Treasury have been taken to enable him to judge whether the public deposits in that institution may be regarded as entirely safe; but as his limited power may prove inadequate to this object, I recommend the subject to the attention of Congress, under the firm belief that it is worthy of their serious investigation. An inquiry into the transactions of the institution, embracing the branches as well as the principal bank, seems called for by the credit which is given throughout the country to many serious charges impeaching its character, and which if true may justly excite the apprehension that it is no longer a safe depository of the money of the people."

2 Mar 1833: Congress revised the tariff law of 1828 [12.2-63, 12.2-64, 12.2-65]. Provisions included **a)** (S. 1) *ad valorem* import duties that were in excess of 20% were to be cut as follows: 1) after 1833, a reduction of 10% of the excess over 20%; 2) in 1836, 1838, and 1840, by an additional 10% of the excess over 20%; 3) in 1842, a reduction of half the remaining excess over 20%; and 4) in 1843, the final reduction to 20% maximum; **b)** (S. 2) increased the *ad valorem* duty on certain wool cloth to 50%; **c)** (S. 3) after 30 Jun 1842, all import duties to be paid in cash; **d)** (S. 4) silk, linens, and shawls to be duty-free starting 1 Jan 1834; and **e)** (S. 5) a large list of items to be duty-free beginning 1 Jan 1843, including indigo, mercury, sulfur, tin, borax, saltpeter, rubber, nuts, and dyes. By 1843, most of the import duties would approximately match the levels that prevailed in 1816 (averaging 14.5 to 16%). It also repealed some of the duties on wool cloth; and after 1842, import duties were to be paid in cash, assessed at point of entry.

18 Sep 1833: President Jackson read a notice to his Cabinet on his rationale for ordering the removal of U. S. Government deposits from the Bank of the United States, effective 1 Oct 1833 [12.2-66]. His reasons are summarized as follows. First, that the Bank had increased its loans from Jan 1831 to May 1832 from $42.402 million to $70.428 million, in order to "bring as large a portion of the people as possible under its power and influence", and granting large loans with suspicious terms (little security and long repayment times) to editors of major newspapers, for the purpose of encouraging them to advocate for Jackson's defeat in the 1832 presidential election. Secondly, it did so to obtain a favorable public opinion when it asked for renewal of the charter in 1832, and spread many notices (at a cost of $80,000) warning of the calamity that would result if the charter were not renewed. Third, the expansion of loans ($28,000,000) was made against Government deposits, when the Bank knew that the Government intended to use those to pay off the national debt. These overextended the Bank to the point that it had to secretly obtain a loan from Holland. Fourth, when the bank obtained the loan, it negotiated an agreement with foreign holders of the debt to delay demand for repayment for one

year; this allowed the Bank to use $5 million of the public's money. Fifth, the Bank did not permit Congress or the Secretary of the Treasury to conduct an audit to determine if public deposits were safe in the Bank. Sixth, the Bank violated its charter because a minority of officers who did not report to the Board of Directors had been allowed to transact business on behalf of the Bank. Seventh, that the president of the Bank (Nicholas Biddle) had too much arbitrary power to manage the Bank outside the knowledge and control of the Board of Directors. Eighth, that:

> "...publications have been prepared and extensively circulated containing the grossest invectives against the officers of the Government, and the money which belongs to the stockholders and to the public has been freely applied in efforts to degrade in public estimation those who were supposed to be instrumental in resisting the wishes of this grasping and dangerous institution. ... It is the desire of the President that the control of the banks and the currency shall, as far as possible, be entirely separated from the political power of the country as well as wrested from an institution which has already attempted to subject the Government to its will. In his opinion the action of the General Government on this subject ought not to extend beyond the grant in the Constitution, which only authorizes Congress to 'coin money and regulate the value thereof'; all else belongs to the States and the people, and must be regulated by public opinion and the interests of trade."

1 Oct 1833: Acting Treasury Secretary Taney removed all the U. S. government deposits from the second Bank of the United States, per President Jackson's order [12.2-67]. This caused considerable anxiety among the banking institutions, and they began to call in their loans, reduce discounting of commercial paper, reduce circulation, which led to a decline in commerce and confidence, with the resulting increase in unemployment [12.2-68]. The State chartered banks increased in number and began to issue notes, which were not always redeemable on demand, and there resulted, as before in 1814, a general depreciation of the money and an increase in prices. The U. S. Government changed its methods of handling public finances [12.2-69]. Instead of relying on banks, all the public funds would be retained within the Treasury in Washington, with sub-treasuries at Philadelphia, New Orleans, New, York, Boston, Charleston, and St. Louis. This method was without the concurrence of Congress, and was continued until legislation was passed on 23 Jun 1836.

3 Dec 1833: Acting Treasury Secretary Taney testified before Congress on his reasons for removing the U. S. government's deposits from the second Bank of the United States. He testified that [12.2-70, 12.2-71, 12.2-72]: a) there was no reason to continue doing business with the Bank of the United States since it seemed unlikely that its charter would be renewed; b) the credit of the Bank was based on the fact that all its notes were receivable for debts due to the Government, which supported the value of the notes, but they would be discounted when the charter expired; c) he was confident the State banks would provide a suitable currency to replace the Bank's notes; and d) recent actions of the Bank indicated that it was involved in politics in violation of the charter.

28 Mar 1834: Congress passed two resolutions: a) censuring President Jackson for his actions regarding the removal of U. S. Government deposits; and b) declaring that the reasons given by Treasury Secretary Taney were an insufficient cause [12.2-73]. John Quincy Adams believed the first resolution was unjustified.

4 Apr 1834: The House of Representatives passed four resolutions [12.2-74]: a) the second Bank of the United States should not be re-chartered; b) U. S. Government deposits having been removed, should not be re-deposited with the second Bank of the United States; c) State banks should continue as depositories of U. S. Government funds; and d) appointed a select banking investigation committee with power to visit banks or any of their branches.

25 Jun 1834: Congress passed legislation [12.2-75] regarding the legal tender status of foreign silver coins: a) dollars of Mexico, Peru, Chile, and Central America to pass at 100 cents by tale if weighing at least 415 grains; b) those of Brazil of weighing 415 grains at fineness at least ten ozt. fifteen pennyweights of silver in twelve ozt. of standard silver (i.e., 0.8958 pure at 415 grains = 371.77 grains, whereas the dollar is 371.25 grains pure silver); c) five franc pieces of France at the value of 93 cents if fineness is at least 10 oz., 16 pennyweights in twelve oz. of silver and weighing at least 384 grains

(i.e., 0.9 pure at 384 grains = 345.6 grains, which corresponds to 93 cents since the dollar is defined as 371.25 grains pure silver).

28 Jun 1834: Congress passed two Coinage Acts. In the first one [12.2-76], section 1 devalued the Eagle coin ($10) from 247.5 to 232 grains of pure gold or from 270 grains to 258 grains of standard gold [12.2-77]. The "standard gold" was redefined from "11 pure to 1 alloy" (22 carat) to 21.58 pure to 2.42 alloy (19.781 carat). The Eagle thus was devalued from $10 to $9.373. The mint ratio of gold to silver was thus 371.35/23.2 = 16.002. This devaluation was made binding as legal tender at $10 on all existing contracts (i.e., the Eagle was devalued from $10 to $9.373 even though the legal tender rate remained at $10). Section 2 specified that all coins minted prior to 1 Jul 1834 to be received at 94.8 per pennyweight. The second act [12.2-78] permitted the use of foreign gold coins as legal tender based on weight [12.2-79]: a) coins of Brazil, Britain, and Portugal with greater than 22 carats at 94.8 cents per pennyweight (24 grains); b) coins of France of 90% fine at 93.1 cents per pennyweight (24 grains); c) those of Mexico, Spain, and Columbia of 20 carats and 3.4375 grains receivable at 89.9 cents per pennyweight (24 grains).

Oct 1834: Treasury Secretary Woodbury made an announcement regarding payment of the national debt [12.2-80]. In his 2 Dec 1834 Annual Report, he stated [12.2-81]:

"In October last [1834], the undersigned gave notice that the whole of this debt, unredeemed after the first of January next [1835], would cease to bear interest, and would be promptly paid after that date, on application to the Commissioners of Loans in the several States."

2 Dec 1834: Treasury Secretary Woodbury, in his annual report commented on the state of the nation's finances [12.2-82]:

"In pursuing this honorable course, the Government of the Union has not only shown good faith abroad to its foreign friends and allies, those who lent assistance when most needed, but it has redeemed, whether at home, or abroad, the entire debt of both the revolution, and the late war, paid the purchase money for Florida and Louisiana; and, with a most scrupulous sense of moral as well as political obligation, administered in various ways to the wants, and atoned for many of the losses, of those who periled life and fortune in the struggle for independence — in which our public debt had its sacred origin. It is an additional source of gratification, that this has been effected without imposing heavy burdens on the people, or leaving their treasury empty, trade languishing, and industry paralyzed; but, on the contrary, with almost every great interest of society flourishing, with taxes reduced, a surplus, of money on hand, valuable stocks and extensive lands still owned by the Government, and with such various other financial resources at command as to give to our country, in this respect, a very enviable superiority. When it is considered that this has been effected by a young and, at first, not very numerous people, within about half a century, and who, during the same period, have provided such other and ample means to sustain their useful systems of government, and to build up great and prosperous communities, we may well be proud of the illustration our country affords of the financial ability of free institutions, and of the high destinies in various respects, not appropriately noticeable on this occasion, but which may await our preservation of these institutions in their original vigor, purity, and republican simplicity."

7 Dec 1835: President Jackson, in his annual address to Congress, announced that the public debt had been fully paid [12.2-83]:

"The condition of our public finances was never more flattering that at the present period. Since my last annual communication all the remains of the public debt have been redeemed, or money has been placed in deposits for this purpose whenever the creditors choose to receive it. All the other pecuniary engagements of the Government have been honorably and promptly fulfilled, and there will be a balance in the Treasury at the close of the present year of about $19,000,000."

18 Feb 1836: The second Bank of the United States obtained a charter from Pennsylvania (13 days before its federal charter expired), retaining its name as the "Bank of the United States". It continued in operation until it failed in 1840 [12.2-84].

15 Jun 1836: Congress repealed [12.2-85] section 14 of the 10 Apr 1816 law that incorporated the subscribers to the Bank of the United States. Section 14 was the provision that made the notes of the Bank acceptable in payments to the U. S.; thus the Bank's notes now could not be used for paying taxes or duties.

23 Jun 1836: Congress passed two laws addressing the banking and finance system [12.2-86, 12.2-87]. The first was "An act to regulate the deposits of public money" (a.k.a. the Deposit and Distribution Act). Among its provisions [12.2-88]: **a)** (S. 1) the Treasury Secretary was responsible for choosing which State-chartered banks were to be depositories of U. S. Government funds; **b)** (S. 3) those chosen were required to provide to the Treasury Secretary a statement of condition as the Secretary deemed appropriate; **c)** (S. 4) selected banks receiving public money to provide condition statements to the Treasury Secretary at intervals not exceeding one week, and to provide all the normal banking services for the U. S. government; **d)** (S. 5) banks so selected for U. S. government deposits must pay their notes in specie on demand; **e)** (S. 5) selected banks are prohibited from issuing notes in denominations less than $5; **f)** (S. 5) other banks that do issue notes in denominations less than $5 shall not be received in taxes due to the U. S.; **g)** (S. 6) Treasury Secretary at discretion may require securities or collateral from the selected banks as insurance against public deposits; **h)** (S. 11) selected banks to pay 2% interest to the U. S. if the public deposits exceed 25% of paid-in capital; **i)** (S. 13) allocated all revenue in the Treasury on 1 Jan 1837, except $5,000,000, to be deposited with the States, to be distributed by population, and to be retained by the States for safekeeping until recalled by the U. S. Treasury for federal payments; and **j)** (S. 14) deposits were to be transferred in 25% increments at 3 month intervals, starting Jan 1837. The second law [12.2-89] directed the Treasury Secretary to handle the transfer of assets and government-owned stock in the second Bank of the United States as the agent for the U. S. government.

Section 13 of the Deposit and Distribution Act was inserted in expectation of large surpluses, and the national debt about to be paid off [12.2-90]. The balance to be distributed on 1 Jan 1837 was $37,468,819.97, and was to be paid in four quarterly installments in 1837. But the nation got into financial trouble in the summer of 1837: excessive imports, unstable State banks that expanded notes without being able to redeem them (which resulted in a loss of the Government's deposits, since they were held in State banks), and a cash-flow problem to importers who could not pay the import duties. Congress was forced to intercede in Oct 1837.

4 Jul 1836: Congress passed a clarification to the Deposit and Distribution Act (cf. 23 Jun 1836) [12.2-91] such that the Treasury Secretary could, at his discretion, move deposits around among the various selected banks so as not to have too great an accumulation in any one place and a general equality of distribution of the public money.

11 Jul 1836: The proliferation of bank notes issued by the State banks led to a large degree of speculation in the sale of Government lands, so much so, that in order to restrain the trend, the "Specie Circular" was issued by the Jackson administration requiring that all purchases of public lands were to be made in gold and silver, with one exception for residents of Virginia. The net result was a decline in the prices of land; banks called in their loans because of fears that this was another "currency experiment" by the administration [12.2-92]. Contrary to predictions made by the administration, gold and silver coin became scarcer than ever.

12.3 Data, 1817-1836

Figures 12.3-1 and 12.3-2 show the revenue and expenditures of the U. S. government from 1817 to 1836.

U. S. Goverment Revenue, 1817 - 1836 (USD)										
			Internal Revenue		Miscellaneous					
Day	Year	Customs	Income and Profits taxes	Misc.	Sales of Public Lands	Direct Tax	Other Misc.	Postal	Public Debt Sales	Total
31 Dec	1817	26,283,348	0	2,678,100	1,991,226	1,834,187	580,006	1,002,973	466,723	34,836,565
31 Dec	1818	17,176,385	0	955,270	2,606,564	264,333	583,030	1,130,202	8,353	22,724,139
31 Dec	1819	20,283,608	0	229,593	3,274,422	83,650	732,098	1,204,737	2,291	25,810,402
31 Dec	1820	15,005,612	0	106,260	1,635,871	31,586	1,061,338	1,111,760	3,040,824	21,993,254
31 Dec	1821	13,004,447	0	69,027	1,212,966	29,349	257,589	1,058,302	5,000,324	20,632,005
31 Dec	1822	17,589,761	0	67,665	1,803,581	20,961	750,457	1,117,555	0	21,349,983
31 Dec	1823	19,088,433	0	34,242	916,523	10,337	491,129	1,130,214	0	21,670,880
31 Dec	1824	17,878,325	0	34,663	984,418	6,201	477,603	1,197,298	5,000,000	25,578,511
31 Dec	1825	20,098,713	0	25,771	1,216,090	2,330	497,951	1,306,253	5,000,000	28,147,111
31 Dec	1826	23,341,331	0	21,589	1,393,785	6,638	497,088	1,447,660	0	26,708,094
31 Dec	1827	19,712,283	0	19,885	1,495,845	2,626	1,735,722	1,524,601	0	24,490,965
31 Dec	1828	23,205,523	0	17,451	1,018,308	2,218	520,126	1,660,276	0	26,423,905
31 Dec	1829	22,681,965	0	14,502	1,517,175	11,335	602,648	1,778,471	0	26,606,099
31 Dec	1830	21,922,391	0	12,160	2,329,356	16,980	563,227	1,919,313	0	26,763,430
31 Dec	1831	24,224,441	0	6,933	3,210,815	10,506	1,074,124	2,105,721	0	30,632,542
31 Dec	1832	28,465,237	0	11,630	2,623,381	6,791	760,410	2,258,570	0	34,126,020
31 Dec	1833	29,032,508	0	2,759	3,967,682	394	945,081	2,617,011	0	36,565,438
31 Dec	1834	16,214,957	0	4,196	4,857,600	19	715,161	2,823,749	0	24,615,682
31 Dec	1835	19,391,310	0	10,459	14,757,600	4,263	1,266,452	2,993,556	0	38,423,643
31 Dec	1836	23,409,940	0	370	24,877,179	728	2,538,576	3,408,323	0	54,235,119

The data for the revenue for 1817 to 1836 is from W. G. McAdoo, "Annual Report of the Secretary of the Treasury on the State of the Finances for the Fiscal Year Ended June 30, 1914", Washington: U. S. Government Printing Office, 1915, pp. 230-241; Treasury Document 2721. This data was modified from 1817 to 1836 per Henry Morgenthau, "Annual Report of the Secretary of the Treasury on the State of the Finances for the Fiscal Year Ended June 30, 1940", Treasury Document 3111, pp. 642-649, which shows "internal revenue" broken out as income taxes and miscellaneous. It is the same data as reported previously (cf. 1914), but shows income taxes and miscellaneous taxes as separate categories.

Figure 12.3-1: U. S. Government Revenue, 1817-1836

U. S. Government Expenditures, 1817 - 1836 (USD)									
		Ordinary Disbursements							
Day	Year	Civil & Misc.	War Dep't	Navy Dep't	Indians	Pensions	Interest on Public Debt	Postal	Public Debt Retired	Total
31 Dec	1817	3,518,936	8,004,236	3,314,598	319,463	297,374	4,536,282	917,128	20,886,753	41,794,774
31 Dec	1818	3,835,839	5,622,715	2,953,695	505,704	890,719	6,209,954	1,031,799	15,086,247	36,136,674
31 Dec	1819	3,067,211	6,506,300	3,847,640	463,181	2,415,939	5,211,730	1,114,032	2,492,195	25,118,232
31 Dec	1820	2,592,021	30,392	4,387,990	315,750	3,208,376	5,151,004	1,163,191	3,477,489	20,326,213
31 Dec	1821	2,223,121	4,461,291	3,319,243	477,005	242,817	5,126,073	1,177,526	3,241,019	20,268,098
31 Dec	1822	1,967,996	3,111,981	2,224,458	575,007	1,948,199	5,172,788	1,167,358	2,676,160	18,843,951
31 Dec	1823	2,022,093	3,096,924	2,503,765	380,781	1,780,588	4,922,475	1,158,777	607,541	16,472,948
31 Dec	1824	7,155,308	3,340,939	2,904,581	429,987	1,499,326	4,943,557	1,190,478	11,624,835	33,089,016
31 Dec	1825	2,748,544	3,659,914	3,049,083	724,106	1,308,810	4,366,757	1,238,912	7,728,587	24,824,717
31 Dec	1826	2,600,177	3,943,194	4,218,902	743,447	1,556,593	3,975,542	1,395,798	7,065,539	25,499,197
31 Dec	1827	2,713,476	3,948,977	4,263,877	750,624	976,138	3,486,071	1,481,619	6,517,596	24,138,383
31 Dec	1828	3,676,052	4,145,544	3,918,786	705,084	850,573	3,098,800	1,679,316	9,064,637	27,138,795
31 Dec	1829	3,082,234	4,724,291	3,308,745	576,344	949,594	2,542,843	1,872,704	9,860,304	26,917,063
31 Dec	1830	3,237,416	4,767,128	3,239,428	622,262	1,363,297	1,912,574	1,950,116	9,443,173	26,535,397
31 Dec	1831	3,064,646	4,841,835	3,856,183	930,738	1,170,665	1,373,748	2,006,742	14,800,629	32,045,188
31 Dec	1832	4,577,141	5,446,034	3,956,370	1,352,419	1,184,422	772,561	2,266,171	17,067,747	36,622,869
31 Dec	1833	5,716,245	6,704,019	3,901,356	1,802,980	4,589,152	303,796	2,930,414	1,239,746	27,187,713
31 Dec	1834	4,404,728	5,696,189	3,956,260	1,003,953	3,364,285	202,152	2,910,605	5,974,412	27,512,587
31 Dec	1835	4,229,698	5,759,156	3,864,939	1,706,444	1,954,711	57,863	2,757,350	328	20,330,491
31 Dec	1836	5,393,279	11,747,345	5,807,718	5,037,022	2,882,797	0	2,841,766	0	33,709,930

The data for the expenditures for 1817 to 1836 is from W. G. McAdoo, "Annual Report of the Secretary of the Treasury on the State of the Finances for the Fiscal Year Ended June 30, 1914", Washington: U. S. Government Printing Office, 1915, pp. 230-241; Treasury Document 2721.

Figure 12.3-2: U. S. Government Expenditures, 1817-1836

Figure 12.3-3 shows the national debt and per-capita national debt for 1817 to 1836. Notice that the debt at the end of 1836 is above zero; the debt was paid off early in the year, but Congress found it necessary to resume deficit spending during the summer. Refer to the Introduction to Part 2 for a sense of wages vs. the per-capita national debt.

U. S. National Debt, 1817-1836 (USD)										
Day	Year	Principal ($) [1]	Population [2]	Debt per Capita ($) [2]	Day	Year	Principal ($) [1]	Population [2]	Debt per Capita ($) [2]	
31 Dec	1817	103,466,633	8,918,881	11.60	31 Dec	1827	67,475,043	11,897,750	5.67	
31 Dec	1818	95,529,648	9,158,739	10.43	31 Dec	1828	58,421,413	12,220,507	4.78	
31 Dec	1819	91,015,566	9,398,596	9.68	31 Dec	1829	48,565,406	12,543,263	3.87	
31 Dec	1820	89,967,427	9,638,453	9.33	31 Dec	1830	39,123,191	12,866,020	3.04	
31 Dec	1821	93,546,676	9,961,210	9.39	31 Dec	1831	24,322,235	13,286,363	1.83	
31 Dec	1822	90,875,877	10,283,966	8.84	31 Dec	1832	7,011,699	13,706,707	0.51	
31 Dec	1823	90,269,777	10,606,723	8.51	31 Dec	1833	4,760,082	14,127,050	0.34	
31 Dec	1824	83,788,432	10,929,480	7.67	31 Dec	1834	37,733	14,547,393	0.00	
31 Dec	1825	81,034,059	11,252,237	7.20	31 Dec	1835	37,513	14,967,737	0.00	
31 Dec	1826	73,967,357	11,574,993	6.39	31 Dec	1836	336,957	15,388,080	0.02	

1. Public debt data from 1837 to 1863 is from the Annual Report of the Secretary of the Treasury, 1980, pp. 61, 62.
2. Population values are based on the dicennial census from the Census Bureau, and linearly interpolated. Per-capita is based on these values.

Figure 12.3-3: National Debt and Per-Capita Share Thereof, 1817-1836

Figures 12.3-4 and 12.3-5 show the combined assets and liabilities of the Bank of the United States and the State banks for 1817 to 1833. Notice there is very little data for the State banks during this interval; not until 1834 did the State banks issue reasonably reliable condition statements.

Assets of the Bank of the United States and State Banks, 1817-1833 (USD)												
	Second Bank of the United States [1]									State Banks [2]		
Year	Loans & Discounts [4]	"Stocks" (i.e, US Securities)	Real Estate	Banking Houses	Due by European Bankers	Due from State banks	Notes of State Banks	Specie	Total Assets	Loans & Discounts [3]	Specie [5]	Total Assets
1817	32,485,195	4,829,234	0	0	0	8,848,315	587,201	1,724,109	48,474,054			
1818	41,181,750	9,475,932	0	175,201	1,033,682	1,203,894	1,837,254	2,515,949	57,423,662			
1819	35,786,263	7,391,823	0	433,808	621,667	2,624,797	1,877,909	2,666,696	51,402,963			
1820	31,401,158	7,192,980	0	1,296,626	261,548	2,727,080	1,443,166	3,392,735	47,715,293	191,329,000	19,820,240	211,149,240
1821	30,905,199	9,155,855	0	1,886,724	83,548	1,178,197	677,022	7,643,140	51,529,685			
1822	28,061,169	13,318,951	563,480	1,855,946	1,107,637	1,717,723	917,629	4,761,299	52,303,834			
1823	30,736,432	11,018,552	626,674	1,956,764	24,599	1,407,573	766,248	4,424,874	50,961,716			
1824	33,432,084	10,874,014	1,302,551	1,871,635	1,434,020	1,287,808	705,173	5,813,694	56,720,979			
1825	31,812,617	18,422,027	1,495,150	1,832,935	24,178	2,130,095	1,056,224	6,746,952	63,520,178			
1826	33,424,621	18,303,501	1,848,354	1,792,870	421,524	747,375	1,114,831	3,960,158	61,613,234			
1827	30,937,866	17,764,359	2,039,226	1,678,192	460,686	1,683,510	1,068,483	6,457,161	62,089,483			
1828	33,682,905	17,624,859	2,295,401	1,634,260	356,740	0	1,447,386	6,170,045	63,211,596			
1829	39,219,602	16,099,099	2,345,539	1,557,356	482,240	1,723,297	1,293,578	6,098,138	68,818,849			
1830	40,663,805	11,610,290	2,886,397	1,444,801	1,530,553	1,199,458	1,465,047	7,608,076	68,408,427	200,451,214	22,114,917	222,566,131
1831	44,032,057	8,674,681	2,629,125	1,344,761	2,383,331	0	1,494,506	10,808,047	71,366,508			
1832	66,293,707	2,200	2,136,525	1,159,637	91,668	3,944,849	2,171,676	7,638,023	83,438,285			
1833	61,695,913	0	1,855,169	1,181,071	3,106,833	3,688,143	2,292,655	8,951,847	82,771,631			

1. Annual Report of the Comptroller of the Currency, 1876, p. LXXXIII. (cf. Annual Report of the Secretary of the Treasury, 1876, p. 193)
2. Annual Report of the Secretary of the Treasury, 1876, p. 158.
3. State bank loans & discounts were not reported for 1820 in the 1876 report. It is estimated here based on the average ratio of loan to total liabilities for 1830 and 1834-1840.
4. The 1876 Comptroller of the Currency Report shows Loans for 1817 as $3,485,195; clearly a misprint. The Annual Report of the Secretary of the Treasury, 1918, Vol 2, p. 834 shows loans in 1817 as 32.2 million. I have assumed the correct number is as shown.
5. Specie was not reported for 1820 in the 1876 report. It is estimated here based on the average ratio of specie to total liabilities for 1830 and 1834-1840.

Figure 12.3-4: Combined Assets of the Bank of the United States and State Banks, 1817-1833

	Second Bank of the United States [1]								State Banks [2]				
Year	Notes in Circulation	Deposits	Due to State Banks	Due to Other Banks	Other Liabilities	Capital	Total Liabilities	Error (%)	Notes in Circulation	Deposits	Capital	Total Liabilities	Error (%)
1817	1,911,200	11,233,021	0	0	0	35,000,000	48,144,221	0.68					
1818	8,339,448	12,270,207	0	1,357,778	0	35,000,000	56,967,433	0.79					
1819	6,563,750	5,792,869	0	1,434,022	0	35,000,000	48,790,641	5.08					
1820	3,580,481	6,568,794	0	2,053,650	0	35,000,000	47,202,925	1.07	44,863,344	35,950,470	137,110,611	217,924,425	-3.21
1821	4,567,053	7,894,985	0	2,053,074	0	35,000,000	49,515,112	3.91					
1822	5,578,782	8,075,152	0	2,040,000	0	35,000,000	50,693,934	3.08					
1823	4,361,658	7,622,340	0	1,292,710	0	35,000,000	48,276,708	5.27					
1824	4,647,077	13,701,936	0	1,020,000	0	35,000,000	54,369,013	4.15					
1825	6,068,394	12,033,364	0	2,407,282	0	35,000,000	55,509,040	12.61					
1826	9,474,987	11,214,640	0	251,494	0	35,000,000	55,941,121	9.21					
1827	8,549,409	14,320,186	0	280,056	0	35,000,000	58,149,651	6.35					
1828	9,855,677	14,497,330	1,697,401	1,467,806	0	35,000,000	62,518,214	1.10					
1829	11,901,656	17,061,918	0	1,447,748	0	35,000,000	65,411,322	4.95					
1830	12,924,145	16,045,782	0	0	0	35,000,000	63,969,927	6.49	61,323,898	55,559,928	145,192,268	262,076,094	-17.75
1831	16,251,267	17,297,041	734,900	0	0	35,000,000	69,283,208	2.92					
1832	21,355,724	22,761,434	1,951,103	0	0	35,000,000	81,068,261	2.84					
1833	17,518,217	20,347,749	2,091,891	0	0	35,000,000	74,957,857	9.44					

Liabilities of the Bank of the United States and State Banks, 1817-1833 (USD)

1. Annual Report of the Comptroller of the Currency, 1876, p. LXXXIII. (cf. Annual Report of the Secretary of the Treasury, 1876, p. 193)
2. Annual Report of the Secretary of the Treasury, 1876, p. 158.

Figure 12.3-5: Combined Liabilities of the Bank of the United States and State Banks, 1817-1833

Figures 12.3-6 and 12.3-7 show the assets and liabilities of the Bank of the United States alone for 1834 to 1836.

Year	Loans & Discounts	"Stocks" (i.e, US Securities)	Real Estate	Banking Houses	Due by European Bankers	Due from State banks	Notes of State Banks	Specie	Total Assets
1834	54,911,461	0	1,741,407	1,189,125	1,801,669	3,058,870	1,982,640	10,039,237	74,724,409
1835	51,808,739	0	1,760,632	1,218,806	1,922,498	4,609,973	1,506,200	15,708,369	78,535,217
1836	59,232,445	0	1,486,561	967,404	73,171	4,088,005	1,736,491	8,417,988	76,002,065

Assets of the Bank of the United States, 1834-1836 (USD) [1]

1. Annual Report of the Comptroller of the Currency, 1876, p. LXXXIII. (cf. 1876 Treasury Report, p. 193)

Figure 12.3-6: Assets of the Bank of the United States, 1834-1836

Year	Notes in Circulation	Deposits	Due to State Banks	Due to Other Banks	Other Liabilities	Capital	Total Liabilities	Error (%)
1834	19,208,379	10,838,555	1,522,124	0	0	35,000,000	66,569,058	10.91
1835	17,339,797	11,756,905	3,119,172	0	0	35,000,000	67,215,874	14.41
1836	23,675,422	5,061,456	2,660,694	0	0	35,000,000	66,397,572	12.64

Liabilities of the Bank of the United States, 1834-1836 (USD) [1]

1. Annual Report of the Comptroller of the Currency, 1876, p. LXXXIII. (cf. 1876 Treasury Report, p. 193)

Figure 12.3-7: Liabilities of the Bank of the United States, 1834-1836

Figure 12.3-8 and 12.3-9 show the assets and liabilities of the State-chartered banks alone for the interval 1833 to 1836.

			"Stocks"							
	No. of	Loans and	(i.e., U. S.	Due from		Notes of	Specie		Other	
Year	Banks	Discounts	Securities)	Other Banks	Real Estate	Other Banks	Funds	Specie	Assets	Total Assets
1834	506	324,119,499	6,113,195	27,329,645	10,850,090	22,154,919	26,641,753	0	1,723,547	418,932,648
1835	704	365,163,834	9,210,579	40,084,038	11,140,167	21,086,301	3,061,819	43,937,625	4,642,124	498,326,487
1836	713	457,506,080	11,709,319	51,876,955	14,194,375	32,115,138	4,800,076	40,019,594	9,975,226	622,196,763

Assets of State Banks, 1834 - 1836 (USD) [1]

1. Annual Report of the Comptroller of the Currency, 1876, p. XCIV. (cf. 1876 Treasury Report, p. 159)

Figure 12.3-8: Assets of the State Banks, 1834-1836

	Notes in		Due to Other		Other		
Year	Circulation	Deposits	Banks	Capital	Liabilities	Total Liabilities	Error (%)
1834	94,839,570	75,666,986	26,602,293	200,005,944	0	397,114,793	5.21
1835	103,692,495	83,081,365	38,972,578	231,250,337	19,320,475	476,317,250	4.42
1836	140,301,038	115,104,440	50,402,369	251,875,292	25,999,234	583,682,373	6.19

Liabilities of State Banks, 1834 - 1836 (USD) [1]

1. Annual Report of the Comptroller of the Currency, 1876, p. XCIV. (cf. 1876 Treasury Report, p. 159)

Figure 12.3-9: Liabilities of the State Banks, 1834-1836

Figures 12.3-10 and 12.3-11 show the combined assets and liabilities of the Bank of the United States and the State chartered banks for the interval 1834 to 1836.

			"Stocks"							
	No. of	Loans and	(i.e., U. S.	Due from		Notes of	Specie		Other	
Year	Banks	Discounts	Securities)	Other Banks	Real Estate	Other Banks	Funds	Specie	Assets	Total Assets
1834	507	379,030,960	6,113,195	32,190,184	12,591,497	24,137,559	26,641,753	10,039,237	2,912,672	493,657,057
1835	705	416,972,573	9,210,579	46,616,509	12,900,799	22,592,501	3,061,819	59,645,994	5,860,930	576,861,704
1836	714	516,738,525	11,709,319	56,038,131	15,680,936	33,851,629	4,800,076	48,437,582	10,942,630	698,198,828

Combined Assets of the Bank of the United States and State Banks, 1834 - 1836 (USD) [1, 2]

1. State banks: Annual Report of the Comptroller of the Currency, 1876, p. XCIV. (cf. 1876 Treasury Report, p. 159)
2. Second Bank of U. S.: Annual Report of the Comptroller of the Currency, 1876, p. LXXXIII. (cf. 1876 Treasury Report, p. 193)

**Figure 12.3-10: Combined Assets of the Bank of the
United States and State Banks, 1834-1836**

	Notes in		Due to Other		Other		
Year	Circulation	Deposits	Banks	Capital	Liabilities	Total Liabilities	Error (%)
1834	114,047,949	86,505,541	28,124,417	235,005,944	0	463,683,851	6.07
1835	121,032,292	94,838,270	42,091,750	266,250,337	19,320,475	543,533,124	5.78
1836	163,976,460	120,165,896	53,063,063	286,875,292	25,999,234	650,079,945	6.89

Combined Liabilities of the Bank of the United States and State Banks, 1834 - 1836 (USD) [1, 2]

1. Annual Report of the Comptroller of the Currency, 1876, p. XCIV. (cf. 1876 Treasury Report, p. 159)
2. 2nd Bank of US: Annual Report of the Comptroller of the Currency, 1876, p. LXXXIII. (cf. 1876 Treasury Report, p. 193)

**Figure 12.3-11: Combined Liabilities of the Bank of the
United States and State Banks, 1834-1836**

Figure 12.3-12 shows the estimated money supply for 1817 to 1836; notice the sharp declines in 1818, 1819, 1825, and 1826; these are the deflationary periods caused by the over-expansion of the money supply in the few years preceding each. Note also the large expansion of the money supply starting in 1834, when the State-chartered banks once again began over-issuing notes, which, as will be shown in chapter 13, led to another recession. The column labeled "Total specie in the U. S." includes foreign coin that circulated as legal tender.

Estimated U. S. Money Supply, 1817-1836 [1] (millions USD)																
1	2	3	4	5	6	7	8	9	10	11	12	13	14	15	16	17
Year (~30 Jun)	Number of Banks [2]	Estimated State Bank Notes [1, 3]	Notes of Bank of U. S. [4]	Total Notes in Circulation	Total Specie in US [1, 5]	Specie in Treasury [1, 6]	Specie Outside Treasury	Total Notes & Specie Outside Treasury	Cash Held in All Banks [5, 10]	Notes & Specie Outside Banks	Estimated State Bank Deposits [8]	Deposits of Bank of U. S. [4]	Total Estimated Deposits	Estimated Interbank Trans- actions [9]	Estimated Deposits Adjusted	Estimated Total Money Supply
1817		65.041	1.911	66.952	19.000	2.300	16.700	83.652	25.932	57.720	91.773	11.233	103.006	10.095	92.911	150.631
1818	27	54.352	8.339	62.692	20.250	2.200	18.050	80.742	25.030	55.712	58.921	12.270	71.191	6.977	64.215	119.926
1819		35.700	6.564	42.264	21.500	2.100	19.400	61.664	19.116	42.548	11.100	5.793	16.893	1.656	15.237	57.785
1820	307	40.600	3.580	44.180	24.300	2.000	22.300	66.480	20.609	45.872	31.200	6.569	37.769	3.701	34.067	79.939
1821	28	44.951	4.567	49.518	25.180	2.370	22.810	72.328	22.422	49.906	81.348	7.895	89.243	8.746	80.498	130.404
1822	33	44.899	5.579	50.477	26.260	2.740	23.520	73.997	22.939	51.058	46.379	8.075	54.454	5.336	49.117	100.176
1823	34	42.979	4.362	47.340	26.940	3.110	23.830	71.170	22.063	49.107	42.883	7.622	50.506	4.950	45.556	94.664
1824	37	50.486	4.647	55.133	27.820	3.480	24.340	79.473	24.637	54.836	68.827	13.702	82.529	8.088	74.441	129.278
1825	41	51.311	6.068	57.379	28.700	3.850	24.850	82.229	25.491	56.738	34.054	12.033	46.087	4.517	41.571	98.309
1826	55	54.342	9.475	63.817	29.580	4.220	25.360	89.177	27.645	61.532	31.493	11.215	42.707	4.185	38.522	100.055
1827	60	56.012	8.549	64.561	30.460	4.590	25.870	90.431	28.034	62.398	33.948	14.320	48.268	4.730	43.538	105.935
1828	108	52.506	9.856	62.361	31.340	4.960	26.380	88.741	27.510	61.232	22.177	14.497	36.674	3.594	33.080	94.311
1829	329	48.200	11.902	60.102	32.220	5.330	26.890	86.992	26.967	60.024	40.700	17.062	57.762	5.661	52.101	112.125
1830	329	61.000	12.924	73.924	33.100	5.756	27.344	101.268	31.393	69.875	39.500	16.046	55.546	5.443	50.102	119.978
1831	91	77.000	16.251	93.251	32.100	6.015	26.085	119.337	36.994	82.342	41.581	17.297	58.878	5.770	53.108	135.450
1832	172	91.500	21.356	112.856	30.400	4.503	25.897	138.753	43.013	95.739	27.762	22.761	50.523	4.951	45.572	141.311
1833	175	91.500	17.518	109.018	30.650	2.012	28.638	137.656	42.673	94.983	35.103	20.348	55.451	5.434	50.017	145.000
1834	506	94.840	19.208	114.048	41.000	11.703	29.297	143.345	44.437	98.908	102.269	10.839	113.108	11.085	102.023	200.931
1835	704	103.692	17.340	121.032	51.000	8.893	42.107	163.139	50.573	112.566	122.054	11.757	133.811	13.113	120.697	233.264
1836	713	140.301	23.675	163.976	65.000	5.000	60.000	223.976	69.433	154.544	165.507	5.061	170.568	16.716	153.853	308.397

1. Values in **bold** are from original sources; all others interpolated or estimated as described.
2. Number of banks from 1817 to 1836 from AR_Comptroller of Currency, 1918, 2 Dec 1918, Vol 2, pp. 835, 836, Table 86, 87.
3. State bank note data from 1817 to 1833 per Introduction to Part 2; for 1834-1836 per Annual Report of the Comptroller of the Currency, 1896, Vol. 1, p. 544
4. Data on notes of the second Bank of the U. S. from the Annual Report of the Secretary of the Treasury, 1876, p. 193.
5. Specie in US 1819 from Annual Report of the Secretary of the Treasury, 1876, p. 153; other years in **bold** from Annual Report of the Comptroller of the Currency, 1896, Vol. 1, p. 544, Table 35.
6. Specie in Treasury from Annual Report of the Comptroller of the Currency, 1896, Vol. 1, p. 544, Table 35.
7. Cash held in banks for 1812 to 1816 estimated based on the average ratio of cash to outstanding currency from 1834 to 1914 (0.31)
8. State bank deposits in 1819, 1820, 1829, 1830 from Annual Report of the Secretary of the Treasury, 1876, pp. 158, 159. Values for 1834 to 1836 from Annual Report of the Comptroller of the Currency, 1931, p. 1018, Table 94. Others are interpolated per Introduction to Part 2.
9. Interbank from 1812 to 1816 based on average of interbank to total deposits from 1914 to 1940 (0.098).
10. Cash in all banks for 1834 to 1836 from the Annual Report of the Comptroller of the Currency, 1931, Table 96, pp. 1023-1025.

Figure 12.3-12: Estimated Money Supply, 1817-1836

Figures 12.3-13 and 12.3-14 show the coinage issued by the U. S. Mint from 1817 to 1836. There was still a fair amount of foreign coins being used in the U. S. as legal tender throughout this period (included in the money supply per Figure 12.3-12).

	Gold Coinage of the U. S. , 1817-1836 ($)						
Year	$20 Double Eagles ($)	$10 Eagles ($)	$5 Half Eagles ($)	Three Dollar ($)	$2.50 Quarter Eagles ($)	Gold Dollars ($)	Total ($)
1817							0.00
1818			242,940.00				242,940.00
1819			258,615.00				258,615.00
1820			1,319,030.00				1,319,030.00
1821			173,205.00		16,120.00		189,325.00
1822			88,980.00				88,980.00
1823			72,425.00				72,425.00
1824			86,700.00		6,500.00		93,200.00
1825			145,300.00		11,085.00		156,385.00
1826			90,345.00		1,900.00		92,245.00
1827			124,565.00		7,000.00		131,565.00
1828			140,145.00				140,145.00
1829			287,210.00		8,507.50		295,717.50
1830			631,755.00		11,350.00		643,105.00
1831			702,970.00		11,300.00		714,270.00
1832			787,435.00		11,000.00		798,435.00
1833			968,150.00		10,400.00		978,550.00
1834			3,660,845.00		293,425.00		3,954,270.00
1835			1,857,670.00		328,505.00		2,186,175.00
1836			2,765,735.00		1,369,965.00		4,135,700.00
Totals	0.00	0.00	14,404,020.00	0.00	2,087,057.50	0.00	16,491,077.50

Source: Annual Report of the Director of the Mint, 1895, 28 Nov 1895, Treasury Document No. 1829, pp. 286-293 (Table XLIV).

Figure 12.3-13: Gold Coins Minted by the U. S., 1817-1836

	Silver and Copper Coinage of the U. S., 1817-1836 ($)									
	Silver ($)								Minor ($)	
Year	Trade Dollars	Dollars	Half Dollars	Quarters	Twenty-cents	Dimes	Half-dimes	Three-cents	Cents & Half-Cents	Total ($)
1817			607,783.50						39,484.00	647,267.50
1818			980,161.00	90,293.50					31,670.00	1,102,124.50
1819			1,104,000.00	36,000.00					26,710.00	1,166,710.00
1820			375,561.00	31,861.00		94,258.70			44,075.50	545,756.20
1821			652,898.50	54,212.75		118,651.20			3,800.00	829,562.45
1822			779,786.50	16,020.00		10,000.00			20,723.00	826,529.50
1823			847,100.00	4,450.00		44,000.00				895,550.00
1824			1,752,477.00						12,620.00	1,765,097.00
1825			1,471,583.00	42,000.00		51,000.00			14,926.00	1,579,509.00
1826			2,002,090.00						16,344.25	2,018,434.25
1827			2,746,700.00	1,000.00		121,500.00			23,577.32	2,892,777.32
1828			1,537,600.00	25,500.00		12,500.00			25,636.24	1,601,236.24
1829			1,856,078.00			77,000.00	61,500.00		16,580.00	2,011,158.00
1830			2,382,400.00			51,000.00	62,000.00		17,115.00	2,512,515.00
1831			2,936,830.00	99,500.00		77,135.00	62,135.00		33,603.60	3,209,203.60
1832			2,398,500.00	80,000.00		52,250.00	48,250.00		23,620.00	2,602,620.00
1833			2,603,000.00	39,000.00		48,500.00	68,500.00		28,160.00	2,787,160.00
1834			3,206,002.00	71,500.00		63,500.00	74,000.00		19,151.00	3,434,153.00
1835			2,676,003.00	488,000.00		141,000.00	138,000.00		39,489.00	3,482,492.00
1836		1,000.00	3,273,100.00	118,000.00		119,000.00	95,000.00		23,100.00	3,629,200.00
Totals	0.00	1,000.00	36,189,653.50	1,197,337.25	0.00	1,081,294.90	609,385.00	0.00	460,384.91	39,539,055.56

Source: Annual Report of the Director of the Mint, 1895, 28 Nov 1895, Treasury Document No. 1829, pp. 286-293 (Table XLIV).

Figure 12.3-14: Silver and Minor (Copper) Coins Minted by the U. S., 1817-1836

Figure 12.3-15 shows the estimated CPI and per-capita money supply for this period.

Year	CPI [1] (1913 = 100)	Total Money Supply [5] (USD)	Population [6]	Per Capita Money Supply (USD)	Annual Rate of Change in CPI (%)	Annual Rate of Change in Per-Capita Money Supply (%)
1817	122.642	150,631,399	8,918,881	16.89	0.042	21.037
1818	119.909	119,926,465	9,158,739	13.09	-2.253	-25.449
1819	106.605	57,785,355	9,398,596	6.15	-11.760	-75.600
1820	92.671	79,938,984	9,638,453	8.29	-14.007	29.933
1821	89.436	130,404,015	9,961,210	13.09	-3.554	45.644
1822	91.768	100,175,544	10,283,966	9.74	2.575	-29.560
1823	89.683	94,663,680	10,606,723	8.92	-2.299	-8.750
1824	87.181	129,277,810	10,929,480	11.83	-2.829	28.166
1825	88.583	98,308,865	11,252,237	8.74	1.595	-30.295
1826	85.931	100,054,501	11,574,993	8.64	-3.039	-1.068
1827	87.983	105,935,269	11,897,750	8.90	2.359	2.961
1828	83.976	94,311,493	12,220,507	7.72	-4.661	-14.299
1829	83.424	112,125,493	12,543,263	8.94	-0.659	14.695
1830	81.191	119,977,519	12,866,020	9.33	-2.713	4.228
1831	85.830	135,450,300	13,286,363	10.19	5.556	8.915
1832	86.731	141,311,135	13,706,707	10.31	1.045	1.121
1833	86.130	144,999,568	14,127,050	10.26	-0.696	-0.444
1834	81.291	200,931,095	14,547,393	13.81	-5.782	29.691
1835	90.588	233,263,646	14,967,737	15.58	10.829	12.072
1836	100.364	308,396,505	15,388,080	20.04	10.248	25.152

1. CPI is the average of L-1 and L-15 data, both re-aligned to 1913 as a reference.
2. L-1 data 1791 to 1938 (Snyder-Tucker) is a general price index (wholesale prices, wages, cost of living and rents).
3. L-15 data 1801 to 1945 includes wholesale prices, all commodities.
4. L1 and L-15 from Historical Statistics of the United States, 1789-1945, A Supplement to the Statistical Abstract of the United States, Bureau of the Census, US Department of Commerce, Washington, DC, 1949.
5. See notes in money supply data for sources.
6. Population is linearly interpolated from Census results.

Figure 12.3-15: Money Supply and CPI, 1817-1836

Figure 12.3-16 shows a summary of the money supply and CPI. Here it is evident that the CPI lags the trend in money supply by about a year (but keep in mind that the source data is only annual). There are three clear trends: 1817 to 1819, 1819 to 1833, and 1833 to 1836. The average annual changes in CPI and money supply for 1817 to 1819 are -7.0% and -50.7% respectively; for 1819 to 1833, -1.52% and +3.66%; and for 1833 to 1836, +7.0% and +12.4%.

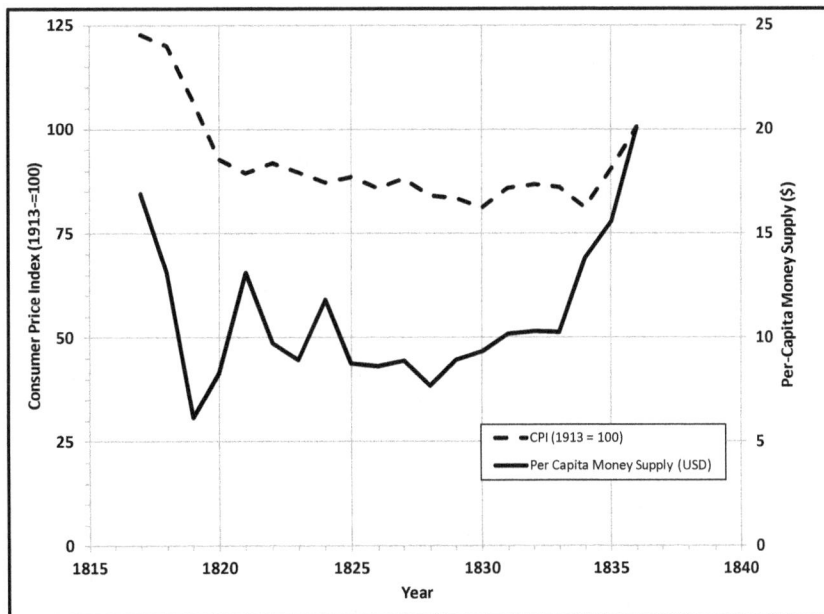

Figure 12.3-16: CPI and Per-Capita Summary, 1817-1836

Figure 12.3-17 shows the approximate median income index, consumer price index, and standard of living index for this period. See the Introduction to Part 2 for cautions regarding these curves.

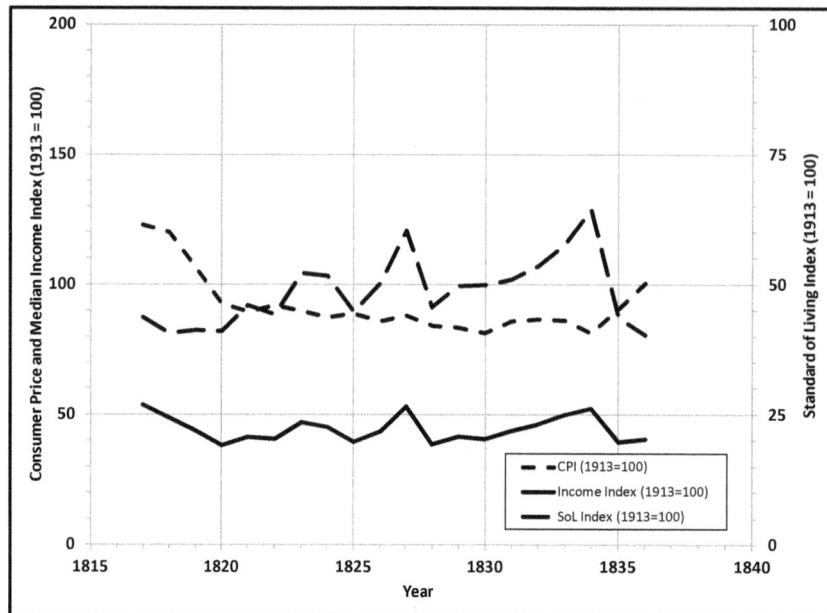

Figure 12.3-17: Median Income, Consumer Price, and Standard of Living Indices, 1817-1836

12.4 Summary, 1817-1836

The second Bank of the United States was successful in five ways, after the early problem caused by the incompetence of William Jones: a) a uniform currency that was widely trusted and accepted everywhere; b) the notes of the Bank were payable in specie on demand; c) even in places where silver was the common medium, the notes of the Bank were not discounted more than 0.25%; d) had handled the U. S. government deposits; and e) was honest and efficient except when it tried to get involved in politics and used U. S. government deposits for its own benefit [12.4-1]. But it could not control the issue of notes by the State banks directly, and once its restraint was gone, the State banks issued profusely. Jackson's claim that the bank did not provide a uniform currency, or that it did not preserve specie on demand is false; notice that his solution, to abolish the Bank, made whatever deficiencies the Bank had much worse. Jackson knew, or should have known, that there was no way that the State banks could be forced to redeem their notes in specie. Most of the people on Jackson's immediate staff (Treasury Secretary Ingham, Treasury Secretary McLane, Treasury Secretary Duane and other members of the Cabinet) were smart enough to realize that removing the deposits to State banks would not work. That said, Jackson was correct in recognizing that the Bank of the United States under Nicholas Biddle had become too powerful, and was attempting to behave like a traditional central bank. He was also correct in stating that the banking industry should be separate from politics.

Hammond [12.4-2] cites two ways in which central banks exert control. First, was the positive function of returning the State banks notes and demanding payment in specie; which served to restrain the volume thereof. The second category, sometimes beneficial and sometimes not, was what he called "discretionary": a) regulating the supply of money based on the balance of trade (since imports greater than exports caused specie to be exported); b) expanding the money supply to compensate for temporary conditions such as crop failures or sudden large payments by the Government; and c) balancing the needs for money at different times in different parts of the country. These functions were probably beneficial at this point in history, only because there was very little U. S. Government debt. Historically the worst activities of a central bank are: a) a monopoly on the issue of paper money; and b) to guarantee a market for excessive Government debt [12.4-3]. Neither of these conditions prevailed during this period.

Jackson contradicted himself about the role of the Bank; on 6 Dec 1830 he desired a bank under the Treasury to handle the fiscal needs of the Government; in his 10 Jul 1832 veto message he criticized the Bank as having a monopoly as the fiscal agent of the Government.

I am inclined to believe Bolles' criticism of Jackson [12.4-4]:

> "He [Jackson] declared that it [Bank of the United States] was corrupt and dangerous. His opposition, in truth, was grounded in no such lofty sentiments. He was opposed to it because he could not control its offices, and convert the institution into a piece of party machinery. ... The secretary [Treasury Secretary Duane] tried to convince the President of the impolicy and injustice of removing the deposits, but in vain. Jackson possessed an indomitable will, which towered vey high above his knowledge, especially of many public questions. He was now straining every fiber to destroy the prosperity of the country, and knew it not, or else he did not care. If so, his sin was still less pardonable. He knew perfectly well that Congress was opposed to the removal of the deposits, and so were the people, and that grave consequences were feared if the event occurred."

The Figures show the increase in the money supply, which caused the depreciation of the currency and the increase in prices. The public began to demand specie payment which the State banks could not do, since they had over-issued their notes. They suspended payment in May 1837 as will be shown in chapter 13.

Former Treasury Secretary Gallatin emphasized the importance of a uniform currency redeemable on demand, and noted that the Bank of United States nearly accomplished that purpose. The main defect is that the notes issued by each branch were not uniformly redeemable [12.4-5]:

> "It has already been observed, that the substitution of paper to gold and silver is a national benefit, in as far as it brings into activity an additional circulating capital, equal to the difference between the amount of paper, and that of the reserve in specie necessary to sustain the par value of that paper. But it is clear that the community derives no other immediate benefit from the substitution, than the accommodation which the banks are thereby enabled to afford, and for which the borrowers pay the usual rate of interest."

> "In order to attain perfect uniformity, the value of a paper currency should, in the United States, be always the same as that of the gold and silver coins, of which it takes the place. It is impossible to fulfill that condition better, than by making that currency payable on demand in specie and at par. This cannot be done but at certain places designated for that purpose. ... When, therefore, it is objected as a want of uniformity, that the notes issued by the Bank of the United States, and its several offices, are not indiscriminately made payable at every one of those places, the objection does not go far enough. In order to attain perfect uniformity, or to render those notes everywhere precisely equal in value to specie, they should be made payable at every town or village in the United States. But, although it may be admitted, that the notes of the Bank of the United States now consist nominally of twenty-four currencies, each payable at a distinct place, they still fulfill the condition of uniformity required by the Constitution; and the defect complained of is not peculiar to them, but would equally attach to any other possible species of bank notes or paper currency."

References

[12.1-1]   Lot M. Morrill, *Annual Report of the Secretary of the Treasury on the State of the Finances for Year 1876*, Appendix containing the Report of the Comptroller of Currency (John Jay Knox), Washington, DC: Government Printing Office, 1876, pp. 125, 126

[12.1-2]   Clifton H. Kreps, Jr., *Money, Banking and Monetary Policy*, NY: The Ronald Press Co., 1962, p. 158

[12.1-3]   Francis A. Walker, *Money*, NY: Henry Holt and Company, 1891, pp. 496-499

[12.1-4]   op. cit., Walker, pp. 480 - 482

[12.2-1]   Albert S. Bolles, *A Financial History of the United States*, NY: Augustus M. Kelley (1969), Vol. 2, pp. 318, 319 (originally published 1884 by D. Appleton & Co., NY)

[12.2-2]   William Graham Sumner, *A History of American Currency*, NY: Henry Holt & Co., 1874, p. 73. (Reprinted 1968 by NY: Augustus M. Kelley)

[12.2-3]   op. cit., Bolles, Vol. 2, pp. 321-325

[12.2-4]   Condy Raguet, *Treatise on Currency and Banking*, Philadelphia, PA: Grigg & Elliot, 1840, p. 156

[12.2-5]   op. cit., Sumner, *History of American Currency*, 1874, p. 74 (Reprinted by Forgotten Books, FB&c Ltd., London)

[12.2-6]   op. cit., Bolles, Vol. 2, pp. 305, 306

[12.2-7]   Text of "An Act supplementary to 'An Act to regulate the duties in imports and tonnage'"; 14th Congress, Session 2, Chapter 51, 3 Mar 1817

[12.2-8]   Text of "An Act to repeal so much of the acts now in force as authorize a loan of money, or an issue of Treasury notes", 14th Congress, Session 2, Chapter 85, 3 Mar 1817

[12.2-9]   Text of "An act to provide for the redemption of the public debt", 14th Congress, Session 2, Chapter 87, 3 Mar 1817

[12.2-10] op. cit., Sumner, p. 73

[12.2-11] op. cit., Sumner, p. 73

[12.2-12] op. cit., Sumner, pp. 76, 77

[12.2-13] Text of "An act to abolish the internal duties", 15th Congress, Session 1, Chapter 1, 23 Dec 1817

[12.2-14] Text of "An Act to increase the duties on certain manufactured articles imported into the United States", 15th Congress, Session 1, Chapter 98, 20 Apr 1818

[12.2-15] Text of "An Act to increase the duties on iron in bars and bolts, iron in pigs, castings, nail, and alum", 15th Congress, Session 1, Chapter 103, 20 Apr 1818

[12.2-16] op. cit., Bolles, Vol. 2, pp. 371, 372

[12.2-17] op. cit., Bolles, Vol. 2, p. 325

[12.2-18] op. cit., Sumner, p. 79

[12.2-19] op. cit., Walker, p. 495

[12.2-20] William M. Malloy, *Treaties, Conventions, International Acts, Protocols, and Agreements Between the United States of America and Other Powers, 1776-1909*, Vol. 2, pp. 1651-1658, Washington, DC: U. S. Government Printing Office, 1910; 61st Congress, Session 2, Senate Document 357. (Republished by Scholarly Press, Grosse Point, MI)

[12.2-21] Text of "An Act to continue in force an act regulating the currency, within the United States, of the gold coins of Great Britain, France, Portugal, and Spain, and the crowns of France and five franc pieces", 15th Congress, Session 2, Chapter 97, 3 Mar 1819

[12.2-22] op. cit., Bolles, Vol. 2, pp. 282, 283

[12.2-23] op. cit., Bolles, Vol. 2, p. 375

[12.2-24] Text of "An Act to regulate the duties on certain wines", 15th Congress, Session 2, Chapter 82, 3 Mar 1819

[12.2-25] op. cit., Bolles, Vol. 2, pp. 325-327

[12.2-26] op. cit., Walker, p. 495

[12.2-27] op. cit., Bolles, Vol. 2, pp. 326-329

[12.2-28] op. cit., Sumner, pp. 78, 79

[12.2-29] op. cit., Bolles, Vol. 2, p. 326

[12.2-30] op. cit., Raguet, Appendix H, pp. 290-305; see also op. cit. Bolles, Vol. 2, pp. 329, 330

[12.2-31] Text of "An Act to authorize the President of the United States to borrow a sum not exceeding three millions of dollars", 16th Congress, Session 1, Chapter 103, 15 May 1820

[12.2-32] Text of "An Act for the relief of purchasers of public lands prior to the first day of July, 1820", 16th Congress, Session 2, Chapter 12, 2 Mar 1821

[12.2-33] Text of "An Act to authorize the President of the United States to borrow a sum not exceeding five millions of dollars", 16th Congress, Session 2, Chapter 38, 3 Mar 1821

[12.2-34] op. cit., Bolles, Vol. 2, p. 283

[12.2-35] Text of "An Act to continue in force and act entitled 'An act regulating the currency, within the United States, of the gold coins of Great Britain, France, Portugal, and Spain', passed on the twenty-ninth day of April, one thousand eight hundred and sixteen, as far as same relates to the crowns and five franc pieces of France", 16th Congress, Session 2, Chapter 53, 3 Mar 1821

[12.2-36] op. cit., Sumner, p. 83

[12.2-37] Text of "An Act relating to treasury notes", 17th Congress, Session 1, Chapter 47, 3 May 1822

[12.2-38] op. cit., Bolles, Vol. 2, p. 283

[12.2-39] Text of " An Act to continue in force and act entitled 'An act regulating the currency, within the United States, of the gold coins of Great Britain, France, Portugal, and Spain', passed on the twenty-ninth day of April, one thousand eight hundred and sixteen, as far as same relates to the crowns and five franc pieces of France", 17th Congress, Session 2, Chapter 50, 3 Mar 1823

[12.2-40] op. cit., Bolles, Vol. 2, p. 308

[12.2-41] Text of "An Act to amend several acts imposing duties on imports", 18th Congress, Session 1, Chapter 136, 22 May 1824

[12.2-42] op. cit., Bolles, Vol. 2, p. 376

[12.2-43] Text of "An Act to authorize the creation of a stock to an amount not exceeding five millions of dollars, to provide for the awards of the commissioners under the treaty with Spain, of the twenty-second of February, one thousand eight hundred and nineteen", 18th Congress, Session 1, Chapter 140, 24 May 1824

[12.2-44] op. cit., Bolles, Vol. 2, p. 312

[12.2-45] op. cit., Sumner, p. 84

[12.2-46] Text of "An Act authorizing the Secretary of the Treasury to borrow a sum not exceeding twelve millions of dollars, or to exchange a stock of four and one half per cent for a certain stock bearing an interest of six per cent.", 18th Congress, Session 2, Chapter 100, 3 Mar 1825

[12.2-47] op. cit., Sumner, pp. 84-86, 303

[12.2-48] op. cit., Sumner, pp. 86, 87

[12.2-49] Text of "An Act in the alteration of the several acts imposing duties on imports", 20th Congress, Session 1, Chapter 55, 19 May 1828

[12.2-50] op. cit., Bolles, Vol. 2, pp. 406, 407

[12.2-51] James D. Richardson, *A Compilation of the Messages and Papers of the Presidents, 1789 - 1897*, Washington, D. C: U. S. Government Printing Office, 1896, Vol. 2, p. 462

[12.2-52] Text of "An Act to authorize the commissioners of the sinking fund to redeem the public debt of the United States", 21st Congress, Session 1, Chapter 78, 24 Apr 1830

[12.2-53] Text of "An Act to reduce the duties on coffee, tea, and cocoa", 21st Congress, Session 1, Chapter 101, 20 May 1830

[12.2-54] Text of "An Act to reduce the duty on molasses, and to allow a drawback on spirits distilled from foreign materials", 21st Congress, Session 1, Chapter 185, 29 May 1830

[12.2-55] Text of "An Act to reduce the duty on salt", 21st Congress, Session 1, Chapter 186, 29 May 1830

[12.2-56] Text of "An Act to repeal the tonnage duties upon ships and vessels of the United States, and upon certain foreign vessels", 21st Congress, Session 1, Chapter 219, 31 May 1830

[12.2-57] op. cit., Richardson, Vol. 2, pp. 528, 529

[12.2-58] op. cit., Richardson, Vol. 2, p. 558

[12.2-59] op. cit., Richardson, Vol. 2, pp. 576 - 591

[12.2-60] Text of "An Act to alter and amend the several acts imposing duties on imports", 22nd Congress, Session 1, Chapter 227, 14 Jul 1832

[12.2-61] op. cit., Bolles, Vol. 2, p. 422

[12.2-62] op. cit., Richardson, Vol. 2, pp. 599, 600

[12.2-63] op. cit., Bolles, Vol. 2, pp. 424, 425

[12.2-64] https://en.wikipedia.org/wiki/Tariff_of_1833

[12.2-65] Text of "An Act to modify the act of the fourteenth of July, one thousand eight hundred and thirty-two, and all other acts imposing duties on imports", 22nd Congress, Session 2, Chapter 55, 2 Mar 1833

[12.2-66] op. cit., Richardson, Vol. 3, pp. 5 - 19

[12.2-67] Lot M. Morrill, *Annual Report of the Secretary of the Treasury on the State of the Finances for Year 1876*, Appendix containing the Report of the Comptroller of Currency (John Jay Knox), Washington, DC: Government Printing Office, 1876, p. 126

[12.2-68] op. cit., Bolles, Vol. 2, pp. 338, 339, 346

[12.2-69] op. cit., Bolles, Vol. 2, p. 352

[12.2-70] op. cit., Bolles, Vol. 2, pp. 338-340

[12.2-71] op. cit., Morrill, p. 126

[12.2-72] R. B. Taney, "Removal of the Public Deposits", in the *Annual Report of the Secretary of the Treasury on the Finances*, 1833, pp. 337-357

[12.2-73] op. cit., Morrill, p. 126, citing the Memoirs of John Quincy Adams

[12.2-74] op. cit., Morrill, p. 127

[12.2-75]   Text of "An Act regulating the value of certain foreign silver coins within the United States", 23rd Congress, Session 1, Chapter 71, 25 Jun 1834

[12.2-76]   Text of "An act concerning the gold coins of the United States and for other purposes", 28 Jun 1834

[12.2-77]   op. cit., Raguet, pp. 44, 45, 178, 179

[12.2-78]   Text of "An act regulating the value of certain foreign gold coins within the United States", 23rd Congress, Session 1, Chapter 96, 28 Jun 1834

[12.2-79]   op. cit., Bolles, Vol. 2, p. 516

[12.2-80]   op. cit., Bolles, Vol. 2, p. 315

[12.2-81]   Jonathan Elliot, *The Funding System of the United States and Great Britain*, Washington, DC: Blair and Rives, 1845, p. 890, quoting L. Woodbury, Annual Report of the Secretary of the Treasury, 1834, 2 Dec 1834

[12.2-82]   L. Woodbury, *Annual Report of the Secretary of the Treasury on the Finances*, 1834, 2 Dec 1834, p. 475

[12.2-83]   op. cit., Richardson, Vol. 3, pp. 160, 161

[12.2-84]   op. cit., Morrill, pp. 128, 129

[12.2-85]   Text of "An Act repealing the fourteenth section of the 'Act to incorporate the subscribers to the bank of the United States', approved April tenth, eighteen hundred and sixteen", 24th Congress, Session 1, Chapter 97, 15 Jun 1836

[12.2-86]   op. cit., Morrill, p. 156

[12.2-87]   op. cit., Bolles, Vol. 2, pp. 352, 353

[12.2-88]   Text of "An act to regulate the deposits of public money", 24th Congress, Session 1, Chapter 115, 23 Jun 1836

[12.2-89]   Text of "An act authorizing the Secretary of the Treasury to act as the agent of the United States in all matters relating to their stock in the Bank of the United States", 24th Congress, Session 1, Chapter 116, 23 Jun 1836

[12.2-90]   op. cit., Bolles, Vol. 2, p. 548

[12.2-91]   Text of "An act supplementary to an act entitled "An act to regulate the deposits of the public money", passed the twenty-third of June, eighteen hundred and thirty-six", 24th Congress, Session 1, Chapter 354, 4 Jul 1836

[12.2-92]   op. cit., Bolles, Vol. 2, pp. 346-350

[12.4-1]   op. cit., Bolles, *A Financial History of the United States*, NY: Augustus M. Kelley (1969), Vol. 2, pp. 331-334 (originally published 1884 by D. Appleton & Co., NY)

[12.4-2]   Bray Hammond, *Banks and Politics in the United States from the Revolution to the Civil War*, Princeton, NJ: Princeton University Press, 1957, p. 301

[12.4-3]   Murray N. Rothbard, *What Has Government Done to Our Money?,* Auburn AL: Ludwig von Mises Institute, 1991 (first published in 1963), pp. 79 - 87

[12.4-4]   op. cit., Bolles, Vol. 2, pp. 334, 335, 337

[12.4-5]   Albert Gallatin, *Considerations on the Currency and Banking System of the United States*, Philadelphia, PA: Carey & Lea, 1831, pp. 85, 88

13

The State Bank/Sub-Treasury System, 1837-1862

13.1 Preview, 1837-1862

This period was characterized by the establishment of a large number of small banks, which posed a risk to the economy because redemption of their notes was not enforced [13.1-1, 13.1-2], a continuation of "wildcat" banking. More notes were issued than could be redeemed, and the banking system was also plagued by some counterfeiting. At the same time there was a mania for over-building of railroads and other infrastructure, cotton, and raw land, with a general appetite for speculation. The banking system did not restrain the speculation by raising discount rates, and it continued until it became a partial cause of the collapse of the banking system in 1837 [13.1-3].

Meanwhile, the federal government was both incompetent and corrupt. Congress continued to spend beyond its means, finally realizing in 1844 that it had to cut expenses in order to restrain the growth of the national debt [13.1-4]. As for corruption, even when the debt was increasing in the 1830's and 1840's, Bolles reported [13.1-5]:

> "Bad enough were these things, but still worse had happened; for corruption, foul and universal, was poisoning every branch, twig, and leaf of the public service. Certainly in no former period, and in no subsequent one, has such a vast mass of corruption in conducting the public business been discovered. Everything, almost, undertaken by the officers of the government, was saturated with it. Every contract and appropriation seemed tainted with fraud."

He goes on to relate some examples: a) military officers drew full pay when not in service; b) obvious travel boondoggles (vacations disguised as training); c) corruption in the contracts regarding the Florida Indian removal; d) outright fraud and mismanagement at the New York customs house; e) a large increase in the number of "useless" offices in the government; and f) a large number of public works, some of which had questionable merit.

There was one important change within the banking system. Until about the mid-1850's, most commercial loans were taken out in bank notes; but afterwards there was a shift toward demand deposits as the means of funding loans. It was about this time that demand deposit liabilities became larger than their bank note liabilities [13.1-6].

13.2 History, 1837-1862

18 Jan 1837: Congress passed legislation [13.2-1] modifying the standards for coins: **a)** (S. 8) standard metal for minting of both gold and silver coins is 90% pure with 10% alloy; **b)** (S. 1) the alloy of the silver coins to be copper, and the alloy of the gold coins to be a mix of copper and silver, but the alloy to be less than half silver; **c)** (S. 9) physical weight of silver dollar coins to be 412.5 grains in standard metal, with corresponding values for the half dollar (206.25), quarter (103.125), dime (41.25), and half-dime (20.625); **d)** (S. 9) the silver coins to be legal tender in any amount; **e)** (S. 10) the $10 gold Eagle to be 258 grains of standard metal, with corresponding weights for the half Eagle

(129.0), and quarter Eagle (64.5); **f)** (S. 10) gold coins to be legal tender (for all sums, Eagle at $10, half Eagle at $5, and quarter Eagle at $2.50; **g)** (S. 11) coins already minted shall pass at full value; **h)** (S. 12) the weight of the cent (1/100th of a dollar) to be 168 grains of copper, and half-cent at 84 grains; and **i)** (S. 14) that bullion may be brought to the mint to be coined at no charge. The $10 gold Eagle was redefined slightly from the 28 Jun 1834 devaluation from 232 grains pure gold to 232.2 grains, or 258 grains of standard metal, the standard now being 90% pure and 10% alloy [13.2-2]. The gold Eagle was thus devalued from its original $10 to $9.38 (247.5 grains pure per 2 Apr 1792; 232.2/247.5 = 0.938) [13.2-3]. The official mint ratio of gold to silver was thus 371.25/23.22 = 15.988.

16 Mar 1837: The 28 Mar 1834 censure of President Jackson was expunged from the Senate Journal [13.2-4].

4 May 1837: Beginning of the Panic of 1837, triggered by a series of runs on the banks. It became a recession that lasted until 1843. Francis Walker [13.2-5] explains the underlying causes:

> "The panic of 1837, the second and heavier shock of 1839, and the long and dreary prostration of industry lasting until 1843, were the result of speculative overtrading, mainly after 1833, leading to a general distortion of productive industry, and to speculative investments, especially in western lands and mines, in railroads and canals, in corner lots and river fronts, which, even had they been intelligently made, would have far outrun the possible growth of the country, locking up in unremunerative enterprises the capital needed to conduct the manufactures and trade of the nation. Language could not well exaggerate the extent to which this misapplication of capital and this distortion of production had been carried. The whole head was sick and the whole heart faint. Even the ordinary commercial machinery of the country was carried away in the crash which followed. The train was wrecked upon the track, and it took years to clear away the debris and get the ordinary agencies of trade, viz., exchanges, commercial correspondence, business goodwill, and in some cases even the facilities of transportation, again in working order.
>
> That the evils of the period 1834 to 1843 were in great measure due to the vices of paper-money banking is not to be questioned. The opening of the "great West" could doubtless have led to much wild adventure, industrially and commercially; and it is of the American genius to take large risks boldly. But the facility of issue, without the reality or scarcely the pretense of redemption, made the banks, even those which had been reasonably well founded, reckless as to the nature of the enterprises which they assisted; while the money thus put into circulation, without "reflux", enhanced prices and still further stimulated both speculative investments and speculative trading. When the audacity of the better institutions failed, hundreds of "wildcat" or "coonbox" banks, without capital, without a constituency, with no past and no future, whose managers risked nothing came forward with offers of notes to speculators who planned to build cities in the wilderness, or contractors who wished to construct roads and bridges without materials, tools, or means of paying wages."

10 May 1837: Nearly all banks in the U. S. suspended payment in specie [13.2-6, 13.2-7]. The State banks had possession of all the U. S. Government deposits (since the Bank of the United States had not been re-chartered), and since the State banks had issued so many bank notes, the public began to demand redemption in specie, which the banks could not do. The government could not regain its deposits, and could not arrange for any of them to be transferred to places were payments had to be made. There was also now no uniform currency: State bank notes were discounted nearly everywhere, and the discounting increased with distance from the issuing bank. President Jackson's elimination of the Bank of the United States had exactly the opposite effect that he intended. President Van Buren then ordered U. S. Government funds be handled using the Treasury system that was in place from 1833 to 1836 [13.2-8].

5 Sep 1837: Treasury Secretary Woodbury issued a report [13.2-9] stating the condition of the Treasury in view of the disbursements of surplus to the States (cf. 23 Jun 1836): a) the surplus in the Treasury as of 1 Jan 1837 was $42,468,860; b) deducting the $5,000,000 to be retained, have a balance of $37,468,860 to be placed in deposit for the several States; c) thus far, in payments made 1 Jan 1837, 1 Apr 1837, and 1 Jun 1837, the amount deposited came to $27,063,431, leaving a balance of $9,367,215 to be paid on 1 Oct 1837. But his estimate for the rest of the year indicated that the

Treasury would not be able to make the last payment, since the projected expenditures were estimated to produce a deficit of $5,876,565 by 1 Jan 1838. The problem was the Congress had appropriated funds without anticipating how to pay for them; secondly, there was a decline in customs duties owing to the economic recession; third, the banks had suspended specie payments and neither the banks nor their customers were able to remit taxes and duties to the Treasury. The Treasury had petitioned Congress to provide some relief, but to no avail. The scheduled 1 Oct 1837 payment to the States was never made.

2 Oct 1837: The Treasury was unable to make the fourth payment to the States on the surplus that had existed on 1 Jan 1837; Congress permitted the Treasury Secretary to withhold the last of the four payments [13.2-10]. Congress postponed until 1 Jan 1839 the fourth installment of federal deposits to be made with the States (cf. 23 Jun 1836) [13.2-11]. It would never be paid.

12 Oct 1837: Congress passed financial legislation [13.2-12] to meet the current expenses of the government, since so much of the government's deposits were tied up in State banks that had suspended payment. Among its provisions: **a)** (S.1) authorized the Treasury Secretary to issue $10,000,000 in Treasury Notes; **b)** (S. 2) the notes were to be redeemed within one year, with the interest rate to be determined by the Treasury Secretary, not to exceed 6%; **c)** (S. 4) notes could be used as payments by the U. S. to creditors who would receive them at par, and authorized the Treasury Secretary to borrow against them; **d)** (S. 6) the notes were to be received for all duties, taxes, and sales of public lands due to the U. S.; **e)** (S. 13) authority to issue notes to expire 31 Dec 1838. This allowed the federal government to meet its immediate obligations. At the same time, Congress was very slow in reducing government expenditures [13.2-13]. The issue of Treasury Notes against future revenues was intended to be temporary until the financial problem with the State bank suspensions abated [13.2-14].

16 Oct 1837: Congress enacted a system to permit importers to delay their duty payments, owing to the cash-flow problem many were experiencing [13.2-15, 13.2-16]. Among its provisions: **a)** (S. 1) Treasury Secretary authorized to grant further extension of credit upon all bonds for duties, up to nine months from the original due date; and **b)** (S. 2) bonds for duties on goods imported prior to 1 Nov 1837 to be payable in three equal installments, at 6% interest.

16 Oct 1837: Congress passed legislation [13.2-17] instructing the Treasury Secretary how to withdraw U. S. funds from the offices of the failed State banks: **a)** (S. 1) "authorized to continue to withdraw public moneys now remaining in any of the former deposit banks, in a manner as gradual and convenient to the institutions as shall be consistent with pecuniary wants of the Government, and the safety of the funds to be withdrawn"; and **b)** (S. 2) the Treasury Secretary authorized to sue any banks that refuse to comply with the requisitions for withdrawals.

5 Dec 1837: Treasury Secretary Woodbury reported [13.2-18] that the amount unavailable to the U. S. Treasury, having been deposited in State banks that had suspended specie payments, was $28,101,645.

23 Apr 1838: Resumption of payments in specie by banks in New York City [13.2-19].

10 May 1838: Resumption of specie payments on demand in other parts of the U. S., including other banks in New York and the New England States [13.2-20, 13.2-21]. Hepburn states [13.2-22] that a general resumption throughout the U. S. did not occur until Feb 1839.

21 May 1838: Congress passed legislation [13.2-23] authorizing the Treasury Secretary to re-issue Treasury Notes that were issued previously and since redeemed (cf. 12 Oct 1837) in order to meet the current expenses of the government.

31 May 1838: Congress passed legislation [13.2-24] repealing the provisos of the 10th and 12th clauses of Section 2 to the import law of 14 Jul 1832. These pertained to manufactures of various metals; this legislation removed the previous requirement that the *ad valorem* duties were to be the same whether fully manufactured or in parts.

7 Jul 1838: Congress passed legislation [13.2-25] instructing the Treasury Secretary to sell two bonds of the Bank of the United States (now chartered in Pennsylvania as a State bank) held by the government for as much as he could get. Each had a face value of $1,986,589.04, to mature in Sep 1839.

7 Jul 1838: Congress passed legislation [13.2-26] prohibiting the circulation or re-issue of notes, bills, and securities of any corporation established by Congress whose charter has expired (meaning the Bank of the United States).

13 Aug 1838: The banks in Philadelphia resumed payments in specie [13.2-27].

31 Dec 1838: Most banks in the U. S. had resumed specie payments [13.2-28].

2 Mar 1839: Congress authorized [13.2-29] the Treasury Secretary to continue issuing Treasury Notes as originally authorized 21 May 1838.

10 Oct 1839: The Bank of the United States (now State-chartered) had engaged in cotton speculation, even though it was deep in debt to European banks. It decided to sell exchanges in New York, then used the notes and checks it obtained to make a run on New York banks in order to finance the export of cotton. It was unable to meet the bills, and on 10 Oct 1839, it suspended specie payments, followed by most of the banks in the South and West that had also speculated in cotton [13.2-30, 13.2-31, 13.2-32]. This was the "bank crash" of 1839.

~15 Oct 1839: The banks in Philadelphia suspended payments in specie, which soon spread throughout the U. S. and continued until 1842 [13.2-33].

31 Mar 1840: Congress passed legislation regarding the Treasury Notes [13.2-34]: **a)** (S. 1) extending the original provisions (cf. 12 Oct 1837); **b)** (S. 2) limited the amount outstanding at any time to be $5,000,000; and **c)** (S. 3) to expire 31 Mar 1841. A total of $31,000,000 were issued and redeemed at various times between 1837 and 1841 [13.2-35].

4 Jul 1840: Congress passed "an act to provide for the collection, safe-keeping, transfer, and disbursement of the public revenue" (a.k.a. the Independent Treasury Act) [13.2-36] to replace the State bank system (cf. 23 Jun 1836) after the demise of the second Bank of the United States, and to formally authorize the treasury system of handling the Government finances [13.2-37]. Provisions include: **a)** (S. 1) all government funds were to be managed by the Treasury Secretary headquartered in Washington, DC; **b)** (S. 2) the Mints at Philadelphia and New Orleans to function as sub-treasuries; **c)** (S. 3 - 5) sub-treasuries to be setup at Boston, New York, Charleston, SC, and St. Louis, led by "receivers-general" to handle the public money; **d)** (S. 6) sub-treasuries to handle public money as directed by the Treasury Secretary; **e)** (S. 7, 8) sub-treasury offices and other authorized depository institutions to provide bonds or other security to the Treasury Secretary as insurance against the public money; **f)** (S. 9 - 11) collectors of taxes and duties to remit payments to the sub-treasuries; **g)** (S. 12, 13, 14) provisions for examinations of sub-treasuries, other depositories, and necessary expenses; **h)** (S. 19) adopted a quarterly payment plan for duties, taxes and receipts from land sales; **i)** (S. 19) all payments due to the U. S. (taxes, import duties, proceeds from government loans and sales of public lands) to be paid in the notes of specie-paying banks; **j)** (S. 20) all debts paid by the federal government must be paid in specie; and **k)** (S. 23) drafts and notes received by the sub-treasuries are to be collected in specie from the banks promptly.

The U. S. Government funds were thus deposited in various banks, rotating monthly. Each bank thus had a short time in which its deposits were very high, which it used to lend out to speculators. It was a defective system because it gave certain institutions unfair advantages and there insufficient guarantee of safety of the public funds.

15 Feb 1841: Congress authorized [13.2-38] a continuation of the issuing of Treasury Notes, limiting the total outstanding to $5,000,000; to expire 4 Mar 1842.

21 Jul 1841: Congress authorized [13.2-39, 13.2-40] Treasury Secretary Ewing to: **a)** (S. 1) obtain a $12,000,000 loan at interest not exceeding 6%, to be redeemable any time after 1 Jan 1845; **b)** (S. 2)

proceeds to be used to fund the redemption of the Treasury Notes; and **c)** (S. 4) Treasury Secretary permitted to use any surplus to purchase existing debt out of proceeds.

13 Aug 1841: Congress repealed the Independent Treasury Act of 1840 (cf. 4 Jul 1840) [13.2-41, 13.2-42, 13.2-43] and the Deposit and Distribution Act of 1836 (cf. 23 Jun 1836) except for sections 13 and 14. The Treasury Secretary went back to depositing federal government funds in State-chartered banks on a rotating basis.

16 Aug 1841: Congress passed a bill authorizing another Bank of the United States. However, President Tyler vetoed it [13.2-44], and the Treasury system continued.

11 Sep 1841: Congress revised the law on import duties [13.2-45], imposing 20% *ad valorem* on all imported items, with a large number items remaining on the free list

31 Jan 1842: Congress extended [13.2-46] the authority to issue Treasury Notes, with the total amount outstanding limited to $5,000,000, expiring 31 Jan 1843.

18 Mar 1842: Banks in Philadelphia resumed payment of their notes in specie [13.2-47, 13.2-48], followed afterward by most banks in the U. S.

15 Apr 1842: Congress authorized [13.2-49]: **a)** (S. 1) an extension of the time for obtaining the loan (cf. 21 Jul 1841) for another year; **b)** (S. 2) to be repaid at the discretion of the Treasury Secretary with six months notice or any time after 20 years; **c)** (S. 3) debt certificates ("stock") to be transferable instead of on the books of the Treasury; **d)** (S. 8) authorized an additional loan of $5,000,000 if the President approves; and **e)** (S. 9) unredeemed Treasury Notes outstanding to carry interest at 6%.

27 Jul 1842: Congress fixed by statute [13.2-50] the value of the British pound sterling at $4.84.

30 Aug 1842: Congress enacted a new tariff law [13.2-51]: **a)** (S. 1) 30% *ad valorem* on raw wool; **b)** (S. 1) 40% *ad valorem* on manufactured wool; import duties; **c)** (S. 1) 30% *ad valorem* on carpets; **d)** (S. 1) 25% on blankets; **e)** (S. 1) 30% on other wool; f) (S. 1) 20% to 50% on cotton goods depending on type; **f)** (S. 2 - 8) duties per weight, or an *ad valorem* up to 30% on raw cotton, silk, hemp, flax, iron, wire, steel, firearms, brass, lead, copper, tin, coal, glass, porcelain, leather, hats, rubber items, clocks, jewelry, wood, marble, roofing slates, toys, brushes, musical strings, paints, books, sugar, molasses, spices, dried fruit, candles, soap, wine, and liquor; **g)** (S. 9) a list of duty-free items, mostly various items essential for certain industries but including tea and coffee if imported on American vessels; **h)** (S. 10) 20% *ad valorem* on items not enumerated; and **i)** (S. 11) an additional 10% for items imported on foreign vessels. It was passed in order to generate more revenue, as the government had been running a deficit since the reduction of tariffs per the 1832 law. It was also intended also to aid the resumption of manufacturing in the U. S. Merchants increased imports so much, anticipating higher prices and profits [13.2-52], that they saturated the market, and prices actually fell. Initially the anticipated revenue did not materialize (it is not clear if it was because the duties were too high, or if the general decline in revenues was from other causes), but by 1844 it was sufficient to meet the expenses of the Government.

31 Aug 1842: Congress directed [13.2-53]: **a)** (S. 1) the Secretary of the Treasury not to issue debt certificates ("stock") for the authorized loan below par (6%); **b)** (S. 2) if sufficient buyers are not found, to issue Treasury Notes up to $6,000,000; and **c)** (S. 2) the total amount of Treasury Notes outstanding was limited to $6,000,000.

3 Mar 1843: Congress passed legislation regulating the value of foreign coins [13.2-54]: **a)** (S. 1) gold coins of Great Britain if 0.9155 fine to be received at $0.946 per pennyweight; b) (S. 1) gold coins of France if 0.899 fine to be received at $0.929 per pennyweight; **c)** (S. 2) silver coins of Spain, Peru, Mexico, and Bolivia if 0.897 fine to be received at $1.00; **d)** (S. 2) 5-franc silver coins of France if 0.900 fine and 384 grains weight to be received at $0.930.

3 Mar 1843: Congress passed legislation on the re-issue of Treasury Notes and payment of interest on them [13.2-55]: **a)** (S. 1) authorized the Treasury Secretary to re-issue Treasury Notes as needed until 1 Jul 1844; **b)** (S.2) interest to be paid on Treasury Notes that were authorized 31 Aug 1842; and

c) (S. 3) if Treasury Notes cannot be issued, the Treasury Secretary was authorized to borrow and issue bonds up to $5,000,000. Treasury Secretary Ewing issued $7,000,000 in Treasury Notes in addition to the $4,656,387 remaining from previous issues [13.2-56].

31 Dec 1843: Sumner states that 1843 had been an especially bad year [13.2-57]:

> "Nor was the fall of prices from 1839 to 1843 due to any forced contraction of the currency. The more correct explanation of the phenomena is that the destruction of the banking system brought with it a collapse of the industry of the country. The revulsion was so complete that it could not be arrested until industry came almost to a standstill and took a fresh start. 1841 was comparatively a year of prosperity. ... The year 1843 was one of the gloomiest in our industrial history. The grand promise of ten years before was now entirely obscured. Mortgaged property was passing into the possession of mortgagees. Factories were idle. Trade was dull, investments slow. All the natural advantages of the country were unimpaired, but the haste to realize them had brought ruin which time only could repair. The year 1843 was one which the ideal of some economists was realized. We exported forty millions more merchandise than we imported, and we imported twenty millions more specie than we exported, but the significance of these facts was simply this: we were paying up for the grand times of the years before. It was like the spendthrift living low to recover his position, and we were doing it by producing mainly for export, at prices low enough to suit the creditors."

~1 Apr 1844: Approximate end of the recession (cf. 4 May 1837) [13.2-58, 13.2-59].

25 Apr 1846: The Thornton Affair, which began of the Mexican War.

8 May 1846: Battle of Palo Alto, TX.

9 May 1846: Battle of Resaca de la Palma, TX.

22 Jul 1846: Congress authorized Treasury Notes, and/or an issue of stock (loan) in lieu thereof, in order to fund the Mexican War [13.2-60, 13.2-61]: **a)** (S. 1) authorized an issue Treasury Notes, not to exceed $10,000,000 outstanding at any one time; **b)** (S. 2) at discretion of the President, the Treasury Secretary may obtain a loan in lieu of issuing Treasury Notes up to $5,000,000 with a 10 year repayment limit; **c)** (S. 2) the combination of Treasury Notes and loan not to exceed $10,000,000; and **d)** (S. 3) maximum interest to be paid on Treasury Notes and loans is 6%.

30 Jul 1846: Congress revised the tariff law [13.2-62]: **a)** (S. 1) divided all the enumerated articles for which duty to be paid to seven schedules A through H; **b)** (S. 1) the *ad valorem* duties per schedule are: A: 100%, B: 40%, C: 30%, D: 25%, E: 20%, F: 15%, G: 10%, H: 5%; and **c)** (S. 11) a long list of items for which *ad valorem* duties to be paid by schedule, with a free list in schedule I. The main idea behind this law was [13.2-63]: a) tariffs should be calibrated to meet the revenue needs of the government (and not a protection; this was a free trade system); b) rates on articles should be calibrated to maximize revenue; c) some exceptions allowed for essential items; d) duties to be maximized on luxuries; e) specific duties to be abolished and replaced entirely with *ad valorem* duties; and f) to be imposed so that they were applied equally in all States. Experience thus far had shown that an *ad valorem* duty of 20% led to the greatest revenue, as it was not worthwhile to risk smuggling. The main problem is that a universal *ad valorem* duty led to fluctuations in revenues, since the values of the commodities tended to vary. Congress now only had the ability to changes the rates. It caused ambiguity among American manufacturers: when prices were high in foreign countries, duties were not protective, and profits increased. When prices were low in foreign countries, the duties also fell, and he gained little protection. There was also a realized risk of fraud due to undervaluation that began to appear in 1849. A fixed duty on most items worked better (as Gallatin had warned in 1801). By 1856 the revenues were triple expectations, but at the expense of many American manufacturing concerns, especially iron and wool [13.2-64].

6 Aug 1846: Congress enacted the Sub-treasury system [13.2-65, 13.2-66], re-invoking most provisions of the law from 1836 (cf. 23 Jun 1836). Among its provisions: **a)** (S. 1) the U. S. Treasury to be headquartered in Washington, DC; **b)** (S. 2) Mints at Philadelphia and New Orleans to be sub-treasuries; **c)** (S. 3, 4) sub-treasuries to be set up in Boston, New York, Charleston, SC, and St. Louis; **d)** (S. 5) President to appoint four assistant treasurers; **e)** (S. 6) treasurers to perform transactions on behalf of the U. S. government; **f)** (S. 7 - 8) treasurers and other depository institutions handling public revenue to provide bonds for security; **g)** (S. 9) collectors of revenue to remit payments to the sub-treasuries; **h)** (S 10) Treasury Secretary authorized to make deposits and withdrawals of public money in any suitable depository institution (bank); **i)** (S. 11 - 13) provisions for examinations and expenses; **j)** (S. 14) Treasury Secretary authorized to transfer public money among depository institutions; **k)** (S. 17, 18) all import duties to be paid in gold and silver, and payments for public lands to be made either in gold and silver or in Treasury Notes; **l)** (S. 19) all debts payable by the U. S. shall be made in gold and silver, or in Treasury Notes if the creditor so agrees; and **m)** (S. 21) all drafts and checks received by the Treasury shall be promptly redeemed for silver and gold, and the Treasury Secretary to prevent as much as possible said paper to be issued as currency or medium of exchange

As implemented, the means of transferring government funds was inefficient (either imposing the expense of transporting specie or using drafts to the bankers) [13.2-67]. The problem with using drafts was that the intermediate banks were permitted, as compensation in lieu of the expense of shipping specie, to use the money for the short period it was in their hands, and this led to a system of corruption and favoritism. The bankers made profits by making unnecessary transfers and timing them such that they had nearly permanent use of government funds. It did, however, provide some benefits. First, government revenues were collected in specie and Treasury Notes, and payments were made accordingly. Secondly, it permitted the Mexican War to be financed without resorting to bank notes, independent of the banking system. Third, it restrained the issue of bank notes by the State banks, since they were returned for payment; this reduced the depreciation of the currency.

21 Sep 1846 - 24 Sep 1846: Battle of Monterrey, TX.

28 Jan 1847: Congress passed a funding law [13.2-68]: **a)** (S. 1) authorized the issue of Treasury Notes up to $23,000,000; **b)** (S. 2) to expire and be redeemed within one or two years from issue; **c)** (S. 2) to bear interest not exceeding 6%, but interest shall cease if the Treasury gives 60 days notice; **d)** (S. 4) permitted the Treasury to borrow against the credit of the Treasury Notes, but only at par; **e)** (S. 6) Treasury Notes to be receivable for all debts to the U. S.; **f)** (S. 13) the Treasury Notes may be converted into long-term public debt bearing 6% interest at the request of the holder; **g)** (S. 15) the previous authorization of $5,000,000 in Treasury Notes was continued until Jan 1849; and **h)** (S. 16) the $23,000,000 or part may be issued directly as public debt in lieu of Treasury Notes, but the total was limited to $23,000,000; This loan was intended to fund the Mexican War [13.2-69].

22, 23 Feb 1847: Battle of Buena Vista.

9 - 29 Mar 1847: Siege of Veracruz.

17, 18 Apr 1847: Battle of Cerro Gordo.

20 Aug 1847: Battles of Contreras and Churubusco.

8 Sep 1847: Battle of Molino del Rey.

12, 13 Sep 1847: Battle of Chapultepec.

2 Feb 1848: The Treaty of Guadalupe Hildago ended the Mexican War.

31 Mar 1848: Congress authorized [13.2-70] the President to borrow up to $16,000,000 at interest not to exceed 6%; payable anytime after 1 Jul 1868. This loan was to pay off debts from the Mexican War [13.2-71].

3 Mar 1849: Congress passed a Coinage Act [13.2-72]. It authorized the Mint to coin double Eagles with a value of $20, and a gold dollar coin, using the existing definitions of a dollar by weight (cf. 28 Jun 1834). It also specified allowable deviations from the standard weights in order to pass for legal tender.

21 Feb 1853: Congress passed the Coinage Act of 1853 [13.2-73]: **a)** (S. 1) defined the weight of the half dollar to 192 grains, and corresponding weights for the quarter, dime, half dime; **b)** (S. 2) the silver

coins of half dollar or less to be legal tender for sums up to $5; **c)** (S. 4) the silver coins can be procured from the Mint only in exchange for gold with a $100 minimum; **d)** (S. 5) ended the free coinage of the half, quarter, dime, and half-dime, reserving it only for the Treasurer of the Mint; **e)** depositors of gold and silver may have their bullion cast into bars or ingots and stamped by the Mint; and **f)** (S. 7) authorized the coining of a $3 gold coin to have proportional weight per the ratios established per 3 Mar 1849. These provisions reduced the amount of silver in the minor coins by about 7%. The purpose was to prevent them from being hoarded or exported [13.2-74]. Since it set the legal tender limit at $5, these silver coins become only subsidiary money. The new coins could only be sold to the public for gold, and prohibited the minting of silver coins less than a dollar to be minted for private individuals. Silver had become worth more relative to gold due to the large influx of gold from the discoveries in California and Australia, and so Congress decided to devalue silver to try to equalize them relative to the dollar. This was a symptom of the bimetallic standard, in which mint ratios are fixed.

21 Feb 1857: Congress passed the Coinage Act of 1857, revising the coinage laws [13.2-75, 13.2-76]: **a)** (S. 1) specified the redemption rate for Spanish and Mexican dollar coins: 1) quarters at 20 cents, 2) eighths at 10 cents, and 3) sixteenths at 5 cents; **b)** (S. 2) any such coins received by the Treasury are not to be re-issued, but melted and re-coined; **c)** (S. 3) repealed the previous laws recognizing them as a legal tender; and **d)** (S. 4) abolished the half-cent U. S. coin, and redefined the one-cent as a coin weighing 72 grains, 88% copper and 12% nickel.

3 Mar 1857: Congress revised the tariff law [13.2-77], changing the *ad valorem* rates called out in the 30 Jul 1846 law per the Schedules defined: **a)** (S. 1) A and B: (30%); **b)** (S. 1) C (24%), D (19%), E (15%), F (12%), G (8%), and H (4%); **c)** (S. 2) transferred some enumerated items to different schedules; and c) (S. 3) expanded the free list. It was desirable to reduce the revenues, but instead of a more protective law on certain items to benefit American manufacturers, Congress universally lowered the *ad valorem* duties to between 20 and 25%, and expanded the free list. This caused a reduction in the revenues sufficient to induce federal deficits leading up to the Civil War [13.2-78].

15 Jun 1857: Approximate beginning of a recession [13.2-79], probably due to decline in stock prices, much of which was bought on credit [13.2-80]. This also began a suspension of payments due to over-issue of paper notes (known as the "Panic of 1857").

12 Dec 1857: The bad loans had been liquidated, and the banks in New York resumed redemption in specie; other banks followed suit soon thereafter [13.2-81]. This marks the end of the "Panic of 1857".

23 Dec 1857: Congress authorized a new issue of Treasury Notes [13.2-82]: **a)** (S. 1) authorized up to $20,000,000 in Treasury Notes to be issued; **b)** (S. 2) $6,000,000 of which to be redeemed one year after issue; **c)** (S. 2) notes to bear interest at 6%; **d)** (S. 4) can be issued to public creditors who agree to accept them at par in exchange for outstanding debt; **e)** (S. 5) are transferable; **f)** (S. 6) to be received for all duties and taxes due to the U. S.; **g)** (S. 10) total outstanding not to exceed $20,000,000; and **h)** (S. 10) authority to issue to expire 1 Jan 1859. This new issue was necessary since revenues had declined due to the national financial panic [13.2-83].

14 Jun 1858: Congress authorized a loan [13.2-84]: **a)** (S. 1) for up to $20,000,000, to be repaid any time after 1 Jan 1874; and **b)** S. 2) at interest not exceeding 5%, payable semi-annually.

15 Dec 1858: Approximate end of the recession (cf. 15 Jun 1857) [13.2-85].

22 Jun 1860: Congress authorized a loan of $21,000,000 at 6% interest, to be repaid between 10 and 20 years to be used for current expenses or redeeming Treasury Notes [13.2-86].

15 Oct 1860: Approximate beginning of a recession [13.2-87].

17 Dec 1860: Congress authorized another issue of $10,000,000 in Treasury Notes bearing 6% interest [13.2-88]: **a)** (S. 1) authorized $10,000,000 in Treasury Notes to be issued; **b)** (S. 2) to be redeemed after one year, and to bear interest at 6%; **c)** (S. 4) notes to be used to pay government debts if the creditor accepts them at par; **d)** (S. 5) are transferable; and **e)** (S. 5) to be received for all debts due to

the U. S. This was necessary generally because Congress had allowed the revenues to sink below what was required for the normal operation of the government (cf. tariff revision in 1857) [13.2-89]. The government's credit was very low at this point.

24 Dec 1860: South Carolina seceded from the Union.

31 Dec 1860: The financial situation was very bad: the Buchanan administration had ruined the nation's credit; Congress had run up large deficits and had increased the public debt; revenues were down, and the government had difficulty borrowing money, even at high interest rates. The treasury was empty, having no money to pay the expenses of the government, including the salaries of members of Congress [13.2-90].

9 Jan 1861: Mississippi seceded from the Union.

10 Jan 1861: Florida seceded from the Union.

11 Jan 1861: Alabama seceded from the Union.

19 Jan 1861: Georgia seceded from the Union.

26 Jan 1861: Louisiana seceded from the Union.

4 Feb 1861: Alabama, Texas, South Carolina, Virginia, Mississippi, and Georgia established the Confederacy, with other States joining by the end of March.

8 Feb 1861: Congress authorized a loan [13.2-91]: **a)** (S. 1) of up to $25,000,000 to either pay the current expenses of the government or pay off the Treasury Notes previously issued; and **b)** (S. 2) the bonds ("stocks") were to bear 6% interest, payable between 1871 and 1881. The bonds were sold at a discount of 8% [13.2-92].

2 Mar 1861: Congress (consisting now of mostly the Northern States) passed a law funding the repayment of Treasury Notes and changing the import duties [13.2-93]: **a)** (S. 1) authorized a loan for $10,000,000 to pay current expenses or to redeem outstanding Treasury Notes; to be paid after 1871; **b)** (S. 2) the loan certificates ("stocks") to bear interest at 6%; **c)** (S. 4) loan certificates only to be sold at par; **d)** (if loan bids are not suitable, then Treasury Notes may be issued instead; **e)** (S. 4) Treasury Notes may be exchanged for loan certificates in amounts greater than $500; **f)** (S. 5) entirely revised the import duties, citing a long list of items, and providing for duties per volume or weight or up to 30% *ad valorem*; **g)** (S. 19 - 22) cites a long list of items at 10%, 20%, 25%, and 30% *ad valorem* respectively; and **h)** (S. 23) a long list of items free from import duties. But the President was allowed to issue Treasury Notes if he could not find sufficient subscribers for the loan. About half of it was issued as Treasury Notes at 6% [13.2-94]. The Treasury Notes were received in payment of taxes, but were not legal tender between individuals (thus was not a forced circulation fiat money). Gallatin pointed out that a loan was better, since the repayment period could be specified, whereas Treasury Notes could be returned immediately as payment in taxes, and the government would not receive the needed revenue. He advised that the power to issue Treasury Notes be reserved for some future emergency [13.2-95].

12 Apr 1861: Battle of Fort Sumter, SC; beginning of the Civil War.

16 May 1861: Tennessee seceded from the Union.

18 May 1861: Arkansas seceded from the Union.

23 May 1861: Virginia seceded from the Union.

15 Jun 1861: Approximate end of the recession (cf. 15 Oct 1860) [13.2-96].

17 Jul 1861: Congress authorized a loan of $250,000,000 to finance the Civil War [13.2-97, 13.2-98]: **a)** (S. 1) authorized a loan or Treasury Notes to be issued up to $250,000,000, at interest not exceeding 7.3%, payable semi-annually, to be redeemed starting in 1881; **b)** (S. 1) debt certificates are referred to as coupon bonds or registered bonds instead of "stocks" that had been used before; **c)** Treasury Notes issued to be payable in three years; **d)** (S. 1) Treasury Notes could be issued in exchange for coin at 3.65% interest payable in one year; **e)** Treasury Notes up to $50,000,000 could be issued in

exchange for coin at no interest but payable on demand; **f)** (S. 4) loan offers to be accepted only at par and above; and **g)** (S. 6) Treasury Notes in denominations less than $50 can be re-issued. Thus Treasury Secretary Chase had several options that could be used in combination: a) issue bonds or coupons at 7%, redeemable after 20 years; b) issue Treasury Notes at 7.3%, payable in three years and convertible into 6% bonds; c) issue Treasury Notes up to $50,000,000 in exchange for coin, bearing no interest [13.2-99], but payable on demand by assistant treasurers at Philadelphia, New York, and Boston (these were the "United States Notes"); or d) issue Treasury Notes at 3.65% payable in one year and exchangeable for 7.3% Treasury Notes as above. This was the first time a Treasury Secretary was authorized to borrow money (had always previously been granted to the President).

21 Jul 1861: First Battle of Bull Run (near Manassas, VA).

5 Aug 1861: Congress passed an additional revenue law [13.2-100]: **a)** (S. 1) imposed import duties either by weight or volume on a list of enumerated items; **b)** (S. 2) imposed *ad valorem* duties on enumerated items; **c)** (S. 3) an additional 10% *ad valorem* if imported in foreign vessels; **d)** (S. 8) laid an annual direct tax of $20,000,000 (including the States that had seceded); **e)** (S. 49) imposed an income tax of 3% on incomes above $800 beginning 1 Jan 1862 and with two exceptions: 1) income from U. S. securities was taxed at 1.5%; and 2) income from stocks and securities owned by Americans living abroad was taxed at 5%; and **f)** (S. 9 to 48, 51 to 58) regulations on assessment and how the taxes are to be collected and recorded. This provided a large array of revenue sources [13.2-101]. First, it permitted bonds to be issued at 6%, payable after 20 years at the government's discretion. Second, import duties on sugar, coffee, tea, spirits, and silk were increased. Third, it imposed a direct tax of $20,000,000 to be apportioned among the States. Fourth, it suspended the sub-treasury system, thus allowing the Treasury Secretary (if desired) to deal with banks directly (although Treasury Secretary Chase refused to do so). Fifth, it imposed the income tax. Bolles comments regarding the income tax [13.2-102]:

> "The objections [by the members of Congress] to an income tax were not so great [as the direct tax]. If honestly collected, this tax is considered by many who have well studied the subject one of the fairest that can be assessed; but as the desire to evade it is strong and general, and the facility for doing so great, the tax, in truth, is very objectionable."

5 Aug 1861: Congress passed a supplementary finance law [13.2-103]: **a)** (S. 1) permitted holders of Treasury Notes bearing 7.3% interest to exchange them for bonds bearing 6% payable in twenty years (cf. 17 Jul 1861); **b)** (S. 3) Treasury Notes may be issued in denominations down to $5 (was $10); **c)** (S. 5) non-interest bearing Treasury Notes receivable for debts due to the government; and **d)** (S. 6) suspended the Sub-Treasury system (cf. 6 Aug 1846) and permitted the Treasury Secretary to select depositories of government funds.

~5 Aug 1861: Secretary Chase began issuing Treasury Notes, non-redeemable demand notes upon the government, to some government employees and creditors. The banks were reluctant to receive them, since they obviously depreciated the value of all other money, but they were received when Chase assured the bankers he would issue only as necessary (although he did not rule out using his authority) [13.2-104].

10 Aug 1861: Battle of Wilson's Creek (Oak Hills, MO).

15 Aug 1861: An agreement was reached by Treasury Secretary Chase and bankers from New York, Boston, and Philadelphia has to how a $150,000,000 loan to the government might be consummated [13.2-105]. The idea was that the banks would form a loose association, combining their assets in order to subscribe to the loan, while reselling portions of it in smaller amounts to the public. The plan was: a) the Treasury Secretary to issue $50,000,000 in Treasury Notes on 15 Aug, bearing 7.3% running for three years; b) the banks would subscribe to the full amount at par; c) the banks would subscribe to additional $50,000,000 at par on 15 Oct 1861 and again on 15 Dec 1861 if necessary; d) in each case, no bank could subscribe to more than 20% of the amounts; e) the banks to pay in 10%

immediately to assistant treasurers in the three cities, and the rest was to be provided as demand deposits on behalf of the government; f) the banks would re-issue the bonds to smaller investors and other institutions who choose to buy them; g) the large banks would pool their coin and assets and issue clearinghouse certificates against specie in order to facilitate payments. This arrangement became necessary because the credit of the government was so low, and the bankers desired to support the Union. The aggregate capital of the banks in New York, Boston, and Philadelphia was $120,000,000, with $63,165,039 in coin against $142,381,956 in liabilities in the form of $125,617,207 in deposits and $16,964,749 in circulating bank notes. Thus the specie reserve was about 44.3%. The purpose of the clearinghouse certificates was to facilitate transfers from the Treasury and by clearing offsetting checks from banks such that the Treasury would not have to make payments solely in coin.

~1 Nov 1861: Treasury Secretary Chase began issuing large amounts of United States Notes (which were Treasury Notes not paying interest), supposedly payable on demand, but not actually backed by coin [13.2-106]. The banks had a problem: they could not refuse them because it would lower the government's credit, but could not pay them because there was no coin in the Treasury to redeem them. Initially they were accepted only as a special deposit, but the public demanded specie for them. The banks acquiesced, paid out in coin and experienced a decline in specie reserves.

7 Dec - 28 Dec 1861: The banks in New York lost about $13,000,000 of its $42,000,000 specie reserve owing to payments on the Treasury Notes, and on 28 Dec 1861 voted to suspend specie payments as of 30 Dec 1861 [13.2-107]. All total, the New York banks lost $25,750,112 in specie from 17 Aug 1861 to 4 Jan 1862. The government also suspended specie payments (since it was dependent on the banks). The amount of Treasury Notes in circulation at this time was estimated at $33,460,000. The banks now had a large amount of U. S. bonds that it could not sell (the 7.3% ones agreed to 15 Aug 1861) [13.2-108]. But the banks did their patriotic duty and held out until the loan was paid (they did make a profit on it). This episode proved that Chase's policy of requiring payments to the Treasury to be paid in coin and in issuing Treasury Notes was a failure, and led to the same result: dependence on a fiat currency. It failed because he expected the banks to pay Treasury Notes in specie, which notes were in competition with their own bank notes, which were adequately covered by reserves; he thus endangered the safety of the banks upon which he was dependent for the implementation of the loans. The core problem was Chase's inability to perceive that a great deal of transactions could be done by offsetting checks without actual transfer of coin. There are some, however who believe that suspension of payments would have happened eventually; Bolles quotes Amasa Walker [13.2-109]:

> "Blame has been thrown upon Mr. Chase for this suspension, but quite unjustly. That he might by some arrangement with the banks, in regard to the circulation of their notes, have postponed the suspension for a short time, we do not doubt; but it could not long have been avoided. Mr. Chase had a broken-down currency to start with. The banks of the United States, on the first of January, 1861, had $459,000,000 of immediate indebtedness, while they held but $87,000,000 of specie, equal to but nineteen cents on the dollar. How was it possible to go through a great war with a currency of so little strength? It could not be done. Suspension was inevitable."

24 Dec 1861: Congress increased the import duties on sugar, tea, and coffee [13.2-110].

30 Dec 1861: The banks suspended redemption of their bank notes in specie [13.2-111]. One result of suspension was the rapid increase in the notes issued by the State banks [13.2-112]: a) small bank notes became necessary for small change since silver coins were hoarded; b) gold was also hoarded, requiring bank notes for transactions; c) since bank notes could not be redeemed, people became accustomed to using them as the best money available and therefore was no penalty for issuing more of them; and d) many bank notes were sent to the West to compensate for the large number of bank failures there. As usual, the greater amount of currency in circulation increased prices.

31 Dec 1861: The U. S. Treasury suspended redemption of its notes; now had a fiat monetary system [13.2-113].

6 Feb 1862: At this point, only $110,000,000 of the $150,000,000 loan from Jul 1861 had been subscribed; the credit of the government was very low, and its bonds would probably have to be sold at a large discount, maybe 40%. Congress had been debating what to do for the past month, and the Treasury was empty [13.2-114].

12 Feb 1862: Congress passed an emergency bill [13.2-115] permitting $10,000,000 in Treasury Notes (United States Notes) to be issued, payable on demand, but considered as part of the $250,000,000 loan that was passed in Jul 1861 [13.2-116].

20, 21 Feb 1862: Battle of Fort Donelson, TN.

25 Feb 1862: Congress passed the "legal tender law" [13.2-117]: **a)** (S. 1) authorized $150,000,000 in United States Notes to be issued not bearing interest, payable to the bearer, at minimum denomination of $5; **b)** (S. 1) $50,000,000 of the $150,000,000 to be issued in lieu of the demand Treasury notes authorized (17 Jul 1861), and the Treasury Notes to be collected as soon as possible and the United States Notes be substituted for them; **c)** (S. 1) the total amount of Treasury Notes and United States Notes limited to $150,000,000; **d)** (S. 1) U. S. Notes receivable for all taxes, internal duties excises and debts to the U. S. except import duties and interest on bonds and notes; **e)** (S. 1) U. S. Notes and Treasury Notes "shall also be lawful money and a legal tender in payment for all debts, public and private, within the United States, except duties on imports and interest"; **f)** U. S. Notes and Treasury Notes convertible into U. S. debt bearing 6% redeemable after 5 years and payable in 20 years; **g)** (S. 2) authorized the Treasury Secretary to issue coupon bonds or registered bonds up to $500,000,000, redeemable after 1867, bearing interest at 6%; **h)** (S. 2) stocks, bonds, and other securities of the U. S. are exempt from State taxes; and **i)** (S. 5) all import duties to be paid in coin or in notes payable on demand. Since the banks and government had already suspended payment, the legal tender provision regarding United States Notes made them a fiat currency [13.2-118]. But the $150,000,000 limitation would not be observed by Congress. It also caused silver coins to be hoarded per Gresham's Law. Also, Chase did not sell any of the bonds unless he could get par for them; since that was not forthcoming, he held onto gradually depreciating bonds, which in turn required the issuing of more U. S. Notes while running up the national debt - incompetence of the first order [13.2-119]. This increase in the money supply also served to depreciate the currency and raise prices, including materials necessary to fight the war. One significant effect of the legal tender law is that the United States Notes were "lawful money", meaning the banks could hold those notes as a reserve against their own notes, using them to redeem their bank notes instead of paying in coin [13.2-120]. Since the banks could sell their gold at a premium for legal tender notes, they could expand the issue of their own notes, depreciating all the currency. The legal tender United States Notes were intended as securities investments, not as circulating currency, but they were used as such [13.2-121].

6 - 8 Mar 1862: Battle of Pea Ridge (Elkhorn Tavern, AR).

17 Mar 1862: Congress passed additional financial legislation [13.2-122]: **a)** (S. 1) authorized the Treasury Secretary to purchase coin with any of the bonds or notes of the U. S;, and may issue certificates of indebtedness; and **b)** (S. 2) the Treasury demand notes (cf. 17 Jul 1861 and 12 Feb 1862) shall also be a legal tender for all public and private debts as the same the U. S. Notes (cf. 25 Feb 1862), in addition to being receivable for duties on imports.

6, 7 Apr 1862: Battle of Shiloh, TN.

27 Jun 1862: Battle of Gaines' Mill (Chickahominy River, VA).

1 Jul 1862: Congress passed a tax law designed to improve the revenue from internal excise taxation, since the previous years' legislation did not produce the anticipated results [13.2-123, 1.2-124]: a) $0.20 per gallon on whiskey, b) *ad valorem* excise taxes on rum (50%), and beer (25%); c) licenses for merchants, banker, brokers, auctioneers, hotels and a few others; d) 15 cents per pound on raw tobacco worth more than 30 cents per pound and 10 cents on lower grades of tobacco; e) *ad valorem*

excise tax on cigars between 20% and 30%; f) 3% on some manufactured goods; g) on gas for lamps; h) on advertising; i) 3% on railroad and steamboat tickets, and 0.2% for each mile traveled by each passenger; and j) stamp taxes on legal some commercial documents. The minimum income subject to the income tax was lowered from $800 to $600, and the rate was increased to 5% on incomes above $5,000. Drawbacks (refund of the excise tax) upon export were permitted on all items except cotton.

1 Jul 1862: Battle of Malvern Hill, VA.

11 Jul 1862: Congress authorized [13.2-125]: **a)** (S. 1) another $150,000,000 in United States Notes to be issued, bearing no interest, payable to the bearer on demand at the Treasury; **b)** (S. 1) receivable for all payments due to the U. S. except import duties, and interest on the debt, and legal tender of all public and private debts except on duties and interest on the debt; **c)** (S. 1) U. S. Notes could be converted to bonds at 6% interest, redeemable after 5 years, and payable in 20 years; and **d)** Treasury Secretary may exchange U. S. Notes for any U. S. bonds bearing interest at 6% payable in 20 years. The conversion provision aided the speculators and bankers: they accepted a U. S. Note, replaced it with a bank note, and then converted the U. S. Note into a 6% bond [13.2-126]. This kept the standard bank notes in circulation, although they were depreciating due to the added U. S. Notes.

14 Jul 1862: Congress passed a law [13.2-127] temporarily increasing import duties on sugar, iron, steel, drugs, and chemicals, plus an increased tonnage duty on goods imported from east of the Cape of Good Hope, unless imported directly from the manufacturing port. There was no opposition to the increase [13.2-128]: a) protection of domestic producers from direct taxation; and b) increased the revenue.

17 Jul 1862: Congress passed a law [13.2-129]: **a)** (S. 1) permitting the use of postage stamps to be receivable in payments to the U. S government for amounts less than $5, and may be exchanged for U. S. Notes in amounts less than $5; and **b)** (S. 2) prohibited banks and private corporations from issuing notes intended to circulate as money in denominations less than $1. The provision regarding stamps was necessary owing to the shortage of small change [13.2-130].

~15 Aug 1862: All specie disappeared from circulation, being replaced by paper notes and postage stamps [13.2-131].

28-30 Aug 1862: Second Battle of Bull Run (Manassas, VA).

17 Sep 1862: Battle of Antietam (Sharpsburg, MD).

13 Dec 1862: Battle of Fredericksburg, VA.

31 Dec 1862: By this time, the U. S. Notes had depreciated against gold (at 23.22 grains) by an average of 13.3%, sometimes as high as 34% [13.2-132].

13.3 Data, 1837-1862

Figures 13.3-1 and 13.3-2 show the U. S. government revenue and expenditures from 1837 to 1862.

			Internal Revenue		Miscellaneous					
			Income and		Sales of				Public Debt	
Day	Year	Customs	Profits taxes	Misc.	Public Lands	Direct Tax	Other Misc.	Postal	Sales	Total
31 Dec	1837	11,169,290	0	5,493	6,776,236	1,687	7,001,444	4,945,668	2,992,989	32,892,810
31 Dec	1838	16,158,800	0	2,467	3,730,945	0	6,410,348	4,238,733	12,716,820	43,258,116
31 Dec	1839	23,137,924	0	2,553	7,361,576	755	979,939	4,484,656	3,857,276	39,824,682
31 Dec	1840	13,499,502	0	1,682	3,411,818	0	2,567,112	4,543,521	5,589,547	29,613,184
31 Dec	1841	14,487,216	0	3,261	1,365,627	0	1,004,054	4,407,726	13,659,317	34,927,203
31 Dec	1842	18,187,908	0	495	1,335,797	0	451,995	4,546,849	14,808,735	39,331,782
30 Jun	1843	7,046,843	0	103	898,158	0	285,895	4,296,225	12,551,409	25,078,635
30 Jun	1844	26,183,570	0	1,777	2,059,939	0	1,075,419	4,237,287	1,877,847	35,435,843
30 Jun	1845	27,528,112	0	3,517	2,077,022	0	361,453	4,289,841	0	34,259,947
30 Jun	1846	26,712,667	0	2,897	2,694,452	0	289,950	3,487,199	0	33,187,167
30 Jun	1847	23,747,864	0	375	2,498,355	0	220,808	3,880,309	28,900,765	59,248,477
30 Jun	1848	31,757,070	0	375	3,328,642	0	612,610	4,555,211	21,293,780	61,547,690
30 Jun	1849	28,346,738	0	0	1,688,969	0	685,379	4,705,176	29,075,815	64,502,069
30 Jun	1850	39,668,686	0	0	1,859,894	0	2,064,308	5,499,984	4,056,500	53,149,373
30 Jun	1851	49,017,567	0	0	2,352,305	0	1,185,166	6,410,604	207,664	59,173,308
30 Jun	1852	47,339,326	0	0	2,043,239	0	464,249	5,184,526	46,300	55,077,642
30 Jun	1853	58,931,865	0	0	1,667,084	0	988,081	5,240,724	16,372	66,844,128
30 Jun	1854	64,224,190	0	0	8,470,798	0	1,105,352	6,255,586	2,001	80,057,929
30 Jun	1855	53,025,794	0	0	11,497,049	0	827,731	6,642,136	800	71,993,510
30 Jun	1856	64,022,863	0	0	8,917,644	0	1,116,190	6,920,821	200	80,977,720
30 Jun	1857	63,875,905	0	0	3,829,486	0	1,259,920	7,353,951	3,900	76,323,164
30 Jun	1858	41,789,620	0	0	3,513,715	0	1,352,029	7,486,792	23,717,300	77,859,458
30 Jun	1859	49,565,824	0	0	1,756,687	0	1,454,596	7,968,484	28,996,857	89,742,449
30 Jun	1860	53,187,511	0	0	1,778,557	0	1,088,530	8,518,067	20,786,808	85,359,475
30 Jun	1861	39,582,125	0	0	870,658	0	1,023,515	8,349,296	41,895,340	91,720,936
30 Jun	1862	49,056,397	0	0	152,203	1,795,331	915,327	8,299,820	529,760,860	589,979,942

1. The data for the revenue for 1837 to 1862 is from W. G. McAdoo, "Annual Report of the Secretary of the Treasury on the State of the Finances for the Fiscal Year Ended June 30, 1914", Washington: U. S. Government Printing Office, 1915, pp. 230-241; Treasury Document 2721. This data was modified from per Henry Morgenthau, "Annual Report of the Secretary of the Treasury on the State of the Finances for the Fiscal Year Ended June 30, 1940", Treasury Document 3111, pp. 642-649, which shows "internal reveune" broken out as income taxes and miscellaneous. It is the same data as reported previously (cf. 1914), but shows income taxes and miscellaneous taxes as separate categories.

2. Figures for 1843 are for a half-year. It is not clear why full year data is not available.

Figure 13.3-1: U. S. Government Revenue, 1837-1862

		Ordinary Disbursements								
							Interest on		Public Debt	
Day	Year	Civil & Misc.	War Dep't	Navy Dep't	Indians	Pensions	Public Debt	Postal	Retired	Total
31 Dec	1837	9,893,370	13,682,730	6,646,914	4,348,036	2,672,162	0	3,288,319	21,822	40,553,356
31 Dec	1838	7,160,664	12,897,224	6,131,580	5,504,191	2,156,057	14,996	4,430,662	5,590,723	43,886,100
31 Dec	1839	5,725,990	8,916,995	6,182,294	2,528,917	3,142,750	399,833	4,636,536	10,718,153	42,251,472
31 Dec	1840	5,995,398	7,095,267	6,113,896	2,331,794	2,603,562	174,598	4,718,235	3,912,015	32,944,769
31 Dec	1841	6,083,224	8,801,610	6,001,076	2,514,837	2,388,434	284,977	4,907,184	5,315,712	36,297,057
31 Dec	1842	6,721,927	6,610,438	8,397,242	1,199,099	1,378,931	773,549	5,728,448	7,801,990	38,611,628
31 Dec	1843	3,181,410	2,908,671	3,727,711	578,371	839,041	523,583	4,396,056	338,012	16,492,858
30 Jun	1844	5,645,183	5,218,183	6,498,199	1,256,532	2,032,008	1,833,452	4,296,512	11,158,450	37,938,523
30 Jun	1845	5,911,760	5,746,291	6,297,177	1,539,351	2,400,788	1,040,458	4,320,731	7,554,580	34,811,140
30 Jun	1846	5,901,052	10,413,370	6,455,013	1,027,693	1,811,097	842,723	4,886,268	371,100	31,708,319
30 Jun	1847	6,349,309	35,840,040	7,900,635	1,430,411	1,744,883	1,119,214	4,515,841	5,600,067	64,500,393
30 Jun	1848	5,628,629	27,688,334	9,408,476	1,252,296	1,227,496	2,390,765	4,349,072	13,036,922	64,981,993
30 Jun	1849	12,885,334	14,558,473	9,786,705	1,374,161	1,328,867	3,565,535	4,479,049	12,887,344	60,865,471
30 Jun	1850	16,043,763	9,687,024	7,904,724	1,663,591	1,866,886	3,782,393	5,212,953	3,656,335	49,817,671
30 Jun	1851	17,888,992	12,161,965	8,880,581	2,829,801	2,293,377	3,696,760	6,278,401	724,625	54,754,505
30 Jun	1852	16,462,727	8,521,506	8,918,842	3,043,576	2,401,858	4,000,297	8,149,894	2,322,356	53,821,058
30 Jun	1853	15,309,318	9,910,498	11,067,789	3,880,494	1,756,300	3,665,832	7,394,474	6,833,072	59,817,786
30 Jun	1854	23,464,799	11,722,282	10,790,096	1,550,339	1,232,665	3,070,926	9,462,931	20,434,715	81,728,756
30 Jun	1855	21,011,611	14,648,074	13,327,095	2,772,990	1,477,612	2,314,464	9,720,950	7,534,113	72,806,912
30 Jun	1856	28,594,920	16,963,160	14,074,834	2,644,263	1,296,229	1,953,822	10,119,939	3,999,991	79,647,163
30 Jun	1857	24,948,615	19,159,150	12,651,694	4,354,418	1,310,380	1,593,265	10,970,834	3,640,178	78,628,539
30 Jun	1858	21,651,093	25,679,121	14,053,264	4,978,266	1,219,768	1,652,055	12,235,715	8,079,693	89,548,979
30 Jun	1859	18,988,985	23,154,720	14,690,927	3,490,534	1,222,222	2,637,649	12,777,042	14,685,043	91,647,126
30 Jun	1860	18,088,432	16,472,202	11,514,649	2,991,121	1,100,802	3,144,120	18,407,613	13,854,250	85,573,193
30 Jun	1861	18,156,392	23,001,530	12,387,156	2,865,481	1,034,599	4,034,157	13,520,191	18,737,100	93,736,609
30 Jun	1862	17,824,134	389,173,562	42,640,353	2,327,948	852,170	13,190,344	11,861,549	96,097,322	573,967,384

1. The data for the expenditures for 1837 to 1862 is from W. G. McAdoo, "Annual Report of the Secretary of the Treasury on the State of the Finances for the Fiscal Year Ended June 30, 1914", Washington: U. S. Government Printing Office, 1915, pp. 230-241; Treasury Document 2721.

2. Figures for 1843 are for a half-year. It is not clear why full year data is not available.

Figure 13.3-2: U. S. Government Expenditures, 1837-1862

Figure 13.3-3 shows the total and per-capita national debt from 1837 to 1862. The increases from 1847 to 1850 and 1860 to 1862 are due to the Mexican and Civil Wars. Refer to the Introduction to Part 2 for a sense of wages vs. per-capita national debt.

	U. S. National Debt, 1837-1862 (USD)
Day	Year	Principal ($) [1]	Population [2]	Debt per Capita ($) [2]	Day	Year	Principal ($) [1]	Population [2]	Debt per Capita ($) [2]
31 Dec	1837	3,308,124	15,808,423	0.21	30 Jun	1850	63,452,774	23,191,876	2.74
31 Dec	1838	10,434,221	16,228,766	0.64	30 Jun	1851	68,304,796	24,017,021	2.84
31 Dec	1839	3,573,344	16,649,110	0.21	30 Jun	1852	66,199,342	24,842,165	2.66
31 Dec	1840	5,250,876	17,069,453	0.31	30 Jun	1853	59,804,661	25,667,310	2.33
31 Dec	1841	13,594,481	17,681,695	0.77	30 Jun	1854	42,243,765	26,492,454	1.59
31 Dec	1842	20,201,226	18,293,938	1.10	30 Jun	1855	35,588,499	27,317,599	1.30
30 Jun	1843	23,461,652	18,906,180	1.24	30 Jun	1856	31,974,081	28,142,743	1.14
30 Jun	1844	23,461,653	19,518,422	1.20	30 Jun	1857	28,701,375	28,967,888	0.99
30 Jun	1845	15,925,303	20,130,665	0.79	30 Jun	1858	44,913,424	29,793,032	1.51
30 Jun	1846	15,550,203	20,742,907	0.75	30 Jun	1859	58,498,381	30,618,177	1.91
30 Jun	1847	38,826,535	21,355,149	1.82	30 Jun	1860	64,843,831	31,443,321	2.06
30 Jun	1848	47,044,862	21,967,391	2.14	30 Jun	1861	90,582,147	32,154,826	2.82
30 Jun	1849	63,661,859	22,579,634	2.82	30 Jun	1862	524,177,955	32,866,331	15.95

1. Public debt data from 1837 to 1862 is from the Annual Report of the Secretary of the Treasury, 1980, pp. 61, 62.
2. Population values are based on the dicennial census from the Census Bureau, and linearly interpolated. Per-capita is based on these values.

Figure 13.3-3: National Debt and Per-Capita Share Thereof, 1837-1862

The next set of Figures show the condition of the banking system. Treasury Secretary Morrill gave an assessment as to the accuracy of this data in 1876 [13.3-1]:

"From the information contained in the reports on the condition of the banks, made annually to Congress in compliance with the resolution of 1832, before mentioned, carefully compiled tables, by States, have been prepared in this Office, which appear in the appendix to this report. These tables, with the exception of that for Massachusetts, commence with the year 1834, which is the first year for which an aggregate statement that is even measurably complete is given, and are brought down to the year 1863, a summary of the condition of all the banks in each year being also given. The statistics derived from these reports are not, however, perfectly reliable, and the aggregates for the Southern States in the years 1862-1863 have been estimated to be the same as for the year 1861.

One source of difficulty in determining for any specified date the condition of the banks of the country under the old system lies in the fact that the dates for which reports were required were not uniform in the several States. Each State determined for itself the time for making these reports; and as a consequence the dates of the returns, which are given in the tables mentioned, differ in certain years and for certain States by a period of six and even of nine months. Nor is it even certain that the returns of a given State include, in any instance, all the banks of that State, unless it be those of New England or of the State of New York."

This is the best data available, as far as I know. Figures 13.3-4 and 13.3-5 show the assets and liabilities of the former second Bank of the United States, which continued operation as a re-chartered State bank until it failed in 1840.

Year	Loans & Discounts	"Stocks" (i.e, US Securities)	Real Estate	Banking Houses	Due by European Bankers	Due from State banks	Notes of State Banks	Specie	Total Assets
	Assets of the former second Bank of the United States, 1837-1840 (USD) [1]
1837	57,393,709	0	816,855	420,244	0	2,284,598	1,206,754	2,638,449	64,760,609
1838	45,256,571	14,862,108	1,061,663	443,100	0	3,657,261	866,597	3,770,842	69,918,142
1839	41,618,637	17,957,497	1,054,523	424,382	0	5,833,000	1,791,580	4,153,607	72,833,226
1840	36,839,593	16,316,419	1,228,630	610,504	0	7,469,422	1,383,686	1,469,674	65,317,928

1. Annual Report of the Comptroller of the Currency, 1876, p. LXXXIII. (cf. 1876 Treasury Report, p. 193)

Figure 13.3-4: Assets of the Former Bank of the United States, 1837-1840

Liabilities of the former second Bank of the United States, 1837 - 1840 (USD) [1]							
Year	Notes in Circulation	Deposits	Due to State Banks	Due to Other Banks	Other Liabilities	Capital	Total Liabilities	Error (%)
1837	11,447,968	2,332,409	2,284,598	6,926,364	0	35,000,000	57,991,339	10.45
1838	6,768,067	2,616,713	4,957,291	12,492,034	7,987,434	35,000,000	69,821,539	0.14
1839	5,982,621	6,770,394	3,061,895	12,770,000	9,260,351	35,000,000	72,845,261	-0.02
1840	6,695,861	3,338,521	4,155,366	4,971,619	8,119,468	35,000,000	62,280,835	4.65
1. Annual Report of the Comptroller of the Currency, 1876, p. LXXXIII. (cf. 1876 Treasury Report, p. 193)								

Figure 13.3-5: Liabilities of the Former Bank of the United States, 1837-1840

Figures 13.3-6 and 13.3-7 show the assets and liabilities of the State-chartered banks from 1837 to 1840.

Assets of State Banks, 1837 - 1840 (USD) [1]									
Year	No. of Banks	Loans and Discounts	"Stocks" (i.e., U. S. Securities)	Due from Other Banks	Real Estate	Notes of Other Banks	Specie Funds	Specie	Other Assets	Total Assets
1837	788	525,115,702	12,407,112	59,663,910	19,064,451	36,533,527	5,366,500	37,915,340	10,423,630	706,490,172
1838	829	485,631,687	33,908,604	58,195,153	19,075,731	24,964,257	904,006	35,184,112	24,194,117	682,057,667
1839	840	492,278,015	36,128,464	52,898,357	16,607,832	27,372,966	3,612,567	45,132,673	28,352,248	702,383,122
1840	901	462,896,523	42,411,750	41,140,184	29,181,919	20,797,892	3,623,874	33,105,155	24,592,580	657,749,877
1. Annual Report of the Comptroller of the Currency, 1876, p. XCIV. (cf. 1876 Treasury Report, p. 159)										

Figure 13.3-6: Assets of the State Banks, 1837-1840

Liabilities of State Banks, 1837 - 1840 (USD) [1]							
Year	Notes in Circulation	Deposits	Due to Other Banks	Capital	Other Liabilities	Total Liabilities	Error (%)
1837	149,185,890	127,397,185	62,421,118	290,772,091	36,560,289	666,336,573	5.68
1838	116,138,910	84,691,184	61,015,692	317,636,778	59,995,679	639,478,243	6.24
1839	135,170,995	90,240,146	53,135,508	327,132,512	62,946,248	668,625,409	4.81
1840	106,968,572	75,696,857	44,159,615	358,442,692	43,275,183	628,542,919	4.44
1. Annual Report of the Comptroller of the Currency, 1876, p. XCIV. (cf. 1876 Treasury Report, p. 159)							

Figure 13.3-7: Liabilities of the State Banks, 1837-1840

Figures 13.3-8 and 13.3-9 show the combined assets and liabilities of the State-chartered banks and the former second Bank of the United States from 1837 to 1840.

Combined Assets of the former second Bank of United States and State Banks, 1837-1840 (USD) [1, 2, 3]									
Year	No. of Banks	Loans and Discounts	"Stocks" (i.e., U. S. Securities)	Due from Other Banks	Real Estate	Notes of Other Banks	Specie Funds	Specie	Other Assets	Total Assets
1837	789	582,509,411	12,407,112	61,948,508	20,301,550	37,740,281	5,366,500	40,553,789	10,423,630	771,250,781
1838	830	530,888,258	48,770,712	61,852,414	20,580,494	25,830,854	904,006	38,954,954	24,194,117	751,975,809
1839	841	533,896,652	54,085,961	58,731,357	18,086,737	29,164,546	3,612,567	49,286,280	28,352,248	775,216,348
1840	902	499,736,116	58,728,169	48,609,606	31,021,053	22,181,578	3,623,874	34,574,829	24,592,580	723,067,805
1. Annual Report of the Comptroller of the Currency, 1876, p. LXXXIII. (cf. 1876 Treasury Report, p. 193)										
2. Annual Report of the Comptroller of the Currency, 1876, p. XCIV. (cf. 1876 Treasury Report, p. 159)										
3. The charter of the second Bank of the US expired in 1836, but it continued operations as State chartered bank until it failed in 1840.										

Figure 13.3-8: Combined Assets of the Former Bank of the United States and State Banks, 1837-1840

Combined Liabilities of the former second Bank of United States and State Banks, 1837-1840 (USD) [1, 2]							
Year	Notes in Circulation	Deposits	Due to Other Banks	Capital	Other Liabilities	Total Liabilities	Error (%)
1837	160,633,858	129,729,594	71,632,080	325,772,091	36,560,289	724,327,912	6.08
1838	122,906,977	87,307,897	78,465,017	352,636,778	67,983,113	709,299,782	5.68
1839	141,153,616	97,010,540	68,967,403	362,132,512	72,206,599	741,470,670	4.35
1840	113,664,433	79,035,378	53,286,600	393,442,692	51,394,651	690,823,754	4.46
1. Annual Report of the Comptroller of the Currency, 1876, p. LXXXIII. (cf. 1876 Treasury Report, p. 193)							
2. Annual Report of the Comptroller of the Currency, 1876, p. XCIV. (cf. 1876 Treasury Report, p. 159)							
3. The charter of the second Bank of the US expired in 1836, but it continued operations as State bank until it failed in 1840.							

Figure 13.3-9: Combined Liabilities of the Former Bank of the United States and State Banks, 1837-1840

Figures 13.3-10 and 13.3-11 show the assets and liabilities of the State-chartered banks for the interval 1841 to 1862, in dollars. The data for 1852 is unreliable.

Assets of State Banks, 1841 - 1862 (USD) [1, 2]									
Year	No. of Banks	Loans and Discounts	"Stocks" (US Securities)	Due from Other Banks	Real Estate	Notes of Other Banks	Specie Funds	Specie	Other Assets	Total Assets
1841	784	386,487,662	64,811,135	47,877,045	33,524,444	25,643,447	3,168,708	34,813,958	11,816,609	608,143,008
1842	692	323,957,569	24,585,540	30,752,496	33,341,988	19,432,744	3,115,327	28,440,423	8,186,317	471,812,404
1843	691	254,544,937	28,380,050	20,666,264	22,826,807	13,306,677	6,578,375	33,515,806	13,343,599	393,162,515
1844	696	264,905,814	22,858,570	35,860,930	22,529,863	11,672,473	6,729,980	49,898,269	12,153,693	426,609,592
1845	707	288,617,131	20,356,070	29,619,272	22,177,270	12,040,760	6,786,026	44,241,242	10,072,466	433,910,237
1846	707	312,114,404	21,486,834	31,689,946	19,099,000	12,914,423	8,386,478	42,012,095	7,913,591	455,616,771
1847	715	310,282,945	20,158,351	31,788,641	21,219,865	13,112,467	13,789,780	35,132,516	12,206,112	457,690,677
1848	751	344,476,582	26,498,054	38,904,525	20,530,955	16,427,716	10,489,822	46,369,765	8,229,682	511,927,101
1849	782	332,323,195	23,571,575	32,228,407	17,491,809	12,708,016	8,680,483	43,619,368	7,965,463	478,588,316
1850	824	364,204,078	20,606,759	41,631,855	20,582,166	16,303,289	11,603,245	45,379,345	11,949,548	532,260,285
1851	879	413,756,799	22,388,389	50,718,015	20,219,724	17,196,083	15,341,196	48,671,048	8,935,972	597,227,226
1852 [3]	913	429,761,000	23,254,000	52,680,000	Note 3	Total: 84,350,000 (Note 3)			30,283,000	620,328,000
1853	750	408,943,758	22,284,692	48,920,258	10,180,071	30,431,189	0	47,138,592	3,873,571	571,772,131
1854	1208	557,397,779	44,359,330	55,516,085	22,367,472	22,659,066	25,579,253	59,410,253	7,589,830	794,879,068
1855	1307	576,144,758	52,727,082	55,738,735	24,073,801	23,429,518	21,935,738	53,944,546	8,734,540	816,728,718
1856	1398	634,183,280	49,485,215	62,639,725	20,865,867	24,779,049	19,937,710	59,314,063	8,882,516	880,087,425
1857	1416	684,456,887	59,272,329	65,849,205	26,124,522	28,124,008	25,081,641	58,349,838	5,920,336	953,178,766
1858	1422	583,165,242	60,305,260	58,052,802	28,755,834	22,447,436	15,380,441	74,412,832	6,075,906	848,595,753
1859	1476	657,183,799	63,502,449	78,244,987	25,976,407	18,858,289	26,808,822	104,537,818	8,323,041	983,435,612
1860	1562	691,945,580	70,344,343	67,235,457	30,782,131	25,502,567	19,331,521	83,594,537	11,123,171	999,859,307
1861	1601	696,778,421	74,004,879	58,793,900	30,748,927	21,903,902	29,297,878	87,674,507	16,657,511	1,015,859,925
1862	1492	646,677,780	99,010,987	65,256,596	32,326,649	25,253,589	27,827,971	102,146,215	13,648,006	1,012,147,793

1. Annual Report of the Comptroller of the Currency, 1876, p. XCIV. (cf. 1876 Treasury Report, p. 159)
2. A note to the table in the 1876 Report states that the returns from 1853 are incomplete. There is no data given for 1852.
3. Data for 1852 estimated per Annual Report of the Comptroller of the Currency, 1931, Table 94 (p. 1018). Real estate is included under "other assets", and notes of other banks, specie funds, and specie are combined as "cash".

Figure 13.3-10: Assets of the State Banks, 1841-1862

Liabilities of State Banks, 1841 - 1862 (USD) [1, 2]							
Year	Notes in Circulation	Deposits	Due to Other Banks	Capital	Other Liabilities	Total Liabilities	Error (%)
1841	107,290,214	64,890,101	42,861,889	313,608,959	42,896,226	571,547,389	6.02
1842	83,734,011	62,408,870	25,863,827	260,171,797	12,775,106	444,953,611	5.69
1843	58,563,608	56,168,628	21,456,523	228,861,948	7,357,033	372,407,740	5.28
1844	75,167,646	84,550,785	31,998,024	210,872,056	5,842,010	408,430,521	4.26
1845	89,608,711	88,020,646	26,337,440	206,045,969	5,853,902	415,866,668	4.16
1846	105,552,427	96,913,070	28,218,568	196,894,309	5,331,572	432,909,946	4.98
1847	105,519,766	91,792,533	28,539,888	203,070,622	4,706,077	433,628,886	5.26
1848	128,596,091	103,226,177	39,414,371	204,838,175	5,501,401	481,576,215	5.93
1849	114,743,415	91,178,623	30,095,366	207,309,361	6,706,357	450,033,122	5.97
1850	131,366,526	109,586,595	36,717,451	217,317,211	8,835,309	503,823,092	5.34
1851	155,165,251	128,957,712	46,416,928	227,807,553	6,438,327	564,785,771	5.43
1852 [3]	161,167,000	182,158,000	Note 3	236,620,000	40,383,000	620,328,000	0.00
1853	146,072,780	145,553,876	49,625,262	207,908,519	28,024,350	577,184,787	-0.95
1854	204,689,207	188,188,744	50,322,162	301,376,071	13,439,276	758,015,460	4.64
1855	186,952,223	190,400,342	45,156,697	332,177,288	15,599,623	770,286,173	5.69
1856	195,747,950	212,705,662	52,719,956	343,874,272	12,227,867	817,275,707	7.14
1857	214,778,822	230,351,352	57,674,333	370,834,686	19,816,850	893,456,043	6.27
1858	155,208,344	185,932,049	51,169,875	394,622,799	14,166,713	801,099,780	5.60
1859	193,306,818	259,568,278	68,215,651	401,976,242	15,048,427	938,115,416	4.61
1860	207,102,477	253,802,129	55,932,918	421,880,095	14,661,815	953,379,434	4.65
1861	202,005,767	257,229,562	61,275,256	429,592,713	23,258,004	973,361,302	4.18
1862	183,792,079	296,322,408	61,144,052	418,139,741	21,633,093	981,031,373	3.07

1. Annual Report of the Comptroller of the Currency, 1876, p. XCIV. (cf. 1876 Treasury Report, p. 159)
2. A note to the 1876 Report table states that the returns from 1853 are incomplete. There is no data given for 1852.
3. Data for 1852 estimated per Annual Report of the Comptroller of the Currency, 1931, Table 94 (p. 1018). "Due to Other Banks" is included under "Other Liabilities".

Figure 13.3-11: Liabilities of the State Banks, 1841-1862

Figure 13.3-12 shows the behavior of the money supply from 1837 to 1862. Column 4 has two purposes: from 1837 to 1840, it shows the notes of the Bank of the United States; in 1862, it shows the combination of United States Notes (a.k.a. "greenback") and Treasury Notes that were issued during the Civil War. The United States Notes were legal tender as "lawful money", and did not bear interest. Note that these figures are in millions of dollars.

Treasury Notes were authorized during this period prior to 1862 (cf. 12 Oct 1837, 31 May 1838, 2 Mar 1839, 31 Mar 1840, 15 Feb 1941, 31 Jan 1842, 31 Aug 1842, 3 Mar 1843, 22 Jul 1846, 28 Jan 1847, and 2 Mar 1861 (repayment)). These were actually interest-bearing bonds (cf. 23 Jul 1846) and did not circulate as currency. Therefore, they do not appear in the tabulation of the money supply. Circulating Treasury Notes do not appear until 1862.

U. S. Money Supply, 1837-1862 (millions USD)																
1	2	3	4	5	6	7	8	9	10	11	12	13	14	15	16	17
Year (~30 Jun)	Number of Banks [1]	Estimated State Bank Notes [1, 2]	Notes of Second Bank of U. S. or Other [3, 4]	Total Notes in Circulation	Total Specie in U.S. [5]	Specie in Treasury [5]	Specie Outside Treasury [6]	Total Notes & Specie Outside Treasury	Cash Held in All Banks [7]	Notes & Specie Outside Banks	Estimated State Bank Deposits [8]	Deposits of Second Bank of U. S. [3]	Total Estimated Deposits	Estimated Interbank Trans-actions [9]	Estimated Deposits Adjusted	Estimated Total Money Supply
1837	788	149.186	11.448	160.634	73.000	5.000	68.000	228.634	79.815	148.819	189.818	2.332	192.150	18.831	173.320	322.139
1838	829	116.139	6.768	122.907	87.500	5.000	82.500	205.407	61.052	144.355	145.707	2.617	148.324	14.536	133.788	278.143
1839	840	135.171	5.983	141.154	87.000	2.467	84.533	225.687	76.118	149.569	143.376	6.770	150.146	14.714	135.432	285.001
1840	901	106.969	6.696	113.664	83.000	3.663	79.337	193.001	57.527	135.474	119.856	3.339	123.195	12.073	111.121	246.596
1841	784	107.290	0.000	107.290	80.000	0.987	79.013	186.303	63.626	122.677	107.752	0.000	107.752	10.560	97.192	219.869
1842	692	83.734	0.000	83.734	80.000	0.230	79.770	163.504	50.988	112.516	88.273	0.000	88.273	8.651	79.622	192.138
1843	691	58.564	0.000	58.564	90.000	1.449	88.551	147.114	53.401	93.713	77.625	0.000	77.625	7.607	70.018	163.731
1844	696	75.168	0.000	75.168	100.000	7.857	92.143	167.310	68.301	99.009	116.549	0.000	116.549	11.422	105.127	204.136
1845	707	89.609	0.000	89.609	96.000	7.658	88.342	177.950	63.068	114.882	114.358	0.000	114.358	11.207	103.151	218.033
1846	707	105.552	0.000	105.552	97.000	9.126	87.874	193.426	63.313	130.113	125.132	0.000	125.132	12.263	112.869	242.982
1847	715	105.520	0.000	105.520	120.000	1.701	118.299	223.819	62.035	161.784	120.332	0.000	120.332	11.793	108.539	270.323
1848	751	128.506	0.000	128.506	112.000	8.101	103.899	232.405	73.287	159.118	142.641	0.000	142.641	13.979	128.662	287.780
1849	782	114.743	0.000	114.743	120.000	2.185	117.815	232.558	65.008	167.550	121.274	0.000	121.274	11.885	109.389	276.940
1850	824	131.367	0.000	131.367	154.000	6.605	147.395	278.762	73.286	205.476	146.304	0.000	146.304	14.338	131.966	337.442
1851	879	155.165	0.000	155.165	186.000	10.912	175.088	330.254	81.208	249.046	175.375	0.000	175.375	17.187	158.188	407.234
1852		171.673	0.000	171.673	204.000	14.632	189.368	361.041	84.350	276.691	182.158	0.000	182.158	17.851	164.307	440.997
1853		188.181	0.000	188.181	236.000	21.943	214.057	402.238	77.570	324.668	195.179	0.000	195.179	19.128	176.051	500.720
1854	1,208	204.689	0.000	204.689	241.000	20.138	220.862	425.551	107.649	317.902	238.511	0.000	238.511	23.374	215.137	533.039
1855	1,307	186.952	0.000	186.952	250.000	18.932	231.068	418.020	99.310	318.710	235.557	0.000	235.557	23.085	212.472	531.183
1856	1,398	195.748	0.000	195.748	250.000	19.901	230.099	425.847	104.031	321.816	265.426	0.000	265.426	26.012	239.414	561.230
1857	1,416	214.779	0.000	214.779	260.000	17.710	242.290	457.069	111.555	345.514	288.026	0.000	288.026	28.227	259.799	605.313
1858	1,422	155.208	0.000	155.208	260.000	6.398	253.602	408.810	112.241	296.569	237.102	0.000	237.102	23.236	213.866	510.435
1859	1,476	193.307	0.000	193.307	250.000	4.339	245.661	438.968	150.205	288.763	327.784	0.000	327.784	32.123	295.661	584.424
1860	1,562	207.102	0.000	207.102	0.000	0.000	228.305	435.407	128.429	306.978	309.735	0.000	309.735	30.354	279.381	586.359
1861	1,601	202.006	0.000	202.006	0.000	0.000	282.400	484.406	138.876	345.530	318.505	0.000	318.505	31.213	287.292	632.821
1862	1,492	183.792	125.915	309.707	0.000	0.000	296.000	605.707	155.228	450.479	357.466	0.000	357.466	35.032	322.434	772.913

1. Number of banks, specie in the U. S. amd specie in Treasury from 1836 to 1859 per Annual Report of the Comptroller of the Currency, 1896, Vol. 1, p. 544.

2. State bank notes for 1837 to 1862 per Annual Report of the Comptroller of the Currency, 1876, p. XCV.

3. Notes and deposits of the second Bank of the United States, 1837-1840 per Annual Report of the Comptroller of the Currency, 1876, p. LXXXIII; Bank of US chartered only in PA after 1837.

4. "Other" bank notes for 1862 include U. S. Notes (greenbacks) and "Other U. S. currency" (Treasury notes). The value for 1862 is from Annual Report of the Secretary of the Treasury, 1947, p. 485.

5. Total specie in the U. S. and specie in the Treasury for 1837 to 1859 from the Annual Report of the Comptroller of the Currency, 1896, Vol. 1, p. 544 (Table 35).

6. Net specie in circulation for 1860 to 1862 from the Annual Report of the Secretary of the Treasury, 1947, p. 485 (Table 90). It includes gold coin, subsidiary silver, and standard silver dollars.

7. Cash held in all banks per the Annual Report of the Comptroller of the Currency, 1931, p. 1023-1025 (Table 96).

8. State bank deposits per the Annual Report of the Comptroller of the Currency, 1931, p. 1018, (Table 94).

9. Interbank from 1837 to 1862 based on average of interbank to total deposits from 1914 to 1940 (0.098).

Figure 13.3-12: Total Money Supply, 1837-1862

Figures 13.3-13 and 13.3-14 show the gold coinage and silver and minor coinage of the U. S. during this period. It was not until 1850 that the $20 double Eagles were coined, although they had been defined by the Coinage Act of 1792 (cf. 2 Apr 1792). Also, gold dollars were not authorized until 1849 (cf. 3 Mar 1849).

Gold Coinage of the U. S. , 1837 - 1862 (USD)							
Year	$20 Double Eagles ($)	$10 Eagles ($)	$5 Half Eagles ($)	Three Dollar ($)	$2.50 Quarter Eagles ($)	Gold Dollars ($)	Total ($)
1837			1,035,605.00		112,700.00		1,148,305.00
1838		72,000.00	1,600,420.00		137,345.00		1,809,765.00
1839		382,480.00	802,745.00		191,622.50		1,376,847.50
1840		473,380.00	1,048,530.00		153,572.50		1,675,482.50
1841		656,310.00	380,945.00		54,602.50		1,091,857.50
1842		1,089,070.00	655,330.00		85,007.50		1,829,407.50
1843		2,506,240.00	4,275,425.00		1,327,132.50		8,108,797.50
1844		1,250,610.00	4,087,715.00		89,345.00		5,427,670.00
1845		736,530.00	2,743,640.00		276,277.50		3,756,447.50
1846		1,018,750.00	2,736,155.00		279,272.50		4,034,177.50
1847		14,337,580.00	5,382,685.00		482,060.00		20,202,325.00
1848		1,813,340.00	1,863,560.00		98,612.50		3,775,512.50
1849		6,775,180.00	1,184,645.00		111,147.50	936,789.00	9,007,761.50
1850	26,225,220.00	3,489,510.00	860,160.00		895,547.50	511,301.00	31,981,738.50
1851	48,043,100.00	4,393,280.00	2,651,955.00		3,867,337.50	3,658,820.00	62,614,492.50
1852	44,860,520.00	2,811,060.00	3,689,635.00		3,283,827.50	2,201,145.00	56,846,187.50
1853	26,645,520.00	2,522,530.00	2,305,095.00		3,519,615.00	4,384,149.00	39,376,909.00
1854	18,052,340.00	2,305,760.00	1,513,235.00	491,214.00	1,896,397.50	1,657,016.00	25,915,962.50
1855	25,046,820.00	1,487,010.00	1,257,090.00	171,465.00	600,700.00	824,883.00	29,387,968.00
1856	30,437,560.00	1,429,900.00	1,806,665.00	181,530.00	1,213,117.50	1,788,996.00	36,857,768.50
1857	28,797,500.00	481,060.00	1,232,970.00	104,673.00	796,235.00	801,602.00	32,214,040.00
1858	21,873,480.00	343,210.00	439,770.00	6,399.00	144,082.50	131,472.00	22,938,413.50
1859	13,782,840.00	253,930.00	361,235.00	46,914.00	142,220.00	193,431.00	14,780,570.00
1860	22,584,400.00	278,830.00	352,365.00	42,465.00	164,360.00	51,234.00	23,473,654.00
1861	74,989,060.00	1,287,330.00	3,322,130.00	18,216.00	3,241,295.00	527,490.00	83,385,521.00
1862	18,926,120.00	234,950.00	69,825.00	17,355.00	300,882.50	1,326,865.00	20,875,997.50
Totals	400,264,480.00	52,429,830.00	47,659,530.00	1,080,231.00	23,464,315.00	18,995,193.00	543,893,579.00
Source: Annual Report of the Director of the Mint, 1895, 28 Nov 1895, Treasury Document No. 1829, pp. 286-293 (Table XLIV).							

Figure 13.3-13: Gold Coins Minted by the U. S., 1837-1862

Silver and Copper Coinage of the U. S., 1837 - 1862 (USD)										
	Silver ($)								Minor ($)	
Year	Trade Dollars	Dollars	Half Dollars	Quarters	Twenty-cents	Dimes	Half-dimes	Three-cents	Cents & Half-Cents	Total ($)
1837			1,814,910.00	63,100.00		104,200.00	113,800.00		55,583.00	2,151,593.00
1838			1,773,000.00	208,000.00		239,493.40	112,750.00		63,702.00	2,396,945.40
1839		300.00	1,748,768.00	122,786.50		229,638.70	103,285.00		31,286.61	2,236,064.81
1840		61,005.00	1,145,054.00	153,331.75		253,358.00	113,954.25		24,627.00	1,751,330.00
1841		173,000.00	355,500.00	143,000.00		363,000.00	98,250.00		15,973.57	1,148,723.57
1842		184,618.00	1,484,882.00	214,250.00		390,750.00	58,250.00		23,833.90	2,356,583.90
1843		165,100.00	3,056,000.00	403,400.00		152,000.00	58,250.00		24,283.20	3,859,033.20
1844		20,000.00	1,885,500.00	290,300.00		7,250.00	32,500.00		23,987.52	2,259,537.52
1845		24,500.00	1,341,500.00	230,500.00		198,500.00	78,200.00		38,948.04	1,912,148.04
1846		169,600.00	2,257,000.00	127,500.00		3,130.00	1,350.00		41,208.00	2,599,788.00
1847		140,750.00	1,870,000.00	275,500.00		24,500.00	63,700.00		61,836.69	2,436,286.69
1848		15,000.00	1,880,000.00	36,500.00		45,150.00	63,400.00		64,157.09	2,104,207.09
1849		62,600.00	1,781,000.00	85,000.00		113,900.00	72,450.00		41,984.32	2,156,934.32
1850		47,500.00	1,341,000.00	150,700.00		244,150.00	82,250.00		44,467.50	1,910,067.50
1851		1,300.00	301,375.00	62,000.00		142,650.00	82,050.00	185,022.00	99,635.43	874,032.43
1852		1,100.00	110,565.00	68,265.00		196,550.00	63,025.00	559,905.00	50,630.04	1,050,040.04
1853		46,110.00	2,430,354.00	4,146,555.00		1,327,301.00	785,251.00	342,000.00	67,059.78	9,144,630.78
1854		33,140.00	4,111,000.00	3,466,000.00		624,000.00	365,000.00	20,130.00	42,638.35	8,661,908.35
1855		26,000.00	2,288,725.00	857,350.00		207,500.00	117,500.00	4,170.00	16,030.79	3,517,275.79
1856		63,500.00	1,903,500.00	2,120,500.00		703,000.00	299,000.00	43,740.00	27,106.78	5,160,346.78
1857		94,000.00	1,482,000.00	2,726,500.00		712,000.00	433,000.00	31,260.00	178,010.46	5,656,770.46
1858			5,998,000.00	2,002,250.00		189,000.00	258,000.00	48,120.00	246,000.00	8,741,370.00
1859		636,500.00	2,074,000.00	421,000.00		97,000.00	45,000.00	10,950.00	364,000.00	3,648,450.00
1860		733,930.00	1,032,850.00	312,350.00		78,700.00	92,950.00	8,610.00	205,660.00	2,465,050.00
1861		78,500.00	2,078,950.00	1,237,650.00		209,650.00	164,050.00	14,940.00	101,000.00	3,884,740.00
1862		12,090.00	802,175.00	249,887.50		102,830.00	74,627.50	10,906.50	280,750.00	1,533,266.50
Totals	0.00	2,790,143.00	48,347,608.00	20,174,175.75	0.00	6,959,201.10	3,831,842.75	1,279,753.50	2,234,400.07	85,617,124.17
Source: Annual Report of the Director of the Mint, 1895, 28 Nov 1895, Treasury Document No. 1829, pp. 286-293 (Table XLIV).										

Figure 13.3-14: Silver and Minor (Copper) Coins Minted by the U. S., 1837-1862

Figure 13.3-15 shows the CPI, total money supply, and per-capita money supply for this period.

Year	CPI [1] (1913 = 100)	Total Money Supply [5] (USD)	Population [6]	Per Capita Money Supply (USD)	Annual Rate of Change in CPI (%)	Annual Rate of Change in Per-Capita Money Supply (%)
1837	99.662	322,138,527	15,808,423	20.38	-0.701	1.665
1838	96.077	278,142,966	16,228,766	17.14	-3.664	-17.309
1839	99.664	285,000,701	16,649,110	17.12	3.665	-0.121
1840	86.531	246,595,807	17,069,453	14.45	-14.130	-16.967
1841	84.951	219,869,173	17,681,695	12.43	-1.843	-14.996
1842	79.363	192,137,773	18,293,938	10.50	-6.805	-16.886
1843	75.619	163,730,886	18,906,180	8.66	-4.832	-19.291
1844	76.234	204,136,464	19,518,422	10.46	0.810	18.869
1845	77.542	218,033,321	20,130,665	10.83	1.701	3.497
1846	79.668	242,982,052	20,742,907	11.71	2.705	7.838
1847	81.390	270,322,979	21,355,149	12.66	2.138	7.754
1848	76.869	287,779,920	21,967,391	13.10	-5.714	3.431
1849	75.402	276,939,599	22,579,634	12.27	-1.928	-6.589
1850	78.586	337,442,190	23,191,876	14.55	4.136	17.084
1851	79.653	407,233,855	24,017,021	16.96	1.350	15.303
1852	78.971	440,997,380	24,842,165	17.75	-0.861	4.587
1853	86.614	500,719,565	25,667,310	19.51	9.239	9.433
1854	87.534	533,039,162	26,492,454	20.12	1.056	3.091
1855	88.455	531,182,661	27,317,599	19.44	1.047	-3.416
1856	87.855	561,229,877	28,142,743	19.94	-0.681	2.527
1857	88.869	605,313,160	28,967,888	20.90	1.147	4.672
1858	80.463	510,435,032	29,793,032	17.13	-9.937	-19.857
1859	79.546	584,423,710	30,618,177	19.09	-1.145	10.804
1860	79.125	586,359,447	31,443,321	18.65	-0.531	-2.329
1861	78.911	632,821,277	32,154,826	19.68	-0.270	5.388
1862	90.861	772,913,411	32,866,331	23.52	14.101	17.809

1. CPI is the average of L-1 and L-15 data, both re-aligned to 1913 as a reference.
2. L-1 data 1791 to 1938 (Snyder-Tucker) is a general price index (wholesale prices, wages, cost of living and rents).
3. L-15 data 1801 to 1945 includes wholesale prices, all commodities.
4. L1 and L-15 from Historical Statistics of the United States, 1789-1945, A Supplement to the Statistical Abstract of the United States, Bureau of the Census, US Department of Commerce, Washington, DC, 1949.
5. See notes in money supply data for sources.
6. Population is linearly interpolated from Census results.

Figure 13.3-15: Money Supply and CPI, 1837-1862

Figure 13.3-16 shows a summary the CPI and per-capita money supply. Three distinct intervals are evident: 1837 to 1843, 1843 to 1857, and 1857 to 1862. The average annual change in CPI and money supply for 1837 to 1843 are -4.6% and -14.2% respectively; for 1843 to 1857, +1.15% and +6.29% respectively, and for 1857 to 1862, 0.4% and 2.36% respectively.

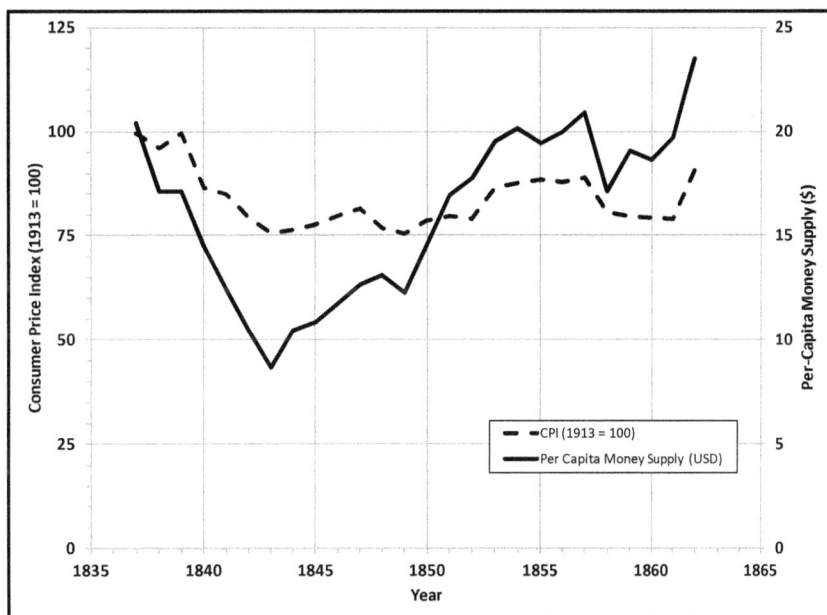

Figure 13.3-16: CPI and Per-Capita Summary, 1837-1862

Figure 13.3-17 shows the approximate median income index, consumer price index, and standard of living index for this period. See the Introduction to Part 2 for cautions regarding these curves.

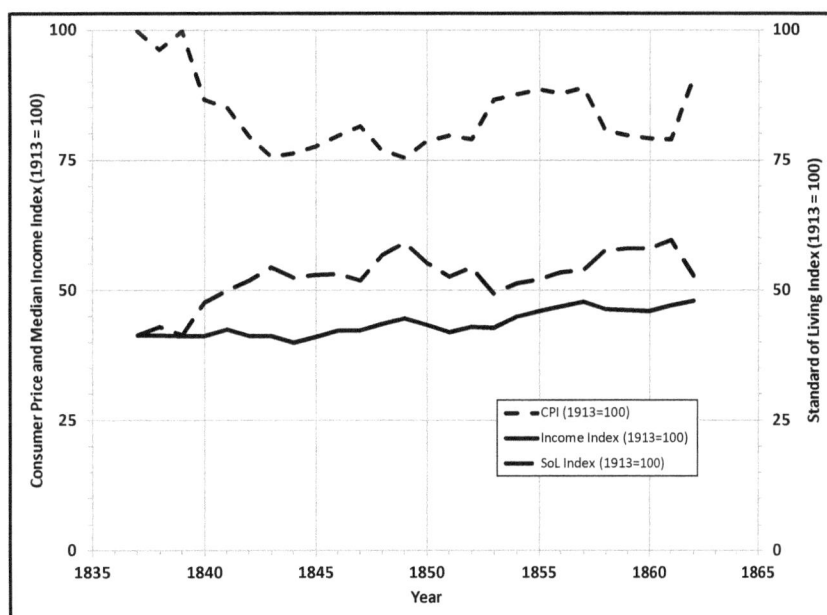

Figure 13.3-17: Median Income, Consumer Price, and Standard of Living Indices, 1837-1862

13.4 Summary, 1837-1862

The amount of loans authorized to fund the Civil War to the end of 1862 came to $500,000,000 (cf. 25 Feb 1862). This is in addition to $300,000,000 in United States Notes (greenbacks): a) $150,000,000 on 25 Feb 1862; and b) $150,000,000 on 11 Jul 1862.

Congress considered absorbing the debts of the States and adding it to the national debt in 1842 [13.4-1]. The States had increased their indebtedness by pursuing building programs, mostly railroads, canals, and paving roads. The States' debts came to about $200,000,000, and most of it was held by foreigners. Some of the States were in default, and many claimed that the federal government should assume the debt for two reasons: a) since it would restore credit and serve to revive industry; and b) an example had been set for doing so in 1790. Ultimately Congress decided not to incorporate those debts since the benefits would have been distributed unequally: some States were in default on large debts, while others were debt-free.

The federal government's credit had been ruined under the Buchanan administration [13.4-2]: increasing debt, and a reduction in revenues, caused mostly by the reduction of tariffs. By 1861 at the start of the Civil War, there was no money in the Treasury, and the government found it necessary to issue unbacked paper money in the form of U. S. Notes and Treasury Notes, the importance of which will be shown in Chapter 15.

References

[13.1-1]   William Graham Sumner, *History of American Currency*, 1874, p. 123

[13.1-2]   Clifton H. Kreps, Jr., *Money, Banking and Monetary Policy*, NY: The Ronald Press Co., 1962, pp. 161, 162

[13.1-3]   op. cit., Sumner, pp. 118, 119, 124

[13.1-4]   Albert S. Bolles, *A Financial History of the United States*, NY: Augustus M. Kelley (1969), Vol. 2, p. 580

[13.1-5]   op. cit., Bolles, Vol. 2, pp. 556, 557

[13.1-6]   op. cit., Kreps, p. 155

[13.2-1]   Text of "An Act supplementary to the act entitled 'An act establishing a mint, and regulating the coin of the United States'", 24th Congress, Session 2, Chapter 3, 18 Jan 1837

[13.2-2]   Fred Rogers Fairchild, Edgar Stevenson Furniss, Norman Sydney Buck, *Elementary Economics*, NY: The Macmillan Company, 1926, Vol. 1, p. 392

[13.2-3]   Condy Raguet, *A Treatise on Money and Banking*, Philadelphia, PA: Briggs & Elliot, (1840), pp. 45, 178 (Reprinted by Forgotten Books, FB&c Ltd., London)

[13.2-4]   Lot M. Morrill, *Annual Report of the Secretary of the Treasury on the State of the Finances for Year 1876*, Appendix containing the Report of the Comptroller of Currency (John Jay Knox), Washington, DC: Government Printing Office, 1876, p. 127

[13.2-5]   Francis A. Walker, *Money*, NY: Henry Holt and Company, 1891, pp. 501 - 503

[13.2-6]   op. cit., Bolles, Vol. 2, p. 351

[13.2-7]   op. cit., Morrill, p. 128

[13.2-8]   op. cit., Bolles, Vol. 2, p. 353

[13.2-9]   Levi Woodbury, *Annual Report of the Secretary of the Treasury of the United States on the Finances*, 5 Sep 1837, pp. 1-9

[13.2-10]   op. cit., Bolles, Vol. 2, pp. 549, 550

[13.2-11]   Text of "An Act to postpone the fourth installment of deposit with the States", 25th Congress, Session 1, Chapter 1, 2 Oct 1837

[13.2-12]   Text of "An act to authorize the issuing of Treasury Notes", 25th Congress, Session 1, Chapter 2, 12 Oct 1837

[13.2-13]   op. cit., Bolles, Vol. 2, p. 556

[13.2-14]   op. cit., Bolles, Vol. 2, p. 550

[13.2-15]   op. cit., Bolles, Vol. 2, p. 550

[13.2-16] Text of "An Act authorizing a further postponement of payment upon duty bonds", 25th Congress, Session 1, Chapter 8, 16 Oct 1837

[13.2-17] Text of "An Act for adjusting the remaining claims upon the late deposit banks", 25th Congress, Session 1, Chapter 19, 16 Oct 1837

[13.2-18] op. cit., Woodbury, pp. 2, 3

[13.2-19] op. cit., Raguet, p. 145

[13.2-20] op. cit., Morrill, p. 128

[13.2-21] op. cit., Sumner, pp. 144, 145

[13.2-22] A. Barton Hepburn, *A History of Currency in the United States*, New York: The Macmillan Co., 1924, p. 138

[13.2-23] Text of "An Act to authorize the issuing of Treasury notes to meet the current expenses of the Government", 25th Congress, Session 2, Chapter 82, 21 May 1838

[13.2-24] Text of "An Act to repeal certain provisions of 'An Act to alter and amend the several acts imposing duties on imports', approved the fourteenth day of July, eighteen hundred and thirty-two", 25th Congress, Session 2, Chapter 93, 31 May 1838

[13.2-25] Text of "An Act to authorize the sale of certain bonds belonging to the United States", 25th Congress, Session 2, Chapter 184, 7 Jul 1838

[13.2-26] Text of "An Act to prevent the issuing and circulation of the bills, notes, and other securities of corporations created by acts of Congress which have expired", 25th Congress, Session 2, Chapter 185, 7 Jul 1838

[13.2-27] op. cit., Sumner, p. 146

[13.2-28] op. cit., Sumner, p. 146

[13.2-29] Text of "An Act to revise and extend 'An act to authorize the issuing of Treasury notes to meet the current expenses of the Government', approved the twenty-first of May, eighteen hundred and thirty-eight", 25th Congress, Session 3, Chapter 37, 2 Mar 1839

[13.2-30] op. cit., Sumner, pp. 148-152

[13.2-31] op. cit., Hepburn, pp. 139-141

[13.2-32] op. cit., Raguet, p. 132 (gives 9 Oct 1839 as the day of suspension).

[13.2-33] op. cit., Raguet, p. 149

[13.2-34] Text of "An Act additional to the act on the subject of Treasury Notes", 26th Congress, Session 1, Chapter 5, 31 Mar 1840

[13.2-35] op. cit., Hepburn, p. 137

[13.2-36] Text of "An act to provide for the collection, safe-keeping, transfer, and disbursement of the public revenue", 26th Congress, Session 1, Chapter 41, 4 Jul 1840

[13.2-37] op. cit., Bolles, Vol. 2, p. 353

[13.2-38] Text of "An Act to authorize the issuing of Treasury notes", 26th Congress, Session 2, Chapter 5, 15 Feb 1841

[13.2-39] op. cit., Bolles, Vol. 2, p. 577

[13.2-40] Text of "An Act authorizing a loan not exceeding the sum of twelve millions of dollars", 27th Congress, Session 1, Chapter 3, 21 Jul 1841

[13.2-41] op. cit., Bolles, Vol. 2, p. 353

[13.2-42] op. cit., Bolles, Vol. 2, p. 354-358

[13.2-43] Text of "An Act to repeal the act entitled "An Act to provide for the collection, safe-keeping, transfer, and disbursement of the public revenue", and to provide for the punishment of embezzlers of public money, and other purposes", 27th Congress, Session 1, Chapter 7, 13 Aug 1841

[13.3-44] op. cit., Bolles, Vol. 2, p. 353

[13.2-45] Text of "An Act relating to duties and drawbacks", 27th Congress, Session 1, Chapter 24, 11 Sep 1841

[13.2-46] Text of "An Act to authorize an issue of Treasury notes", 27th Congress, Session 2, Chapter 2, 31 Jan 1842

[13.2-47] op. cit., Morrill, p. 128

[13.2-48] op. cit., Sumner, p. 152

[13.2-49] Text of "An Act for the extension of the loan of eighteen hundred and forty-one, and for an additional five millions of dollars thereto; and for allowing interest on Treasury notes due", 27th Congress, Session 2, Chapter 26, 15 Apr 1842

[13.2-50] Text of "An Act to regulate the value to be affixed to the pound sterling by the Treasury Department", 27th Congress, Session 2, Chapter 66, 27 Jul 1842

[13.2-51] Text of "An Act to provide revenue from imports, and to change and modify existing laws imposing duties on imports, and for other purposes", 27th Congress, Session 2, Chapter 270, 30 Aug 1842

[13.2-52] op. cit., Bolles, Vol. 2, pp. 439-443

[13.2-53] Text of "An Act to limit the sale of the public stock to par, and to authorize the issue of Treasury notes, in lieu thereof, to a certain amount", 27th Congress, Session 2, Chapter 287, 31 Aug 1842

[13.2-54] Text of "An Act regulating the currency of foreign gold and silver coins in the United States", 27th Congress, Session 3, Chapter 69, 3 Mar 1843

[13.2-55] Text of "An Act authorizing the reissue of Treasury notes and for other purposes", 27th Congress, Session 3, Chapter 81, 3 Mar 1843

[13.2-56] op. cit., Bolles, Vol. 2, p. 577

[13.2-57] op. cit., Sumner, pp. 153, 154

[13.2-58] op. cit., Bolles, Vol. 2, p. 589

[13.2-59] op. cit., F. A. Walker, p. 501

[13.2-60] op. cit., Bolles, Vol. 2, p. 590

[13.2-61] Text of "An Act to authorize an issue of Treasury Notes and a Loan", 29th Congress, Session 1, Chapter 65, 22 Jul 1846

[13.2-62] Text of "An Act reducing duties on imports, and for other purposes", 29th Congress, Session 1, Chapter 74, 30 Jul 1846

[13.2-63] op. cit., Bolles, Vol. 2, pp. 449-454, 461

[13.2-64] op. cit., Bolles, Vol. 2, pp. 458, 459

[13.2-65] op. cit., Bolles, p. 353

[13.2-66] Text of "An Act to provide for the better Organization of the Treasury, and for the Collection, Safe-Keeping, Transfer, and Disbursement of the public Revenue", 29th Congress, Chapter 90, 6 Aug 1846

[13.2-67] op. cit., Bolles, Vol. 2, p. 355-358

[13.2-68] Text of "An Act authorizing the issue of Treasury notes, a loan, and for other purposes", 29th Congress, Session 2, Chapter 5, 28 Jan 1847

[13.2-69] op. cit., Bolles, Vol. 2, pp. 590-592

[13.2-70] Text of "An Act to authorize a loan not to exceed a sum of sixteen millions of dollars", 30th Congress, Session 1, Chapter 26, 31 Mar 1848

[13.2-71] op. cit., Bolles, Vol. 2, p. 593

[13.2-72] Text of "An Act to authorize the coinage of gold dollars and double eagles", 30th Congress, Session 2, Chapter 109, 3 Mar 1849

[13.2-73] Text of "An Act amendatory of existing laws relative to the half dollar, quarter dollar, dime, and half dime"; 32nd Congress, Session 2, Chapter 79, 21 Feb 1853

[13.2-74] op. cit., Kreps, p. 80

[13.2-75] op. cit., Bolles, Vol. 2, p. 516

[13.2-76] Text of "An act relating to foreign coins and to the coinage of cents at the Mint of the United States", 34th Congress, Session 3, Chapter 57, 21 Feb 1857

[13.2-77] Text of "An Act reducing the duty on imports, and for other purposes", 34th Congress, Session 3, Chapter 98, 3 Mar 1857

[13.2-78] op. cit., Bolles, Vol. 2, pp. 460, 461

[13.2-79] National Bureau of Economic Research, Cambridge, MA (see website below)

[13.2-80] op. cit., Sumner, pp. 180-184

[13.2-81] op. cit., Sumner, pp. 186, 187

[13.2-82] Text of "An Act to authorize the issue of Treasury notes", 35th Congress, Session 1, Chapter 1, 23 Dec 1857

[13.2-83] op. cit., Bolles, Vol. 2, p. 599; Vol. 3, p. 44

[13.2-84] Text of "An Act to authorize a loan not exceeding the sum of twenty millions of dollars", 35th Congress, Session 1, Chapter 165, 14 Jun 1858

[13.2-85] op. cit., National Bureau of Economic Research

[13.2-86] Text of "An Act authorizing a loan and providing for the redemption of Treasury notes", 36th Congress, Session1, Chapter 180, 22 Jun 1860

[13.2-87] op. cit., National Bureau of Economic Research

[13.2-88] Text of "An Act to authorize the issue of Treasury notes, and for other purposes", 36th Congress, Session 2, Chapter 1, 17 Dec 1860

[13.2-89] op. cit., Bolles, Vol. 2, pp. 601, 602

[13.2-90]   op. cit., Bolles, Vol. 3, p. 4

[13.2-91]   Text of "An Act authorizing a loan", 36th Congress, Session 2, Chapter 29, 8 Feb 1861

[13.2-92]   op. cit., Bolles, Vol. 3, p. 8

[13.2-93]   Text of "An Act to provide for the payment of outstanding Treasury notes, to authorize a loan, to regulate and fix the duties on imports, and for other purposes", 36th Congress, Session 2, Chapter 68, 2 Mar 1861

[13.2-94]   op. cit., Bolles, Vol. 2, pp. 603-605

[13.2-95]   op. cit., Bolles, Vol. 3, pp. 7, 8

[13.2-96]   op. cit., National Bureau of Economic Research

[13.2-97]   Text of "An Act to authorize a national loan and for other purposes", 37th Congress, Session 1, Chapter 5, 17 Jul 1861

[13.2-98]   op. cit., Bolles, Vol. 3, p. 16

[13.2-99]   op. cit., Bolles, Vol. 3, p. 49

[13.2-100]   Text of "An Act to provide increased revenue from imports, to pay interest on the public debt, and for other purposes", 37th Congress, Session 1, Chapter 45, 5 Aug 1861

[13.2-101]   op. cit., Bolles, Vol. 3, pp. 16-18, 26

[13.2-102]   op. cit., Bolles, Vol. 3, p. 18

[13.2-103]   Text of "An Act supplementary to an Act entitled 'An Act to authorize a National Loan' and for other purposes"; 37th Congress, Session 1, Chapter 46, 5 Aug 1861

[13.2-104]   op. cit., Bolles, Vol. 3, pp. 29-31

[13.2-105]   op. cit., Bolles, Vol. 3, pp. 20-25

[13.2-106]   op. cit., Bolles, Vol. 3, pp. 34, 35

[13.2-107]   op. cit., Bolles, Vol. 3, pp. 35, 36

[13.2-108]   op. cit., Bolles, Vol. 3, p. 42

[13.2-109]   op. cit. Bolles, Vol. 3, p. 38, quoting Amasa Walker

[13.2-110]   Text of "An Act to increase the duties on tea, coffee, and sugar", 37th Congress, Session 2, Chapter 2, 24 Dec 1861

[13.2-111]   op. cit., Kreps, p. 79

[13.2-112]   op. cit., Bolles, Vol. 3, pp. 132-134

[13.2-113]   op. cit., Bolles, Vol. 3, p. 36

[13.2-114]   op. cit., Bolles, Vol. 3, pp. 47-61

[13.2-115]   Text of "An Act to authorize an additional issue of United States Notes", 37th Congress, Session 2, Chapter 20, 12 Feb 1862

[13.2-116]   op. cit., Bolles, Vol. 3, p. 61

[13.2-117]   Text of "An Act to authorize the issue of United States Notes, and for the redemption or funding thereof, and for funding the floating debt of the United States", 37th Congress, Session 2, Chapter 33, 25 Feb 1862

[13.2-118]   op. cit., Bolles, Vol. 3, pp. 43, 57-67

[13.2-119]   op. cit., Bolles, Vol. 3, pp. 97, 98

[13.2-120]   op. cit., Bolles, Vol. 3, pp. 208-211

[13.2-121]   op. cit., Bolles, Vol. 3, pp. 265, 266

[13.2-122]   Text of "An Act to authorize the purchase of coin, and for other purposes", 37th Congress, Session 2, Chapter 45, 17 Mar 1862

[13.2-123]   op. cit., Bolles, Vol. 3, pp. 168-176

[13.2-124]   Text of "An Act to provide internal revenue to support the Government and to pay interest on the public debt", 37th Congress, Session 2, Chapter 119, 1 Jul 1862

[13.2-125]   Text of "An Act to authorize an additional issue of United States Notes and for other purposes", 37th Congress, Session 2, Chapter 142, 11 Jul 1862

[13.2-126]   op. cit., Bolles, Vol. 3, pp. 78-83

[13.2-127]   Text of "An Act increasing, temporarily, the duties on imports, and for other purposes", 37th Congress, Session 2, Chapter 163, 14 Jul 1862

[13.2-128]   op. cit., Bolles, Vol. 3, pp. 176, 177

[13.2-129]   Text of "An Act to authorize payments in stamps, and to prohibit circulation of notes of less denomination than one dollar", 37th Congress, Session 2, Chapter 196, 17 Jul 1862

[13.2-130]   op. cit., Bolles, Vol. 3, p. 83

[13.2-131]   op. cit., Sumner, p. 205

[13.2-132]   op. cit., Kreps, p. 80

[13.3-1]   op. cit., Morrill, p. 157

[13.4-1]   op. cit., Bolles, Vol. 2, pp. 580-582
[13.4-2]   op. cit., Bolles, Vol. 3, p. 4

NBER website: https://www.nber.org/research/data/us-business-cycle-expansions-and-contractions

14

A Digression on the National Banking System

The U. S. banking system changed in 1863 with the advent of the "national banking association" system. This change was made for two reasons. The first reason was to correct some problems with the competing bank notes issued by the State-chartered banks, and produce a uniform, commonly-recognized paper currency throughout the nation. The second motivation was to promote stability in the banking system by ensuring that bank notes issued by national banks were fully redeemable, thus reducing losses due to bankruptcy of the individual issuing banks.

The national bank system was not designed to operate as a central bank; in fact it was deliberately designed to be a diversified system, but one operating under a consistent set of rules. It was also designed to permit any group of five persons to establish a banking association, subject to capitalization requirements; therefore it prevented the formation of a banking cartel. Every national bank, after certification by the Comptroller of the Currency, was permitted to issue national bank notes as circulating currency. As mentioned, these were fully guaranteed for payment. But here comes the big change: the bank notes were indirectly "insured" by U. S. securities. Each national bank, before it could issue its bank notes, was required to buy U. S. securities out of its capital fund and deposit the securities with the U. S. Treasury. The value of the securities thus deposited was to be equal to 110% of the amount of national bank notes to be issued. The idea was that if a National Bank failed, the Treasury department would then sell the securities that backed the notes, and use the proceeds to pay the holders of the notes. But why use U. S. securities as backing instead of gold or silver? Simple: the U. S. government had a great deal of securities to sell in order to finance the Civil War. Figure 14-1 shows the transactions between the national bank associations and the U. S. Treasury.

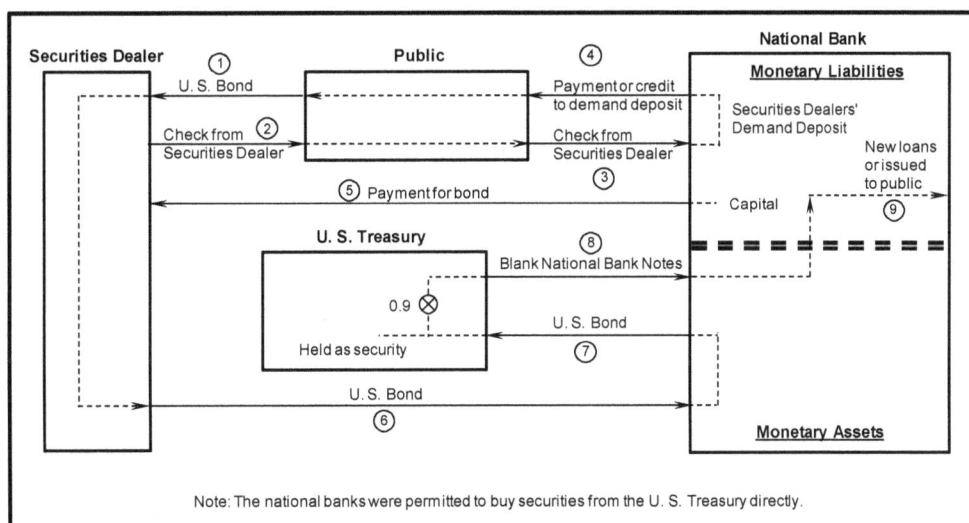

Figure 14-1: The National Banking System

But the national bank law did not permit an unlimited amount of national bank notes to be issued, backed by an unlimited amount of U. S. securities; in fact the total amount of national bank notes to be issued for circulation was limited to $300,000,000 (it was later increased). It soon became apparent that this was insufficient to finance the war, and the federal government resorted to issuing United States Notes (a.k.a. "greenbacks") as legal tender notes. There were some other conditions imposed by the banking law, namely that the distribution of national bank notes was to be fairly uniform throughout the States, and that the redemption was of notes was permitted only at the main office of the issuing national bank. Also, State-chartered banks were allowed to convert to the national bank system under certain conditions. The conversion from State to national banks accelerated when Congress imposed a 10% annual tax on bank notes issued by State banks. The number of State banks declined dramatically until the 1890's, and then increased again when the State banks realized that loans could be issued via demand deposits instead of issuing bank notes.

The national banks were divided into three classes: a) central reserve city banks (i.e., initially those in New York City, but in 1887, also included Chicago and St. Louis); b) regional reserve city banks (those located in 16 other cities listed in the authorizing law), and c) country banks (all those not in the first two categories). Each category of bank was required to hold reserves against its demand and time deposits (the bank notes already being secured by the bonds held by the Treasury). The banks in the central reserve cities were required to hold all its reserves in its vaults. The regional banks were required to hold part of theirs in their vaults, but part could be held in the banks in central reserve cities. Meanwhile, the country banks were required to hold a different fraction in their vaults and a part in the regional banks; but the regional banks could also hold part of the country banks' reserves as accounts with the central reserve banks. Interest could be paid for all reserve deposits as a means of compensating for services rendered; the regional banks paid interest on reserves it held for the country banks; for example, the banks in New York paid interest to the regional banks for regional reserves deposited in New York. This scheme became known as the "pyramiding of reserves" [14-1]. "Pyramiding" is an unfortunate name; it implies that somehow that the total amount of reserves is being increased because it is built upon other reserves. That is not the case: "pyramiding" in this instance means only that reserves tended to be concentrated in the banks in New York (and other central reserve cities), not that reserves were being multiplied. Meade [14-2] has given a good description of how the "pyramiding" actually worked, as shown on Figure 14-2.

The country banks were required to maintain 15% in reserves against the sum of deposits and notes in circulation, but only 40% of that had to be held in the vault, and 60% could be held as accounts in a regional reserve bank. Banks in regional reserve cities were required to maintain a 25% reserve against the sum of deposits and note circulation, half of which had to be in the vault and half could be held as accounts in the banks in central reserve cities. Thus the reserves in the regional banks amounted to 12.5% of its notes and deposits plus 9% of the reserves of the country banks (which was 60% of the 15% country bank reserves). The banks in the central reserve cities were required to maintain 25% reserves against the sum of notes and deposits, all of which had to be held in the vault; once again, part of the deposits were fractions of the reserves of country and regional banks.

To summarize, the permissible fraction of cash held in the vaults against deposits and circulation came to:

a. Country banks: $0.4(0.15) = 0.06 = 6\%$ of its notes and deposits
b. Regional reserve banks: $0.125(0.6)(0.15) = 1.125\%$ of country bank notes and deposits plus 12.5% of its deposits and reserves
c. Central reserve banks: $0.25(0.125)(0.6)(0.15) = 0.28\%$ of country bank notes and deposits plus $0.25(0.125) = 3.125\%$ of regional banks notes and deposits, plus 25% of its notes and deposits.

The regional and country banks did not always send the maximum permitted to the other banks as deposits; this analysis shows only what was permitted. If they did maximize the transfer of reserves, then the situation was as follows. The total cash on hand in country banks against their bank notes and deposits was thus 6% in their vaults plus 1.125% in regional bank vaults plus 0.28% in central reserve vaults = 7.4%. Likewise, the total cash on hand vs. regional reserve notes and deposits was 12.5% in their vaults plus 3.125% in the central reserve vaults = 15.6%. For the central reserve city banks, it was 25% of their notes and deposits, all in its vault. Far from a 'pyramid' of reserves, it was a method that reduced the actual cash on hand below the statutory reserve levels.

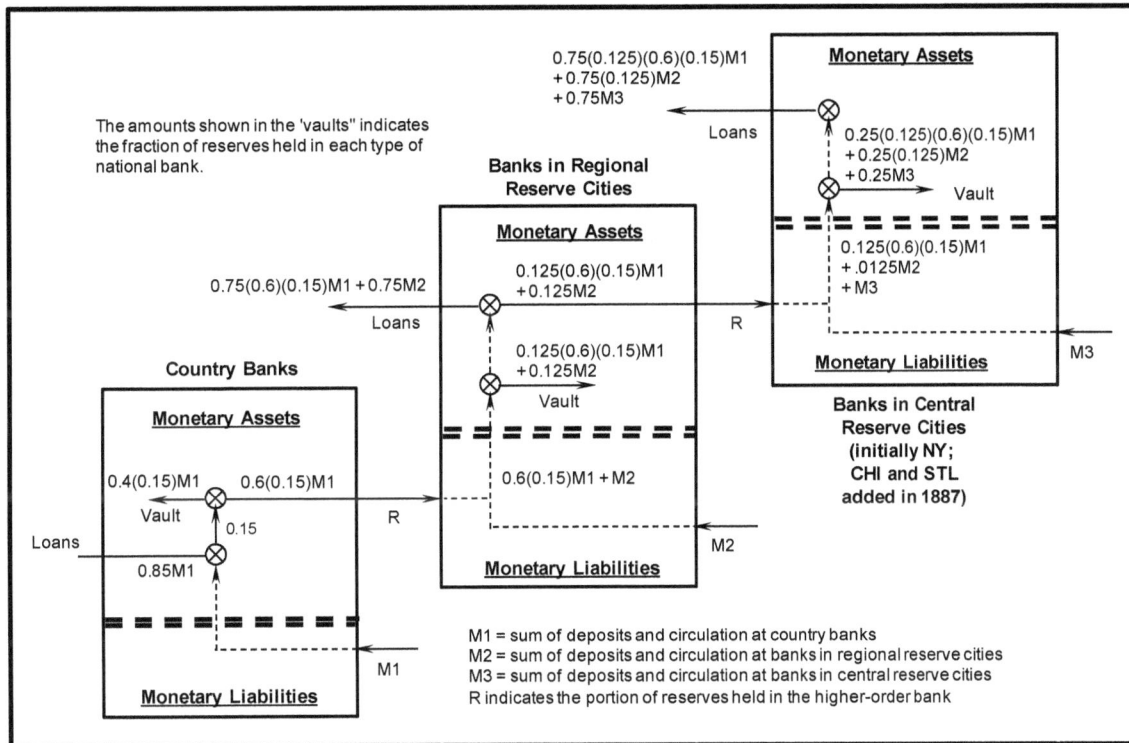

Figure 14-2: "Pyramiding" of Reserves under the National Bank Law

This "pyramiding" did end up being one of the weaknesses of the national bank system. The reason is, since interest was being paid on the reserves, and reserves were being somewhat concentrated in New York, the New York banks had reserves in excess of what was required against their deposits. The New York banks then issued loans upon these excess reserves to stock brokers, who used the proceeds to invest in the stock market [14-3]. It is easy to see what happens when there is a downturn in the market: losses in the market means that the loans are not repaid, which means the New York banks had to take losses which reduced their reserves. Thus the regional and country banks also ended up with a reduction in their reserves even though they did not make the bad loans.

A problem could also occur from the other direction: suppose business suddenly picked up in the country banks, and they decided to issue loans or decided to withdraw their reserves. With the concentration in New York, the New York banks found they had to call in the stock loans; if they could not be repaid, the New York banks sold off the collateral at a loss. That could cause a cash-flow problem in the New York banks, and several undesirable emergency remedies became necessary.

References

[14-1]   Clifton H. Kreps, Jr., *Money, Banking and Monetary Policy*, NY: The Ronald Press Co., 1962, p. 168

[14-2]   Edward S. Meade, "The Deposit-Reserve System of the National Bank Law", Journal of Political Economy, Vol. 6, No. 2, Mar 1898, pp. 209-224

[14-3]   Albert S. Bolles, *A Financial History of the United States*, NY: Augustus M. Kelley (1969), Vol. 3, pp. 348-351 (originally published 1884 by D. Appleton & Co., NY)

15

The National Banking System
Under Fiat Currency,
1863-1878

15.1 Preview, 1863-1878

This period in U. S history is characterized by three major phenomena: a) the advent of the national bank system; b) the continued issue of unbacked legal tender paper money during the Civil War, and c) the planned resumption of payment in specie. The legal tender paper money was formally named "United States Notes" (U. S. Notes), but its popular name was "greenbacks". They were authorized by Congress in 1862 under the Legal Tender Act to generate enough circulating currency to pay expenses of the Civil War (for the Northern States). This chapter only reports on the banking system in place in the Union.

Congress enacted a tax on the issue of State bank notes, which in effect put the State banks out of the note-issuing business, since they could not obtain sufficient interest on loans to cover the tax. Many State banks voluntarily converted to national banks under the National Bank Act, and there was little disruption in banking throughout the country [15.1-1]. Banks still made most of their money in acquiring assets by issuing notes, although as mentioned in chapter 13, the trend was toward issuing loans in the form of demand deposits. The reason is that the public had become used to making transactions by checks instead of by notes [15.1-2].

There were a series of financial panics during this period; they are similar to the previous ones that occurred in 1819 and 1837, and, contrary to later claims, were not in fact due to the national banking system per se. They were due as always to a financial expansion followed by a contraction. I have included in the history the details of these financial problems as documented by Sprague [15.1-3].

As mentioned in chapter 14, the national banks were permitted per an act of Congress in 1863 to issue National Bank Notes as circulating money. They were no different than any other bank note. The main difference between the National Bank Notes and the ones issued by the State banks is that the National Bank Notes had to be backed by bonds submitted to the U. S. Treasury. The idea was that if a national bank failed to pay its notes, the bonds could be sold to compensate the holders thereof.

The national banks had three sources of profits [15.1-4]: a) interest on bonds deposited with the U. S. Treasury against note circulation; b) on the note circulation itself (but was very small); and c) interest on loans issued in the form of demand deposits.

The phrase "lawful money" is found in many places in the legislation during this period. "Lawful money" meant [15.1-5, 15.1-6, 15.1-7]: a) gold coin; b) silver coin; c) U. S. Notes; d) gold certificates; e) silver certificates; f) clearinghouse certificates (used only between banks); g) 3% certificates; and h) "compound interest notes". National Bank Notes could not be used as reserves against those same notes. However, the public regarded the National Bank Notes as good as any other, and they passed hand-to-hand as money. The last two types above were issued by the U. S. Treasury and only the compound interest notes circulated to any extent; the clearinghouse certificates were used only between banks as a way to offset accounts. "Lawful money" is very different from "legal tender". "Legal tender" meant: a) U. S. Notes, b) gold coin, c) silver coin; and d) compound interest notes. The 3% certificates and compound interest notes were all redeemed by 1872 [15.1-8].

15.2 History, 1863-1878

17 Jan 1863: Congress passed a joint resolution approving another $100,000,000 in United States Notes, for a total of $400,000,000 [15.2-1]. The provisions were [15.2-2]: a) authorized the Secretary of the Treasury to issue up to $100,000,000 in United States Notes on the credit of the United States; b) not to bear interest, c) payable on demand; d) to be lawful money and legal tender for all debts, public and private, except for duties on imports and interest on the public debt; and e) the amount authorized here shall be considered part of the amount to be called out in a future law. No mention is made of what "payment on demand" meant, since these were both legal tender and lawful money, and the U. S. Treasury has already stopped paying in specie (cf. 31 Dec 1861).

25 Feb 1863: Congress passed the National Currency Act. It created a new class of banks called National Banks, to be supervised by the Office of the Comptroller. National Banks could issue National Bank Notes based on U. S. securities. The bank notes were to be backed by U. S. securities, to be purchased with the bank's paid-in capital [15.2-3]. The process was: a) a National Bank bought U. S. government securities eligible for "circulation privilege" (which was all of them); b) the U. S. securities were deposited with the U. S. Treasury; c) the Treasury then issued National Bank Notes up to 90% of the value of the securities; and d) these notes were given to the bank's customers. The total volume of National Bank Notes was limited to $300,000,000 [15.2-4].

Specific provisions of the law were [15.2-5]: a) (S. 5 and 6) a bank may be established by five or more persons with capital not less than $50,000 increments; b) (S. 7) 30% of the capital stock is to be paid in at start of business, with the rest to be paid in at 10% every two months; c) (S. 12) shareholders are liable for twice the value of their shares; d) (S. 15) upon starting operations, the bank was to deliver to the Treasury 6% interest-bearing U. S. bonds not less than one-third of the paid in capital, to be retained by the Treasury Secretary; e) (S. 16, 30) in return for the bonds, the Treasury to issue National Bank Notes in various denominations to the bank for circulation, up to 90% of the par value of the bonds if the bonds bearing interest at 6% or more (lower percentage for lower interest bonds), and the amount of bonds not to exceed the current paid-in capital; f) (S. 17) the total quantity of notes to be issued is limited to $300,000,000, half of which to be apportioned to the States by population, and the other half distributed as the Treasury Secretary sees fit based on local needs; g) (S. 20) the notes to indicate: 1) that they are secured by United States bonds; and 2) that the issuing bank promises to pay on demand; h) (S. 18) circulating notes permitted in denominations of $5, $10, $20, $50, $100, $500, and $1,000; i) (S. 19) banks to be taxed 2% in lawful money annually on circulation to reimburse the Treasury for the expense of printing the notes and enforcing the law; j) (S. 20) the notes are to circulate as money, and to be received at par by the U. S. government for taxes, excises, and public lands, but not import duties; k) (S. 20) the notes are to be received at par by individual and corporate creditors of the government except for payment of interest on public debt; l) (S. 20) the banks cannot issue any other notes; m) (S. 24, 45) the banks to submit quarterly statements of condition; n) (S. 25-29) if the bank does not redeem its notes in lawful money, the bonds with the Treasury are to be forfeited or sold and used to make payment (after 30 days); o) (S. 41) each bank shall have on hand in lawful money an amount of at least 25% of the total of its circulation and deposits, except banks outside Boston, Providence, New York, Philadelphia, Baltimore, Cincinnati, Chicago, St. Louis, and New Orleans (i.e., regional reserve banks) may hold 60% of their reserves as deposits in banks on those cities; **p)** (S. 41) clearinghouse certificates representing lawful money or specie count as lawful money to fulfill the 25% reserve obligation; **q)** (S. 42) the debts of the bank shall not exceed its net paid-in capital (excluding normal liabilities of circulation, deposits, and profits); **r)** (S. 61) existing State chartered banks may convert to the national system if 50% of its capital stock is in U. S. bonds, and upon transfer as above, may receive notes for circulation up to 80% of the par value thereof; and **s)** (S. 54) such banks may be used to deposit U. S. government funds.

The purposes of the national banking system, as Secretary Chase described it, were: a) to bring about a uniformity in the currency (there being many types of State bank notes in circulation), issued on good security, with reasonable safeguards against depreciation; b) stimulate a large demand for government securities (to finance the Civil War); and c) benefit industry by a decline in the interest rate [15.2-6].

3 Mar 1863: Congress passed a funding law [15.2-7]. Among its provisions: **a)** (S. 1) authorized a loan for $300,000,000 at 6% or less, payable between 10 and 40 years for expenses in 1863 (called the ten-forty bonds); and a loan of $600,000,000 for 1864 under the same terms; **b)** (S. 2) authorized the Treasury Secretary to issue an additional $400,000,000 in Treasury Notes bearing interest not exceeding 6%, payable at the pleasure of the U. S. and not exceeding three years from the date of issue; **c)** (S. 2) the Treasury Notes were legal tender at face value excluding interest; **d)** (S. 2) Treasury Secretary may issue up to $150,000,000 of U. S. Notes to be exchanged for Treasury Notes, and the Treasury Notes destroyed; **e)** (S. 3) authorized the Treasury Secretary to issue up to $150,000,000 of Treasury Notes not bearing interest, which shall be legal tender except for import duties and interest on the debt, and may be re-issued; **f)** (S. 4) authorized the Treasury Secretary to issue up to $50,000,000 of fractional currency, in denominations of 3, 5, 10, 15, 25, and 50 cents, to relieve the shortage of small change in lieu of postage stamps (cf. 17 Jul 1862); **g)** (S. 5) authorized the Treasury Secretary to receive gold coin and bullion for which he can issue gold certificates up to 120% of the coin and bullion received, and the coin and bullion to remain in the Treasury for payment on demand; **h)** (S. 5) gold certificates to be legal tender for import duties and interest on the debt; **i)** (S. 7) banks issuing currency for circulation to pay 2% tax on the average circulation of their notes (sliding scale based on paid-in capital: 90% for capital under $100,000 down to 25% for capital above $2,000,000); and **j)** (S. 7) banks to pay 0.25% annual tax on average demand deposits (excluding savings deposits). The fractional currency was to replace the small-denomination notes that had been issued by cities receivable for local taxes that had begun earlier in the year. Ultimately $368,720,079.21 in fractional currency would be issued between 1863 and 1876 [15.2-8]. The rate of interest on bonds was thus set by the Secretary of the Treasury (S. 2), which created great uncertainty as to the true value of the U. S. Notes (since they were originally convertible into bonds bearing 6%) [15.2-9]. No gold certificates were issued until Nov 1865 [15.2-10]. The new taxes on bank note circulation and deposits were in addition to the existing 3% tax on earnings and stamp duties [15.2-11].

3 Mar 1863: Congress revised [15.2-12] the previous law (cf. 1 Jul 1862) on import duties and licenses: **a)** (S. 1) increasing license fees and expanding the occupations requiring licenses; **b)** (S. 1) changing duty rates on many enumerated items and the stamp duty; **c)** (S. 3) imposed a 1% tax on the premiums paid for travelers insurance; **d)** (S. 4) required a stamp duty of 0.5% plus interest at 6% prorated to be paid on contracts, sales, or loans of gold or silver coin or bullion to take place 3 days after contract, and contracts can only be made for the par value thereof; **e)** (S. 14) banks that do not issue dividends or add to surplus to pay a 3% tax on profits; and **f)** (S. 23) lard, lubricating oil and linseed oil subject to the same duties as on liquor.

3 Mar 1863: Congress passed [15.2-13] another modification to the import duties: **a)** (S. 2) reduced the additional duties on cotton and silk (cf. 14 Jul 1862); **b)** (S. 5) changed the duty on printing paper to 20% *ad valorem*; and **c)** (S. 6) added a 20% *ad valorem* duty on petroleum and illuminating oil.

18 May - 4 Jul 1863: Siege of Vicksburg, MS.

30 May - 6 Apr 1863: Battle of Chancellorsville, VA.

1 - 3 Jul 1863: Battle of Gettysburg, PA.

19, 20 Sep 1863: Battle of Chickamauga, GA.

24 Nov 1863: Battle of Lookout Mountain, TN.

25 Nov 1863: Battle of Missionary Ridge, TN.

31 Dec 1863: The U. S. Notes had depreciated against gold (at 23.22 grains) between 22.23% and 72.5%, at an average depreciation of 45.2% [15.2-14].

3 Mar 1864: Congress authorized [15.2-15, 15.2-16] a loan: **a)** (S. 1) in lieu of the $600,000,000 previously authorized (cf. 3 Mar 1863), a loan for $200,000,000 by issuing bonds at 6%, redeemable at the discretion of the government after five years and payable in coin after forty years, referred to as the 5-40 bonds (i.e. 1869 to 1904); **b)** (S. 1) Treasury Secretary may dispose of the bonds in lawful money (Treasury Notes, certificates of indebtedness, or certificates of deposit); **c)** (S. 1) such bonds are exempt from taxation by the States; and **d)** (S. 4) permitted the Treasury Secretary to issue 5-20 bonds to certain investors who subscribed to the previous loan prior to 1 Jan 1864.

7 Mar 1864: Congress increased the duties on liquor and cotton [15.2-17].

11 Apr 1864: Secretary Chase wrote a letter to Congressman E. G. Spaulding [15.2-18], complaining that it was difficult to sell the "ten-forty" bonds (cf. 3 Mar 1863). No wonder: they originally were subscribed at 6% running for between 10 and forty years, but Chase had tried to sell them at 5% for five years. He also mentions that because they could not be sold, it was necessary to issue $400,000,000 more in U. S. Notes, depreciating the currency. Chase chose to depreciate the currency by insisting on limiting the interest to 5% instead of the permitted 6%; the greater amount of money in circulations gave the public the illusion of wealth which made them reluctant to buy bonds.

22 Apr 1864: Congress revised the 1857 Coinage Act (cf. 21 Feb 1857) regarding the one-cent coin [15.2-19]: **a)** (S. 1) redefined the one-cent coin to be a coin of 48 grains, 95% copper and 5% tin and zinc; **b)** (S. 1) permitted a two-cent coin to be made at proportional weight; and **c)** (S. 4) specified that each coin was legal tender to ten times their face values.

5 - 7 May 1864: Battles in the Wilderness and Port Walthall Junction, VA.

18 - 21 May 1864: Battle of Spotsylvania Courthouse, VA.

3 Jun 1864: Congress passed the National Banking Act, a modification of the 1863 Act [15.2-20]. First (S. 7), it established capitalization requirements for a national bank based on population of the location: a) for population less than 6,000, minimum capitalization is $50,000; b) 6,000 to 49,000: $100,000; c) for 50,000 and above, $200,000. Second (S. 16), the bank was required to deposit U. S. bonds with the U. S. Treasury, the amount being the greater of $30,000 or one-third of the paid-in capital. Third, (S. 14), 50% of the capital was to be paid in before starting business, the rest payable in 10% increments monthly. Fourth (S. 21), reserve requirements on National Bank Notes issued against U. S. bonds bearing at least 5% interest was changed from 80% of the amount of deposited U. S. bonds to 90% of the lower of current value or par value. Fifth (S. 23), national bank notes were to circulate as money, were payable on demand, and receivable for all taxes excise, duties, to the U. S. except for import duties. Sixth (S. 22), the total amount of notes that could be issued was limited to $300,000,000. Seventh, (S. 20) the volume of national bank notes was limited to 90% of the current value of the deposited bonds, but in no case in excess of 100% of paid-in capital. Eighth (S. 31), the national banks were required to maintain reserves in "lawful money" against the sum of deposits (time and demand) and notes issued: a) 25% for central reserve city banks, all held in the bank; b) 25% for banks in reserve cities (at least half in the bank, up to half as deposits in a central reserve city bank); and c) 15% in banks "country banks" (at least 40% in the bank, up to 60% could be held as a deposit in a reserve or central reserve bank). Interest could be paid for deposits representing reserves. If the reserves fell below the required minimum, the bank was prohibited from making further loans and discounts except by discounting or purchasing bills of exchange payable on sight. Ninth (S. 31) a total of 16 regional cities were defined, with the bank at New York as the

"central reserve city". The sixteen reserve cities were: St. Louis, MO, Louisville, KY, Chicago, IL, Detroit, MI, Milwaukee, WI, New Orleans, LA, Cincinnati, OH, Cleveland, OH, Pittsburg, PA, Baltimore, MD, Philadelphia, PA, Boston, MA, Albany, NY, Leavenworth, KS (was deleted from the list 1 Mar 1872); San Francisco, CA, and Washington DC. Tenth (S. 32) the 16 reserve cities may keep half of its reserves in the central reserve city at NY. Eleventh (S. 31), it defined clearinghouse certificates as lawful money for the purposes of reserves if "representing specie or lawful money specially deposited for the purpose of and clearinghouse association". Twelfth (S. 47), if a national bank fails to redeem its notes in "lawful money", the bank shall be declared in default, the deposited bonds are forfeited, and the Treasury will pay the holders of the notes. Thirteenth (S. 41), taxes were imposed on notes, deposits, and capital: a) 1% annual tax on average notes in circulation; b) 0.5% annual tax on deposits; c) 0.5% annual tax on capital invested in other than U. S. government securities, and States were permitted to tax shares of the national banking associations. Fourteenth (S. 32), every national bank was required to accept the notes of every other national bank at par, regardless of location; this provided the desired "uniform currency" [15.2-21, 15.2-22]. Fifteenth (S. 30), interest was limited to 7% unless a different rate prevailed in the State where the bank was located. Sixteenth (S. 26), a bank that chose to reduce its circulation could do so by returning the notes and retrieving the bonds. Seventeenth (S. 34), each bank was to submit quarterly statements of condition. Eighteenth (S. 44), State banks may become national banks.

One of the problems with this system was that interest was paid on reserve deposits; this often caused the regional banks to deposit their reserves with the banks in New York City, which in turn loaned the money to stockbrokers [15.2-23]. This is part of the issue with "pyramiding of reserves" discussed in chapter 14.

15-18 Jun 1864: Second Battle of Petersburg, VA.

17 Jun 1864: Congress passed the "Gold Act" [15.2-24]: a) (S. 1) contracts specifying delivery of gold at any future day illegal; b) (S. 2) gold sales were to be made on a cash basis on the same day in the usual place of business; and c) (S. 2) the same restrictions applied to foreign exchange. It was passed as an attempt to prevent speculators from driving up the price of gold, failing to realize that increased price of gold was a result of a depreciating paper currency, not a change in gold [15.2-25]. The behavior of the speculators was a minor influence. But the law caused so much uncertainty that the price of gold increased 30% in one week.

30 Jun 1864: Congress passed a law increasing import duties [15.2-26].

30 Jun 1864: Congress passed a funding bill [15.2-27]: a) (S. 1) authorized a loan of $400,000,000 by issuing bonds at 6% interest, payable between 5 and 30 years at the discretion of the government, or if expedient, payable in 40 years; b) (S. 1) interest not to exceed 6%, payable semi-annually in coin; c) (S. 1) Treasury Secretary may dispose of (sell) these bonds and the 5-20's remaining unsold in Europe on terms he thinks appropriate for lawful U. S. money, Treasury Notes, certificates of indebtedness, or certificates of deposit; d) (S. 2) Treasury Secretary may issue up to $200,000,000 in Treasury Notes in lieu of the bonds, at 7.3% interest, redeemable in three years in lawful money, to be legal tender; e) (S. 2) the total amount of newly issued bonds and Treasury Notes not to exceed $400,000,000; f) (S. 4) authorized the Treasury Secretary to obtain a 30-day loan from national banking associations for $150,000,000; and g) (S. 5) authorized an issue up to $50,000,000 in fractional currency. The Treasury Secretary was given the option [15.2-28] obtain half of this amount by issuing Treasury Notes, payable after three years at 7.3%.

30 Jun 1864: Congress passed a general revision of the import duties and licensing, and regulations for collecting thereof [15.2-29]. It increased the excise taxes on tobacco (20 cents per pound on raw tobacco, and 5 to 12% on manufactured tobacco items); and a 0.05% duty on insurance policies (50 cents per $1000 insured) [15.2-30].

1 Jul 1864: Fessenden succeeded Chase as Treasury Secretary. At this time, the Treasury had a cash balance of $18,842,558, unpaid requisitions were $71,814,000, the outstanding bonds and debt certifi-

cates came to $161,796,000, and daily expenses were estimated at $2,250,000 [15.2-31]. Monthly revenue was about $15,000,000. By this time, a large amount of interest-bearing Treasury Notes were being used as money (instead of investments), and this caused a depreciation in the value of all money in general [15.2-32].

2 Jul 1864: The Gold Act (cf. 17 Jun 1864) was repealed [15.2-33, 15.2-34].

19 Sep 1864: Battle of Opequon, VA.

27 Sep 1864: Battle of Fort Davidson (Pilot Knob, MO).

~1 Oct 1864: Treasury Secretary Fessenden recognized that the government had insufficient coin to pay the interest on the Treasury Notes and bonds, and that in the future it would be necessary to pay the interest in currency, but convertible into other bonds that paid in coin [15.2-35]. The annual interest payments due in coin was about $56,000,000. The idea was to use bonds maturing in three to five years paying higher interest, but paid in currency, then permit them to be converted at maturity into twenty-year bonds at 5%.

19 Oct 1864: Battle of Cedar Creek, VA.

10 Dec 1864: Treasury Secretary Fessenden notified bondholders that the Treasury would be able to pay either in lawful money or by conversion into new bonds, the three-year Treasury Notes from Jul 1861 [15.2-36]. It was necessary for Fessenden to obtain a $25,000,000 loan to redeem them.

31 Dec 1864: The U. S. Notes had depreciated against gold (at 23.22 grains) between 51.5% and 185%, at an average depreciation of 103% ($100 in gold required between $151.50 and $285.00 in greenbacks, averaging $203.3) [15.2-37].

28 Jan 1865: Congress passed financial legislation [15.2-38] authorizing the Treasury Secretary to issue Treasury Notes in lieu of any bonds remaining unsold that were authorized previously (cf. 30 Jun 1864), with the caveat that the total of new bonds and Treasury Notes is not to exceed $400,000,000

3 Mar 1865: Congress passed the National Bank Act of 1865 [15.2-39] amending a section of the National Banking Act of 1864 (cf. 3 Jun 1864): **a)** (S. 21) national banks to be able to issue notes per 90% of the bonds deposited with the Treasury if bearing more than 5% interest; **b)** (S. 21) adopted a sliding scale of the volume of bank notes a bank could issue, based on the amount of paid-in capital: 1) paid-in capital less than $500,000: 90%; 2) paid-capital between $500,000 and $999,999, 80%; 3) paid-in capital between $1,000,000 and $3,000,000, 75%; 4) paid-in capital greater than $3,000,000, 60%; and **c)** (S. 21) that $150,000,000 of National Bank Notes is to be apportioned by the Treasury Secretary to institutions in the States and territories by population, and the remainder of bank notes distributed by banking capital, resources, and businesses of the States and territories.

3 Mar 1865: Congress passed a finance bill [15.2-40]: **a)** (S. 1) authorized Treasury Secretary Fessenden to borrow $600,000,000, issuing bonds or Treasury Notes; **b)** (S. 1) the bonds are payable at any time but not more than 40 years from issue or redeemable between 5 and 40 years; **c)** (S. 1) the portion issued in Treasury Notes to be convertible into bonds; **d)** (S. 1) the Treasury Notes would be redeemable at the Secretary's discretion at not more than 40 years from issue; **e)** (S. 1) interest on notes and bonds at 6% when payable in coin, and at interest of 7.3% when payable in currency; **f)** the interest and principal on the Treasury Notes may be made payable in coin or other lawful money; and **g)** (S. 2) the Treasury Secretary may sell the bonds either domestically or in foreign countries for coin, other lawful money of the U. S. Treasury Notes, certificates of indebtedness, or certificates of deposits issued by authority of Congress. A total of $500,000,000 was subscribed by Jun 1865 [15.2-41].

3 Mar 1865: Congress passed a tariff law [15.2-42]: **a)** (S. 1) changed the *ad valorem* rates: 1) cotton, 20%; 2) spools of thread, 20%; **b)** (S. 3) 40 cents per gallon on petroleum, 15 cents per gallon on coal-oil, 60% *ad valorem* on silk, 15% *ad valorem* on mercury; **c)** (S. 2) increased the excise taxes on wine, brandy, and beer; **d)** (S. 4) tonnage duty of 30 cents per ton; and **e)** (S. 6) an additional 10% *ad valorem* on the products imported from east of Good Hope.

3 Mar 1865: Congress passed a revenue act [15.2-43, 15.2-44]: **a)** (S. 1) called out regulations for collection of import duties and taxes; **b)** (S. 1) changed the income tax: 1) 5% income tax on incomes between $500 and $5,000, 2) 10% on income above $5,000; **c)** (S. 1) granted a $100 income deduction for husband, wife, and each minor child; **d)** (S. 1) income to include interest on public debt and gains from sales; **e)** (S. 6) levied a 10% annual tax on bank notes issued after 1 Jul 1866 by State-chartered banks; **f)** (S. 7) preference over new national bank applications was to be given to State banks that agreed to convert to the national system before 1 Jul 1865; and **g)** (S. 8) imposed a $1 per barrel tax on petroleum. The objective of the 10% tax on notes issued by State-chartered banks was to either to drive them out of business or force them to join the national bank system [15.2-45, 15.2-46]. It initially caused the number of State-chartered banks to decline, but by 1892, the number of State-chartered banks exceeded the federally-chartered ones. The State-chartered banks found that they did not have to issue notes, since a great deal of business was then done with demand deposits and checks.

3 Mar 1865: Congress authorized [15.2-47] coinage of a 3-cent coin: **a)** (S. 1) to be composed of copper and nickel, with nickel not more than 25%, of total weight 30 grains; **b)** (S. 3) to be legal tender up to 60 cents; **c)** (S. 3) prohibited fractional paper currency under 5 cents face value; **d)** (S. 5) "In God We Trust" to be imprinted on all coinage in the future, if the coin is large enough to permit it; and **e)** (S. 6) the one cent and two-cent coins to be legal tender only up to four cents.

25 Mar 1865: Battle of Fort Stedman, VA.

1 Apr 1865: Battle of Five Forks, VA.

2 Apr 1865: Third Battle of Petersburg, VA.

9 Apr 1865: Battle of Appomattox Courthouse, VA; Confederate General Robert E. Lee surrendered to Union General Ulysses S. Grant.

~10 Apr 1865: The amount of National Bank Notes in circulation is estimated at $100,000,000 [15.2-48].

15 Apr 1865: Approximate beginning of a recession [15.2-49].

12, 13 May 1865: Battle of Palomino Ranch, TX, this was the last battle of the Civil War.

1 Nov 1865: There were at this time 1,600 national banks in operation, of which 922 were converted State banks [15.2-50].

31 Dec 1865: The U. S. Notes had depreciated against gold (at 23.22 grains) between 28.5% and 133%, at an average depreciation of 57.3% ($100 in gold required between $128.62 and $233.75 in greenbacks, averaging $157.30) [15.2-51].

12 Apr 1866: Congress began a plan to reduce the number of legal tender notes in circulation [15.2-52]. The provisions were: **a)** the interest-bearing legal tender notes would no longer be a legal tender once they reached maturity, and the Treasury could then retire them; **b)** the Treasury Secretary was authorized to sell bonds bearing interest at 6% or less, redeemable at the convenience of the government, as a means of retiring the compound interest Treasury Notes and the United States Notes, (Treasury Notes not bearing interest); and **c)** not more than $10,000,000 in U. S. Notes could be retired in the next 6 months, and afterward no more than $4,000,000 in any one month.

This was the culmination of a long debate in Congress, and it enacted this plan as a first step toward reducing the volume of legal-tender notes and return gradually to payment of notes in specie on demand [15.2-53]. Treasury Secretary McCulloch's view was that the depreciated currency was harmful because it was in excess of what was needed, therefore it increased prices and the excess was used for speculation. The volume of notes in circulation injured the poorer classes, who had to pay high prices for necessities. But he recognized that the reduction of the currency had to be done slowly, so as not to shock the system; otherwise, people would have to pay their debts in money that was more valuable than when they contracted the debt. One result was that the interest-bearing notes stopped circulating, and were held by the banks as a reserve. At the same time, as the banks increased their circulation and deposits, they kept the legal tender notes as reserves against them. By this means the total volume of U. S. Notes (greenbacks) was reduced to $356,000,000, by the end of 1867 [15.2-54, 15.2-55].

16 May 1866: Congress authorized coinage of 5-cent pieces [15.2-56]: **a)** (S. 1) to weigh 77.16 grains, made of copper and nickel, with the nickel not exceeding 5%; **b)** (S. 3) to be legal tender up to $1; and **c)** (S. 3) paper fractional currency smaller than 10 cents prohibited, and old issues to be collected and destroyed.

13 Jul 1866: Congress revised [15.2-57] the internal duties and taxes that had been imposed as a war measure (cf. 3 Mar 1865), reducing licensing fees, lowering import duties, setting the tax on banks at a flat rate, and repealed the 20% tax on manufactures. Treasury Secretary Boutwell estimated in 1872 that the total reduction in revenue to 1872 came to $65,000,000 [15.2-58, 15.2-59].

28 Jul 1866: Congress revised the law on import duties [15.2-60], **a)** (S. 1) altered the duties on cotton, cigars, and liquor; **b)** (S. 4) repealed the fishing bounties; **c)** (S. 11) machines to make beet sugar exempt for one year; and **d)** (S. 14) extended the period for the collection of the direct tax (cf. 5 Aug 1861) in the Southern States until 1 Jan 1868.

2 Mar 1867: Congress passed a revision of the revenue laws [15.2-61]: **a)** (S. 1) 2.5 cents per pound on cotton; **b)** (S. 2) a special tax on apothecaries, butchers, plumbers, confectioners, and gasfitters; **c)** (S. 9) changed procedural rules for collecting and assessing duties and internal taxes, and modifying some of the rates; **d)** (S. 13) changed the income tax: 1) the exemption on the income tax from $600 to $1,000; and 2) a uniform tax rate of 5% over $1,000; **e)** (S. 13) income to include profits on sales of real estate and farm products, interest on U. S. bonds, but allowing deductions for national, State, county, and municipal taxes paid; eliminating the individual deductions; **f)** (S. 13) income taxes to levied until 1870 and no longer; and **g)** (S. 14) $2 per gallon excise tax on liquor. In 1872 Treasury Secretary Boutwell estimated the total decline in revenue to 1872 at $40,000,000 [15.2-62, 15.2-63].

2 Mar 1867: Congress passed legislation regarding the compound interest notes [15.2-64]: **a)** (S. 1) authorized the Treasury Secretary to issue $50,000,000 of temporary loan certificates bearing 3% interest, principal and interest payable in lawful money on demand; **b)** (S. 1) authorized the national banks to hold the certificates as part of their reserves so long as two-thirds of reserves were held as lawful money; and **c)** (S. 1) the amount of temporary certificates outstanding not to exceed $50,000,000. This was a way to pay off and redeem the compound interest notes that were about to mature [15.2-65]. Compound interest notes were Treasury Notes payable at 6% interest after three years, issued in 1863 and 1864; cf. 3 Mar 1863 and 30 Jun 1864.

2 Mar 1867: Congress revised [15.2-66] the import duties on wool: a) on carpets: 3 cents per pound if costing less than 12 cents per pound, 6 cents per pound for higher valued carpets; b) clothing: 10 cents per pound on goods costing 32 cents per pound, 11% *ad valorem* if valued higher; c) combing wool: 12 cents per pound if costing 32 cents, and for higher valued, 10% *ad valorem*. These changes did not seem like much but actually increased the import duties significantly owing to the change in classification [15.2-67]. The wool growers and manufacturers gained some protection from this measure.

26 Mar 1867: Congress passed a revenue exemption and banking law [15.2-68]: **a)** (S. 1) wrapping paper made from cornstalk to be exempt from duty; **b)** (S. 2) national banking associations, State banks, and other bankers to pay a 10% tax on notes of cities and towns paid out since 1 May 1867, to be collected in the same way as the tax on State bank notes; and **c)** (S. 4) ladders made of wood exempt from internal duties. This was one method used to reduce the local notes that had been issued by cities to be used as small change (cf. 17 Jul 1862).

15 Dec 1867: Approximate end of the recession (cf. 15 Apr 1865) [15.2-69].

3 Feb 1868: Congress repealed [15.2-70] the 3% tax on raw cotton (domestic and imported), to which Treasury Secretary Boutwell in 1872 attributed a decline in total revenue of $23,000,000 [15.2-71, 15.2-72].

4 Feb 1868: Congress enacted legislation to suspend the process of retiring and contracting the amount of legal tender notes [15.2-73]. The reason was that the prices of commodities had declined with the contraction of the currency, and producers complained about it [15.2-74].

31 Mar 1868: Congress revised the internal revenue law [15.2-75]: **a)** (S. 1) repealed the remainder of the tax on manufactures except tobacco and lubricating oils and coal oil; **b)** (S. 1) reduced the tax on petroleum by half; and **c)** (S. 4) imposed a tax of $2 per $1000 in sales above $5000 on manufacturers of any goods not otherwise taxed. In 1872 Treasury Secretary Boutwell estimated this led to a total reduction of $45,000,000 in revenue [15.2-76, 15.2-77].

25 Jun 1868: Congress passed legislation [15.2-78] declaring 8 hours to be a normal workday for all employees and contractors to the federal government.

20 Jul 1868: Congress changed the revenue law [15.2-79]: **a)** (S. 1-108) changing the excise taxes on liquor and tobacco, and also specifying records to be kept, work rules, and rules for storage and transportation for distilleries and tobacco growers and manufacturers; and **b)** (S. 109) repealed the taxes on mineral oil and other illuminating oils, petroleum, and oils produced by distilling peat, asphalt, or coal.

25 Jul 1868: Congress authorized [15.2-80] an additional issue of $25,000,000 of temporary loan certificates to retire the remaining compound interest notes outstanding; the temporary certificates to bear interest at 3%, with principal and interest to be payable in lawful money on demand, and may be used as reserves of national banking associations as before (cf. 2 Mar 1867).

19 Feb 1869: Congress passed legislation [15.2-81] prohibiting the national banking associations from receiving United States Notes or National Bank Notes as security or collateral for a loan of money, or agreeing to withhold either from use as an indirect way of using as collateral for a loan of money.

3 Mar 1869: Congress passed legislation [15.2-82] requiring all national banking associations to provide reports to the Comptroller of the Currency, and to have same published in their local newspaper, detailing the resources and liabilities of the associations. The reports are to be made at least five times annually.

18 Mar 1869: Congress clarified [15.2-83] that promises made in 1863 and 1864 that debt payments would be paid in coin, would be respected, stating:

> "it is hereby provided and declared that the faith of the United States is solemnly pledged to the payment in coin or its equivalent of all the obligations of the United States not bearing interest, known as United States Notes, and all of the interest-bearing obligations of the United States, except in cases where the law authorizing the issue of any such obligation has expressly provided that the same may be paid in lawful money or other currency than gold and silver".

This came about because some factions desired that interest on the national debt either be repudiated or paid in legal tender notes (since the reduction of the debt through the sinking fund had not progressed as quickly as desired), although they were supposed to be paid in coin [15.2-84, 15.2-85].

15 Jun 1869: Approximate beginning of a recession [15.2-86].

29 Jan 1870: The U. S. Supreme Court ruled, in Hepburn v. Griswold, that the law establishing the U. S. Notes as legal tender was unconstitutional [15.2-87]. Chief Justice Chase, who wrote the majority opinion, was Secretary of the Treasury when the legal tender law was passed, and he approved of it then. It is not clear why he changed his mind. Most of the legal tender notes were still in circulation, and continued to be circulated and accepted even when not a legal tender since this ruling did not make them void.

12 Jul 1870: Congress passed financial legislation [15.2-88]: **a)** (S. 1) increased the limit on the total circulation of National Bank Notes from $300,000,000 to $354,000,000; **b)** (S. 1) limited the amount of National Bank Notes that could be issued by an individual national bank to $500,000; **c)** (S. 2) the Comptroller of the Currency to report to the Treasury Secretary each month as to how much in National Bank Notes was issued, and the Treasury Secretary to cancel a like amount of 3% temporary

loan certificates issued per 2 Mar 1867 and 25 Jul 1868, in order to obtain the 3% notes in exchange for the new National Bank Notes, and stop paying interest on them; **d)** (S. 2) said 3% notes no longer eligible to be counted as national bank reserves; **e)** (S. 3) any new national banking associations depositing U. S. bonds paying interest in gold per the National Currency Act (cf. 25 Feb 1863) shall be eligible to receive notes from the Treasury for circulation, and the notes thereof to state they are redeemable in gold, and such associations to have a circulation less than $1,000,000; **f)** (S. 4) the new banking associations to keep on hand 25% reserves in gold or silver coin and receive at par any gold notes of other national bank associations; **g)** (S. 5) new banking associations using gold notes shall interpret "lawful money" as gold and silver only; and **h)** (S. 6) the Treasury Secretary was authorized to redistribute National Bank Notes per population or business conditions, but the amount withdrawn is limited to $25,000,000.

The new national banking associations dealing in gold as authorized by this legislation (S. 3, 4, and 5) were called the "gold banks".

This law was passed as a compromise method of supplying currency to the Southern States [15.2-89], while at the same time reducing the 3% loan certificates from circulation. The increase in the National Bank Notes was designed to supply those States with a deficiency of them (South), and withdraw from those States that had a surplus (Rhode Island, Massachusetts, and Connecticut).

14 Jul 1870: Congress revised the customs and income tax laws [15.2-90]: **a)** (S. 1, 2, 21) reduced duties on imports (tea, coffee, sugar, molasses, spices, pig iron); **b)** (S. 3) repealed the sales tax; **c)** (S. 4) repealed most stamp duties on tobacco, mortgages, and liquor; **d)** (S. 6, 7) changed the income tax law: 1) exemption was raised to $2,000; 2) the tax rate was lowered from 5% to 2.5%, 3) income tax to expire in 1871; **d)** (S. 15) imposed a 2.5% dividends of insurance companies; and **e)** (S. 22) expanded the free list. In 1872 Treasury Secretary Boutwell estimated [15.2-91, 15.2-92] the resulting total decline in customs revenue as $29,526,410, and from income, receipts, and sales taxes, as $55,000,000.

14 Jul 1870: Congress passed a law to fund the public debt [15.2-93]: **a)** (S. 1) authorized the Treasury Secretary to issue three kinds of bonds against the credit of the U. S.: 1) $200,000,000 at 5%, payable semi-annually in coin, redeemable after ten years; 2) $300,000,000 at 4.5% payable semi-annually in coin, redeemable after 15 years; 3) $1,000,000,000 at 4% payable in coin semi-annually, redeemable after 30 years; **b)** (S. 1) interest on all bonds exempt from federal and State taxes; **c)** (S. 2) Treasury Secretary may sell the bonds at not less than par, or exchange them for 5-20 bonds at par; **d)** (S. 4) proceeds from the new bond sales may be used to pay off the 5-20 bonds bearing 6% interest that become due; **e)** (S. 5) the Treasury Secretary may receive gold coin and issue certificates of deposits at 2.5% annual for a period not exceeding 30 days, and redeemable in gold; and **f)** (S. 6) U. S. bonds purchased and held by the Treasury as part of the sinking fund to be destroyed.

~ Oct 1870: Treasury Secretary Boutwell issued $1,500,000 in legal tender notes to relieve a cash flow problem among stock market traders and their bankers [15.2-94].

15 Dec 1870: Approximate end of the recession (cf. 15 Jun 1869) [15.2-95].

20 Jan 1871: Congress amended the refunding law (cf. 14 Jul 1870) [15.2-96] to permit the total of bonds issued at 5% be increased to $500,000,000, but the overall total bonds issued to be limited to the original $1,500,000,000; and also permitted interest on such bonds to be paid quarterly.

3 Mar 1871: Congress authorized [15.2-97] the Treasury Secretary to redeem copper coins and other base metal coins in lawful money when presented in sums less than $20.

1 May 1871: The U. S. Supreme Court reversed itself, overturning Hepburn v. Griswold (cf. 29 Jan 1870), deciding in Knox v. Lee that the legal tender law did not violate the Constitution. It held that that the government does have a power to issue legal tender notes, at least in time of emergency (specifically the Civil War). The majority opinion (Justice Strong) stated [15.2-98]:

"If it be held by this court that Congress has no constitutional power, under any circumstances, or in any emergency, to make treasury-notes a legal tender for the payment of all debts (a power confessedly possessed by every independent sovereignty other than the Unites States), the government is without those means of self-preservation, which, all must admit, may, in certain contingencies, become indispensable, even if they were not when the Acts of Congress now called into question were enacted. It is also clear that if we hold the Acts invalid as applicable to debts incurred, or transactions which have taken place since their enactment, our decision must cause, throughout the country, great business derangement, wide-spread distress, and the rankest injustice."

1 May 1872: Congress revised the customs law [15.2-99], eliminating all duties on tea and coffee.

6 Jun 1872: Congress revised the internal revenue and customs law [15.2-100]: a) reduced duties on salt by 50% and on coal by 40%, b) reduced excise taxes on liquor and tobacco, and c) expanded of the free list. Treasury Secretary Boutwell in 1872 estimated that the total reduction in revenue due to this change and the 1 May 1872 change came to $31,172 671 [15.2-101, 15.2-102].

12 Feb 1873: Congress passed the Coinage Act [15.2-103], abolishing the coinage of silver by the Mint, thus eliminating it as standard money. Provisions include: **a)** (S. 1 - 12) called out the offices, duties, and salaries of the affected employees; **b)** (S. 13) specified that standard metal is 90% pure and 10% alloy; the alloy for silver is copper, and the alloy for gold is either copper or copper and silver, but the silver shall be no more than 10% of the alloy; **c)** (S. 14) specified the gold coins authorized in terms of weight of standard metal: 1) gold dollar (25.8 grains); 2) $2.50 quarter Eagle (64.5 grains); 3) 3-dollar (77.4 grains); 4) $5 half Eagle (129 grains); 5) $10 Eagle (258 grains); and 6) $20 double Eagle (516 grains); all legal tender at any amount; **d)** (S. 15) specified the authorized silver coins by standard weight: 1) trade dollar (420 grains); 2) half dollar (12.5 grams = 192.9 grains); 3) quarter dollar (6.25 grams = 96.45 grains); 4) dime (2.5 grams = 38.58 grains); and are legal tender up to $5 in one payment; **e)** (S. 16) specified the authorized minor coins by weight of standard metal: a) 5-cent (77.16 grains, 75% copper and 25% nickel); b) 3-cent (30 grains, 75% copper, 25% nickel); and c) one-cent (48 grains, 95% copper and 5% zinc and tin); all are legal tender up to 25 cents in any one payment; and **f)** (S. 17) stated that no other coins were be minted. It is silent on the legal tender status of existing coins, and they were regarded as such [15.2-104]. The rest of the law is administrative. This abolished the silver dollar and reduced silver to a subsidiary status, tending away from a bimetallic standard toward a gold standard. The market price of silver had been above the mint price for a long time, and silver coins had not circulated since 1834 [15.2-105]; and this demonetization was a formality of the existing situation [15.2-106]. It had no effect on prices, since silver coins were not in common use (few had been coined since 1806, few had circulated since 1834, and duties were paid in gold), and had been replaced by greenbacks and National Bank Notes [15.2-107]. The "trade dollar" was not intended for circulation, but for trade with China.

3 Mar 1873: Congress passed legislation [15.2-108]: **a)** (S. 1) requiring national banking associations to restore their capital when they have incurred losses by assessment upon the shares of stockholders; **b)** (S. 1) required the Treasury Secretary to withhold interest on bonds for notes until the capital position is restored; and **c)** (S. 3) prohibited the use of the word 'national' in the name of any financial institution that is not a national bank.

~15 Sep - ~ 30 Oct 1873: The banks in the U. S. experienced a financial panic. Bolles wrote [15.2-109]: "a financial cyclone struck the country. Prices suddenly went down, great houses failed, and Wall Street raged like a maelstrom". Treasury Secretary Richardson issued $12,000,000 in legal tender notes to relieve the stress, arguing that the $400,000,000 limitations allowed during the Civil War had never been repealed. The problem was that many country banks called in their reserves, but were not available, since they had been loaned out by the central reserve bank in New York to stock brokers on call loans; $60,000,000 could not be called in because the stock market was depressed [15.2-110]. The banks also greatly expanded the use of clearinghouse exchanges as money to be used between the banks (approximately $22,000,000 [15.2-111]). There was a widespread suspension of specie payment in the last week of Sep 1873 [15.2-112]. The NY stock exchange was closed from

20 Sep to 30 Sep 1873. The banks resumed payment in specie at various times toward the end of Oct 1873. Sprague [15.2-113] attributes the problem to several causes: a) expansion of bank loans between 1869 and 1873, especially for speculation in railroad bonds; b) a concentration of reserves in the large cities, which was attractive because some of them paid interest; consequently the sudden demands of depositors in smaller cities led to the inability to respond for demands for cash; and c) the New York banks used the smaller banks' reserves to lend out call loans, which could not be repaid due to a decline in the stock market. Sprague [15.2-114] cites the 1873 Report of the Comptroller of the Currency, which stated that the bank failures were due to "the criminal mismanagement of their officers or to the neglect or violation of the national bank act on the part of their directors". Sprague, writing in 1910, states that this banking panic only affected the banks [15.2-115] referring to conditions at the end of Oct 1873:

> "At that time, the more permanent causes of business depression were beginning to make themselves felt. The transition from business activity was gradual and seems to have extended beyond the close of the year [1873]. There was no sudden and universal trade prostration such as occurred in November and December 1907, lasting during the period of suspension and then followed by considerable recovery to a condition of less severe though more prolonged depression. It is, therefore, reasonable to conclude that the temporary suspension of payments in 1873 had relatively little influence upon the course of trade."

15 Oct 1873: Approximate beginning of a recession [15.2-116].

17 Dec 1873: Congress passed legislation regarding the public debt [15.2-117]: **a)** (S. 1) that the bonds issued as part of the loan obtained in 1858 (cf. 14 Jun 1858 and 2 Mar 1859) are to be redeemed as of 1 Jan 1874, and all interest payments to end; and **b)** (S. 2) authorized the Treasury Secretary to issue bonds at 5% (per 14 Jul 1870 and 20 Jan 1871) to those holding the 1858 bonds if they wish to exchange them at par.

23 Mar - 22 Apr 1874: After a long debate, Congress revised the limitation on the issue of legal tender notes, upwards from $354,000,000 to $400,000,000 [15.2-118], and authorized $46,000,000 in new bank notes to be distributed to banks in the southern and western States. This was intended as a new injection of currency designed to relieve the financial panic, but would have depreciated the currency. It was passed by Congress 14 Apr 1874, but vetoed by President Grant on 22 Apr 1874; a victory for those opposed to depreciation of the money.

18 Jun 1874: Congress clarified [15.2-119] a provision in the banking law (cf. 30 Jun 1864), that institutions doing business only as savings banks, even holding capital, are exempt from taxation of deposits and dividends, so long as profits are divided among the depositors, and the capital stock is invested in the same class of securities as the deposits, and paying at least 4.5% interest to their depositors.

20 Jun 1874: Congress passed legislation on bank regulation [15.2-120]: **a)** (S. 2) removed the requirement that a national bank maintain cash reserves against National Bank Note circulation; **b)** (S. 3) required national banks to keep on deposit in lawful money with the Treasury an amount equal to 5% of its note circulation for redeeming notes or replacing mutilated notes, and counting against the legal reserve; **c)** (S. 4) national banks were permitted to reduce the volume of National Bank Notes; to do so, it was required to deposit money with the Treasury ($9,000 minimum), and the Treasury was to redeem and destroy the U. S. bonds initially used to secure the notes; **d)** (S. 4) the minimum amount of bonds for security against circulation is set at $50,000,000; **e)** (S. 6) limited the total amount of legal tender notes (United States Notes) that could be outstanding at $382,000,000, none of which can be held as a bank reserve, and is to be included in the public debt; **f)** (S. 7, 9) directed the Treasury Secretary to withdraw and re-allocate $55,000,000 from the banks with an excess circulation and provide to places with a deficiency; and **g)** (S. 8) Comptroller of the Currency authorized to sell any deposited bonds if a bank fails to meet the 5% deposit vs. circulation requirement. The purpose of the withdrawal of the $55,000,000 from the east and provide them to the banks in the south and west was to obtain a more uniform distribution of the currency [15.2-121]. The "5% fund" was actually a reserve against circulation (since cash in vault was no longer required for it) [15.2-

122]. The "5% fund" was also used to redeem mutilated notes; Bolles [15.2-123] states that a total of $286,310,153 mutilated notes were redeemed by the Comptroller between 1874 and 1876 inclusive; and $113,898,356 had been replaced between 1869 and 1873 inclusive. In addition, Revised Statute 3586 [15.2-124] limited all silver coins as a legal tender to $5, including ones then in circulation (cf. 12 Feb 1873). There were, however very few in circulation. This completely demonetized silver (but see 28 Feb 1878, when silver was once again made legal tender).

22 Jun 1874: Congress clarified the rule on taxation of savings banks (cf. 18 Jun 1874, permitting savings banks to be taxed) [15.2-125]: that no internal revenue tax is to be levied against the earning of savings banks that have no capital and do business only as receiving deposits and making loans for the benefit of the parties making deposits.

14 Jan 1875: Congress passed a law specifying the process for resumption of specie payments (i.e. redemption of the legal tender U. S. Notes) [15.2-126]. The provisions were: a) (S. 1) silver coins of 10, 25 and 50 cents to be coined to entirely replace the fractional paper currency, and issued at par among the sub-treasuries and post offices; b) (S. 2) repealed the 0.2% charge for coining gold from bullion; c) (S. 3) removed the limitation on the total quantity of National Bank Notes that could be issued (was $354,000,000), and permitted them to increase their notes per the existing laws regarding capital and reserves; d) (S. 3) repealed the requirement for redistribution of the National Bank Notes (cf. 20 Jun 1874); e) (S. 3) Treasury Secretary to permit the increase the number National Bank Notes by $102,500,000 while retiring $82,000,000 of legal tender notes (U. S. Notes = greenbacks) so as to bring the total of legal tender notes down to $300,000,000; f) (S. 3) resumption of payment in specie at par of the United States Notes to begin on 1 Jan 1879, when presented in sums of $50 or more; and g) (S. 3) the specie was to be obtained by using any surplus revenue and selling bonds as authorized on 14 Jul 1870 to obtain the gold and silver. There were many who questioned how effective this might be, given that the advocates of fiat money would probably find ways to circumvent it [15.2-127]. The Democratic Party was opposed to specie redemption, although it had in the past opposed the paper legal tender notes. But as shown later (cf. 1 Jan 1879), the resumption succeeded.

8 Feb 1875: Congress repealed [15.2-128] some of the 10% reduction on import duties that had been enacted 1 May 1872 (since revenues had fallen too low) [15.2-129].

3 Mar 1875: Congress increased import duties [15.2-130] on spirits, tobacco, sugar, and certain cloth since the current rates did not generate enough revenue.

3 Mar 1875: Congress authorized [15.2-131] the coining of a twenty-cent silver piece, to weight 5 grams (77.16 grains) of standard metal (cf. 12 Feb 1873) and to be legal tender up to $5.

22 Jul 1876: Congress passed a joint resolution regarding silver coin [15.2-132]: a) (S. 1) authorized the Treasury Secretary to redeem $10,000,000 in legal tenders with silver coin; b) (S. 1) the legal tender notes to kept in a separate fund and used to redeem fractional currency notes, and the fractional currency notes are to be destroyed; c) (S. 2) eliminated the legal tender status of the "trade dollars", and permitted the Treasury Secretary to coin only as much as is required for export requirements; d) (S. 3) authorized the minting of an additional $50,000,000 in subsidiary silver coins; e) (S. 4) silver bullion for the coinage to be procured at market rate so long as there are no losses to the Treasury; and f) (S. 4) the total amount invested in silver bullion at any time to not exceed $200,000.

May - Nov 1877: The Treasury Secretary sold $40,000,000 in bonds at 4 or 4.5% interest to obtain gold necessary for resumption of specie [15.2-133].

28 Feb 1878: Congress passed (over President Hayes' veto) a law (Bland-Allison Act) [15.2-134]: a) (S. 1) Treasury required to buy between $2,000,000 and $4,000,000 of silver each month to be coined at 412.5 grains of standard silver (cf. 18 Jan 1837) to be legal tender for all debts public and private except where negated by contract; b) (S. 1) silver could not be coined on private account; and c) (S. 1) the amount invested in silver to comply with this requirement not to exceed $5,000,000. The limitations on private coining and the amount the Treasury could buy was due to the fact that under free coinage, a great deal of bullion would be brought in at $0.70 per oz. and coined into $1.29 in money,

which would have generated an enormous depreciation in the purchasing power thereof [15.2-135]. The Treasury made a profit on the silver purchased at the market price (then about $0.70 per oz.) and coined into $1.29 in coins. Debtors believed it would make repayment of debts easier. This was an attempt to return to the bimetallic free coinage system in order to aid the silver miners in the western States. But the law did not achieve its objectives since the price of silver continued to fall owing to the large amount produced, and the additional coin that was minted was not enough to induce the public to use the coins or to depreciate the currency. It had very little effect on prices, although farmers believed that a greater amount of money would increase the prices of their products.

11 Apr 1878: The Treasury Secretary sold $50,000,000 in bonds at 4% interest to obtain gold necessary to resume redemption of paper in specie beginning 1 Jan 1879 [15.2-136].

2 May 1878: Congress repealed [15.2-137] the law that authorized the coining of a 20-cent silver coin (cf. 3 Mar 1875).

31 May 1878: Congress passed a law [15.2-138] prohibiting the Treasury Secretary from retiring any more legal tender notes. The amount of legal tenders in circulation at this time was $346,681,016. The total reduction of legal tenders since 1875 was $35,318,984 (including the $10,000,000 per the law passed 22 Jul 1876) [15.2-139, 15.2-140].

31 Dec 1878: The Treasury possessed $113,508,804.50 in gold coin in preparation for resumption of payments, starting the next day [15.2-141]. The U. S. had also benefitted from a crop failure in Europe, and the U. S. surplus was sold there for gold.

15.3 Data, 1863-1878

Figures 15.3-1 and 15.3-2 show the U. S. government revenue and expenditures for 1863 to 1878.

Day	Year	Panama Canal Proceeds of Bonds	Customs	Internal Revenue		Miscellaneous			Postal	Public Debt Sales	Excess of deposits to retire national bank notes over redemption	Total
				Income and Profits taxes	Misc.	Sales of Public Lands	Direct Tax	Other Misc.				
30 Jun	1863	0	69,059,642	2,741,858	34,898,930	167,617	1,485,103	3,741,794	11,163,789	775,185,707	0	898,444,442
30 Jun	1864	0	102,316,152	20,294,732	89,446,402	588,333	475,648	49,590,595	12,438,253	1,088,188,103	0	1,363,338,222
30 Jun	1865	0	84,928,260	60,979,329	148,484,886	996,553	1,200,573	30,693,916	14,556,158	1,474,495,997	0	1,816,335,674
30 Jun	1866	0	179,046,651	72,982,159	236,244,654	665,031	1,974,754	66,903,980	14,436,986	612,250,667	0	1,184,504,884
30 Jun	1867	0	176,417,810	66,014,429	200,013,108	1,163,575	4,200,233	29,192,365	15,297,026	486,657,277	0	978,955,827
30 Jun	1868	0	164,464,599	41,455,598	149,631,991	1,348,715	1,788,145	39,680,390	16,292,600	544,368,616	0	959,030,658
30 Jun	1869	0	180,048,426	34,791,856	123,564,605	4,020,344	765,685	26,373,628	18,344,510	101,448,272	0	489,357,328
30 Jun	1870	0	194,538,374	37,775,874	147,123,882	3,350,481	229,102	28,236,255	19,772,220	31,571,422	0	462,597,614
30 Jun	1871	0	206,270,408	19,162,651	123,935,503	2,388,646	580,355	30,986,381	20,037,045	91,603,212	0	494,964,202
30 Jun	1872	0	216,370,286	14,436,862	116,205,316	2,575,714	0	24,518,688	21,915,426	173,717,750	0	569,740,043
30 Jun	1873	0	188,089,522	5,062,312	108,667,002	2,882,312	315,254	28,721,800	22,996,741	38,681,450	0	395,416,396
30 Jun	1874	0	163,103,833	139,472	102,270,313	1,852,428	0	37,612,708	26,471,071	183,235,866	0	514,685,693
30 Jun	1875	0	157,167,722	233	110,007,261	1,413,640	0	19,411,195	26,791,360	133,118,500	0	447,909,911
30 Jun	1876	0	148,071,984	588	116,700,144	1,129,466	93,798	27,794,148	28,644,197	133,234,684	0	455,669,012
30 Jun	1877	0	130,956,493	98	118,630,310	976,253	0	30,687,068	27,531,585	141,290,845	0	450,072,653
30 Jun	1878	0	130,170,680	0	110,581,624	1,079,743	0	15,931,830	29,277,516	198,850,250	0	485,891,645

1. The data for the revenue for 1863 to 1878 is from W. G. McAdoo, "Annual Report of the Secretary of the Treasury on the State of the Finances for the Fiscal Year Ended June 30, 1914", Washington: U. S. Government Printing Office, 1915, pp. 230-241; Treasury Document 2721. This data was modified from per Henry Morgenthau, "Annual Report of the Secretary of the Treasury on the State of the Finances for the Fiscal Year Ended June 30, 1940", Treasury Document 3111, pp. 642-649, which shows "internal reveune" broken out as income taxes and miscellaneous. It is the same data as reported previously (cf. 1914), but shows income taxes and miscellaneous taxes as separate categories.

Figure 15.3-1: U. S. Government Revenue, 1863-1878

			U. S. Government Expenditures, 1863-1878 (USD)									
			Ordinary Disbursements									
Day	Year	Panama Canal Disburse-ments	Civil & Misc.	War Dep't	Navy Dep't	Indians	Pensions	Interest on Public Debt	Postal	Public Debt Retired	Excess of National Bank Notes Retired Over Deposits	Total
30 Jun	1863	0	22,449,068	603,314,411	63,261,235	3,152,032	1,078,513	24,729,700	11,913,103	178,982,635	0	908,880,700
30 Jun	1864	0	26,572,236	690,391,048	85,704,963	2,629,975	4,985,473	53,685,421	13,438,233	388,010,965	0	1,265,418,320
30 Jun	1865	0	42,739,383	1,030,690,400	122,617,434	5,059,360	16,347,621	77,395,090	14,806,158	607,174,211	0	1,916,829,660
30 Jun	1866	0	40,613,114	283,154,676	43,285,662	3,295,729	15,605,549	133,067,624	14,436,986	530,287,590	0	1,063,746,933
30 Jun	1867	0	47,593,557	95,224,415	31,034,011	4,642,531	20,936,551	143,781,591	18,813,693	586,933,849	0	948,960,202
30 Jun	1868	0	48,956,676	123,246,648	25,775,502	4,100,682	23,782,386	140,424,045	20,345,792	610,450,237	0	997,081,972
30 Jun	1869	0	51,078,551	78,501,990	20,000,757	7,042,923	28,476,621	130,694,242	23,740,021	140,385,928	0	479,921,036
30 Jun	1870	0	48,392,882	57,655,675	21,780,229	3,407,938	28,340,202	129,235,498	24,616,799	156,807,197	0	470,236,423
30 Jun	1871	0	55,350,666	35,799,991	19,431,027	7,426,997	34,443,894	125,576,565	25,168,295	216,694,334	0	519,891,773
30 Jun	1872	0	55,809,757	35,372,157	21,249,809	7,061,728	28,533,402	117,357,839	27,090,426	292,836,270	0	585,311,392
30 Jun	1873	0	67,837,635	46,323,138	23,526,256	7,951,704	29,359,426	104,750,688	28,487,216	101,659,405	0	409,895,472
30 Jun	1874	0	80,427,548	42,313,927	30,932,587	6,692,462	29,038,414	107,119,815	31,185,116	177,818,564	0	505,528,436
30 Jun	1875	0	63,859,056	41,120,645	21,497,626	8,384,656	29,456,216	103,093,544	34,003,006	151,150,636	0	452,565,389
30 Jun	1876	0	68,507,120	38,070,888	18,963,309	5,966,558	28,257,395	100,243,271	33,736,737	166,128,514	0	459,873,796
30 Jun	1877	0	52,756,193	37,082,735	14,959,935	5,277,007	27,963,752	97,124,511	33,701,924	151,239,525	0	420,105,585
30 Jun	1878	0	47,424,309	32,154,147	17,365,301	4,629,280	27,137,019	102,500,874	35,030,910	143,997,993	0	410,239,837

The data for the expenditures for 1863 to 1878 is from W. G. McAdoo, "Annual Report of the Secretary of the Treasury on the State of the Finances for the Fiscal Year Ended June 30, 1914", Washington: U. S. Government Printing Office, 1915, pp. 230-241; Treasury Document 2721.

Figure 15.3-2: U. S. Government Expenditures, 1863-1878

Figure 15.3-3 shows the national debt and per-capita debt for this period. Refer to the Introduction to Part 2 for a sense of wages vs. per-capita national debt.

		U. S. National Debt, 1863-1878 (USD)							
Day	Year	Principal ($) [1]	Population [2]	Debt per Capita ($) [2]	Day	Year	Principal ($) [1]	Population [2]	Debt per Capita ($) [2]
30 Jun	1863	1,119,773,681	33,577,836	33.35	30 Jun	1871	2,322,052,141	39,639,668	58.58
30 Jun	1864	1,815,830,814	34,289,341	52.96	30 Jun	1872	2,209,990,838	40,720,965	54.27
30 Jun	1865	2,677,929,012	35,000,846	76.51	30 Jun	1873	2,151,210,345	41,802,262	51.46
30 Jun	1866	2,755,763,929	35,712,351	77.17	30 Jun	1874	2,159,932,730	42,883,559	50.37
30 Jun	1867	2,650,168,223	36,423,856	72.76	30 Jun	1875	2,156,276,649	43,964,856	49.05
30 Jun	1868	2,583,446,456	37,135,361	69.57	30 Jun	1876	2,130,845,778	45,046,152	47.30
30 Jun	1869	2,545,110,590	37,846,866	67.25	30 Jun	1877	2,107,759,903	46,127,449	45.69
30 Jun	1870	2,436,453,269	38,558,371	63.19	30 Jun	1878	2,159,418,315	47,208,746	45.74

1. Public debt data from 1863 to 1878 is from the Annual Report of the Secretary of the Treasury, 1980, pp. 61, 62.
2. Population values are based on the dicennial census from the Census Bureau, and linearly interpolated. Per-capita is based on these values.

Figure 15.3-3: National Debt and Per-Capita Share Thereof, 1863-1878

Figures 15.3-4 and 15.4-5 show the assets and liabilities of all State and private banks, including savings, savings and loan, and trust companies on the 30 Jun call dates.

			Assets of Reporting State & Private Banks, 1863-1878 (millions USD)					
Day	Year	Number of Banks	Loans & Discounts, incl. Overdrafts	U. S. Gov't and Other Securities	Cash	Due from Banks	Other Assets	Total Assets
~30 Jun	1863	1,466	648.602	180.508	205.563	96.934	60.143	1,191.750
~30 Jun	1864	1,089	483.906	57.183	99.633	50.409	29.530	720.661
~30 Jun	1865	349	155.081	18.326	31.930	16.155	9.464	230.956
~30 Jun	1866	297	131.974	15.595	27.173	13.748	8.054	196.544
~30 Jun	1867	272	120.866	14.282	24.885	12.591	7.376	180.000
~30 Jun	1868	247	109.757	12.970	22.598	11.433	6.698	163.456
~30 Jun	1869	259	115.089	13.600	23.696	11.989	7.023	171.397
~30 Jun	1870	325	144.416	17.066	29.734	15.044	8.813	215.073
~30 Jun	1871	452	200.850	23.734	41.354	20.923	12.256	299.117
~30 Jun	1872	566	251.507	29.720	51.783	26.200	15.348	374.558
~30 Jun	1873	1,330	514.319	276.436	19.704	28.071	41.581	880.111
~30 Jun	1874	1,569	638.187	280.797	42.822	37.482	39.346	1,038.634
~30 Jun	1875	1,260	775.083	359.164	49.588	45.068	62.524	1,291.427
~30 Jun	1876	1,357	793.491	390.797	50.951	51.781	70.236	1,357.256
~30 Jun	1877	1,306	819.307	420.569	55.634	56.753	77.402	1,429.665
~30 Jun	1878	1,173	726.141	414.265	51.810	53.195	84.792	1,330.203

Condition of State and private banks (including savings and savings & loan and trust companies) on 30 Jun call dates from from Annual Report of the Comptroller of the Currency, 1931 (7 Dec 1931), Table 94; pp. 1018, 1019.

Figure 15.3-4: Assets of State and Private Banks, 30 Jun Call Date, 1863-1878

				Liabilities of Reporting State & Private Banks, 1863-1878 (millions USD)				
Day	Year	Number of Banks	Capital	Surplus and Net Undivided Profits	Notes in Circulation	Total Deposits	Bills Payable & Rediscounts	Other Liabilities	Total Liabilities
~30 Jun	1863	1,466	405.046	0.000	238.677	494.213	0.000	53.814	1,191.750
~30 Jun	1864	1,089	311.554	0.000	150.431	233.155	0.000	25.521	720.661
~30 Jun	1865	349	71.182	0.000	48.210	74.721	0.000	36.843	230.956
~30 Jun	1866	297	66.479	0.000	41.026	63.588	0.000	25.451	196.544
~30 Jun	1867	272	65.204	0.000	37.573	58.235	0.000	18.988	180.000
~30 Jun	1868	247	66.364	0.000	34.120	52.883	0.000	10.089	163.456
~30 Jun	1869	259	66.969	0.000	35.777	55.452	0.000	13.199	171.397
~30 Jun	1870	325	86.513	0.000	44.894	69.582	0.000	14.084	215.073
~30 Jun	1871	452	111.444	0.000	62.438	96.773	0.000	28.462	299.117
~30 Jun	1872	566	122.129	0.000	78.185	121.180	0.000	53.064	374.558
~30 Jun	1873	1,330	42.706	43.485	0.175	788.956	0.000	4.789	880.111
~30 Jun	1874	1,569	59.306	54.520	0.153	912.121	0.000	12.534	1,038.634
~30 Jun	1875	1,260	90.939	68.922	0.178	1,111.233	0.000	20.155	1,291.427
~30 Jun	1876	1,357	101.961	83.127	0.388	1,151.314	0.000	20.466	1,357.256
~30 Jun	1877	1,306	133.297	85.390	0.388	1,187.839	0.000	22.751	1,429.665
~30 Jun	1878	1,173	117.280	79.151	0.388	1,107.004	0.000	26.380	1,330.203

Condition of State and private banks (including savings and savings & loan and trust companies) on 30 Jun call dates from from Annual Report of the Comptroller of the Currency, 1931 (7 Dec 1931), Table 94; pp. 1018, 1019.

Figure 15.3-5: Liabilities of State and Private Banks, 30 Jun Call Date, 1863-1878

Figures 15.3-6 and 15.3-7 show the assets and liabilities of all national banks on the 30 Jun call date for this period.

			Loans & Discounts, incl.	U. S. Gov't and Other		Due from	Other	
Day	Year	Number of Banks	Overdrafts	Securities	Cash	Banks	Assets	Total Assets
~30 Jun	1863	66	5.466	5.665	2.212	3.118	0.337	16.798
~30 Jun	1864	467	70.747	92.531	47.628	38.330	3.038	252.274
~30 Jun	1865	1,294	362.443	393.988	199.515	144.370	26.139	1,126.455
~30 Jun	1866	1,634	550.353	467.601	231.921	206.756	19.764	1,476.395
~30 Jun	1867	1,636	588.450	521.967	130.334	230.284	23.050	1,494.085
~30 Jun	1868	1,640	655.730	507.307	136.338	247.153	25.639	1,572.167
~30 Jun	1869	1,619	686.348	466.204	112.718	269.225	29.679	1,564.174
~30 Jun	1870	1,612	719.341	452.668	144.201	216.629	32.918	1,565.757
~30 Jun	1871	1,723	789.417	455.689	163.325	259.051	35.933	1,703.415
~30 Jun	1872	1,853	871.531	449.790	165.574	246.098	37.844	1,770.837
~30 Jun	1873	1,968	925.558	444.912	179.290	259.500	41.975	1,851.235
~30 Jun	1874	1,983	926.196	451.203	199.026	230.504	44.912	1,851.841
~30 Jun	1875	2,076	972.926	442.780	180.646	251.285	65.602	1,913.239
~30 Jun	1876	2,091	933.687	427.417	166.396	233.450	64.811	1,825.761
~30 Jun	1877	2,078	901.731	431.044	165.008	205.907	70.663	1,774.353
~30 Jun	1878	2,056	835.078	460.213	155.474	232.028	67.672	1,750.465

Condition of national banks on 30 Jun call dates from from Annual Report of the Comptroller of the Currency, 1931 (7 Dec 1931), Table 95; p. 1021

Figure 15.3-6: Assets of National Banks, 30 Jun Call Date, 1863-1878

				Surplus and Net Undivided	Notes in	Total	Bills Payable &	Other	Total
Day	Year	Number of Banks	Capital	Profits	Circulation	Deposits	Rediscounts	Liabilities	Liabilities
~30 Jun	1863	66	7.189	0.128	0.000	9.479	0.000	0.002	16.798
~30 Jun	1864	467	75.214	4.224	25.826	146.796	0.000	0.214	252.274
~30 Jun	1865	1,294	325.835	54.463	131.452	614.242	0.000	0.463	1,126.455
~30 Jun	1866	1,634	414.270	79.438	267.799	694.892	0.000	19.996	1,476.395
~30 Jun	1867	1,636	418.558	93.889	291.770	685.384	0.000	4.484	1,494.085
~30 Jun	1868	1,640	420.105	109.383	294.908	744.607	0.000	3.164	1,572.167
~30 Jun	1869	1,619	422.659	126.032	292.753	716.044	4.127	2.559	1,564.174
~30 Jun	1870	1,612	427.236	134.552	291.184	705.518	5.045	2.222	1,565.757
~30 Jun	1871	1,723	450.331	143.857	307.794	791.066	8.399	1.968	1,703.415
~30 Jun	1872	1,853	470.543	155.416	327.093	805.397	10.687	1.701	1,770.837
~30 Jun	1873	1,968	490.110	172.154	338.789	836.227	12.731	1.224	1,851.235
~30 Jun	1874	1,983	491.004	184.572	338.539	827.928	8.789	1.009	1,851.841
~30 Jun	1875	2,076	501.569	185.329	318.148	897.387	10.019	0.787	1,913.239
~30 Jun	1876	2,091	500.394	178.506	294.445	841.716	10.041	0.659	1,825.761
~30 Jun	1877	2,078	481.045	175.222	290.002	818.360	9.202	0.522	1,774.353
~30 Jun	1878	2,056	470.393	158.662	299.621	813.894	7.477	0.418	1,750.465

Condition of National banks on 30 Jun call dates from from Annual Report of the Comptroller of the Currency, 1931 (7 Dec 1931), Table 95; p. 1021

Figure 15.3-7: Liabilities of National Banks, 30 Jun Call Date, 1863-1878

Figures 15.3-8 and 15.3-9 show the assets and liabilities of the combined State, private, and national banks on the 30 Jun call date for this period. Keep in mind the State and private applies only to the ones required by State law to provide reports.

Combined Assets of National, State, and Private Banks, 1863-1878 (millions USD)								
Day	Year	Number of Banks	Loans & Discounts, incl. Overdrafts	U. S. Gov't and Other Securities	Cash	Due from Banks	Other Assets	Total Assets
~ 30 Jun	1863	1,532	654.068	186.173	207.775	100.052	60.480	1,208.548
~ 30 Jun	1864	1,556	554.653	149.714	147.261	88.739	32.568	972.935
~ 30 Jun	1865	1,643	517.524	412.314	231.445	160.525	35.603	1,357.411
~ 30 Jun	1866	1,931	682.327	483.196	259.094	220.504	27.818	1,672.939
~ 30 Jun	1867	1,908	709.316	536.249	155.219	242.875	30.426	1,674.085
~ 30 Jun	1868	1,887	765.487	520.277	158.936	258.586	32.337	1,735.623
~ 30 Jun	1869	1,878	801.437	479.804	136.414	281.214	36.702	1,735.571
~ 30 Jun	1870	1,937	863.757	469.734	173.935	231.673	41.731	1,780.830
~ 30 Jun	1871	2,175	990.267	479.423	204.679	279.974	48.189	2,002.532
~ 30 Jun	1872	2,419	1,123.038	479.510	217.357	272.298	53.192	2,145.395
~ 30 Jun	1873	3,298	1,439.877	721.348	198.994	287.571	83.556	2,731.346
~ 30 Jun	1874	3,552	1,564.383	732.000	241.848	267.986	84.258	2,890.475
~ 30 Jun	1875	3,336	1,748.009	801.944	230.234	296.353	128.126	3,204.666
~ 30 Jun	1876	3,448	1,727.178	818.214	217.347	285.231	135.047	3,183.017
~ 30 Jun	1877	3,384	1,721.038	851.613	220.642	262.660	148.065	3,204.018
~ 30 Jun	1878	3,229	1,561.219	874.478	207.284	285.223	152.464	3,080.668
Condition of all reporting banks (National, State, savings, and savings & loan and trust companies) per Annual Report of the Comptroller of the Currency, 1931 (7 Dec 1931), Table 96; pp. 1023, 1024.								

Figure 15.3-8: Combined Assets of National, State, and Private Banks, 30 Jun, 1863-1878

Combined Liabilities of National, State, and Private Banks, 1863-1878 (millions USD)								
Day	Year	Number of Banks	Capital	Surplus and Net Undivided Profits	Notes in Circulation	Total Deposits	Bills Payable & Rediscounts	Other Liabilities	Total Liabilities
~ 30 Jun	1863	1,532	412.235	0.128	238.677	503.692	0.000	53.816	1,208.548
~ 30 Jun	1864	1,556	386.768	4.224	176.257	379.951	0.000	25.735	972.935
~ 30 Jun	1865	1,643	397.017	54.463	179.662	688.963	0.000	37.306	1,357.411
~ 30 Jun	1866	1,931	480.749	79.438	308.825	758.480	0.000	45.447	1,672.939
~ 30 Jun	1867	1,908	483.762	93.889	329.343	743.619	0.000	23.472	1,674.085
~ 30 Jun	1868	1,887	486.469	109.383	329.028	797.490	0.000	13.253	1,735.623
~ 30 Jun	1869	1,878	489.628	126.032	328.530	771.496	4.127	15.758	1,735.571
~ 30 Jun	1870	1,937	513.749	134.552	336.078	775.100	5.045	16.306	1,780.830
~ 30 Jun	1871	2,175	561.775	143.857	370.232	887.839	8.399	30.430	2,002.532
~ 30 Jun	1872	2,419	592.672	155.416	405.278	926.577	10.687	54.765	2,145.395
~ 30 Jun	1873	3,298	532.816	215.639	338.964	1,625.183	12.731	6.013	2,731.346
~ 30 Jun	1874	3,552	550.310	239.092	338.692	1,740.049	8.789	13.543	2,890.475
~ 30 Jun	1875	3,336	592.508	254.251	318.326	2,008.620	10.019	20.942	3,204.666
~ 30 Jun	1876	3,448	602.355	261.633	294.833	1,993.030	10.041	21.125	3,183.017
~ 30 Jun	1877	3,384	614.342	260.612	290.390	2,006.199	9.202	23.273	3,204.018
~ 30 Jun	1878	3,229	587.673	237.813	300.009	1,920.898	7.477	26.798	3,080.668
Condition of all reporting banks (National, State, savings, and savings & loan and trust companies) per Annual Report of the Comptroller of the Currency, 1931 (7 Dec 1931), Table 96; pp. 1023, 1024.								

Figure 15.3-9: Combined Liabilities of National, State, and Private Banks, 30 Jun, 1863-1878

Figures 15.3-10 through 15.3-17 show the condition statements (assets and liabilities) of the national banks on each of the reporting dates, in 4-year increments. The exact dates are shown, as there was no regular schedule. Some of the source data contains errors and misprints; these have been corrected as shown in bold type. There is no corresponding data for the State and private banks.

National Banking System Assets, 1863-1868 (millions USD) [1]

Day	Year	Loans & Discounts [2]	U.S. Bonds (Circulation) [4]	5% Redemption Fund with Treasury [3]	U.S. Bonds (Deposit)	U.S. Bonds, Other Bonds, and Stocks	Real Estate	Due from National and State Banks	Due from Reserve Agents	Specie	Legal Tender Notes [5]	Clearing-house exchanges	Fractional Currency	Compound Interest Notes & 3% Certificates	Checks & Other Cash Items	Miscellaneous [6]	Due from U.S. Treasury [7]	Total Assets
5 Oct	1863	5.466	5.663	0.000	0.000	0.106	0.178	2.626	0.000	1.447	0.000	0.000	0.000	0.000	0.492	0.821	0.000	16.798
4 Jan	1864	10.666	15.112	0.000	0.000	0.075	0.381	4.786	0.000	5.019	0.000	0.000	0.000	0.000	0.578	1.014	0.000	37.631
4 Apr	1864	31.594	41.175	0.000	0.000	0.432	0.756	13.237	0.000	22.961	0.000	0.000	0.000	0.000	2.652	2.013	0.000	114.820
4 Jul	1864	70.747	92.531	0.000	0.000	0.842	1.694	33.273	0.000	42.284	0.000	0.000	0.000	0.000	5.057	5.847	0.000	252.274
3 Oct	1864	93.239	108.064	0.000	0.000	1.435	2.202	34.017	0.000	44.801	0.000	0.000	0.000	0.000	7.640	5.709	0.000	297.108
2 Jan	1865	166.449	176.579	0.000	0.000	3.295	4.083	50.656	0.000	4.482	72.536	0.000	0.000	0.000	17.837	16.652	0.000	512.569
3 Apr	1865	252.404	277.620	0.000	0.000	4.276	6.525	63.518	0.000	6.660	112.999	0.000	0.000	0.000	29.681	17.832	0.000	771.515
3 Jul	1865	362.443	391.745	0.000	0.000	12.569	11.231	103.056	0.000	9.437	168.426	0.000	0.000	0.000	41.315	26.234	0.000	1,126.455
2 Oct	1865	487.170	427.731	0.000	0.000	19.049	14.703	107.372	0.000	18.072	189.988	0.000	0.000	0.000	72.310	23.372	0.000	1,359.768
1 Jan	1866	500.650	298.377	0.000	142.004	17.484	15.436	107.913	0.000	19.205	187.847	0.000	0.000	0.000	89.838	26.024	0.000	1,404.777
2 Apr	1866	528.081	315.850	0.000	125.626	17.380	15.896	101.247	0.000	17.530	189.868	0.000	0.000	0.000	105.491	25.441	0.000	1,442.408
2 Jul	1866	550.353	326.483	0.000	121.153	17.566	16.731	110.679	0.000	12.629	201.425	0.000	0.000	0.000	96.077	23.298	0.000	1,476.395
1 Oct	1866	603.315	331.843	0.000	94.975	15.887	17.134	122.861	0.000	9.227	205.794	0.000	0.000	0.000	**100.684**	25.243	0.000	1,526.963
7 Jan	1867	608.772	339.571	0.000	36.186	**68.022**	18.925	105.548	0.000	19.726	104.872	0.000	0.000	82.047	101.430	26.123	0.000	1,511.223
1 Apr	1867	597.648	338.864	0.000	38.466	66.834	**19.653**	104.859	0.000	11.445	92.861	0.000	0.000	84.066	87.951	22.805	0.000	1,465.451
1 Jul	1867	588.450	337.684	0.000	38.369	67.086	19.801	101.972	0.000	11.129	102.535	0.000	0.000	75.488	128.312	23.258	0.000	1,494.085
7 Oct	1867	609.675	338.640	0.000	37.862	63.969	20.640	103.607	0.000	12.798	100.551	0.000	0.000	56.888	134.603	20.236	0.000	1,499.469
6 Jan	1868	616.603	339.064	0.000	37.316	63.530	21.126	107.792	0.000	20.982	114.306	0.000	1.928	48.242	109.390	22.368	0.000	1,502.648
6 Apr	1868	628.029	339.687	0.000	**37.449**	65.833	22.083	102.975	0.000	18.374	84.390	0.000	1.826	63.172	114.993	20.858	0.000	1,499.669
6 Jul	1868	655.730	339.569	0.000	37.853	63.076	22.700	123.077	0.000	20.756	100.166	0.000	1.863	64.378	124.076	18.923	0.000	1,572.167
5 Oct	1868	657.669	340.487	0.000	37.360	57.511	22.748	110.127	0.000	13.005	92.453	0.000	2.263	63.594	143.241	19.164	0.000	1,559.622

1. Source: Annual Report, Comptroller of the Currency, 1914, Vol. 2, Table 56 (p. 220 ff)
2. Includes overdrafts
3. Required in 1874, but not cited separately on statements until 1887.
4. Bonds for security against circulation and deposits were combined until 1866.
5. These are the U.S. Notes (greenbacks).
6. Includes premiums on bonds, current expenses, and bills of national and other banks.
7. Includes certificates of deposits and other deposits with the U.S. Treasury.

Figure 15.3-10: National Bank System Assets, 1863-1868

National Banking System Liabilities, 1863-1868 (millions USD) [1]

Day	Year	Number of Banks	Paid-in Capital	Other Liabilities [2]	Due to Other Banks	Due to Reserve Agents	U.S. Deposits [3]	Individual and Other Deposits	National Bank Notes in Circulation	State Bank Notes in Circulation	Bills & Notes Rediscounted	Total Liabilities
5 Oct	1863	66	7.188	0.130	0.981	0.000	0.000	8.498	0.000	0.000	0.000	16.798
4 Jan	1864	139	14.741	1.256	2.154	0.000	0.000	19.450	0.030	0.000	0.000	37.631
4 Apr	1864	307	42.204	4.728	6.815	0.000	0.000	51.275	9.798	0.000	0.000	114.820
4 Jul	1864	467	75.214	4.438	27.382	0.000	0.000	119.414	25.826	0.000	0.000	252.274
3 Oct	1864	508	86.783	8.036	34.862	0.000	0.000	122.167	45.261	0.000	0.000	297.108
2 Jan	1865	638	135.619	21.213	67.723	0.000	37.765	183.480	66.769	0.000	0.000	512.569
3 Apr	1865	907	215.326	35.707	100.994	0.000	57.630	262.961	98.896	0.000	0.000	771.515
3 Jul	1865	1,294	325.835	54.926	157.853	0.000	58.033	398.358	131.452	0.000	0.000	1,126.455
2 Oct	1865	1,513	393.157	72.008	174.200	0.000	48.170	500.911	171.322	0.000	0.000	1,359.768
1 Jan	1866	1,582	403.357	71.973	118.503	0.000	29.747	522.508	213.240	45.449	0.000	1,404.777
2 Apr	1866	1,612	409.274	75.652	110.909	0.000	29.151	534.735	248.886	33.801	0.000	1,442.408
2 Jul	1866	1,634	414.270	79.438	122.448	0.000	39.105	533.338	267.799	19.996	0.000	1,476.395
1 Oct	1866	1,644	415.472	85.953	137.518	0.000	33.401	564.617	280.254	9.748	0.000	1,526.963
7 Jan	1867	1,648	420.230	86.954	117.179	0.000	29.762	558.700	291.437	6.961	0.000	1,511.223
1 Apr	1867	1,642	419.399	91.337	114.296	0.000	30.124	512.046	292.789	5.460	0.000	1,465.451
1 Jul	1867	1,636	418.558	93.889	112.481	0.000	33.313	539.599	291.761	4.484	0.000	1,494.085
7 Oct	1867	1,642	420.073	100.447	112.756	0.000	27.414	540.798	293.888	4.092	0.000	1,499.469
6 Jan	1868	1,642	420.261	101.986	120.012	0.000	27.514	534.705	294.377	3.792	0.000	1,502.648
6 Apr	1868	1,643	420.676	105.211	115.397	0.000	27.727	532.011	295.336	3.310	0.000	1,499.669
6 Jul	1868	1,640	420.105	109.383	140.662	0.000	28.103	575.842	294.908	3.164	0.000	1,572.167
5 Oct	1868	1,643	420.635	114.092	123.135	0.000	22.144	580.941	295.769	2.906	0.000	1,559.622

1. Source: Annual Report, Comptroller of the Currency, 1914, Vol. 2, Table 56 (p. 220 ff)
2. Includes surplus fund, undivided profits, unpaid dividends, bills payable, reserved for taxes, and miscellaneous.
3. Includes deposits of U.S. disbursing officers.

Figure 15.3-11: National Bank System Liabilities, 1863-1868

| | | | U. S. Obligations Deposited with Treasury as Security for: | | | Investments | | Balances | | | Lawful Money for Reserves | | | | Other Assets | | | |
| | | | Circulation | | Deposit | | | | | | | | | | | | | |
Day	Year	Loans & Discounts [2]	U. S. Bonds	5% Redemption Fund with Treasury [3]	U. S. Bonds	U. S. Bonds, Other Bonds, and Stocks	Real Estate	Due from National and State Banks	Due from Reserve Agents	Specie	Legal Tender Notes [4]	Clearing-house exchanges	Fractional Currency	Compound Interest Notes & 3% Certificates	Checks & Other Cash Items	Miscellaneous [5]	Due from U. S. Treasury [6]	Total Assets
4 Jan	1869	644.945	338.540	0.000	34.538	55.138	23.290	43.783	65.727	29.627	88.239	0.000	2.280	52.075	142.606	19.605	0.000	1,540.394
17 Apr	1869	662.085	338.379	0.000	29.721	50.301	23.798	38.596	57.554	9.945	80.875	0.000	2.089	51.190	154.137	19.083	0.000	1,517.753
12 Jun	1869	686.348	338.700	0.000	27.625	48.254	23.859	44.697	62.913	18.455	80.934	0.000	1.805	49.815	161.615	19.154	0.000	1,564.174
9 Oct	1869	682.883	339.480	0.000	18.704	48.155	25.169	44.184	56.670	23.002	83.719	0.000	2.091	45.845	108.810	18.515	0.000	1,497.227
22 Jan	1870	688.875	339.351	0.000	17.592	45.760	26.003	41.314	71.641	48.345	87.709	0.000	2.477	43.820	111.625	21.750	0.000	1,546.261
24 Mar	1870	710.849	339.251	0.000	16.102	47.816	26.331	39.749	73.435	37.097	82.486	75.318	2.285	43.570	11.268	23.591	0.000	1,529.148
9 Jun	1870	719.341	338.845	0.000	15.704	51.577	26.593	46.560	74.635	31.099	94.574	83.937	2.185	43.465	11.498	25.744	0.000	1,565.757
8 Oct	1870	715.928	340.857	0.000	15.382	45.939	27.471	43.151	66.276	18.460	79.325	79.090	2.078	43.345	12.537	20.876	0.000	1,510.713
28 Dec	1870	725.516	344.104	0.000	15.190	46.580	28.022	47.302	64.805	26.307	80.581	76.209	2.151	41.845	13.229	27.159	0.000	1,538.998
18 Mar	1871	767.858	351.557	0.000	15.232	46.675	28.806	40.473	83.809	25.769	91.072	100.694	2.103	37.570	11.643	23.771	0.000	1,627.032
29 Apr	1871	779.322	354.427	0.000	15.237	44.903	29.243	49.811	85.061	22.732	106.219	130.856	2.136	33.935	12.749	27.811	0.000	1,694.441
10 Jun	1871	789.417	357.389	0.000	15.251	47.333	29.638	51.490	92.369	19.925	122.138	102.091	2.161	30.690	13.101	30.423	0.000	1,703.415
2 Oct	1871	831.552	364.476	0.000	28.088	42.271	30.090	56.298	86.879	13.253	109.415	101.166	2.095	25.075	14.058	25.852	0.000	1,730.567
16 Dec	1871	818.996	366.840	0.000	23.155	40.737	30.070	56.383	77.986	29.595	93.943	114.539	2.062	21.400	13.784	26.372	0.000	1,715.862
27 Feb	1872	839.665	370.925	0.000	15.870	44.162	30.638	50.553	89.548	25.508	97.865	93.154	2.278	18.980	12.143	28.127	0.000	1,719.416
19 Apr	1872	844.902	374.428	0.000	15.169	40.831	30.809	48.997	82.120	24.434	105.732	114.196	2.143	15.365	12.461	32.063	0.000	1,743.652
10 Jun	1872	871.531	377.030	0.000	15.410	38.729	31.124	52.483	91.564	24.257	122.994	88.593	2.069	12.005	13.459	29.590	0.000	1,770.837
3 Oct	1872	877.198	382.046	0.000	15.480	35.676	32.276	47.463	80.717	10.230	105.121	110.086	2.152	7.140	14.917	28.645	6.710	1,755.857
27 Dec	1872	885.653	384.459	0.000	16.305	33.467	33.015	54.716	86.401	19.047	102.922	90.145	2.271	4.185	13.697	34.623	12.650	1,773.557

National Banking System Assets, 1869-1872 (millions USD) [1]

1. Source: Annual Report, Comptroller of the Currency, 1914, Vol. 2, Table 56 (p. 220 ff)
2. Includes overdrafts
3. Required in 1874, but not cited separately on statements until 1887.
4. These are the U. S. Notes (greenbacks).
5. Includes premiums on bonds, current expenses, national bank notes, bills of national banks.
6. Includes certificates of deposits and other deposits with the U. S. Treasury.

Figure 15.3-12: National Bank System Assets, 1869-1872

Day	Year	Number of Banks	Paid-in Capital	Other Liabilities [2]	Due to Other Banks	Due to Reserve Agents	U. S. Deposits [3]	Individual and Other Deposits	National Bank Notes in Circulation	State Bank Notes in Circulation	Bills & Notes Rediscounted	Total Liabilities
4 Jan	1869	1,628	419.041	116.488	122.438	0.000	16.685	568.531	294.477	2.735	0.000	1,540.394
17 Apr	1869	1,620	420.819	122.014	115.681	0.000	13.779	547.922	292.457	2.615	2.465	1,517.753
12 Jun	1869	1,619	422.659	127.767	128.981	0.000	12.756	574.307	292.753	2.559	2.392	1,564.174
9 Oct	1869	1,617	426.399	128.993	118.917	0.000	11.629	511.400	293.594	2.455	3.839	1,497.227
22 Jan	1870	1,615	426.075	128.318	137.256	0.000	9.342	546.237	292.839	2.352	3.843	1,546.261
24 Mar	1870	1,615	427.504	137.696	139.435	0.000	11.203	516.058	292.509	2.279	2.463	1,529.148
9 Jun	1870	1,612	427.236	138.372	148.469	0.000	13.271	542.262	291.184	2.223	2.742	1,565.757
8 Oct	1870	1,615	430.399	139.725	130.042	0.000	11.358	501.408	291.799	2.139	3.844	1,510.713
28 Dec	1870	1,648	435.356	147.843	135.291	0.000	10.230	507.369	296.205	2.092	4.612	1,538.998
18 Mar	1871	1,688	444.233	147.258	156.216	0.000	11.128	561.191	301.713	2.036	3.257	1,627.032
29 Apr	1871	1,707	446.925	150.372	164.151	0.000	10.279	611.025	306.131	1.983	3.574	1,694.441
10 Jun	1871	1,723	450.331	150.545	176.388	0.000	11.159	602.111	307.794	1.968	3.120	1,703.415
2 Oct	1871	1,767	458.256	152.190	171.943	0.000	25.906	600.868	315.519	1.921	3.965	1,730.567
16 Dec	1871	1,790	460.226	156.972	156.775	0.000	20.229	596.586	318.265	1.887	4.922	1,715.862
27 Feb	1872	1,814	464.082	154.612	167.653	0.000	12.140	593.646	321.635	1.831	3.819	1,719.416
19 Apr	1872	1,843	467.924	158.125	155.761	0.000	9.772	620.775	325.306	1.764	4.226	1,743.652
10 Jun	1872	1,853	470.543	162.813	172.684	0.000	12.457	618.802	327.093	1.701	4.745	1,770.837
3 Oct	1872	1,919	479.629	166.072	143.836	0.000	12.418	613.291	333.495	1.567	5.549	1,755.857
27 Dec	1872	1,940	482.606	176.476	159.013	0.000	13.000	598.115	336.289	1.511	6.545	1,773.557

National Banking System Liabilities, 1869-1872 (millions USD) [1]

1. Source: Annual Report, Comptroller of the Currency, 1914, Vol. 2, Table 56 (p. 220 ff)
2. Includes surplus fund, undivided profits, unpaid dividends, bills payable, reserved for taxes, and miscellaneous.
3. Includes deposits of U. S. disbursing officers.

Figure 15.3-13: National Bank System Liabilities, 1869-1872

| | | | U. S. Obligations Deposited with Treasury as Security for: | | | Investments | | Balances | Lawful Money for Reserves | | | | | | Other Assets | | | |
| | | | Circulation | | Deposit | | | | | | | | | | | | | |
Day	Year	Loans & Discounts [2]	U. S. Bonds	5% Redemption Fund with Treasury [3]	U. S. Bonds	U. S. Bonds, Other Bonds, and Stocks	Real Estate	Due from National and State Banks	Due from Reserve Agents	Specie	Legal Tender Notes [4]	Clearing-house exchanges	Fractional Currency	3% Certificates	Checks & Other Cash Items	Miscellaneous [5]	Due from U. S. Treasury [6]	Total Assets
28 Feb	1873	913.265	384.675	0.000	15.035	32.500	34.023	53.079	95.773	17.778	97.142	131.384	2.290	1.805	11.762	30.182	18.460	1,839.153
25 Apr	1873	912.064	386.764	0.000	16.235	32.063	34.217	51.554	88.816	16.869	100.605	94.132	2.199	0.710	11.425	34.280	18.370	1,800.303
13 Jun	1873	925.558	388.080	0.000	15.935	32.702	34.821	57.402	97.143	27.950	106.381	91.919	2.198	0.305	13.036	35.440	22.365	1,851.235
12 Sep	1873	944.220	388.330	0.000	14.805	32.534	34.662	53.437	96.134	19.868	92.523	88.926	2.303	0.000	11.434	30.842	20.610	1,830.628
26 Dec	1873	856.817	389.384	0.000	14.815	32.989	35.557	51.590	73.032	26.907	108.720	62.882	2.287	0.000	12.322	38.069	24.010	1,729.380
27 Feb	1874	897.860	389.615	0.000	14.600	36.349	36.044	48.121	101.503	32.366	102.718	63.768	2.310	0.000	10.270	35.743	37.235	1,808.501
1 May	1874	923.347	389.249	0.000	14.890	35.612	36.708	53.665	94.018	32.570	101.693	94.878	2.187	0.000	11.949	36.901	40.135	1,867.803
26 Jun	1874	**926.195**	390.282	0.000	14.890	37.468	37.271	58.240	97.872	22.326	103.108	63.896	2.284	0.000	10.496	39.641	47.871	1,851.841
2 Oct	1874	954.395	383.255	0.000	14.692	41.121	38.113	50.892	83.885	21.241	80.022	97.384	2.225	0.000	12.296	34.485	63.175	1,877.181
31 Dec	1874	955.863	382.976	0.000	14.714	43.604	39.191	59.756	80.489	22.437	82.605	112.995	2.393	0.000	14.006	36.669	54.713	1,902.410
1 Mar	1875	956.486	380.683	0.000	14.492	46.331	39.431	57.445	89.991	16.667	78.508	81.128	3.009	0.000	11.735	35.707	58.208	1,869.820
1 May	1875	971.835	378.027	0.000	14.372	43.400	40.312	58.134	80.621	10.620	84.016	116.971	2.702	0.000	13.122	35.646	60.069	1,909.848
30 Jun	1875	972.927	375.128	0.000	14.147	44.763	40.969	60.139	89.789	18.960	87.493	88.924	2.621	0.000	12.433	37.996	66.951	1,913.239
1 Oct	1875	984.691	370.322	0.000	14.097	47.495	42.367	58.993	89.701	8.050	76.459	75.143	2.596	0.000	12.759	35.040	68.497	**1,886.209**
17 Dec	1875	962.572	363.618	0.000	13.982	47.758	41.583	56.727	81.463	17.071	70.725	67.887	2.901	0.000	11.239	35.827	50.207	**1,823.560**
10 Mar	1876	950.206	354.548	0.000	14.217	56.336	41.938	53.522	99.068	29.077	76.768	58.863	3.216	0.000	9.518	37.779	49.284	**1,834.340**
12 May	1876	939.895	344.537	0.000	14.128	57.482	42.184	55.591	86.769	21.715	79.859	56.807	2.772	0.000	9.693	37.583	44.292	1,793.306
30 Jun	1876	933.687	339.142	0.000	14.328	63.325	42.722	58.407	87.990	25.218	90.837	75.329	1.988	0.000	11.725	36.046	45.018	1,825.761
2 Oct	1876	931.305	337.170	0.000	14.698	67.587	43.122	59.586	87.327	21.361	84.251	87.871	1.417	0.000	12.043	33.613	45.914	1,827.265
22 Dec	1876	929.066	336.705	0.000	14.757	63.504	43.498	56.428	83.789	33.000	66.221	68.027	1.147	0.000	10.659	38.151	42.454	1,787.407

1. Source: Annual Report, Comptroller of the Currency, 1914, Vol. 2, Table 56 (p. 220 ff)
2. Includes overdrafts
3. Required in 1874, but not cited separately on statements until 1887.
4. These are the U. S. Notes (greenbacks).
5. Includes premiums on bonds, current expenses, national bank notes, bills of national banks.
6. Includes certificates of deposits and other deposits with the U. S. Treasury.

Figure 15.3-14: National Bank System Assets, 1873-1876

National Banking System Liabilities, 1873-1876 (millions USD) [1]

Day	Year	Number of Banks	Paid-in Capital	Other Liabilities [2]	Due to Other Banks	Due to Reserve Agents	U. S. Deposits [3]	Individual and Other Deposits	National Bank Notes in Circulation	State Bank Notes in Circulation	Bills & Notes Rediscounted	Total Liabilities
28 Feb	1873	1,947	484.552	170.398	172.357	0.000	12.881	656.188	336.292	1.368	5.118	1,839.153
25 Apr	1873	1,962	487.891	176.742	161.668	0.000	12.306	616.848	338.164	1.280	5.403	1,800.303
13 Jun	1873	1,968	490.110	180.769	178.598	0.000	15.107	641.122	338.789	1.224	5.516	1,851.235
12 Sep	1873	1,976	491.073	181.713	**172.961**	0.000	15.928	622.686	339.082	1.189	5.998	1,830.628
26 Dec	1873	1,976	490.267	188.360	151.595	0.000	12.386	540.511	341.320	1.131	3.811	1,729.380
27 Feb	1874	1,975	490.859	**179.301**	186.548	0.000	12.312	595.350	339.603	1.079	3.449	1,808.501
1 May	1874	1,978	490.077	186.925	184.324	0.000	11.292	649.286	340.268	**1.049**	4.581	1,867.803
26 Jun	1874	1,983	491.004	190.167	193.261	0.000	10.561	622.863	338.539	1.009	4.436	1,851.841
2 Oct	1874	2,004	493.765	188.910	175.820	0.000	11.230	669.069	333.225	0.965	4.197	1,877.181
31 Dec	1874	2,027	495.802	193.451	180.818	0.000	11.072	682.847	331.193	0.860	6.366	1,902.410
1 Mar	1875	2,029	496.273	189.287	**193.020**	0.000	13.302	647.746	324.525	0.825	4.842	1,869.820
1 May	1875	2,046	498.717	196.094	180.318	0.000	9.564	695.348	323.321	0.815	5.671	1,909.848
30 Jun	1875	2,076	501.569	197.193	194.629	0.000	10.173	686.479	318.148	0.787	4.261	1,913.239
1 Oct	1875	2,088	504.830	197.915	179.729	0.000	10.779	664.580	318.350	0.772	5.254	1,882.209
17 Dec	1875	2,086	505.486	200.700	166.892	0.000	10.885	618.517	314.979	0.753	5.257	1,823.470
10 Mar	1876	2,091	504.819	191.724	193.410	0.000	10.920	620.674	307.476	0.715	4.632	1,834.370
12 May	1876	2,089	500.982	188.810	174.587	0.000	10.999	612.355	300.252	0.667	4.653	1,793.306
30 Jun	1876	2,091	500.394	190.796	183.106	0.000	11.061	641.433	294.445	0.659	3.868	1,825.761
2 Oct	1876	2,089	499.802	188.651	179.786	0.000	11.004	651.385	291.544	0.629	4.464	1,827.265
22 Dec	1876	2,082	497.482	190.888	171.037	0.000	11.477	619.350	292.012	0.609	4.553	1,787.407

1. Source: Annual Report, Comptroller of the Currency, 1914, Vol. 2, Table 56 (p. 220 ff)
2. Includes surplus fund, undivided profits, unpaid dividends, bills payable, reserved for taxes, and miscellaneous.
3. Includes deposits of U. S. disbursing officers.

Figure 15.3-15: National Bank System Liabilities, 1873-1876

Day	Year	Loans & Discounts [2]	U.S. Bonds	5% Redemption Fund with Treasury [3]	U.S. Bonds	U.S. Bonds, Other Bonds, and Stocks	Real Estate	Due from National and State Banks	Due from Reserve Agents	Specie	Legal Tender Notes [4]	Clearing-house exchanges	Fractional Currency	3% Certificates	Checks & Other Cash Items	Miscellaneous [5]	Due from U.S. Treasury [6]	Total Assets
20 Jan	1877	920.561	337.591	0.000	14.782	63.809	43.704	58.526	88.698	49.709	72.690	81.118	1.238	0.000	10.295	33.542	41.912	1,818.175
14 Apr	1877	911.947	339.658	0.000	15.084	65.519	44.737	53.939	84.943	27.070	72.352	85.159	1.115	0.000	10.411	36.279	48.391	1,796.603
22 Jun	1877	901.731	337.754	0.000	14.971	67.998	44.819	55.814	82.132	21.336	78.004	57.861	1.055	0.000	10.100	38.414	62.363	1,774.353
1 Oct	1877	891.921	336.811	0.000	14.903	64.525	45.230	56.633	73.284	22.659	66.921	74.525	0.901	0.000	11.675	31.666	48.432	1,740.085
28 Dec	1877	881.857	343.870	0.000	13.538	60.649	45.512	55.604	75.960	32.908	70.568	64.664	0.778	0.000	10.265	38.114	43.009	1,737.295
15 Mar	1878	854.751	343.871	0.000	13.329	69.556	45.792	51.375	86.017	54.730	64.035	66.499	0.697	0.000	10.108	31.843	36.863	1,729.466
1 May	1878	847.620	345.256	0.000	19.536	68.313	45.902	52.959	71.331	46.024	67.246	95.525	0.661	0.000	10.989	33.177	37.359	1,741.899
29 Jun	1878	835.078	347.332	0.000	28.371	77.175	46.153	54.130	78.875	29.251	71.643	87.498	0.610	0.000	11.525	29.118	53.704	1,750.465
1 Oct	1878	833.988	347.557	0.000	47.937	83.645	46.702	53.808	85.083	30.689	64.429	82.373	0.516	0.000	10.982	30.337	49.234	1,767.279
6 Dec	1878	826.017	347.812	0.000	49.111	80.073	46.728	55.404	81.733	34.355	64.673	61.998	0.497	0.000	9.985	33.979	50.461	1,742.827

1. Source: Annual Report, Comptroller of the Currency, 1914, Vol. 2, Table 56 (p. 220 ff)
2. Includes overdrafts
3. Required in 1874, but not cited separately on statements until 1887.
4. These are the U. S. Notes (greenbacks).
5. Includes premiums on bonds, current expenses, national bank notes, bills of national banks.
6. Includes certificates of deposits and other deposits with the U. S. Treasury.

Figure 15.3-16: National Bank System Assets, 1877, 1878

Day	Year	Number of Banks	Paid-in Capital	Other Liabilities [2]	Due to Other Banks	Due to Reserve Agents	U.S. Deposits [3]	Individual and Other Deposits	National Bank Notes in Circulation	State Bank Notes in Circulation	Bills & Notes Rediscounted	Total Liabilities
20 Jan	1877	2,083	493.635	176.613	180.259	0.000	10.343	659.892	292.851	0.581	4.000	1,818.175
14 Apr	1877	2,073	489.685	181.226	174.027	0.000	10.661	641.773	294.710	0.536	3.985	1,796.603
22 Jun	1877	2,078	481.045	182.870	169.796	0.000	10.898	636.268	290.002	0.522	2.953	1,774.353
1 Oct	1877	2,080	479.468	177.110	161.606	0.000	10.350	616.404	291.874	0.482	3.791	1,741.085
28 Dec	1877	2,074	477.129	180.397	160.582	0.000	10.310	604.513	299.240	0.471	4.655	1,737.295
15 Mar	1878	2,063	473.953	171.334	167.219	0.000	10.247	602.883	300.926	0.439	2.465	1,729.466
1 May	1878	2,059	471.972	169.372	153.727	0.000	16.204	625.480	301.885	0.427	2.834	1,741.899
29 Jun	1878	2,056	470.393	169.150	161.206	0.000	25.590	621.632	299.621	0.418	2.454	1,750.465
1 Oct	1878	2,053	466.147	165.455	165.133	0.000	44.998	620.236	301.888	0.414	3.007	1,767.279
6 Dec	1878	2,055	464.875	166.442	162.030	0.000	43.721	598.806	303.325	0.401	3.228	1,742.827

1. Source: Annual Report, Comptroller of the Currency, 1914, Vol. 2, Table 56 (p. 220 ff)
2. Includes surplus fund, undivided profits, unpaid dividends, bills payable, reserved for taxes, and miscellaneous.
3. Includes deposits of U. S. disbursing officers.

Figure 15.3-17: National Bank System Liabilities, 1877, 1878

Figures 15.3-18 through 15.3-21 show the reserve position of the national banks on the reporting dates, using the definitions of "lawful" money described in section 15.1.

Day	Year	U. S. Bonds for Circ. & Deposit	Paid-in Capital	Ratio, Securing Bonds to Capital	U. S. Bonds v. Circulation	Nat'l Bank Note Circulation	Ratio, Securing Bonds to Circulation	Total, N. B. Notes & Deposits	Reserve Agent Net	Total "Lawful Money"	Total Reserves	Avg. Ratio, Reserves to Notes Plus Deposits
5 Oct	1863	5.663	7.188	0.788	5.663	0.000	0.000	8.498	0.000	1.447	1.447	0.170
4 Jan	1864	15.112	14.741	1.025	15.112	0.030	0.002	19.481	0.000	5.019	5.019	0.258
4 Apr	1864	41.175	42.204	0.976	41.175	9.798	0.238	61.073	0.000	22.961	22.961	0.376
4 Jul	1864	92.531	75.214	1.230	92.531	25.826	0.279	145.240	0.000	42.284	42.284	0.291
3 Oct	1864	108.064	86.783	1.245	108.064	45.261	0.419	167.427	0.000	44.801	44.801	0.268
2 Jan	1865	176.579	135.619	1.302	176.579	66.769	0.378	288.014	0.000	77.017	77.017	0.267
3 Apr	1865	277.620	215.326	1.289	277.620	98.896	0.356	419.488	0.000	119.659	119.659	0.285
3 Jul	1865	391.745	325.835	1.202	391.745	131.452	0.336	587.842	0.000	177.863	177.863	0.303
2 Oct	1865	427.731	393.157	1.088	427.731	171.322	0.401	720.403	0.000	208.061	208.061	0.289
1 Jan	1866	298.377	403.357	0.740	298.377	213.240	0.715	765.495	0.000	207.052	207.052	0.270
2 Apr	1866	315.850	409.274	0.772	315.850	248.886	0.788	812.772	0.000	207.398	207.398	0.255
2 Jul	1866	326.483	414.270	0.788	326.483	267.799	0.820	840.242	0.000	214.054	214.054	0.255
1 Oct	1866	331.843	415.472	0.799	331.843	280.254	0.845	878.271	0.000	215.020	215.020	0.245
7 Jan	1867	339.571	420.230	0.808	339.571	291.437	0.858	879.899	0.000	206.646	206.646	0.235
1 Apr	1867	338.864	419.399	0.808	338.864	292.789	0.864	834.959	0.000	188.372	188.372	0.226
1 Jul	1867	337.684	418.558	0.807	337.684	291.761	0.864	864.672	0.000	189.152	189.152	0.219
7 Oct	1867	338.640	420.073	0.806	338.640	293.888	0.868	862.100	0.000	170.237	170.237	0.197
6 Jan	1868	339.064	420.261	0.807	339.064	294.377	0.868	856.597	0.000	185.458	185.458	0.217
6 Apr	1868	339.687	420.676	0.807	339.687	295.336	0.869	855.075	0.000	167.762	167.762	0.196
6 Jul	1868	339.569	420.105	0.808	339.569	294.908	0.868	898.853	0.000	187.164	187.164	0.208
5 Oct	1868	340.487	420.635	0.809	340.487	295.769	0.869	898.854	0.000	171.314	171.314	0.191

(Table title: Reserve Position of National Banks, 1863-1868 (millions USD, except ratios))

Figure 15.3-18: Reserve Position of National Banks, 1863-1868

Day	Year	U. S. Bonds for Circ. & Deposit	Paid-in Capital	Ratio, Securing Bonds to Capital	U. S. Bonds v. Circula-tion	Nat'l Bank Note Circula-tion	Ratio, Securing Bonds to Circula-tion	Total, N. B. Notes & Deposits	Reserve Agent Net	Total "Lawful Money"	Total Reserves	Avg. Ratio, Reserves to Notes Plus Deposits
4 Jan	1869	338.540	419.041	0.808	338.540	294.477	0.870	879.692	65.727	172.222	237.949	0.270
17 Apr	1869	338.379	420.819	0.804	338.379	292.457	0.864	854.159	57.554	144.098	201.653	0.236
12 Jun	1869	338.700	422.659	0.801	338.700	292.753	0.864	879.817	62.913	151.009	213.922	0.243
9 Oct	1869	339.480	426.399	0.796	339.480	293.594	0.865	816.623	56.670	154.657	211.327	0.259
22 Jan	1870	339.351	426.075	0.796	339.351	292.839	0.863	848.418	71.641	182.351	253.992	0.299
24 Mar	1870	339.251	427.504	0.794	339.251	292.509	0.862	819.770	73.435	240.756	314.191	0.383
9 Jun	1870	338.845	427.236	0.793	338.845	291.184	0.859	846.716	74.635	255.259	329.895	0.390
8 Oct	1870	340.857	430.399	0.792	340.857	291.799	0.856	804.564	66.276	222.297	288.573	0.359
28 Dec	1870	344.104	435.356	0.790	344.104	296.205	0.861	813.804	64.805	227.092	291.897	0.359
18 Mar	1871	351.557	444.233	0.791	351.557	301.713	0.858	874.032	83.809	257.209	341.018	0.390
29 Apr	1871	354.427	446.925	0.793	354.427	306.131	0.864	927.436	85.061	295.878	380.939	0.411
10 Jun	1871	357.389	450.331	0.794	357.389	307.794	0.861	921.064	92.369	277.005	369.374	0.401
2 Oct	1871	364.476	458.256	0.795	364.476	315.519	0.866	942.293	86.879	251.004	337.883	0.359
16 Dec	1871	366.840	460.226	0.797	366.840	318.265	0.868	935.081	77.986	261.538	339.524	0.363
27 Feb	1872	370.925	464.082	0.799	370.925	321.635	0.867	927.420	89.548	237.786	327.334	0.353
19 Apr	1872	374.428	467.924	0.800	374.428	325.306	0.869	955.853	82.120	261.871	343.991	0.360
10 Jun	1872	377.030	470.543	0.801	377.030	327.093	0.868	958.351	91.564	249.918	341.483	0.356
3 Oct	1872	382.046	479.629	0.797	382.046	333.495	0.873	959.203	80.717	234.729	315.446	0.329
27 Dec	1872	384.459	482.606	0.797	384.459	336.289	0.875	947.404	86.401	218.571	304.972	0.322

(Table title: Reserve Position of National Banks, 1869-1872 (millions USD, except ratios))

Figure 15.3-19: Reserve Position of National Banks, 1869-1872

		U. S. Bonds for Circ. & Deposit	Paid-in Capital	Ratio, Securing Bonds to Capital	U. S. Bonds v. Circula-tion	Nat'l Bank Note Circula-tion	Ratio, Securing Bonds to Circula-tion	Total, N. B. Notes & Deposits	Reserve Agent Net	Total "Lawful Money"	Total Reserves	Avg. Ratio, Reserves to Notes Plus Deposits
\multicolumn{13}{	c	}{Reserve Position of National Banks, 1873-1876 (millions USD, except ratios)}
Day	Year											
28 Feb	1873	384.675	484.552	0.794	384.675	336.292	0.874	1,005.361	95.773	250.398	346.171	0.344
25 Apr	1873	386.764	487.891	0.793	386.764	338.164	0.874	967.318	88.816	214.515	303.331	0.314
13 Jun	1873	388.080	490.110	0.792	388.080	338.789	0.873	995.018	97.143	228.753	325.896	0.328
12 Sep	1873	388.330	491.073	0.791	388.330	339.082	0.873	977.695	96.134	203.620	299.754	0.307
26 Dec	1873	389.384	490.267	0.794	389.384	341.320	0.877	894.217	73.032	200.796	273.828	0.306
27 Feb	1874	389.615	490.859	0.794	389.615	339.603	0.872	947.265	101.503	201.161	302.664	0.320
1 May	1874	389.249	490.077	0.794	389.249	340.268	0.874	1,000.846	94.018	231.328	325.345	0.325
26 Jun	1874	390.282	491.004	0.795	390.282	338.539	0.867	971.963	97.872	191.615	289.486	0.298
2 Oct	1874	383.255	493.765	0.776	383.255	333.225	0.869	1,013.524	83.885	200.872	284.757	0.281
31 Dec	1874	382.976	495.802	0.772	382.976	331.193	0.865	1,025.112	80.489	220.430	300.918	0.294
1 Mar	1875	380.683	496.273	0.767	380.683	324.525	0.852	985.574	89.991	179.312	269.303	0.273
1 May	1875	378.027	498.717	0.758	378.027	323.321	0.855	1,028.233	80.621	214.309	294.930	0.287
30 Jun	1875	375.128	501.569	0.748	375.128	318.148	0.848	1,014.800	89.789	197.997	287.786	0.284
1 Oct	1875	370.322	504.830	0.734	370.322	318.350	0.860	993.709	89.701	162.248	251.949	0.254
17 Dec	1875	363.618	505.486	0.719	363.618	314.979	0.866	944.382	81.463	158.584	240.047	0.254
10 Mar	1876	354.548	504.819	0.702	354.548	307.476	0.867	939.071	99.068	167.925	266.993	0.284
12 May	1876	344.537	500.982	0.688	344.537	300.252	0.871	923.606	86.769	161.152	247.921	0.268
30 Jun	1876	339.142	500.394	0.678	339.142	294.445	0.868	946.938	87.990	193.372	281.362	0.297
2 Oct	1876	337.170	499.802	0.675	337.170	291.544	0.865	953.933	87.327	194.900	282.227	0.296
22 Dec	1876	336.705	497.482	0.677	336.705	292.012	0.867	922.839	83.789	168.395	252.184	0.273

Figure 15.3-20: Reserve Position of National Banks, 1873-1876

		U. S. Bonds for Circ. & Deposit	Paid-in Capital	Ratio, Securing Bonds to Capital	U. S. Bonds v. Circula-tion	Nat'l Bank Note Circula-tion	Ratio, Securing Bonds to Circula-tion	Total, N. B. Notes & Deposits	Reserve Agent Net	Total "Lawful Money"	Total Reserves	Avg. Ratio, Reserves to Notes Plus Deposits
\multicolumn{13}{	c	}{Reserve Position of National Banks, 1877, 1878 (millions USD, except ratios)}
Day	Year											
20 Jan	1877	337.591	493.635	0.684	337.591	292.851	0.867	963.086	88.698	204.755	293.453	0.305
14 Apr	1877	339.658	489.685	0.694	339.658	294.710	0.868	947.144	84.943	185.696	270.639	0.286
22 Jun	1877	337.754	481.045	0.702	337.754	290.002	0.859	937.167	82.132	158.257	240.389	0.257
1 Oct	1877	336.811	479.468	0.702	336.811	291.874	0.867	918.628	73.284	165.006	238.290	0.259
28 Dec	1877	343.870	477.129	0.721	343.870	299.240	0.870	914.063	75.960	168.918	244.879	0.268
15 Mar	1878	343.871	473.953	0.726	343.871	300.926	0.875	914.056	86.017	185.961	271.978	0.298
1 May	1878	345.256	471.972	0.732	345.256	301.885	0.874	943.568	71.331	209.456	280.787	0.298
29 Jun	1878	347.332	470.393	0.738	347.332	299.621	0.863	946.843	78.875	189.003	267.878	0.283
1 Oct	1878	347.557	466.147	0.746	347.557	301.888	0.869	967.122	85.083	178.005	263.089	0.272
6 Dec	1878	347.812	464.875	0.748	347.812	303.325	0.872	945.852	81.733	161.523	243.256	0.257

Figure 15.3-21: Reserve Position of National Banks, 1877, 1878

Figure 15.3-22 shows the total money supply for this period. All of these values apply to approximately 30 Jun of each year. Professors Friedman and Schwartz did an extensive bottom-up analysis of the money supply, and the values they have for most of this period differ from the ones shown in Figure 15.3-22. Their total money supply values in millions, corresponding to column 15 in Figure 15.3-22 are [15.3-1]: Jan 1867: 1,590; Jan 1868: 1,568; Jan 1869: 1,638; Jan 1870: 1,725; Jan 1871: 1,911; Jan 1872: 2,105; Feb 1873: 2,306; Feb 1874: 2,337; Aug 1875: 2,532; Aug 1876: 2,505; Aug 1877: 2,435; and Aug 1878: 2,327. One source of error is that Freidman and Schwartz used seasonally adjusted values, and they show mutual savings banks as a separate class. It is not clear why there is such a large discrepancy from 1863 to 1872, after which they begin to converge.

Estimated U. S. Money Supply, 1863-1878 (millions USD)														
1	2	3	4	5	6	7	8	9	10	11	12	13	14	15
Year (~30 Jun)	Number of Banks [1]	State Bank Notes [2]	US Notes, Treasury Notes, National Bank Notes [3]	Total Notes in Circulation	Net Specie in Circulation [4]	Notes & Specie Outside Treasury	Cash Held in All Banks [5]	Currency & Coin Outside Banks	State Bank Deposits [6]	National Bank Deposits and Other Deposits Outside State Banks [7]	Total Deposits	Estimated Interbank Trans-actions [8]	Deposits Adjusted	Total Money Supply
1863	1,532	238.677	421.595	660.272	271.000	931.272	207.775	723.497	494.213	9.479	503.692	49.362	454.330	1,177.827
1864	1,556	150.431	634.736	785.167	193.721	978.888	147.261	831.627	233.155	146.796	379.951	37.235	342.716	1,174.343
1865	1,643	48.210	783.351	831.561	157.270	988.831	231.445	757.386	74.721	614.242	688.963	67.518	621.445	1,378.831
1866	1,931	41.026	801.736	842.762	117.946	960.708	259.094	701.614	63.588	694.892	758.480	74.331	684.149	1,385.763
1867	1,908	37.573	774.913	812.486	79.964	892.450	155.219	737.231	58.235	685.384	743.619	72.875	670.744	1,407.975
1868	1,887	34.120	698.442	732.562	70.278	802.840	158.936	643.904	52.883	744.607	797.490	78.154	719.336	1,363.240
1869	1,878	35.777	670.258	706.035	67.824	773.859	136.414	637.445	55.452	716.044	771.496	75.607	695.889	1,333.334
1870	1,937	44.894	682.582	727.476	90.161	817.637	173.935	643.702	69.582	705.518	775.100	75.960	699.140	1,342.842
1871	2,175	62.438	707.775	770.213	84.413	854.626	204.679	649.947	96.773	791.066	887.839	87.008	800.831	1,450.778
1872	2,419	78.185	738.870	817.055	88.639	905.694	217.357	688.337	121.180	805.397	926.577	90.805	835.772	1,524.109
1873	3,298	0.175	760.454	760.629	76.397	837.026	198.994	638.032	788.956	836.227	1,625.183	159.268	1,465.915	2,103.947
1874	3,552	0.153	768.556	768.709	93.888	862.597	241.848	620.749	912.121	827.928	1,740.049	170.525	1,569.524	2,190.273
1875	3,336	0.178	746.238	746.416	86.587	833.003	230.234	602.769	1,111.233	897.387	2,008.620	196.845	1,811.775	2,414.544
1876	3,448	0.388	705.182	705.570	100.894	806.464	217.347	589.117	1,151.314	841.716	1,993.030	195.317	1,797.713	2,386.830
1877	3,384	0.388	692.184	692.572	120.996	813.568	220.642	592.926	1,187.839	818.360	2,006.199	196.608	1,809.591	2,402.517
1878	3,229	0.388	674.331	674.719	144.867	819.586	207.284	612.302	1,107.004	813.894	1,920.898	188.248	1,732.650	2,344.952

1. Number of banks (includes National, State, Private, and Loan & Trust Companies) from Annual Report of the Comptroller of the Currency, 1931, pp. 1023, 1024 (Table 96).
2. State Bank notes per Annual Report of the Comptroller of the Currency, 1931, pp. 1018, 1019 (Table 94).
3. Includes fractional currency, U. S. Notes, National Bank Notes, "Other U. S. currency" (Treasury notes), gold certificates, and silver certificates. Data is from the Annual Report of the Secretary of the Treasury, 1947, p. 485, (Table 90).
4. This is the sum of gold coin, standard silver dollars, and subsidiary silver. Data is from the Annual Report of the Secretary of the Treasury, 1947, p. 485, (Table 90).
5. From the Annual Report of the Comptroller of the Currency, 1931, pp. 1023-1025, (Table 96).
6. From the Annual Report of the Comptroller of the Currency, 1931, pp. 1018, 1019, (Table 94).
7. From the Annual Report of the Comptroller of the Currency, 1931, pp. 1018, 1024 (Tables 94 and 96). The values shown here are the difference between "all banks" per Table 96 and "State banks" per Table 94.
8. Interbank from 1863 to 1878 based on average of interbank to total deposits from 1914 to 1940 (0.098).

Figure 15.3-22: Total Money Supply, 1863-1878

Figures 15.3-23 and 15.3-24 show the coinage of the U. S. during this period.

Gold Coinage of the U. S., 1863-1878 (USD)							
Year	$20 Double Eagles ($)	$10 Eagles ($)	$5 Half Eagles ($)	Three Dollar ($)	$2.50 Quarter Eagles ($)	Gold Dollars ($)	Total ($)
1863	22,187,200.00	112,480.00	97,360.00	15,117.00	27,075.00	6,250.00	22,445,482.00
1864	19,958,900.00	60,800.00	40,540.00	8,040.00	7,185.00	5,950.00	20,081,415.00
1865	27,874,000.00	207,050.00	144,535.00	3,495.00	62,302.50	3,725.00	28,295,107.50
1866	30,820,500.00	237,800.00	253,200.00	12,090.00	105,175.00	7,180.00	31,435,945.00
1867	23,436,300.00	121,400.00	179,600.00	7,950.00	78,125.00	5,250.00	23,828,625.00
1868	18,722,000.00	241,550.00	288,625.00	14,625.00	94,062.50	10,525.00	19,371,387.50
1869	17,238,100.00	82,850.00	163,925.00	7,575.00	84,612.50	5,925.00	17,582,987.50
1870	22,819,480.00	164,430.00	143,550.00	10,605.00	51,387.50	9,335.00	23,198,787.50
1871	20,456,740.00	254,650.00	245,000.00	3,990.00	68,375.00	3,930.00	21,032,685.00
1872	21,230,600.00	244,500.00	275,350.00	6,090.00	52,575.00	3,530.00	21,812,645.00
1873	55,456,700.00	173,680.00	754,605.00	75.00	512,562.50	125,125.00	57,022,747.50
1874	33,917,700.00	799,270.00	203,530.00	125,460.00	9,850.00	198,820.00	35,254,630.00
1875	32,737,820.00	78,360.00	105,240.00	60.00	30,050.00	420.00	32,951,950.00
1876	46,386,920.00	104,280.00	61,820.00	135.00	23,052.50	3,245.00	46,579,452.50
1877	43,504,700.00	211,490.00	182,660.00	4,464.00	92,630.00	3,920.00	43,999,864.00
1878	45,916,500.00	1,031,440.00	1,427,470.00	246,972.00	1,160,650.00	3,020.00	49,786,052.00
Totals	482,664,160.00	4,126,030.00	4,567,010.00	466,743.00	2,459,670.00	396,150.00	494,679,763.00

Source: Annual Report of the Director of the Mint, 1895, 28 Nov 1895, Treasury Document No. 1829, pp. 286-293 (Table XLIV).

Figure 15.3-23: Gold Coins Minted by the U. S., 1863-1878

Silver and Copper Coinage of the U. S., 1863-1878 (USD)									
	Silver ($)							Minor ($)	
Year	Trade Dollars	Dollars	Half Dollars	Quarters	Twenty-cents	Dimes	Half-dimes	Three-cents	Cents	Total ($)
1863		27,660.00	709,830.00	48,015.00		17,196.00	5,923.00	643.80	498,400.00	1,307,667.80
1864		31,170.00	518,785.00	28,517.50		26,907.00	4,523.50	14.10	926,687.14	1,536,604.24
1865		47,000.00	593,450.00	25,075.00		18,550.00	6,675.00	255.00	968,552.86	1,659,557.86
1866		49,625.00	899,812.50	11,381.25		14,372.50	6,536.25	681.75	1,042,960.00	2,025,369.25
1867		60,325.00	810,162.50	17,156.25		14,662.50	6,431.25	138.75	1,819,910.00	2,728,786.25
1868		182,700.00	769,100.00	31,500.00		72,625.00	18,295.00	123.00	1,697,150.00	2,771,493.00
1869		424,300.00	725,950.00	23,150.00		70,660.00	21,930.00	153.00	963,000.00	2,229,143.00
1870		445,462.00	829,758.50	23,935.00		52,150.00	26,830.00	120.00	350,325.00	1,728,580.50
1871		1,117,136.00	1,741,655.00	53,255.50		109,371.00	82,493.00	127.80	99,890.00	3,203,928.30
1872		1,118,600.00	866,775.00	68,762.50		261,045.00	180,247.50	58.50	369,380.00	2,864,868.50
1873	1,225,000.00	296,600.00	1,593,780.00	414,190.50		443,329.10	51,830.00	18.00	379,455.00	4,404,202.60
1874	4,910,000.00		1,406,650.00	215,975.00		319,151.70			342,475.00	7,194,251.70
1875	6,279,600.00		5,117,750.00	1,278,375.00	265,598.00	2,406,570.00			246,970.00	15,594,863.00
1876	6,102,150.00		7,451,575.00	7,839,287.50	5,180.00	3,015,115.00			210,800.00	24,624,107.50
1877	13,092,710.00		7,540,255.00	6,024,927.50	102.00	1,735,051.00			8,525.00	28,401,570.50
1878	4,259,900.00	22,495,550.00	726,200.00	849,200.00	120.00	187,880.00			58,186.50	28,577,036.50
Totals	35,869,360.00	26,296,128.00	32,301,488.50	16,952,703.50	271,000.00	8,764,635.80	411,714.50	2,333.70	9,982,666.50	130,852,030.50

Source: Annual Report of the Director of the Mint, 1895, 28 Nov 1895, Treasury Document No. 1829, pp. 286-293 (Table XLIV).

Figure 15.3-24: Silver and Minor (Copper) Coins Minted by the U. S., 1863-1878

Figure 15.3-25 shows the CPI, total money supply, and per-capita money supply during this period.

Year	CPI [1] (1913 = 100)	Total Money Supply [5] (USD)	Population [6]	Per Capita Money Supply (USD)	Annual Rate of Change in CPI (%)	Annual Rate of Change in Per-Capita Money Supply (%)
1863	112.828	1,177,827,402	33,577,836	35.08	21.653	39.984
1864	147.595	1,174,342,802	34,289,341	34.25	26.860	-2.393
1865	158.056	1,378,830,626	35,000,846	39.39	6.848	13.999
1866	144.809	1,385,762,960	35,712,351	38.80	-8.753	-1.511
1867	133.643	1,407,975,338	36,423,856	38.66	-8.024	-0.383
1868	126.986	1,363,239,980	37,135,361	36.71	-5.110	-5.163
1869	122.477	1,333,334,392	37,846,866	35.23	-3.615	-4.116
1870	113.106	1,342,842,200	38,558,371	34.83	-7.960	-1.152
1871	108.812	1,450,777,778	39,639,668	36.60	-3.870	4.965
1872	111.530	1,524,109,454	40,720,965	37.43	2.467	2.240
1873	109.957	2,103,947,066	41,802,262	50.33	-1.420	29.620
1874	106.023	2,190,273,198	42,883,559	51.07	-3.643	1.467
1875	101.659	2,414,544,240	43,964,856	54.92	-4.203	7.258
1876	95.076	2,386,830,060	45,046,152	52.99	-6.695	-3.584
1877	90.352	2,402,517,498	46,127,449	52.08	-5.096	-1.717
1878	83.198	2,344,951,996	47,208,746	49.67	-8.250	-4.742

1. CPI is the average of L-1 and L-15 data, both re-aligned to 1913 as a reference.
2. L-1 data 1791 to 1938 (Snyder-Tucker) is a general price index (wholesale prices, wages, cost of living and rents).
3. L-15 data 1801 to 1945 includes wholesale prices, all commodities.
4. L1 and L-15 from Historical Statistics of the United States, 1789-1945, A Supplement to the Statistical Abstract of the United States, Bureau of the Census, US Department of Commerce, Washington, DC, 1949.
5. See notes in money supply data for sources.
6. Population is linearly interpolated from Census results.

Figure 15.3-25: Money Supply and CPI, 1863-1878

Figure 15.3-26 shows a summary of the CPI and per-capita money supply. Three distinct intervals are evident: 1863 to 1865, 1865 to 1872, and 1872 to 1878. The average annual change in CPI and money supply for 1863 to 1865 are 16.8 and 5.8% respectively; for 1865 to 1872, -4.98 and -0.7% respectively, and for 1872 to 1878, -4.88 and +4.71% respectively.

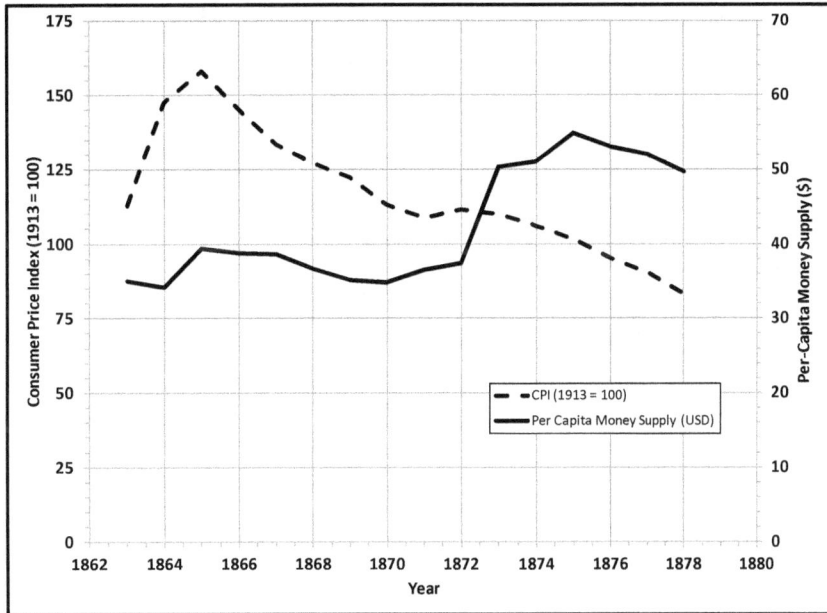

Figure 15.3-26: CPI and Per-Capita Summary, 1863-1878

Figure 15.3-27 shows the approximate median income index, consumer price index, and standard of living index for this period. See the Introduction to Part 2 for cautions regarding these curves.

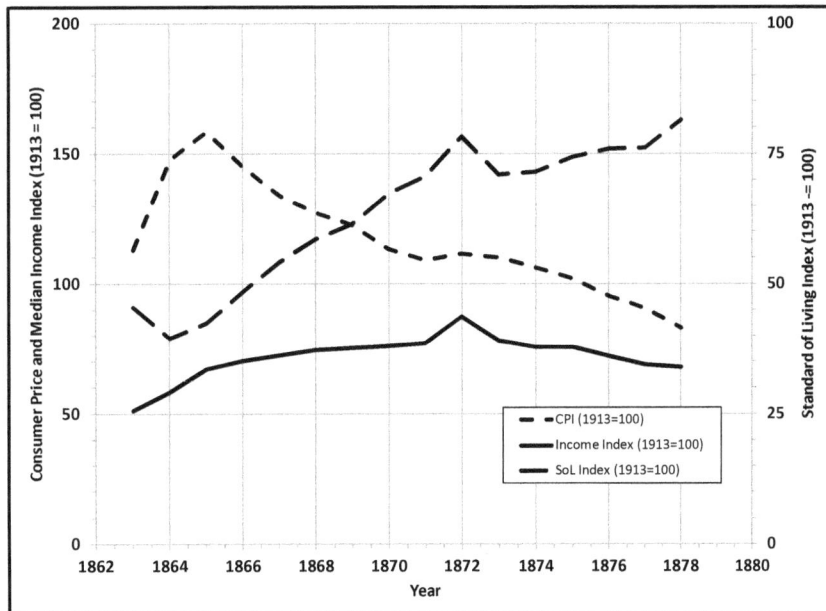

Figure 15.3-27: Median Income, Consumer Price, and Standard of Living Indices, 1863-1878

Figure 15.3-28 shows the prime interest rates for commercial paper prevailing in New York City between 1863 and 1878 [15.3-2].

Approximate Monthly Average, Prime Commercial Paper Rate, 60-90 Days (%) [1]											
Year	Jan	Feb	Mar	Apr	May	Jun	Jul	Aug	Sep	Oct	Nov	Dec
1863	5.30	5.70	5.30	5.30	5.20	5.40	5.60	5.30	5.60	5.70	6.60	6.80
1864	7.30	6.50	5.60	6.70	6.90	6.80	6.50	7.70	9.00	9.20	8.30	7.80
1865	8.00	8.50	9.00	8.50	7.20	6.70	7.30	7.70	7.10	7.60	8.00	7.80
1866	7.37	7.28	7.32	6.69	6.05	5.56	5.89	5.89	5.25	5.45	6.69	6.88
1867	7.40	7.06	7.19	7.17	6.67	7.38	6.55	6.50	7.12	8.40	8.56	7.94
1868	7.06	6.50	7.67	8.00	6.62	5.72	6.50	6.62	6.75	7.44	10.00	8.25
1869	8.31	7.69	9.40	9.88	7.81	9.65	10.25	9.56	10.94	10.38	11.94	10.17
1870	9.00	7.38	7.50	7.19	6.38	5.46	6.38	7.18	7.25	7.28	7.25	8.75
1871	7.22	6.62	6.25	6.78	5.50	5.06	4.90	5.52	6.66	10.03	9.28	9.94
1872	8.30	7.56	8.62	8.66	7.20	6.00	6.45	7.56	10.00	10.80	11.62	10.83
1873	9.28	9.38	10.12	11.40	8.12	6.83	6.44	7.06	14.28	16.50	14.50	9.80
1874	7.44	6.00	6.14	6.25	5.66	5.56	5.61	5.44	6.25	5.81	5.62	6.00
1875	5.25	5.19	5.90	5.44	4.56	4.55	4.31	4.94	5.89	6.31	6.39	6.61
1876	6.44	5.33	5.39	5.50	5.05	4.75	3.81	3.60	4.75	5.67	5.44	5.88
1877	5.55	4.50	4.44	4.38	4.00	4.06	4.14	5.64	6.38	7.25	6.19	5.62
1878	5.85	5.31	5.12	5.36	4.53	3.81	3.60	3.81	4.62	5.45	5.12	5.06

1. Source: Frederick R. Macaulay, *Some Theoretical Problems Suggested by the Movements of Interest Rates, Bond Yields and Stock Prices in the United States Since 1856*, New York: National Bureau of Economic Research (NBER), 1938, Appendix A, Table 10 (pp. A143-A147). This data applies to New York City. Copyright 1938 by National Bureau of Economic Research, Inc. Used with permission.

Figure 15.3-28: Commercial Paper Prime Interest Rate, New York City, 1863-1878

15.4 Summary, 1863-1878

The National Bank system demonstrated two major advantages. First, once the notes of the State-chartered banks were eliminated by taxation, the national banks were able to produce a uniform currency. There were two major types of currency in use in this period: the National Bank Notes, and the legal tender U. S. notes (greenbacks) issued by the North to finance the Civil War. Clearinghouse certificates were commonly used as legal tender among the banks to offset balances, but were not in general circulation. The total amount of notes in circulation was limited for most of this period, a vast improvement over the previous system in which State banks issued notes in excess, confident they would not be returned for payment. Secondly, the national bank system did provide better regulation and reporting by the national banks, although it did not extend to the State-chartered banks. The State-chartered banks provided data per the State guidelines, which were inconsistent and irregular. It was not until about 1900 or so that the State banks provided sufficient data to enable an overall assessment of the banking system in general.

The first main disadvantage of the national bank system was the pyramiding of reserves, which is a euphemism for the concentration of reserves in the New York banks. Since the "country banks" were allowed to keep some of their reserves with "reserve city" banks, and those in turn were permitted to keep half of their reserves in "central city reserve banks" (New York, St. Louis, and Chicago), reserves tended to concentrate in the larger cities. The problem then was that the central reserve city banks did not have access to high-quality U. S. bonds as security (since the government was running a surplus after the late 1860's); instead those banks lent out the excess reserves to stock brokers as "call loans". When reserves were called for by the lower-tier banks, calling in the loans was not an issue so long as stock prices were reasonably stable. But when the stock market was lower than expected, the call loans defaulted, and the central reserve city banks could not return the reserves where they were needed. This defect is considered to be the main source of the "Panics" of 1873 and 1907. It should be recalled however, that the motivation for placing reserves in higher-order banks is that they paid interest instead of lying in the vault. Several potential remedies for this have been pointed out. Bolles [15.4-1] suggested a prohibition on the payment of interest on reserve deposits. Friedman [15.4-2] noted that reserve problem could be avoided by three other means: a) a central reserve of idle cash set aside as reserves; b) an emergency currency per the future Aldrich-Vreeland Act; and c) a guarantee of deposits in order to enhance public confidence in the banking system. Kreps [15.4-3] claims that the only real solution was a central bank. Sprague [15.4-

4] recommended two remedies for the national bank system: a) prohibit paying of interest on bankers' deposits (reserves); and b) require banks holding bankers' deposits to have a higher reserve ratio so they can accommodate high demand for cash when needed.

The second main disadvantage of the national bank system was that it intimately linked the banking system with the federal government [15.4-5]. The banks could only issue bank notes if it deposited U. S. securities with the Treasury; thus the banks' capital was used as a market for the federal obligations. Secondly, the banks also had to buy U. S. securities as security against both deposits they received as well as notes issued; initially this was done by direct purchase of U. S. debt obligations. The National Bank Notes were technically liabilities of the national banks, but in reality were liabilities of the federal government since bonds had to be purchased in order to issue the notes [15.4-6]. If a bank failed, the Treasury had the first lien on its assets, and paid any deficiency; therefore the quality of the National Bank Notes did not depend on the financial health of the bank that issued them. After 1874, the U. S. bonds as security against note circulation was augmented by a "5% Redemption Fund". Prior to 1863, banks held their own specie reserves or bonds as they saw fit against their notes, now they were indirectly holding U. S. debt as "security". Thus the federal government potentially had a ready market for its debt obligations.

In 1878, the federal government took action to fund the resumption and payment in specie, unlike Jackson in 1836, who talked a good game, but did nothing to ensure adequate supplies of metal were available. That is why the 1878 resumption was successful, aided by unfortunate circumstances in Europe (a crop failure, which forced Europeans to buy grain, paid for with gold). Bolles [15.4-7] also notes that the banks aided the government in promoting a smooth transition to resumption. On 1 Jan 1879, the banks in New York held $40,000,000 in legal tender notes, for which they could have demanded immediate payment. But, they did not demand any; instead, they obtained payment in gold over a period of time only as needed.

Bolles [15.4-8] points out that the redistribution of national bank notes in 1873 and 1874 was intended to provide currency to the Southern States; however, those States needed capital, not currency. Government cannot create capital out of nothing; the best that could have been done for the Southern States is to borrow the capital and lend it.

Last, Sprague [15.4-9] gave a warning on the on risks of allowing greater ability to issue notes without better management. It leads to an unrestrained expansion of credit. That was not the problem during this period, but was will be shown in chapter 16, it became a problem in 1893.

The de-monetization of silver in 1874 proved to be temporary, as silver was again monetized with the Bland-Allison Act of 1878, and again in 1890, as will be shown in chapter 16.

This chapter covered the first half of the first unusual period in U. S. history mentioned in the Introduction to Part 2, in which the standard of living index increased dramatically. Figures 15.3-25 and 15.3-26 seem to contradict the basic premise that a rise in the money supply leads to a rise in prices. The interval from 1872 to 1878 shows the opposite: money supply increased, but prices decreased. The reason is that there was a very large increase in output during this period [15.4-10, 15.4-11]. The increased money supply was put to good use in such a way that production efficiency caused prices to decline. It was true not only of industrial processes, but also the improvements in transportation that led to reductions in overall production costs. It is possible that the "recession" of 1873 to 1879 is more fiction than truth, or if the recession is true, that it probably ended in 1877. Unfortunately recordkeeping on wage and unemployment is unreliable, and it is difficult to give a general picture.

The total amount of loans authorized to fund the Civil War came to $2,000,000,000: a) $500,000,000 on 25 Feb 1862; b) $300,000,000 on 3 Mar 1863; c) $200,000,000 on 3 Mar 1864; d) $400,000,000 on 30 Jun 1864; and e) $600,000,000 on 3 Mar 1865. This is in addition to $550,000,000 in United States Notes (greenbacks): a) $150,000,000 on 25 Feb 1862; b) $150,000,000 on 11 Jul 1862; c) $100,000,000 on 17 Jan 1863; and d) $150,000,000 on 3 Mar 1863, the last increment to be used for exchanging Treasury Notes. Also, Secretary Chase found it necessary to issue $400,000,000 in U. S. Notes (cf. 11 Apr

1864) because he couldn't find buyers for the 10-40 bonds. At least $50,000,000 in fractional currency was issued (probably much more), as authorized 3 Mar 1863. Bolles commented [15.4-12]:

> "Since the beginning of the special session of Congress, in 1861, said [Treasury Secretary] Mr. McCulloch, in his first annual report, the most important subject which had demanded and received the attention of Congress, had been that of providing the means to prosecute the war; and the success of the government in raising money was evidence of the wisdom of the measures devised for that purpose, as well as of the loyalty of the people, and the resources of the country. No nation, within the same period, had ever borrowed so largely, or with so much facility."

The next chapter describes the events that occurred when the U. S. had a true gold coin monetary regime under the national bank system; it extends to 1914.

References

[15.1-1]   Albert S. Bolles, *A Financial History of the United States*, NY: Augustus M. Kelley (1969), Vol. 3, p. 226 (originally published 1884 by D. Appleton & Co., NY)

[15.1-2]   Clifton H. Kreps, Jr., *Money, Banking and Monetary Policy*, NY: The Ronald Press Co., 1962, p. 166

[15.1-3]   Oliver M. W. Sprague, *History of Crises under the National Bank System*, National Monetary Commission, 61st Congress, Senate Document 538, Washington DC: U. S. Government Printing Office, 1910

[15.1-4]   op. cit., Bolles, Vol. 3, pp. 359, 360

[15.1-5]   Bruce Champ, *The National Banking System: A Brief Summary*, Working Paper 07-23, Dec 2007, Federal Reserve Bank of Cleveland, p. 32

[15.1-6]   A. T. Huntington and R. J. Mawhinney, *Laws of the United States Concerning Money, Banking, and Loans, 1778-1909*, Washington, D. C.: Publications of the National Monetary Commission, Vol. 2, (1911) p. 345

[15.1-7]   Milton Friedman, Anna Jacobson Schwartz, *A Monetary History of the United States, 1867 - 1960*, A Study by the National Bureau of Economic Research, NY, Princeton, NJ: Princeton University Press, 1963, pp. 21, 25

[15.1-8]   op. cit., Friedman and Schwartz, p. 25

[15.2-1]   op. cit., Bolles, Vol. 3, p. 85

[15.2-2]   Text of "Joint Resolution to provide for the immediate Payment of the Army and Navy of the United States", 37th Congress, Session 3, Resolution 9, 17 Jan 1863

[15.2-3]   op. cit., Kreps, p. 164

[15.2-4]   op. cit., Champ, p. 30

[15.2-5]   Text of "An Act to provide for a national Currency secured by a Pledge of United States Stocks, and to provide for the Circulation and Redemption Thereof", 37th Congress, Session 3, Chapter 58, 25 Feb 1863

[15.2-6]   op. cit., Bolles, Vol. 3, pp. 199-201

[15.2-7]   Text of "An Act to provide ways and means for the support of the Government", 37th Congress, Session 3, Chapter 73, 3 Mar 1863

[15.2-8]   op. cit., Bolles, Vol. 3, pp. 83, 84

[15.2-9]   op. cit., Bolles, Vol. 3, pp. 111-113

[15.2-10]   op. cit., Friedman and Schwartz, p. 25

[15.2-11]   op. cit., Bolles, Vol. 3, pp. 182, 183

[15.2-12]   Text of "An Act to amend an act entitled 'An Act to provide internal revenue to support the Government and pay interest on the public debt', approved July first, eighteen hundred and sixty-two, and for other purposes", 37th Congress, Session 3, Chapter 74, 3 Mar 1863

[15.2-13]   Text of "An Act to modify existing laws imposing duties on imports, and for other purposes", 37th Congress, Session 3, Chapter 77, 3 Mar 1863

[15.2-14]   op. cit., Kreps, p. 80

[15.2-15]   op. cit., Bolles, Vol. 3, pp. 114, 128

[15.2-16]   Text of "An Act supplementary to the Act entitled 'An Act to provide ways and means for the support of the Government', approved March third, eighteen hundred and sixty-three", 38th Congress, Session 1, Chapter 17, 3 Mar 1864

[15.2-17]   Text of "An Act to increase the internal revenue, and for other purposes", 38th Congress, Session 1, Chapter 20, 7 Mar 1864

[15.2-18]   op. cit., Bolles, Vol. 3, pp. 105, 106

[15.2-19]   Text of "An act in amendment to an Act entitled 'An act relating to foreign coins and the coinage of cents at the Mint of the United States', approved February twenty-one, eighteen hundred and fifty-seven", 38th Congress, Session 1, Chapter 66, 22 Apr 1864

[15.2-20]   Text of "An Act to provide for a National Currency, secured by a pledge of United States Bonds, and to provide for the circulation and redemption thereof", 38th Congress, Session 1, Chapter 106, 3 Jun 1864

[15.2-21]   op. cit., Champ, p. 3

[15.2-22]   op. cit., Kreps, p. 167

[15.2-23]   op. cit., Bolles, Vol. 3, pp. 346-350

[15.2-24]   Text of "An Act to prohibit certain sales of gold and foreign exchange", 38th Congress, Session 1, Chapter 127, 17 Jun 1864

[15.2-25]   op. cit., Bolles, Vol. 3, pp. 142-148

[15.2-26]   Text of "An Act to increase duties on imports, and for other purposes", 38th Congress, Session 1, Chapter 171, 30 Jun 1864

[15.2-27]   Text of "An Act to provide ways and means for the support of the Government, and for other purposes", 38th Congress, Session 1, Chapter 172, 30 Jun 1864

[15.2-28]   op. cit., Bolles, Vol. 3, pp. 119, 120

[15.2-29]   Text of "An Act to provide internal revenue to support the Government, to pay interest on the public debt, and for other purposes", 38th Congress, Session 1, Chapter 173, 30 Jun 1864

[15.2-30]   op. cit., Bolles, Vol. 3, pp. 184, 185

[15.2-31]   op. cit., Bolles, Vol. 3, p. 119

[15.2-32]   op. cit., Bolles, Vol. 3, p. 124

[15.2-33]   op. cit., Bolles, Vol. 3, p. 145

[15.2-34]   Text of "An Act to repeal the Act of the seventeenth of June, eighteen hundred and sixty-four, prohibiting the sales of gold and foreign exchange", 38th Congress, Session 1, Chapter 209, 2 Jul 1864

[15.2-35]   op. cit., Bolles, Vol. 3, pp. 125, 126

[15.2-36]   op. cit., Bolles, Vol. 3, p. 126

[15.2-37]   op. cit., Kreps, p. 80

[15.2-38]   Text of "An Act to amend an Act entitled 'An Act to provide ways and means for the support of the Government, and for other purposes', approved June thirtieth, eighteen hundred and sixty-four", 38th Congress, Session 2, Chapter 22, 28 Jan 1865

[15.2-39]   Text of "An Act to amend an Act entitled 'An Act to provide a National Currency, secured by a pledge of United States Bonds, and to provide for the circulation and redemption thereof", 38th Congress, Session 2, Chapter 82, 3 Mar 1865

[15.2-40]   Text of "An Act to Provide for the Ways and Means in Support of the Government", 38th Congress, Chapter 77, 3 Mar 1865

[15.2-41]   op. cit., Bolles, Vol. 3, pp. 126-128

[15.2-42]   Text of "An Act amendatory of certain Acts imposing duties upon foreign imports", 38th Congress, Session 2, Chapter 80, 3 Mar 1865

[15.2-43]   Text of "An Act to amend an Act entitled 'An Act to provide internal revenue to support the Government, to pay interest on the public debt, and for other purposes', approved Jun thirtieth, eighteen hundred and sixty-four", a.k.a., the Revenue Act of 1865, 38th Congress, Session 2, Chapter 78, 3 Mar 1865

[15.2-44]   op. cit., Bolles, Vol. 3, pp. 194-196

[15.2-45]   op. cit., Kreps, p. 166

[15.2-46]   op. cit., Bolles, Vol. 3, pp. 194, 341

[15.2-47]   Text of "An Act to authorize the coinage of three-cent pieces, and for other purposes", 38th Congress, Session 2, Chapter 100, 3 Mar 1865

[15.2-48]   op. cit., Kreps, p. 165

[15.2-49]   National Bureau of Economic Research, Cambridge, MA (see website below)

[15.2-50]   op. cit., Bolles, Vol. 3, p. 341

[15.2-51]   op. cit., Kreps, p. 80

[15.2-52]   Text of "An Act to amend an Act entitled 'An Act to provide ways and means to support the Government,' approved March third, eighteen hundred and sixty-five", 39th Congress, Session 1, Chapter 39, 12 Apr 1866
[15.2-53]   op. cit., Bolles, Vol. 3, pp. 263-277
[15.2-54]   op. cit., Friedman and Schwartz, p. 24
[15.2-55]   op. cit., Kreps, pp. 82, 83
[15.2-56]   Text of "An Act to authorize the coinage of five-cent pieces", 39th Congress, Session 1, Chapter 81, 16 May 1866
[15.2-57]   Text of "An Act to reduce internal taxation and to amend an Act entitled 'An Act to provide internal revenue to support the Government, to pay interest on the public debt, and for other purposes,' approved Jun thirtieth, eighteen hundred and sixty-four, and Acts amendatory thereof", 39th Congress, Session 1, Chapter 184, 13 Jul 1866
[15.2-58]   op. cit., Bolles, Vol. 3, pp. 409, 569
[15.2-59]   George S. Boutwell, *Annual Report of the Secretary of the Treasury for the Year 1872*, 2 Dec 1872, Washington DC: Government Printing Office, 1872, p. IX
[15.2-60]   Text of "An Act to protect the revenue, and for other purposes", 39th Congress, Session 1, Chapter 298, 28 Jul 1866
[15.2-61]   Text of "An Act to amend existing laws related to internal revenue, and for other purposes", 39th Congress, Session 2, Chapter 169, 2 Mar 1867
[15.2-62]   op. cit., Bolles, Vol. 3, pp. 411, 412, 569
[15.2-63]   op. cit., Boutwell, p. IX
[15.2-64]   Text of "An Act to provide ways and means for the payment of compound interest notes", 39th Congress, Chapter 194, 2 Mar 1867
[15.2-65]   op. cit., Bolles, Vol. 3, pp. 277, 278
[15.2-66]   Text of "An Act to provide increased revenue from imported wool and other purposes", 39th Congress, Session 2, Chapter 197, 2 Mar 1867
[15.2-67]   op. cit., Bolles, Vol. 3, pp. 450, 451
[15.2-68]   Text of "An Act to exempt wrapping paper, made from wood, from internal tax, and for other purposes", 40th Congress, Session 1, Chapter 8, 26 Mar 1867
[15.2-69]   op. cit., National Bureau of Economic Research
[15.2-70]   Text of "An Act to provide for the exemption of cotton from internal tax", 40th Congress, Session 2, Chapter 5, 3 Feb 1868
[15.2-71]   op. cit., Bolles, Vol. 3, pp. 409, 569
[15.2-72]   op. cit., Boutwell, p. IX
[15.2-73]   Text of "An Act to suspend further reduction of the currency", 40th Congress, Session 2, Chapter 6, 4 Feb 1868
[15.2-74]   op. cit., Bolles, Vol. 3, pp. 278-280
[15.2-75]   Text of "An Act to exempt certain manufactures from internal tax, and for other purposes", 40th Congress, Session 2, Chapter 41, 31 Mar 1868
[15.2-76]   op. cit., Bolles, Vol. 3, pp. 410, 569
[15.2-77]   op. cit., Boutwell, p. IX
[15.2-78]   Text of "An Act constituting eight hours a day's work for all laborers, workmen, and mechanics employed by or on behalf of the Government of the United States", 40th Congress, Session 2, Chapter 72, 25 Jun 1868
[15.2-79]   Text of "An Act imposing taxes on distilled spirits and tobacco, and for other purposes", 40th Congress, Session 2, Chapter 186, 20 Jul 1868
[15.2-80]   Text of "An Act to provide for a further issue of temporary loan certificates, for the purpose of redeeming and retiring the remainder of the compound interest notes", 40th Congress, Session 2, Chapter 237, 25 Jul 1868
[15.2-81]   Text of "An Act to prevent loaning money upon United States Notes", 40th Congress, Session 3, Chapter 32, 19 Feb 1869
[15.2-82]   Text of "An Act regulating the reports of the National Banking Associations", 40th Congress, Session 3, Chapter 130, 3 Mar 1869
[15.2-83]   Text of "An Act to strengthen the public credit", 41st Congress, Session 1, Chapter 1, 18 Mar 1869
[15.2-84]   op. cit., Bolles, Vol. 3, p. 319
[15.2-85]   op. cit., Friedman and Schwartz, p. 45

[15.2-86]   op. cit., National Bureau of Economic Research
[15.2-87]   op. cit., Bolles, Vol. 3, pp. 254-257
[15.2-88]   Text of "An Act to provide for the redemption of the three per cent temporary loan certificates, and for an increase in national bank notes", 41st Congress, Session 2, Chapter 252, 12 Jul 1870
[15.2-89]   op. cit., Bolles, Vol. 3, pp. 354, 355
[15.2-90]   Text of "An Act to reduce internal taxes, and for other purposes", 41st Congress, Session 2, Chapter 255, 14 Jul 1870
[15.2-91]   op. cit., Bolles, Vol. 3, pp. 412, 453, 569
[15.2-92]   op. cit., Boutwell, p. IX
[15.2-93]   Text of "An Act to authorize the refunding of the national debt", 41st Congress, Session 2, Chapter 256, 14 Jul 1870
[15.2-94]   op. cit., Bolles, Vol. 3, p. 282
[15.2-95]   op. cit., National Bureau of Economic Research
[15.2-96]   Text of "An Act to amend an Act entitled 'An Act to authorize the refunding of the national debt'", 41st Congress, Session 3, Chapter 23, 20 Jan 1871
[15.2-97]   Text of "An Act to provide for the redemption of copper and other token coins", 41st Congress, Session 3, Chapter 124, 3 Mar 1871
[15.2-98]   op. cit., Bolles, Vol. 3, pp. 257-260
[15.2-99]   Text of "An Act repealing the duty on tea and coffee", 42nd Congress, Session 2, Chapter 131, 1 May 1872
[15.2-100] Text of "An Act to reduce duties on imports, and to reduce internal taxes, and for other purposes", 42nd Congress, Session 2, Chapter 315, 20 Jun 1872
[15.2-101] op. cit., Bolles, Vol. 3, pp. 412, 472, 543
[15.2-102] op. cit., Boutwell, p. IX
[15.2-103] Text of "An act revising and amending the laws relative to the Mints, assay-offices, and coinage of the United States, 42nd Congress, Session 3, Chapter 131, 12 Feb 1873
[15.2-104] op. cit., Bolles, Vol. 3, pp. 377-380
[15.2-105] op. cit., Kreps, pp. 83, 84
[15.2-106] op. cit., Friedman and Schwartz, pp. 113, 114
[15.2-107] op. cit., Bolles, Vol. 3, pp. 377-380, 389
[15.2-108] Text of "An Act to require national banks to restore their capital when impaired, and to amend the national currency act", 42nd Congress, Session 3, Chapter 269, 3 Mar 1873
[15.2-109] op. cit., Bolles, Vol. 3, p. 283
[15.2-110] op. cit., Bolles, Vol. 3, pp. 349, 350
[15.2-111] op. cit., Sprague, p. 54
[15.2-112] op. cit., Sprague, pp. 63-67
[15.2-113] op. cit., Sprague, pp. 1-107
[15.2-114] op. cit., Sprague, p. 81, citing the *Annual Report of the Comptroller of the Currency for 1873*, p. XXXV
[15.2-115] op. cit., Sprague, p. 77
[15.2-116] op. cit., National Bureau of Economic Research
[15.2-117] Text of "An Act to provide for the redemption of the loan of eighteen hundred and fifty-eight", 43rd Congress, Session 1, Chapter 1, 17 Dec 1873
[15.2-118] op. cit., Bolles, Vol. 3, pp. 283-289
[15.2-119] Text of "An act explanatory of the act of June thirtieth, eighteen hundred and sixty-four", 43rd Congress, Session 1, Chapter 304, 18 Jun 1874
[15.2-120] Text of "An act fixing the amount of United States notes, providing for a redistribution of the national bank currency, and for other purposes", 43rd Congress, Session 1, Chapter 343, 20 Jun 1874
[15.2-121] op. cit., Bolles, Vol. 3, p. 290
[15.2-122] op. cit., Friedman and Schwartz, pp. 20, 21
[15.2-123] op. cit., Bolles, Vol. 3, pp. 345, 346
[15.2-124] op. cit., Friedman and Schwartz, p. 113
[15.2-125] Text of "An act for the relief of savings institutions having no capital and doing business solely for the benefit of its depositors", 43rd Congress, Session 1, Chapter 399, 22 Jun 1874
[15.2-126] Text of "An act to provide for the resumption of specie payments", 43rd Congress, Session 2, Chapter 15, 14 Jan 1875
[15.2-127] op. cit., Bolles, Vol. 3, pp. 291-304, 352

[15.2-128] Text of "An act to amend existing customs and internal revenue laws, and for other purposes", 43rd Congress, Session 2, Chapter 36, 8 Feb 1875

[15.2-129] op. cit., Bolles, Vol. 3, p. 474

[15.2-130] Text of "An Act to further protect the sinking fund and provide for the exigencies of the Government", 43rd Congress, Session 2, Chapter 127, 3 Mar 1875

[15.2-131] Text of "An act authorizing the coinage of a twenty cent piece of silver at the mints of the United States", 43rd Congress, Session 2, Chapter 143, 3 Mar 1875

[15.2-132] Text of "Joint Resolution for the issue of silver coin", 44th Congress, Joint Resolution 17, 22 Jul 1876

[15.2-133] op. cit., Bolles, Vol. 3, p. 298

[15.2-134] Text of "An act to authorize the coinage of the standard silver dollar, and to restore its legal-tender status", 45th Congress, Session 2, Chapter 20, 28 Feb 1878

[15.2-135] op. cit., Kreps, pp. 85, 86

[15.2-136] op. cit., Bolles, Vol. 3, p. 298

[15.2-137] Text of "An act to prohibit the coinage of the twenty cent piece of silver", 45th Congress, Session 2, Chapter 79, 2 May 1878

[15.2-138] Text of "An act to forbid the further retirement of United States legal-tender notes", 45th Congress, Session 2, Chapter 146, 31 May 1878

[15.2-139] op. cit., Bolles, Vol. 3, p. 297

[15.2-140] op. cit., Friedman and Schwartz, pp. 24, 49

[15.2-141] op. cit., Bolles, Vol. 3, pp. 298, 299

[15.3-1]   op. cit., Friedman and Schwartz, Appendix A, p. 704

[15.3-2]   Frederick R. Macaulay, *Some Theoretical Problems Suggested by the Movements of Interest Rates, Bond Yields and Stock Prices in the United States Since 1856*, New York: National Bureau of Economic Research, 1938, Appendix A, Table 10 (pp. A143-A147). Copyright 1938, by National Bureau of Economic Research, Inc. Used with permission.

[15.4-1]   op. cit., Bolles, Vol. 3, pp. 349-351

[15.4-2]   op. cit., Friedman and Schwartz, pp. 108, 169-173

[15.4-3]   op. cit., Kreps, p. 170

[15.4-4]   op. cit., Sprague, p. 186

[15.4-5]   Murray N. Rothbard, *A History of Money and Banking in the United States: From the Colonial Era to World War II*, Auburn, AL: Ludwig von Mises Institute, 2003, p. 142

[15.4-6]   op. cit., Friedman and Schwartz, pp. 20, 21

[15.4-7]   op. cit., Bolles, Vol. 3, pp. 299-303

[15.4-8]   op. cit., Bolles, Vol. 3, pp. 361, 362

[15.4-9]   op. cit., Sprague, pp. 213-215

[15.4-10] op. cit., Friedman and Schwartz, pp. 32-34, 86-88

[15.4-11] op. cit., Rothbard, pp. 152-159

[15.4-12] op. cit., Bolles, Vol. 3, p. 129

NBER website: https://www.nber.org/research/data/us-business-cycle-expansions-and-contractions

16

The National Banking System Under the Gold Standard, 1879-1914

16.1 Preview, 1879-1914

Several important trends will be observed during this period: a) resumption of payment in specie and the redemption of the legal tender notes; b) a resurgence in the number of State banks in the 1890's; c) the resurgence of monetary silver and its ultimate replacement by a gold dollar; d) several "panics" that ultimately became the justification for the Federal Reserve; e) changes to the tariff system, generally trending toward a "free-trade" regime; and f) a reduction of the national debt by half, and the per-capita liability thereof falling by 75%.

The "depression" of 1873 to 1879 is probably a myth. Many writers have claimed that there must have been a sharp decline in the economy because of the decline in retail on prices. But actually this period was characterized by a growth in the money supply, an expansion of industry and more efficient production, which led to both rising incomes and falling stable prices [16.1-1], at least for the first half of this period. Prices then rose slowly afterward. If there was a recession, it probably ended in 1876 or so.

The government began to get involved in the operation and regulation of the economy, passing several pieces of legislation regulating work hours, and the establishment of a Department of Labor to compile statistics on workers.

The transition from fiat money to a commodity standard changed the behavior of money [16.1-2]. First, under a fiat system the amount of money is controlled by the government; in a commodity standard is controlled by external forces such as mining and foreign trade balances. Secondly, in a fiat system the exchange rate floats against other currencies depending on confidence in the currency and the balance of trade; in a commodity system the exchange rate varies only within narrow limits.

16.2 History, 1879-1914

1 Jan 1879: Resumption of specie payments began, but the banks made arrangements to make payments among themselves in clearinghouse certificates and legal tender notes, and not call upon the Treasury to redeem the legal tender notes, although the banks in New York held $40,000,000 in legal tenders [16.2-1]. By Nov 1879, only $11,256,678 had been presented for redemption. But the fact that redemption was required increased the confidence of the public in the money supply, and business expanded accordingly.

26 Feb 1879: Congress authorized [16.2-2] the Treasury Secretary to issue certificates of deposit bearing 4% interest, in exchange for lawful money, and convertible into the 4% bonds; and the proceeds to be used to make payments on the bonds paying interest up to 5%.

1 Mar 1879: Congress revised [16.2-3] the internal duties, mostly on liquor, tobacco, and imported-liquor stamps.

15 Mar 1879: Approximate end of the recession (cf. 15 Oct 1873) [16.2-4].

9 Jun 1879: Congress revised [16.2-5] the legal tender laws regarding silver coins: **a)** (S. 1, 2) silver coins of denominations less than $1 may be redeemed for lawful money when presented in sums greater than $20 to the Treasurer or assistant Treasurer; and **b)** (S. 3) silver coins of denominations less than $1 shall be legal tender for all payments, public and private, for amounts up to $10.

14 Feb 1880: Congress authorized [16.2-6] "gold banks" (cf. 12 Jul 1870) to convert to national banking associations.

15 Mar 1882: Approximate beginning of a recession [16.2-7].

4 May 1882: Congress repealed [16.2-8] the discriminating duties on items produced in places east of the Cape of Good Hope, so long as they are imported from places west of it; except wool, raw cotton, and raw silk.

26 May 1882: Congress authorized [16.2-9] the assay office in New York to issue gold bars at par value in return for gold coin in sums not less than $5,000.

12 Jul 1882: Congress revised the national banking law [16.2-10]: **a)** (S. 1) any national banking association established per 25 Feb 1863, 3 Jun 1864, or 14 Feb 1880 may apply within two years to have their charters extended another 20 years; **b)** (S. 2) application requires consent of the board of directors and the holders of two-thirds of the capital; **c)** (S. 8) national banks having a paid-in capital of $150,000 or less were required to deposit at least one-fourth of that amount in U. S. bonds with the U. S. Treasury as security for the circulating notes, and the amount of circulating notes shall not exceed 90% of the face value of the deposited bonds; **d)** (S. 9) banks that choose to reduce their circulation cannot increase it again until six months have elapsed; **e)** (S. 9) any reduction of bank notes was limited to $3,000,000 per month; **f)** (S. 10) circulation of national banking association notes is limited to 90% of paid-in capital stock; **g)** (S. 12) the Treasury Secretary was authorized to issue gold certificates only up to the actual amount of gold on hand; **h)** (S. 12) gold and silver certificates held by a national bank shall count toward the legal reserves; and **i)** (S. 12) national banks are prohibited from membership in any clearinghouse where the gold and silver certificates are not accepted. The gold certificates mentioned here are warehouse receipts for gold [16.2-11].

3 Mar 1883: Congress passed a general revision [16.2-12] to the tariff law: **a)** (S. 1) repealed the taxes on capital and deposits of banks, bankers, and national banking associations; **b)** (S. 1) repealed the stamp tax on bank checks, drafts, orders, and vouchers, matches, perfumes, and medicine; and **c)** (S. 2-13) [16.2-13] changed the tariff rates on 144 items: 98 were lowered and 46 were increased.

3 Mar 1884: The U. S. Supreme Court, in Juilliard v. Greenman, upheld the constitutionality of issuing legal tender notes during peacetime, thus extending the ruling in Knox v. Lee (1 May 1871), and upholding the legal tender laws of 25 Feb 1862 and 3 Mar 1863. Justice Gray wrote the majority ruling [16.2-14]:

> "The power to make the notes of the government a legal tender in payment of private debts being one of the powers belonging to sovereignty in other civilized nations, and not expressly withheld from Congress by the constitution, we are irresistibly impelled to the conclusion that the impressing upon the treasury-notes of the United States the quality of being a legal tender in payment of private debts is an appropriate means, conducive and plainly adapted to the execution of the undoubted powers of Congress, consistent with the letter and spirit of the constitution, and therefore within the meaning of that instrument necessary and proper for carrying into execution the powers vested by this constitution in the government of the United States. Whether at any particular time in war or in peace, the exigency is such, by reason of universal and pressing demand on the resources of the government, or of the inadequacy of the supply of gold and silver coin to

furnish the currency needed for the uses of the government and of the people, that it is, as a matter of fact, wise and expedient to resort to this means, is a political question, to be determined by Congress when a question of exigency arises, and not a judicial question, to be afterward passed upon by the courts."

3 May - 10 Jun 1884: There was a local money panic in New York [16.2-15, 16.2-16] due to several causes: a) a reduction in the reserve position of several New York banks due to an outflow of gold to Europe between Mar and Apr 1884; b) falling prices of commodities over the past year that in turn reduced prices of the stocks in those companies, putting speculators' call loans at risk; c) failure of the Marine National Bank on 6 May due to corruption; d) failure on 8 May of the brokerage firm Grant and Ward due to corruption and incompetence (one of its partners was the president of the Marine National Bank); e) on 13 May it was found that the president of the Second National Bank had stolen $3,000,000 of securities from the vault; f) the Metropolitan National Bank failed on 14 May, and several other local banks and brokerage houses failed in the next few days owing to an inability to obtain ready cash. Call rates for money became very high, and banks were unable to collect on their call loans. These events caused a crisis of confidence in the banks, although there was not actually a money shortage or any question as to the general health of the banking system. This was resolved within two weeks because the other banks used $24,000,000 in clearinghouse loan certificates to offset transactions among the banks.

27 Jun 1884: Congress established a Bureau of Labor [16.2-17]; duties to include:

> "the subject of labor, its relation to capital, hours worked, the earnings of laboring men and women, and the means of promoting their material, social, intellectual, and moral prosperity."

10 Aug 1884: There was an earthquake in New York City, probably centered near Coney Island, estimated at a magnitude between 4.9 and 5.5.

15 May 1885: Approximate end of the recession (cf. 15 Mar 1882) [16.2-18].

4 Feb 1887: Congress passed the Interstate Commerce Act [16.2-19] designed to regulate transportation by railroad and water. The goal was to restrain monopolies and prevent price-fixing or preferential treatment by the railroads to certain customers. Provisions included: **a)** (S. 1 - 4) prohibited railroads from preferential pricing or accommodations; **b)** (S. 5) prohibited railroads from pooling freight resources by contract (i.e., collusion); **c)** (S. 6 - 8) required the railroads to publish regular schedules and charges; **d)** (S. 6) schedules and fares to be filed with the Interstate Commerce Commission; and **e)** (S. 11 - 24) created the Interstate Commerce Commission.

3 Mar 1887: Congress revised [16.2-20] the regulations for regional reserve city and central reserve city banks: **a)** (S. 1) cities with populations of 50,000 could become "reserve cities" if 75% of the national banks in operation there concurred, and those banks are to keep 25% reserves in their vaults; and **b)** (S. 2) cities with populations of 200,000 could become "central reserve cities" if 75% of the national banks in operation there concurred, those banks to keep 25% of reserves in their vaults; and **c)** (S. 3) legal tender notes may be redeemed at San Francisco, in addition to New York. By this means Chicago and St. Louis were upgraded to "central reserve cities" [16.2-21, 16.2-22].

3 Mar 1887: Congress altered the banking laws [16.2-23]: **a)** (S. 1) permitted all trade dollars to be redeemed at par in standard silver dollars or of subsidiary coins if presented by Sep 1887; **b)** (S. 2) trade dollars received by the Treasurer to be re-coined into standard silver dollars or subsidiary coin, but the recoined trade dollars not to count against the bullion and new silver coinage per the Allison-Bland Act (cf. 28 Feb 1878); and **c)** (S. 3) prohibited further coining of trade dollars.

15 Mar 1887: Approximate beginning of a recession [16.2-24].

15 Apr 1888: Approximate end of the recession (cf. 15 Mar 1887) [16.2-25].

13 Jun 1888: Congress established the Department of Labor [16.2-26]. The duties of the Commissioner of Labor include:

"to ascertain, at as early a date as possible, and whenever industrial changes shall make it essential, the cost of producing articles at the time dutiable in the United States, in leading countries where such articles are produced, by fully-specified units of production, and under a classification showing the different elements of cost, or approximate cost, of such articles of production, including the wages paid in such industries per day, week, month, or year, or by the piece; and hours employed per day; and the profits of the manufacturers and producers of such articles; and the comparative cost of living, and the kind of living. It shall be the duty of the Commissioner also to ascertain and report as to the effect of the customs laws, and the effect thereon of the state of the currency, in the United States, on the agricultural industry, especially as to its effect on mortgage indebtedness of farmers; and what articles are controlled by Trusts, or other combinations of capital, business operations, or labor and what effect said trusts, or other combinations of capital, business operations, or labor have on production and prices. He shall also establish a system of reports by which, at intervals of not less than two years, he can report the general condition, so far as production is concerned, of the leading industries of the country. The Commissioner of Labor is also specially charged to investigate the causes of, and facts relating to, all controversies and disputes between employers and employees as they may occur, and which may tend to interfere with the welfare of the people of the different States, and report thereon to Congress. The Commissioner of Labor shall also obtain such information upon the various subjects committed to him as he may deem desirable from different foreign nations, and what, if any, convict made goods are imported into this country, and if so from whence."

1 Jul - 30 Nov 1890: The large banks in New York, Boston, and Philadelphia experienced a money panic [16.2-27]. Good business conditions in the West and South caused banks there to make loans, instead of sending their cash to the eastern banks to be held as reserves. By Jun 1890, the banks in New York had considerably less excess reserves than normal. Rather than contract their loans to restore the normal position, they increased the issues of call loans to stock market speculators. In late Jun 1890 British banks with offices in New York began selling off their stocks to generate cash in order to support other investments in England. Between 15 Jun and 7 Aug the New York banks exported gold amounting to about 15% of their reserves. By 23 Aug the New York banks found it necessary to liquidate their call loans, which in turn depressed stock prices since the stocks had to be sold to repay the loans. This cash flow problem was made worse since the New York banks were about begin the usual shipment of money to the West and South to finance the normal agricultural cycle. The federal government was running surpluses at this time, so the Treasury stepped in and offered to redeem $76,000,000 worth of 4.5% notes held by the bank between 20 Aug and 7 Sep. On 17 Sep the Treasury offered 17,000,000 in bonds, subscribed to by other Eastern banks; those proceeds went directly into the banks at New York, Boston, and Philadelphia to shore up their reserves. In addition, the banks resumed the use of clearinghouse loan certificates ($31,365,000) to make offsetting payments among themselves. This was not quite enough; the banks began to send cash to the West and South, and continued loan contractions until 1 Nov. On 7 Nov the Bank of England raised its discount rate from 5 to 6%; this led to a selloff in the English stock market until 30 Nov, with the failure of several prominent investment houses (most notable Baring & Co. on 15 Nov). At that point, the situation stabilized, and the panic ended. Throughout this episode, there were no domestic bank failures: they continued to make loans to solvent borrowers, and continued to make cash payments on demand to depositors.

2 Jul 1890: Congress passed legislation [16.2-28] outlawing monopolies and conspiracies to create monopolies. Sections 1 and 2 state:

"SEC. 1. Every contract, combination in the form of trust or otherwise, or conspiracy, in restraint of trade or commerce among the several States, or with foreign nations, is hereby declared to be illegal. Every person who shall make any such contract or engage in any such combination or conspiracy, shall be deemed guilty of a misdemeanor, and, on conviction thereof, shall be punished by fine not exceeding five thousand dollars, or by imprisonment not exceeding one year, or by both said punishments, in the discretion of the court.

SEC. 2. Every person who shall monopolize, or attempt to monopolize, or combine or conspire with any other person or persons, to monopolize any part of the trade or commerce among the several States, or with foreign nations, shall be deemed guilty of a misdemeanor, and, on conviction thereof, shall be punished by fine not exceeding five thousand dollars, or by imprisonment not exceeding one year, or by both said punishments, in the discretion of the court."

14 Jul 1890: Congress passed the Sherman Silver Purchase Act in order to keep parity between gold and silver [16.2-29]: **a)** (S. 1) directed the Treasury to buy silver 4,500,000 ozt. of silver at the market price not exceeding 371.25 grains per dollar; **b)** (S. 1) issue in payment for the silver Treasury Notes (i.e., the "Treasury Notes of 1890") against the silver at $1.29/ozt. (which was the statutory value of silver); **c)** (S. 2) the Treasury Notes to be payable in coin on demand, and were legal tender for all public and private debts except where a contract specified otherwise; **d)** (S. 2) the volume of Treasury Notes was limited to the cost of the bullion and coinage; **e)** (S. 2) Treasury Notes to be redeemable in either gold or silver at the discretion of the Treasury Secretary in order to maintain parity between gold and silver; **f)** (S. 3) Treasury required to coin 2,000,000 ozt. into standard silver dollars each month until 1 Jul 1891, and afterwards per the amount of bullion purchased; **g)** (S. 5) repealed the Bland-Allison Act (cf. 28 Feb 1878) insofar as the requirement to coin between 2 and 4 million dollars worth of bullion; and **h)** changed the accounting rules regarding national bank notes: redemption of notes to be destroyed and not replaced to be covered by Treasury cash, and not against the 5% deposited for security by the banks.

Regarding section 1, the current market price was about 70 cents per ozt., and 371.25 grains would sell for about 54 cents. The market value of silver was steadily declining, and note holders preferred gold for redemption per section 2 [16.2-30]. This led to a drain on the Treasury's gold reserves from $200,000,000 in 1890 to about $100,000,000 by Apr 1893. The drain on gold was caused by Treasury Secretary Carlisle's insistence that the notes be redeemed in gold, instead of using his option to redeem in silver. The addition of the Treasury Notes of 1890 contributed to an unnecessary expansion of the money supply, and led indirectly to the recession in 1893.

This was the culmination of a long debate on the use of silver [16.2-31]. First, because many farms had been ruined in the South during the Civil War, and because many farms in the West were new, farmers had to go into debt to resume operations. There was a demand for an increase in the money supply, as it would serve to increase farm prices. Secondly, the price of silver had been falling since the mid-1870's, since several European nations had also adopted the gold standard. That meant that silver was cheaper, and the Treasury could mint more money. Third, the coinage due to the Bland-Allison Act in 1878 had not been well-received by the public; many of the standard silver coins had gone out of circulation. The Sherman Act was designed to stimulate silver production, increase the money supply, and issue more convenient paper notes in the form of the Treasury Notes of 1890.

15 Jul 1890: Approximate beginning of a recession [16.2-32].

26 Sep 1890: Congress discontinued [16.2-33] the coinage of the one-dollar and three-dollar gold coins, and also the three-cent coin. The existing ones were to be withdrawn from circulation as they came into the Treasury, to be recoined into other denominations.

1 Oct 1890: Congress passed the McKinley Tariff law [16.2-34]: a) increased average duties on most imports from 38% to 49%; and b) eliminated duties on sugar, molasses, tea, and coffee. The addition of sugar to the free list caused a sharp decline in revenue from import duties [16.2-35], and lowered demand for other items. It was mostly a protection measure for tin and wool producers, and was replaced by the Wilson-Gorman Tariff of 1894.

15 May 1891: Approximate end of the recession (cf. 15 Jul 1890) [16.2-36].

1 Aug 1892: Congress extended [16.2-37] the 8-hour workday (cf. 25 Jun 1868) to all federal contractors and sub-contractors employed on public works.

15 Jan 1893: Approximate beginning of a recession [16.2-38, 16.2-39]. Europeans began selling off U. S. securities to pay for food imports, owing to disastrous crop failures in Europe in 1891 and 1892. The stock market began a slow decline, and the Philadelphia and Reading Railroad failed on 26 Feb 1893. The banks reduced the volume of loans throughout Mar and Apr. At the same time, prices

were low in Europe, and Americans imported heavily, causing an export of gold from the U. S. There was also a drain on gold from the Treasury, since the Treasury Notes of 1890 issued under the Sherman Act could be redeemed for either silver or gold at the Treasury Secretary's discretion. Secretary Carlisle chose to redeem them all in gold [16.2-40].

4 May - 9 Sep 1893: This was the period of the Panic of 1893 [16.2-41, 16.2-42]. The U. S. experienced a stock market crash on 4 May; the National Cordage Company failed in early May; the stock market continued to decline; there was a decline in volume of loans; and exportation of gold and shipments of cash from New York to the banks in the West and South occurred as part of the normal agricultural cycle. There was some question in the minds of foreign investors as to whether the U. S. would stay on the gold standard, given the expansion of money backed by the purchases of silver under the Sherman Act. In May and June, a total of 158 banks, mostly small, and mostly in the South and West failed due to run on them, which in turn was caused by a lack of confidence in the banking system. Of the 158 suspended banks, 65 were insolvent, 86 were eventually allowed to re-open, and 7 went into investigation. There were a total of 3,401 business failures between Jan and Jul 1893, with liabilities totaling $169,000,000 which naturally took a toll on some banks. The drains on the New York banks caused them to experience a problem with their reserve position; they continued to liquidate their call loans, further suppressing stock prices. On 17 Jun the New York banks started issuing clearinghouse loan certificates in lieu of cash to settle balances between them. On 8 Jul the New York banks had reserves below the legal limit. Beginning on 21 Jul, there was another set of bank failures, mostly in the Midwest; 33 national banks suspended cash payments between 14 Jul and 1 Aug. By late Jul, there was a widespread suspension of payment through the nation. On 2 Aug the banks in New York suspended cash payments. On 12 Aug the New York banks had reserves against deposits of only 20.55% (legal requirements was 25%). The reserves were restored by large gold imports from Europe, paid for with commercial bills. By 7 Sep, the reserve position was restored, and the banks resumed cash payments shortly thereafter. The shortage of cash was a consequence, not a cause of the panic. A total of $300,000,000 in money substitutes was used throughout the U. S during Aug. The total amount of clearinghouse loan certificates in use came to $41.9 M.

~10 Sep 1893: Resumption of specie payments of notes, end of the panic [16.2-43].

1 Nov 1893: Congress amended the Sherman Silver Act (cf. 14 Jul 1890) [16.2-44]: **a)** (S. 1) repealed the portion requiring the Treasury to purchase 4,500,000 ozt. of silver; **b)** (S. 1) declared that both silver and gold should be the circulating medium of the U. S. with equal parity of value; and **c)** (S. 1) endorsed a bimetallic system, stating: "the efforts of the Government should be steadily directed to the establishment of such a safe system of bimetallism as will maintain at all times the equal power of every dollar coined or issued by the United States, in the markets, and in the payment of debts".

~1 Jan 1894 to Jan 1896: It became necessary for the Treasury Department to issue bonds totaling $275,000,000 in order to buy enough gold to redeem the remaining Treasury Notes of 1890, since they were being redeemed in gold, instead of either gold or silver per Carlisle. But the gold that was obtained with the proceeds of these bond sales was either exported or hoarded [16.2-45].

15 Jun 1894: Approximate end of the recession (cf. 15 Jan 1893) [16.2-46].

13 Aug 1894: Congress passed legislation [16.2-47] authorizing the States to levy a tax on: a) National Bank Notes; b) United States legal tender notes ("greenbacks"); c) other notes and certificates of the United States that circulate and are payable on demand, and d) gold and silver coin as money on hand or deposit, provided the taxation is the same as on other money circulating in the State.

27 Aug 1894: Congress passed the Wilson-Gorman Tariff Act [16.2-48]: **a)** (S. 1, 2) revised tariffs on 362 items, mostly reducing what had been increased in 1890 except imposing an import duty on sugar; **b)** (S. 2) a list of 323 items on the free list (including iron ore lumber, and coal); **c)** (S. 3, 4) 10% *ad valorem* duty on any items not listed; **d)** (S. 17) prohibited importation of meat or cattle unless the Treasury Secretary verifies there is no risk from disease that could spread to domestic cattle; **e)** (S. 27, 28) imposed a 2% income tax on incomes over $4,000 with a $1,000 family deduction between

1895 and 1900; **f)** (S. 28) income to include interest income, sales of real estate and other items, and gifts; **g)** (S. 27, 33) federal employees, military, and members of Congress exempt from filing a return because their salaries were subject to 2% withholding, **h)** (S. 33) salaries of State, county, and municipal employees exempt from income tax; **i)** (S. 32) imposed a 2% profits tax on corporations; exempting States, municipalities, charitable organizations, and mutual insurance companies; and **j)** made it illegal for a revenue officer to divulge any information on income or taxes of individuals or corporations. Notice that this legislation made certain public employees first-class citizens, exempt from income taxes.

8 Apr 1895: The U. S. Supreme Court ruled in Pollock vs. Farmers' Loan and Trust that the income tax provision of the Wilson-Gorman Tariff Act was unconstitutional [16.2-49] on the grounds that it did not apportion the tax among the States as required by the Constitution.

15 Dec 1895: Approximate beginning of a recession [16.2-50].

15 Jun 1897: Approximate end of the recession (cf. 15 Dec 1895) [16.2-51].

24 Jul 1897: Congress passed the Dingley Tariff Act [16.2-52] increasing duties on many items, in order to counteract the Wilson-Gorman Tariff of 1894, and reducing the number of items on the free list from 323 to 242. It re-imposed duties on woolen goods, linen, silk, and sugar. The *ad valorem* duties ranged from 25% to 60%.

15 Feb 1898: Sinking of the USS Maine at Havana, later shown to be a boiler accident.

23 Apr 1898: Spain declared war on the U. S.

25 Apr 1898: Congress declared war on Spain; beginning of the Spanish-American War.

1 May 1898: Battle of Manila Bay.

8 - 11 May 1898: First and Second Battles of Cardenas.

6 - 10 Jun 1898: Battle of Guantanamo Bay.

13 Jun 1898: Congress passed tax legislation [16.2-53] to fund the war: **a)** (S. 1) imposed a $2 per gallon excise on beer and liquor; **b)** (S. 2) imposed annual taxes on certain businesses: 1) $25 for banks with a capital up to $25,000, plus $2 for every thousand above $25,000, 2) $50 on brokers, 3) $25 on pawnbrokers, 4) $20 on commercial brokers, 5) $10 on customs brokers, 6) $100 on theaters, museums, and concert halls, 7) $100 on proprietors of circuses, 8) $10 on all others not enumerated, and 9) $5 per individual bowling alley and pool table; **c)** (S. 3) excise taxes on tobacco; **d)** (S. 4) annual tax of $6 on tobacco dealers per 50,000 pounds sold; **e)** (S. 6) stamp tax on certain documents (bonds, debentures, stock certificates, telegrams; **f)** (S. 20) stamp tax on medicines; **g)** (S. 32) authorized the Treasury Secretary to borrow up to $100,000,000 and issue certificates of indebtedness at 3% interest, payable within one years; **h)** (S. 33) authorized the Treasury Secretary to borrow up to $400,000,000 and issue bonds at 3% to fund the war, redeemable in coin after 10 years, and payable after 20 years; **i)** (S. 34) directed the Treasury Secretary to coin all the bullion in the Treasury at a rate of $1,500,000 in silver dollars each month to be used to pay interest on certificates and bonds; **j)** (S. 35) $12 annual tax on producers of flour; and **k)** (S. 50) 10 cents per pound duty on imported tea.

20, 21 Jun 1898: Battle of Guam.

22 - 28 Jun 1898: Second and Third Battles of San Juan.

30 Jun 1898: Battle of Tayacoba.

1 Jul 1898: Battle of San Juan Hill.

3 - 17 Jul 1898: Siege of Santiago de Cuba.

23 Jul 1898: Battle of Mani-Mani.

8, 9 Aug 1898: Battle of Coamo.

9 - 13 Aug 1898: Battle of Asomante.

13 Aug 1898: Battle of Manila.

10 Dec 1898: Treaty of Paris, end of the Spanish-American War.

15 Jun 1899: Approximate beginning of a recession [16.2-54].

14 Mar 1900: Congress revised the national banking system and currency laws [16.2-55]: **a)** (S. 1) the dollar was defined as 25.8 grains of gold, 90% fine (i.e., 23.22 grains pure gold), and to be the standard of value for the dollar; **b)** (S. 2) the United States Notes (greenbacks) and Treasury Notes of 1890 (cf. 14 Jul 1890) to be redeemable in gold coin, and the Treasury Secretary directed to set aside $150,000,000 in gold coin and bullion for redemption thereof; **c)** (S. 2) the Treasury Secretary to borrow on the credit of the U. S. if necessary to obtain a sufficient amount of gold by issuing bonds at interest not exceeding 3%, interest payable quarterly and bonds payable anytime after one year in gold; **d)** (S. 2) said bonds to be exempt from federal, State, and municipal taxes; **e)** (S. 2) redeemed United States Notes may be re-issued, but to be held in reserve until exchanged for gold; **f)** (S. 2) the total amount of United States Notes plus gold held in reserve limited to $150,000,000; **g)** (S. 3) the silver dollar to retain its existing legal tender status; **h)** (S. 4) directed the Treasury to establish a gold and silver reserves as trust funds, and authorized it to issue gold and silver certificates at par against the coin and bullion; **i)** (S. 5) Treasury Notes to be retired and cancelled after being redeemed either with gold and silver coin, or by exchange for silver certificates; **j)** (S. 6) authorized the Treasury to receive gold coin and issue gold certificates in return; the gold coin to be held as security for the certificates for payment on demand; **k)** (S. 6) the issuing of gold certificates is to be suspended if the Treasury's gold fund falls below $100,000,000, and the issuing of silver certificates is to be suspended if the total of United States Notes and silver certificates in the Treasury general fund exceeds $60,000,000; **l)** (S. 8) the Treasury was authorized to coin subsidiary silver coins to an amount not exceeding $100,000,000; **m)** (S. 10) national banks could be established in locations with a population less than 3,000; the required capitalization is $25,000; **n)** (S. 11) Treasury Secretary authorized to exchange 2% bonds in exchange for old 5%, 4%, or 3% bonds with compensation for the reduction of interest; **o)** (S. 12) the amount of National Bank Notes that could be issued was increased to 100% of the deposited bonds (but the lower of current value or par); **p)** (S. 12) national banks could issue National Bank Notes in denominations less than $5, but only in aggregate up to one-third of the total issued; and **q)** (S. 13) the tax on bank notes in circulation was revised: 1) notes backed by the new 2% coupon bonds to be taxed at 0.5% annually; 2) notes backed by all other bonds to remain taxed at 1% annual. The definition of the dollar defined only as gold formalized the de facto standard that had existed since 1837; this formally demonetized silver, isolating the dollar from silver altogether [16.2-56].

15 Dec 1900: Approximate end of the recession (cf. 15 Jun 1899) [16.2-57].

2 Mar 1901: Congress passed a revision [16.2-58] to the tax law of 13 Jun 1898: **a)** (S. 1) reduced taxes on beer and liquor; **b)** (S. 3, 4) reduced taxes on tobacco and tobacco dealers; **c)** (S. 5) replaced the tax on medicine with a tax on wine; and **d)** (S. 32) repealed the stamp tax on telegrams.

12 Apr 1902: Congress reduced [16.2-59] the war taxes previously enacted (cf. 13 Jun 1898, 2 Mar 1901); among its provisions: **a)** (S. 1) reduced tax on liquor to $1 per barrel; **b)** (S. 2) repealed all of S. 2 of 13 Jun 1898; **c)** (S. 3) reduced the taxes on tobacco to 6 cents per pound; **d)** (S. 5) repealed the dealers tax (cf. 18 Jun 1898, S. 4); **e)** (S. 7) repealed the stamp taxes; and **f)** (S. 10) repealed S. 50 of 13 Jun 1898.

12 Apr 1902: Congress extended [16.2-60] the charters of the national banking associations for another 20 years.

15 Sep 1902: Approximate beginning of a recession [16.2-61].

14 Jan 1903: Congress enacted a law [16.2-62] regarding Hawaiian money: **a)** (S. 1, 2) full-weight Hawaiian silver coins to be accepted at par value, but once received, are to be recoined into U. S. coins; **b)** (S. 3) full-weight Hawaiian silver coins may be exchanged for standard silver dollars at par value; **c)** below-weight Hawaiian coins to be exchanged for U. S. coins per their true weight in silver; **d)** Hawaiian silver coins to be legal tender in Hawaii only until 1 Jan 1904; **e)** (S. 5) silver certificates

issued by the government of Hawaii shall be redeemed by the Hawaiian government by 1 Jan 1905, and thereafter not to circulate as money; and **f)** (S. 7) the U. S. shall not redeem Hawaiian silver certificates.

14 Feb 1903: Congress established the Department of Commerce and Labor [16.2-63]. Section 3 spelled out its duties:

> "That it shall be the province and duty of said Department to foster, promote, and develop the foreign and domestic commerce, the mining, manufacturing, shipping, and fishery industries, the labor interests, and the transportation facilities of the United States; and to this end it shall be vested with jurisdiction and control of the departments, bureaus, offices, and branches of the public service hereinafter specified, and with such other powers and duties as may be prescribed by law."

3 Mar 1903: Congress revised [16.2-64] the rules for reserve city status: **a)** (S. 1) cities with a population of 25,000 could become a "reserve city" if 75% of the national banks operating there concurred; and **b)** (S. 2) national banks in such cities then required to keep on hand a reserve in lawful money equal to 25% of its deposits.

15 Aug 1904: Approximate end of the recession (cf. 15 Sep 1902) [16.2-65].

26 May 1906: Congress passed legislation [16.2-66] regarding the issuing of gold certificates. It changed S. 6 of the 14 Mar 1900 law, reducing the threshold at which gold certificate issues are to be suspended, from $100,000,000 in the gold fund to $50,000,000.

22 Jun 1906: Congress passed legislation [16.2-67] regarding liabilities of national banks: **a)** (S. 1) the total amount of money borrowed not to exceed 10% of the combined paid-in capital and unimpaired surplus; and **b)** (S. 1) subject to an overall limit of 30% of its capital stock, but the discounts on bills of exchange and discounts of commercial paper are not to be counted as borrowed money.

4 Mar 1907: Congress revised the banking laws [16.2-68]; among its provisions: **a)** (S. 1) reversed the threshold as to when issuing gold certificates is to be suspended, restoring it from $50,000,000 (cf. 26 May 1906) back to the original $100,000,000 (cf. 14 Mar 1900); **b)** (S. 2) authorized the Treasury Secretary to issue $1, $2, and $5 United States Notes if the outstanding amount of $1, $2, and $5 silver certificates is insufficient, in the Secretary's opinion, to meet public demand, but: 1) larger denominations of United States Notes are to be destroyed if they come into the Treasury, and 2) the total amount of Unites States Notes outstanding is limited to the same extent as currently provided [$346,681,016, cf. 31 May 1875]; **c)** (S. 3) national banks may be depositories of public money, shall provide bonds for the security of public deposits, and shall receive at par all national currency bills; and **d)** (S. 4) increased the amount by which a national bank may deposit lawful money with the Treasury and have its bonds returned, thus to reduce its note circulation to $9,000,000 per month.

~10 Mar 1907: Large decline in stock prices, especially among the large corporations whose stock had been used as collateral for "finance bills" used in foreign trade [16.2-69]. There was a recovery of stock prices between Apr and Jul 1907.

15 May 1907: Approximate beginning of a recession [16.2-70].

~10 Aug 1907: Stock prices declined again, accompanied by a decline in savings, making it difficult for businesses to obtain loans [16.2-71].

19 Oct 1907 to 2 Jan 1908: The U. S. experienced a banking panic [16.2-72, 16.2-73]. The economy was in decline: a) a large decline in stock prices in Mar 1907; and b) 11% decline in industrial production beginning in May 1907 which continued until Jun 1908. The panic per se began with a lack of trust among prominent bankers in New York (F. A. Heinze and C. F. Morse); Heinze had tried to corner the copper market, and Morse had a reputation for bad management although he was on the board of directors of six large New York banks (City, Commerce, First, Park, Hanover, and Chase). At this point six major banks held 75% of the total banker's deposits (i.e., reserves of other banks in the national bank system); this concentration amounted to a concentration of liability, which required large cash reserves to meet emergencies, but they retained only the legally required 25%. At this time a

great deal of banking business was conducted by trust companies; they generally did not keep cash reserves and most of them were not members of the clearinghouse. Runs on the National Bank of North America and Mercantile National Bank began 19 Oct; Knickerbocker Trust Company experienced a run starting on 21 Oct; a run on the Trust Company of America and Lincoln Trust Company began 23 Oct, and many other smaller banks and trusts as well. The trust companies then had to liquidate their call loans, and those customers had to appeal to the national banks to avoid insolvency. Therefore the New York national banks had to issue new loans in order for the trust company customers to avoid insolvency (loans actually increased during this period). There was no standing organization to deal with large scale runs on the banks. By late Oct many New York banks suspended cash payments, accepted checks only for collection, limited the amounts of withdrawals, and imposed 60 days notice for withdrawal of savings. The New York clearinghouse began the use of clearinghouse loan certificates (a total of $101,060,000 issued, $88,420,000 maximum outstanding on 16 Dec 1907) for balancing payments among the banks, which freed up cash for depositors. By mid-Nov, clearinghouse loan certificates were used in 60 of the 106 clearinghouses as a means to preserve cash. The Treasury injected $36,000,000 into the New York banks between 19 and 31 Oct. By 2 Nov, the distrust of banks had spread nationwide owing to the events in New York, and most banks adopted the same suspension policies as the banks in New York. A total of $96,000,000 in gold was imported during Nov and Dec 1907, which restored the reserve balances. The New York banks continued to ship currency to the interior banks in response to their demands, but those smaller institutions decided to suspend payments in an effort to maintain their cash reserve balances. A general decline in business in the rest of the nation caused currency to return to the banks, and cash flowed back to the New York banks. Cash payments resumed 2 Jan 1908 after the reserve positions were restored and the public once again gained confidence in the banking system. The early suspension of payments (defined as refusal by the banks to convert deposits into currency) preserved the reserves of the banks, and caused the contraction to be shortened. This Panic was used as the justification to examine a reform of the banking system.

30 May 1908: Congress passed the Aldrich-Vreeland Act [16.2-74]: **a)** (S. 1) permitted a group of national banks (at least ten), with a combined capital and surplus of $5,000,000 to form a "currency association"; **b)** (S. 1) the "currency association" was to be a separate corporation from the national banks that formed it; **c)** (S. 1) only one currency association could be established in a city, although the member banks could be located outside and across State lines; **d)** (S. 1) the currency association to be managed by one representative from each member national bank; **e)** (S. 1) any member bank, having notes outstanding less than 40% of its capital, and an unimpaired capital and surplus of at least 20%, may deposit securities or commercial paper with the currency association, and may make application to the Comptroller of the Currency for additional circulating notes in amount up to 75% of the cash value of the securities and paper; **f)** (S. 1) the additional circulating notes to be limited to 90% of the value of any State or municipal securities and 30% of unimpaired capital in the case of commercial paper deposited; **g)** (S. 1) the member banks to be liable for redemption of the additional notes; **h)** (S. 2, 6) Treasury Secretary to sell bonds deposited by the banks if they fail to maintain the 5% redemption fund; **i)** (S. 3) national banks may, with concurrence of the Treasury, issue notes based on securities other than those of the United States, up to 90% of face value; **j)** (S. 9) all circulating notes subject to an annual tax of 0.5% if secured by 2% bonds; **k)** (S. 9) all circulating notes secured by bonds other than U. S. bonds shall pay a tax: 1) 5% annual rate for the first month, 2) 1% annual rate monthly thereafter until the total is 10%, 3) afterward at 10%; **l)** (S. 10) reduction of circulating notes secured by bonds other than those of the U. S. subject to the same rules, but the bonds are to be retained by the Treasury for redemption of the notes, instead of being returned to the bank; **m)** (S. 15) national banks designated as depositories of public funds shall pay interest not less than 1%, as determined by the Treasury Secretary, and shall be uniform throughout the U. S.; and **n)** (S. 17 - 19) formation of a National Monetary Commission study group to suggest banking reform.

This law permitted groups of national banks to issue emergency currency if there was a run on the banks, but imposed penalties for maintaining the emergency currency in circulation after it was no longer needed [16.2-75]. The Commission issued a report in 1912 with a plan that became the basis for the Federal Reserve System (cf. 23 Dec 1913).

15 Jun 1908: Approximate end of the recession (cf. 15 May 1907) [16.2-76].

5 Aug 1909: Congress passed the Payne-Aldrich Tariff Act [16.2-77], completely re-writing the tariff law. Among its provisions: **a)** Schedule A (Chemical, oils, and paints), up to 25% *ad valorem*; **b)** Schedule B (earthenware), up to 35% *ad valorem*; **c)** Schedule C (metals and manufactures thereof), up to 45% *ad valorem*, but some by weight; **d)** Schedule D (wood and manufactures thereof), up to 45% *ad valorem*; **e)** Schedule E (sugar, molasses, and manufactures thereof), up to 20% *ad valorem*; **f)** Schedule F (tobacco and manufactures thereof), up to 55 cents per pound; **g)** Schedule G (agricultural products), some by weight, others up to 30% *ad valorem*; **h)** Schedule H (spirits and wines), up to $2.75 per gallon or 45% *ad valorem*; **i)** Schedule I (cotton manufactures), some by weight or size, or up to 50% *ad valorem*; **j)** Schedule J (hemp, flax, etc.), some by weight, others up to 60% *ad valorem*; **k)** Schedule K (wool and manufactures thereof), up to 40% *ad valorem*; **l)** Schedule L (silk, etc.), up to 60% *ad valorem*; **m)** Schedule M (paper), up to 35% *ad valorem*; **n)** Schedule N (sundries), up to 45% *ad valorem*; **o)** 237 items on the free list; **p)** (S. 2 - 5) exemptions for imports from Cuba and the Philippines; **q)** (S. 15) 10% additional duty if imported on foreign vessels; **r)** (S. 38) imposed a 1% excise tax on net income over $5,000 on corporations, joint stock companies, and insurance companies, but excluding agricultural, labor, religious, and charitable organizations; **s)** (S. 39) authorized the Treasury Secretary to borrow $290,569,000 to defray expenditures on the Panama Canal, at 3%, payable in 50 years; and **t)** (S. 40) authorized the Treasury Secretary to borrow up to $200,000,000 at 3% as necessary to meet current expenses of the Government.

5 Aug 1909: Congress passed a tariff bill regarding imports into the Philippines [16.2-78], but also includes export duties from the Philippines.

15 Jan 1910: Approximate beginning of a recession [16.2-79].

4 Feb 1910: Congress passed legislation [16.2-80] regarding the payment of principal and interest on U. S. debt: **a)** (S. 1) the principal and interest on U. S. bonds and certificates of indebtedness issued hereafter shall be payable in gold coin at present standard of value (cf. 14 Mar 1900); **b)** (S. 2) that certificates of indebtedness of the United States are exempt from federal, State, and local or municipal taxes; and **c)** (S. 3) repealed any existing provisions in law that were contrary.

25 Jun 1910: Congress established [16.2-81] the postal savings system: **a)** (S. 1) established a Postal Savings Board of Trustees, consisting of designees appointed by the Postmaster-General, Treasury Secretary and Attorney General; **b)** (S. 3) certain post offices to be designated as savings depository offices, and to receive savings deposits by the public; **c)** (S. 4) postal savings account may be opened by anyone ten years of age, and by married women separate from her husband; **d)** (S. 5) deposits to be recorded in a passbook or equivalent; **e)** (S. 7) 2% annual interest to be paid on deposits; **f)** (S. 7) maximum balance is $500; **g)** (S. 9) postal savings to be deposited in local solvent banks, and the banks to pay 2.25% interest on balances, and the Board to obtain bonds from the bank as security; **h)** (S. 9) the Board shall reserve 5% as security against deposits; **i)** (S. 10) withdrawals from postal savings account to be paid in U. S. bonds bearing 2.5% interest, principal and interest payable in gold, redeemable after one year and payable after 20 years; and **j)** (S. 16) faith of the United States is pledged for repayment of postal savings accounts.

2 Mar 1911: Congress amended [16.2-82] the laws (cf. 14 Mar 1900, section 6 and 4 Mar 1907) regarding gold certificates: a) Treasury Secretary authorized to receive gold coin and issue gold certificates in denominations greater than $10; b) coin for which certificates are issued to be retained in the Treasury and used only for payment of certificates; c) gold certificates are receivable for all customs, taxes, and dues, and may be re-issued; d) if received by a national bank association, may be used to count against reserves; e) issue of gold certificates to be suspended if the gold coin and bullion held

in the Treasury for redemption falls below $100,00,00; f) Treasury Secretary may suspend issue of gold certificates if the aggregate of U. S. notes and silver bullion is above $60,000,000; g) permitted foreign gold coin to be received, and gold certificates to issued; h) permitted gold certificates to be issued against bullion bearing the stamp of U. S. Mints; and i) but the total amount of foreign gold and stamped bullion shall not exceed one-third of the gold certificates outstanding.

2 Mar 1911: Congress prohibited [16.2-83] Panama Canal bonds to be used as security against circulating National Bank Notes.

22 Aug 1911: Congress directed [16.2-84] the National Monetary Commission (cf. 30 May 1908, S. 17 - 19) to issue its report on or before 8 Jan 1912.

31 Dec 1911: By this time about 90% of business transactions were done with checks, according to an estimate by economist Irving Fisher [16.2-85].

15 Jan 1912: Approximate end of the recession (cf. 15 Jan 1910) [16.2-86].

15 Jan 1913: Approximate beginning of a recession [16.2-87].

3 Feb 1913: The 16th Amendment to the Constitution was ratified, permitting an income tax:

"The Congress shall have power to lay and collect taxes on incomes, from whatever source derived, without apportionment among the several States, and without regard to any census or enumeration."

4 Mar 1913: Congress passed legislation [16.2-88] splitting the Department of Commerce and Labor into two: the Department of Labor and the Department of Commerce. The stated purpose of the Department of Labor:

"shall be to foster, promote, and develop the welfare of the wage earners of the United States, to improve their working conditions, and to advance their opportunities for profitable employment. The Department of Labor is to have a Bureau of Labor Statistics, which 'shall collect, collate, and report at least once each year, or oftener if necessary, full and complete statistics of the conditions of labor and the products and distribution of the products of the same.' "

3 Oct 1913: Congress passed a revision to the tariff law [16.2-89], generally reducing import duties from about 40% to about 25%, and establishing an income tax (now legitimate after ratification of the 16th Amendment to the Constitution). Among its tariff provisions: **a)** Schedule A (chemicals, oils, and paints), 15% to 25% *ad valorem*; **b)** Schedule B (earthenware), up to 20% *ad valorem*; **c)** Schedule C (metals and manufactures thereof), up to 30% *ad valorem*, but some by weight; **d)** Schedule D (wood and manufactures thereof), up to 25% *ad valorem*, but many items added to the free list; **e)** Schedule E (sugar, molasses, and manufactures thereof), up to 20% *ad valorem*; **f)** Schedule F (tobacco and manufactures thereof), up to 55 cents per pound; **g)** Schedule G (agricultural products), some by weight, others up to 25% *ad valorem*; **h)** Schedule H (spirits and wines), up to $2.60 per gallon or 45% *ad valorem*; **i)** Schedule I (cotton manufactures), some by weight or size, or up to 30% *ad valorem*; **j)** Schedule J (hemp, flax, etc.), some by weight, others up to 30% *ad valorem*; **k)** Schedule K (wool and manufactures thereof), up to 30% *ad valorem*, except carpets at 50%; **l)** Schedule L (silk, etc.), up to 60% *ad valorem*; **m)** Schedule M (paper), up to 30% *ad valorem*; **n)** Schedule N (sundries), up to 60% *ad valorem*; and **o)** 271 items on the free list in addition to some from Schedule E.

The income tax applied to both personal and business income. The personal income tax permitted a deduction of $4,000 for a married couple ($3,000 if single), and deductions for all business expenses for business returns. There was imposed a "normal" tax of 1% on net income, plus progressive "additional taxes" on the net income lying between certain limits: a) 1%, if between $20,000 and $50,000; b) 2%, if between $50,000 and $75,000; c) 3%, if between $75,000 and $100,000; d) 4%, if between $100,000 and $250,000; e) 5%, if between $250,00 and $500,000; and f) 6%, if above $500,000. (For a married couple with net income of $55,000, the tax was 1% of $55,000, plus 2% of $30,000, plus 3% of $5,000, which comes to $550 + $600 + $150 = $1,300, or 2.3% on gross income). The income tax laws have been frequently revised since 1913, but the changes are beyond the scope of this book.

23 Dec 1913: Congress passed the Federal Reserve Act [16.2-90], replacing the National Bank system. The details of the system's structure and operation will be described in chapter 17. As a short summary, the main provisions are: **a)** (S. 2) directs the Secretary of Agriculture, Treasury Secretary, and Comptroller of the Currency to establish between eight and twelve Federal reserve cities [twelve were designated]; **b)** (S. 2) all national banks are required to join the Federal Reserve system by subscribing 6% of their capital to stock in the district Federal Reserve Bank; **c)** (S. 1) national banks that refuse to join to lose their charter; **d)** (S. 1) member banks holding stock in the Reserve Bank do not get voting powers in the Bank; **e)** (S. 1) minimum capital requirements for each Reserve Bank is $4,000,000; **f)** (S. 3) Reserve Banks may set up branch offices; **g)** (S. 4) Federal Reserve Banks to have normal corporate powers; **h)** (S. 4) upon deposit of bonds with the Treasury, Federal Reserve Banks may receive circulating currency notes equal to the value of the bonds, except the issue of notes is not limited to the capital stock of the Bank; **i)** (S. 4) Federal Reserve Banks to be led by three classes of directors (A, B, C); **j)** (S. 5) member banks to subscribe to additional stock if they increase their capital (6%); **k)** (S. 6) insolvent member banks to have their stock canceled and the proceeds used to pay any liabilities; **l)** (S. 7) member banks to receive 6% annual interest on the stock in the Federal Reserve Bank after expenses, and remaining earnings of the Federal Reserve Bank to be paid to the U. S. as a franchise tax; **m)** (S. 7) Federal Reserve Banks are exempt from federal, State, and local taxes, except for real estate; **n)** (S. 8, 9) State-chartered banks may become members of the Federal Reserve system unless prohibited by State laws, although upon a majority vote, State-chartered banks may first convert to national banks and then join the Federal Reserve; **o)** (S. 9) State banks may join the Federal Reserve system under the same conditions as national banks; **p)** (S. 10) created a Federal Reserve Board to consist of seven members (Secretary of the Treasury, Comptroller of the Currency, and five appointed by the President); **q)** (S. 1) one of the Presidential appointees shall be Governor of the Board; **r)** (S. 1) the Federal Reserve Board shall provide an annual report to Congress; **s)** (S. 11) the powers of the Federal Reserve Board are: 1) examine each Federal Reserve Bank and member banks, 2) upon a vote of five, permit a Federal Reserve Bank to rediscount the discounted paper of other Federal Reserve Banks, 3) to suspend for a period not exceeding 30 days any reserve requirements, 4) to impose a graduated tax upon a Reserve Bank if the gold reserve against Federal Reserve Notes falls below 40%, 5) regulate the handling of Federal Reserve Notes by the Comptroller's office, 6) add Federal Reserve cities, 7) to remove officers of Federal Reserve Banks for cause, 8) to write off worthless assets held by Federal Reserve Banks, and 9) perform general supervision of Federal Reserve Banks; **t)** (S. 12) created a Federal Advisory Council to meet quarterly with the Board to discuss business matters and provide advice; **u)** (S. 13) Federal Reserve Banks may receive deposits from member banks in the form of lawful money, national bank notes, Federal Reserve Notes, checks or drafts of solvent member banks payable upon presentation; **v)** (S. 13) Federal Reserve Banks may discount notes, drafts, and bills of exchange arising out of normal commercial transactions of any member bank upon endorsement by the member bank, with maximum maturity of 90 days; **w)** (S. 13) Federal Reserve Banks may discount acceptances of member banks that are based on exports, with a maximum maturity of 90 days; the amount of acceptances is limited to half the member bank's paid-up capital; **x)** (S. 13) rediscounts not to exceed 10% of member bank's paid-up capital; **y)** (S. 13) debts of national banks are limited to its capital stock, with some exceptions; **z)** (S. 14) Federal Reserve Banks have powers of open-market operations to 1) buy and sell in the open market, from domestic or foreign entities, acceptances and bills of exchange; 2) deal in gold coin or bullion; 3) buy and sell at home and abroad any bonds and notes of the United States; 4) buy and sell notes, bonds, and warrants issued by States, counties, and districts with maturities not exceeding 6 months; 5) to establish, with concurrence of the Board, discount rates for member bank paper; and 6) establish accounts with other Federal Reserve Banks and foreign banks; **aa)** (S. 15) Treasury Secretary may deposit funds in Federal Reserve Banks and the Bank

to be a fiscal agent of the U. S. Government, but the Secretary may also make deposits in member banks; **ab)** (S. 16) Federal Reserve Notes to be issued by the Board to Federal Reserve Banks, are obligations of the United States, shall be receivable by all national and member banks, and are receivable for taxes, customs, and other public dues, and shall be redeemed on demand in gold or lawful money at any Federal Reserve Bank; **ac)** (S. 16) 100% collateral required for Federal Reserve Notes, to be in the form of notes and bills rediscounted under S. 13; **ad)** (S. 16) Federal Reserve Banks shall maintain reserves in gold or lawful money 35% against its deposits (i.e., deposits of member banks); **ae)** (S. 16) Federal Reserve Banks to maintain 40% reserves in gold against Federal Reserve Notes in circulation, and to maintain at least 5% in gold on deposit at the U. S. Treasury for Federal Reserve Note redemption, counted as part of the 40%; **af)** (S. 16) Federal Reserve Banks may reduce their Note liabilities by returning Notes and by depositing notes, gold, or gold certificates with the Federal Reserve agent; **ag)** (S. 16) Federal Reserve Banks to participate in a check clearinghouse function; **ah)** (S. 17) member banks may, during the next 20 years, retire any amount of its circulating notes by arranging with the Treasury Secretary to sell the bonds securing them; **ai)** (S. 18) Treasury Secretary may issue to Federal Reserve Banks one-year gold notes in exchange for 2% gold bonds, subject to approval by the Board; **aj)** (S. 18) Treasury Secretary authorized to issue Treasury Notes bearing 3% interest to facilitate the gold note exchanges; **ak)** (S. 19) "demand deposits" defined to mean deposits payable within 30 days; time deposits defined to mean deposit payable after 30 days (including savings); **al)** (S. 19) member banks shall maintain reserves at the Federal Reserve Bank (via deposits there): 1) for banks not in reserve or reserve cities, 12% against demand and 5% against time deposits; 2) in reserve cities, 15% against demand and 5% against time deposits; 3) central reserve cities, 18% against demand and 5% against time deposits; **am)** (S. 19) national bank redemption funds not to be counted as reserves; **an)** (S. 21) regulations regarding bank examinations; **ao)** (S. 22) restrictions on bank officials and penalties for violations; **ap)** (S. 23) national bank stockholders individually liable for debts and obligations up to the amount of stock; **aq)** (S. 24) national banks not in reserve cities may make loans on farm land with term limited to 5 years and only up to 25% of its capital; **ar)** (S. 25) national banks may open foreign branches under certain conditions; **as)** (S. 26) previous laws contrary to this Act are repealed; **at)** (S. 27) National Currency Associations extended to 30 Jun 1915, and the tax rates on circulation not secured by U. S. bonds modified (3% annual for first 3 months, and additional 0.5% for each month afterward); **au)** (S. 28) capital of national banks may be reduced, but not below its note circulation; and **av)** (S. 29) severability clause regarding each provision.

31 Jul 1914: The NY stock market was closed due a stock sell-off by Europeans owing to the start of World War I [16.2-91]. It became necessary for the banks to invoke the powers granted under the Aldrich-Vreeland Act (cf. 30 May 1908): it issued $400,000,000 in substitute emergency currency in the form of clearinghouse loan certificates, which probably prevented a panic.

4 Aug 1914: Congress passed a law [16.2-92] amending Section 27 to the Federal Reserve Act (cf. 23 Dec 1913): a) National Currency Associations (national banks) authorized per 30 May 1908 to continue until 30 Jun 1915; b) the National Monetary Commission extended to 30 Jun 1915; c) circulating notes issued by a National Banking Association secured by other than U. S. bonds to be taxed between 3 and 6% annually; d) the Treasury Secretary is authorized to remove limitations on issues of notes by national banks, but are still required to maintain in the Treasury gold equaling 5% on deposits; and e) Treasury Secretary is authorized to extend the same benefits to State-chartered banks and trust companies that have joined the Federal Reserve system.

15 Aug 1914: Congress passed a law amending Section 19 of the Federal Reserve Act (cf. 23 Dec 1913) [16.2-93] providing a sliding scale in the location of legal reserves. For member banks in reserve cities: legal reserves 15% on demand deposits and 5% on time deposits; after 3 years, one-third of reserves to be held in the bank vault, with the other two-thirds either in their vaults or on deposit at the Federal Reserve bank in its district. For member banks in a central reserve city, legal reserves are

18% of its demand deposits and 5% of time deposits; 33.3% in its vault, 38.9% on deposits at the Federal Reserve Bank, and the remaining 27.8% either in its vault or at the Federal Reserve bank.

26 Sep 1914: Congress established the Federal Trade Commission [16.2-94] to ensure fair competition. Section 5 states:

> "That unfair methods of competition in commerce are hereby declared unlawful. The commission is hereby empowered and directed to prevent persons, partnerships, or corporations, except banks, and common carriers subject to the Acts to regulate commerce, from using unfair methods of competition in commerce."

Notice that "unfair methods" are not defined, being left to the discretion of the Federal Trade Commission, and that banks are exempt. The commission was granted power to serve notice and order a hearing on any suspected unfair practices, and to issue cease-and-desist orders as follows:

> "Whenever the commission shall have reason to believe that any such person, partnership, or corporation has been or is using any unfair method of competition in commerce, and if it shall appear to the commission that a proceeding by it in respect thereof would be to the interest of the public, it shall issue and serve upon such person, partnership, or corporation a complaint stating its charges in that respect, and containing a notice of a hearing upon a day and at a place therein fixed at least thirty days after the service of said complaint."

16 Nov 1914: The Federal Reserve system began operations [16.2-95]. The Federal Reserve Act had revised the entire banking system. First it divided the nation into twelve "reserve regions", each with a Federal Reserve Bank and branches (Reserve Cities). Second, it specified the reserve ratios for Federal Reserve Banks, Reserve City Banks, and "country banks", which meant all commercial banks that were members of the Federal Reserve System not included in the first two classifications. The two Central Reserve banks (at New York and Chicago) were required to maintain 13% reserves against demand deposits and 3% against time deposits. The Reserve City Banks (all the other Federal Reserve Banks and their branches, 24 in total), were required to maintain 10% reserves against demand deposits and 3% against time deposits. The "country banks" were required to maintain 7% reserves against demand deposits and 3% against time deposits. Third, all the reserves of member banks were to be held in one of the 12 Federal Reserve Banks. (The structure of the Federal Reserve will be described in chapter 17). The Federal Reserve Banks were required to pay a "franchise tax" to the Treasury amounting to 90% of net earnings after its surplus had accumulated to be equal to its paid-in capital [16.2-96].

12 Dec 1914: The NY stock exchange re-opened to restricted trading [16.2-97].

15 Dec 1914: Approximate end of the recession (cf. 15 Jan 1913) [16.2-98].

16.3 Data, 1879-1914

Figures 16.2-1 and 16.3-2 show the U. S. government revenue and expenditures for 1879 to 1914.

				Internal Revenue		Miscellaneous					Excess of Deposits to Retire National Bank Notes Over	
Day	Year	Panama Canal proceeds of bonds	Customs	Income and Profits taxes	Misc.	Sales of Public Lands	Direct Tax	Other Misc.	Postal	Public Debt Sales	Redemption	Total
30 Jun	1879	0	137,250,047	0	113,561,610	924,781	0	20,593,801	30,041,982	619,074,953	0	921,447,177
30 Jun	1880	0	186,522,064	0	124,009,373	1,016,506	30	21,978,525	33,315,479	73,065,650	0	439,907,630
30 Jun	1881	0	198,159,676	3,022	135,261,364	2,201,863	1,516	25,154,850	36,785,397	678,200	0	398,245,890
30 Jun	1882	0	220,410,730	0	146,497,595	4,753,140	160,141	31,703,642	41,876,410	225,300	0	445,626,960
30 Jun	1883	0	214,706,496	0	144,720,368	7,955,864	108,156	30,796,695	45,508,692	304,372,850	0	748,169,124
30 Jun	1884	0	195,067,489	55,628	121,530,445	9,810,705	70,720	21,984,881	43,325,958	1,404,650	0	393,250,478
30 Jun	1885	0	181,471,939	0	112,498,725	5,705,986	0	24,014,055	42,560,843	58,150	0	366,309,700
30 Jun	1886	0	192,905,023	0	116,805,936	5,630,999	108,239	20,989,527	43,948,422	39,850	0	380,428,000
30 Jun	1887	0	217,286,893	0	118,823,391	9,254,286	32,892	26,005,814	48,837,609	40,900	0	420,281,787
30 Jun	1888	0	219,091,173	0	124,296,871	11,202,017	1,565	24,674,446	52,695,176	48,650	0	432,009,901
30 Jun	1889	0	223,832,741	0	130,881,513	8,038,651	0	24,297,151	56,175,611	24,350	0	443,250,020
30 Jun	1890	0	229,668,584	0	142,606,705	6,358,272	0	24,447,419	60,882,097	21,650	0	463,984,730
30 Jun	1891	0	219,522,205	0	145,686,249	4,029,535	0	23,374,457	65,931,785	13,750	40,018,392	498,576,375
30 Jun	1892	0	177,452,964	0	153,971,072	3,261,875	0	20,251,871	70,930,475	15,250	0	425,883,510
30 Jun	1893	0	203,355,016	0	161,027,623	3,182,089	0	18,254,898	75,896,993	22,900	0	461,739,521
30 Jun	1894	0	131,818,530	0	147,111,232	1,673,637	0	17,118,618	75,080,479	58,647,545	5,708,247	437,158,291
30 Jun	1895	0	152,158,617	77,131	143,344,541	1,103,347	0	16,706,438	76,983,128	92,504,394	0	482,877,597
30 Jun	1896	0	160,021,751	0	146,762,864	1,005,523	0	19,186,060	82,499,208	142,335,046	0	551,810,455
30 Jun	1897	0	176,554,126	0	146,688,574	864,581	0	23,614,422	82,665,462	3,250	4,356,614	434,747,032
30 Jun	1898	0	149,575,062	0	170,900,641	1,243,129	0	83,602,501	89,012,618	5,950	6,034,510	500,374,413
30 Jun	1899	0	206,128,481	0	273,437,161	1,678,246	0	34,716,730	95,021,384	199,201,210	5,324,234	815,507,448
30 Jun	1900	0	233,164,871	0	295,327,926	2,836,882	0	35,911,170	102,354,579	117,770	0	669,713,201
30 Jun	1901	0	238,585,455	0	307,180,663	2,965,119	0	38,954,098	111,631,193	3,700	0	699,320,230
30 Jun	1902	0	254,444,708	0	271,880,122	4,144,122	0	32,009,280	121,848,047	2,370	12,650,160	696,978,810
30 Jun	1903	0	284,479,581	0	230,810,124	8,926,311	0	36,180,657	134,224,443	1,486,098	0	696,107,215
30 Jun	1904	0	261,274,564	0	232,904,119	7,453,479	0	38,084,749	143,582,624	457,936	0	683,757,474
30 Jun	1905	0	261,798,856	0	234,095,740	4,859,249	0	43,852,911	152,826,585	2,750	0	697,436,093
30 Jun	1906	0	300,251,877	0	249,150,212	4,879,833	0	40,436,017	167,932,782	532,374	10,408,537	773,591,636
30 Jun	1907	31,210,817	332,233,362	0	269,666,772	7,878,811	0	53,346,713	183,585,005	1,514,334	5,023,165	884,458,982
30 Jun	1908	25,367,768	286,113,130	0	251,711,126	9,731,560	0	53,504,906	191,478,663	15,436,500	24,797,980	858,141,635
30 Jun	1909	30,731,008	300,711,933	0	246,212,643	7,700,567	0	48,964,344	203,562,383	0	0	837,882,881
30 Jun	1910	0	333,683,445	20,951,781	268,981,738	6,355,797	0	45,538,953	224,128,657	0	0	899,640,372
30 Jun	1911	18,102,170	314,497,071	33,516,977	289,012,224	5,731,636	0	58,614,466	237,879,823	0	5,255,715	962,610,083
30 Jun	1912	33,189,104	311,321,672	28,583,304	293,028,896	5,392,796	0	53,451,796	246,744,015	459,280	0	972,170,865
30 Jun	1913	0	318,891,395	35,006,300	309,410,666	2,910,204	0	57,892,663	266,619,525	1,929,840	0	992,660,595
30 Jun	1914	0	292,320,014	71,381,275	308,659,733	2,571,774	0	59,740,370	287,934,565	3,118,940	0	1,025,726,672

1. The data for the revenue for 1879 to 1914 is from W. G. McAdoo, "Annual Report of the Secretary of the Treasury on the State of the Finances for the Fiscal Year Ended June 30, 1914", Washington: U. S. Government Printing Office, 1915, pp. 230-241; Treasury Document 2721. This data was modified from 1879 to 1914 per Henry Morgenthau, "Annual Report of the Secretary of the Treasury on the State of the Finances for the Fiscal Year Ended June 30, 1940", Treasury Document 3111, pp. 642-649, which shows "internal reveune" broken out as income taxes and miscellaneous. It is the same data as reported previously (cf. 1914), but shows income taxes and miscellaneous taxes as separate categories.

Figure 16.3-1: U. S. Government Revenue, 1879-1914

			Ordinary Disbursements								Excess of	
Day	Year	Panama Canal Disburse-ments	Civil & Misc.	War Dep't	Navy Dep't	Indians	Pensions	Interest on Public Debt	Postal	Public Debt Retired	National Bank Notes Retired Over Deposits	Total
30 Jun	1879	0	60,968,031	40,425,660	15,125,126	5,206,109	35,121,482	105,327,949	34,815,507	479,882,226	0	776,872,092
30 Jun	1880	0	51,642,529	38,116,916	13,536,984	5,945,457	56,777,174	95,757,575	36,386,479	283,230,257	0	581,393,374
30 Jun	1881	0	60,520,686	40,466,460	15,686,671	6,514,161	50,059,279	82,508,741	40,681,036	87,171,829	0	383,608,866
30 Jun	1882	0	57,219,750	43,570,494	15,032,046	9,736,747	61,345,193	71,077,206	41,876,410	166,505,255	0	466,363,105
30 Jun	1883	0	68,603,519	48,911,382	15,283,437	7,362,590	66,012,573	59,160,131	45,583,195	438,430,756	0	749,347,587
30 Jun	1884	0	70,920,433	39,429,603	17,292,601	6,475,999	55,429,228	54,578,378	43,325,958	101,266,334	0	388,718,537
30 Jun	1885	0	82,952,647	42,670,578	16,021,079	6,552,494	56,102,267	51,386,256	47,102,454	46,042,635	0	348,830,414
30 Jun	1886	0	65,973,277	34,324,152	13,907,887	6,099,158	63,404,864	50,580,145	52,142,074	44,583,843	0	331,015,404
30 Jun	1887	0	78,763,578	38,561,025	15,141,126	6,194,522	75,029,101	47,741,577	55,338,856	127,959,368	0	444,729,157
30 Jun	1888	0	69,896,223	38,522,436	16,926,437	6,249,307	80,288,508	44,715,007	55,751,213	83,133,055	0	395,482,190
30 Jun	1889	0	76,795,144	44,435,270	21,378,809	6,892,207	87,624,779	41,001,484	60,044,530	138,581,151	0	476,753,377
30 Jun	1890	0	74,528,219	44,582,838	22,006,206	6,708,046	106,936,855	36,099,284	67,757,134	124,968,023	0	483,586,608
30 Jun	1891	0	105,306,395	48,720,065	26,113,896	8,527,469	124,415,951	37,547,135	70,673,557	111,404,276	0	532,708,747
30 Jun	1892	0	95,790,498	46,895,456	29,174,138	11,150,577	134,583,052	23,378,116	74,981,965	24,348,086	13,254,883	453,556,776
30 Jun	1893	0	97,786,004	49,641,773	30,136,084	13,345,347	159,357,557	27,264,392	81,843,788	709,903	6,100,071	466,184,922
30 Jun	1894	0	93,693,884	54,567,929	31,701,293	10,293,481	141,177,284	27,841,405	83,330,479	256,447	0	442,862,206
30 Jun	1895	0	82,263,188	51,804,759	28,797,795	9,939,754	141,395,228	30,978,030	87,999,669	2,494,549	1,012,196	436,685,172
30 Jun	1896	0	77,916,234	50,830,920	27,147,732	12,165,528	139,434,000	35,385,028	91,799,208	7,294,103	5,257,466	447,230,224
30 Jun	1897	0	79,252,061	48,950,267	34,561,546	13,016,802	141,053,164	37,791,110	93,814,668	11,378,502	0	459,818,124
30 Jun	1898	0	86,016,464	91,992,000	58,823,984	10,994,667	147,452,368	37,585,056	99,516,658	29,942,062	0	562,323,263
30 Jun	1899	0	110,979,685	229,841,254	63,942,104	12,805,711	139,394,929	39,896,925	103,232,954	14,622,363	0	714,715,927
30 Jun	1900	0	98,542,411	134,774,767	55,953,077	10,175,106	140,877,316	40,160,333	109,585,358	55,937,113	669,503	646,674,987
30 Jun	1901	0	117,327,240	144,615,697	60,506,978	10,896,073	139,323,621	32,342,979	116,585,955	50,762,371	5,743,569	678,104,487
30 Jun	1902	0	111,067,171	112,272,216	67,803,128	10,049,584	138,488,559	29,108,044	124,250,199	70,267,309	0	663,306,214
30 Jun	1903	9,985	122,165,385	118,619,520	82,618,034	12,935,168	138,425,646	28,556,348	136,993,362	27,515,952	2,001,161	669,840,564
30 Jun	1904	50,164,500	130,099,672	115,035,410	102,956,101	10,438,350	142,559,266	24,646,489	150,085,155	19,880,308	4,526,766	750,392,020
30 Jun	1905	3,918,819	127,968,471	122,175,074	117,550,308	14,236,073	141,773,964	24,590,944	167,891,842	605,230	3,299,440	724,010,169
30 Jun	1906	19,379,373	130,221,177	117,946,692	110,474,264	12,746,859	141,034,561	24,308,576	180,606,077	1,662,191	0	738,379,773
30 Jun	1907	27,198,618	145,416,530	122,576,465	97,128,469	15,163,608	139,309,514	24,481,158	191,214,388	30,598,138	0	793,086,892
30 Jun	1908	38,093,929	162,532,367	137,746,523	118,037,097	14,579,755	153,892,467	21,426,138	204,366,704	34,356,750	0	885,031,733
30 Jun	1909	31,419,442	167,001,087	161,067,462	115,546,011	15,694,618	161,710,367	21,803,836	223,063,445	15,434,687	43,937,843	956,678,800
30 Jun	1910	33,911,673	171,580,829	155,911,705	123,173,716	18,504,131	160,696,415	21,342,978	232,624,269	760,925	614,478	919,121,125
30 Jun	1911	37,063,515	173,838,599	160,135,975	119,937,644	20,933,869	157,980,575	21,311,334	237,660,705	246,496	0	929,108,715
30 Jun	1912	35,327,370	172,256,794	148,795,421	135,591,955	20,134,839	153,590,456	22,616,300	248,312,210	120,616	8,449,346	945,195,312
30 Jun	1913	41,741,258	169,802,304	160,387,452	133,262,861	20,306,158	175,085,450	22,899,108	263,136,243	102,575	2,618,025	989,341,438
30 Jun	1914	34,826,941	170,530,235	173,522,804	139,682,186	20,215,075	173,440,231	22,863,956	283,558,102	109,127	6,949,917	1,025,698,578

The data for the expenditures for 1863 to 1878 is from W. G. McAdoo, "Annual Report of the Secretary of the Treasury on the State of the Finances for the Fiscal Year Ended June 30, 1914", Washington: U. S. Government Printing Office, 1915, pp. 230-241; Treasury Document 2721.

Figure 16.3-2: U. S. Government Expenditures, 1879-1914

Figure 16.3-3 shows the national debt and per-capita debt for this period. Refer to the Introduction to Part 2 for a sense of wages vs. per-capita national debt.

Day	Year	Principal ($) [1]	Population [2]	Debt per Capita ($) [2]	Day	Year	Principal ($) [1]	Population [2]	Debt per Capita ($) [2]
30 Jun	1879	2,298,912,643	48,290,043	47.61	30 Jun	1897	1,226,793,713	72,242,447	16.98
30 Jun	1880	2,090,908,872	49,371,340	42.35	30 Jun	1898	1,232,743,063	73,565,688	16.76
30 Jun	1881	2,019,285,728	50,732,183	39.80	30 Jun	1899	1,436,700,704	74,888,928	19.18
30 Jun	1882	1,856,915,644	52,093,025	35.65	30 Jun	1900	1,263,416,913	76,212,168	16.58
30 Jun	1883	1,721,958,918	53,453,868	32.21	30 Jun	1901	1,221,572,245	77,813,804	15.70
30 Jun	1884	1,625,307,444	54,814,710	29.65	30 Jun	1902	1,178,031,357	79,415,441	14.83
30 Jun	1885	1,578,551,169	56,175,553	28.10	30 Jun	1903	1,159,405,913	81,017,077	14.31
30 Jun	1886	1,555,659,550	57,536,396	27.04	30 Jun	1904	1,136,259,016	82,618,713	13.75
30 Jun	1887	1,465,485,294	58,897,238	24.88	30 Jun	1905	1,132,357,095	84,220,350	13.45
30 Jun	1888	1,384,631,656	60,258,081	22.98	30 Jun	1906	1,142,522,970	85,821,986	13.31
30 Jun	1889	1,249,470,511	61,618,923	20.28	30 Jun	1907	1,147,178,193	87,423,622	13.12
30 Jun	1890	1,122,396,584	62,979,766	17.82	30 Jun	1908	1,177,690,403	89,025,258	13.23
30 Jun	1891	1,005,806,561	64,303,006	15.64	30 Jun	1909	1,148,315,372	90,626,895	12.67
30 Jun	1892	968,218,841	65,626,246	14.75	30 Jun	1910	1,146,939,969	92,228,531	12.44
30 Jun	1893	961,431,766	66,949,487	14.36	30 Jun	1911	1,153,984,937	93,607,835	12.33
30 Jun	1894	1,016,897,817	68,272,727	14.89	30 Jun	1912	1,193,838,505	94,987,138	12.57
30 Jun	1895	1,096,913,120	69,595,967	15.76	30 Jun	1913	1,193,047,745	96,366,442	12.38
30 Jun	1896	1,222,729,350	70,919,207	17.24	30 Jun	1914	1,188,235,400	97,745,746	12.16

1. Public debt data from 1879 to 1914 is from the Annual Report of the Secretary of the Treasury, 1980, pp. 61, 62.
2. Population values are based on the dicennial census from the Census Bureau, and linearly interpolated. Per-capita is based on these values.

Figure 16.3-3: National Debt and Per-Capita Share Thereof, 1879-1914

Figures 16.3-4 and 16.3-5 show the assets and liabilities of all reporting State and private banks, including savings, savings and loan, and trust companies for this period.

			Loans & Discounts, incl.	U. S. Gov't and Other		Due from	Other	
Day	Year	Number of Banks	Overdrafts	Securities	Cash	Banks	Assets	Total Assets
~30 Jun	1879	1,287	671.479	423.906	55.787	51.061	90.563	1,292.796
~30 Jun	1880	1,279	667.543	452.699	75.479	62.403	105.328	1,363.452
~30 Jun	1881	1,312	757.048	500.995	59.075	95.266	130.907	1,543.291
~30 Jun	1882	1,333	841.520	583.771	60.158	96.951	104.402	1,686.802
~30 Jun	1883	1,418	947.947	563.062	59.513	111.455	161.294	1,843.271
~30 Jun	1884	1,488	990.841	592.409	72.668	117.713	165.059	1,938.690
~30 Jun	1885	1,661	1,014.580	609.786	84.231	128.646	167.735	2,004.978
~30 Jun	1886	1,529	1,035.232	644.154	70.352	109.597	208.516	2,067.851
~30 Jun	1887	3,156	1,382.937	682.129	161.337	160.906	168.738	2,556.047
~30 Jun	1888	3,527	1,533.091	774.776	161.496	156.574	113.073	2,739.010
~30 Jun	1889	4,005	1,698.541	806.225	201.264	185.883	115.018	3,006.931
~30 Jun	1890	4,717	1,920.024	862.505	185.861	207.185	120.280	3,295.855
~30 Jun	1891	4,989	2,067.319	869.994	165.634	212.521	133.317	3,448.785
~30 Jun	1892	5,577	2,209.132	936.327	197.789	261.279	147.122	3,751.649
~30 Jun	1893	5,685	2,348.193	1,009.605	205.645	250.701	164.865	3,979.009
~30 Jun	1894	5,738	2,140.628	1,010.248	229.373	309.015	179.211	3,868.475
~30 Jun	1895	6,103	2,252.283	1,118.159	227.743	320.721	220.085	4,138.991
~30 Jun	1896	5,780	2,279.515	1,210.827	169.199	295.862	244.722	4,200.125
~30 Jun	1897	5,847	2,238.424	1,248.150	193.094	335.794	243.215	4,258.677
~30 Jun	1898	5,918	2,488.597	1,304.890	194.914	400.566	242.361	4,631.328
~30 Jun	1899	6,149	2,669.639	1,527.595	210.884	515.892	272.167	5,196.177
~30 Jun	1900	6,650	3,013.450	1,723.830	220.667	582.032	301.680	5,841.659
~30 Jun	1901	7,241	3,444.378	1,935.626	240.146	659.799	401.618	6,681.567
~30 Jun	1902	7,889	3,942.593	2,094.496	250.816	742.494	324.712	7,355.111
~30 Jun	1903	8,745	4,296.676	2,334.330	275.814	768.653	340.709	8,016.182
~30 Jun	1904	9,519	4,360.209	2,522.891	301.578	963.048	395.113	8,542.839
~30 Jun	1905	10,742	5,097.761	2,748.448	314.248	974.930	455.014	9,590.401
~30 Jun	1906	11,852	5,656.832	2,790.160	334.938	983.619	597.802	10,363.351
~30 Jun	1907	13,317	6,099.898	2,931.506	391.848	1,005.211	740.052	11,168.515
~30 Jun	1908	14,522	5,797.612	2,873.227	479.116	1,131.786	587.605	10,869.346
~30 Jun	1909	15,598	6,385.523	3,009.481	525.238	1,405.890	400.039	11,726.171
~30 Jun	1910	15,950	7,065.907	3,111.410	558.356	1,219.434	598.589	12,553.696
~30 Jun	1911	17,115	7,412.154	3,289.468	556.086	1,489.242	501.085	13,248.035
~30 Jun	1912	17,823	7,979.853	3,497.602	576.811	1,532.726	537.887	14,124.879
~30 Jun	1913	18,520	8,464.738	3,517.531	591.608	1,407.994	693.373	14,675.244
~30 Jun	1914	19,240	8,893.923	3,670.036	616.656	1,481.522	827.070	15,489.207

Assets of Reporting State & Private Banks, 1879 - 1914 (millions USD)

Condition of State and private banks (including savings and savings & loan and trust companies) on 30 Jun call dates from from Annual Report of the Comptroller of the Currency, 1931 (7 Dec 1931), Table 94; pp. 1018, 1019.

Figure 16.3-4: Assets of Reporting State and Private Banks, 30 Jun Call Date, 1879-1914

				Surplus and Net Undivided	Notes in	Total	Bills Payable &	Other	Total
Day	Year	Number of Banks	Capital	Profits	Circulation	Deposits	Rediscounts	Liabilities	Liabilities
~30 Jun	1879	1,287	125.227	86.043	0.389	1,059.082	0.000	22.055	1,292.796
~30 Jun	1880	1,279	109.319	91.751	0.283	1,136.966	0.000	25.133	1,363.452
~30 Jun	1881	1,312	112.111	110.711	0.275	1,284.676	0.000	35.518	1,543.291
~30 Jun	1882	1,333	113.362	126.854	0.286	1,412.461	0.000	33.839	1,686.802
~30 Jun	1883	1,418	125.233	141.175	0.188	1,546.615	0.000	30.060	1,843.271
~30 Jun	1884	1,488	133.959	163.314	0.177	1,615.793	0.000	25.447	1,938.690
~30 Jun	1885	1,661	151.687	163.202	0.098	1,658.559	0.000	31.432	2,004.978
~30 Jun	1886	1,529	141.284	174.680	0.103	1,726.939	0.000	24.845	2,067.851
~30 Jun	1887	3,156	227.526	225.230	0.231	2,068.490	0.000	34.570	2,556.047
~30 Jun	1888	3,527	265.368	240.411	0.169	2,174.881	0.000	58.181	2,739.010
~30 Jun	1889	4,005	288.861	263.513	0.120	2,390.937	0.000	63.500	3,006.931
~30 Jun	1890	4,717	331.289	292.295	0.120	2,597.662	0.000	74.489	3,295.855
~30 Jun	1891	4,989	356.749	304.624	0.111	2,708.609	0.000	78.692	3,448.785
~30 Jun	1892	5,577	386.395	323.715	0.137	2,970.209	0.000	71.193	3,751.649
~30 Jun	1893	5,685	406.007	346.206	0.010	3,126.187	0.000	100.599	3,979.009
~30 Jun	1894	5,738	398.735	352.425	0.005	3,039.359	0.000	77.951	3,868.475
~30 Jun	1895	6,103	422.053	370.397	0.000	3,259.742	0.000	86.799	4,138.991
~30 Jun	1896	5,780	400.831	362.603	0.000	3,345.229	0.000	91.462	4,200.125
~30 Jun	1897	5,847	380.091	382.437	0.000	3,401.520	0.000	94.629	4,258.677
~30 Jun	1898	5,918	370.074	399.766	0.000	3,755.417	0.000	106.071	4,631.328
~30 Jun	1899	6,149	368.747	418.798	0.000	4,361.691	0.000	46.941	5,196.177
~30 Jun	1900	6,650	403.193	490.655	0.000	4,891.488	0.000	56.323	5,841.659
~30 Jun	1901	7,241	430.402	538.866	0.000	5,645.841	0.000	66.458	6,681.567
~30 Jun	1902	7,889	499.621	614.510	0.000	6,157.534	0.000	83.446	7,355.111
~30 Jun	1903	8,745	578.419	731.314	0.000	6,617.260	0.000	89.189	8,016.182
~30 Jun	1904	9,519	625.117	779.242	0.000	7,028.901	0.000	109.579	8,542.839
~30 Jun	1905	10,742	671.599	824.243	0.000	7,925.346	0.000	169.213	9,590.401
~30 Jun	1906	11,852	739.163	893.680	0.000	8,514.624	0.000	215.884	10,363.351
~30 Jun	1907	13,317	807.178	924.655	0.000	9,167.830	0.000	268.852	11,168.515
~30 Jun	1908	14,522	838.058	1,012.811	0.000	8,786.342	0.000	232.135	10,869.346
~30 Jun	1909	15,598	866.057	1,039.548	0.000	9,658.994	64.811	96.761	11,726.171
~30 Jun	1910	15,950	890.377	1,094.196	0.000	10,327.137	83.743	158.243	12,553.696
~30 Jun	1911	17,115	932.778	1,152.074	0.000	10,905.735	89.388	168.060	13,248.035
~30 Jun	1912	17,823	977.273	1,215.331	0.000	11,655.095	91.009	186.171	14,124.879
~30 Jun	1913	18,520	1,039.930	1,261.092	0.000	11,994.624	113.112	266.486	14,675.244
~30 Jun	1914	19,240	1,073.882	1,284.995	0.000	12,796.091	141.349	192.890	15,489.207

Liabilities of Reporting State & Private Banks, 1879-1914 (millions USD)

Condition of State and private banks (including savings and savings & loan and trust companies) on 30 Jun call dates from from Annual Report of the Comptroller of the Currency, 1931 (7 Dec 1931), Table 94; pp. 1018, 1019.

Figure 16.3-5: Liabilities of Reporting State and Private Banks, 30 Jun Call Date, 1879-1914

Figures 16.3-6 and 16.3-7 show the assets and liabilities of all national banks on the 30 Jun call date during this period.

Day	Year	Number of Banks	Loans & Discounts, incl. Overdrafts	U. S. Gov't and Other Securities	Cash	Due from Banks	Other Assets	Total Assets
~30 Jun	1879	2,048	835.875	714.717	151.704	246.258	71.331	2,019.885
~30 Jun	1880	2,076	994.713	451.494	198.783	318.746	71.757	2,035.493
~30 Jun	1881	2,115	1,144.989	484.303	218.912	408.307	69.322	2,325.833
~30 Jun	1882	2,239	1,208.933	471.138	208.539	389.448	66.285	2,344.343
~30 Jun	1883	2,417	1,285.592	464.729	226.607	314.166	73.739	2,364.833
~30 Jun	1884	2,625	1,269.863	448.726	230.644	257.327	76.039	2,282.599
~30 Jun	1885	2,689	1,257.656	432.238	305.568	357.508	68.882	2,421.852
~30 Jun	1886	2,809	1,398.552	407.405	276.467	316.701	75.419	2,474.544
~30 Jun	1887	3,014	1,560.372	328.970	270.982	405.836	71.116	2,637.276
~30 Jun	1888	3,120	1,628.125	356.331	297.579	373.623	75.790	2,731.448
~30 Jun	1889	3,239	1,779.055	322.983	313.731	443.449	78.758	2,937.976
~30 Jun	1890	3,484	1,933.509	310.698	302.887	427.454	87.223	3,061.771
~30 Jun	1891	3,652	1,963.705	309.399	332.297	414.185	93.829	3,113.415
~30 Jun	1892	3,759	2,127.757	347.366	388.616	530.309	99.747	3,493.795
~30 Jun	1893	3,807	2,020.484	356.546	310.343	422.994	102.895	3,213.262
~30 Jun	1894	3,770	1,944.441	435.204	459.624	475.307	107.520	3,422.096
~30 Jun	1895	3,715	2,016.640	447.171	403.368	490.195	113.179	3,470.553
~30 Jun	1896	3,689	1,971.642	463.820	362.657	438.627	117.051	3,353.797
~30 Jun	1897	3,610	1,977.554	484.268	435.107	547.093	119.386	3,563.408
~30 Jun	1898	3,582	2,163.682	554.993	492.883	635.988	130.129	3,977.675
~30 Jun	1899	3,583	2,507.955	651.543	512.415	915.812	121.109	4,708.834
~30 Jun	1900	3,732	2,644.237	774.551	529.273	871.069	125.036	4,944.166
~30 Jun	1901	4,165	2,981.053	885.570	567.371	1,114.131	127.785	5,675.910
~30 Jun	1902	4,535	3,246.517	944.930	597.287	1,088.142	131.879	6,008.755
~30 Jun	1903	4,939	3,442.305	1,025.464	581.446	1,051.619	186.101	6,286.935
~30 Jun	1904	5,331	3,621.814	1,096.301	688.997	1,051.999	196.878	6,655.989
~30 Jun	1905	5,668	3,929.537	1,204.576	679.888	1,302.996	210.809	7,327.806
~30 Jun	1906	6,053	4,236.925	1,241.338	681.509	1,390.195	234.261	7,784.228
~30 Jun	1907	6,429	4,664.014	1,362.280	721.895	1,436.026	292.286	8,476.501
~30 Jun	1908	6,824	4,640.380	1,519.647	889.213	1,375.923	288.901	8,714.064
~30 Jun	1909	6,926	5,061.199	1,612.978	932.447	1,572.375	292.734	9,471.733
~30 Jun	1910	7,145	5,455.902	1,576.343	865.453	1,684.412	314.515	9,896.625
~30 Jun	1911	7,227	5,634.236	1,725.529	998.062	1,694.263	330.959	10,383.049
~30 Jun	1912	7,372	5,973.754	1,823.033	996.143	1,719.306	349.528	10,861.764
~30 Jun	1913	7,473	6,162.034	1,846.475	969.102	1,690.840	368.469	11,036.920
~30 Jun	1914	7,525	6,445.555	1,871.401	1,022.564	1,749.057	393.614	11,482.191

Condition of national banks on 30 Jun call dates from Annual Report of the Comptroller of the Currency, 1931 (7 Dec 1931), Table 95; pp. 1021, 1022

Figure 16.3-6: Assets of National Banks, 30 Jun Call Date, 1879-1914

				Liabilities of National Banks, 1879-1914 (millions USD)					
Day	Year	Number of Banks	Capital	Surplus and Net Undivided Profits	Notes in Circulation	Total Deposits	Bills Payable & Rediscounts	Other Liabilities	Total Liabilities
~ 30 Jun	1879	2,048	455.245	160.124	307.329	1,090.110	6.737	0.340	2,019.885
~ 30 Jun	1880	2,076	455.909	168.546	318.088	1,085.140	7.519	0.291	2,035.493
~ 30 Jun	1881	2,115	460.228	181.364	312.223	1,364.386	7.389	0.243	2,325.833
~ 30 Jun	1882	2,239	477.185	183.208	308.922	1,364.960	9.833	0.235	2,344.343
~ 30 Jun	1883	2,417	500.298	206.686	311.963	1,337.362	8.335	0.189	2,364.833
~ 30 Jun	1884	2,625	522.516	216.361	295.175	1,232.761	15.606	0.180	2,282.599
~ 30 Jun	1885	2,689	526.274	198.754	269.148	1,419.594	7.938	0.144	2,421.852
~ 30 Jun	1886	2,809	539.109	221.306	244.893	1,459.240	9.864	0.132	2,474.544
~ 30 Jun	1887	3,014	571.649	234.643	166.626	1,650.149	14.111	0.098	2,637.276
~ 30 Jun	1888	3,120	588.384	253.403	155.313	1,716.215	18.051	0.082	2,731.448
~ 30 Jun	1889	3,239	605.852	269.445	128.867	1,919.579	14.152	0.081	2,937.976
~ 30 Jun	1890	3,484	642.074	292.469	126.324	1,978.771	22.056	0.077	3,061.771
~ 30 Jun	1891	3,652	672.904	314.647	123.916	1,974.086	27.788	0.074	3,113.415
~ 30 Jun	1892	3,759	684.678	326.467	141.062	2,327.251	13.763	0.574	3,493.795
~ 30 Jun	1893	3,807	685.787	343.083	155.071	1,939.235	61.322	28.764	3,213.262
~ 30 Jun	1894	3,770	671.091	330.297	171.715	2,228.310	18.195	2.488	3,422.096
~ 30 Jun	1895	3,715	658.224	329.004	178.816	2,278.892	21.949	3.668	3,470.553
~ 30 Jun	1896	3,689	651.145	331.852	199.214	2,140.953	27.768	2.865	3,353.797
~ 30 Jun	1897	3,610	632.153	330.267	196.591	2,385.668	15.075	3.654	3,563.408
~ 30 Jun	1898	3,582	622.017	332.972	189.866	2,798.748	14.648	19.424	3,977.675
~ 30 Jun	1899	3,583	604.865	342.322	199.358	3,538.612	8.233	15.444	4,708.834
~ 30 Jun	1900	3,732	621.536	391.548	265.303	3,621.542	16.872	27.365	4,944.166
~ 30 Jun	1901	4,165	645.719	416.740	319.009	4,250.281	17.652	26.509	5,675.910
~ 30 Jun	1902	4,535	701.991	482.377	309.337	4,468.058	22.739	24.253	6,008.755
~ 30 Jun	1903	4,939	743.506	542.184	359.261	4,561.884	28.759	51.341	6,286.935
~ 30 Jun	1904	5,331	767.378	581.638	399.584	4,836.024	30.596	40.769	6,655.989
~ 30 Jun	1905	5,668	791.567	615.291	445.456	5,407.455	27.164	40.873	7,327.806
~ 30 Jun	1906	6,053	826.130	665.163	510.861	5,692.805	37.403	51.866	7,784.228
~ 30 Jun	1907	6,429	883.691	720.413	547.919	6,190.385	39.140	94.953	8,476.501
~ 30 Jun	1908	6,824	919.101	748.702	613.664	6,330.521	42.327	59.749	8,714.064
~ 30 Jun	1909	6,926	937.004	807.071	641.312	7,009.225	34.133	42.988	9,471.733
~ 30 Jun	1910	7,145	989.567	861.403	675.633	7,257.038	69.702	43.282	9,896.625
~ 30 Jun	1911	7,227	1,019.633	913.501	681.740	7,675.740	45.999	46.436	10,383.049
~ 30 Jun	1912	7,372	1,033.571	950.827	708.691	8,064.193	58.606	45.876	10,861.764
~ 30 Jun	1913	7,473	1,056.920	988.748	722.125	8,143.929	72.907	52.291	11,036.920
~ 30 Jun	1914	7,525	1,058.192	991.522	722.555	8,563.751	91.212	54.959	11,482.191

Condition of national banks on 30 Jun call dates from Annual Report of the Comptroller of the Currency, 1931 (7 Dec 1931), Table 95; pp. 1021, 1022

Figure 16.3-7: Liabilities of National Banks, 30 Jun Call Date, 1879-1914

Figures 16.3-8 and 16.3-9 show the assets and liabilities of the combined State, private, and national banks on the 30 Jun call date for this period. Keep in mind the State and private data applies only to the ones required by State law to provide reports.

			Combined Assets of National, State, and Private Banks, 1879-1914 (millions USD)					
Day	Year	Number of Banks	Loans & Discounts, incl. Overdrafts	U. S. Gov't and Other Securities	Cash	Due from Banks	Other Assets	Total Assets
~30 Jun	1879	3,335	1,507.354	1,138.623	207.491	297.319	161.894	3,312.681
~30 Jun	1880	3,355	1,662.256	904.193	274.262	381.149	177.085	3,398.945
~30 Jun	1881	3,427	1,902.037	985.298	277.987	503.573	200.229	3,869.124
~30 Jun	1882	3,572	2,050.453	1,054.909	268.697	486.399	170.687	4,031.145
~30 Jun	1883	3,835	2,233.539	1,027.791	286.120	425.621	235.033	4,208.104
~30 Jun	1884	4,113	2,260.704	1,041.135	303.312	375.040	241.098	4,221.289
~30 Jun	1885	4,350	2,272.236	1,042.024	389.799	486.154	236.617	4,426.830
~30 Jun	1886	4,338	2,433.784	1,051.559	346.819	426.298	283.935	4,542.395
~30 Jun	1887	6,170	2,943.309	1,011.099	432.319	566.742	239.854	5,193.323
~30 Jun	1888	6,647	3,161.216	1,131.107	459.075	530.197	188.863	5,470.458
~30 Jun	1889	7,244	3,477.596	1,129.208	514.995	629.332	193.776	5,944.907
~30 Jun	1890	8,201	3,853.533	1,173.203	488.748	634.639	207.503	6,357.626
~30 Jun	1891	8,641	4,031.024	1,179.393	497.931	626.706	227.146	6,562.200
~30 Jun	1892	9,336	4,336.889	1,283.693	586.405	791.588	246.869	7,245.444
~30 Jun	1893	9,492	4,368.677	1,366.151	515.988	673.695	267.760	7,192.271
~30 Jun	1894	9,508	4,085.069	1,445.452	688.997	784.322	286.731	7,290.571
~30 Jun	1895	9,818	4,268.923	1,565.330	631.111	810.916	333.264	7,609.544
~30 Jun	1896	9,469	4,251.157	1,674.647	531.856	734.489	361.773	7,553.922
~30 Jun	1897	9,457	4,215.978	1,732.418	628.201	882.887	362.601	7,822.085
~30 Jun	1898	9,500	4,652.279	1,859.883	687.797	1,036.554	372.490	8,609.003
~30 Jun	1899	9,732	5,177.594	2,179.138	723.299	1,431.704	393.276	9,905.011
~30 Jun	1900	10,382	5,657.687	2,498.381	749.940	1,453.101	426.716	10,785.825
~30 Jun	1901	11,406	6,425.431	2,821.196	807.517	1,773.930	529.403	12,357.477
~30 Jun	1902	12,424	7,189.110	3,039.426	848.103	1,830.636	456.591	13,363.866
~30 Jun	1903	13,684	7,738.981	3,359.794	857.260	1,820.272	526.810	14,303.117
~30 Jun	1904	14,850	7,982.023	3,619.192	990.575	2,015.047	591.991	15,198.828
~30 Jun	1905	16,410	9,027.298	3,953.024	994.136	2,277.926	665.823	16,918.207
~30 Jun	1906	17,905	9,893.757	4,031.498	1,016.447	2,373.814	832.063	18,147.579
~30 Jun	1907	19,746	10,763.912	4,293.786	1,113.743	2,441.237	1,032.338	19,645.016
~30 Jun	1908	21,346	10,437.992	4,392.874	1,368.329	2,507.709	876.506	19,583.410
~30 Jun	1909	22,524	11,446.722	4,622.459	1,457.685	2,978.265	692.773	21,197.904
~30 Jun	1910	23,095	12,521.809	4,687.753	1,423.809	2,903.846	913.104	22,450.321
~30 Jun	1911	24,342	13,046.390	5,014.997	1,554.148	3,183.505	832.044	23,631.084
~30 Jun	1912	25,195	13,953.607	5,320.635	1,572.954	3,252.032	887.415	24,986.643
~30 Jun	1913	25,993	14,626.772	5,364.006	1,560.710	3,098.834	1,061.842	25,712.164
~30 Jun	1914	26,765	15,339.478	5,541.437	1,639.220	3,230.579	1,220.684	26,971.398

Condition of all reporting banks (National, State, savings, and savings & loan and trust companies) per Annual Report of the Comptroller of the Currency, 1931 (7 Dec 1931), Table 96; pp. 1023, 1024.

Figure 16.3-8: Combined Assets of National, State, and Private Banks, 30 Jun, 1879-1914

| | | | | Combined Liabilities of National, State, and Private Banks, 1879-1914 (millions USD) | | | | | |
Day	Year	Number of Banks	Capital	Surplus and Net Undivided Profits	Notes in Circulation	Total Deposits	Bills Payable & Rediscounts	Other Liabilities	Total Liabilities
~ 30 Jun	1879	3,335	580.472	246.167	307.718	2,149.192	6.737	22.395	3,312.681
~ 30 Jun	1880	3,355	565.228	260.297	318.371	2,222.106	7.519	25.424	3,398.945
~ 30 Jun	1881	3,427	572.339	292.075	312.498	2,649.062	7.389	35.761	3,869.124
~ 30 Jun	1882	3,572	590.547	310.062	309.208	2,777.421	9.833	34.074	4,031.145
~ 30 Jun	1883	3,835	625.531	347.861	312.151	2,883.977	8.335	30.249	4,208.104
~ 30 Jun	1884	4,113	656.475	379.675	295.352	2,848.554	15.606	25.627	4,221.289
~ 30 Jun	1885	4,350	677.961	361.956	269.246	3,078.153	7.938	31.576	4,426.830
~ 30 Jun	1886	4,338	680.393	395.986	244.996	3,186.179	9.864	24.977	4,542.395
~ 30 Jun	1887	6,170	799.175	459.873	166.857	3,718.639	14.111	34.668	5,193.323
~ 30 Jun	1888	6,647	853.752	493.814	155.482	3,891.096	18.051	58.263	5,470.458
~ 30 Jun	1889	7,244	894.713	532.958	128.987	4,310.516	14.152	63.581	5,944.907
~ 30 Jun	1890	8,201	973.363	584.764	126.444	4,576.433	22.056	74.566	6,357.626
~ 30 Jun	1891	8,641	1,029.653	619.271	124.027	4,682.695	27.788	78.766	6,562.200
~ 30 Jun	1892	9,336	1,071.073	650.182	141.199	5,297.460	13.763	71.767	7,245.444
~ 30 Jun	1893	9,492	1,091.794	689.289	155.081	5,065.422	61.322	129.363	7,192.271
~ 30 Jun	1894	9,508	1,069.826	682.722	171.720	5,267.669	18.195	80.439	7,290.571
~ 30 Jun	1895	9,818	1,080.277	699.401	178.816	5,538.634	21.949	90.467	7,609.544
~ 30 Jun	1896	9,469	1,051.976	694.455	199.214	5,486.182	27.768	94.327	7,553.922
~ 30 Jun	1897	9,457	1,012.244	712.704	196.591	5,787.188	15.075	98.283	7,822.085
~ 30 Jun	1898	9,500	992.091	732.738	189.866	6,554.165	14.648	125.495	8,609.003
~ 30 Jun	1899	9,732	973.612	761.120	199.358	7,900.303	8.233	62.385	9,905.011
~ 30 Jun	1900	10,382	1,024.729	882.203	265.303	8,513.030	16.872	83.688	10,785.825
~ 30 Jun	1901	11,406	1,076.121	955.606	319.009	9,896.122	17.652	92.967	12,357.477
~ 30 Jun	1902	12,424	1,201.612	1,096.887	309.337	10,625.592	22.739	107.699	13,363.866
~ 30 Jun	1903	13,684	1,321.925	1,273.498	359.261	11,179.144	28.759	140.530	14,303.117
~ 30 Jun	1904	14,850	1,392.495	1,360.880	399.584	11,864.925	30.596	150.348	15,198.828
~ 30 Jun	1905	16,410	1,463.166	1,439.534	445.456	13,332.801	27.164	210.086	16,918.207
~ 30 Jun	1906	17,905	1,565.293	1,558.843	510.861	14,207.429	37.403	267.750	18,147.579
~ 30 Jun	1907	19,746	1,690.869	1,645.068	547.919	15,358.215	39.140	363.805	19,645.016
~ 30 Jun	1908	21,346	1,757.159	1,761.513	613.664	15,116.863	42.327	291.884	19,583.410
~ 30 Jun	1909	22,524	1,803.061	1,846.619	641.312	16,668.219	98.944	139.749	21,197.904
~ 30 Jun	1910	23,095	1,879.944	1,955.599	675.633	17,584.175	153.445	201.525	22,450.321
~ 30 Jun	1911	24,342	1,952.411	2,065.575	681.740	18,581.475	135.387	214.496	23,631.084
~ 30 Jun	1912	25,195	2,010.844	2,166.158	708.691	19,719.288	149.615	232.047	24,986.643
~ 30 Jun	1913	25,993	2,096.850	2,249.840	722.125	20,138.553	186.019	318.777	25,712.164
~ 30 Jun	1914	26,765	2,132.074	2,276.517	722.555	21,359.842	232.561	247.849	26,971.398

Condition of all reporting banks (National, State, savings, and savings & loan and trust companies) per Annual Report of the Comptroller of the Currency, 1931 (7 Dec 1931), Table 96; pp. 1023, 1024.

Figure 16.3-9: Combined Liabilities of National, State, and Private Banks, 1879-1914

Figures 16.3-10 through 16.3-29 show the condition statements (assets and liabilities) of the national banks on each of the reporting dates. The exact dates are shown, as there was no regular schedule. Some of the source data contains errors and misprints, these have been corrected as shown in bold type. There is no corresponding data for the State and private banks.

			Circulation		Deposit	Investments		Balances		Lawful Money for Reserves						Other Assets			
Day	Year	Loans & Discounts [2]	U. S. Bonds	5% Redemption Fund with Treasury [3]	U. S. Bonds	U. S. Bonds, Other Bonds, and Stocks	Real Estate	Due from National and State Banks	Due from Reserve Agents	Specie	Legal Tender Notes [4]	Clearing-house exchanges	Frac-tional Currency	3% Cer-tificates	Checks & Other Cash Items	Miscel-laneous [5]	Due from U. S. Treasury [6]	Total Assets
1 Jan	1879	823.907	347.118	0.000	66.507	79.827	47.092	56.054	77.925	41.500	70.561	100.035	0.476	0.000	13.565	29.935	46.090	1,800.592
4 Apr	1879	814.653	348.488	0.000	309.348	91.349	47.462	49.679	74.004	41.149	64.461	63.712	0.467	0.000	10.011	30.372	38.914	1,984.069
14 Jun	1879	835.875	352.208	0.000	257.038	99.797	47.796	59.451	93.443	42.333	67.059	83.152	0.446	0.000	10.210	29.273	41.801	2,019.885
2 Oct	1879	878.503	357.313	0.000	18.205	92.614	47.817	60.324	107.024	42.174	69.197	**122.965**	0.396	0.000	11.306	27.151	43.799	1,868.787
12 Dec	1879	933.544	364.273	0.000	14.789	79.514	47.992	69.778	102.742	79.013	54.715	112.173	0.374	0.000	10.377	28.031	27.915	1,925.230
21 Feb	1880	974.295	361.902	0.000	14.917	78.022	47.846	67.731	117.791	89.442	55.229	166.736	0.397	0.000	10.320	25.682	27.754	2,038.066
23 Apr	1880	992.971	361.275	0.000	14.722	72.005	47.808	67.787	103.964	86.430	61.049	99.357	0.396	0.000	9.858	31.864	25.116	1,974.600
11 Jun	1880	994.713	359.512	0.000	14.727	73.553	47.979	70.440	115.936	99.507	64.471	122.390	0.387	0.000	9.980	32.389	29.509	2,035.493
1 Oct	1880	1,040.977	357.789	0.000	14.827	77.657	48.046	78.905	134.563	109.347	56.640	121.095	0.367	0.000	12.729	28.086	24.759	2,105.787
31 Dec	1880	1,071.356	358.043	0.000	14.727	73.645	47.784	86.191	126.155	107.173	59.217	229.734	0.390	0.000	14.714	29.280	23.276	2,241.684

National Banking System Assets, 1879, 1880 (millions USD) [1]

U. S. Obligations Deposited with Treasury as Security for:

1. Source: Annual Report, Comptroller of the Currency, 1914, Vol. 2, Table 56 (p. 220 ff)
2. Includes overdrafts
3. Required in 1874, but not cited separately on statements until 1887.
4. These are the U. S. Notes (greenbacks).
5. Includes premiums on bonds, current expenses, and bills of other banks.
6. Includes certificates of deposits and other deposits with the U. S. Treasury.

Figure 16.3-10: National Bank System Assets, 1879, 1880

Day	Year	Number of Banks	Paid-in Capital	Other Liabilities [2]	Due to Other Banks	Due to Reserve Agents	U. S. Deposits [3]	Individual and Other Deposits	National Bank Notes in Circula-tion	State Bank Notes in Circula-tion	Bills & Notes Redis-counted	Total Liabilities
1 Jan	1879	2,051	462.031	162.796	162.347	0.000	63.258	643.338	303.506	0.388	2.926	1,800.592
4 Apr	1879	2,048	455.611	162.247	154.191	0.000	306.153	598.823	304.467	0.352	2.224	1,984.069
14 Jun	1879	2,048	455.244	165.944	187.763	0.000	252.104	648.934	307.329	0.340	2.226	2,019.885
2 Oct	1879	2,048	454.067	162.954	201.223	0.000	14.488	719.738	313.786	0.326	2.205	1,868.787
12 Dec	1879	2,052	454.499	168.350	211.716	0.000	10.817	755.460	321.949	0.323	2.116	1,925.230
21 Feb	1880	2,061	454.549	165.454	235.684	0.000	10.927	848.927	320.304	0.303	1.919	2,038.066
23 Apr	1880	2,075	456.098	171.598	220.527	0.000	11.147	791.555	320.759	0.300	2.617	1,974.600
11 Jun	1880	2,076	455.910	175.136	239.401	0.000	10.708	833.701	318.089	0.291	2.259	2,035.493
1 Oct	1880	2,090	457.554	175.142	267.860	0.000	10.893	873.538	317.350	0.271	3.178	2,105.787
31 Dec	1880	2,095	458.540	180.606	263.599	0.000	11.388	1,006.453	317.484	0.258	3.355	2,241.684

National Banking System Liabilities, 1879, 1880 (millions USD) [1]

1. Source: Annual Report, Comptroller of the Currency, 1914, Vol. 2, Table 56 (p. 220 ff)
2. Includes surplus fund, undivided profits, unpaid dividends, bills payable, reserved for taxes, and miscellaneous.
3. Includes deposits of U. S. disbursing officers.

Figure 16.3-11: National Bank System Liabilities, 1879, 1880

National Banking System Assets, 1881-1884 (millions USD) [1]																		
			U. S. Obligations Deposited with Treasury as Security for:															
			Circulation		Deposit	Investments		Balances			Lawful Money for Reserves						Other Assets		
Day	Year	Loans & Discounts [2]	U. S. Bonds	5% Redemption Fund with Treasury [3]	U. S. Bonds	U. S. Bonds, Other Bonds, and Stocks	Real Estate	Due from National and State Banks	Due from Reserve Agents	Specie	Legal Tender Notes [4]	C. H. exchanges & C. H. loan certificates [5]	Fractional Currency	3% Certificates	Checks & Other Cash Items	Miscellaneous [6]	Due from U. S. Treasury [7]	Total Assets
11 Mar	1881	1,073.787	339.812	0.000	14.852	96.181	47.526	79.328	120.821	105.156	52.156	147.762	0.387	0.000	10.145	29.074	23.135	2,140.121
6 May	1881	1,093.649	352.654	0.000	15.240	97.025	47.791	80.115	128.018	122.629	62.516	196.634	0.387	0.000	11.827	35.242	26.502	2,270.227
30 Jun	1881	1,144.989	358.288	0.000	15.265	106.634	47.834	94.554	156.259	128.639	58.729	143.960	0.372	0.000	13.534	29.984	26.792	2,325.833
1 Oct	1881	1,173.796	363.386	0.000	15.540	102.819	47.329	97.812	132.968	114.335	53.158	189.222	0.374	0.000	14.832	28.603	24.213	2,358.387
31 Dec	1881	1,169.178	368.736	0.000	15.715	94.547	47.445	95.279	123.530	113.681	60.104	217.215	0.366	0.000	17.338	32.729	26.028	2,381.891
11 Mar	1882	1,182.662	367.334	0.000	16.093	92.954	47.073	84.223	117.453	109.984	56.634	162.088	0.390	0.000	13.308	31.697	27.166	2,309.057
19 May	1882	1,189.095	360.154	0.000	15.920	94.938	46.957	83.774	124.190	112.416	65.970	107.270	0.390	0.000	12.295	37.063	27.494	2,277.925
1 Jul	1882	1,208.933	355.790	0.000	15.920	93.934	46.425	91.712	118.455	111.694	64.020	159.114	0.374	0.000	20.167	29.930	27.875	2,344.343
3 Oct	1882	1,243.203	357.632	0.000	16.111	87.484	46.537	85.622	113.277	102.858	63.314	208.367	0.396	0.000	14.784	34.443	25.806	2,399.834
30 Dec	1882	1,230.456	357.048	0.000	16.344	82.491	46.993	94.479	122.066	106.427	68.478	155.951	0.401	0.000	16.281	36.948	26.429	2,360.793
13 Mar	1883	1,249.115	354.747	0.000	16.799	86.279	47.962	84.257	121.024	97.962	60.848	107.790	0.432	0.000	11.361	36.110	25.131	2,298.918
1 May	1883	1,262.340	354.480	0.000	16.949	84.211	47.156	87.860	109.307	103.607	68.256	145.991	0.446	0.000	15.461	38.209	25.918	2,360.192
22 Jun	1883	1,285.592	354.003	0.000	17.116	85.530	47.502	85.616	126.647	115.354	73.832	90.792	0.456	0.000	11.110	43.189	28.093	2,364.833
2 Oct	1883	1,309.245	351.413	0.000	17.081	84.707	48.338	83.981	124.919	107.818	70.673	96.353	0.444	0.000	13.581	37.548	26.557	2,372.656
31 Dec	1883	1,307.491	345.596	0.000	16.846	84.761	49.541	97.305	127.000	114.276	80.560	134.545	0.428	0.000	17.492	42.335	27.706	2,445.881
7 Mar	1884	1,321.548	339.816	0.000	16.850	91.828	49.419	82.576	138.705	122.080	75.847	68.403	0.491	0.000	11.384	41.042	30.511	2,390.501
24 Apr	1884	1,333.433	337.343	0.000	17.135	88.985	49.667	86.177	122.492	114.745	77.713	83.531	0.490	0.000	11.238	44.406	29.459	2,396.814
20 Jun	1884	1,269.863	334.346	0.000	17.060	86.715	50.149	81.198	95.247	109.662	76.917	79.834	0.473	0.000	11.382	42.859	26.893	2,282.599
30 Sep	1884	1,245.294	327.435	0.000	16.840	84.943	49.901	82.170	111.993	128.609	77.045	67.947	0.469	0.000	13.103	41.805	31.940	2,279.494
20 Dec	1884	1,234.202	317.586	0.000	16.740	85.755	49.890	87.790	121.162	139.747	77.066	77.066	0.457	0.000	11.924	43.972	34.482	2,297.143

1. Source: Annual Report, Comptroller of the Currency, 1914, Vol. 2, Table 56 (p. 220 ff)
2. Includes overdrafts
3. Required in 1874, but not cited separately on statements until 1887.
4. These are the U. S. Notes (greenbacks).
5. Clearinghouse loan certificates used in conjunction with exchanges from 1884 to 1891
6. Includes premiums on bonds, current expenses, and bills of other banks.
7. Includes certificates of deposits and other deposits with the U. S. Treasury.

Figure 16.3-12: National Bank System Assets, 1881-1884

National Banking System Liabilities, 1881-1884 (millions USD) [1]												
Day	Year	Number of Banks	Paid-in Capital	Other Liabilities [2]	Due to Other Banks	Due to Reserve Agents	U. S. Deposits [3]	Individual and Other Deposits	National Bank Notes in Circulation	State Bank Notes in Circulation	Bills & Notes Rediscounted	Total Liabilities
11 Mar	1881	2,094	458.255	182.527	253.257	0.000	11.220	933.392	298.591	0.253	2.616	2,140.111
6 May	1881	2,102	459.039	186.423	271.951	0.000	12.876	1,027.041	309.737	0.253	2.908	2,270.227
30 Jun	1881	2,115	460.228	192.404	314.539	0.000	12.244	1,031.731	312.223	0.243	2.220	2,325.833
1 Oct	1881	2,132	463.822	193.013	294.910	0.000	12.108	1,070.997	320.200	0.244	3.091	2,358.387
31 Dec	1881	2,164	465.860	194.944	276.633	0.000	12.392	1,102.679	325.018	0.242	4.122	2,381.891
11 Mar	1882	2,187	469.390	197.247	265.793	0.000	12.226	1,036.595	323.652	0.242	3.913	2,309.057
19 May	1882	2,224	473.819	198.537	270.986	0.000	13.234	1,001.682	315.671	0.241	3.754	2,277.925
1 Jul	1882	2,239	477.184	195.480	278.934	0.000	12.685	1,066.707	308.922	0.235	4.195	2,344.343
3 Oct	1882	2,269	483.104	201.160	259.961	0.000	12.445	1,122.473	314.721	0.221	5.748	2,399.834
30 Dec	1882	2,308	484.883	201.936	271.522	0.000	13.409	1,066.902	315.231	0.207	6.703	2,360.793
13 Mar	1883	2,343	490.457	201.314	271.549	0.000	13.401	1,004.111	312.778	0.207	5.101	2,298.918
1 May	1883	2,375	493.963	204.729	258.990	0.000	15.243	1,067.962	313.550	0.198	5.557	2,360.192
22 Jun	1883	2,417	500.298	211.278	278.895	0.000	13.874	1,043.138	311.963	0.189	5.198	2,364.833
2 Oct	1883	2,501	509.700	216.835	264.431	0.000	14.163	1,049.438	310.518	0.184	7.388	2,372.656
31 Dec	1883	2,529	511.838	214.727	285.644	0.000	13.796	1,106.453	304.994	0.181	8.249	2,445.881
7 Mar	1884	2,563	515.725	213.778	295.928	0.000	13.813	1,046.050	298.792	0.181	6.234	2,390.501
24 Apr	1884	2,589	518.472	218.108	279.647	0.000	14.822	1,060.778	297.506	0.181	7.299	2,396.814
20 Jun	1884	2,625	522.516	222.008	226.266	0.000	14.195	979.020	295.175	0.180	23.239	2,282.599
30 Sep	1884	2,664	524.271	218.556	246.387	0.000	14.072	975.244	289.775	0.180	11.009	2,279.494
20 Dec	1884	2,664	524.089	222.325	259.869	0.000	14.406	987.649	280.197	0.175	8.434	2,297.143

1. Source: Annual Report, Comptroller of the Currency, 1914, Vol. 2, Table 56 (p. 220 ff)
2. Includes surplus fund, undivided profits, unpaid dividends, bills payable, reserved for taxes, and miscellaneous.
3. Includes deposits of U. S. disbursing officers.

Figure 16.3-13: National Bank System Liabilities, 1881-1884

		Loans & Discounts [2]	U.S. Obligations Deposited with Treasury as Security for:			Investments		Balances		Lawful Money for Reserves					Other Assets			Total Assets
			Circulation		Deposit													
Day	Year		U.S. Bonds	5% Redemption Fund with Treasury [3]	U.S. Bonds	U.S. Bonds, Other Bonds, and Stocks	Real Estate	Due from National and State Banks	Due from Reserve Agents	Specie	Legal Tender Notes [4]	C.H. exchanges & C.H. loan certificates [5]	Fractional Currency	Trade Dollars	Checks & Other Cash Items	Miscellaneous [6]	Due from U.S. Treasury [7]	
10 Mar	1885	1,232.327	313.106	0.000	16.815	89.761	49.700	84.015	136.462	167.116	71.017	60.616	0.520	0.000	11.229	42.221	37.840	2,312.744
6 May	1885	1,241.451	312.169	0.000	16.740	89.788	49.886	85.216	130.903	177.433	77.337	73.689	0.513	0.000	11.277	45.672	34.608	2,346.682
1 Jul	1885	1,257.656	310.102	0.000	17.607	91.838	50.730	94.401	132.734	177.612	79.701	114.539	0.490	0.000	17.214	39.690	37.538	2,421.852
1 Oct	1885	1,306.144	307.657	0.000	17.457	91.825	51.294	96.956	138.379	174.873	69.738	86.037	0.477	1.606	14.348	42.427	33.697	2,432.913
24 Dec	1885	1,343.518	304.777	0.000	18.012	90.200	51.963	98.006	139.239	165.354	67.585	92.981	0.415	1.671	12.810	44.397	26.746	2,457.675
1 Mar	1886	1,367.705	296.661	12.953	18.637	96.807	52.263	95.768	142.806	171.616	67.015	100.429	0.470	1.682	15.136	40.447	13.943	2,494.337
3 Jun	1886	1,398.552	279.414	12.199	18.810	95.883	53.118	95.353	133.027	157.460	79.657	76.345	0.452	1.713	12.181	47.113	13.267	2,474.544
27 Aug	1886	1,421.547	270.316	11.869	19.985	96.809	53.835	96.479	143.715	149.000	64.040	62.560	0.451	1.857	10.409	41.081	9.714	2,453.667
7 Oct	1886	1,450.957	258.499	11.358	20.106	94.152	54.090	100.667	140.765	156.388	62.812	95.537	0.434	1.890	13.277	44.476	8.447	2,513.855
28 Dec	1886	1,470.158	228.384	10.056	21.041	92.007	54.764	109.737	142.118	166.984	67.740	70.525	0.448	1.827	13.219	51.576	7.170	2,507.754
4 Mar	1887	1,515.535	211.537	9.281	22.977	97.162	55.129	108.187	163.161	171.679	66.228	89.239	0.578	1.804	13.309	45.837	9.501	2,581.143
13 May	1887	1,560.292	200.452	8.811	24.991	96.188	55.729	128.323	148.068	167.316	79.595	86.829	0.556	0.184	13.066	49.776	9.139	2,629.314
1 Aug	1887	1,560.372	189.032	8.342	26.402	96.183	56.955	120.440	140.270	165.104	74.477	128.212	0.564	0.064	16.914	45.475	8.471	2,637.276
5 Oct	1887	1,587.549	189.083	8.310	27.757	95.745	57.968	115.406	140.874	165.085	73.751	88.775	0.541	0.001	14.691	47.481	7.175	2,620.193
7 Dec	1887	1,583.941	186.432	8.169	42.203	97.764	58.825	120.222	132.960	159.241	75.362	85.097	0.555	0.000	13.326	52.845	7.233	**2,624.176**
14 Feb	1888	1,584.170	181.845	7.993	56.863	100.604	59.366	114.861	155.341	173.831	82.318	73.418	0.683	0.000	12.256	49.456	11.360	2,664.366
30 Apr	1888	1,606.398	181.043	7.888	56.643	102.936	60.111	118.229	146.478	172.074	83.574	117.271	0.663	0.000	14.645	53.779	10.691	2,732.423
30 Jun	1888	1,628.125	177.544	7.766	55.788	104.096	61.102	124.404	158.134	181.292	81.996	74.230	0.633	0.000	16.856	45.932	13.552	2,731.448
4 Oct	1888	1,684.181	171.867	7.555	54.208	106.259	62.635	123.588	170.459	178.098	81.099	102.440	0.684	0.000	15.071	47.715	9.891	2,815.751
12 Dec	1888	1,676.555	162.821	7.141	48.949	108.651	63.436	131.393	156.587	172.734	82.555	91.765	0.628	0.001	14.141	49.752	10.466	2,777.576

Title: National Banking System Assets, 1885-1888 (millions USD) [1]

1. Source: Annual Report, Comptroller of the Currency, 1914, Vol. 2, Table 56 (p. 220 ff)
2. Includes overdrafts
3. Required in 1874, but not cited separately on statements until 1887.
4. These are the U.S. Notes (greenbacks).
5. Clearinghouse loan certificates used in conjunction with exchanges from 1884 to 1891
6. Includes premiums on bonds, current expenses, and bills of other banks.
7. Includes certificates of deposits and other deposits with the U. S. Treasury.

Figure 16.3-14: National Bank System Assets, 1885-1888

National Banking System Liabilities, 1885-1888 (millions USD) [1]

Day	Year	Number of Banks	Paid-in Capital	Other Liabilities [2]	Due to Other Banks	Due to Reserve Agents	U.S. Deposits [3]	Individual and Other Deposits	National Bank Notes in Circulation	State Bank Notes in Circulation	Bills & Notes Rediscounted	Total Liabilities
10 Mar	1885	2,671	524.255	209.357	288.068	0.000	14.047	996.502	274.054	0.163	6.300	2,312.744
6 May	1885	2,678	525.196	210.033	281.047	0.000	15.021	1,035.802	273.703	0.144	5.736	2,346.682
1 Jul	1885	2,689	526.274	207.242	292.780	0.000	14.023	1,106.377	269.148	0.144	5.864	2,421.852
1 Oct	1885	2,714	527.524	211.660	299.650	0.000	14.267	1,102.372	268.870	0.137	8.433	2,432.913
24 Dec	1885	2,732	529.361	222.698	301.625	0.000	15.065	1,111.430	267.431	0.134	9.933	2,457.675
1 Mar	1886	2,768	533.361	214.959	312.442	0.000	15.434	1,152.660	256.972	0.134	8.376	2,494.337
3 Jun	1886	2,809	539.109	223.978	294.996	0.000	16.470	1,146.247	244.893	0.132	8.719	2,474.544
27 Aug	1886	2,849	545.523	222.460	308.694	0.000	17.181	1,113.459	238.274	0.128	7.949	2,453.667
7 Oct	1886	2,852	548.241	228.048	308.642	0.000	16.563	1,172.968	228.673	0.125	10.594	2,513.855
28 Dec	1886	2,875	550.699	242.907	315.097	0.000	17.982	1,169.716	202.078	0.115	9.159	2,507.754
4 Mar	1887	2,909	555.352	235.110	352.350	0.000	19.511	1,224.926	186.231	0.106	7.557	2,581.143
13 May	1887	2,955	565.629	242.110	346.665	0.000	21.336	1,266.571	176.772	0.099	10.133	2,629.314
1 Aug	1887	3,014	571.649	239.869	339.570	0.000	23.262	1,285.077	166.626	0.099	11.125	2,637.276
5 Oct	1887	3,049	578.463	252.748	329.587	0.000	25.224	1,249.477	167.283	0.099	17.313	2,620.193
7 Dec	1887	3,070	580.733	261.595	321.898	0.000	42.931	1,235.758	164.904	0.099	16.268	2,624.186
14 Feb	1888	3,077	582.194	251.471	346.578	0.000	59.449	1,251.958	159.750	0.099	12.867	2,664.366
30 Apr	1888	3,098	585.449	264.486	341.560	0.000	59.481	1,309.731	158.898	0.095	12.724	2,732.423
30 Jun	1888	3,120	588.384	265.740	358.120	0.000	58.370	1,292.342	155.313	0.082	13.096	2,731.448
4 Oct	1888	3,140	592.622	271.949	375.634	0.000	56.134	1,350.321	151.703	0.082	17.306	2,815.751
12 Dec	1888	3,150	593.848	282.571	360.293	0.000	51.123	1,331.266	143.549	0.082	14.844	2,777.576

1. Source: Annual Report, Comptroller of the Currency, 1914, Vol. 2, Table 56 (p. 220 ff)
2. Includes surplus fund, undivided profits, unpaid dividends, bills payable, reserved for taxes, and miscellaneous.
3. Includes deposits of U. S. disbursing officers.

Figure 16.3-15: National Bank System Liabilities, 1885-1888

National Banking System Assets, 1889-1892 (millions USD) [1]																		
			U.S. Obligations Deposited with Treasury as Security for:			Investments		Balances		Lawful Money for Reserves					Other Assets			
			Circulation		Deposit													
Day	Year	Loans & Discounts [2]	U.S. Bonds	5% Redemption Fund with Treasury [3]	U.S. Bonds	U.S. Bonds, Other Bonds, and Stocks	Real Estate	Due from National and State Banks	Due from Reserve Agents	Specie	Legal Tender Notes [4]	C.H. exchanges & C.H. loan certificates [5]	Fractional Currency	Trade Dollars	Checks & Other Cash Items	Miscellaneous [6]	Due from U.S. Treasury [7]	Total Assets
26 Feb	1889	1,704.067	156.728	6.860	46.384	108.610	66.248	125.979	192.702	182.285	88.625	84.112	0.718	0.000	12.677	46.559	14.852	2,837.406
13 May	1889	1,739.652	149.521	6.565	44.882	109.721	66.855	134.016	187.372	185.176	97.838	101.453	0.698	0.000	15.049	51.766	14.357	2,904.923
12 Jul	1889	1,779.055	147.502	6.458	44.832	113.523	67.377	134.956	192.590	175.904	97.457	101.552	0.719	0.000	14.351	45.649	16.052	2,937.976
30 Sep	1889	1,817.258	146.472	6.405	44.063	113.752	69.377	146.287	189.136	164.326	86.752	136.783	0.682	0.000	17.060	46.015	13.922	2,998.291
11 Dec	1889	1,811.687	143.435	6.277	41.681	115.085	70.694	146.350	164.890	171.089	84.491	103.719	0.720	0.000	15.135	48.139	10.285	2,933.677
28 Feb	1890	1,844.978	142.532	6.192	31.620	122.719	72.567	143.180	188.064	181.546	86.552	112.614	0.807	0.000	15.187	45.092	9.685	3,003.335
17 May	1890	1,904.167	143.791	6.302	29.893	122.643	74.212	141.946	183.206	178.165	88.089	68.428	0.746	0.000	15.444	44.181	9.002	3,010.216
18 Jul	1890	1,933.509	144.625	6.305	29.663	122.094	75.658	139.519	185.822	178.604	92.480	88.238	0.794	0.000	13.875	39.758	10.827	3,061.771
2 Oct	1890	1,986.058	139.969	6.124	28.387	117.826	76.835	146.775	189.452	195.909	80.605	106.767	0.767	0.000	17.202	41.840	6.972	3,141.487
19 Dec	1890	1,932.393	139.688	6.069	27.859	118.685	78.060	140.008	160.221	190.063	82.177	102.214	0.755	0.000	15.057	46.836	6.854	3,046.939
26 Feb	1891	1,927.655	140.183	6.134	27.905	124.565	79.097	138.807	182.646	201.240	89.400	78.438	0.865	0.000	13.349	41.964	12.755	3,065.002
4 May	1891	1,969.846	140.498	6.159	27.955	126.103	80.875	140.673	180.005	194.939	96.375	126.567	0.830	0.000	17.602	46.823	12.244	3,167.495
9 Jul	1891	1,963.705	142.586	6.130	25.151	127.311	81.919	142.215	175.591	190.770	100.400	80.306	0.863	0.000	16.073	40.396	20.000	3,113.415
25 Sep	1891	2,005.463	150.036	6.537	20.433	129.619	83.270	144.669	193.990	183.515	97.616	122.040	0.867	0.000	13.273	44.576	17.178	3,213.080
2 Dec	1891	2,001.033	153.838	6.682	19.187	132.721	84.049	157.253	196.320	207.898	93.854	108.243	0.837	0.000	17.939	48.200	9.813	3,237.866
1 Mar	1892	2,058.925	158.109	6.898	17.417	142.694	85.127	163.430	256.751	230.148	99.446	129.516	0.925	0.000	17.644	44.512	25.131	3,436.672
17 May	1892	2,108.360	160.635	6.991	16.386	149.470	86.563	162.131	250.249	239.044	107.981	99.954	0.924	0.000	15.037	47.979	27.331	3,479.035
12 Jul	1892	2,127.757	161.940	7.093	15.447	155.980	86.678	170.622	252.474	229.320	113.915	90.364	0.939	0.000	16.849	39.891	24.524	3,493.795
30 Sep	1892	2,171.041	163.275	7.140	15.282	159.418	87.862	173.089	236.434	209.116	104.268	105.523	0.935	0.000	17.706	43.904	15.102	3,510.095
9 Dec	1892	2,166.616	166.449	7.282	15.321	157.797	88.221	177.026	204.948	209.895	102.276	110.523	0.894	0.000	16.755	48.607	7.738	3,480.350

1. Source: Annual Report, Comptroller of the Currency, 1914, Vol. 2, Table 56 (p. 220 ff)
2. Includes overdrafts.
3. Required in 1874, but not cited separately on statements until 1887.
4. These are the U.S. Notes (greenbacks).
5. Clearinghouse loan certificates used in conjunction with exchanges from 1884 to 1891.
6. Includes premiums on bonds, current expenses, and bills of other banks.
7. Includes certificates of deposits and other deposits with the U.S. Treasury.

Figure 16.3-16: National Bank System Assets, 1889-1892

National Banking System Liabilities, 1889-1892 (millions USD) [1]												
Day	Year	Number of Banks	Paid-in Capital	Other Liabilities [2]	Due to Other Banks	Due to Reserve Agents	U.S. Deposits [3]	Individual and Other Deposits	National Bank Notes in Circulation	State Bank Notes in Circulation	Bills & Notes Redis-counted, C.H. Loans [4]	Total Liabilities
26 Feb	1889	3,170	596.569	273.712	417.505	0.000	48.099	1,354.974	137.216	0.082	9.250	2,837.406
13 May	1889	3,206	599.473	283.794	410.961	0.000	47.102	1,422.042	131.128	0.082	10.341	2,904.923
12 Jul	1889	3,239	605.852	276.981	427.225	0.000	46.699	1,442.138	128.867	0.081	10.133	2,937.976
30 Sep	1889	3,290	612.584	293.058	425.342	0.000	46.525	1,475.468	128.451	0.080	16.783	2,998.291
11 Dec	1889	3,326	617.840	302.820	390.873	0.000	43.898	1,436.403	126.040	0.081	15.723	2,933.677
28 Feb	1890	3,383	626.598	295.797	434.166	0.000	32.473	1,479.986	123.862	0.081	10.371	3,003.335
17 May	1890	3,438	635.055	310.218	414.460	0.000	30.720	1,480.474	125.792	0.077	13.420	3,010.216
18 Jul	1890	3,834	642.074	302.342	423.602	0.000	30.578	1,521.746	126.324	0.077	15.028	3,061.771
2 Oct	1890	3,540	650.447	323.749	426.432	0.000	29.348	1,564.845	122.928	0.077	23.660	3,141.487
19 Dec	1890	3,573	657.877	339.407	374.520	0.000	29.379	1,485.096	123.039	0.077	37.543	3,046.939
26 Feb	1891	3,601	662.518	326.428	422.839	0.000	29.247	1,483.450	123.113	0.077	17.331	3,065.002
4 May	1891	3,633	667.787	334.866	420.016	0.000	29.193	1,575.506	123.448	0.074	16.605	3,167.495
9 Jul	1891	3,652	672.904	327.361	408.472	0.000	25.911	1,535.059	123.916	0.074	19.720	3,113.415
25 Sep	1891	3,677	677.427	343.094	430.595	0.000	20.267	1,588.318	131.323	0.074	21.982	3,213.080
2 Dec	1891	3,692	677.357	347.014	441.816	0.000	18.434	1,602.053	134.793	0.074	16.326	3,237.866
1 Mar	1892	3,711	679.970	337.005	554.673	0.000	16.563	1,702.241	137.627	0.075	8.517	3,436.672
17 May	1892	3,734	682.232	345.134	543.131	0.000	15.536	1,743.788	140.052	0.072	9.090	3,479.035
12 Jul	1892	3,759	684.678	335.452	555.827	0.000	14.180	1,753.340	141.062	0.075	9.182	3,493.795
30 Sep	1892	3,773	686.573	352.942	530.653	0.000	13.873	1,765.423	143.423	0.075	17.132	3,510.095
9 Dec	1892	3,784	689.698	366.851	484.118	0.000	13.708	1,764.456	145.669	0.074	15.776	3,480.350

1. Source: Annual Report, Comptroller of the Currency, 1914, Vol. 2, Table 56 (p. 220 ff).
2. Includes surplus fund, undivided profits, unpaid dividends, bills payable, reserved for taxes, and miscellaneous.
3. Includes deposits of U.S. disbursing officers.
4. Includes bills and notes rediscounted (1869-1914) and clearinghouse loan certificates (1890, 1891).

Figure 16.3-17: National Bank System Liabilities, 1889-1892

				U. S. Obligations Deposited with Treasury as Security for:				Investments		Balances		Lawful Money for Reserves						Other Assets			
			Circulation			Deposit															
Day	Year	Loans & Discounts [2]	U. S. Bonds	5% Redemption Fund with Treasury	U. S. Bonds	U. S. Bonds, Other Bonds, and Stocks	Real Estate	Due from National and State Banks	Due from Reserve Agents	Specie	Legal Tender Notes [3]	Clearing-house exchanges	Frac-tional Currency	Trade Dollars	Checks & Other Cash Items	Miscel-laneous [4]	Due from U. S. Treasury [5]	Total Assets
6 Mar	1893	2,159.614	170.097	7.402	15.351	157.793	89.710	154.511	202.612	208.342	90.936	125.143	0.946	0.000	18.755	42.512	15.997	3,459.721
4 May	1893	2,161.402	172.413	7.468	15.261	154.267	90.034	154.356	174.312	207.222	103.511	114.977	0.953	0.000	17.547	44.767	13.687	3,432.177
12 Jul	1893	2,020.484	176.588	7.601	15.256	152.769	89.383	139.168	159.353	186.761	95.834	107.766	0.953	0.000	16.708	36.961	7.679	3,213.262
3 Oct	1893	1,843.634	206.464	8.977	14.816	151.331	89.152	118.969	158.500	224.704	114.709	106.181	1.027	0.000	15.360	47.456	8.283	3,109.563
19 Dec	1893	1,871.575	204.809	8.876	14.436	162.798	92.322	136.948	212.631	251.254	131.627	71.943	0.989	0.000	13.519	35.304	33.284	3,242.315
28 Feb	1894	1,872.403	200.809	8.751	14.445	191.556	94.289	140.008	246.892	256.167	142.769	70.300	1.062	0.000	12.634	35.473	37.178	3,324.735
4 May	1894	1,926.687	200.469	8.713	14.720	200.130	95.978	148.932	257.854	259.942	146.131	76.002	1.014	0.000	12.550	35.888	48.331	3,433.342
18 Jul	1894	1,944.441	201.335	8.792	14.926	204.013	96.807	138.839	258.089	250.671	138.216	66.512	1.042	0.000	11.866	34.581	51.966	3,422.096
2 Oct	1894	2,007.122	199.643	8.723	15.226	203.962	97.892	150.453	248.850	237.251	120.544	88.524	0.953	0.000	15.577	33.205	45.998	3,473.922
19 Dec	1894	1,991.913	195.736	8.542	15.051	218.089	98.660	155.761	234.331	218.041	119.513	80.869	0.885	0.000	13.051	34.653	38.379	3,423.475
5 Mar	1895	1,965.375	195.787	8.528	26.405	222.043	101.269	143.976	222.468	220.932	113.282	77.344	1.002	0.000	12.425	34.949	32.735	3,378.521
7 May	1895	1,989.411	203.648	8.748	28.616	211.576	102.015	147.969	218.799	218.647	118.529	83.833	1.008	0.000	12.558	36.698	27.948	3,410.002
11 Jul	1895	2,016.640	206.227	9.094	15.878	208.626	102.939	158.419	235.309	214.427	123.185	82.868	1.023	0.000	13.599	35.843	46.476	3,470.553
28 Sep	1895	2,059.408	208.683	9.086	15.328	205.818	103.772	154.352	222.287	196.237	93.947	57.507	0.936	0.000	13.056	32.006	51.206	3,423.629
13 Dec	1895	2,041.499	210.480	9.195	15.358	202.039	104.272	164.349	203.002	206.712	99.209	86.558	0.925	0.000	12.939	33.813	33.184	3,423.534
28 Feb	1896	1,966.212	215.637	9.231	34.922	205.247	105.244	144.109	189.345	196.017	112.508	89.996	1.019	0.000	12.276	35.627	30.455	3,347.844
7 May	1896	1,982.886	225.018	9.775	25.573	203.430	104.985	142.360	195.753	202.373	118.972	85.504	0.986	0.000	12.295	38.059	29.670	3,377.639
14 Jul	1896	1,971.642	227.214	9.923	15.929	203.099	105.449	144.717	204.384	203.835	113.213	75.926	0.999	0.000	13.601	35.024	28.842	3,353.797
6 Oct	1896	1,893.269	237.292	10.374	15.793	198.338	105.450	141.414	190.078	200.809	110.495	76.760	0.967	0.000	13.913	35.686	33.049	3,263.685
17 Dec	1896	1,901.160	239.346	10.412	15.868	198.108	106.061	157.524	219.967	225.541	118.894	84.976	0.925	0.000	13.138	36.225	38.970	3,367.116

National Banking System Assets, 1893-1896 (millions USD) [1]

1. Source: Annual Report, Comptroller of the Currency, 1914, Vol. 2, Table 56 (p. 220 ff)
2. Includes overdrafts
3. These are the U. S. Notes (greenbacks).
4. Includes premiums on bonds, current expenses (to 1892), and bills of other banks.
5. Includes certificates of deposits and other deposits with the U. S. Treasury.

Figure 16.3-18: National Bank System Assets, 1893-1896

National Banking System Liabilities, 1893-1896 (millions USD) [1]

Day	Year	Number of Banks	Paid-in Capital	Other Liabilities [2]	Due to Other Banks	Due to Reserve Agents	U. S. Deposits [3]	Individual and Other Deposits	National Bank Notes in Circula-tion	State Bank Notes in Circula-tion	Bills & Notes Redis-counted	Total Liabilities
6 Mar	1893	3,806	688.643	370.990	471.686	0.000	13.742	1,751.439	149.125	0.075	14.022	3,459.721
4 May	1893	3,830	688.701	380.243	428.628	0.000	13.951	1,749.931	151.694	0.075	18.953	3,432.177
12 Jul	1893	3,807	685.787	407.033	364.893	0.000	13.701	1,556.761	155.071	0.075	29.940	3,213.262
3 Oct	1893	3,781	678.540	412.159	349.315	0.000	14.323	1,451.124	182.960	0.075	21.067	3,109.563
19 Dec	1893	3,787	681.813	365.608	450.120	0.000	13.861	1,539.400	179.973	0.075	11.466	3,242.315
28 Feb	1894	3,777	678.537	346.505	517.086	0.000	13.569	1,586.800	174.436	0.071	7.730	3,324.735
4 May	1894	3,774	675.869	349.579	542.477	0.000	13.856	1,670.959	172.626	0.071	7.906	3,433.342
18 Jul	1894	3,770	671.091	345.305	533.794	0.000	14.129	1,677.801	171.715	0.066	8.196	3,422.096
2 Oct	1894	3,755	668.862	352.188	526.860	0.000	13.741	1,728.419	172.332	0.066	11.453	3,473.922
19 Dec	1894	3,737	666.271	355.647	514.965	0.000	14.017	1,695.489	169.337	0.066	7.683	3,423.475
5 Mar	1895	3,728	662.100	348.447	495.401	0.000	28.055	1,667.843	169.755	0.066	6.853	3,378.521
7 May	1895	3,711	659.147	354.307	493.675	0.000	27.248	1,690.961	175.654	0.066	8.945	3,410.002
11 Jul	1895	3,715	658.224	347.887	526.673	0.000	13.167	1,736.022	178.816	0.066	9.698	3,470.553
28 Sep	1895	3,712	657.135	360.418	494.937	0.000	13.541	1,701.654	182.482	0.066	13.396	3,423.629
13 Dec	1895	3,706	656.956	365.669	470.025	0.000	13.759	1,720.550	185.151	0.064	11.360	3,423.534
28 Feb	1896	3,699	653.995	364.854	448.371	0.000	33.787	1,648.093	187.217	0.061	11.466	3,347.844
7 May	1896	3,694	652.090	361.187	443.295	0.000	24.432	1,687.630	197.382	0.060	11.564	3,377.639
14 Jul	1896	3,689	651.145	353.411	454.302	0.000	15.404	1,668.414	199.214	0.060	11.847	3,353.797
6 Oct	1896	3,676	648.540	362.095	415.102	0.000	15.171	1,597.891	209.944	0.060	14.881	3,263.685
17 Dec	1896	3,661	647.186	359.475	486.496	0.000	15.420	1,639.688	210.690	0.060	8.100	3,367.116

1. Source: Annual Report, Comptroller of the Currency, 1914, Vol. 2, Table 56 (p. 220 ff)
2. Includes surplus fund, undivided profits, unpaid dividends, bills payable, reserved for taxes, and miscellaneous.
3. Includes deposits of U. S. disbursing officers.

Figure 16.3-19: National Bank System Liabilities, 1893-1896

| | | | U. S. Obligations Deposited with Treasury as Security for: | | | Investments | Balances | | Lawful Money for Reserves | | | | | | | Other Assets | | | |
| | | | Circulation | | Deposit | | | | | | | | | | | | | | |
Day	Year	Loans & Discounts [2]	U.S. Bonds	5% Redemption Fund with Treasury	U.S. Bonds	U.S. Bonds, Other Bonds, and Stocks	Real Estate	Due from National and State Banks	Due from Reserve Agents	Specie	Legal Tender Notes [3]	Clearing-house exchanges	Fractional Currency	Internal Revenue Stamps	Checks & Other Cash Items	Miscellaneous [4]	Due from U.S. Treasury [5]	Total Assets
9 Mar	1897	1,898.009	231.611	10.310	16.178	212.530	106.646	166.834	258.430	233.949	118.638	74.831	1.020	0.000	11.635	36.429	68.988	3,446.039
14 May	1897	1,934.152	229.420	10.083	16.533	219.282	107.204	176.912	251.949	236.076	120.555	84.351	0.967	0.000	12.000	37.104	55.825	3,492.412
23 Jul	1897	1,977.554	228.439	10.004	16.724	221.671	107.561	169.863	275.755	240.923	126.511	89.457	0.982	0.000	12.018	38.042	47.905	3,563.408
5 Oct	1897	2,066.776	227.484	10.022	17.003	224.319	108.417	197.391	297.018	239.388	107.220	112.306	0.963	0.000	15.535	37.837	43.456	3,705.134
15 Dec	1897	2,100.350	222.021	9.762	45.367	232.499	109.107	216.838	309.570	252.164	112.565	118.416	0.925	0.000	14.933	37.415	47.283	3,829.214
18 Feb	1898	2,152.172	212.425	9.316	34.761	243.531	109.014	218.902	360.277	271.378	120.265	113.591	1.041	0.000	13.100	36.390	50.785	3,946.947
5 May	1898	2,109.773	216.158	9.521	28.631	252.390	109.789	197.841	300.962	317.183	119.059	126.235	1.057	0.000	16.719	39.610	25.039	3,869.967
14 Jul	1898	2,163.682	218.106	9.601	53.519	264.421	109.495	204.388	320.015	335.677	114.915	94.276	1.094	0.000	17.309	39.759	31.418	3,977.675
20 Sep	1898	2,172.520	224.629	9.795	83.926	285.813	109.871	205.453	320.002	293.874	110.038	110.287	1.024	0.000	16.829	38.621	20.830	4,003.511
1 Dec	1898	2,237.069	238.586	10.484	95.528	288.359	110.156	250.134	359.371	328.601	117.846	194.981	1.017	0.000	19.223	41.952	20.087	4,313.395
4 Feb	1899	2,318.584	235.209	10.287	89.100	301.733	109.757	263.466	432.036	371.843	116.003	75.673	1.108	0.000	17.057	39.712	22.315	4,403.883
5 Apr	1899	2,421.357	233.731	10.307	89.201	322.436	109.907	271.554	412.677	364.163	110.235	212.818	1.110	0.000	18.807	39.281	21.556	4,639.138
30 Jun	1899	2,507.955	228.870	10.096	78.497	326.460	109.383	280.508	406.668	356.822	116.338	203.004	1.108	0.000	25.632	37.273	20.220	4,708.834
7 Sep	1899	2,515.983	229.640	10.116	80.977	339.765	109.319	271.720	414.127	338.571	111.215	154.801	1.121	0.000	17.415	37.704	17.881	4,650.355
2 Dec	1899	2,513.501	234.403	10.299	81.266	343.208	109.109	258.766	345.556	314.825	101.676	90.515	1.013	0.000	21.432	34.897	14.876	4,475.344
13 Feb	1900	2,505.083	236.284	10.306	111.516	346.080	108.222	254.778	375.117	339.578	122.466	186.012	1.226	0.000	22.517	39.628	16.096	4,674.911
26 Apr	1900	2,585.100	265.341	11.942	112.252	356.772	107.200	258.584	404.957	358.051	139.838	147.355	1.220	1.346	16.170	37.434	8.396	4,811.956
29 Jun	1900	2,644.237	282.424	13.326	107.349	373.903	107.404	277.962	412.781	356.014	143.757	159.189	1.230	1.425	21.136	35.954	6.075	4,944.166
5 Sep	1900	2,709.890	294.890	14.244	102.811	378.303	107.212	285.646	450.714	373.328	145.046	124.517	1.241	1.471	19.749	35.368	3.705	5,048.138
13 Dec	1900	2,748.217	306.622	14.833	101.415	383.505	108.382	318.260	417.723	359.672	141.285	183.476	1.258	1.448	19.343	33.192	3.461	5,142.090

1. Source: Annual Report, Comptroller of the Currency, 1914, Vol. 2, Table 56 (p. 220 ff)
2. Includes overdrafts
3. These are the U. S. Notes (greenbacks).
4. Includes premiums on bonds and bills of other banks.
5. Includes certificates of deposits and other deposits with the U. S. Treasury.

Figure 16.3-20: National Bank System Assets, 1897-1900

Day	Year	Number of Banks	Paid-in Capital	Other Liabilities [2]	Due to Other Banks	Due to Reserve Agents	U. S. Deposits [3]	Individual and Other Deposits	National Bank Notes in Circulation	State Bank Notes in Circulation	Bills & Notes Rediscounted	Total Liabilities
9 Mar	1897	3,534	642.424	348.190	563.438	0.000	15.330	1,669.220	202.655	0.060	4.721	3,446.039
14 May	1897	3,614	637.002	349.719	558.220	0.000	15.629	1,728.084	198.278	0.060	5.419	3,492.412
23 Jul	1897	3,610	632.153	345.287	596.995	0.000	16.391	1,770.481	196.591	0.060	5.450	3,563.408
5 Oct	1897	3,610	631.488	352.259	645.708	0.000	16.142	1,853.349	198.921	0.060	7.206	3,705.134
15 Dec	1897	3,607	629.655	364.032	677.939	0.000	43.951	1,916.630	193.784	0.060	3.162	3,829.214
18 Feb	1898	3,594	628.890	352.166	764.952	0.000	31.434	1,982.661	184.106	0.056	2.681	3,946.947
5 May	1898	3,586	624.472	356.366	669.848	0.000	27.025	1,999.308	188.425	0.056	4.468	3,869.967
14 Jul	1898	3,582	622.017	364.328	719.817	0.000	52.869	2,023.357	189.866	0.056	5.365	3,977.675
20 Sep	1898	3,585	621.518	376.414	698.335	0.000	75.165	2,031.455	194.484	0.056	6.085	4,003.511
1 Dec	1898	3,590	620.516	367.469	794.954	0.000	93.905	2,225.270	207.093	0.055	4.132	4,313.395
4 Feb	1899	3,579	608.301	358.223	894.049	19.051	86.623	2,232.193	203.636	0.053	1.753	4,403.883
5 Apr	1899	3,583	607.263	369.628	911.998	20.351	87.173	2,437.223	203.829	0.053	1.620	4,639.138
30 Jun	1899	3,583	604.865	371.527	910.838	21.566	76.313	2,522.158	199.358	0.053	2.155	4,708.834
7 Sep	1899	3,595	605.773	381.344	909.427	19.440	78.880	2,450.726	200.346	0.053	4.366	4,650.355
2 Dec	1899	3,602	606.725	401.686	796.317	0.000	80.025	2,380.610	204.925	0.053	5.001	4,475.344
13 Feb	1900	3,604	613.084	406.180	855.873	0.000	109.266	2,481.847	204.913	0.053	3.695	4,674.911
26 Apr	1900	3,631	617.051	421.640	953.573	21.898	108.467	2,449.213	236.250	0.053	3.811	4,811.956
29 Jun	1900	3,732	621.536	433.165	1,032.977	29.927	98.872	2,458.093	265.303	0.053	4.239	4,944.166
5 Sep	1900	3,871	630.299	429.205	1,069.357	27.209	93.818	2,508.249	283.949	0.052	6.001	5,048.138
13 Dec	1900	3,942	632.353	442.831	1,005.734	38.902	94.378	2,623.998	298.917	0.052	4.925	5,142.090

(Title row: National Banking System Liabilities, 1897-1900 (millions USD) [1])

1. Source: Annual Report, Comptroller of the Currency, 1914, Vol. 2, Table 56 (p. 220 ff)
2. Includes surplus fund, undivided profits, unpaid dividends, bills payable, reserved for taxes, and miscellaneous.
3. Includes deposits of U. S. disbursing officers.

Figure 16.3-21: National Bank System Liabilities, 1897-1900

| | | | U. S. Obligations Deposited with Treasury as Security for: | | | Investments | | Balances | Lawful Money for Reserves | | | | | | | Other Assets | | | |
| | | | Circulation | | Deposit | | | | | | | | | | | | | | |
Day	Year	Loans & Discounts [2]	U. S. Bonds	5% Redemption Fund with Treasury	U. S and other bonds [3]	U. S. Bonds, Other Bonds, and Stocks	Real Estate	Due from National and State Banks	Due from Reserve Agents	Specie	Legal Tender Notes [4]	Clearing-house exchanges	Fractional Currency	Internal Revenue Stamps	Checks & Other Cash Items	Miscellaneous [5]	Due from U. S. Treasury [6]	Total Assets
5 Feb	1901	2,851.082	317.916	15.423	101.750	402.512	107.961	318.976	472.178	399.956	152.386	238.846	1.376	1.273	18.611	33.216	2.444	5,435.906
24 Apr	1901	2,939.563	323.512	15.811	102.111	431.365	108.994	327.572	480.032	386.774	159.324	290.162	1.346	1.117	21.694	34.986	6.430	5,630.794
15 Jul	1901	2,981.054	326.971	15.934	105.327	444.383	108.539	334.150	454.077	371.086	164.930	300.690	1.312	0.681	25.214	34.147	7.416	5,675.910
30 Sep	1901	3,051.702	329.373	16.105	107.107	456.511	109.241	328.394	456.639	376.682	151.019	236.656	1.315	0.600	26.707	33.698	13.599	5,695.347
10 Dec	1901	3,081.612	324.507	2.344	110.258	459.534	110.054	351.516	432.959	369.652	151.118	253.420	1.320	0.553	22.625	35.321	15.937	5,722.731
25 Feb	1902	3,160.942	320.978	15.628	114.055	468.827	110.128	344.645	490.304	407.082	154.683	196.618	1.476	0.472	20.437	34.223	2.550	5,843.049
30 Apr	1902	3,199.969	316.271	15.245	120.561	475.121	112.601	339.389	467.418	398.761	159.484	290.652	1.490	0.416	26.237	35.931	2.590	5,962.135
16 Jul	1902	3,246.517	316.139	15.376	124.408	492.853	113.330	347.027	471.696	404.764	164.854	247.113	1.498	0.359	22.306	37.701	2.814	6,008.755
15 Sep	1902	3,314.239	324.254	15.800	124.685	501.118	114.211	354.610	465.641	366.236	141.758	327.763	1.378	0.287	24.501	35.080	2.369	6,113.929
25 Nov	1902	3,346.671	341.329	16.662	151.082	497.286	116.609	364.126	436.821	391.282	142.310	236.990	1.407	0.211	21.332	36.952	3.022	6,104.092
6 Feb	1903	3,386.619	342.071	16.661	152.004	520.675	121.409	364.454	479.725	417.572	153.026	214.496	1.633	0.149	23.846	37.583	2.848	6,234.773
9 Apr	1903	3,433.138	343.119	16.581	152.349	527.454	122.949	357.889	454.803	389.082	147.133	201.934	1.579	0.097	22.328	39.399	2.958	6,212.792
9 Jun	1903	3,442.304	368.941	17.804	152.589	530.004	124.090	364.121	437.792	388.616	163.593	227.580	1.611	0.064	22.126	41.864	3.834	6,286.935
9 Sep	1903	3,508.639	381.569	18.605	158.940	522.984	128.536	365.234	454.908	397.556	156.750	147.696	1.597	0.042	23.436	41.201	2.737	6,310.430
17 Nov	1903	3,476.485	380.645	18.497	171.606	520.110	130.579	397.164	437.180	378.290	142.325	179.111	1.597	0.030	24.527	41.323	2.717	6,302.187
22 Jan	1904	3,511.597	387.499	18.859	170.903	538.319	132.795	398.707	494.706	453.192	161.435	234.896	1.840	0.022	22.357	44.815	4.936	6,576.878
28 Mar	1904	3,575.725	394.118	19.073	178.526	546.003	134.515	384.237	503.985	464.417	153.098	181.824	1.709	0.018	23.624	41.903	3.218	6,605.996
9 Jun	1904	3,621.814	409.977	19.894	121.158	583.788	137.830	381.745	498.104	488.664	169.729	147.705	1.809	0.015	24.445	45.231	4.081	6,655.989
6 Sep	1904	3,757.929	418.409	20.308	120.261	602.452	140.084	399.699	562.610	504.749	156.798	213.167	1.793	0.010	30.534	43.038	3.246	6,975.087
10 Nov	1904	3,827.581	425.759	20.706	114.324	610.757	142.758	450.377	543.145	484.188	157.943	341.998	1.759	0.007	29.204	43.263	3.222	7,196.992

1. Source: Annual Report, Comptroller of the Currency, 1914, Vol. 2, Table 56 (p. 220 ff)
2. Includes overdrafts
3. Bonds other than U. S. obligations were authorized as security vs. deposits in 1902.
4. These are the U. S. Notes (greenbacks).
5. Includes premiums on bonds and bills of other banks.
6. Includes certificates of deposits and other deposits with the U. S. Treasury.

Figure 16.3-22: National Bank System Assets, 1901-1904

National Banking System Liabilities, 1901-1904 (millions USD) [1]

Day	Year	Number of Banks	Paid-in Capital	Other Liabilities [2]	Due to Other Banks	Due to Reserve Agents	U. S. Deposits [3]	Individual and Other Deposits	National Bank Notes in Circulation	State Bank Notes in Circulation	Bills & Notes Rediscounted & Bonds [4]	Total Liabilities
5 Feb	1901	3,999	634.697	434.185	1,176.380	28.685	95.033	2,753.970	309.466	0.052	3.439	5,435.906
24 Apr	1901	4,064	640.779	452.191	1,196.768	30.100	96.002	2,893.665	317.202	0.052	4.035	5,630.794
15 Jul	1901	4,165	645.719	457.504	1,171.190	35.626	99.072	2,941.837	319.009	0.052	5.900	5,675.910
30 Sep	1901	4,221	655.342	475.221	1,152.019	33.266	106.860	2,937.753	323.864	0.052	10.971	5,695.347
10 Dec	1901	4,291	665.341	489.122	1,136.552	32.086	109.749	2,964.418	319.437	0.052	5.974	5,722.731
25 Feb	1902	4,357	667.381	482.633	1,248.431	30.507	112.297	2,982.489	314.439	0.052	4.820	5,843.049
30 Apr	1902	4,423	671.176	495.231	1,216.529	32.193	120.105	3,111.690	309.782	0.052	5.378	5,962.135
16 Jul	1902	4,535	701.991	524.897	1,209.057	33.842	123.966	3,098.876	309.337	0.043	6.746	6,008.755
15 Sep	1902	4,601	705.535	547.759	1,169.328	31.014	123.944	3,209.274	317.992	0.043	9.041	6,113.929
25 Nov	1902	4,666	714.616	551.442	1,118.157	36.736	146.818	3,152.879	336.506	0.043	46.895	6,104.092
6 Feb	1903	4,766	731.275	540.305	1,241.471	30.795	147.835	3,159.535	335.226	0.043	48.288	6,234.773
9 Apr	1903	4,845	734.903	559.019	1,189.434	28.490	148.028	3,168.275	335.094	0.043	49.507	6,212.792
9 Jun	1903	4,939	743.506	575.211	1,178.801	33.445	147.102	3,200.994	359.261	0.043	48.572	6,286.935
9 Sep	1903	5,042	753.723	594.218	1,197.231	29.252	149.615	3,156.333	375.038	0.043	54.978	6,310.430
17 Nov	1903	5,118	758.315	608.709	1,126.932	36.828	162.513	3,176.202	376.239	0.043	56.408	6,302.187
22 Jan	1904	5,180	765.862	590.285	1,288.679	34.236	163.295	3,300.620	380.992	0.043	52.867	6,576.878
28 Mar	1904	5,232	765.975	599.128	1,350.481	32.404	160.233	3,254.471	385.908	0.043	57.353	6,605.996
9 Jun	1904	5,331	767.378	610.267	1,378.635	33.515	110.343	3,312.440	399.584	0.043	43.784	6,655.989
6 Sep	1904	5,412	770.778	616.633	1,529.916	31.336	110.767	3,458.217	411.231	0.043	46.166	6,975.087
10 Nov	1904	5,477	776.089	629.013	1,473.838	38.793	110.303	3,707.707	419.120	0.043	42.087	7,196.992

1. Source: Annual Report, Comptroller of the Currency, 1914, Vol. 2, Table 56 (p. 220 ff)
2. Includes surplus fund, undivided profits, unpaid dividends, bills payable, reserved for taxes, and miscellaneous.
3. Includes deposits of U. S. disbursing officers.
4. Includes bills and notes rediscounted and bonds borrowed (1902-1914).

Figure 16.3-23: National Bank System Liabilities, 1901-1904

| | | | U.S. Obligations Deposited with Treasury as Security for: | | | Investments | | Balances | Lawful Money for Reserves | | | | | | Other Assets | | | |
| | | | Circulation | | Deposit | | | | | | | | | | | | | |
Day	Year	Loans & Discounts [2]	U.S. Bonds	5% Redemption Fund with Treasury	U.S and other bonds [3]	U.S. Bonds, Other Bonds, and Stocks	Real Estate	Due from National and State Banks	Due from Reserve Agents	Specie	Legal Tender Notes [4]	C.H. exchanges & loan certificates [5]	Frac-tional Currency	Internal Revenue Stamps	Checks & Other Cash Items	Miscel-laneous [6]	Due from U.S. Treasury [7]	Total Assets
11 Jan	1905	3,771.916	431.777	21.007	110.767	620.226	144.608	449.371	542.194	491.849	178.123	268.375	1.938	0.000	31.443	48.250	5.960	7,117.801
14 Mar	1905	3,888.234	440.801	21.461	100.205	660.338	148.664	452.623	594.094	483.249	157.905	287.122	1.854	0.000	25.261	42.546	3.772	7,308.128
29 May	1905	3,929.538	457.503	22.209	81.816	685.654	150.161	444.532	562.495	479.635	169.630	267.856	1.799	0.000	28.112	43.315	3.553	7,327.806
25 Aug	1905	4,028.415	477.593	23.280	68.156	679.219	152.914	434.210	605.464	495.479	170.074	265.081	1.860	0.000	23.032	43.558	4.017	7,472.351
9 Nov	1905	4,071.209	493.679	24.048	65.183	668.481	156.581	473.416	569.122	460.934	161.158	340.428	1.817	0.000	28.261	44.911	3.927	7,563.156
29 Jan	1906	4,118.298	505.724	24.722	64.998	661.796	159.226	465.845	598.697	492.568	175.735	421.600	2.103	0.000	30.036	43.509	4.970	7,769.827
6 Apr	1906	4,175.980	511.842	24.988	76.117	668.319	160.608	447.708	588.640	459.179	161.315	320.559	2.119	0.000	27.721	41.609	3.913	7,670.618
18 Jun	1906	4,236.925	516.872	25.247	93.990	659.330	163.097	457.934	587.669	485.987	165.246	313.378	1.993	0.000	31.214	41.456	3.891	7,784.228
4 Sep	1906	4,331.459	524.037	25.527	109.850	682.511	163.978	457.649	616.148	464.437	161.575	395.340	1.992	0.000	36.449	42.000	3.068	8,016.021
12 Nov	1906	4,419.780	544.202	26.546	147.391	672.699	166.677	534.404	605.237	482.276	152.274	376.672	1.995	0.000	37.517	42.419	3.788	8,213.878
26 Jan	1907	4,505.184	551.887	26.942	165.492	665.643	172.198	503.372	662.435	521.723	173.781	128.250	2.249	0.000	28.897	41.780	4.979	8,154.812
22 Mar	1907	4,572.607	548.788	26.916	158.284	690.277	174.204	495.929	624.972	500.086	156.135	262.867	2.241	0.000	28.477	41.427	5.080	8,288.290
20 May	1907	4,664.014	554.029	27.097	191.240	685.940	177.274	501.644	628.784	530.714	160.877	273.101	2.203	0.000	32.497	42.509	4.577	8,476.501
22 Aug	1907	4,709.027	557.278	27.306	163.827	707.743	181.088	457.592	614.496	531.108	170.516	190.602	2.315	0.000	26.905	45.794	4.732	8,390.328
3 Dec	1907	4,622.882	619.330	28.490	257.849	710.232	187.571	401.317	523.828	509.685	151.099	298.514	2.401	0.000	36.305	56.545	1.941	8,407.988

1. Source: Annual Report, Comptroller of the Currency, 1914, Vol. 2, Table 56 (p. 220 ff)
2. Includes overdrafts
3. Bonds other than U.S. obligations were authorized as security vs. deposits in 1902.
4. These are the U.S. Notes (greenbacks).
5. Clearinghouse certificates used in conjunction with exchanges in 1907 and 1908.
6. Includes premiums on bonds and bills of other banks.
7. Includes certificates of deposits and other deposits with the U.S. Treasury.

Figure 16.3-24: National Bank System Assets, 1905-1907

National Banking System Liabilities, 1905-1907 (millions USD) [1]

Day	Year	Number of Banks	Paid-in Capital	Other Liabilities [2]	Due to Other Banks	Due to Reserve Agents	U.S. Deposits [3]	Individual and Other Deposits	National Bank Notes in Circula-tion	State Bank Notes in Circula-tion	Bills & Notes Redis-counted & Bonds [4]	Total Liabilities
11 Jan	1905	5,528	776.916	622.099	1,493.043	41.565	106.394	3,612.500	424.345	0.040	40.898	7,117.801
14 Mar	1905	5,587	782.488	627.408	1,517.711	37.916	93.222	3,777.474	430.955	0.040	40.912	7,308.128
29 May	1905	5,668	791.567	644.149	1,509.596	37.573	75.298	3,783.658	445.456	0.031	40.477	7,327.806
25 Aug	1905	5,757	799.870	650.423	1,590.515	34.363	62.090	3,820.682	468.980	0.031	45.397	7,472.351
9 Nov	1905	5,833	808.329	670.470	1,464.909	39.127	61.286	3,989.523	485.522	0.031	43.959	7,563.156
29 Jan	1906	5,911	814.988	668.198	1,558.178	37.317	62.017	4,088.420	498.238	0.031	42.440	7,769.827
6 Apr	1906	5,975	819.307	686.221	1,520.457	36.800	73.523	3,978.468	505.457	0.031	50.353	7,670.618
18 Jun	1906	6,053	826.130	706.545	1,509.148	36.120	89.910	4,055.874	510.861	0.031	49.611	7,784.228
4 Sep	1906	6,137	835.067	719.705	1,558.187	30.814	107.832	4,199.938	517.965	0.031	46.482	8,016.021
12 Nov	1906	6,199	847.515	733.378	1,555.937	44.007	140.402	4,289.774	536.110	0.030	66.726	8,213.878
26 Jan	1907	6,288	860.931	723.748	1,638.461	38.466	157.362	4,115.650	545.482	0.030	74.682	8,154.812
22 Mar	1907	6,344	873.670	743.287	1,598.116	39.043	153.359	4,269.512	543.320	0.030	67.954	8,288.290
20 May	1907	6,429	883.691	763.340	1,645.210	40.330	180.688	4,322.880	547.919	0.030	92.413	8,476.501
22 Aug	1907	6,544	896.451	791.920	1,557.353	38.140	161.038	4,319.035	551.949	0.030	74.410	8,390.328
3 Dec	1907	6,625	901.682	844.137	1,351.210	36.676	234.729	4,176.874	601.806	0.030	260.844	8,407.988

1. Source: Annual Report, Comptroller of the Currency, 1914, Vol. 2, Table 56 (p. 220 ff)
2. Includes surplus fund, undivided profits, unpaid dividends, bills payable, reserved for taxes, and miscellaneous.
3. Includes deposits of U.S. disbursing officers.
4. Includes bills and notes rediscounted and bonds borrowed (1902-1914).

Figure 16.3-25: National Bank System Liabilities, 1905-1907

| | | | U. S. Obligations Deposited with Treasury as Security for: | | | Investments | Balances | | Lawful Money for Reserves | | | | | | Other Assets | | | |
| | | | Circulation | | Deposit | | | | | | | | | | | | | |
Day	Year	Loans & Discounts [2]	U. S. Bonds	5% Redemption Fund with Treasury	U.S and other bonds [3]	U. S. Bonds, Other Bonds, and Stocks	Real Estate	Due from National and State Banks	Due from Reserve Agents	Specie	Legal Tender Notes [4]	C. H. exchanges & loan certificates [5]	Fractional Currency	Internal Revenue Stamps	Checks & Other Cash Items	Miscellaneous [6]	Due from U. S. Treasury [7]	Total Assets
14 Feb	1908	4,451.979	636.283	30.612	256.201	720.931	189.439	436.322	598.537	614.385	174.011	196.042	2.881	0.000	30.228	54.252	4.771	8,396.872
14 May	1908	4,551.683	624.919	30.350	206.601	740.783	194.318	449.052	612.969	677.142	184.184	233.481	2.813	0.000	25.358	53.832	7.138	8,594.623
15 Jul	1908	4,640.381	624.705	30.512	157.214	774.545	198.279	464.071	640.388	656.458	192.561	244.556	2.714	0.000	26.908	53.732	7.042	8,714.064
23 Sep	1908	4,781.522	628.073	30.739	138.783	807.760	203.431	491.395	711.949	680.186	188.239	276.557	2.684	0.000	25.430	54.344	6.169	9,027.260
27 Nov	1908	4,879.279	614.221	29.809	134.531	809.568	207.671	549.533	701.705	656.529	188.231	330.711	2.593	0.000	32.476	54.139	6.080	9,197.076
5 Feb	1909	4,869.844	630.763	29.985	116.209	853.913	209.954	530.944	750.598	664.583	195.534	274.196	2.903	0.000	26.886	56.463	8.421	9,221.194
28 Apr	1909	4,987.695	649.390	31.329	78.915	885.406	215.967	505.544	727.012	679.659	198.898	303.590	2.807	0.000	34.743	60.758	7.172	9,368.884
23 Jun	1909	5,061.199	655.258	31.502	81.569	896.694	218.959	522.531	720.198	694.141	191.775	303.697	2.716	0.000	25.950	58.634	6.911	9,471.733
1 Sep	1909	5,158.435	668.680	32.489	57.214	921.534	221.282	507.890	719.351	666.398	187.674	329.726	2.757	0.000	38.287	54.926	7.312	9,573.954
16 Nov	1909	5,190.695	676.149	32.746	53.936	888.928	226.076	595.491	689.514	628.835	176.026	337.905	2.693	0.000	32.752	53.515	6.134	9,591.395
31 Jan	1910	5,263.531	678.232	32.493	51.350	861.666	229.910	557.041	707.434	660.679	172.400	407.440	2.965	0.000	44.185	52.251	8.943	9,730.519
29 Mar	1910	5,464.008	680.447	32.485	49.819	861.484	233.708	557.747	727.763	661.800	173.096	305.632	2.855	0.000	28.465	56.021	6.596	9,841.924
30 Jun	1910	5,455.903	683.990	32.984	54.423	862.323	236.463	541.255	660.352	644.344	176.429	428.654	2.936	0.000	54.151	52.969	9.450	9,896.625
1 Sep	1910	5,496.702	685.692	33.121	51.785	868.170	236.814	526.209	688.716	672.627	179.058	284.963	2.907	0.000	39.331	52.440	7.647	9,826.181
10 Nov	1910	5,497.711	690.057	33.439	51.323	866.083	244.498	630.935	686.469	646.146	169.924	339.861	2.843	0.000	35.988	54.676	6.524	9,956.477
7 Jan	1911	5,443.149	691.774	33.620	49.924	893.808	245.222	633.484	717.463	667.871	168.396	163.783	3.129	0.000	40.816	55.559	12.485	9,820.484
7 Mar	1911	5,588.091	692.843	33.024	49.445	936.597	248.206	625.064	814.271	735.762	172.275	248.023	3.156	0.000	31.092	55.627	7.300	10,240.774
7 Jun	1911	5,634.236	694.215	33.643	52.937	1,005.329	253.009	611.100	765.686	761.112	185.220	286.322	3.139	0.000	31.155	58.499	7.448	10,383.049
1 Sep	1911	5,690.562	707.204	34.374	57.803	1,034.866	256.417	561.781	744.614	711.522	183.953	298.180	3.266	0.000	35.323	51.422	8.151	10,379.439
5 Dec	1911	5,695.060	713.620	34.503	70.642	1,040.373	257.254	652.594	751.993	681.550	181.245	263.726	3.211	0.000	34.648	55.187	7.851	10,443.457

National Banking System Assets, 1908-1911 (millions USD) [1]

1. Source: Annual Report, Comptroller of the Currency, 1914, Vol. 2, Table 56 (p. 220 ff)
2. Includes overdrafts
3. Bonds other than U. S. obligations were authorized as security vs. deposits in 1902.
4. These are the U. S. Notes (greenbacks).
5. Clearinghouse certificates used in conjunction with exchanges in 1907 and 1908.
6. Includes premiums on bonds and bills of other banks.
7. Includes certificates of deposits and other deposits with the U. S. Treasury.

Figure 16.3-26: National Bank System Assets, 1908-1911

Day	Year	Number of Banks	Paid-in Capital	Other Liabilities [2]	Due to Other Banks	Due to Reserve Agents	U. S. Deposits [3]	Individual and Other Deposits	National Bank Notes in Circulation	State Bank Notes in Circulation	Bills & Notes Rediscounted & Bonds [4]	Total Liabilities
14 Feb	1908	6,698	905.550	790.368	1,551.141	33.285	232.734	4,105.814	627.642	0.030	150.307	8,396.872
14 May	1908	6,778	912.362	795.673	1,656.532	35.890	181.657	4,312.657	614.089	0.030	85.733	8,594.623
15 Jul	1908	6,824	919.101	791.789	1,783.244	39.610	130.266	4,374.551	613.664	0.030	61.810	8,714.064
23 Sep	1908	6,853	921.463	816.937	1,903.989	37.676	126.372	4,548.135	613.726	0.030	58.932	9,027.260
27 Nov	1908	6,865	921.019	821.946	1,919.884	38.947	124.429	4,720.285	599.319	0.030	51.216	9,197.076
5 Feb	1909	6,887	927.722	800.066	1,996.416	38.754	99.670	4,699.683	615.316	0.030	43.538	9,221.194
28 Apr	1909	6,893	933.980	824.932	1,995.496	41.257	70.402	4,826.060	636.368	0.030	40.359	9,368.884
23 Jun	1909	6,926	937.004	842.429	1,993.855	40.808	74.485	4,898.577	641.312	0.030	43.232	9,471.733
1 Sep	1909	6,977	944.642	846.925	1,980.175	38.639	48.705	5,009.893	658.040	0.030	46.905	9,573.954
16 Nov	1909	7,006	953.963	869.163	1,838.116	48.144	49.068	5,120.443	668.394	0.030	44.072	9,591.395
31 Jan	1910	7,043	960.125	855.989	1,925.876	40.719	48.134	5,190.835	667.501	0.030	**41.309**	9,730.519
29 Mar	1910	7,082	972.820	893.604	1,949.118	38.882	47.916	5,227.852	669.182	0.030	42.519	9,841.924
30 Jun	1910	7,145	989.567	939.865	1,858.895	41.240	54.541	5,287.216	675.633	0.030	49.636	9,896.625
1 Sep	1910	7,173	1,002.735	955.644	1,906.044	37.647	50.161	5,145.658	674.822	0.028	53.442	9,826.181
10 Nov	1910	7,264	1,004.288	963.944	1,864.473	41.888	48.422	5,304.788	680.440	0.028	48.206	9,956.477
7 Jan	1911	7,218	1,007.335	933.858	1,949.011	42.177	46.718	5,113.222	684.136	0.028	43.999	9,820.484
7 Mar	1911	7,216	1,011.570	934.034	2,185.950	38.770	45.524	5,304.624	680.727	0.028	39.548	10,240.774
7 Jun	1911	7,277	1,019.633	961.592	2,108.583	38.858	48.456	5,477.991	681.741	0.028	46.167	10,383.049
1 Sep	1911	7,301	1,025.441	979.229	2,050.662	37.525	48.344	5,489.995	696.982	0.028	51.233	10,379.439
5 Dec	1911	7,328	1,026.441	994.999	2,038.466	46.640	53.056	5,536.042	702.647	0.028	45.138	10,443.457

National Banking System Liabilities, 1908-1911 (millions USD) [1]

1. Source: Annual Report, Comptroller of the Currency, 1914, Vol. 2, Table 56 (p. 220 ff)
2. Includes surplus fund, undivided profits, unpaid dividends, bills payable, reserved for taxes, and miscellaneous.
3. Includes deposits of U. S. disbursing officers.
4. Includes bills and notes rediscounted and bonds borrowed (1902-1914).

Figure 16.3-27: National Bank System Liabilities, 1908-1911

| | | | U. S. Obligations Deposited with Treasury as Security for: | | | Investments | | Balances | Lawful Money for Reserves | | | | | | | Other Assets | | | |
| | | | Circulation | | Deposit | | | | | | | | | | | | | | |
Day	Year	Loans & Discounts [2]	U.S. and Misc. Bonds [3]	5% Redemption Fund with Treasury	U.S and other bonds [4]	U.S. Bonds, Other Bonds, and Stocks	Real Estate	Due from National and State Banks	Due from Reserve Agents	Specie	Legal Tender Notes [5]	Clearinghouse exchanges	Fractional Currency	Internal Revenue Stamps	Checks & Other Cash Items	Miscellaneous [6]	Due from U.S. Treasury [7]	Total Assets
20 Feb	1912	5,834.416	718.697	34.586	72.535	1,041.491	261.116	698.841	859.562	769.029	181.468	245.106	3.518	0.000	28.181	56.579	7.303	10,812.428
18 Apr	1912	5,901.986	719.571	34.643	75.308	1,038.373	264.502	664.054	809.940	743.868	187.821	255.123	3.452	0.000	27.225	56.699	9.585	10,792.149
14 Jun	1912	5,973.754	721.396	34.488	77.437	1,054.992	266.625	645.183	778.908	756.763	188.440	266.040	3.376	0.000	29.175	55.020	10.166	10,861.764
4 Sep	1912	6,061.009	724.086	35.028	78.708	1,047.791	268.505	640.917	812.152	713.461	182.490	296.017	3.300	0.000	37.343	55.685	6.908	10,963.401
26 Nov	1912	6,085.475	728.483	35.486	79.195	1,044.679	274.876	695.471	786.191	682.321	176.778	278.672	3.300	0.000	34.101	53.178	7.583	10,965.789
4 Feb	1913	6,147.336	730.755	34.989	82.149	1,050.079	278.700	682.791	850.478	749.732	183.685	288.820	3.783	0.000	36.722	56.470	9.110	11,185.599
4 Apr	1913	6,198.174	730.424	35.020	85.123	1,059.381	280.504	646.069	808.365	712.906	175.377	249.894	3.895	0.000	32.681	54.766	9.395	11,081.974
4 Jun	1913	6,162.034	735.227	35.395	90.660	1,056.926	280.222	634.011	762.177	724.075	189.908	257.560	3.580	0.000	37.092	58.415	9.637	11,036.920
9 Aug	1913	6,186.934	735.809	35.597	103.178	1,046.942	283.569	601.136	769.214	728.267	170.902	123.507	3.650	0.000	29.860	49.243	9.043	10,876.852
21 Oct	1913	6,288.339	737.481	35.809	118.727	1,045.171	286.061	748.200	791.671	710.894	178.738	258.499	3.868	0.000	34.817	54.140	9.143	11,301.558
13 Jan	1914	6,197.243	736.601	35.372	118.221	1,025.608	289.621	733.150	802.787	780.490	201.429	263.296	3.960	0.000	37.244	56.869	14.464	11,296.355
4 Mar	1914	6,378.872	733.564	35.402	109.617	1,032.803	291.501	744.504	881.703	792.694	175.373	282.344	3.965	0.000	40.184	53.037	8.934	11,564.497
30 Jun	1914	6,445.555	734.897	35.510	105.187	1,070.746	307.085	613.676	777.499	791.585	177.490	309.321	3.829	0.000	48.560	53.718	7.533	11,482.191
12 Sep	1914	6,417.910	1,129.349	44.324	120.684	990.180	310.449	602.345	673.959	746.199	157.508	171.406	3.592	0.000	34.205	77.468	3.952	11,483.529

National Banking System Assets, 1912-1914 (millions USD) [1]

1. Source: Annual Report, Comptroller of the Currency, 1914, Vol. 2, Table 56 (p. 220 ff)
2. Includes overdrafts
3. Securities other than US bonds used as security vs. circulation 12 Sep 1914 ($392.663 M)
4. Bonds other than U. S. obligations were authorized as security vs. deposits in 1902.
5. These are the U. S. Notes (greenbacks).
6. Includes premiums on bonds and bills of other banks.
7. Includes certificates of deposits and other deposits with the U. S. Treasury.

Figure 16.3-28: National Bank System Assets, 1912-1914

Day	Year	Number of Banks	Paid-in Capital	Other Liabilities [2]	Due to Other Banks	Due to Reserve Agents	U.S. Deposits [3]	Individual and Other Deposits [4]	National Bank Notes in Circulation	State Bank Notes in Circulation	Bills & Notes Rediscounted & Bonds [5]	Total Liabilities
20 Feb	1912	7,339	1,031.193	969.579	2,336.811	44.403	54.745	5,630.559	704.226	0.028	40.884	10,812.428
18 Apr	1912	7,355	1,036.125	990.424	2,204.950	43.268	53.938	5,712.051	706.979	0.028	44.387	10,792.149
14 Jun	1912	7,372	1,033.571	1,010.985	2,134.451	43.712	58.946	5,825.461	708.691	0.028	45.920	10,861.764
4 Sep	1912	7,397	1,046.013	1,021.522	2,137.943	39.546	59.227	5,891.670	713.823	0.028	53.629	10,963.401
26 Nov	1912	7,420	1,045.093	1,041.312	2,058.006	43.799	46.287	5,960.210	721.502	0.028	49.551	10,965.789
4 Feb	1913	7,425	1,048.899	1,012.574	2,266.435	44.155	46.025	6,002.441	717.468	0.028	47.575	11,185.599
4 Apr	1913	7,440	1,052.266	1,035.179	2,151.555	40.790	46.203	5,986.475	718.977	0.028	50.503	11,081.974
4 Jun	1913	7,473	1,056.920	1,058.156	2,074.666	45.886	49.725	5,972.123	722.125	0.022	57.296	11,036.920
9 Aug	1913	7,488	1,056.346	1,087.493	2,069.027	39.523	57.304	5,781.129	724.460	0.028	61.542	10,876.852
21 Oct	1913	7,509	1,059.403	1,103.720	2,128.770	52.266	90.570	6,073.178	727.079	0.028	66.544	11,301.558
13 Jan	1914	7,493	1,057.676	1,065.841	2,166.872	43.631	84.298	6,094.308	725.326	0.028	58.375	11,296.355
4 Mar	1914	7,493	1,056.482	1,057.730	2,428.504	43.938	66.383	6,134.897	720.640	0.028	55.896	11,564.497
30 Jun	1914	7,525	1,058.192	1,099.402	2,143.242	42.661	66.655	6,292.533	722.555	0.028	56.924	11,482.191
12 Sep	1914	7,538	1,060.332	1,151.550	1,910.028	39.871	69.712	6,166.708	918.270	0.028	167.031	11,483.529

National Banking System Liabilities, 1912-1914 (millions USD) [1]

1. Source: Annual Report, Comptroller of the Currency, 1914, Vol. 2, Table 56 (p. 220 ff)
2. Includes surplus fund, undivided profits, unpaid dividends, bills payable, reserved for taxes, and miscellaneous.
3. Includes deposits of U. S. disbursing officers.
4. Includes postal savings deposits 1912 ff.
5. Includes bills and notes rediscounted and bonds borrowed (1902-1914).

Figure 16.3-29: National Bank System Liabilities, 1912-1914

Figures 16.3-30 through 16.3-39 show the reserve positions of the national banks for this period.

Day	Year	U. S. Bonds for Circ. & Deposit	Paid-in Capital	Ratio, Securing Bonds to Capital	U. S. Bonds v. Circulation	Nat'l Bank Note Circulation	Ratio, Securing Bonds to Circulation	Total, N. B. Notes & Deposits	Reserve Agent Net	Total "Lawful Money"	Total Reserves	Avg. Ratio, Reserves to Notes Plus Deposits
1 Jan	1879	347.118	462.031	0.751	347.118	303.506	0.874	1,010.102	77.925	212.572	290.497	0.288
4 Apr	1879	348.488	455.611	0.765	348.488	304.467	0.874	1,209.443	74.004	169.789	243.793	0.202
14 Jun	1879	352.208	455.244	0.774	352.208	307.329	0.873	1,208.366	93.443	192.991	286.434	0.237
2 Oct	1879	357.313	454.067	0.787	357.313	313.786	0.878	1,048.012	107.024	234.731	341.755	0.326
12 Dec	1879	364.273	454.499	0.801	364.273	321.949	0.884	1,088.226	102.742	246.275	349.017	0.321
21 Feb	1880	361.902	454.549	0.796	361.902	320.304	0.885	1,180.157	117.791	311.805	429.596	0.364
23 Apr	1880	361.275	456.098	0.792	361.275	320.759	0.888	1,123.461	103.964	247.231	351.196	0.313
11 Jun	1880	359.512	455.910	0.789	359.512	318.089	0.885	1,162.497	115.936	286.755	402.691	0.346
1 Oct	1880	357.789	457.554	0.782	357.789	317.350	0.887	1,201.781	134.563	287.449	422.012	0.351
31 Dec	1880	358.043	458.540	0.781	358.043	317.484	0.887	1,335.325	126.155	396.514	522.669	0.391

Reserve Position of National Banks, 1879, 1880 (millions USD, except ratios)

Figure 16.3-30: Reserve Position of National Banks, 1879, 1880

Day	Year	U. S. Bonds for Circ. & Deposit	Paid-in Capital	Ratio, Securing Bonds to Capital	U. S. Bonds v. Circula-tion	Nat'l Bank Note Circula-tion	Ratio, Securing Bonds to Circula-tion	Total, N. B. Notes & Deposits	Reserve Agent Net	Total "Lawful Money"	Total Reserves	Avg. Ratio, Reserves to Notes Plus Deposits
11 Mar	1881	339.812	458.255	0.742	339.812	298.591	0.879	1,243.204	120.821	305.461	426.281	0.343
6 May	1881	352.654	459.039	0.768	352.654	309.737	0.878	1,349.653	128.018	382.165	510.183	0.378
30 Jun	1881	358.288	460.228	0.779	358.288	312.223	0.871	1,356.199	156.259	331.700	487.959	0.360
1 Oct	1881	363.386	463.822	0.783	363.386	320.200	0.881	1,403.306	132.968	357.089	490.058	0.349
31 Dec	1881	368.736	465.860	0.792	368.736	325.018	0.881	1,440.090	123.530	391.366	514.896	0.358
11 Mar	1882	367.334	469.390	0.783	367.334	323.652	0.881	1,372.472	117.453	329.095	446.548	0.325
19 May	1882	360.154	473.819	0.760	360.154	315.671	0.876	1,330.587	124.190	286.046	410.236	0.308
1 Jul	1882	355.790	477.184	0.746	355.790	308.922	0.868	1,388.314	118.455	335.202	453.657	0.327
3 Oct	1882	357.632	483.104	0.740	357.632	314.721	0.880	1,449.639	113.277	374.934	488.211	0.337
30 Dec	1882	357.048	484.883	0.736	357.048	315.231	0.883	1,395.541	122.066	331.258	453.324	0.325
13 Mar	1883	354.747	490.457	0.723	354.747	312.778	0.882	1,330.291	121.024	267.032	388.057	0.292
1 May	1883	354.480	493.963	0.718	354.480	313.550	0.885	1,396.755	109.307	318.301	427.608	0.306
22 Jun	1883	354.003	500.298	0.708	354.003	311.963	0.881	1,368.975	126.647	280.435	407.082	0.297
2 Oct	1883	351.413	509.700	0.689	351.413	310.518	0.884	1,374.119	124.919	275.288	400.207	0.291
31 Dec	1883	345.596	511.838	0.675	345.596	304.994	0.883	1,425.243	127.000	329.809	456.809	0.321
7 Mar	1884	339.816	515.725	0.659	339.816	298.792	0.879	1,358.655	138.705	266.822	405.527	0.298
24 Apr	1884	337.343	518.472	0.651	337.343	297.506	0.882	1,373.107	122.492	276.479	398.971	0.291
20 Jun	1884	334.346	522.516	0.640	334.346	295.175	0.883	1,288.391	95.247	266.886	362.133	0.281
30 Sep	1884	327.435	524.271	0.625	327.435	289.775	0.885	1,279.091	111.993	274.070	386.063	0.302
20 Dec	1884	317.586	524.089	0.606	317.586	280.197	0.882	1,282.252	121.162	293.639	414.801	0.323

Figure 16.3-31: Reserve Position of National Banks, 1881-1884

Day	Year	U. S. Bonds for Circ. & Deposit	Paid-in Capital	Ratio, Securing Bonds to Capital	U. S. Bonds v. Circula-tion	Nat'l Bank Note Circula-tion	Ratio, Securing Bonds to Circula-tion	Total, N. B. Notes & Deposits	Reserve Agent Net	Total "Lawful Money"	Total Reserves	Avg. Ratio, Reserves to Notes Plus Deposits
10 Mar	1885	313.106	524.255	0.597	313.106	274.054	0.875	1,284.602	136.462	299.269	435.731	0.339
6 May	1885	312.169	525.196	0.594	312.169	273.703	0.877	1,324.526	130.903	328.972	459.876	0.347
1 Jul	1885	310.102	526.274	0.589	310.102	269.148	0.868	1,389.547	132.734	372.342	505.076	0.363
1 Oct	1885	307.657	527.524	0.583	307.657	268.870	0.874	1,385.509	138.379	332.730	471.109	0.340
24 Dec	1885	304.777	529.361	0.576	304.777	267.431	0.877	1,393.925	139.239	328.007	467.247	0.335
1 Mar	1886	309.615	533.361	0.580	309.615	256.972	0.830	1,425.066	142.806	341.211	484.017	0.340
3 Jun	1886	291.613	539.109	0.541	291.613	244.893	0.840	1,407.610	133.027	315.628	448.655	0.319
27 Aug	1886	282.185	545.523	0.517	282.185	238.274	0.844	1,368.914	143.715	277.908	421.623	0.308
7 Oct	1886	269.857	548.241	0.492	269.857	228.673	0.847	1,418.204	140.765	317.061	457.826	0.323
28 Dec	1886	238.440	550.699	0.433	238.440	202.078	0.847	1,389.777	142.118	307.524	449.642	0.324
4 Mar	1887	220.818	555.352	0.398	220.818	186.231	0.843	1,430.668	163.161	329.528	492.689	0.344
13 May	1887	209.263	565.629	0.370	209.263	176.772	0.845	1,464.678	148.068	334.481	482.548	0.329
1 Aug	1887	197.374	571.649	0.345	197.374	166.626	0.844	1,474.964	140.270	368.421	508.691	0.345
5 Oct	1887	197.394	578.463	0.341	197.394	167.283	0.847	1,441.984	140.874	328.153	469.027	0.325
7 Dec	1887	194.600	580.733	0.335	194.600	164.904	0.847	1,443.593	132.960	320.255	453.215	0.314
14 Feb	1888	189.839	582.194	0.326	189.839	159.750	0.842	1,471.157	155.341	330.250	485.591	0.330
30 Apr	1888	188.931	585.449	0.323	188.931	158.898	0.841	1,528.109	146.478	373.582	520.060	0.340
30 Jun	1888	185.310	588.384	0.315	185.310	155.313	0.838	1,506.026	158.134	338.151	496.284	0.330
4 Oct	1888	179.423	592.622	0.303	179.423	151.703	0.846	1,558.158	170.459	362.322	532.780	0.342
12 Dec	1888	169.962	593.848	0.286	169.962	143.549	0.845	1,525.938	156.587	347.684	504.271	0.330

Figure 16.3-32: Reserve Position of National Banks, 1885-1888

Day	Year	U.S. Bonds for Circ. & Deposit	Paid-in Capital	Ratio, Securing Bonds to Capital	U.S. Bonds v. Circula-tion	Nat'l Bank Note Circula-tion	Ratio, Securing Bonds to Circula-tion	Total, N.B. Notes & Deposits	Reserve Agent Net	Total "Lawful Money"	Total Reserves	Avg. Ratio, Reserves to Notes Plus Deposits
26 Feb	1889	163.588	596.569	0.274	163.588	137.216	0.839	1,540.289	192.702	355.739	548.441	0.356
13 May	1889	156.086	599.473	0.260	156.086	131.128	0.840	1,600.272	187.372	385.166	572.538	0.358
12 Jul	1889	153.960	605.852	0.254	153.960	128.867	0.837	1,617.704	192.590	375.632	568.222	0.351
30 Sep	1889	152.877	612.584	0.250	152.877	128.451	0.840	1,650.443	189.136	388.544	577.680	0.350
11 Dec	1889	149.711	617.840	0.242	149.711	126.040	0.842	1,606.340	164.890	360.020	524.910	0.327
28 Feb	1890	148.723	626.598	0.237	148.723	123.862	0.833	1,636.321	188.064	381.519	569.583	0.348
17 May	1890	150.092	635.055	0.236	150.092	125.792	0.838	1,636.986	183.206	335.429	518.635	0.317
18 Jul	1890	150.930	642.074	0.235	150.930	126.324	0.837	1,678.648	185.822	360.116	545.938	0.325
2 Oct	1890	146.093	650.447	0.225	146.093	122.928	0.841	1,717.121	189.452	384.048	573.499	0.334
19 Dec	1890	145.757	657.877	0.222	145.757	123.039	0.844	1,637.513	160.221	375.209	535.429	0.327
26 Feb	1891	146.317	662.518	0.221	146.317	123.113	0.841	1,635.809	182.646	369.944	552.589	0.338
4 May	1891	146.657	667.787	0.220	146.657	123.448	0.842	1,728.146	180.005	418.712	598.717	0.346
9 Jul	1891	148.716	672.904	0.221	148.716	123.916	0.833	1,684.885	175.591	372.338	547.929	0.325
25 Sep	1891	156.573	677.427	0.231	156.573	131.323	0.839	1,739.909	193.990	404.038	598.028	0.344
2 Dec	1891	160.520	677.357	0.237	160.520	134.793	0.840	1,755.279	196.320	410.833	607.153	0.346
1 Mar	1892	165.007	679.970	0.243	165.007	137.627	0.834	1,856.431	256.751	460.034	716.785	0.386
17 May	1892	167.625	682.232	0.246	167.625	140.052	0.836	1,899.376	250.249	447.904	698.153	0.368
12 Jul	1892	169.032	684.678	0.247	169.032	141.062	0.835	1,908.581	252.474	434.539	687.013	0.360
30 Sep	1892	170.415	686.573	0.248	170.415	143.423	0.842	1,922.719	236.434	419.842	656.276	0.341
9 Dec	1892	173.732	689.698	0.252	173.732	145.669	0.838	1,923.833	204.948	423.588	628.536	0.327

Reserve Position of National Banks, 1889-1892 (millions USD, except ratios)

Figure 16.3-33: Reserve Position of National Banks, 1889-1892

Day	Year	U.S. Bonds for Circ. & Deposit	Paid-in Capital	Ratio, Securing Bonds to Capital	U.S. Bonds v. Circula-tion	Nat'l Bank Note Circula-tion	Ratio, Securing Bonds to Circula-tion	Total, N.B. Notes & Deposits	Reserve Agent Net	Total "Lawful Money"	Total Reserves	Avg. Ratio, Reserves to Notes Plus Deposits
6 Mar	1893	177.498	688.643	0.258	177.498	149.125	0.840	1,914.306	202.612	425.366	627.978	0.328
4 May	1893	179.881	688.701	0.261	179.881	151.694	0.843	1,915.576	174.312	426.663	600.976	0.314
12 Jul	1893	184.189	685.787	0.269	184.189	155.071	0.842	1,725.533	159.353	391.313	550.666	0.319
3 Oct	1893	215.441	678.540	0.318	215.441	182.960	0.849	1,648.407	158.500	446.621	605.121	0.367
19 Dec	1893	213.685	681.813	0.313	213.685	179.973	0.842	1,733.234	212.631	455.812	668.443	0.386
28 Feb	1894	209.560	678.537	0.309	209.560	174.436	0.832	1,774.806	246.892	470.297	717.189	0.404
4 May	1894	209.183	675.869	0.310	209.183	172.626	0.825	1,857.440	257.854	483.089	740.943	0.399
18 Jul	1894	210.127	671.091	0.313	210.127	171.715	0.817	1,863.644	258.089	456.440	714.530	0.383
2 Oct	1894	208.366	668.862	0.312	208.366	172.332	0.827	1,914.492	248.850	447.272	696.121	0.364
19 Dec	1894	204.278	666.271	0.307	204.278	169.337	0.829	1,878.843	234.331	419.309	653.640	0.348
5 Mar	1895	204.315	662.100	0.309	204.315	169.755	0.831	1,865.653	222.468	412.560	635.027	0.340
7 May	1895	212.396	659.147	0.322	212.396	175.654	0.827	1,893.863	218.799	422.017	640.816	0.338
11 Jul	1895	215.321	658.224	0.327	215.321	178.816	0.830	1,928.005	235.309	421.504	656.813	0.341
28 Sep	1895	217.768	657.135	0.331	217.768	182.482	0.838	1,897.676	222.287	348.627	570.915	0.301
13 Dec	1895	219.674	656.956	0.334	219.674	185.151	0.843	1,919.460	203.002	393.405	596.407	0.311
28 Feb	1896	224.868	653.995	0.344	224.868	187.217	0.833	1,869.097	189.345	399.541	588.885	0.315
7 May	1896	234.793	652.090	0.360	234.793	197.382	0.841	1,909.444	195.753	407.835	603.588	0.316
14 Jul	1896	237.137	651.145	0.364	237.137	199.214	0.840	1,883.032	204.384	393.974	598.358	0.318
6 Oct	1896	247.665	648.540	0.382	247.665	209.944	0.848	1,823.007	190.078	389.031	579.108	0.318
17 Dec	1896	249.758	647.186	0.386	249.758	210.690	0.844	1,865.798	219.967	430.336	650.302	0.349

Reserve Position of National Banks, 1893-1896 (millions USD, except ratios)

Figure 16.3-34: Reserve Position of National Banks, 1893-1896

Day	Year	U. S. Bonds for Circ. & Deposit	Paid-in Capital	Ratio, Securing Bonds to Capital	U. S. Bonds v. Circula-tion	Nat'l Bank Note Circula-tion	Ratio, Securing Bonds to Circula-tion	Total, N. B. Notes & Deposits	Reserve Agent Net	Total "Lawful Money"	Total Reserves	Avg. Ratio, Reserves to Notes Plus Deposits
9 Mar	1897	241.921	642.424	0.377	241.921	202.655	0.838	1,887.205	258.430	428.437	686.868	0.364
14 May	1897	239.502	637.002	0.376	239.502	198.278	0.828	1,941.991	251.949	441.949	693.897	0.357
23 Jul	1897	238.443	632.153	0.377	238.443	196.591	0.824	1,983.462	275.755	457.873	733.628	0.370
5 Oct	1897	237.506	631.488	0.376	237.506	198.921	0.838	2,068.412	297.018	459.876	756.894	0.366
15 Dec	1897	231.782	629.655	0.368	231.782	193.784	0.836	2,154.365	309.570	484.070	793.640	0.368
18 Feb	1898	221.741	628.890	0.353	221.741	184.106	0.830	2,198.201	360.277	506.275	866.552	0.394
5 May	1898	225.679	624.472	0.361	225.679	188.425	0.835	2,214.758	300.962	563.533	864.495	0.390
14 Jul	1898	227.708	622.017	0.366	227.708	189.866	0.834	2,266.093	320.015	545.962	865.977	0.382
20 Sep	1898	234.424	621.518	0.377	234.424	194.484	0.830	2,301.104	320.002	515.223	835.225	0.363
1 Dec	1898	249.071	620.516	0.401	249.071	207.093	0.831	2,526.268	359.371	642.444	1,001.816	0.397
4 Feb	1899	245.496	608.301	0.404	245.496	203.636	0.829	2,522.453	412.984	564.627	977.611	0.388
5 Apr	1899	244.038	607.263	0.402	244.038	203.829	0.835	2,728.226	392.327	688.326	1,080.653	0.396
30 Jun	1899	238.966	604.865	0.395	238.966	199.358	0.834	2,797.829	385.102	677.272	1,062.374	0.380
7 Sep	1899	239.756	605.773	0.396	239.756	200.346	0.836	2,729.951	394.686	605.708	1,000.394	0.366
2 Dec	1899	244.702	606.725	0.403	244.702	204.925	0.837	2,665.561	345.556	508.029	853.585	0.320
13 Feb	1900	246.590	613.084	0.402	246.590	204.913	0.831	2,796.026	375.117	649.282	1,024.400	0.366
26 Apr	1900	277.282	617.051	0.449	277.282	236.250	0.852	2,793.930	383.058	647.809	1,030.868	0.369
29 Jun	1900	295.750	621.536	0.476	295.750	265.303	0.897	2,822.268	382.854	661.615	1,044.469	0.370
5 Sep	1900	309.134	630.299	0.490	309.134	283.949	0.919	2,886.015	423.505	645.604	1,069.109	0.370
13 Dec	1900	321.455	632.353	0.508	321.455	298.917	0.930	3,017.293	378.821	687.139	1,065.960	0.353

Figure 16.3-35: Reserve Position of National Banks, 1897-1900

Day	Year	U. S. Bonds for Circ. & Deposit	Paid-in Capital	Ratio, Securing Bonds to Capital	U. S. Bonds v. Circula-tion	Nat'l Bank Note Circula-tion	Ratio, Securing Bonds to Circula-tion	Total, N. B. Notes & Deposits	Reserve Agent Net	Total "Lawful Money"	Total Reserves	Avg. Ratio, Reserves to Notes Plus Deposits
5 Feb	1901	333.340	634.697	0.525	333.340	309.466	0.928	3,158.469	443.494	793.837	1,237.330	0.392
24 Apr	1901	339.323	640.779	0.530	339.323	317.202	0.935	3,306.870	449.932	838.724	1,288.655	0.390
15 Jul	1901	342.905	645.719	0.531	342.905	319.009	0.930	3,359.919	418.451	838.697	1,257.148	0.374
30 Sep	1901	345.478	655.342	0.527	345.478	323.864	0.937	3,368.477	423.372	766.272	1,189.645	0.353
10 Dec	1901	326.851	665.341	0.491	326.851	319.437	0.977	3,393.604	400.873	776.064	1,176.937	0.347
25 Feb	1902	336.606	667.381	0.504	336.606	314.439	0.934	3,409.224	459.796	760.331	1,220.127	0.358
30 Apr	1902	331.516	671.176	0.494	331.516	309.782	0.934	3,541.577	435.225	850.803	1,286.028	0.363
16 Jul	1902	331.515	701.991	0.472	331.515	309.337	0.933	3,532.178	437.854	818.589	1,256.443	0.356
15 Sep	1902	340.053	705.535	0.482	340.053	317.992	0.935	3,651.210	434.627	837.421	1,272.048	0.348
25 Nov	1902	357.990	714.616	0.501	357.990	336.506	0.940	3,636.203	400.085	772.201	1,172.286	0.322
6 Feb	1903	358.732	731.275	0.491	358.732	335.226	0.934	3,642.596	448.930	786.876	1,235.806	0.339
9 Apr	1903	359.700	734.903	0.489	359.700	335.094	0.932	3,651.397	426.313	739.825	1,166.138	0.319
9 Jun	1903	386.745	743.506	0.520	386.745	359.261	0.929	3,707.357	404.347	781.465	1,185.812	0.320
9 Sep	1903	400.174	753.723	0.531	400.174	375.038	0.937	3,680.986	425.656	703.640	1,129.296	0.307
17 Nov	1903	399.142	758.315	0.526	399.142	376.239	0.943	3,714.954	400.352	701.354	1,101.706	0.297
22 Jan	1904	406.359	765.862	0.531	406.359	380.992	0.938	3,844.907	460.471	851.384	1,311.855	0.341
28 Mar	1904	413.191	765.975	0.539	413.191	385.908	0.934	3,800.613	471.581	801.067	1,272.648	0.335
9 Jun	1904	429.871	767.378	0.560	429.871	399.584	0.930	3,822.367	464.589	807.923	1,272.511	0.333
6 Sep	1904	438.717	770.778	0.569	438.717	411.231	0.937	3,980.215	531.274	876.517	1,407.791	0.354
10 Nov	1904	446.465	776.089	0.575	446.465	419.120	0.939	4,237.129	504.352	985.894	1,490.246	0.352

Figure 16.3-36: Reserve Position of National Banks, 1901-1904

Day	Year	U. S. Bonds for Circ. & Deposit	Paid-in Capital	Ratio, Securing Bonds to Capital	U. S. Bonds v. Circulation	Nat'l Bank Note Circulation	Ratio, Securing Bonds to Circulation	Total, N. B. Notes & Deposits	Reserve Agent Net	Total "Lawful Money"	Total Reserves	Avg. Ratio, Reserves to Notes Plus Deposits

Reserve Position of National Banks, 1905-1907 (millions USD, except ratios)

Day	Year	U. S. Bonds for Circ. & Deposit	Paid-in Capital	Ratio, Securing Bonds to Capital	U. S. Bonds v. Circulation	Nat'l Bank Note Circulation	Ratio, Securing Bonds to Circulation	Total, N. B. Notes & Deposits	Reserve Agent Net	Total "Lawful Money"	Total Reserves	Avg. Ratio, Reserves to Notes Plus Deposits
11 Jan	1905	452.784	776.916	0.583	452.784	424.345	0.937	4,143.239	500.629	940.284	1,440.913	0.348
14 Mar	1905	462.261	782.488	0.591	462.261	430.955	0.932	4,301.652	556.178	930.130	1,486.308	0.346
29 May	1905	479.711	791.567	0.606	479.711	445.456	0.929	4,304.413	524.923	918.920	1,443.842	0.335
25 Aug	1905	500.873	799.870	0.626	500.873	468.980	0.936	4,351.752	571.102	932.494	1,503.596	0.346
9 Nov	1905	517.727	808.329	0.640	517.727	485.522	0.938	4,536.330	529.995	964.338	1,494.332	0.329
29 Jan	1906	530.445	814.988	0.651	530.445	498.238	0.939	4,648.675	561.380	1,092.006	1,653.386	0.356
6 Apr	1906	536.830	819.307	0.655	536.830	505.457	0.942	4,557.448	551.840	943.173	1,495.013	0.328
18 Jun	1906	542.119	826.130	0.656	542.119	510.861	0.942	4,656.644	551.549	966.604	1,518.153	0.326
4 Sep	1906	549.564	835.067	0.658	549.564	517.965	0.943	4,825.735	585.334	1,023.345	1,608.679	0.333
12 Nov	1906	570.748	847.515	0.673	570.748	536.110	0.939	4,966.286	561.230	1,013.217	1,574.447	0.317
26 Jan	1907	578.829	860.931	0.672	578.829	545.482	0.942	4,818.494	623.970	826.002	1,449.972	0.301
22 Mar	1907	575.704	873.670	0.659	575.704	543.320	0.944	4,966.191	585.929	921.328	1,507.258	0.304
20 May	1907	581.126	883.691	0.658	581.126	547.919	0.943	5,051.487	588.454	966.895	1,555.350	0.308
22 Aug	1907	584.584	896.451	0.652	584.584	551.949	0.944	5,032.023	576.356	894.540	1,470.897	0.292
3 Dec	1907	647.820	901.682	0.718	647.820	601.806	0.929	5,013.409	487.152	961.699	1,448.851	0.289

Figure 16.3-37: Reserve Position of National Banks, 1905-1907

Reserve Position of National Banks, 1908-1911 (millions USD, except ratios)

Day	Year	U. S. Bonds for Circ. & Deposit	Paid-in Capital	Ratio, Securing Bonds to Capital	U. S. Bonds v. Circulation	Nat'l Bank Note Circulation	Ratio, Securing Bonds to Circulation	Total, N. B. Notes & Deposits	Reserve Agent Net	Total "Lawful Money"	Total Reserves	Avg. Ratio, Reserves to Notes Plus Deposits
14 Feb	1908	666.895	905.550	0.736	666.895	627.642	0.941	4,966.191	565.252	987.318	1,552.569	0.313
14 May	1908	655.269	912.362	0.718	655.269	614.089	0.937	5,108.403	577.079	1,097.620	1,674.699	0.328
15 Jul	1908	655.217	919.101	0.713	655.217	613.664	0.937	5,118.481	600.778	1,096.288	1,697.067	0.332
23 Sep	1908	658.812	921.463	0.715	658.812	613.726	0.932	5,288.234	674.272	1,147.666	1,821.938	0.345
27 Nov	1908	644.030	921.019	0.699	644.030	599.319	0.931	5,444.033	662.758	1,178.063	1,840.821	0.338
5 Feb	1909	660.748	927.722	0.712	660.748	615.316	0.931	5,414.669	711.844	1,137.215	1,849.060	0.341
28 Apr	1909	680.718	933.980	0.729	680.718	636.368	0.935	5,532.830	685.755	1,184.954	1,870.709	0.338
23 Jun	1909	686.760	937.004	0.733	686.760	641.312	0.934	5,614.374	679.390	1,192.329	1,871.719	0.333
1 Sep	1909	701.169	944.642	0.742	701.169	658.040	0.938	5,716.638	680.713	1,186.554	1,867.267	0.327
16 Nov	1909	708.895	953.963	0.743	708.895	668.394	0.943	5,837.905	641.370	1,145.458	1,786.828	0.306
31 Jan	1910	710.725	960.125	0.740	710.725	667.501	0.939	5,906.470	666.715	1,243.484	1,910.199	0.323
29 Mar	1910	712.932	972.820	0.733	712.932	669.182	0.939	5,944.950	688.880	1,143.383	1,832.263	0.308
30 Jun	1910	716.974	989.567	0.725	716.974	675.633	0.942	6,017.390	619.112	1,252.363	1,871.475	0.311
1 Sep	1910	718.813	1,002.735	0.717	718.813	674.822	0.939	5,870.641	651.068	1,139.555	1,790.623	0.305
10 Nov	1910	723.496	1,004.288	0.720	723.496	680.440	0.940	6,033.650	644.581	1,158.775	1,803.356	0.299
7 Jan	1911	725.393	1,007.335	0.720	725.393	684.136	0.943	5,844.016	675.286	1,003.180	1,678.466	0.287
7 Mar	1911	725.866	1,011.570	0.718	725.866	680.727	0.938	6,030.875	775.501	1,159.216	1,934.717	0.321
7 Jun	1911	727.858	1,019.633	0.714	727.858	681.741	0.937	6,208.187	726.828	1,235.792	1,962.620	0.316
1 Sep	1911	741.579	1,025.441	0.723	741.579	696.982	0.940	6,235.321	707.089	1,196.921	1,904.010	0.305
5 Dec	1911	748.123	1,026.441	0.729	748.123	702.647	0.939	6,291.745	705.353	1,129.731	1,835.084	0.292

Figure 16.3-38: Reserve Position of National Banks, 1908-1911

Reserve Position of National Banks, 1912-1914 (millions USD, except ratios)

Day	Year	U. S. Bonds for Circ. & Deposit	Paid-in Capital	Ratio, Securing Bonds to Capital	U. S. Bonds v. Circulation	Nat'l Bank Note Circulation	Ratio, Securing Bonds to Circulation	Total, N. B. Notes & Deposits	Reserve Agent Net	Total "Lawful Money"	Total Reserves	Avg. Ratio, Reserves to Notes Plus Deposits
20 Feb	1912	753.282	1,031.193	0.730	753.282	704.226	0.935	6,389.530	815.159	1,199.121	2,014.280	0.315
18 Apr	1912	754.214	1,036.125	0.728	754.214	706.979	0.937	6,472.968	766.672	1,190.264	1,956.936	0.302
14 Jun	1912	755.884	1,033.571	0.731	755.884	708.691	0.938	6,593.098	735.196	1,214.619	1,949.815	0.296
4 Sep	1912	759.114	1,046.013	0.726	759.114	713.823	0.940	6,664.720	772.606	1,195.268	1,967.875	0.295
26 Nov	1912	763.969	1,045.093	0.731	763.969	721.502	0.944	6,727.999	742.392	1,141.071	1,883.463	0.280
4 Feb	1913	765.744	1,048.899	0.730	765.744	717.468	0.937	6,765.934	806.323	1,226.020	2,032.344	0.300
4 Apr	1913	765.444	1,052.266	0.727	765.444	718.977	0.939	6,751.654	767.574	1,142.073	1,909.647	0.283
4 Jun	1913	770.622	1,056.920	0.729	770.622	722.125	0.937	6,743.973	716.291	1,175.124	1,891.415	0.280
9 Aug	1913	771.406	1,056.346	0.730	771.406	724.460	0.939	6,562.893	729.691	1,026.327	1,756.017	0.268
21 Oct	1913	773.290	1,059.403	0.730	773.290	727.079	0.940	6,890.827	739.405	1,152.000	1,891.404	0.274
13 Jan	1914	771.972	1,057.676	0.730	771.972	725.326	0.940	6,903.932	759.156	1,249.175	2,008.331	0.291
4 Mar	1914	768.966	1,056.482	0.728	768.966	720.640	0.937	6,921.920	837.765	1,254.376	2,092.140	0.302
30 Jun	1914	770.407	1,058.192	0.728	770.407	722.555	0.938	7,081.743	734.838	1,282.225	2,017.063	0.285
12 Sep	1914	1,173.673	1,060.332	1.107	1,173.673	918.270	0.782	7,154.690	634.088	1,078.705	1,712.793	0.239

Figure 16.3-39: Reserve Position of National Banks, 1912-1914

Figure 16.3-40 shows the money supply from 1879 to 1914. The average error between these values and those per Friedman and Schwartz [16.3-1], assuming theirs is correct, is 0.491% with a standard deviation of 5.282%. If the truth lies halfway between these values and Friedman and Schwartz, then the average error is 0.245% and the standard deviation is 2.641%.

U. S. Money Supply, 1879-1914 (millions USD)														
1	2	3	4	5	6	7	8	9	10	11	12	13	14	15
Year (~30 Jun)	Number of Banks [1]	State Bank Notes [2]	U.S. Notes, Treasury Notes, National Bank Notes, etc. [3]	Total Notes in Circulation	Net Specie in Circulation [4]	Notes & Specie Outside Treasury	Cash Held in All Banks [5]	Currency & Coin Outside Banks	State Bank Deposits [6]	National Bank Deposits and Other Deposits Outside State Banks [7]	Total Deposits	Estimated Interbank Transactions [8]	Deposits Adjusted	Total Money Supply
1879	3,335	0.389	638.743	639.132	179.888	819.020	207.491	611.529	1,059.082	1,090.110	2,149.192	210.621	1,938.571	2,550.100
1880	3,355	0.283	679.064	679.347	294.319	973.666	274.262	699.404	1,136.966	1,085.140	2,222.106	217.766	2,004.340	2,703.744
1881	3,427	0.275	722.744	723.019	391.494	1,114.513	277.987	836.526	1,284.676	1,364.386	2,649.062	259.608	2,389.454	3,225.980
1882	3,572	0.286	737.255	737.541	437.035	1,174.576	268.697	905.879	1,412.461	1,364.960	2,777.421	272.187	2,505.234	3,411.113
1883	3,835	0.188	803.526	803.714	426.778	1,230.492	286.120	944.372	1,546.615	1,337.362	2,883.977	282.630	2,601.347	3,545.719
1884	4,113	0.177	816.951	817.128	426.975	1,244.103	303.312	940.791	1,615.793	1,232.761	2,848.554	279.158	2,569.396	3,510.187
1885	4,350	0.098	868.111	868.209	424.458	1,292.667	389.799	902.868	1,658.559	1,419.594	3,078.153	301.659	2,776.494	3,679.362
1886	4,338	0.103	795.638	795.741	457.063	1,252.804	346.819	905.985	1,726.939	1,459.240	3,186.179	312.246	2,873.933	3,779.918
1887	6,170	0.231	836.865	837.096	480.674	1,317.770	432.319	885.451	2,068.490	1,650.149	3,718.639	364.427	3,354.212	4,239.663
1888	6,647	0.169	875.168	875.337	497.003	1,372.340	459.075	913.265	2,174.881	1,716.215	3,891.096	381.327	3,509.769	4,423.034
1889	7,244	0.120	897.946	898.066	482.416	1,380.482	514.995	865.487	2,390.937	1,919.579	4,310.516	422.431	3,888.085	4,753.572
1890	8,201	0.120	944.681	944.801	484.571	1,429.372	488.748	940.624	2,597.662	1,978.771	4,576.433	448.490	4,127.943	5,068.567
1891	8,641	0.111	973.076	973.187	524.364	1,497.551	497.931	999.620	2,708.609	1,974.086	4,682.695	458.904	4,223.791	5,223.411
1892	9,336	0.137	1,072.668	1,072.805	528.680	1,601.485	586.405	1,015.080	2,970.209	2,327.251	5,297.460	519.151	4,778.309	5,793.389
1893	9,492	0.010	1,065.766	1,065.776	530.936	1,596.712	515.988	1,080.724	3,126.187	1,939.235	5,065.422	496.411	4,569.011	5,649.735
1894	9,508	0.005	1,053.757	1,053.762	607.053	1,660.815	688.997	971.818	3,039.359	2,228.310	5,267.669	516.232	4,751.437	5,723.255
1895	9,818	0.000	1,009.994	1,009.994	591.974	1,601.968	631.111	970.857	3,259.742	2,278.892	5,538.634	542.786	4,995.848	5,966.705
1896	9,469	0.000	939.208	939.208	567.226	1,506.434	531.856	974.578	3,345.229	2,140.953	5,486.182	537.646	4,948.536	5,923.114
1897	9,457	0.000	1,010.837	1,010.837	629.146	1,639.983	628.201	1,011.782	3,401.520	2,385.668	5,787.188	567.144	5,220.044	6,231.826
1898	9,500	0.000	1,057.370	1,057.370	780.490	1,837.860	687.797	1,150.063	3,755.417	2,798.748	6,554.165	642.308	5,911.857	7,061.920
1899	9,732	0.000	1,093.787	1,093.787	810.285	1,904.072	723.299	1,180.773	4,361.691	3,538.612	7,900.303	774.230	7,126.073	8,306.846
1900	10,382	0.000	1,302.295	1,302.295	778.936	2,081.231	749.940	1,331.291	4,891.488	3,621.542	8,513.030	834.277	7,678.753	9,010.044
1901	11,406	0.000	1,399.361	1,399.361	803.837	2,203.198	807.517	1,395.681	5,645.841	4,250.281	9,896.122	969.820	8,926.302	10,321.983
1902	12,424	0.000	1,462.529	1,462.529	816.586	2,279.115	848.103	1,431.012	6,157.534	4,468.058	10,625.592	1,041.308	9,584.284	11,015.296
1903	13,684	0.000	1,585.315	1,585.315	814.419	2,399.734	857.260	1,542.474	6,617.260	4,561.884	11,179.144	1,095.556	10,083.588	11,626.062
1904	14,850	0.000	1,706.483	1,706.483	846.423	2,552.906	990.575	1,562.331	7,028.901	4,836.024	11,864.925	1,162.763	10,702.162	12,264.493
1905	16,410	0.000	1,761.798	1,761.798	861.544	2,623.342	994.136	1,629.206	7,925.346	5,407.455	13,332.801	1,306.614	12,026.187	13,655.393
1906	17,905	0.000	1,879.360	1,879.360	895.329	2,774.689	1,016.447	1,758.242	8,514.624	5,692.805	14,207.429	1,392.328	12,815.101	14,573.343
1907	19,746	0.000	2,007.771	2,007.771	806.091	2,813.862	1,113.743	1,700.119	9,167.830	6,190.385	15,358.215	1,505.105	13,853.110	15,553.229
1908	21,346	0.000	2,224.265	2,224.265	854.891	3,079.156	1,368.329	1,710.827	8,786.342	6,330.521	15,116.863	1,481.453	13,635.410	15,346.237
1909	22,524	0.000	2,302.582	2,302.582	846.243	3,148.825	1,457.685	1,691.140	9,658.994	7,009.225	16,668.219	1,633.485	15,034.734	16,725.874
1910	23,095	0.000	2,303.462	2,303.462	845.223	3,148.685	1,423.809	1,724.876	10,327.137	7,257.038	17,584.175	1,723.249	15,860.926	17,585.802
1911	24,392	0.000	2,413.839	2,413.839	849.213	3,263.052	1,554.148	1,708.904	10,905.735	7,675.740	18,581.475	1,820.985	16,760.490	18,469.394
1912	25,195	0.000	2,458.415	2,458.415	876.805	3,335.220	1,572.954	1,762.266	11,655.095	8,064.193	19,719.288	1,932.490	17,786.798	19,549.064
1913	25,993	0.000	2,528.753	2,528.753	889.940	3,418.693	1,560.710	1,857.983	11,994.624	8,143.929	20,138.553	1,973.578	18,164.975	20,022.958
1914	26,150	0.000	2,560.205	2,560.205	899.230	3,459.435	1,639.220	1,820.215	12,796.091	8,563.751	21,359.842	2,698.000	18,661.842	20,482.057

1. Number of banks from the Annual Report of the Comptroller of the Currency, 1931, pp. 1024, 1025 (Table 96).

2. State Bank notes form the Annual Report of the Comptroller of the Currency, 1931, pp. 1018, 1019 (Table 94).

3. Includes gold certificates, silver certificates, U. S. Notes, Treasury Notes of 1890, and National Bank Notes (fractional and "Other" obsolete) per Annual Report of the Secretary of the Treasury, 1947, pp. 485, 486 (Table 90).

4. This is the sum of gold coin, standard silver dollars, and subsidiary silver. Data is from the Annual Report of the Secretary of the Treasury, 1947, p. 485, (Table 90).

5. From the Annual Report of the Comptroller of the Currency, 1931, pp. 1023-1025, (Table 96).

6. From the Annual Report of the Comptroller of the Currency, 1931, pp. 1018, 1019, (Table 94).

7. From the Annual Report of the Comptroller of the Currency, 1931, pp. 1018, 1024 (Tables 94 and 96). The values shown here are the difference between "all banks" per Table 96 and "State banks" per Table 94.

8. Interbank from 1879 to 1913 based on average of interbank to total deposits from 1914 to 1940 (0.098). Value for 1914 from from Bank and Monetary Statistics, 1914-1941, Table 2, p. 18.

Figure 16.3-40 Total Money Supply, 1879-1914

Figures 16.3-41 and 16.3-42 show the coinage of the U. S. during this period.

	Gold Coinage of the U. S. , 1879-1914 (USD)						
Year	$20 Double Eagles ($)	$10 Eagles ($)	$5 Half Eagles ($)	Three Dollar ($)	$2.50 Quarter Eagles ($)	Gold Dollars ($)	Total ($)
1879	28,880,260.00	6,120,320.00	3,727,155.00	9,090.00	331,225.00	3,030.00	39,071,080.00
1880	17,749,120.00	21,715,160.00	22,831,765.00	3,108.00	7,490.00	1,636.00	62,308,279.00
1881	14,585,200.00	48,796,250.00	33,458,430.00	1,650.00	1,700.00	7,660.00	96,850,890.00
1882	23,295,400.00	24,740,640.00	17,831,885.00	4,620.00	10,100.00	5,040.00	65,887,685.00
1883	24,980,040.00	2,595,400.00	1,647,990.00	2,820.00	4,900.00	10,840.00	29,241,990.00
1884	19,944,200.00	2,110,800.00	1,922,250.00	3,318.00	4,982.00	6,206.00	23,991,756.00
1885	13,875,560.00	4,815,270.00	9,065,030.00	2,730.00	2,217.50	12,205.00	27,773,012.50
1886	22,120.00	10,621,600.00	18,282,160.00	3,426.00	10,220.00	6,016.00	28,945,542.00
1887	5,662,420.00	8,706,800.00	9,560,435.00	18,480.00	15,705.00	8,543.00	23,972,383.00
1888	21,717,320.00	8,030,310.00	1,560,080.00	15,873.00	40,245.00	16,080.00	31,379,908.00
1889	16,995,120.00	4,298,850.00	37,825.00	7,287.00	44,120.00	30,729.00	21,413,931.00
1890	19,399,080.00	755,430.00	290,640.00		22,032.00		20,467,182.00
1891	25,891,340.00	1,956,000.00	1,347,065.00		27,600.00		29,222,005.00
1892	19,238,760.00	9,817,400.00	5,724,700.00		6,362.50		34,787,222.50
1893	27,178,320.00	20,132,450.00	9,610,985.00		75,265.00		56,997,020.00
1894	48,350,800.00	26,032,780.00	5,152,275.00		10,305.00		79,546,160.00
1895	45,163,120.00	7,148,260.00	7,289,680.00		15,297.50		59,616,357.50
1896	43,931,760.00	2,000,980.00	1,072,315.00		48,005.00		47,053,060.00
1897	57,070,220.00	12,774,090.00	6,109,415.00		74,760.00		76,028,485.00
1898	54,912,900.00	12,857,970.00	10,154,475.00		60,412.50		77,985,757.50
1899	73,593,680.00	21,403,520.00	16,278,645.00		68,375.00		111,344,220.00
1900	86,681,680.00	3,749,600.00	8,673,650.00		168,012.50		99,272,942.50
1901	34,150,520.00	46,036,160.00	21,320,200.00		228,307.50		101,735,187.50
1902	35,697,580.00	5,520,130.00	5,557,810.00		334,332.50	75,000.00	47,184,852.50
1903	24,828,560.00	7,766,970.00	10,410,120.00		503,142.50	175,000.00	43,683,792.50
1904	227,819,440.00	2,709,880.00	2,445,680.00		402,400.00	25,000.00	233,402,400.00
1905	37,440,220.00	5,763,280.00	5,915,040.00		544,860.00	35,000.00	49,698,400.00
1906	55,113,800.00	16,903,920.00	6,334,100.00		441,225.00		78,793,045.00
1907	96,656,620.00	26,838,790.00	7,570,960.00		841,100.00		131,907,470.00
1908	109,263,200.00	14,813,360.00	6,149,430.00		1,412,642.50		131,638,632.50
1909	59,774,140.00	5,987,530.00	21,910,490.00		1,104,747.50		88,776,907.50
1910	60,788,340.00	34,863,440.00	7,840,250.00		1,231,705.00		104,723,735.00
1911	36,392,000.00	5,866,950.00	12,018,195.00		1,899,677.50		56,176,822.50
1912	2,996,480.00	7,050,830.00	5,910,720.00		1,540,492.50		17,498,522.50
1913	11,926,760.00	5,080,710.00	6,620,495.00		1,805,412.50		25,433,377.50
1914	40,926,400.00	7,025,500.00	3,785,625.00		1,720,292.50		53,457,817.50
Totals	1,522,892,480.00	453,407,330.00	315,417,965.00	72,402.00	15,059,669.00	417,985.00	2,307,267,831.00

Source (1879-1894): Annual Report of the Director of the Mint, 1895, 28 Nov 1895, Treasury Document No. 1829, pp. 286-293 (Table XLIV).
Source (1895-1914): Annual Report of the Director of the Mint, 1915, 1 Nov 1915, Treasury Document No. 2757, pp. 102-106 (Table 20).

Figure 16.3-41: Gold Coins Minted by the U. S., 1879-1914

Silver and Copper Coinage of the U. S., 1879-1914 (USD)										
	Silver ($)								Minor ($)	
Year	Trade Dollars	Dollars	Half Dollars	Quarters	Twenty-cents	Dimes	Half-dimes	Three-cents	Cents	Total ($)
1879	1,541.00	27,560,100.00	2,950.00	3,675.00		1,510.00			165,003.00	27,734,779.00
1880	1,987.00	27,397,355.00	4,877.00	3,738.75		3,735.50			391,395.95	27,803,089.20
1881	960.00	27,927,975.00	5,487.50	3,243.75		2,497.50			428,151.75	28,368,315.50
1882	1,097.00	27,574,100.00	2,750.00	4,075.00		391,110.00			960,400.00	28,933,532.00
1883	979.00	28,470,039.00	4,519.50	3,859.75		767,571.20			1,604,770.41	30,851,738.86
1884		28,136,875.00	2,637.50	2,218.75		393,134.90			796,483.78	29,331,349.93
1885		28,697,767.00	3,065.00	3,632.50		257,711.70			191,622.04	29,153,798.24
1886		31,423,886.00	2,943.00	1,471.50		658,409.40			343,186.10	32,429,896.00
1887		33,611,710.00	2,855.00	2,677.50		1,573,838.90			1,215,686.26	36,406,767.66
1888		31,990,833.00	6,416.50	306,708.25		721,648.70			912,200.78	33,937,807.23
1889		34,651,811.00	6,355.50	3,177.75		835,338.90			1,283,408.49	36,780,091.64
1890		38,043,004.00	6,295.00	20,147.50		1,133,461.70			1,384,792.14	40,587,700.34
1891		23,562,735.00	100,300.00	1,551,150.00		2,304,671.60			1,312,441.00	28,831,297.60
1892		6,333,245.00	1,652,136.50	2,960,331.00		1,695,365.50			961,480.42	13,602,558.42
1893		1,455,792.00	4,003,948.50	2,583,837.50		759,219.30			1,134,931.70	9,937,729.00
1894		3,093,972.00	3,667,831.00	2,233,448.25		205,099.60			438,177.92	9,638,528.77
1895		862,880.00	2,354,652.00	2,255,390.25		225,088.00			882,430.56	6,580,440.81
1896		19,876,762.00	1,507,855.00	1,386,760.25		318,581.80			832,718.93	23,922,677.98
1897		12,651,731.00	2,023,315.50	2,524,440.00		1,287,810.80			1,526,100.05	20,013,397.35
1898		14,426,735.00	3,094,642.50	3,497,331.75		2,015,324.20			1,124,835.14	24,158,868.59
1899		15,182,846.00	4,474,628.50	3,994,211.50		2,409,833.90			1,837,451.86	27,898,971.76
1900		25,010,912.00	5,033,617.00	3,822,874.25		2,477,918.20			2,031,137.39	38,376,458.84
1901		22,566,813.00	3,119,928.50	2,644,369.25		2,507,350.00			2,120,122.08	32,958,582.83
1902		18,160,777.00	4,454,723.50	4,617,589.00		2,795,077.70			2,445,796.17	32,473,963.37
1903		10,343,755.00	3,149,763.50	3,551,516.00		2,829,405.50			2,251,281.18	22,125,721.18
1904		8,812,650.00	2,331,654.00	3,011,203.25		1,540,102.70			1,683,529.35	17,379,139.30
1905			1,830,863.50	2,020,562.50		2,480,754.90			2,298,555.43	8,630,736.33
1906			5,426,414.50	2,248,108.75		2,976,504.60			2,890,908.80	13,541,936.65
1907			5,825,587.50	3,899,143.75		3,453,704.50			3,042,126.18	16,220,561.93
1908			5,819,686.50	4,262,136.25		2,309,954.50			1,468,738.72	13,860,515.97
1909			2,529,025.00	4,110,662.50		1,448,165.00			1,756,388.93	9,844,241.43
1910			1,183,275.50	936,137.75		1,625,055.10			3,036,929.83	6,781,398.18
1911			1,686,811.50	1,410,535.75		3,359,954.30			3,156,726.47	9,614,028.02
1912			2,610,750.00	1,277,175.00		3,453,070.00			2,577,386.30	9,918,381.30
1913			663,313.50	493,853.25		2,027,062.20			4,667,335.47	7,851,564.42
1914			558,305.00	2,388,652.50		3,136,865.50			2,208,071.22	8,291,894.22
Totals	6,564.00	547,827,060.00	69,154,180.00	64,040,046.25	0.00	56,381,907.80	0.00	0.00	57,362,701.80	794,772,459.85

Source (1879-1894): Annual Report of the Director of the Mint, 1895, 28 Nov 1895, Treasury Document No. 1829, pp. 286-293 (Table XLIV).
Source (1895-1914): Annual Report of the Director of the Mint, 1915, 1 Nov 1915, Treasury Document No. 2757, pp. 102-106 (Table 20).

Figure 16.3-42: Silver and Minor (Copper) Coins Minted by the U. S., 1879-1914

Figure 16.3-43 shows the CPI, total money supply, and per-capita money supply during this period.

Year	CPI [1] (1913 = 100)	Total Money Supply [5] (USD)	Population [6]	Per Capita Money Supply (USD)	Annual Rate of Change in CPI (%)	Annual Rate of Change in Per-Capita Money Supply (%)
1879	80.620	2,550,100,184	48,290,043	52.81	-3.147	6.122
1880	87.633	2,703,743,612	49,371,340	54.76	8.341	3.636
1881	88.632	3,225,979,924	50,732,183	63.59	1.133	14.941
1882	90.850	3,411,112,742	52,093,025	65.48	2.471	2.933
1883	88.275	3,545,719,254	53,453,868	66.33	-2.875	1.291
1884	82.838	3,510,186,708	54,814,710	64.04	-6.357	-3.521
1885	79.044	3,679,362,006	56,175,553	65.50	-4.688	2.255
1886	78.115	3,779,918,458	57,536,396	65.70	-1.183	0.303
1887	78.901	4,239,663,378	58,897,238	71.98	1.002	9.140
1888	80.117	4,423,033,592	60,258,081	73.40	1.530	1.950
1889	79.617	4,753,572,432	61,618,923	77.14	-0.626	4.974
1890	79.258	5,068,566,566	62,979,766	80.48	-0.453	4.232
1891	78.471	5,223,410,890	64,303,006	81.23	-0.997	0.930
1892	75.393	5,793,388,920	65,626,246	88.28	-4.003	8.320
1893	75.752	5,649,734,644	66,949,487	84.39	0.476	-4.507
1894	69.812	5,723,255,438	68,272,727	83.83	-8.166	-0.664
1895	70.957	5,966,704,868	69,595,967	85.73	1.626	2.246
1896	68.809	5,923,114,164	70,919,207	83.52	-3.073	-2.617
1897	69.381	6,231,825,576	72,242,447	86.26	0.827	3.232
1898	71.242	7,061,919,830	73,565,688	95.99	2.647	10.690
1899	75.893	8,306,846,306	74,888,928	110.92	6.323	14.454
1900	79.686	9,010,044,060	76,212,168	118.22	4.878	6.374
1901	80.113	10,321,983,044	77,813,804	132.65	0.534	11.514
1902	84.192	11,015,295,984	79,415,441	138.70	4.966	4.463
1903	85.693	11,626,061,888	81,017,077	143.50	1.768	3.400
1904	85.765	12,264,493,350	82,618,713	148.45	0.084	3.388
1905	87.052	13,655,392,502	84,220,350	162.14	1.489	8.823
1906	89.769	14,573,342,958	85,821,986	169.81	3.074	4.622
1907	93.205	15,553,228,930	87,423,622	177.91	3.756	4.658
1908	90.557	15,346,237,426	89,025,258	172.38	-2.882	-3.155
1909	95.424	16,725,873,538	90,626,895	184.56	5.235	6.826
1910	98.930	17,585,801,850	92,228,531	190.68	3.608	3.262
1911	94.490	18,469,394,450	93,607,835	197.31	-4.592	3.418
1912	99.499	19,549,063,776	94,987,138	205.81	5.165	4.218
1913	100.000	20,022,957,806	96,366,442	207.78	0.503	0.954
1914	98.782	20,482,057,000	97,745,746	209.54	-1.225	0.846

1. CPI is the average of L-1 and L-15 data, both re-aligned to 1913 as a reference.
2. L-1 data 1791 to 1938 (Snyder-Tucker) is a general price index (wholesale prices, wages, cost of living and rents).
3. L-15 data 1801 to 1945 includes wholesale prices, all commodities.
4. L1 and L-15 from Historical Statistics of the United States, 1789-1945, A Supplement to the Statistical Abstract of the United States, Bureau of the Census, US Department of Commerce, Washington, DC, 1949.
5. See notes in money supply data for sources.
6. Population is linearly interpolated from Census results.

Figure 16.3-43: Money Supply and CPI, 1879-1914

388 | The Control and Manipulation of Money

Figure 16.3-44 shows a summary of the CPI and per-capita money supply. Three distinct intervals are evident: 1879 to 1885, 1885 to 1897, and 1897 to 1914. The average annual change in CPI and money supply for 1879 to 1885 are -8.8 and +3.50% respectively; for 1885 to 1897, -1.08 and +2.29% respectively, and for 1897 to 1914, 2.07 and 5.22% respectively.

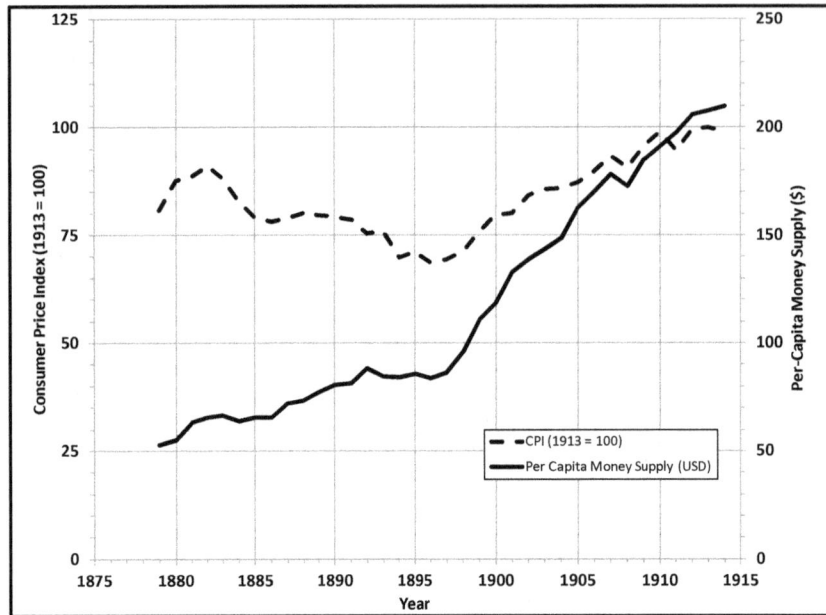

Figure 16.3-44: CPI and Per-Capita Summary, 1879-1914

Figure 16.3-45 shows the approximate median income index, consumer price index, and standard of living index for this period. See the Introduction to Part 2 for cautions regarding these curves. This is the second half of the first unusual period in U. S. history, in which the standard of living index increased dramatically in a short period.

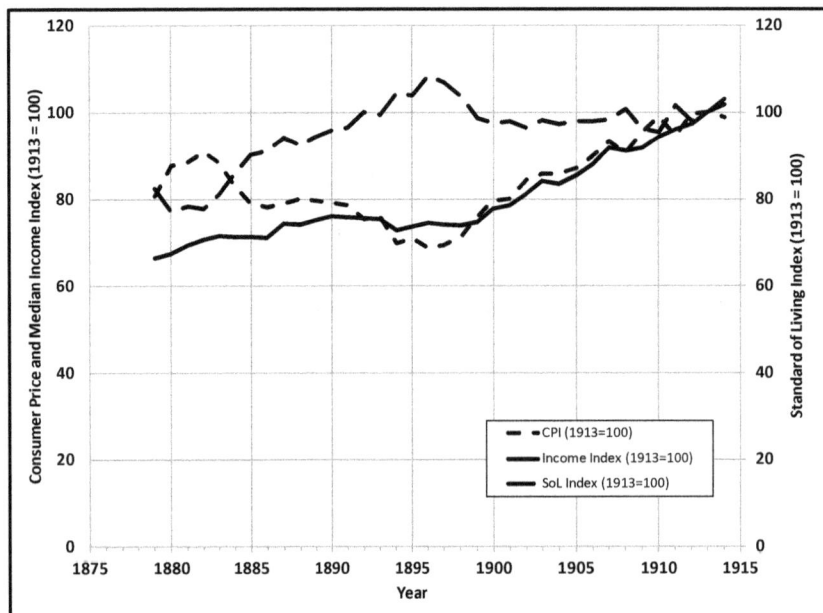

Figure 16.3-45: Median Income, Consumer Price, and Standard of Living Indices, 1879-1914

Figure 16.3-46 shows the approximate monthly interest rates for prime commercial paper loans in New York City for 1879-1889 [16.3-2].

Approximate Monthly Average, Prime Commercial Paper Rate, 60-90 Days (%) [1]											
Year	Jan	Feb	Mar	Apr	May	Jun	Jul	Aug	Sep	Oct	Nov	Dec
1879	4.33	3.81	5.06	5.45	4.44	4.25	3.90	5.56	5.78	5.94	6.25	5.95
1880	5.38	5.31	5.50	5.50	5.19	4.55	4.44	5.03	5.25	5.12	5.44	6.00
1881	5.25	5.38	5.55	5.19	4.06	3.50	4.00	4.95	5.69	6.25	6.30	6.25
1882	5.50	5.47	5.64	5.06	4.85	5.12	4.62	5.65	6.75	6.67	6.50	5.88
1883	5.50	5.38	6.38	5.81	5.35	5.50	4.78	5.61	6.00	6.00	5.69	5.50
1884	4.89	4.75	4.62	4.72	5.06	5.75	5.95	5.50	5.50	5.50	5.19	5.00
1885	4.69	4.50	4.47	3.97	3.68	3.55	3.50	3.68	3.75	4.00	4.44	4.50
1886	4.31	3.90	3.87	4.25	4.06	3.85	3.94	5.19	5.81	6.06	5.92	5.97
1887	5.50	4.81	5.35	5.38	5.21	5.13	6.19	6.35	6.94	6.38	5.75	6.00
1888	5.60	4.85	5.22	5.40	4.82	4.25	4.08	4.36	5.28	5.07	4.75	4.97
1889	4.65	4.25	4.50	4.29	3.85	3.88	4.40	5.16	5.28	6.00	6.00	6.09

1. Source: Frederick R. Macaulay, *Some Theoretical Problems Suggested by the Movements of Interest Rates, Bond Yields and Stock Prices in the United States Since 1856*, New York: National Bureau of Economic Research (NBER), 1938, Appendix A, Table 10 (pp. A147-A150). This data applies to New York City. Copyright 1938 by National Bureau of Economic Research, Inc. Used with permission.

Figure 16.3-46: Interest Rates on Prime Commercial Paper Loans, New York City, 1879-1889

Figures 16.3-47 and 16.3-48 show the approximate monthly interest rates for prime commercial paper loans (4 to 6 months) and 90-day stock market loans. This data applies to loans in New York City.

Approximate Monthly Average, Prime Commercial Paper Rate, 4 to 6 Month (%) [1]											
Year	Jan	Feb	Mar	Apr	May	Jun	Jul	Aug	Sep	Oct	Nov	Dec
1890	6.45	6.13	6.75	6.65	6.38	6.28	6.25	6.50	6.75	7.25	8.88	8.63
1891	7.28	6.38	6.50	6.25	6.50	6.50	6.60	6.75	6.60	6.41	6.25	5.75
1892	5.45	4.94	5.35	4.81	4.56	4.40	5.13	5.28	6.07	6.44	6.00	6.38
1893	6.06	6.00	6.80	6.13	8.35	9.75	9.75	9.70	10.14	7.69	5.80	5.50
1894	5.35	5.19	4.94	4.81	4.75	4.94	4.94	4.98	5.50	5.75	5.75	5.75
1895	5.89	6.79	6.50	6.25	4.85	4.31	4.55	5.50	6.44	6.44	5.50	6.80
1896	8.90	7.31	6.56	6.31	5.75	5.75	6.40	8.33	9.10	8.56	6.19	5.10
1897	4.69	4.50	4.50	4.63	4.75	4.30	4.38	4.81	5.20	5.25	4.63	5.00
1898	4.63	4.56	6.10	7.58	6.10	5.00	5.00	5.20	5.50	4.94	4.75	4.69
1899	4.50	4.50	5.20	5.25	4.80	4.50	5.06	5.70	6.29	6.00	6.80	7.38
1900	6.60	6.00	6.13	5.69	5.25	5.00	5.25	5.60	5.56	6.08	5.50	5.81
1901	5.44	5.00	4.83	5.44	5.50	5.25	5.40	5.75	5.79	5.35	5.38	5.63
1902	5.55	5.25	5.50	5.28	5.50	5.33	5.65	5.75	6.17	6.93	6.29	6.50
1903	5.71	5.60	6.08	5.91	5.66	5.81	6.00	6.75	6.75	6.50	6.57	6.55
1904	5.53	5.75	5.55	4.75	4.75	4.63	4.63	4.75	5.38	5.75	5.15	5.06
1905	4.71	4.71	4.75	4.75	4.75	4.75	4.75	4.85	5.63	5.75	6.00	6.75
1906	5.75	5.79	6.00	5.92	5.81	5.75	5.93	6.50	7.21	6.85	6.69	6.75
1907	6.69	6.50	6.81	6.47	5.71	6.25	6.36	6.60	7.17	7.83	NA	NA
1908	6.70	5.80	NA	5.25	4.25	4.64	4.58	4.43	4.75	NA	NA	4.69
1909	4.40	4.22	4.28	4.25	4.29	4.21	4.15	4.56	4.75	NA	5.98	5.59
1910	5.28	5.16	5.23	5.59	5.45	5.50	6.16	6.30	6.31	6.21	6.15	5.28
1911	4.61	4.72	4.59	4.28	4.33	4.63	4.79	4.86	5.33	4.93	4.72	5.25
1912	4.63	4.50	4.91	5.00	5.00	4.50	5.08	5.69	6.13	6.50	6.50	6.50
1913	5.50	5.50	6.25	6.20	5.88	6.38	6.66	6.63	6.45	6.38	6.25	6.30
1914	5.09	4.38	4.44	4.28	4.50	4.50	5.03	7.00	7.60	7.56	6.44	4.85

1. Source: Board of Governors of the Federal Reserve System, Bank and Monetary Statistics 1914-1941, Washington DC: Nov 1943, Table 120, pp. 448-451
2. "NA" means data not available

Figure 16.3-47: Interest Rates on Prime Commercial Paper Loans, 1890-1914

Approximate Monthly Average, Stock Exchange Time Loan Rate, 90 days (%) [1]											
Year	Jan	Feb	Mar	Apr	May	Jun	Jul	Aug	Sep	Oct	Nov	Dec
1890	5.12	4.94	5.05	4.50	4.75	5.00	4.81	5.60	6.00	6.00	6.00	6.00
1891	4.17	4.38	4.80	4.25	5.19	4.50	4.50	5.40	5.60	5.62	5.00	4.50
1892	3.45	3.12	3.55	3.00	2.63	2.62	3.00	3.25	4.87	5.20	5.38	5.50
1893	4.88	4.12	5.69	5.90	6.00	5.44	6.00	6.00	5.80	4.87	3.56	2.65
1894	2.58	2.62	2.50	2.50	2.00	1.90	2.00	2.44	2.40	2.00	2.25	2.45
1895	2.34	3.19	3.35	3.41	2.50	2.00	2.34	2.50	2.69	2.94	2.50	4.12
1896	6.00	5.35	3.88	3.87	3.10	3.12	3.62	6.40	7.00	8.10	4.45	3.10
1897	2.62	2.50	2.38	2.50	2.50	2.25	2.00	2.69	3.12	3.25	3.00	3.40
1898	2.88	2.69	4.50	5.65	3.81	2.87	2.55	2.62	3.70	2.55	2.87	3.00
1899	2.88	2.94	3.97	3.87	3.41	3.00	3.31	4.44	5.25	5.25	6.00	6.00
1900	5.00	3.12	4.55	3.50	3.00	3.05	3.33	3.60	3.88	5.00	4.44	4.78
1901	3.97	3.34	3.22	4.12	4.35	3.55	4.31	4.37	5.06	4.69	4.65	5.19
1902	4.62	4.00	4.00	4.25	4.69	4.34	4.62	4.67	6.44	6.47	6.13	6.37
1903	4.97	4.59	4.25	5.14	4.06	4.31	4.52	4.90	5.12	5.15	5.81	5.22
1904	4.03	3.69	3.22	2.75	2.56	2.25	2.42	2.31	3.10	3.50	3.69	3.67
1905	2.94	3.03	3.25	3.44	3.25	3.02	3.09	3.19	4.17	4.90	5.69	5.87
1906	5.19	5.00	5.30	5.69	4.97	4.47	4.50	5.30	7.19	5.97	7.10	7.87
1907	5.84	5.31	6.02	4.50	3.95	4.44	5.00	6.22	5.72	6.66	13.60	10.75
1908	5.83	4.22	3.84	2.94	2.87	2.34	2.27	2.56	2.56	3.00	3.31	3.20
1909	2.65	2.78	2.65	2.50	2.59	2.59	2.37	3.20	3.65	4.57	4.87	4.65
1910	4.37	3.63	3.83	4.06	3.94	3.37	3.88	3.75	4.17	4.66	4.69	4.00
1911	3.50	3.19	2.94	2.78	2.78	2.78	2.85	3.19	3.45	3.63	3.59	4.00
1912	3.13	2.88	3.36	3.56	3.28	3.13	3.50	4.10	5.34	5.70	5.93	6.00
1913	4.28	4.31	5.32	4.56	4.00	4.25	4.47	4.60	4.65	5.03	4.97	5.18
1914	3.90	3.06	3.00	2.91	2.73	2.59	3.03	6.98	7.88	6.75	5.53	4.05

1. Source: Board of Governors of the Federal Reserve System, Bank and Monetary Statistics 1914-1941, Washington DC: Nov 1943, Table 120, pp. 448-451

Figure 16.3-48: Interest Rates on 90-Day Stock Market Loans, 1890-1914

16.4 Summary, 1879-1914

The stock of money increased from 1879 to 1897, but at the same time, the CPI was decreasing; this was a continuation of the trend observed earlier from 1872 to 1878: increased productivity. From 1897 to 1914 the situation changed: now have a steadily increasing money supply and CPI. Professors Friedman and Schwartz [16.4-1] attribute the increase in the money supply to two factors: a) a large growth in the production of gold in South America, Colorado, and Alaska, coupled with improved mining techniques; and b) crop failures in Europe that caused the Europeans to import grain from the U. S., paying for it in gold. It is likely, though not certain, that the increase in CPI was lower than the increase in the money supply between 1897 and 1914 due to continued improvements in productivity that lowered prices faster than the increase in money. Friedman and Schwartz quote [16.4-2] a much larger growth in money supply for 1897 to 1914 (7.5%); the difference is that their analysis applies to total money supply, whereas the money supply growth (5.22%) in section 16.3 has been normalized to a per capita basis.

The three "panics" in this period became a justification for the Federal Reserve. The "Panic" of 1884 was caused by a sell-off of U. S. stocks by Europeans, and was generally confined only to a few banks in New York [16.4-3]. Likewise, the Panics of 1893 and 1907 were caused by a stock market crash followed by a run on the New York banks, and a spreading lack of confidence in the banking system [16.4-4]. When the runs on banks reached the reserve city and country banks, they were not able to obtain their reserves from the New York banks in sufficient time to convert the deposits into currency as demanded by their customer. Hence, they had to suspend redemption.

There was a temporary surge of interest in silver as money in this period (Sherman Act, 1890) as there was in the 1870's. Both caused some increase in the money supply, but the effect was tempered by the fact that most commerce by the 1890's was being done with checks, not notes or coin. Figure 16.3-42 shows that the ratio of coin and currency in the public hands to total deposits was about 1:4 in 1879; but 1914, it was about 1:12. The legislation of 1900 divorced silver from the dollar altogether, although silver coins continued to be minted; after 1904 it was relegated to subsidiary coinage of half-dollars and lesser denominations. Gold coinage increased after 1900, except the $3 and $1 gold coin were phased out. But this represented the beginning of a shift away from commodity money, since there was no reason why paper money, if considered more convenient in the pocket, could not be backed entirely by gold and silver. In fact, the trend away from commodity money will accelerate from 1915 to 1932, and will be complete by 1933 as will be shown in chapters 19 and 20.

There is one important point to be made about changes in America's economy during this period, and how it affected money. All of my grandparents were born in the latter portion of this period (1899-1907). One of my grandfathers was the son of a sharecropper, growing up in very rural conditions. The other grandfather was the son of a railroad worker, and grew up in a major large industrial city. The sharecropper's son did not see much money passing hand-to-hand; there was a great deal of economic activity among the farmers, but a lot of was accomplished without money (barn-raising, cooperative planting and harvesting, barter for common items, the self-reliance of many agricultural families). It was the opposite for the son of the railroad worker: money was essential since basic necessities in the cities were obtained with money. Both of my grandmothers worked until they got married (in the 1920's); afterward they stayed home and raised the children and ran the households. This was a transition period from the U. S. from a mostly agricultural society to a mostly urban one. The behavior of money changed as a result: more of it was required because more transactions were necessary. At the same time, better recordkeeping about income was done, and it is possible from this point to compare the CPI to median income levels, at least for urban workers. As the 20th century progressed, my grandparent's generation passed to my parents and their siblings. Whereas neither of my grandmothers worked outside the home, about one-third of my aunts did (my mother did, starting when the oldest child was old enough to look after the younger ones). All of the members of the second generation in my family were urban residents.

References

[16.1-1]   Murray N. Rothbard, *A History of Money and Banking in the United States: From the Colonial Era to World War II*, Auburn, AL: Ludwig von Mises Institute, 2002, pp. 153-157

[16.1-2]   Milton Friedman, Anna Jacobson Schwartz, *A Monetary History of the United States, 1867 - 1960*, A Study by the National Bureau of Economic Research, NY, Princeton, NJ: Princeton University Press, 1963, pp. 89, 90

[16.2-1]   Albert S. Bolles, *A Financial History of the United States*, NY: Augustus M. Kelley (1969), Vol. 3, pp. 301-303 (originally published 1884 by D. Appleton & Co., NY)

[16.2-2]   Text of "An act to authorize the issue of certificates of deposit in aid of the refunding of the public debt" 45th Congress, Session 3, Chapter 101, 26 Feb 1879

[16.2-3]   Text of "An act to amend the laws relating to internal revenue", 45th Congress, Session 3, Chapter 125, 1 Mar 1879

[16.2-4]   National Bureau of Economic Research, Cambridge, MA, (see website below)

[16.2-5]   Text of "An act to provide for the exchange of subsidiary coins for lawful money of the United States under certain circumstances, and to make such coins a legal tender in all sums not exceeding ten dollars, and for other purposes", 46th Congress, Session 1, Chapter 12, 9 Jun 1879

[16.2-6]   Text of "An act authorizing the conversion of the national gold banks", 46th Congress, Session 2, Chapter 25, 14 Feb 1880

[16.2-7]   op. cit., National Bureau of Economic Research

[16.2-8]   Text of "An act to repeal the discriminating duties on goods produced east of the Cape of Good Hope", 47th Congress, Session 1, Chapter 120, 4 May 1882

[16.2-9]   Text of "An act to authorize the receipt of United States gold coin in exchange for gold bars", 47th Congress, Session 1, Chapter 190, 26 May 1882

[16.2-10]   Text of "An act to enable national banking associations to extend their corporate existence, and for other purposes", 47th Congress, Session 1, Chapter 290, 12 Jul 1882

[16.2-11]   op. cit., Friedman and Schwartz, p. 25

[16.2-12]   Text of "An act to reduce internal revenue taxation, and for other purposes", 47th Congress, Session 2, Chapter 121, 3 Mar 1883

[16.2-13]   op. cit., Bolles, Vol. 3, pp. 480, 481

[16.2-14]   op. cit., Bolles, Vol. 3, pp. 260-262

[16.2-15] Oliver M. W. Sprague, *History of Crises under the National Bank System*, National Monetary Commission, 61st Congress, Senate Document 538, Washington DC: U. S. Government Printing Office, 1910, pp. 108-123, 345-353

[16.2-16] op. cit., Friedman and Schwartz, pp. 100, 101

[16.2-17] Text of "An Act to establish a Bureau of Labor", 48th Congress, Session 1, Chapter 127, 27 Jun 1884

[16.2-18] op. cit., National Bureau of Economic Research

[16.2-19] Text of "An act to regulate commerce", 49th Congress, Session 2, Chapter 104, Public Law 49-104, 4 Feb 1887

[16.2-20] Text of "An act to amend sections five thousand one hundred and ninety-one and five thousand one hundred and ninety-two of the Revised Statutes of the United States, and for other purposes", 49th Congress, Session 2, Chapter 378, 3 Mar 1887

[16.2-21] op. cit., Friedman and Schwartz, p. 123

[16.2-22] Bruce Champ, *The National Banking System: A Brief Summary*, Working Paper 07-23, Dec 2007, Federal Reserve Bank of Cleveland, p. 32

[16.2-23] Text of "An act for the retirement and recoinage of the trade dollar", 49th Congress, Session 2, Chapter 396, 3 Mar 1887

[16.2-24] op. cit., National Bureau of Economic Research

[16.2-25] op. cit., National Bureau of Economic Research

[16.2-26] Text of "An act to establish a department of Labor", 50th Congress, Session 1, Chapter 389, 13 Jun 1888

[16.2-27] op. cit., Sprague, pp. 124-152, 387-392

[16.2-28] Text of "An act to protect trade and commerce against unlawful restraints and monopolies", 51st Congress, Session 1, Chapter 647, 2 Jul 1890

[16.2-29] Text of "An act directing the purchase of silver bullion and the issue of Treasury notes, and for other purposes", a.k.a. the Sherman Silver Purchase Act, 51st Congress, Session 1, Chapter 708, 14 Jul 1890

[16.2-30] Clifton H. Kreps, Jr., *Money, Banking and Monetary Policy*, NY: The Ronald Press Co., 1962, p. 87

[16.2-31] op. cit., Kreps, pp. 85-87

[16.2-32] op. cit., National Bureau of Economic Research

[16.2-33] Text of "An act to discontinue the coinage of the three-dollar and one-dollar gold pieces and three-cent nickel piece", 51st Congress, Session 1, Chapter 945, 26 Sep 1890

[16.2-34] Text of "An act to reduce the revenue and equalize duties on imports, and for other purposes", a.k.a. the McKinley Tariff Act, 51st Congress, Session 1, Chapter 1244, 1 Oct 1890

[16.2-35] op. cit., Friedman and Schwartz, p. 106

[16.2-36] op. cit., National Bureau of Economic Research

[16.2-37] Text of "An act relating to the limitation of the hours of daily service of laborers and mechanics employed upon the public works of the United States and the District of Columbia", 52nd Congress, Session 1, Chapter 352, 1 Aug 1892

[16.2-38] op. cit., National Bureau of Economic Research

[16.2-39] op. cit., Sprague, pp. 153-162, 400-412

[16.2-40] op. cit., Kreps, p. 88

[16.2-41] op. cit., Sprague, pp. 163-215, 400-412

[16.2-42] op. cit., Friedman and Schwartz, p. 108

[16.2-43] op. cit. Friedman and Schwartz, p. 111

[16.2-44] Text of "An act to repeal a part of an act approved July fourteenth, eighteen hundred and ninety, entitled 'An act directing purchase silver bullion and the issue of Treasury notes thereon, and for other purposes'", 53rd Congress, Session 1, Chapter 8, 1 Nov 1893

[16.2-45] op. cit., Kreps, p. 88

[16.2-46] op. cit., National Bureau of Economic Research

[16.2-47] Text of "An Act to subject to State taxation national bank notes and United States Treasury notes", 53rd Congress, Session 2, Chapter 281, 13 Aug 1894

[16.2-48] Text of "An Act to reduce taxation, to provide revenue for the Government, and for other purposes", a.k.a. Wilson-Gorman Tariff Act, 53rd Congress, Session 2, Chapter 349, 27 Aug 1894

[16.2-49] Edward S. Corwin, ed., *The Constitution of the United States of America, Annotations of Cases Decided by the Supreme Court of the United States to June 30th, 1952*, 82nd Congress, Document No. 170, U. S. Government Printing Office, 1953, pp. 319-321, 1191-1193

[16.2-50] op. cit., National Bureau of Economic Research

[16.2-51]   op. cit., National Bureau of Economic Research

[16.2-52]   Text of "An Act to provide revenue for the Government and to encourage the industries of the United States", a.k.a. Dingley Tariff Act, 55th Congress, Session 1, Chapter 11, 24 Jul 1897

[16.2-53]   Text of "An Act to provide ways and means to meet war expenditures, and for other purposes", 55th Congress, Session 2, Chapter 448, 13 Jun 1898

[16.2-54]   op. cit., National Bureau of Economic Research

[16.2-55]   Text of "An Act to define and fix the standard of value, to maintain the parity of all forms of money issued or coined by the United States, to refund the public debt, and for other purposes", a.k.a. the Gold Act, 56th Congress, Session 1, Chapter 41, 14 Mar 1900

[16.2-56]   op. cit., Kreps, p. 84

[16.2-57]   op. cit., National Bureau of Economic Research

[16.2-58]   Text of "An Act to amend an Act entitled 'An Act to provide ways and means to meet war expenditures, and for other purposes', approved June thirteenth, eighteen hundred and ninety-eight, and to reduce taxation thereunder", 56th Congress, Session 2, Chapter 806, 2 Mar 1901

[16.2-59]   Text of "An Act to repeal war-revenue taxation, and for other purposes", 57th Congress, Session 1, Chapter 500, 12 Apr 1902

[16.2-60]   Text of "An Act to provide for the extension of the charters of national banks", 57th Congress, Session 1, Chapter 503, 12 Apr 1902

[16.2-61]   op. cit., National Bureau of Economic Research

[16.2-62]   Text of "An Act relating to Hawaiian silver coinage and silver certificates", 57th Congress, Session 2, Chapter 186, 14 Jan 1903

[16.2-63]   Text of "An Act to establish the Department of Commerce and Labor", 57th Congress, Session 2, Chapter 552, 14 Feb 1903

[16.2-64]   Text of "An Act to amend section one of an Act entitled 'An Act to amend sections fifty-one hundred and ninety-one and fifty-one hundred and ninety-two of the Revised Statutes of the United States, and for other purposes", 57th Congress, Session 2, Chapter 1014, 3 Mar 1903

[16.2-65]   op. cit., National Bureau of Economic Research

[16.2-66]   Text of "An Act to amend section six of an Act entitled 'An Act to define and fix the standard of value, to maintain the parity of all forms of money issued or coined by the United States, to refund the public debt, and for other purposes', approved March fourteenth, nineteen hundred", 59th Congress, Session 1, Chapter 2558, 26 May 1906

[16.2-67]   Text of "An Act to amend section fifty-two hundred, Revised Statutes of the United States, relating to national banks", 59th Congress, Session 1, Chapter 3516, 22 Jun 1906

[16.2-68]   Text of "An Act to amend the national banking Act, and for other purposes", 59th Congress, Session 2, Chapter 2913, 4 Mar 1907

[16.2-69]   op. cit., Sprague, pp. 240-242

[16.2-70]   op. cit., National Bureau of Economic Research

[16.2-71]   op. cit. Sprague, pp. 242-244

[16.2-72]   op. cit., Friedman and Schwartz, pp. 156-168

[16.2-73]   op. cit., Sprague, pp. 244-320, 429, 430

[16.2-74]   Text of "An Act to amend the banking laws", a.k.a. the Aldrich-Vreeland Act, 60th Congress, Session 1, Chapter 229, 30 May 1908

[16.2-75]   op. cit., Friedman and Schwartz, pp. 170, 171

[16.2-76]   op. cit., National Bureau of Economic Research

[16.2-77]   Text of "An Act to provide revenue, equalize duties and encourage the industries of the United States, and for other purposes", 61st Congress, Session 1, Chapter 6, 5 Aug 1909

[16.2-78]   Text of "An Act to raise revenue for the Philippine Islands, and for other purposes", 61st Congress, Session 1, Chapter 8, 5 Aug 1909

[16.2-79]   op. cit., National Bureau of Economic Research

[16.2-80]   Text of "An Act prescribing certain conditions under which bonds and certificates of indebtedness of the United States may be issued, and for other purposes", 61st Congress, Session 1, Chapter 25, 4 Feb 1910

[16.2-81]   Text of "An Act to establish postal savings depositories for depositing savings at interest with the security of the Government for repayment thereof, and for other purposes", 61st Congress, Session 2, Chapter 386, 25 Jun 1910

[16.2-82] Text of "An Act to amend section six of the currency act of March fourteenth, nineteen hundred, as amended by the Act approved March fourth, nineteen hundred and seven", 61st Congress, Session 3, Chapter 190, 2 Mar 1911

[16.2-83] Text of "An Act to restrain the Secretary of the Treasury from receiving bonds issued to provide money for the building of the panama Canal as security for the issue of circulating notes to national banks, and for other purposes", 61st Congress, Session 3, Chapter 195, 2 Mar 1911

[16.2-84] Text of "An Act to require the National Monetary Commission to make final reports on or before January eighth, nineteen hundred and twelve, and to repeal sections seventeen, eighteen, and nineteen of the Act entitled 'An Act to amend the national banking laws,' approved May thirtieth, nineteen hundred and eight, the repeal to take effect March thirty-first, nineteen hundred and twelve", 62nd Congress, Session 1, Chapter 36, 22 Aug 1911

[16.2-85] op. cit., Kreps, p. 167

[16.2-86] op. cit., National Bureau of Economic Research

[16.2-87] op. cit., National Bureau of Economic Research

[16.2-88] Text of "An Act to Create a Department of Labor", 62nd Congress, Session 3, Chapter 141, 4 Mar 1913

[16.2-89] Text of "An Act to reduce tariff duties and to provide revenue for the Government, and for other purposes", 63rd Congress, Session 1, Chapter 16, Public Law 63-16, 3 Oct 1913

[16.2-90] Text of "An Act to provide for the establishment of Federal reserve banks, to furnish an elastic currency, to afford a means of rediscounting commercial paper, to establish a more effective supervision of banking in the United States, and for other purposes", a.k.a. "The Federal Reserve Act", 63rd Congress, Session 2, Chapter 6, Public Law 63-43, 23 Dec 1913

[16.2-91] op. cit., Friedman and Schwartz, p. 172

[16.2-92] Text of "An Act to amend section twenty-seven of an Act approved December twenty-third, nineteen hundred and thirteen, and known as the Federal Reserve Act", 63rd Congress, Session 2, Chapter 225, Public Law 63-163, 4 Aug 1914

[16.2-93] Text of "An Act proposing an amendment to section nineteen of the Federal Reserve Act relating to reserves, and for other purposes", Public Law 63-171, 15 Aug 1914

[16.2-94] Text of "An Act to create a federal trade commission, to define its powers and duties, and for other purposes", Public Law 63-203, 26 Sep 1914

[16.2-95] op. cit., Kreps, p. 511

[16.2-96] op. cit., Friedman and Schwartz, p. 578

[16.2-97] op. cit., Friedman and Schwartz, p. 172

[16.2-98] op. cit., National Bureau of Economic Research

[16.3-1] op. cit., Friedman Schwartz, Appendix A, pp. 704-708

[16.3-2] Frederick R. Macaulay, *Some Theoretical problems Suggested by the Movements of Interest Rates, Bond Yields and Stock Prices in the United Sates Since 1856*, New York: National Bureau of Economic Research, 1838, Appendix A, Table 10 (pp. A147-A150). Copyright 1938, by National Bureau of Economic Research, Inc. Used with permission.

[16.4-1] op. cit., Friedman and Schwartz, pp. 137, 140

[16.4-2] op. cit., Friedman and Schwartz, p. 138

[16.4-3] op. cit., Friedman and Schwartz, pp. 100, 101

[16.4-4] op. cit., Friedman and Schwartz, pp. 108, 156-162

NBER website: https://www.nber.org/research/data/us-business-cycle-expansions-and-contractions

A Digression on the Federal Reserve System and Commercial Banks

17.1 Introduction

This chapter describes the structure and operation of the Federal Reserve (the U. S. central bank) and the relations between it, the U. S. Treasury, and the commercial banking system. The first three topics are the rationale for the Federal Reserve, its structure, and operational control. Next is considered the operation of the Federal Reserve and its relation to the U. S. Treasury and the commercial banking institutions, showing how the system works as a unified whole under the Federal Reserve central bank. Last is a description of the several means utilized to control the quantity of money.

17.2 Rationale for the Federal Reserve

The Federal Reserve Act was signed into law by President Wilson on 23 Dec 1913 and went into operation on 16 Nov 1914. Congress had previously set up other "Banks of the United States" (1791 to 1811, 1817 to 1837), but they operated only as the fiscal agent for the government, and served as a restraint on the volume of notes issued by State-chartered banks. Otherwise they were commercial banks. Those institutions attempted to provide a uniform currency, mostly by requiring other banks to redeem their notes in coin. The Federal Reserve is the first true central bank in the U. S. because it has a monopoly on the issuing of bank notes (called Federal Reserve Notes), and has supervisory authority over all the commercial banks in the U. S. that choose to become members of the Federal Reserve system. The establishment of the Federal Reserve was justified by its promoters under six categories.

The first justification was the protection of the commercial banking system, i.e., to provide liquidity to the commercial banks if they experienced a run. This is commonly called being "lender of last resort" [17.2-1]: if the commercial banks were to experience an unusual demand for cash, the central bank would provide it, and thus protect otherwise solvent banks from failure. In the course of aiding commercial banks, it would provide the means for an elastic currency by being granted the authority to discount commercial paper directly. That means it could buy the assets of banks [17.2-2], transforming those assets into money, in order to accommodate seasonal variations in the demand for cash or demand deposits. The goal of "protecting the banks" was also a means to prevent the "financial panics" that had occurred periodically in the U. S. (most notably in 1837, 1839, 1857, 1866, 1872, 1884, 1893, and 1907).

A financial panic is defined as a local shortage of money. The logic behind the Federal Reserve was to centralize reserves under one institution such that they would be available to all the banks that chose to become members of the Federal Reserve System. The goal was to correct a defect in the existing National Bank system [17.2-3], wherein banks kept a large amount of money in the vault that was not usable, since it functioned as its local reserve. It is true that banks held reserves as deposits in other banks, but those banks often made loans against those deposits, sometimes on call loans, and sometimes to still other banks. When a large demand for cash occurred, the national bank used up all of its cash in the vault, but then had to call in loans and its reserves that it held in other banks. Call loans against stocks meant that the stocks had to be sold quickly, which caused the price of stocks to fall and, depending on the level of the market, sometimes did not result in sufficient revenue to pay back the loan. The consequence was both a decline in stock prices and an apparent shortage of money-in-hand. That caused a shortage of cash, and cast suspicion on the entire banking system, which sometimes led to further demands for cash. The underlying problem was that although the national bank system had sufficient overall "reserves" to meet occasional large demand for cash, they were not always in the proper location to actually accommodate those demands when they occurred.

The Federal Reserve did not in fact eliminate the "panics"; the problem of "runs" on the banks was resolved by the Federal Deposit Insurance Corporation (FDIC). Once the public was assured that their deposits would be returned, there was little motivation to demand payment en masse from the banks. Whether the FDIC is adequately funded is another matter entirely (it is not).

The second justification was that the Federal Reserve would promote stability in the banking system under a uniform system of financial requirements, supervision, and regulation [17.2-4]. The objective is to make sure that the banks are able to perform their function without undue risk to either their customers or the banking system generally. Since banks are profit-seeking institutions, their viability must be maintained while allowing for competition among the various banks. This includes examination of banks' financial records, regulation of mergers and acquisitions, evaluating the prevention of local banking monopolies. Also, a central bank would bring all the commercial banks under a uniform supervisory regime such that an accurate assessment of money and debt could be reported.

The third justification was to protect the nation's monetary reserves (then consisting of gold) by centralizing the control over it. It was believed at the time that the gold coinage system would continue, and could operate efficiently so long as its movements could be monitored to prevent a drain out of the nation. Once the reserves are controlled, the money supply can be controlled, thus to bring the banking system under the leadership of the central bank.

The fourth justification was that the central bank would perform a host of banking functions as a public service without profit motive, including operating a nationwide check clearinghouse and providing loans and discounts to banks. A central bank could provide an elastic currency and a more efficient overall operation of the money supply [17.2-5]. It could accomplish this goal by operating a nation-wide check clearing system, thus improving and thus expanding the use of checks, which in turn would reduce the dependence on bank notes transferred hand-to-hand in transactions. A central bank clearinghouse would also reduce the time delay in collecting checks and balancing accounts. Also, with the reserves and clearinghouse operating smoothly, a central bank could respond to seasonal variations in the demand for money, whether bank notes or deposits; this would correct the defect of a fixed amount of notes that prevailed under the National Bank system. Since it earns it interest on securities that it buys, and on loans to banks, the Federal Reserve does earn a profit, but these are transferred to the U. S. Treasury after expenses are deducted.

A fifth justification was that a central bank could manage foreign exchange more efficiently [17.2-6]. The idea here was that an U. S. central bank could bypass London as the financier of foreign exchange, and by doing so, could prevent trading partners from gaining inside information on U. S. importers and exporters. Secondly, a U. S. central bank should be able to reduce the expenses of shipping gold and insurance.

The sixth justification was that a central bank could more efficiently handle the government's financial interests and payments [17.2-7]. A central bank could dispense with the inefficiencies of the National Bank system, in which government funds were dispersed among many banks (1,514 in 1914), leading to large amounts of government funds lying in vaults, for which no interest was earned, but requiring accounting expenses. Secondly, the government funds tended to vary periodically during the year. When the government had large payments to make, it made large withdrawals that contracted the currency; when it made large deposits in the collection of taxes, it made large deposits which expanded the currency. The net effect was to cause changes in interest rates on certain types of loans. Third, the national banks had to rely on the government, specifically the Secretary of the Treasury, to supply them with government deposits when there was a large local requirement for cash or demand deposits. Generally the growth and contraction of government assets in the national banks did not correlate with demands from the public for cash or deposits, and the Treasury was responsible for smoothing out the fluctuations; which in turn raised suspicion that the Treasury Secretary exercised too much power.

The banking system was still in the process of transitioning from the National Bank system to the Federal Reserve when World War I broke out. Benjamin Strong, first Governor of the Federal Reserve Bank of New York, was a major force within the Federal Reserve until his death in 1928. He had been selected to attend the secret meeting at the Jekyll Island Hunt Club in 1910 that formulated the Aldrich Plan, a revised banking system for the U. S. to be called the National Reserve Association. The other attendees were Senator Nelson Aldrich of Rhode Island; A. Piatt Andrew, Assistant Secretary of the Treasury; Paul Warburg, a partner in the Kuhn, Loeb & Co. bank of New York; Frank A. Vanderlip, president of the National City Bank of New York; Henry P. Davison, partner in J. P. Morgan; and Charles D. Norton, president of the First National Bank of New York [17.2-8]. Congress regarded the Aldrich Plan to be too heavily weighted toward the bankers' interests, and adopted a modified version of it that ultimately became the Federal Reserve Act. The main difference was that the Federal Reserve System consisted of regional banks as a way to "decentralize" a central bank (or to give the illusion thereof); ensured that the top officers were publicly appointed; and that other interests were represented in the operation of the system. Strong gives an additional rationale for the development of the Federal Reserve besides those cited above [17.2-9]:

> "It was the influence of the war which demanded that the federal reserve banks be organized as promptly as possible. The best banking machinery and the best banking talent in the country seemed to be required to protect the interests of both bankers and business men. Much was expected from the new system, once it was started. Very shortly, however, immense imports of gold from abroad, general business prosperity stimulated by war profits, and reasonably comfortable conditions in credit and banking, appeared to put the federal reserve banks for the first two and one-half years of their existence into the class of expensive luxuries; in fact, they were regarded as examples of governmental interference with business which were tolerated but, nevertheless, were not appreciated by many bankers.
>
> During this interval, November 1914 to April 1917, the system, by slow stages of progress, found itself. The machinery for conducting actual operations was designed and developed far beyond the requirements of the moment. The terms of the Act were perfected where need was discovered, the men engaged in the work became better acquainted with their duties and with each other, skilled clerks were engaged and trained, and accounting methods perfected, so that when the test came as a result of our entry into the war, in April 1917, the federal reserve banks were in large measure prepared for the grave tasks and responsibilities at once to be assumed.
>
> During the first twelve months of our country's participation in the war the reserve system became established upon a basis of confidence and respect, even in fact of admiration, among both bankers and business men; and its future therefore seems assured so long as good management deserves the support now enjoyed."

Kemmerer amplified this notion [17.2-10]:

> "The Secretary of the Treasury said in his report of 1918: 'Much of the great work has been done by the federal reserve banks. The federal reserve system has been of incalculable value during this period of war financing on the most extensive scale ever undertaken by any nation in the history of the world. It would have been impossible to carry through these unprecedented financial operations under our old banking system. Great credit is due to the federal reserve banks for their broad grasp of the situation and their intelligent, comprehensive cooperation.'
>
> One shudders when he thinks what might have happened if the war had found us with our former decentralized and antiquated banking system. Think of pouring the crisis of 1914-1918 into bottles that broke with the crisis of 1907!"

It's a good thing Congress did not adopt the Aldrich plan; the U. S. would have been prepared to get embroiled in World War I on the every first day (28 Jul 1914).

17.3 Structure of the Federal Reserve

The Federal Reserve System was set up as twelve regional Federal Reserve banks rather than a single central bank as is the case in England and France. The nation was divided into twelve regions, each of which was to have a Federal Reserve Bank (some with branches) that would collect data from all the banks in its jurisdiction. Supposedly each of them could conduct its operations in accordance with the needs of the district; sort of a decentralized, diffused central bank. That seemed like a good idea, so long as the twelve Federal Reserve Banks could operate independently in accordance with the needs of their district. Most likely this was a fiction added to the law to pacify those who saw the danger of central banks. Although advertised as a decentralized system responsive to the needs of differing areas of the country, the authors knew, or should have known, that an institution with central bank powers has to be centrally controlled. Leadership of the Federal Reserve initially lay with the Federal Reserve Bank in New York, since its officers had the most knowledge and experience, but power was transferred by the 1920's to the headquarters in Washington D. C. under a Board of Governors such that the system operates as a one-size-fits-all central bank. The structure of the system in the 1913 law made the transfer seamless through the rules regarding the appointment of officers and by rules on transactions. It is curious that the first two decades of the 20th century saw a movement to break up the large business monopolies, but at the same time, to turn the banking business into a unified cartel by creating a central bank.

The U. S. commercial banking system under Federal Reserve consists of three types of institutions: a) the twelve regional Federal Reserve Banks and their branches, b) federally-chartered commercial banks; and c) (optionally) State-chartered commercial banks. The twelve regional Federal Reserve Banks and their branches are:

District 1: Boston, MA
District 2: New York City, NY, with a branch in Buffalo, NY
District 3: Philadelphia, PA
District 4: Cleveland, OH, with branches in Pittsburgh, PA, and Cincinnati, OH
District 5: Richmond, VA, with branches in Baltimore, MD, and Charlotte, NC
District 6: Atlanta, GA, with branches in Nashville, TN, Birmingham, AL, New Orleans, LA, and Jacksonville, FL
District 7: Chicago, IL, with a branch in Detroit, MI
District 8: St. Louis, MO, with branches in Louisville, KY, Memphis, TN, and Little Rock, AR
District 9: Minneapolis, MN, with a branch in Helena, MT
District 10: Kansas City, MO, with branches in Omaha, NE, Denver, CO, and Oklahoma City, OK
District 11: Dallas, TX, with branches in Houston, TX, San Antonio, TX, and El Paso, TX
District 12: San Francisco, CA, with branches in Seattle, WA, Portland, OR, Los Angeles, CA, and Salt Lake City, UT

Figure 17.3-1 shows the rules for federally chartered vs. State chartered commercial banks in relation to the Federal Reserve. Federally-chartered commercial banks (called "national banks") are required to become members of the Federal Reserve and the Federal Deposit Insurance Corporation (FDIC). They are subject to triple supervision (Federal Reserve, FDIC, and Comptroller of the Currency) and examined by the Comptroller of the Currency. A State-chartered commercial bank may choose to become a member of the Federal Reserve. If so, it must also join the FDIC, and is also subject to triple supervision (State, Federal Reserve, and the FDIC) while being examined by both the State banking authorities and the FDIC. If a State-chartered bank chooses not to become a member of the Federal Reserve, it may still join the FDIC. It is then supervised by the Federal Reserve and examined by the State banking authority and by the FDIC (if it is a member).

Federal Charter	State Charter	
Naming convention: "national bank"	Naming convention: Arbitrary or as designated by the State	
Must be member of Federal Reserve	If a member of the Federal Reserve	If not a member of the Federal Reserve
Must be member of FDIC	Must be a member of FDIC	FDIC membership optional
Supervised by:	Supervised by:	Supervised by:
Comptroller of the Currency	State banking authorities	State banking authorities
Federal Reserve	Federal Reserve	FDIC (if a member)
FDIC	FDIC	
Examined by:	Examined by:	Examined by:
Comptroller of the Currency	State banking authorities	State banking authorities
	Federal Reserve	FDIC (if a member)

Figure 17.3-1: Federal vs. State Chartered Banks In Relation to Federal Reserve

Banks that choose to become members of the Federal Reserve are required to subscribe 6% of their total capital into stock in the Federal Reserve regional or branch bank. Therefore, technically, the Federal Reserve banks are privately owned (private in the sense of not being government agencies), since the only stockholders are commercial banks. Commercial banks are U. S. institutions and are either privately owned or publicly traded. The member banks as shareholders receive 6% dividend on their stock annually. But the "ownership" is a fiction: although the member banks own all the shares in the Federal Reserve regional and branch Banks, they have no control over the operations at those Banks. All policies and activities are decided and performed by officers of the Federal Reserve Banks, not by a Board of Directors elected by the shareholders as in a normal corporation. The "owners" only choose a minority of the Directors of the Federal Reserve regional or branch Banks, and even then they have limited powers. The main benefits of being a member bank are [17.3-1]: a) access to the clearinghouse function; b) the ability to obtain reserves through the discount power; and c) the ability to obtain Federal Reserve Notes, which are the same as any other bank notes used as currency by the public.

The Federal Reserve was granted powers to provide services for, and to regulate, commercial banks; and also to indirectly control the money supply. The services provided to its member banks fall into four categories: a) access to the Federal Reserve's check clearing and collection service; b) print and provide Federal Reserve Notes to member banks when required; c) provide discounts (loans) to member banks; and d) handle member bank accounts at the Federal Reserve (i.e., the reserve accounts). The discount service amounts to the Federal Reserve buying assets from a commercial banks at a discount, which amounts to a loan from the Federal Reserve to the bank, usually done to provide liquidity to the commercial banks. The proceeds of the loan are added to the commercial bank's reserve account at the Federal Reserve. The discount, like any loan, has to be repaid.

The Federal Reserve is the fiscal agent for the federal government, handling interactions with the U. S. Treasury and managing accounts for receipts of taxes and disbursements by the federal government. It controls the overall money supply using four powers initially granted to each of the twelve regional Banks. The four powers are: a) set margin requirements for loans on securities sold on exchanges; b) set maximum interest rates payable on savings and time deposits; c) set reserve requirements for member banks; and d) permitted the Federal Reserve to engage in "open market operations", in which it is authorized to buy and sell U. S. government securities of any denomination and term. This last power was centralized by the Banking Acts of 1933 and 1935 [17.3-2] into the Federal Open Market Committee (FOMC). The Federal Reserve eventually migrated from the initial plan of using commercial discounting as the basis for reserves into the use of U. S. government securities for reserves [17.3-3].

17.4 Operations of the Federal Reserve

The Federal Reserve is headquartered in Washington, DC, and is led by a Board of Governors. The structure has changed somewhat since 1913. In its current configuration, the Board of Governors consists of seven members, serving 14 year terms, all of whom are appointed by the President of the U. S. and approved by the U. S. Senate. They are appointed by the President, but are not part of the Executive branch of the government. The chairman and vice-chairman of the Board are designated by the President, and serve four-year terms, and may be re-appointed. A member may not be re-appointed after serving the full 14-year term. The terms are staggered such that one vacancy occurs every two years. Each member of the Board of Governors must come from different Federal Reserve region. All the expenses of the Board are paid by the twelve regional Banks, including the salaries of the Board members, the staff of analysts, auditors, and examiners. An annual report is sent to Congress, not to the President or the Secretary of the Treasury. This arrangement was established in order to give the illusion that the Federal Reserve is independent of political considerations. It advertises itself as "an independent agency of the federal government" [17.4-1].

The Board currently has several administrative divisions: a) Inspector General; b) Currency (handles bank payments, risk analysis, some oversight functions, and printing of Federal Reserve Notes); c) Research and Statistics; d) International Finance; e) Monetary Affairs; f) Financial Stability; g) Supervision and Regulation; h) Consumer and Community Affairs; i) Legal; j) Reserve Bank Operations and Payment Systems; and k) the Chief Operating Officer, which has three sub-divisions: Information Technology, Management, and Financial Management.

The Board of Governors has four primary functions. First, it determines the reserve ratio requirements for all member banks. For each member commercial bank, the reserve ratio is the fraction of reserves to be kept on deposit in a Federal Reserve Bank as necessary to meet day-to-day transactions. It is called the primary reserve ratio, and is intended to provide "liquidity" at each commercial bank, i.e., the ability to meet immediate demand deposit withdrawals. It is the means to ensure that the bank can meet its immediate liabilities day-to-day. Second, it sets margin rates on loans made by commercial banks to customers who use the loans to buy securities listed on stock exchanges. The margin rate is the fraction that must be provided by the borrower to buy those securities; if the margin rate is 75%, it means that the borrower, who intends to use the loan to buy open-market securities, must provide 75% of the funds; i.e., the maximum loan amount is limited to 25% of the value of the securities. The idea is to control the amount of demand deposits created in the course of making the loan that is subject to risk of default from a steep decline stock market prices. Federal Reserve Regulation T applies to loans made by stock brokers and dealers to their customers; Regulation U applies to loans on stocks made by the member banks. Regulation X applies Regulations T and U to any person subject to U. S. laws on obtaining loans for stock purchases anywhere, inside or outside the U. S. The third function of the Board is to set the maximum interest rates at the member banks may pay on savings and time accounts. Payment of interest is prohibited on demand deposit accounts (since 1935). The rationale for limiting interest rates is to control competition among member banks, i.e., to prevent them from paying higher interest rates in order to attract deposits [17.4-2]. The fourth function of the Board is to sit on the Federal Open-Market Committee (FOMC); the seven member of the Board of Governors constitutes a majority of the twelve-member FOMC. The operation of the FOMC is probably the most important function of the Federal Reserve, as it exerts the greatest amount of control over the money supply and the interest rate. One of its important functions is to set the target rate for the "Federal Funds Rate", which is the interest rate charged for overnight loans between commercial banks. The amounts that can be lent are limited to the excess reserves held by the commercial banks at the Federal Reserve Banks. The target rate is set by the Federal Reserve Open Market Committee, revised 8 times each year, although the actual rate depends on agreement between the banks. The Federal Funds Rate is an important determinate of interest rates for commercial, home, and car loans by the banking system. The economy is indirectly stimulated by a decrease in the Federal Funds Rate, which increases the demand for short-term loans; the economy is indirectly slowed by increasing the Federal Funds Rate, which reduces the demand for short-term loans.

America's money supply is actually controlled, albeit indirectly, by the activities of the Federal Open Market Committee (FOMC). It consists of twelve members, seven of whom are the Federal Reserve Board of Governors. The Chairman of the Board of Governors is also Chairman of the FOMC. By tradition, the President of the Federal Reserve Bank of New York is the vice-chairman of the FOMC (and also handles the actual transactions). Remaining seats on the FOMC are occupied by four Presidents of the other Federal Reserve regional Banks, each serving one-year rotating terms. The FOMC has the authority to buy and sell on the open market any type of U. S. government security of any amount or maturity. All transaction decisions made by the FOMC are binding on all twelve regional Federal Reserve Banks and their branches, and the amounts of ownership are assigned to each Federal Reserve Bank on a pro-rata basis per the relative size of those banks. They are held on the FOMC's security portfolio on behalf of the twelve banks and branches, and the Banks earn interest on those securities. But the profits of the regional banks, after expenses, are provided to the U. S. Treasury, since the Federal Reserve is intended to operate as a non-profit public service.

The Board of Governors consults quarterly with an Advisory Council, consisting of one representative elected by the Board of Directors of each of the twelve regional banks. The Advisory Council is designed to give advice to the Board regarding the state of commercial banks and policies of the Reserve system.

Each of the twelve regional Federal Reserve Banks is led by nine Directors, divided into three classes, called A, B, and C. All nine Directors serve three-year terms. The "Class A" Directors are bankers, and the "Class B" Directors are businessmen, all of whom are elected by the member banks within the Regional Banks' district. "Class C" Directors are appointed by the Board of Governors; one of these is the Chairman of the Board of the regional Federal Reserve Bank, and one is the vice-Chairman. This Board of Directors performs general supervision of the Federal Reserve Bank. Additionally, with the approval of the Board of Governors, these nine directors: a) set the discount rate for member banks in the Federal Reserve district; b) appoint other bank officers such as the President and vice-President; c) manage the other personnel of the bank; and d) set the salaries of all employees in the regional Bank.

Not every commercial bank chooses to become a member of the Federal Reserve, but all of them do business with a member. The reason is that every commercial bank requires access to the Federal Reserve's check clearinghouse, and access to the physical Federal Reserve Notes. In order to do so, a non-member bank will keep a demand deposit account in a member bank (referred to as a correspondent bank); that account is used to pay or receive payment on checks made against or to the non-member bank. That same account can be used to pay for any notes that the non-member bank requires for its customers, and it is also constitutes the primary reserves of the non-member bank (along with the cash in its vault) [17.4-3]. Secondly, although only a minority of commercial banks chose to become members, those member banks hold the vast majority of deposits. Each commercial bank is primarily concerned with five operations: liquidity reserves, demand deposits, secondary deposits, loans, and its investment portfolio.

A commercial bank holds reserves for four purposes: a) to meet legal requirements per the bank regulations; b) to make payments to other banks for clearinghouse services rendered; c) to have cash on hand for customers in the form of Federal Reserve Notes; and d) to hold additional reserves to accommodate future loan requests. "Liquidity reserves" is the sum of the primary and secondary reserves plus some additional factor for day-to-day working cash at the discretion of the bank management [17.4-4] as described in section 5.6. "Primary reserves" is the sum of the legal and working reserves held against current demand deposits. A revision to the banking laws in 1959 permitted cash held in the vault to be counted against legal reserve requirements. Primary reserves are held to meet anticipated near-term withdrawals [17.4-5]. For banks that are members of the Federal Reserve, primary reserves are the sum of cash in the vault and their deposits as the Federal Reserve Bank. For non-members, primary reserves are the sum of cash in the vault plus their account at a "correspondent bank" that is a member of the Federal Reserve.

"Secondary" reserves [17.4-6] are held to accommodate new loan requests and withdrawals that the banker anticipates to occur within a year or so. They are mostly held in the form of open-market securities, usually having less than a year to run to maturity, of the highest quality, and thus easily marketed. They generally consist of U. S. government securities, although they could consist of commercial paper and acceptances. They are used the same as primary reserves (to provide liquidity), but with two distinctions: they are liquidity requirements that are not immediate but expected in the short-term, and they do earn some income. Each banker makes choices based on his experience about how much to keep in secondary reserves (since primary reserves are the combination of required legal reserves and day-to-day operations).

Commercial banks accept two types of "primary deposits": demand, and time. Demand deposits include: a) deposits owned by other banks; b) the U. S. government (usually in the form of Tax and Loan accounts); c) State and local government entities (fire, water, and school districts, etc.); d) businesses; e) non-profit organizations; and f) private individuals. All of these are checking accounts owned by those entities and individuals upon which checks may be written on demand; all of them are counted as part of the money supply. Commercial banks were prohibited from paying interest on demand deposit accounts until 2011 (Regulation Q). Banks were required to keep a legal reserve (part of primary reserves) against all of these as determined by the Federal Reserve primary reserve ratio.

Time deposits fall into three categories: a) passbook savings, b) certificates of deposits (CD), and c) open-account time deposits. Passbook savings are typically used only by individuals, and the balances are recorded in passbooks or coupons. Technically, savings deposits are subject to a 30 day notification of intent to make a withdrawal, but the notification provision is never enforced. If the notification provision were enforced, savings deposits would be included as "near-money" (presuming the bank would have to sell assets to provide the withdrawal). But since the notification is always waived, savings deposits are actually part of the money supply. A CD is a deposit that does have an enforced notification provision for withdrawals, or withdrawals may not occur until maturity. It is used by individuals and sometimes by businesses and local governments that have cash not required immediately. An open account time deposit is the same as a CD, also requiring notification of withdrawal, but the depositor is allowed to add deposits as desired. Interest is paid on all three types of time deposits, varying with local conditions, but subject to maximums set by the Federal Reserve. Banks were required to keep a reserve against all of these as determined by the Federal Reserve until 1990 when Regulation D set it to zero. The reserve ratio was generally less for time deposits than for primary deposits.

The process of money creation by a commercial bank was described in section 5.6. By way of review, consider a case where a commercial bank has a certain amount of primary deposits backed by the required primary reserves (plus working reserves). If a customer makes a demand deposit, the bank then has more primary deposits and thus his primary reserves have fallen below the required level. To correct it, he takes a portion of the new deposit corresponding to the reserve ratio and allocates it to his reserve account. The remaining portion of the new deposit is called "excess primary reserves" [17.4-7]. The term "excess primary reserves" is somewhat of a misnomer: this residual from the new deposit, after subtracting out the necessary reserves, is actually excess money that the banker may now use as he sees fit. The excess primary reserves can be used for three purposes: a) secondary deposits from which new near-term loans can be extended; b) investments as secondary reserves, and c) additional working reserves. Only the portion allocated to secondary deposits contributes to the expansion of the money supply. So: an initial new deposit has been reduced by the legal reserve ratio, and the residual is available for creating new deposits. Suppose the banker decides to use all the excess primary reserves to issue loans. If the reserve ratio is 20%, one would think that a $10,000 primary deposit, leaving $8,000 after allocating $2,000 as primary reserves against it, would allow the banker to issue $40,000 in new loans. After all, he can create new deposits up to the reciprocal of the reserve ratio, so the logic goes. But actually, the banker cannot do so. The reason is that there is no reason to assume that the new deposit will remain in his bank; it is likely to be transferred by checks written against it. Therefore, he requires 100% reserves against the "secondary deposits". The total of $40,000 that could theoretically be created lies within the banking system as a whole as checks are written to other banks. Therefore, the banker can only lend or create new deposits up to the $8,000 residual; other banks down the line will create deposits against any residual from this account deposited in their banks and so on until the total potential created money sums to the $40,000 as shown in section 5.6. Every bank in the chain can only lend or create deposits up to the "secondary deposit" level.

This process ends when the total "excess primary reserves" throughout the banking system are required to support the primary deposits. This multiplier effect is valid for the entire banking system as a whole, since the total banking system does not lose deposits to other banking systems (except for a small amount held by foreigners). But the multiplier effect of fractional reserves does not usually approach the maximum because bankers may not lend out or create deposits to the maximum theoretical extent: there may not be sufficient loan opportunities available. The same thing occurs if the public removes cash from the banks. Bankers do tend to maximize their loans as much as possible; if commercial loans cannot be made, bankers typically will create the secondary deposits and use those to buy U. S. government securities. Thus the money supply volume is maintained; if government debt or commercial paper was not available, and without good commercial opportunities, the money supply would contract [17.4-8].

The other method by which commercial banks can create excess primary reserves is by issuing its promissory note to a Federal Reserve Bank in return for a credit to its account at the Bank. This is the process of "discounting", which is actually a loan from the Federal Reserve that has to be repaid. But, the bank has additional excess primary reserves that it can use temporarily.

It is easy to see that, from the banking system as a whole, a deposit in one bank that represents a withdrawal from another bank does not affect the primary reserve position of the banking system overall. It changes the deposit and reserve positions of different banks; it may lead to different banks allocating their secondary deposits according to their experience and financial position; but does not affect the overall money supply. This discussion about expansion of the money supply and the creation of new money within the banking system overall applies only when money from outside the system is inserted into the banking system. That primary mechanism is the infusion of new primary reserves by the Federal Reserve in the course of buying U. S. government debt securities [17.4-9]. A contraction of the money supply is the reverse of the creation process (all that is necessary is to add minus signs to the charts in section 5.6).

Loans can be issued by the commercial banks (either as notes or as demand deposits) because the bank finds itself with excess primary reserves, which in turn was caused by new deposits. They are the banks' "earning assets" aside from its permanent investment portfolio. Typically commercial banks issue seven types of loans: a) to businesses (usually for capital expansion, and for terms less than five years); b) to farmers, to finance planting and carry the farmer until harvest; c) for buying open-market securities, subject to margin requirements; d) real estate; e) to other financial institutions; f) consumer credit; and g) to churches and other non-profit institutions.

In modern times, banks generally make two kinds of business loans: a) short-term, self-liquidating; and b) long-term working capital, in which the repayment is to come from future earnings. Prior to WW II the first type was most often used, based on the traditional notion of "real bills"; the "real bills" concept is one in which the loan proceeds would be used to invest in products or inventory that would generate enough revenue to make the repayment directly. The classic example is lending to a farmer expecting that the sale of the harvest would be sufficient to repay the loan, or lending to a merchant with a high probability that the inventory purchased could be sold in a certain time [17.4-10]. These types of loans were considered to provide adequate short-term liquidity, but have now been replaced by the large availability of U. S. government securities since WWII. Many banks now make loans to businesses that are continuously renewed as long-term working capital. The banker's expectation is that the future earnings of the business due to the capital improvements will generate the revenue necessary to repay the loan. In each case the banker has to evaluate the risk of repayment (which in turn depends on the borrowers' credit history), and the term of the loan with regard to fluctuations in the interest rate. Bankers generally prefer to lend to long-standing customers with good credit, and prefer to make the term of the loan as short as practical [17.4-11].

Bankers develop permanent investment portfolios as a means of generating additional income. These are paid for out of any excess primary reserves as described in section 5.6, and these investments are only made after all the viable loans have already been extended and the banks' liquidity position is satisfactory [17.4-12]. In the U. S. the permanent investment portfolio consists mostly of short term U. S. government securities, government-guaranteed securities, corporate bonds, and municipal bonds, usually maturing in more than one year. It is called permanent on the grounds that the banker intends to hold them to maturity in the belief that they will not be called upon to provide liquidity. Banks also have a secondary investment portfolio consisting of similar assets with maturities less than one year; these are readily available to provide liquidity if necessary. All the investments are intended to provide the bank with some income, since the more profitable loans have already been extended as much as the banker believes is prudent. Bankers generally make investments based on expectations of future interest rates, and how they are likely to change over the long and short term [17.4-13]. The banker makes his decisions based on a calculation of an asset to risk ratio, which is the ratio of capital to total assets, excluding cash and U. S. securities.

To review, demand deposits are regarded as part of the money supply since checks written against those accounts can be used in making transactions. Demand deposits are normally created in the course of granting a loan (upon collateral) to a business or other entity. The demand deposit is an exchange of the banks' liabilities (checks against the demand deposit are payable on demand) for an earning asset (i.e., the repayment of the loan). When commercial banks create demand deposits upon injection of new deposits into the banking system, and withhold enough in reserves to meet legal requirements and immediate anticipated needs, the banking system as a whole creates money. The potential total of created money, given that there are other uses besides loans is as shown in section 5.6. Once again, the "new deposits into the banking system" as a whole is mostly a result of Federal Reserve purchases of U. S. government securities through the FOMC.

Commercial banks conduct their business based on a set of priorities. The highest priority is to maintain liquidity: a) maintain the ability to pay all the demands upon them from checks written against demand deposits, and any other withdrawals in notes; b) control the risks of their loans so as to maintain a suitably low asset-to-risk ratio; and c) maintain all their legally required reserve levels. The second priority is to maximize earnings by lending to high-quality customers. The third priority, after all viable loans have been made, it to use any remaining funds to make earning investments, usually in high-quality securities, those issued by the U. S. government being regarded as the safest.

There are four categories of money in the U. S. The first is Treasury cash, consisting of gold and silver owned and held by the U. S. Treasury against which it has not issued gold certificates or silver certificates to the Federal Reserve. It is controlled entirely by the U. S. Treasury. The second category is Treasury Currency; in modern times it consists of two types: a) minor coins issued to the public; and b) silver and gold certificates issued only to the Federal Reserve. The third category of money is controlled by the Federal Reserve, and consists of two variants: a) reserves of commercial banks as a basis for primary demand deposits; and b) circulating Federal Reserve Notes. The fourth category of money is created by the commercial banks in the form of demand deposits against loans, based on excess primary reserves (a.k.a. secondary deposits).

Figure 17.4-1 illustrates the balance sheet of the overall U. S. monetary system as intended by the original Federal Reserve Act and the flow of money in and out of the three principal entities, namely the U. S. Treasury, the Federal Reserve System, and the commercial banking system. This description will follow the Figure left-to-right. The U. S. Treasury holds gold and silver that it buys from miners, the public, or foreigners. Part of it is devoted to monetary uses as shown starting in the boxes labeled "gold and silver" as Monetary Assets in the U. S. Treasury. The remainder is part of "Treasury Cash"; it consists of "free" gold for which no gold certificates have been issued, and "free" silver that has not been coined. Treasury Cash is regarded as a non-monetary liability of the U. S. Treasury. Treasury Currency in 1913 consisted of silver dollars, silver coins (dollar, half-dollar, quarter, dime), minor coins (nickel and penny), Silver Certificates, United States Notes (a.k.a. "greenbacks" issued during the Civil War), Federal Reserve Bank Notes, National Bank Notes, and Treasury Notes of 1890 [17.4-14]. The Federal Reserve Bank Notes referred to here are not the Federal Reserve Notes that are in common circulation today. They were a form of paper currency issued from 1914 to 1934, intended to take the place of National Bank Notes, but failed to do so. The U. S. Treasury also buys other metals such as copper, zinc, and nickel that are used in the manufacture of U. S. coins (none of which contain any silver now). Silver Certificates were issued between 1878 and 1964. United States Notes (greenbacks) were issued by the U. S. Treasury between 1861 and 1863 as an emergency measure during the Civil War. National Bank Notes were issued by the National Banks starting in the mid-1860's. Treasury Notes of 1890 were issued between 1890 and 1893 as part of the Sherman Silver Purchase Act; nearly all of them were redeemed in coin, and only a few are known to exist. All these types of currency were in circulation at the start of the Federal Reserve. All were tabulated as monetary liabilities of the U. S. Treasury, and assets of the Federal Reserve System.

Physical gold for monetary purposes is held by the Treasury, but it issues Gold Certificates against it, and they are provided to the Federal Reserve Banks. The Gold Certificates were initially backed 100% by physical gold (until 1916), and were used as partial backing for Federal Reserve Notes. The Gold Certificates are issued as monetary liabilities of the U. S. Treasury and are assets of the Federal Reserve System. Federal Reserve Notes were initially liabilities of the Treasury. Under the initial Federal Reserve Act, the Federal Reserve Banks were required to deposits bonds for the Federal Reserve Notes, same as the transactions that prevailed under the national banking system. Those transactions are not shown on Figures 17.4-1 for clarity, but are the same as shown on Figure 14-1. Federal Reserve Notes are now liabilities of the Federal Reserve Banks.

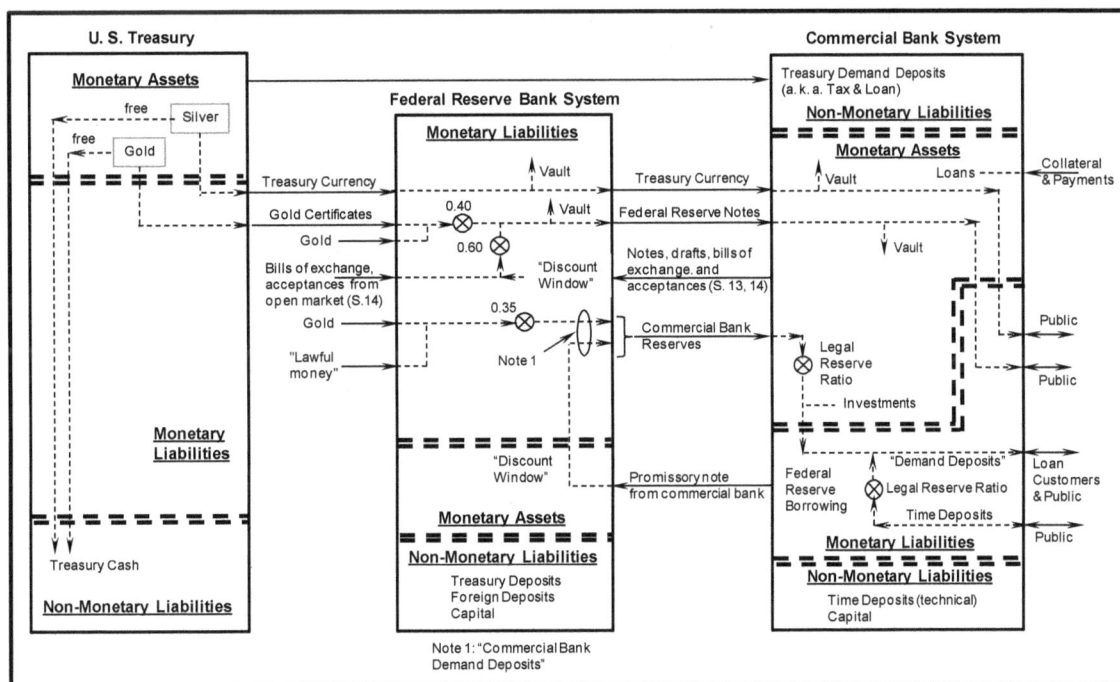

Figure 17.4-1: The Federal Reserve System (Original Design, 1913)

Activities of the Federal Reserve Bank System are shown in the center of the Figure. Treasury Currency received from the U. S. Treasury may be purchased by and sent to the Commercial Banking system; and some may be kept in the vaults of both types of banks. Eventually the Treasury Currency finds its place in the hand of the public, in the tills of the banks, or in their vaults. This simply passes through the Federal Reserve as liabilities of the Treasury, and liabilities of the commercial banks when in circulation. Treasury Currency does not count as any part of reserves. The second monetary asset of the Federal Reserve System, being the Gold Certificates, was utilized within the Federal Reserve System in two ways. First, they were used as reserve backing for the issuance of Federal Reserve Notes. Per section 16 of the original Federal Reserve Act, Federal Reserve Notes must be fully secured as indicated by the circles with X's: a) 40% in gold or gold certificates; and b) the remaining 60% in "eligible paper", meaning: a) bills of exchange; or b) acceptances purchased on the open market per section 13 and 14 of the Federal Reserve Act. Federal Reserve Notes are liabilities of the Federal Reserve, and are also indirect liabilities of the commercial banks when they go into circulation. The Federal Reserve Notes may be passed to the Commercial Banking system as a liability of the Federal Reserve, after some are retained in the Federal Reserve vaults; and from there passed to the public by the commercial banks after withholding some in their vaults. Federal Reserve Notes are not held as reserve deposits in the Federal Reserve Banks as part of commercial reserve accounts. Last, the Federal Reserve Banks may issue loans to member banks upon suitable collateral at the 'discount window', as shown at the bottom of the Monetary Assets of the Federal Reserve System.

Section 16 of the original Federal Reserve Act required a 35% reserve in the form of gold and "lawful money" to be held by the Federal Reserve against deposits held there by the commercial banks. Recall that the deposits of commercial banks at the Federal Reserve are the reserves upon which they can issue demand deposits as indicated by Note 1 at the bottom. At the time of the Federal Reserve Act, "lawful money" included all the various types cited above, except for the minor coins. The reserve accounts at the Federal Reserve are monetary liabilities of the Federal Reserve, and monetary assets of the commercial banks. When those reserves are used to create demand deposits (subject to the reserve ratio as shown at right), the demand deposits become liabilities of the commercial banks; the loans for which the demand deposits were created are the corresponding assets of the commercial banks.

So far two of the three components of commercial bank demand deposits at the Federal Reserve Banks are addressed. The third one, "commercial bank borrowing" from the Federal Reserve, is shown at right as a liability of the commercial banking system; the promissory note given by the commercial banks are an asset to the Federal Reserve. Amounts borrowed at this "discount window" are applied to the Commercial Banking System's demand deposits at the Federal Reserve. These three components are the crucial part of the Federal Reserve System and its influence on the money supply. The "demand deposits" owned by the commercial banking system at the Federal Reserve Banking System are known on the commercial bank side as its "reserve account"; it is the fractional reserve backing for loans and investments made by the commercial banking system. Last, the Federal Reserve Banks hold non-monetary liabilities of deposits owned by foreign persons, and foreign governments, Treasury deposits and its own capital account.

The commercial banking system holds some Treasury Currency in their vaults, and passes some of it to the public as noted above. Federal Reserve Notes within the commercial banking system operate in a similar fashion. The degree to which cash held in bank vaults is counted against reserves has changed twice. Originally section 19 of the Federal Reserve Act permitted both cash in vaults and demand deposits at the Federal Reserve Banks to be counted toward reserves; in 1917 it was changed such that only the demand deposits at the Federal Reserve counted as reserves; in 1959 it was changed back such that Federal Reserve Notes in bank vaults is permitted to count against reserves. The combination of cash in vault in the commercial banks and their demand deposits at the Federal Reserve form the reserves that the commercial banks can use to issue loans via demand deposits and make new investments. As shown in the Figure, the allowable demand deposits based on the reserves is regulated by the legal reserve ratio. If the ratio is 20%, then the Commercial banking system as a whole could theoretically create $4 for every $1 in new reserves (i.e., the increase is $1/r - 1$, where r is the reserve ratio). The exact mechanism, including other considerations about the effective reserve ratio, was described in section 5.6.

Commercial banks also handle time deposits in the form of savings, checking accounts, and certificates of deposit. Those also can be used, subject to the legal reserve ratio, to create demand deposits, although the reserve ratio for time deposits is different than the one for the demand deposits at the Federal Reserve Banks. Last, the commercial banking system has non-monetary liabilities in the form of Treasury demand deposits and it own capital accounts. The lower right of Figure 17.4-1 indicates that time deposits are technically part of the commercial banking systems' non-monetary liabilities. This is true only if notification for withdrawal is enforced. It is never enforced for savings accounts, but is nearly always enforced for certificates of deposit. I have chosen to include it as part of the liabilities.

We've all seen that cartoon where two identical-looking pictures are shown, and the task is to find a certain number of differences between them. The same can be done with Figure 17.4-1 (the original Federal Reserve design) against 17.4-2, which shows how the system operates at present.

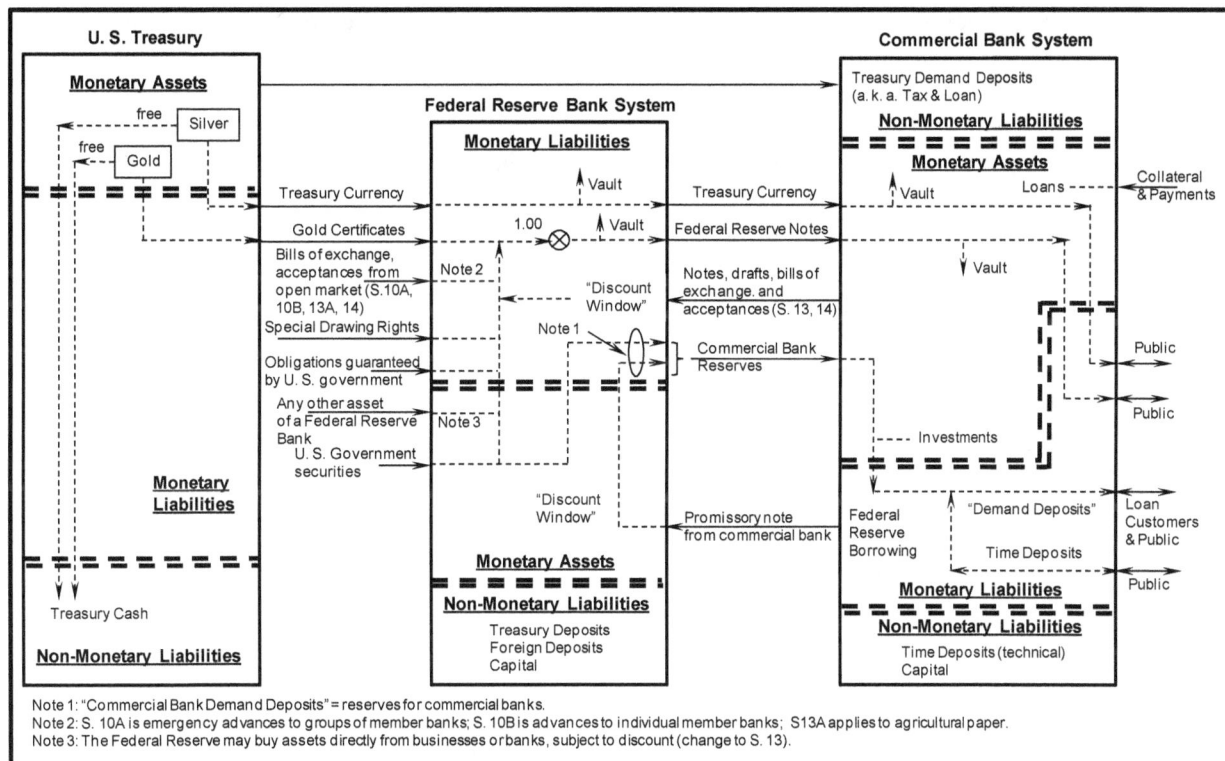

Figure 17.4-2: The Federal Reserve System (2020 Operation)

Treasury cash is the same as before: the Treasury holds some free gold and silver for which no certificates or coins are made. Treasury Currency operates the same, although its form has changed considerably. Silver Certificates were issued until 1964, but were withdrawn from circulation in 1967, and are redeemable only in Federal Reserve Notes since 1968. I saw a few of them when I was younger, even occasionally into the 1970's, but they are mostly out of circulation now. United States Notes (greenbacks) were mostly redeemed by the 1930's in Federal Reserve Notes, and are no longer in circulation. National Bank Notes were issued by the National Banks until 1933, and have since been removed from circulation, redeemable in Federal Reserve Notes. Nearly all of the Treasury Notes of 1890 have been redeemed and no longer circulate. So, "Treasury Currency" now means only dollar, half-dollar, quarter, dime, nickel, and penny coins; i.e., small change; plus whatever small amounts of standard silver coins that may still be in circulation. These minor coins are issued to the Federal Reserve Banks and are tabulated as monetary liabilities of the U. S. Treasury, and assets of the Federal Reserve System. Mostly they pass through the Federal Reserve System into the commercial banks, and onto the public for circulation.

The last monetary liability of the U. S. Treasury is U. S. Government securities issued by the Treasury to the Federal Reserve Banks upon authorization from Congress. This is the same as the U. S. public debt. They are tabulated as shown in the Figure as monetary assets of the Federal Reserve System.

Federal Reserve Notes still maintain a 100% reserve, but the form is different. Whereas originally gold and gold certificates comprised 40% of the reserve with the rest in eligible paper, now Federal Reserve Notes are backed by a) gold certificates, b) commercial, agricultural, and industrial loans; c) loans secured by U. S. securities rediscounted by member banks; d) loans to members banks secured by paper eligible for rediscount or secured by U. S. government securities; e) bankers' acceptances (a. k. a. bills bought); and f) U. S. government securities in Reserve bank portfolio. These changes were made gradually by legislation starting in 1932. There is no specified portion that has to be covered by gold certificates, and no gold per se can be used as backing for them (since all the monetary gold was given to the Treasury in 1933).

It is easy to see that the big change is that the backing for Federal Reserve deposits (the commercial bank reserve accounts) are now backed only by paper, mostly U. S. government securities, and there is no fixed reserve ratio. The requirement for gold backing of Federal Reserve deposits was abolished in 1965.

Another important difference is in the commercial bank side: there is no longer a legal reserve requirement for either time or demand deposits. Technically, the Federal Reserve has the authority to impose a reserve requirement (Regulation D), but it was reduced to zero in 2020. So, what regulates the amount of demand deposits (and thus the money supply), now that the formula $(1/r - 1)$ equals infinity? It comes down to the experience, common sense, and risk assessment capabilities of the bankers. Now don't laugh too hard: this technically appears to give the bankers license to create as much money as possible, and maybe they will; but recall that the Bank of England has never imposed a legal reserve requirement. The growth of the money supply will depend on the prudence and insight of the banking industry, for good or bad.

Figure 17.4-3 shows a summary of the overall banking system balance sheet as well as the portions that constitute the total money supply [17.4-15]. By convention, the Treasury's holding of non-gold metal is accounted for as Treasury Currency rather than as silver coin or bullion. The total monetary assets, considered as a systematic whole, consists of Treasury currency, gold stock in the U. S. Treasury, loans and investments held by the Federal Reserve Banking System, and loans and investments held by the commercial banks. Keep in mind that these "investments" consist mostly of U. S. Government securities. The overall monetary liabilities are Treasury Currency and Federal Reserve Notes held outside the banking systems, plus demand deposits at the commercial banks. I have also included as liabilities (although is only partially correct) time deposits held in the commercial banks, since these are partly payable on demand. The non-monetary liabilities remain the same as indicated. A more detailed description of the overall balance sheet is given in Appendix A. Chapters 18 through 23 will show the condition of the overall banking system based on this description.

The total privately-held money supply can be calculated by observing that several of the assets and liabilities partly cancel out. Only the portion of Treasury Currency and Federal Reserve Notes held by the public in circulation is counted as part of the privately-owned money supply. Therefore, the total money supply is the sum of Treasury currency outside the banks, Federal Reserve Notes outside the banks, and demand deposits at the commercial banks. Some time deposits at the commercial banks are also included (the portion subject to payment on demand). In 1973 the Federal Reserve developed three measures of the money supply. They have specific technical definitions that will be described in the proper place, but to first order, they are: a) M0 is the Treasury Currency and Federal Reserve Notes in circulation (see upper right of Figure 17.4-3), b) M1 is M0 plus demand deposits (representing loans to commercial customers) and non-enforced time deposits (i.e., savings accounts); and c) M3 is M2 plus all time deposits with enforced notification (i.e., money market mutual funds and certificates of deposit). These definitions were significantly revised in 1980 and many other minor changes were made over the years.

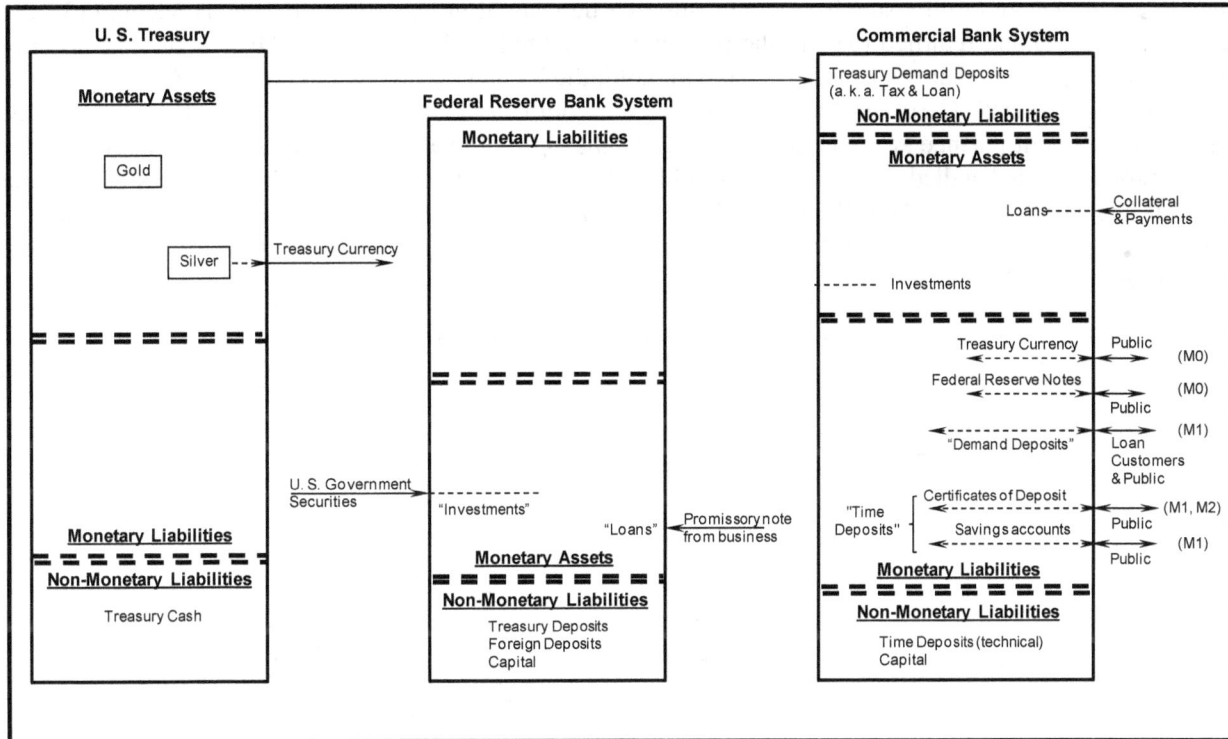

Figure 17.4-3: Overall U. S. Banking System Balance Sheet and Money Supply

17.5 Control of the Money Supply

This section presents the seven methods by which the U. S. Treasury, the Federal Reserve, and the commercial banks control the money supply. In the description that follows, the use of reserve ratios is retained in order to see the effects of the transactions. There are many occasions in which the legal reserve requirements no longer exist.

The first method used to control the money supply is when the U. S. Treasury buys gold and silver and allocates it for monetary use, as illustrated on Figure 17.5-1. In the case of gold, it obtains the gold from a miner or other seller (1), and pays for it with a check drawn on its account at the Federal Reserve Bank (2). The mining company or other seller then deposits the check at its commercial bank (3); the commercial bank pays the seller either directly or by increasing its demand deposit account (4). The commercial bank then sends the Treasury check to the Federal Reserve Bank for collection as usual (5), and the check is paid by the Federal Reserve by increasing the reserve account of the commercial bank held at the Federal Reserve (6). Now the Treasury's account with the Federal Reserve is depleted by the amount of the check, and ordinarily that would be the end of it, with no change in the money supply. However, the U. S. Treasury is allowed to issue gold certificates (7), backed by the gold itself, to the Federal Reserve Bank. The Federal Reserve now holds the gold certificate, and can be used to meet its reserve requirement against the issue of Federal Reserve Notes and its deposit liabilities (8) subject to the reserve requirement (25% shown here as an example). Also, the Federal Reserve Bank then usually restores the balance in the U. S. Treasury's account (9) at the Federal Reserve [17.5-1]. In the end, procurement of gold by the U. S. Treasury increases the money supply because the Treasury's Federal Reserve account is restored to its balance after payment of the check to the miner, and the gold certificates, provided to the Federal Reserve, become reserves against Federal Reserve Note and deposit liabilities (which are reserves to the commercial banks).

Procurement of silver by the U. S. Treasury operates differently. The process of buying the silver and paying for it is the same as with gold: a check is written by the Treasury against its Federal Reserve demand deposit account to the supplier (2); the supplier deposits it in his commercial bank account (3), the check is paid (4) and returned (5) and the payment is credited to the commercial banks' reserve account (6). Here the process changes from the case with gold: the U. S. Treasury issues Treasury Currency to the Federal Reserve Bank (10), and the Federal Reserve compensates the Treasury by restoring the U. S. Treasury's account balance at the Federal Reserve to the amount of the check given to the silver supplier (11). Silver is thus handled differently than gold: instead of the silver being used as reserves against the Federal Reserve Note liabilities, the value of the silver is added as a monetary liability of the Federal Reserve Bank, and the silver coin is provided directly to the commercial banks for issue to their customers when required [17.5-2].

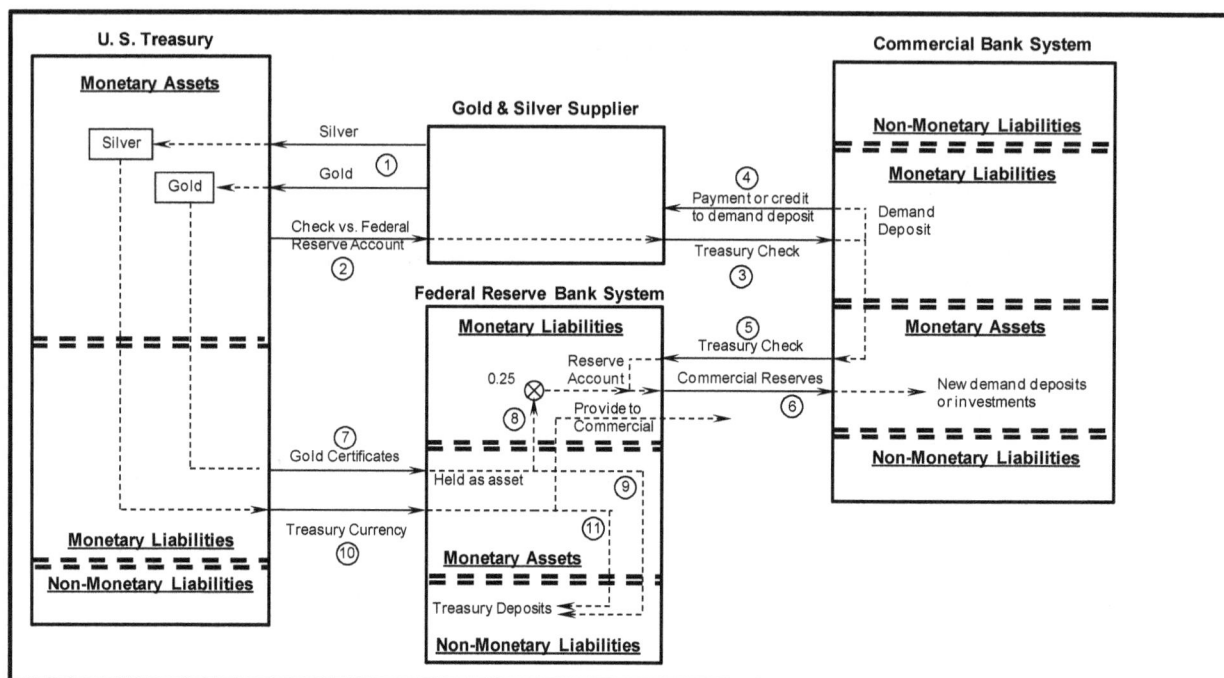

Figure 17.5-1: Effect on Money Supply When the U. S. Treasury Buys Gold and Silver

The second means of controlling the money supply is the setting of commercial bank reserve ratios on demand deposits and time deposits by the Federal Reserve. Reserve ratios at commercial banks apply at the points indicated by symbol shown as an X inside a circle on the right side of Figure 17.4-1. The total amount of potential demand deposits that can be created by the Commercial Banking System was explained in section 5.6. The same principle applies to the reserve ratio on time deposits.

The third general method of money supply control is accomplished by Federal Reserve by adjusting the discount rate at the Federal Reserve discount window as shown on Figure 17.4-1. The "discount rate" is the interest rate the Federal Reserve charges member commercial banks for borrowing against its assets (i.e., the amount "borrowed" is credited to the commercial bank's reserve account at the Federal Reserve). (Borrowed reserves must be paid back to the Federal Reserve Bank.) The original idea of a discount window was to make the discount rate higher than normal as a disincentive to borrow (i.e., a "penalty rate"), but the Federal Reserve has not usually taken that approach [17.5-3]. The discount rate is only effective when the commercial banks must borrow to maintain their primary reserve; otherwise, the rate is immaterial insofar as a control mechanism because the commercial banks are not in need of loans from the Federal Reserve. The Federal Reserve has a related power to adjust interest rates, known as the "Federal Funds Rate", mentioned above in connection with the powers of the FOMC. It is a target rate by which commercial banks can lend their excess reserves; that rate in turn affects the interest rates that banks charge their customers. When the Federal Reserve desires to reduce the rate of growth in the money supply, it increases the Federal Funds Rate, which leads to higher interest rates in the commercial sector, which reduces the demand for loans, which reduces the creation of demand deposits. Those demand deposits constitute a significant portion of the overall money supply, as mentioned in section 5.6 and as seen on the far right side of Figure 17.4-3. Likewise, when the Federal Reserve desires to increase the rate of growth in the money supply, it lowers the Federal Funds Rate, causing lower interest rates, a higher demand for loans, increased demand deposits, and a consequent increase in the money supply.

The fourth general method of money supply control is by open-market purchases and sales of U. S. Government securities through the Federal Open Market Committee (FOMC). All of the actions agreed to by the FOMC are actually implemented by the Federal Reserve Bank of New York. The process is illustrated on Figure 17.5-2. Here the Federal Reserve buys an existing bond from the public through a securities dealer. In the first four transactions the dealer buys the bond from the public. Next the bond is provided to the Federal Reserve (5) and is paid for by a check drawn on the Federal Reserve (6), then cleared to the securities dealer by his commercial bank (7, 8). The check is returned to the Federal Reserve (9), and payment is made by crediting the commercial banks' demand deposit account, which is part of the commercial bank's reserves (10). The increase in the reserves permits the commercial bank to expand its demand deposits upon loans (11). After withholding the required legal reserve 25% (example) shown at right, the remaining 75% of the increase is available as "excess primary reserves" for uses as described in section 5.6. The transactions (3, 4, 7, 8) occur within the securities' dealers demand deposit account (which may be at a different bank), and these deposits/withdrawals are part of the excess reserve accounting by the banks. Notice, however, they nearly cancel out except for the dealers' commission, and do not affect the money supply. This is the means of increasing the money supply but without increasing the national debt. The reason is: the existing bond, in the hands of the public, has already been paid for out of individual savings. It is true that the interest payments have to be made, but they were in effect before the Federal Reserve bought the existing bond from the securities dealer, who bought it from a member of the public.

Figure 17.5-2 shows the process of monetary expansion when the Federal Reserve buys existing U. S. government securities, but the money supply contracts in the same way when it sells securities. To see how it works, reverse the arrows in Figure 17.5-2.

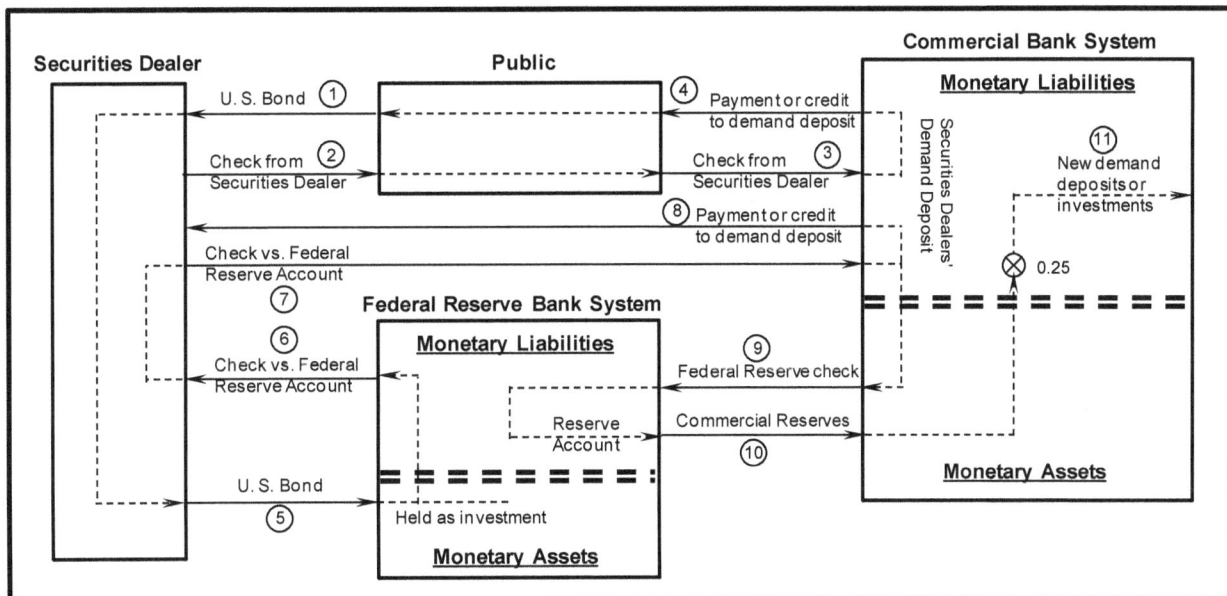

Figure 17.5-2: Money Supply Expansion from Buying Existing U. S. Government Securities

There is a fifth way to increase the money supply, known as "monetizing the debt", as shown on Figure 17.5-3 [17.5-4]. It occurs when the commercial banking system buys new U. S. Government securities directly from the U. S. Treasury. But, the commercial banks may not have the finances to do so directly; first, the Federal Reserve must buy existing securities and use them to create commercial bank reserves in order for the commercial banks to buy the new bonds, and steps 1 through 11 inclusive are the same in Figure 17.5-3 as in Figure 17.5-2. "Monetizing the debt" actually occurs in steps 12 through 16: the new addition to the commercial demand deposits at the Federal Reserve (11) are used to buy new U. S. securities from the Treasury directly. The commercial banks send a check for the new bonds against their reserves (12) in exchange for the bonds (13) to be held as an asset (14); the bond amount is credited to the Treasury's demand deposits at the commercial banks (15), and is available to the Treasury (16) as a demand deposit at commercial banks. This is how the money supply can be expanded as a consequence of an increasing the national debt. Keep in mind that the amount of the increased reserves permits an expansion in accordance with the reserve ratio: in $100 million in new reserves are created because the Federal Reserve bought existing securities, the commercial banking system can procure $400 million in U. S. securities if the reserve ratio is 20%. This is a "pyramiding of reserves", since existing U. S. government securities are used to create reserves that allow for additional new U. S. government securities to be issued. The end result is an increase in the Treasury's demand deposit account at commercial banks; this is a monetary asset of the Treasury, but is a non-monetary liability of the commercial banks.

But notice the taxpayer's position in all of this: not only is the money supply increased, which causes a depreciation of the money, but the taxpayers now have to pay the principal and interest on the bonds issued by the Treasury [17.5-5].

It could be worse [17.5-6]: the Federal Reserve could buy U. S. government securities from the U. S. Treasury directly; it would mean that the U. S. Treasury would have demand deposits at the Federal Reserve that could be spent subject to the legal reserve ratio. This would be a much greater expansion of the money supply, and of course, an expansion of the national debt. It was permitted intermittently between World War II and 1981. Since then, the Federal Reserve cannot buy Treasury debt issued today, but of course, it can buy those that were issued yesterday. The limitation of "existing bills" is not really much of a restraint.

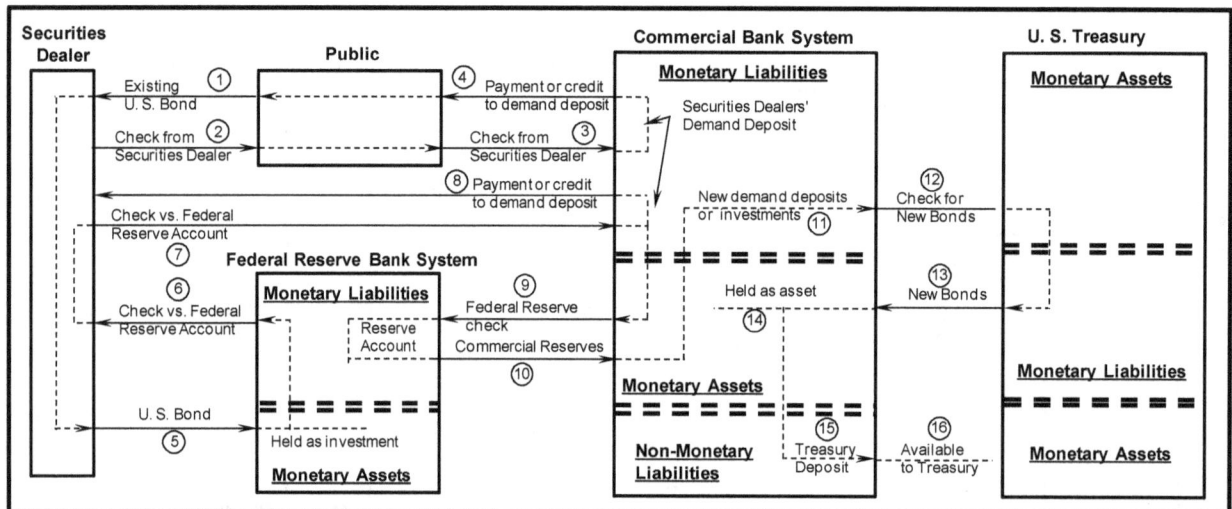

Figure 17.5-3: Process for "Monetizing Debt"

The growth of the money supply and an annual U. S. government deficit are not necessarily related. The government could run a deficit, and pay for it by selling bonds to the public. The money is then simply transferred from private savings to the government. That does increase the national debt, but does not affect the money supply and does not contribute to depreciation of the money. Money spent by the public to buy bonds to finance government spending is that much less that can be used to finance private businesses, which is the larger problem with government deficits [17.5-7].

The sixth means of control is to set margin rates on loans for stock purchases on the public exchanges as described earlier. The main effect is to reduce the portion of the money supply that is devoted to stock speculation and a possible decline in stock market prices.

The seventh means of money supply control is to issue Federal Reserve Notes or increase commercial bank reserve accounts backed by commercial paper (short term promissory notes, which was credit extended to businesses and farmers) [17.5-8]. This power was prohibited by the National Bank System. A commercial bank may sell any commercial paper that it holds to the Federal Reserve, and the Federal Reserve credits the commercial banks reserve account; which in turn permits the commercial banks to expand demand deposits. This falls under the category of acceptances, usually bankers' acceptances, purchased on the open market by the Federal Reserve Banks directly. This provides the commercial banks with a supply of reserves, but does not require any repayment (unlike loans from the discount window). Normally the acceptances are procured by the Federal Reserve from the commercial banks by a special group of dealers granted a monopoly for this purpose.

These seven methods showed the process by which the Federal Reserve can affect the money supply. But not every influence on the money supply is directly controllable by the Federal Reserve. Figure 17.5-4 shows the factors that tend to increase the reserves of the member banks and the degree to which the Federal Reserve can control them [17.5-9, 17.5-10]. Opposite actions from those listed lead to decreases in the bank reserves.

No.	Factor Leading to Increased Reserves	Controlled by Federal Reserve	Comment
1	Procurement of gold and silver by the U. S. Treasury	No	But the Federal Reserve has some influence.
2	Purchase of assets (U. S. government securities) other than gold by Federal Reserve, proceeds to commercial bank demand deposit accounts	Yes	The effect is reduced by any amount the seller takes in Federal Reserve Notes.
3	Increase Federal Reserve Float (uncollected checks by Federal Reserve)	No	Float is the period when checks are not yet collected.
4	New bills discounted at the Federal Reserve (discount window)	Yes	But repayment of discounted bills is uncontrolled, and leads to a decrease in reserves
5	Decline in public demand for Federal Reserve Notes (circulation outside banking system)	No	Is a shift from cash to demand deposits; thus an increase in reserves.
6	Decrease in Treasury deposits at Federal Reserve Banks	No	Controlled by the U. S. Treasury; spending by Treasury increases demand deposits.
7	Decrease in Treasury cash	No	Controlled by the U. S. Treasury
8	Decrease in foreign deposits at Federal Reserve Banks	No	
9	Increase in Treasury currency in circulation	No	Controlled by the U. S. Treasury
10	Decrease in non-member bank deposits at the Federal Reserve Banks	No	
11	Reduction in legal reserve ratio	Yes	

Figure 17.5-4: Factors and Federal Reserve Controllability that Increase Bank Reserves

We know that the U. S. Treasury issues gold certificates to the Federal Reserve as partial backing for the money supply. But how much physical gold does the U. S. Treasury actually possess? Are the vaults in Fort Knox and in the basement of the Federal Reserve Bank of New York full of gold? Who knows? They may be full of U. S. gold, or of gold owned by other governments; or they completely empty; or they may be full of lead bars painted gold. It is in fact a trick question: it doesn't matter because neither the U. S. government nor the Federal Reserve is going to tell us about it. You and I will never see any of it. If it becomes necessary to release it in an economic collapse, any gold will be given to the ruling elite, not chumps like us. We get to pay the debts. The important thing to keep in mind is: even if there is no gold at all, the current U. S. monetary system will continue to function as a fiat system until the growth of the debt and the expenditures of the government exceed the taxpayers' ability to make interest payments. Then the system will collapse under the weight of debt. That is because the real reserves are not so much gold, but are in fact your labor, your home, your car, your business, your retirement accounts, and all the assets of the industrial base. Professor Kreps proposed in 1962 [17.5-11] that gold no longer has any significance as the ultimate monetary reserve, and could safely be abolished.

Federal Reserve officials often testify in Congress and give interviews in which they comment on the state of the U. S. economy and the actions of the Federal Reserve. As always, their comments are full of obscurities; done either because there is something to hide, or to avoid being accused of favoring one economic group. Herewith is a short list of historical Federal Reserve BankSpeak euphemisms to help alleviate the confusion issued by their spokespersons.

1. Deflation: This has three possible meanings. First, it refers to an appreciation of the purchasing power of the U. S. dollar; i.e., a decline in prices. Second, it can refer to a decline in business activity and an increase in unemployment. Third, it can refer to a decline in the volume of the money supply. The second meaning is most commonly used, as it justifies a further expansion of the money supply.

2. Devaluation of the dollar: Since the U. S. dollar is a fiat currency, it cannot be "devalued", since it has no inherent defined value. "Devaluation" now means that the U. S. dollar is suffering a lowered exchange rate against foreign currencies, (or to put it more directly, the U. S. dollar is depreciating faster than the others).

3. Inflation: Depreciation of the purchasing power of the U. S. dollar, and an increase in the cost of living. But what is not said is that it is caused by an excessive increase in the money supply.

4. Monetizing the debt: the expansion of the money supply financed entirely by procurement of additional U. S. government securities [U. S. taxpayer liabilities] by commercial banks using new reserves provided by Federal Reserve procurement of old U. S. government securities, all in order to increase the reserve accounts of commercial banks.

5. Quantitative Easing: the expansion of the money supply financed by procurement of existing U. S. government securities [U. S. taxpayer liabilities] or commercial paper (usually mortgage-backed securities) from the public or other institutions in order to increase the reserve accounts of commercial banks.

6. Stagflation: An increase in the money supply resulting in deprecation of the dollar, but without the intended expansion of the economy, usually accompanied by an increase in the interest rate plus an increase in unemployment. It occurs when the government or Federal Reserve attempts to use monetary policy to maintain economic growth after it has stopped because capital industries have become unprofitable due to high wages and prices caused by previous monetary expansions. It can also be caused by regulation that increases costs and makes them unprofitable. Interest rates increase because it is riskier to lend, and unemployment increases because only profitable labor can be employed (in a free market).

References

[17.2-1] Clifton H. Kreps, Jr., *Money, Banking and Monetary Policy*, NY: The Ronald Press Co., 1962, pp. 295, 296
[17.2-2] op. cit., Kreps, p. 510
[17.2-3] Edwin Walter Kemmerer, *The ABC of the Federal Reserve System*, Princeton, NJ: Princeton University Press, 1918, pp. 4, 5
[17.2-4] Board of Governors of the Federal Reserve System, *The Federal Reserve System: Purposes and Functions*, Washington, DC: U. S. Government Printing Office, 1963, pp. 257-266
[17.2-5] op. cit., Kemmerer, pp. 8, 9, 11-18
[17.2-6] op. cit., Kemmerer, pp. 23, 24
[17.2-7] op. cit., Kemmerer, pp. 25-27
[17.2-8] cf. https://en.wikipedia.org/wiki/Benjamin_Strong_Jr.
[17.2-9] Benjamin Strong, Jr., in the Preface to op. cit., Kemmerer, pp. v - vii

[17.2-10]   op. cit., Kemmerer, p. 100

[17.3-1]   op. cit., Kreps, pp. 370, 373, 374
[17.3-2]   op. cit., Kreps, p. 376
[17.3-3]   Allan H. Meltzer, *A History of the Federal Reserve*, Chicago, IL; University of Chicago Press, 2003, Vol. 1, pp. 726, 727

[17.4-1]   https://www.federalreserve.gov/aboutthefed/structure-federal-reserve-system.htm
[17.4-2]   op. cit., Kreps, pp. 182-184
[17.4-3]   op. cit., Kreps, p. 261
[17.4-4]   op. cit., Kreps, pp. 216, 217, 260
[17.4-5]   op. cit., Kreps, p. 262
[17.4-6]   op. cit., Kreps, pp. 262, 273, 276-278
[17.4-7]   op. cit., Kreps, pp. 216, 217
[17.4-8]   op. cit., Kreps, p. 359
[17.4-9]   op. cit., Kreps, pp. 358, 471, 472
[17.4-10]   op. cit., Kreps, pp. 289, 290
[17.4-11]   op. cit., Kreps, pp. 307, 308
[17.4-12]   op. cit., Kreps, pp. 225, 327, 328
[17.4-13]   op. cit., Kreps, pp. 230-232, 334-344
[17.4-14]   op. cit., Kreps, p. 34
[17.4-15]   op. cit., Kreps, pp. 42-44. Kreps states that he relied on Edward S. Shaw, *Money Income, and Monetary Policy*, Homewood, IL: Richard D. Irwin, Inc. 1950, chapters 2 and 3; Morris A. Copeland and Daniel H. Brill, "Banking Assets and the Money Supply Since 1929", Federal Reserve Bulletin, Jan, 1948, pp. 24-32; and William J. Abbott, "A New Measure of the Money Supply", Federal Reserve Bulletin, Oct 1960, pp. 1102, 1103. The main difference between Kreps and Figures 17.4-1 and 17.4-2 is that time deposits are shown as liabilities of the commercial banks; Kreps shows them as non-monetary liabilities. Technically, Kreps is correct since time deposits are "near money" if the notice is enforced, but it never is.

[17.5-1]   op. cit., Kreps, pp. 473, 474
[17.5-2]   op. cit., Kreps, pp. 35, 36, 38, 475
[17.5-3]   op. cit., Kreps, pp. 499, 502
[17.5-4]   Murray N. Rothbard, *The Mystery of Banking,* Auburn, AL: Ludwig von Mises Institute, 2008 pp. 172-174 (originally published 1983)
[17.5-5]   op. cit., Rothbard, p. 172
[17.5-6]   op. cit., Rothbard, pp. 174-176
[17.5-7]   op. cit., Rothbard, pp. 170, 171
[17.5-8]   op. cit., Kreps, pp. 277, 278
[17.5-9]   op. cit., Kreps, p. 483
[17.5-10]   Murray N. Rothbard, *America's Great Depression,* Auburn, AL: Ludwig von Mises Institute, 2000, pp. 101-106 (originally published 1963)
[17.5-11]   op. cit., Kreps, p. 109

18

Federal Reserve Under the Gold Standard, 1915-1932

18.1 Preview, 1915-1932

The period from 1915 to 1932 is the last period of the gold coin standard in the U. S. The Federal Reserve Act had been passed in late 1913, but the system did not get up and running until late 1914. The national banking system was absorbed into the Federal Reserve System; all the national bank associations became members of the Federal Reserve and continued operations as usual.

This period saw the attack on gold, even going so far as to criticize the public for giving gold coins to children at Christmas. The first example is from the Federal Reserve in late 1917 [18.1-1]:

> "The following circular letter, issued by a large national bank in New York on November 16 to its customers, affords a statement of the policy that is being pursued by many institutions regarding the use of gold as holiday gifts."

> *"To our customers and friends:*
> The use of gold coins as holiday presents during the war period is being discouraged by the Government—not for the purpose of abolishing a time-honored custom, but, to put it plainly, to conserve its supply of gold and thus help win the war. That a hearty and willing response from everyone will be forthcoming goes without saying. It occurs to us that excellent substitutes can be found, through the use of Liberty bonds, war-savings certificates, and United State's thrift cards. These should not only prove to be acceptable presents, but their use would encourage the further development of thrift - to the importance of which the people of this country are slowly awakening. "Easy to come, easy to go" as the saying is, can be safely applied to money presents. Why not introduce the investment feature into your Christmas gifts? You will serve three purposes: The spirit of the holiday time will be gratified. The necessity for saving and thrift will be emphasized. Your country will be backed in its fight for right. We will gladly furnish full details regarding Liberty bonds, war-saving certificates, or United States thrift cards, and are in a position to supply them at face value. No charge for our services. Your cooperation in this will be direct support to a noble cause."

The same issue [18.1-2] mentioned that the Federal Reserve approved of substituting war certificates in lieu of gold as Christmas presents:

"Referring further to your letter of October 29, in which you enclose a letter from _____, dated October 27, with reference to the use of gold as Christmas holiday gifts, I beg to advise you that at a meeting of the Federal Reserve Board, held November 16, the committee to which this matter had been referred reported:

That -- in view of the general opinion that gold should be concentrated, the attention of bankers, employers of labor, and of individuals should be directed to the new war savings certificate plan as being an entirely suitable and patriotic method of handling the matter. These war savings stamps will be on sale by December 1, descriptive literature is now on the press, and the Treasury circular will be issued within a few days.

This report was approved by the Board, 19 Nov 1917"

That was a patriotic appeal, but the Federal Reserve's tone changed by the following year, after WWI ended [18.1-3]:

"Use of gold coin for Christmas presents. The Board has been asked for an expression of its views as to the propriety of using gold coin for Christmas presents. About a year ago the Board issued a statement giving some reasons why, in its opinion, it was not desirable to use gold coin for such purposes. There are still some objections to the use of gold coin for gifts, for we are not yet through with war financing, and the problems which grow out of the war and reconstruction will be live ones for many years. There is a worldwide movement to discourage the use of gold coin as a circulating medium upon the ground that gold should be concentrated in the banks as reserve and used in the settlement of balances growing out of international transactions. New bills can be obtained readily for use as presents, and Liberty bonds, war savings certificates, and United States thrift cards can be used, in the same way to good advantage. We should continue to encourage habits of thrift and should frown upon extravagance and the wasteful employment of anything which can be diverted to a useful purpose.

November 26, 1918"

It should come as no surprise that the government found a way to confiscate all the gold in 1933 to be used as monetary reserves. Unfortunately, the American public was willing to hand it in, since they had already become accustomed to using paper money, and actually only a fairly small amount of gold was in circulation.

The economic condition of the U. S. was affected by World War I in two ways: a) an influx of gold from Europe, and b) a selling off of U. S. securities by Europeans to generate revenue to fight the war. After the war ended, there was a severe depression that began in 1920 and lasted for a year or so. This was an industrial collapse, very different from the "money panics" of 1893 and 1907; it included widespread unemployment and approximately a 50% decline in industrial production. But, to their credit, neither the Wilson nor Harding administrations nor the Federal Reserve attempted to intervene in the economy; wages and prices fell, the bad investments were written off and liquidated at bankruptcy sales, and the economy recovered within 18 months.

The period from 1921 to 1929 is known as the "Roaring '20's", characterized by stable economic conditions and stable prices. But the apparent prosperity masked two problems: a) a decline in the prices of agricultural products, putting many farmers and their small local banks into financial difficulty; and b) the extension of call loans for stock market speculation, perhaps as a result of excessive optimism and the belief that the Federal Reserve had solved the "money panic" problem. A fairly large number of small rural banks serving agricultural communities failed during the 1920's, and the Federal Reserve took no action to stabilize them. Since there was no deposit insurance at this time, the depositors in those banks lost their savings. The Federal Reserve engineered a large expansion of the money supply starting in 1924, but did not show up as a general increase in prices because increased productivity was providing countering price reductions. So the stage was set for a recession: weakness in the agricultural sector, speculation driving up stock prices (and loan liabilities) showing profits that existed only on paper, and the prior expansion of the money supply that led to bad investments. A fairly mild recession began in the summer of 1929, but turned into the Great Depression with the collapse of the stock market in Oct 1929. This time, the Hoover administration adopted an entirely different policy than Wilson and Harding in 1920 and 1921: it attempted by legislation to maintain prices and wages, which caused even more businesses to become unprofitable, and thus made the situation worse.

Congress gradually gave the Federal Reserve more power throughout the 1920's, as will be seen by the modifications to the original Federal Reserve Act. There was a gradual shift in power at the Federal Reserve from the Federal Reserve Bank in New York to Washington DC. The bankers in New York, being the financial center of the U. S., had better policies than the people in Washington, but were routinely overruled until it was too late for the policy to work. As a result of this change in the power structure the Federal Reserve became a one-size-fits-all system. The entire banking system operated uniformly even though different policies in different areas were necessary.

Although the industrial decline after the stock market crash in 1929 was less severe than in 1920, this recession became the Great Depression, partly because the federal government and the Federal Reserve pursued counteracting policies. The net result was a collapse of the banking system as it attempted to continue to pay its notes in cash (gold).

By 1932 a great many banks had failed, and at the close of this period, many of the States had declared "banking holidays". The "holidays" were actual closing of banks, ceasing all business and personal transactions. This was the first time in U. S. history that even the solvent banks were actually closed. In all the previous "money panics" and recessions, banks "suspended payment" of their notes in coin, but continued to operate normally, still conducting business by checks, issuing loans, and paying out deposits (in notes, not specie). Now it was different: the banks held out as long as they could until the entire system collapsed. Professors Friedman and Schwartz [18.1-4] have suggested that the Depression could have been aborted if the banks had suspended specie payments temporarily in late 1930. Meanwhile, the Federal Reserve allowed the total money supply to decline starting in 1931, which created "deflation". Each money unit became more valuable, and thus debts in real terms increased, causing a further erosion of profitability among businesses. For individuals, unemployment increased because the continuation of high wages (encouraged by federal government policy) caused businesses to cut costs by layoffs and closing of factories.

The Federal Reserve published a definition of "lawful money" in 1915 [18.1-5]. It was published under the rubric of "Informal Rulings of the Board" (the Federal Reserve Board), and is in the form of responses to letters received by the Board. The contents of the original letters are not provided. Here is the answer to a letter inquiring as to the meaning of "lawful money":

> "Below are reproduced letters sent out from time to time over the signatures of the officers of the Federal Reserve Board, which contain information believed to be of general interest to Federal Reserve Banks and member banks of the system:
>
> **Lawful money, January 12, 1915**
>
> The Federal Reserve Board has carefully considered your letter of December 22, addressed to the secretary. In reply you are advised that the primary meaning of the term "lawful money" would seem to be legal tender. Silver certificates and gold certificates, however, have been specifically made available for reserves of national banks. Inasmuch as these reserves have to consist, under the law, of lawful money, it would seem clear that the statutes authorizing such silver and gold certificates for use in reserves would bring them within the meaning of the term "lawful money of the United States. The Board, therefore; is of opinion that Federal reserve agents should receive silver certificates deposited to reduce its liability for outstanding Federal reserve notes by the Federal reserve bank."

Translation: "lawful money" is anything the government decides is "legal tender", but it also means gold and silver certificates when legislation authorizes them to be used as part of member bank reserves. Notice it says nothing about what constitutes "lawful" money for the public. You know it's getting bad when the central bank can't or won't define what "lawful money" is. The following chapters will show that gold certificates were never allowed to circulate as money, and that although silver certificates did circulate, they were payable in silver only up to the early 1930's. The silver certificates were withdrawn from circulation in the 1970's, to be exchanged for Federal Reserve Notes.

18.2 History, 1915-1932

3 Mar 1915: Congress passed a law amending Section 13 of the Federal Reserve Act (cf. 23 Dec 1913) [18.2-1]: a) Federal Reserve banks may discount bankers' acceptances on foreign trade so long as it matures in less than 90 days and has been endorsed by at least one member bank; b) the value of acceptances shall not exceed half the paid-in capital and surplus of the bank for which rediscounts are made; c) the aggregate of rediscounts for any one person or corporations is not to exceed 10% of paid-up capital and surplus of the bank for which rediscounts are made; and d) drafts and bills of exchange accepted by member banks not to exceed 50% of paid-in capital and surplus, and shall have less than 6 months to run.

1 Apr 1915: The NY stock exchanged re-opened for normal trading [18.2-2] (cf. 31 Jul 1914 and 12 Dec 1914).

12 Jun 1916: Congress modified [18.2-3] section 6 of the currency law (cf. 2 Mar 1911) such that the amount of gold bullion and foreign coin held by the Treasury shall not exceed 2/3's of the face value of gold certificates (i.e., gold certificates only backed by 2/3 in gold).

17 Jul 1916: Congress passed the Federal Farm Loan Act of 1916 [18.2-4] to provide credit to farmers for both land and improvements: **a)** (S. 3) established a Federal Farm Loan Bureau (FFLB); **b)** (S. 4) required the FFLB to divide the continental U. S. into 12 districts, and establish a Federal Land Bank in each; **c)** (S. 5) Land Bank permitted to begin operations when $750,000 in capital has been subscribed by individuals, corporations, or State or federal government, so long as shares not owned by a government paid dividends; **d)** (S. 5) Land Banks to hold reserves equal to at least 25% of its capital, with 20% of those reserves in the form of U. S. government bonds, and the other 80% of reserves either as cash in vault or as deposits in a Federal Reserve Bank; **e)** (S. 6) the Land Banks to accept deposits as a depository institution; **f)** (S. 7) national farm loan associations may be established by individuals or corporations desiring to borrow from the Land Banks with farm mortgages as security; **g)** (S. 7) associations may borrow between $100 and $10,000 on farm mortgages from the Land Banks and lend to members of the association upon good mortgage security; **h)** (S. 8) the farm loan associations to operate as mutual associations, each borrower required to be a shareholder; **i)** (S. 12) interest rates on loan made by the Land Banks not to exceed 6%, and the principal not to exceed 50% of the appraised value of land and improvements for which the loan is made; **j)** (S. 14) loans to be made only on first mortgages; **k)** (S. 16) permitted joint stock Land Banks to be established on the same terms and same powers as the Federal Land Banks, except the U. S. government is prohibited from investing; **l)** (S. 19) both types of Land Banks may issue Farm Loan bonds, secured either by the mortgages or by U. S. government bonds; **m)** (S. 26) Federal Land banks and national farm loan associations to be exempt from taxation except real estate taxes, since mortgages are to be considered debt instruments of the U. S. government; and **n)** (S. 27) the Federal Reserve may buy and sell Farm Loan bonds as desired.

7 Sep 1916: Congress passed an amendment [18.2-5] to the Federal Reserve Act (FRA): **a)** FRA Section 11 was changed to permit the Federal Reserve Board to allow member banks to maintain all their required reserves as deposits in the Federal Reserve Bank in their district; **b)** FRA Section 13 was modified such that 1) Federal Reserve Banks may receive deposits from member banks in any form of lawful money; 2) Federal Reserve Banks may discount commercial paper related to commercial, industrial, and agricultural, but excludes notes, drafts, and bills issued or drawn for the purpose of speculation in stocks or non-U. S. government bonds; 3) Federal Reserve Banks may make advances to member banks on their promissory notes for duration not to exceed 15 days at rates to be set by the Federal Reserve Board; 4) national banks may not incur debts exceeding their paid-in capital and surplus; 5) member banks may accept bills of currency exchange; **c)** FRA Section 14 was modified to permit Federal Reserve Banks to open accounts in foreign countries for the purpose of dealing in bills of exchange; **d)** FRA Section 16 was modified to expand the type of paper that can be used as

collateral for Federal Reserve Notes, now included notes, drafts, bills of exchange and acceptances discounted per Federal Reserve Act Section 14; **e)** FRA Section 24 was modified to permit national banks to make loans on real estate within 100 miles of its location, subject to a maximum term of 5 years, not more than 50% of assessed value, so long as the total loans did not exceed 25% of capital plus surplus or one-third of time deposits; and **f)** FRA Section 25 was modified to permit member banks to invest in foreign banks for the purpose of furthering commerce, limited to 10% of its paid-in capital and surplus.

6 Apr 1917: The U. S. entered World War I.

24 Apr 1917: Congress passed a law to fund WWI, a.k.a. the First Liberty Bond Act [18.2-6]: **a)** (S. 1) authorized the Treasury Secretary to borrow up to $5,000,000,000 and issue bonds, at an interest not exceeding 3.5%; **b)** (S. 1); principal and interest on bonds to be payable in U. S. gold coin at current value; **c)** (S. 1) principal and interest to be exempt from federal, State, and local taxes, except inheritance and estate; **d)** bonds not to have circulation privilege; **e)** (S. 2) authorized the Treasury Secretary to purchase bonds of foreign nations allied with the U. S., up to $3,000,000,000; **f)** (S. 4) authorized the Treasury Secretary to borrow up to $63,945,460 in order to redeem the 3% loan of 1908; **g)** (S. 6) authorized the Treasury Secretary to borrow up to $2,000,000,000 and issue certificates of indebtedness with interest up to 3.5% annual, payable in one year as the Secretary may prescribe; **h)** (S. 6) certificates of indebtedness not to have circulation privilege; **i)** (S. 6) certificates of indebtedness to be exempt from federal State, and local taxes except inheritance and estate; and **j)** that public money may be deposited in national and member banks of the Federal Reserve, but those banks are not required to keep reserves against those deposits.

21 Jun 1917: Congress revised the Federal Reserve Act [18.2-7, 18.2-8]. Among its provisions: **a)** (S. 2, modifying FRA S. 3) Federal Reserve Board may authorize branches of Federal Reserve Banks in their districts; **b)** (S. 2, modifying FRA S. 3) changed method of appointing Class C directors of a Federal Reserve Bank and makes one of them a "federal reserve agent" for handling of reserves; **c)** (S. 3, modifying FRA S. 9) permitted State banks to become members of the Federal Reserve under the same stock subscription and capital requirement as for national banks; **d)** (S. 4, modifying FRA S. 13) permitted Federal Reserve Banks to receive deposits from nonmember banks; **e)** (S. 7, modifying FRA S. 16) added gold to the allowable collateral for Federal Reserve Notes; **f)** (S. 7, modifying FRA S. 13) Federal Reserve Banks to maintain reserves in gold or lawful money 35% against deposits; **g)** (S. 7, modifying FRA S. 16) permitted gold held by a federal reserve agent to count against the 40% gold reserve against Federal Reserve Notes in circulation; **h)** (S. 7, modifying FRA S. 16) permitted drafts, bills of exchange and bankers acceptances was well as gold or gold certificates as reserves against Federal Reserve Notes; **i)** (S. 10, modifying FRA S. 19) prohibited member banks from counting cash in their vaults against their reserve requirements (now had to be entirely as deposits in Federal Reserve Banks); and **j)** (S. 10, modifying FRA S. 19) reduced reserve requirements from the 1913 original levels [18.2-9]: a) for central reserve city banks, from 18% to 13% on demand deposits; b) for reserve city banks, from 15% to 10% on demand deposits; c) for country banks, from 12% to 7% on demand deposits; and d) for all banks, from 5% to 3% on time deposits.

7 Sep 1917: President Wilson issued an Executive Order [18.2-10] prohibiting exportation of gold except with permission of the Treasury and the Federal Reserve Board. This kept the stock of gold approximately constant.

24 Sep 1917: Congress passed a funding law, a.k.a. the Second Liberty Bond Act [18.2-11]: **a)** (S. 1) authorized the Treasury Secretary to borrow up to $7,538,945,460 in addition to the $2,000,000,000 authorized previously (cf. 24 Apr 1917) and to issue bonds therefor; **b)** (S. 1) bonds not to exceed 4% interest, with principal and interest payable in U. S. gold coin at current value; **c)** (S. 2) authorized the Treasury Secretary to purchase at par up to $4,000,000,000 in bonds of foreign government allied with the U. S.; **d)** (S. 3) authorized conversion of existing foreign bonds to a higher interest rate; **e)** authorized the Treasury Secretary to convert old bonds into new issues at higher interest

rates; **f)** (S. 5) authorized the Treasury Secretary to borrow and issue certificates of indebtedness within one year at interest on terms per the Secretary's discretion, but the total outstanding at any time to be limited to $4,000,000,000; and **g)** (S. 6) authorized the Treasury Secretary to borrow up to $2,000,000,000 and issue war-savings certificates, payable within five years and at interest per the Secretary's discretion.

5 Oct 1917: Congress authorized [18.2-12] national banks to issue notes in denominations less than $5, except each national bank was limited to issuing no more than $25,000 in $1 and $2 notes (cf. 25 Feb 1863 and 14 Mar 1900).

4 Apr 1918: Congress passed a funding law (a.k.a. the Third Liberty Bond Act) [18.2-13]: **a)** (S. 1) authorized the Treasury Secretary to borrow up to $12,000,000,000 and issue bonds therefor (in addition to the $2,000,000,00 authorized 24 Apr 1917); **b)** (S. 1) the bonds to be limited to 4.25% interest rate, **c)** (S. 1) principal and interest on bonds to be payable in gold; **d)** (S. 3) holder of current bonds bearing more than 4% are not convertible; and **e)** (S. 4) total certificates of indebtedness outstanding at any one time not to exceed $8,000,000,000 (cf. 24 Sep 1917). The limitation of the 4.25% interest rate that could be paid on U. S. Government securities for those maturing in more than 5 years was not a problem (since market rates were below this level) until 1959, when market rates went above 4.5% for a short time [18.2-14].

23 Apr 1918: Congress passed a law regarding the use of gold and silver (a.k.a. the Pittman Act) [18.2-15]. Among its provisions: **a)** (S. 1) The Treasury authorized to melt down $350 M worth of silver dollars, cast into bullion, and sold at not less than $1 per ozt., and the silver certificates having been issued against the silver dollars to be retired at face value; **b)** (S. 2) upon sales of bullion the Director of the Mint is to buy newly mined silver at $1 per fine ozt., partly to be resold and partly to be coined; **c)** (S. 3) the sales of silver is intended to be used to conserve the gold stock, and to assist American allies and to pay foreign trade imbalances; **d)** (S. 5) the Federal Reserve Board "may be either permitted or required" to issue Federal Reserve Bank Notes up to the amount of silver coins melted down (i.e., up to $350 M) in order to replace the retired silver certificates and prevent a contraction of the currency; **e)** (S. 5) the Federal Reserve Bank Notes to be insured by depositing with the Treasurer either U. S. certificates of indebtedness or United States one-year gold notes; and **f)** (S. 6) the amount of Federal Reserve Bank Notes issued to be reduced if the new silver is coined. The main purposes of this legislation were to use silver exports to settle trade balances due to the gold embargo (cf. 7 Sep 1917), and to provide aid to Great Britain. About $270 M of silver dollars were melted and sold off [18.2-16].

15 Aug 1918: Approximate beginning of a recession [18.2-17].

7 Nov 1918: Congress passed a law [18.2-18] permitting national banks located in the same district to merge.

11 Nov 1918: World War I ended.

15 Mar 1919: Approximate end of the recession (cf. 15 Aug 1918) [18.2-19].

9 Jun 1919: President Wilson rescinded the previous prohibition on gold exports (cf. 7 Sep 1917) [18.2-20]. There was a subsequent outflow of gold as the Federal Reserve desired, since a declining gold-to-monetary liabilities ratio indicated a need to raise interest rates. The gold-to-monetary liability ratio went from 50.6 to 47.3 between Jun and Sep 1918 [18.2-21].

24 Dec 1919: Congress passed the Edge Act of 1919 [18.2-22] to permit U. S. banks to compete with foreign banks. Among its provisions (which became Section 25A of the Federal Reserve Act) are: **a)** permitted subsidiaries of U. S. national banks to establish subsidiaries for the purpose of conducting international banking business (called Edge Corporations); **b)** Edge Corporations can receive deposits and make loan to companies as necessary for the conduct of international trade; **c)** may establish branches in foreign nations; **d)** may own stock in other domestic or foreign companies, so long as such companies are engaged in foreign trade; **e)** Edge corporations prohibited from engaging in any domestic business except related to foreign trade; **f)** minimum capital requirements for an Edge Cor-

poration is $2,000,000; and **g**) prohibits Edge Corporations from becoming members of the Federal Reserve.

31 Dec 1919: A total of 63 banks failed in 1919 [18.2-23].

15 Jan 1920: Approximate beginning of a recession [18.2-24].

15 May 1920: The recession in the U. S. turned into a severe depression as monetary growth of 1915-1919 and depreciation ended [18.2-25]; falling farm prices, many farm foreclosures, and bank failures in rural areas. The industrial decline was one of the most severe contractions in our history [18.2-26]. The Federal Reserve had raised the rediscount rate to 6% in Jan 1920 (too late, but then too severe) in order to stem the expansion of the money supply [18.2-27]. Raising the discount rates made it less profitable for member banks to borrow, and thus could not profitably extend or renew loans. Otherwise the federal government and the Federal Reserve allowed the economy to recover on its own. The depression ended in the summer of 1921.

31 Dec 1920: 155 banks failed in 1920 [18.2-28], but there was no loss of confidence in the banking system by the public.

14 Jun 1921: Congress increased the initial capital requirements for Edge Corporations to $2,000,000 [18.2-29], but can only be up to 10% of a national bank's capital.

15 Jul 1921: Approximate end of the depression (cf. 15 Jan 1920) [18.2-30].

31 Dec 1921: 506 banks failed in 1921, with losses to depositors totaling $59.967 M. [18.2-31].

3 Jun 1922: Congress passed an amendment to the Federal Reserve Act [18.2-32]: **a**) created a Federal Reserve Board, consisting of the Secretary of the Treasury, Comptroller of the Currency, and six others, to be appointed by the President and subject to approval by the Senate; **b**) the six members to be from different Federal Reserve districts, and to serve for 10 year terms; **c**) the six appointed members chosen to "have a due regard to a fair representation of the financial, agricultural, industrial, and commercial interests, and geographical divisions of the country"; **d**) Treasury Secretary to be ex officio chairman of the Federal Reserve Board; **e**) no member of the Board shall be an officer or director of any bank, banking institution, trust company, or Federal Reserve Bank, nor hold stock in any of those institutions; and **f**) created the office of the Comptroller of the Currency within the Treasury Department. The Federal Reserve Board was to be headquartered in Washington, DC, but its duties and authority was not specified.

22 Sep 1922: Congress passed a law [18.2-33] declaring a coal and fuel emergency: **a**) (S. 1) declared a national emergency in coal and fuel caused by prolonged interruption of the coal mining industry and economic disturbances caused by World War I leading to unreasonably high prices and shortages; **b**) (S. 2) granted the Interstate Commerce Commission additional powers to set priorities in the distribution of coal and fuel to ensure equal distribution, subjecting all vessels carrying fuel to the jurisdiction of the ICC; **c**) (S. 3) created the office of Federal Fuel Distributor (FFD); **d**) (S. 4) the FFD to determine if a shortage exists, where supplies are located and means of transportation, whether prices are too high, and to provide advice to the ICC for equitable distribution; **e**) (S. 5) FFD to make rules as necessary to carry out his duties and coordinate with other agencies on fuel supplies and distribution; **f**) (S. 6) the emergency powers to continue for one year unless terminated earlier by the President; and **g**) (F. 7) specified penalties for providing false information or violating price controls, or evading the distribution plan.

31 Dec 1922: 366 banks failed in 1922, with losses to depositors totaling $38.223 M [18.2-34].

15 May 1923: Approximate beginning of a recession [18.2-35].

31 Dec 1923: 646 banks failed in 1923, with losses to depositors totaling $62.142 M [18.2-36].

15 Jul 1924: Approximate end of the recession (cf. 15 May 1923) [18.2-37].

31 Dec 1924: 775 banks failed in 1924, with losses to depositors totaling $79.381 M [18.2-38].

31 Dec 1925: 617 banks failed in 1925, with losses to depositors totaling $60.799 M [18.2-39].

15 Oct 1926: Approximate beginning of a recession [18.2-40].

31 Dec 1926: 975 banks failed in 1926, with losses to depositors totaling $83.066 M [18.2-41].

25 Feb 1927: Congress passed the McFadden Act [18.2-42]: **a)** (S. 18) chartered the Federal Reserve permanently (was only chartered for 20 years under Section 4 the original Federal Reserve Act); **b)** (S. 7) permitted national banks to open branches in States where it was allowed; **c)** (S. 9) prohibited interstate banking by a State bank that becomes a member of the Federal Reserve; **d)** (S. 16) permitted banks that were members of the Federal Reserve to make loans on real estate and improved farm land, up to 50% of the appraised value for terms up to 5 years; **e)** (S. 10) national banks are prohibited from making loans or otherwise permitting a single customer to have obligations to the such bank in excess of 10% of the bank's paid-in capital plus 10% of its surplus, and **f)** (S. 4) revised the capital conditions under which national bank may be organized: 1) $50,000 in locations with a population less than 6,000; 2) $25,000 in locations with a population less than 3,000; 3) $200,000 in locations with a population greater than 50,000; and $100,000 for all others.

15 Nov 1927: Approximate end of the recession (cf. 15 Oct 1926) [18.2-43].

31 Dec 1927: 669 banks failed in 1927, with losses to depositors totaling $60.681 M [18.2-44].

28 Dec 1928: Banks that were members of the Federal Reserve had about 40% of their loan portfolios (about $9 billion) in stock market call loans [18.2-45]; $3.6 billon held by central reserve city banks (NY); $3.2 billion held by reserve city banks, and $2.2 billion held by country banks.

31 Dec 1928: 498 banks failed in 1928, with losses to depositors totaling $43.813 M [18.2-46].

15 Jun 1929: Congress passed the Agricultural Marketing Act [18.2-47] designed to "protect, control, and stabilize the currents of interstate and foreign commerce in the marketing of agricultural commodities and their food products -- 1) by minimizing speculation, 2) by preventing inefficient and wasteful methods of distribution, 3) encouraging the organization of producers..., 4) aiding in preventing and controlling surpluses in any agricultural commodity ...". Among the provisions: **a)** (S. 2) established a Federal Farm Board (FFB), to be staffed by people knowledgeable in agricultural commodities; **b)** (S. 3) the FFB to make recommendations on marketing of food products; **c)** (S. 5) promote education in marketing, make reports of crop prices, issue reports on land utilizations, etc.; **d)** (S. 6) FFB to be appropriated $500 M as a revolving fund for use in making loans to cooperative agricultural associations and stabilization corporations; **e)** (S. 9) stabilization corporations to act as marketing agencies for associations, controlling surpluses, and making loans to associations; and **f)** (S. 11) FFB authorized to administer price insurance programs against declines in crop prices.

15 Aug 1929: Approximate beginning of a recession [18.2-48].

29 Oct 1929: The stock market crashed, setting off the Great Depression [18.2-49]. The collapse of stock prices caused a run on the banks, and the banks were forced to call in the call loans, mostly used to invest in stocks (cf. 31 Dec 1928). Stock prices had been inflated through optimism, an increase in the money supply since 1924, and speculation funded by call loans. Now, with stock prices declining, the borrowers defaulted on the loans. The heavy reliance on call loans, secured by stocks, was not included as a possibility by the architects of the Federal Reserve. These loans did not qualify for rediscounting by the Federal Reserve, so the banks in New York were left with a liquidity problem. The rush to cash spread throughout the nation and the lack of adequate reserves caused many bank failures since they could not meet depositors' demands for cash. This is the traditional start of the Great Depression, although Rothbard [18.2-50] shows that it probably began in Aug 1929 as a business downturn that occurred after the stimulating inflation ended in 1928.

31 Dec 1929: 659 banks failed in 1929, with losses to depositors totaling $76.659 M [18.2-51].

17 Jun 1930: Congress passed the "Smoot-Hawley" Tariff Act of 1930 [18.2-52], a general revision of the tariff laws, consisting of 174 pages of details on duties and administrative regulations regarding imports of merchandise and commodities. It increased average tariffs overall to a high level. Title I contained 15 sections, each specifying duties on a category of imports. The percentages below indi-

cate *ad valorem* rates, usually in addition to duties per weight or per-item: **a)** Schedule 1, Chemicals (1% to 60%); **b)** Schedule 2: Earthenware and glassware (15% to 60%); **c)** Schedule 3, Metals and manufactures of (20% to 60%); **d)** Schedule 4, Wood and manufactures of (15% to 45%); **e)** Schedule 5, Sugar and manufactures of (up to 50%); **f)** Schedule 6, Tobacco and manufactures of (up to 35%); **g)** Schedule 7, Agricultural products (25% to 50%); **h)** Schedule 8, Spirits and wines (no *ad valorem*); **i)** Schedule 9, Cotton manufactures (25% to 75%); **j)** Schedule 10, Flax, hemp, etc. (15% to 45%).; **k)** Schedule 11, Wool and manufactures (30% to 60%); **l)** Schedule 12, Silk (20% to 65%); **m)** Schedule 13, Rayon and synthetics (10% to 65%); **n)** Schedule 14, Paper and books (10% to 30%); and **o)** Schedule 15, Sundries (25% to 90%). Title II contained 214 sections specifying items on the free list, which included diamonds, gold, silver, certain drugs, coal, bananas, cyanide, radium, tapioca, and art works made before 1830. Title III contained 81 pages of administrative regulations regarding documentation, sales, storage, etc.

11 Dec 1930: The Bank of the United States failed, with deposits of $200 M [18.2-53]. Although it was a normal bank, this failure had a psychological effect on the public, and produced some anxiety about the safety of the banking system.

20 Dec 1930: Congress passed a supplemental appropriations bill [18.2-54] for public works and to increase employment: **a)** national forests, $3 M; **b)** national forest highways, $3 M; **c)** roads on unreserved public land, $3 M; **d)** federal highway system, $80 M; **e)** rivers and harbors, $22.5 M; **f)** trails in national parks, $1.5 M; and **g)** Mississippi River flood control, $3 M.

31 Dec 1930: 1,350 banks failed in 1930, with losses to depositors totaling $237.359 M [18.2-55].

21 Sep 1931: Britain abandoned the gold standard; the result was an outflow of gold from the U. S. The Federal Reserve decided to raise the discount rate in order to counteract the gold flow. But the bigger problem was the rush to cash by the public, resulting in a decrease in bank reserves, and a general trend toward a declining money supply [18.2-56].

31 Dec 1931: 2,293 banks failed in 1931, with losses to depositors totaling $390.476 M [18.2-57].

22 Jan 1932: Congress passed an emergency financing law [18.2-58] to provide emergency relief for farms and industry. Among its provisions: **a)** (S. 1) created the Reconstruction Finance Corporation (RTC); **b)** (S. 2) the capital stock of the RTC to be $500 M, to be subscribed by the U. S. government; **c)** (S. 2) $50 M of the RTC funding to be used by the Secretary of Agriculture to make loans to farmers; **d)** (S. 4) the RTC charter to expire after ten years; e) $200 M of RTC funding authorized for loans to depository institutions (savings banks, trust companies, savings and loan associations, insurance companies, federal land banks, credit unions, and others) that are either closed or in the process of being liquidated, the loans to have a term not exceeding three years, and to be secured by assets held by the institutions except no foreign securities are to be used as collateral; and **e)** (S. 9) the RTC (with concurrence of the Treasury Secretary) was authorized to issue bonds and other U. S. obligations to fund the RTC, not to exceed three times the subscribed capital stock.

27 Feb 1932: Congress passed the Glass-Steagall Act [18.2-59, 18.2-60]: **a)** (S. 1) created a new Section 10A of the Federal Reserve Act, permitting the Federal Reserve: 1) to grant advances to groups of five member banks on any time or demand promissory notes offered by the member banks if they cannot obtain credit from them through the normal channels of new Section 10B; 2) advances may be made to banks in groups less than five if the their deposit liability is at least 10% of the total deposits liabilities within the Federal Reserve District; 3) the interest rate on such advances to be at least 1% higher than the normal discount rate; 4) the notes upon which advances are made cannot be used as security for Federal Reserve Notes; 5) obligations of foreign entities, including foreign governments are not eligible for advances under Section 10A; **b)** (S. 2) created a new Section 10B of the Federal Reserve Act, permitting the Federal Reserve, until 3 Mar 1933, to extend advances in emergency circumstances, with the approval of five members of the Federal Reserve Board: 1) to banks with less than $5,000,000 in capital and not having sufficient assets to obtain discounts; 2) based on time or demand promissory notes of those banks; 3) at interest at least 1% higher than the normal

discount rate; 3) classes of acceptable promissory notes as determined by the Federal Reserve Board; 4) notes accepted are not eligible for collateral against Federal Reserve Notes; and 5) obligations of foreign entities, including foreign governments were not eligible for advances under Section 10B; and **c)** (S. 3) modified Section 16 of the Federal Reserve Act, permitting, until 3 Mar 1933, the use of U. S. government bonds in a Reserve Bank portfolio to be used as collateral against the required 60% eligible paper reserves against Federal Reserve Notes. The provisions for using U. S. government bonds as a reserve against the Federal Reserve Notes was intended to be temporary, but became permanent. Meltzer reports that it was by this action and the later expansion prior to WWII that caused U. S. government securities to become the dominant source of credit at the Federal Reserve Banks [18.2-61].

21 Jul 1932: Congress passed the Emergency Relief and Construction Act [18.2-62]: **a)** (S. 1) authorized the RFC to allocate $300,000,000 to make loans to States and territories to "provide relief and work relief to needy and distressed people and relieving the hardship resulting from unemployment"; **b)** (S. 201) authorized the RFC to make loans to corporations and railroads (since they were near default on their bonds); **c)** (S. 205) the amount of notes or bonds issued by the RFC is increased to 6.6 times its subscribed capital stock; **d)** (S. 210) (modifying FRA Section 13) authorized the Federal Reserve to loan (discount) to banks, individuals, and corporations as an emergency measure to relieve the liquidity problem owing to a run on the banks by the public, and to also make discounts to corporations as deemed necessary by the Federal Reserve Board; **e)** (S. 301) authorized $322.224 M for public works ($136 M for highway construction, $30 M for river and harbors; $15.5 M for flood control projects, and a long list of other miscellaneous projects). Friedman and Schwartz [18.2-63] note that these measures did not have the intended effects: a) agricultural land values and income continued to fall; and b) the rate of farm foreclosures and distress sales due to delinquent tax liabilities continued unabated.

22 Jul 1932: Congress passed the Federal Home Loan Bank Act [18.2-64, 18.2-65] designed to extend loans to banks and other finance companies using mortgages they held as collateral. The idea was to provide liquidity to institutions holding mortgages that could not be sold. Among its provisions were: **a)** (S. 2) created the Federal Home Loan Bank Board (FHLBB); **b)** (S. 3) directed the FHLBB divide the U. S. into 12 geographic districts and establish a Federal Home Loan Banks (FHLB) in each; **c)** (S. 17) the FHLBB to supervise the operations of the FHLB's; **d)** (S. 4, 10) savings banks, savings and loans, cooperative banks, and building and loan institutions appropriately chartered by a State could borrow from an FHLB to finance home mortgages when the homeowner cannot get financing elsewhere (up to 15 years term, mortgage less than $20,000); **e)** (S. 6) initial capital of each FHLB to be not less than $5,000,000, subscribed by institutions that choose to become a member; and **f)** (S. 6) authorized the Treasury Secretary to invest up to $125,000,000. This was the beginning of federal government involvement in housing financing.

31 Oct 1932: State-wide "banking holiday" (banks closed) in Nevada [18.2-66].

31 Dec 1932: 1,463 banks failed in 1932, with losses to depositors totaling $168.302 M [18.2-67]. This makes a total of 5,096 banks that had failed since 1 Jan 1930 [18.2-68].

18.3 Data, 1915-1932

Figures 18.3-1 and 18.3-2 show the U. S. government revenue and expenditures for 1915 to 1932.

			U. S. Government Revenue, 1915-1932 (USD)									
			Internal Revenue			Miscellaneous						
Day	Year	Customs	Income and Profits Taxes	Social Security Tax	Misc.	Sales of Public Lands	Surplus Postal Covered Into Treasury	Direct Tax Plus Other Misc.	Postal	Refunds of Receipts	Capital Transfers	Total
30 Jun	1915	209,786,672	80,201,759	0	335,467,887	2,167,136	3,500,000	66,787,373	283,748,165	0	0	981,658,992
30 Jun	1916	213,185,846	124,937,253	0	387,764,776	1,887,662	0	54,759,011	312,057,689	0	0	1,094,592,237
30 Jun	1917	225,962,393	359,681,228	0	449,684,980	1,892,893	5,200,000	81,903,301	324,526,116	0	0	1,448,850,911
30 Jun	1918	179,998,385	2,314,006,292	0	872,028,020	1,969,455	48,630,701	247,950,012	295,845,261	0	0	3,960,428,126
30 Jun	1919	184,457,867	3,018,783,687	0	1,296,501,292	1,404,705	89,906,000	561,203,585	274,941,126	0	0	5,427,198,262
30 Jun	1920	322,902,650	3,944,949,288	0	1,460,082,287	1,910,140	5,213,000	959,508,024	431,937,212	0	0	7,126,502,601
30 Jun	1921	308,564,391	3,206,046,158	0	1,390,379,823	1,530,439	0	718,412,150	463,491,275	0	0	6,088,424,236
30 Jun	1922	356,443,387	2,068,128,193	0	1,145,125,064	895,391	81,494	538,430,622	484,772,047	0	0	4,593,876,198
30 Jun	1923	561,928,867	1,678,607,428	0	945,865,333	656,508	0	820,077,345	532,827,925	0	0	4,539,963,406
30 Jun	1924	545,637,504	1,842,144,418	0	953,012,618	522,223	0	670,727,939	572,948,778	0	0	4,584,993,480
30 Jun	1925	547,561,226	1,760,537,824	0	828,638,068	623,534	0	642,788,033	599,591,477	0	0	4,379,740,162
30 Jun	1926	579,430,093	1,982,040,088	0	855,599,289	754,253	0	544,931,967	659,819,801	0	0	4,622,575,491
30 Jun	1927	605,499,983	2,224,992,800	0	644,421,542	621,187	0	653,858,929	683,121,989	0	0	4,812,516,430
30 Jun	1928	568,986,188	2,173,952,557	0	621,018,666	384,651	0	678,006,094	693,633,921	0	0	4,735,982,077
30 Jun	1929	602,262,786	2,330,711,823	0	607,307,549	314,568	0	492,653,499	696,947,578	0	0	4,730,197,803
30 Jun	1930	587,000,903	2,410,986,978	0	628,308,036	395,744	0	551,250,041	705,484,098	0	0	4,883,425,800
30 Jun	1931	378,354,005	1,860,394,295	0	569,386,721	230,302	0	381,273,309	656,463,383	-74,081,709	0	3,772,020,306
30 Jun	1932	327,754,969	1,057,335,853	0	503,670,481	170,339	0	116,793,795	588,171,923	-81,812,320	0	2,512,085,040

1. The data for the revenue and expenditures for 1915 to 1932 is from Henry Morgenthau, "Annual Report of the Secretary of the Treasury on the State of the Finances for the Fiscal Year Ended June 30, 1940", Washington: U. S. Government Printing Office, 1940, pp. 645, 648, 649. However, the 1956 Annual Treasury Report, p. 322 calls out refunds of receipts and capital transfers for 1931 and 1932; these have been included here. The 1956 total receipts also excludes Postal revenue, which is included here.

Figure 18.3-1: U. S. Government Revenue, 1915-1932

			U. S. Government Expenditures, 1915-1932 (USD)								
		Ordinary Disbursements									
Day	Year	Civil & Misc.	War Dep't, (including Rivers, Canals, and Panama Canal)	Navy Dep't	Indians	Pensions	Postal Deficiencies	Interest on Public Debt	Public Debt Retirement Chargeable vs. Ordinary Receipts	Postal Expenditures Exclusive of Postal Deficiencies	Total
30 Jun	1915	200,533,231	202,160,134	141,835,654	22,130,351	164,387,942	6,636,593	22,902,897	0	291,944,881	1,052,531,683
30 Jun	1916	191,752,692	183,176,439	153,853,567	17,570,284	159,302,351	5,500,000	22,900,869	0	300,728,453	1,034,784,655
30 Jun	1917	1,144,448,923	377,940,870	239,632,757	30,598,093	160,318,406	0	24,742,702	0	319,889,904	2,297,571,655
30 Jun	1918	6,143,916,172	4,869,955,286	1,278,840,487	30,888,400	181,137,754	2,221,095	189,743,277	1,134,234	322,628,094	13,020,464,799
30 Jun	1919	6,627,726,263	9,009,075,789	2,002,310,785	34,593,257	221,614,781	343,511	619,215,569	8,014,750	362,160,763	18,885,055,468
30 Jun	1920	2,771,141,778	1,621,953,095	736,021,456	40,516,832	213,344,204	114,854	1,020,251,622	78,746,350	418,607,441	6,900,697,632
30 Jun	1921	1,916,122,018	1,118,076,423	650,373,836	41,470,808	260,611,416	130,128,458	999,144,731	422,281,500	489,506,490	6,027,715,680
30 Jun	1922	1,091,652,312	457,756,139	476,775,194	38,500,413	252,576,848	64,346,235	991,000,759	422,694,600	481,316,006	4,276,618,506
30 Jun	1923	1,166,634,334	397,050,596	333,201,362	45,142,763	264,147,869	32,526,915	1,055,923,690	402,850,491	524,366,214	4,221,844,234
30 Jun	1924	1,131,154,606	357,016,878	332,249,137	46,754,026	228,261,555	12,638,850	940,602,913	457,999,750	574,773,905	4,081,451,620
30 Jun	1925	1,183,882,296	370,980,708	346,142,001	38,755,457	218,321,424	23,216,784	881,806,662	466,538,114	616,119,721	4,145,763,167
30 Jun	1926	1,293,702,536	364,089,945	312,743,410	48,442,120	207,189,622	39,506,490	831,937,700	487,376,051	640,285,690	4,225,273,564
30 Jun	1927	1,204,375,973	369,114,122	318,909,096	36,791,649	230,556,065	27,263,191	787,019,578	519,554,845	687,364,998	4,180,949,518
30 Jun	1928	1,340,702,732	400,989,683	331,335,492	36,990,808	229,401,462	32,080,202	731,764,476	540,255,020	693,674,815	4,337,194,690
30 Jun	1929	1,471,452,939	425,947,194	364,561,544	34,086,586	229,781,079	94,699,744	678,330,400	549,603,704	687,709,010	4,536,172,200
30 Jun	1930	1,597,512,107	464,853,515	374,165,639	32,066,628	220,608,931	91,714,451	659,347,613	553,883,603	711,985,635	4,706,138,122
30 Jun	1931	1,800,641,110	478,418,974	354,071,004	26,778,585	234,402,722	145,643,613	611,559,704	440,082,000	656,885,960	4,748,483,672
30 Jun	1932	2,639,280,132	477,449,816	357,617,834	26,125,092	232,521,292	202,876,341	599,276,631	412,629,750	590,846,193	5,538,623,081

1. The data for the expenditures for 1915 to 1932 is from Henry Morgenthau, "Annual Report of the Secretary of the Treasury on the State of the Finances for the Fiscal Year Ended June 30, 1940", Washington: U. S. Government Printing Office, 1940, pp. 645, 648, 649.

2. The 1956 Annual Treasury Report excludes Postal disbursements from the total expenditures; but they are included here per the 1940 Treasury Report.

Figure 18.3-2: U. S. Government Expenditures, 1915-1932

Figure 18.3-3 shows the national debt and per-capita debt for this period. Refer to the Introduction to Part 2 for a sense of wages vs. per-capita national debt.

				U. S. National Debt, 1915-1932 (USD)						
Day	Year	Principal ($) [1]	Population [2]	Debt per Capita ($) [2]	Day	Year	Principal ($) [1]	Population [2]	Debt per Capita ($) [2]
30 Jun	1915	1,191,264,068	99,125,050	12.02	30 Jun	1924	21,250,812,989	112,894,005	188.24
30 Jun	1916	1,225,145,568	100,504,353	12.19	30 Jun	1925	20,516,193,888	114,612,114	179.01
30 Jun	1917	2,975,618,585	101,883,657	29.21	30 Jun	1926	19,643,216,315	116,330,223	168.86
30 Jun	1918	12,455,225,365	103,262,961	120.62	30 Jun	1927	18,511,906,932	118,048,332	156.82
30 Jun	1919	25,484,506,160	104,642,264	243.54	30 Jun	1928	17,604,293,201	119,766,442	146.99
30 Jun	1920	24,299,321,467	106,021,568	229.19	30 Jun	1929	16,931,088,484	121,484,551	139.37
30 Jun	1921	23,977,450,553	107,739,677	222.55	30 Jun	1930	16,185,309,831	123,202,660	131.37
30 Jun	1922	22,963,381,708	109,457,786	209.79	30 Jun	1931	16,801,281,492	124,098,907	135.39
30 Jun	1923	22,349,707,365	111,175,896	201.03	30 Jun	1932	19,487,002,444	124,995,154	155.90

1. Public debt data from 1915 to 1932 is from the Annual Report of the Secretary of the Treasury, 1980, pp. 61, 62.
2. Population values are based on the dicennial census from the Census Bureau, and linearly interpolated. Per-capita is based on these values.

Figure 18.3-3: National Debt and Per-Capita Share Thereof, 1915-1932

Figures 18.3-4 through 18.3-11 show the balance sheet assets and liabilities of the Federal Reserve and commercial banking system as a whole, as described in Appendix A. It should be noted that the available data as published by the Federal Reserve, which was supposed to improve reporting standards above what prevailed during the national bank system, is actually greatly inferior to the national bank system. A fair amount of the data had to be interpolated as indicated by the values in italics. Also, the "currency outside banks" excludes gold and gold certificates [18.3-1].

		Assets of the Federal Reserve & Commercial System, 1915-1918 (millions USD)								
				Federal Reserve Loans & Investments		Commercial Bank Loans and Investments				
Day	Year	Gold Stock [3, 5]	Treasury Currency Outstanding [3, 5]	U. S. Government Securities [3, 5]	Discounts & Advances [3, 5]	Loans [4, 5]	U. S. Government Securities [4, 5]	Other [4, 5]	Total Assets	Note
31 Mar	1914									
30 Jun	1914									
30 Sep	1914									
31 Dec	1914	1,526	2,197	0	0					
31 Mar	1915	1,582	2,061	7	33					
30 Jun	1915	1,699	1,981	8	36	13,519	802	3,152	21,197	1, 2
30 Sep	1915	1,837	1,950	9	45	14,081	790	3,337	22,049	1, 6
31 Dec	1915	2,025	1,938	16	56	14,644	777	3,522	22,977	1, 6
31 Mar	1916	2,036	1,925	40	61	15,206	765	3,706	23,739	1, 6
30 Jun	1916	2,158	1,912	57	92	15,768	752	3,891	24,630	1, 2
30 Sep	1916	2,343	1,902	53	117	16,372	950	3,952	25,689	1, 6
31 Dec	1916	2,556	1,901	55	158	16,977	1,149	4,012	26,807	1, 6
31 Mar	1917	2,818	1,903	105	107	17,581	1,347	4,073	27,933	1, 6
30 Jun	1917	2,933	1,899	66	405	18,185	1,545	4,133	29,166	1, 2
30 Sep	1917	2,864	1,907	99	416	18,657	1,962	4,124	30,028	1, 6
31 Dec	1917	2,868	1,923	122	933	19,129	2,378	4,115	31,468	1, 6
31 Mar	1918	2,878	1,939	326	915	19,601	2,795	4,105	32,559	1, 6
30 Jun	1918	2,876	1,880	255	1,105	20,073	3,211	4,096	33,496	1, 2
30 Sep	1918	2,866	1,825	81	1,982	20,646	3,695	4,135	35,230	1, 6
31 Dec	1918	2,873	1,795	239	2,053	21,218	4,179	4,173	36,530	1, 6

1. BMS1943, Table 102 is end-of-month call dates.
2. BMS1943, Table 3 is per end-of month call date.
3. These are end-of-month call date figures per BMS1943, Table 102 (1915 to 1921).
4. Commercial Bank data per BMS1943, Table 3 (end-of-month call dates).
5. A footnote to BMS1943, Table 3 states that some of these are "rough approximations" prior to 1930.
6. Items in italics linearly interpolated from adjacent data.
7. BMS1943 is: Board of Governors of the Federal Reserve, Banking and Monetary Statistics, 1914-1941, Washington DC: Publication Services, Division of Administrative Services, Board of Governors of the Federal Reserve System, Nov 1943

Figure 18.3-4: Banking System Assets, 1915-1918

		Liabilities of the Federal Reserve and Commercial System, 1915-1918 (millions USD)										
				At Federal Reserve Banks		At Commercial Banks						
Day	Year	Currency Outside Banks [2]	Treasury Cash [4]	Treasury Demand Deposits [1]	Foreign Demand Deposits [1]	Demand Deposits [2]	Treasury Demand Deposits [2]	Time Deposits [2]	Capital [3]	Total Liabilities	Error (%)	Note
31 Mar	1914											
30 Jun	1914											
30 Sep	1914											
31 Dec	1914	1,533	416	0	0	10,082	66	4,441	2,093	18,631		5, 6
31 Mar	1915	1,554	384	0	0	9,955	57	4,853	2,109	18,911		7
30 Jun	1915	1,575	352	0	0	9,828	48	5,264	2,124	19,191	9.46	
30 Sep	1915	1,650	339	0	0	10,364	46	5,470	2,129	19,998	9.30	7
31 Dec	1915	1,726	325	0	0	10,901	44	5,676	2,134	20,804	9.46	7
31 Mar	1916	1,801	312	0	0	11,437	41	5,882	2,138	21,611	8.96	7
30 Jun	1916	1,876	298	0	0	11,973	39	6,088	2,143	22,417	8.98	
30 Sep	1916	1,976	284	72	1	12,355	238	6,326	2,184	23,435	8.77	7
31 Dec	1916	2,076	270	145	1	12,737	437	6,563	2,225	24,453	8.78	7
31 Mar	1917	2,176	256	217	2	13,119	635	6,801	2,266	25,471	8.81	7
30 Jun	1917	2,276	242	289	2	13,501	834	7,038	2,307	26,489	9.18	
30 Sep	1917	2,532	252	64	1	13,837	1,017	7,080	2,481	27,262	9.21	7
31 Dec	1917	2,787	261	153	5	14,172	1,200	7,123	2,655	28,355	9.89	7
31 Mar	1918	3,043	271	85	71	14,508	1,382	7,165	2,828	29,352	9.85	7
30 Jun	1918	3,298	280	142	100	14,843	1,565	7,207	3,002	30,437	9.13	
30 Sep	1918	3,372	301	152	101	15,538	1,415	7,536	3,089	31,504	10.58	7
31 Dec	1918	3,446	321	101	92	16,234	1,265	7,865	3,089	32,413	11.27	7

1. The Treasury and Foreign Demand Deposits are monthly averages of daily figures per BMS1943, Table 93.
2. Currrency Outside Banks, Demand Deposits, Treasury Demand Deposits, and Time Deposits are end-of-month call date figures per BMS1943, Table 9.
3. Capital figures are for all Federal Reserve Member Banks (not all commercial banks) on call dates (30 June and 31 Dec) per BMS1943, Table 18.
4. Treasury Cash is annual average of daily figures per BMS1943, Table 100.
5. All except capital accounts are actually Jun 1914 figures.
6. Items in italics are linearly interpolated from adjacent data.
7. BMS1943 is: Board of Governors of the Federal Reserve, Banking and Monetary Statistics, 1914-1941, Washington DC: Publication Services, Division of Administrative Services, Board of Governors of the Federal Reserve System, Nov 1943

Figure 18.3-5: Banking System Liabilities, 1915-1918

				Federal Reserve Loans & Investments		Commercial Bank Loans and Investments				
Day	Year	Gold Stock [3, 6]	Treasury Currency Outstanding [3, 6]	U.S. Government Securities [3, 6]	Discounts & Advances [3, 6]	Loans [4]	U.S. Government Securities [4]	Other [4]	Total Assets	Note
31 Mar	1919	2,878	1,727	203	2,135	21,791	4,663	4,212	37,609	7
30 Jun	1919	2,826	1,709	292	2,116	22,363	5,147	4,250	38,703	
30 Sep	1919	2,860	1,705	283	2,274	23,798	4,797	4,298	40,016	7
31 Dec	1919	2,707	1,707	300	2,789	25,233	4,448	4,347	41,530	7
31 Mar	1920	2,563	1,687	289	2,883	26,668	4,098	4,395	42,583	7
30 Jun	1920	2,578	1,687	341	2,853	28,103	3,748	4,443	43,753	
30 Sep	1920	2,585	1,702	300	3,027	27,596	3,658	4,522	43,389	7
31 Dec	1920	2,639	1,709	287	2,947	27,088	3,567	4,602	42,839	7
31 Mar	1921	2,799	1,726	277	2,352	26,581	3,477	4,681	41,892	7
30 Jun	1921	2,988	1,750	259	1,791	26,073	3,386	4,760	41,007	
30 Sep	1921	3,232	1,789	228	1,458	25,718	3,535	4,885	40,845	7
31 Dec	1921	3,373	1,842	234	1,289	25,363	3,684	5,010	40,794	7
29 Mar	1922	3,459	1,841	441	739	25,007	3,832	5,135	40,455	7
28 Jun	1922	3,497	1,862	557	623	24,652	3,981	5,260	40,432	
27 Sep	1922	3,583	1,890	451	658	25,220	4,162	5,315	41,279	7
27 Dec	1922	3,637	1,946	458	876	25,788	4,343	5,370	42,418	7
28 Mar	1923	3,682	1,983	249	954	26,355	4,524	5,425	43,172	7
27 Jun	1923	3,761	1,980	204	979	26,923	4,705	5,480	44,032	
26 Sep	1923	3,846	2,001	172	1,034	27,070	4,583	5,550	44,255	7
26 Dec	1923	3,948	2,010	336	1,193	27,216	4,460	5,620	44,783	1

Assets of the Federal Reserve & Commercial System, 1919-1923 (millions USD)

1. BMS1943, Table 3 does not distinguish between US Gov't and other securities. Split is estimated from adjacent data.
2. BMS1943, Table 102 is end-of month call date; Table 3 is call date data.
3. Figures per BMS1943, Table 102 (1915 to 1921), Table 103 for 1922 ff.
4. Commercial Bank data per BMS1943, Table 3 (end-of-month call dates).
5. A footnote to BMS1943, Table 3 states that some of these are "rough approximations" prior to 1930.
6. BMS1943, Table 103 (1922 ff) is Wednesday data.
7. Items in italics are linearly interpolated from adjacent data.
8. BMS1943 is: Board of Governors of the Federal Reserve, Banking and Monetary Statistics, 1914-1941, Washington DC: Publication Services, Division of Administrative Services, Board of Governors of the Federal Reserve System, Nov 1943

Figure 18.3-6: Banking System Assets, 1919-1923

				At Federal Reserve Banks		At Commercial Banks						
Day	Year	Currency Outside Banks [2]	Treasury Cash [4]	Treasury Demand Deposits [1]	Foreign Demand Deposits [1]	Demand Deposits [2]	Treasury Demand Deposits [2]	Time Deposits [2]	Capital [3]	Total Liabilities	Error (%)	Note
31 Mar	1919	3,519	344	177	95	16,929	1,115	8,193	3,263	33,635	10.57	6
30 Jun	1919	3,593	365	112	95	17,624	965	8,522	3,350	34,626	10.53	
30 Sep	1919	3,721	338	54	82	18,122	800	9,019	3,476	35,611	11.01	6
31 Dec	1919	3,849	311	70	73	18,620	635	9,516	3,602	36,675	11.69	6
31 Mar	1920	3,977	284	57	76	19,118	469	10,012	3,727	37,721	11.42	6
30 Jun	1920	4,105	257	34	59	19,616	304	10,509	3,853	38,737	11.46	
30 Sep	1920	3,998	247	57	20	18,990	333	10,611	3,923	38,179	12.01	6
31 Dec	1920	3,891	238	39	6	18,365	361	10,713	3,993	37,605	12.22	6
31 Mar	1921	3,784	228	80	9	17,739	390	10,815	4,063	37,107	11.42	6
30 Jun	1921	3,677	218	29	10	17,113	418	10,917	4,133	36,515	10.95	
30 Sep	1921	3,594	220	59	10	17,346	356	11,086	4,153	36,824	9.84	6
31 Dec	1921	3,512	221	54	11	17,579	294	11,255	4,174	37,099	9.06	6
29 Mar	1922	3,429	223	44	8	17,812	232	11,423	4,194	37,364	7.64	6
28 Jun	1922	3,346	224	39	5	18,045	170	11,592	4,214	37,635	6.92	
27 Sep	1922	3,444	223	32	5	18,273	209	12,038	4,252	38,476	6.79	6
27 Dec	1922	3,543	221	23	2	18,502	249	12,483	4,291	39,312	7.32	6
28 Mar	1923	3,641	220	66	2	18,730	288	12,929	4,329	40,203	6.88	6
27 Jun	1923	3,739	218	36	3	18,958	327	13,374	4,367	41,022	6.84	
26 Sep	1923	3,733	218	38	3	19,051	291	13,623	4,373	41,328	6.61	6
26 Dec	1923	3,726	218	28	4	19,144	254	13,871	4,378	41,623	7.06	

Liabilities of the Federal Reserve and Commercial System, 1919-1923 (millions USD)

1. The Treasury and Foreign Demand Deposits are monthly averages of daily figures per BMS1943, Table 93.
2. Currrency Outside Banks, Demand Deposits, Treasury Demand Deposits, and Time Deposits are end-of-month call date figures per BMS1943, Table 9.
3. Capital figures are for all Federal Reserve Member Banks (not all commercial banks) on call dates (30 June and 31 Dec) per BMS1943, Table 18.
4. Treasury Cash is annual average of daily figures per BMS1943, Table 100.
5. All except capital accounts are actually Jun 1914 figures.
6. Items in italics are linearly interpolated from adjacent data.
7. BMS1943 is: Board of Governors of the Federal Reserve, Banking and Monetary Statistics, 1914-1941, Washington DC: Publication Services, Division of Administrative Services, Board of Governors of the Federal Reserve System, Nov 1943

Figure 18.3-7: Banking System Liabilities, 1919-1923

				Federal Reserve Loans & Investments		Commercial Bank Loans and Investments				
Day	Year	Gold Stock [3, 5]	Treasury Currency Outstanding [3, 5]	U. S. Government Securities [3, 5]	Discounts & Advances [3, 5]	Loans [4]	U. S. Government Securities [4]	Other [4]	Total Assets	Note
26 Mar	1924	4,067	2,014	257	684	27,430	4,446	5,838	44,736	6
25 Jun	1924	4,194	2,019	430	395	27,644	4,432	6,055	45,169	
24 Sep	1924	4,223	2,017	575	352	28,000	4,570	6,414	46,151	6
31 Dec	1924	4,212	2,025	540	707	28,356	4,707	6,773	47,320	1
25 Mar	1925	4,048	2,016	344	695	28,958	4,670	6,907	47,638	6
24 Jun	1925	4,075	1,997	325	708	29,560	4,632	7,041	48,338	
30 Sep	1925	4,095	1,985	343	911	30,422	4,585	7,115	49,456	6
30 Dec	1925	4,111	1,977	377	1,121	31,284	4,538	7,189	50,597	1
31 Mar	1926	4,155	1,983	330	891	31,367	4,545	7,366	50,636	6
30 Jun	1926	4,160	1,986	385	770	31,449	4,551	7,542	50,843	
29 Sep	1926	4,188	1,988	302	993	31,706	4,465	7,564	51,206	6
29 Dec	1926	4,203	1,993	317	1,090	31,962	4,379	7,586	51,530	1
30 Mar	1927	4,310	1,996	353	693	32,070	4,485	7,970	51,877	6
29 Jun	1927	4,302	2,003	376	693	32,178	4,591	8,354	52,497	
28 Sep	1927	4,290	2,002	494	672	32,687	4,714	8,551	53,410	6
28 Dec	1927	4,098	2,006	603	995	33,196	4,836	8,748	54,482	1
28 Mar	1928	4,021	2,006	386	870	33,616	4,999	9,037	54,935	6
27 Jun	1928	3,816	2,007	212	1,255	34,035	5,162	9,325	55,812	
26 Sep	1928	3,842	2,009	229	1,274	34,579	5,137	9,215	56,285	6
26 Dec	1928	3,862	2,013	232	1,657	35,123	5,111	9,105	57,103	1

Title: Assets of the Federal Reserve & Commercial System, 1924-1928 (millions USD)

1. BMS1943, Table 3 does not distinguish between US Gov't and other securities. Split is estimated from adjacent data.
2. BMS1943, Tables 3 and 102 are end-of-month call date data.
3. Figures per BMS1943, Table 103 (Wednesday date).
4. Commercial Bank data per BMS1943, Table 3 (end-of-month call dates).
5. A footnote to BMS1943, Table 3 states that some of these are "rough approximations" prior to 1930.
6. Items in italics are linearly interolated from adjacent data.
7. BMS1943 is: Board of Governors of the Federal Reserve, Banking and Monetary Statistics, 1914-1941, Washington DC: Publication Services, Division of Administrative Services, Board of Governors of the Federal Reserve System, Nov 1943

Figure 18.3-8: Banking System Assets, 1924-1928

		At Federal Reserve Banks				At Commercial Banks						
Day	Year	Currency Outside Banks [2]	Treasury Cash [4]	Treasury Demand Deposits [1]	Foreign Demand Deposits [1]	Demand Deposits [2]	Treasury Demand Deposits [2]	Time Deposits [2]	Capital [3]	Total Liabilities	Error (%)	Note
26 Mar	1924	3,688	218	54	3	19,278	222	14,182	4,432	42,077	5.94	5
25 Jun	1924	3,650	218	43	4	19,412	189	14,492	4,486	42,494	5.92	
24 Sep	1924	3,673	218	37	13	20,155	224	14,886	4,509	43,715	5.28	5
31 Dec	1924	3,696	218	42	14	20,898	258	15,280	4,532	44,938	5.03	
25 Mar	1925	3,635	216	26	9	21,137	219	15,627	4,611	45,479	4.53	5
24 Jun	1925	3,573	213	42	6	21,376	180	15,974	4,690	46,054	4.73	
30 Sep	1925	3,672	213	27	7	21,832	249	16,272	4,611	46,883	5.20	5
30 Dec	1925	3,771	213	31	11	22,288	318	16,570	4,532	47,734	5.66	
31 Mar	1926	3,686	212	53	7	22,144	273	16,848	4,682	47,904	5.40	5
30 Jun	1926	3,601	210	12	6	22,000	228	17,125	4,832	48,014	5.56	
29 Sep	1926	3,714	210	32	11	21,861	238	17,317	4,888	48,270	5.73	5
29 Dec	1926	3,827	210	40	14	21,721	247	17,508	4,944	48,511	5.86	
30 Mar	1927	3,692	208	22	6	21,852	236	17,907	5,046	48,968	5.61	5
29 Jun	1927	3,556	205	21	5	21,983	225	18,306	5,147	49,448	5.81	
28 Sep	1927	3,628	205	20	6	22,357	253	18,644	5,244	50,356	5.72	5
28 Dec	1927	3,700	205	10	5	22,730	280	18,982	5,341	51,253	5.93	
28 Mar	1928	3,661	205	23	5	22,495	276	19,392	5,483	51,539	6.18	5
27 Jun	1928	3,622	204	13	8	22,259	271	19,802	5,625	51,804	7.18	
26 Sep	1928	3,608	204	18	7	22,670	280	19,782	5,762	52,330	7.03	5
26 Dec	1928	3,593	204	19	6	23,081	288	19,761	5,899	52,851	7.45	

Title: Liabilities of the Federal Reserve and Commercial System, 1924-1928 (millions USD)

1. The Treasury and Foreign Demand Deposits are monthly averages of daily figures per BMS1943, Table 93.
2. Currrency Outside Banks, Demand Deposits, Treasury Demand Deposits, and Time Deposits are end-of-month call date figures per BMS1943, Table 9.
3. Capital figures are for all Federal Reserve Member Banks (not all commercial banks) on call dates (30 June and 31 Dec) per BMS1943, Table 18.
4. Treasury Cash is annual average of daily figures per BMS1943, Table 100.
5. Items in italics linearly interpolated from adjacent data.
6. BMS1943 is: Board of Governors of the Federal Reserve, Banking and Monetary Statistics, 1914-1941, Washington DC: Publication Services, Division of Administrative Services, Board of Governors of the Federal Reserve System, Nov 1943

Figure 18.3-9: Banking System Liabilities, 1924-1928

| Assets of the Federal Reserve & Commercial System, 1929-1932 (millions USD) | | | | | | | | | | |
| | | | | Federal Reserve Loans & Investments | | Commercial Bank Loans and Investments | | | | |
Day	Year	Gold Stock [3, 5]	Treasury Currency Outstanding [3, 5]	U. S. Government Securities [3, 5]	Discounts & Advances [3, 5]	Loans [4]	U. S. Government Securities [4]	Other [4]	Total Assets	
27 Mar	1929	3,887	2,012	170	1,232	35,431	5,026	8,925	56,683	6
26 Jun	1929	4,040	2,019	150	1,100	35,738	4,941	8,745	56,733	
25 Sep	1929	4,088	2,009	152	1,208	35,852	4,864	8,730	56,903	6
31 Dec	1929	3,997	2,022	511	1,024	35,966	4,786	8,715	57,021	1
26 Mar	1930	4,133	2,022	529	463	35,253	4,882	9,046	56,327	6
25 Jun	1930	4,246	2,025	577	334	34,539	4,977	9,376	56,074	
24 Sep	1930	4,219	2,026	602	365	33,287	5,167	9,338	55,003	6
31 Dec	1930	4,306	2,027	729	615	32,034	5,357	9,299	54,367	1
25 Mar	1931	4,402	2,027	599	248	30,600	5,686	9,486	53,048	6
24 Jun	1931	4,628	2,023	619	320	29,166	6,014	9,673	52,443	
30 Sep	1931	4,454	2,023	742	802	27,196	5,965	9,093	50,274	6
30 Dec	1931	4,171	2,035	803	1,351	25,226	5,915	8,512	48,013	1
30 Mar	1932	4,101	2,060	872	699	23,516	6,066	8,290	45,604	6
29 Jun	1932	3,633	2,057	1,801	534	21,806	6,217	8,068	44,116	
28 Sep	1932	3,897	2,152	1,854	374	20,944	6,747	7,897	43,864	6
28 Dec	1932	4,218	2,203	1,851	300	20,081	7,276	7,726	43,655	1

1. BMS1943, Table 3 does not distinguish between US Gov't and other securities. Split is estimated from adjacent data.
2. BMS1943, Table 3 is end-of month call date data.
3. Figures per BMS1943, Table 103 (Wednesday date).
4. Commercial Bank data per BMS1943, Table 3 (end-of-month call dates).
5. A footnote to BMS1943, Table 3 states that some of these are "rough approximations" prior to 1930.
6. Items in italics linearly interpolated from adjacent data.
7. BMS1943 is: Board of Governors of the Federal Reserve, Banking and Monetary Statistics, 1914-1941, Washington DC: Publication Services, Division of Administrative Services, Board of Governors of the Federal Reserve System, Nov 1943

Figure 18.3-10: Banking System Assets, 1929-1932

| Liabilities of the Federal Reserve and Commercial System, 1929-1932 (millions USD) | | | | | | | | | | | | |
| | | | | At Federal Reserve Banks | | At Commercial Banks | | | | | | |
Day	Year	Currency Outside Banks [2]	Treasury Cash [4]	Treasury Demand Deposits [1]	Foreign Demand Deposits [1]	Demand Deposits [2]	Treasury Demand Deposits [2]	Time Deposits [2]	Capital [3]	Total Liabilities	Error (%)	Note
27 Mar	1929	3,616	206	17	9	22,811	335	19,659	6,122	52,775	6.89	5
26 Jun	1929	3,639	207	30	7	22,540	381	19,557	6,345	52,706	7.10	
25 Sep	1929	3,598	207	33	7	22,675	270	19,375	6,527	52,691	7.40	5
31 Dec	1929	3,557	207	16	6	22,809	158	19,192	6,709	52,654	7.66	
26 Mar	1930	3,463	209	16	7	22,258	240	19,449	6,718	52,359	7.04	5
25 Jun	1930	3,369	211	39	6	21,706	322	19,705	6,726	52,084	7.12	
24 Sep	1930	3,487	211	28	6	21,337	314	19,359	6,660	51,400	6.55	5
31 Dec	1930	3,605	211	26	6	20,967	305	19,012	6,593	50,725	6.70	
25 Mar	1931	3,628	215	33	6	20,400	372	18,852	6,512	50,017	5.71	5
24 Jun	1931	3,651	219	44	12	19,832	439	18,691	6,430	49,318	5.96	
30 Sep	1931	4,061	219	31	173	18,622	452	17,014	6,215	46,785	6.94	5
30 Dec	1931	4,470	219	28	115	17,412	464	15,336	5,999	44,043	8.27	
30 Mar	1932	4,543	228	39	16	16,519	441	14,693	5,830	42,308	7.23	5
29 Jun	1932	4,616	236	39	34	15,625	418	14,049	5,661	40,678	7.79	
28 Sep	1932	4,643	236	51	11	15,677	463	13,840	5,535	40,455	7.77	5
28 Dec	1932	4,669	236	31	18	15,728	508	13,631	5,409	40,230	7.85	

1. The Treasury and Foreign Demand Deposits are monthly averages of daily figures per BMS1943, Table 93.
2. Currrency Outside Banks, Demand Deposits, Treasury Demand Deposits, and Time Deposits are end-of-month call date figures per BMS1943, Table 9.
3. Capital figures are for all Federal Reserve Member Banks (not all commercial banks) on call dates (30 June and 31 Dec) per BMS1943, Table 18.
4. Treasury Cash is annual average of daily figures per BMS1943, Table 100.
5. Items in italics linearly interpolated from adjacent data.
6. BMS1943 is: Board of Governors of the Federal Reserve, Banking and Monetary Statistics, 1914-1941, Washington DC: Publication Services, Division of Administrative Services, Board of Governors of the Federal Reserve System, Nov 1943

Figure 18.3-11: Banking System Liabilities, 1929-1932

Figure 18.3-12 shows the money supply for this period. All of the values apply to approximately 30 Jun of each year. The average error between Figure 18.3-12 and that reported by Friedman and Schwartz [18.3-2] (if they are correct) is -5.23% (i.e., the values shown here are higher than Friedman), and the standard deviation is 1.90%. If it is assumed that the truth lies halfway between Friedman and these numbers, then the average error is -2.54% and the standard deviation is 0.91%.

Estimated U. S. Money Supply, 1915-1932 (millions USD)														
1	2	3	4	5	6	7	8	9	10	11	12	13	14	15
Year (~30 Jun)	Number of Banks [1]	Federal Reserve Notes and Bank Notes [2]	U.S. Notes, Treasury Notes, National Bank Notes, etc. [3]	Total Notes in Circulation	Net Specie in Circulation [4]	Notes & Specie Outside Treasury	Cash Held in All Banks [5]	Currency & Coin Outside Banks	State Bank Deposits [6, 7]	National Bank Deposits and Other Deposits Outside State Banks [8]	Total Deposits	Estimated Interbank Trans- actions [9]	Deposits Adjusted	Total Money Supply
1915	27,062	70.810	2,379.177	2,449.987	869.595	3,319.582	1,457.702	1,861.880	12,310.428	9,721.241	22,031.669	2,761.000	19,270.669	21,132.549
1916	27,513	150.835	2,573.074	2,723.909	925.349	3,649.258	1,486.118	2,163.140	15,499.471	10,963.030	26,462.501	3,463.000	22,999.501	25,162.641
1917	27,923	510.458	2,555.491	3,065.949	1,000.455	4,066.404	1,502.502	2,563.902	17,671.244	12,798.915	30,470.159	3,917.000	26,553.159	29,117.061
1918	28,880	1,709.160	1,866.656	3,575.816	905.881	4,481.697	896.571	3,585.126	18,567.619	14,047.849	32,615.468	3,578.000	29,037.468	32,622.594
1919	29,123	2,605.292	1,406.333	4,011.625	865.012	4,876.637	997.353	3,879.284	21,744.046	15,941.926	37,685.972	3,902.000	33,783.972	37,663.256
1920	30,139	3,250.173	1,326.020	4,576.193	891.392	5,467.585	1,076.378	4,391.207	24,558.654	17,166.570	41,725.224	3,674.000	38,051.224	42,442.431
1921	30,812	2,729.540	1,341.592	4,071.132	839.859	4,910.991	946.567	3,964.424	23,516.468	15,148.519	38,664.987	2,858.000	35,806.987	39,771.411
1922	30,389	2,210.583	1,460.211	3,670.794	792.377	4,463.171	829.892	3,633.279	24,799.532	16,328.820	41,128.352	3,302.000	37,826.352	41,459.631
1923	30,178	2,254.629	1,765.999	4,020.628	802.647	4,823.275	797.101	4,026.174	27,342.975	16,906.549	44,249.524	3,366.000	40,883.524	44,909.698
1924	29,348	1,853.172	2,198.843	4,052.015	797.292	4,849.307	911.500	3,937.807	29,351.735	18,357.293	47,709.028	3,996.000	43,713.028	47,650.835
1925	28,841	1,643.029	2,353.277	3,996.306	818.902	4,815.208	951.286	3,863.922	32,073.263	19,921.796	51,995.059	4,203.000	47,792.059	51,655.981
1926	28,146	1,684.860	2,382.861	4,067.721	817.546	4,885.267	996.529	3,888.738	33,414.213	20,655.044	54,069.257	4,139.000	49,930.257	53,818.995
1927	27,061	1,707.449	2,326.462	4,033.911	817.411	4,851.322	1,007.896	3,843.426	34,960.735	21,790.572	56,751.307	4,292.000	52,459.307	56,302.733
1928	26,213	1,630.462	2,353.680	3,984.142	812.486	4,796.628	887.845	3,908.783	35,773.790	22,657.271	58,431.061	4,304.000	54,127.061	58,035.844
1929	25,330	1,696.337	2,238.350	3,934.687	811.608	4,746.295	819.928	3,926.367	36,312.553	21,598.088	57,910.641	3,978.000	53,932.641	57,859.008
1930	24,079	1,405.272	2,322.184	3,727.456	794.532	4,521.988	865.979	3,656.009	36,578.311	23,268.884	59,847.195	5,125.000	54,722.195	58,378.204
1931	22,071	1,711.358	2,322.689	4,034.047	787.886	4,821.933	884.327	3,937.606	34,666.504	22,198.240	56,864.744	5,133.000	51,731.744	55,669.350
1932	19,163	2,782.975	2,059.480	4,842.455	852.717	5,695.172	791.627	4,903.545	27,929.356	17,460.913	45,390.269	3,318.000	42,072.269	46,975.814

1. Number of banks from Annual Report of the Comptroller of the Currency, 1937, p. 766 (Table 81).
2. Includes Federal Reserve Notes and Federal Reserve Bank Notes; data from Annual Report of the Secretary of the Treasury, 1947, p. 486 (Table 90).
3. Includes gold certificates, silver certificates, U. S. Notes, Treasury Notes of 1890, and National Bank Notes per Annual Report of the Secretary of the Treasury, 1947, pp. 485, 486 (Table 90).
4. This is the sum of gold coin, standard silver dollars, subsidiary silver, and minor coin. Data is from the Annual Report of the Secretary of the Treasury, 1947, p. 485, (Table 90).
5. From the Annual Report of the Comptroller of the Currency, 1931, pp. 1023-1025, (Table 96).
6. State bank deposits for 1915 to 1931 from Annual Report of the Comptroller of the Currency, 1931, p. 1020 (Table 94).
7. State bank deposits for 1932 from the Annual Report of the Comptroller of the Currency, 1937, p. 764 (Table 79).
8. Deposits in all banks except State derived by subtracting all banks deposits from State banks deposits per Annual Report of the Comptroller of the Currency, 1937, pp. 764, 766 (Tables 79 and 81).
9. Interbank deposits for 1915 to 1932 from Bank and Monetary Statistics, 1914-1941, Table 2, p. 18.

Figure 18.3-12: Total Money Supply, 1915-1932

Figures 18.3-13 and 18.3-14 show the coinage of the U. S. during this period.

	$20 Double Eagles ($)	$10 Eagles ($)	$5 Half Eagles ($)	Three Dollar ($)	$2.50 Quarter Eagles ($)	Gold Dollars ($)	Total ($)
Gold Coinage of the U. S. , 1915-1932 (USD)							
Year							
1915 [2]	14,391,000.00	4,100,750.00	3,760,375.00		1,540,292.50	25,034.00	23,817,451.50
1916	15,920,000.00	1,385,000.00	1,200,000.00			20,026.00	18,525,026.00
1917						10,014.00	10,014.00
1918							0.00
1919							0.00
1920	15,725,000.00	1,265,000.00					16,990,000.00
1921	10,570,000.00						10,570,000.00
1922	80,670,000.00					10,016.00	80,680,016.00
1923	45,365,000.00						45,365,000.00
1924	206,010,000.00						206,010,000.00
1925	190,935,000.00				1,445,000.00		192,380,000.00
1926	66,785,000.00	10,140,000.00			1,615,000.00		78,540,000.00
1927	124,675,000.00				970,000.00		125,645,000.00
1928	176,320,000.00				1,040,000.00		177,360,000.00
1929	35,595,000.00		3,310,000.00		1,330,000.00		40,235,000.00
1930	1,480,000.00	960,000.00					2,440,000.00
1931	60,895,000.00						60,895,000.00
1932	22,035,000.00	44,630,000.00					66,665,000.00
Totals	1,067,371,000.00	62,480,750.00	8,270,375.00	0.00	7,940,292.50	65,090.00	1,146,127,507.50

1. Source: Annual Report of the Director of the Mint, 1940, 3 Sep 1940, Treasury Document 3109, p. 67
2. The mint coined $150,950 in $50 gold pieces in 1915.

Figure 18.3-13: Gold Coins Minted by the U. S., 1915-1932

Silver and Copper Coinage of the U. S., 1915-1932 (USD)										
	Silver ($)								Minor ($)	
Year	Trade Dollars	Dollars	Half Dollars	Quarters	Twenty-cents	Dimes	Half-dimes	Three-cents	Nickels and Cents	Total ($)
1915			1,486,440.00	1,969,612.50		658,045.00			2,062,839.70	6,176,937.20
1916			1,065,200.00	2,095,200.00		5,720,400.00			6,337,550.07	15,218,350.07
1917			10,751,700.00	9,464,400.00		9,196,200.00			6,118,089.30	35,530,389.30
1918			10,434,549.00	8,173,000.00		6,865,480.00			5,972,662.04	31,445,691.04
1919			1,839,500.00	3,776,000.00		5,452,900.00			7,909,000.00	18,977,400.00
1920			6,398,570.00	9,456,000.00		9,202,100.00			8,166,650.00	33,223,320.00
1921		87,736,473.00	611,062.50	479,000.00		231,000.00			1,155,310.00	90,212,845.50
1922		84,275,000.00	50,030.50						71,600.00	84,396,630.50
1923		56,631,000.00	1,226,038.50	2,769,000.00		5,657,000.00			2,927,080.00	69,210,118.50
1924		13,539,000.00	71,040.00	4,223,000.00		3,794,000.00			2,309,690.00	23,936,730.00
1925		11,808,000.00	1,338,518.00	3,070,000.00		3,657,700.00			4,202,645.00	24,076,863.00
1926		11,267,700.00	574,306.50	3,933,000.00		4,050,800.00			4,461,630.00	24,287,436.50
1927		2,982,900.00	1,216,017.00	3,321,100.00		3,766,200.00			4,215,910.00	15,502,127.00
1928		1,992,649.00	1,000,018.00	2,651,000.00		3,104,100.00			3,664,670.00	12,412,437.00
1929			1,451,600.00	3,565,500.00		3,573,400.00			5,399,900.00	13,990,400.00
1930				1,797,000.00		861,300.00			3,632,210.00	6,290,510.00
1931						621,000.00			307,420.00	928,420.00
1932				1,562,200.00					195,620.00	1,757,820.00
Totals	0.00	270,232,722.00	39,514,590.00	62,305,012.50	0.00	66,411,625.00	0.00	0.00	69,110,476.11	507,574,425.61
1. Source: Annual Report of the Director of the Mint, 1940, 3 Sep 1940, Treasury Document 3109, pp. 69, 73										

Figure 18.3-14: Silver and Minor (Copper) Coins Minted by the U. S., 1915-1932

Figure 18.3-15 shows the CPI, total money supply, and per-capita money supply during this period.

Year	CPI [1] (1913 = 100)	Total Money Supply [5] (USD)	Population [6]	Per Capita Money Supply (USD)	Annual Rate of Change in CPI (%)	Annual Rate of Change in Per-Capita Money Supply (%)
1915	101.285	21,132,549,000	99,125,050	213.19	2.502	1.725
1916	119.746	25,162,641,000	100,504,353	250.36	16.744	16.073
1917	153.669	29,117,061,000	101,883,657	285.79	24.942	13.233
1918	172.554	32,622,594,000	103,262,961	315.92	11.591	10.023
1919	185.784	37,663,256,000	104,642,264	359.92	7.387	13.041
1920	207.102	42,442,431,000	106,021,568	400.32	10.863	10.637
1921	151.414	39,771,411,000	107,739,677	369.14	-31.319	-8.108
1922	148.269	41,459,631,000	109,457,786	378.77	-2.099	2.575
1923	154.563	44,909,698,000	111,175,896	403.95	4.157	6.436
1924	153.272	47,650,835,000	112,894,005	422.08	-0.839	4.391
1925	159.140	51,655,981,000	114,612,114	450.70	3.757	6.560
1926	157.133	53,818,995,000	116,330,223	462.64	-1.269	2.614
1927	153.838	56,302,733,000	118,048,332	476.95	-2.119	3.046
1928	157.269	58,035,844,000	119,766,442	484.58	2.206	1.587
1929	157.766	57,859,008,000	121,484,551	476.27	0.316	-1.730
1930	145.891	58,378,204,000	123,202,660	473.84	-7.826	-0.511
1931	127.292	55,669,350,000	124,098,907	448.59	-13.637	-5.476
1932	112.418	46,975,814,000	124,995,154	375.82	-12.426	-17.699
1. CPI is the average of L-1 and L-15 data, both re-aligned to 1913 as a reference.						
2. L-1 data 1791 to 1938 (Snyder-Tucker) is a general price index (wholesale prices, wages, cost of living and rents).						
3. L-15 data 1801 to 1945 includes wholesale prices, all commodities.						
4. L1 and L-15 from Historical Statistics of the United States, 1789-1945, A Supplement to the Statistical Abstract of the United States, Bureau of the Census, US Department of Commerce, Washington, DC, 1949.						
5. See notes in money supply data for sources.						
6. Population is linearly interpolated from Census results.						

Figure 18.3-15: Money Supply and CPI, 1915-1932

Figure 18.3-16 shows a summary of the CPI and per-capita money supply. Four distinct intervals are evident: 1915 to 1920, 1920 to 1921, 1921 to 1929, and 1929 to 1932. The average annual changes in CPI and per-capita money supply for 1915 to 1920 are 15.3 and 12.6% respectively; for 1920 to 1921, are -31.3 and -8.1% respectively; for 1921 to 1929, 0.5 and 3.1% respectively, and for 1929 to 1932, -11.2 and -7.8% respectively.

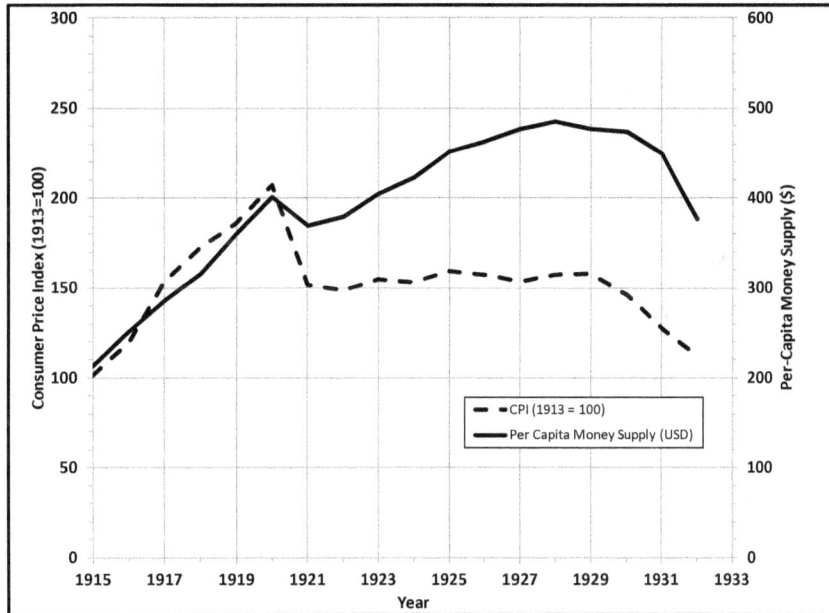

Figure 18.3-16: CPI and Per-Capita Summary, 1915-1932

Figure 18.3-17 shows the approximate median income index, consumer price index, and standard of living index for this period. See the Introduction to Part 2 for cautions regarding these curves.

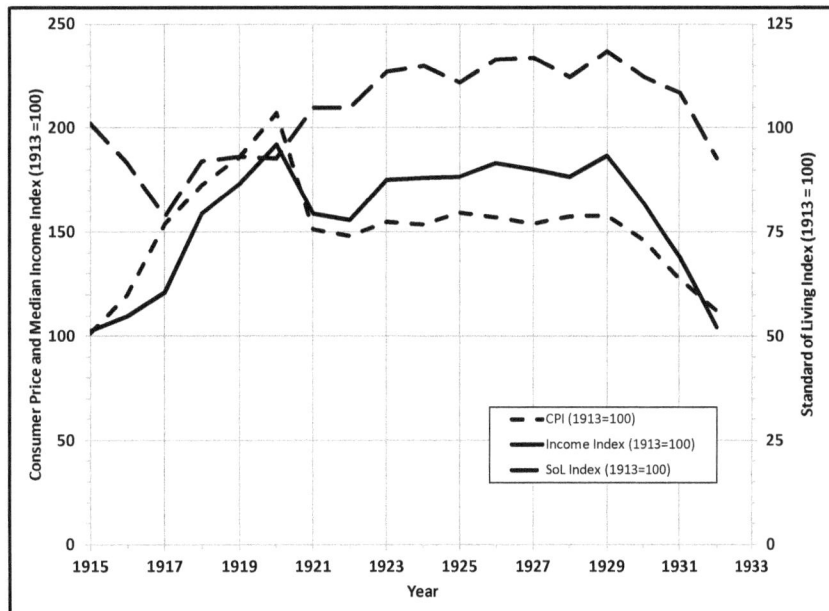

Figure 18.3-17: Median Income, Consumer Price, and Standard of Living Indices, 1915-1932

Figure 18.3-18 shows the changes in the legal reserve ratios for demand and time deposits at commercial banks during this period.

Legal Reserve Ratio Changes, 1913-1932									
vs. Demand Deposits (%)							vs. Time Deposits (%)		
Day	Year	Central Reserve City Banks	Reserve City banks	Day	Year	Country Banks	Day	Year	All Banks
23 Dec	1913	18.00	15.00	23 Dec	1913	12.00	23 Dec	1913	5.00
21 Jun	1917	13.00	10.00	21 Jun	1917	7.00	21 Jun	1917	3.00
Source: Joshua N. Feinman, Reserve Requirements: History, Current Practice, and Potential Reform, Federal Reserve Bulletin, June 1993, p. 569-589									

Figure 18.3-18: Legal Reserve Ratio Changes, 1913-1932

Figures 18.3-19 through 18.3-22 show some miscellaneous statistics of the banking system, including total reserves, and ratios of demand deposits to reserves and demand deposits to currency.

Miscellaneous Statistics of the Federal Reserve and Commercial System, 1914-1918 (millions USD)										
		Federal Reserve	At Commercial Banks							
Day	Year	Member Bank Reserves [1]	Demand Deposits [2]	Time Deposits [2]	Total Deposits	Reserve Ratio, Demand Deposits	Reserve Ratio, Total Deposits	Currency Outside Banks [3]	Ratio, Demand Deposits to Reserves	Ratio, Demand Deposits to Currency
31 Mar	1914									
30 Jun	1914									
30 Sep	1914									
31 Dec	1914		10,082	4,441	14,523			1,533		
31 Mar	1915		9,955	4,853	14,808			1,554		
30 Jun	1915		9,828	5,264	15,092			1,575		
30 Sep	1915		10,364	5,470	15,834			1,650		
31 Dec	1915		10,901	5,676	16,577			1,726		
31 Mar	1916		11,437	5,882	17,319			1,801		
30 Jun	1916		11,973	6,088	18,061			1,876		
30 Sep	1916		12,355	6,326	18,681			1,976		
31 Dec	1916		12,737	6,563	19,300			2,076		
31 Mar	1917	742	13,119	6,801	19,920	0.057	0.037	2,176	17.681	6.029
30 Jun	1917	1,045	13,501	7,038	20,539	0.077	0.051	2,276	12.920	5.932
30 Sep	1917	1,157	13,837	7,080	20,917	0.084	0.055	2,532	11.959	5.466
31 Dec	1917	1,447	14,172	7,123	21,295	0.102	0.068	2,787	9.794	5.085
31 Mar	1918	1,511	14,508	7,165	21,672	0.104	0.070	3,043	9.601	4.768
30 Jun	1918	1,564	14,843	7,207	22,050	0.105	0.071	3,298	9.490	4.501
30 Sep	1918	1,556	15,538	7,536	23,074	0.100	0.067	3,372	9.986	4.608
31 Dec	1918	1,636	16,234	7,865	24,099	0.101	0.068	3,446	9.923	4.711
1. Member bank reserves per BMS1943, Table 102 (end of month data).										
2. Demand deposits and time deposits are end-of-month call date figures per BMS1943, Table 9.										
3. Currrency Outside Bank data is end-of-month call date figures per BMS1943, Table 9.										
4. BMS1943 is: Board of Governors of the Federal Reserve, Banking and Monetary Statistics, 1914-1941, Washington DC: Publication Services, Division of Administrative Services, Board of Governors of the Federal Reserve System, Nov 1943										
5. Items in italics linearly interpolated from adjacent data.										

Figure 18.3-19: Miscellaneous Statistics of the Banking System, 1914-1918

Miscellaneous Statistics of the Federal Reserve and Commercial System, 1919-1923 (millions USD)									
		Federal Reserve	At Commercial Banks							
Day	Year	Member Bank Reserves [1]	Demand Deposits [2]	Time Deposits [2]	Total Deposits	Reserve Ratio, Demand Deposits	Reserve Ratio, Total Deposits	Currency Outside Banks [3]	Ratio, Demand Deposits to Reserves	Ratio, Demand Deposits to Currency
31 Mar	1919	1,614	16,929	8,193	25,122	0.095	0.064	3,519	10.489	4.811
30 Jun	1919	1,758	17,624	8,522	26,146	0.100	0.067	3,593	10.025	4.905
30 Sep	1919	1,762	18,122	9,019	27,141	0.097	0.065	3,721	10.285	4.870
31 Dec	1919	1,890	18,620	9,516	28,136	0.102	0.067	3,849	9.852	4.838
31 Mar	1920	1,856	19,118	10,012	29,130	0.097	0.064	3,977	10.301	4.807
30 Jun	1920	1,822	19,616	10,509	30,125	0.093	0.060	4,105	10.766	4.779
30 Sep	1920	1,807	18,990	10,611	29,601	0.095	0.061	3,998	10.509	4.750
31 Dec	1920	1,781	18,365	10,713	29,078	0.097	0.061	3,891	10.311	4.720
31 Mar	1921	1,659	17,739	10,815	28,554	0.094	0.058	3,784	10.692	4.688
30 Jun	1921	1,604	17,113	10,917	28,030	0.094	0.057	3,677	10.669	4.654
30 Sep	1921	1,581	17,346	11,086	28,432	0.091	0.056	3,594	10.972	4.826
31 Dec	1921	1,753	17,579	11,255	28,834	0.100	0.061	3,512	10.028	5.006
29 Mar	1922	1,668	17,812	11,423	29,235	0.094	0.057	3,429	10.679	5.195
28 Jun	1922	1,865	18,045	11,592	29,637	0.103	0.063	3,346	9.676	5.393
27 Sep	1922	1,798	18,273	12,038	30,311	0.098	0.059	3,444	10.163	5.305
27 Dec	1922	1,861	18,502	12,483	30,985	0.101	0.060	3,543	9.942	5.223
28 Mar	1923	1,871	18,730	12,929	31,658	0.100	0.059	3,641	10.011	5.144
27 Jun	1923	1,868	18,958	13,374	32,332	0.099	0.058	3,739	10.149	5.070
26 Sep	1923	1,852	19,051	13,623	32,674	0.097	0.057	3,733	10.287	5.104
26 Dec	1923	1,874	19,144	13,871	33,015	0.098	0.057	3,726	10.216	5.138

1. Member bank reserves 1919-1921 per BMS1943, Table 102 (end of month data); 1922-1923 per BMS1943, Table 103.
2. Demand deposits and time deposits are end-of-month call date figures per BMS1943, Table 9.
3. Currrency Outside Bank data is end-of-month call date figures per BMS1943, Table 9.
4. BMS1943 is: Board of Governors of the Federal Reserve, Banking and Monetary Statistics, 1914-1941, Washington DC: Publication Services, Division of Administrative Services, Board of Governors of the Federal Reserve System, Nov 1943
5. Items in italics linearly interpolated from adjacent data.

Figure 18.3-20: Miscellaneous Statistics of the Banking System, 1919-1923

Miscellaneous Statistics of the Federal Reserve and Commercial System, 1924-1928 (millions USD)									
		Federal Reserve	At Commercial Banks							
Day	Year	Member Bank Reserves [1]	Demand Deposits [2]	Time Deposits [2]	Total Deposits	Reserve Ratio, Demand Deposits	Reserve Ratio, Total Deposits	Currency Outside Banks [3]	Ratio, Demand Deposits to Reserves	Ratio, Demand Deposits to Currency
26 Mar	1924	1,912	19,278	14,182	33,460	0.099	0.057	3,688	10.083	5.227
25 Jun	1924	2,035	19,412	14,492	33,904	0.105	0.060	3,650	9.539	5.318
24 Sep	1924	2,120	20,155	14,886	35,041	0.105	0.061	3,673	9.507	5.487
31 Dec	1924	2,220	20,898	15,280	36,178	0.106	0.061	3,696	9.414	5.654
25 Mar	1925	2,119	21,137	15,627	36,764	0.100	0.058	3,635	9.975	5.816
24 Jun	1925	2,140	21,376	15,974	37,350	0.100	0.057	3,573	9.989	5.983
30 Sep	1925	2,210	21,832	16,272	38,104	0.101	0.058	3,672	9.879	5.946
30 Dec	1925	2,309	22,288	16,570	38,858	0.104	0.059	3,771	9.653	5.910
31 Mar	1926	2,215	22,144	16,848	38,992	0.100	0.057	3,686	9.997	6.008
30 Jun	1926	2,229	22,000	17,125	39,125	0.101	0.057	3,601	9.870	6.109
29 Sep	1926	2,249	21,861	17,317	39,177	0.103	0.057	3,714	9.720	5.886
29 Dec	1926	2,264	21,721	17,508	39,229	0.104	0.058	3,827	9.594	5.676
30 Mar	1927	2,274	21,852	17,907	39,759	0.104	0.057	3,692	9.609	5.920
29 Jun	1927	2,342	21,983	18,306	40,289	0.107	0.058	3,556	9.386	6.182
28 Sep	1927	2,337	22,357	18,644	41,001	0.105	0.057	3,628	9.566	6.162
28 Dec	1927	2,432	22,730	18,982	41,712	0.107	0.058	3,700	9.346	6.143
28 Mar	1928	2,357	22,495	19,392	41,887	0.105	0.056	3,661	9.544	6.144
27 Jun	1928	2,345	22,259	19,802	42,061	0.105	0.056	3,622	9.492	6.145
26 Sep	1928	2,316	22,670	19,782	42,452	0.102	0.055	3,608	9.788	6.284
26 Dec	1928	2,409	23,081	19,761	42,842	0.104	0.056	3,593	9.581	6.424

1. Member bank reserves per BMS1943, Table 103 (Wedneday call date).
2. Demand deposits and time deposits are end-of-month call date figures per BMS1943, Table 9.
3. Currrency Outside Bank data is end-of-month call date figures per BMS1943, Table 9.
4. BMS1943 is: Board of Governors of the Federal Reserve, Banking and Monetary Statistics, 1914-1941, Washington DC: Publication Services, Division of Administrative Services, Board of Governors of the Federal Reserve System, Nov 1943
5. Items in italics linearly interpolated from adjacent data.

Figure 18.3-21: Miscellaneous Statistics of the Banking System, 1924-1928

Miscellaneous Statistics of the Federal Reserve and Commercial System, 1929-1932 (millions USD)										
		Federal Reserve	At Commercial Banks							
Day	Year	Member Bank Reserves [1]	Demand Deposits [2]	Time Deposits [2]	Total Deposits	Reserve Ratio, Demand Deposits	Reserve Ratio, Total Deposits	Currency Outside Banks [3]	Ratio, Demand Deposits to Reserves	Ratio, Demand Deposits to Currency
27 Mar	1929	2,332	22,811	19,659	42,470	0.102	0.055	3,616	9.782	6.308
26 Jun	1929	2,344	22,540	19,557	42,097	0.104	0.056	3,639	9.616	6.194
25 Sep	1929	2,364	22,675	19,375	42,049	0.104	0.056	3,598	9.592	6.302
31 Dec	1929	2,355	22,809	19,192	42,001	0.103	0.056	3,557	9.685	6.412
26 Mar	1930	2,340	22,258	19,449	41,706	0.105	0.056	3,463	9.512	6.427
25 Jun	1930	2,386	21,706	19,705	41,411	0.110	0.058	3,369	9.097	6.443
24 Sep	1930	2,416	21,337	19,359	40,695	0.113	0.059	3,487	8.831	6.119
31 Dec	1930	2,471	20,967	19,012	39,979	0.118	0.062	3,605	8.485	5.816
25 Mar	1931	2,357	20,400	18,852	39,251	0.116	0.060	3,628	8.655	5.623
24 Jun	1931	2,457	19,832	18,691	38,523	0.124	0.064	3,651	8.072	5.432
30 Sep	1931	2,364	18,622	17,014	35,636	0.127	0.066	4,061	7.877	4.586
30 Dec	1931	2,323	17,412	15,336	32,748	0.133	0.071	4,470	7.495	3.895
30 Mar	1932	1,911	16,519	14,693	31,211	0.116	0.061	4,543	8.644	3.636
29 Jun	1932	2,034	15,625	14,049	29,674	0.130	0.069	4,616	7.682	3.385
28 Sep	1932	2,269	15,677	13,840	29,517	0.145	0.077	4,643	6.909	3.377
28 Dec	1932	2,482	15,728	13,631	29,359	0.158	0.085	4,669	6.337	3.369

1. Member bank reserves per BMS1943, Table 103 (Wednday call date).
2. Demand deposits and time deposits are end-of-month call date figures per BMS1943, Table 9.
3. Currrency Outside Bank data is end-of-month call date figures per BMS1943, Table 9.
4. BMS1943 is: Board of Governors of the Federal Reserve, Banking and Monetary Statistics, 1914-1941, Washington DC: Publication Services, Division of Administrative Services, Board of Governors of the Federal Reserve System, Nov 1943
5. Items in italics linearly interpolated from adjacent data.

Figure 18.3-22: Miscellaneous Statistics of the Banking System, 1929-1932

Figures 18.3-23 and 18.3-24 show the approximate monthly interest rates for prime commercial paper loans (4 to 6 months) and 90-day stock market loans. This data applies to loans in New York City.

Approximate Monthly Average, Prime Commercial Paper Rate, 4 to 6 Month (%) [1]												
Year	Jan	Feb	Mar	Apr	May	Jun	Jul	Aug	Sep	Oct	Nov	Dec
1915	4.38	4.38	3.93	4.25	4.34	4.33	3.81	4.01	3.88	3.91	3.45	3.50
1916	3.50	3.50	3.50	3.50	3.50	4.00	4.38	4.13	4.00	3.95	3.94	4.19
1917	3.98	4.47	4.50	4.63	5.18	5.28	5.15	5.19	5.44	5.63	5.69	5.75
1918	5.83	5.88	6.00	6.08	6.13	6.03	6.10	6.22	6.00	6.00	6.00	6.00
1919	5.25	5.13	5.50	5.38	5.25	5.38	5.38	5.38	5.38	5.25	5.25	5.88
1920	6.00	6.38	6.88	6.88	7.38	7.88	8.13	8.13	8.13	8.13	8.13	8.00
1921	7.88	7.63	7.63	7.63	6.88	6.75	6.38	6.13	6.00	5.88	5.50	5.13
1922	5.00	4.88	4.75	4.50	4.38	4.38	4.13	4.13	4.13	4.38	4.75	4.88
1923	4.50	4.63	5.13	5.38	5.00	5.00	5.13	5.13	5.38	5.38	5.13	5.00
1924	4.88	4.88	4.88	4.63	4.50	4.13	3.50	3.25	3.13	3.13	3.25	3.63
1925	3.63	3.63	4.00	4.00	3.88	3.88	3.88	4.00	4.25	4.38	4.38	4.38
1926	4.38	4.25	4.38	4.38	4.00	4.00	4.00	4.38	4.63	4.63	4.50	4.50
1927	4.25	4.13	4.13	4.13	4.13	4.25	4.25	4.00	4.00	4.00	4.00	4.00
1928	4.00	4.00	4.13	4.38	4.50	4.75	5.13	5.38	5.63	5.50	5.38	5.38
1929	5.38	5.50	5.88	6.00	6.00	6.00	6.00	6.13	6.25	6.25	5.75	5.00
1930	4.88	4.75	4.25	3.88	3.75	3.50	3.25	3.00	3.00	3.00	2.88	2.88
1931	2.88	2.63	2.50	2.38	2.25	2.00	2.00	2.00	2.00	3.13	4.00	3.88
1932	3.88	3.88	3.63	3.50	3.13	2.75	2.50	2.25	2.13	2.00	1.63	1.50

1. Source: Board of Governors of the Federal Reserve System, Bank and Monetary Statistics 1914-1941, Washington DC: Nov 1943, Table 120, pp. 448-451

Figure 18.3-23: Interest Rates on Prime Commercial Paper Loans, 1915-1932

Approximate Monthly Average, Stock Exchange Time Loan Rate, 90 days (%) [1]											
Year	Jan	Feb	Mar	Apr	May	Jun	Jul	Aug	Sep	Oct	Nov	Dec
1915	3.40	2.88	2.88	2.91	2.90	2.63	2.68	2.88	2.78	2.83	2.78	2.68
1916	2.73	2.75	2.88	2.85	2.94	3.31	3.95	3.31	3.33	3.38	3.22	4.22
1917	3.22	3.75	3.85	3.97	4.56	4.95	4.75	4.38	5.35	5.44	5.44	5.83
1918	5.81	5.81	6.00	5.94	5.88	5.83	5.75	6.00	6.00	6.00	6.00	5.73
1919	5.25	5.25	5.38	5.50	5.50	5.75	6.00	6.00	5.88	6.00	6.50	7.00
1920	7.50	8.00	8.00	8.00	8.25	8.00	8.50	8.75	8.38	7.88	8.00	7.50
1921	7.00	6.75	6.75	6.75	6.50	6.63	6.00	5.88	5.63	5.38	5.38	5.13
1922	4.75	4.88	4.75	4.38	4.25	4.13	4.00	4.13	4.38	4.88	5.00	4.88
1923	4.63	4.88	5.25	5.38	5.13	4.88	5.13	5.25	5.50	5.38	5.13	5.13
1924	4.88	4.75	4.63	4.50	4.00	3.25	2.75	2.63	2.75	2.75	3.25	3.50
1925	3.63	3.88	4.13	4.00	3.88	3.88	4.00	4.25	4.50	4.75	4.94	4.94
1926	4.75	4.69	4.75	4.31	4.00	4.13	4.44	4.75	4.94	5.00	4.75	4.69
1927	4.50	4.44	4.44	4.50	4.38	4.50	4.44	4.19	4.13	4.31	4.19	4.19
1928	4.38	4.56	4.63	4.94	5.25	5.69	6.00	6.25	7.00	7.13	6.94	7.50
1929	7.75	7.63	7.88	8.75	8.75	8.25	7.75	8.88	8.88	8.13	5.50	4.88
1930	4.75	4.75	4.25	4.13	3.50	2.88	2.75	2.63	2.63	2.50	2.13	2.25
1931	2.13	1.88	2.13	2.00	1.75	1.50	1.38	1.38	1.63	3.25	3.50	3.25
1932	3.75	3.63	3.13	2.50	1.75	1.50	1.38	1.38	1.38	1.00	0.50	0.50

1. Source: Board of Governors of the Federal Reserve System, Bank and Monetary Statistics 1914-1941, Washington DC: Nov 1943, Table 120, pp. 448-451

Figure 18.3-24: Interest Rates on 90-Day Stock Market Loans, 1915-1932

18.4 Summary, 1915-1932

The stock market crash of 1929 followed by the collapse of the banking system in 1930-1932 was preceded by a string of bank failures, with considerable losses to depositors, throughout the 1920's. The economics experts have concluded that a variety of causes were at work. Friedman and Schwartz [18.4-1], in a paragraph contributed by Clark Warburton, states that many of the bank failures early in the decade were small banks that were not members of the Federal Reserve, and for which the Federal Reserve took little responsibility. As for the failures among larger banks in 1930, the Federal Reserve regarded those as symptoms of bad management. The failure of small banks is supported by Kreps [18.4-2], referencing Ross Robertson, who points out that many of the small banks were in rural areas, and their portfolios were injured by falling values of farmland after WWI. Meltzer observed that as the smaller banks' portfolio declined, they became reluctant to issue new loans [18.4-3]. A decline in the value of bond portfolios made some banks insolvent [18.4-4]. Friedman and Schwartz [18.4-5] cite a lack of leadership when it mattered; the Federal Reserve should have pursued an open-market policy to prevent a decline in the overall supply of money. A countering theory [18.4-6] is that a decline in the money supply during a depression is acceptable as a means of liquidating the bad investments during a preceding expansion. But this is true if and only if wages and prices are both allowed to fall.

There are a great many theories as to what caused the stock market crash of 1929 and what caused that to pervade throughout the entire economy into a depression that lasted for a decade. The most likely train of events was the large increase in the money supply in the mid-1920's and a rise in stock prices fueled partly by optimism and partly by the speculative tendency of the easy money policy [18.4-7] (although Friedman dismisses this claim [18.4-8]). At the same time, there was no obvious indication of risk to the economy since prices were relatively stable [18.4-9]. But stable price levels do not mean there isn't a problem: the oversupply of money distorts the production of capital goods [18.4-10]. When the Federal Reserve recognized the expansionary money policy error in 1928, it did too little to correct it [18.4-11]. Most likely the expansion of industrial production became unprofitable as wages rose or as selling prices declined. That trend in turn caused stock prices to fall, losses on margin loans mounted, and the banks took on heavy losses. That would explain a financial problem in New York, same as had occurred in 1893 and 1907. But this time industrial sector began to contract, partly because highly leveraged large holding companies experienced a decline in income [18.4-12] which caused them to proceed with commensurate layoffs. The general decline in employment led to a need for cash instead of deposits, although there was at this time no particular distrust of the banking system [18.4-13]. The run on the banks (mostly in the Midwest) was out of necessity. The run on the banks caused a liquidity problem, and the banks, instead of suspending payments in gold as had been done in previous panics, chose to keep going until they were insolvent. The change from deposits to cash caused a decline in the overall money supply (not advisable in a recession), and the Federal Reserve did nothing to correct it. Thus as the money unit became more valuable, the real cost of doing business, i.e., the real cost of repayment of loans and interest, and the real losses, increased, leading to a further decline in output and employment. In this case, the Federal Reserve permitted the money supply to decline (1930 to 1932) when it should have been maintained at stable levels. The depreciation induced by the expansion of the 1920's should have been recognized as permanent, especially if government policy was to maintain wages and prices. Eventually the public did lose confidence in the banking system, which accelerated the runs on the banks [18.4-14].

Meltzer [18.4-15] provides some insight into what the Federal Reserve could have done to prevent the collapse of the banking system. He relates that there had been a proposal in 1931 by which the large stable banks should fund a new entity called the National Credit Commission, which would in turn buy assets of banks that were close to insolvency, thus freeing up cash or credit. But the Federal Reserve supposedly refused to accept the bonds offered by the proposed National Credit Commission as suitable paper for issuing credit to the banks, and the plan was never implemented.

Friedman alludes to a similar problem: thinking at the time was that the existence of the Federal Reserve was a guaranteed preventative for the type of panics in 1893 and 1907 [18.4-16]. Thus there was overconfidence in the Federal Reserve, which failed to prevent the continuing decline by allowing the money supply to contract; while at the same time, there was no alternate emergency currency such as had been used in 1907 under the Aldrich-Vreeland Act [18.4-17].

It is instructive to compare the deep depression of 1920-1921 to the depression that began in 1929. In the former one, there was a 50% decline in industrial activity (a larger decline than in 1929-1930), yet the government and the Federal Reserve did very little to intervene in the economy in 1920. By mid-1921 the economy had recovered to its previous level. In the 1929 collapse, the government interfered while the Federal Reserve pursued a traditional policy; it was the opposing forces that caused the collapse of 1929 to last until 1940. During this period, the Federal Reserve was pursuing a deflationary policy while the federal government was doing what it could to maintain high wages and prices. It should be one or the other; you would think that a central bank and the government would have consistent policies. These counteracting policies served only to increase the anxiety among the public, this led to some distrust of the banks, and a continuing demand for cash instead of leaving money in the banks in the form of deposits.

To summarize to origin of the Great Depression: a) had a boom in the growth of capital-goods industries the 1920's followed by a crash [18.4-18]; b) the Federal Reserve pursued an expansion of the money supply in the 1920's partly to aid Britain [18.4-19]; c) the Federal Reserve expanded the money supply during the 1920's by keeping the discount rate too low, continuing the silver purchase policy, and buying bankers' acceptances at subsidized rates [18.4-20]; and d) in 1930 the Federal Reserve pursued a deflationary policy inconsistent with the government's approach of maintaining prices and wages [18.4-21]. The expansion in the capital-goods industries should have caused prices to decrease, but the expansion of the money supply caused them to be stable in the 1920's; thus camouflaging an underlying problem.

It is easy to see from Figure 18.3-15 that the money supply and prices generally were decreasing rapidly between 1930 and 1932. But because the government was interfering in wage rates (keeping them high instead of allowing them to fall), unemployment increased and average income declined as shown on Figure 18.3-17. So, although interest rates were low per Figure 18.3-23, there was little demand for loans, since labor was likely too expensive to employ profitably. Thus there was a decline in demand deposits as seen from Figure 18.3-22, combined with an increase in cash held by the public outside the banks; which served to also reinforce the decline in the money supply.

This monetary deflation, in the presence of continued artificially high wage rates, only injured further the people who had been injured by the previous inflation. Fortunately, the Federal Reserve has not allowed this deflationary trend to occur again in the past 90 years. It has in fact pursued a continuous policy of inflation.

President Hoover's bad policies were expanded and intensified under President Roosevelt, which is why the Great Depression, although started by a milder downturn than the 1920 depression, continued until 1940.

References

[18.1-1]   Federal Reserve Board, *Federal Reserve Bulletin*, Dec 1917, p. 931

[18.1-2]   Federal Reserve Board, *Federal Reserve Bulletin*, Dec 1917, p. 951

[18.1-3]   Federal Reserve Board, *Federal Reserve Bulletin*, Dec 1918, p. 1216

[18.1-4]   Milton Friedman, Anna Jacobson Schwartz, *A Monetary History of the United States, 1867 - 1960*, A Study by the National Bureau of Economic Research, NY, Princeton, NJ: Princeton University Press, 1963, pp. 167, 168, 311

[18.1-5]   Federal Reserve Board, *Federal Reserve Bulletin*, 1 May 1915, p. 12

[18.2-1]   Text of "An Act proposing an amendment to the Federal Reserve Act relative to acceptances, and for other purposes", 63rd Congress, Session 1, Chapter 93, Public Law 63-281, 3 Mar 1915

[18.2-2]   op. cit., Friedman and Schwartz, p. 172

[18.2-3]   Text of "An Act to amend section six of an Act to define and fix the standard of value, to maintain the parity of all forms of money issued or coined by the United States, to refund the public debt, and for other purposes, approved 14 Mar 1900, as amended by the Act of March 2nd, nineteen hundred and eleven", 64th Congress, Session 1, Chapter 142, Public Law 64-90, 12 Jun 1916

[18.2-4]   Text of "An Act to provide capital for agricultural development, to create standard form of investment based on farm mortgage, to equalize rates of interest upon farm loans, to furnish a market for United States bonds, to create Government depositaries and financial agents for the United States, and for other purposes", a.k.a. the Federal Farm Loan Act of 1916, 64th Congress, Session 1, Chapter 245, Public Law 64-158, 17 Jul 1916

[18.2-5]   Text of "An Act to amend certain sections of the Act entitled "Federal Reserve Act", approved December twenty-third, nineteen hundred and thirteen", 64th Congress, Session 1, Chapter 461, Public Law 64-270, 7 Sep 1916

[18.2-6]   Text of "An Act to authorize an issue of bonds to meet expenditures for the national security and defense, and, for the purpose of assisting in the prosecution of the war, to extend credit to foreign government, and for other purposes"; a.k.a. First Liberty Bond Act, 65th Congress, Session 1, Chapter 4, Public Law 65-3, 24 Apr 1917

[18.2-7]   op. cit., Friedman and Schwartz, pp. 194, 208

[18.2-8]   Text of "An Act to amend the Act approved December twenty-third, nineteen hundred and thirteen, known as the Federal Reserve Act, as amended by the Acts of August fourth, nineteen hundred and fourteen, August fifteenth, nineteen hundred and fourteen, March third, nineteen hundred and fifteen, and September seventh, nineteen hundred and sixteen", 65th Congress, Session 1, Chapter 32, Public Law 65-25, 21 Jun 1917

[18.2-9]   Joshua N. Feinman, *Reserve Requirements: History, Current Practice, and Potential Reform, Federal Reserve Bulletin*, Jun 1993, pp. 569-589

[18.2-10] op. cit., Friedman and Schwartz, p. 220

[18.2-11] Text of "An Act to authorize an additional issue of bonds to meet expenditures for the national security and defense, and, for the purpose of assisting in the prosecution of the war, to extend additional credit to foreign governments, and for other purposes", a.k.a. Second Liberty Bond Act, 65th Congress, Session 1, Chapter 56, Public Law 65-43, 24 Sep 1917

[18.2-12] Text of "An Act to amend the laws relating to denominations of circulating notes by national banks and to permit the issuance of notes of small denominations", 65th Congress, Session 1, Chapter 74, Public Law 65-61, 5 Oct 1917

[18.2-13] Text of "An Act to amend an Act approved September twenty-fourth, nineteen hundred and seventeen, entitled 'An Act to authorize an additional issue of bonds to meet expenditures for the national security and defense, and for the purpose of assisting in the prosecution of the war, to extend additional credit to foreign government, and for other purposes'"; 65th Congress, Session 2, Chapter 44, Public Law 65-120, 4 Apr 1918

[18.2-14] op. cit., Friedman and Schwartz, p. 635

[18.2-15] Text of "An Act to conserve the gold supply of the United States; to permit the settlement in silver of trade balances adverse to the United States; to provide silver for subsidiary coinage and for commercial use; to assist foreign governments at war with the enemies of the United States; and for the above purposes to stabilize the price and encourage the production of silver"; 65th Congress, Session 2, Chapter 63, Public Law 65-139, 23 Apr 1918

[18.2-16] Clifton H. Kreps, Jr., *Money, Banking and Monetary Policy*, NY: The Ronald Press Co., 1962, p. 90

[18.2-17] National Bureau of Economic Research, Cambridge, MA (see website below)

[18.2-18] Text of "An Act to provide for the consolidation of national banking associations", 65th Congress, Session 2, Chapter 209, Public Law 65-240, 7 Nov 1918

[18.2-19] op. cit., National Bureau of Economic Research

[18.2-20] op. cit., Friedman and Schwartz, p. 222

[18.2-21] Allan H. Meltzer, *A History of the Federal Reserve*, Chicago, IL: University of Chicago Press, 2003, Vol. 1, p. 95

[18.2-22] Text of "An Act to amend the Act approved December 23, 1913, known as the Federal Reserve Act", 66th Congress, Session 2, Chapter 18, Public Law 66-106, 24 Dec 1919

[18.2-23] op. cit., Friedman and Schwartz, p. 235

[18.2-24] op. cit., National Bureau of Economic Research

[18.2-25] op. cit., Kreps, p. 513

[18.2-26] op. cit., Friedman and Schwartz, pp. 231, 232

[18.2-27] op. cit., Friedman and Schwartz, pp. 229-235

[18.2-28] op. cit., Friedman and Schwartz, p. 235

[18.2-29] Text of "An Act to amend the Act of December 23, 1913, known as the Federal Reserve Act", 67th Congress, Session 1, Chapter 22, Public Law 67-86, 14 Jun 1921

[18.2-30] op. cit., National Bureau of Economic Research

[18.2-31] Federal Deposit Insurance Corporation, Division of Research and Statistics, *A Brief History of Deposit Insurance in the United States*, Sep 1998, p. 21

[18.2-32] Text of "An Act to amend the Federal Reserve Act approved December 23, 1913", 67th Congress, Session 2, Chapter 205, Public law 67-230, 3 Jun 1922

[18.2-33] Text of "An Act to declare a national emergency to exist in the production, transportation, and distribution of coal and other fuel, granting additional powers to the Interstate Commerce Commission, providing for the appointment of a Federal Fuel Distributor, providing for the declaration of car-service priorities during the present emergency, and to prevent the sale of fuel at unjust and unreasonably high prices", 67th Congress, Session 2, Chapter 413, Public Law 67-348, 22 Sep 1922

[18.2-34] op. cit., Federal Deposit Insurance Corporation, p. 21

[18.2-35] op. cit., National Bureau of Economic Research

[18.2-36] op. cit., Federal Deposit Insurance Corporation, p. 21

[18.2-37] op. cit., National Bureau of Economic Research

[18.2-38] op. cit., Federal Deposit Insurance Corporation, p. 21

[18.2-39] op. cit., Federal Deposit Insurance Corporation, p. 21

[18.2-40] op. cit., National Bureau of Economic Research

[18.2-41] op. cit., Federal Deposit Insurance Corporation, p. 21

[18.2-42] Text of "An Act to further amend the national banking laws and the Federal Reserve Act, as amended", a.k.a. the McFadden Act, 69th Congress, Session 1, Chapter 191, Public Law 69-639, 25 Feb 1927

[18.2-43] op. cit., National Bureau of Economic Research

[18.2-44] op. cit., Federal Deposit Insurance Corporation, p. 21

[18.2-45] op. cit., Kreps, pp. 176, 517, 518

[18.2-46] op. cit., Federal Deposit Insurance Corporation, p. 21

[18.2-47] Text of "An Act to establish a Federal Farm Board to promote the effective merchandising of agricultural commodities in interstate and foreign commerce, and to place agriculture on a basis of economic equality with other industries", a.k.a. the Agricultural Marketing Act, 71st Congress, Session 1, Chapter 24, Public Law 71-24, 15 Jun 1929

[18.2-48]   op. cit., National Bureau of Economic Research

[18.2-49]   op. cit., Kreps, pp. 176, 177

[18.2-50]   Murray N. Rothbard, *America's Great Depression,* Auburn, AL: Ludwig von Mises Institute, 2000, pp. 161-163 (originally published 1963)

[18.2-51]   op. cit., Federal Deposit Insurance Corporation, p. 21

[18.2-52]   Text of "An Act to provide revenue, to regulate commerce with foreign countries, to encourage the industries of the United States, to protect American labor, and for other purposes", a.k.a. the Tariff Act of 1930, 71st Congress, Session 2, Chapter 497, Public Law 71-361, 17 Jun 1930

[18.2-53]   op. cit., Friedman and Schwartz, pp. 308-311

[18.2-54]   Text of "An Act making supplemental appropriations to provide for emergency construction on certain public works during the remainder of the fiscal year ending June 30, 1931, with a view to increasing employment", 71st Congress, Session 3, Chapter 19, Public Law 71-550, 20 Dec 1930

[18.2-55]   op. cit., Federal Deposit Insurance Corporation, p. 21

[18.2-56]   op. cit., Friedman and Schwartz, pp. 380-382

[18.2-57]   op. cit., Federal Deposit Insurance Corporation, p. 21

[18.2-58]   Text of "An Act to provide emergency financing facilities for financial institutions, to aid in financing agriculture, commerce, and industry, and other purposes", 72nd Congress, Session 1, Chapter 8, 22 Jan 1932

[18.2-59]   op. cit., Friedman and Schwartz, pp. 191, 321, 400

[18.2-60]   Text of "An Act to improve the facilities of the Federal reserve system for the service of commerce, industry, and agriculture, to provide means for meeting the needs of member banks in exceptional circumstances, and for other purposes", a.k.a. Glass-Steagall Act, 72nd Congress, Session 1, Chapter 58, Public Law 72-44, 27 Feb 1932

[18.2-61]   op. cit., Meltzer, Vol. 1, p. 417

[18.2-62]   Text of "An Act to relieve destitution, to broaden the lending powers of the Reconstruction Finance Corporation, and to create employment by providing for and expediting a public works program", a.k.a. the Emergency Relief and Construction Act of 1932, 72nd Congress, Session 1, Chapter 520, Public Law 72-302, 21 Jul 1932

[18.2-63]   op. cit., Friedman and Schwartz, p. 320

[18.2-64]   op. cit., Friedman and Schwartz, pp. 321, 322

[18.2-65]   Text of "An Act to create Federal Home Loan banks, to provide for the supervision thereof, and for other purposes", a.k.a. the Federal Home Loan Bank Act, 72nd Congress, Session 1, Chapter 522, Public Law 72-304, 22 Jul 1932

[18.2-66]   op. cit., Friedman and Schwartz, p. 325

[18.2-67]   op. cit., Federal Deposit Insurance Corporation, p. 21

[18.2-68]   op. cit., Kreps, p. 177

[18.3-1]   Board of Governors of the Federal Reserve, *Banking and Monetary Statistics, 1914-1941*, Washington, DC: Publication Services, Division of Administrative Services, Board of Governors of the Federal reserve, Nov 1943, Table 110.

[18.3-2]   op. cit., Friedman and Schwartz, pp. 709-713

[18.4-1]   op. cit., Friedman and Schwartz, pp. 358, 359

[18.4-2]   op. cit., Kreps, p. 93, citing Ross M. Robertson, *History of the American Economy*, NY: Harcourt, Brace, & World, 1955, p. 459

[18.4-3]   op. cit., Meltzer, Vol. 1, pp. 272, 332

[18.4-4]   op. cit., Friedman and Schwartz, p. 312

[18.4-5]   op. cit., Friedman and Schwartz, pp. 409-415

[18.4-6]   op. cit., Meltzer, Vol. 1, pp. 277, 278; here Meltzer is citing the views of Oliver M. W. Sprague as expressed in speeches he gave in 1931.

[18.4-7]   op. cit., Rothbard, p. 163

[18.4-8]   op. cit., Friedman and Schwartz, p. 298

[18.4-9]   op. cit., Friedman and Schwartz, pp. 242-244

[18.4-10]   op. cit., Rothbard, pp. 169-171

[18.4-11]   op. cit., Friedman and Schwartz, pp. 297, 298
[18.4-12]   op. cit., Kreps, pp. 522, 523
[18.4-13]   op. cit., Friedman and Schwartz, p. 392
[18.4-14]   op. cit., Kreps, pp. 177, 178
[18.4-15]   op. cit., Meltzer, Vol. 1, p. 425
[18.4-16]   op. cit., Friedman and Schwartz, p. 411
[18.4-17]   op. cit., Friedman and Schwartz, p. 172
[18.4-18]   op. cit., Rothbard, p. 171
[18.4-19]   op. cit., Rothbard, pp. 142, 143
[18.4-20]   op. cit., Rothbard, p. 137
[18.4-21]   Henry Hazlitt, *What You Should Know About Inflation*, NY: Funk & Wagnalls, 1968, pp. 104-107 (originally published 1960 by D. von Nostrand)

NBER website: https://www.nber.org/research/data/us-business-cycle-expansions-and-contractions

19

Federal Reserve Under the Gold Bullion Standard, Part 1, 1933-1950

19.1 Preview, 1933-1950

The first part of this period covers the rest of the Great Depression. It was also during this period that the U. S. abandoned the gold standard. Kreps [19.1-1] gives several reasons. First, the goal, given the federal government's policy of maintaining high wages, was to increase prices domestically without causing gold to flow out of the U. S. as would normally be the case under a gold standard. Second, if the U. S. dollar were depreciated, foreign nations will find it attractive to increase their imports from the U. S., thus stimulating industry in the U. S. The underlying idea here was that the U. S. could use depreciation of the currency as a way to revive industry. These objectives led to the need for a double standard: fiat currency at home (immune from foreign price movements) and a gold standard for international trade.

It was shown earlier (sections 1.9 and 2.3) that a policy of depreciation works in the short run, but is only an illusion that fails in the long run. Depreciation did not resolve the Depression, but it did stimulate exports; when that realization came about, there could be no going back to the gold standard. If the gold standard had been revived, the U. S. would again be subject to an inconvenient gold flow mechanism (a decline in the money supply), and so the U. S. went to a gold bullion system. American people were prohibited from possessing or trading in gold, and gold bullion was only used in large transactions involving foreign trade. All the gold coin and bullion possessed by the American people was called in, and the people, desperate at the depths of the Depression and willing to believe Roosevelt's fairy tales, handed it over. A handful of patriots kept their gold. A lesson for us now as Americans: surrender nothing, concede nothing, and tell them nothing.

President Roosevelt also devalued the dollar in terms of gold after the gold was confiscated. That increased the dollar value of bank reserves and permitted an expansion of the money supply. This was in addition to the importation of gold from Europe due to concerns about Hitler's intentions.

President Hoover was a well-meaning but incompetent do-gooder, who meddled with economic policy in an effort to help the people after the market and industrial crash of 1929. If we're going to have a central bank (not a good idea), the least we should expect is that central bank policy be consistent with the government's economic policy. The leaders of the Federal Reserve believed that the best remedy for a recession was to do nothing (which worked well in 1920-1921) and let the economy liquidate the bad investments. Hoover and Congress, on the other hand, proceeded to prop up prices and wages. The two policies counteracted each other; not only that, but as Friedman [19.1-2] has pointed out, allowed the situation with the banks to linger far too long: they should have suspended specie payments in early 1931, and would have avoided the banking collapse. The bank "suspensions" of the early 1930's were an entirely new phenomenon. In suspensions before 1932, it meant the banks were still open and did normal business using checks; "suspension" meant limited or no ability to convert deposits to specie. But in the early 1930's "suspension" meant the entire banking system was closed entirely, including banks that were fully solvent [19.1-3].

Roosevelt expanded Hoover's erroneous notion of maintaining "purchasing power" by maintaining high wages during an economic decline. The only thing Roosevelt ever wanted was absolute power, and he realized (correctly) that the control and manipulation of money was an efficient way to obtain it. He therefore expanded and intensified the failed policies that Hoover had started, thus prolonging what could have been a short recession into a decade-long depression. The economy revived only with the advent of World War II; Hitler and Hirohito rescued Roosevelt. Meanwhile, the Federal Reserve continued to fail in one of its main objectives of maintaining public confidence in the banking system. The Federal Deposit Insurance Corporation (FDIC), established as a temporary measure in 1933, restored public confidence that their savings were safe and prevented runs on the banks; thus FDIC succeeded where the Federal Reserve had failed. The FDIC managed the Federal Deposit Insurance Fund (FDIF), which actually compensated the depositors of failed banks.

The government continued its involvement in the farming industry and passed several legislative initiatives to "support agriculture". The net result of the Agricultural Adjustment Acts of 1933 and 1938 (cf. also U. S. vs. Butler, 6 Jan 1936) was to benefit large farmers at the expense of small farmers and sharecroppers, which led to food shortages and hunger. These types of results are typical of government attempts at price fixing and control of the economy.

Having failed in its basic mission of preventing bank runs and promoting economic stability, the Federal Reserve took a secondary place behind the Treasury Department from the mid-1930's to 1951. The goal of the Treasury Department was to keep interest rates at a minimum such that the interest payments on the ever-increasing national debt would not pose a cash-flow problem for the government.

19.2 History, 1933-1950

20 Jan 1933: State-wide "banking holidays" (banks closed) imposed in IA [19.2-1].

3 Feb 1933: State-wide "banking holidays" (banks closed) imposed in LA [19.2-2].

3 Feb 1933: Congress extended the authority of the Federal Reserve Banks to accept U. S. obligations as security for Federal Reserve Notes [19.2-3] until 3 Mar 1934.

14 Feb 1933: State-wide "banking holidays" (banks closed) imposed in MI [19.2-4].

3 Mar 1933: The Federal Reserve Board suspended reserve requirements for 30 days [19.2-5].

4 Mar 1933: State-wide "banking holidays" (banks closed) imposed in NY, IL, MA, NJ, and PA [19.2-6]; by this time bank holidays had been declared in about half the States.

6 Mar 1933: President Roosevelt issued a Proclamation imposing a nationwide three-day "bank holiday" to formulate an economic policy on the banks and the Depression in general [19.2-7]. The banks were prohibited from exporting or paying obligations in gold. Many of the banks were already closed per State orders (beginning in Oct 1932) as a means to stop the runs on the banks.

9 Mar 1933: Congress passed the Emergency Banking Act (Public Law 73-1) [19.2-8, 19.2-9] to improve the capital positions of banks. Its provisions included: **a)** (S. 1) confirmed Roosevelt's actions of 6 Mar 1933; b) (S. 2) granted emergency regulatory powers to the President regarding foreign trade or trade in gold or gold bullion; **b)** (S. 3) modified Section 11 of the Federal Reserve Act, authorizing the Treasury Secretary to order all gold coin, gold bullion, and gold certificates owned by organizations and individuals, to be turned in to the Treasury, and be paid for in another form of coin or currency as the Secretary may determine; **c)** (S. 3) makes hoarding of gold a crime, punishable by twice the value of the gold; **d)** (S. 4) suspended all bank operations during any emergency declared by the President except under rules prescribed by the Treasury Secretary; **e)** (S. 202) conservators appointed by the Comptroller of the Currency to aid re-opening of banks with non-

marketable assets; **f)** (S. 204) authorized the Comptroller of the Currency to permit re-opening of solvent banks; **g)** (S. 206) directed the conservators to determine how much may be withdrawn from accounts; **h)** (S. 301, 304) permitted, with Comptroller of the Currency's approval, preferred stock of national banks to be sold to the public or to the Reconstruction Finance Corporation, and holders of preferred stock to receive 6% annual dividends; **i)** (S. 401) modified Section 18 of the Federal Reserve Act to permit the Federal Reserve to issue Federal Reserve Notes to banks based on 90% of the face value of eligible paper or bankers' acceptances (over $200,000,000 were issued), or 100% of the face value of U. S. securities; **j)** (S. 401) changed Section 18 of the Federal Reserve Act to make Federal Reserve Notes an obligation of the Federal Reserve (was the U. S. Treasury); **k)** (S. 401) Federal Reserve Notes subject to the same tax as national bank notes that are secured by 2% U. S. securities; **l)** modified Section 10B of the Federal Reserve Act, to permit the Federal Reserve Banks' authority to issue advances to member banks even if assets are not eligible for rediscount (the member banks' time or demand notes), limited to 3 Mar 1934 (later extended to 3 Mar 1935); and **m)** (S. 403) added a paragraph to Section 13 of the Federal Reserve Act, permitting Federal Reserve Banks to make advances up to 90 days on promissory notes of individuals, or organizations, secured by U. S. securities. These provisions gave new powers to the Federal Reserve to act as "the banker of last resort" by permitting discounts and advances on the notes of member banks, so long as they were in turn secured on appropriate assets. Solvent banks were to begin re-opening on 13 Mar 1933 per a radio address by President Roosevelt designed to instill confidence in the banking system [19.2-10].

10 Mar 1933: Roosevelt issued an Executive Order [19.2-11] prohibiting exportation of gold except by license from the Treasury Department, and authorizing banks to re-open per regulations to be established by the Secretary of the Treasury.

13 Mar 1933: The banks began to gradually re-open [19.2-12], starting with licensed banks in the Federal Reserve cities. Re-opening continued at a slow pace, and about 4,000 that had closed between 1929 and 1933 never re-opened.

15 Mar 1933: Approximate end of first phase of the Great Depression (cf. 15 Aug 1929) [19.2-13].

24 Mar 1933: Congress passed an amendment [19.2-14] to the Emergency Banking Act (cf. 9 Mar 1933): **a)** (S. 1) permitted State-chartered banks and trust companies that are not members of the Federal Reserve to borrow from the Federal Reserve in the district where located; **b)** (S. 2) permitted the Reconstruction Finance Corporation to invest in State-charted institutions and trust companies unless the laws of the State precluded double indemnity; and **c)** (S. 3) permitted the RTC to buy and sell notes, bonds and debt obligations of State banks and trust companies. This policy was to continue for one year unless ended by proclamation by the President.

5 Apr 1933: President Roosevelt issued an Executive Order [19.2-15] regarding the "hoarding" of gold: a) prohibited private possession of gold except for jewelry; b) all gold coin, gold bullion, and gold certificates held by individuals and banks to be turned in to the Treasury or Federal Reserve Banks by 1 May 1933 except for a few collectors' coins; c) the gold received to be paid for with an equivalent amount of other coin or currency. The purpose of nationalizing gold was to let the U. S. dollar fall against foreign currencies as a way to increase domestic prices [19.2-16, 19.2-17].

20 Apr 1933: President Roosevelt issued an Executive Order [19.2-18] prohibiting the Treasury Secretary from issuing any licenses to export gold, except to settle existing claims by foreign governments. This action removed the U. S. from the gold standard entirely [19.2-19].

12 May 1933: Congress passed the Agricultural Adjustment Act [19.2-20] to control agriculture prices by manipulating both production and consumption through actions by the RTC and the Secretary of Agriculture. This was the beginning of direct federal government interference in farming. Sections 3 through 41 contain all the regulations on price control for cotton, other agricultural commodities (S. 11) especially wheat, cotton, field corn, hogs, rice, milk and its products, and tobacco; and the processing thereof, taxation, and exportation. Section 21 authorized the Federal Farm Loan Banks to is-

sue up to $2,000 M in bonds not exceeding 4% to purchase farm mortgages. The rationale for agricultural control is stated in Sections 1 and 2, is worth quoting in full:

> (S. 1) "That the present acute economic emergency being in part the consequence of a severe and increasing disparity between the prices of agricultural and other commodities, which disparity has largely destroyed the purchasing power of farmers for industrial products, has broken down the orderly exchange of commodities, and has seriously impaired the agricultural assets supporting the national credit structure, it is hereby declared that these conditions in the basic industry of agriculture have affected transactions in agricultural commodities with a national public interest, have burdened and obstructed the normal currents of commerce in such commodities, and render imperative the immediate enactment of title I of this Act."

> (S. 2) "DECLARATION OF POLICY: It is hereby declared to be the policy of Congress -- (1) To establish and maintain such balance between the production and consumption of agricultural commodities, and such marketing conditions therefor, as will reestablish prices to farmers at a level that will give agricultural commodities a purchasing power with respect to articles that farmers buy, equivalent to the purchasing power of agricultural commodities in the base period. The base period in the case of all agricultural commodities except tobacco shall be the prewar period, August 1909-July 1914. In the case of tobacco, the base period shall be the postwar period, August 1919-July 1929. (2) To approach such equality of purchasing power by gradual correction of the present inequalities therein at as rapid a rate as is deemed feasible in view of the current consumptive demand in domestic and foreign markets. (3) To protect the consumers' interest by readjusting farm production at such level as will not increase the percentage of the consumers' retail expenditures for agricultural commodities, or products derived therefrom, which is returned to the farmer, above the percentage which was returned to the farmer in the prewar period, August 1909-July 1914."

12 May 1933: Congress passed the "Emergency Farm Mortgage Act", [19.2-21] which was Title III of the Agricultural Adjustment Act. It contained the "Thomas amendments" that affected the banking system [19.2-22]. The rationale for it falls under four categories, namely if the:

> "President finds, upon investigation that: 1) the foreign commerce of the United States is adversely affected by reason of the depreciation in the value of the currency of any other government or governments in relation to the present standard value of gold, or 2) action under this section is necessary in order to regulate and maintain the parity of currency issues of the United States, or 3) an economic emergency requires an expansion of credit, or 4) an expansion of credit is necessary to secure by international agreement a stabilization at proper levels of the currencies of various governments"

then the President may direct the Treasury Secretary to take the following actions: **a)** (S. 43) Federal Reserve Banks to conduct open-market purchases of U. S. securities up to $3,000,000,000; **b)** (S. 48) adjust reserve requirements for demand and time deposits accounts; **c)** (S. 43) permitted the Treasury Secretary to issue up to $3,000,000,000 in U. S. Notes (the Civil War era "greenbacks"); **d)** (S. 45) permitted foreign governments to pay interest and principal due to the U. S. in silver at $0.50 per ozt.; **e)** (S. 43) permitted the President by proclamation to change the definitions of the dollar as weights of gold and silver, limiting the depreciation to 50%; and **f)** (S. 45) permitted the Treasury to coin gold and silver without limitation. Only two of these powers were used: paying in silver by foreign governments, and devaluation of the dollar. The explicit goal of the "Thomas amendments", as explained by Roosevelt, was to expand the money supply and thus increase prices; the provisions permitting adjustment of the gold dollar caused the price of gold to rise as well as the price of foreign currencies [19.2-23].

18 May 1933: Congress passed the Tennessee Valley Authority Act [19.2-24] to provide flood control and promote agricultural and industrial development of the area.

5 Jun 1933: Congress passed a joint resolution [19.2-25, 19.2-26] declaring that all contracts calling for payment in gold were invalid, and instead required them to be paid in Federal Reserve Notes and other currency. National Bank Notes and Federal Reserve Notes were made legal tender for all debts public and private. The Supreme Court held in 1935 [19.2-27] that existing government contracts, in which the government was obligated to pay in gold, were still valid.

13 Jun 1933: Congress passed the Homeowners Loan Act of 1933 [19.2-28] as a means to prevent home foreclosures. Among its provisions: **a)** (S. 2) created a Home Owners' Loan Corporation (HOLC); **b)** (S. 3) repealed the portion of the Federal Home Loan Bank Act (cf. 22 Jul 1932) that permitted direct loans to homeowners; **c)** (S. 4) authorized the Federal Home Loan Bank Board (FHLBB) to determine the capital requirements of the Home Owners' Loan Corporation, not to exceed $200 M; **d)** (S. 4) authorized the Treasury to subscribe to the stock in the HOLC with financing made available by the Reconstruction Finance Corporation; **e)** (S. 4) authorized the HOLC to issue bonds to be sold in order to finance the HOLC; **f)** (S. 4) the HOLC authorized for the next three years to finance mortgages and obligations from existing lien holders secured by real estate up to the smaller of $14,000 or 80% of the appraised value at an interest rate to the homeowner not to exceed 3%; **g)** (S. 4) authorized the HOLC for the next three years to advance cash to homeowners unable to obtain financing elsewhere up to 40% of appraised value at 6% interest; **h)** (S. 5) authorized the FHLBB to establish and charter institutions to be known as "savings and loan associations" (S&L); **i)** (S. 5) S&L's are to be mutual operations and members of a Federal Home Loan Bank; **j)** (S. 5) S&L's are permitted to make loans secured either by their shares or mortgages up to $20,000 within 50 miles of their location; **k)** (S. 5) assets of S&L's may be invested in stock of a Federal Home Loan Bank or obligations of the U. S.; and **l)** (S. 5) the U. S. Treasury authorized to subscribe to shares in S&L's up to $100 M.

16 Jun 1933: Congress passed the Banking Act of 1933 [19.2-29, 19.2-30]: **a)** (S. 3) modified Section 9 of the Federal Reserve Act (FRA) (cf. 23 Dec 1913) to grant the Board power to review issue rules on discounts and advances based on the lending practices of member banks (i.e., loans on securities, real estate or agriculture); **b)** (S. 3) modified Section 9 of the FRA to permit mutual savings banks to apply for membership in the Federal Reserve; **c)** (S. 7) modified Section 11 of the FRA, granting power to the Federal Reserve Board to determine what percentage of capital and surplus that may be lent with stock or bonds as collateral; **d)** (S. 8) added Section 12A to the FRA, which established the Federal Open Market Committee, and Federal Reserve Banks to engage in open-market operations under FRA Section 14 only by regulations set by the Federal Reserve Board; **e)** (S. 8) added Section 12B to the FRA, which created the Federal Deposit Insurance Corporation (FDIC) to insure depositors as a temporary measure (deposits insured to $2,500); **f)** (S. 8) Federal Reserve Banks to subscribe to FDIC stock in an amount equal to half their surplus on 1 Jan 1933; **g)** (S. 8) member banks to subscribe to the FDIC in the amount of 0.5% of its deposits; **h)** (S. 11) modified Section 19 of the FRA to prohibit member banks from paying of interest on demand deposits, except for existing Certificates of Deposit; **i)** (S. 11) modified Section 19 of the FRA to grant the Federal Reserve authority to set maximum interest rates on savings and time deposits (allowing different rates for varying duration of time deposits); **j)** (S. 9) modified Section 13 of the FRA, to penalize member banks for continuing to lend on stocks after a warning from the District Bank: 1) no access to the discount window for a period to be determined by the Federal Reserve Board, and 2) all existing discount advances are due and payable; **k)** (S. 10) modified Section 14 of the FRA to prohibit Federal Reserve Banks from negotiating with foreign banks or bankers without supervision by the Federal Reserve Board; **l)** (S. 11) modified Section 19 of the FRA to prohibit member banks from acting as an agent of any other entity making loans on the security of stocks, bonds or other investment securities; **m)** (S. 11) modified the Postal Savings system provisions such that interest on deposits to accrue only to the date of this Banking Act; **n)** (S. 13) added section 23A to the FRA, limiting loans to banks holding companies or other financial institutions based on the stock or promissory notes thereof: 1) such loans not to exceed 10% of capital of the lending member bank, and 2) can loan only up to 80% of the value of securities offered as collateral; **o)** (S. 14) added Section 24A to the FRA, prohibiting national banks from investing in any bank premises, or in any holding company holding bank premises, or making loans upon the stock of such holding companies; **p)** (S. 16) restricted national bank investment of securities (other than U. S. securities) on their own account to a maximum of either: 1) 10% of the amount issued by one obligor, or 2) the sum of 15% of paid-in capital plus 25% of unimpaired sur-

plus; **q)** (S. 17) doubled capital requirements for national banks; **r)** (S. 20) prohibited member banks from being affiliated with any organization that is in the business of issuing, floating, underwriting, sale or distribution of stocks, bonds, debentures, notes or other securities; **s)** (S. 21) prohibited organizations engaged in stock or bond operations (per S. 20) to accept demand or savings deposits; **t)** (S. 22) additional liabilities to shareholders in national banks repealed; **u)** (S. 23) permitted national banks to establish branches within certain limitations; and **v)** (S. 32) created a system of permits and regulation of companies that are engaged in purchasing, selling or negotiating securities. The goal of most of these was to reduce the level of competition among the banks [19.2-31], to separate commercial from investment banking so as to reduce exposure to stock market events, to return to the real-bills method, and to provide a means of insuring deposits to prevent bank runs [19.2-32].

16 Jun 1933: Congress passed the National Industrial Recovery Act [19.2-33]. Among its provisions: **a)** (S. 2) established an industrial planning and research agency controlled by the President; **b)** (S. 3) authorized the President to establish Code of Fair Competition with trade unions and businesses but not allowing monopolies; **c)** (S. 4) permitted the President to establish licensing requirements to prevent "destructive wage or price cutting", ensuring only those businesses that conform to the "code of fair competition" to be allowed to do business; **d)** (S. 6) Federal Trade Commission was authorized to arbitrate wages and working conditions when agreement between unions and corporations was not achieved; **e)** (S. 7) defined "code of fair competition" as 1) employees to have the right to organize and bargain collectively; 2) employees are not to be forced to join a union or be prevented from joining a union; and 3) employers to comply with maximum hours of labor, minimum pay, and other conditions of employment, "as approved or prescribed by the President"; **f)** (S. 9) Interstate Commerce commission authorized to regulate transportation of oil; **g)** (S. 201) created a Federal Emergency Administration of Public Works to create work for the unemployed; and **h)** (S. 302) the funding for the RTC was decreased by $400 M.

8 Sep 1933: President Roosevelt began a daily fixing of the price of gold [19.2-34] based on world price estimates. The Treasury bought gold at the established price such that miners could sell to U. S. Treasury at prices competitive with foreign buyers. The objective was to raise domestic prices, especially on raw materials and agricultural products.

25 Oct 1933: The Reconstruction Finance Corporation began buying gold at $31.36/ozt., and continued until the price rose to $35 per ozt. as a means to expand the money supply [19.2-35]. The idea was to expand the money supply and increase wages and prices, and reduce unemployment. It did not work in this case because the core problem was an industrial collapse, not a banking problem.

21 Dec 1933: President Roosevelt issued the Silver Purchase Proclamation, based on the London Silver Agreement agreed to in June, in which the U. S. was to buy 24,421,000 ozt. of silver at $0.6464 (market price was $0.45) [19.2-36]. The objective was to inject money into the system and revive the use of silver as money (a return to the bimetal system).

28 Dec 1933: The Treasury Secretary issued an order [19.2-37] that all private gold except for rare coins (held outside the Federal Reserve) was to be turned in to the Treasury not later than 17 Jan 1934, to be paid at $20.67 per ozt. (i.e., at 23.22 grains of gold per 14 Mar 1900), although the market price was about $33/ozt.

31 Dec 1933: 4,000 banks suspended in 1933, with losses to depositors totaling $540.396 M [19.2-38]. A total of 9,056 banks had closed since 1 Jan 1930, which was about 40% of the institutions that had existed in 1930 [19.2-39].

30 Jan 1934: Congress passed the Gold Reserve Act [19.2-40]: **a)** (S. 12) confirmed the President's authority to adjust the definition of the dollar in terms of gold and silver (cf. 12 May 1933) but his authority to expire in two years; **b)** (S. 12) devaluation of the dollar limited to 60%; **c)** (S. 3, 4) completed nationalization of all the gold in the U. S.; **d)** (S. 5) gold to be used for monetary purposes only in the course of foreign trade; **e)** (S. 7) no U. S. currency (including Federal Reserve Notes authorized by FRA section 16) can be redeemed for gold; currency can only be redeemed for "lawful mon-

Chapter 19: Federal Reserve Under the Gold Bullion Standard, Part 1, 1933-1950 | 451

ey"; **f)** (S. 2) required the Federal Reserve Banks to turn all the gold acquired from individuals (cf. 5 Apr 1933) to the Treasury for which gold certificates were issued to the Federal Reserve Banks; **g)** (S. 10) appropriated $2,000 M as a "gold stabilization fund" to the Treasury to purchase gold and carry out the confiscation of gold; and **h)** (S. 2) (modifying section 16 of the Federal Reserve Act) required Federal Reserve banks to maintain reserves in gold certificates or lawful money of 35% against deposits and 40% against Federal Reserve Notes, counting gold certificates held as collateral by a Federal Reserve agent. The Treasury subsequently converted all the coin into bullion. This legislation placed the U. S. formally on a fiat money standard domestically, although gold was still used in foreign transactions. This put the U. S. on the "gold bullion standard". Possession of gold by individuals was now formally prohibited, except it was legal for collectors to possess two of each type previously minted; Friedman and Schwartz have concluded that $287 M was illegally retained [19.2-41]. The President's authority to change the gold content of the dollar eventually expired on 30 Jun 1943 [19.2-42].

31 Jan 1934: President Roosevelt officially devalued the dollar 40.94% from $20.67 to $35.00 per ozt. [19.2-43]: from 23.22 grains to 13.714 grains of fine gold (officially from 25.8 grains at 90% fine to 15.238 grains 90% fine).

31 Jan 1934: Congress passed the Federal Farm Mortgage Corporation Act [19.2-44] to refinance debts of farmers. Among its provisions: **a)** (S. 1) created the Federal Farm Mortgage Corporation (FFMC); **b)** (S. 3) the FFMC to be initially capitalized with $200 M; **c)** (S. 4) FFMC authorized to sell bonds up to $2 B, to be guaranteed by the United States; **d)** (S. 4) the Treasury Secretary authorized to buy FFMC bonds in the open market; **e)** (S. 5) the FFMC to replace the Federal Land Bank, except for refinancing of existing loans; and **f)** (S. 16) authorized the Federal Reserve Banks to make advances to member banks using FFMC bonds as collateral (FRA S. 13a) as open-market transactions (FRA S. 14b).

2 Feb 1934: President Roosevelt issued an Executive Order [19.2-45] establishing an Export-Import Bank. Generally it was a banking organization designed to "aid in financing and to facilitate exports and imports and the exchange of commodities between the United States and other nations or the agencies of nationals thereof" in order to implement the National Recovery Act (cf. 16 Jun 1933), the Reconstruction Finance Corporation Act (cf. 22 Jan 1932), and the Bank Conservation Act (cf. 9 Mar 1933). The initial capital stock was $11 M, $1 M of which came from funding per the National Industrial Recovery Act. The idea was to provide loans to imports and exporters and foreign governments, to promote trade with Russia and South America, and was later expanded to promote trade worldwide when Congress formalized it (cf. 31 Jul 1945) [19.2-46].

6 Mar 1934: Congress extended [19.2-47] the period for which U. S. obligations can be used as security against Federal Reserve Notes (FRA, S. 16) until 3 Mar 1935 or until 3 Mar 1937 if the President so desires.

6 Jun 1934: Congress passed the Securities Exchange Act [19.2-48]. It contained the following provisions: **a)** (S. 4) created the Securities and Exchange Commission; **b)** (S. 5) required registration of securities exchanges; and **c)** (S. 7) limited the ability of banks to lend on stock securities (applied to member banks, national banks, and State-chartered non-member banks), accomplished by setting margin rates (the fraction that must be supplied by the borrower) for stock loans. The initial margin requirement for stock loans was set at the higher of: a) 55% of the current market price; or b) 100% of the lowest price in the past 36 months but not more than 75% of the current price. The objective was to reduce the banks' exposure to large stock market changes, which had been a problem in the crash of 1929 [19.2-49].

19 Jun 1934: Congress passed the Silver Purchase Act [19.2-50]: **a)** (S. 3) directed the Treasury Secretary to buy silver until 25% of the total gold and silver monetary stock consisted of silver; **b)** (S. 10) this ratio to be determined using silver at $1.29 per ozt. and gold at $35 per ozt.; and **c)** (S. 5) Treasury Secretary to issue silver certificates with face value equal to the cost of the silver; and **d)** (S. 6, 7)

prohibits the hoarding of silver and requires silver to be turned over to the Treasury if the President deems it appropriate. The Treasury procured 2,596,300,000 fine ozt. (2.5963 B) of silver between 1934 and Dec 1941, costing $1,399.8 M ($1.3998 B), and issued silver certificates to the Federal Reserve Banks. Due to large gold inflows, the 25% ratio was never achieved; by 1941 it was only 15.7% [19.2-51].

26 Jun 1934: Congress passed the Federal Credit Union Act [10.2-52]. Among its provisions: **a)** (S. 2) approved creation of federal credit unions to "promote thrift among its members"; **b)** (S. 6) to be supervised by the Farm Credit Administration; **c)** (S. 7) federal credit unions authorized to make loans to its members for term not exceeding two years, to make investments only in loans to members and in securities of the United States, and to borrow up to 50% of its paid-in capital; **d)** (S. 12) to retain 20% reserve against losses; and **e)** (S. 17) may act as a fiscal agent of the Treasury if requested by the Treasury Secretary. As the title says, it was also designed to "establish a further market for securities of the United States".

27 Jun 1934: Congress passed the National Housing Act [19.2-53] intended to stop the increase in foreclosures on homes and to improve home mortgage affordability. Among its provisions: **a)** (S. 1) created the Federal Housing Administration (FHA); **b)** (S. 2) authorized the FHA administrator to extend credit insurance against losses to banks, trust companies, personal finance companies, mortgage companies, building and loan associations, and installment lending companies up to an aggregate of $200 M; **c)** (S. 3) authorized the FHA administrator to issue loans to the same institutions; **d)** (S. 201-203) created a Mutual Mortgage Insurance Fund (MMIF) to insure mortgages on low-income housing (up to 80% of the face value, financed by annual premiums between 0.5 and 5% of the mortgage face value) up to an aggregate liability of $1,000 M ($1 B); **e)** (S. 206) excess funds to be invested in securities of the United States; **f)** (S. 301) permitted the establishment of national mortgage associations to buy and sell mortgages; **g)** (S. 402) established the Federal Savings and Loan Insurance Corporation (FSLIC) with an initial capital of $100 M, the capital of which is to be subscribed by the Home Owners' Loan Corporation; **h)** (S. 404) insurance premiums charged by the FSLIC to insured institutions to be 0.25% of the sum of accounts and creditor obligations; **i)** (S. 405) the FSLIC to insure depositors at Savings and Loan institutions up to $5,000; and **j)** (S. 406) the liquidation process for failed institutions was either to contract with healthy Savings and Loans to take over the deposits, or organize a new Savings and Loan institution to do so. This law did reduce the risk of owning S&L shares, but the process sometimes caused depositors to wait up to three years to be compensated [19.2-54].

1 Jul 1934: The FDIC insurance limit on deposits was raised from $2,500 (cf. 16 Jun 1933) to $5,000 [19.2-55].

9 Aug 1934: President Roosevelt issued an Executive Order [19.2-56] based on the Silver Purchase Act (cf. 19 Jun 1934), requiring individuals holding silver to turn it into the Treasury within 90 days in return for $0.5001 per ozt., with exceptions for industrial and artistic uses in order for the U. S. government to realize a profit on the recent increase in the price of silver. Silver coins were excluded from this order, since the market value of the silver in the coins was less than the face value [19.2-57].

31 Dec 1934: Nine banks failed in 1934, with net losses to the FDIC FDIF totaling $207,000 [19.2-58].

14 Jun 1935: Congress passed a Joint Resolution [19.2-59]: **a)** (S. 1) extended Title I, S. 2(c) of the National Industrial Recovery Act to 1 Apr 1936; and **b)** (S. 2) repealed the President's powers under the National Industrial recovery Act to prescribe "codes of fair competition", except provisions enacted relating to minimum wages, maximum hours, and child labor to remain per section 7 of the National Industrial Recovery Act (cf. 16 Jun 1933).

1 Aug 1935: The issues of U. S. bonds that had been deposited with the U. S. Treasury as "circulation privilege" for National Bank Notes were redeemed, so the authority to issue further National Bank

Notes terminated. From this point, National Bank Notes became a liability of the Treasury, were exchanged for Federal Reserve Notes, and retired from circulation [19.2-60].

14 Aug 1935: Congress passed the Social Security Act [19.2-61] to provide federal old-age benefits and to assist the States to "provide for the blind, dependent and crippled children, maternal and child welfare", and administration of unemployment laws

23 Aug 1935: Congress passed the Banking Act of 1935 (Public Law 74-305) [19.2-62]. Section 101 was a complete re-write of the Federal Reserve Act (FRA) section 12B (FDIC); Section 201 modified FRA Section 4; Section 202 modified FRA section 9; sections 203 and 204 modified FRA section 10; section 205 modified FRA section 12A; section 206 modified FRA section 14; section 207 modified FRA section 19; and section 208 modified FRA section 14. Among its provisions: **a)** (S. 101) directed the Comptroller of Currency to supervise national and District banks; **b)** (S. 101) made the FDIC permanent (cf. 16 Jun 1933) and established the Federal Deposit Insurance Fund (FDIF) to insure depositors with an initial funding of $150 M; **c)** (S. 101) insurance to be funded by 1% assessment on deposits; **d)** (S. 101) set the maximum insurance on deposits in FDIC insured banks to $5,000; **e)** (S. 101) prohibited payment of interest on demand deposits in insured banks that were not members of the Federal Reserve; **f)** (S. 201) changed the staffing of Federal Reserve Banks (president of a Federal Reserve Bank to be appointed by the Federal Reserve Board); **g)** (S. 203, modifying FRA S. 10) changed the name of the Federal Reserve Board to the Board of Governors of the Federal Reserve System: 1) seven members of the Board of Governors, 2) all appointed to 14-year terms; **h)** (S. 204) the Federal Reserve was granted new powers to lend to member banks through rediscounting commercial paper; **i)** (S. 205) the decisions of the Federal Open Market Committee (FOMC) were made binding on all Federal Reserve Banks; **j)** (S. 207) permitted the FOMC to buy and sell U. S. securities but only in the open market; **k)** (S. 207) permitted the Board of Governors to change reserve requirements for member banks (now between original levels and twice the original levels); and **l)** (S. 208) changed the makeup of the FOMC from the presidents of the twelve Federal Reserve Banks to the seven members of the Board of Governors plus five Bank presidents on a rotating schedule. The new reserve ratios became: a) for central reserve city banks (New York and Chicago), 13 to 26% on demand deposits and from 3% to 6% on time deposits; b) for reserve city banks, 10% to 20% on demand deposits, and from 3% to 6% on time deposits; and c) for "country banks", 7% to 14% on demand deposits, and 3% to 6% on time deposits. The additional Federal Reserve powers were: a) Federal Reserve to regulate acquisition of commercial bank earning assets, allowing it to do so at any time on any type of assets (cf. 27 Feb 1932); and b) Federal Reserve to act as the lender of last resort in order to provide ultimate liquidity using open market operations. The open market provisions included: a) authorized the purchase and sale of U. S. Government securities; b) centralized monetary policy by making Open Market Committee decisions binding on all Federal Reserve Banks; c) permitted purchase and sale of all securities guaranteed by the U. S. government; d) established regular open-market operations; and e) the Federal Reserve powers to lend to member banks through rediscounting commercial paper was expanded. The open-market operations thus became the principal operational method of influencing the money supply. These provisions expanded the powers of the Federal Reserve as a central bank [19.2-63] and made previous temporary powers permanent [19.2-64].

31 Dec 1935: Twenty-five banks failed in 1935; net losses to the FDIC FDIF totaled $2.685 M [19.2-65].

20 May 1936: Congress passed the Rural Electrification Act of 1936 [19.2-66] to provide electricity to rural areas with an initial allocation of $50 M.

6 Jul 1935: Congress passed the National Labor Relations Act [19.2-67]. Among its provisions: **a)** (S. 3) created a National Labor Relations Board (NLRB) to enforce the following provisions; **b)** (S. 7) employees to have the right to self-organization, and to bargain collectively; **c)** (S. 8) made it illegal for an employer to: 1) interfere with or restrain employees from joining labor organization for collective bargaining, 2) interfere with the affairs of any labor organization, 3) discriminate in regard to hiring

or continuing employment based on membership in any labor organization, 4) discriminate against or fire an employee for labor complaints, or 5) refuse to engage in collective bargaining with a labor organization; **d)** (S. 10, 11) the NLRB has power to hold hearings, obtain evidence, compel testimony by subpoena upon complaints of unfair labor practices, and the normal rules of evidence prevailing in courts of law to not apply; **e)** (S. 10) the NRLB may petition a court for an injunction if it finds the complaint is valid, and the court shall judge the merits; and **f)** (S. 13) no provision of this law impedes or diminishes the right to strike.

31 Dec 1936: Sixty-nine banks failed in 1936; net losses to the FDIC FDIF totaled $2.333 M [19.2-68].

1 Mar 1937: Congress extended [19.2-69] the period for which U. S. obligations can be used as security against Federal Reserve Notes (FRA, S. 16) until 30 Jun 1939.

15 May 1937: Approximate beginning of a recession [19.2-70]. There is no consensus on whether the Federal Reserve's actions were a factor, except it possibly was too late in lowering reserve requirements (they had been raised in 1936) and using its open-market powers [19.2-71, 19.2-72]. The other problem was the labor policies of the 1930's New Deal (maintaining high wages and depreciating the currency to do so, although Kreps regards this as 'specious').

1 Sep 1937: Congress passed the U. S. Housing Act of 1937 [19.2-73] in order to "promote the general welfare of the Nation by employing its funds and credit, as provided in this Act, to assist the several States and their political subdivisions to alleviate present and recurring unemployment and to remedy the unsafe and insanitary housing conditions and the acute shortage of decent, safe, and sanitary dwellings for families of low income, in rural or urban communities, that are injurious to the health, safety, and morals of the citizens of the Nation." Among its provisions: **a)** (S. 3) created a United States Housing Authority (USHA) within the Department of the Interior; **b)** (S. 9) the USHA authorized to make loans for low-rent housing projects and to clear slums; **c)** (S. 10) USHA authorized to make annual contributions to organization managing low-income rental properties; **d)** (S. 11) USHA authorized to make capital grants to public housing agencies to maintain low-income housing or clear slums; **e)** (S. 12) the USHA was directed as soon as practical to dispose of any properties it acquired by sale or lease; **f)** (S. 18) USHA initially funded at $26 M; and **g)** (S. 20) USHA authorized to issue bonds and notes not exceeding 4% interest up to $400 M through 1 Jul 1939, such obligations to be guaranteed by the U. S. government.

1 Nov 1937: The Federal Reserve modified margin requirements [19.2-74]: a) brokers loans on listed stocks = 40%; b) broker loans for short sales = 50%; c) bank loans on stocks = 40%.

31 Dec 1937: Seventy-five banks failed in 1937; net losses to the FDIC FDIF totaled $3.672 M [19.2-75].

16 Feb 1938: Congress passed the Agricultural Adjustment Act of 1938 [19.2-76] as a means of controlling land allocation and providing support for farm prices by paying farmers not to grow crops. Section 2 states the objectives:

> "It is hereby declared to be the policy of Congress to continue the Soil Conservation and Domestic Allotment Act, as amended, for the purpose of conserving national resources, preventing the wasteful use of soil fertility, and of preserving, maintaining, and rebuilding the farm and ranch land resources in the national public interest; to accomplish these purposes through the encouragement of soil-building and soil-conserving crops and practices; to assist in the marketing of agricultural commodities for domestic consumption and for export; and to regulate interstate and foreign commerce in cotton, wheat, corn, tobacco, and rice to the extent necessary to provide an orderly, adequate, and balanced flow of such commodities in interstate and foreign commerce through storage of reserve supplies, loans, marketing quotas, assisting farmers to obtain, insofar as practicable, parity prices for such commodities and parity of income, and assisting consumers to obtain an adequate and steady supply of such commodities at fair prices."

8 Mar 1938: Congress passed a law [19.2-77]: **a)** (S. 1) requiring the Treasury Secretary to maintain the capital of the Commodity Credit Corporation at $100,000,000; and **b)** (S. 4) authorized the Commodity Credit Corporation to issue and maintain outstanding up to $500,000,000 in bonds, notes, debentures and other obligations.

21 Mar 1938: Congress passed a law [19.2-78] amending the Federal Trade Commission Act (cf. 14 Sep 1914): **a)** (S. 5) expanded the FTC's powers to investigate and prevent "unfair methods of competition in commerce, and unfair or deceptive acts or practices in commerce"; **b)** (S. 5) granted the FTC power to issue a cease-and-desist order if a corporation or person engages in unfair competition, subject to review by a court; and **c)** (S. 12, 13) permits the FTC to sue a corporation for false advertising.

15 Jun 1938: Approximate end of the recession (cf. 15 May 1937) [19.2-79].

25 Jun 1938: Congress passed the Fair Labor Standards Act of 1938 [19.2-80], which established the first minimum wage level. Among its provisions: **a)** (S. 6) imposed hourly minimum wages: 1) 24 Oct 1938 to 23 Oct 1939, $0.25; 2) 24 Oct 1939 to 23 Oct 1945: $0.30; 3) 24 Oct 1945 to 23 Oct 1952: $0.40; and **b)** (S. 7) made 40 hours the standard workweek, after which workers must be paid time and a half, with some exceptions for collective bargaining contracts. These rates have been continuously updated, the last change being made in 2009. Section 2 states the rationale:

> "(a) The Congress hereby finds that the existence, in industries engaged in commerce or in the production of goods for commerce, of labor conditions detrimental to the maintenance of the minimum standard of living necessary for health, efficiency, and general well-being of workers (1) causes commerce and the channels and instrumentalities of commerce to be used to spread and perpetuate such labor conditions among the workers of the several States; (2) burdens commerce and the free flow of goods in commerce; (3) constitutes an unfair method of competition in commerce; (4) leads to labor disputes burdening and obstructing commerce and the free flow of goods in commerce; and (5) interferes with the orderly and fair marketing of goods in commerce.

> (b) It is hereby declared to be the policy of this Act, through the exercise by Congress of its power to regulate commerce among the several States, to correct and as rapidly as practicable to eliminate the conditions above referred to in such industries without substantially curtailing employment or earning power."

31 Dec 1938: Seventy-four banks failed in 1938; net losses to the FDIC FDIF totaled $2.425 M [19.2-81].

30 Jun 1939: Congress extended the period for which direct obligations of the U. S. can be used as collateral for Federal Reserve Notes until 30 Jun 1941 [19.2-82].

6 Jul 1939: Congress passed a law [19.2-83] revising the Gold Reserve Act (cf. 30 Jan 1934): **a)** (S. 2) terminated the President's power to adjust the definition of the dollar in term of gold, effective 30 Jun 1941; **b)** (S. 3) terminates President's authority per S. 12 of Gold Reserve Act effective 30 Jun 1941; and **c)** (S. 4) the official purchase price by the Treasury for silver was adjusted from $0.6464 to $0.7095 per ozt. (i.e., the seigniorage decreased from 50 to 45%, since the official mint value is $1.29 per ozt.) [19.2-84].

31 Dec 1939: Sixty banks failed in 1939, with net losses to the FDIC FDIF totaling $7.152 M [19.2-85].

30 Jun 1940 - 31 Dec 1945: The Federal Reserve began open-market operations to fund the World War II (the U. S. was aiding Britain at this time) [19.2-86]. The method was: a) the Treasury issued new securities that were purchased by the commercial banks; b) when the commercial banks needed reserves to do so, the Federal Reserve bought some of the old bonds from the commercial banks through the Open Market Account; these were added to the commercial banks reserve account. This permitted the commercial banks to buy as much as the Treasury needed, while being assured by the Federal Reserve that they would always have a continuous availability of reserves. Between 30 Jun 1940 and 31 Dec 1945, the commercial banks purchased $75,000 M ($75 B) and the Federal Reserve about $21,000 M ($21 B). The Federal Reserve established a minimum price for the Treasury securities, buying enough to ensure the price never went below the minimum. The purpose of maintaining prices (between 0.375% on 91 day Treasury bills to 2.5% on long-term Treasury bonds) was to prevent high interest payments on the national debt. This policy was continued until Mar 1951. Secondly, this process enabled the commercial banks to obtain excess reserves that paid interest.

31 Dec 1940: Forty-three banks failed in 1940; net losses to the FDIC FDIF totaled $3.706 M [19.2-87].

30 Jun 1941: Congress extended the period for which direct obligations of the U. S. can be used as collateral for Federal Reserve Notes until 30 Jun 1943 [19.2-88].

9 Aug 1941: President Roosevelt issued an Executive Order [19.2-89] permitting the Federal Reserve to control access to consumer credit in order to reduce demand for consumer goods and aid the war effort [19.2-90].

1 Sep 1941: The Federal Reserve Board imposed consumer credit controls via Regulation W, based on the Executive Order of 9 Aug 1941 [19.2-91]. Consumer goods were mostly unavailable during the war, and this credit control had little effect. This control took the form of specifying minimum down payments and maximum duration of the credit extended for purchase of durable goods [19.2-92].

1 Nov 1941: The Federal Reserve Board raised reserve requirements to the maximum allowed [19.2-93].

7 Dec 1941: Japan attacked the U. S. naval base at Pearl Harbor, HI (then a territory); formal entrance of the U. S. into World War II.

8 Dec 1941: Declaration of war against Japan.

11 Dec 1941: Declaration of war against Germany and Italy.

15 Dec 1941: Approximate end of the Great Depression, with the expansion of industry to support the war effort; the unemployment rate was finally under 10%.

31 Dec 1941: Fifteen banks failed in 1941, with net losses to the FDIC FDIF totaling $591,000 [19.2-94].

7 Jan 1942 - 9 Apr 1942: Battle of Bataan.

30 Jan 1942: Congress passed the Emergency Price Control Act of 1942 [19.2-95] to establish price controls during the war: **a)** (S. 1) price controls to end 30 Jun 1943 unless extended by proclamation of the President; **b)** (S. 2) granted the Price Administrator power to set prices as follows: 1) for agricultural commodities per the prices prevailing 1-15 Oct 1941; and 2) for rent, per prices prevailing 1 Apr 1941; **c)** (S. 2) granted power to the Price Administrator: 1) to enact regulations to prevent hoarding and speculation, 2) to purchase necessary supplies and provide subsidies to producers; **d)** (S. 3) granted power to the Price Administrator to set minimum prices on agricultural commodities; **e)** (S. 201) established the Office of Price Administrator; and **f)** (S. 202) authorized the Price Administrator to require record-keeping by all commodity producers, landlords, and brokers, and to compel testimony in the course of obtaining any information desired by the Price Administrator.

Freidman and Schwartz [19.2-96] observed that the shortages produced by this policy, especially motor vehicles, washing machines, refrigerators, and other durable goods were a more important factor than the price controls themselves. Also, some of these were easily evaded, and there were shortages that led to rationing of certain foods. But it also led to a large increase in personal saving, which helped the economy stabilize after price controls were lifted in mid-1947.

4 - 8 May 1942: Battle of the Coral Sea.

3 - 7 Jun 1942: Battle of Midway.

7 Jul 1942: Congress passed an amendment to the Federal Reserve Act [19.2-97]: **a)** (S. 1) changed the membership of five the Federal Open Market Committee (i.e., in addition to the seven members of the Board of Governors) to be presidents or first vice-presidents of Federal Reserve Banks, on a rotating basis; **b)** (S. 2) authorized the Federal Reserve Board of Governors, upon a vote of four members, to adjust reserve requirements separately on demand and time deposits for all three classes of member banks (those in central reserve cities, reserve cities, in neither central reserve or reserve cities); **c)** (S. 2) the legal reserve requirement must lie between those specified in the Banking Act of 1935 and twice those amounts; and **d)** (S. 3) permitted member banks to write checks against their reserve balances to "meet existing liabilities", subject to penalties determined by the Federal Reserve Board. It was through this legislation that the legal reserve requirement applying to the central reserve city banks was lowered separately from other banks [19.2-98].

7 Aug 1942 - 9 Feb 1943: Battle of Guadalcanal.

2 Oct 1942: Congress passed an amendment to the Emergency Price Control Act of 1942 (cf. 30 Jan 1942) [19.2-99]: **a)** (S. 1) authorized the President to fix prices by proclamation; **b)** (S. 3) authorized the Secretary of Agriculture to set maximum and parity prices on agricultural products; **c)** (S. 4) permitted the President to set wages and salaries, so long as they do not conflict with the Fair Labor Standards Act of 1938 or the National Labor Relations Act; **d)** (S. 5) prohibited employers from offering or employees receiving compensation above that ordered by the President; **e)** (S. 5) permitted private employers to reduce salaries to $5,000; and **f)** (S. 7) extended the price control system to 30 Jun 1944.

8 Nov - 10 Nov 1942: Operation Torch (battles in Algeria and Morocco).

31 Dec 1942: Twenty banks failed in 1942, with net losses to the FDIC FDIF totaling $688,000 [19.2-100].

19 Feb - 25 Feb 1943: Battle of the Kasserine Pass (Tunisia).

~30 Apr 1943: The U. S. Treasury's War Loan Accounts became exempt from reserve requirements at the commercial banks [19.2-101]; this caused a reduction in required reserves, and freed up money for loans and investments.

25 May 1943: Congress extended the period for which direct obligations of the U. S. can be used as collateral for Federal Reserve Notes until 30 Jun 1945 [19.2-102].

31 Dec 1943: Five banks failed in 1943, with net losses to the FDIC FDIF totaling $123,000 [19.2-103].

22 Jan - 5 Jun 1944: Battle of Anzio (Italy).

6 Jun - 24 Jul 1944: Battle of Normandy (a.k.a. D-Day) (France).

15 Jun - 9 Jul 1944: Battle of Saipan.

23 Oct - 26 Oct 1944: Battle of Leyte Gulf.

16 Dec 1944 - 25 Jan 1945: Battle of the Bulge.

31 Dec 1944: Two banks failed in 1944, with net losses to the FDIC FDIF totaling $40,000 [19.2-104].

5 Feb 1945: The Federal Reserve modified margin requirements [19.2-105]: a) brokers loans on listed stocks = 50%; b) broker loans for short sales = 50%; and c) bank loans on stocks = 40%.

15 Feb 1945: Approximate beginning of a recession [19.2-106].

19 Feb - 26 Mar 1945: Battle of Iwo Jima.

26 Mar - 29 Mar 1945: Battle of Frankfurt.

1 Apr - 22 Jun 1945: Battle of Okinawa.

16 Apr - 20 Apr 1945: Battle of Nuremberg.

8 May 1945: V-E Day: the last German army is defeated; end of the war in Europe.

12 Jun 1945: Congress passed an amendment to the Federal Reserve Act (FRA) [19.2-107]: **a)** (S. 1) modified FRA S. 16, paragraph 3 such that Federal Reserve Banks are to maintain reserves in the form of gold certificates (was gold or lawful money) of 25% (was 35%) against deposits; **b)** (S. 1) modified FRA S. 16, paragraph 3 such that Federal Reserve Banks are to maintain reserves of 25% (was 40%) in the form of gold certificates (originally was gold) against Federal Reserve Notes in circulation (with the other 75% collateralized by any combination of gold certificates, U. S. government securities, or commercial paper eligible for rediscount by member banks); **c)** (S. 1) changed FRA S. 11(c) to impose graduated taxation of Federal Reserve Banks (by the Federal Reserve Board) if reserves fell below prescribed levels (now 25% vs. 40%); **d)** (S. 2) modified FRA S. 16, paragraph 2 such that gold was eliminated as a type of collateral against Federal Reserve Notes; **e)** (S. 3) abolished the authority of the Federal Reserve to issue Federal Reserve Bank Notes; and **f)** (S. 5) abolished the authority of the Treasury Secretary or President to issue United States Notes (greenbacks) (cf. 12 May 1933). This made the use of direct U. S. government obligations as collateral for Federal Reserve Notes permanent (cf. 25 May 1943). The Federal Reserve Banks now must maintain 25%

reserves for both Federal Reserve Notes and deposits; although Federal Reserve Notes are to be fully backed: 1) by 25% in gold certificates, and 2) 75% in a combination of gold certificates, U. S. government securities, and eligible commercial paper rediscounted [19.2-108].

30 Jun 1945: Congress passed joint resolution as an amendment to the Emergency Price Control Act of 1942 [19.2-109]: **a)** (S. 2) extended price controls until 30 Jun 1946; **b)** (S. 3) changed procedures for determining parity and maximum prices and rents by the Price Administrator; and **c)** (S. 5) price controls on agricultural products was expanded to include livestock.

5 Jul 1945: The Federal Reserve modified margin requirements [19.2-110]: a) brokers loans on listed stocks = 75%; b) broker loans for short sales = 75%; and c) bank loans on stocks = 75%.

31 Jul 1945: Congress passed the Export-Import Bank Act [19.2-111] (cf. 2 Feb 1934). Among its provisions: **a)** (S. 2) continued the Export-Import Bank as an official independent agency of the United States government, but increased its powers to include making loans, discounts, rediscount, guarantor of notes and bills of exchange to promote foreign trade; **b)** (S. 1) as a matter of policy, to supplement private capital and not compete with it; **c)** (S. 3) the Export-Import Bank to be managed by the Administrator of Foreign Economic Administration, the Secretary of State, and three others to be appointed by the President; **d)** (S. 4) the U. S. is to subscribe to $1 B of capital stock in the Export-Import Bank; and **e)** (S. 6) the Export-Import Bank was authorized to issue bonds, notes, and debt instruments, but only up to 2.5 times its authorized capital.

31 Jul 1945: Congress passed the Bretton Woods Agreement Act [19.2-112, 19.2-113]. Among its provisions: **a)** (S. 2) authorized the President to accept U. S. membership in the International Monetary Fund (IMF) and International Bank for Reconstruction and Development (IBRD) per the United Nations Monetary and Financial Conference of 22 Jul 1944; **b)** (S. 3) the President to appoint directors of the IMF and IBRD; **c)** (S. 4) created a National Advisory Council on International Monetary and Financial Problems, consisting of: Treasury Secretary, Secretary of State, Secretary of Commerce, Chairman of the Board of the Governors of the Federal Reserve System, and the Chairman of the Board of the Export-Import Bank to coordinate policies and operations of the U. S. members of the IMF and IBRD; **d)** (S. 5) requires Congressional approval to: 1) change the U. S. quota of the IMF; 2) make change to the value of the dollar expressed in gold (replaces President's authority per the Banking Act of 1935, which expired in 1943); 3) subscribe to additional shares in the IMF; 4) accept any amendments to either the IMF of IBRD charter; or 5) make any loan to the IMF or IBRD; and **e)** (S. 7) authorized the Treasury Secretary to pay $4.125 B in gradual subscriptions to the IMF or the IRBD.

The main objective of the Bretton Woods Agreement was to recognize the U. S. dollar as a de facto reserve currency, which was pegged to gold at $35 per ozt., and the other 43 nations that signed up agreed to maintain their currencies within 1% of the existing exchange rate. This provision thus fixed exchange rates among the 44 currencies, and required the other 43 nations to buy dollars in order to support their exchange rate. The purposes of the IMF [19.2-114] were to assist nations that were experiencing balance of payments difficulties and make loans to them as appropriate, and attempted to institutionalize the system of fiat currencies domestically and a gold standard for foreign trade. "Drawing rights" was method by which a nation could access the International Monetary Fund in order to cover short-term balance-of-payment deficits (using its own currency to buy needed currency on a temporary basis, subject to certain conditions).

2 Sep 1945: V-J Day: Japan surrendered, the war in the Pacific ended; the end of WWII.

15 Oct 1945: Approximate end of the recession (cf. 15 Feb 1945) [19.2-115].

31 Dec 1945: One bank failed in 1945, with no losses to the FDIC FDIF [19.2-116].

21 Jan 1946: The Federal Reserve modified margin requirements [19.2-117]: a) brokers loans on listed stocks = 100%; b) broker loans for short sales = 100%; and c) bank loans on stocks = 100% (i.e., no lending at all on these categories).

20 Feb 1946: Congress passed the Employment Act of 1946 [19.2-118] in which the government assumed responsibility for maintaining a healthy economy. Among its provisions: **a)** (S. 2) required the President to submit an "Economic Report" to Congress within 60 days of each Congressional session, providing data on employment, production, purchasing power, trends thereof, an assessment of how current federal economic policy will affect each, and recommendations for carrying out the general policy per Section 2; **b)** (S. 4) established a Council of Economic Advisors to the President to make assessments and recommendations; and **c)** (S. 5) Congress to establish a Joint Committee to study the Economic Report and make recommendations on legislation. This legislation confirmed the government's view that it had responsibility for maintain full employment by controlling production and the value of money [19.2-119]. It is worth quoting the Section 2 policy statement in its entirety:

> "Sec. 2. The Congress hereby declares that it is the continuing policy and responsibility of the Federal Government to use all practicable means consistent with its needs and obligations and other essential considerations of national policy, with the assistance and cooperation of industry, agriculture, labor, and State and local governments, to coordinate and utilize all its plans, functions, and resources for the purpose of creating and maintaining, in a manner calculated to foster and promote free competitive enterprise and the general welfare, conditions under which there will be afforded useful employment opportunities, including self-employment, for those able, willing, and seeking to work, and to promote maximum employment, production, and purchasing power."

25 Jul 1946: Congress passed a joint resolution [19.2-120]: **a)** (S. 2) extended the Emergency Price Control Act of 1942 and the Stabilization Act to 30 Jun 1947; **b)** (S. 3) required the President before 15 Jan 1947 to provide a transition plan to end the price controls; and **c)** (S. 3) all price controls on non-agricultural products to end 31 Dec 1947.

31 Jul 1946: The official Treasury purchase price for silver was adjusted from $0.7095 to $0.905 per ozt. (i.e., reduction of seigniorage from 45 to 30%) [19.2-121]. The market price of silver ranged from $0.71 to $0.87 per ozt. between 1946 and 1955, after which it rose to about $0.90. The Treasury bought very little after 1955 [19.2-122].

31 Dec 1946: One bank failed in 1946, with no losses to the FDIC FDIF [19.2-123].

1 Feb 1947: The Federal Reserve modified margin requirements [19.2-124]: a) brokers loans on listed stocks = 75%; b) broker loans for short sales = 75%; and c) bank loans on stocks = 75%.

23 Apr 1947: The Federal Reserve Board adopted a new method of turning over profits to the Treasury [19.2-125]. It now turned over 90% of its net earnings.

28 Apr 1947: Congress passed an amendment to the Federal Reserve Act [19.2-126]; modifying section 14(b) to permit the Federal Reserve banks to purchase U. S. government securities directly from the U. S. Treasury. This authority was limited to an aggregate of $5,000 M ($5 B), and the authority to do so was limited to 30 Jun 1950. However, this authority has routinely been extended.

9 Jun 1947: Congress passed an act re-incorporating the Export-Import Bank [19.2-127].

30 Jun 1947: The exemption of Treasury's War Loan Accounts from reserve requirements at the commercial banks expired (cf. 30 Apr 1943) [19.2-128].

5 Aug 1947: Congress passed a law [19.2-129] modifying the Federal Reserve and FDIC: **a)** (S. 1) retired the stock of the existing Federal Deposit Insurance Corporation (cf. 16 Jun 1933, 23 Aug 1935), transferring it to the Treasury (repaid the initial funding provided by the Federal Reserve and Treasury); and **b)** (S. 4) authorized the FDIC to borrow up to $3,000 M ($3 B) from the Treasury for insurance purposes to finance its operations.

30 Oct 1947: The U. S. signed onto the General Agreement on Tariffs and Trade (GATT), to go into effect 1 Jan 1948. It was intended to restore international trade after World War II. It was ultimately absorbed into the World Trade Organization 1 Jan 1995.

1 Nov 1947: The authority of the Federal Reserve Board to regulate consumer credit (Regulation W) (cf. 9 Aug 1941) was terminated [19.2-130].

31 Dec 1947: Two banks failed in 1947, with net losses to the FDIC FDIF totaling $59,000 [19.2-131].

1 Jan 1948: The GATT agreement went into effect.

14 Jun 1948: The U. S. joined the World Health Organization (WHO) [19.2-132].

16 Aug 1948: Congress passed legislation "to aid in protecting the nation's economy against inflationary pressures" [19.2-133]: **a)** (S. 1) authorized the Federal Reserve Board to resume implementation of Regulation W (cf. 1 Nov 1941), which controlled terms and conditions of consumer credit, supposedly to restrain the growth in prices; **b)** (S. 2) permitted the Federal Reserve Board to adjust legal reserve requirements within the following limits: 1) for banks in central reserve cities, up to 7.5% against time deposits, and up to 30% against demand deposits; 2) for banks in reserve cities; up to 7.5% against time deposits and up to 24% against demand deposits; and 3) for all others, up to 7.5% against time deposits and up to 18% against demand deposits; and **c)** (S. 2) the reserve requirement changes limited to 30 Jun 1949 (after which they would revert back to the old limits).

The commercial banks began selling their government securities holdings in order to obtain the higher reserves [19.2-134], and because the Federal Reserve policy was to maintain prices of government bonds, it was obligated to buy all of them; about $2,000 M ($2 B).

15 Nov 1948: Approximate beginning of a recession [19.2-135].

31 Dec 1948: Three banks failed in 1948, with net losses to the FDIC FDIF totaling $641,000 [19.2-136].

30 Jun 1949: Regulation W expired (cf. 16 Aug 1948).

15 Oct 1949: Approximate end of the recession (cf. 15 Nov 1948) [19.2-137].

31 Oct 1949: Congress passed the Agricultural Act of 1949 [19.2-138] providing federal government price supports and regulation for a variety of agricultural products, to be administered by the Secretary of Agriculture. Generally the government was to assign production quotas via acreage limitations and to buy excess production in order to maintain prices at 90% of parity.

31 Dec 1949: Four banks failed in 1949, with net losses to the FDIC FDIF totaling $369,000 [19.2-139].

27 Jun 1950: President Truman ordered U. S. forces to Korea as a "police action" under U. N. auspices after North Korea invaded South Korea. This led to an expansion of Federal Reserve credit through the purchase by the Federal Reserve of U. S. bonds to fund the war effort [19.2-140].

30 Jun 1950: Congress extended [19.2-141] the authority of Federal Reserve banks to buy U. S. securities directly from the U. S. Treasury until 30 Jun 1952 (cf. 28 Apr 1947).

5 Jul 1950: Battle of Osan.

17 Aug 1950: Congress passed a revision to the banking laws [19.2-142]: **a)** (S. 2) permitted national banks to merge or consolidate with a State-chartered bank in the same State; **b)** (S. 3) the merged organization then becomes a bank regulated by the State; **c)** (S. 4) such mergers permitted only if permitted by the State; **d)** (S. 6, 7) if the State bank was a member of the Federal Reserve, the merged organization to continue as an insured bank unless it withdraws from the Federal Reserve system; and **e)** (S. 7) if the State bank was not a member of the Federal Reserve, the merged organization may apply to become a member.

8 Sep 1950: Congress passed the Defense Production Act [19.2-143]. Most of it involves defense procurement, but a few provisions pertain to banking and regulation: **a)** (S. 402) granted the President authority to issue price and wage controls, except for real property, professional services, insurance, newspapers, and common carriers; **b)** (S. 501) authorized the President or designees to intervene and resolve labor disputes in order to maintain uninterrupted production; **c)** (S. 601, 602) resume control of consumer credit with regard to real estate credit (loans, mortgages, rental agreements, deeds of trust, discounts, and conditional sales); and **d)** (S. 716) authorities to terminate 30 Jun 1951. This was done supposedly to restrain the growth in prices due to the Korean War [19.2-144].

15 Sep 1950: Battle of Inchon.

21 Sep 1950: Congress passed the Federal Deposit Insurance Act [19.2-145, 19.2-146], amending the previous law (cf. 5 Aug 1947). Among its provisions: **a)** (S. 1) formally established the FDIC as an independent agency, separate from the Federal Reserve; **b)** (S. 3, 10) the maximum insured deposits for accounts in Savings and Loans also increased to $10,000; **c)** (S. 4) all banks that are members of the Federal Reserve fall under the jurisdiction of the FDIC; **d)** (S. 5) banks that are not members of the Federal Reserve may join the FDIC; **e)** (S. 7) annual assessment rate for membership is 0.0833% of deposit liabilities (with some deductions allowed); **f)** (S. 11) the Temporary Federal Deposit Insurance Fund and Fund for Mutuals that was established per Section 12B of the Federal Reserve Act as amended by the 1933 Banking Act (cf. 16 Jul 1933) was consolidated into a Permanent Insurance Fund under the FDIC; **g)** (S. 11) the limit on insured deposits was increased from $5,000 (cf. 1 Jul 1934) to $10,000; **h)** (S. 14) permitted the FDIC to borrow up to $3 B from the Treasury for carrying out insurance provisions; **i)** (S. 15) required permission from the FDIC before insured banks could merge, or consolidate with a non-insured bank, or assume liability for non-insured bank deposits; and **j)** (S. 18) prohibited payment of interest on demand deposits held in insured banks that are not members of the Federal Reserve.

27 Nov - 13 Dec 1950: Battle of Chosin Reservoir.

31 Dec 1950: Four banks failed in 1950, with net losses to the FDIC FDIF totaling $1.385 M [19.2-147].

19.3 Data, 1933-1950

Figures 19.3-1 and 19.3-2 show the U. S. government revenue and expenditures for 1933 to 1940. Figures 19.3-3 and 19.3-4 show the same for 1941 to 1950. The split in the figures is due to a difference in the reporting method. Notice that the units have changed to millions USD.

			U. S. Government Revenue, 1933-1940 (millions USD)									
			Internal Revenue			Miscellaneous						
Day	Year	Customs	Income and Profits taxes	Social Security Tax	Misc.	Sales of Public Lands	Surplus Postal Covered Into Treasury	Direct Tax Plus Other Misc.	Postal	Refunds of Receipts	Capital Transfers	Total
30 Jun	1933	250.750	746.206	0.000	858.218	0.103	0.000	224.420	587.631	-58.484	0.000	2,608.844
30 Jun	1934	313.434	817.961	0.000	1,822.642	0.099	0.000	161.417	586.733	-51.286	0.000	3,651.001
30 Jun	1935	343.353	1,099.119	0.000	2,178.571	0.087	0.000	179.337	630.795	-70.553	0.000	4,360.709
30 Jun	1936	386.812	1,426.575	0.000	2,086.276	0.074	0.000	216.219	665.343	-47.020	0.000	4,734.280
30 Jun	1937	486.357	2,157.527	252.161	1,922.452	0.071	0.000	210.272	726.201	-49.990	0.250	5,705.302
30 Jun	1938	359.187	2,634.618	604.449	2,048.252	0.096	0.000	208.060	728.634	-93.037	0.000	6,490.258
30 Jun	1939	318.837	2,182.300	631.224	1,844.697	0.248	0.000	187.517	745.955	-61.427	0.000	5,849.352
30 Jun	1940	348.591	2,125.325	712.218	1,927.880	0.072	0.000	273.039	766.949	-78.705	43.757	6,119.125

1. The data for the revenue and expenditures for 1933 to 1940 is from Henry Morgenthau, "Annual Report of the Secretary of the Treasury on the State of the Finances for the Fiscal Year Ended June 30, 1940", Washington: U. S. Government Printing Office, 1940, pp. 645, 648, 649. However, the 1956 Annual Treasury Report, p. 322 calls out refunds of receipts and capital transfers for 1933 and 1940; these have been included here. The 1956 total receipts also excludes Postal revenue, which is included here.

Figure 19.3-1: U. S Government Revenue, 1933-1940

			U. S. Government Expenditures, 1933-1940 (millions USD)								
			Ordinary Disbursements								
Day	Year	Civil & Misc.	War Dep't, (including Rivers, Canals, and Panama Canal)	Navy Dep't	Indians	Pensions	Postal Deficiencies	Interest on Public Debt	Public Debt Retirement Chargeable vs. Ordinary Receipts	Postal Expenditures Exclusive of Postal Deficiencies	Total
30 Jun	1933	2,000.130	449.395	349.562	22.722	234.990	117.380	689.365	461.605	582.626	4,907.776
30 Jun	1934	4,153.844	408.895	297.029	23.373	319.322	52.003	756.617	359.864	578.764	6,949.711
30 Jun	1935	4,797.652	489.155	436.448	27.919	373.805	63.970	820.926	573.558	632.633	8,216.066
30 Jun	1936	6,254.318	618.919	529.032	28.876	399.066	86.039	749.397	403.240	667.621	9,736.506
30 Jun	1937	5,650.914	628.348	556.884	36.933	396.047	41.897	866.384	103.971	730.919	9,012.299
30 Jun	1938	4,591.321	644.525	596.278	33.378	402.779	44.259	926.281	65.465	728.187	8,032.474
30 Jun	1939	5,892.880	695.780	672.969	46.964	416.721	41.237	940.540	58.246	743.410	9,508.748
30 Jun	1940	5,650.600	907.160	891.625	37.821	429.178	40.870	1,040.936	129.184	767.035	9,894.409

1. The data for the expenditures for 1933 to 1940 is from Henry Morgenthau, "Annual Report of the Secretary of the Treasury on the State of the Finances for the Fiscal Year Ended June 30, 1940", Washington: U. S. Government Printing Office, 1940, pp. 645, 648, 649.
2. The 1956 Annual Treasury Report excludes Postal dispursements from the total expenditures; but they are included here per the 1940 Treasury Report.

Figure 19.3-2: U. S. Government Expenditures, 1933-1940

			Income taxes				Social Insurance				
Day	Year	Customs Duties	Individual	Corporate	Excise Taxes	Estate and Gift Taxes	OASDI & Disability (Off-Budget)	Medicare & Retirements (on-budget)	Federal Reserve Deposits	Other Misc.	Net Receipts
30 Jun	1941	365	1,314	2,124	2,552	403	688	1,252	0	14	8,712
30 Jun	1942	369	3,263	4,719	3,399	420	896	1,557	0	11	14,634
30 Jun	1943	308	6,505	9,557	4,096	441	1,130	1,913	0	50	24,001
30 Jun	1944	417	19,705	14,838	4,759	507	1,292	2,181	0	48	43,747
30 Jun	1945	341	18,372	15,988	6,265	637	1,310	2,141	0	105	45,159
30 Jun	1946	424	16,098	11,883	6,998	668	1,238	1,877	0	109	39,296
30 Jun	1947	477	17,935	8,615	7,211	771	1,459	1,963	15	69	38,514
30 Jun	1948	403	19,315	9,678	7,356	890	1,616	2,134	100	68	41,560
30 Jun	1949	367	15,552	11,192	7,502	780	1,690	2,091	187	54	39,415
30 Jun	1950	407	15,755	10,449	7,550	698	2,106	2,232	192	55	39,443

U. S. Government Revenue, 1941-1950 (millions USD)

1. The revenue data for 1941 to 1950 is from the OMB White House, file = HIST_FY21.pdf, Tables 2.1 and 2.5

Figure 19.3-3: U. S. Government Revenue, 1941-1950

Day	Year	National Defense	Education, Training, Employment, Social Services	Health	Medicare	Income Security	Social Security [1]	Veterans	Physical Resources [2]	Interest on Debt	International Affairs	Agriculture	Other [3]	Undistributed Offsetting Receipts [4]	Total
30 Jun	1941	6,435	1,592	60	0	1,855	91	560	1,782	943	145	339	398	-547	13,653
30 Jun	1942	25,658	1,062	71	0	1,828	137	501	3,892	1,052	968	344	518	-894	35,137
30 Jun	1943	66,699	375	92	0	1,739	177	276	6,433	1,529	1,286	343	828	-1,221	78,555
30 Jun	1944	79,143	160	174	0	1,503	217	-126	5,471	2,219	1,449	1,275	1,140	-1,320	91,304
30 Jun	1945	82,965	134	211	0	1,137	267	110	1,747	3,112	1,913	1,635	870	-1,389	92,712
30 Jun	1946	42,681	85	201	0	2,384	358	2,465	836	4,111	1,935	610	1,035	-1,468	55,232
30 Jun	1947	12,808	102	177	0	2,820	466	6,344	1,227	4,204	5,791	814	1,295	-1,552	34,496
30 Jun	1948	9,105	191	162	0	2,499	558	6,457	2,243	4,341	4,566	69	1,216	-1,643	29,764
30 Jun	1949	13,150	178	197	0	3,174	657	6,599	3,104	4,523	6,052	1,924	1,056	-1,779	38,835
30 Jun	1950	13,724	241	268	0	4,097	781	8,834	3,667	4,812	4,673	2,049	1,233	-1,817	42,562

U. S. Government Expenditures, 1941-1950 (millions USD)

1. Social Security expenditures during this period were all "off-budget".
2. "Physical Resources" includes Energy, Natural Resources and Environment, Commerce and Housing Credit, Transportation, and Community & Regional Development.
3. "Other" includes General Science, Space & Technology, Administration of Justice, General Government and Allowances.
4. "Offsetting Receipts" is a combination of new debt and intra-government transfers from Trust Funds.
5. The expenditure data for 1941 to 1950 is from the OMB White House, file = HIST_FY21.pdf, Table 3.1.

Figure 19.3-4: U. S. Government Expenditures, 1941-1950

Figure 19.3-5 shows the national debt and per-capita debt for 1933 to 1950. Refer to the Introduction to Part 2 for a sense of wages vs. per-capita national debt.

Day	Year	Principal ($) [1]	Population [2]	Debt per Capita ($) [2]	Day	Year	Principal ($) [1]	Population [2]	Debt per Capita ($) [2]
30 Jun	1933	22,538,672,560	125,891,401	179.03	30 Jun	1942	72,422,445,116	135,997,263	532.53
30 Jun	1934	27,053,141,414	126,787,648	213.37	30 Jun	1943	136,696,090,330	137,913,330	991.17
30 Jun	1935	28,700,892,625	127,683,895	224.78	30 Jun	1944	201,003,387,221	139,829,397	1,437.49
30 Jun	1936	33,778,543,494	128,580,141	262.70	30 Jun	1945	258,682,187,410	141,745,464	1,824.98
30 Jun	1937	36,424,613,732	129,476,388	281.32	30 Jun	1946	269,422,099,173	143,661,530	1,875.39
30 Jun	1938	37,164,740,315	130,372,635	285.07	30 Jun	1947	256,562,383,109	145,577,597	1,762.38
30 Jun	1939	40,439,532,411	131,268,882	308.07	30 Jun	1948	251,131,246,513	147,493,664	1,702.66
30 Jun	1940	42,967,531,038	132,165,129	325.10	30 Jun	1949	251,707,359,860	149,409,731	1,684.68
30 Jun	1941	48,961,443,536	134,081,196	365.16	30 Jun	1950	256,087,352,351	151,325,798	1,692.29

U. S. National Debt, 1933-1950 (USD)

1. Public debt data from 1933 to 1950 is from the Annual Report of the Secretary of the Treasury, 1980, pp. 61, 62.
2. Population values are based on the dicennial census from the Census Bureau, and linearly interpolated. Per-capita is based on these values.

Figure 19.3-5: National Debt and Per-Capita Share Thereof, 1933-1950

Figures 19.3-6 through 19.3-13 show the balance sheet assets and liabilities of the Federal Reserve and commercial banking system as a whole for 1933 to 1950, as described in Appendix A. The sources for the data are cited in Appendix B.

Assets of the Federal Reserve & Commercial System, 1933-1937 (millions USD)										
				Federal Reserve Loans & Investments		Commercial Bank Loans and Investments				
Day	Year	Gold Stock [3]	Treasury Currency Outstanding [3]	U. S. Government Securities [3]	Discounts & Advances [2]	Loans [5]	U. S. Government Securities [5]	Other [5]	Total Assets	Note
29 Mar	1933	3,983	2,287	1,838	869	*18,215*	*7,376*	*7,129*	*41,697*	8
28 Jun	1933	4,031	2,296	1,975	199	16,349	7,476	6,532	38,858	
27 Sep	1933	4,037	2,279	2,274	140	16,298	7,879	6,397	*39,303*	8
27 Dec	1933	4,036	2,304	2,432	222	16,246	8,282	6,261	39,783	1
28 Mar	1934	7,681	2,356	2,432	82	15,973	9,295	6,498	44,317	8
27 Jun	1934	7,846	2,364	2,430	32	15,700	10,307	6,735	45,414	
26 Sep	1934	7,976	2,409	2,430	26	*14,894*	*11,022*	6,873	*45,630*	8
26 Dec	1934	8,228	2,504	2,430	15	14,088	11,736	7,011	46,012	1
27 Mar	1935	8,563	2,535	2,430	13	*14,499*	*12,226*	6,987	47,253	8
26 Jun	1935	9,109	2,508	2,430	12	14,909	12,716	6,963	48,647	
25 Sep	1935	9,297	2,382	2,430	15	*15,014*	*13,196*	7,075	49,409	8
31 Dec	1935	10,125	2,476	2,431	10	15,119	13,676	7,187	51,024	1
25 Mar	1936	10,777	2,502	2,430	11	*15,339*	*14,443*	7,449	*52,951*	8
24 Jun	1936	10,600	2,500	2,430	9	15,559	15,210	7,711	54,019	
30 Sep	1936	10,845	2,512	2,430	12	*15,959*	*15,272*	7,746	*54,775*	6, 8
30 Dec	1936	11,251	2,530	2,430	8	16,358	15,334	7,780	55,691	6
31 Mar	1937	11,574	2,541	2,430	15	*16,895*	*14,949*	7,629	*56,032*	6, 8
30 Jun	1937	12,318	2,550	2,526	14	17,432	14,563	7,477	56,880	6
29 Sep	1937	12,734	2,596	2,526	27	*17,266*	*14,360*	7,277	*56,786*	6, 8
29 Dec	1937	12,760	2,634	2,564	16	17,100	14,156	7,077	56,307	6

1. BMS1943 Table 3 (call date) does not distinguish between US Gov't and other securities. Split is estimated from adjacent data.
2. Discounts and Advances by Federal Reserve per BMS1943, Table 103 to Jun 1936; per Federal Reserve Bulletins afterward.
3. Gold Stock, Treasury Currency Outstanding, U. S. Securities by Federal Reserve per BMS1943, Table 103 (Wednesday dates).
4. Commercial Bank data per BMS1943, Table 3 to Dec 1941; per Federal Reserve Bulletins on Wednesday dates afterward.
5. Commercial Bank data estimated per adjacent values (ratios of preceding and following figures).
6. BMS1943 does not distinguish "US Securities" from "Other" for 1936 ff; data in Federal Reserve Bulletins used for these dates.
7. Increase in gold stock in Mar 1934 due to devaluation of the dollar from $20.67 per troy oz. to $35.00 per troy oz.
8. Items in italics linearly interpolated from adjacent data.
9. BMS1943 is: Board of Governors of the Federal Reserve, Banking and Monetary Statistics, 1914-1941, Washington DC: Publication Services, Division of Administrative Services, Board of Governors of the Federal Reserve System, Nov 1943

Figure 19.3-6: Banking System Assets, 1933-1937

Liabilities of the Federal Reserve and Commercial System, 1933-1937 (millions USD)											
				At Federal Reserve Banks		At Commercial Banks					
Day	Year	Currency Outside Banks [1]	Treasury Cash [3]	Treasury Demand Deposits [5]	Foreign Demand Deposits [5]	Demand Deposits [1]	Treasury Demand Deposits [1]	Time Deposits [1]	Capital [4]	Total Liabilities	Error (%)	Note
29 Mar	1933	*4,715*	*250*	56	30	*15,070*	680	*12,240*	5,123	*38,164*	8.47	7
28 Jun	1933	*4,761*	*264*	81	15	14,411	852	10,849	4,837	36,070	7.17	6
27 Sep	1933	*4,772*	*290*	56	22	*14,723*	934	*10,934*	4,900	36,630	6.80	7
27 Dec	1933	*4,782*	315	71	7	15,035	1,016	11,019	4,962	37,207	6.48	6
28 Mar	1934	*4,721*	*1,696*	42	6	*15,965*	1,375	11,504	5,034	41,327	8.97	7
27 Jun	1934	*4,659*	3,077	115	5	16,894	1,733	11,988	5,105	43,576	4.05	6
26 Sep	1934	*4,657*	*3,129*	138	11	*17,677*	*1,724*	12,101	5,080	44,516	2.44	7
26 Dec	1934	*4,655*	3,181	136	18	18,459	1,715	12,213	5,054	45,431	1.26	6
27 Mar	1935	*4,719*	3,086	202	17	*19,446*	*1,263*	12,517	5,084	46,334	1.94	7
26 Jun	1935	*4,783*	2,991	81	27	20,433	811	12,820	5,114	47,060	3.26	6
25 Sep	1935	*4,850*	*3,051*	102	18	*21,274*	860	*12,995*	5,130	48,279	2.29	7
31 Dec	1935	4,917	3,110	324	33	22,115	909	13,170	5,145	49,723	2.55	6
25 Mar	1936	*5,070*	*3,344*	760	63	*22,948*	1,026	13,438	5,190	*51,837*	2.10	7
24 Jun	1936	*5,222*	3,577	793	58	23,780	1,142	13,706	5,235	53,513	0.94	6
30 Sep	1936	*5,369*	2,973	233	59	24,632	1,067	13,876	5,287	53,495	2.34	7
30 Dec	1936	*5,516*	2,368	154	73	25,483	991	14,046	5,339	53,970	3.09	6
31 Mar	1937	*5,503*	*2,907*	205	93	*25,341*	829	14,280	5,520	*54,675*	2.42	7
30 Jun	1937	5,489	3,445	131	148	25,198	666	14,513	5,700	55,290	2.80	
29 Sep	1937	*5,564*	*3,533*	189	219	*24,579*	745	14,646	5,700	55,174	2.84	7
29 Dec	1937	5,638	3,620	187	226	23,959	824	14,779	5,700	54,933	2.44	

1. These figures per BMS1943, Table 9 (call dates), from 1933 to 1941; per Federal Reserve Bulletins on Wednesday dates afterward.
2. BMS1976, Table 1.3 (single-date) had Demand Deposits and Treasury Demand Deposits combined; split estimated per adjacent data.
3. Treasury Cash figures from Federal Reserve Bulletins as noted. Increase in Jun 1934 due to devaluation of dollar from $20.66 to $35.00 per oz. 31 Jan 1934.
4. Capital data from BMS1943, Table 18 (call dates) for 1933 to 1936, and Jun 1940; from BMS1976, Table 1.3 for Dec 1942, from Federal Reserve Bulletins otherwise.
5. Treasury and Foreign Demand Deposits at Federal Reserve per BMS1943, Table 93 (monthly averages of daily figures) from 1933 to 1941.
6. Capital figures are from BMS1943, Table 18 (call dates); they do not correspond with later figures from Jan 1948 and Feb 1953 Federal Reserve Bulletins.
7. Items in italics linearly interpolated from adjacent data.
8. BMS1943 is: Board of Governors of the Federal Reserve, Banking and Monetary Statistics, 1914-1941, Washington DC: Publication Services, Division of Administrative Services, Board of Governors of the Federal Reserve System, Nov 1943

Figure 19.3-7: Banking System Liabilities, 1933-1937

				Federal Reserve Loans & Investments		Commercial Bank Loans and Investments				
Day	Year	Gold Stock [3]	Treasury Currency Outstanding [3]	U. S. Government Securities [3]	Discounts & Advances [2]	Loans [5]	U. S. Government Securities [5]	Other [5]	Total Assets	Note
30 Mar	1938	12,794	2,680	2,564	13	16,577	14,099	7,046	55,773	6, 8
29 Jun	1938	12,962	2,712	2,564	11	16,053	14,042	7,014	55,358	6
28 Sep	1938	13,714	2,738	2,564	10	16,209	14,557	7,124	56,915	6, 8
28 Dec	1938	14,508	2,790	2,564	8	16,364	15,071	7,234	58,539	6
29 Mar	1939	15,160	2,837	2,564	4	16,394	15,386	7,239	59,583	6, 8
28 Jun	1939	16,093	2,879	2,551	6	16,423	15,700	7,244	60,896	6
27 Sep	1939	16,925	2,914	2,804	7	16,833	16,000	7,184	62,667	6, 8
27 Dec	1939	17,620	2,963	2,489	8	17,243	16,300	7,124	63,747	6
27 Mar	1940	18,413	2,990	2,475	2	17,329	16,427	7,153	64,788	6, 8
26 Jun	1940	19,871	3,012	2,473	2	17,414	16,553	7,181	66,506	6
25 Sep	1940	21,166	3,041	2,434	5	18,103	17,156	7,276	69,181	6, 8
31 Dec	1940	21,995	3,087	2,184	3	18,792	17,759	7,371	71,191	6
26 Mar	1941	22,359	3,108	2,184	1	19,573	18,927	7,274	73,426	6, 8
25 Jun	1941	22,620	3,148	2,184	2	20,353	20,095	7,177	75,579	6
24 Sep	1941	22,749	3,194	2,184	12	21,032	20,942	7,200	77,313	6, 8
31 Dec	1941	22,737	3,247	2,254	3	21,711	21,788	7,223	78,963	6
25 Mar	1942	22,684	3,274	2,244	6	20,980	24,099	7,102	80,389	6, 8
24 Jun	1942	22,735	3,313	2,583	5	20,249	26,410	6,980	82,275	6
30 Sep	1942	22,754	3,353	3,567	8	20,050	33,474	6,991	90,197	5, 6, 8
30 Dec	1942	22,726	3,628	5,989	5	19,217	41,373	6,801	99,739	6

Assets of the Federal Reserve & Commercial System, 1938-1942 (millions USD)

1. BMS1943 Table 3 (call date) does not distinguish between US Gov't and other securities. Split is estimated from adjacent data.
2. Discounts and Advances by Federal Reserve per BMS1943, Table 103 to Jun 1936; per Federal Reserve Bulletins afterward.
3. Gold Stock, Treasury Currency Outstanding, U. S. Securities by Federal Reserve per BMS1943, Table 103 (Wednesday dates).
4. Commercial Bank data per BMS1943, Table 3 to Dec 1941; per Federal Reserve Bulletins on Wednesday dates afterward.
5. Commercial Bank data estimated per adjacent values (ratios of preceding and following figures).
6. BMS1943 does not distinguish "US Securities" from "Other" for 1936 ff; data in Federal Reserve Bulletins used for these dates.
7. Increase in gold stock in Mar 1934 due to devaluation of the dollar from $20.67 per troy oz. to $35.00 per troy oz.
8. Items in italics linearly interpolated from adjacent data.
9. BMS1943 is: Board of Governors of the Federal Reserve, Banking and Monetary Statistics, 1914-1941, Washington DC: Publication Services, Division of Administrative Services, Board of Governors of the Federal Reserve System, Nov 1943

Figure 19.3-8: Banking System Assets, 1938-1942

				At Federal Reserve Banks		At Commercial Banks						
Day	Year	Currency Outside Banks [1]	Treasury Cash [3]	Treasury Demand Deposits [5]	Foreign Demand Deposits [5]	Demand Deposits [1]	Treasury Demand Deposits [1]	Time Deposits [1]	Capital [4]	Total Liabilities	Error (%)	Note
30 Mar	1938	5,528	2,960	220	115	24,136	712	14,777	5,700	54,148	2.91	9
29 Jun	1938	5,417	2,299	966	139	24,313	599	14,776	5,700	54,209	2.08	
28 Sep	1938	5,596	2,503	704	164	25,150	744	14,776	5,650	55,287	2.86	9
28 Dec	1938	5,775	2,707	723	202	25,986	889	14,776	5,600	56,658	3.21	
29 Mar	1939	5,890	2,633	1,155	258	26,671	841	14,937	5,750	58,134	2.43	9
28 Jun	1939	6,005	2,559	929	336	27,355	792	15,097	5,900	58,973	3.16	
27 Sep	1939	6,203	2,484	610	437	28,574	819	15,193	6,356	60,676	3.18	9
27 Dec	1939	6,401	2,409	616	398	29,793	846	15,288	6,812	62,563	1.86	
27 Mar	1940	6,550	2,298	612	370	30,878	837	15,414	6,210	63,168	2.50	9
26 Jun	1940	6,699	2,186	286	545	31,962	828	15,540	5,608	63,654	4.29	6
25 Sep	1940	7,012	2,200	781	989	33,454	791	15,659	5,954	66,838	3.39	9
31 Dec	1940	7,325	2,213	337	1,130	34,945	753	15,777	6,300	68,780	3.39	
26 Mar	1941	7,765	2,330	906	1,141	36,131	753	15,853	6,703	71,581	2.51	7, 9
25 Jun	1941	8,204	2,275	1,081	1,240	37,317	753	15,928	7,106	73,904	2.22	7
24 Sep	1941	8,910	2,350	379	1,111	38,155	1,324	15,906	7,466	75,600	2.22	7, 9
31 Dec	1941	9,615	2,215	867	774	38,992	1,895	15,884	7,826	78,068	1.13	7
25 Mar	1942	10,276	2,175	472	727	40,446	3,184	15,775	7,532	80,586	-0.25	9
24 Jun	1942	10,936	2,191	139	965	41,900	4,473	15,665	7,237	83,506	-1.50	2
30 Sep	1942	12,441	2,222	661	947	45,400	6,437	16,030	7,069	91,206	-1.12	9
30 Dec	1942	13,946	2,194	811	806	48,900	8,400	16,395	6,900	98,352	1.39	8

Liabilities of the Federal Reserve and Commercial System, 1938-1942 (millions USD)

1. These figures per BMS1943, Table 9 (call dates), from 1933 to to 1941; per Federal Reserve Bulletins on Wednesday dates afterward.
2. BMS1976, Table 1.3 (single-date) had Demand Deposits and Treasury Demand Deposits combined; split estimated per adjacent data.
3. Treasury Cash figures from Federal Reserve Bulletins as noted.
4. Capital data from BMS1943, Table 18 (call dates) for 1933 to 1936, and Jun 1940; from BMS1976, Table 1.3 for Dec 1942, from Federal Reserve Bulletins otherwise.
5. Treasury and Foreign Demand Deposits at Federal Reserve per BMS1943, Table 93 (monthly averages of daily figures) from 1933 to 1941.
6. Capital figures are from BMS1943, Table 18 (call dates); they do not correspond with later figures from Jan 1948 and Feb 1953 Federal Reserve Bulletins.
7. The Treasury Demand Deposits for 1941 do not match to the ones in BMS1943, Table 93. The cause for the discrepancy is unclear.
8. Time Deposits for Dec 1940 from BMS1976, Table 1.3 (single-date figure).
9. Items in italics are linearly interpolated from adjacent data.
10. BMS1943 is: Board of Governors of the Federal Reserve, Banking and Monetary Statistics, 1914-1941, Washington DC: Publication Services, Division of Administrative Services, Board of Governors of the Federal Reserve System, Nov 1943
11. BMS1976 is: Board of Governors of the Federal Reserve, Banking and Monetary Statistics, 1941-1970, Washington DC: Publication Services, Division of Administrative Services, Board of Governors of the Federal Reserve System, Sep 1976

Figure 19.3-9: Banking System Liabilities, 1938-1942

Assets of the Federal Reserve & Commercial System, 1943-1947 (millions USD)										
				Federal Reserve Loans & Investments		Commercial Bank Loans and Investments				
Day	Year	Gold Stock	Treasury Currency Outstanding	U. S. Government Securities	Discounts & Advances	Loans	U. S. Government Securities	Other	Total Assets	Note
31 Mar	1943	22,576	3,989	5,919	13	18,565	46,752	6,695	104,509	1
30 Jun	1943	22,388	4,077	7,202	5	17,660	52,458	6,516	110,306	
29 Sep	1943	22,175	4,096	9,186	13	18,401	56,110	6,353	116,334	1
29 Dec	1943	22,044	4,096	11,615	101	19,117	59,842	6,136	122,951	
29 Mar	1944	21,600	4,092	12,297	83	20,007	64,106	6,230	128,415	1
28 Jun	1944	21,193	4,107	15,081	52	21,010	68,431	6,290	136,164	
27 Sep	1944	20,825	4,114	16,501	88	21,372	72,945	6,324	142,169	1
27 Dec	1944	20,639	4,131	19,064	153	21,664	77,558	6,329	149,538	
28 Mar	1945	20,419	4,118	19,516	218	22,665	80,815	6,548	154,299	1
27 Jun	1945	20,263	4,144	21,693	203	23,672	84,069	6,764	160,808	
26 Sep	1945	20,093	4,222	23,186	422	24,866	87,349	7,047	167,185	1
26 Dec	1945	20,065	4,334	24,037	492	26,076	90,613	7,331	172,948	
27 Mar	1946	20,257	4,478	22,974	683	26,622	87,516	7,596	170,126	1
26 Jun	1946	20,269	4,539	23,385	231	27,130	84,473	7,845	167,872	
25 Sep	1946	20,301	4,547	23,866	294	29,189	79,557	7,975	165,729	1
31 Dec	1946	20,529	4,562	23,350	163	31,122	74,780	8,091	162,597	
26 Mar	1947	20,438	4,556	22,810	287	32,408	72,650	8,316	161,465	1
25 Jun	1947	21,174	4,553	21,582	132	33,679	70,539	8,538	160,197	
24 Sep	1947	21,950	4,552	22,118	119	35,908	69,862	8,748	163,257	1
31 Dec	1947	22,754	4,562	22,559	85	38,190	69,130	8,960	166,240	

1. Commercial Bank data (Loans, U. S. Gov't Securities, and Other) estimated per adjacent values (ratios of preceding and following figures).
2. All data from is Federal Reserve Bulletins; se Appendix B for references.

Figure 10.3-10: Banking System Assets, 1943-1947

Liabilities of the Federal Reserve and Commercial System, 1943-1947 (millions USD)												
				At Federal Reserve Banks			At Commercial Banks					
Day	Year	Currency Outside Banks	Treasury Cash [2]	Treasury Demand Deposits [2]	Foreign Demand Deposits [2]	Demand Deposits	Treasury Demand Deposits	Time Deposits	Capital	Total Liabilities	Error (%)	Note
31 Mar	1943	15,814	2,224	55	879	55,000	3,000	16,900	7,201	101,073	3.29	1
30 Jun	1943	17,421	2,268	455	1,114	56,039	8,048	17,543	7,501	110,389	-0.08	3
29 Sep	1943	17,200	2,274	682	1,208	54,800	16,300	18,400	7,551	118,415	-1.79	1
29 Dec	1943	18,837	2,316	764	1,513	60,815	10,424	19,213	7,600	121,482	1.19	3
29 Mar	1944	19,500	2,329	753	1,564	59,600	14,700	20,100	7,791	126,337	1.62	1
28 Jun	1944	20,900	2,314	561	1,577	60,100	19,100	21,200	7,982	133,734	1.78	3
27 Sep	1944	22,200	2,373	483	1,262	65,500	13,500	22,800	8,341	136,459	4.02	1
27 Dec	1944	23,505	2,377	901	1,210	66,930	20,763	24,074	8,700	148,460	0.72	
28 Mar	1945	24,200	2,356	310	1,186	70,900	13,400	25,700	8,950	147,002	4.73	1
27 Jun	1945	25,097	2,314	687	1,298	69,053	24,381	27,171	9,200	159,201	1.00	
26 Sep	1945	26,200	2,263	961	1,051	75,400	14,300	29,100	10,090	159,365	4.68	1
26 Dec	1945	26,490	2,283	1,199	863	75,851	24,608	30,135	10,979	172,408	0.31	
27 Mar	1946	26,100	2,298	1,397	772	75,000	22,400	31,300	10,690	169,957	0.10	1
26 Jun	1946	26,516	2,262	970	519	79,476	13,416	32,429	10,400	165,988	1.12	
25 Sep	1946	26,800	2,279	928	668	80,900	8,700	33,200	11,100	164,575	0.70	1
31 Dec	1946	26,730	2,258	547	520	83,314	3,103	33,808	11,800	162,080	0.32	
26 Mar	1947	26,000	1,355	1,600	458	80,400	3,800	34,300	11,350	159,263	1.36	1
25 Jun	1947	26,299	1,329	642	405	82,500	1,000	34,700	10,900	157,775	1.51	
24 Sep	1947	26,300	1,319	800	401	84,200	1,600	34,900	11,850	161,370	1.16	1
31 Dec	1947	26,476	1,336	870	392	87,123	1,452	35,233	12,800	165,682	0.34	

1. Capital Data interpolated from adjacent figures.
2. Figures from BMS1976, Table 10.1D (Wednesday figures).
3. Commercial bank capital accounts from BMS1976, Table 1.3 (single date) for these dates; otherwise Wednesday dates from Federal Reserve Bulletins.
4. BMS1976 is: Board of Governors of the Federal Reserve, Banking and Monetary Statistics, 1941-1970, Washington DC: Publication Services, Division of Administrative Services, Board of Governors of the Federal Reserve System, Sep 1976

Figure 19.3-11: Banking System Liabilities, 1943-1947

Assets of the Federal Reserve & Commercial System, 1948-1950 (millions USD)									
				Federal Reserve Loans & Investments		Commercial Bank Loans and Investments			
Day	Year	Gold Stock	Treasury Currency Outstanding	U. S. Government Securities	Discounts & Advances	Loans	U. S. Government Securities	Other	Total Assets	Note
31 Mar	1948	23,137	4,559	20,887	430	39,041	66,949	9,078	164,081	1
30 Jun	1948	23,532	4,565	21,336	265	39,865	64,798	9,192	163,553	
29 Sep	1948	23,872	4,573	23,282	357	41,720	62,460	9,420	165,684	
29 Dec	1948	24,236	4,585	23,347	255	42,690	62,500	9,120	166,733	
30 Mar	1949	24,311	4,591	21,828	298	42,370	60,880	9,250	163,528	
29 Jun	1949	24,466	4,597	19,517	150	41,025	63,220	9,528	162,503	
28 Sep	1949	24,602	4,590	17,852	300	41,780	66,880	10,170	166,174	
28 Dec	1949	24,427	4,598	18,789	142	43,300	67,280	10,250	168,786	
29 Mar	1950	24,246	4,599	17,516	365	43,650	65,820	10,850	167,046	
28 Jun	1950	24,230	4,608	18,217	69	44,796	65,751	11,221	168,892	
27 Sep	1950	23,474	4,614	19,353	120	49,030	62,540	12,090	171,221	
27 Dec	1950	22,795	4,631	20,337	301	52,830	62,390	12,330	175,614	

1. Commercial Bank data (Loans, U. S. Gov't Securities, and Other) estimated per adjacent values (ratios of preceding and following figures).
2. All data from is Federal Reserve Bulletins; see Appendix B for references.

Figure 19.3-12: Banking System Assets, 1948-1950

Liabilities of the Federal Reserve and Commercial System, 1948-1950 (millions USD)												
				At Federal Reserve Banks		At Commercial Banks						
Day	Year	Currency Outside Banks	Treasury Cash [2]	Treasury Demand Deposits [2]	Foreign Demand Deposits [2]	Demand Deposits	Treasury Demand Deposits	Time Deposits	Capital	Total Liabilities	Error (%)	Note
31 Mar	1948	25,600	1,325	1,972	486	81,500	2,400	35,500	11,544	160,327	2.29	1
30 Jun	1948	25,638	1,327	1,822	377	82,697	2,180	35,788	10,287	160,116	2.10	3
29 Sep	1948	25,700	1,324	1,660	410	83,900	2,800	35,700	11,728	163,222	1.49	1
29 Dec	1948	26,079	1,329	1,283	614	85,520	2,451	35,804	13,168	166,248	0.29	
30 Mar	1949	25,100	1,320	1,678	694	81,100	3,400	36,000	11,974	161,266	1.38	1
29 Jun	1949	25,266	1,324	497	507	81,877	2,304	36,292	10,780	158,847	2.25	3
28 Sep	1949	24,900	1,311	1,170	517	83,300	3,700	36,100	12,586	163,584	1.56	1
28 Dec	1949	25,415	1,314	987	763	85,750	3,249	36,146	14,392	168,016	0.46	
29 Mar	1950	24,600	1,321	997	879	83,200	4,300	36,500	14,505	166,302	0.45	1
28 Jun	1950	25,185	1,306	886	1,140	85,040	3,801	36,719	14,618	168,695	0.12	
27 Sep	1950	24,500	1,307	1,144	910	88,100	3,600	36,200	14,621	170,382	0.49	1
27 Dec	1950	25,398	1,295	786	921	88,960	2,989	36,314	14,624	171,287	2.46	

1. Capital Data interpolated from adjacent figures.
2. Figures from BMS1976, Table 10.1D (Wednesday figures).
3. Commercial bank capital accounts from BMS1976, Table 1.3 (single date) for these dates; otherwise Wednesday dates from Federal Reserve Bulletins.
4. BMS1976 is: Board of Governors of the Federal Reserve, Banking and Monetary Statistics, 1941-1970, Washington DC: Publication Services, Division of Administrative Services, Board of Governors of the Federal Reserve System, Sep 1976

Figure 19.3-13: Banking System Liabilities, 1948-1950

Figure 19.3-14 shows the total money supply for this period. The tabulation has a new format starting in 1948, in which data from the Federal Reserve Bulletins are used instead of the reports of the Comptroller of the Currency. The syntax for the Federal Reserve Bulletin references is: M/Y, xx = Month/Year, xx is the page number of the pdf document (not the page number of the Bulletin). Please note that the data for 1948 to 1950 does not correspond to the definitions of M1, M2, and M3; they were not defined until 1973, and backward calculations extended only back to 1959. All of the values apply to approximately 30 Jun of each year. The average error between Figure 19.3-14 and that reported by Friedman and Schwartz [19.3-1] (assuming they are correct) is -2.23% (i.e., the values shown here are higher than Friedman's), and the standard deviation is 3.5%. If it is assumed that the truth lies halfway between Friedman and these numbers, then the average error is -1.07% and the standard deviation is 1.72%.

								Estimated U. S. Money Supply, 1933-1950 (milions USD)						
1	2	3	4	5	6	7	8	9	10	11	12	13	14	15
Year (~30 Jun)	Number of Banks [1]	Federal Reserve Notes and Bank Notes [2]	U.S. Notes, Treasury Notes, National Bank Notes, etc. [3]	Total Notes in Circulation	Net Specie in Circulation [4]	Notes & Specie Outside Treasury	Cash Held in All Banks [5]	Currency & Coin Outside Banks	State Bank Deposits [6]	National Bank Deposits and Other Deposits Outside State Banks [7, 8]	Total Deposits [9]	Estimated Interbank Trans-actions [9]	Deposits Adjusted	Total Money Supply
1933	14,624	3,186.638	1,815.795	5,002.433	718.331	5,720.764	672.556	5,048.208	24,759.355	16,774.115	41,533.470	3,443.000	38,090.470	43,138.678
1934	15,894	3,210.049	1,733.865	4,943.914	429.555	5,373.469	713.968	4,659.501	26,692.381	19,932.660	46,625.041	4,560.000	42,065.041	46,724.542
1935	16,053	3,304.383	1,809.503	5,113.886	453.206	5,567.092	784.576	4,782.516	29,067.877	22,518.246	51,586.123	5,657.000	45,929.123	50,711.639
1936	15,803	4,054.170	1,700.835	5,755.005	486.196	6,241.201	1,018.951	5,222.250	32,139.362	26,200.453	58,339.815	6,886.000	51,453.815	56,676.065
1937	15,580	4,437.642	1,717.680	6,155.322	522.980	6,678.302	958.317	5,719.985	33,056.457	26,765.913	59,822.370	6,332.000	53,490.370	59,210.355
1938	15,341	4,331.779	1,789.421	6,121.200	527.013	6,648.213	1,044.251	5,603.962	32,563.656	26,815.894	59,379.550	6,831.000	52,548.550	58,152.512
1939	15,146	4,670.032	1,979.111	6,649.143	558.485	7,207.628	1,042.408	6,165.220	35,107.225	29,469.469	64,576.694	8,232.000	56,344.694	62,509.914
1940	15,017	5,328.439	2,062.660	7,391.099	599.184	7,990.283	1,148.589	6,841.694	38,079.051	33,074.407	71,153.458	10,188.000	60,965.458	67,807.152
1941	14,919	6,834.669	2,227.515	9,062.184	680.440	9,742.624	1,408.306	8,334.318	41,198.026	37,351.303	78,549.329	10,948.000	67,601.329	75,935.647
1942	14,815	9,449.266	2,270.829	11,720.095	783.184	12,503.279	1,446.780	11,056.499	42,370.458	40,659.117	83,029.575	10,647.575	72,382.000	83,438.499
1943	14,661	13,878.742	2,161.108	16,039.850	929.378	16,969.228	1,606.564	15,362.664	53,014.738	54,769.361	107,784.099	11,455.099	96,329.000	111,691.664
1944	14,598	18,876.088	2,090.989	20,967.077	1,066.122	22,033.199	1,623.191	20,410.008	63,533.994	65,833.253	129,367.247	33,585.247	95,782.000	116,192.008
1945	14,587	22,987.471	2,146.522	25,133.993	1,205.457	26,339.450	1,649.487	24,689.963	75,107.154	76,825.537	151,932.691	38,626.691	113,306.000	137,995.963
1946	14,626	24,086.954	2,507.241	26,594.195	1,300.435	27,894.630	1,729.034	26,165.596	79,854.647	80,494.758	160,349.405	29,044.405	131,305.000	157,470.596
1947	14,755	24,105.433	2,536.501	26,641.934	1,355.462	27,997.396	1,986.836	26,010.560	76,793.973	77,397.149	154,191.122	16,350.122	137,841.000	163,851.560

Year	Number of Banks [1]	Currency Outside Banks	Demand Deposits, Adjusted	Time Deposits	Total Deposits Adjusted	Total Money Supply	Federal Reserve Bulletin Reference (M/Y, PDF page)
1948	14,735	25,638.000	82,697.000	57,360.000	140,057.000	165,695.000	8/50, 96
1949	14,705	25,266.000	81,877.000	58,483.000	140,360.000	165,626.000	8/50, 96
1950	14,666	25,185.000	85,040.000	59,739.000	144,779.000	169,964.000	10/51, 51

1. Number of banks from the Annual Reports of the Comptroller of the Currency as follows: 1933-1937: 1937, p. 766; 1938-1947: 1947, p. 160; 1848-1951: 1954, pp. 205, 206
2. Includes Federal Reserve Notes and Federal Reserve Bank Notes per the Annual Report of the Secretary of the Treasury, 1947, pp. 486, 487, (Table 90).
3. Includes gold certificates, silver certificates, Treasury Notes of 1890, U. S. Notes, and National bank Notes per Annual Report of the Secretary of the Treasury, 1947, pp. 486, 487 (Table 90).
4. This is the sum of gold coin, standard silver, subsidiary silver, and minor coin. Data is from the Annual Report of the Secretary of the Treasury, 1947, pp. 486, 487 (Table 90).
5. For 1933 to 1937: from the Annual Report of the Comptroller of the Currency, 1937, p. 766 (Table 81); for 1938 to 1947, from the Annual Report of the Comptroller of the Currency, 1947, p. 160 (Table 39).
6. State bank deposits for 1933 to 1937 from the Annual Report of the Comptroller of the Currency, 1937, p. 764 (Table 79); for 1938 to 1947 from Annual Report of the Comptroller of the Currency, 1947, pp. 160, 162, (Tables 39, 41).
7. Deposits in all banks except State for 1933 to 1937 derived by subtracting all banks deposits from State banks deposits per Annual Report of the Comptroller of the Currency, 1937, pp. 764, 766 (Tables 79 and 81).
8. Total deposits in all active banks from 1936 to 1947 per the Annual Report of the Comptroller of the Currency, 1947, p. 160 (Table 39).
9. The total adjusted deposits for 1942 to 1947 are from FRB (1/43, 60; 1/44, 70; 11/45, 49; 8/50, 96). The interbank values are calculated for these years.

Figure 19.3-14: Total Money Supply, 1933-1950

Previous chapters showed the amount of gold coinage for the period, but since gold was confiscated in 1933, no gold coins were made. The U. S. did manufacture some gold coinage in 1933 prior to the confiscation [19.3-1]: a) $8,910,000 in $20 Double Eagles, and b) $3,125,000 in $10 Eagles.

Figure 19.3-15 shows the silver and minor coinage of the U. S. during this period.

			Silver and Copper Coinage of the U. S., 1933-1950 (USD)							
	Silver ($)								Minor ($)	
Year	Trade Dollars	Dollars	Half Dollars	Quarters	Twenty-cents	Dimes	Half-dimes	Three-cents	Nickels and Cents	Total ($)
1933			895,625.00						205,600.00	1,101,225.00
1934			6,612,270.50	8,859,813.00		3,085,200.00			3,859,910.15	22,417,193.65
1935			8,201,523.50	10,981,000.00		8,514,700.00			7,343,700.00	35,040,923.50
1936			10,745,882.50	12,626,459.25		11,284,613.00			11,731,146.69	46,388,101.44
1937			6,824,600.50	7,135,785.50		8,075,175.60			9,088,431.65	31,123,993.25
1938			2,337,909.00	3,078,011.25		3,582,572.80			3,719,685.59	12,718,178.64
1939			6,827,967.00	10,817,198.75		10,268,332.10			10,375,671.95	38,289,169.80
1940			6,858,639.50	11,689,211.50		10,811,982.70			20,798,016.62	50,157,850.32
1941			21,776,906.00	27,960,521.75		26,383,055.70			26,089,027.00	102,209,510.45
1942			35,760,460.00	34,747,080.75		31,547,232.90			17,229,026.00	119,283,799.65
1943			38,993,000.00	34,373,900.00		32,405,900.00			30,464,336.70	136,237,136.70
1944			23,439,500.00	33,029,200.00		34,312,400.00			30,142,330.00	120,923,430.00
1945			25,812,400.00	25,929,400.25		24,129,500.00			5,260,785.00	81,132,085.25
1946			9,897,047.50	16,678,200.00		34,419,350.00			26,052,860.00	87,047,457.50
1947			4,147,325.50	10,856,600.00		20,319,500.00			12,720,150.00	48,043,575.50
1948			3,547,714.50	16,980,700.00		16,331,100.00			12,988,525.00	49,848,039.50
1949			6,757,306.00	4,845,100.00		7,048,400.00			9,695,275.00	28,346,081.00
1950			8,180,604.00	14,082,779.00		11,742,450.00			7,885,284.00	41,891,117.00
Totals	0.00	0.00	227,616,681.00	284,670,961.00	0.00	294,261,464.80	0.00	0.00	245,649,761.35	1,052,198,868.15

1. Source, 1933-1939: Annual Report of the Director of the Mint, 1940, 3 Sep 1940, Treasury Document 3109, pp. 69, 73
2. Source, 1940-1950: Annual Report of the Director of the Mint, 1966, 15 Feb 1967, Treasury Document 3241, pp. 85, 87, 91, 93

Figure 19.3-15: Silver and Minor (Copper) Coins Minted by the U. S., 1933-1950

Figure 19.3-16 shows the CPI, money supply, and per-capita money supply during this period. The CPI data changes from the average of L-1 and L-15 to the Bureau of Labor Statistics data in 1946 for "urban, all commodities, not seasonally adjusted", normalized to 1913, which appears to be reasonably consistent with the previous data.

Year	CPI [1, 7] (1913 = 100)	Total Money Supply [5] (USD)	Population [6]	Per Capita Money Supply (USD)	Annual Rate of Change in CPI (%)	Annual Rate of Change in Per-Capita Money Supply (%)
1933	111.706	43,138,678,000	125,891,401	342.67	-0.635	-9.236
1934	122.153	46,724,542,000	126,787,648	368.53	8.940	7.276
1935	129.807	50,711,639,000	127,683,895	397.17	6.077	7.484
1936	134.880	56,676,065,000	128,580,141	440.78	3.834	10.420
1937	142.319	59,210,355,000	129,476,388	457.31	5.369	3.680
1938	133.304	58,152,512,000	130,372,635	446.05	-6.544	-2.493
1939	130.760	62,509,914,000	131,268,882	476.20	-1.927	6.541
1940	133.304	67,807,152,000	132,165,129	513.05	1.927	7.454
1941	148.059	75,935,647,000	134,081,196	566.34	10.498	9.883
1942	167.562	83,438,499,000	135,997,263	613.53	12.375	8.003
1943	174.855	111,691,664,000	137,913,330	809.87	4.260	27.764
1944	176.382	116,192,008,000	139,829,397	830.96	0.869	2.570
1945	179.434	137,995,963,000	141,745,464	973.55	1.716	15.837
1946	196.970	157,470,596,000	143,661,530	1,096.12	9.324	11.859
1947	225.253	163,851,560,000	145,577,597	1,125.53	13.417	2.647
1948	243.434	165,695,000,000	147,493,664	1,123.40	7.763	-0.189
1949	240.404	165,626,000,000	149,409,731	1,108.54	-1.253	-1.332
1950	243.434	169,964,000,000	151,325,798	1,123.17	1.253	1.311

1. CPI is the average of L-1 and L-15 data, both re-aligned to 1913 as a reference.
2. L-1 data 1791 to 1938 (Snyder-Tucker) is a general price index (wholesale prices, wages, cost of living and rents).
3. L-15 data 1801 to 1945 includes wholesale prices, all commodities.
4. L1 and L-15 from Historical Statistics of the United States, 1789-1945, A Supplement to the Statistical Abstract of the United States, Bureau of the Census, US Department of Commerce, Washington, DC, 1949.
5. See notes in money supply data for sources.
6. Population is linearly interpolated from Census results.
7. CPI data from 1946 ff from Bureau of Labor Statistics, series CUUR0000AA0R (urban, all commodities, not seasonally adjusted), referenced to 1913

Figure 19.3-16: Money Supply and CPI, 1933-1950

Figure 19.3-17 shows a summary of the CPI and per-capita money supply. Four distinct trends are evident: 1933 to 1937, 1937 to 1942, 1942 to 1947, and 1947 to 1950. The average annual change in CPI and money supply for 1933 to 1937 are 6.0 and 7.2% respectively; for 1937 to 1942, 3.2 and 5.8% respectively; for 1942 to 1947, 5.9 and 12.1% respectively, and for 1947 to 1950, 2.5 and 0.0% respectively.

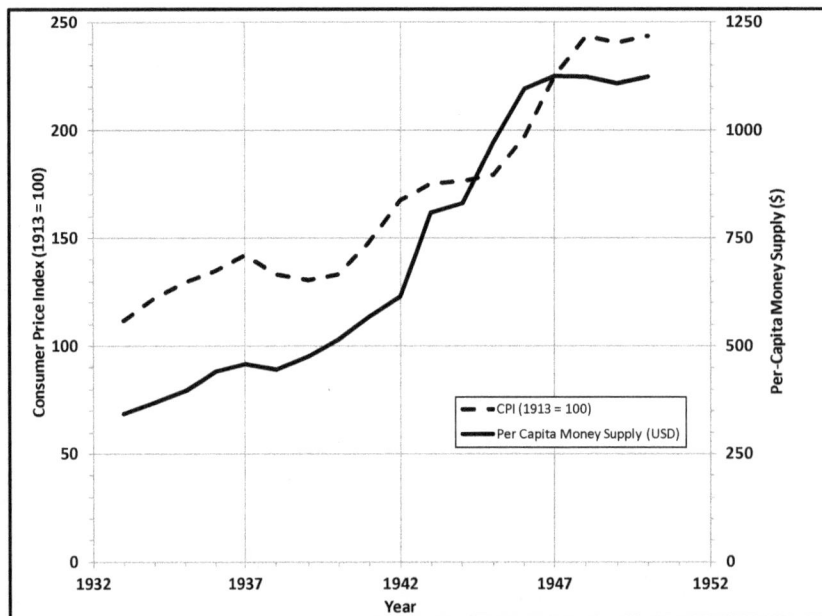

Figure 19.3-17: CPI and Per-Capita Summary, 1933-1950

Figure 19.3-18 shows the approximate median income index, consumer price index, and standard of living index for this period. See the Introduction to Part 2 for cautions regarding these curves.

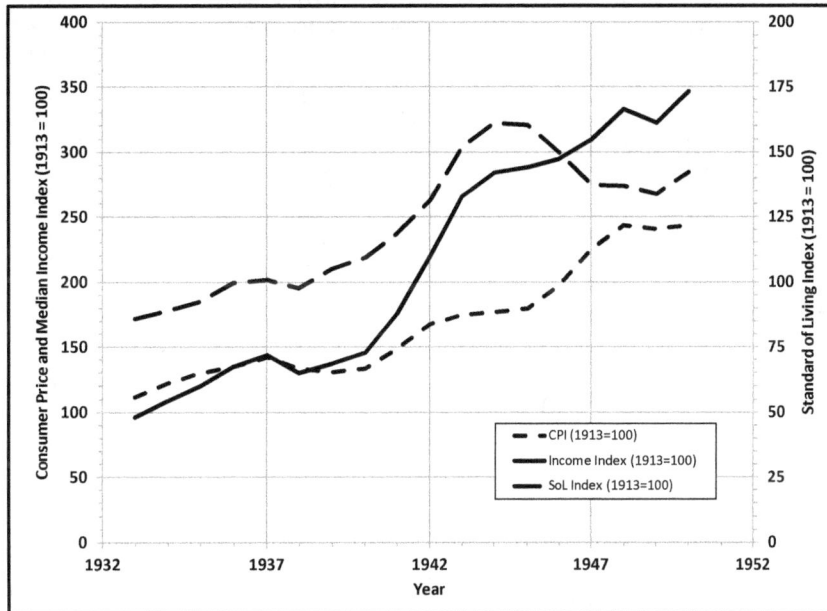

Figure 19.3-18: Median Income, Consumer Price, and Standard of Living Indices, 1933-1950

Figure 19.3-19 shows the changes in the legal reserve ratios for demand and time deposits at commercial banks during this period.

Legal Reserve Ratio Changes, 1933-1950									
vs. Demand Deposits (%)							vs. Time Deposits (%)		
Day	Year	Central Reserve City Banks	Reserve City Banks	Day	Year	Country Banks	Day	Year	All Banks
16 Aug	1936	19.50	15.00	16 Aug	1936	10.50	16 Aug	1936	4.50
1 Mar	1937	22.75	17.50	1 Mar	1937	22.50	1 Mar	1937	5.25
1 May	1937	26.00	20.00	1 May	1937	14.00	1 May	1937	6.00
16 Apr	1938	22.75	17.50	16 Apr	1938	12.00	16 Apr	1938	5.00
1 Nov	1941	26.00	20.00	1 Nov	1941	14.00	1 Nov	1941	6.00
20 Aug	1942	24.00	20.00	20 Aug	1942	14.00	20 Aug	1942	6.00
14 Sep	1942	22.00	20.00	14 Sep	1942	14.00	14 Sep	1942	6.00
3 Oct	1942	20.00	20.00	3 Oct	1942	14.00	3 Oct	1942	6.00
27 Feb	1948	22.00	20.00	27 Feb	1948	14.00	27 Feb	1948	6.00
11 Jun	1948	24.00	20.00	11 Jun	1948	14.00	11 Jun	1948	6.00
24 Sep	1948	26.00	22.00	24 Sep	1948	16.00	16 Sep	1948	7.50
5 May	1949	24.00	21.00	1 May	1949	15.00	5 May	1949	7.00
30 Jun	1949	24.00	20.00	1 Jul	1949	14.00	30 Jun	1949	6.00
1 Aug	1949	24.00	20.00	1 Aug	1949	13.00	1 Aug	1949	6.00
11 Aug	1949	23.50	19.50	16 Aug	1949	12.00	11 Aug	1949	5.00
18 Aug	1949	23.00	19.00	18 Aug	1949	12.00	18 Aug	1949	5.00
25 Aug	1949	22.50	18.50	25 Aug	1949	12.00	25 Aug	1949	5.00
1 Sep	1949	22.00	18.00	1 Sep	1949	12.00	1 Sep	1949	5.00
Source: Joshua N. Feinman, Reserve Requirements: History, Current Practice, and Potential Reform, Federal Reserve Bulletin, June 1993, p. 569-589									

Figure 19.3-19: Legal Reserve Requirements, 1933-1950

Figures 19.3-20 through 19.3-23 show some miscellaneous statistics for the banking system, including reserve levels, and ratios of demand deposits to reserves and demand deposits to currency.

| | | Miscellaneous Statistics of the Federal Reserve and Commercial System, 1933-1937 (millions USD) | | | | | | | | |
| | | Federal Reserve | At Commercial Banks | | | | | | | |
Day	Year	Member Bank Reserves [1]	Demand Deposits [2]	Time Deposits [2]	Total Deposits	Reserve Ratio, Demand Deposits	Reserve Ratio, Total Deposits	Currency Outside Banks [3]	Ratio, Demand Deposits to Reserves	Ratio, Demand Deposits to Currency
29 Mar	1933	1,987	15,070	12,240	27,310	0.132	0.073	4,715	7.584	3.196
28 Jun	1933	2,286	14,411	10,849	25,260	0.159	0.090	4,761	6.304	3.027
27 Sep	1933	2,596	14,723	10,934	25,657	0.176	0.101	4,772	5.671	3.086
27 Dec	1933	2,675	15,035	11,019	26,054	0.178	0.103	4,782	5.621	3.144
28 Mar	1934	3,439	15,965	11,504	27,468	0.215	0.125	4,721	4.642	3.382
27 Jun	1934	3,837	16,894	11,988	28,882	0.227	0.133	4,659	4.403	3.626
26 Sep	1934	3,970	17,677	12,101	29,777	0.225	0.133	4,657	4.453	3.796
26 Dec	1934	3,961	18,459	12,213	30,672	0.215	0.129	4,655	4.660	3.965
27 Mar	1935	4,285	19,446	12,517	31,963	0.220	0.134	4,719	4.538	4.121
26 Jun	1935	5,029	20,433	12,820	33,253	0.246	0.151	4,783	4.063	4.272
25 Sep	1935	5,236	21,274	12,995	34,269	0.246	0.153	4,850	4.063	4.386
31 Dec	1935	5,587	22,115	13,170	35,285	0.253	0.158	4,917	3.958	4.498
25 Mar	1936	5,059	22,948	13,438	36,386	0.220	0.139	5,070	4.536	4.527
24 Jun	1936	5,308	23,780	13,706	37,486	0.223	0.142	5,222	4.480	4.554
30 Sep	1936	6,357	24,632	13,876	38,508	0.258	0.165	5,369	3.875	4.588
30 Dec	1936	6,572	25,483	14,046	39,529	0.258	0.166	5,516	3.878	4.620
31 Mar	1937	6,639	25,341	14,280	39,620	0.262	0.168	5,503	3.817	4.605
30 Jun	1937	6,900	25,198	14,513	39,711	0.274	0.174	5,489	3.652	4.591
29 Sep	1937	7,035	24,579	14,646	39,225	0.286	0.179	5,564	3.494	4.418
29 Dec	1937	6,983	23,959	14,779	38,738	0.291	0.180	5,638	3.431	4.250

1. Member bank reserves per BMS1943, Table 103 (Wedneday call date).
2. Demand and time deposits per BMS1943, Table 9 (Wednesday call dates).
3. Currency outside banks per BMS1943, Table 9 (Wednesday call dates).
4. BMS1943 is: Board of Governors of the Federal Reserve, Banking and Monetary Statistics, 1914-1941, Washington DC: Publication Services, Division of Administrative Services, Board of Governors of the Federal Reserve System, Nov 1943

Figure 19.3-20: Miscellaneous Statistics of the Banking System, 1933-1937

| | | Miscellaneous Statistics of the Federal Reserve and Commercial System, 1938-1942 (millions USD) | | | | | | | | |
| | | Federal Reserve | At Commercial Banks | | | | | | | |
Day	Year	Member Bank Reserves [1]	Demand Deposits [2]	Time Deposits [2]	Total Deposits	Reserve Ratio, Demand Deposits	Reserve Ratio, Total Deposits	Currency Outside Banks [3]	Ratio, Demand Deposits to Reserves	Ratio, Demand Deposits to Currency
30 Mar	1938	7,312	24,136	14,777	38,913	0.303	0.188	5,528	3.301	4.366
29 Jun	1938	8,041	24,313	14,776	39,089	0.331	0.206	5,417	3.024	4.488
28 Sep	1938	8,197	25,150	14,776	39,926	0.326	0.205	5,596	3.068	4.494
28 Dec	1938	8,577	25,986	14,776	40,762	0.330	0.210	5,775	3.030	4.500
29 Mar	1939	9,125	26,671	14,937	41,607	0.342	0.219	5,890	2.923	4.528
28 Jun	1939	10,116	27,355	15,097	42,452	0.370	0.238	6,005	2.704	4.555
27 Sep	1939	11,621	28,574	15,193	43,767	0.407	0.266	6,203	2.459	4.606
27 Dec	1939	11,493	29,793	15,288	45,081	0.386	0.255	6,401	2.592	4.654
27 Mar	1940	12,294	30,878	15,414	46,292	0.398	0.266	6,550	2.512	4.714
26 Jun	1940	13,723	31,962	15,540	47,502	0.429	0.289	6,699	2.329	4.771
25 Sep	1940	13,703	33,454	15,659	49,112	0.410	0.279	7,012	2.441	4.771
31 Dec	1940	14,026	34,945	15,777	50,722	0.401	0.277	7,325	2.491	4.771
26 Mar	1941	13,633	36,131	15,853	51,984	0.377	0.262	7,765	2.650	4.653
25 Jun	1941	12,985	37,317	15,928	53,245	0.348	0.244	8,204	2.874	4.549
24 Sep	1941	13,273	38,155	15,906	54,061	0.348	0.246	8,910	2.875	4.282
31 Dec	1941	12,450	38,992	15,884	54,876	0.319	0.227	9,615	3.132	4.055
25 Mar	1942	12,527	40,446	15,775	56,221	0.310	0.223	10,276	3.229	3.936
24 Jun	1942	12,523	41,900	15,665	57,565	0.299	0.218	10,936	3.346	3.831
30 Sep	1942	11,592	45,400	16,030	61,430	0.255	0.189	12,441	3.916	3.649
30 Dec	1942	12,788	48,900	16,395	65,295	0.262	0.196	13,946	3.824	3.506

1. Member bank reserves to 1941, per BMS1943, Table 103 (Wedneday call dates); for 1941 ff, per BMS1976, Table 10.1D
2. Demand and time deposits per BMS1943, Table 9 (call dates), from 1933 to 1941; per Federal Reserve Bulletins on Wednesday dates afterward.
3. Currency outside banks per BMS1943, Table 9 (call dates), from 1933 to 1941; per Federal Reserve Bulletins on Wednesday dates afterward.
4. BMS1976 is: Board of Governors of the Federal Reserve, Banking and Monetary Statistics, 1941-1970, Washington DC: Publication Services, Division of Administrative Services, Board of Governors of the Federal Reserve System, Sep 1976
5. BMS1943 is: Board of Governors of the Federal Reserve, Banking and Monetary Statistics, 1914-1941, Washington DC: Publication Services, Division of Administrative Services, Board of Governors of the Federal Reserve System, Nov 1943

Figure 19.3-21: Miscellaneous Statistics of the Banking System, 1938-1942

		Miscellaneous Statistics of the Federal Reserve and Commercial System, 1943-1947 (millions USD)								
		Federal Reserve	At Commercial Banks							
Day	Year	Member Bank Reserves [1]	Demand Deposits [2]	Time Deposits [2]	Total Deposits	Reserve Ratio, Demand Deposits	Reserve Ratio, Total Deposits	Currency Outside Banks [3]	Ratio, Demand Deposits to Reserves	Ratio, Demand Deposits to Currency
31 Mar	1943	12,759	55,000	16,900	71,900	0.232	0.177	15,814	4.311	3.478
30 Jun	1943	12,085	56,039	17,543	73,582	0.216	0.164	17,421	4.637	3.217
29 Sep	1943	12,054	54,800	18,400	73,200	0.220	0.165	17,200	4.546	3.186
29 Dec	1943	12,769	60,815	19,213	80,028	0.210	0.160	18,837	4.763	3.228
29 Mar	1944	12,053	59,600	20,100	79,700	0.202	0.151	19,500	4.945	3.056
28 Jun	1944	13,081	60,100	21,200	81,300	0.218	0.161	20,900	4.594	2.876
27 Sep	1944	13,355	65,500	22,800	88,300	0.204	0.151	22,200	4.905	2.950
27 Dec	1944	13,969	66,930	24,074	91,004	0.209	0.153	23,505	4.791	2.847
28 Mar	1945	14,305	70,900	25,700	96,600	0.202	0.148	24,200	4.956	2.930
27 Jun	1945	14,760	69,053	27,171	96,224	0.214	0.153	25,097	4.678	2.751
26 Sep	1945	15,274	75,400	29,100	104,500	0.203	0.146	26,200	4.936	2.878
26 Dec	1945	15,658	75,851	30,135	105,986	0.206	0.148	26,490	4.844	2.863
27 Mar	1946	15,395	75,000	31,300	106,300	0.205	0.145	26,100	4.872	2.874
26 Jun	1946	15,910	79,476	32,429	111,905	0.200	0.142	26,516	4.995	2.997
25 Sep	1946	15,975	80,900	33,200	114,100	0.197	0.140	26,800	5.064	3.019
31 Dec	1946	16,530	83,314	33,808	117,122	0.198	0.141	26,730	5.040	3.117
26 Mar	1947	15,658	80,400	34,300	114,700	0.195	0.137	26,000	5.135	3.092
25 Jun	1947	16,081	82,500	34,700	117,200	0.195	0.137	26,299	5.130	3.137
24 Sep	1947	16,831	84,200	34,900	119,100	0.200	0.141	26,300	5.003	3.202
31 Dec	1947	17,899	87,123	35,233	122,356	0.205	0.146	26,476	4.867	3.291

1. Member bank reserves per BMS1976, Table 10.1D (Wednesday call dates).
2. Demand and time deposits per Federal Reserve Bulletins on Wednesday dates; see Appendix B.
3. Currency outside banks per Federal Reserve Bulletins on Wednesday dates; see Appendix B.
4. BMS1976 is: Board of Governors of the Federal Reserve, Banking and Monetary Statistics, 1941-1970, Washington DC: Publication Services, Division of Administrative Services, Board of Governors of the Federal Reserve System, Sep 1976

Figure 19.3-22: Miscellaneous Statistics of the Banking System, 1943-1947

		Miscellaneous Statistics of the Federal Reserve and Commercial System, 1948-1950 (millions USD)								
		Federal Reserve	At Commercial Banks							
Day	Year	Member Bank Reserves [1]	Demand Deposits [2]	Time Deposits [2]	Total Deposits	Reserve Ratio, Demand Deposits	Reserve Ratio, Total Deposits	Currency Outside Banks [3]	Ratio, Demand Deposits to Reserves	Ratio, Demand Deposits to Currency
31 Mar	1948	16,639	81,500	35,500	117,000	0.204	0.142	25,600	4.898	3.184
30 Jun	1948	17,389	82,697	35,788	118,485	0.210	0.147	25,638	4.756	3.226
29 Sep	1948	19,884	83,900	35,700	119,600	0.237	0.166	25,700	4.219	3.265
29 Dec	1948	20,238	85,520	35,804	121,324	0.237	0.167	26,079	4.226	3.279
30 Mar	1949	19,019	81,100	36,000	117,100	0.235	0.162	25,100	4.264	3.231
29 Jun	1949	18,013	81,877	36,292	118,169	0.220	0.152	25,266	4.545	3.241
28 Sep	1949	16,016	83,300	36,100	119,400	0.192	0.134	24,900	5.201	3.345
28 Dec	1949	16,299	85,750	36,146	121,896	0.190	0.134	25,415	5.261	3.374
29 Mar	1950	15,782	83,200	36,500	119,700	0.190	0.132	24,600	5.272	3.382
28 Jun	1950	15,988	85,040	36,719	121,759	0.188	0.131	25,185	5.319	3.377
27 Sep	1950	16,699	88,100	36,200	124,300	0.190	0.134	24,500	5.276	3.596
27 Dec	1950	17,174	88,960	36,314	125,274	0.193	0.137	25,398	5.180	3.503

1. Member bank reserves per BMS1976, Table 10.1D (Wednesday call dates).
2. Demand and time deposits per Federal Reserve Bulletins on Wednesday dates; see Appendix B.
3. Currency outside banks per Federal Reserve Bulletins on Wednesday dates; see Appendix B.
4. BMS1976 is: Board of Governors of the Federal Reserve, Banking and Monetary Statistics, 1941-1970, Washington DC: Publication Services, Division of Administrative Services, Board of Governors of the Federal Reserve System, Sep 1976

Figure 19.3-23: Miscellaneous Statistics of the Banking System, 1948-1950

Figures 19.3-24 and 19.3-25 show the approximate monthly interest rates for prime commercial paper loans (4 to 6 months) and Federal Funds Rate.

Approximate Monthly Average, Prime Commercial Paper Rate, 4 to 6 Month (%) [1, 2]											
Year	Jan	Feb	Mar	Apr	May	Jun	Jul	Aug	Sep	Oct	Nov	Dec
1933	1.38	1.38	3.00	2.63	2.13	1.88	1.63	1.50	1.38	1.25	1.25	1.38
1934	1.50	1.38	1.25	1.00	1.00	0.88	0.88	0.88	0.88	0.88	0.88	0.88
1935	0.88	0.75	0.75	0.75	0.75	0.75	0.75	0.75	0.75	0.75	0.75	0.75
1936	0.75	0.75	0.75	0.75	0.75	0.75	0.75	0.75	0.75	0.75	0.75	0.75
1937	0.75	0.75	0.75	1.00	1.00	1.00	1.00	1.00	1.00	1.00	1.00	1.00
1938	1.00	1.00	0.88	0.88	0.88	0.88	0.75	0.75	0.69	0.69	0.69	0.63
1939	0.56	0.56	0.56	0.56	0.56	0.56	0.56	0.56	0.69	0.69	0.63	0.56
1940	0.56	0.56	0.56	0.56	0.56	0.56	0.56	0.56	0.56	0.56	0.56	0.56
1941	0.56	0.56	0.56	0.56	0.56	0.56	0.50	0.50	0.50	0.50	0.50	0.55
1942	0.59	0.63	0.63	0.63	0.63	0.67	0.69	0.69	0.69	0.69	0.69	0.69
1943	0.69	0.69	0.69	0.69	0.69	0.69	0.69	0.69	0.69	0.69	0.69	0.69
1944	0.69	0.69	0.69	0.72	0.75	0.75	0.75	0.75	0.75	0.75	0.75	0.75
1945	0.75	0.75	0.75	0.75	0.75	0.75	0.75	0.75	0.75	0.75	0.75	0.75
1946	0.75	0.75	0.75	0.75	0.75	0.75	0.77	0.81	0.81	0.89	0.94	1.00
1947	1.00	1.00	1.00	1.00	1.00	1.00	1.00	1.00	1.02	1.06	1.10	1.22
1948	1.30	1.38	1.38	1.38	1.38	1.38	1.38	1.47	1.54	1.56	1.56	1.56
1949	1.56	1.56	1.56	1.56	1.56	1.56	1.56	1.43	1.38	1.38	1.38	1.33
1950	1.31	1.31	1.31	1.31	1.31	1.31	1.31	1.42	1.65	1.72	1.69	1.72

1. Source for Jan 1933 to Dec 1940: Board of Governors of the Federal Reserve System, Bank and Monetary Statistics 1914-1941, Washington DC: Nov 1943, Table 120, pp. 448-451

2. Source for Jan 1941 to Dec 1950: Board of Governors of the Federal Reserve System, Bank and Monetary Statistics 1941-1970, Washington DC: Sep 1976, Table 12.5, p. 671

Figure 19.3-24: Interest Rates on Prime Commercial Paper Loans, 1933-1950

Approximate Monthly Average Federal Funds Rate (%) [1, 2, 3]											
Year	Jan	Feb	Mar	Apr	May	Jun	Jul	Aug	Sep	Oct	Nov	Dec
1933	0.25	0.63	2.44	0.33	0.20	0.21	0.31	0.19	0.19	0.19	0.19	0.19
1934	0.19	0.19	0.19	0.19	0.19	0.19	0.19	0.19	0.19	0.19	0.19	0.19
1935	0.19	0.19	0.19	0.19	0.19	0.19	0.19	0.19	0.19	0.19	0.19	0.19
1936	0.19	0.19	0.19	0.19	0.19	0.19	0.19	0.19	0.19	0.19	0.19	0.19
1937	0.19	0.19	0.23	0.25	0.38	0.38	0.38	0.38	0.38	0.38	0.38	0.38
1938	0.38	0.38	0.38	0.25	0.25	0.25	0.25	0.25	0.25	0.25	0.25	0.25
1939	0.25	0.25	0.25	0.25	0.25	0.25	0.25	0.25	0.25	0.25	0.25	0.25
1940	0.25	0.25	0.25	0.25	0.25	0.25	0.25	0.25	0.25	0.25	0.25	0.25
1941	0.25	0.25	0.25	0.25	0.25	0.25	0.25	0.25	0.25	0.25	0.25	0.25
1942	0.25	0.25	0.25	0.25	0.25	0.25	0.25	0.25	0.25	0.25	0.25	0.25
1943	0.25	0.25	0.25	0.25	0.25	0.25	0.25	0.25	0.25	0.25	0.25	0.25
1944	0.25	0.25	0.25	0.25	0.25	0.25	0.25	0.25	0.25	0.25	0.25	0.25
1945	0.25	0.25	0.45	0.45	0.40	0.60	0.60	0.45	0.40	0.35	0.40	0.40
1946	0.40	0.40	0.70	0.75	0.55	0.45	0.80	0.55	0.55	0.95	0.45	0.50
1947	0.35	0.80	0.50	0.75	0.80	0.65	0.55	0.20	0.75	1.15	1.10	1.00
1948	0.75	0.75	0.76	0.77	0.78	0.79	0.80	1.50	1.40	1.30	1.40	1.45
1949	1.50	1.40	1.30	1.20	1.10	1.00	0.98	1.15	0.81	0.64	0.95	1.05
1950	0.62	1.22	1.11	1.26	0.95	0.64	1.20	1.20	1.19	0.84	1.37	0.82

1. Source for 1933 to Mar 1938: Board of Governors of the Federal Reserve System, Federal Funds Effective Rate, Federal Reserve Bank of St. Louis; series FFHTLOW and FFHTHIGH (https://fred.stlouisfed.org/series/FFHTLOW and FFHTHIGH). These are averages calculated from data published in the New York Herald-Tribune.

2. Source for Apr 1938 to Jun 1949 from: S. Anbil, M. Carlson, C. Hanes, D. C. Wheelock, "A New Daily Federal Funds Rate Series and the History of the Federal Funds Market, 1928-1954, Figures 4 and 6. Federal Reserve Bank of St. Louis Review, First Quarter 2021, 103(1), pp. 45-70. The data shown here are approximate values read from Figures 4 and 6. Use the data from Mar 1945 to Jun 1949 with caution; they are crude estimates from Figure 6.

3. Source for Jul 1949 to Dec 1950: Board of Governors of the Federal Reserve System, Federal Funds Effective Rate, Federal Reserve Bank of St. Louis; series FFWSHLOW and FFWSJHIGH (https://fred.stlouisfed.org/series/FFWSJLOW and FFWSJHIGH). These are averages calculated from data published in the Wall Street Journal.

Figure 19.3-25: Federal Funds Rate, 1933-1950

19.4 Summary, 1933-1950

There was a local grocery store owner in my neighborhood that started in business sometime in the 1920's, although I didn't meet him until the 1960's. Teddy Dombrowski had a store at the corner of E. Lovejoy and Ideal Streets. Mr. Dombrowski did what many Americans did during the Great Depression: he did not wait for the government to dictate conditions: he did for his friends, neighbors, and customers.

My father, who knew Mr. Dombrowski well, told me that during the Depression, when money was scarce, Teddy extended credit to his regular customers, and by doing so, built up enormous good will in the neighborhood. In fact, my grandmother refused to do her grocery shopping anywhere else, even when the large supermarkets came along in the 1950's: "if Teddy doesn't carry it, I don't need it". It is guys like Teddy Dombrowski that made America great; doing what is right by the local people.

The Depression lasted throughout the 1930's because the federal government got involved directly in the economy by creating public works programs to stimulate employment, regulating farmland, regulating working conditions, and propping up prices and wages artificially. In other words, the government did what it could to prevent the economy from the natural liquidation that should have occurred after the excesses of the 1920's, and restricting personal freedom at the same time. The government confiscated all the gold, ending the gold coin system in the U. S. on the grounds that the only way out of the Depression was to depreciate the currency. That did improve exports, but did not make the necessary corrections to revive industry. With the regulating influence of the gold standard removed, the U. S. government was able to issue as much new debt as necessary to finance the public works, a system that prevails today. It was during this period that government debt came to be seen as an asset, and the monetary system became founded on, and reliant upon, increasing debt.

Credit controls and commodity rationing were imposed during World War II, which increased the personal savings of the public. After the war, the pent-up demand for items that had been restricted during the war and the large amount of savings available caused an increase in prices. A second effect was the increased demand for loans, and many commercial banks sold off their U. S. securities, creating excess reserves, which increased the money-creating capacity of the banking system; i.e., an increase in the money supply until about 1948 [19.4-1]. The Federal Reserve tried to raise reserve requirements in the late 1940's, but was prevented by Congress from doing so [19.4-2].

The Federal Reserve continued to support the prices of U. S. securities after the war. It continued until the "accord" of 1951, after which the Federal Reserve once again pursued an independent policy [19.4-3]. It returned to the "bills only" policies.

References

[19.1-1]   Clifton H. Kreps, Jr., *Money, Banking and Monetary Policy*, NY: The Ronald Press Co., 1962, pp. 105, 106

[19.1-2]   Milton Friedman, Anna Jacobson Schwartz, *A Monetary History of the United States, 1867 - 1960*, A Study by the National Bureau of Economic Research, NY, Princeton, NJ: Princeton University Press, 1963, p. 168

[19.1-3]   op. cit., Friedman and Schwartz, pp. 328-330

[19.2-1]   op. cit., Friedman and Schwartz, p. 325

[19.2-2]   op. cit., Friedman and Schwartz, p. 325

[19.2-3]   Text of "An Act to extend the time during which certain provisions of the Act of February 27, 1932, relating to improving the facilities of the Federal reserve system to meet the needs of the member banks in exceptional circumstances, shall be effective", 72nd Congress, Session 2, Chapter 34, Public Law 72-326, 3 Feb 1933

[19.2-4]   op. cit., Friedman and Schwartz, p. 325

[19.2-5]   op. cit., Friedman and Schwartz, p. 327

[19.2-6]   op. cit., Friedman and Schwartz, p. 327

[19.2-7]   op. cit., Kreps, pp. 94, 177

[19.2-8]   Text of "An Act to provide relief in the existing national emergency in banking, and for other purposes", 73rd Congress, Session 1, Chapter 1, Public Law 73-1, 9 Mar 1933

[19.2-9]   op. cit., Friedman and Schwartz, pp. 328, 421, 422

[19.2-10]   op. cit., Kreps, pp. 177, 178

[19.2-11]   Text of Executive Order 6073, Reopening Banks, 10 Mar 1933

[19.2-12]   Allan H. Meltzer, *A History of the Federal Reserve*, Chicago, IL: University of Chicago Press, (2003), Vol. 1, pp. 423, 424

[19.2-13]   National Bureau of Economic Research (NBER), Cambridge, MA (see website below)

[19.2-14]   Text of "An Act to provide for direct loans by Federal reserve Banks to State banks and trust companies in certain cases, and for other purposes", 73rd Congress, Session 1, Chapter 8, 24 Mar 1933

[19.2-15]   Executive Order 6102, forbidding the hoarding of gold coin, gold bullion, and gold certificates, 5 Apr 1933

[19.2-16]   op. cit., Meltzer, Vol. 1, p. 426

[19.2-17]   op. cit., Friedman and Schwartz, pp. 463-465

[19.2-18]   Executive Order 6111, On Transactions in Foreign Exchange, 20 Apr 1933

[19.2-19]   op. cit., Meltzer, Vol. 1, p. 426

[19.2-20]   Text of Titles I and II from "An Act To relieve the existing national economic emergency by increasing agricultural purchasing power, to raise revenue for extraordinary expenses incurred by reason of such emergency, to provide emergency relief with respect to agricultural indebtedness, to provide for the orderly liquidation of joint-stock land banks, and for other purposes", 73rd Congress, Session 1, Chapter 25, 12 May 1933

[19.2-21]   Text of "The Emergency Farm Mortgage Act of 1933", Title III of "An Act To relieve the existing national economic emergency by increasing agricultural purchasing power, to raise revenue for extraordinary expenses incurred by reason of such emergency, to provide emergency relief with respect to agricultural indebtedness, to provide for the orderly liquidation of joint-stock land banks, and for other purposes", 73rd Congress, Session 1, Chapter 25, 12 May 1933

[19.2-22]   op. cit., Kreps, pp. 96, 97

[19.2-23]   op. cit., Friedman and Schwartz, pp. 464, 465

[19.2-24]   Text of "An Act to improve the navigability and to provide for the flood control of the Tennessee River, to provide for the reforestation and the proper use of marginal lands in the Tennessee valley; to provide for the agricultural and industrial development of said valley; to provide for the national defense by the creation of a corporation for the operation of government properties at an near Muscle Shoals in the State of Alabama, and for other purposes", a.k.a. the Tennessee Valley Authority Act, 73rd Congress, Session 1, Chapter 32, Public Law 73-17, 18 May 1838

[19.2-25]   Text of "A Joint Resolution to assure uniform value to the coins and currencies of the United States", 73rd Congress, Session 1, Public Resolution 10, 5 Jun 1933

[19.2-26]   op. cit., Kreps, p. 95

[19.2-27]   op. cit., Friedman and Schwartz, p. 469

[19.2-28]   Text of "An Act to provide emergency relief to home mortgage indebtedness, to refinance home mortgages, to extend relief to the owners of homes occupied by them and who are unable to amortize their debt elsewhere, to amend the Federal Home Loan Bank, to increase the market for obligations of the United States, and for other purposes", a.k.a. the Home Owners Loan Act of 1933, 72nd Congress, Session 1, Chapter 64, Public Law 73-43, 13 Jun 1933

[19.2-29]   op. cit., Friedman and Schwartz, pp. 578, 579, 646

[19.2-30]   Text of "An Act to provide for the safer and more effective use of the assets of banks, to regulate interbank control, to prevent the undue diversion of funds into speculative operations, and for other purposes", a.k.a. the Banking Act of 1933, 73rd Congress, Session 1, Chapter 89, Public Law 73-66, 16 Jun 1933

[19.2-31]   op. cit., Kreps, pp. 180-186

[19.2-32]   op. cit., Meltzer, Vol. 1, p. 417

[19.2-33]   Text of "The National Industrial Recovery Act", 73rd Congress, Session 1, Chapter 90, 16 Jun 1933

[19.2-34]   op. cit., Friedman and Schwartz, p. 465

[19.2-35]   op. cit., Kreps, pp. 98, 99

[19.2-36]   op. cit., Kreps, p. 109

[19.2-37]   op. cit., Friedman and Schwartz, p. 463

[19.2-38]   Federal Deposit Insurance Corporation, Division of Research and Statistics, *A Brief History of Deposit Insurance in the United States*, Sep 1998, p. 21

[19.2-39]   op. cit., Kreps, p. 177

[19.2-40]   Text of "An Act to protect the currency system of the United States, to provide for the better use of the monetary gold stock of the United States, and for other purposes", a.k.a. the Gold Reserve Act of 1934, 73rd Congress, Public Law 73-87, 30 Jan 1934

[19.2-41] op. cit., Friedman and Schwartz, p. 464

[19.2-42] op. cit., Kreps, pp. 99, 100

[19.2-43] op. cit., Kreps, p. 99

[19.2-44] Text of "An Act to provide for the establishment of a corporation to aid in the refinancing of farm debts, and for other purposes", a.k.a. the Federal Farm Mortgage Corporation Act, 73rd Congress, Session 2, Chapter 7, Public Law 73-88, 31 Jan 1934

[19.2-45] Text of Executive Order 6581, Creating the Export-Import Bank of Washington, 2 Feb 1934

[19.2-46] op. cit., Kreps, p. 115

[19.2-47] Text of "An Act to extend the period during which direct obligations of the United States may be used as collateral security for Federal Reserve notes", 73rd Congress, Session 2, Chapter 47, Public Law 73-115, 6 Mar 1934

[19.2-48] Text of " An Act to provide for the regulation of securities exchanges and of over-the-counter markets operating in interstate and foreign commerce and through the mails, to prevent inequitable and unfair practices on such exchanges and markets, and for other purposes", a.k.a. the Securities Exchange Act of 1934, 73rd Congress, Session 2, Chapter 404, Public Law 73-291, 6 Jun 1934

[19.2-49] op. cit., Kreps, pp. 184, 185

[19.2-50] Text of "An Act to authorize the Secretary of the Treasury to purchase silver, issue silver certificates, and for other purposes", 73rd Congress, Session 2, Chapter 694, Public Law 73-438, 19 Jun 1934

[19.2-51] op. cit., Kreps, pp. 109-111

[19.2-52] Text of "An Act to establish a Federal Credit Union System, to establish a further market for securities of the United States and to make more available to people of small means credit for provident purposes through a national system of cooperative credit, thereby helping to stabilize the credit structure of the United States, a.k.a. the Federal Credit Union Act, 73rd Congress, Session 2, Chapter 750, Public Law 73-467, 26 Jun 1934

[19.2-53] Text of "An Act to encourage improvement in housing standards and conditions, to provide a system of mutual mortgage insurance, and for other purposes", a.k.a. the National Housing Act, 73rd Congress, Session 2, Chapter 847, Public Law 73-479, 27 Jun 1934

[19.2-54] op. cit., Friedman and Schwartz, pp. 668, 669

[19.2-55] op. cit., Friedman and Schwartz, p. 435

[19.2-56] Text of Executive Order 6814, Requiring the Delivery of All Silver to the United States for Coinage, 9 Aug 1934

[19.2-57] op. cit., Friedman and Schwartz, p. 485

[19.2-58] op. cit., Federal Deposit Insurance Corporation, p. 67

[19.2-59] Text of "Joint Resolution to extend until April 1, 1936 certain provisions of the National Industrial Recovery Act, and for other purposes", 74th Congress, Session 1, Chapter 246, Joint Resolution 74-35, 14 Jun 1935

[19.2-60] op. cit., Friedman and Schwartz, pp. 21, 442

[19.2-61] Text of "An Act to provide for the general welfare by establishing a system of Federal old-age benefits, and by enabling the several States to make more adequate provision for aged persons, blind persons, dependent and crippled children, maternal and child welfare, public health, and the administration of their unemployment compensation laws; to establish a Social Security Board; to raise revenues, and for other purposes", a.k.a. the Social Security Act, 74th Congress, Session 1, Chapter 531, Public Law 73-271, 14 Aug 1935

[19.2-62] Text of "An Act to provide for the sound, effective, and uninterrupted operation of the banking system, and for other purposes", a.k.a. the Banking Act of 1935, 74th Congress, Session 1, Chapter 614, Public Law 74-305, 23 Aug 1935

[19.2-63] op. cit., Kreps, pp. 180, 186-189

[19.2-64] op. cit., Friedman and Schwartz, pp. 191, 435, 646

[19.2-65] op. cit., Federal Deposit Insurance Corporation, p. 67

[19.2-66] Text of "An Act to provide for rural electrification, and for other purposes", a.k.a. the Rural Electrification Act of 1936, 74th Congress, Session 2, Chapter 432, Public Law 74-605, 20 May 1936

[19.2-67] Text of "An Act to diminish the causes of labor disputes burdening or obstructing interstate and foreign commerce, to create a National Labor relations Board, and for other purposes", a.k.a. the "National Labor Relations Act", 74th Congress, Session 1, Chapter 372, Public Law 74-198, 5 Jul 1935

[19.2-68] op. cit., Federal Deposit Insurance Corporation, p. 67

[19.2-69] Text of "An Act to extend the period during which direct obligations of the United States may be used as collateral security for Federal Reserve notes", 75th Congress, Session 1, Chapter 20, Public Law 75-9, 1 Mar 1937

[19.2-70] op. cit., National Bureau of Economic Research

[19.2-71] op. cit., Kreps, p. 528

[19.2-72] op. cit., Meltzer, Vol. 1, pp. 517-519, 572

[19.2-73] Text of "An Act to provide financial assistance to the States and political subdivisions thereof for the elimination of unsafe and unsanitary housing conditions, for the eradication of slums, for the provisions of decent, safe, and sanitary dwellings for families of low income, and for the reduction of unemployment and the stimulation of business activity, to create a United States Housing Authority, and for other purposes", a.k.a. the United States Housing Act of 1937, 75th Congress, Session 1, Chapter 896, Public Law 75-412, 1 Sep 1937

[19.2-74] op. cit., Kreps, p. 536

[19.2-75] op. cit., Federal Deposit Insurance Corporation, p. 67

[19.2-76] Text of "An Act to provide for the conservation of national soil resources and to provide an adequate and balanced flow of agricultural commodities in interstate and foreign commerce and for other purposes", a.k.a. the Agricultural Adjustment Act of 1938, 75th Congress, Session 3, Chapter 30, Public Law 75-430, 16 Feb 1938

[19.2-77] Text of "An Act to maintain unimpaired the capital of the Commodity Credit Corporation at $100,000,000, and for other purposes", 75th Congress, Session 3, Chapter 44, Public Law 75-442, 8 Mar 1938

[19.2-78] Text of "An Act to amend the Act creating the Federal Trade Commission, to define its powers and duties, and for other purposes", a.k.a. the Federal Trade Commission Act, 75th Congress, Session 3, Chapter 49, Public Law 75-447, 21 Mar 1938

[19.2-79] op. cit., National Bureau of Economic Research

[19.2-80] Text of "An Act to provide for the establishment of fair labor standards in employments in and affecting interstate commerce, and for other purposes", a.k.a. the Fair Labor Standards Act of 1938, 75th Congress, Session 3, Chapter 676, Public Law 75-718, 25 Jun 1938

[19.2-81] op. cit., Federal Deposit Insurance Corporation, p. 67

[19.2-82] Text of An Act to extend the period during which direct obligations of the United States may be used as collateral security for Federal Reserve Notes", 76th Congress, Session 1, Chapter 256, Public Law 76-162, 30 Jun 1939

[19.2-83] Text of "An Act to extend the time within which the powers relating to the stabilization fund and alteration of the weight of the dollar may be exercised", 76th Congress, Session 1, Chapter 260, Public Law 76-165, 6 Jul 1939

[19.2-84] op. cit., Friedman and Schwartz, p. 486

[19.2-85] op. cit., Federal Deposit Insurance Corporation, p. 67

[19.2-86] op. cit., Kreps, pp. 529-532, 539

[19.2-87] op. cit., Federal Deposit Insurance Corporation, p. 67

[19.2-88] Text of "An Act to extend the period during which direct obligations of the United States may be used as collateral security for Federal Reserve notes", 77th Congress, Session 1, Chapter 264, Public Law 77-141, 30 Jun 1941

[19.2-89] Text of Executive Order 8843, Directing the Federal Reserve Board to Curb Installment Purchasing, 9 Aug 1941

[19.2-90] op. cit., Kreps, p. 535

[19.2-91] op. cit., Friedman and Schwartz, pp. 553, 555

[19.2-92] op. cit., Kreps, p. 535

[19.2-93] op. cit., Friedman and Schwartz, p. 556

[19.2-94] op. cit., Federal Deposit Insurance Corporation, p. 67

[19.2-95] Text of "An Act to further the national defense and security by checking speculative and excessive price rises, price dislocations, and inflationary tendencies, and for other purposes", a.k.a. the Emergency Price Control Act of 1942, 77th Congress, Session 2, Chapter 26, Public Law 77-421, 30 Jan 1942

[19.2-96] op. cit., Friedman and Schwartz, pp. 557-559

[19.2-97] Text of "An Act to amend sections 12A and 19 of the Federal Reserve Act, as amended", 77th Congress, Session 2, Chapter 488, Public Law 77-656, 7 Jul 1942

[19.2-98] op. cit., Friedman and Schwartz, p. 563

[19.2-99]   Text of "An Act to amend the Emergency Price Control Act of 1942, to aid in preventing inflation, and for other purposes", 77th Congress, Session 2, Chapter 578, Public Law 77-729, 2 Oct 1942

[19.2-100]   op. cit., Federal Deposit Insurance Corporation, p. 67

[19.2-101]   op. cit., Friedman and Schwartz, p. 573

[19.2-102]   Text of "An Act to extend the period during which direct obligations of the United States may be used as collateral security for Federal Reserve notes", 78th Congress, Session 1, Chapter 102, Public Law 78-58, 25 May 1943

[19.2-103]   op. cit., Federal Deposit Insurance Corporation, p. 67

[19.2-104]   op. cit., Federal Deposit Insurance Corporation, p. 67

[19.2-105]   op. cit., Kreps, p. 536

[19.2-106]   op. cit., National Bureau of Economic Research

[19.2-107]   Text of "An Act to amend sections 11(c) and 16 of the Federal Reserve Act, as amended, and for other purposes", 79th Congress, Session 1, Chapter 186, Public Law 78-84, 12 Jun 1945

[19.2-108]   op. cit., Kreps, pp. 107, 108

[19.2-109]   Text of "A Joint Resolution Extending the effective period of the Emergency Price Control Act of 1942, as amended, and the Stabilization Act of 1942, as amended", 79th Congress, Session 1, Chapter 14, Public Law 79-108, 30 Jun 1945

[19.2-110]   op. cit., Kreps, p. 536

[19.2-111]   Text of "The Export-Import Bank Act of 1945", 79th Congress, Session 1, Chapter 341, Public Law 79-173, 31 Jul 1945

[19.2-112]   op. cit., Friedman and Schwartz, p. 509

[19.2-113]   Text of "The Bretton Woods Agreement Act", 79th Congress, Session 1, Chapter 339, Public Law 79-171, 31 Jul 1945

[19.2-114]   op. cit., Kreps, pp. 116-121

[19.2-115]   op. cit., National Bureau of Economic Research

[19.2-116]   op. cit., Federal Deposit Insurance Corporation, p. 67

[19.2-117]   op. cit., Kreps, p. 536

[19.2-118]   Text of "An Act to declare a national policy on employment, production, and purchasing power, and for other purposes", a.k.a. the Employment Act of 1946, 79th Congress, Session 2, Chapter 33, Public Law 79-304, 20 Feb 1946

[19.2-119]   op. cit., Friedman and Schwartz, p. 596

[19.2-120]   Text of "Joint Resolution extending the effective period of the Emergency Price Control Act of 1942, as amended and the Stabilization Act of 1942, as amended", 79th Congress, Session 2, Chapter 671, Public Law 79-548, 25 Jul 1946

[19.2-121]   op. cit., Friedman and Schwartz, p. 486

[19.2-122]   op. cit., Kreps, p. 111

[19.2-123]   op. cit., Federal Deposit Insurance Corporation, p. 67

[19.2-124]   op. cit., Kreps, p. 536

[19.2-125]   op. cit., Friedman and Schwartz, p. 578

[19.2-126]   Text of "An Act to amend the Federal Reserve Act and for other purposes", 80th Congress, Session 1, Chapter 44, Public Law 80-41, 28 Apr 1947

[19.2-127]   Text of "An Act to provide for the reincorporation of the Export-Import bank of Washington, and for other purposes", 80th Congress, Session 1, Chapter 101, Public Law 80-89, 9 Jun 1947

[19.2-128]   op. cit. Friedman and Schwartz, p. 582

[19.2-129]   Text of "An Act to provide for the cancellation of the capital stock of the Federal Deposit Insurance Corporation and the refund of moneys received for such stock, and for other purposes", 80th Congress, Session 1, Chapter 492, Public Law 80-363, 5 Aug 1947

[19.2-130]   op. cit., Friedman and Schwartz, p. 577

[19.2-131]   op. cit., Federal Deposit Insurance Corporation, p. 67

[19.2-132]   Text of "Joint Resolution for membership and participation of the United States in the World Health organization and authorizing an appropriation therefor", 80th Congress, Session 2, Chapter 469, Public Law 80-643, 14 Jun 1948

[19.2-133]   Text of "Joint Resolution to aid in protecting the Nation's economy against inflationary pressures", 80th Congress, Session 2, Chapter 836, Public Law 80-905, 16 Aug 1948

[19.2-134]   op. cit., Friedman and Schwartz, pp. 580, 604

[19.2-135]   op. cit., National Bureau of Economic Research

[19.2-136] op. cit., Federal Deposit Insurance Corporation, p. 67
[19.2-137] op. cit., National Bureau of Economic Research
[19.2-138] Text of "An Act to stabilize prices of agricultural commodities", a.k.a. the Agricultural Act of 1949, 81st Congress, Session 1, Chapter 792, Public Law 81-439, 31 Oct 1949
[19.2-139] op. cit., Federal Deposit Insurance Corporation, p. 67
[19.2-140] op. cit., Friedman and Schwartz, pp. 610, 611
[19.2-141] Text of "An Act to amend section 14(b) of the Federal Reserve Act, as amended", 81st Congress, Session 2, Chapter 425, Public Law 81-589, 30 Jun 1950
[19.2-142] Text of "An Act to provide for the conversion of national banking associations into and their merger or consolidation with State banks, and for other purposes", 81st Congress, Session 2, Chapter 729, Public Law 81-706, 17 Aug 1950
[19.2-143] Text of "An Act to establish a system of priorities and allocations for materials and facilities, authorize the requisitioning thereof, provide financial assistance for expansion of productive capacity and supply, provide for wage and price stabilization, provide for the settlement of labor disputes, strengthen controls over credit, and by these measures facilitate the production of goods and services necessary for the national security, and for other purposes", a.k.a. the Defense Production Act of 1950, 81st Congress, Session 2, Chapter 932, Public Law 81-774, 8 Sep 1950
[19.2-144] op. cit., Friedman and Schwartz, pp. 610, 611
[19.2-145] op. cit., Friedman and Schwartz, p. 435
[19.2-146] Text of "An Act to amend the Federal Deposit Insurance Act (U. S. C. title 12, sec. 264)", a.k.a. the Federal Deposit Insurance Act, 81st Congress, Session 2, Chapter 967, Public Law 81-797, 21 Sep 1950
[19.2-147] op. cit., Federal Deposit Insurance Corporation, p. 67

[19.3-1] op. cit., Friedman, and Schwartz, Appendix A, pp. 740-742
[19.3-2] Annual Report of the Director of the Mint, 1940, 3 Sep 1940, Treasury Document 3109, p. 67

[19.4-1] op. cit., Kreps, pp. 540, 541
[19.4-2] op. cit., Kreps, p. 543
[19.4-3] op. cit., Kreps, pp. 539, 547-549

NBER website: https://www.nber.org/research/data/us-business-cycle-expansions-and-contractions

20

Federal Reserve Under the Gold Bullion Standard, Part 2, 1951-1971

20.1 Preview, 1951-1971

The U. S. had been on the "gold bullion" system since 1933, in which gold was used only for foreign transactions, and fiat money was used domestically. The U. S. had also now become the de facto reserve currency after the Bretton Woods Agreement in 1945. These two factors led to a drain on America's gold reserve in the 1950's. First, some foreign nations held a surplus of U. S. dollars and decided to hand them in for gold. They had surpluses of dollars due to: a) U. S. foreign aid; b) large imports of foreign goods into the U. S. to help those foreign economies recover), and c) exportation of American capital to help rebuild the ruined industrial base in Europe [20.1-1].

William McChesney Martin, Jr., Chairman of the Board of Governors of the Federal Reserve System, gave a speech before the Economic Club of Detroit, MI, 13 Apr 1953. He stated in part [20.1-2]:

> "If we handle our fiscal, monetary, and debt management problems wisely, we will not have to worry very much about the value of the dollar."

The Federal Reserve and the U. S. government did handle the economy and money supply wisely until about 1967. This was the second unusual period in U. S. economic history, in which the standard of living rose quickly in a short time. It was caused by the fact that the U. S. was the dominant industrial power, having the largest completely intact industrial base after World War II.

In the history that follows, I have indicated the legislation passed under President Johnson's "Great Society" programs. I do not give the description of them since they are well-known. I mention them in passing only to remind you that they were a major factor in the increase in the government expenditures as will be seen in the tabulated data. The entire "Great Society" initiative was designed to: a) eliminate poverty, b) improve education; c) improve access to medical care; d) solve urban problems; e) end racial injustice; and f) improve transportation. You may judge for yourself as to whether these were effective or not. My own opinion is that the "Great Society" did more harm than good. It served to destroy the family unit among Americans of African descent; the third great attack on them at the hands of the Democratic Party (the first two being slavery and Jim Crow).

Europeans continued to demand gold in return for the dollars they held, and the U. S. gold supply dwindled. This banking period ended when President Nixon abandoned the Bretton Woods Agreement in 1971, removing the ability of foreign nations to obtain gold in exchange for U. S. dollars. The U. S. dollar then become an entirely fiat currency internationally, as it had been domestically since 1933. President Kennedy brought many Keynesian economists into his administration [20.1-3], and they remained throughout the Johnson and Nixon administrations. As President Nixon later observed, "We're all Keynesians now".

20.2 History, 1951-1971

4 Mar 1951: The Federal Reserve and the U. S. Treasury issued an "Accord" [20.2-1]:

> "The Treasury and the Federal Reserve System have reached full accord with respect to debt management and monetary policies to be pursued in furthering their common purpose to assure the financing of the Government's requirements and, at the same time, to minimize monetization of the public debt."

> Translation: The Federal Reserve would no longer use the Open Market Account to provide all the reserves necessary to buy government debt at minimum prices; U. S. security prices would change per market conditions. The Federal Reserve could now pursue monetary policy with the prices of U. S. securities only as a secondary consideration.

6 - 15 Mar 1951: Fourth Battle of Seoul (a.k.a. Operation Ripper).

17 Aug - 5 Sep 1951: Battle of Bloody Ridge.

31 Dec 1951: Two banks failed in 1951, with no losses to the FDIC FDIF [20.2-2].

23 Jun 1952: Congress extended [20.2-3] the authority of Federal Reserve banks to buy U. S. securities directly from the U. S. Treasury until 30 Jun 1954 (cf. 30 Jun 1950).

30 Jun 1952: The power of the Federal Reserve to control consumer credit under Regulation W expired (cf. 8 Sep 1950) [20.2-4].

14 Jul 1952: Congress passed legislation [20.2-5] on bank mergers: **a)** (S. 4) permitted two national banking associations to merge within one State; and **b)** (S. 4) permitted two State banks to merge and become a national bank.

13 Sep - 15 Oct 1952: Battle of Heartbreak Ridge.

31 Dec 1952: Three banks failed in 1952, with net losses to the FDIC FDIF totaling $792,000 [20.2-6].

5 Mar 1953: The Open Market Committee adopted a bills-only approach to open market operations (until Jul 1958) [20.2-7]. The Federal Reserve Open Market Committee adopted a policy [20.2-8, 20.2-9] of buying only short-term Treasury bills (called "bills preferably") on the grounds that short-term bills are subject to a more competitive market and thus Federal Reserve transactions interferes least with the rest of the securities market. The Federal Reserve policy was based on the concept that its activities then would mostly affect bank reserves and total stock of money and less on what kind of securities it bought. The decision was stated in the Federal Reserve's 1953 Annual Report [20.2-10]:

> "It is not now the policy of the Committee to support any pattern of prices and yields in the Government securities market, and intervention in the Government securities market is solely to effectuate the objectives of monetary and credit policy (including correction of disorderly markets)."

28, 29 May 1953: Battle of the Hook.

27 Jun 1953: Active hostilities ended in Korea with a truce (still in effect).

30 Jun 1953: The Federal Reserve Board's authority to regulate residential mortgages per Regulation X (cf. 8 Sep 1950) formally expired [20.2-11], although it had not been used since Sep 1952.

15 Jul 1953: Approximate beginning of a recession [20.2-12].

31 Dec 1953: Two banks failed in 1953, with no losses to the FDIC FDIF [20.2-13].

15 May 1954: Approximate end of the recession (cf. 15 Jul 1953) [20.2-14].

29 Jun 1954: Congress extended [20.2-15] the authority of Federal Reserve Banks to buy U. S. securities directly from the U. S. Treasury until 30 Jun 1956 (cf. 23 Jun 1952).

14 Jul 1954: The Treasury Secretary issued a regulation declaring all gold coins minted before 5 Apr 1933 to be owned legally (i.e., were all now "collectors' coins") [20.2-16].

19 Jul 1954: Congress repealed [20.2-17] part of Section 16 of the Federal Reserve Act (cf. 23 Dec 1913) that required each Federal Reserve Bank to either return for payment any Federal Reserve Notes issued by another Federal Reserve Bank, or send them to the Treasury for redemption, upon penalty of a 10% tax on the face value. This meant that all Federal Reserve Notes are treated in common. Secondly, the "payment" provision had been irrelevant since 1933, since Federal Reserve Notes are "redeemable" only in other Federal Reserve Notes or in subsidiary coin.

31 Dec 1954: Two banks failed in 1954, with net losses to the FDIC FDIF totaling $258,000 [20.2-18].

31 Dec 1955: Five banks failed in 1955, with net losses to the FDIC FDIF totaling $230,000 [20.2-19].

9 May 1956: Congress passed the Bank Holding Company Act (Public Law 84-511) [20.2-20]: **a)** (S. 3) all bank holding companies were to required to be regulated by the Federal Reserve, in order to end the current practice of holding companies controlling branches in States where its branches were not permitted directly; **b)** (S. 3) new holding companies to require approval from the Federal Reserve before beginning operations; **c)** (S. 4) required approval from the Federal Reserve before any holding company could acquire more than 5% equity in any bank; and **d)** (S. 4) bank holding companies were restricted to owning and voting shares only in bank institutions. The objective was to prevent the banking industry from being too concentrated in a small number of large organizations, and to ensure there was adequate competition among banks [20.2-21].

28 May 1956: Congress passed the Agricultural Act of 1956 [20.2-22] to regulate the U. S. agricultural industry. Section 102, stating the finding of Congress, reads in part:

> "The Congress hereby finds that the production of excessive supplies of agricultural commodities depresses the prices and income of farm families; constitutes improper land use and brings about soil erosion, depletion of soil fertility, and too rapid release of water from lands where it falls, thereby adversely affecting the national welfare, impairing the productive facilities necessary for a continuous and stable supply of agricultural commodities, and endangering an adequate supply of water for agricultural and nonagricultural use; overtaxes the facilities of interstate and foreign transportation; congests terminal markets and handling and processing centers in the flow of commodities from producers to consumers; depresses prices in interstate and foreign commerce; disrupts the orderly marketing of commodities in such commerce; and otherwise affects, burdens, and obstructs interstate and foreign commerce. It is in the interest of the general welfare that the soil and water resources of the Nation be not wasted and depleted in the production of such burdensome surpluses and that interstate and foreign commerce in agricultural commodities be protected from excessive supplies. It is hereby declared to be the policy of the Congress and the purposes of this title to protect and increase farm income, to protect the national soil, water, and forest and wildlife resources from waste and depletion, to protect interstate and foreign commerce from the burdens and obstructions which result from the utilization of farmland for the production of excessive supplies of agricultural commodities, and to provide for the conservation of such resources and an adequate, balanced, and orderly flow of such agricultural commodities in interstate and foreign commerce."

Provisions include, as an amendment and expansion of the Agricultural Adjustment Act of 1938 (cf. 16 Feb 1938): **a)** (S. 103-105) acreage controls ("acreage reserve program") through 1959 for wheat, cotton, corn, peanuts, rice, and tobacco, reducing the amount of land that can be used for planting, and to compensate farmers accordingly; **b)** (S. 107) conditions on grazing etc. on land set aside as fallow; **c)** (S. 108) authorized the Agriculture Secretary to determine conservation goals for each year; and **d)** S. 201) provisions for disposing of agricultural surpluses. The rest is administrative.

25 Jun 1956: Congress extended [20.2-23] the authority of Federal Reserve Banks to buy U. S. securities directly from the U. S. Treasury until 30 Jun 1958 (cf. 29 Jun 1954).

31 Dec 1956: Two banks failed in 1956, with net losses to the FDIC FDIF totaling $213,000 [20.2-24].

15 Aug 1957: Approximate beginning of the recession [20.2-25].

31 Dec 1957: One bank failed in 1957, with no losses to the FDIC FDIF [20.2-26].

15 Apr 1958: Approximate end of a recession (cf. 15 Aug 1957) [20.2-27].

30 Jun 1958: Congress extended [20.2-28] the authority of Federal Reserve Banks to buy U. S. securities directly from the U. S. Treasury until 30 Jun 1960 (cf. 25 Jun 1956).

28 Aug 1958: Congress passed the Agricultural Act of 1958 [20.2-29] (cf. 31 Oct 1949, 28 May 1956), modifying the acreage and quotas of various crops, and providing for price supports at 90% parity on wool, cotton, grains (oats, barley, and rye), and rice, but eliminating acreage allotments on corn.

31 Dec 1958: Four banks failed in 1958, with net losses to the FDIC FDIF totaling $28,000 [20.2-30].

17 Jun 1959: Congress passed an amendment to the Bretton Woods Act [20.2-31] (cf. 31 Jul 1945), increasing the value of U. S. shares in the IDBF and IMF from $4,125 M ($4.125 B) to $8,675 M ($8.675 B).

28 Jul 1959: Congress passed revisions to the National Bank Act and Federal Reserve Act [20.2-32]: **a)** (S. 1) member banks can include cash in vault against primary legal reserves on a graduated scale (100% counted as reserves effective after Nov 1960); **b)** (S. 2) reduced demand deposit reserve range in central reserve bank cities from [13 to 26%] to [10 to 22%]; **c)** (S. 2) reserve cities: from [10 to 20%] to new range of [10 to 22%]; **d)** (S. 1) member banks in the same city as a central reserve or reserve city to carry lower reserves if authorized by Board of Governors; **e)** (S. 3) deleted "central reserve city" designation effective 28 Jul 1962; and **f)** (S. 3) all member banks will be classified either reserve city banks or country banks (based on the type of business rather than geographical location). The rationale was that the correspondent banking function in the reserve cities had become increasingly important, and there was no reason to distinguish the reserve requirements between banks in central reserve and reserve cities [20.2-33].

8 Sep 1959: Congress passed legislation [20.2-34] clarifying and updating provisions regarding national banks within the Federal Reserve System. The main provisions include: **a)** (S. 1) deleted the Home Owners Loan Association, substituting Federal Home Loan Banks, from the powers granted to the Federal Reserve under Section 23A; **b)** (S. 4) required all capital stock to be paid into a national banking association before beginning operation; and **c)** (S. 20) permitted national banks within a single State to consolidate if permitted by State laws and with the approval of the Comptroller of the Currency.

31 Dec 1959: Three banks failed in 1959, with net losses to the FDIC FDIF totaling $97,000 [20.2-35].

15 Apr 1960: Approximate beginning of a recession [20.2-36].

13 May 1960: Congress passed a revision [20.2-37] to the Federal Deposit Insurance Act (cf. 21 Sep 1950): **a)** banks insured by the FDIC can merge only approval from either the Comptroller of the Currency (national banks), Federal Reserve Board of Governors (State-chartered banks), or FDIC (banks that are not members of the Federal Reserve); and **b)** approval to be based on an analysis of public interest and necessity, and the goal of maintaining competition. The objective was to control the pace of bank mergers and preserve competition among the banks [20.2-38].

1 Jul 1960: Congress extended [20.2-39] the authority of Federal Reserve Banks to buy U. S. securities directly from the U. S. Treasury until 30 Jun 1962 (cf. 30 Jun 1958).

1 Dec 1960: Banks were now permitted to count 100% of their cash in vault against legal reserves, based on the 28 Jul 1959 law [20.2-40].

31 Dec 1960: One bank failed in 1960, with no losses to the FDIC FDIF [20.2-41].

15 Feb 1961: Approximate end of a recession (cf. 15 Apr 1960) [20.2-42].

20 Feb 1961: The Federal Reserve Open Market Committee abandoned the bills-only approach [20.2-43, 20.2-44]. This was done to increase short-term interest rates and stem the flow of gold out of the U. S. (since the foreign holders of short-term dollar accounts had begun converting them into gold and exporting the gold out of the U. S.). The Federal Reserve also announced that part of the reason was to obtain the lowest prices on securities and to assist in the U. S. balance of payments. The Treasury

announced that it would offer discounts on government securities, if necessary, when the market interest rate exceeded the 4.5% legal yield limit on bonds maturing in more than 5 years (cf. 4 Apr 1918).

30 Jun 1961: Congress passed the Old Series Currency Adjustment Act [20.2-45] providing direction on retirement of old series currency: **a)** (S. 2) defined "U. S. Notes" as those issued per 25 Feb 1862, 11 Jul 1862, 17 Jan 1863, 3 Mar 1863; **b)** (S. 2) defined "Treasury Notes of 1890" as notes issued per 14 Jul 1890; **c)** (S. 3) authorized and directed to transfer three types of currency to the general fund, and credited as a receipt against the public debt: 1) gold held as security for gold certificates issued prior to 30 Jan 1934; 2) standard silver dollars held as security for and redemption of silver certificates issued prior to 1 Jul 1929; and 3) standard silver dollars held as security for and redemption of Treasury Notes of 1890; **d)** (S. 4) authorized the Board of Governors of the Federal Reserve to determine, with approval of the Treasury Secretary, if any Federal Reserve Notes issued prior to 1928 should be returned to the Treasury and counted as a receipt against the public debt; **e)** (S. 5) five types of notes to be carried on Treasury accounts as public debt bearing no interest: 1) gold certificates issued prior to 30 Jan 1934, 2) Treasury Notes of 1890, 3) United States Notes issued prior to 1 Jul 1929, 4) silver certificates issued prior to 1 Jul 1929, and 5) any Federal Reserve Notes paid under section 4; **f)** (S. 6) Treasury Secretary to determine the amount gold certificates, Treasury Notes of 1890, United States Notes, silver certificates, Federal Reserve Bank Notes issued prior to 1 Jul 1929, and National Bank Notes issued prior to 1 Jul 1929 that have been lost or destroyed and will never be presented for redemption, and to reduce the amounts on the Treasury account accordingly; **g)** (S. 7) reduced the amount of National Bank Notes that can circulate by the amount of reduction estimated per section 6; **h)** (S. 8) modified Federal Reserve Act section 16 to permit withdrawal of securities commensurate with the reduction of Federal Reserve Notes; and **i)** (S. 9) this act does not affect the redeemability of "any currency of the United States as now provided by law". (Only silver certificates were redeemable in silver coin at this time.)

26 Sep 1961: Congress authorized [20.2-46] up to $1,000 M ($1 B) in credit to be extended by the Export-Import Bank, requiring 25% reserves for guarantees, insurance, and reinsurance.

4 Oct 1961: Congress passed legislation [20.2-47] to abolish the Federal Farm Mortgage Corporation, and transfer its titles and interest in real property to the Federal Land Bank in the same district, except cash and accounts receivable are transferred to the Treasury, and mineral rights to the Department of the Interior.

31 Dec 1961: Five banks failed in 1961, with net losses to the FDIC FDIF totaling $1.502 M [20.2-48].

19 Jun 1962: Congress passed an amendment [20.2-49] to the Bretton Woods Act (cf. 31 Jul 1945), authorizing the Treasury Secretary to issue loans up $2,000 M ($2 B) to the IMF.

28 Jun 1962: Congress extended [20.2-50] the authority of Federal Reserve Banks to buy U. S. securities directly from the U. S. Treasury until 30 Jun 1964 (cf. 1 Jul 1960).

23 Oct 1962: Congress passed legislation [20.2-51]: **a)** (S. 1) permitted banks to invest in corporations that provide clerical services for them, including sorting of checks and deposits, payment of interest, preparation and mailing of bills and statement, bookkeeping, and accounting; **b)** (S. 2) banks permitted to invest up to 10% of capital and surplus in service corporations; **c)** (S. 4) bank service corporations are restricted only to that business; and **d)** (S. 5) banks and service corporations required to provide assurance of only authorized activity to: 1) national banks in Washington DC to the Comptroller of the Currency; 2) banks that are members of the Federal Reserve, to the Board of Governors; and 3) banks insured by FDIC, to the Board of Directors of the FDIC.

31 Dec 1962: There were no bank failures in 1962 [20.2-52].

4 Jun 1963: Congress passed legislation regarding the purchase of silver [20.2-53]: **a)** (S. 1) repealed the Silver Purchase Act of 1934 (cf. 19 Jun 1934); **b)** (S. 1) repealed section 4 of the Act of 6 Jul 1939; **c)** (S. 1) repealed the Act of 31 Jul 1946; **d)** (S. 2) required the Treasury to maintain enough silver to

fully back the existing silver certificates; e) (S. 3) authorized Federal Reserve Notes to be issued in denominations of $1 and $2; and f) (S. 201) repealed the tax on silver bullion. The net result was the exchange of silver certificates for Federal Reserve Notes, ultimately leading to the temporary elimination of redemption by Mar 1964 and permanently in Jun 1968.

20 Aug 1963: Congress increased [20.2-54] the lending authority of the Export-Import Bank to $9,000 M ($9 B), and extended its operation until 30 Jun 1968.

31 Dec 1963: Two banks failed in 1963, with net losses to the FDIC FDIF totaling $286,000 [20.2-55].

25 Mar 1964: Silver certificates were no longer were redeemable in coin, only in silver granules per order of the Treasury Secretary (cf. 4 Jun 1963).

30 Jun 1964: Congress extended [20.2-56] the authority of Federal Reserve banks to buy U. S. securities directly from the U. S. Treasury until 30 Jun 1966 (cf. 28 Jun 1962).

30 Jun 1964: Congress authorized [20.2-57] national banks (per a modification to the Federal Reserve Act, section 24) to make loans on "properly managed" forest tracts, up to 60% of appraised value at interest rate not to exceed 6.66% and for terms not to exceed 15 years.

2 Aug 1964: A minor engagement occurred between the USS Maddox and three North Vietnamese torpedo boats at Tonkin Gulf. There were subsequent reports, later proven false, of an additional confrontation on 4 Aug 1964. However, this gave President Lyndon Johnson the excuse he needed to involve the U. S. in the Vietnamese Civil War.

10 Aug 1964: Congress passes a Joint Resolution [20.2-58] authorizing the President to take "all necessary measures to repel any armed attack against the forces of the United States and to prevent further aggression".

20 Aug 1964: Congress passed the Economic Opportunity Act of 1964 [20.2-59] as part of the Great Society: a) established the Job Corps, including work training and work-study programs; b) Urban and Rural Community Action Programs to "provide services, assistance and other activities ... to give promise toward elimination of poverty", including Adult Basic Education and Voluntary Assistance to Needy Children; c) Special Programs to Combat Poverty in Rural Areas, including loans to low-income rural families and assistance for migrant and other seasonally employed agricultural employees, d) Employment and Investment Incentives including loans for small businesses; and e) Work Experience Programs. The programs begun here ended up as 85 types of block grants; later consolidated into 17 per the Community Services Block Grants under the Omnibus Reconciliation Act of 1981 (P. L. 97-35), and then amended by the Coates Human Services Reauthorization Act of 1998 (P. L. 105-285).

31 Aug 1964: Congress passed the Food Stamp Act of 1964 [20.2-60] as part of the Great Society; established food stamps and the school lunch program.

31 Dec 1964: Seven banks failed in 1964, with net losses to the FDIC FDIF totaling $1.541 M [20.2-61].

3 Mar 1965: Congress passed legislation altering Section 16 of the Federal Reserve Act [20.2-62]: a) (S. 1) eliminated the requirement of Federal Reserve Banks to hold 25% in gold certificates against deposits (i.e., these deposits are the reserve accounts of member banks); but b) (S. 2) retained the requirement for Federal Reserve Banks (via gold deposits with the Board of Governors) to maintain gold reserves against Federal Reserve Notes in circulation per existing law.

11 Apr 1965: Congress passed the Elementary and Secondary Education Act of 1965 [20.2-63] as part of the Great Society, providing federal grant for a variety of purposes: a) school districts with low income students; b) allocations for libraries; c) Supplementary Educational Centers and Service, d) Educational Research and Training; and e) to "Strengthen State Departments of Education". The provisions of this legislation were ultimately incorporated into the No Child Left Behind Act of 8 Jan 2002 (P. L. 110-110), then repealed 10 Dec 2015.

23 Jul 1965: Congress passed the Coinage Act of 1965 [20.2-64]: a) (S. 101) revised the metallic standard for the minor coins: redefined the composition (core and cladding) of half-dollars, quarters and

dimes: 1) half-dollars to consist of 4.6 grams silver and 6.9 grams of copper; 2) quarter to consist of a copper core and a cladding of 75% copper and 25% nickel, and the full weight to be 5.67 grams, and 3) dime to consist of a copper core and a cladding of 75% copper and 25% nickel, and the full weight to be 2.268 grams; **b)** (S. 101) authorized the Mint to continue coining standard 90% silver coins (half-dollar, quarter, and dime) until enough of the new ones were made or five years, whichever came first; **c)** (S. 101) prohibited minting of standard silver dollars; **d)** (S. 102) declared that "all coins and currencies of the United States (including Federal Reserve Notes and circulating notes of Federal Reserve banks and national banking associations), regardless of when coined or issued, shall be legal tender for all debts, public and private, public charges, taxes, duties, and dues"; **e)** (S. 104) permitted the Treasury Secretary to purchase silver at $1.25 per ozt. at his discretion; **f)** (S. 105) granted the Treasury Secretary the power to "prohibit, curtail, or regulate the exportation, melting or treating of any coin of the United States" to "protect the coinage of the United States"; **g)** (S. 209) authorized the Treasury Secretary to sell silver in excess of required reserves against silver certificates at $1.2929 per ozt.; and **h)** (S. 301) created a Joint Commission on the Coinage to advise the President and Congress on future coinage issues. The change in coinage was done in response to a shortage of silver [20.2-65].

30 Jul 1965: Congress passed the "Social Security Amendments of 1965" [20.2-66], which created Medicare, a health insurance program for those 65 and over, and Medicaid, a health insurance program for the poor. It also increased Social Security benefits for eligible retired and disabled persons.

10 Aug 1965: Congress passed the Housing and Urban Development Act of 1965 [20.2-67] as part of the Great Society under 11 categories: a) Special Provisions for Disadvantaged Persons; b) FHA Insurance Operation; c) Urban Renewal; d) Lease Guarantees; e) Compensation of Condemnees; f) Low Rent Public Housing; g) College Housing; h) Community Facilities; i) Federal National Mortgage Association; j) Open-Space Land and Urban Beautification and Improvement; and k) Rural Housing.

9 Oct 1965: Congress passed the Economic Opportunity Amendments of 1965 [20.2-68] as part of the Great Society, emulating and expanding the provision of the original law (cf. 20 Aug 1964).

8 Nov 1965: Congress passed the Higher Education Act of 1965 [20.2-69] as part of the Great Society under seven categories: a) Community Service and Continuing Education Programs; b) College Library Assistance and Library Training and Research; c) Strengthening Developing Institutions; d) Student Assistance (grants and student loans); e) Teacher Programs; f) Financial Assistance for the Improvement of Undergraduate Education; and g) Amendments to Higher Education Facilities Act of 1963.

14 - 18 Nov 1965: Battle of la Drang Valley.

31 Dec 1965: Five banks failed in 1965, with net losses to the FDIC FDIF totaling $663,000 [20.2-70].

28 Mar 1966: Congress passed legislation [20.2-71] abolishing the Postal Savings System (cf. 25 Jun 1910).

30 Jun 1966: Congress extended [20.2-72] the authority of Federal Reserve Banks to buy U. S. securities directly from the U. S. Treasury until 30 Jun 1968 (cf. 30 Jun 1964).

1 Jul 1966: Congress passed an amendment to the Bank Holding Company Act of 1956 [20.2-73], changing administrative and tax rules of holding companies.

21 Sep 1966: Congress passed legislation on the banking system [20.2-74], effective for one year: **a)** (S. 1) directed the "Secretary of the Treasury, the Board of Governors of the Federal Reserve System, the Board of Directors of the Federal Deposit Insurance Corporation, and the Federal Home Loan Bank Board, in implementation of their respective powers under existing law and this Act, shall take action to bring about the reduction of interest rates to the maximum extent feasible in the light of prevailing money market and general economic conditions"; **b)** (S. 2) authorized the Board of Governors to set maximum interest rates; **c)** (S. 2) changed reserve requirements on deposits: 1) for reserve cities, between 10 and 22% on demand deposits, but permitted the Board to make exceptions

as necessary; 2) for "country banks", between 7 and 14% on demand deposits; and 3) between 3 and 10% on time deposits for all banks; **d)** (S. 3) authorized the FDIC to set maximum interest rates on demand and time deposits held in insured banks that are not members of the Federal Reserve; **e)** (S. 4) authorized the Board of Governors and FDIC to set maximum interest rates on deposits and shares of Savings and Loan institutions; **f)** (S. 6) modified Section 14b of the Federal Reserve Act to permit the Federal Reserve to buy and sell U. S. securities and any securities for which the principal and interest are guaranteed by any federal agency; and **g)** (S. 7) authorities to expire 21 Sep 1967.

11 Oct 1966: Congress passed the Child Nutrition Act of 1966 [20.2-75] as part of the Great Society: a) school breakfast program, b) milk program, and c) preschool provisions.

15 Oct 1966: Congress authorized [20.2-76] the use of foreign currencies on hand to pay current expenditures in lieu of dollars, in order to relieve the current negative balance of payments.

16 Oct 1966: Congress passed the Financial Institutions Supervisory Act [20.2-77]: **a)** (S. 101) permitted the Federal Home Loan Bank Board (FHLBB) to issue cease-and-desist orders against any institution (Federal Home Loan Bank or Savings and Loan) that the Board believes has engaged in unsound banking practices, or has or is about to violate either its charter or the regulations; **b)** (S. 101) FHLBB may remove officers and directors of such institutions; **c)** (S. 101) FHLBB to appoint conservators or receiver for insolvent institutions; **d)** (S. 101) granted the FHLBB power to make rules for liquidating or converting any institutions whose deposits are insured by the FSLIC; **e)** (S. 201) same provisions as above apply to national banking association or Federal Reserve Bank (Comptroller of the Currency), State insured member bank (Federal Reserve Board), and State nonmember insured bank (FDIC); and **f)** (S. 301, 302) increased the amount of the insured deposits from $10,000 to $15,000 for all FDIC and FSLIC insured banks.

3 Nov 1966: Congress passed the Demonstration Cities and Metropolitan Development Act [20.2-78] as part of the Great Society: a) Comprehensive City Demonstration Programs, b) Planned Metropolitan Development, c) FHA Insurance Operations, d) Land Development and New Communities, e) Mortgage Insurance for Group Practice Facilities, f) Preservation of Historic Structures, g) Urban Renewal, h) Rural Housing, and i) Urban Information and Technical Services Assistance.

5 Nov 1966: Congress passed a modification [20.2-79] to Section 11(j) of the Federal Reserve Act permitting the Board of Governors authority to delegate any of its functions related to "exercising general supervision over Federal Reserve Banks" to employees of the Board, hearing examiners, or the Federal Reserve Banks themselves. The delegation does not apply to rulemaking, or any decisions related principally to monetary or credit policy.

31 Dec 1966: Seven banks failed in 1966, with net losses to the FDIC FDIF totaling $245,000 [20.2-80].

24 Jun 1967: Congress passed legislation regarding silver [20.2-81]: **a)** (S. 1) authorized the Treasury Secretary to determine what amount of silver certificates will never be redeemed (up to $200 M), and credit accounts accordingly, and reduce the estimated number outstanding; **b)** (S. 2) silver certificates to be redeemable in silver bullion until 24 Jun 1968, after which they will be redeemable only in "other moneys in the general fund of the Treasury not otherwise appropriated" (i.e. Federal Reserve Notes); **c)** (S. 3) authorized the Treasury Secretary to buy or sell silver at $1.2929 per ozt.; and **d)** (S. 4) required the Treasury Secretary to hold in reserve 165 M ozt. of fine silver, and after one year, to transfer it to the Strategic and Critical Materials Stockpile.

21 Sep 1967: Congress extended the provisions [20.2-82] of the 21 Sep 1966 law to 21 Sep 1968.

31 Dec 1967: Four banks failed in 1967, with net losses to the FDIC FDIF totaling $1.010 M [20.2-83].

2 Jan 1968: Congress passed the Social Security Amendments of 1967 [20.2-84] as part of the Great Society; amended and expanded Social Security, Medicare, Medicaid, and aid to children.

21 Jan 1968 - 9 Apr 1968: Battle of Khe Sanh.

31 Jan 1968 - 28 Feb 1968: Battle of Hue.

16 Mar 1968: Congress increased [20.2-85] the lending authority of the Export-Import Bank to $13,500 M ($13.5 B), and extended its operation until 30 Jun 1973; changed its name from the Export-Import Bank of Washington to the Export-Import Bank of the United States; and prohibited it from doing any business in a Communist nation.

18 Mar 1968: Congress passed legislation [20.2-86] modifying the Federal Reserve Act (FRA): **a)** (S. 1, 9) abolished the tax on member banks that could be imposed if their reserves fell below the legal requirement (FRA 11(c)); **b)** (S. 2) abolished the 5% reserve to be held in the general fund of the Treasury against Federal Reserve Notes; **c)** (S. 3) required Federal Reserve Notes to bear a unique serial number; **d)** (S. 4, 5, 7) abolished the requirement (per FRA 16 original paragraphs 3 and 18) for Federal Reserve Banks to maintain on deposit with the Treasury a sufficient amount of gold as reserve for the redemption for Federal Reserve Notes (was 40% total, with 5% on deposit; now no gold reserve was required); **e)** (S. 6) permitted Federal Reserve Notes to be re-issued (modifying FRA section 16, original paragraph 7); and **f)** (S. 8, 10, 11, and 12) abolished the requirement to hold any gold reserves for United States Notes (greenbacks), Treasury Notes of 1890, and Federal Reserve Notes.

4 May 1968: Congress extended [20.2-87] the authority of Federal Reserve Banks to buy U. S. securities directly from the U. S. Treasury until 30 Jun 1970 (cf. 30 Jun 1966).

19 Jun 1968: Congress passed legislation [20.2-88] permitting the U. S. to participate in the Special Drawing Rights of the International Monetary Fund. Among its provisions: **a)** (S. 2) authorized the President to accept the amendment to the articles of the International Monetary Fund that established the Special Drawing Rights facility; **b)** (S. 3) Special Drawing Rights for the U. S. to be administered by the "Stabilization Fund" (cf. Gold Reserve Act of 1934, section 10, 30 Jan 1934); **c)** (S. 4) Treasury Secretary authorized to issue to the Federal Reserve Banks, and the Federal Reserve Banks shall purchase, Special Drawing Rights certificates held to the credit of the Exchange Stabilization Fund; and **d)** modified S. 16 of the Federal Reserve Act such that Special Drawing Rights may be used as collateral against Federal Reserve Notes.

28 Jun 1968: All redemption of silver certificates for silver coin or granules was abolished by order of the Treasury Secretary (cf. 4 Jun 1963).

21 Sep 1968: Congress extended the provisions [20.2-89] of the 21 Sep 1966 law to 22 Sep 1969.

31 Dec 1968: Three banks failed in 1968, with net losses to the FDIC FDIF totaling $12,000 [20.2-90].

28 Jan 1969 - 28 Mar 1969: The Tet Offensive.

10 May 1969 - 20 May 1969: Battle of Hamburger Hill.

22 Sep 1969: Congress extended the provisions [20.2-91] of the 21 Sep 1966 law to 22 Dec 1969 (cf. 21 Sep 1968).

15 Dec 1969: Approximate beginning of a recession [20.2-92].

23 Dec 1969: Congress passed legislation modifying the banking laws [20.2-93]. The provisions of Title I include: **a)** (S. 2) made permanent the authority of the FDIC to control interest rates on savings and time deposits, and expanded it to control interest rates on savings and time deposits in uninsured State banks until 31 Jul 1970; **b)** (S. 2) authorized the FDIC to determine maximum interest rates on savings and time deposits in insured savings and loan institutions permanently; and **c)** (S. 7) FDIC and FSLIC insurance limit increased to $20,000. Title II is called the Credit Control Act; among its provisions: **a)** (S. 202) granted the Board of Governors of the Federal Reserve the authority to set credit controls on corporations and individuals; and **b)** (S. 204, 205, 207) regulatory authority includes: 1) interest rates on loans; 2) the total volume of credit; 3) may require licensing of lender and borrowers; 4) maximum amount of credit on any transaction; 5) rates of interest, maturity, and other conditions of credit; 6) determine formulas for purchase prices or down payment requirements; and 7) to prohibit any extension of credit the Board "deems inappropriate".

31 Dec 1969: Nine banks failed in 1969, with net losses to the FDIC FDIF totaling $162,000 [20.2-94].

31 Jul 1970: Congress extended [20.2-95] the authority of Federal Reserve Banks to buy U. S. securities directly from the U. S. Treasury until 31 Jul 1971 (cf. 4 May 1968).

15 Aug 1970: Congress passed the Economic Stabilization Act of 1970 [20.2-96]: **a)** (S. 202): granted the President authority to "issue orders and regulations as he may deem appropriate to stabilize prices, rents, wages, and salaries at levels not less than those prevailing on May 25, 1970"; **b)** (S. 202) the President may delegate his authority other officers, departments, and agencies as he sees fit; **c)** (S. 204) the penalty for violating a control order is to be $5,000; and **d)** the authority to issue such orders to expire 28 Feb 1971.

26 Oct 1970: Congress passed the Currency and Foreign Transactions Act [20.2-97], it requires each FDIC-insured bank to create a record of: **a)** the identity of every account holder; **b)** every check or draft presented to it for payment; **c)** each check, draft, or similar instrument received by it for deposit or collection along with the identity of the account holder; and **d)** a record of any transactions that fall under the Currency and Foreign Transactions Act. This was passed because such records have a "high degree of usefulness in criminal, tax, and regulatory investigations and proceedings". It requires the filing of a Currency Transaction Report if a person makes cash transactions totaling more than $10,000 in one day; and must retain for five years a report on any person making cash purchases between $3,000 and $10,000 of money orders, traveler's checks, or cashier's checks.

15 Nov 1970: Approximate end of a recession (cf. 15 Dec 1969) [20.2-98].

17 Dec 1970: Congress extended the President's authority to impose wage and price controls until 31 Mar 1971 (cf. 15 Aug 1970) [20.2-99].

31 Dec 1970: Seven banks failed in 1970, with net losses to the FDIC FDIF totaling $272,000 [20.2-100].

31 Mar 1971: Congress passed economic legislation [20.2-101]: **a)** (S. 1) extended the authority of the Board of Governors to control interest rates on deposits until 1 Jun 1971; and **b)** (S. 2) extended the President's authority to impose wage and price controls until 31 May 1971.

18 May 1971: Congress passed legislation [20.2-102] that **a)** (S. 1) extended the authority of the Board of Governors to regulate interest rates (cf. 31 Mar 1971) until 1 Jun 1973, and **b)** (S. 3) extended the President's authority to implement wage and price controls until 30 Apr 1972 (cf. 31 Mar 1971).

2 Jul 1971: Congress extended [20.2-103] the authority of Federal Reserve Banks to buy U. S. securities directly from the U. S. Treasury until 30 Jun 1973 (cf. 31 Jul 1970).

15 Aug 1971: President Nixon issued Executive Order 11615 [20.2-104], which created the Cost of Living Council. This began Phase 1 of price controls, a 90-day freeze on wages and prices, expiring 13 Nov 1971.

15 Aug 1971: President Nixon announced a "new economic policy" regarding wage and price controls, and that the dollar was no longer convertible into gold for foreign transactions ("closing the gold window") [20.2-105]. This ended the Bretton Woods system, and made the U. S. dollar entirely a fiat currency, with exchange rates floating against other currencies. This caused a depreciation of the dollar, and negatively affected the oil-producing nations, who had priced their oil in dollars.

15 Oct 1971: President Nixon issued Executive Order 11627 [20.2-106]:, which created the Office of Wage Stabilization and Office of Price Stabilization, in order to enforce the Economic Stabilization Act of 1970 (cf. 15 Aug 1970).

14 Nov 1971: Beginning of Phase 2 of wage and price controls per EO 11627, expiring 10 Jan 1973.

22 Dec 1971: Congress passed the Economic Stabilization Act Amendments of 1971 [20.2-107]: **a)** (S. 203) authorized the President to freeze wages, salaries, prices, and rents as prevailed on 15 Aug 1971 (cf. 15 Aug 1970); and **b)** (S. 217) authority to expire 30 Apr 1973. The remaining provisions were the same as the original law (cf. 15 Aug 1970).

31 Dec 1971: Six banks failed in 1971, with net losses to the FDIC FDIF totaling $193,000 [20.2-108].

20.3 Data, 1951-1971

Figures 20.3-1 and 20.3-2 show the U. S. government revenue and expenditures for 1951 to 1971.

			Income taxes				Social Insurance				
Day	Year	Customs Duties	Individual	Corporate	Excise Taxes	Estate and Gift Taxes	OASDI & Disability (Off-Budget)	Medicare & Retirements (On-Budget)	Federal Reserve Deposits	Other Misc.	Net Receipts
30 Jun	1951	609	21,616	14,101	8,648	708	3,120	2,554	189	72	51,616
30 Jun	1952	533	27,934	21,226	8,852	818	3,594	2,851	278	81	66,167
30 Jun	1953	596	29,816	21,238	9,877	881	4,097	2,723	298	81	69,608
30 Jun	1954	542	29,542	21,101	9,945	934	4,589	2,619	341	88	69,701
30 Jun	1955	585	28,747	17,861	9,131	924	5,081	2,781	251	90	65,451
30 Jun	1956	682	32,188	20,880	9,929	1,161	6,425	2,896	287	140	74,587
30 Jun	1957	735	35,620	21,167	10,534	1,365	6,789	3,208	434	139	79,990
30 Jun	1958	782	34,724	20,074	10,638	1,393	8,049	3,190	664	123	79,636
30 Jun	1959	925	36,719	17,309	10,578	1,333	8,296	3,427	491	171	79,249
30 Jun	1960	1,105	40,715	21,494	11,676	1,606	10,641	4,042	1,093	119	92,492
30 Jun	1961	982	41,338	20,954	11,860	1,896	12,109	4,331	788	130	94,388
30 Jun	1962	1,142	45,571	20,523	12,534	2,016	12,271	4,776	718	125	99,676
30 Jun	1963	1,205	47,588	21,579	13,194	2,167	14,175	5,629	828	194	106,560
30 Jun	1964	1,252	48,697	23,493	13,731	2,394	16,366	5,597	947	139	112,613
30 Jun	1965	1,442	48,792	25,461	14,570	2,716	16,723	5,519	1,372	222	116,817
30 Jun	1966	1,767	55,446	30,073	13,062	3,066	19,085	6,460	1,713	163	130,835
30 Jun	1967	1,901	61,526	33,971	13,719	2,978	24,401	8,217	1,805	302	148,822
30 Jun	1968	2,038	68,726	28,665	14,079	3,051	24,917	9,007	2,091	400	152,973
30 Jun	1969	2,319	87,249	36,678	15,222	3,491	28,953	10,062	2,662	247	186,882
30 Jun	1970	2,430	90,412	32,829	15,705	3,644	33,459	10,903	3,266	158	192,807
30 Jun	1971	2,591	86,230	26,785	16,614	3,735	35,845	11,481	3,533	325	187,139

Table title: **U. S. Government Revenue, 1951-1971 (millions USD)**

1. The revenue data for 1951 to 1971 is from the OMB White House, file = HIST_FY21.pdf, Tables 2.1 and 2.5

Figure 20.3-1: U. S. Government Revenue, 1951-1971

Day	Year	National Defense	Education, Training, Employment, Social Services	Health	Medicare	Income Security	Social Security [1]	Veterans	Physical Resources [2]	Interest on Debt	International Affairs	Agri-culture	Other [3]	Undistributed Offsetting Receipts [4]	Total
30 Jun	1951	23,566	235	323	0	3,352	1,565	5,526	3,924	4,665	3,647	-323	1,366	-2,332	45,514
30 Jun	1952	46,089	339	347	0	3,655	2,063	5,341	4,182	4,701	2,691	176	1,479	-3,377	67,686
30 Jun	1953	52,802	441	336	0	3,823	2,717	4,519	4,005	5,156	2,119	2,253	1,501	-3,571	76,101
30 Jun	1954	49,266	370	307	0	4,434	3,352	4,613	2,584	4,811	1,596	1,817	1,102	-3,397	70,855
30 Jun	1955	42,729	445	291	0	5,071	4,427	4,675	2,732	4,850	2,223	3,514	981	-3,493	68,444
30 Jun	1956	42,523	591	359	0	4,734	5,478	4,891	3,092	5,079	2,414	3,486	1,582	-3,589	70,640
30 Jun	1957	45,430	590	479	0	5,427	6,661	5,005	4,559	5,354	3,147	2,288	1,785	-4,146	76,578
30 Jun	1958	46,815	643	541	0	7,535	8,219	5,350	5,188	5,604	3,364	2,411	1,121	-4,385	82,405
30 Jun	1959	49,015	789	685	0	8,239	9,737	5,443	7,813	5,762	3,144	4,509	1,576	-4,613	92,098
30 Jun	1960	48,130	968	795	0	7,378	11,602	5,441	7,991	6,947	2,988	2,623	2,149	-4,820	92,191
30 Jun	1961	49,601	1,063	913	0	9,683	12,474	5,705	7,754	6,716	3,184	2,641	2,796	-4,807	97,723
30 Jun	1962	52,345	1,241	1,198	0	9,198	14,365	5,628	8,831	6,889	5,639	3,562	3,200	-5,274	106,821
30 Jun	1963	53,400	1,458	1,451	0	9,304	15,788	5,521	8,013	7,740	5,308	4,384	4,745	-5,797	111,316
30 Jun	1964	54,757	1,555	1,788	0	9,650	16,620	5,682	9,528	8,199	4,945	4,609	6,904	-5,708	118,528
30 Jun	1965	50,620	2,140	1,791	0	9,462	17,460	5,723	11,264	8,591	5,273	3,954	7,859	-5,908	118,228
30 Jun	1966	58,111	4,363	2,543	64	9,671	20,694	5,923	13,410	9,386	5,580	2,447	8,884	-6,542	134,532
30 Jun	1967	71,417	6,453	3,351	2,748	10,253	21,725	6,743	14,674	10,268	5,566	2,990	8,570	-7,294	157,464
30 Jun	1968	81,926	7,634	4,390	4,649	11,806	23,854	7,042	16,002	11,090	5,301	4,544	7,941	-8,045	178,134
30 Jun	1969	82,497	7,548	5,162	5,695	13,066	27,298	7,642	11,869	12,699	4,600	5,826	7,725	-7,986	183,640
30 Jun	1970	81,692	8,634	5,907	6,213	15,645	30,270	8,679	15,574	14,380	4,330	5,166	7,790	-8,632	195,649
30 Jun	1971	78,872	9,849	6,843	6,622	22,936	35,872	9,778	18,286	14,841	4,159	4,290	7,930	-10,107	210,172

Table title: **U. S. Government Expenditures, 1951-1971 (millions USD)**

1. Social Security expenditures were "off-budget" up to and including 1966. The values for 1967 ff are the totals of on- and off- budget.
2. "Physical Resources" includes Energy, Natural Resources and Environment, Commerce and Housing Credit, Transportation, and Community & Regional Development.
3. "Other" includes General Science, Space & Technology, Administration of Justice, General Government, and Allowances.
4. "Offsetting Receipts" is a combination of new debt and intra-government transfers from Trust Funds.
5. The expenditure data for 1951 to 1971 is from the OMB White House, file = HIST_FY21.pdf, Table 3.1.

Figure 20.3-2: U. S. Government Expenditures, 1951-1971

Figure 20.3-3 shows the national debt and per-capita debt for this period. It is easy to see the acceleration of the per-capita national debt beginning in 1968. Refer to the Introduction to Part 2 for a sense of wages vs. per-capita national debt.

U. S. National Debt, 1951-1971 (USD)									
Day	Year	Principal ($) [1]	Population [2]	Debt per Capita ($) [2]	Day	Year	Principal ($) [1]	Population [2]	Debt per Capita ($) [2]
30 Jun	1951	253,938,976,815	154,125,536	1,647.61	30 Jun	1962	295,363,518,321	184,100,925	1,604.36
30 Jun	1952	257,831,178,785	156,925,273	1,643.02	30 Jun	1963	302,683,676,396	186,489,800	1,623.06
30 Jun	1953	264,769,061,639	159,725,011	1,657.66	30 Jun	1964	308,131,638,257	188,878,675	1,631.37
30 Jun	1954	269,848,599,108	162,524,749	1,660.35	30 Jun	1965	313,818,898,984	191,267,551	1,640.73
30 Jun	1955	272,807,222,803	165,324,487	1,650.13	30 Jun	1966	316,097,587,795	193,656,426	1,632.26
30 Jun	1956	271,008,813,649	168,124,224	1,611.96	30 Jun	1967	322,892,937,795	196,045,301	1,647.03
30 Jun	1957	269,459,171,896	170,923,962	1,576.49	30 Jun	1968	345,369,406,426	198,434,176	1,740.47
30 Jun	1958	275,725,217,746	173,723,700	1,587.15	30 Jun	1969	352,895,253,841	200,823,051	1,757.24
30 Jun	1959	282,726,657,078	176,523,437	1,601.64	30 Jun	1970	370,093,706,950	203,211,926	1,821.22
30 Jun	1960	284,092,760,848	179,323,175	1,584.25	30 Jun	1971	397,304,744,455	205,545,314	1,932.93
30 Jun	1961	286,417,286,410	181,712,050	1,576.22					
1. Public debt data from 1951 to 1971 is from the Annual Report of the Secretary of the Treasury, 1980, pp. 61, 62.									
2. Population values are based on the dicennial census from the Census Bureau, and linearly interpolated. Per-capita is based on these values.									

Figure 20.3-3: National Debt and Per-Capita Share Thereof, 1951-1971

Figures 20.3-4 through 20.3-11 show summaries of assets and liabilities of the Federal Reserve and commercial banking system for this period.

				Federal Reserve Loans & Investments		Commercial Bank Loans and Investments				
Day	Year	Gold Stock	Treasury Currency Outstanding	U.S. Government Securities	Discounts & Advances	Loans	U.S. Government Securities	Other	Total Assets	Note
28 Mar	1951	21,885	4,637	22,606	471	54,420	58,770	12,550	175,339	
27 Jun	1951	21,755	4,650	22,843	220	54,821	58,521	12,783	175,593	
26 Sep	1951	22,013	4,676	23,474	216	55,960	59,690	12,900	178,929	
26 Dec	1951	22,621	4,704	23,503	797	58,300	61,910	13,160	184,995	
26 Mar	1952	23,291	4,731	22,528	170	57,840	61,120	13,570	183,250	
25 Jun	1952	23,436	4,752	22,564	304	59,233	61,178	14,026	185,493	
24 Sep	1952	23,343	4,781	23,715	400	61,200	61,610	14,170	189,219	
24 Dec	1952	23,187	4,812	24,697	156	64,290	63,230	14,080	194,452	
25 Mar	1953	22,562	4,826	23,869	705	65,220	60,470	14,310	191,962	
24 Jun	1953	22,487	4,851	24,837	317	65,025	58,644	14,287	190,448	
30 Sep	1953	22,128	4,872	25,235	329	66,260	62,200	14,530	195,554	
30 Dec	1953	22,029	4,889	25,902	100	68,260	63,590	14,550	199,320	
31 Mar	1954	21,965	4,928	24,649	190	67,050	60,650	15,090	194,522	
30 Jun	1954	21,926	4,956	25,113	157	67,337	63,508	15,538	198,535	
29 Sep	1954	21,810	4,968	23,868	191	67,250	67,330	16,000	201,417	
29 Dec	1954	21,712	4,982	24,918	377	71,150	69,460	16,240	208,839	
30 Mar	1955	21,719	4,997	23,604	745	72,310	64,180	17,000	204,555	
29 Jun	1955	21,677	5,001	23,554	456	75,183	63,271	16,809	205,951	
28 Sep	1955	21,683	5,006	23,598	901	78,390	62,020	16,850	208,448	
28 Dec	1955	21,690	5,008	24,767	753	82,760	61,810	16,510	213,298	

1. All data is from the Federal Reserve Bulletins; see Appendix B for references.

Figure 20.3-4: Banking System Assets, 1951-1955

				At Federal Reserve Banks		At Commercial Banks					
Day	Year	Currency Outside Banks	Treasury Cash [3]	Treasury Demand Deposits [3]	Foreign Demand Deposits [3]	Demand Deposits [1]	Treasury Demand Deposits [1]	Time Deposits [1]	Capital [1]	Total Liabilities	Error (%)
28 Mar	1951	24,600	1,299	1,052	898	90,600	6,400	36,200	14,900	175,949	-0.35
27 Jun	1951	25,776	1,286	418	947	88,960	6,332	36,781	14,820	175,320	0.16
26 Sep	1951	25,400	1,288	816	769	92,000	5,100	37,200	15,700	178,273	0.37
26 Dec	1951	26,303	1,289	289	610	98,234	3,615	37,859	15,320	183,519	0.80
26 Mar	1952	25,700	1,282	7	545	94,800	5,800	38,500	15,900	182,534	0.39
25 Jun	1952	26,474	1,290	134	595	94,754	6,121	39,302	16,120	184,790	0.38
24 Sep	1952	26,660	1,274	264	728	96,400	6,500	39,800	16,700	188,326	0.47
24 Dec	1952	27,494	1,270	389	550	101,508	5,259	40,666	16,647	193,783	0.34
25 Mar	1953	26,900	1,306	7	511	97,400	5,800	41,200	17,000	190,124	0.96
24 Jun	1953	27,369	1,272	8	615	96,898	3,942	42,245	17,234	189,583	0.45
30 Sep	1953	27,500	1,283	642	512	97,700	6,200	42,800	18,000	194,637	0.47
30 Dec	1953	28,091	773	377	474	102,451	4,457	43,659	17,538	197,820	0.75
31 Mar	1954	26,900	819	722	494	96,700	5,400	44,500	17,800	193,335	0.61
30 Jun	1954	27,093	811	875	545	98,132	5,895	45,653	18,161	197,165	0.69
29 Sep	1954	26,900	796	769	489	101,200	4,400	46,400	19,000	199,954	0.73
29 Dec	1954	27,852	809	465	577	106,550	4,510	46,844	18,806	206,413	1.16
30 Mar	1955	26,700	829	851	356	102,400	4,400	47,200	19,100	201,836	1.33
29 Jun	1955	27,375	818	344	407	103,234	5,418	47,846	18,956	204,398	0.75
28 Sep	1955	27,200	791	512	383	104,900	4,500	48,100	19,800	206,186	1.09
28 Dec	1955	28,285	778	522	468	109,914	4,038	48,359	19,193	211,557	0.82

1. Some of these figures are not Wednesday dates; used best available as referenced in Appendix B.
2. BMS1976, Table 10.1D and Federal Reserve Bulletin data is per Wednesday dates.
3. Treasury cash, treasury demand deposits, and foreign demand deposits per BMS1976, Table 10.1D.
4. BMS1976 is: Board of Governors of the Federal Reserve, Banking and Monetary Statistics, 1941-1970, Washington DC: Publication Services, Division of Administrative Services, Board of Governors of the Federal Reserve System, Sep 1976

Figure 20.3-5: Banking System Liabilities, 1951-1955

				Federal Reserve Loans & Investments		Commercial Bank Loans and Investments				
Day	Year	Gold Stock	Treasury Currency Outstanding	U. S. Government Securities	Discounts & Advances	Loans	U. S. Government Securities	Other	Total Assets	Note
28 Mar	1956	21,715	5,015	23,508	1,196	84,730	58,540	16,640	211,344	
27 Jun	1956	21,799	5,033	23,748	756	86,887	56,620	16,502	211,345	
26 Sep	1956	21,884	5,044	23,576	705	88,480	56,950	16,600	213,239	
26 Dec	1956	21,949	5,066	24,906	667	91,240	58,300	16,150	218,278	
27 Mar	1957	22,305	5,083	23,094	844	90,630	55,740	15,490	213,186	
26 Jun	1957	22,622	5,106	22,951	1,003	93,280	55,500	16,820	217,282	
25 Sep	1957	22,628	5,123	23,178	1,106	93,400	55,870	17,050	218,355	
25 Dec	1957	22,770	5,145	23,950	786	94,280	57,850	17,710	222,491	
26 Mar	1958	22,498	5,180	23,552	167	92,980	59,550	18,880	222,807	
25 Jun	1958	21,374	5,204	25,002	99	95,571	64,194	20,140	231,584	
24 Sep	1958	20,895	5,216	24,893	433	94,230	64,720	20,560	230,947	
31 Dec	1958	20,526	5,232	26,437	808	97,980	66,180	20,420	237,583	
25 Mar	1959	20,442	5,246	23,510	619	99,190	63,160	20,590	232,757	
24 Jun	1959	20,017	5,280	25,970	894	104,450	60,860	20,610	238,081	
30 Sep	1959	19,493	5,287	26,563	722	107,830	59,230	20,730	239,855	
30 Dec	1959	19,456	5,313	26,829	933	112,000	58,600	20,380	243,511	
30 Mar	1960	19,408	5,340	25,239	608	111,390	54,160	20,130	236,275	
29 Jun	1960	19,325	5,356	26,129	412	114,840	54,210	19,850	240,122	
28 Sep	1960	18,731	5,375	26,539	244	115,430	57,690	20,150	244,159	
28 Dec	1960	17,882	5,398	27,074	56	118,160	61,320	20,830	250,720	

1. All data is from the Federal Reserve Bulletins; see Appendix B for references.

Figure 20.3-6: Banking System Assets, 1956-1960

				At Federal Reserve Banks				At Commercial Banks				
Day	Year	Currency Outside Banks	Treasury Cash [3]	Treasury Demand Deposits [3]	Foreign Demand Deposits [3]	Demand Deposits [1]	Treasury Demand Deposits [1]	Time Deposits [1]	Capital [1]	Total Liabilities	Error (%)
28 Mar	1956	27,200	787	512	343	104,400	6,500	48,800	20,100	208,642	1.28
27 Jun	1956	28,284	785	576	293	104,744	5,537	49,698	19,807	209,724	0.77
26 Sep	1956	27,400	780	583	331	105,400	5,400	50,100	20,900	210,894	1.10
26 Dec	1956	28,335	766	533	382	111,391	4,038	50,577	20,246	216,268	0.92
27 Mar	1957	27,400	811	490	345	105,200	3,800	52,600	20,900	211,546	0.77
26 Jun	1957	28,018	770	456	410	105,706	3,625	53,605	21,605	214,195	1.42
25 Sep	1957	27,800	780	605	370	105,500	3,900	55,100	21,900	215,955	1.10
25 Dec	1957	28,301	761	481	356	110,254	4,179	56,139	21,023	221,494	0.45
26 Mar	1958	27,400	730	623	256	104,600	5,800	58,800	22,200	220,409	1.08
25 Jun	1958	27,790	700	524	268	106,169	9,471	61,473	22,880	229,275	1.00
24 Sep	1958	27,900	686	490	314	108,100	4,500	62,700	23,900	228,590	1.02
31 Dec	1958	28,740	683	358	272	115,507	4,558	63,166	22,829	236,113	0.62
25 Mar	1959	27,900	714	517	340	110,300	3,900	64,100	23,900	231,671	0.47
24 Jun	1959	28,300	412	532	337	110,700	4,700	65,400	24,200	234,581	1.47
30 Sep	1959	28,500	377	704	312	111,400	6,400	65,700	24,800	238,193	0.69
30 Dec	1959	29,422	409	518	383	115,402	5,319	65,884	24,186	241,523	0.82
30 Mar	1960	28,100	436	511	223	108,800	4,700	66,000	25,100	233,870	1.02
29 Jun	1960	28,300	405	495	289	107,800	6,657	67,400	26,200	237,546	1.07
28 Sep	1960	28,300	404	554	184	109,300	7,700	69,400	27,300	243,142	0.42
28 Dec	1960	29,356	403	416	265	115,102	6,194	71,380	26,783	249,899	0.33

1. Some of these figures are not Wednesday dates; used best available as referenced in Appendix B.
2. BMS1976, Table 10.1D and Federal Reserve Bulletin data is per Wednesday dates.
3. Treasury cash, treasury demand deposits, and foreign demand deposits per BMS1976, Table 10.1D
4. BMS1976 is: Board of Governors of the Federal Reserve, Banking and Monetary Statistics, 1941-1970, Washington DC: Publication Services, Division of Administrative Services, Board of Governors of the Federal Reserve System, Sep 1976

Figure 20.3-7: Banking System Liabilities, 1956-1960

Assets of the Federal Reserve & Commercial System, 1961-1965 (millions USD)										
				Federal Reserve Loans & Investments		Commercial Bank Loans and Investments				
Day	Year	Gold Stock	Treasury Currency Outstanding	U. S. Government Securities	Discounts & Advances	Loans	U. S. Government Securities	Other	Total Assets	Note
29 Mar	1961	17,389	5,408	26,724	87	116,640	59,670	21,680	247,598	
28 Jun	1961	17,553	5,434	26,820	84	117,953	61,824	22,071	251,739	
27 Sep	1961	17,451	5,560	27,200	29	120,520	66,130	23,260	260,150	
27 Dec	1961	16,889	5,584	28,893	218	125,230	66,480	23,900	267,194	
28 Mar	1962	16,666	5,587	28,679	151	126,490	64,610	26,160	268,343	
27 Jun	1962	16,433	5,600	29,320	216	129,123	64,443	27,034	272,169	
26 Sep	1962	16,068	5,548	29,340	152	132,480	63,250	28,180	275,018	
26 Dec	1962	15,978	5,564	30,510	308	139,860	65,870	29,240	287,330	
27 Mar	1963	15,878	5,576	30,635	271	139,360	64,840	30,660	287,220	
26 Jun	1963	15,779	5,582	31,583	234	145,049	63,562	32,423	294,212	
25 Sep	1963	15,582	5,587	32,040	418	148,870	61,810	34,160	298,467	
25 Dec	1963	15,552	5,586	33,586	350	155,720	62,690	34,860	308,344	
25 Mar	1964	15,462	5,579	33,384	279	156,810	61,500	35,570	308,584	
24 Jun	1964	15,461	5,582	34,427	232	164,463	59,322	36,394	315,881	
30 Sep	1964	15,461	5,556	35,186	280	167,640	60,630	37,790	322,543	
30 Dec	1964	15,388	5,397	36,936	535	175,550	62,000	38,430	334,236	
31 Mar	1965	14,562	5,397	37,419	502	179,040	59,040	40,270	336,230	
30 Jun	1965	14,227	5,413	38,870	500	188,641	56,853	42,229	346,733	
29 Sep	1965	13,858	5,474	39,074	559	191,690	55,930	43,850	350,435	
29 Dec	1965	13,786	5,585	40,852	592	201,030	58,520	44,600	364,965	

1. All data is from the Federal Reserve Bulletins; see Appendix B for references.

Figure 20.3-8: Banking System Assets, 1961-1965

Liabilities of the Federal Reserve and Commercial System, 1961-1965 (millions USD)										
				At Federal Reserve Banks		At Commercial Banks				
Day	Year	Currency Outside Banks	Treasury Cash [3]	Treasury Demand Deposits [3]	Foreign Demand Deposits [3]	Demand Deposits	Treasury Demand Deposits	Time Deposits	Capital	Total Liabilities	Error (%)
29 Mar	1961	28,000	437	489	268	110,300	4,400	74,200	27,700	245,794	0.73
28 Jun	1961	29,361	410	649	200	110,288	6,638	79,092	27,212	253,850	-0.84
27 Sep	1961	28,600	416	485	353	112,400	8,400	80,800	28,500	259,954	0.08
27 Dec	1961	29,300	425	264	237	119,900	6,700	81,700	28,200	266,726	0.18
28 Mar	1962	28,900	437	462	217	113,000	6,500	87,700	28,900	266,116	0.83
27 Jun	1962	30,433	411	578	342	112,089	9,841	91,734	28,275	273,703	-0.56
26 Sep	1962	29,400	405	511	251	114,100	8,300	94,000	29,500	276,467	-0.53
26 Dec	1962	30,700	395	602	229	121,700	7,000	96,700	29,000	286,326	0.35
27 Mar	1963	30,100	440	851	184	115,400	7,600	102,200	29,900	286,675	0.19
26 Jun	1963	31,832	402	1,054	182	115,312	11,306	105,648	29,732	295,468	-0.43
25 Sep	1963	31,100	388	940	141	117,000	9,100	108,100	31,700	298,469	0.00
25 Dec	1963	32,900	361	880	171	124,500	7,000	110,800	30,300	306,912	0.46
25 Mar	1964	32,100	415	1,101	143	118,800	8,100	115,800	31,400	307,859	0.23
24 Jun	1964	33,020	446	967	139	120,311	10,502	119,330	31,915	316,630	-0.24
30 Sep	1964	33,200	434	933	148	122,600	9,400	122,100	33,700	322,515	0.01
30 Dec	1964	34,300	642	754	228	130,000	6,600	125,600	33,500	331,624	0.78
31 Mar	1965	33,800	702	867	162	123,000	8,600	132,800	35,300	335,231	0.30
30 Jun	1965	34,524	747	672	179	124,354	12,062	137,088	35,814	345,440	0.37
29 Sep	1965	34,900	804	852	195	126,300	7,600	141,800	36,900	349,351	0.31
29 Dec	1965	36,200	820	533	159	135,700	5,600	145,600	36,500	361,112	1.06

1. Some of these figures are not Wednesday dates; used best available as referenced in Appendix B.
2. BMS1976, Table 10.1D and Federal Reserve Bulletin data is per Wednesday dates.
3. Treasury cash, treasury demand deposits, and foreign demand deposits per BMS1976, Table 10.1D
4. BMS1976 is: Board of Governors of the Federal Reserve, Banking and Monetary Statistics, 1941-1970, Washington DC: Publication Services, Division of Administrative Services, Board of Governors of the Federal Reserve System, Sep 1976

Figure 20.3-9: Banking System Liabilities, 1961-1965

				Federal Reserve Loans & Investments		Commercial Bank Loans and Investments				
Day	Year	Gold Stock	Treasury Currency Outstanding	U.S. Government Securities	Discounts & Advances	Loans	U.S. Government Securities	Other	Total Assets	Note
30 Mar	1966	13,632	5,734	40,505	528	203,490	55,430	45,430	364,749	
29 Jun	1966	13,432	5,933	41,795	776	211,980	53,503	48,755	376,174	
28 Sep	1966	13,257	6,086	42,493	662	212,500	53,610	48,810	377,418	
28 Dec	1966	13,159	6,297	43,947	559	218,100	55,600	48,240	385,902	
29 Mar	1967	13,108	6,496	44,659	138	216,750	57,830	51,990	390,971	
28 Jun	1967	13,108	6,610	45,940	165	223,952	54,233	56,671	400,679	
27 Sep	1967	13,006	6,759	46,452	74	227,430	60,090	58,260	412,071	
27 Dec	1967	12,434	6,783	48,937	345	235,720	62,540	60,300	427,059	
27 Mar	1968	10,484	6,800	49,621	597	233,570	61,200	63,140	425,412	
26 Jun	1968	10,367	6,766	52,009	820	244,580	58,604	64,376	437,522	
25 Sep	1968	10,367	6,742	51,844	475	251,680	62,540	67,620	451,268	
25 Dec	1968	10,367	6,812	52,232	859	264,480	64,640	70,580	469,970	
26 Mar	1969	10,367	6,826	52,015	997	264,970	58,510	71,420	465,105	
25 Jun	1969	10,367	6,750	53,206	1,384	283,850	54,044	72,385	481,986	
24 Sep	1969	10,367	6,761	53,828	1,106	284,300	53,200	71,170	480,732	
31 Dec	1969	10,367	6,848	57,491	1,104	293,630	54,570	70,610	494,620	
25 Mar	1970	11,367	6,900	55,621	1,594	288,230	51,520	72,660	487,892	
24 Jun	1970	11,367	7,008	57,005	841	296,091	51,569	75,579	499,460	
30 Sep	1970	11,300	7,060	60,555	853	301,530	55,750	79,510	516,558	
30 Dec	1970	11,105	7,147	60,632	253	314,300	61,100	85,720	540,257	
31 Mar	1971	10,732	7,263	64,345	391	310,380	61,620	91,500	546,231	
30 Jun	1971	10,332	7,434	65,518	446	322,886	60,254	97,383	564,253	
29 Sep	1971	10,132	7,547	67,661	381	331,000	58,740	99,900	575,361	
29 Dec	1971	10,132	7,619	71,759	1,338	343,530	64,550	103,590	602,518	

1. All data is from the Federal Reserve Bulletins; see Appendix B for references.

Figure 20.3-10: Banking System Assets, 1966-1971

				At Federal Reserve Banks		At Commercial Banks					
Day	Year	Currency Outside Banks	Treasury Cash [3]	Treasury Demand Deposits [3]	Foreign Demand Deposits [3]	Demand Deposits	Treasury Demand Deposits	Time Deposits	Capital	Total Liabilities	Error (%)
30 Mar	1966	35,800	940	546	142	130,300	5,400	151,000	37,800	361,928	0.77
29 Jun	1966	37,128	1,086	825	132	130,961	11,237	154,798	38,454	374,621	0.41
28 Sep	1966	36,800	1,091	1,313	159	129,300	6,200	156,900	42,200	373,963	0.92
28 Dec	1966	38,300	1,196	249	168	136,900	5,400	157,700	41,700	381,613	1.11
29 Mar	1967	37,600	1,335	677	134	132,100	5,800	167,500	42,200	387,346	0.93
28 Jun	1967	39,681	1,369	1,215	127	134,647	5,427	173,566	43,567	399,599	0.27
27 Sep	1967	38,700	1,523	711	159	136,800	7,300	178,300	46,600	410,093	0.48
27 Dec	1967	40,400	1,386	352	131	146,200	6,900	181,100	45,700	422,169	1.15
27 Mar	1968	39,800	1,131	965	161	140,200	5,700	187,800	46,000	421,757	0.86
26 Jun	1968	42,261	905	1,017	198	144,301	5,298	189,144	48,901	432,025	1.26
25 Sep	1968	41,500	797	1,027	134	143,800	8,900	196,100	51,700	443,958	1.62
25 Dec	1968	43,500	763	168	226	162,500	5,400	202,200	48,100	462,857	1.51
26 Mar	1969	42,800	715	502	137	147,900	4,600	201,800	54,900	453,354	2.53
25 Jun	1969	44,478	675	1,547	106	149,518	5,997	199,516	68,705	470,542	2.37
24 Sep	1969	44,100	682	1,203	149	148,800	7,900	193,600	66,200	462,634	3.76
31 Dec	1969	46,300	596	1,312	134	167,300	5,200	192,400	64,500	477,742	3.41
25 Mar	1970	45,400	581	1,479	194	151,600	6,300	196,200	66,300	468,054	4.07
24 Jun	1970	47,032	475	1,136	246	154,582	8,285	203,916	68,501	484,173	3.06
30 Sep	1970	47,300	447	1,238	136	154,900	8,800	219,500	68,800	501,121	2.99
30 Dec	1970	49,779	403	1,271	135	169,643	8,409	230,622	64,020	524,282	2.96
31 Mar	1971	48,800	467	783	139	159,400	5,000	247,000	66,000	527,589	3.41
30 Jun	1971	50,491	491	652	155	164,519	8,939	253,651	66,324	545,222	3.37
29 Sep	1971	50,500	466	1,621	151	161,900	9,500	261,400	67,600	553,138	3.86
29 Dec	1971	53,141	453	1,926	290	181,735	10,698	271,760	64,423	584,426	3.00

1. Some of these figures are not Wednesday dates; used best available as referenced in Appendix B.
2. BMS1976, Table 10.1D and Federal Reserve Bulletin data is per Wednesday dates.
3. Treasury cash, treasury demand deposits, and foreign demand deposits to 1970 per BMS1976, Table 10.1D
4. BMS1976 is: Board of Governors of the Federal Reserve, Banking and Monetary Statistics, 1941-1970, Washington DC: Publication Services, Division of Administrative Services, Board of Governors of the Federal Reserve System, Sep 1976

Figure 20.3-11: Banking System Liabilities, 1966-1971

Figure 20.3-12 shows the money supply for this period. Columns 1 through 7 continue the series per the previous periods, and columns 8 through 12 shows the estimated money supply per the definitions of M1, M2, and M3 developed by the Federal Reserve in 1973. Although they were defined in 1973, the Federal Reserve performed a back-calculation estimate to 1959 as shown here. Column 6 is most closely comparable to column 11 (M2). But there is a large discrepancy between these two values in this period; the reason is that the data in column 6 (going back to 1935) does not include deposits at Savings and Loan institutions. As far as I know, that data is not available. All of the values apply to approximately 30 Jun of each year. The average error between column 6 of Figure 20.3-12 and that reported by Friedman and Schwartz [20.3-1] (assuming they are correct) for 1951 to 1960 is 1.15% (i.e., the values shown here are lower than Friedman's), and the standard deviation is 0.43%. If it is assumed that the truth lies halfway between Friedman and these numbers, then the average error is 0.58% and the standard deviation is 0.22%.

Estimated U. S. Money Supply, 1951-1971 (millions USD)							U. S. Money Supply per F. R. H.6 Data [1, 2], 1959-1971 (millions USD)				
1	2	3	4	5	6	7	8	9	10	11	12
Year (~30 Jun)	Currency Outside Banks	Demand Deposits Adjusted	Time Deposits	Total Deposits Adjusted	Total Money Supply	Reserve Bulletin Reference (M/Y, PDF page)	Currency Outside Banks	Adjusted Commercial Demand Deposits	M1 [3]	M2 [4]	M3 [5]
1951	25,776	88,960	59,948	148,908	174,684	10/51, 51					
1952	26,474	94,754	63,676	158,430	184,904	10/52, 34					
1953	27,369	96,898	68,293	165,191	192,560	11/53, 29					
1954	27,093	98,132	73,292	171,424	198,517	11/54, 23					
1955	27,375	103,234	77,129	180,363	207,738	11/55, 24					
1956	28,284	104,744	80,615	185,359	213,643	11/56, 49					
1957	28,018	105,706	85,715	191,421	219,439	12/58, 35					
1958	27,790	106,169	95,524	201,693	229,483	12/58, 35					
1959	28,563	112,351	100,838	213,189	241,752	12/59, 49	28,700	110,300	139,400	292,500	294,800
1960	28,544	110,024	103,056	213,080	241,624	10/60, 46	28,700	108,900	137,900	300,900	303,100
1961	29,361	110,288	117,280	227,568	256,929	10/61, 66	28,600	112,100	141,200	322,700	327,500
1962	30,433	114,000	132,106	246,106	276,539	10/62, 55	29,800	114,700	144,800	347,700	355,000
1963	31,832	115,312	149,322	264,634	296,466	10/63, 67	31,100	117,000	148,700	376,700	387,400
1964	33,020	120,311	166,627	286,938	319,958	10/64, 57	33,100	120,300	153,900	405,300	420,800
1965	34,524	124,354	188,348	312,702	347,226	11/65, 63	34,600	125,300	160,500	438,400	458,500
1966	37,128	130,961	208,647	339,608	376,736	1/67, 103	36,900	132,400	170,000	469,600	495,700
1967	39,681	134,647	231,780	366,427	406,108	11/67, 87	38,800	136,100	175,600	500,900	532,000
1968	42,261	144,301	251,913	396,214	438,475	11/68, 79	41,400	146,000	188,200	542,200	575,400
1969	44,478	149,318	266,171	415,489	459,967	12/69, 79	44,300	155,000	200,200	578,700	612,000
1970	47,032	154,582	273,109	427,691	474,723	11/70, 89	47,200	158,700	206,900	597,500	629,000
1971	50,491	164,519	331,873	496,392	546,883	11/71, 105	50,500	171,200	222,900	675,900	732,100

1. F. R. = Federal Reserve. M1, M2, and M3 were defined in 1973, and back-calculated to 1959; cf. Federal Reserve Bulletin, Feb 1973, p. 71.
2. The discrepancy between the data shown in columns 6 and 11 is that the values comprising column 6 (and all previous years dating back to 1935) did not include deposits at Savings and Loan institutions.
3. M1 is defined: "includes (1) demand deposits at all commercial banks other than those due to domestic commercial banks, and the U. S. government, less cash items in the process of collection, and the Federal Reserve float; (2) foreign demand balances at Federal Reserve Banks; and (3) currency outside the Treasury, Federal Reserve Banks, and vaults of all commercial banks".
4. M2 is defined: "includes, in addition to currency and demand deposits, savings deposits, time deposits open account, and time certificates of deposit (CD's) other than negotiable time CD's issued in denominations of $100,000 or more by large weekly reporting commercial banks. Excludes time deposits of the U. S. government, and of domestic commercial banks." In other words, M2 = M1 plus savings deposits, time deposits, and CD's greater than $100,000.
5. M3 is defined: "includes M2 plus the average of the beginning and end-of-month deposits of mutual savings banks and savings capital at savings and loan associations."

Figure 20.3-12: U. S. Money Supply, 1951-1971

No gold coins have been minted since 1933 (after which they were confiscated anyway), and silver coinage continued only until the 1960's. The Coinage Act of 1965 eliminated silver from quarters and dimes, and reduced it to 40% in half-dollars. This revision caused all the vending machines to be re-calibrated. To a first approximation, although some full-silver coins were permitted until 1970, silver coinage in the U. S. ended in 1965, and we can consider all subsequent coins to be "token". Figure 20.3-13 shows the silver coinage from 1951 to 1965.

Silver and Copper Coinage of the U. S., 1951-1965 (USD)										
	Silver ($)								Minor ($)	
Year	Trade Dollars	Dollars	Half Dollars	Quarters	Twenty-cents	Dimes	Half-dimes	Three-cents	Nickels and Cents	Total ($)
1951			20,347,459.00	21,977,100.50		19,109,660.20			13,302,260.00	74,736,479.70
1952			27,108,988.50	25,591,268.25		26,564,157.30			16,471,868.84	95,736,282.89
1953			13,984,673.00	22,198,330.00		22,923,192.00			17,685,453.00	76,791,648.00
1954			22,003,259.50	27,196,431.25		24,350,050.30			13,918,054.00	87,467,795.05
1955			1,438,190.50	5,435,195.25		4,529,738.10			13,524,772.00	24,927,895.85
1956			2,350,692.00	19,286,971.00		21,732,448.40			20,351,571.04	63,721,682.44
1957			13,164,401.00	31,426,028.00		27,476,228.20			22,175,542.12	94,242,199.32
1958			14,440,032.00	21,340,138.00		16,935,025.20			19,854,178.12	72,569,373.32
1959			10,201,520.50	21,896,880.75		25,184,908.10			28,363,019.46	85,646,328.81
1960			12,965,707.00	23,463,981.50		27,224,200.20			34,174,295.12	97,828,183.82
1961			15,797,343.00	30,930,293.00		30,590,479.40			40,396,949.64	117,715,065.04
1962			24,202,650.00	41,732,193.75		41,061,639.90			43,064,001.14	150,060,484.79
1963			46,154,468.50	53,169,957.25		54,820,217.50			48,096,115.70	202,240,758.95
1964			102,905,187.00	96,471,017.50		81,487,519.20			73,919,621.72	354,783,345.42
1965			92,987,919.00	219,487,985.00		130,804,712.00			131,451,797.00	574,732,413.00
Totals	0.00	0.00	420,052,490.50	661,603,771.00	0.00	554,794,176.00	0.00	0.00	536,749,498.90	2,173,199,936.40

1. Source, 1940-1950: Annual Report of the Director of the Mint, 1966, 15 Feb 1967, Treasury Document 3241, pp. 87, 93

Figure 20.3-13: Silver and Copper (Minor) Coins Minted by the U. S., 1951-1965

Figure 20.3-14 shows the CPI, total money supply, and per-capita money supply during this period. As mentioned earlier, there are two competing money supply values, the traditional one, and the back-calculated M-series. I have chosen to use the M2 data in Figure 20.3-14 in order to be consistent with the next three chapters, but doing so causes a large jump in the money supply in 1959. The reason is the fact that data previous to 1959, and going back to 1935, excludes Savings and Loan data.

Year	CPI [1] (1913 = 100)	Total Money Supply [2, 3] (USD)	Population [4]	Per Capita Money Supply (USD)	Annual Rate of Change in CPI (%)	Annual Rate of Change in Per-Capita Money Supply (%)
1951	262.626	174,684,000,000	154,125,536	1,133.39	7.588	0.906
1952	267.677	184,904,000,000	156,925,273	1,178.29	1.905	3.886
1953	269.697	192,560,000,000	159,725,011	1,205.57	0.752	2.289
1954	271.717	198,517,000,000	162,524,749	1,221.46	0.746	1.309
1955	270.707	207,738,000,000	165,324,487	1,256.55	-0.372	2.832
1956	274.747	213,643,000,000	168,124,224	1,270.74	1.482	1.124
1957	283.838	219,439,000,000	170,923,962	1,283.84	3.255	1.025
1958	291.919	229,483,000,000	173,723,700	1,320.97	2.807	2.851
1959	293.939	292,500,000,000	176,523,437	1,657.00	0.690	22.665
1960	298.990	300,900,000,000	179,323,175	1,677.98	1.704	1.258
1961	302.020	322,700,000,000	181,712,050	1,775.89	1.008	5.671
1962	305.051	347,700,000,000	184,100,925	1,888.64	0.998	6.156
1963	309.091	376,700,000,000	186,489,800	2,019.95	1.316	6.722
1964	313.131	405,300,000,000	188,878,675	2,145.82	1.299	6.045
1965	318.182	438,400,000,000	191,267,551	2,292.08	1.600	6.594
1966	327.273	469,600,000,000	193,656,426	2,424.91	2.817	5.634
1967	337.374	500,900,000,000	196,045,301	2,555.02	3.040	5.227
1968	351.515	542,200,000,000	198,434,176	2,732.39	4.106	6.712
1969	370.707	578,700,000,000	200,823,051	2,881.64	5.316	5.318
1970	391.919	597,500,000,000	203,211,926	2,940.28	5.564	2.014
1971	409.091	675,900,000,000	205,545,314	3,288.33	4.288	11.187

1. CPI data from Bureau of Labor Statistics, series CUUR0000AA0R (urban, all commodities, not seasonally adjusted), referenced to 1913
2. See notes in money supply data for sources.
3. Large change in per-capita money supply in 1959 is artificial; due to use of back-calculated M2.
4. Population is linearly interpolated from Census results.

Figure 20.3-14: Money Supply and CPI, 1951-1971

Figure 20.3-15 shows a summary of the CPI and per-capita money supply. Keeping in mind that the 1959 money supply jump is artificial, there are two relevant intervals: 1951 to 1958, and 1960 to 1971. The average annual change in CPI and per-capita money supply for 1951 to 1958 are 1.5 and 2.1% respectively; and for 1960 to 1971, 2.85 and 6.1% respectively.

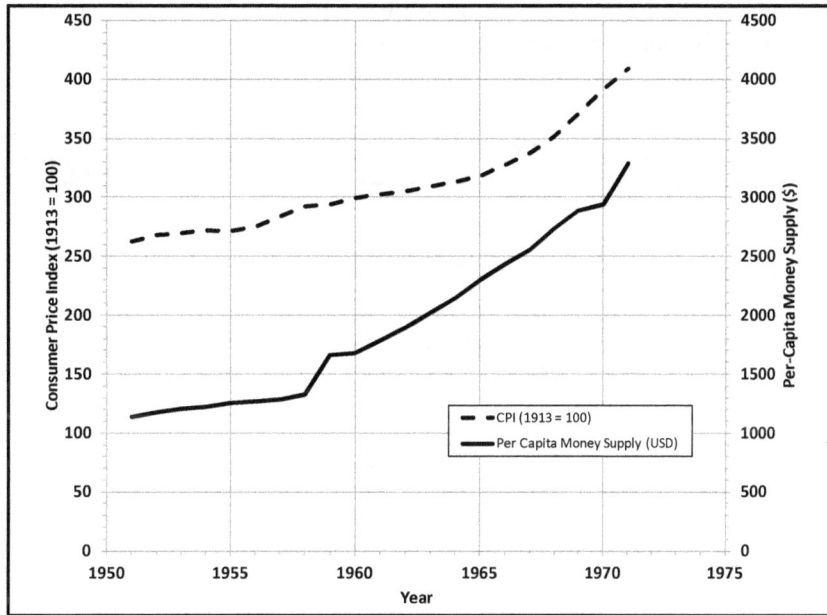

Figure 20.3-15: CPI and Per-Capita Summary, 1951-1971

Figure 20.3-16 shows the approximate median income index, consumer price index, and standard of living index for this period. There was a rapid increase in the standard of living index (owing mostly to the dominance of the U. S. industrial base) while the per-capita national debt remained fairly stable until it began to accelerate starting in 1968. See the Introduction to Part 2 for cautions regarding these curves.

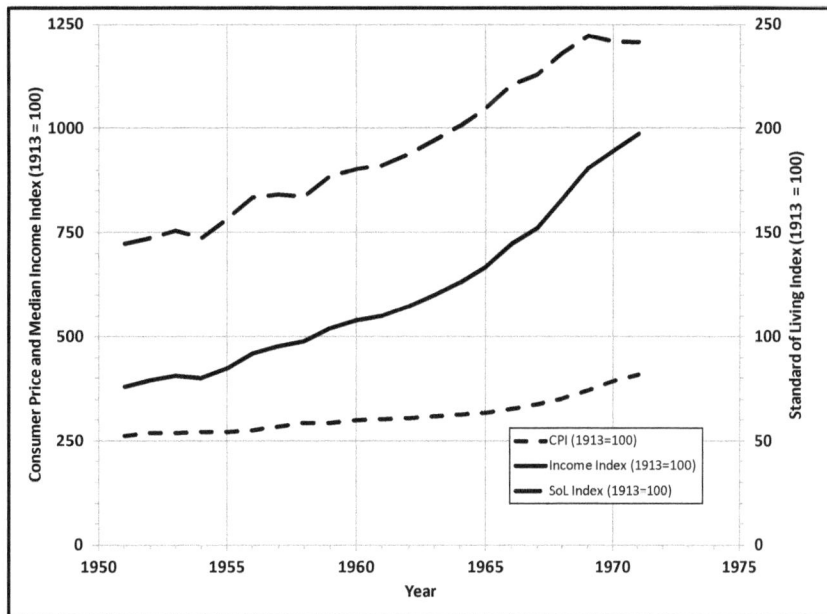

Figure 20.3-16: Median Income, Consumer Price, and Standard of Living Indices, 1951-1971

Figures 20.3-17 and 20.3-18 show the changes in the legal reserve ratios during this period. The scheme changed in 1963, in which the reserve ratio depended on the total amount of deposits at the institution; those are shown on Figure 20.3-18.

Legal Reserve Ratio Changes, 1951-1962									
vs. Demand Deposits (%)							vs. Time Deposits (%)		
Day	Year	Central Reserve City Banks	Reserve City Banks	Day	Year	Country Banks	Day	Year	All Banks
11 Jan	1951	23.00	19.00	16 Jan	1951	13.00	11 Jan	1951	6.00
25 Jan	1951	24.00	20.00	1 Feb	1951	14.00	25 Jan	1951	6.00
9 Jul	1953	22.00	19.00	1 Jul	1953	13.00	9 Jul	1953	6.00
24 Jun	1954	21.00	19.00	16 Jun	1954	13.00	24 Jun	1954	5.00
29 Jul	1954	20.00	18.00	1 Aug	1954	12.00	29 Jul	1954	5.00
27 Feb	1958	19.50	17.50	1 Mar	1958	11.50	27 Feb	1958	5.00
20 Mar	1958	19.00	17.00	1 Apr	1958	11.00	20 Mar	1958	5.00
17 Apr	1958	18.50	17.00	17 Apr	1958	11.00	17 Apr	1958	5.00
24 Apr	1958	18.00	16.50	24 Apr	1958	11.00	24 Apr	1958	5.00
1 Sep	1960	17.50	16.50	1 Sep	1960	11.00	1 Sep	1960	5.00
24 Nov	1960	17.50	16.50	24 Nov	1960	12.00	24 Nov	1960	5.00
1 Dec	1960	16.50	16.50	1 Dec	1960	12.00	1 Dec	1960	5.00
28 Jul	1962	16.50	16.50	28 Jul	1962	12.00	28 Jul	1962	5.00
25 Oct	1962	16.50	16.50	1 Nov	1962	12.00	25 Oct	1962	4.00

Source: Joshua N. Feinman, Reserve Requirements: History, Current Practice, and Potential Reform, Federal Reserve Bulletin, June 1993, p. 569-589

Figure 20.3-17: Legal Reserve Ratios, 1951-1962

Legal Reserve Ratio Changes, 1966-1971												
vs. Demand Deposits								vs. Time Deposits				
		Reserve City Bank Deposit Levels ($)				Country Bank Deposit Levels ($)					Magnitude of Other Time Accounts ($)	
Day	Year	Zero to 5 M	More than 5 M	Day	Year	Zero to 5 M	More than 5 M	Day	Year	Savings	Zero to 5 M	More than 5 M
21 Jul	1966	16.5	16.5	21 Jul	1966	12.0	12.0	21 Jul	1966	4.0	4.0	5.0
8 Sep	1966	16.5	16.5	11 Sep	1966	12.0	12.0	11 Sep	1966	4.0	4.0	6.0
2 Mar	1967	16.5	16.5	2 Mar	1967	12.0	12.0	2 Mar	1967	3.5	3.5	6.0
16 Mar	1967	16.5	16.5	16 Mar	1967	12.0	12.0	16 Mar	1967	3.0	3.0	6.0
11 Jan	1968	16.5	17.0	18 Jan	1968	12.0	12.5	11 Jan	1968	3.0	3.0	6.0
17 Apr	1969	17.0	17.5	17 Apr	1969	12.5	13.0	17 Apr	1969	3.0	3.0	6.0
1 Oct	1970	17.0	17.5	1 Oct	1970	12.5	13.0	1 Oct	1970	3.0	3.0	5.0

Source: Joshua N. Feinman, Reserve Requirements: History, Current Practice, and Potential Reform, Federal Reserve Bulletin, June 1993, p. 569-589

Figure 20.3-18: Legal Reserve Ratios, 1963-1971

Figures 20.3-19 through 20.3-22 show some miscellaneous statistics of the banking system, including total reserves, demand deposits to reserve ratio, and demand deposits to currency ratio.

		Federal Reserve	At Commercial Banks							
Day	Year	Member Bank Reserves [1]	Demand Deposits [2]	Time Deposits [2]	Total Deposits	Reserve Ratio, Demand Deposits	Reserve Ratio, Total Deposits	Currency Outside Banks [2]	Ratio, Demand Deposits to Reserves	Ratio, Demand Deposits to Currency
28 Mar	1951	19,023	90,600	36,200	126,800	0.210	0.150	24,600	4.763	3.683
27 Jun	1951	19,102	88,960	36,781	125,741	0.215	0.152	25,776	4.657	3.451
26 Sep	1951	19,369	92,000	37,200	129,200	0.211	0.150	25,400	4.750	3.622
26 Dec	1951	20,028	98,234	37,859	136,093	0.204	0.147	26,303	4.905	3.735
26 Mar	1952	20,276	94,800	38,500	133,300	0.214	0.152	25,700	4.675	3.689
25 Jun	1952	20,006	94,754	39,302	134,056	0.211	0.149	26,474	4.736	3.579
24 Sep	1952	20,581	96,400	39,800	136,200	0.213	0.151	26,660	4.684	3.616
24 Dec	1952	19,950	101,508	40,666	142,174	0.197	0.140	27,494	5.088	3.692
25 Mar	1953	20,148	97,400	41,200	138,600	0.207	0.145	26,900	4.834	3.621
24 Jun	1953	20,173	96,898	42,245	139,143	0.208	0.145	27,369	4.803	3.540
30 Sep	1953	19,309	97,700	42,800	140,500	0.198	0.137	27,500	5.060	3.553
30 Dec	1953	20,066	102,451	43,659	146,110	0.196	0.137	28,091	5.106	3.647
31 Mar	1954	19,914	96,700	44,500	141,200	0.206	0.141	26,900	4.856	3.595
30 Jun	1954	19,011	98,132	45,653	143,785	0.194	0.132	27,093	5.162	3.622
29 Sep	1954	18,331	101,200	46,400	147,600	0.181	0.124	26,900	5.521	3.762
29 Dec	1954	19,233	106,550	46,844	153,394	0.181	0.125	27,852	5.540	3.826
30 Mar	1955	18,388	102,400	47,200	149,600	0.180	0.123	26,700	5.569	3.835
29 Jun	1955	18,595	103,234	47,846	151,080	0.180	0.123	27,375	5.552	3.771
28 Sep	1955	18,475	104,900	48,100	153,000	0.176	0.121	27,200	5.678	3.857
28 Dec	1955	18,890	109,914	48,359	158,273	0.172	0.119	28,285	5.819	3.886

1. Member bank reserves per BMS1976, Table 10.1D (Wednesday call dates).
2. See Appendix B for references.
3. BMS1976 is: Board of Governors of the Federal Reserve, Banking and Monetary Statistics, 1941-1970, Washington DC: Publication Services, Division of Administrative Services, Board of Governors of the Federal Reserve System, Sep 1976

Figure 20.3-19: Miscellaneous Statistics of the Banking System, 1951-1955

		Federal Reserve	At Commercial Banks							
Day	Year	Member Bank Reserves [1]	Demand Deposits [2]	Time Deposits [2]	Total Deposits	Reserve Ratio, Demand Deposits	Reserve Ratio, Total Deposits	Currency Outside Banks [2]	Ratio, Demand Deposits to Reserves	Ratio, Demand Deposits to Currency
28 Mar	1956	18,445	104,400	48,800	153,200	0.177	0.120	27,200	5.660	3.838
27 Jun	1956	18,560	104,744	49,698	154,442	0.177	0.120	28,284	5.644	3.703
26 Sep	1956	18,656	105,400	50,100	155,500	0.177	0.120	27,400	5.650	3.847
26 Dec	1956	19,140	111,391	50,577	161,968	0.172	0.118	28,335	5.820	3.931
27 Mar	1957	18,350	105,200	52,600	157,800	0.174	0.116	27,400	5.733	3.839
26 Jun	1957	18,628	105,706	53,605	159,311	0.176	0.117	28,018	5.675	3.773
25 Sep	1957	18,594	105,500	55,100	160,600	0.176	0.116	27,800	5.674	3.795
25 Dec	1957	19,444	110,254	56,139	166,393	0.176	0.117	28,301	5.670	3.896
26 Mar	1958	18,426	104,600	58,800	163,400	0.176	0.113	27,400	5.677	3.818
25 Jun	1958	18,568	106,169	61,473	167,642	0.175	0.111	27,790	5.718	3.820
24 Sep	1958	18,101	108,100	62,700	170,800	0.167	0.106	27,900	5.972	3.875
31 Dec	1958	18,504	115,507	63,166	178,673	0.160	0.104	28,740	6.242	4.019
25 Mar	1959	18,194	110,300	64,100	174,400	0.165	0.104	27,900	6.062	3.953
24 Jun	1959	18,188	110,700	65,400	176,100	0.164	0.103	28,300	6.086	3.912
30 Sep	1959	17,760	111,400	65,700	177,100	0.159	0.100	28,500	6.273	3.909
30 Dec	1959	18,297	115,402	65,884	181,286	0.159	0.101	29,422	6.307	3.922
30 Mar	1960	18,010	108,800	66,000	174,800	0.166	0.103	28,100	6.041	3.872
29 Jun	1960	17,863	107,800	67,400	175,200	0.166	0.102	28,300	6.035	3.809
28 Sep	1960	18,996	109,300	69,400	178,700	0.174	0.106	28,300	5.754	3.862
28 Dec	1960	19,558	115,102	71,380	186,482	0.170	0.105	29,356	5.885	3.921

1. Member bank reserves per BMS1976, Table 10.1D (Wednesday call dates).
2. See Appendix B for references.
3. BMS1976 is: Board of Governors of the Federal Reserve, Banking and Monetary Statistics, 1941-1970, Washington DC: Publication Services, Division of Administrative Services, Board of Governors of the Federal Reserve System, Sep 1976

Figure 20.3-20: Miscellaneous Statistics of the Banking System, 1956-1960

		Miscellaneous Statistics of the Federal Reserve and Commercial System, 1961-1965 (millions USD)								
		Federal Reserve	At Commercial Banks							
Day	Year	Member Bank Reserves [1]	Demand Deposits [2]	Time Deposits [2]	Total Deposits	Reserve Ratio, Demand Deposits	Reserve Ratio, Total Deposits	Currency Outside Banks [2]	Ratio, Demand Deposits to Reserves	Ratio, Demand Deposits to Currency
29 Mar	1961	18,713	110,300	74,200	184,500	0.170	0.101	28,000	5.894	3.939
28 Jun	1961	18,953	110,288	79,092	189,380	0.172	0.100	29,361	5.819	3.756
27 Sep	1961	19,240	112,400	80,800	193,200	0.171	0.100	28,600	5.842	3.930
27 Dec	1961	21,214	119,900	81,700	201,600	0.177	0.105	29,300	5.652	4.092
28 Mar	1962	19,597	113,000	87,700	200,700	0.173	0.098	28,900	5.766	3.910
27 Jun	1962	20,304	112,089	91,734	203,823	0.181	0.100	30,433	5.521	3.683
26 Sep	1962	20,314	114,100	94,000	208,100	0.178	0.098	29,400	5.617	3.881
26 Dec	1962	20,166	121,700	96,700	218,400	0.166	0.092	30,700	6.035	3.964
27 Mar	1963	19,597	115,400	102,200	217,600	0.170	0.090	30,100	5.889	3.834
26 Jun	1963	20,050	115,312	105,648	220,960	0.174	0.091	31,832	5.751	3.623
25 Sep	1963	20,105	117,000	108,100	225,100	0.172	0.089	31,100	5.819	3.762
25 Dec	1963	21,026	124,500	110,800	235,300	0.169	0.089	32,900	5.921	3.784
25 Mar	1964	20,123	118,800	115,800	234,600	0.169	0.086	32,100	5.904	3.701
24 Jun	1964	20,701	120,311	119,330	239,641	0.172	0.086	33,020	5.812	3.644
30 Sep	1964	20,947	122,600	122,100	244,700	0.171	0.086	33,200	5.853	3.693
30 Dec	1964	22,188	130,000	125,600	255,600	0.171	0.087	34,300	5.859	3.790
31 Mar	1965	21,176	123,000	132,800	255,800	0.172	0.083	33,800	5.808	3.639
30 Jun	1965	22,226	124,354	137,088	261,442	0.179	0.085	34,524	5.595	3.602
29 Sep	1965	21,842	126,300	141,800	268,100	0.173	0.081	34,900	5.782	3.619
29 Dec	1965	23,388	135,700	145,600	281,300	0.172	0.083	36,200	5.802	3.749

1. Member bank reserves per BMS1976, Table 10.1D (Wednesday call dates).
2. See Appendix B for references.
3. BMS1976 is: Board of Governors of the Federal Reserve, Banking and Monetary Statistics, 1941-1970, Washington DC: Publication Services, Division of Administrative Services, Board of Governors of the Federal Reserve System, Sep 1976

Figure 20.3-21: Miscellaneous Statistics of the Banking System, 1961-1965

		Miscellaneous Statistics of the Federal Reserve and Commercial System, 1966-1971 (millions USD)								
		Federal Reserve	At Commercial Banks							
Day	Year	Member Bank Reserves [1]	Demand Deposits [2]	Time Deposits [2]	Total Deposits	Reserve Ratio, Demand Deposits	Reserve Ratio, Total Deposits	Currency Outside Banks [2]	Ratio, Demand Deposits to Reserves	Ratio, Demand Deposits to Currency
30 Mar	1966	22,245	130,300	151,000	281,300	0.171	0.079	35,800	5.857	3.640
29 Jun	1966	22,762	130,961	154,798	285,759	0.174	0.080	37,128	5.753	3.527
28 Sep	1966	22,625	129,300	156,900	286,200	0.175	0.079	36,800	5.715	3.514
28 Dec	1966	24,934	136,900	157,700	294,600	0.182	0.085	38,300	5.490	3.574
29 Mar	1967	23,304	132,100	167,500	299,600	0.176	0.078	37,600	5.669	3.513
28 Jun	1967	23,757	134,647	173,566	308,213	0.176	0.077	39,681	5.668	3.393
27 Sep	1967	24,986	136,800	178,300	315,100	0.183	0.079	38,700	5.475	3.535
27 Dec	1967	26,580	146,200	181,100	327,300	0.182	0.081	40,400	5.500	3.619
27 Mar	1968	26,166	140,200	187,800	328,000	0.187	0.080	39,800	5.358	3.523
26 Jun	1968	26,116	144,301	189,144	333,445	0.181	0.078	42,261	5.525	3.415
25 Sep	1968	26,853	143,800	196,100	339,900	0.187	0.079	41,500	5.355	3.465
25 Dec	1968	26,919	162,500	202,200	364,700	0.166	0.074	43,500	6.037	3.736
26 Mar	1969	26,442	147,900	201,800	349,700	0.179	0.076	42,800	5.593	3.456
25 Jun	1969	25,635	149,518	199,516	349,034	0.171	0.073	44,478	5.833	3.362
24 Sep	1969	27,167	148,800	193,600	342,400	0.183	0.079	44,100	5.477	3.374
31 Dec	1969	27,272	167,300	192,400	359,700	0.163	0.076	46,300	6.134	3.613
25 Mar	1970	27,078	151,600	196,200	347,800	0.179	0.078	45,400	5.599	3.339
24 Jun	1970	26,215	154,582	203,916	358,498	0.170	0.073	47,032	5.897	3.287
30 Sep	1970	28,271	154,900	219,500	374,400	0.183	0.076	47,300	5.479	3.275
30 Dec	1970	28,005	169,643	230,622	400,265	0.165	0.070	49,779	6.058	3.408
31 Mar	1971	31,014	159,400	247,000	406,400	0.195	0.076	48,800	5.140	3.266
30 Jun	1971	29,911	164,519	253,651	418,170	0.182	0.072	50,491	5.500	3.258
29 Sep	1971	30,811	161,900	261,400	423,300	0.190	0.073	50,500	5.255	3.206
29 Dec	1971	35,154	181,735	271,760	453,495	0.193	0.078	53,141	5.170	3.420

1. Member bank reserves to 1970 per BMS1976, Table 10.1D (Wednesday call dates); for 1971, per Federal Reserve Bulletins (see Appendix B).
2. See Appendix B for references.
3. BMS1976 is: Board of Governors of the Federal Reserve, Banking and Monetary Statistics, 1941-1970, Washington DC: Publication Services, Division of Administrative Services, Board of Governors of the Federal Reserve System, Sep 1976

Figure 20.3-22: Miscellaneous Statistics of the Banking System, 1966-1971

Figures 20.3-23 and 20.3-24 show the approximate monthly commercial bank prime interest rates and the Federal Funds Rate.

Approximate Monthly Average Bank Prime Rate (%) [1]											
Year	Jan	Feb	Mar	Apr	May	Jun	Jul	Aug	Sep	Oct	Nov	Dec
1951	2.44	2.50	2.50	2.50	2.50	2.50	2.50	2.50	2.50	2.62	2.75	2.85
1952	3.00	3.00	3.00	3.00	3.00	3.00	3.00	3.00	3.00	3.00	3.00	3.00
1953	3.00	3.00	3.00	3.03	3.25	3.25	3.25	3.25	3.25	3.25	3.25	3.25
1954	3.25	3.25	3.13	3.00	3.00	3.00	3.00	3.00	3.00	3.00	3.00	3.00
1955	3.00	3.00	3.00	3.00	3.00	3.00	3.00	3.23	3.25	3.40	3.50	3.50
1956	3.50	3.50	3.50	3.65	3.75	3.75	3.75	3.84	4.00	4.00	4.00	4.00
1957	4.00	4.00	4.00	4.00	4.00	4.00	4.00	4.42	4.50	4.50	4.50	4.50
1958	4.34	4.00	4.00	3.83	3.50	3.50	3.50	3.50	3.83	4.00	4.00	4.00
1959	4.00	4.00	4.00	4.00	4.23	4.50	4.50	4.50	5.00	5.00	5.00	5.00
1960	5.00	5.00	5.00	5.00	5.00	5.00	5.00	4.85	4.50	4.50	4.50	4.50
1961	4.50	4.50	4.50	4.50	4.50	4.50	4.50	4.50	4.50	4.50	4.50	4.50
1962	4.50	4.50	4.50	4.50	4.50	4.50	4.50	4.50	4.50	4.50	4.50	4.50
1963	4.50	4.50	4.50	4.50	4.50	4.50	4.50	4.50	4.50	4.50	4.50	4.50
1964	4.50	4.50	4.50	4.50	4.50	4.50	4.50	4.50	4.50	4.50	4.50	4.50
1965	4.50	4.50	4.50	4.50	4.50	4.50	4.50	4.50	4.50	4.50	4.50	4.92
1966	5.00	5.00	5.35	5.50	5.50	5.52	5.75	5.88	6.00	6.00	6.00	6.00
1967	5.96	5.75	5.71	5.50	5.50	5.50	5.50	5.50	5.50	5.50	5.68	6.00
1968	6.00	6.00	6.00	6.20	6.50	6.50	6.50	6.50	6.45	6.25	6.25	6.60
1969	6.95	7.00	7.24	7.50	7.50	8.23	8.50	8.50	8.50	8.50	8.50	8.50
1970	8.50	8.50	8.39	8.00	8.00	8.00	8.00	8.00	7.83	7.50	7.28	6.92
1971	6.29	5.88	5.44	5.28	5.46	5.50	5.91	6.00	6.00	5.90	5.53	5.49

1. Source: Board of Governors of the Federal Reserve System, Bank Prime Loan Rate [MPRIME], Federal Reserve Bank of St. Louis; series MPRIME (https://fred.stlouisfed.org/series/MPRIME). These are averages of daily figures, not seasonally adjusted. The data is listed as "observation dates" on the first of the month; it is assumed they apply for the entire month, since the Federal Reserve cites them as monthly averages.

Figure 20.3-23: Monthly Average Bank Prime Rates, 1951-1971

Approximate Monthly Average Federal Funds Rate (%) [1, 2]											
Year	Jan	Feb	Mar	Apr	May	Jun	Jul	Aug	Sep	Oct	Nov	Dec
1951	1.12	1.42	0.94	0.54	1.46	0.69	1.51	1.63	1.58	0.69	1.38	1.52
1952	0.79	1.42	1.04	1.51	1.67	1.59	1.65	1.69	1.27	1.64	1.72	1.70
1953	1.83	1.98	1.98	1.93	1.94	0.90	1.39	1.91	1.33	1.11	1.84	1.56
1954	0.68	1.54	1.37	0.75	0.91	0.79	0.80	1.22	1.07	0.85	0.83	1.28
1955	1.39	1.29	1.35	1.43	1.43	1.64	1.68	1.96	2.18	2.24	2.35	2.48
1956	2.45	2.50	2.50	2.62	2.75	2.71	2.75	2.73	2.95	2.96	2.88	2.94
1957	2.84	3.00	2.96	3.00	3.00	3.00	2.99	3.24	3.47	3.50	3.28	2.98
1958	2.72	1.67	1.20	1.26	0.63	0.93	0.68	1.53	1.76	1.80	2.27	2.42
1959	2.48	2.43	2.80	2.96	2.90	3.39	3.47	3.50	3.76	3.98	4.00	3.99
1960	3.99	3.97	3.84	3.92	3.85	3.32	3.23	2.98	2.60	2.47	2.44	1.98
1961	1.45	2.54	2.02	1.49	1.98	1.73	1.17	2.00	1.88	2.26	2.61	2.33
1962	2.15	2.37	2.85	2.78	2.36	2.68	2.71	2.93	2.90	2.90	2.94	2.93
1963	2.92	3.00	2.98	2.90	3.00	2.99	3.02	3.49	3.48	3.50	3.48	3.38
1964	3.48	3.48	3.43	3.47	3.50	3.50	3.42	3.50	3.45	3.36	3.52	3.85
1965	3.90	3.98	4.05	4.09	4.10	4.05	4.09	4.12	4.02	4.08	4.10	4.32
1966	4.42	4.60	4.66	4.67	4.90	5.17	5.30	5.53	5.40	5.53	5.76	5.40
1967	4.94	5.00	4.53	4.05	3.94	3.98	3.79	3.90	3.99	3.88	4.13	4.51
1968	4.61	4.71	5.05	5.76	6.12	6.07	6.03	6.03	5.78	5.91	5.82	6.02
1969	6.30	6.61	6.79	7.41	8.67	8.90	8.61	9.19	9.15	9.00	8.85	8.97
1970	8.98	8.98	7.76	8.10	7.95	7.60	7.21	6.62	6.29	6.20	5.60	4.90
1971	4.14	3.72	3.71	4.16	4.63	4.91	5.31	5.57	5.55	5.20	4.91	4.14

1. Source for Jan 1951 to Jun 1954: Board of Governors of the Federal Reserve System; Federal Reserve Bank of St. Louis; series FFWSJLOW and FFWSJHIGH (https://fred.stlouisfed.org/series/FFWSJLOW and FFWSJHIGH). These are averages calculated from data published in the Wall Street Journal.
2. Source for Jul 1954 ff: Board of Governors of the Federal Reserve System, Federal Funds Effective Rate, Federal Reserve Bank of St. Louis, series = FEDFUNDS; https://fred.stlouisfed.org/series/FEDFUNDS. They are cited as "observed dates" always on the first of the month; it is assumed they apply as averages to the entire month, since the Federal Reserve cites them as "averages of daily figures".

Figure 20.3-24: Monthly Average Federal Funds Rate, 1951-1971

20.4 Summary, 1951-1971

The federal government began a program of wage and price controls in 1971. No surprise; once the government "takes responsibility" for employment and prosperity, the government proceeds to "fix" problems in the economy. In this case, the problem was the increasing prices due to the inflation created by the Federal Reserve (an independent agency of the federal government), which Nixon tried to correct by creating another independent agency of the government and give it powers to treat the symptoms (increasing prices) of the problem caused by the other independent agency. In other words, the strategy was to impose new government initiatives to address errors made by existing government initiatives. It is illogical to believe that the core problem of depreciation of the currency (inflation) can be cured by limiting the symptom of prices and wages. Apparently no thought was given to fixing the core problem, which was the inflationary policy of the Federal Reserve. Can't have that; it would require policy makers to admit that they made a mistake. But in fairness to the Federal Reserve, it was only following the lead of Congress, which increased the debt due to the Great Society programs and the Vietnam War, which required an expansion of the money supply, which depreciated the currency. The Federal Reserve is ultimately the servant of Congress.

The per-capita money supply and CPI began to increase rapidly from 1968 to 1970 as shown on Figure 20.3-14; to counteract it, the Federal Reserve dramatically increased the Federal Funds Rate in those years as shown on Figure 20.3-24.

References

[20.1-1]   Clifton H. Kreps, Jr., *Money, Banking and Monetary Policy*, NY: The Ronald Press Co., 1962, pp. 540, 541

[20.1-2]   Federal Reserve Board, *Federal Reserve Bulletin*, Apr 1953, p. 335

[20.1-3]   Allan H. Meltzer, *A History of the Federal Reserve*, Chicago, IL: University of Chicago Press, (2003), Vol. 2, Book 1, p. 6

[20.2-1]   op. cit., Kreps, pp. 547, 548

[20.2-2]   Federal Deposit Insurance Corporation, Division of Research and Statistics, *A Brief History of Deposit Insurance in the United States*, Sep 1998, p. 67

[20.2-3]   Text of "An Act to amend section 14(b) of the Federal Reserve Act, as amended", 82nd Congress, Session 2, Chapter 454, Public Law 82-405, 23 Jun 1952

[20.2-4]   op. cit., Kreps, p. 535

[20.2-5]   Text of "An Act to provide for the merger of two or more national banking associations and for the merger of State banks with national banking associations, and for other purposes", 82nd Congress, Session 2, Chapter 722, Public Law 82-530, 14 Jul 1952

[20.2-6]   op. cit., Federal Deposit Insurance Corporation, p. 67

[20.2-7]   Federal Reserve Board, *Federal Reserve Bulletin*, Mar 1953, pp. 231-235

[20.2-8]   op. cit., Kreps, Jr., pp. 550-554

[20.2-9]   Milton Friedman, Anna Jacobson Schwartz, *A Monetary History of the United States, 1867 - 1960*, A Study by the National Bureau of Economic Research, NY, Princeton, NJ: Princeton University Press, 1963, pp. 593-596, 632, 633

[20.2-10]   op. cit., Friedman and Schwartz, p. 613, quoting the Federal Reserve System *Annual Report*, 1953, p. 88

[20.2-11]   op. cit., Kreps, p. 535

[20.2-12]   National Bureau of Economic Research (NBER), Cambridge, MA (see website below)

[20.2-13]   op. cit., Federal Deposit Insurance Corporation, p. 67

[20.2-14]   op. cit., National Bureau of Economic Research

[20.2-15]   Text of "An Act to amend section 14(b) of the Federal Reserve Act, as amended", 83rd Congress, Session 2, Chapter 422, Public Law 83-450, 29 Jun 1954

[20.2-16]   op. cit., Friedman and Schwartz, p. 464

[20.2-17]   Text of "An Act to repeal the provisions of section 16 of the Federal Reserve Act which prohibits a Federal Reserve bank from paying out notes of another Federal Reserve bank", 83rd Congress, Session 2, Chapter 547, Public Law 83-514, 19 Jul 1954

[20.2-18]   op. cit., Federal Deposit Insurance Corporation, p. 67

[20.2-19]   op. cit., Federal Deposit Insurance Corporation, p. 66

[20.2-20]   Text of "An Act to define bank holding companies, control their future expansion, and require divest-
            ment of their nonbanking interests", a.k.a. the Bank Holding Company Act of 1956, 84th Congress Ses-
            sion 2, Chapter 240, Public Law 84-511, 9 May 1956

[20.2-21]   op. cit., Kreps, pp. 194-196

[20.2-22]   Text of "An Act to enact the Agricultural Act of 1956, 84th Congress, Session 2, Chapter 327, Public
            Law 84-520, 28 May 1956

[20.2-23]   Text of "An Act to amend section 14(b) of the Federal Reserve Act, so as to extend for two more years
            the authority of the Federal Reserve banks to purchase United States obligations directly from the
            Treasury", 84th Congress, Chapter 447, Public Law 84-622, 25 Jun 1956

[20.2-24]   op. cit., Federal Deposit Insurance Corporation, p. 66

[20.2-25]   op. cit., National Bureau of Economic Research

[20.2-26]   op. cit., Federal Deposit Insurance Corporation, p. 66

[20.2-27]   op. cit., National Bureau of Economic Research

[20.2-28]   Text of " An Act to amend section 14(b) of the Federal Reserve Act, so as to extend for two more years
            the authority of the Federal Reserve Banks to purchase United States obligations directly from the
            Treasury", 85th Congress, Session 2, Public Law 85-476, 30 Jun 1958

[20.2-29]   Text of "An Act to provide more effective price, production adjustment, and marketing programs for
            various agricultural commodities", a.k.a. the Agricultural Act of 1958, 85th Congress, Public Law 85-
            835, 28 Aug 1958

[20.2-30]   op. cit., Federal Deposit Insurance Corporation, p. 66

[20.2-31]   Text of "An Act to amend the Bretton Woods Agreements Act", 86th Congress, Public Law 86-48, 17
            Jun 1959

[20.2-32]   Text of "An Act to amend the National Bank Act and the Federal Reserve Act with respect to the re-
            serves required to be maintained by member banks of the Federal reserve System against deposits and
            to eliminate the classification 'central reserve city'", 86th Congress, Public Law 86-114, 28 Jul 1959

[20.2-33]   op. cit., Kreps, pp. 268, 269

[20.2-34]   Text of "An Act to amend the national banking laws to clarify or eliminate ambiguities, to repeal certain
            laws which have become obsolete, and for other purposes", 86th Congress, Public Law 86-230, 8 Sep
            1959

[20.2-35]   op. cit., Federal Deposit Insurance Corporation, p. 66

[20.2-36]   op. cit., National Bureau of Economic Research

[20.2-37]   Text of "An Act to amend the Federal Deposit Insurance Act to require approval for mergers and con-
            solidations of insured banks", 86th Congress, Public Law 86-463, 13 May 1960

[20.2-38]   op. cit., Kreps, pp. 197-199

[20.2-39]   Text of " An Act to amend section 14(b) of the Federal Reserve Act, so as to extend for two more years
            the authority of the Federal Reserve banks to purchase United States obligations directly from the
            Treasury", 86th Congress, Public Law 86-567, 1 Jul 1960

[20.2-40]   op. cit., Friedman and Schwartz, p. 604

[20.2-41]   op. cit., Federal Deposit Insurance Corporation, p. 66

[20.2-42]   op. cit., National Bureau of Economic Research

[20.2-43]   op. cit., Kreps, pp. 556, 557

[20.2-44]   op. cit., Friedman and Schwartz, pp. 635, 636, citing the Federal Reserve System *Annual Report*, 1961,
            p. 43

[20.2-45]   Text of "An Act to authorize adjustments in accounts of outstanding old series currency, and for other
            purposes", a.k.a. the Old Series Currency Adjustment Act, 87th Congress, Public Law 87-66, 30 Jun
            1961

[20.2-46]   Text of "An Act to amend the Export-Import Bank Act of 1945", 87th Congress, Public Law 87-311, 26
            Sep 1961

[20.2-47]   Text of "An Act to abolish the Federal Farm Mortgage Corporation", 87th Congress, Public Law 87-
            353, 4 Oct 1961

[20.2-48]   op. cit., Federal Deposit Insurance Corporation, p. 66

[20.2-49]   Text of "An Act to amend the Bretton Woods Agreements Act to authorize the United States to partici-
            pate in loans to the International Monetary Fund to strengthen the International monetary system", 87th
            Congress, Public Law 87-490, 19 Jun 1962

[20.2-50] Text of " An Act to amend section 14(b) of the Federal Reserve Act, so as to extend for two more years the authority of the Federal Reserve banks to purchase United States obligations directly from the Treasury", 87th Congress, Public Law 87-506, 28 Jun 1962

[20.2-51] Text of "An Act to authorize certain banks to invest in corporations whose purpose is to provide clerical services for them and for other purposes", 87th Congress, Public Law 87-856, 23 Oct 1962

[20.2-52] op. cit., Federal Deposit Insurance Corporation, p. 66

[20.2-53] Text of "An Act to repeal certain legislation relating to the purchase of silver, and for other purposes", 88th Congress, Public Law 88-36, 4 Jun 1963

[20.2-54] Text of "An Act to increase the lending authority of the Export-Import bank of Washington, to extend the period within which the Export-Import Bank of Washington may exercise its functions, and for other purposes", 88th Congress, Public Law 88-101, 20 Aug 1963

[20.2-55] op. cit., Federal Deposit Insurance Corporation, p. 66

[20.2-56] Text of " An Act to amend section 14(b) of the Federal Reserve Act, so as to extend for two more years the authority of the Federal Reserve banks to purchase United States obligations directly from the Treasury", 88th Congress, Public Law 88-344, 30 Jun 1964

[20.2-57] Text of "An Act to amend section 24 of the Federal Reserve Act (12 U. S. C. 371) to liberalize the conditions of loans by national banks on forest tracts", 88th Congress, Public Law 88-341, 30 Jun 1964

[20.2-58] Text of "Joint Resolution to promote the maintenance of international peace and security in Southeast Asia", 88th Congress, Public Law 88-408, 10 Aug 1964

[20.2-59] Text of "An Act to mobilize the human and financial resources of the Nation to combat poverty in the United States", a.k.a. the Economic Opportunity Act of 1964, 88th Congress, Public Law 88-452, 20 Aug 1964

[20.2-60] Text of "An Act to strengthen the agricultural economy; to help achieve a fuller and more effective use of food abundances; to provide improved levels of nutrition among low-income households through a cooperative Federal-State program of food assistance to be operated through normal channels of trade; and for other purposes", a.k.a. the Food Stamp Act of 1964, 88th Congress, Public Law 88-525, 31 Aug 1964

[20.2-61] op. cit., Federal Deposit Insurance Corporation, p. 66

[20.2-62] Text of "An Act to eliminate the requirement that Federal Reserve banks maintain certain reserves in gold certificates against deposit liabilities", 89th Congress, Public Law 89-3, 3 Mar 1965

[20.2-63] Text of "An Act to strengthen and improve educational quality and educational opportunities in the Nation's elementary and secondary schools", a.k.a. the Elementary and Secondary Education Act of 1965, 89th Congress, Public Law 89-10, 11 Apr 1965

[20.2-64] Text of "An Act to provide for the coinage of the United States", a.k.a. Coinage Act of 1965, 89th Congress, 89th Congress, Public Law 89-81, 23 Jul 1965

[20.2-65] The Federal Reserve Bank of Atlanta website states that the Coinage Act of 1965 was in response to a shortage of silver. Quarters and dimes no longer contained any silver (were 90% silver), and the half-dollar silver content was reduced from 90% to 40%; cf.:
https://www.atlantafed.org/education/publications/dollars-and-cents/us-coins.aspx

[20.2-66] Text of "An Act to provide a hospital insurance program for the aged under the Social Security Act with a supplementary medical benefits program and an expanded program of medical assistance, to increase benefits under the Old Age, Survivors, and Disability Insurance System, to improve the Federal-State public assistance programs, and for other purposes", 89th Congress, Public Law 89-97, 30 Jul 1965

[20.2-67] Text of "An Act to assist in the provision of housing for low- and moderate-income families, to promote orderly urban development, to improve living environment in urban areas, and to extend and amend laws related to housing, urban renewal, and community facilities", a.k.a. the Housing and Urban Development Act of 1965, 89th Congress, Public Law 89-117, 10 Aug 1965

[20.2-68] Text of "An Act to expand the war on poverty and enhance the effectiveness of programs under the "Economic Opportunity Act of 1964", a.k.a. the Economic Opportunity Amendments of 1965, 89th Congress, Public Law 89-253, 9 Oct 1965

[20.2-69] Text of "An Act to strengthen the educational resources of our colleges and universities and to provide financial assistance for students in postsecondary and higher education", a.k.a. the Higher Education Act of 1965, 89th Congress, Public Law 89-329, 8 Nov 1965

[20.2-70] op. cit., Federal Deposit Insurance Corporation, p. 66

[20.2-71] Text of "An Act to provide for the discontinuance of the Postal Savings System, and for other purposes", 89th Congress, Public Law 89-377, 28 Mar 1966

[20.2-72]   Text of " An Act to amend section 14(b) of the Federal Reserve Act, so as to extend for two more years the authority of the Federal Reserve banks to purchase United States obligations directly from the Treasury", 89th Congress, Public Law 89-484, 30 Jun 1966

[20.2-73]   Text of "An Act to amend the bank Holding Company Act of 1956", 89th Congress, Public Law 89-485, 1 Jul 1966

[20.2-74]   Text of "An Act to provide for the more flexible regulation of maximum rates of interest or dividends payable by banks and certain other financial institutions on deposits or share accounts, to authorize higher reserve requirements on time deposits at member banks, to authorize open market operations in agency issues by Federal reserve banks, and for other purposes", 89th Congress, Public Law 89-597, 21 Sep 1966

[20.2-75]   Text of "An Act to strengthen and expand food service programs for children", 89th Congress, Public Law 89-642, 11 Oct 1966

[20.2-76]   Text of "An Act to improve the balance-of-payments position of the United States by permitting the use of reserved foreign currencies in lieu of dollars for current expenditures", 89th Congress, Public Law 89-677, 15 Oct 1966

[20.2-77]   Text of "An Act to strengthen the regulatory and supervisory authority of Federal agencies over insured banks and insured savings and loan associations, and for other purposes", a.k.a. the Financial Institutions Supervisory Act, 89th Congress, Public Law 89-695, 16 Oct 1966

[20.2-78]   Text of "An Act to assist comprehensive city demonstration programs for rebuilding slum and blighted areas and for providing the public facilities and services necessary to improve the general welfare of the people who live in those areas, to assist and encourage planned metropolitan development, and for other purposes", 89th Congress, Public Law 89-754, 3 Nov 1966

[20.2-79]   Text of "An Act to authorize the Board of Governors of the Federal Reserve System to delegate certain of its functions, and for other purposes", Public Law 89-765, 5 Nov 1966

[20.2-80]   op. cit., Federal Deposit Insurance Corporation, p. 66

[20.2-81]   Text of "An Act to authorize adjustments in the amount of outstanding silver certificates, and for other purposes", 90th Congress, Public Law 90-29, 24 Jun 1967

[20.2-82]   Text of "An Act to extend for one year the authority for more flexible regulation of maximum rates of interest or dividends, higher reserve requirements, and open market operation in agency issues", 90th Congress, 90th Congress, Public Law 90-87, 21 Sep 1967

[20.2-83]   op. cit., Federal Deposit Insurance Corporation, p. 66

[20.2-84]   Text of "An Act to amend the Social Security Act to provide an increase in benefits under the old-age, survivors, and disability insurance system, to provide benefits for additional categories of individuals, to improve the public assistance programs relating to the welfare and health of children, and for other purposes", a.k.a. the Social Security Amendments of 1967, 90th Congress, Public Law 90-248, 2 Jan 1968

[20.2-85]   Text of "An Act to amend the Export-Import Bank Act of 1945, as amended, to change the name of the Bank, to extend for five years the period within which the Bank is authorized to exercise its functions, to increase the Bank's lending authority and its authority to issue, against fractional reserves, export credit insurance and guarantees, to restrict the financing by the Bank of certain transactions, and for other purposes", 90th Congress, Public Law 90-267, 13 Mar 1968

[20.2-86]   Text of "An Act to eliminate the reserve requirements for Federal Reserve notes and for United States notes, and Treasury notes of 1890", 90th Congress, Public Law 90-269, 18 Mar 1968

[20.2-87]   Text of " An Act to amend section 14(b) of the Federal Reserve Act, as amended, to extend for two years the authority of the Federal Reserve banks to purchase United States obligations directly from the Treasury", 90th Congress, Public Law 90-300, 4 May 1968

[20.2-88]   Text of "An Act to provide for United States participation in the facility based on Special Drawing Rights in the International Monetary Funds, and for other purposes", 90th Congress, Public Law 90-349, 19 Jun 1968

[20.2-89]   Text of "An Act to extend for one year the authority to limit the rates of interest or dividends payable on time and savings deposits and accounts, and for other purposes", 90th Congress, Public Law 90-505, 21 Sep 1968

[20.2-90]   op. cit., Federal Deposit Insurance Corporation, p. 66

[20.2-91]   Text of "An Act to extend for three months the authority to limit the rates of interest or dividends payable on time and savings deposits and accounts", 91st Congress, Public Law 91-71, 22 Sep 1969

[20.2-92]   op. cit., National Bureau of Economic Research

[20.2-93]   Text of "An Act to lower interest rates and fight inflation; to help housing, small business, and employment; to increase the availability of mortgage credit; and for other purposes", 91st Congress, Public Law 91-151, 23 Dec 1969

[20.2-94]   op. cit., Federal Deposit Insurance Corporation, p. 66

[20.2-95]   Text of " An Act to amend section 14(b) of the Federal Reserve Act, as amended, to extend for one year the authority of the Federal Reserve banks to purchase United States obligations directly from the Treasury", 91st Congress, Public Law 91-360, 31 Jul 1970

[20.2-96]   Text of "Economic Stabilization Act of 1970", Title II of "An Act to amend the Defense Production Act of 1950, and for other purposes", 91st Congress, Public Law 91-379, 15 Aug 1970

[20.2-97]   Text of "An Act to Amend the Federal Deposit Insurance Act to require insured banks to maintain certain records, to require that certain transactions in United States currency by reported to the Department of the Treasury, and for other purposes", a.k.a. the Currency and Foreign Transactions Reporting Act, 91st Congress, Public Law 91-508, 26 Oct 1970

[20.2-98]   op. cit., National Bureau of Economic Research

[20.2-99]   Text of Title II (S. 201) of "An Act to amend the Small Business Act", Public Law 91-558, 17 Dec 1970

[20.2-100] op. cit., Federal Deposit Insurance Corporation, p. 66

[20.2-101] Text of "Joint Resolution to provide a temporary extension of certain provisions of law relating to interest rates and cost-of-living stabilization", 92nd Congress, Public Law 92-8, 31 Mar 1971

[20.2-102] Text of "An act to extend certain laws relating to the payment of interest on time and savings deposits and economic stabilization, and for other purposes", 92nd Congress, Public Law 92-15, 18 May 1971

[20.2-103] Text of " An Act to amend section 14(b) of the Federal Reserve Act, as amended, to extend for two years the authority of the Federal Reserve banks to purchase United States obligations directly from the Treasury", 92nd Congress, Public Law 92-45, 2 Jul 1971

[20.2-104] Text of Executive Order 11615, Providing for the Stabilization of Prices, Rents, Wages, and Salaries, 15 Aug 1971

[20.2-105] op. cit., Meltzer, Vol. 2, Book 2, pp. 764-766, 770

[20.2-106] Text of Executive Order 11627, Further Providing for the Stabilization of the Economy, 15 Oct 1971

[20.2-107] Text of "The Economic Stabilization Act Amendments of 1971", 92nd Congress, Public Law 92-210, 22 Dec 1971

[20.2-108] op. cit., Federal Deposit Insurance Corporation, p. 66

[20.3-1]   op. cit., Friedman and Schwartz, Appendix A, pp. 719-722

NBER website: https://www.nber.org/research/data/us-business-cycle-expansions-and-contractions

21

Federal Reserve, Fiat System, Part 1, 1972-1986

21.1 Preview, 1972-1986

This period runs from the end of the Bretton Woods system to the collapse of the Savings and Loan system. It was the period of the oil crisis, wage and price controls, the defeat in Vietnam, high unemployment, rapid depreciation of the dollar, and finally, the collapse of the Savings and Loan industry. But it did have one redeeming feature: the U. S. military buildup that eventually led to the end of the Cold War with the Soviet Union. There was a great deal of legislation ordering studies and plans to correct economic problems, most of which were caused by previous government initiatives.

Although economic conditions were worst from 1975 to 1980, the U. S. was not technically in a recession until early 1980. But it felt like a depression to most people in the major cities in the Northeast. I can recall occasions in the late 1970's when men with accounting degrees, dressed in 3-piece suits and carrying briefcases, were applying for minimum-wage bookkeeping positions.

The Federal Reserve has made many changes to the definitions of M1, M2, and M3 monetary measures; the most significant one in 1980. Anderson and Kavajecz inform us [21.1-1]:

> "Since monetary aggregates data first appeared on the J.3 statistical release in 1960, the broad monetary aggregates (known and M1, M2, M3) have been redefined about a dozen times. Changes have ranged in magnitude from the massive redefinition in February 1980 to small additions and subtractions such as the inclusion of nonbank travelers checks in June 1981."

The U. S. Department of Education was established during this period, the fourth economic attack against black Americans (after slavery, Jim Crow, and the Great Society).

21.2 History, 1972-1986

15 Mar 1972 - 15 Oct 1972: The Easter Offensive.

31 Mar 1972: Congress passed the Par Value Modification Act [21.2-1]: **a)** (S. 2) devalued the U. S. dollar as the basis for issuing gold certificates from $35 per ozt. of gold to $38 per ozt. of gold; and **b)** (S. 3) the Secretary of the Treasury was directed to maintain this new value in terms of gold of the holdings of the U. S. in the IMF and IBRD and other international banks.

31 Dec 1972: One bank failed in 1972, with net losses to the FDIC FDIF totaling $1.696 M [21.2-2].

10 Jan 1973: Phase 2 of wage and price controls expired.

11 Jan 1973: President Nixon issued Executive Order 11695, urging voluntary price controls. This was the beginning of Phase 3 of wage and price controls, lasting until 13 Jun 1973 [21.2-3].

30 Apr 1973: Congress passed the "Economic Stabilization Act Amendments of 1973" [21.2-4]. Among its provisions: **a)** (S. 2) authorized the President to develop a means to ensure adequate supplies of petroleum, and to provide for "rational and equitable distribution"; and **b)** extended the authority of the President to impose wage and price controls until 30 Apr 1974.

13 Jun 1973: President Nixon issued Executive Order 11723, imposing price a 60-day price freeze [21.2-5]. This was the second half of Phase 3 of wage and price controls.

18 Jul 1973: President Nixon issued Executive Order 11730 [21.2-6], extending wage and price controls, but with gradual reduction. This was the beginning of Phase 4 of wages and price controls.

12 Aug 1973: Phase 3 of wage and price controls expired (cf. 13 Jun 1973).

14 Aug 1973: Congress re-authorized [21.2-7] the Federal Reserve to buy U. S. securities directly from the U. S. Treasury until 31 Oct 1973 (cf. 2 Jul 1971, which expired 30 Jun 1973).

16 Aug 1973: Congress passed legislation on the banking system [21.2-8]: **a)** (S. 1) extended the authority of the Board of Governors to regulate interest rates on deposits (cf. 21 Sep 1966) until 31 Dec 1974; **b)** (S. 2) prohibited owners of deposits to make withdrawals by negotiable or transferable instrument for the purpose of making transfers to third parties, except such withdrawals may be made in New Hampshire and Massachusetts; **c)** (S. 4) prohibited, until 30 Jun 1974, conversion of an FDIC-insured mutual institution into a stock institution; **d)** (S. 5) authorized federal savings and loan institutions and national banks to invest in housing projects for low- and moderate-income families operated by a State-sponsored housing corporation; **e)** (S. 6) required insured savings and loan institutions to pay an annual premium of 0.0833% of the total of all accounts to the FSLIC; **f)** authorized the FSLIC to assess additional premiums as necessary to cover losses; **g)** (S. 7) prohibited States and political subdivisions from taxing federally insured bank institutions on the basis of income or receipts, unless the institution's principal office is located within the State; and **h)** (S. 7) tasked the Advisory Commission on Intergovernmental relations to perform a study, due 31 Dec 1974, to make recommendations on the taxation by States of out-of-State commercial banks.

21 Sep 1973: Congress passed an amendment to the Par Value Modification Act [21.2-9]. Among its provisions: **a)** (S. 1) devalued the dollar, now defined as 0.828948 Special Drawing Right, and in terms of gold, forty-two and two-ninths dollars per fine ozt. ($42.2222 per ozt. of gold) (cf. 31 Mar 1972); **b)** (S. 3) repealed sections 3 and 4 of the Gold Reserve Act of 1934 (cf. 30 Jan 1934); **c)** (S. 3) restored American's right to purchase, hold, sell or otherwise deal in gold, but not to go into effect until the President certifies that the private ownership of gold will not adversely affect the United States' international monetary position; and **d)** (S. 202) authorized the Treasury Secretary to develop standards for reporting foreign currency transactions as a way to monitor capital flows.

20 Oct 1973: The Organization of Petroleum Exporting Countries (OPEC), consisting of Saudi Arabia, Iraq, Venezuela, Iran, Kuwait, Libya, Algeria, Indonesia, Nigeria, and Qatar, imposed an oil embargo on the U. S., Canada, Japan, the Netherlands, and Great Britain in retribution for the latter groups' support of Israel in the Yom Kippur War. Oil prices gradually increased from $3 per barrel to $12 per barrel by early 1974. This caused a recession in the U. S. as the costs of energy increased dramatically, along with gas lines, odd/even purchasing days (last digit of license plates), and a general decline in the stock market.

15 Nov 1973: Approximate beginning of a recession [21.2-10].

27 Nov 1973: Congress passed the Emergency Petroleum Allocation Act [21.2-11]: **a)** (S. 2) "the purpose of this Act is to grant to the President of the United States and direct him to exercise specific temporary authority to deal with shortages of crude oil, residual fuel oil, and refined petroleum products or dislocations in their national distribution system"; **b)** (S. 4) required the President to issue within 15 days a regulation on mandatory allocation of domestic and imported crude oil, residual fuel oil and

petroleum products, specifying amounts and prices thereof; **c)** (S. 4) the regulation shall take into account the protection of health, safety and welfare, maintenance of public services, maintenance of agricultural operations, preservation of the petroleum industry, equitable distribution of fuels, economic efficiency, and minimizing economic distortion; and **d)** (S. 4) the regulations to expire 28 Feb 1975.

29 Dec 1973: Congress passed the Federal Financing Bank Act [21.2-12] as a way to coordinate the financing of federal programs among the various agencies that are authorized to borrow money. Among its provisions: **a)** (S. 4) the Federal Financing Bank is established as a separate agency of the federal government, and supervised by the Treasury Department; **b)** (S. 6) the Bank is authorized to purchase and sell any debt obligation that is issued by a federal agency, and said obligations may be issued to or sold directly to the Bank; **c)** (S. 8) initial capital of the Bank shall be $100 M; **d)** (S. 9) the Bank is authorized to issue and have outstanding not more than $15,000 M ($15 B) of federal debt obligations at interest rates and maturities determined by the Bank; **e)** (S. 9) the Bank is authorized to issue its obligations directly to the Secretary of the Treasury; **f)** (S. 9) the Bank may require the Treasury Secretary to purchase obligations of the Bank; and **g)** (S. 14) obligations of the Bank are eligible for purchase by the national banks. Section 2 states the rationale for the Bank:

> "The Congress finds that demands for funds through Federal and federally assisted borrowing programs are increasing faster than the total supply of credit and that such borrowings are not adequately coordinated with overall Federal fiscal and debt management policies. The purpose of this Act is to assure coordination of these programs with the overall economic and fiscal policies of the Government, to reduce the costs of Federal and federally assisted borrowings from the public, and to assure that such borrowings are financed in a manner least disruptive of private financial markets and institutions."

31 Dec 1973: Six banks failed in 1973, with net losses to the FDIC FDIF totaling $67.487 M [21.2-13].

17 Mar 1974: OPEC announced the end of the oil embargo against the U. S., a result of Israel withdrawing its troops from areas west of the Suez Canal.

30 Apr 1974: Phase 4 of wage and price controls expired (cf. 30 Apr 1973). This was the end of the wage and price controls first initiated 15 Aug 1970.

9 Aug 1974: Richard M. Nixon resigned as President of the United States, and was succeeded by Gerald R. Ford.

24 Aug 1974: Congress passed the Council on Wage and Price Stability Act [21.2-14]: **a)** (S. 2) authorized the President to create a Council on Wage and Price Stability to advise the President on, but not to enact, wage and price controls; **b)** (S. 3) its duties were: "1) … review and analyze industrial capacity, demand, supply, and the effect of economic concentration and anticompetitive practices, and supply in various sectors of the economy, working with the industrial groups concerned and appropriate governmental agencies to encourage price restraint; 2) work with labor and management in the various sectors of the economy having special economic problems, as well as with appropriate government agencies, to improve the structure of collective bargaining and the performance of those sectors in restraining prices; 3) improve wage and price data bases for the various sectors of the economy to improve collective bargaining and encourage price restraint; 4) conduct public hearings necessary to provide for public scrutiny of inflationary problems in various sectors of the economy; 5) focus attention on the need to increase productivity in both the public and private sectors of the economy; 6) monitor the economy as a whole by acquiring as appropriate, reports on wages, costs, productivity, prices, sales, profits, imports, and exports; and 7) review and appraise the various programs, policies, and activities of the departments and agencies of the United States for the purpose of determining the extent to which those programs and activities are contributing to inflation"; **c)** (S. 3) prohibited any re-imposition of mandatory economic controls on prices, wages, rents, salaries, corporate dividends, or other transfers; and **d)** (S. 3) this act did not affect the powers conferred under the Emergency Petroleum Allocation Act of 1973 (cf. 27 Nov 1973); and **e)** (S. 7) the Council to terminate on 15 Aug 1975.

8 Sep 1974: President Ford granted Richard Nixon a full and unconditional pardon.

17 Oct 1974: President Ford testified before Congress regarding his rationale for pardoning Richard Nixon. It reads in part:

> "As a people we have a long record of forgiving even those who have been our country's most destructive foes. Yet, to forgive is not to forget the lessons of evil in whatever ways evil has operated against us. And certainly the pardon granted the former President will not cause us to forget the evils of Watergate-type offenses or to forget the lessons we have learned that a government which deceives its supporters and treats its opponents as enemies must never, never be tolerated."

How charming; how naïve. This set the precedent by which all future abuses of power by government employees would be tolerated at every level of government in the United States.

28 Oct 1974: Congress passed the Depository Institutions Amendments of 1974 [21.2-15]. Among its provisions: **a)** (S. 101) increased insurance limit to $100,000 for accounts held by political entities; **b)** (S. 102, 104) FDIC deposit insurance increased to $40,000 for individual deposits in credit unions and federally insured banks; **c)** (S. 103) FSLIC deposit insurance increased to $40,000 for individual deposits in S&L's; **d)** (S. 107) extended the authority to regulate interest rates per 21 Sep 1966 to 31 Dec 1975; **e)** (S. 109) extended the authority of the Federal Reserve Banks to purchase U. S. securities directly from the Treasury until 31 Oct 1975; **f)** (S. 112) increased the authority of the U. S. Treasury to purchase securities from the Federal Home Loan Banks to $2,000 M ($2 B); **g)** (S. 201 ff, Title II) established a commission to make recommendations on electronic fund transfer regulations; and **h)** (S. 301 ff, Title III, "The Fair Credit Billing Act") established regulations for credit reporting and billing.

27 Nov 1974: President Ford issued Executive Order 11821 [21.2-16] requiring legislative proposals originating in the Executive Branch be evaluated by the Office of Management and Budget as to the inflationary impact of such proposals: a) cost impact on consumers, b) effect on productivity, c) effect on competition, and d) effect on supplies of important products.

31 Dec 1974: Four banks failed in 1974, with net losses to the FDIC FDIF totaling $40,000 [21.2-17].

15 Mar 1975: Approximate end of a recession (cf. 15 Nov 1973) [21.2-18].

9 Apr 1975 - 20 Apr 1975: Battle of Xuan Loc.

27 Apr - 30 Apr 1975: Battle of Saigon, evacuation of Americans, and end of the U. S. involvement in Vietnam.

9 Aug 1975: Congress passed the Council and Wage and Price Stability Act Amendments of 1975 [21.2-19]: **a)** (S. 2) expanded the authority of the Council to call witnesses and obtain data on wages, costs, productivity, prices, sales, profits, imports and exports by product line or other categories determined by the Council, applicable to businesses with gross revenues in excess of $5 M; **b)** (S. 4) permitted the Council to intervene and provide their opinion on the effects of inflation due to actions of other agencies; and **c)** (S. 7) extended its existence until 30 Sep 1977.

29 Sep 1975: Congress passed the Emergency Petroleum Allocation Act of 1975 [21.2-20], extending the original until 15 Nov 1975 (cf. 27 Nov 1973). The purpose of the extension was to allow time for Congress and the President to achieve consensus on "long-term petroleum pricing policy".

12 Nov 1975: Congress re-authorized [21.2-21] Federal Reserve Banks to buy U. S. securities directly from the U. S. Treasury until 31 Jun 1976 (cf. 28 Oct 1974, which expired 31 Oct 1975).

14 Nov 1975: Congress extended the Emergency Petroleum Allocation Act provisions until 15 Dec 1975 [21.2-22] (cf. 29 Sep 1975).

31 Dec 1975: Thirteen banks failed in 1975, with net losses to the FDIC FDIF totaling $16.312 M [21.2-23].

31 Dec 1976: Sixteen banks failed in 1976, with net losses to the FDIC FDIF totaling $247,000 [21.2-24].

19 Apr 1977: Congress passed legislation [21.2-25]: **a)** (S. 101) re-authorizing the powers granted 21 Sep 1966 (reserve ratios and interest rates) until 15 Dec 1977; **b)** (S. 201) extended the authority of the Federal Reserve Banks to buy and sell U. S securities, or those guaranteed by any federal agency until 31 Oct 1978; and **c)** (S. 301) modified the provisions of the Federal Credit Union Act regarding requirements for loans.

7 Sep 1977: The U. S. ceded the Panama Canal to Panama.

6 Oct 1977: Congress passed a law [21.2-26] extending the Council on Wage and Price Stability to 30 Sep 1979; it also added as two justifications: 1) "focus attention on the need to move toward full employment", and 2) "for the purpose of controlling inflation".

12 Oct 1977: Congress passed the Community Reinvestment Act [21.2-27] in an effort to reduce the incidence of discrimination against residential home and business borrowers in low and moderate income neighborhoods. It required: **a)** the credit practices of all FDIC-insured banking institutions be reviewed by the Federal Reserve, FDIC, or the Comptroller of the Currency to ensure credit was being offered on an equal basis to all potential borrowers, consistent with sound lending practices; **b)** publish the results of the evaluations; and **c)** use the results of the evaluation in approving mergers or acquisitions. No specific criteria was called out by which the institutions were to be evaluated.

28 Oct 1977: Congress passed legislation [21.2-28]: **a)** (S. 1) permitted the Treasury Secretary to invest, for up to 90 days, any excess funds in securities of the U. S. or in obligations of depository institutions secured by collateral suitable as collateral for Tax and Loan Accounts; **b)** (S. 2) permitted the Treasury Secretary to use several types of institutions as depositories of public funds: 1) Federal Home Loan Banks, 2) federal credit unions, State-chartered banks, savings banks, savings and loan and building and loan institutions insured by an organization chartered by the State; **c)** (S. 4) modified rules for making deposits in the International Monetary Fund; **d)** (S. 4) limited loans and credits to foreign governments or entities through the IMF to 6 months unless approved by the President; **e)** (S. 4) modified section 10(b) of the Gold Reserve Act (cf. 30 Jan 1934) such that gold transactions are no longer for the purpose of stabilizing the dollar; and **f)** (S. 4) permitted transactions with the IMF to be done in gold (i.e., exempt from provisions of Resolution 73-10, 5 Jun 1933).

7 Nov 1977: Congress extended [21.2-29] until 30 Apr 1978 the authority of the Federal Reserve Banks to buy and sell U. S. securities directly from the U. S. Treasury (cf. 19 Apr 1977).

16 Nov 1977: Congress passed the Federal Reserve Reform Act [21.2-30]: **a)** (S. 101) extended the authority of the Board of Governors to regulate interest rates on savings and deposit accounts until 15 Dec 1978; **b)** (S. 202) added section 2A to the Federal Reserve Act to require the Federal Reserve to testify before Congress regarding its monetary, credit, and open-market policies; **c)** (S. 204) required Senate confirmation of Chairman and Vice-Chairman of the Board of Governors; and **d)** (S. 301-303) made some regulatory changes to the Bank Holding Acts of 1956 and 1966.

28 Dec 1977: Congress passed the International Emergency Economic Powers Act [21.2-31] to grant the President certain economic powers during a declared national emergency: **a)** (S. 202) regulate: 1) foreign exchange transactions, 2) credit or payments between a banking institution and any foreign entity, and 3) import or export of currency or securities; **b)** (S. 203) regulate transfer of any property in which a foreign country or national has an interest; and **c)** (S. 203) powers do not apply to charitable donations or personal communications in which no value is attached.

31 Dec 1977: Six banks failed in 1977, with net losses to the FDIC FDIF totaling $2.093 M [21.2-32].

21 Jul 1978: Congress passed the Federal Banking Agency Audit Act [21.2-33]: **a)** (S. 2) required the Comptroller General of the U. S. to conduct, or authorize the General Accounting Office (GAO) to conduct, audits of: 1) the Federal Reserve Board, 2) all Federal Reserve Banks, 3) Federal Deposit Insurance Corporation, and 4) Office of the Comptroller of the Currency; **b)** (S. 2) audits not to include transactions with foreign central banks, decisions relating to monetary policy (discount window, reserves, securities credit, interest on deposits, and open market operations), open market trans-

actions, or communications among the Federal Reserve Board members regarding these; **c)** (S. 2) required written consent of an insured bank or holding company before the GAO can conduct an on-site examination thereof; and **d)** (S. 2) Comptroller General to report to Congress as practical.

20 Aug 1978: Congress passed the National Consumer Cooperative Bank Act [21.2-34] to finance and promote, through a National Consumer Cooperative Bank, non-profit organizations to provide goods and services at lower costs. Section 2 states the rationale:

> "The economic and financial structure of this country in combination with the Nation's natural resources and the productivity of the American people has produced one of the highest average standards of living in the world. However, the Nation has been experiencing inflation and unemployment together with an increasing gap between producers' prices and consumers' purchasing power. This has resulted in a growing number of our citizens, especially the elderly, the poor, and the inner city resident, being unable to share in the fruits of our Nation's highly efficient economic system. The Congress finds that user-owned cooperatives are a proven method for broadening ownership and control of economic organizations, increasing the number of market participants, narrowing price spreads, raising the quality of goods and services available to their members, and building bridges between producers and consumers, and their members and patrons."

It failed to mention the real source of the problem: depreciation of the currency by the Federal Reserve, and the resulting inability of businesses to estimate costs and thus to estimate profitability.

17 Sep 1978: Congress passed the International Banking Act [21.2-35] to modify the provisions of the Edge Act (cf. 24 Dec 1919): **a)** brought foreign banks operating in the U. S. under federal supervision (previously were only under State supervision); **b)** defined categories of permitted foreign institutions (representative offices, agencies, branches, banking subsidiaries, or investment subsidiaries, each with different set of permitted banking capabilities); **c)** permitted foreign-owned banks to operate in the U. S. subject to the same State laws where they are located, if permitted by the State; and **d)** required capital and reserve requirements to be the same as members of the FDIC.

5 Oct 1978: Congress authorized [21.2-36] the Treasury Secretary to bail out New York City by guaranteeing $1,650 M ($1.65 B) in loans and interest currently in default.

27 Oct 1978: Congress extended [21.2-37] until 30 Apr 1979 the authority of the Federal Reserve Banks to buy and sell U. S. securities directly from the U. S. Treasury (cf. 7 Nov 1977)

10 Nov 1978: Congress passed the Financial Institutions Regulatory and Interest Rate Control Act of 1978 [21.2-38]. Among its provisions: **a)** (S. 101-103) created a new section 28 of the Federal Reserve Act (FRA), imposing penalties on any member bank or individual found to be in violation of FRA section 22 or 23A; **b)** (S. 104, modifying FRA S. 22) prohibited member banks from lending to any of its executive officers; **c)** (S. 105) provided for cases of termination of a bank holding company charter if the Board of Governors believes it's activities are a risk to its financial stability; **d)** (S. 202) prohibited individuals from being directors in more than one depository institution, with some exceptions; **e)** (S. 301) prohibited State FDIC-insured banks that are not members of the Federal Reserve from opening branches in foreign nations except by permission; **f)** (S. 501) created a National Credit Union Administration to regulate credit unions; **g)** (S. 1002, 1006) created a Financial Institutions Examination Council to develop uniform rules for examination of banking institutions; **h)** (S. 1102) required banking institutions to keep their customers' financial record private, except by court order, search warrant, or subpoena; **i)** (S. 1401) FDIC insurance of Keogh and IRA accounts increased to $100,000; **j)** (S. 1601) authority of the Board of Governors to control interest rates on deposits and savings was extended to 15 Dec 1980; **k)** (S. 1802) created a National Credit Union Central Liquidity Facility to maintain the financial stability of credit unions; and **l)** (S. 1902) extended the lending authority of the Export-Import Bank to $40,000 M ($40 B) and extended its charter to 30 Sep 1983.

31 Dec 1978: Seven banks failed in 1978, with net losses to the FDIC FDIF totaling $9.015 M [21.2-39].

16 Jan 1979: The Shah of Iran was overthrown by the Ayatollah Khomeini; this led to a decline in oil production, and precipitated another "oil crisis" in the U. S. The oil shortage was made worse during

the 1980 Iran-Iraq War. The price of oil increased from $15.85 per barrel in Feb 1979 to $39.50 per barrel in Feb 1980. The amount of oil sold in the U. S. declined only slightly, since overall oil production only declined by about 10%.

10 May 1979: Congress passed a law [21.2-40] regarding the Council on Wage and Price Stability. Among its provisions: **a)** (S. 1) extended the Council on Wage and Price Stability to 30 Sep 1980, and **b)** (S. 5) required the Council to issue a report, setting a goal and modifying the Employment of Act of 1946 (cf. 20 Feb 1946) such that the share of the nation's gross national product due to federal outlays to be reduced to 21% or less by 1981, and to 20% or less by 1983, so long as doing so does not impede the goals for the reduction of unemployment.

8 Jun 1979: Congress passed legislation on the banking system [21.2-41]: **a)** modified section 14 of the Federal Reserve Act (FRA) to permit the Federal Reserve to lend securities to the U. S. Treasury; **b)** modified section 14 of the FRA to permit, for 30 days, and with approval of five members of the Board of Governors, the Federal Reserve to buy and sell directly to or from the United States any obligations that are either direct obligations of the United States, or for which principal and interest are guaranteed by a federal agency, and the transactions to be performed in the open market per section 12 of the FRA; **c)** total of obligations acquired from or loaned to the Treasury not to exceed $5,000 M ($5 B); **d)** added a new paragraph to section 14 of the FRA to permit the Treasury Secretary to borrow and sell any obligation from any Federal Reserve Bank in order to meet short-term cash flow problems at Treasury, and the Treasury required to repurchase them within six months; **e)** these authorities to continue until 8 Jun 1981; and **f)** after 8 Jun 1981, the Federal Reserve to buy and sell U. S. securities only in the open market.

31 Dec 1979: Ten banks failed in 1979, with net losses to the FDIC FDIF totaling $10.867 M [21.2-42]. There were a total of 143 S&L failures between 1934 and 1979 inclusive (46 years), causing total losses to the FSLIC of $306.0 M [21.2-43].

7 Jan 1980: Congress passed the Chrysler Corporation Loan Guarantee Act of 1979 [21.2-44], authorizing the Treasury Secretary and Board of Governors to provide up to $1,430 M ($1.43 B) in loan guarantees to bail out the Chrysler Corporation, which they did.

15 Jan 1980: Approximate beginning of a recession [21.2-45].

31 Mar 1980: Congress passed the Depository Institutions Deregulation and Monetary Control Act, supposedly in response to the high inflation of the 1970's. Its provisions included [21.2-46]: **a)** (S. 102) required all banks (including ones that are not members of the Federal Reserve) to submit regular reports on the status of their deposits and reserves; **b)** (S. 103) established a two-tiered legal reserve requirements to apply to all banking institutions that accept demand or time deposits, including commercial, savings, mutual savings banks, savings and loan institutions, and credit unions; **c)** (S. 103) permitted all depository institutions that are not members of the Federal Reserve to access the Federal Reserve discount window; **d)** (S. 106) abolished the discount window penalty rate provision of section 10 of the Federal Reserve Act; **e)** (S. 107) required the Federal Reserve to establish a fee schedule for services rendered to member banks; **f)** (S. 204) enacted a gradual phasing out of interest rate ceilings on time deposits at member banks; and **g)** (S. 308) increased the insurance limit on deposits in federally insured banks, savings and loans, and credit unions from $40,000 to $100,000.

~15 Apr 1980: The FDIC bailed out the First Pennsylvania Bank with assets of $8,000 M ($8 B) on the grounds that its failure would pose a systemic risk to the banking system. This was the first time that the authority granted in 1950 was used [21.2-47].

4 May 1980: The U. S. Department of Education began operations, having been split off from the Department of Health and Human Services.

15 Jul 1980: Approximate end of a recession (cf. 15 Jan 1980) [21.2-48].

8 Dec 1980: Congress extended [21.2-49] the Council on Wage and Price Stability to 30 Jun 1982, and required it to tabulate numerous statistics on the nation's economy.

17 Dec 1980: Congress increased [21.2-50] the U. S. quota in the International Monetary Fund (IMF) by appropriating $4,202.5 M in Special Drawing Rights (SDR), equivalent to $5,537,839,000 USD to the IMF.

31 Dec 1980: Eleven banks failed in 1980, with net losses to the FDIC FDIF totaling $30.680 M [21.2-51]. Eleven S&L's failed in 1980, with net losses to the FSLIC of $158.193 M [21.2-52].

15 Jul 1981: Approximate beginning of a recession [21.2-53].

31 Dec 1981: Ten banks failed in 1981, with net losses to the FDIC FDIF totaling $781.778 M [21.2-54], as did 34 S&L's, with net losses to the FSLIC of $1,887.709 M ($1.8877 B) [21.2-55].

8 Oct 1982: Congress passed the Export Trading Company Act [21.2-56] in order to streamline the financial handling of exports, by allowing export service companies to facilitate exports. It permitted banks to invest in export trading companies, defined as those that:

> "provide consulting, international market research, advertising, marketing, insurance, product research and design, legal assistance, transportation, including trade documentation and freight forwarding, communication and processing of foreign orders to and for exporters and foreign purchasers, warehousing, foreign exchange, financing, and taking title to goods, when provided in order to facilitate the export of goods or services produced in the United States".

15 Oct 1982: Congress passed the Garn-St. Germain Depository Institutions Act [21.2-57]: **a)** (Title I, S. 111) FDIC was authorized to make loans to, and make deposits or purchase assets or securities as required to prevent an FDIC-insured bank from closing or to restore it to normal operating condition, or to reduce overall risk to the FDIC by a spreading of failures, so long as the cost thereof is less than liquidation; **b)** (Title I, S.112) permitted an FDIC-insured State-chartered savings bank to be converted to a federally chartered savings bank if not precluded by State law, whereupon the deposits thereof are regarded as insured under FSLIC; **c)** (Title I, S. 112) FDIC-insured banks are prohibited from merging with non-insured institutions; **d)** (Title I, S. 116) established procedures for liquidating FDIC-insured banks having assets in excess of $500 M; **e)** (Title I, S. 123) established provisions for emergency assistance to institutions under the National Housing Act of 1933 (cf. 27 Jun 1934), the failure of which would impair the stability of a large number of other institutions; **f)** (Title I, S. 125) Federal Home Loan Banks are authorized to lend to the FSLIC; **g)** (Title I, S. 131) permitted the FDIC to authorize the merger of an insolvent credit union with a stable one; **h)** (Title II) permitted the FDIC to support the capital positions of FDIC-insured banks by purchasing capital instruments, whereupon the bank could issue "Net Worth Certificates"; **i)** (Title III, S. 311) permitted conversions of Federal Home Loan Banks into federal savings and loan or federal savings banks; **j)** (Title III, S. 341) permitted transfer of real estate into trusts without triggering the due-on-sale provision in mortgage contracts; **k)** (Title IV, S. 411) reduced to zero the reserve ratio of the first $2 M in deposits of Federal Reserve member banks; **l)** (Title V) enacted minor rule changes to credit union operations; and **m)** (Title VIII) permitted alternative forms of mortgages: 1) adjustable rate over the term of the mortgage; 2) fixed rate, but implicit rate changes by termination of the loan period (i.e., balloon mortgages); 3) those in which variations in equity, appreciation, type of rate, term, or method of determining return that differs from traditional fixed-rate, fixed term contracts.

15 Nov 1982: Approximate end of a recession (cf. 15 Jul 1981) [21.2-58].

31 Dec 1982: Forty-two banks failed in 1982, with net losses to the FDIC FDIF of $1,168.571 M ($1.168 B) [21.2-59]; as did 73 S&L's, with net losses to the FSLIC of $1,499.584 M ($1.499 B) [21.2-60].

25-29 Oct 1983: The U. S. invasion of Grenada.

31 Dec 1983: Forty-eight banks failed in 1983, with net losses to the FDIC FDIF totaling $1,376.609 M ($1.376 B) [21.2-61]; as did 51 S&L's, with net losses to the FSLIC of $418.425 M [21.2-62].

26 Jul 1984: The FDIC bailed out the Continental Illinois National Bank, having assets of $45,000 M ($45 B), on the grounds that its failure would endanger public confidence [21.2-63]. It was the se-

cond time the authority granted in 1950 was used. The FDIC agreed to buy $4,500 M ($4.5 B) in bad loans, and this event also gave rise to the term "too big to fail" [21.2-64].

3 Oct 1984: Congress passed the Secondary Mortgage Market Enhancement Act of 1984 [21.2-65]. The objective was to improve the marketability of mortgage-backed securities. Among its provisions are: **a)** (Title I, S. 101) defined a "mortgage related security" as a security that is rated at one of the two highest rating categories by at least one nationally recognized statistical rating organization and either: 1) represents ownership of notes or certificates denoting: A) secured by first mortgages on residential property, and B) originated by a federal or State chartered savings and loan, credit union, savings, banks, commercial banks or insurance company; OR 2) secured by other such promissory notes that conform to the provisions as above; **b)** (Title I, S. 106) these mortgage backed securities were to be treated as the equivalent of U. S. Treasury bonds for the purpose of investments by federally chartered depository institutions; **c)** (Title 1, S. 106) to be treated the same by State chartered savings banks and financial institutions unless superseded by State law; and **d)** (Title II, S. 201) permitted Federal Home Loan Mortgage Association (FREDDIE MAC) and Federal National Mortgage Association (FANNIE MAE) to invest in these mortgage-backed securities.

A total of 21 States decided to exercise exemption provision [21.2-66]: Alaska, Arkansas, Colorado, Connecticut, Delaware, Florida, Georgia, Illinois, Kansas, Maryland, Michigan, Missouri, Nebraska, New Hampshire, New York, North Carolina, Ohio, South Dakota, Utah, West Virginia, and Virginia.

This legislation, aided by corruption, contributed indirectly over the next twenty years to the collapse of the financial system in 2007: **a)** development of a sub-prime mortgage market: 1) residential loans were issued by mortgage brokers customers who did not have sufficient income to repay them, and 2) some mortgage brokers used illegal means to issue "predatory " loans; **b)** solid mortgages and these sub-prime mortgages were bundled together into mortgage-backed securities by securities firms with no way to unravel them; **c)** were given unjustified higher investment grade ratings by the rating agencies (Moody's, Standard & Poor); **d)** these were sold to investors as collateralized mortgage obligations (CMO), collateralized debt obligations (CDO) etc.; **e)** FREDDIE MAC and FANNIE MAE invested in these securities as part of the government's low-income housing initiatives or lowered their underwriting standards to compete with the private mortgage-backed securities; **f)** led to a boom in the residential mortgage market, with home prices rising steadily; **g)** when the sub-prime mortgages began to go into default, the value of the securities fell also, causing a run on the stock market and banks; and **h)** the securities themselves could not be sorted out because of the peculiar bundling process, thus they could not be priced accurately which led to a steep price decline in all of them due to a collapse of investor confidence.

31 Dec 1984: Eighty banks failed in 1984, with net losses to the FDIC FDIF totaling $1,640.571 M ($1.640 B) [21.2-67], as did 26 S&L's, with net losses to the FSLIC of $886.518 M [21.2-68].

17 Dec 1985: Congress passed the Gold Bullion Coin Act [21.2-69] as a convenient way for people to buy and hold gold, to be issued in denominations of $50 (1 ozt. fine gold), $25 (0.5 ozt.), $10 (0.25 ozt.), and $5 (0.10 ozt.). They were to be marketed to the public, and sold at a price that covers all costs of materials, tools, and labor.

31 Dec 1985: A total of 120 banks failed in 1985, with net losses to the FDIC FDIF totaling $1,007.152 M ($1.007 B) [21.2-70]; as did 54 S&L's, with net losses to the FSLIC totaling $7,420.153 M ($7.420 B) [21.2-71].

15 Oct 1986: Congress passed the Export-Import Bank Act Amendments of 1986 [21.2-72]. Among its provisions: **a)** (S. 3) enhancement of the medium-term program (181 days to five years); **b)** (S. 6) provided for risk insurance for medium-term financing; and **c)** (S. 8) prohibited providing any assistance for trade with Marxist-Leninist countries, defined as either: "1) maintains a centrally planned economy based on the principles of Marxist-Leninism, or 2) is economically and militarily dependent on the Union of Soviet Socialist Republics or on any other Marxist-Leninist country." Thirty nations are specifically mentioned as fitting this description.

27 Oct 1986: Congress passed the Anti-Drug Abuse Act [21.2-73], prescribing the federal governments 'war on drugs'. One of the provisions involved 'money laundering': **a)** (S. 1352) prohibited financial transactions by a person who knows it is the proceeds of an illegal activity, including any attempt to conceal such fact (penalty: $500,000 fine and/or 20 years imprisonment, regardless of the amount in question); **b)** (S. 1352) same for attempting to transport a financial instrument that is the proceeds of illegal activity across State lines or outside the United States; **c)** (S. 1352) 'illegal activity' means the illicit drug trade, concealment of assets, bribery, counterfeiting, smuggling, theft of public property, embezzlement by bank officers or employees, espionage, hostage taking, and bank fraud, among others; and **d)** (S. 1353) if ordered by a court, prohibited notification to a person by a financial institution that a subpoena has been issued for their financial records.

31 Dec 1986: A total of 145 banks failed in 1986, with net losses to the FDIC FDIF totaling $1,781.742 M ($1.781 B) [21.2-74]; as did 65 S&L's, with net losses to the FSLIC totaling $9,130.022 M ($9.130 B) [21.2-75].

21.3 Data, 1972-1986

Figure 21.3-1 and 21.3-2 show the U. S. government revenue and expenditures for 1972 to 1986.

U. S. Government Revenue, 1972-1986 (millions USD)										
			Income taxes				Social Insurance Taxes			
Day	Year	Customs Duties	Individual	Corporate	Excise Taxes	Estate and Gift Taxes	OASDI & Disability (Off-Budget)	Medicare & Retirements (On-Budget)	Federal Reserve Deposits	Other Misc.	Net Receipts
30 Jun	1972	3,287	94,737	32,166	15,477	5,436	39,907	12,667	3,252	380	207,309
30 Jun	1973	3,188	103,246	36,153	16,260	4,917	46,084	17,031	3,495	425	230,799
30 Jun	1974	3,334	118,952	38,620	16,844	5,035	53,925	21,146	4,845	523	263,224
30 Jun	1975	3,676	122,386	40,621	16,551	4,611	62,458	22,077	5,777	935	279,090
30 Jun	1976	4,074	131,603	41,409	16,963	5,216	66,389	24,381	5,451	2,576	298,060
30 Sep	1976 TQ	1,212	38,801	8,460	4,473	1,455	18,016	7,203	1,500	111	81,232
30 Sep	1977	5,150	157,626	54,892	17,548	7,327	76,817	29,668	5,908	623	355,559
30 Sep	1978	6,573	180,988	59,952	18,376	5,285	85,391	35,576	6,641	778	399,561
30 Sep	1979	7,439	217,841	65,677	18,745	5,411	97,994	40,945	8,327	925	463,302
30 Sep	1980	7,174	244,069	64,600	24,329	6,389	113,209	44,594	11,767	981	517,112
30 Sep	1981	8,083	285,917	61,137	40,839	6,787	130,176	52,545	12,834	956	599,272
30 Sep	1982	8,854	297,744	49,207	36,311	7,991	143,467	58,031	15,186	975	617,766
30 Sep	1983	8,655	288,938	37,022	35,300	6,053	147,320	61,674	14,492	1,108	600,562
30 Sep	1984	11,370	298,415	56,893	37,361	6,010	166,075	73,301	15,684	1,328	666,438
30 Sep	1985	12,079	334,531	61,331	35,992	6,422	186,170	78,992	17,059	1,460	734,037
30 Sep	1986	13,327	348,959	63,143	32,919	6,958	200,228	83,673	18,374	1,574	769,155

1. The revenue data for 1972 to 1986 is from the OMB White House, file = HIST_FY21.pdf, Tables 2.1 and 2.5
2. https://www.whitehouse.gov/omb/historical-tables/

Figure 21.3-1: U. S. Government Revenue, 1972-1986

Day	Year	National Defense	Education, Training, Employ-ment, Social Services	Health	Medicare	Income Security	Social Security [1]	Veterans	Physical Resources [1, 2]	Interest on Debt [1]	Inter-national Affairs	Agri-culture	Other [3]	Undistrib-uted Offsetting Receipts [1, 4]	Total
30 Jun	1972	79,174	12,529	8,674	7,479	27,638	40,157	10,732	19,574	15,478	4,781	5,227	8,820	-9,583	230,681
30 Jun	1973	76,681	12,744	9,356	8,052	28,265	49,090	12,015	20,614	17,349	4,149	4,821	15,980	-13,409	245,707
30 Jun	1974	79,347	12,455	10,733	9,639	33,700	55,867	13,388	25,106	21,449	5,710	2,194	16,519	-16,749	269,359
30 Jun	1975	86,509	16,022	12,930	12,875	50,161	64,658	16,599	35,449	23,244	7,097	2,997	17,393	-13,602	332,332
30 Jun	1976	89,619	18,910	15,734	15,834	60,784	73,899	18,433	39,188	26,727	6,433	3,109	17,508	-14,386	371,792
30 Sep	1976 TQ	22,269	5,159	3,929	4,264	14,981	19,763	3,963	9,512	6,949	2,458	972	5,958	-4,206	95,975
30 Sep	1977	97,241	21,104	17,302	19,345	61,045	85,061	18,038	40,746	29,901	6,353	6,734	21,228	-14,879	409,218
30 Sep	1978	104,495	26,706	18,524	22,768	61,492	93,861	18,978	52,590	35,458	7,482	11,301	20,811	-15,720	458,746
30 Sep	1979	116,342	30,218	20,494	26,495	66,364	104,073	19,931	54,559	42,633	7,459	11,176	21,761	-17,476	504,028
30 Sep	1980	133,995	31,835	23,169	32,090	86,548	118,547	21,185	65,985	52,533	12,714	8,774	23,508	-19,942	590,941
30 Jun	1981	157,513	33,146	26,866	39,149	100,286	139,584	22,991	70,886	68,766	13,104	11,241	22,750	-28,041	678,241
30 Jun	1982	185,309	26,609	27,445	46,567	108,138	155,964	23,958	61,752	85,032	12,300	15,866	22,902	-26,099	745,743
30 Jun	1983	209,903	26,192	28,643	52,588	123,018	170,724	24,846	57,603	89,808	11,848	22,807	24,360	-33,976	808,364
30 Jun	1984	227,411	26,913	30,420	57,540	113,378	178,223	25,601	57,960	111,102	15,869	13,477	25,868	-31,957	851,805
30 Jun	1985	252,743	28,584	33,546	65,822	129,002	188,623	26,281	56,804	129,478	16,169	25,427	26,564	-32,698	946,344
30 Jun	1986	273,373	29,771	35,935	70,164	120,656	198,756	26,343	58,722	136,017	14,146	31,319	28,187	-33,007	990,382

1. The totals of "on budget and off-budget" are shown here.
2. "Physical Resources" includes Energy, Natural Resources and Environment, Commerce and Housing Credit, Transportation, and Community & Regional Development.
3. "Other" includes General Science, Space & Technology, Administration of Justice, General Government, and Allowances.
4. "Offsetting Receipts" is a combination of new debt and intra-government transfers from Trust Funds.
5. The expenditure data for 1972 to 1986 is from the OMB White House, file = HIST_FY21.pdf, Table 3.1.
6. https://www.whitehouse.gov/omb/historical-tables/

Figure 21.3-2: U. S. Government Expenditures, 1972-1986

Figure 21.3-3 shows the national debt and per-capita debt for this period. Refer to the Introduction to Part 2 for a sense of wages vs. per-capita national debt.

Day	Year	Principal ($) [1, 3]	Population [2]	Debt Per Capita ($) [2]	Day	Year	Principal ($) [1, 3]	Population [2]	Debt Per Capita ($) [2]
30 Jun	1972	426,435,460,940	207,878,702	2,051.37	30 Sep	1980	907,701,290,900	226,545,805	4,006.70
30 Jun	1973	457,316,605,312	210,212,090	2,175.50	30 Sep	1981	997,855,000,000	228,762,212	4,361.97
30 Jun	1974	474,234,815,732	212,545,478	2,231.22	30 Sep	1982	1,142,034,000,000	230,978,619	4,944.33
30 Jun	1975	533,188,976,772	214,878,866	2,481.35	30 Sep	1983	1,377,210,000,000	233,195,025	5,905.83
30 Jun	1976	620,432,971,265	217,212,253	2,856.34	30 Sep	1984	1,572,266,000,000	235,411,432	6,678.80
30 Sep	1977	698,839,928,356	219,545,641	3,183.12	30 Sep	1985	1,823,103,000,000	237,627,839	7,672.09
30 Sep	1978	771,544,478,952	221,879,029	3,477.32	30 Sep	1986	2,125,302,616,658	239,844,246	8,861.18

1. Public debt data from 1972 to 1980 is from the Annual Report of the Secretary of the Treasury, 1980, pp. 61, 62.
2. Population values are based on the dicennial census from the Census Bureau, and linearly interpolated. Per-capita is based on these
3. The total debt data for 1981 to 1986 is from: https://fiscaldata.treasury.gov/datasets/historical-debt-outstanding/historical-debt-outstanding

Figure 21.3-3: National Debt and Per-Capita Share Thereof, 1972-1986

Figures 21.3-4 through 21.3-9 show summaries of assets and liabilities of the Federal Reserve and commercial banking system for this period.

Assets of the Federal Reserve & Commercial System, 1972-1976 (millions USD)										
				Federal Reserve Loans & Investments		Commercial Bank Loans and Investments				
Day	Year	Gold Stock	Treasury Currency Outstanding	U. S. Government Securities	Discounts & Advances	Loans	U. S. Government Securities	Other	Total Assets	Note
29 Mar	1972	9,588	7,889	70,689	1,030	351,800	62,500	108,490	611,986	
28 Jun	1972	10,410	8,057	72,094	475	370,910	60,258	111,521	633,725	
27 Sep	1972	10,410	8,196	70,018	842	381,740	60,290	113,720	645,216	
27 Dec	1972	10,410	8,302	69,545	1,434	409,790	64,670	115,530	679,681	
28 Mar	1973	10,410	8,422	75,193	2,028	429,400	61,180	117,740	704,373	
27 Jun	1973	10,410	8,535	75,865	1,587	456,780	57,877	121,099	732,153	
26 Sep	1973	10,410	8,595	76,969	4,520	466,420	54,800	123,930	745,644	
26 Dec	1973	11,567	8,675	76,740	485	490,680	58,180	126,960	773,287	
27 Mar	1974	11,567	8,772	80,920	1,713	500,100	57,510	133,470	794,052	
26 Jun	1974	11,567	8,892	83,555	2,978	528,951	52,114	137,648	825,705	
25 Sep	1974	11,567	9,016	84,982	3,531	531,210	50,630	136,720	827,656	
25 Dec	1974	11,652	9,208	89,258	426	546,660	54,360	138,750	850,314	
26 Mar	1975	11,620	9,386	86,867	155	531,440	59,330	140,920	839,718	
25 Jun	1975	11,620	9,553	93,269	1,100	535,493	68,191	143,868	863,094	
24 Sep	1975	11,599	9,811	90,530	395	522,580	75,440	144,280	854,635	
31 Dec	1975	11,599	10,218	94,124	211	542,090	84,220	145,070	887,532	
31 Mar	1976	11,599	10,442	95,638	36	534,530	89,260	143,470	884,975	
30 Jun	1976	11,598	10,573	101,528	314	543,740	90,800	145,280	903,833	
29 Sep	1976	11,598	10,757	106,276	326	550,820	92,630	146,950	919,357	
29 Dec	1976	11,598	10,884	100,959	375	576,000	99,800	148,000	947,616	
1. See Appendix B for references.										

Figure 21.3-4: Banking System Assets, 1972-1976

Liabilities of the Federal Reserve and Commercial System, 1972-1976 (millions USD)										
				At Federal Reserve Banks			At Commercial Banks			
Day	Year	Currency Outside Banks	Treasury Cash	Treasury Demand Deposits	Foreign Demand Deposits	Demand Deposits	Treasury Demand Deposits	Time Deposits	Capital	Total Liabilities	Error (%)
29 Mar	1972	52,600	388	933	170	175,100	9,200	282,100	65,200	585,691	4.30
28 Jun	1972	55,144	356	2,673	153	179,977	9,575	292,021	66,184	606,083	4.36
27 Sep	1972	53,700	320	938	190	181,400	10,000	301,900	68,200	616,648	4.43
27 Dec	1972	57,900	350	1,449	272	205,100	7,400	311,800	52,658	636,929	6.29
28 Mar	1973	57,400	384	3,598	338	198,100	10,400	332,600	53,300	656,120	6.85
27 Jun	1973	59,400	386	2,408	266	204,100	7,100	344,500	55,740	673,900	7.96
26 Sep	1973	60,100	349	792	332	203,800	5,300	359,200	55,570	685,443	8.07
26 Dec	1973	62,600	323	1,892	406	215,500	6,300	361,800	56,920	705,741	8.73
27 Mar	1974	62,700	338	2,094	355	209,800	6,400	379,100	59,310	720,097	9.31
26 Jun	1974	64,800	303	2,693	282	213,100	6,100	397,900	61,623	746,801	9.56
25 Sep	1974	65,800	318	3,347	611	213,200	5,400	410,200	61,730	760,606	8.10
25 Dec	1974	68,900	212	2,671	450	222,800	4,600	417,700	63,070	780,403	8.22
26 Mar	1975	68,800	306	3,554	428	236,900	3,950	429,500	65,220	808,658	3.70
25 Jun	1975	71,200	370	5,497	294	264,027	3,117	433,389	66,557	844,451	2.16
24 Sep	1975	71,900	356	7,249	234	240,080	3,220	438,920	66,990	828,949	3.01
31 Dec	1975	75,000	425	7,285	353	278,280	3,170	446,830	68,510	879,853	0.87
31 Mar	1976	75,100	519	7,144	305	256,930	2,430	457,950	70,070	870,448	1.64
30 Jun	1976	77,800	500	11,972	349	266,400	4,700	462,900	72,100	896,721	0.79
29 Sep	1976	79,000	425	12,212	245	252,900	5,800	469,900	73,100	893,582	2.80
29 Dec	1976	82,200	475	9,684	257	275,900	3,400	484,800	75,000	931,716	1.68
1. See Appendix B for references.										

Figure 21.3-5: Banking System Liabilities, 1972-1976

| Assets of the Federal Reserve & Commercial System, 1977-1981 (millions USD) | | | | | | | | | | |
| | | | | Federal Reserve Loans & Investments | | Commercial Bank Loans and Investments | | | | |
Day	Year	Gold Stock	Treasury Currency Outstanding	U. S. Government Securities	Discounts & Advances	Loans	U. S. Government Securities	Other	Total Assets	Note
30 Mar	1977	11,636	10,990	96,112	149	551,000	103,600	148,400	921,887	
29 Jun	1977	11,620	11,116	101,864	606	572,400	105,200	152,900	955,706	
28 Sep	1977	11,595	11,246	104,275	1,292	592,200	100,100	156,100	976,808	
28 Dec	1977	11,718	11,364	105,682	1,909	612,900	93,500	159,000	996,073	
29 Mar	1978	11,718	11,480	102,443	364	677,800	98,600	159,600	1,062,005	
28 Jun	1978	11,706	11,594	110,508	2,648	707,800	95,900	163,200	1,103,356	
27 Sep	1978	11,668	11,695	116,363	1,158	733,600	95,000	167,700	1,137,184	
27 Dec	1978	11,671	11,846	111,639	3,110	770,900	92,600	171,200	1,172,966	
28 Mar	1979	11,481	12,085	104,705	1,498	771,100	94,900	179,400	1,175,169	
27 Jun	1979	11,323	12,409	109,341	2,922	810,300	93,100	183,100	1,222,495	
26 Sep	1979	11,228	12,645	115,005	1,820	846,700	93,500	188,300	1,269,198	
26 Dec	1979	11,112	12,947	113,057	1,982	862,600	94,500	192,200	1,288,398	
26 Mar	1980	11,172	13,146	117,830	4,651	865,000	96,200	195,400	1,303,399	
25 Jun	1980	11,172	13,285	119,841	364	857,400	97,200	202,400	1,301,662	
24 Sep	1980	11,168	13,341	120,713	3,617	877,000	104,500	207,700	1,338,039	
31 Dec	1980	11,161	13,838	121,328	1,809	910,100	109,600	214,300	1,382,136	
25 Mar	1981	11,155	13,502	119,606	3,229	921,200	117,100	217,500	1,403,292	
24 Jun	1981	11,154	13,575	119,360	1,803	950,000	119,700	219,600	1,435,192	
30 Sep	1981	11,152	14,315	124,740	2,486	976,600	115,600	224,000	1,468,893	
30 Dec	1981	11,151	13,687	131,493	1,237	982,900	111,400	233,300	1,485,168	
1. See Appendix B for references.										

Figure 21.3-6: Banking System Assets, 1977-1981

| Liabilities of the Federal Reserve and Commercial System, 1977-1981 (millions USD) | | | | | | | | | | |
| | | | | At Federal Reserve Banks | | At Commercial Banks | | | | |
Day	Year	Currency Outside Banks	Treasury Cash	Treasury Demand Deposits	Foreign Demand Deposits	Demand Deposits	Treasury Demand Deposits	Time Deposits	Capital	Total Liabilities	Error (%)
30 Mar	1977	82,200	471	7,769	288	263,100	3,100	504,400	77,100	938,428	-1.79
29 Jun	1977	84,000	441	14,058	259	288,100	2,800	515,600	81,800	987,058	-3.28
28 Sep	1977	86,100	429	11,197	300	272,500	8,000	526,100	80,100	984,726	-0.81
28 Dec	1977	90,000	390	7,664	327	307,000	7,200	541,100	81,600	1,035,281	-3.94
29 Mar	1978	89,900	396	4,389	276	281,200	4,900	567,100	83,400	1,031,561	2.87
28 Jun	1978	92,900	370	12,173	209	317,500	8,000	580,800	89,900	1,101,852	0.14
27 Sep	1978	94,900	297	13,543	253	297,100	11,000	588,300	87,100	1,092,493	3.93
27 Dec	1978	99,100	241	3,540	285	327,100	2,300	600,300	87,300	1,120,166	4.50
28 Mar	1979	98,600	374	3,178	271	355,700	7,800	638,300	99,800	1,204,023	-2.46
27 Jun	1979	101,800	365	3,597	270	376,400	10,800	639,200	99,800	1,232,232	-0.80
26 Sep	1979	104,500	306	5,483	275	383,200	12,400	660,400	104,200	1,270,764	-0.12
26 Dec	1979	108,000	430	2,883	216	400,500	9,500	675,800	115,400	1,312,729	-1.89
26 Mar	1980	107,900	566	2,998	368	373,600	7,400	699,900	130,900	1,323,632	-1.55
25 Jun	1980	111,000	534	2,951	295	379,100	10,000	709,600	124,100	1,337,580	-2.76
24 Sep	1980	113,700	467	3,928	301	391,200	14,100	731,000	130,600	1,385,296	-3.53
31 Dec	1980	118,500	441	3,062	411	453,600	9,000	786,300	135,500	1,506,814	-9.02
25 Mar	1981	116,800	476	2,609	244	367,400	10,200	823,200	137,200	1,458,129	-3.91
24 Jun	1981	119,900	505	2,909	237	389,400	12,400	847,300	140,700	1,513,351	-5.45
30 Sep	1981	121,000	456	3,520	420	417,300	11,100	881,900	153,300	1,588,996	-8.18
30 Dec	1981	125,400	442	3,402	319	378,400	11,300	911,300	135,600	1,566,163	-5.45
1. See Appendix B for references.										

Figure 21.3-7: Banking System Liabilities, 1977-1981

| Assets of the Federal Reserve & Commercial System, 1982-1986 (millions USD) | | | | | | | | | | |
| | | | | Federal Reserve Loans & Investments | | Commercial Bank Loans and Investments | | | | |
Day	Year	Gold Stock	Treasury Currency Outstanding	U. S. Government Securities	Discounts & Advances	Loans	U. S. Government Securities	Other	Total Assets	Note
31 Mar	1982	11,150	13,734	125,589	2,646	989,600	116,300	233,100	1,492,119	
30 Jun	1982	11,149	13,781	127,005	1,638	1,014,600	116,100	235,600	1,519,873	
29 Sep	1982	11,148	13,786	130,305	1,154	1,035,600	117,800	237,700	1,547,493	
29 Dec	1982	11,148	13,786	138,148	1,813	1,050,700	131,400	240,700	1,587,695	
30 Mar	1983	11,138	13,786	134,660	1,985	1,049,500	153,200	242,300	1,606,569	
29 Jun	1983	11,131	13,786	140,729	2,080	1,068,000	171,600	245,900	1,653,226	
28 Sep	1983	11,128	13,786	149,370	2,359	1,098,200	176,300	247,100	1,698,243	
28 Dec	1983	11,123	13,786	152,750	1,311	1,140,700	188,900	248,500	1,757,070	
28 Mar	1984	11,114	15,889	145,670	718	1,190,300	189,800	250,700	1,804,191	
27 Jun	1984	11,100	16,113	152,907	3,332	1,245,500	248,200	133,000	1,810,152	
26 Sep	1984	11,097	16,280	153,748	4,786	1,277,300	243,500	133,800	1,840,511	
26 Dec	1984	11,096	16,415	161,529	2,423	1,336,800	242,500	134,900	1,905,663	
27 Mar	1985	11,093	16,602	159,169	385	1,347,400	250,800	132,800	1,918,249	
26 Jun	1985	11,090	16,770	166,282	776	1,388,900	255,300	136,800	1,975,918	
25 Sep	1985	11,090	16,924	174,646	2,121	1,417,900	254,400	142,600	2,019,681	
25 Dec	1985	11,090	17,043	177,730	1,362	1,465,000	249,900	163,600	2,085,725	
26 Mar	1986	11,090	17,216	176,712	895	1,491,300	250,900	171,200	2,119,313	
25 Jun	1986	11,084	17,329	181,893	797	1,515,800	295,500	176,400	2,198,803	
24 Sep	1986	11,084	17,450	187,958	1,555	1,542,500	276,600	192,800	2,229,947	
31 Dec	1986	11,084	17,567	211,316	1,565	1,638,100	292,600	187,000	2,359,232	
1. See Appendix B for references.										

Figure 21.3-8: Banking System Assets, 1982-1986

| Liabilities of the Federal Reserve and Commercial System, 1982-1986 (millions USD) | | | | | | | | | | |
| | | At Federal Reserve Banks | | | | At Commercial Banks | | | | |
Day	Year	Currency Outside Banks	Treasury Cash	Treasury Demand Deposits	Foreign Demand Deposits	Demand Deposits	Treasury Demand Deposits	Time Deposits	Capital	Total Liabilities	Error (%)
31 Mar	1982	123,800	484	2,866	421	350,800	15,600	944,200	135,000	1,573,171	-5.43
30 Jun	1982	128,300	460	4,099	586	357,400	10,800	968,400	140,800	1,610,845	-5.99
29 Sep	1982	130,200	421	8,320	295	335,100	12,400	1,006,800	143,800	1,636,836	-5.77
29 Dec	1982	135,200	435	3,620	261	376,200	10,900	1,033,400	148,400	1,708,416	-7.60
30 Mar	1983	135,400	495	2,116	250	345,700	13,200	1,073,800	141,100	1,712,061	-6.57
29 Jun	1983	140,300	531	4,026	241	356,400	13,200	1,087,300	142,300	1,744,298	-5.51
28 Sep	1983	142,600	468	14,253	205	340,000	18,000	1,108,800	142,300	1,766,626	-4.03
28 Dec	1983	148,700	462	3,686	263	383,200	10,800	1,141,700	158,600	1,847,411	-5.14
28 Mar	1984	148,900	503	14,045	251	440,900	17,500	1,053,600	176,300	1,851,999	-2.65
27 Jun	1984	154,900	523	3,533	243	445,900	12,400	1,086,900	173,800	1,878,199	-3.76
26 Sep	1984	156,500	465	8,814	196	442,300	17,500	1,107,600	142,300	1,875,675	-1.91
26 Dec	1984	160,900	511	3,587	182	490,500	12,500	1,139,500	196,200	2,003,880	-5.15
27 Mar	1985	159,800	554	4,204	216	457,600	12,800	1,167,600	177,000	1,979,774	-3.21
26 Jun	1985	165,200	588	3,892	243	473,800	14,900	1,183,900	179,300	2,021,823	-2.32
25 Sep	1985	167,600	544	8,009	230	474,900	16,800	1,208,600	183,600	2,060,283	-2.01
25 Dec	1985	173,100	554	3,286	209	536,400	14,600	1,227,100	178,500	2,133,749	-2.30
26 Mar	1986	172,300	617	2,394	187	502,100	15,700	1,252,000	187,500	2,132,798	-0.64
25 Jun	1986	177,400	636	2,846	240	523,300	13,100	1,268,700	168,500	2,154,722	2.00
24 Sep	1986	179,600	493	7,744	208	537,400	18,200	1,293,400	177,500	2,214,545	0.69
31 Dec	1986	186,100	447	7,588	287	689,700	19,200	1,325,400	200,300	2,429,022	-2.96
1. See Appendix B for references.										

Figure 21.3-9: Banking System Liabilities, 1982-1986

I have stopped showing coinage data at this point since all U. S. coinage is now "token" in the sense that it contains only base materials. Figure 21.3-10 shows the total money supply for this period; it is based on the M-series data published by the Federal Reserve. The M-series data was not defined until 1973; the prior values are back-calculated. Also, the definitions of the M-series data were radically changed in 1979 and took effect in 1980. The money supply values shown are from the Federal Reserve H.6 data.

U. S. Money Supply per Federal Reserve H.6 Data [1], 1972-1986 (millions USD)					
1	2	3	4	5	6
Year (~30 Jun)	Currency Outside Banks	Adjusted Commercial Demand Deposits	M1 [2], Redefined in Nov 1979 [5]	M2 [3], Redefined in Nov 1979 [6]	M3 [4], Redefined in Nov 1979 [7]
1972	53,800	181,000	236,100	753,200	827,800
1973	58,700	196,000	256,400	837,200	943,500
1974	63,900	202,400	268,300	881,900	1,040,400
1975	70,300	209,300	282,300	966,900	1,121,200
1976	76,600	214,800	295,600	1,080,800	1,237,900
1977	83,100	228,300	317,700	1,219,800	1,388,200
1978	91,600	245,500	345,200	1,319,000	1,553,700
1979	100,500	253,100	371,900	1,422,500	1,725,100
1980	109,700	253,500	387,300	1,527,400	1,880,300
1981	118,900	232,500	422,800	1,667,100	2,112,000
1982	127,700	226,300	446,200	1,822,700	2,353,000
1983	140,100	236,800	503,500	2,051,800	2,579,800
1984	152,700	242,900	541,400	2,214,300	2,845,800
1985	162,500	254,500	585,200	2,413,400	3,100,000
1986	174,400	280,800	662,800	2,605,300	3,348,800

1. M1, M2, and M3 were defined by the Federal Reserve in 1973, cf. Federal Reserve Bulletin, Feb 1973, p. 71.

2. M1 was defined in 1973: "includes (1) demand deposits at all commercial banks other than those due to domestic commercial banks, and the U. S. government, less cash items in the process of collection, and the Federal Reserve float; (2) foreign demand balances at Federal Reserve Banks; and (3) currency outside the Treasury, Federal Reserve Banks, and vaults of all commercial banks".

3. M2 was defined in 1973: "includes, in addition to currency and demand deposits, savings deposits, time deposits open account, and time certificates of deposit (CD's) other than negotiable time CD's issued in denominations of $100,000 or more by large weekly reporting commercial banks. Excludes time deposits of the U. S. government, and of domestic commercial banks." In other words, M2 = M1 plus savings deposits, time deposits, and CD's greater than $100,000.

4. M3 was defined in 1973: "includes M2 plus the average of the beginning and end-of-month deposits of mutual savings banks and savings capital at savings and loan associations."

5. M1 was redefined effective Nov 1979 per Federal Reserve Bulletin, Feb 1980, p. 98: Currency outside banks, demand deposits excluding those due to foreign commercial banks and U. S. government, plus other checkable deposits, (NOW, ATS, credit union share balances, and demand deposits at thrift institutions).

6. M2 was redefined in Nov 1979 as M1 plus overnight repurchase agreements and overnight Eurodollars held by non-bank U. S. residents, plus money market mutual fund shares, and savings and small denomination time deposits at all institutions (formerly was commercial banks only).

7. M3 was redefined in Nov 1979 as M2 plus large denomination time deposits at all depositary institutions including negotiable CD's, plus term repurchase agreements issued by commercial banks and savings and loan institutions.

Figure 21.3-10: Total Money Supply, 1972-1986

Figure 21.3-11 shows the CPI, total money supply, and per-capita money supply during this period.

Year	CPI (1913 = 100)	Total Money Supply M2 [2] (USD)	Population [3]	Per Capita Money Supply (USD)	Annual Rate of Change in CPI (%)	Annual Rate of Change in Per- Capita Money Supply (%)
1972	422.222	753,200,000,000	207,878,702	3,623.27	3.159	9.700
1973	448.485	837,200,000,000	210,212,090	3,982.64	6.034	9.457
1974	497.980	881,900,000,000	212,545,478	4,149.23	10.468	4.098
1975	543.434	966,900,000,000	214,878,866	4,499.74	8.735	8.110
1976	574.747	1,080,800,000,000	217,212,253	4,975.78	5.602	10.056
1977	612.121	1,219,800,000,000	219,545,641	5,556.02	6.300	11.030
1978	658.586	1,319,000,000,000	221,879,029	5,944.68	7.316	6.761
1979	733.333	1,422,500,000,000	224,212,417	6,344.43	10.751	6.508
1980	832.323	1,527,400,000,000	226,545,805	6,742.12	12.662	6.080
1981	918.182	1,667,100,000,000	228,762,212	7,287.48	9.817	7.778
1982	974.747	1,822,700,000,000	230,978,619	7,891.21	5.978	7.959
1983	1,006.061	2,051,800,000,000	233,195,025	8,798.64	3.162	10.885
1984	1,049.495	2,214,300,000,000	235,411,432	9,406.09	4.227	6.676
1985	1,086.869	2,413,400,000,000	237,627,839	10,156.22	3.499	7.673
1986	1,107.071	2,605,300,000,000	239,844,246	10,862.47	1.842	6.723

1. CPI data from Bureau of Labor Statistics, series CUUR0000AA0R (urban, all commodities, not seasonally adjusted), referenced to 1913

2. See notes in money supply data for sources.

3. Population is linearly interpolated from Census results.

Figure 21.3-11: Money Supply and CPI, 1972-1986

Figure 21.3-12 shows a summary of the CPI and per-capita money supply. Three distinct intervals are evident: 1972 to 1978, 1978 to 1983, and 1983 to 1986. The average annual change in CPI and money supply for 1972 to 1978 are 7.4% and 8.2% respectively; for 1978 to 1983, 8.4% and 7.8% respectively; and for 1983 to 1986, 3.2% and 7.0% respectively. For the entire period from 1972 to 1986, the average annual increase in CPI and money supply were 6.88% and 7.84% respectively. The policies of the Federal Reserve reduced the 1978-1983 rate of monetary depreciation by about 62% during 1983 to 1986.

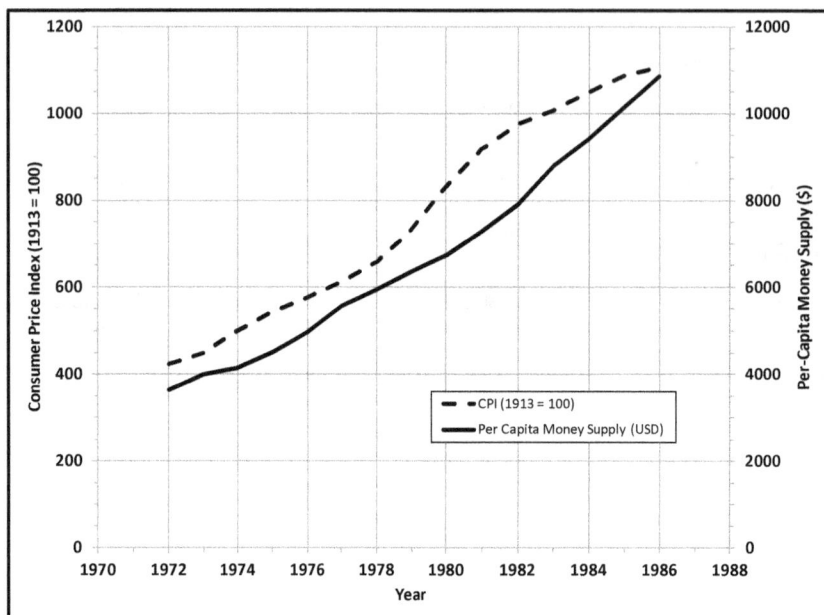

Figure 21.3-12: CPI and Per-Capita Summary, 1972-1986

Figure 21.3-13 shows the approximate median income index, consumer price index, and standard of living index for this period. See the Introduction to Part 2 for cautions regarding these curves.

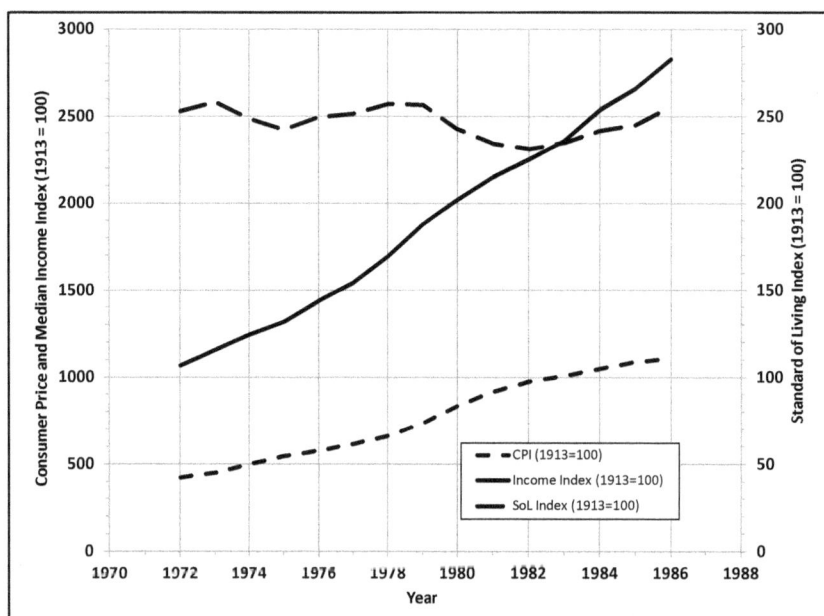

Figure 21.3-13: Median Income, Consumer Price, and Standard of Living Indices, 1972-1986

Figures 21.3-14 and 21.3-15 show the changes in the legal reserve ratio made during this period.

Legal Reserve Ratio Changes, 1972-1976												
		Demand Deposit Reserve Requirements (%)						Time Deposit Reserve Requirements (%)				
		By Aggregate Deposit Levels ($)						Zero to $5 M			More than $5 M		
Day	Year	Zero to $2 M	$2 to $4 M	$10 to $100 M	$100 to $400 M	More than $400 M	Savings Deposits	Maturing Less Than 180 Days	Maturing 0.5 to 4 Years	Maturing More than 4 Years	Maturing Less Than 180 Days	Maturing 0.5 to 4 Years	Maturing More than 4 Years
9 Nov	1972	8.00	10.00	12.00	16.50	17.50	3.00	3.00	3.00	3.00	5.00	5.00	5.00
16 Nov	1972	8.00	10.00	12.00	13.00	17.50	3.00	3.00	3.00	3.00	5.00	5.00	5.00
19 Jul	1973	8.00	10.50	12.50	13.50	18.00	3.00	3.00	3.00	3.00	5.00	5.00	5.00
12 Dec	1974	8.00	10.50	12.50	13.50	17.50	3.00	3.00	3.00	3.00	6.00	3.00	3.00
13 Feb	1975	7.50	10.00	12.00	13.00	16.50	3.00	3.00	3.00	3.00	6.00	3.00	3.00
30 Oct	1975	7.50	10.00	12.00	13.00	16.50	3.00	3.00	3.00	1.00	6.00	3.00	1.00
8 Jan	1976	7.50	10.00	12.00	13.00	16.50	3.00	3.00	2.50	1.00	6.00	2.50	1.00
30 Dec	1976	7.00	9.50	11.75	12.50	16.25	3.00	3.00	2.50	1.00	6.00	2.50	1.00

Source: Joshua N. Feinman, Reserve Requirements: History, Current Practice, and Potential Reform, Federal Reserve Bulletin, June 1993, p. 569-589

Figure 21.3-14: Legal Reserve Ratios, 1972-1976

Legal Reserve Ratio Changes, 1977-1986					
		Demand Deposits			
Day	Year	Lower Threshold ($ M)	Upper Threshold ($ M)	Between Thresholds (%)	Above Upper Threshold	Savings & Time Deposits
13 Nov	1980	None	None	12	12	3.0
14 Jan	1982	0.0	26.0	3	10	3.0
23 Dec	1982	2.1	26.0	3	10	3.0
13 Jan	1983	2.1	26.3	3	10	3.0
12 Jan	1984	2.2	28.9	3	10	3.0
3 Jan	1985	2.4	29.8	3	10	3.0
2 Jan	1986	2.6	31.7	3	10	3.0

Source: Joshua N. Feinman, Reserve Requirements: History, Current Practice, and Potential Reform, Federal Reserve Bulletin, June 1993, p. 569-589

Figure 21.3-15: Legal Reserve Ratios, 1977-1986

Figures 21.3-16 through 21.3-18 show some miscellaneous statistics of the banking system, including the reserve ratio and the ratios of demand deposits to reserves and demand deposits to currency.

Miscellaneous Statistics of the Federal Reserve and Commercial System, 1972-1976 (millions USD)										
		Federal Reserve	At Commercial Banks							
Day	Year	Member Bank Reserves [1]	Demand Deposits	Time Deposits	Total Deposits	Reserve Ratio, Demand Deposits	Reserve Ratio, Total Deposits	Currency Outside Banks	Ratio, Demand Deposits to Reserves	Ratio, Demand Deposits to Currency
29 Mar	1972	32,253	175,100	282,100	457,200	0.184	0.071	52,600	5.429	3.329
28 Jun	1972	32,299	179,977	292,021	471,998	0.179	0.068	55,144	5.572	3.264
27 Sep	1972	32,448	181,400	301,900	483,300	0.179	0.067	53,700	5.590	3.378
27 Dec	1972	28,946	205,100	311,800	516,900	0.141	0.056	57,900	7.086	3.542
28 Mar	1973	32,672	198,100	332,600	530,700	0.165	0.062	57,400	6.063	3.451
27 Jun	1973	30,968	204,100	344,500	548,600	0.152	0.056	59,400	6.591	3.436
26 Sep	1973	37,362	203,800	359,200	563,000	0.183	0.066	60,100	5.455	3.391
26 Dec	1973	31,953	215,500	361,800	577,300	0.148	0.055	62,600	6.744	3.442
27 Mar	1974	34,736	209,800	379,100	588,900	0.166	0.059	62,700	6.040	3.346
26 Jun	1974	36,763	213,100	397,900	611,000	0.173	0.060	64,800	5.797	3.289
25 Sep	1974	40,041	213,200	410,200	623,400	0.188	0.064	65,800	5.325	3.240
25 Dec	1974	37,030	222,800	417,700	640,500	0.166	0.058	68,900	6.017	3.234
26 Mar	1975	34,819	236,900	429,500	666,400	0.147	0.052	68,800	6.804	3.443
25 Jun	1975	34,706	264,027	433,389	697,416	0.131	0.050	71,200	7.608	3.708
24 Sep	1975	34,617	240,080	438,920	679,000	0.144	0.051	71,900	6.935	3.339
31 Dec	1975	35,611	278,280	446,830	725,110	0.128	0.049	75,000	7.814	3.710
31 Mar	1976	34,236	256,930	457,950	714,880	0.133	0.048	75,100	7.505	3.421
30 Jun	1976	34,789	266,400	462,900	729,300	0.131	0.048	77,800	7.658	3.424
29 Sep	1976	34,577	252,900	469,900	722,800	0.137	0.048	79,000	7.314	3.201
29 Dec	1976	35,834	275,900	484,800	760,700	0.130	0.047	82,200	7.699	3.356

1. Member bank reserves is the sum of reserve deposits at Federal Reserve Banks and applied vault cash per Bulletins (to 1974) and H.3 (1975 ff).
2. See Appendix B for references.

Figure 21.3-16: Miscellaneous Statistics of the Banking System, 1972-1976

| Miscellaneous Statistics of the Federal Reserve and Commercial System, 1977-1981 (millions USD) | | | | | | | | | |
| Day | Year | Federal Reserve Member Bank Reserves [1] | Demand Deposits | Time Deposits | Total Deposits | Reserve Ratio, Demand Deposits | Reserve Ratio, Total Deposits | Currency Outside Banks | Ratio, Demand Deposits to Reserves | Ratio, Demand Deposits to Currency |
			At Commercial Banks							
30 Mar	1977	34,758	263,100	504,400	767,500	0.132	0.045	82,200	7.569	3.201
29 Jun	1977	35,064	288,100	515,600	803,700	0.122	0.044	84,000	8.216	3.430
28 Sep	1977	35,614	272,500	526,100	798,600	0.131	0.045	86,100	7.651	3.165
28 Dec	1977	36,807	307,000	541,100	848,100	0.120	0.043	90,000	8.341	3.411
29 Mar	1978	36,450	281,200	567,100	848,300	0.130	0.043	89,900	7.715	3.128
28 Jun	1978	37,503	317,500	580,800	898,300	0.118	0.042	92,900	8.466	3.418
27 Sep	1978	38,441	297,100	588,300	885,400	0.129	0.043	94,900	7.729	3.131
27 Dec	1978	41,357	327,100	600,300	927,400	0.126	0.045	99,100	7.909	3.301
28 Mar	1979	39,941	355,700	638,300	994,000	0.112	0.040	98,600	8.906	3.608
27 Jun	1979	40,181	376,400	639,200	1,015,600	0.107	0.040	101,800	9.368	3.697
26 Sep	1979	41,545	383,200	660,400	1,043,600	0.108	0.040	104,500	9.224	3.667
26 Dec	1979	43,969	400,500	675,800	1,076,300	0.110	0.041	108,000	9.109	3.708
26 Mar	1980	42,972	373,600	699,900	1,073,500	0.115	0.040	107,900	8.694	3.462
25 Jun	1980	43,240	379,100	709,600	1,088,700	0.114	0.040	111,000	8.767	3.415
24 Sep	1980	41,643	391,200	731,000	1,122,200	0.106	0.037	113,700	9.394	3.441
31 Dec	1980	41,146	453,600	786,300	1,239,900	0.091	0.033	118,500	11.024	3.828
25 Mar	1981	39,590	367,400	823,200	1,190,600	0.108	0.033	116,800	9.280	3.146
24 Jun	1981	40,691	389,400	847,300	1,236,700	0.104	0.033	119,900	9.570	3.248
30 Sep	1981	41,551	417,300	881,900	1,299,200	0.100	0.032	121,000	10.043	3.449
30 Dec	1981	42,362	378,400	911,300	1,289,700	0.112	0.033	125,400	8.933	3.018

1. Member bank reserves is the sum of reserve deposits at Federal Reserve Banks and applied vault cash per H.3.
2. See Appendix B for references.

Figure 21.3-17: Miscellaneous Statistics of the Banking System, 1977-1981

| Miscellaneous Statistics of the Federal Reserve and Commercial System, 1982-1986 (millions USD) | | | | | | | | | |
| Day | Year | Federal Reserve Member Bank Reserves [1] | Demand Deposits | Time Deposits | Total Deposits | Reserve Ratio, Demand Deposits | Reserve Ratio, Total Deposits | Currency Outside Banks | Ratio, Demand Deposits to Reserves | Ratio, Demand Deposits to Currency |
			At Commercial Banks							
31 Mar	1982	39,288	350,800	944,200	1,295,000	0.112	0.030	123,800	8.929	2.834
30 Jun	1982	40,332	357,400	968,400	1,325,800	0.113	0.030	128,300	8.861	2.786
29 Sep	1982	40,557	335,100	1,006,300	1,341,400	0.121	0.030	130,200	8.262	2.574
29 Dec	1982	42,008	376,200	1,033,400	1,409,600	0.112	0.030	135,200	8.955	2.783
30 Mar	1983	38,288	345,700	1,073,800	1,419,500	0.111	0.027	135,400	9.029	2.553
29 Jun	1983	39,042	356,400	1,087,300	1,443,700	0.110	0.027	140,300	9.129	2.540
28 Sep	1983	38,375	340,000	1,108,800	1,448,800	0.113	0.026	142,600	8.860	2.384
28 Dec	1983	39,003	383,200	1,141,700	1,524,900	0.102	0.026	148,700	9.825	2.577
28 Mar	1984	36,007	440,900	1,053,600	1,494,500	0.082	0.024	148,900	12.245	2.961
27 Jun	1984	37,679	445,900	1,086,900	1,532,800	0.085	0.025	154,900	11.834	2.879
26 Sep	1984	38,222	442,300	1,107,600	1,549,900	0.086	0.025	156,500	11.572	2.826
26 Dec	1984	41,805	490,500	1,139,500	1,630,000	0.085	0.026	160,900	11.733	3.048
27 Mar	1985	40,168	457,600	1,167,600	1,625,200	0.088	0.025	159,800	11.392	2.864
26 Jun	1985	42,608	473,800	1,183,900	1,657,700	0.090	0.026	165,200	11.120	2.868
25 Sep	1985	44,814	474,900	1,208,600	1,683,500	0.094	0.027	167,600	10.597	2.834
25 Dec	1985	48,911	536,400	1,227,100	1,763,500	0.091	0.028	173,100	10.967	3.099
26 Mar	1986	47,107	502,100	1,252,000	1,754,100	0.094	0.027	172,300	10.659	2.914
25 Jun	1986	49,983	523,300	1,268,700	1,792,000	0.096	0.028	177,400	10.470	2.950
24 Sep	1986	53,664	537,400	1,293,400	1,830,800	0.100	0.029	179,600	10.014	2.992
31 Dec	1986	61,289	689,700	1,325,400	2,015,100	0.089	0.030	186,100	11.253	3.706

1. Member bank reserves is the sum of reserve deposits at Federal Reserve Banks and applied vault cash per H.3.
2. See Appendix B for references.

Figure 21.3-18: Miscellaneous Statistics of the Banking System, 1982-1986

Figures 21.3-19 and 21.3-20 show the approximate monthly commercial bank prime interest rates and the Federal Funds Rate. The Federal Funds Rate is the interest rate charged for overnight loans between commercial banks.

Approximate Monthly Average Bank Prime Rate (%) [1]											
Year	Jan	Feb	Mar	Apr	May	Jun	Jul	Aug	Sep	Oct	Nov	Dec
1972	5.18	4.75	4.75	4.97	5.00	5.04	5.25	5.27	5.50	5.73	5.75	5.79
1973	6.00	6.02	6.30	6.61	7.01	7.49	8.30	9.23	9.86	9.94	9.75	9.75
1974	9.73	9.21	8.85	10.02	11.25	11.54	11.97	12.00	12.00	11.68	10.83	10.50
1975	10.05	8.96	7.93	7.50	7.40	7.07	7.15	7.66	7.88	7.96	7.53	7.26
1976	7.00	6.75	6.75	6.75	6.75	7.20	7.25	7.01	7.00	6.77	6.50	6.35
1977	6.25	6.25	6.25	6.25	6.41	6.75	6.75	6.83	7.13	7.52	7.75	7.75
1978	7.93	8.00	8.00	8.00	8.27	8.63	9.00	9.01	9.41	9.94	10.94	11.55
1979	11.75	11.75	11.75	11.75	11.75	11.65	11.54	11.91	12.90	14.39	15.55	15.30
1980	15.25	15.63	18.31	19.77	16.57	12.63	11.48	11.12	12.23	13.79	16.06	20.35
1981	20.16	19.43	18.05	17.15	19.61	20.03	20.39	20.50	20.08	18.45	16.84	15.75
1982	15.75	16.56	16.50	16.50	16.50	16.50	16.26	14.39	13.50	12.52	11.85	11.50
1983	11.16	10.98	10.50	10.50	10.50	10.50	10.50	10.89	11.00	11.00	11.00	11.00
1984	11.00	11.00	11.21	11.93	12.39	12.60	13.00	13.00	12.97	12.58	11.77	11.06
1985	10.61	10.50	10.50	10.50	10.31	9.78	9.50	9.50	9.50	9.50	9.50	9.50
1986	9.50	9.50	9.10	8.83	8.50	8.50	8.16	7.90	7.50	7.50	7.50	7.50

1. Source: Board of Governors of the Federal Reserve System, Bank Prime Loan Rate [MPRIME], Federal Reserve Bank of St. Louis; series MPRIME (https://fred.stlouisfed.org/series/MPRIME). These are averages of daily figures, not seasonally adjusted. The data is listed as "observation dates" on the first of the month; it is assumed they apply for the entire month, since the Federal Reserve cites them as monthly averages.

Figure 21.3-19: Monthly Average Bank Prime Rates, 1972-1986

Approximate Monthly Average Federal Funds Rate (%) [1]											
Year	Jan	Feb	Mar	Apr	May	Jun	Jul	Aug	Sep	Oct	Nov	Dec
1972	3.51	3.30	3.83	4.17	4.27	4.46	4.55	4.81	4.87	5.05	5.06	5.33
1973	5.94	6.58	7.09	7.12	7.84	8.49	10.40	10.50	10.78	10.01	10.03	9.95
1974	9.65	8.97	9.35	10.51	11.31	11.93	12.92	12.01	11.34	10.06	9.45	8.53
1975	7.13	6.24	5.54	5.49	5.22	5.55	6.10	6.14	6.24	5.82	5.22	5.20
1976	4.87	4.77	4.84	4.82	5.29	5.48	5.31	5.29	5.25	5.02	4.95	4.65
1977	4.61	4.68	4.69	4.73	5.35	5.39	5.42	5.90	6.14	6.47	6.51	6.56
1978	6.70	6.78	6.79	6.89	7.36	7.60	7.81	8.04	8.45	8.96	9.76	10.03
1979	10.07	10.06	10.09	10.01	10.24	10.29	10.47	10.94	11.43	13.77	13.18	13.78
1980	13.82	14.13	17.19	17.61	10.98	9.47	9.03	9.61	10.87	12.81	15.85	18.90
1981	19.08	15.93	14.70	15.72	18.52	19.10	19.04	17.82	15.87	15.08	13.31	12.37
1982	13.22	14.78	14.68	14.94	14.45	14.15	12.59	10.12	10.31	9.71	9.20	8.95
1983	8.68	8.51	8.77	8.80	8.63	8.98	9.37	9.56	9.45	9.48	9.34	9.47
1984	9.56	9.59	9.91	10.29	10.32	11.06	11.23	11.64	11.30	9.99	9.43	8.38
1985	8.35	8.50	8.58	8.27	7.97	7.53	7.88	7.90	7.92	7.99	8.05	8.27
1986	8.14	7.86	7.48	6.99	6.85	6.92	6.56	6.17	5.89	5.85	6.04	6.91

1. Source: Board of Governors of the Federal Reserve System, Federal Funds Effective Rate, Federal Reserve Bank of St. Louis, series = FEDFUNDS; https://fred.stlouisfed.org/series/FEDFUNDS. They are cited as "observed dates" always on the first of the month; it is assumed they apply as averages to the entire month, since the Federal Reserve cites them as "averages of daily figures".

Figure 21.3-20: Monthly Average Federal Funds Rates, 1972-1986

21.4 Summary, 1972-1986

The early 1970's saw several "shortages". The gasoline shortage was real due to the embargo by OPEC, but many of the other shortages were due to price controls. One of the more prominent shortages was that of sugar (which is why the price of a Three Musketeers bar jumped to 50 cents during this period). My father was in the gourmet food importing business in the early 1970's, and I worked making deliveries for his company. One of the items that he imported was some sort of specialty sugar from somewhere in South America. We made regular deliveries to the major sugar distributors because the amounts called for were not worth their trouble. Anyway, during the height of the "sugar shortage", in the course of making deliveries of specialty sugars, it was easy to see that the sugar distributors' warehouses were bulging with standard white granulated and confectioners' sugar. Yet there was little being sent to the grocery stores. Why was that? I don't know for sure, but I suspect that the prices set per the price controls were below the cost of the sugar (once the cost of transportation was included). Maybe the thinking was: why give it away; maybe it's better to hold onto it until the price controls come off. I don't suppose we'll ever know, but this is the type of thing that happens when the government attempts to inject itself into the economy, especially when it comes to common commodities.

How would price controls on sugar affect your management of Granny's Sublime Tarts? The biggest problem may be that sugar becomes unavailable, especially, since it is likely to be allocated based on the highest priority need (such as bread and breakfast cereals). In that case, you may not be able to obtain sugar at all (since Granny's special tarts are not "essential"). Then you would have to re-work the recipe to use available substitutes, such as carob, sorbital, malitol, sucralose, saccharine, or corn syrup. Maybe those ingredients would cost just as much, or make the product taste different, or not maintain freshness as well, or interact with some other ingredient to give the customer a bitter after-taste. On the other hand, sugar may be available, but at a much higher cost, which may make the tarts unprofitable. It is generally better for an economy to tolerate the higher costs due to actual supply problems, than to have the government allocate supplies based (usually) on political considerations. After all, if there was an actual failure of the sugar crop, the public understands the problem and why sugar-based products will cost more.

The government also imposed "even-odd" gas rationing during this period; if your license plate ended in an odd number, you could buy gas on odd-numbered days and likewise for even license plate numbers on even days. Commercial and government vehicles were exempt. Anyone with an IQ above 30 could figure out how to beat that system, and it is pretty easy to change license plates. But it wasn't even necessary in my neighborhood: Frank M., who ran the local Exxon station at the corner of E. Lovejoy and N. Ogden, sold his regular customers all the gas they wanted regardless of even/odd plates and days. The cops (supposed to be monitoring and enforcing the rationing) stood by and watched because either their 10-year-olds were changing license plates on the family cars, or they were regulars at Frank's. Once again, the best solution is to let the economy sort things out; if the shortage is real, then the prices will increase until demand levels off and the prices stabilize. This initial gas shortage led to the production of smaller, more fuel-efficient cars in the mid- to late-1970's.

This period also saw the growth of the government's involvement in the housing industry in an effort to improve the housing conditions of the poor and lower-income families. The disastrous public-housing projects built by or sponsored by the government are well-known: most of them became dangerous (due partly to lack of maintenance and partly due to uncontrolled criminal activity among the residents). Most of those facilities were torn down in the 1980's and 1990's as a monument to abject failure. But the growth of the mortgage industry, spurred on by the government's interest, did partly contribute to the continuing failure of the savings and loan industry, which is detailed in the next chapter. It is easy but unfair to blame the government for the entire problem; there was also a certain amount of over-confidence and incompetence within both industries.

As shown on Figure 21.3-11, the CPI was above 5% annually for the period 1973-1982, and was caused partly by the increase in energy costs (in 1973 and 1974), and partly by the increase in the money supply. It rose to 10% and 12% in 1979 and 1980. Increases in federal spending led to an increase in the money supply, and it can be observed from Figure 21.2-12 that the CPI tracked fairly closely with the growth of the per-capita money supply. Figure 21.3-20 shows that it became necessary for the Federal Reserve to increase the Federal Funds Rate dramatically in 1973 and 1974, 1979 through 1982, and again in 1984. The objective was to reduce the rate of growth of the monetary inflation (by reducing the demand for money) that was the primary cause of the CPI increases, at least in the late 1970's.

References

[21.1-1] Richard G. Anderson, Kenneth A. Kavajecz, "A Historical Perspective on the Federal Reserve's Monetary Aggregates: Definition, Construction, and Targeting", Federal Reserve Bank of St. Louis Review, Mar/Apr 1994, p. 21

[21.2-1] Text of "An Act to provide for a modification in the par value of the dollar, and for other purposes", a.k.a. the Par Value Modification Act, 92nd Congress, Public Law 92-268, 31 Mar 1972

[21.2-2]   Federal Deposit Insurance Corporation, Division of Research and Statistics, *A Brief History of Deposit Insurance in the United States*, Sep 1998, p. 66

[21.2-3]   Text of Executive Order 11695, "Further providing for the stabilization of the economy", 11 Jan 1973

[21.2-4]   Text of "An Act to extend and amend the Economic Stabilization Act of 1970", 93rd Congress, Public Law 93-28, 30 Apr 1973

[21.2-5]   Text of Executive Order 11723, "Further providing for the stabilization of the economy", 13 Jun 1973

[21.2-6]   Text of Executive Order 11730, "Further providing for the stabilization of the economy", 18 Jul 1973

[21.2-7]   Text of " An Act to amend section 14(b) of the Federal Reserve Act, as amended, to extend for three months the authority of the Federal Reserve banks to purchase United States obligations directly from the Treasury", 93rd Congress, Public Law 93-93, 14 Aug 1973

[21.2-8]   Text of "An Act To extend certain laws relating to the payment of interest on time and savings deposits, to prohibit depository institutions from permitting negotiable orders of withdrawal to be made with respect to any deposit or account on which any interest or dividend is paid, to authorize Federal savings and loan associations and national banks to own stock in and invest in loans to certain State housing corporations, and for other purposes", 93rd Congress, Public Law 93-100, 16 Aug 1973

[21.2-9]   Text of "An Act to amend the Par Value Modification Act, and for other purposes", 93rd Congress, Public Law 93-110, 21 Sep 1973

[21.2-10]   National Bureau of Economic Research (NBER), Cambridge, MA (see website below)

[21.2-11]   Text of "An Act to authorize and require the President of the United States to allocate crude oil, residual fuel oil, and refined petroleum products to deal with existing or imminent shortages and dislocations in the national distribution system which jeopardize the public health, safety, or welfare; to provide for the delegation of authority; and for other purposes", 93rd Congress, Public Law 93-159, 27 Nov 1973

[21.2-12]   Text of "An Act to establish a Federal Financing Bank, to provide for coordinated and more efficient financing of Federal and federally assisted borrowings from the public, and for other purposes", a.k.a. the "Federal Financing Bank Act of 1973", 93rd Congress, Public Law 93-224, 29 Dec 1973

[21.2-13]   op. cit., Federal Deposit Insurance Corporation, p. 66

[21.2-14]   Text of "An Act to authorize the establishment of a Council on Wage and Price Stability", a.k.a. the Council on Wage and Price Stability Act, 93rd Congress, Public Law 93-387, 24 Aug 1974

[21.2-15]   Text of "An Act to increase deposit insurance from $20,000 to $40,000, to provide full insurance for public unit deposits of $100,000 per account, to establish a National Commission on Electronic Fund Transfers, and for other purposes", 93rd Congress, Public Law 93-495, 28 Oct 1974

[21.2-16]   Text of Executive Order 11821, Inflation Impact Statements, 27 Nov 1974

[21.2-17]   op. cit., Federal Deposit Insurance Corporation, p. 66

[21.2-18]   op. cit., National Bureau of Economic Research

[21.2-19]   Text of "An Act to increase the authorization for the Council on Wage and Price Stability, and to extend the duration of the Council", 94th Congress, Public Law 94-78, 9 Aug 1975

[21.2-20]   Text of "An Act to extend the Emergency Petroleum Allocation Act of 1973", a.k.a. the Emergency Petroleum Allocation Act of 1975, 94th Congress, Public Law 94-99, 29 Sep 1975.

[21.2-21]   Text of "Joint Resolution to extend the authority for the direct purchase of United States obligations by the Federal Reserve banks", 94th Congress, Public Law 94-125, 12 Nov 1975

[21.2-22]   Text of "An Act to extend the Emergency Petroleum Allocation Act of 1973", 94th Congress, Public Law 94-133, 14 Nov 1975

[21.2-23]   op. cit., Federal Deposit Insurance Corporation, p. 66

[21.2-24]   op. cit., Federal Deposit Insurance Corporation, p. 66

[21.2-25]   Text of "An Act to extend the authority for the flexible regulation of interest rates on deposits and accounts in depository institutions", 95th Congress, Public Law 95-22, 19 Apr 1977

[21.2-26]   Text of "An Act to amend the Council on Wage and Price Stability to extend its termination date, and for other purposes", 95th Congress, Public Law 95-121, 6 Oct 1977

[21.2-27]   Text of "An Act to amend certain Federal laws pertaining to community development, housing, and related programs", a.k.a. the Community Reinvestment Act, 95th Congress, Public Law 95-128, 12 Oct 1977

[21.2-28]   Text of "An Act to authorize the Secretary of the Treasury to invest public moneys, and for other purposes", 95th Congress, Public Law 95-147, 28 Oct 1977

[21.2-29]   Text of "An Act to extend the authority of the Federal Reserve banks to buy and sell certain obligations", 95th Congress, Public Law 95-154, 7 Nov 1977

[21.2-30] Text of "An Act to extend the authority for the flexible regulation of interest rates on deposits and accounts in depository institutions, to promote the accountability of the Federal Reserve System, and for other purposes", a.k.a. the Federal Reserve Reform Act of 1977, 95th Congress, Public Law 95-188, 16 Nov 1977

[21.2-31] Text of "An Act with respect to the powers of the President in time of war or national emergency", 95th Congress, Public Law 95-223, 28 Dec 1977

[21.2-32] op. cit., Federal Deposit Insurance Corporation, p. 66

[21.2-33] Text of "An Act to amend the Accounting and Auditing Act of 1950 to provide for the audit, by the Comptroller General of the United States, of the Federal Reserve System, the Federal Deposit Insurance Corporation, and the Office of the Comptroller of the Currency, and for other purposes", a.k.a. the Federal Banking Agency Audit Act, 95th Congress, Public Law 95-320, 21 Jul 1978

[21.2-34] Text of "An Act to provide for consumers a further means of minimizing the impact of inflation and economic depression by narrowing the price spread between costs to the producer and the consumer of needed goods, services, facilities, and commodities through the development and funding of specialized credit sources or, and technical assistance to, self-help, not-for-profit cooperatives, and for other purposes", 95th Congress, Public Law 95-351, 20 Aug 1978

[21.2-35] Text of "An Act to provide for Federal regulation of participation by foreign banks in domestic financial markets", a.k.a. the International Banking Act of 1978, 95th Congress, Public Law 95-369, 17 Sep 1978

[21.2-36] Text of "Joint Resolution providing financial assistance for the city of New York", 95th Congress, Public Law 95-45, 5 Oct 1978

[21.2-37] Text of "Joint Resolution to extend the authority of the Federal reserve banks to buy and sell certain obligations", 95th Congress, Public Law 95-534, 27 Oct 1978

[21.2-38] Text of "An Act to extend the authority for the flexible regulation of interest rates on deposits and accounts at depository institutions", a.k.a. the Financial Institutions Regulatory and Interest Rate Control Act of 1978, 95th Congress, Public Law 95-630, 10 Nov 1978

[21.2-39] op. cit., Federal Deposit Insurance Corporation, p. 66

[21.2-40] Text of "An Act to amend the Council on Wage and Price Stability Act to extend the authority granted by such Act to September 30, 1980, and for other purposes", 96th Congress, Public Law 96-10, 10 May 1979

[21.2-41] Text of "An Act to amend the Federal Reserve Act to authorize Federal Reserve banks to lend certain obligations to the Secretary of the Treasury to meet short term cash requirements of the Treasury and for other purposes", 96th Congress, Public Law 96-18, 8 Jun 1979

[21.2-42] op. cit., Federal Deposit Insurance Corporation, p. 66

[21.2-43] Alane Moysich, *The Savings and Loan Crisis and Its Relationship to Banking*, Chapter 4 in: Federal Deposit Insurance Corporation (FDIC, *History of the Eighties: Lessons for the Future, Vol. 1, An Examination of the Banking Crises of the 1980s and Early 1990s*, Washington, DC, 1997.

[21.2-44] Text of "An Act to authorize loan guarantees to the Chrysler Corporation", 96th Congress, Public Law 96-185, 7 Jan 1980

[21.2-45] op. cit., National Bureau of Economic Research

[21.2-46] Text of "An Act to facilitate the implementation of monetary policy, to provide for the gradual elimination of all limitations on the rates of interest which are payable on deposits and accounts, and to authorize interest-bearing transaction accounts, and for other purposes", a.k.a. the Depository Institutions Deregulation and Monetary Control Act of 1980, 96th Congress, Public Law 96-221, 31 Mar 1980

[21.2-47] op. cit., Federal Deposit Insurance Corporation, p. 55

[21.2-48] op. cit., National Bureau of Economic Research

[21.2-49] Text of "An Act to increase the authorization for the Council on Wage and Price Stability, to extend the duration of such Council, and for other purposes", 96th Congress, Public Law 96-508, 8 Dec 1980

[21.2-50] Text of "Joint Resolution making an appropriation for the International Monetary Fund for the fiscal year ending September 30, 1981", 96th Congress, Public Law 96-544, 17 Dec 1980

[21.2-51] op. cit., Federal Deposit Insurance Corporation, p. 66

[21.2-52] op. cit., Moysich, p. 169

[21.2-53] op. cit., National Bureau of Economic Research

[21.2-54] op. cit., Federal Deposit Insurance Corporation, p. 66

[21.2-55] op. cit., Moysich, p. 169

[21.2-56]   Text of "An Act to encourage exports by facilitating the formation and operation of trading companies, export trade associations, and the expansion of export trade services generally", 97th Congress, Public Law 97-290, 8 Oct 1982

[21.2-57]   Text of "An Act to revitalize the housing industry by strengthening the financial stability of home mortgage lending institutions and ensuring the availability of home mortgage loans", a.k.a. the Garn-St. Germain Depository Institutions Act of 1982, 97th Congress, Public Law 97-320, 15 Oct 1982

[21.2-58]   op. cit., National Bureau of Economic Research

[21.2-59]   op. cit., Federal Deposit Insurance Corporation, p. 66

[21.2-60]   op. cit., Moysich, p. 169

[21.2-61]   op. cit., Federal Deposit Insurance Corporation, p. 66

[21.2-62]   op. cit., Moysich, p. 169

[21.2-63]   op. cit., Federal Deposit Insurance Corporation, p. 55

[21.2-64]   An essay by the staff of the Federal Reserve available at:
            https://www.federalreservehistory.org/essays/failure-of-continental-illinois

[21.2-65]   Text of "An Act to amend the Securities Exchange Act of 1934 with respect to the treatment of mortgage backed securities, to increase the authority of the Federal National Mortgage Association and the Federal Home Loan Mortgage Association, and for other purposes", a.k.a. the Secondary Mortgage Market Act of 1984, 98th Congress, Public Law 98-440, 3 Oct 1984

[21.2-66]   https://wiki2.org/en/Secondary_Mortgage_Market_Enhancement_Act

[21.2-67]   op. cit., Federal Deposit Insurance Corporation, p. 66

[21.2-68]   op. cit., Moysich, p. 169

[21.2-69]   Text of "An Act to authorize the minting of gold bullion coins", 99th Congress, Public Law 99-185, 17 Dec 1985

[21.2-70]   op. cit., Federal Deposit Insurance Corporation, p. 66

[21.2-71]   op. cit., Moysich, p. 169

[21.2-72]   Text of "An Act to amend the Export-Import Bank Act of 1945", a.k.a. the Export-Import Bank Act Amendments of 1986", 99th Congress, Public Law 99-472, 15 Oct 1986

[21.2-73]   Text of "An Act to strengthen Federal efforts to encourage foreign cooperation in eradicating illicit drug crops and in halting international drug traffic, to improve enforcement of Federal drug laws and enhance interdiction of illicit drug shipments, to provide strong federal leadership in establishing effective drug use prevention and education programs, to expand Federal support for drug abuse treatment and rehabilitation efforts, and for other purposes", 99th Congress, Public Law 99-570, 27 Oct 1986

[21.2-74]   op. cit., Federal Deposit Insurance Corporation, p. 66

[21.2-75]   op. cit., Moysich, p. 169

NBER website: https://www.nber.org/research/data/us-business-cycle-expansions-and-contractions

22

Federal Reserve, Fiat System, Part 2, 1987-2003

22.1 Preview, 1987-2003

This period is characterized by two major financial problems: the collapse of the savings and loan industry, and the advent of the World Trade Organization.

The savings and loan (S&L) industry had started to have problems in 1980 or so, but it was not until the latter part of the 1980's that the collapse accelerated. Between 1986 and 1995, 1,043 out of 3,234 S&L's failed; they had to be liquidated and depositors compensated by the federal deposit insurance agencies (FSLIC and FDIC). This collapse was the largest financial fiasco since the Great Depression, and would be exceeded in magnitude only by the housing collapse of 2007 (which will be considered in chapter 23). A great many economists have developed a list of the causes of the S&L problem, and the FDIC has provided a summary paper on the subject [22.1-1]. First, the S&L's were set up in the 1930's as a means to finance homes at reasonably low interest rates. At the same time, the S&L's took deposits and paid fairly low interest rates, as regulated by the Federal Reserve Regulation Q. That was a workable system until the early 1980's when the Federal Reserve decided to stop the high depreciation rate on the dollar, and to do so, increased interest rates. Keep in mind that the depreciation of the dollar was the result of the expansion of the money supply spurred on by the domestic spending of the Great Society programs of the 1960's, most of which was financed by debt. The undue expansion of the money supply continued into the 1970's until the rate of depreciation became too large for the government to tolerate because the public was finally catching on. Now the S&L's had a problem: their income was based on long-term low-interest mortgages, but now had to pay higher rates to obtain financing. When the interest rates increased, savers decided to look elsewhere, especially to the new negotiable order of withdrawal (NOW) accounts to obtain higher return on their money. That left the S&L's with a capital problem due to a decline in deposits. The federal government did permit higher interest rates on savings accounts, but was too late. It did help the S&L's remain solvent in the short term, but did not solve the cash flow problem, since they were still paying higher interest than they were receiving from the mortgages.

The second cause was that the federal government went the wrong way in deregulating the S&L's. Instead of permitting competitive interest rates, Congress permitted S&L's to engage in a wider variety of investments, including especially commercial construction. It also reduced capital requirements. The main legislative forces were the Monetary Control Act of 1980 (cf. 31 Mar 1980) and the Garn-St. Germain Act (cf. 15 Oct 1982). The idea was that the S&L's could earn more and improve their position by taking larger risks and reaping larger rewards. Many S&L's did so, increasing risk, and assuming the economy would be stable. But the higher interest rates in the early 1980's caused many of their higher-risk investments to fail, resulting in losses to the S&L's for which they did not have sufficient capital to cover.

The third reason was that the insurance premiums that the S&L's paid to the FSLIC were the same for all institutions; there was no adjustment of premiums based on a risk assessment of their portfolios. That meant that the FSLIC was always under-capitalized. Rather than accept that fact and deal with it in the early 1980's, Congress was tempted was to avoid the problem and allow the S&L's to continue in operation in the hope that they would improve their positions. Unfortunately, it only made the bailout problem worse, since the losses in the industry continued to accelerate. By 1989 Congress had no choice but to pursue a bailout/liquidation scheme, when in fact the problem could have been corrected at a lower cost five years earlier.

The fourth cause was a combination of overbuilding, which led to a decline in real estate prices and losses to S&L's holding those mortgages. Another, more local cause was a collapse of the oil industry that affected parts of Texas, Oklahoma, and Louisiana that also negatively affected real estate prices. At the same time, the recession caused a decline in the number of home buyers, which reduced the opportunities for S&L's to generate new business.

The fifth cause was competition from the federally-sponsored FREDDIE MAC and FANNIE MAE mortgage programs, which undercut the S&L's in the competition for mortgages, since the rates offered by those two were partly subsidized by the taxpayers. So the taxpayers paid twice: once to assist the customers of FREDDIE MAC and FANNIE MAE, and once to pay off the depositors of the S&L's that could not compete due to the subsidies. The taxpayers will pay a third time in 2008 when FREDDIE MAC and FANNEI MAE themselves had to be bailed out, as will be shown in chapter 23.

The sixth cause was the traditionally weak supervision and examination of the S&L's that had been performed by different agencies, due mainly to the fact that historically the S&L's were engaged in routine residential mortgages and taking of deposits. Because the S&L's were limited in the types of investments they could make until the 1980's, there were only occasional failures and little cause for broad supervision. The supervision and examination did not increase when the S&L's began to engage in higher-risk investments.

The seventh reason was some degree of accounting fraud when evaluating the conditions of S&L's; community "good will" was sometimes listed as a capital asset.

The World Trade Organization was established in 1995 as an independent entity to enforce trade rules as negotiated by its members, and attempts to resolve disputes between them. It is the successor to the General Agreement on Tariffs and Trade (GATT). The stated goal of the WTO is to encourage a unified free trade regime (open markets), suppress the trend of some nations to provide subsidies to their industries (regarded as "unfair" practices), encourage movements of capital, assist with workers' rights, and provide a transparent enforcement method. The utility of the WTO may be debated on many grounds, some for it and some against. The U. S. is certainly capable of competing against any set of reciprocal rules. But one fiasco did occur during this portion of our history: the admission of Communist China into the WTO on an equal basis with honest nations. It was quite a collection of naïve gullible politicians in the U. S. who actually thought that Communists would see the light and participate in trade under a mutually honest competitive regime. But it hasn't worked that way: China continues to steal U. S. technology (or even worse, intimidates U. S. companies to hand over their technology). At the same time, many U. S. companies (actually U. S.-based multinational corporations) have moved their operations to China in order to take advantage of the slave labor; we have in fact exported our industrial base at the expense of the American worker. We are now importing a great deal of low-quality products made of "Chinesium", assembled by five-year olds in the same slave labor sweatshops where their parents and grandparents work. Meanwhile, unemployment remains persistently high in our (former) industrial cities (like Flint and Cleveland).

22.2 History, 1987-2003

10 Aug 1987: Congress passed the Competitive Equality Banking Act of 1987 [22.2-1]. Title I modified the Bank Holding Company Act of 1956, mostly eliminating a loophole that permitted commercial companies from offering banking services; it defined all federally insured depositories as banks, but allowed the 'nonbank banks' in operation to continue. Title 2 imposed a moratorium on the investment activities of foreign banks. The most important provisions are in Titles 3, 4, and 9: a) (S. 302) established a Financing Corporation to assist in re-capitalizing the FSLIC; b) (S. 302) Federal Home Loan Banks are now required to invest in capital stock of the Financing Corporation, with allocations

by geographic area; **c)** (S. 302) the total investments not to exceed $3,000 M ($3 B); **d)** (S. 302) proceeds to be invested in capital of the FSLIC (i.e., invest in any security offered by the FSLIC); **e)** (S. 302) the obligations of the Financing Corporation are not backed by the faith and credit of the United States; **f)** (S. 302) Financing Corporation obligations (bonds, etc.) are tax-exempt; **g)** (S. 402) improved and standardized the accounting principles to be applied to thrift institutions; **h)** (S. 406) permitted the Financing Board to determine capitalization requirements of S&L's on a case-by-case basis; and **i)** (S. 901) re-affirms that "deposits up to the statutorily prescribed amount in federally insured depository institutions are backed with the full faith and credit of the United States". This was a method to restore the capitalization of the FSLIC, now faced with mounting losses due to failures of S&L's. This approach only worked in the short term (cf. 9 Aug 1989).

31 Dec 1987: A total of 203 banks failed in 1987, with net losses to the FDIC FDIF totaling $2,022.996 M ($2.022 B) [22.2-2]; as did 59 S&L's, with net losses to the FSLIC totaling $5,666.729 M ($5.666 B) [22.2-3].

28 Sep 1988: Congress passed the United States-Canada Free-Trade Agreement Implementation Act of 1988 [22.2-4] to improve trade between the U. S. and Canada per the agreement reached 2 Jan 1988.

9 Dec 1988: The Silverado Savings and Loan failed; Neil Bush, son of then Vice-President George H. W. Bush, was on the Board of Directors at the time; the net losses to the FSLIC totaled about $1,300 M ($1.3 B).

31 Dec 1988: A total of 280 banks failed in 1988, with net losses to the FDIC FDIF totaling $6,949.197 M ($6.949 B) [22.2-5]; as did 190 S&L's, with net losses to the FSLIC totaling $46,688.466 M ($46.688 B) [22.2-6].

14 Apr 1989: The Lincoln Savings and Loan failed, with assets of $5,400 M ($5.4 B), then led by Charles Keating; this failure caused losses of about $3,400 M ($3.4 B) to the FSLIC.

9 Aug 1989: Congress passed the Financial Institutions Reform, Recovery, and Enforcement Act (FIRREA) of 1989 [22.2-7] in order to restore confidence in the savings and loan system after their collapse. Among its provisions: **a)** (Title IV, S. 401) abolished the Federal Savings and Loan Insurance Corporation (FSLIC) and Federal Home Loan Bank Board (FHLBB); **b)** (Title V, S. 501) established a Resolution Trust Corporation (RTC) to oversee the liquidation or resolution of accounts of the failed Savings and Loan institutions insured by the FSLIC; **c)** (Title VII, S. 703) replaced the Federal Home Loan Bank Board with a Federal Housing Finance Board and an Office of Thrift Supervision (OTS) to charter, supervise and examine S&L's and savings banks; **d)** (Title II, S. 203) changed the membership of the FDIC board of directors; **e)** (Title II, S. 208, Title IV, S.401) established the Savings Association Insurance Fund (SAIF), administered by the FDIC to take over the insurance function formerly performed by the FSLIC for S&L's, credit unions, and mutual savings banks; **f)** (Title II, S. 202 ff) FDIC to have control of deposit insurance of all depositary institutions (BIF, SAIF, FRF); **g)** (Title V, S. 501) established a Resolution Funding Corporation (RFC) to provide funding for the activities of the RTC ($18,900 M ($18.9 B) in 1989); **h)** (Title II, S. 215) authorized the Treasury Secretary to provide additional funding to RFC if necessary; **i)** (Title II, S. 211) increased the amount of FDIC deposit insurance to $100,000; **j)** (Title II, S. 208) renamed the Federal Deposit Insurance Fund (FDIF) to Bank Insurance Fund (BIF) to administer deposit insurance for commercial banks and savings institutions supervised by FDIC, Office of the Comptroller of the Currency (OCC), or Federal Reserve; **k)** (Title V, S. 511) authorized the RTC to issue bonds up to $30,000 M ($30 B) in funding from the sale of bonds; **l)** (Title II, S. 215) established the FSLIC Resolution Fund (FRF), administered by FDIC, to manage the assets and liabilities of S&L's not in conservatorship to RTC and otherwise wind up the affairs of the former FSLIC; and **m)** (Title V, S. 501) Federal National Mortgage Association (FANNIE MAE) & Federal Home Loan Mortgage Association (FREDDIE MAC) given additional responsibility to support mortgages for low and moderate income families.

The RTC handled the liquidation [22.2-8] of the S&L's assets using "equity partnerships", accomplished under three programs: a) Multiple Investor Fund (MIF); b) N-Series Mortgage Trusts; and c) S-Series Mortgage Trusts. In all three cases, the RTC bundled commercial and residential mortgages (mostly in default or close to being in default) into portfolios that were sold to private investors, with the RTC providing up to 75% seller financing, and priced per an estimate of the current value. The RTC retained an equity share in the subsequent liquidation of the assets by the portfolio buyers. The main difference among these methods were: a) the mortgages contained in the MIF portfolios were not listed; b) the specific mortgages were listed in the N-Series and S-Series portfolios; and c) the S-Series portfolio mortgages were generally located in the same geographic area. The RTC also operated a Land Fund under much the same terms, except the mortgages were for raw land or were mortgages secured by land, and were sold with the intention of development. The RTC ultimately liquidated 747 S&Ls with assets of $394,000 M ($394 B) between 1989 and 1995. The RTC issued a total of $31,200 M ($31.2 B) in bonds to finance the equity partnerships [22.2-9], and the interest paid on them totaled $10,400 M ($10.4 B) from 2016 to 2019 alone.

20 Dec 1989: The U. S. invaded Panama to overthrow its leader Manual Noriega (accused of drug-trafficking charges).

31 Dec 1989: A total of 207 FDIC-BIF insured banks failed in 1989 with net losses to the FDIC BIF totaling $8,491.286 M ($8.491 B) [22.2-10]; and RTC liquidation of 318 failed S&L's led to a net loss to the RTC of $49,308.118 M ($49.308 B) [22.2-11].

3 Jan 1990: Capture of Manuel Noriega, end of the Panama invasion.

15 Jul 1990: Approximate beginning of a recession [22.2-12].

2 Aug 1990: Iraq invaded Kuwait, and the U. S. decided to intervene; beginning of the First Gulf War.

31 Dec 1990: A total of 169 FDIC-BIF insured banks and 213 FDIC-SAIF insured S&L's failed in 1990, with combined net losses to the FDIC BIF and SAIF totaling $5,109.489 M ($5.109 B) [22.2-13]. RTC liquidation of the 213 S&L's assets led to net losses to the RTC of $19,258.655 M ($19.258 B) [22.2-14].

14 Jan 1991: Congress authorized use of force against Iraq [22.2-15] to enforce a United Nations Resolution.

17 Jan - 23 Feb 1991: U. S air campaign vs. Iraq.

18, 19 Jan 1991: Battle of Ad-Dawrah (Iraq).

29 Jan - 1 Feb 1991: Battle of Khafji (Iraq).

16 Feb 1991: Battle of Wadi Al-Batin (Iraq).

24-28 Feb 1991: Liberation of Kuwait.

26 Feb 1991: Battles of 73 Easting and Al Busayyah (Iraq).

27 Feb 1991: Battles at Jalibah Airfield and Medina Ridge (Iraq).

2 Mar 1991: Battle of Rumaila (Iraq).

15 Mar 1991: Approximate end of a recession (cf. 15 Jul 1990) [22.2-16].

12 Dec 1991: Congress passed the Resolution Trust Corporation Refinancing, Restructuring, and Improvement Act of 1991 [22.2-17]. Among its provisions: a) (Title 1, S. 101) authorized the Treasury to provide an additional $25,000 M ($25 B) in funding to the RTC; b) (Title I, S. 103) extended the RTC's liquidation activities until 1998; c) (Title 1, S. 106) required the RTC to provide reports on the disposition of assets, how disposed, and condition of loans; d) (Title II, S. 201) required the RTC to use advice from employees of the FDIC; e) (Title III, S. 302, 305) the Oversight Board of the Federal Farm Loan system was renamed the "Thrift Depositor Protection Oversight Board" (TDPOB), and was tasked with reviewing the plans and strategies of the RTC with respect to policies and finances of the RTC; f) (Title III, S. 312) required the TDPOB to establish a National Housing Advisory Board to develop strategies to address affordable housing; g) (Title V, S. 501) permitted the RTC to

provide additional mortgage credit to low and moderate income and to non-profit organizations supporting same; and **h)** (Title VI, S. 601) expanded eligibility for residential credit to buildings with more than four units.

19 Dec 1991: Congress passed the Federal Deposit Insurance Corporation Improvement Act of 1991 [22.2-18]: **a)** (Title I, S. 101) increased funding for the FDIC from $5,000 M ($5 B) to $30,000 M ($30 B); **b)** (Title I, S. 111 to 127) increased reporting and audit duties of the FDIC; **c)** (Title I, S. 102) permitted the FDIC to borrow directly from the Treasury to rescue troubled banks; **d)** (Title I, S. 131) required the FDIC to put banks with a capital-to-asset ratio below 2% into immediate receivership; **e)** (Title I, S. 141) required the FDIC to pursue compensation to depositors of insolvent banks by the most cost-effective manner; **f)** (Title III, S. 305) required the FDIC to establish new capital requirements for insured banks; **g)** (Title II, S. 202, 207) required foreign banks to obtain approval from the Federal Reserve to open banks or agencies or acquire shares in U. S. banks; **h)** (Title II, S. 263) required depository institutions to disclose interest rates and fees on deposit accounts ("Truth in Savings"); and **i)** (Title III, S. 302) required the FDIC to develop a risk-based assessment system for insured banks.

Title IV, S. 456 indicates the findings and sense of Congress regarding the current credit condition:

> "FINDINGS: The Congress finds that: (1) during the past year and a half a credit crunch of crisis proportions has taken hold of the economy and grown increasingly severe, particularly for real estate; (2) to date the credit crisis has shown no sign of improvement with its effects being felt broadly throughout the Nation as business failures soar, financial institutions weaken, real estate values decline, and State and local property tax bases further erode; (3) approximately $200,000,000,000 of the nearly $4,000,000,000,000 in commercial real estate loans now held by commercial banks are coming due within the next 2 years; (4) banks for a variety of reasons, are reluctant to renew these maturing real estate loans; (5) both pension funds in the United States, with assets of nearly $2,000,000,000,000, and a stronger and more active secondary market for commercial real estate debt and equity could play a more significant role in providing liquidity and credit to the real estate and banking sectors of the economy; (6) many regulatory practices encourage banks to reduce their real estate lending without regard to long-term historical risk; and (7) the stability of real estate has suffered during the past decade first from tax rules that in 1981 stimulated excessive investment in real estate, and then in 1986 when rules were adopted that discourage capital investment in real estate, artificially eroding real estate values.
>
> SENSE OF THE CONGRESS: (1) immediate and carefully-coordinated action should be taken by the Congress and the President to arrest the credit crisis referred to in subsection (a) and provide a healthy and efficient marketplace that works for owners, lenders, and investors; and (2) that efforts should be undertaken to explore measures that (A) modernize and simplify the rules that apply to pension investment in real estate to remove unnecessary barriers to pension funds seeking to invest in real estate; (B) strengthen the secondary market for commercial real estate debt and equity by removing arbitrary obstacles to private forms of credit enhancement; (C) restore balance to the regulatory environment by considering the impact of risk-based capital standards on commercial, multifamily and single-family real estate; ending mark-to-market, liquidation-based, appraisals; encouraging loan renewals; and, fully communicating the supervisory policy to bank examiners in the field; and (D) rationalize the tax system for real estate owners and operators by modifying the passive loss rules and encouraging loan restructures."

25 Dec 1991: The Union of Soviet Socialist Republics (U.S.S.R.) collapsed, the culmination of a movement in which many of the slave-state "republics" had declared their independence (starting with Azerbaijan on 23 Sep 1989). But its successor, the Russian Federation, is controlled by the old guard of the KGB.

31 Dec 1991: A total of 127 FDIC BIF insured banks and 144 FDIC SAIF insured S&L's failed in 1991, with combined net losses to the FDIC BIF and SAIF totaling $9,025.595 M ($9.025 B) [22.2-19]. RTC liquidation of the 144 S&L's assets incurred net losses to the RTC of $9,126.190 M ($9.126 B) [22.2-20].

28 Oct 1992: Congress passed the Housing and Community Development Act of 1992 [22.2-21]: **a)** (Title I, S. 101) changed many provisions and funding procedures per the United States Housing Act of

1937 (cf. 1 Sep 1937) relating to rent ceilings and rehabilitation of sub-standard housing in low-income neighborhoods; **b)** (Title VIII, S. 1332) required the Secretary of Housing and Urban Development to devise plans for financing residential mortgages for low and moderate income families; **c)** (Title VIII, S. 1333) authorized an initial $2,000 M ($2 B) to the FNMA and $1,500 M ($1.5 B) to FHLMC for purchases of mortgages under the affordable housing objectives; and **d)** (Title XV) established penalties for banks found to engage in money-laundering (a.k.a. the Annunzio-Wylie Anti-Money Laundering Act).

The direction given to HUD, FNMA, and FHLMA represent a general federal government policy of direct involvement in housing for low and moderate income families, as well as various community development initiatives. It was the beginning of policies that ultimately were partly responsible for the housing bubble in 2006 and the financial collapse in 2008 [22.2-22].

The anti-money-laundering provision required banks and deposit institutions to keep records of certain cash transactions and established a requirement for "suspicious activity reports" (SAR), which banks are required to file if any of their customers engage in "suspicious activities", specifically: a) cash transactions exceeding a certain dollar amount; b) transactions that are unusual for the customer; c) customers who have control over foreign accounts totaling a certain dollar amount; or d) businesses transactions greater than a certain dollar amount in currency. The implementing regulations used $10,000 as the threshold "dollar amount" for SAR reports. Institutions are prohibited from informing a customer that a SAR has been filed. It also prohibits any money-transmitting business to be operated without a State or federal license.

31 Dec 1992: A total of 122 FDIC BIF insured banks and 59 FDIC SAIF insured S&L's failed in 1992, with combined net losses to the FDIC BIF and SAIF totaling $3,674.399 M ($3.674 B) [22.2-23]. RTC liquidation of the 59 S&L's assets incurred net losses to the RTC of $3,780.121 M ($3.780 B) [22.2-24].

31 Dec 1992: The RTC had disposed of assets worth $330,000 M ($330 B) book value, about 75% of the assets of the failed S&L's that the RTC took over [22.2-25]. Of the remaining assets totaling $103,000 M ($103 B) book value, about 75% are regarded by the RTC as "hard to sell". "Book value" here refers to the amount on the failed S&L balance sheet, which may be very different from the market or appraised value.

5 Mar 1993: By this time, the RTC had closed 654 S&L's and covered $196,000 M ($196 B) in deposit liabilities [22.2-26].

17 Dec 1993: Congress passed the Resolution Trust Completion Act [22.2-27]: **a)** (S. 2 and 8) provided $18,000 M ($18 B) in final funding for the Resolution Trust Corporation (cf. 9 Aug 1989); **b)** (S. 6, 7) directed the RTC to transfer all its assets to the FSLIC Resolution Fund administered by the FDIC by 1 Jan 1996; and **c)** (S. 12 to 17) expanded provisions for affordable housing.

31 Dec 1993: A total of 41 FDIC BIF insured banks and 10 FDIC SAIF insured S&L's failed in 1993, with combined net losses to the FDIC BIF and SAIF totaling $632.646 M [22.2-28]. RTC liquidation of the 10 S&L's assets incurred net losses to the RTC of $65.212 M [22.2-29].

1 Jan 1994: The North American Free Trade Agreement (NAFTA) went into effect. Mexico and Canada are important trading partners with the U. S. and this agreement did streamline some transactions. However, NAFTA did promote the loss of the industrial base in the Northern States, especially Ohio, Michigan, and Pennsylvania, since many of those operations relocated to Mexico.

29 Sep 1994: Congress passed the Riegle-Neal Interstate Banking and Branching Efficiency Act [22.2-30]: **a)** (S. 101) permitted, with approval of the Federal Reserve Board and/or FDIC: 1) suitably capitalized bank holding companies to acquire banks in any of the States, but approval to be withheld if either: a) the bank holding company would holding or control more than 30% of the deposits within any State (unless a State changed the limit), or b) the bank holding company would control more than 10% of the total deposits in the U. S.; **b)** (S. 101) permitted banks in different States to merge under the same bank holding company; **c)** (S. 102) permitted States to opt-out of the interstate bank-

ing provisions (none did); **d)** (S. 103) authorized the Comptroller of the Currency to permit a national bank to expand into a State where it has no branches, if State law allows it (called 'opt-in'); and **d)** (S. 104) permitted foreign banks to open branches in other States other than where currently operating, subject to approval by the Federal Reserve Board and the Comptroller of the Currency. This legislation mostly repealed the McFadden Act of 1927 (cf. 25 Feb 1927). By the time this was enacted in 1994, about 46 States already had allowed some form of interstate banking [22.2-31]. This legislation provided a uniform set of rules.

8 Dec 1994: Congress confirmed the Uruguay Round Agreements Act [22.2-32], agreed to on 15 Apr 1994, which established the World Trade Organization, and established rules on tariffs, procedures for resolving trade disputes, etc.

31 Dec 1994: A total of 13 FDIC BIF insured banks and 2 FDIC SAIF insured S&L's failed in 1994, with combined net losses to the FDIC BIF and SAIF totaling $179.051 M [22.2-33]. RTC liquidation of the 2 S&L's assets incurred net losses to the RTC of $14.599 M [22.2-34].

1 Jan 1995: The World Trade Organization (WTO) began operations; it was a multilateral agreement on goods, services, and intellectual property (unlike GATT, which dealt only with goods).

30 Jun 1995: The authority of the Resolution Trust Corporation, instituted to resolve the problem of failed and failing Savings and Loans, expired. The Government Accounting Office estimated that the total cost of the liquidation of 747 S&L's was [22.2-35]: **a)** direct costs to taxpayers: 1) $81,900 M ($81.9 B) for RTC (i.e., the FSLIC Resolution Fund (FRF)) and 2) $42,700 M ($42.7 B) for FSLIC for a total of $124,600 M ($124.6 B); **b)** direct costs from private sources: 1) $6,000 M ($6.0 B) for RTC and 2) $22,000 M ($22.0 B) for FSLIC for a total of $28,000 M ($28.0 B); **c)** indirect costs to taxpayer in the form of tax benefits under FSLIC assistance, $7,500 M ($7.5 B); **d)** taxpayer interest expenses: 1) known interest on REFCORP bonds, $76,200 M ($76.2 B); 2) estimated interest expense on appropriations, $209,000 M ($209.0 B), for a total interest costs to the taxpayers of $285,200 M ($285.2 B); and **e)** private interest expense: 1) known interest on FICO bonds, $23,800 M ($23.8 B); 2) known interest expense on REFCORP bonds, $11,800 M ($11.8 B), for a total of $35,600 M ($35.6 B) in private known interest expenses. The total direct, indirect, and interest expense to the taxpayers comes to $417,300 M ($417.3 B); the total private direct, indirect, and interest expenses comes to $63,600 M ($63.6 B). It is possible that the costs will actually be higher.

30 Aug 1995: The U. S. began active military involvement in the Bosnian War (a bombing campaign), although it had been supporting European allies since 1992.

14 Dec 1995: End of the war in Bosnia (the Dayton Agreement).

29 Dec 1995: Congress passed the ICC Termination Act of 1995 [22.2-36], abolishing the Interstate Commerce Commission, requiring modifications to U. S. Code Titles 5, 11, 18, 28, 31, 39, 49, and the Internal Revenue Code of 1986; as well as a great number of other amendments to various laws, mostly relating to railroads and waterways. The ICC was replaced by a Surface Transportation Board within the Department of Transportation, with the same powers as the ICC.

31 Dec 1995: A total of 6 FDIC BIF-insured banks and 2 FDIC SAIF-insured S&L's failed in 1995, with combined net losses to the FDIC BIF and SAIF totaling $84.472 M [22.2-37]. RTC liquidation of the 2 S&L's assets incurred net losses to the RTC of $27.750 M [22.2-38].

1 Jan 1996: All RTC assets and liabilities were transferred to the FDIC FSLIC Resolution Fund (FRF) (cf. 17 Dec 1993).

31 Dec 1996: A total of 5 FDIC BIF/SAIF insured institutions failed in 1996, with combined net losses to the FDIC BIF and SAIF totaling $60.615 M [22.2-39].

19 Nov 1997: Congress passed the "Savings are Vital to Everyone's Retirement Act of 1997" [22.2-40]: **a)** S. 3) directed the Secretary of Labor to establish an educational program to encourage people to save for retirement; and **b)** (S. 4) required the President to convene a National Summit on Retirement Income Savings in 2001 and 2005 "to advance the public's knowledge and understanding of retire-

ment savings and its critical importance to the future well-being of American workers and their families".

26 Nov 1997: Congress passed legislation [22.2-41]: **a)** (S. 2) extended the Export-Import Bank until 30 Sep 2001; and **b)** (S. 3) did not impose a limit on Export-Import Bank credit, revising 12 U.S.C. 635i-3(e) to state "There are authorized to be appropriated to the Fund such sums as may be necessary to carry out the purposes of this section."

31 Dec 1997: One FDIC BIF/SAIF insured institution failed in 1997, with combined net losses to the FDIC BIF and SAIF totaling $5.026 M [22.2-42].

31 Dec 1998: Three FDIC BIF/SAIF insured institutions failed in 1998, with combined net losses to the FDIC BIF and SAIF totaling $221.606 M [22.2-43].

12 Nov 1999: Congress passed the Financial Services Modernization Act (a.k.a. Gramm-Leach-Bliley) [22.2-44]: **a)** (S. 101) repealed the portion of the Glass-Steagall Act (cf. 16 Jun 1933) that prohibited a bank from engaging in both investment and commercial banking (investment banks, commercial banks, securities companies were now allowed to merge); **b)** (S. 103) permitted holding companies to engage in transactions involving financial products (insurance and underwriting of securities); **c)** (S. 108) required the Federal Reserve and Treasury Secretary to study ways to use subordinated debt to protect depositors and institutions that were "too big to fail"; **d)** (S. 118) repealed the section of the Bank Holding Company Act of 1956 (cf. 9 May 1956) that applied to savings banks; **e)** (S. 121) permitted national banks to operate or control subsidiaries; **f)** (S. 151) permitted national banks to underwrite municipal bonds; **g)** (S. 206) permitted banks and holding companies to make transactions (except to retail customers) of credit and equity swap agreements in commodities, securities, currencies, and other assets; **h)** (S. 301) required States to functionally regulate insurance activities of persons and banks; **i)** (S. 302) permitted national banks to sell insurance under certain conditions if permitted by State law, but prohibited title insurance (unless already doing so under State law) and annuity contracts; **j)** (S. 312) specified rules by which a mutual insurance company may reorganize into a mutual holding company, but only if there is no State law that currently provides for it; **k)** (S. 401) prohibited new mergers between S&L's and commercial bank holding companies, but existing S&L holding companies are permitted to continue; **l)** (S. 503) required banking institutions to provide customers with their privacy policy; **m)** (S. 602) permitted member banks with less than $500 M in assets to issue loans to small business and agriculture based on long-term advances from the Federal Home Loan Bank; **n)** (S. 606) revised the management structure of Federal Home Loan Banks; **o)** (S. 608) revised the capital structure of Federal Home Loan Banks (5% of total assets or as necessary to meet evaluated risks); and **p)** (S. 702) required disclosure of automated teller machine (ATM) fees.

6 Dec 1999: Congress passed legislation [22.2-45] modifying section 16 of the Federal Reserve Act (FRA) that permitted a wider range of collateral to be used by Federal Reserve Banks to obtain Federal Reserve Notes. It now permitted promissory notes issued by member banks upon an emergency advance (FRA S. 10A), promissory notes from member banks backed by mortgages (FRA S. 10B), and discounts backed by agricultural paper or issued by agricultural marketing associations (FRA S. 13A).

31 Dec 1999: Eight FDIC BIF/SAIF insured institutions failed in 1999, with combined net losses to the FDIC BIF and SAIF totaling $586.027 M [22.2-46].

31 Dec 2000: Seven FDIC BIF/SAIF insured institutions failed in 2000, with combined net losses to the FDIC BIF and SAIF totaling $32.138 M [22.2-47].

15 Mar 2001: Approximate beginning of a recession [22.2-48].

11 Sep 2001: An attack on the World Trade Towers in New York and on the Pentagon using hijacked commercial aircraft was committed by members of al Qaeda. This began the war in Afghanistan, since the Taliban regime that ruled Afghanistan had permitted al Qaeda to train there.

7 Oct 2001: Beginning of the aerial bombardment of Kabul (Afghanistan).

26 Oct 2001: Congress passed the USA PATRIOT Act [22.2-49]. It expanded the "Bank Secrecy" provisions of the "Money Laundering Control Act of 1986" (cf. 27 Oct 1986), and required financial institutions to make reports on "suspicious activity". Section 365 requires a report to be generated as follows:

> "Coin and currency receipts of more than $10,000 -- any person -- (1) who is engaged in a trade or business; and (2) who, in the course of such trade or business, receives more than $10,000 in coins or currency in 1 transactions (or 2 or more related transactions), shall file a report described in subsection (b) with respect to such transaction (or related transactions) with the Financial Crimes Enforcement Network, at such time and such manner as the Secretary may, by regulations, prescribe". Subsection b) requires the name and address of the person making the transactions, the amount of coins and currency received, date and nature of the transaction."

Carrying more than $10,000 outside the U. S. is now a criminal offense called "bulk cash smuggling" per Section 371:

> "Whoever, with the intent to evade a currency reporting requirement under section 5316, knowingly conceals more than $10,000 in currency or other monetary instruments on the person of such individual or in any conveyance, article of luggage, merchandise, or other container, and transports or transfers or attempts to transport or transfer such currency or monetary instruments from a place within the United States to a place outside of the United States, or from a place outside the United States to a place within the United States, shall be guilty of a currency smuggling offense and subject to punishment pursuant to subsection (b)."

The penalty per subsection (b) is 5 years in prison and confiscation of "any property real or personal, and any property traceable to such property."

Title IV ("Protecting the Border") contains provisions under Subtitle A for "Protecting the Northern Border"; but the law is entirely silent on protecting the Southern border.

(We certainly would not want to offend the *National Council of La Raza* (now renamed *UnidosUS*) or inconvenience the drug cartels and their associates in the Mexican government.)

9 - 11 Nov 2001: Battle of Mazar-i Sharif (Afghanistan).

12, 13 Nov 2001: Fall of Kabul (Afghanistan).

15 Nov 2001: Approximate end of the recession (cf. 15 Mar 2001) [22.2-50].

25 - 27 Nov 2001: Battle of Qala-i-Jangi (Afghanistan).

5 - 7 Dec 2001: Battle of Kandahar (Afghanistan).

6 - 17 Dec 2001: Battle of Tora Bora (Afghanistan).

11 Dec 2001: China joined the World Trade Organization, and this marked the beginning of the exportation of the U. S. industrial base to Communist China. China was expected to transition to a market economy, and was granted a 15-year transition period to do so, but has never changed. Allowing a Communist regime to enter into trade agreements as an equal member shows how naive and gullible the WTO negotiators were, not to mention the American political class.

31 Dec 2001: Four FDIC BIF/SAIF insured institutions failed in 2001, with combined net losses to the FDIC BIF and SAIF totaling $292.465 M [22.2-51].

31 Mar 2002: Congress extended [22.2-52] the authorization for the Export-Import Bank until 30 Apr 2002.

1 May 2002: Congress extended [22.2-53] the authorization for the Export-Import Bank until 31 May 2002.

30 May 2002: Congress extended [22.2-54] the authorization for the Export-Import Bank until 14 Jun 2002.

14 Jun 2002: Congress extended [22.2-55] the authorization for the Export-Import Bank until 31 Dec 2006. It was given an additional objective per Section 2:

"The Bank's objective in authorizing loans, guarantees, insurance, and credits shall be to contribute to or maintain or increasing employment of United States workers."

31 Dec 2002: Eleven FDIC BIF/SAIF insured institutions failed in 2002, with combined net losses to the FDIC BIF and SAIF totaling $413.989 M [22.2-56].

19 Mar 2003: Beginning of Operation Iraqi Freedom (a.k.a. Second Gulf War) to enforce a U. N. resolution against Iraq and under the belief by the U. S. intelligence services that Iraqi dictator Saddam Hussein's regime possessed "weapons of mass destruction" (WMD's).

21 - 25 Mar 2003: Battle of Umm Qasr (Iraq).

3 - 12 Apr 2003: Battle of Baghdad (Iraq).

28 Oct 2003: Congress passed the Check Clearing for the 21st Century Act [22.2-57], which permits physical checks to be deposited and cleared by purely electronic means (creating a digital image and making deposits remotely).

13 Dec 2003: Operation Red Dawn, capture of Iraqi dictator Saddam Hussein.

31 Dec 2003: Three FDIC BIF/SAIF insured institutions failed in 2003, with combined net losses to the FDIC BIF and SAIF totaling $62.647 M [22.2-58].

22.3 Data, 1987-2003

Figures 22.3-1 and 22.3-2 show the U. S. government revenue and expenditures for 1987 to 2003.

U. S. Government Revenue, 1987-2003 (millions USD)										
			Income taxes				Social Insurance Taxes				
Day	Year	Customs Duties	Individual	Corporate	Excise Taxes	Estate and Gift Taxes	OASDI & Disability (Off-Budget)	Medicare & Retirements (On-Budget)	Federal Reserve Deposits	Other Misc.	Net Receipts
30 Sep	1987	15,085	392,557	83,926	32,457	7,493	213,401	89,916	16,817	2,635	854,287
30 Sep	1988	16,198	401,181	94,508	35,227	7,594	241,491	92,845	17,163	3,031	909,238
30 Sep	1989	16,334	445,690	103,291	34,386	8,745	263,666	95,751	19,604	3,639	991,104
30 Sep	1990	16,707	466,884	93,507	35,345	11,500	281,656	98,392	24,319	3,647	1,031,958
30 Sep	1991	15,949	467,827	98,086	42,402	11,138	293,885	102,131	19,158	4,412	1,054,988
30 Sep	1992	17,359	475,964	100,270	45,569	11,143	302,426	111,263	22,920	4,293	1,091,208
30 Sep	1993	18,802	509,680	117,520	48,057	12,577	311,900	116,366	14,908	4,491	1,154,334
30 Sep	1994	20,099	543,055	140,385	55,225	15,225	335,026	126,450	18,023	5,081	1,258,566
30 Sep	1995	19,301	590,244	157,004	57,484	14,763	351,079	133,394	23,378	5,143	1,351,790
30 Sep	1996	18,670	656,417	171,824	54,014	17,189	367,492	141,922	20,477	5,048	1,453,053
30 Sep	1997	17,928	737,466	182,293	56,924	19,845	391,990	147,381	19,636	5,769	1,579,232
30 Sep	1998	18,297	828,586	188,677	57,673	24,076	415,799	156,032	24,540	8,048	1,721,728
30 Sep	1999	18,336	879,480	184,680	70,414	27,782	444,468	167,365	25,917	9,010	1,827,452
30 Sep	2000	19,914	1,004,462	207,289	68,865	29,010	480,584	172,268	32,293	10,506	2,025,191
30 Sep	2001	19,369	994,339	151,075	66,232	28,400	507,519	186,448	26,124	11,576	1,991,082
30 Sep	2002	18,602	858,345	148,044	66,989	26,507	515,321	185,439	23,683	10,206	1,853,136
30 Sep	2003	19,862	793,699	131,778	67,524	21,959	523,842	189,136	21,878	12,636	1,782,314

1. The revenue data for 1987 to 2003 is from the OMB White House, file = HIST_FY21.pdf, Tables 2.1 and 2.5
2. https://www.whitehouse.gov/omb/historical-tables/

Figure 22.3-1: U. S. Government Revenue, 1987-2003

			Education, Training, Employ-ment, Social			Income	Social Security		Physical Resources	Interest on	Inter-national	Agri-		Undistrib-uted Offsetting Receipts	
Day	Year	National Defense	Services	Health	Medicare	Security	[1]	Veterans	[1, 2]	Debt [1]	Affairs	culture	Other [3]	[1, 4]	Total
30 Jun	1987	281,996	28,915	39,967	75,120	124,105	207,352	26,761	55,132	138,611	11,645	26,466	24,402	-36,455	1,004,017
30 Jun	1988	290,360	30,939	44,471	78,878	130,387	219,341	29,409	68,625	151,803	10,466	17,088	29,615	-36,967	1,064,416
30 Jun	1989	303,555	35,314	48,390	84,964	137,554	232,542	30,038	81,553	168,981	9,583	16,698	31,782	-37,212	1,143,743
30 Jun	1990	299,321	37,167	57,700	98,102	148,783	248,623	29,088	126,011	184,347	13,758	11,637	35,073	-36,615	1,252,993
30 Jun	1991	273,285	41,260	71,139	104,489	172,589	269,014	31,319	135,159	194,448	15,846	14,886	40,147	-39,356	1,324,226
30 Jun	1992	298,346	42,807	89,415	119,024	199,657	287,584	34,112	75,586	199,344	16,090	14,922	43,922	-39,280	1,381,529
30 Jun	1993	291,084	47,455	99,321	130,552	210,088	304,585	35,690	46,841	198,713	17,218	20,081	45,144	-37,386	1,409,386
30 Jun	1994	281,640	43,337	107,051	144,747	217,233	319,565	37,617	70,677	202,932	17,067	14,795	42,863	-37,772	1,461,752
30 Jun	1995	272,063	51,067	115,352	159,855	223,758	335,846	37,910	59,113	232,134	16,429	9,671	46,999	-44,455	1,515,742
30 Jun	1996	265,748	48,334	119,342	174,225	229,699	349,671	37,003	64,170	241,053	13,487	9,035	46,337	-37,620	1,560,484
30 Jun	1997	270,502	49,014	123,790	190,016	234,986	365,251	39,332	59,852	243,984	15,173	8,889	50,300	-49,973	1,601,116
30 Jun	1998	268,194	50,534	131,403	192,822	237,698	379,215	41,793	74,669	241,118	13,054	12,077	57,075	-47,194	1,652,458
30 Jun	1999	274,769	50,608	141,045	190,447	242,417	390,037	43,216	81,892	229,755	15,239	22,879	59,983	-40,445	1,701,842
30 Jun	2000	294,363	53,766	154,502	197,113	253,673	409,423	47,040	84,925	222,949	17,213	36,458	60,106	-42,581	1,788,950
30 Jun	2001	304,732	57,089	172,238	217,384	269,724	432,958	45,024	97,492	206,167	16,485	26,252	64,312	-47,011	1,862,846
30 Jun	2002	348,456	70,592	196,471	230,855	312,670	455,980	50,979	104,308	170,949	22,315	21,965	72,746	-47,392	2,010,894
30 Jun	2003	404,733	82,733	219,605	249,433	334,574	474,680	56,832	115,588	153,073	21,199	22,496	79,335	-54,382	2,159,899

U. S. Government Expenditures, 1987-2003 (millions USD)

1. The totals of "on budget and "off-budget" are shown here.
2. "Physical Resources" includes Energy, Natural Resources and Environment, Commerce and Housing Credit, Transportation, and Community & Regional Development.
3. "Other" includes General Science, Space & Technology, Administration of Justice, General Government, and Allowances.
4. "Offsetting Receipts" is a combination of new debt and intra-government transfers from Trust Funds.
5. The expenditure data for 1987 to 2003 is from the OMB White House, file = HIST_FY21.pdf, Table 3.1.
6. https://www.whitehouse.gov/omb/historical-tables/

Figure 22.3-2: U. S. Government Expenditures, 1987-2003

Figure 22.3-3 shows the national debt and per-capita debt for this period. Refer to the Introduction to Part 2 for a sense of wages vs. per-capita national debt.

U. S. National Debt, 1987-2003 (USD)

Day	Year	Principal ($) [1]	Population [2]	Debt per Capita ($) [2]	Day	Year	Principal ($) [1]	Population [2]	Debt per Capita ($) [2]
30 Sep	1987	2,350,276,890,953	242,060,653	9,709.45	30 Sep	1996	5,224,810,939,136	268,337,093	19,471.07
30 Sep	1988	2,602,337,712,041	244,277,059	10,653.22	30 Sep	1997	5,413,146,011,397	271,608,296	19,929.97
30 Sep	1989	2,857,430,960,187	246,493,466	11,592.32	30 Sep	1998	5,526,193,008,898	274,879,499	20,104.06
30 Sep	1990	3,233,313,451,777	248,709,873	13,000.34	30 Sep	1999	5,656,270,901,615	278,150,703	20,335.27
30 Sep	1991	3,665,303,351,697	251,981,076	14,545.95	30 Sep	2000	5,674,178,209,887	281,421,906	20,162.53
30 Sep	1992	4,064,620,655,522	255,252,280	15,923.93	30 Sep	2001	5,807,463,412,200	284,154,269	20,437.71
30 Sep	1993	4,411,488,883,139	258,523,483	17,064.17	30 Sep	2002	6,228,235,965,597	286,886,632	21,709.75
30 Sep	1994	4,692,749,910,013	261,794,686	17,925.31	30 Sep	2003	6,783,231,062,744	289,618,996	23,421.22
30 Sep	1995	4,973,982,900,709	265,065,890	18,765.08					

1. The total debt data for 1987 to 2003 is from: https://fiscaldata.treasury.gov/datasets/historical-debt-outstanding/historical-debt-outstanding.
2. Population values are based on the dicennial census from the Census Bureau, and linearly interpolated. Per-capita is based on these values.

Figure 22.3-3: National Debt and Per-Capita Share Thereof, 1987-2003

Figures 22.3-4 through 22.3-11 show a summary of the asset and liability condition statements of the Federal Reserve and commercial banking system for this period. Unless otherwise stated, all the values are from references shown in Appendix B. I do not have an explanation as to why the error between assets and liabilities is so large from Mar 1994 to Sep 2001.

				Federal Reserve Loans & Investments		Commercial Bank Loans and Investments				
Day	Year	Gold Stock	Treasury Currency Outstanding	U. S. Government Securities	Discounts & Advances	Loans	U. S. Government Securities	Other [1, 2]	Total Assets	Note
25 Mar	1987	11,082	17,735	194,544	573	1,613,500	299,500	186,700	2,323,634	
24 Jun	1987	11,069	17,889	216,671	760	1,657,500	304,600	188,000	2,396,489	
30 Sep	1987	11,075	18,006	211,941	1,941	1,696,200	313,800	187,900	2,440,863	
30 Dec	1987	11,078	18,177	222,383	951	1,727,200	321,400	193,100	2,494,289	
30 Mar	1988	11,063	18,339	215,160	2,134	1,743,900	324,700	193,700	2,508,996	
29 Jun	1988	11,063	18,501	228,438	2,244	1,807,300	328,800	191,600	2,587,946	
28 Sep	1988	11,063	18,637	228,858	2,664	1,823,500	336,500	190,500	2,611,722	
28 Dec	1988	11,060	18,799	237,268	1,603	1,874,300	345,900	187,100	2,676,030	
29 Mar	1989	11,061	18,961	227,924	2,305	1,901,800	357,100	181,600	2,700,751	
28 Jun	1989	11,062	19,201	231,062	1,759	1,941,800	360,900	180,000	2,745,784	
27 Sep	1989	11,065	19,386	220,505	585	1,975,300	365,100	176,300	2,768,241	
27 Dec	1989	11,059	19,606	233,951	2,159	2,016,000	374,100	174,900	2,831,775	
28 Mar	1990	11,059	19,823	220,529	1,895	2,017,700	401,800	171,700	2,844,506	
27 Jun	1990	11,065	20,033	230,978	608	2,055,900	422,200	167,600	2,908,384	
26 Sep	1990	11,063	20,213	236,575	501	2,073,000	434,500	167,200	2,943,052	
26 Dec	1990	11,058	20,378	241,569	4,979	2,105,300	439,600	166,000	2,988,884	
27 Mar	1991	11,058	20,562	241,238	173	2,087,300	463,300	165,100	2,988,731	
26 Jun	1991	11,062	20,738	247,352	363	2,108,800	477,500	163,100	3,028,915	
25 Sep	1991	11,062	20,877	256,361	354	2,093,500	500,600	162,900	3,045,654	
25 Dec	1991	11,058	21,008	275,934	182	2,111,500	538,500	166,400	3,124,582	

Table title: Assets of the Federal Reserve & Commercial System, 1987-1991 (millions USD)

1. "Trading account assets" were shown separately from "other securities" in FRB's prior to Apr 1994 and was combined into "other securities" starting May 1994.
2. "H.8" data is used for "other securities" from Mar 1994 ff since it excludes the trading accounts.

Figure 22.3-4: Banking System Assets, 1987-1991

				At Federal Reserve Banks		At Commercial Banks					
Day	Year	Currency Outside Banks	Treasury Cash	Treasury Demand Deposits	Foreign Demand Deposits	Demand Deposits	Treasury Demand Deposits [2]	Time Deposits	Capital [1]	Total Liabilities	Error (%)
25 Mar	1987	186,000	515	2,953	226	568,800	17,200	1,330,900	188,700	2,295,294	1.22
24 Jun	1987	191,900	499	16,356	208	578,300	25,500	1,345,500	200,500	2,358,763	1.57
30 Sep	1987	194,300	460	9,120	456	610,700	25,500	1,357,700	224,800	2,423,036	0.73
30 Dec	1987	199,400	454	4,773	207	623,200	22,400	1,389,000	231,800	2,471,234	0.92
30 Mar	1988	199,200	475	3,190	207	587,600	22,300	1,416,400	209,500	2,438,872	2.79
29 Jun	1988	205,800	452	8,216	203	602,300	21,000	1,436,100	215,000	2,489,071	3.82
28 Sep	1988	207,900	389	14,694	331	588,300	24,500	1,470,500	213,100	2,519,714	3.52
28 Dec	1988	214,800	390	5,822	216	641,300	22,900	1,500,300	227,300	2,613,028	2.35
29 Mar	1989	213,900	457	5,254	224	582,000	18,100	1,538,100	219,900	2,577,935	4.55
28 Jun	1989	218,500	481	19,244	287	580,500	26,200	1,551,600	218,400	2,615,212	4.76
27 Sep	1989	218,600	440	9,768	335	588,500	24,800	1,586,800	221,400	2,650,643	4.25
27 Dec	1989	225,300	447	5,029	269	643,300	19,600	1,621,800	239,100	2,754,845	2.72
28 Mar	1990	227,000	540	6,218	285	593,900	16,700	1,652,700	228,100	2,725,443	4.19
27 Jun	1990	234,700	580	5,915	189	598,500	21,000	1,675,400	234,300	2,770,584	4.74
26 Sep	1990	240,800	521	5,402	198	596,300	31,000	1,701,800	236,800	2,812,821	4.43
26 Dec	1990	249,400	553	11,375	183	638,100	23,000	1,721,200	265,000	2,908,811	2.68
27 Mar	1991	255,600	623	6,156	299	602,800	28,400	1,779,700	278,200	2,951,778	1.24
26 Jun	1991	259,100	613	5,419	233	611,200	23,600	1,794,900	264,100	2,959,165	2.30
25 Sep	1991	261,800	607	5,324	243	613,700	26,900	1,816,600	265,200	2,990,374	1.82
25 Dec	1991	270,000	634	9,834	268	682,300	25,400	1,808,400	295,700	3,092,536	1.03

Table title: Liabilities of the Federal Reserve and Commercial System, 1987-1991 (millions USD)

1. Used "other liabilities" from H.8 for Mar 1994 ff.

Figure 22.3-5: Banking System Liabilities, 1987-1991

| | | | | Federal Reserve Loans & Investments | | Commercial Bank Loans and Investments | | | | |
| | | | | | | | | | | |
Day	Year	Gold Stock	Treasury Currency Outstanding	U. S. Government Securities	Discounts & Advances	Loans	U. S. Government Securities	Other [1, 2]	Total Assets	Note
25 Mar	1992	11,058	21,128	266,994	59	2,090,000	557,300	162,700	3,109,239	
24 Jun	1992	11,060	21,252	279,196	237	2,083,400	586,800	158,000	3,139,945	
30 Sep	1992	11,058	21,342	296,397	609	2,098,200	611,100	160,200	3,198,906	
30 Dec	1992	11,056	21,469	301,342	56	2,123,685	635,476	162,998	3,256,082	
31 Mar	1993	11,054	21,584	305,317	752	2,085,977	672,074	163,089	3,259,847	
30 Jun	1993	11,057	21,741	328,199	1,534	2,113,578	676,925	163,178	3,316,212	
29 Sep	1993	11,057	21,864	326,938	269	2,158,431	684,415	165,642	3,368,616	
29 Dec	1993	11,053	22,039	344,321	47	2,195,330	699,806	165,526	3,438,122	
30 Mar	1994	11,052	22,268	342,254	74	2,208,400	760,200	165,192	3,509,440	
29 Jun	1994	11,052	22,517	351,622	380	2,242,000	749,400	166,555	3,543,526	
28 Sep	1994	11,054	22,716	349,846	570	2,314,500	734,900	170,817	3,604,403	
28 Dec	1994	11,051	22,990	370,962	167	2,400,400	712,600	171,428	3,689,598	
29 Mar	1995	11,053	23,185	369,324	115	2,441,200	704,700	151,819	3,701,396	
28 Jun	1995	11,054	23,416	375,686	228	2,515,600	706,000	184,283	3,816,267	
27 Sep	1995	11,051	23,724	376,139	340	2,577,600	707,500	193,912	3,890,266	
27 Dec	1995	11,050	23,937	387,965	63	2,617,500	701,500	189,009	3,931,024	
27 Mar	1996	11,053	24,179	385,787	38	2,641,300	711,200	193,208	3,966,765	
26 Jun	1996	11,050	24,484	386,748	258	2,674,700	706,800	193,172	3,997,212	
25 Sep	1996	11,050	24,679	396,783	385	2,725,900	706,200	192,514	4,057,511	
25 Dec	1996	11,048	24,964	407,289	105	2,801,700	695,700	195,869	4,136,675	

Assets of the Federal Reserve & Commercial System, 1992-1996 (millions USD)

1. "Trading account assets" were shown separately from "other securities" in FRB's prior to Apr 1994 and was combined into "other securities" starting May 1994.
2. "H.8" data is used for "other securities" from Mar 1994 ff since it excludes the trading accounts.

Figure 22.3-6: Banking System Assets, 1992-1996

| | | At Federal Reserve Banks | | | At Commercial Banks | | | | | |
| | | | | | | | | | | |
Day	Year	Currency Outside Banks	Treasury Cash	Treasury Demand Deposits	Foreign Demand Deposits	Demand Deposits	Treasury Demand Deposits [2]	Time Deposits	Capital [1]	Total Liabilities	Error (%)
25 Mar	1992	271,100	711	4,631	172	663,600	20,100	1,690,300	290,700	2,941,314	5.40
24 Jun	1992	277,300	612	7,649	213	665,700	25,100	1,674,000	307,700	2,958,274	5.79
30 Sep	1992	284,700	527	24,586	546	727,700	28,700	1,760,500	329,328	3,156,587	1.32
30 Dec	1992	295,100	508	7,270	254	799,332	19,500	1,742,304	342,903	3,207,171	1.50
31 Mar	1993	297,900	515	6,752	318	757,336	17,300	1,734,250	352,502	3,166,873	2.85
30 Jun	1993	307,500	432	28,386	286	795,187	21,600	1,712,222	359,176	3,224,789	2.76
29 Sep	1993	314,800	384	11,438	294	791,887	28,800	1,699,674	379,360	3,226,637	4.21
29 Dec	1993	324,900	377	5,407	286	852,224	21,400	1,698,656	383,758	3,287,008	4.40
30 Mar	1994	330,700	370	5,562	198	801,600	32,000	1,701,700	203,340	3,075,470	12.37
29 Jun	1994	340,600	353	6,435	163	791,900	48,400	1,688,900	207,836	3,084,587	12.95
28 Sep	1994	347,100	363	6,658	399	782,200	45,100	1,710,300	185,300	3,077,420	14.62
28 Dec	1994	357,700	335	7,677	173	846,100	28,800	1,728,600	213,394	3,182,779	13.74
29 Mar	1995	361,400	361	4,389	185	765,200	17,800	1,756,700	248,815	3,154,850	14.77
28 Jun	1995	368,100	319	7,721	260	764,300	46,900	1,795,200	264,175	3,246,975	14.92
27 Sep	1995	369,200	322	6,553	170	780,400	48,700	1,853,600	289,073	3,348,018	13.94
27 Dec	1995	376,000	270	5,779	178	815,000	35,900	1,864,900	280,141	3,378,168	14.06
27 Mar	1996	374,200	314	4,593	172	743,200	29,000	1,929,600	286,958	3,368,037	15.09
26 Jun	1996	380,500	280	7,290	163	729,800	38,200	1,955,200	275,165	3,386,598	15.28
25 Sep	1996	386,800	286	6,846	165	704,800	40,100	2,018,400	281,910	3,439,307	15.24
25 Dec	1996	397,900	249	6,479	214	764,600	29,600	2,151,000	293,267	3,643,309	11.93

Liabilities of the Federal Reserve and Commercial System, 1992-1996 (millions USD)

1. Used "other liabilities" from H.8 for Mar 1994 ff.
2. Treasury Demand Deposits not shown after Dec 1993 in FRB's; used US government total cash balance at commercial banks (series GDTCBW, H.6).

Figure 22.3-7: Banking System Liabilities, 1992-1996

| Assets of the Federal Reserve & Commercial System, 1997-2001 (millions USD) | | | | | | | | | | |
| | | | | Federal Reserve Loans & Investments | | Commercial Bank Loans and Investments | | | | |
Day	Year	Gold Stock	Treasury Currency Outstanding	U. S. Government Securities	Discounts & Advances	Loans	U. S. Government Securities	Other [1, 2]	Total Assets	Note
26 Mar	1997	11,051	25,149	404,489	54	2,846,800	715,000	203,510	4,206,053	
25 Jun	1997	11,050	25,343	422,859	702	2,910,700	719,500	206,531	4,296,685	
24 Sep	1997	11,050	25,474	423,549	383	2,944,100	725,700	219,948	4,350,204	
31 Dec	1997	11,047	25,644	451,924	2,036	3,042,000	755,000	241,537	4,529,188	
25 Mar	1998	11,049	25,744	439,854	38	3,075,200	733,600	245,167	4,530,652	
24 Jun	1998	11,049	25,836	452,990	196	3,135,600	747,400	262,150	4,635,221	
30 Sep	1998	11,044	25,972	458,182	1,055	3,240,000	768,100	284,633	4,788,986	
30 Dec	1998	11,046	26,267	470,321	1,669	3,335,600	794,900	308,204	4,948,007	
31 Mar	1999	11,049	26,564	478,516	245	3,291,900	814,500	287,740	4,910,514	
30 Jun	1999	11,046	26,930	493,966	220	3,323,000	813,200	300,439	4,968,801	
29 Sep	1999	11,048	27,354	496,239	418	3,382,800	805,100	314,895	5,037,854	
29 Dec	1999	11,048	27,978	483,417	2,872	3,545,000	806,900	342,417	5,219,632	
29 Mar	2000	11,048	28,728	502,762	124	3,564,500	821,200	332,470	5,260,832	
28 Jun	2000	11,047	29,727	507,884	526	3,713,900	811,900	346,974	5,421,958	
27 Sep	2000	11,046	30,749	512,472	407	3,834,800	797,000	372,284	5,558,758	
27 Dec	2000	11,046	31,593	515,491	117	3,929,100	784,300	398,319	5,669,966	
28 Mar	2001	11,046	32,235	524,946	15	3,921,000	761,300	410,516	5,661,058	
27 Jun	2001	11,044	32,644	535,191	152	3,925,900	758,500	428,311	5,691,742	
26 Sep	2001	11,043	32,999	526,817	95	3,920,400	792,600	431,187	5,715,141	
26 Dec	2001	11,045	33,181	555,997	45	3,961,900	817,100	459,268	5,838,536	

1. "Trading account assets" were shown separately from "other securities" in FRB's prior to Apr 1994 and was combined into "other securities" starting May 1994.

2. "H.8" data is used for "other securities" from Mar 1994 ff since it excludes the trading accounts.

Figure 22.3-8: Banking System Assets, 1997-2001

| Liabilities of the Federal Reserve and Commercial System, 1997-2001 (millions USD) | | | | | | | | | | |
| | | | | At Federal Reserve Banks | | At Commercial Banks | | | | |
Day	Year	Currency Outside Banks	Treasury Cash	Treasury Demand Deposits	Foreign Demand Deposits	Demand Deposits	Treasury Demand Deposits [2]	Time Deposits	Capital [1]	Total Liabilities	Error (%)
26 Mar	1997	401,000	313	4,420	162	681,400	39,700	2,192,300	295,983	3,615,278	14.05
25 Jun	1997	408,400	343	19,285	468	675,800	48,100	2,261,100	286,964	3,700,460	13.88
24 Sep	1997	414,300	255	7,328	162	657,500	40,100	2,325,800	291,811	3,737,256	14.09
31 Dec	1997	429,000	225	5,444	457	768,000	37,300	2,408,200	316,216	3,964,842	12.46
25 Mar	1998	431,500	265	4,819	159	670,300	37,800	2,483,300	322,897	3,951,040	12.79
24 Jun	1998	438,300	204	22,464	154	655,300	68,000	2,509,400	304,014	3,997,836	13.75
30 Sep	1998	448,200	92	4,952	347	708,400	53,500	2,559,400	362,505	4,137,396	13.61
30 Dec	1998	464,100	85	10,174	166	746,600	53,700	2,619,700	370,227	4,264,752	13.81
31 Mar	1999	471,300	135	5,374	166	702,500	15,600	2,677,200	317,951	4,190,226	14.67
30 Jun	1999	483,200	90	6,720	410	695,400	61,300	2,696,000	321,693	4,264,813	14.17
29 Sep	1999	493,400	93	8,232	191	637,400	66,600	2,744,300	352,352	4,302,568	14.60
29 Dec	1999	523,100	109	25,923	234	691,800	88,100	2,869,900	397,628	4,596,794	11.93
29 Mar	2000	517,000	174	5,288	80	630,500	16,900	2,936,500	410,235	4,516,677	14.15
28 Jun	2000	521,200	76	6,613	117	625,800	84,600	3,001,700	418,474	4,658,580	14.08
27 Sep	2000	522,400	184	7,986	75	602,700	54,400	3,107,900	447,747	4,743,392	14.67
27 Dec	2000	535,800	450	5,320	83	671,100	17,300	3,238,200	466,744	4,934,997	12.96
28 Mar	2001	539,100	478	4,764	145	622,800	9,300	3,309,300	490,415	4,976,302	12.10
27 Jun	2001	549,100	444	6,857	73	616,600	37,600	3,359,400	485,877	5,055,951	11.17
26 Sep	2001	566,000	422	9,668	635	646,700	45,900	3,444,300	553,233	5,266,858	7.84
26 Dec	2001	585,600	425	4,856	233	695,600	54,100	3,563,600	462,823	5,367,237	8.07

1. Used "other liabilities" from H.8 for Mar 1994 ff

2. Treasury Demand Deposits not shown after Dec 1993 in FRB's; used US government total cash balance at commercial banks (series GDTCBW, H.6).

Figure 22.3-9: Banking System Liabilities, 1997-2001

Assets of the Federal Reserve & Commercial System, 2002, 2003 (millions USD)										
				Federal Reserve Loans & Investments		Commercial Bank Loans and Investments				
Day	Year	Gold Stock	Treasury Currency Outstanding	U. S. Government Securities	Discounts & Advances	Loans	U. S. Government Securities	Other [1, 2]	Total Assets	Note
27 Mar	2002	11,044	33,591	576,093	22	3,939,800	843,800	458,293	5,862,643	
26 Jun	2002	11,044	33,913	592,390	180	3,992,200	882,800	456,005	5,968,532	
25 Sep	2002	11,042	34,289	606,248	176	4,099,900	959,000	437,585	6,148,240	
25 Dec	2002	11,043	34,566	629,402	59	4,220,800	1,013,300	464,961	6,374,131	
26 Mar	2003	11,043	34,752	666,401	7	4,206,200	1,055,200	465,478	6,439,081	
25 Jun	2003	11,044	35,018	684,003	95	4,300,700	1,143,600	455,542	6,630,002	
24 Sep	2003	11,043	35,279	682,003	341	4,190,200	1,044,600	498,616	6,462,082	
24 Dec	2003	11,043	35,461	702,716	175	4,213,752	1,096,349	508,540	6,568,036	

1. "Trading account assets" were shown separately from "other securities" in FRB's prior to Apr 1994 and was combined into "other securities" starting May 1994.
2. "H.8" data is used for "other securities" from Mar 1994 ff since it excludes the trading accounts.

Figure 22.3-10: Banking System Assets, 2002, 2003

Liabilities of the Federal Reserve and Commercial System, 2002, 2003 (millions USD)											
				At Federal Reserve Banks		At Commercial Banks					
Day	Year	Currency Outside Banks	Treasury Cash	Treasury Demand Deposits,	Foreign Demand Deposits	Demand Deposits	Treasury Demand Deposits [2]	Time Deposits	Capital [1]	Total Liabilities	Error (%)
27 Mar	2002	595,000	412	5,009	71	644,400	33,800	3,664,800	421,983	5,365,475	8.48
26 Jun	2002	610,700	395	7,620	74	634,100	28,000	3,725,700	515,819	5,522,408	7.47
25 Sep	2002	615,800	380	7,209	75	598,500	59,300	3,804,400	586,222	5,671,886	7.75
25 Dec	2002	630,300	367	4,662	139	676,800	32,100	3,868,600	598,142	5,811,110	8.83
26 Mar	2003	638,900	373	5,927	162	633,600	10,300	3,919,400	556,638	5,765,300	10.46
25 Jun	2003	647,600	365	5,306	404	660,900	36,100	3,989,200	618,923	5,958,798	10.12
24 Sep	2003	651,000	341	6,837	82	646,700	48,700	4,063,600	574,074	5,991,334	7.28
24 Dec	2003	723,150	319	4,670	128	4,690,954	38,400		572,530	6,030,151	8.19

1. Used "other liabilities" from H.8 for Mar 1994 ff.
2. Treasury Demand Deposits not shown after Dec 1993 in FRB's; used US government total cash balance at commercial banks (series GDTCBW, H.6).
3. Time deposits included in demand deposits per H.8 in Dec 2003 ff.

Figure 22.3-11: Banking System Liabilities, 2002, 2003

Figure 22.3-12 shows the total money supply for this period; it is based on the M-series data published by the Federal Reserve.

U. S. Money Supply Per Federal Reserve H.6 Data, 1987-2003 (millions USD)					
1	2	3	4	5	6
Year (~30 Jun)	Currency Outside Banks	Adjusted Commercial Demand Deposits	M1 [1]	M2 [2]	M3 [3]
1987	188,400	294,300	743,800	2,773,400	3,588,000
1988	205,500	290,800	778,500	2,935,300	3,827,800
1989	218,200	276,100	772,800	3,022,600	3,987,500
1990	234,400	274,700	809,000	3,210,800	4,111,300
1991	258,500	279,700	856,700	3,349,700	4,205,200
1992	276,800	310,800	951,000	3,388,700	4,211,400
1993	306,800	358,900	1,071,800	3,439,500	4,238,400
1994	340,200	382,000	1,141,800	3,477,400	4,294,900
1995	368,200	381,800	1,141,000	3,545,500	4,510,200
1996	380,600	409,700	1,115,000	3,721,100	4,807,100
1997	408,500	396,900	1,064,800	3,899,800	5,166,800
1998	438,400	382,700	1,075,200	4,175,100	5,711,800
1999	483,200	359,100	1,098,200	4,495,400	6,219,700
2000	521,000	331,100	1,101,800	4,758,300	6,805,100
2001	549,000	314,600	1,126,300	5,160,300	7,631,700
2002	610,600	311,400	1,194,700	5,537,900	8,184,900
2003	647,600	335,100	1,284,700	5,992,300	8,792,300

1. M1 (new definition, cf. 1979): Currency outside banks, demand deposits excluding those due to foreign commercial banks and U. S. government, plus other checkable deposits, (NOW, ATS, credit union share balances, and demand deposits at thrift institutions).

2. M2 (new definition, cf. 1979): M1 plus overnight repurchase agreements and overnight Eurodollars held by non bank U. S. residents, plus money market mutual fund shares, and savings and small denomination time deposits at all institutions (formerly was commercial banks only).

3. M3 (new definition, cf. 1979): M2 plus large denomination time deposits at all depositary institutions including negotiable CD's, plus term repurchase agreements issued by commercial banks and savings and loan institutions.

Figure 22.3-12: Total Money Supply, 1987-2003

Figure 22.3-13 shows the CPI, total money supply, and per-capita money supply during this period.

Year	CPI [1] (1913 = 100)	Total Money Supply M2 [2] (USD)	Population [3]	Per Capita Money Supply (USD)	Annual Rate of Change in CPI (%)	Annual Rate of Change in Per-Capita Money Supply (%)
1987	1,147.475	2,773,400,000,000	242,060,653	11,457.46	3.585	5.333
1988	1,194.949	2,935,300,000,000	244,277,059	12,016.27	4.054	4.762
1989	1,252.525	3,022,600,000,000	246,493,466	12,262.39	4.706	2.028
1990	1,320.202	3,210,800,000,000	248,709,873	12,909.82	5.262	5.145
1991	1,375.758	3,349,700,000,000	251,981,076	13,293.46	4.122	2.928
1992	1,417.172	3,388,700,000,000	255,252,280	13,275.89	2.966	-0.132
1993	1,459.596	3,439,500,000,000	258,523,483	13,304.40	2.950	0.215
1994	1,496.970	3,477,400,000,000	261,794,686	13,282.93	2.528	-0.162
1995	1,539.394	3,545,500,000,000	265,065,890	13,375.92	2.795	0.698
1996	1,584.848	3,721,100,000,000	268,337,093	13,867.26	2.910	3.607
1997	1,621.212	3,899,800,000,000	271,608,296	14,358.18	2.269	3.479
1998	1,646.465	4,175,100,000,000	274,879,499	15,188.84	1.546	5.624
1999	1,682.828	4,495,400,000,000	278,150,703	16,161.74	2.185	6.209
2000	1,739.394	4,758,300,000,000	281,421,906	16,908.07	3.306	4.514
2001	1,788.889	5,160,300,000,000	284,154,269	18,160.21	2.806	7.144
2002	1,817.172	5,537,900,000,000	286,886,632	19,303.44	1.569	6.105
2003	1,858.586	5,992,300,000,000	289,618,996	20,690.29	2.253	6.938

1. CPI data from Bureau of Labor Statistics, series CUUR0000AA0R (urban, all commodities, not seasonally adjusted), referenced to 1913

2. See notes in money supply data for sources.

3. Population is linearly interpolated from Census results.

Figure 22.3-13: Money Supply and CPI, 1987-2003

Figure 22.3-14 shows a summary of the CPI and per-capita money supply. Three distinct intervals are evident: 1987 to 1991, 1991 to 1995, and 1995 to 2003. The average annual change in CPI and per-capita money supply for 1987 to 1991 are 4.5% and 3.7% respectively; for 1991 to 1995, 2.8% and 0.1% respectively, and for 1995 to 2003, 2.3% and 5.4% respectively. For the entire period from 1987 to 2003, the average annual growth rates of CPI and per-capita money supply are 3.0% and 3.9% respectively.

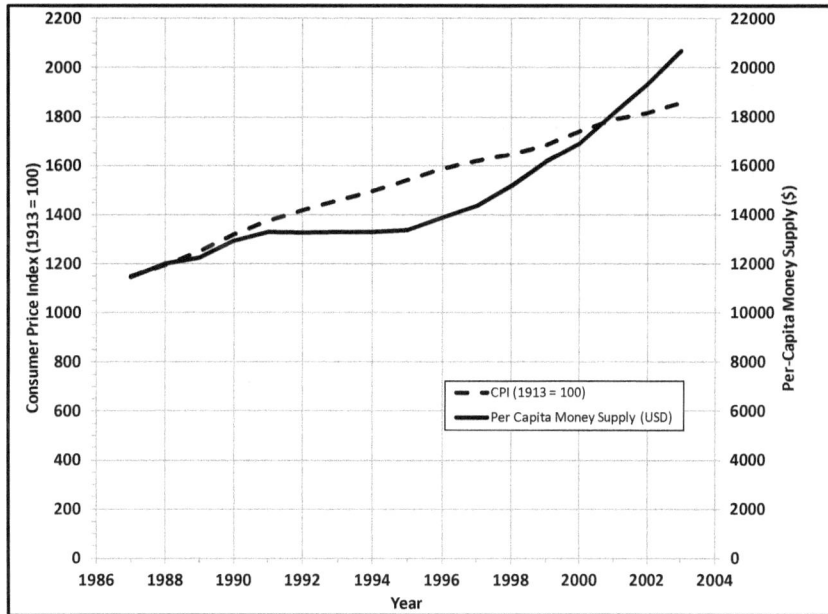

Figure 22.3-14: CPI and Per-Capita Summary, 1987-2003

Figure 22.3-15 shows the approximate median income index, consumer price index, and standard of living index for this period. See the Introduction to Part 2 for cautions regarding these curves.

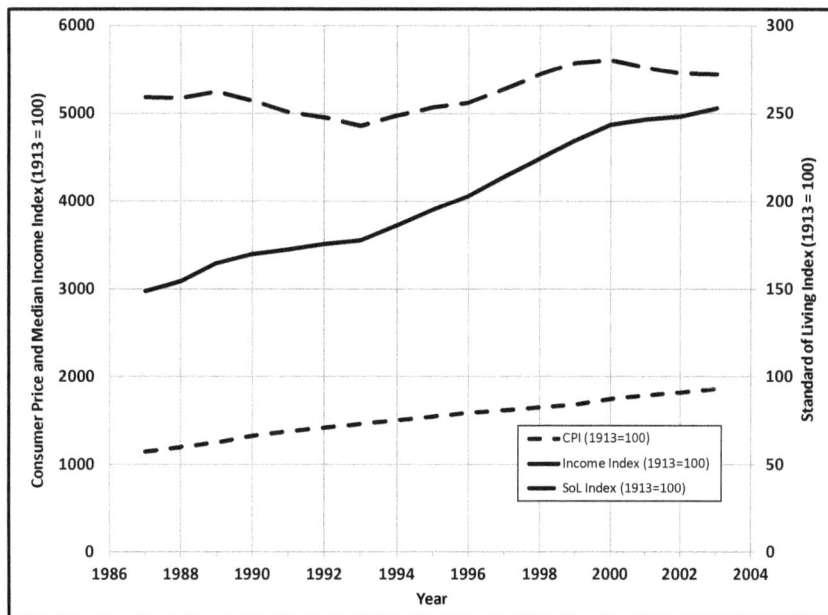

Figure 22.3-15: Median Income, Consumer Price, and Standard of Living Indices, 1987-2003

Figure 22.3-16 shows the changes in legal reserves on demand and time deposits at commercial banks during this period.

Legal Reserve Ratio Changes, 1987-2003						
		Demand Deposits				
Day	Year	Lower Threshold ($ M)	Upper Threshold ($ M)	Between Thresholds (%)	Above Upper Threshold	Savings & Time Deposits
1 Jan	1987	2.9	36.7	3	10	3.0
31 Dec	1987	3.2	40.5	3	10	3.0
29 Dec	1988	3.4	41.5	3	10	3.0
28 Dec	1989	3.4	40.4	3	10	3.0
26 Dec	1990	3.4	41.1	3	10	0.0
26 Dec	1991	3.6	42.2	3	10	0.0
24 Dec	1992	3.8	46.8	3	10	0.0
23 Dec	1993	4.0	51.9	3	10	0.0
22 Dec	1994	4.2	54.0	3	10	0.0
21 Dec	1995	4.3	52.0	3	10	0.0
31 Dec	1996	4.4	49.3	3	10	0.0
1 Jan	1998	4.7	47.8	3	10	0.0
31 Dec	1998	4.9	46.5	3	10	0.0
30 Dec	1999	5.0	44.3	3	10	0.0
28 Dec	2000	5.5	42.8	3	10	0.0
27 Dec	2001	5.7	41.3	3	10	0.0
26 Dec	2002	6.0	42.1	3	10	0.0
25 Dec	2003	6.6	45.4	3	10	0.0
1.: Joshua N. Feinman, Reserve Requirements: History, Current Practice, and Potential Reform, Federal Reserve Bulletin, June 1993, p. 569-589						
2. Federal Reserve Board, https://www.federalreserve.gov/monetarypolicy/reservereq.htm						

Figure 22.3-16: Legal Reserve Ratios, 1987-2003

Figures 22.3-17 through 22.3-20 show some miscellaneous statistics of the banking system, including the reserve ratio, and ratios of demand deposits to reserves and demand deposits to currency.

Miscellaneous Statistics of the Federal Reserve and Commercial System, 1987-1991 (millions USD)									
		Federal Reserve	At Commercial Banks						
Day	Year	Member Bank Reserves [1]	Demand Deposits	Time Deposits	Total Deposits	Reserve Ratio, Demand Deposits	Reserve Ratio, Total Deposits	Currency Outside Banks	Ratio, Demand Deposits to Reserves	Ratio, Demand Deposits to Currency
25 Mar	1987	56,839	568,800	1,330,900	1,899,700	0.100	0.030	186,000	10.007	3.058
24 Jun	1987	58,547	578,300	1,345,500	1,923,800	0.101	0.030	191,900	9.878	3.014
30 Sep	1987	60,093	610,700	1,357,700	1,968,400	0.098	0.031	194,300	10.163	3.143
30 Dec	1987	62,208	623,200	1,389,000	2,012,200	0.100	0.031	199,400	10.018	3.125
30 Mar	1988	60,529	587,600	1,416,400	2,004,000	0.103	0.030	199,200	9.708	2.950
29 Jun	1988	61,765	602,300	1,436,100	2,038,400	0.103	0.030	205,800	9.751	2.927
28 Sep	1988	61,583	588,300	1,470,500	2,058,800	0.105	0.030	207,900	9.553	2.830
28 Dec	1988	63,552	641,300	1,500,300	2,141,600	0.099	0.030	214,800	10.091	2.986
29 Mar	1989	60,167	582,000	1,538,100	2,120,100	0.103	0.028	213,900	9.673	2.721
28 Jun	1989	59,103	580,500	1,551,600	2,132,100	0.102	0.028	218,500	9.822	2.657
27 Sep	1989	59,333	588,500	1,586,800	2,175,300	0.101	0.027	218,600	9.919	2.692
27 Dec	1989	62,920	643,300	1,621,800	2,265,100	0.098	0.028	225,300	10.224	2.855
28 Mar	1990	60,695	593,900	1,652,700	2,246,600	0.102	0.027	227,000	9.785	2.616
27 Jun	1990	61,074	598,500	1,675,400	2,273,900	0.102	0.027	234,700	9.800	2.550
26 Sep	1990	60,887	596,300	1,701,800	2,298,100	0.102	0.026	240,800	9.794	2.476
26 Dec	1990	58,038	638,100	1,721,200	2,359,300	0.091	0.025	249,400	10.995	2.559
27 Mar	1991	48,907	602,800	1,779,700	2,382,500	0.081	0.021	255,600	12.325	2.358
26 Jun	1991	50,387	611,200	1,794,900	2,406,100	0.082	0.021	259,100	12.130	2.359
25 Sep	1991	50,177	613,700	1,816,600	2,430,300	0.082	0.021	261,800	12.231	2.344
25 Dec	1991	55,705	682,300	1,808,400	2,490,700	0.082	0.022	270,000	12.248	2.527
1. Member bank reserves is the sum of reserve deposits at Federal Reserve Banks and applied vault cash per H.3.									
2. See Appendix B for references.									

Figure 22.3-17: Miscellaneous Statistics of the Banking System, 1987-1991

		Federal Reserve	At Commercial Banks							
		Member Bank Reserves [1]	Demand Deposits	Time Deposits	Total Deposits	Reserve Ratio, Demand Deposits	Reserve Ratio, Total Deposits	Currency Outside Banks	Ratio, Demand Deposits to Reserves	Ratio, Demand Deposits to Currency
Day	Year									
25 Mar	1992	56,399	663,600	1,690,300	2,353,900	0.085	0.024	271,100	11.766	2.448
24 Jun	1992	49,707	665,700	1,674,000	2,339,700	0.075	0.021	277,300	13.392	2.401
30 Sep	1992	51,420	727,700	1,760,500	2,488,200	0.071	0.021	284,700	14.152	2.556
30 Dec	1992	57,706	799,332	1,742,304	2,541,636	0.072	0.023	295,100	13.852	2.709
31 Mar	1993	53,850	757,336	1,734,250	2,491,586	0.071	0.022	297,900	14.064	2.542
30 Jun	1993	57,526	795,187	1,712,222	2,507,409	0.072	0.023	307,500	13.823	2.586
29 Sep	1993	58,597	791,887	1,699,674	2,491,561	0.074	0.024	314,800	13.514	2.516
29 Dec	1993	63,637	852,224	1,698,656	2,550,880	0.075	0.025	324,900	13.392	2.623
30 Mar	1994	58,859	801,600	1,701,700	2,503,300	0.073	0.024	330,700	13.619	2.424
29 Jun	1994	59,826	791,900	1,688,900	2,480,800	0.076	0.024	340,600	13.237	2.325
28 Sep	1994	59,327	782,200	1,710,300	2,492,500	0.076	0.024	347,100	13.185	2.254
28 Dec	1994	61,624	846,100	1,728,600	2,574,700	0.073	0.024	357,700	13.730	2.365
29 Mar	1995	57,137	765,200	1,756,700	2,521,900	0.075	0.023	361,400	13.392	2.117
28 Jun	1995	56,460	764,300	1,795,200	2,559,500	0.074	0.022	368,100	13.537	2.076
27 Sep	1995	56,753	780,400	1,853,600	2,634,000	0.073	0.022	369,200	13.751	2.114
27 Dec	1995	58,881	815,000	1,864,900	2,679,900	0.072	0.022	376,000	13.841	2.168
27 Mar	1996	54,506	743,200	1,929,600	2,672,800	0.073	0.020	374,200	13.635	1.986
26 Jun	1996	53,491	729,800	1,955,200	2,685,000	0.073	0.020	380,500	13.643	1.918
25 Sep	1996	50,819	704,800	2,018,400	2,723,200	0.072	0.019	386,800	13.869	1.822
25 Dec	1996	52,092	764,600	2,151,000	2,915,600	0.068	0.018	397,900	14.678	1.922

Miscellaneous Statistics of the Federal Reserve and Commercial System, 1992-1996 (millions USD)

1. Member bank reserves is the sum of reserve deposits at Federal Reserve Banks and applied vault cash per H.3.
2. See Appendix B for references.

Figure 22.3-18: Miscellaneous Statistics of the Banking System, 1992-1996

		Federal Reserve	At Commercial Banks							
		Member Bank Reserves [1]	Demand Deposits	Time Deposits	Total Deposits	Reserve Ratio, Demand Deposits	Reserve Ratio, Total Deposits	Currency Outside Banks	Ratio, Demand Deposits to Reserves	Ratio, Demand Deposits to Currency
Day	Year									
26 Mar	1997	46,991	681,400	2,192,300	2,873,700	0.069	0.016	401,000	14.501	1.699
25 Jun	1997	46,751	675,800	2,261,100	2,936,900	0.069	0.016	408,400	14.455	1.655
24 Sep	1997	45,355	657,500	2,325,800	2,983,300	0.069	0.015	414,300	14.497	1.587
31 Dec	1997	49,356	768,000	2,408,200	3,176,200	0.064	0.016	429,000	15.560	1.790
25 Mar	1998	45,121	670,300	2,483,300	3,153,600	0.067	0.014	431,500	14.856	1.553
24 Jun	1998	45,026	655,300	2,509,400	3,164,700	0.069	0.014	438,300	14.554	1.495
30 Sep	1998	44,503	708,400	2,559,400	3,267,800	0.063	0.014	448,200	15.918	1.581
30 Dec	1998	46,126	746,600	2,619,700	3,366,300	0.062	0.014	464,100	16.186	1.609
31 Mar	1999	43,435	702,500	2,677,200	3,379,700	0.062	0.013	471,300	16.174	1.491
30 Jun	1999	42,282	695,400	2,696,000	3,391,400	0.061	0.012	483,200	16.447	1.439
29 Sep	1999	41,030	637,400	2,744,300	3,381,700	0.064	0.012	493,400	15.535	1.292
29 Dec	1999	42,230	691,800	2,869,900	3,561,700	0.061	0.012	523,100	16.382	1.323
29 Mar	2000	40,519	630,500	2,936,500	3,567,000	0.064	0.011	517,000	15.561	1.220
28 Jun	2000	39,925	625,800	3,001,700	3,627,500	0.064	0.011	521,200	15.674	1.201
27 Sep	2000	40,073	602,700	3,107,900	3,710,600	0.066	0.011	522,400	15.040	1.154
27 Dec	2000	39,455	671,100	3,238,200	3,909,300	0.059	0.010	535,800	17.009	1.253
28 Mar	2001	38,657	622,800	3,309,300	3,932,100	0.062	0.010	539,100	16.111	1.155
27 Jun	2001	38,974	616,600	3,359,400	3,976,000	0.063	0.010	549,100	15.821	1.123
26 Sep	2001	42,776	646,700	3,444,300	4,091,000	0.066	0.010	566,000	15.118	1.143
26 Dec	2001	42,000	695,600	3,563,600	4,259,200	0.060	0.010	585,600	16.562	1.188

Miscellaneous Statistics of the Federal Reserve and Commercial System, 1997-2001 (millions USD)

1. Member bank reserves is the sum of reserve deposits at Federal Reserve Banks and applied vault cash per H.3.
2. See Appendix B for references.

Figure 22.3-19: Miscellaneous Statistics of the Banking System, 1997-2001

		Federal Reserve	At Commercial Banks							
		Member Bank Reserves [1]	Demand Deposits	Time Deposits	Total Deposits	Reserve Ratio, Demand Deposits	Reserve Ratio, Total Deposits	Currency Outside Banks	Ratio, Demand Deposits to Reserves	Ratio, Demand Deposits to Currency
Day	Year									
27 Mar	2002	40,974	644,400	3,664,800	4,309,200	0.064	0.010	595,000	15.727	1.083
26 Jun	2002	39,451	634,100	3,725,700	4,359,800	0.062	0.009	610,700	16.073	1.038
25 Sep	2002	41,426	598,500	3,804,400	4,402,900	0.069	0.009	615,800	14.447	0.972
25 Dec	2002	40,785	676,800	3,868,600	4,545,400	0.060	0.009	630,300	16.594	1.074
26 Mar	2003	41,663	633,600	3,919,400	4,553,000	0.066	0.009	638,900	15.208	0.992
25 Jun	2003	42,573	660,900	3,989,200	4,650,100	0.064	0.009	647,600	15.524	1.021
24 Sep	2003	46,133	646,700	4,063,600	4,710,300	0.071	0.010	651,000	14.018	0.993
24 Dec	2003	42,635	4,690,954		4,690,954	0.009	0.009	723,150	110.026	6.487

Miscellaneous Statistics of the Federal Reserve and Commercial System, 2002-2003 (millions USD)

1. Member bank reserves is the sum of reserve deposits at Federal Reserve Banks and applied vault cash per H.3.
2. See Appendix B for references.
3. Time deposits included in demand deposits per H.8 in Dec 2003 ff.

Figure 22.3-20: Miscellaneous Statistics of the Banking System, 2002, 2003

Figures 22.3-21 and 22.3-22 show the approximate monthly average commercial bank prime interest rates and the Federal Funds Rates.

Year	Jan	Feb	Mar	Apr	May	Jun	Jul	Aug	Sep	Oct	Nov	Dec
1987	7.50	7.50	7.50	7.75	8.14	8.25	8.25	8.25	8.70	9.07	8.78	8.75
1988	8.75	8.51	8.50	8.50	8.84	9.00	9.29	9.84	10.00	10.00	10.05	10.50
1989	10.50	10.93	11.50	11.50	11.50	11.07	10.98	10.50	10.50	10.50	10.50	10.50
1990	10.11	10.00	10.00	10.00	10.00	10.00	10.00	10.00	10.00	10.00	10.00	10.00
1991	9.52	9.05	9.00	9.00	8.50	8.50	8.50	8.50	8.20	8.00	7.58	7.21
1992	6.50	6.50	6.50	6.50	6.50	6.50	6.02	6.00	6.00	6.00	6.00	6.00
1993	6.00	6.00	6.00	6.00	6.00	6.00	6.00	6.00	6.00	6.00	6.00	6.00
1994	6.00	6.00	6.06	6.45	6.99	7.25	7.25	7.51	7.75	7.75	8.15	8.50
1995	8.50	9.00	9.00	9.00	9.00	9.00	8.80	8.75	8.75	8.75	8.75	8.65
1996	8.50	8.25	8.25	8.25	8.25	8.25	8.25	8.25	8.25	8.25	8.25	8.25
1997	8.25	8.25	8.30	8.50	8.50	8.50	8.50	8.50	8.50	8.50	8.50	8.50
1998	8.50	8.50	8.50	8.50	8.50	8.50	8.50	8.50	8.49	8.12	7.89	7.75
1999	7.75	7.75	7.75	7.75	7.75	7.75	8.00	8.06	8.25	8.25	8.37	8.50
2000	8.50	8.73	8.83	9.00	9.24	9.50	9.50	9.50	9.50	9.50	9.50	9.50
2001	9.05	8.50	8.32	7.80	7.24	6.98	6.75	6.67	6.28	5.53	5.10	4.84
2002	4.75	4.75	4.75	4.75	4.75	4.75	4.75	4.75	4.75	4.75	4.35	4.25
2003	4.25	4.25	4.25	4.25	4.25	4.22	4.00	4.00	4.00	4.00	4.00	4.00

Approximate Monthly Average Bank Prime Rate (%) [1]

1. Source: Board of Governors of the Federal Reserve System, Bank Prime Loan Rate [MPRIME], Federal Reserve Bank of St. Louis; series MPRIME (https://fred.stlouisfed.org/series/MPRIME). These are averages of daily figures, not seasonally adjusted. The data is listed as "observation dates" on the first of the month; it is assumed they apply for the entire month, since the Federal Reserve cites them as monthly averages.

Figure 22.3-21: Monthly Average Bank Prime Rates, 1987-2003

Approximate Monthly Average Federal Funds Rate (%) [1]											
Year	Jan	Feb	Mar	Apr	May	Jun	Jul	Aug	Sep	Oct	Nov	Dec
1987	6.43	6.10	6.13	6.37	6.85	6.73	6.58	6.73	7.22	7.29	6.69	6.77
1988	6.83	6.58	6.58	6.87	7.09	7.51	7.75	8.01	8.19	8.30	8.35	8.76
1989	9.12	9.36	9.85	9.84	9.81	9.53	9.24	8.99	9.02	8.84	8.55	8.45
1990	8.23	8.24	8.28	8.26	8.18	8.29	8.15	8.13	8.20	8.11	7.81	7.31
1991	6.91	6.25	6.12	5.91	5.78	5.90	5.82	5.66	5.45	5.21	4.81	4.43
1992	4.03	4.06	3.98	3.73	3.82	3.76	3.25	3.30	3.22	3.10	3.09	2.92
1993	3.02	3.03	3.07	2.96	3.00	3.04	3.06	3.03	3.09	2.99	3.02	2.96
1994	3.05	3.25	3.34	3.56	4.01	4.25	4.26	4.47	4.73	4.76	5.29	5.45
1995	5.53	5.92	5.98	6.05	6.01	6.00	5.85	5.74	5.80	5.76	5.80	5.60
1996	5.56	5.22	5.31	5.22	5.24	5.27	5.40	5.22	5.30	5.24	5.31	5.29
1997	5.25	5.19	5.39	5.51	5.50	5.56	5.52	5.54	5.54	5.50	5.52	5.50
1998	5.56	5.51	5.49	5.45	5.49	5.56	5.54	5.55	5.51	5.07	4.83	4.68
1999	4.63	4.76	4.81	4.74	4.74	4.76	4.99	5.07	5.22	5.20	5.42	5.30
2000	5.45	5.73	5.85	6.02	6.27	6.53	6.54	6.50	6.52	6.51	6.51	6.40
2001	5.98	5.49	5.31	4.80	4.21	3.97	3.77	3.65	3.07	2.49	2.09	1.82
2002	1.73	1.74	1.73	1.75	1.75	1.75	1.73	1.74	1.75	1.75	1.34	1.24
2003	1.24	1.26	1.25	1.26	1.26	1.22	1.01	1.03	1.01	1.01	1.00	0.98

1. Source: Board of Governors of the Federal Reserve System, Federal Funds Effective Rate, Federal Reserve Bank of St. Louis, series = FEDFUNDS; https://fred.stlouisfed.org/series/FEDFUNDS. They are cited as "observed dates" always on the first of the month; it is assumed they apply as averages to the entire month, since the Federal Reserve cites them as "averages of daily figures".

Figure 22.3-22: Monthly Average Federal Funds Rates, 1987-2003

22.4 Summary, 1987-2003

The growth of CPI and money supply was fairly stable during this period, and the CPI tracked the per-capita money supply fairly closely as shown on Figure 22.3-14. There was some growth in the money supply between 2001 and 2003, mostly due to an increase in federal spending to fight the wars in Iraq and Afghanistan (cf. Figure 22.3-2).

The per-capita national debt continued to increase steadily from about $9,700 in 1987 to about $23,400 in 2003. Referring back to Figure I2-9 in the Introduction to Part 2, the median annual family income in 1987 was about $31,000 and in 2003 was about $52,600. If so, the per-capita debt was about 31% of family median income in 1987, and rose to about 44% in 2003. Referring back to Figure 21.3-3, the per-capita debt in 1975 was about $2,500 and the median family income per Figure I2-9 was about $13,700. Thus the ratio of per-capita debt to family median income was only 18% as recently as 1975. The debt continued to grow since the federal government cannot control its spending. But it will get much worse in the period from 2004 to 2020, as will be shown in the next chapter.

This period saw the colossal failure of public policy regarding the banking system culminating in the savings and loan fiasco from 1987 to 1995. That was bad enough, and you would think adequate safeguards would be in place by now, but no -- the banking system, encouraged by public policy and government intervention, was already at work setting up the U. S. economy for an even larger disaster, namely the housing collapse of 2007-2009.

The exportation of the industrial base to China was only in its infancy during this period; it will accelerate through the final period, as will be shown in chapter 23.

References

[22.1-1]   Alane Moysich, *The Savings and Loan Crisis and Its Relationship to Banking*, Chapter 4 in: Federal Deposit Insurance Corporation (FDIC), *History of the Eighties: Lessons for the Future, Vol. 1, An Examination of the Banking Crises of the 1980s and Early 1990s*, Washington, DC, 1997.

[22.2-1]   Text of "An Act to regulate nonbank banks, impose a moratorium on certain securities and insurance activities by banks, recapitalize the Federal Savings and Loan Insurance Corporation, allow emergency interstate bank acquisitions, streamline credit union operations, regulate consumer checkholds, and for other purposes", a.k.a. the Competitive Equality Banking Act of 1987, 100th Congress, Public Law 100-86, 10 Aug 1987

[22.2-2] Federal Deposit Insurance Corporation, Division of Research and Statistics, *A Brief History of Deposit Insurance in the United States*, Sep 1998, p. 66

[22.2-3] op. cit., Alane Moysich, p. 169

[22.2-4] Text of "An Act to implement the United-States-Canada Free Trade Agreement", 100th Congress, Public Law 100-449, 28 Sep 1988

[22.2-5] Federal Deposit Insurance Corporation, Division of Research and Statistics, *A Brief History of Deposit Insurance in the United States*, Sep 1998, p. 66

[22.2-6] op. cit., Moysich, p. 169

[22.2-7] Text of "An Act to reform, recapitalize, and consolidate the Federal deposit insurance system, to enhance the regulatory and enforcement powers of Federal financial institutions regulatory agencies, and for other purposes", a.k.a. the Financial Institutions Reform, Recovery, and Enforcement Act of 1989, 101st Congress, Public Law 101-73, 9 Aug 1989

[22.2-8] https://en.wikipedia.org/wiki/Resolution_Trust_Corporation

[22.2-9] https://www.cbo.gov/publication/56910

[22.2-10] Jelena McWilliams, *Federal Deposit Insurance Corporation 2020 Annual Report*, 18 Feb 2021, pp. 145, 146

[22.2-11] Sheila C. Bair, *Federal Deposit Insurance Corporation 2010 Annual Report*, 31 Mar 2011, p. 139

[22.2-12] National Bureau of Economic Research (NBER), Cambridge, MA (see website below)

[22.2-13] op. cit., McWilliams, pp. 145, 146

[22.2-14] op. cit., Bair, p. 139

[22.2-15] Text of "Joint Resolution to authorize the use of United States Armed Forces pursuant to United Nations Security Council Resolution 678", Public Law 102-1, 14 Jan 1991

[22.2-16] op. cit., National Bureau of Economic Research

[22.2-17] Text of "An Act to provide funding for the resolution of failed savings associations and working capital for the Resolution Trust Corporation, to restructure the Oversight Board and the Resolution Trust Corporation, and for other purposes", a.k.a. the Resolution Trust Corporation Refinancing, Restructuring, and Improvement Act of 1991, 102nd Congress, Public Law 102-233, 12 Dec 1991

[22.2-18] Text of "An Act to require the least-cost resolution of insured depository institutions, to improve supervision and examinations, to provide additional resources to the Bank Insurance Fund, and for other purposes", a.k.a. the Federal Deposit Insurance Corporation Improvement Act of 1991, 102nd Congress, Public Law 102-242, 19 Dec 1991

[22.2-19] op. cit., McWilliams, pp. 145, 146

[22.2-20] op. cit., Bair, p. 139

[22.2-21] Text of "An Act to amend and extend certain laws relating to housing and community development, and for other purposes", a.k.a. the Housing and Community Development Act of 1992, 102nd Congress, Public Law 102-550, 28 Oct 1992

[22.2-22] Financial Crisis Inquiry Commission (Phil Angelides, Chairman), *The Financial Crisis Inquiry Report*, NY: Public Affairs, 2011, pp. 425, 444

[22.2-23] op. cit., McWilliams, pp. 145, 146

[22.2-24] op. cit., Bair, p. 139

[22.2-25] Charles A. Bowsher, Comptroller General of the United States, *Testimony before the House Committee on Banking, Finance, and Urban Affairs, on the Resolution Trust Corporation, Funding, Organization, and Performance*, 18 Mar 1993, GAO/T-GGD-93-13, pp. 4, 10-12

[22.2-26] op. cit., Bowsher, GAO/T-GGD-93-13, p. 4

[22.2-27] Text of "An Act to provide for the remaining funds needed to assure that the United States fulfills its obligation for the protection of depositors at savings and loan institutions, to improve the management of the Resolution Trust Corporation ("RTC") in order to assure taxpayers the fairest and most efficient disposition of savings and loan assets, to provide for a comprehensive transition plan to assure an orderly transfer of RTC resources to the Federal Deposit Insurance Corporation, to abolish the RTC, and for other purposes", a.k.a. the Resolution Trust Completion Act, 103rd Congress, Public Law 103-204, 17 Dec 1993

[22.2-28] op. cit., McWilliams, p. 145

[22.2-29] op. cit., Bair, p. 139

[22.2-30] Text of "An Act to amend the Bank Holding Company Act of 1956, the Revised Statutes of the United States, and the Federal Deposit Insurance Act to provide for interstate banking and branching", a.k.a.

the Riegle-Neal Interstate Banking and Branching Efficiency Act of 1994, 103rd Congress, Public Law 103-328, 29 Sep 1994

[22.2-31]   Bill Medley, Federal Reserve Bank of Kansas City, "Riegle-Neal Interstate Banking and Branching Efficiency Act of 1994", Sep 1994, https://www.federalreservehistory.org/essays/riegle-neal-act-of-1994

[22.2-32]   Text of "An Act to approve and implement the trade agreements concluded in the Uruguay Round of multilateral trade negotiations", 103rd Congress, Public Law 103-465, 8 Dec 1994

[22.2-33]   op. cit., McWilliams, p. 145

[22.2-34]   op. cit., Bair, p. 139

[22.2-35]   Charles A. Bowsher, Comptroller General of the United States, *Financial Audit of the Resolution Trust Corporation's 1994 and 1995 Financial Statements,* GAO/AIMD-96-123, Jul 1996, pp. 12 - 19

[22.2-36]   Text of "An Act to abolish the Interstate Commerce Commission, to amend subtitle IV of title 49, United States Code, to reform economic regulation of transportation, and for other purposes", 104th Congress, Public Law 104-88, 29 Dec 1995

[22.2-37]   op. cit., McWilliams, p. 145

[22.2-38]   op. cit., Bair, p. 139

[22.2-39]   op. cit., McWilliams, p. 145

[22.2-40]   Text of "An Act to amend Title I of the Employee Retirement Income Security Act of 1974 to encourage retirement income savings", 105th Congress, Public Law 105-92, 19 Nov 1997

[22.2-41]   Text of "An Act to reauthorize the Export-Import Bank of the United States", 105th Congress, Public Law 105-121, 26 Nov 1997

[22.2-42]   op. cit., McWilliams, p. 145

[22.2-43]   op. cit., McWilliams, p. 145

[22.2-44]   Text of "An Act to enhance competition in the financial services industry by providing a prudential framework for the affiliation of banks, securities firms, insurance companies, and other financial service providers, and for other purposes", a.k.a. Gramm-Leach-Bliley or the Financial Services Modernization Act, 106th Congress, Public Law 106-102, 12 Nov 1999

[22.2-45]   Text of "An Act to amend the Federal Reserve Act to broaden the range of discount window loans which may be used as collateral for Federal Reserve notes", 106th Congress, Public Law 106-122, 6 Dec 1999

[22.2-46]   op. cit., McWilliams, p. 145

[22.2-47]   op. cit., McWilliams, p. 145

[22.2-48]   op. cit., National Bureau of Economic Research

[22.2-49]   Text of "An Act to deter and punish terrorist acts in the United States and around the world, to enhance law enforcement investigatory tools, and for other purposes", a.k.a. the USA PATRIOT Act, 107th Congress, Public Law 107-56, 26 Oct 2001

[22.2-50]   op. cit., National Bureau of Economic Research

[22.2-51]   op. cit., McWilliams, p. 145

[22.2-52]   Text of "An Act to extend the authority of the Export-Import Bank until April 30, 2002", 107th Congress, Public Law 107-156, 31 Mar 2002

[22.2-53]   Text of "An Act to extend the authority of the Export-Import Bank until May 31, 2002", 107th Congress, Public Law 107-168, 1 May 2002

[22.2-54]   Text of "An Act to extend the authority of the Export-Import Bank until June 14, 2002", 107th Congress, Public Law 107-186, 30 May 2002

[22.2-55]   Text of "An Act to reauthorize the Export-Import Bank of the United States", 107th Congress, Public Law 107-189, 14 Jun 2002

[22.2-56]   op. cit., McWilliams, p. 145

[22.2-57]   Text of "An Act to facilitate check truncation by authorizing substitute checks, to foster innovation in the check collection system without mandating receipt of checks in electronic form, and to improve the overall efficiency of the nation's payments system, and for other purposes", 108th Congress, Public Law 108-100, 28 Oct 2003

[22.2-58]   op. cit., McWilliams, p. 145

NBER website: https://www.nber.org/research/data/us-business-cycle-expansions-and-contractions

23

Federal Reserve, Fiat System, Part 3, 2004-2020

23.1 Preview, 2004-2020

There was another change in the definitions of the money supply per the Federal Reserve H.6 data in 2006. Quoting Ben Bernanke, Chairman of the Board of Governors of the Federal Reserve [23.1-1]:

> "In 1971, M1 was currency and demand deposits at commercial banks. M2 was M1 plus commercial bank savings and small time deposits, and M3 was M2 plus deposits at mutual savings banks, savings and loans, and credit unions; data from the latter type of institution were available only monthly. M4 was M2 plus large time deposits, and M5 was M3 plus large time deposits. Changes in definitions make it difficult to track the historical development of the various monetary aggregates. Approximately, the 2006 definition of M1 is equivalent to this older definition, the 2006 definition of M2 is equivalent to the older definition of M3, and the definition of M3 at its date of last publication was equivalent to the older definition of M5. M4 and M5 were dropped in a 1980 redefinition of the monetary aggregates. See Board of Governors of the Federal Reserve System (1976), pp. 10-11 and Anderson and Kavajecz (1994)."

23.2 History, 2004-2020

4 Apr 2004: Battle of Fallujah (Iraq).

6 - 10 Apr 2004: Battle of Ramadi (Iraq).

5 - 27 Aug 2004: Battle of Najaf (Iraq).

10 - 16 Nov 2004: Battle of Mosul (Iraq).

31 Dec 2004: Four FDIC BIF/SAIF insured institutions failed in 2004, with combined net losses to the FDIC BIF and SAIF totaling $3.917 M [23.2-1].

1 Aug - 3 Aug 2005: Battle of Haditha (Iraq).

1 Sep - 18 Sep 2005: Battle of Tal Afar (Iraq).

31 Dec 2005: There were no bank or S&L failures in 2005 [23.2-2].

8 Feb 2006: Congress passed the Federal Deposit Insurance Reform Act of 2005 [23.2-3] (Title II of the Deficit Reduction Act of 2005): **a)** (Title II, S. 2102) merged the Savings Association Insurance Fund (SAIF) and the Bank Insurance Fund (BIF) into a single insurance fund, called the Depositor Insurance Fund (DIF); **b)** (Title II, S. 2103(c)) increased the amount of deposit insurance for certain retirement accounts from $100,000 to $250,000, and is to be indexed for inflation; and **c)** (Title II, S. 2103(a)) tasked the FDIC to calculate the inflation factor for standard deposit accounts, and recommend an adjustment to the standard deposit insurance level accordingly.

13 Oct 2006: Congress passed the Financial Services Regulatory Relief Act of 2006 [23.2-4]; among its provisions are: **a)** (Title II, S. 201, 203) permitted the Federal Reserve Banks to pay interest beginning 1 Oct 2011 on member bank balances held as legally-required reserves, and the rate of interest to be not more than "general level of short-term interest rates"; **b)** (Title II, S. 202) permitted the Federal Reserve to reduce reserve requirements on the first $25 M in demand deposits to between zero and 3%; **c)** (Title II, S. 202) permitted the Federal Reserve to reduce reserve requirements on demand deposits in excess of $25 M to between zero and 14%; **d)** (Title VI, S. 602) permitted FDIC-insured banks to invest in bank service companies (check clearing, interest calculations, check sorting and depositing, mailing services, miscellaneous accounting services); **e)** (Title VI, S. 605) increased the examination interval to 18 months for community banks with deposits less than $500,000,000; and **f)** (Title VI, S. 608) changed procedures of a federal savings association to become a national or State bank.

15, 16 Nov 2006: Battle of Turki (Iraq).

20 Dec 2006: Congress extended [23.2-5] the authorization for the Export-Import Bank until 31 Dec 2011.

31 Dec 2006: There were no bank or S&L failures in 2006 [23.2-6].

6 Jun - 9 Jan 2007: Battle of Haifa Street (Iraq).

15 Jun - 19 Jun 2007: Battle of Chora (Afghanistan).

7 Dec - 12 Dec 2007: Battle of Musa Qala (Afghanistan).

12 Dec 2007: The Federal Reserve Open Market Committee (FOMC) announced the formation of central bank liquidity swap lines (a.k.a. reciprocal currency arrangements) with several foreign central banks in order to provide dollar liquidity to those institutions. Quoting from the Federal Reserve [23.2-7]:

> "When a foreign central bank draws on its dollar liquidity swap line with the Federal Reserve, the foreign central bank sells a specified amount of its currency to the Federal Reserve in exchange for dollars at the prevailing market exchange rate. At the same time, the Federal Reserve and the foreign central bank enter into an agreement for a second transaction that obligates the foreign central bank to buy back its currency on a specified future date, which could be the next day or as much as three months later, at the same exchange rate used in the initial leg of the transaction. Because both legs of the transaction are conducted at the same exchange rate, the recorded value of the foreign currency amount is not affected by changes in the market exchange rate, and the Federal Reserve bears no exchange rate risk. At the conclusion of the second leg of the transaction, the foreign central bank pays interest to the Federal Reserve on the dollars drawn.

> The foreign central bank lends the dollars it obtained via the swap line to institutions in its jurisdiction. The foreign central bank is obligated to return the dollars to the Federal Reserve under the terms of the agreement; the Federal Reserve is not a counterparty to the loan extended by the foreign central bank to depository institutions. The foreign central bank therefore bears the credit risk associated with the loans that it makes to institutions in its jurisdiction."

15 Dec 2007: Approximate beginning of a recession [23.2-8]. This was the beginning of the collapse of the residential mortgage system due to investment banks and insurance companies buying and selling mortgage-backed securities they did not understand (or pretended not to understand) over the past few years (cf. 3 Oct 1984 and 28 Oct 1992).

17 - 20 Dec 2007: The Federal Reserve began the Term Auction Facility (TAF) [23.2-9] with $40,000 M ($40 B) of short-term loans to solvent depository institutions at rates below the discount rates [23.2-10]. It was devised as a way to provide additional liquidity to the banks under Section 10B of the Federal Reserve Act at rates below the standard discount rate. Banks were hesitant to borrow directly at the discount window for fear that the public would regard those institutions as unsound. The funds were actually distributed through an auction process in which banks placed bids for the loans. This policy was adopted in order to inject liquidity into banking system by permitting banks to borrow from the Federal Reserve on assets they could not readily sell (mostly securities backed by mortgages). All of the borrowing institutions were required to fully collateralize the loans. At first

the loans had terms of 28 days, and were extended to 84 days in Aug 2008. This program was continued until 8 Mar 2010.

Quoting from the Federal Reserve [23.2-11]:

"Bank funding markets, especially term funding markets (funding longer than overnight), came under severe pressure at the start of the financial crisis in 2007. Amid widespread concerns about the condition of many financial institutions, investors became very reluctant to lend, especially at maturities beyond the very shortest terms. To address these funding pressures, the Federal Reserve first took steps to increase the amount of liquidity available to financial institutions through the discount window. However, many banks were reluctant to borrow at the discount window out of fear that their borrowing would become known and would be erroneously taken as a sign of financial weakness. To meet the demands for term funding more directly, the Federal Reserve established the Term Auction Facility (TAF) in December 2007.

Under the program, the Federal Reserve auctioned 28-day loans, and, beginning in August 2008, 84-day loans, to depository institutions [commercial savings, savings and loans, and credit unions] in generally sound financial condition. The TAF enabled the Federal Reserve to provide term funds to a broader range of counterparties and against a broader range of collateral than it could through open market operations. As a result, the TAF helped promote the distribution of liquidity when unsecured bank funding markets were under stress. It also provided access to term credit without the stigma that had been associated with use of the discount window.

All depository institutions that were eligible to borrow under the Federal Reserve's primary credit program [lending to depository institutions on a very short-term basis, typically at a higher interest rate than the short-term market rate] were eligible to participate in the TAF. All U.S. depository institutions and U.S. branches and agencies of foreign institutions that maintain deposits subject to reserve requirements are eligible to borrow from the Federal Reserve's discount window. Of those institutions, primary credit, and thus also the TAF, is available only to institutions that are financially sound.

All loans extended under the TAF were fully collateralized, and the funds were allocated through an auction, in which participating depository institutions placed bids specifying an amount of funds, up to a pre-specified limit, and an interest rate that they would be willing to pay for such funds. The funds were allocated beginning with the highest interest rate offered until either all funds were allocated or all bids were satisfied. All borrowing institutions paid the same interest rate, either the rate associated with the bid that would fully subscribe the auction, or in the case that total bids were less than the amount of funds offered, the lowest rate that was bid. The TAF was created under the Federal Reserve's standard discount window lending authority granted under Section 10B of the Federal Reserve Act. The auctions were administered by the Federal Reserve Bank of New York, with loans granted through the 12 Federal Reserve Banks.

The facility was announced on December 12, 2007. The final TAF auction was held on March 8, 2010, with credit extended under that auction maturing on April 8, 2010. All loans made under the facility were repaid in full, with interest, in accordance with the terms of the facility."

31 Dec 2007: Three FDIC DIF insured institutions failed in 2007, with net losses to the FDIC DIF totaling $158.065 M [23.2-12].

13 Feb 2008: Congress passed the Economic Stimulus Act of 2008 [23.2-13]: **a)** (S. 101) provided tax credits of $600 ($1,200 for joint tax returns); **b)** (S. 102, 103) made changes to expensing depreciation and property acquisitions between 2001 and 2007; **c)** (S. 201) increased the loan limit on mortgages that can be purchased by FREDDIE MAC and FANNIE MAE up to 175% of the original loan amount; **d)** (S. 202) increased the loan limit on FHA mortgages to $125% of the median home prices in the area; and **e)** (S. 301) stated that S. 201 and 202 are intended as temporary emergency provisions.

16 Mar 2008: The Bear Stearns investment bank failed [23.2-14]. It was taken over in a cooperative venture by JPMorgan and the Federal Reserve, in which JPMorgan would invest $1,200 M ($1.2 B) and the Federal Reserve would purchase $29,970 M ($29.97 B) of Bear Stearns' assets, mostly mortgage-based securities of various types. The Federal Reserve's purchases were accomplished through a new firm called Maiden Lane LLC. This was the beginning of a string of failures due high-risk in-

vestments in sub-prime mortgages and bundling them into obscure security types that were poorly understood.

The Federal Reserve announced its actions [23.2-15]:

> "Despite the receipt by Bear Stearns of Federal Reserve funding through a bridge loan on March 14, 2008, market pressures on Bear Stearns worsened that day and during the weekend. Bear Stearns likely would have been unable to avoid bankruptcy on Monday, March 17, without either very large injections of liquidity from the Federal Reserve or an acquisition by a stronger firm. JPMorgan Chase and Co. (JPMC) emerged as the only viable bidder for Bear Stearns, and on Sunday, March 16, Bear Stearns accepted an offer to merge with JPMC.
>
> However, JPMC was concerned about its ability to absorb a portion of Bear Stearns' mortgage trading portfolio, given the uncertainty about the scale of potential losses facing the financial system at the time and strained credit markets.
>
> To facilitate a prompt acquisition of Bear Stearns by JPMC, the FRBNY [Federal Reserve Bank of New York] created a limited liability company Maiden Lane LLC, to acquire that set of assets of Bear Stearns. The FRBNY extended credit to the LLC, which would then manage those assets through time to maximize the repayment of credit extended to the LLC and to minimize disruption to financial markets. Maiden Lane LLC purchased approximately $30 billion in assets from Bear Stearns with a loan of approximately $29 billion from the FRBNY. Under the terms of the agreement, JPMC also lent roughly $1 billion to Maiden Lane in a loan that is subordinated to the loan from the FRBNY for repayment purposes. The interest rate on the loan extended by the FRBNY is the primary credit rate, and the interest rate on the subordinated loan is the primary credit rate plus 450 basis points. Payments from the proceeds from the assets held by the LLC are to be used in the following order: operating expenses of the LLC, principal due to the FRBNY, interest due to the FRBNY, principal due to JPMC, and interest due to JPMC. Any remaining funds will be paid to the FRBNY. The loan to Maiden Lane LLC was extended under the authority of Section 13(3) of the Federal Reserve Act, which permitted the Board, in unusual and exigent circumstances, to authorize Reserve Banks to extend credit to individuals, partnerships, and corporations."

6 Apr 2008: Battle of Shok Valley (Afghanistan).

18, 19 Jun 2008: Battle of Arghandab (Afghanistan).

13 Jul 2008: Battle of Wanat (Afghanistan).

30 Jul 2008: Congress passed the Housing and Economic Recovery Act of 2008 [23.2-16]. Among its provisions: **a)** (S. 1101) established a Federal Housing Finance Agency (FHFA), tasked with regulating the government sponsored enterprises (GSE) FANNIE MAE, FREDDIE MAC, the Federal Home Loan Banks, and the Office of Finance; **b)** (S. 1109) FHFA to review the portfolio of the GSE's to ensure adequate risk-based capitalization, and to monitor their transactions; **c)** (S. 1124) increased loan limits for single-family homes to $147,000; **d)** (S. 1301) abolished the Office of Federal Housing Enterprise Oversight (OFHEO); **e)** (S. 1311) abolished the Federal Housing Finance Board (FHFB); **f)** (S. 1402) established the HOPE for Homeowners program, designed to: 1) establish an FHA program (until the housing market stabilizes), to be voluntary on the part of homeowners and existing loan holders, "to insure refinanced loans for distressed borrowers", and 2) avoid foreclosure by reducing principal and interest on mortgage loans; **g)** (S. 1502 - 1505) required persons who originate mortgage loans be licensed: 1) those who work for banks must register with the National Mortgage Licensing System and Registry, and 2) those who work for non-bank institutions are to be licensed and register per State laws; **h)** (S. 2112) changed the FHA loan limit on single-family homes to the lesser of 115% of median prices and 150% of the previous statutory standard; and **i)** (S. 2502) improved mortgage loan disclosure requirements.

7 Sep 2008: Both the Federal National Mortgage Association (FANNIE MAE) and Federal Home Loan Mortgage Association (FREDDIE MAC) were placed into conservatorship by the Federal Housing Finance Agency (FHFA) [23.2-17]. These two government-sponsored enterprises (GSE) had ignored risk assessment procedures by reducing credit quality standards and had authorized many subprime mortgages (although at Congressional direction (cf. 28 Oct 1992) as part of the federal gov-

ernment's low-income housing objectives). At this time it held and guaranteed about $5,300,000 M ($5,300 T) in mortgages with only 2% capital to back it up.

15 Sep 2008: The Lehman Brothers investment bank filed for Chapter 11 bankruptcy protection, made necessary because it had invested too heavily in sub-prime mortgage-backed securities, and did not adhere to standard risk assessment procedures [23.2-18].

16 Sep 2008: A money market mutual fund called the Reserve Primary Fund experienced a run by investors and subsequently traded for less than $1.00, indicating that its investments had lost money [23.2-19]. The Federal Reserve also extended an emergency loan [23.2-20] to the American International Insurance Group (AIG) for $85,000 M ($85 B) to keep it afloat because of concerns that its failure would lead to a contagion in the financial services industry. AIG had been a major player in the sale of credit default swaps to financial firms. The concern was that if AIG failed, it could lead to large markdowns in the assets held by those firms and a chain-effect reaction among other businesses with financial connections to them.

16 Sep 2008: The Federal Reserve announced its actions regarding AIG [23.2-21], stating in part:

> "The Federal Reserve announced that it would lend to AIG to provide the company with the time and flexibility to execute a plan that would allow it to restructure to maximize its value. Initially, the Federal Reserve Bank of New York (FRBNY) extended a line of credit to AIG for up to $85 billion. The revolving credit facility was established to assist AIG in meeting its obligations as they came due and to facilitate a process under which AIG would sell certain of its businesses in an orderly manner, with the least possible disruption to the overall economy. ... In consideration for the establishment of the credit facility, the AIG Credit Facility Trust, a trust established for the sole benefit of the U.S. Department of the Treasury, received a 79.9 percent equity interest in AIG."

21 Sep 2008: The Federal Reserve agreed to recognize the investment banks Goldman Sachs and Morgan Stanley as bank holding companies to preclude their failure [23.2-22], which brought them under regular bank regulation.

25 Sep 2008: Washington Mutual, the largest Savings and Loan institution in the U. S., failed due to a run on deposits, and was placed into receivership of the FDIC by the Office of Thrift Supervision (OTS) (cf. 9 Aug 1989) [23.2-23].

3 Oct 2008: Congress passed the Emergency Economic Stabilization Act of 2008 [23.2-24] in response to the financial problems caused by the collapse of the subprime mortgage market. The idea was to provide liquidity to a large number of institutions that held securities that had fallen in value, or could not be priced and therefore could not be sold, because they consisted partly of sub-prime mortgages that were in default. Among its provisions: **a)** (Title I, S. 101) created a Troubled Asset Relief Program (TARP), and authorized the Treasury Secretary to purchase "troubled assets" from financial institutions; **b)** (Title I, S. 101) required the TARP program to be managed by the Treasury Secretary with consultation from the Federal Reserve Board, Comptroller of the Currency, FDIC, Office of Thrift Supervision, and the Secretary of Housing and Urban Development; **c)** (Title I, S. 101) authorized the Treasury Secretary, as part of the TARP program, to purchase non-voting stock in any corporations that participated in the TARP program; **d)** (Title I, S. 102) authorized the Treasury Secretary to set up an insurance program to guarantee principal and interest payments on the troubled assets, including mortgage-backed securities, in which premiums would be collected from participating corporations; **e)** (Title I, S. 104) created a Financial Stability Oversight Board (FSOB) to advise the Treasury Secretary on the management of the TARP program (consisting of Chairman of the Federal Reserve Board of Governors, Chairman of the Securities and Exchange Commission, the Secretary of Housing and Urban Development, and the director of the Federal Housing Finance Agency (FHFA); **f)** (Title I, S. 109, 110, 124) required the Treasury Secretary to develop a plan to assist homeowners behind on their mortgages and to work with mortgage underwriters to reduce foreclosures; **g)** (Title I, S. 111) provided that, if the Treasury purchased an equity stake in participating corporations, the Treasury Secretary was permitted to limit senior executive compensation if their

actions increased risk, and prohibited payment of "golden parachutes" while the Treasury held an equity stake; **h)** (Title I, S. 114) required the Treasury Secretary to publish a description, price, and amounts of assets acquired under the TARP program; **i)** (Title I, S. 115) established graduated funding up to $700,000 M ($700 B) total: 1) $250,000 M ($250 B) would become available immediately, 2) an additional $100,000 M ($100 B) could be authorized by the President, and 3) the remaining $350,000 M ($350 B) by consent of Congress; **j)** (Title I, S. 116, 121) required the Comptroller General of the United Stated and a Special Inspector General to provide general oversight and audits of the TARP program; and **k)** (Title I, S. 136) temporarily increased FDIC and credit union deposit insurance to $250,000 (to expire 31 Dec 2009).

The injection of money from the TARP program provided the bank institutions with the cash they needed to meet other obligations, and at the same time, the Treasury would receive the monthly mortgage payments from the homeowners. Eventually, the Treasury would be able to sell these securities once they could be priced. Thus the taxpayers bailed out the banks from their failure to perform accurate risk assessment, or their knowing ignorance of true contents of the "mortgage backed securities". But there was some possibility that the funds could be recovered. The institutions that were in the most trouble from these "toxic assets" were the Federal National Mortgage Association (FANNIE MAE), Federal Home Loan Mortgage Association (FREDDIE MAC), American International Insurance Group (AIG), Bank of America, Citigroup, Wells Fargo, and Bear Stearns (now JP Morgan).

6 Oct 2008: The Federal Reserve announced [23.2-25] that it will begin paying interest on depository institutions required and excess reserve accounts, as authorized by the Emergency Economic Stabilization Act of 2008 (cf. 3 Oct 2008). The interest rate on the required reserves was set at the FOMC federal funds rate less 0.0010%; the rate on excess reserves was set at the lowest federal funds rate per maintenance period less 0.0075%. This announcement also extended loans under the Term Auction Facility (TAF) (cf. 17 Dec 2007) program to 84 days.

8 Oct 2008: AIG had utilized $62,000 M ($62 B) of the revolving credit issued by the Federal Reserve [23.2-26], and had used the cash to settle with institutions that had borrowed securities from AIG. But there was some concern that the other institutions might discontinue borrowing of securities from AIG, and since the credit markets and AIG were still unstable, the Federal Reserve extended credit directly to some AIG subsidiaries in exchange for securities. The Federal Reserve began to borrow investment grade, fixed-income securities from AIG in return for cash collateral under section 13(3) of the Federal Reserve Act. This preserved AIG's cash position. This was continued until the restructuring of 10 Nov 2008, which created Maiden Lane II and III.

27 Oct 2008: The Federal Reserve announced the Commercial Paper Funding Facility (CPFF) [23.2-27], stating in part:

> "Commercial paper is a critical source of funding for many businesses. In the fall of 2008, the commercial paper market was under considerable strain as money market mutual funds and other investors--themselves often facing liquidity pressures--became increasingly reluctant to purchase commercial paper. As a result, the volume of outstanding commercial paper fell, interest rates on longer-term commercial paper increased significantly, and an increasingly high percentage of outstanding commercial paper needed to be refinanced each day. This restriction in the availability of credit made it more difficult for businesses to obtain credit during a critical period of economic stress.

> To address these strains, the Federal Reserve established the Commercial Paper Funding Facility (CPFF) to provide liquidity to U.S. issuers of commercial paper in the event that credit was not available in the market. By providing liquidity to the commercial paper market, the CPFF encouraged investors to resume lending in the market.

> Under the program, the Federal Reserve Bank of New York (FRBNY) provided three-month loans to the CPFF LLC, a specially created limited liability company (LLC) that used the funds to purchase commercial paper directly from eligible issuers. The commercial paper that was eligible for purchase was highly rated, U.S. dollar-denominated, unsecured and asset-backed commercial with a three-month maturity. To manage

its risk, the Federal Reserve required issuers whose commercial paper was purchased by the CPFF LLC to pay fees at the time of each purchase. Additionally, at the time of the initial registration, each issuer was required to pay a facility fee equal to 10 basis points of the maximum amount of commercial paper that it could issue to the CPFF LLC. A total of $849 million in fees were collected by the CPFF LLC. The FRBNY's loan to the CPFF LLC was secured by all of the LLC's assets, including its commercial paper holdings, accumulated fees, and proceeds from investments.

The CPFF was created by the Federal Reserve under the authority of Section 13(3) of the Federal Reserve Act, which permitted the Board, in unusual and exigent circumstances, to authorize Reserve Banks to extend credit to individuals, partnerships, and corporations. The facility was administered by the FRBNY.

The facility was announced on October 7, 2008, began purchases of commercial paper on October 27, 2008, and was closed on February 1, 2010. The last of the CPFF LLC's commercial paper holdings matured on April 26, 2010, and the CPFF LLC was dissolved on August 30, 2010. All loans that were made to the CPFF LLC were repaid in full, in accordance with the terms of the facility, and all of the commercial paper that the CPFF LLC purchased was repaid in accordance with the stated terms."

The loans were provided mainly to four AIG affiliates.

10 Nov 2008: The Federal Reserve provided the status of the AIG bailout [23.2-28], stating in part:

"The Federal Reserve and the Treasury announced a restructuring of the government's support for AIG to enhance AIG's ability to repay the credit extension while retaining adequate time to dispose of its assets to achieve favorable returns. As part of the restructuring, the Treasury acquired $40 billion in newly issued preferred stock in AIG, using funding from the Troubled Asset Relief Program (TARP). In addition, the maturity of the loan from the FRBNY was extended to five years, and the maximum amount of credit available under the facility was reduced from $85 billion to $60 billion."

The Maiden Lane II LLC and Maiden Lane III LLC's were created (cf. 25 Nov 2008 and 12 Dec 2008).

24 Nov 2008: Citicorp, one of the four largest banks in the U. S., had experienced heavy losses on its subprime mortgage CDO portfolio and was about to fail, although it had received $24,300 M ($24.3 B) under the TARP program. The FDIC, Treasury Department, and Federal Reserve implemented a plan to save Citicorp by investing $19,500 M ($19.5 B) directly in company stock, providing an additional $20,000 M ($20 B) from TARP, and providing guarantees for about $306,000 M ($306 B) of Citigroup's portfolio [23.2-29].

25 Nov 2008: The Federal Reserve announced the creation of the Term Asset Backed Securities Loan facility (TALF) [23.2-30]. It was administered by the Federal Reserve Bank of New York, and made loans to holders of eligible asset-backed securities to be used as collateral. The loans had terms up to five years. The eligible collateral securities included those backed by student loans, auto loans, credit card loans, and loans guaranteed by the Small Business Administration.

25 Nov 2008: Maiden Lane III had been established to purchase multi-sector collateralized debt obligations on which AIG had written credit default swaps [23.2-31]. The Federal Reserve began extending credit to Maiden Lane III using a $24,300 M ($24.3 B) senior loan with a six-year term from the Federal Reserve Bank of New York and $5,000 M ($5 B) from AIG. The assets held by Maiden Lane III, as procured from the AIG subsidiaries was collateral for the Federal Reserve loan, and is to be repaid from the sale of those assets. The authority for this transaction was permitted under section 13(3) of the Federal Reserve Act.

12 Dec 2008: Maiden Lane II had been established to purchase asset-backed securities from AIG subsidiaries [23.2-32]. The Federal Reserve began extending credit to Maiden Lane II using a $19,500 M ($19.5 B) senior loan from the Federal Reserve Bank of New York and $1,000 M ($1 B) from AIG. The assets held by Maiden Lane II, as procured from the AIG subsidiaries is collateral for the Federal Reserve loan, and was to be repaid from the sale of those assets. The agreement of 8 Oct 2008 was terminated; all securities were returned to AIG, and cash returned to the Federal Reserve. The authority for this transaction was justified under section 13(3) of the Federal Reserve Act.

31 Dec 2008: A total of 25 FDIC DIF insured institutions failed in 2008, with net losses to the FDIC DIF totaling $17,817.916 M ($17.817 B) [23.2-33].

1 Jan 2009: Merrill Lynch had incurred large losses on its portfolios of subprime mortgage-backed CDO's in the last quarter of 2008. The Bank of America had previously agreed to acquire Merrill Lynch on 14 Sep 2008, but tried to terminate the agreement on the grounds that Merrill Lynch had hidden losses. However, Merrill Lynch had in fact informed the Bank of America, and the merger went through under pressure from federal regulators [23.2-34].

15 Jan 2009: The Federal Reserve and FDIC assisted the Bank of America [23.2-35] by purchasing $20,000 M ($20 B) of company stock under the TARP program, and the Treasury Department, FDIC, and Federal Reserve agreed to share anticipated losses of up to $118,000 M ($118 B) from the Merrill Lynch portfolio assumed by Bank of America. Bank of America later terminated the agreement on the grounds it could not afford to take the first $10,000 M ($10 B) in losses under the agreement.

10 Feb 2009: The Federal Reserve announced [23.2-36] an expansion of the TALF program to $1,000,000 M ($1 T), and expanded the list of eligible asset-backed securities to include AAA-rated securities backed by commercial mortgages and private label securities backed by residential mortgages.

17 Feb 2009: Congress passed the American Recovery and Reinvestment Act of 2009 [23.2-37]. Among its provisions: **a)** (S. 5) allocated emergency appropriations to all federal departments; **b)** (S.1001) enacted a $400 individual income tax rebate ($800 if filing jointly); **c)** (S. 1011 - 1131) defined various tax incentives (alternative minimum tax, clean energy, energy conservation etc.); **d)** (S. 1201 - 1404) provided tax incentives for businesses; **e)** (S. 2001, 2005) extended unemployment insurance; **f)** (S. 2205) provided $250 economic recovery payments to certain individuals; **g)** (S. 3001) provided premium assistance for those covered under COBRA health insurance; **h)** (S. 4101) defined Medicare incentives; **i)** (S. 5000) provided compensation to States to maintain their Medicaid programs; and **j)** (S. 6000) expanded broadband technology to underserved areas. The total spending for this stimulus package was $787,000 M ($787 B), and was increased to $831,000 M ($831 B) in 2009 and 2010.

19 Mar 2009: The Federal Reserve announced [23.2-38] that the TALF program would be expanded to include as eligible collateral: a) asset backed securities backed by loans or leases for business equipment, b) leases of vehicle fleets, c) floor plan loans, and d) mortgage servicing.

15 Jun 2009: Approximate end of a recession (cf. 15 Dec 2007) [23.2-39].

12 - 15 Aug 2009: Battle of Dananeh (Afghanistan).

8 Sep 2009: Battle of Ganjal (Afghanistan).

3 Oct 2009: Battle of Kamdesh (Afghanistan).

1 Dec 2009: Two special purpose vehicles (SPV's) were created to provide $8,500 M ($8.5 B) in credit to assist AIG's foreign insurance subsidiaries [23.2-40]. AIA Aurora LLC was created to hold the outstanding common stock of the American International Assurance Company Ltd., and the ALICO Holding LLC was created for the same purpose for the American Life Insurance Company. The two LLC's were to repay the loan from the Federal Reserve from cash generated by existing life insurance policies. The Federal Reserve received preferred stock in both companies; the idea was, as separate holding companies, they would be easier to sell.

31 Dec 2009: A total of 140 FDIC DIF insured institutions failed in 2009, with net losses to the FDIC DIF totaling $25,979.466 M ($25.979 B) [23.2-41].

1 Feb 2010: The Central Bank Liquidity Swap program was terminated [23.2-42].

8 Mar 2010: The Federal Reserve held the last auction under the Term Auction Facility (TAF) program (cf. 17 Dec 2007), with the loans negotiated to mature on 8 Apr 2010 [23.2-43]. The TAF program

lent a total of $3,800,000 ($3.8 T) to 416 various institutions from 2007 to 2010. All of the loans were repaid in full.

21 Jul 2010: Congress passed the Wall Street Reform and Consumer Protection Act [23.2-44] (a.k.a. the Dodd-Frank Act) in response to the housing collapse of 2007-2008, which occurred due to lax risk assessment among certain banking institutions. Among its provisions: **a)** (Title III) abolished the Office of Thrift Supervision (OTS), and transferred its activities to the FDIC (State savings banks), the Federal Reserve (bank holding companies), or Comptroller of the Currency (other savings institutions); **b)** (Title X) created the Consumer Financial Protection Bureau (CFPB); **c)** (Title I) created two research organizations within the Treasury Department (Financial Stability Oversight Council and Office of Financial Research) to evaluate the general health of, and threats to, the financial and banking systems; **d)** (Title I) defined "systemically important institutions" that affect the overall economy, and directed the Federal Reserve to regulate them; **e)** (Title V) created the Federal Insurance Office under the Treasury Department to monitor the insurance industry; **f)** (Title II) created the Orderly Liquidation Authority to liquidate the assets of failed institutions (banks by FDIC, brokers by SEC or Federal Reserve, insurance companies by the Federal Insurance Office under Treasury); **g)** (Title VI) imposed the "Volcker Rule", prohibiting banks from investing more than 3% of capital in hedge funds or private equity institutions; **h)** (Title VII) required credit-default swaps to be cleared through clearinghouses or exchanges instead of over the counter, regulated various types of swaps, and prohibited swaps from being considered as "insurance" under State laws; **i)** (Title IX) changed some rules for credit-reporting agencies; **j)** (Title IX) established rules on executive compensation; **k)** (Title XIV) established "Ability to Repay" assessment requirements on residential mortgage lenders, and included limits on points and fees; **l)** (Title IV) required all investment advisors to be registered with the SEC while permitting advisors managing less than $100 M to be regulated by the States (if doing business in 15 States or less); **m)** (Title XI) required the Federal Reserve to establish emergency lending procedures to at-risk (but not insolvent) institutions; **n)** (Title III, S. 335) increased the amount of deposits insured by the FDIC and National Credit Union Insurance Fund from $100,000 to $250,000 (made permanent the temporary provision of 3 Oct 2008); **o)** (Title IV) required the SEC to establish standards for "fiduciary duty" designation of brokers and dealers; **p)** (Title IX) required issuers of asset-backed securities retain an economic interest therein through a minimum 5% risk retention on those securities (including collateralized mortgage, debt, and bond obligations (CMO, CDO, CBO) as well as "doubled" securities (collateralized debt obligations of asset-backed securities and CDO's of CDO's)); **q)** (Title XI) required the Federal Reserve to establish standards for financial institution regulation (liquidity, overall risk management, capital position); **r)** (Title XIII) reduced the amount allocated to the Troubled Asset Relief Program (TARP) (cf. 3 Oct 2008) from $700,000 M ($700 B) to $475,000 M ($475 B), with a prohibition on program expansion; **s)** (Title VII) prohibited federal assistance to any entity engaged in swap transactions, except it does permit assistance to insured depositary institutions (FDIC-insured institutions); **t)** (Title III) required the FDIC to take steps as necessary to bring the Deposit Insurance Fund to 1.35% of insured deposits by 30 Sep 2020; **u)** (Title VI) established rules for conflicts of interest on transactions between banks and equity funds or hedge funds; and **v)** (Title VI, S. 627) modified the Federal Reserve Act section 19 to authorize payment of interest on demand deposit accounts (which would repeal Regulation Q).

The Financial Stability Oversight Council was given authority (Title I, section 121, Title VIII, sections 804 to 808) to place bank or non-bank financial institutions or subsidiaries foreign banks under Federal Reserve supervision if they are believed to be a threat to the stability of the U. S. financial system. This regulation is applicable to bank institutions holding more than $50,000 M ($50 B) in assets. The first four options if an institution is designated to be a "grave threat to the financial stability of the United States" are: a) limit the ability of the company to merge with, acquire, consolidate with, or otherwise become affiliated with another company; b) restrict the ability of the company to offer a financial product or products; c) require the company to terminate one or more activities; and d) impose conditions on the manner in which the company conducts one or more activities. If those do not reduce risk sufficiently, then the Federal Reserve can require the company to sell or otherwise transfer assets or off-balance-sheet items to unaffiliated entities. For non-bank financial institutions, the Financial Stability Oversight Council has authority (Title VIII, section 804) to act if the institution is a threat to the financial stability of the U. S.

Two of the stated goals of the Wall Street Reform Act were to prevent banks from becoming "too big to fail" and end the bailouts of the banking system. Those are patently false, since the entire financial industry is now part of the protected political class. The reason is simple: the financial system is based on debt, and the expansion of the debt is the means by which the political class maintains power. Therefore, the political class must protect the financial industry in order to ensure its own viability.

22 Jul 2010: Congress passed the Unemployment Compensation Extension Act of 2010 [23.2-45], extending unemployment benefits until 1 Dec 2010 due to the continuing economic problems (although technically the U. S. was not in a recession at this time).

10 - 13 Sep 2010: Battle of the Palm Grove (Iraq).

17 Dec 2010: Congress passed the Tax Relief, Unemployment Insurance Reauthorization, and Job Creation Act of 2010 [23.2-46]. Among its provisions: **a)** (S. 101-103) extended tax relief granted previously in 2001, 2003, and 2009 until 31 Dec 2012; **b)** (S. 201, 202) extended the alternative minimum tax relief until 2011; **c)** (S. 301-304) extended estate tax relief for all years after 2009; **d)** (S. 401, 402) extended investment incentives until 2013; **e)** (S. 505-505) extended unemployment insurance payments until Dec 2012; and **f)** (S. 501-802) contained miscellaneous tax provisions.

31 Dec 2010: A total of 157 FDIC DIF insured institutions failed in 2010, with net losses to the FDIC DIF totaling $15,810.522 M ($15.810 B) [23.2-47].

21 Jul 2011: Regulation Q (originally section 19(i) of the Federal Reserve Act) was terminated as authorized by section 627 the Wall Street Reform Act (cf. 21 Jul 2010) [23.2-48].

31 Dec 2011: A total of 92 FDIC DIF insured institutions failed in 2011, with net losses to the FDIC DIF totaling $6,411.680 M ($6.411 B) [23.2-49].

3 Jan 2012: Congress directed [23.2-50] the FDIC to conduct a study on the impact of the failure of insured financial institutions.

22 Feb 2012: Congress passed the Middle Class Tax Relief and Job Creation Act of 2012 [23.2-51], which extended some unemployment insurance payments and made some changes to Medicare, federal employee retirement, and auction procedures for the electromagnetic spectrum.

30 May 2012: Congress extended [23.2-52] the authorization for the Export-Import Bank until 30 Sep 2014.

13 Dec 2012: The Central Bank Liquidity Swap program (cf. 12 Dec 2007) was restarted per an agreement between the Federal Reserve and the Bank of Canada, the Bank of England, the European Central Bank, and the Swiss National Bank [23.2-53].

31 Dec 2012: A total of 51 FDIC DIF insured institutions failed in 2012, with net losses to the FDIC DIF totaling $2,391.530 M ($2.391 B) [23.2-54].

2 Jan 2013: Congress passed the American Taxpayer Relief Act of 2012 [23.2-55]. Among its provisions: **a)** (S. 101 - 103) made permanent the tax reductions enacted in 2001 and 2003, and extended the tax reductions made in 2009 until 2018; **b)** (S. 104) made permanent the reductions in the alternative minimum tax enacted previously; **c)** (S. 201 - 209) extended miscellaneous individual tax deductions to 2013 or 2014; **d)** (S. 301 - 331) extended various business tax deductions to 2013 or 2014; **e)** (S. 401 - 412) extended various clean energy tax deductions and incentives to 2013; **f)** (S. 501 - 504) extended unemployment benefits to 30 Jun 2014; and **g)** (S. 601 - 644) extended various tax deductions and incentives for Medicare and other health services.

31 Dec 2013: A total of 24 FDIC DIF insured institutions failed in 2013, with net losses to the FDIC DIF totaling $1,212.465 M ($1.212 B) [23.2-56].

19 Sep 2014: Congress, as part of a funding bill, [23.2-57], re-authorized (per. S. 147) the Export-Import Bank until 30 Jun 2015.

31 Dec 2014: A total of 18 FDIC DIF insured institutions failed in 2014, with net losses to the FDIC DIF totaling $378.283 M [23.2-58].

4 Dec 2015: Congress passed the FAST Act [23.2-59], a highway and railroad funding bill that included some banking legislation: **a)** (S. 32202) limited the surplus funds in a Federal Reserve Bank to $10,000 M ($10 B), and any surplus over that to be transferred to the Board of Governors to be forwarded to the U. S. Treasury; **b)** (S. 32203) modified the dividend payments to stockholders in Federal Reserve banks: 1) for banks with assets over $10,000 M ($10 B), the smaller of 6% or rate equal to the high yield of the 10-year Treasury note at the most recent auction; 2) for banks with assets less than $10,000 M ($10 B) to receive 6%; **c)** (S. 54001) reauthorized the Export-Import Bank until 30 Sep 2019; and **d)** (S. 50001) authorized the Export-Import Bank to finance up to up to $135,000 M ($135 B) annually.

31 Dec 2015: A total of eight FDIC DIF insured institutions failed in 2015, with net losses to the FDIC DIF totaling $850.588 M [23.2-60].

31 Dec 2016: A total of five FDIC DIF insured institutions failed in 2016, with net losses to the FDIC DIF totaling $42.474 M [23.2-61].

31 Dec 2017: A total of eight FDIC DIF insured institutions failed in 2017, with net losses to the FDIC DIF totaling $1,107.455 M ($1.107 B) [23.2-62].

24 May 2018: Congress passed the Economic Growth, Regulatory Relief, and Consumer Protection Act [23.2-63]. It was a mostly reduction in the rules called out by Dodd-Frank (cf. 21 Jul 2010). Among its provisions are: **a)** provided certain exemptions and relaxation of the rules applicable to home mortgage lending (relaxing criteria, but requiring the lender to hold the loan for the life of the loan (was three years)); **b)** modified rules regarding the banking systems involvement in proprietary trading (a.k.a. the Volcker rule, involving trading securities held in the bank's portfolio to take advantage of price changes); **c)** increased regulation of certain large bank institutions; **d)** reduced capital requirements for certain small "community banks"; **e)** modified the "Ability to Repay" rule for credit union and bank institutions with less than $10,000 M ($10 B) in assets; **f)** expanded reporting requirements for credit reporting agencies, making allowances for victims of fraud and identity theft (modifying part of the Fair Credit Reporting Act of 1997); **g)** changed the criteria by which bank institutions constitute "global systemically important banks" and thus were subject to greater regulation (now required 5% or 6% supplementary leverage ratio (capital to assets aside from adjustment for risk)), depending on the type of institution; **h)** required the Federal Reserve to transfer $675 M from its surplus to the Treasury; and **i)** extended examination intervals for small banks from 12 to 18 months. Revised regulations for large banks include: a) banks with $250,000 M ($250 B) in assets still subject to enhanced regulation; b) those with assets between $100,000 M ($100 B) and $250,000 M ($250 B) subject only to stress tests, but the Federal Reserve may choose to apply the enhanced regulations; and c) institutions with assets between $50,000 M ($50 B) and $100,000 M ($100 B) are now exempt from enhanced regulation. The relaxation of the Volcker Rule permits proprietary trading for: a) banks with less than $10,000 M ($10 B) in assets; or b) any size bank trading an amount less than 5% of total assets.

31 Dec 2018: There were no bank failures in 2018 [23.2-64].

20 Dec 2019: Congress, under an omnibus appropriations bill [23.2-65] reauthorized (per S. 401) the Export-Import Bank until 31 Dec 2026.

31 Dec 2019: A total of four FDIC DIF insured institutions failed in 2019, with net losses to the FDIC DIF totaling $30.576 M [23.2-66].

29 Jan 2020: Congress passed legislation [23.2-67] implementing the United States-Mexico-Canada Agreement (USMCA), which replaced NAFTA.

15 Mar 2020: Approximate beginning of a recession due to the Wuhan virus, and many restrictions imposed by State governors under the guise of "public health". These restrictions were mostly in the interest of gaining power, since it divided the public into "essential" and "non-essential" workers. The directives mostly ordered "non-essential" workers to stay at home, and to work from home if possible. These were referred to as "lockdown orders", prohibiting those running small businesses from making a living ostensibly to control the spread of the Wuhan virus, but probably because small businesses cannot finance political campaigns the way large corporations can. The only States that never imposed restrictions were North Dakota, South Dakota, Iowa, Wyoming, Arkansas, and Nebraska.

17 Mar 2020: The Federal Reserve issued a press release [23.2-68] stating in part:

"The Federal Reserve Board established a Primary Dealer Credit Facility (PDCF) on March 17, 2020, to support the credit needs of American households and businesses. The facility allowed primary dealers to support smooth market functioning and facilitate the availability of credit to businesses and households. [Per a later update] The PDCF ceased extending credit on March 31, 2021".

17 Mar 2020: The Federal Reserve made an announcement on the CPFF [23.2-69], stating in part:

"The Federal Reserve Board established a Commercial Paper Funding Facility (CPFF) on March 17, 2020, to support the flow of credit to households and businesses. Commercial paper markets directly finance a wide range of economic activity, supplying credit and funding for auto loans and mortgages as well as liquidity to meet the operational needs of a range of companies. By ensuring the smooth functioning of this market, particularly in times of strain, the Federal Reserve provided credit that supported families, businesses, and jobs across the economy.

[Per a later update] The CPFF program was established by the Federal Reserve under the authority of Section 13(3) of the Federal Reserve Act, with approval of the Treasury Secretary. The CPFF ceased purchasing commercial paper on March 31, 2021."

18 Mar 2020: Congress passed the "Families First Coronavirus Response Act" [23.2-70] in response to the Wuhan pandemic. Among its provisions: **a)** (Division A, Title I) appropriated $500 M for the "Special Supplemental Nutrition Program for Women, Infants, and Children"; **b)** (Division A, Title I) appropriated $400 M for the "Commodity Assistance program" (emergency food and assistance program); **c)** (Division A, Title II) appropriated $82 M for the "Defense Health Program"; **d)** (Division A, Title III) appropriated $15 M to the Treasury Department Internal Revenue Service for "Taxpayer Services"; **e)** (Division A, Title IV) appropriated $64 M for "Indian Health Services"; **f)** (Division A, Title V) appropriated $250 M for "Aging and Disability programs"; **g)** (Division A, Title V) appropriated $1,000 M ($1 B) for "Public Health and Social Services Emergency Fund to pay claims for Wuhan virus treatment; **h)** (Division A, Title VI) appropriated $30 M for Veterans health services; **i)** (Division A, Title VI) appropriated $30 M for "Medical Community Care"; **j)** (Division B) waived regulations relating to student meals for schoolchildren and low-income unemployed adults; **k)** (Division C) expanded emergency medical leave, permitting individual payments up to $10,000; **l)** (Division D) expanded emergency unemployment insurance, appropriating $1,000 M ($1 B) therefor; **m)** (Division E) extended emergency sick leave benefits, up to $5,110 per person; **n)** (Division F) provided for government-paid testing and treatment for persons who become ill from the Wuhan virus, and allocating approximately $3,300 M ($3.3 B) to Medicaid; and **o)** enacted a tax credit provision for paid sick and family medical leave.

18 Mar 2020: The Federal Reserve issued a press release [23.2-71], stating in part:

"The Federal Reserve established the Money Market Mutual Fund Liquidity Facility, or (MMLF) to broaden its program of support for the flow of credit to households and businesses. The Federal Reserve Bank of Boston made loans available to eligible financial institutions secured by high-quality assets purchased by the financial institution from money market mutual funds. Money market funds are common investment tools for families, businesses, and a range of companies. The MMLF assisted money market funds in meeting demands for redemptions by households and other investors, enhancing overall market functioning and credit provision to the broader economy."

19 Mar 2020: Lockdown restrictions were imposed in California. The "lockdowns" divided workers into "essential" and "non-essential", which mostly meant closing down restaurants, most small businesses, and houses of worship. The lockdown provisions were similar in most States. The duration of the lockdowns also varied by State; Arizona and Florida ended it for practical purposes in May 2020 but others such as California and New York continued them throughout 2020.

20 Mar 2020: Lockdown restrictions were imposed in Nevada.

21 Mar 2020: Lockdown restrictions were imposed in Illinois and New Jersey.

22 Mar 2020: Lockdown restrictions were imposed in Louisiana and New York.

23 Mar 2020: Lockdown restrictions were imposed in Connecticut, Hawaii, Maryland, Ohio, Oregon, Massachusetts, and New Mexico. New York Governor Andrew Cuomo issued an Executive Order [3.2-72] prohibiting the use of hydroxychloroquine for the treatment of the Wuhan virus. He thus not only gave himself a medical degree, but also appointed himself personal doctor to all 20 million residents of New York State. It makes you wonder where people as incompetent as Cuomo get this level of arrogance.

24 Mar 2020: Lockdown restrictions were imposed in Delaware, Michigan, Washington, and West Virginia.

25 Mar 2020: Lockdown restrictions were imposed in Idaho, Indiana, Wisconsin, and Vermont.

26 Mar 2020: The Federal Reserve reduced reserve ratios for commercial banks to zero, which eliminated reserve requirements for all depository institutions [23.2-73]. Lockdown restrictions were imposed in Colorado and Kentucky.

27 Mar 2020: Congress passed the Coronavirus Aid, Relief, and Economic Security Act (CARES) [23.2-74] to provide financial support to individuals and businesses due to the impact of the Wuhan virus. Among its provisions: **a)** (S. 1102) created the Paycheck Protection Program, which is a loan program up to $349,000 M ($349 B) with terms up to ten years to small businesses (less than 500 employees) that will permit them to keep their employees on the payroll during the lockdowns; **b)** (S. 4003, 4027) created the Main Street Lending Program (MSLP) authorizing up to $500,000 M ($500 B) in loans to businesses, cities and States, of which $29,000 M ($29 B) was devoted to the airline industry and $17,000 M ($17 B) to businesses critical to national security; **c)** (S. 5001) authorized $150,000 M ($150 B) in loans to State, tribal, and local governments; **d)** (S. 1107) expanded lending authority to $349,000 M ($349 B) by the Small Business Administration to extend emergency loans to eligible businesses and non-profit institutions; **e)** (S. 2201) provided one-time grants to individuals totaling $300,000 M ($300 B); mostly in the form of $1,200 grants to individuals that had filed an income tax return in 2019; **f)** (S. 2104, 2107) $260,000 M ($260 B) was appropriated to increased benefits to the unemployed mostly in the form of a $600 increase in monthly benefits; **g)** (S. 3211) appropriated $1,320 M ($1.32 B) in grants to community health centers; and **h)** (S. 2202, 2203) permitted emergency withdrawals from certain retirement accounts without penalties. All total, the appropriations came to about $2,100,000 M ($2.1 T).

27 Mar 2020: Lockdown restrictions were imposed in Minnesota, New Hampshire, and Utah.

28 Mar 2020: Lockdown restrictions were imposed in Alaska, Rhode Island, and Montana.

29 Mar 2020: Lockdown restrictions were imposed in Kansas.

30 Mar 2020: Lockdown restrictions were imposed in North Carolina and Virginia.

31 Mar 2020: Lockdown restrictions were imposed in Arizona and Texas.

1 Apr 2020: Lockdown restrictions were imposed in Washington, DC.

2 Apr 2020: Lockdown restrictions were imposed in Maine, Oklahoma, Pennsylvania, and Tennessee.

3 Apr 2020: Lockdown restrictions were imposed in Florida, Georgia, and Mississippi.

4 Apr 2020: Lockdown restrictions were imposed in Alabama.

6 Apr 2020: Lockdown restrictions were imposed in Missouri.

7 Apr 2020: Lockdown restrictions were imposed in South Carolina.

9 Apr 2020: The Federal Reserve began extending loans under the Paycheck Protection Program (PPP) [23.2-75]. The Federal Reserve set up a Paycheck Protection Program Lending Facility (PPPLF) to issue credit to depository institutions that in turn issued paycheck protection loans to small businesses. The ultimate purpose of the PPP program is to allow businesses to retain their employees on the payroll during the Wuhan virus pandemic.

9 Apr 2020: The Federal Reserve announced a lending program [23.2-76] through the Federal Reserve Bank of Boston called the Main Street Lending Program, designed to provide loans to small and medium sized businesses in difficulty due to the Wuhan pandemic. These loans are intended for businesses that are either not eligible for the Paycheck Protection Program or needed additional funding after receiving PPP assistance. The Main Street LLC is an umbrella organization that manages funding for five special purpose vehicles: a) Main Street New Loan Facility (MSNLF); b) Main Street Priority Loan Facility (MSPLF); c) Main Street Expanded Loan Facility (MSELF); d) Nonprofit Organization New Loan Facility (NONLF); and e) Nonprofit Organization Expanded Loan Facility (NOELF). Loans issued under the program have a five year maturity, deferral of principal for two years, and deferral of interest for one year.

13 Apr 2020: The Federal Reserve began lending to individuals and businesses under the Term Asset Backed Securities Loan Facility 2 (TALF II) to assist with finances during the Wuhan virus pandemic. Quoting an auditor's report [23.2-77]:

> "In accordance with section 13(3) of the Federal Reserve Act and with prior approval from the Secretary of the Treasury, the Board of Governors of the Federal Reserve System authorized the Federal Reserve Bank of New York ("FRBNY") to establish the Term Asset-Backed Securities Loan Facility ("Facility") in order to support the flow of credit to consumers and businesses. TALF's purpose is to provide credit to eligible borrowers by making three-year loans ("TALF Loans" or "Loans to eligible borrowers") secured by eligible collateral, which includes asset-backed securities ("ABS") backed by student loans, auto loans, credit card loans, loans guaranteed by the Small Business Administration ("SBA"), leveraged loans, commercial mortgages, and certain other assets. The authorization to extend TALF Loans through the Facility expired on December 31, 2020.

> TALF II LLC ("TALF II") is a Delaware limited liability company ("LLC") formed in connection with the implementation of the Facility on April 13, 2020. TALF II has two members: FRBNY, which is TALF II's managing member and the U.S. Department of the Treasury ("Treasury"), which is TALF II's preferred equity member. The managing member has the exclusive rights to manage TALF II. The preferred equity member contributed capital to TALF II using funds from the Exchange Stabilization Fund under section 4027 of the Coronavirus Aid, Relief, and Economic Security Act.

> FRBNY also serves as the lender to TALF II. FRBNY extended $4.4 billion in loans to TALF II to enable TALF II to make Loans to eligible borrowers ("TALF Borrowers") during the period of June 25, 2020 to December 31, 2020. The loans made by FRBNY are with full recourse to TALF II and are secured by all the assets of TALF II. TALF II records a liability in the Statement of Financial Condition when FRBNY funds the loans. Interest on loans from FRBNY is paid on the maturity date or upon any repayment or prepayment of the loans.

> TALF Loans may be made only against eligible ABS collateral, as set forth in the Facility's terms and conditions and Master Loan and Security Agreement. As described in more detail therein, the underlying credit exposures for eligible ABS collateral must be one of the following: 1) auto loans and leases; 2) student loans; 3) credit card receivables (both consumer and corporate); 4) equipment loans; 5) floorplan loans; 6) premium finance loans for property and casualty insurance; 7) certain small business loans that are guaranteed by the Small Business Administration (SBA); 8) leveraged loans; or 9) commercial mortgages.

> TALF II's recourse against TALF Borrowers is limited to the ABS collateral securing a TALF Loan, absent breaches of representations, warranties, or covenants by a TALF Borrower. The ABS collateral pledged to

TALF II by TALF Borrowers is subject to haircuts, based on the ABS type and weighted average life. A TALF Borrower is entitled to prepay its loan, in whole or in part, without penalty. A TALF Borrower may also surrender the ABS collateral to TALF II at any time in full satisfaction of its loan.

TALF Borrowers are required to pay a non-refundable administrative fee equal to 10 basis points of the loan amount on the loan settlement date.

All available cash receipts of TALF II are used to pay its obligations as described in Note 7. Distributions of residual proceeds to the members will occur after all loans from FRBNY are repaid in full. During the life of TALF II, undistributed net residual income or loss is reported as "Undistributed net operating income" in the Statement of Changes in Members' Equity."

Note 7 (Distribution of Proceeds) reads:

"Amounts available for distribution, due to interest, fees, payments on investments and other receipts of income are applied on the dates and in the order of priority set forth in the credit agreement between TALF II and FRBNY.

At the conclusion of the Facility, when the credit agreement has been terminated and all obligations of TALF II repaid, the remaining net assets will be allocated and distributed in accordance with the limited liability company agreement of TALF II. That agreement contemplates the distribution, upon TALF II's liquidation, 1) to Treasury of the preferred equity account balance inclusive of any investment earnings accrued on those amounts, and 2) 90 percent of the remaining net assets to the preferred equity member and 10 percent of the remaining net assets to the managing member.

The following table presents the allocation of undistributed net operating income to equity members as of December 31, 2020 (in thousands):

Managing member: $1,104; Preferred equity member: $13,264; Total undistributed net operating income: $14,368."

13 Apr 2020: The Federal Reserve announced the formation of the Corporate Credit Facility LLC. Per an auditor's report [23.2-78] the facility was an umbrella corporation to manage two lending programs: a) the Primary Market Corporate Credit Facility (PMCCF), and b) the Secondary Market Corporate Credit Facility (SMCCF). The PMCCF provided loans to issuers of corporate debt to maintain liquidity through the Wuhan virus pandemic. The SMCCF was designed to issue loans to maintain liquidity for corporate debt by purchasing corporate bonds and exchange-traded funds (ETF) listed on the U. S. exchanges.

24 Apr 2020: Congress passed the Paycheck Protection Program and Healthcare Enhancement Act [23.2-79] to address the Wuhan pandemic (cf. 27 Mar 2020). Among its provisions: **a)** (S. 101) increased the funding for the Paycheck Protection Program from $349,000 M ($349 B) to $659,000 M ($659 B); **b)** (S. 101) increased the funding the Small Business Administration emergency loan program from $349,000 M ($349 B) to $670,335 M ($670.335 B); and **c)** (S. 102) appropriated money to the Department of Health and Human Services for testing research.

27 Apr 2020: The Federal Reserve announced it would begin lending to municipalities under the Municipal Liquidity Facility [23.2-80]. It had been authorized under sections 4003 and 4027 of the CARES Act (cf. 27 Mar 2020). The Federal Reserve Bank of New York is to issue a special purpose vehicle (SPV) which will, in turn, issue loans to cities with populations over 250,000, counties with populations exceeding 500,000, and States. Eligible collateral for the loans include: a) tax anticipation notes, b) tax and revenue anticipation notes, and c) bond anticipation notes, all of which must have maturities less than three years. The SPV is authorized to issue up to $500,000 M ($500 B) in loans.

5 Jun 2020: Congress passed the "Paycheck Protection Program Flexibility Act of 2020" [23.2-81]. It modified conditions under which the Paycheck Protection Loans (cf. 27 Mar 2020) can be forgiven, and delayed the payments on employer-paid payroll taxes.

1 Jul 2020: The North American Free Trade Agreement (NAFTA) (cf. 1 Jan 1994) was replaced by the United States-Mexico-Canada Agreement (CAFTA).

4 Jul 2020: Congress changed [23.2-82] the funding for the emergency Small Business Administration (cf. 27 Mar 2020) from $679,000 M to $659,000 M ($659 B).

11 Dec 2020: The FDA approved the Pfizer COVID-19 vaccine for emergency use.

18 Dec 2020: The FDA approved the Moderna COVID-19 vaccine for emergency use.

27 Dec 2020: Congress passed the Consolidated Appropriations Act of 2021, parts N and M of which included additional appropriations to address the Wuhan pandemic. Among its provisions [23.2-83]: **a)** an additional $284,000 M ($284 B) in loans under the Paycheck Protection Program (cf. 27 Mar 2020); **b)** $20,000 M ($20 B) for businesses in low-income areas; **c)** additional stimulus grants to individuals making under $75,000 (totaling $166,000 M ($166 B)); **d)** additional unemployment benefits totaling $120,000 M ($120 B); and **e)** $25,000 M ($25 B) in loans and grants to State and local governments.

31 Dec 2020: A total of four FDIC DIF insured institutions failed in 2020, with net losses to the FDIC DIF totaling $99.455 M [23.2-84]. Also, some level of lockdown restrictions were still in place in many States, including New York, New Jersey, Michigan, Maine, Illinois, New Mexico, Connecticut, Maryland, Maine, Rhode Island, California, Oregon, and Pennsylvania.

23.3 Data, 2004-2020

Figures 23.3-1 and 23.3-2 show the U. S. government revenue and expenditures for 2004 to 2020.

			Income taxes				Social Insurance Taxes				
Day	Year	Customs Duties	Individual	Corporate	Excise Taxes	Estate and Gift Taxes	OASDI & Disability (Off-Budget)	Medicare & Retirements (On-Budget)	Federal Reserve Deposits	Other Misc.	Net Receipts
30 Sep	2004	21,083	808,959	189,371	69,855	24,831	534,745	198,662	19,652	12,956	1,880,114
30 Sep	2005	23,379	927,222	278,282	73,094	24,764	577,476	216,649	19,297	13,448	2,153,611
30 Sep	2006	24,810	1,043,908	353,915	73,961	27,877	608,382	229,439	29,945	14,632	2,406,869
30 Sep	2007	26,010	1,163,472	370,243	65,069	26,044	635,089	234,518	32,043	15,497	2,567,985
30 Sep	2008	27,568	1,145,747	304,346	67,334	28,844	658,046	242,109	33,598	16,399	2,523,991
30 Sep	2009	22,453	915,308	138,229	62,483	23,482	654,009	236,908	34,318	17,799	2,104,989
30 Sep	2010	25,298	898,549	191,437	66,909	18,885	631,687	233,127	75,845	20,969	2,162,706
30 Sep	2011	29,519	1,091,473	181,085	72,381	7,399	565,788	253,004	82,546	20,271	2,303,466
30 Sep	2012	30,307	1,132,206	242,289	79,061	13,973	569,501	275,813	81,957	24,883	2,449,990
30 Sep	2013	31,815	1,316,405	273,506	84,007	18,912	673,274	274,546	75,767	26,874	2,775,106
30 Sep	2014	33,926	1,394,568	320,731	93,368	19,300	735,565	287,893	99,235	36,905	3,021,491
30 Sep	2015	35,041	1,540,802	343,797	98,279	19,232	770,372	294,885	96,468	51,014	3,249,890
30 Sep	2016	34,838	1,546,075	299,571	95,026	21,354	810,180	304,885	115,672	40,364	3,267,965
30 Sep	2017	34,574	1,587,120	297,048	83,823	22,768	850,618	311,279	81,287	47,667	3,316,184
30 Sep	2018	41,299	1,683,538	204,733	94,986	22,983	854,747	315,954	70,750	40,917	3,329,907
30 Sep	2019	70,784	1,717,857	230,245	99,452	16,672	914,303	329,069	52,793	32,986	3,464,161
30 Sep	2020	68,551	1,608,661	211,845	86,780	17,624	965,428	344,527	81,880	35,866	3,421,162

U. S. Government Revenue, 2004-2020 (millions USD)

1. The revenue data for 2004 to 2020 is from the OMB White House, file = HIST_FY21.pdf, Tables 2.1 and 2.5
2. The revenue data for 2020 is from the OMB White House, files = hist02z1_fy22.xlsx and hist02z5_fy22.xlsx
3. https://www.whitehouse.gov/omb/historical-tables/

Figure 23.3-1: U. S. Government Revenue, 2004-2020

		National Defense	Education, Training, Employ-ment, Social Services	Health	Medicare	Income Security	Social Security [1]	Veterans	Physical Resources [1, 2]	Interest on Debt [1]	Inter-national Affairs	Agri-culture	Other [3]	Undistrib-uted Offsetting Receipts [1, 4]	Total
Day	Year														
30 Jun	2004	455,813	87,997	240,148	269,360	333,027	495,548	59,729	116,259	160,245	26,870	15,439	90,943	-58,537	2,292,841
30 Jun	2005	495,294	97,553	250,605	298,638	345,800	523,305	70,112	130,145	183,986	34,565	26,565	80,613	-65,224	2,471,957
30 Jun	2006	521,820	118,473	252,779	329,868	352,425	548,549	69,832	164,706	226,603	29,499	25,969	82,777	-68,250	2,655,050
30 Jun	2007	551,258	91,647	266,425	375,407	365,931	586,153	72,828	133,828	237,109	28,482	17,662	84,194	-82,238	2,728,686
30 Jun	2008	616,066	91,304	280,626	390,758	431,211	617,027	84,711	161,889	252,757	28,857	18,387	95,193	-86,242	2,982,544
30 Jun	2009	661,012	79,744	334,368	430,093	533,080	682,963	95,545	443,828	186,902	37,529	22,237	103,015	-92,639	3,517,677
30 Jun	2010	693,485	128,595	369,081	451,636	622,106	706,737	108,478	88,835	196,194	45,195	21,356	107,497	-82,116	3,457,079
30 Jun	2011	705,554	101,256	372,481	485,653	597,269	730,811	127,269	161,932	229,962	45,685	20,662	112,998	-88,467	3,603,065
30 Jun	2012	677,852	90,822	346,755	471,793	541,248	773,290	124,679	215,287	220,408	36,802	17,791	113,372	-103,536	3,526,563
30 Jun	2013	633,446	72,860	358,264	497,826	536,411	813,551	139,038	89,997	220,885	46,464	29,678	109,246	-92,785	3,454,881
30 Jun	2014	603,457	90,610	409,497	511,688	513,596	850,533	149,621	59,165	228,956	46,879	24,386	105,940	-88,044	3,506,284
30 Jun	2015	589,659	122,035	482,257	546,202	508,800	887,753	159,781	115,171	223,181	52,040	18,500	102,274	-115,803	3,691,850
30 Jun	2016	593,372	109,709	511,325	594,536	514,098	916,067	174,557	121,432	240,033	45,306	18,344	109,088	-95,251	3,852,616
30 Sep	2017	598,722	143,953	533,152	597,307	503,443	944,878	176,584	133,526	262,551	46,309	18,872	112,159	-89,826	3,981,630
30 Sep	2018	631,130	95,503	551,219	588,706	495,289	987,791	178,895	166,783	324,975	48,996	21,789	115,837	-97,869	4,109,044
30 Sep	2019	686,003	136,752	584,816	650,996	514,787	1,044,409	199,843	141,162	375,158	52,739	38,257	121,586	-98,192	4,448,316
30 Sep	2020	724,645	237,754	747,582	776,225	1,263,639	1,095,816	218,655	845,901	345,470	67,666	47,298	286,107	-106,362	6,550,396

U. S. Government Expenditures, 2004-2020 (millions USD)

1. The totals of "on budget and "off-budget" are shown here.
2. "Physical Resources" includes Energy, Natural Resources and Environment, Commerce and Housing Credit, Transportation, and Community & Regional Development.
3. "Other" includes General Science, Space & Technology, Administration of Justice, General Government and Allowances.
4. "Offsetting Receipts" is a combination of new debt and intra-government transfers from Trust Funds.
5. The expenditure data for 2004 to 2019 is from the OMB White House, file = HIST_FY21.pdf, Table 3.1; for 2020, from OMB White House, file = hist03z1_fy22.xlsx, Table 3.1.
6. https://www.whitehouse.gov/omb/historical-tables/

Figure 23.3-2: U. S. Government Expenditures, 2004-2020

Figure 23.3-3 shows the national debt and per-capita debt for this period. Refer to the Introduction to Part 2 for a sense of wages vs. per-capita national debt.

Day	Year	Principal ($) [1]	Population [2]	Debt per Capita ($) [2]	Day	Year	Principal ($) [1]	Population [2]	Debt per Capita ($) [2]
30 Sep	2004	7,379,052,696,330	292,351,359	25,240.36	30 Sep	2013	16,738,183,526,697	314,967,114	53,142.64
30 Sep	2005	7,932,709,661,724	295,083,722	26,882.91	30 Sep	2014	17,824,071,380,734	317,040,972	56,220.09
30 Sep	2006	8,506,973,899,215	297,816,085	28,564.52	30 Sep	2015	18,150,617,666,484	319,114,831	56,878.01
30 Sep	2007	9,007,653,372,262	300,548,448	29,970.72	30 Sep	2016	19,573,444,713,937	321,188,689	60,940.64
30 Sep	2008	10,024,724,896,912	303,280,812	33,054.27	30 Sep	2017	20,244,900,016,054	323,262,548	62,626.80
30 Sep	2009	11,909,829,003,512	306,013,175	38,919.33	30 Sep	2018	21,516,058,183,180	325,336,406	66,134.80
30 Sep	2010	13,561,623,030,892	308,745,538	43,924.92	30 Sep	2019	22,719,401,753,434	327,410,265	69,391.23
30 Sep	2011	14,790,340,328,557	310,819,397	47,585.00	30 Sep	2020	26,945,391,194,615	329,484,123	81,780.55
30 Sep	2012	16,066,241,407,386	312,893,255	51,347.36					

U. S. National Debt, 2004-2020 (USD)

1. The total debt data for 2004 to 2020 is from: https://fiscaldata.treasury.gov/datasets/historical-debt-outstanding/historical-debt-outstanding
2. Population values are based on the dicennial census from the Census Bureau, and linearly interpolated. The 2020 census data is estimated. Per-capita is based on these values.

Figure 23.3-3: National Debt and Per-Capita Share Thereof, 2004-2020

Figures 23.3-4 through 23.3-11 show a summary of the asset and liability condition statements of the Federal Reserve and commercial banking system for this period. I do not have an explanation as to why the error between assets and liabilities are so large in the period from 2004 to 2007 and the latter half of 2020.

				Federal Reserve Loans & Investments		Commercial Bank Loans and Investments				
Day	Year	Gold Stock	Treasury Currency Outstanding	U.S. Government Securities	Discounts & Advances	Loans	U.S. Government Securities	Other	Total Assets	Note
31 Mar	2004	11,045	35,643	693,745	48	4,268,862	1,209,292	528,614	6,747,249	
30 Jun	2004	11,045	35,825	717,177	165	4,408,393	1,197,965	521,958	6,892,528	
29 Sep	2004	11,043	36,197	728,117	251	4,517,955	1,155,174	547,831	6,996,568	
29 Dec	2004	11,045	36,476	750,813	57	4,677,743	1,158,383	565,634	7,200,151	
30 Mar	2005	11,041	36,546	749,286	62	4,770,936	1,207,552	634,244	7,409,667	
29 Jun	2005	11,041	36,657	752,022	247	4,903,781	1,186,335	680,007	7,570,090	
28 Sep	2005	11,041	36,485	766,332	353	5,095,564	1,161,357	693,743	7,764,875	
28 Dec	2005	11,041	36,541	789,460	114	5,262,859	1,137,937	697,615	7,935,567	
29 Mar	2006	11,041	36,651	778,029	251	5,341,966	1,167,983	709,001	8,044,922	
28 Jun	2006	11,041	38,048	788,849	300	5,499,984	1,201,574	721,172	8,260,968	
27 Sep	2006	11,041	38,138	796,415	366	5,616,753	1,170,157	736,396	8,369,266	
27 Dec	2006	11,041	38,245	809,043	488	5,909,942	1,200,290	773,747	8,742,796	
28 Mar	2007	11,041	38,366	816,890	28	5,851,097	1,218,917	805,329	8,741,668	
27 Jun	2007	11,041	38,526	810,497	187	6,028,499	1,183,777	858,178	8,930,705	
26 Sep	2007	11,041	38,653	835,633	207	6,298,401	1,159,390	926,589	9,269,914	
26 Dec	2007	11,041	38,807	797,112	4,535	6,525,728	1,122,001	958,870	9,458,094	
26 Mar	2008	11,041	38,778	719,055	37,607	6,606,045	1,144,338	936,478	9,493,342	
25 Jun	2008	11,041	38,847	608,546	13,713	6,585,526	1,146,495	940,410	9,344,578	
24 Sep	2008	11,041	38,774	572,578	39,447	6,740,006	1,153,657	952,000	9,507,503	
31 Dec	2008	11,041	38,843	576,892	84,941	6,926,237	1,260,361	835,641	9,733,956	

1. See Appendix B for references.

Figure 23.3-4: Banking System Assets, 2004-2008

				At Federal Reserve Banks			At Commercial Banks				
Day	Year	Currency Outside Banks [1]	Treasury Cash [1]	Treasury Demand Deposits [1]	Foreign Demand Deposits	Demand Deposits	Treasury Demand Deposits [3]	Time Deposits [4]	Capital [2]	Total Liabilities	Error (%)
31 Mar	2004	714,914	347	4,404	80	4,833,596	24,400		568,390	6,146,131	8.91
30 Jun	2004	727,776	307	7,202	82	4,964,822	45,800		528,961	6,274,950	8.96
29 Sep	2004	738,856	291	5,436	81	5,004,322	40,900		562,151	6,352,037	9.21
29 Dec	2004	758,397	270	5,934	87	5,175,511	31,000		571,913	6,543,112	9.13
30 Mar	2005	755,241	284	5,198	102	5,275,282	39,600		599,314	6,675,021	9.91
29 Jun	2005	763,437	237	4,173	83	5,348,084	52,300		603,044	6,771,358	10.55
28 Sep	2005	768,115	237	4,479	83	5,461,905	66,800		620,869	6,922,488	10.85
28 Dec	2005	794,900	203	4,243	85	5,644,245	44,500		584,605	7,072,781	10.87
29 Mar	2006	788,785	209	4,619	84	5,720,719	24,500		597,820	7,136,736	11.29
28 Jun	2006	795,479	174	4,879	90	5,791,045	58,300		651,705	7,301,672	11.61
27 Sep	2006	792,276	150	4,585	91	5,857,625	71,900		662,873	7,389,500	11.71
27 Dec	2006	819,930	252	4,470	92	6,136,138	51,300		698,519	7,710,701	11.81
28 Mar	2007	807,386	301	4,772	91	6,211,271	29,200		705,570	7,758,591	11.25
27 Jun	2007	812,339	306	4,039	97	6,248,045	59,600		724,816	7,849,242	12.11
26 Sep	2007	812,059	336	4,943	96	6,396,948	91,700		759,492	8,065,574	12.99
26 Dec	2007	829,913	246	4,529	97	6,718,067	57,300		792,882	8,403,034	11.16
26 Mar	2008	817,761	331	4,944	239	6,811,865	26,700		900,300	8,562,140	9.81
25 Jun	2008	825,203	279	4,208	100	6,792,636	38,400		751,336	8,412,162	9.98
24 Sep	2008	836,437	270	5,175	150	7,042,687	103,200		768,571	8,756,490	7.90
31 Dec	2008	886,651	233	118,058	1,190	7,330,679	393,300		977,080	9,707,191	0.27

1. Some of these figures are one week prior to the listed date.
2. Used "other liabilities" from H.8 for Mar 1994 ff.
3. Treasury Demand Deposits nots shown separately; used US government total cash balance at commercial banks (series GDTCBW, H.6).
4. Time deposits included in demand deposits per H.8 after Dec 2003.

Figure 23.3-5: Banking System Liabilities, 2004-2008

				Federal Reserve Loans & Investments		Commercial Bank Loans and Investments				
Day	Year	Gold Stock	Treasury Currency Outstanding	U. S. Government Securities	Discounts & Advances	Loans	U. S. Government Securities	Other	Total Assets	Note
25 Mar	2009	11,041	38,774	572,578	39,407	6,816,298	1,298,139	872,575	9,648,812	
24 Jun	2009	11,041	42,417	749,818	49,216	6,744,270	1,326,627	924,867	9,848,256	
30 Sep	2009	11,041	42,579	765,633	29,213	6,515,090	1,382,711	906,922	9,653,189	
30 Dec	2009	11,041	42,719	776,587	20,135	6,465,138	1,465,244	867,374	9,648,238	
31 Mar	2010	11,041	42,825	776,667	9,560	6,703,107	1,497,101	808,411	9,848,712	
30 Jun	2010	11,041	42,913	776,970	361	6,620,226	1,500,607	792,013	9,744,131	
29 Sep	2010	11,041	43,378	811,669	176	6,568,268	1,615,552	810,436	9,860,520	
29 Dec	2010	11,041	43,567	1,016,102	98	6,600,143	1,646,850	773,019	10,090,820	
30 Mar	2011	11,041	43,710	1,333,445	32	6,458,173	1,656,813	779,004	10,282,218	
29 Jun	2011	11,041	43,966	1,617,060	75	6,490,713	1,635,008	767,409	10,565,272	
28 Sep	2011	11,041	44,121	1,664,655	132	6,550,056	1,673,351	794,939	10,738,295	
28 Dec	2011	11,041	44,250	1,672,092	70	6,680,290	1,711,059	793,708	10,912,510	
28 Mar	2012	11,041	44,366	1,664,911	4	6,693,766	1,787,810	797,891	10,999,789	
27 Jun	2012	11,041	44,557	1,666,530	84	6,771,829	1,805,980	798,080	11,098,101	
26 Sep	2012	11,041	44,685	1,648,403	219	6,816,296	1,843,635	834,618	11,198,897	
26 Dec	2012	11,041	44,803	1,656,930	56	6,965,833	1,886,675	865,742	11,431,080	
27 Mar	2013	11,041	44,919	1,794,459	4	6,917,554	1,848,142	869,094	11,485,213	
26 Jun	2013	11,041	45,139	1,928,416	126	6,990,254	1,829,764	881,927	11,686,667	
25 Sep	2013	11,041	45,315	2,062,004	167	7,024,385	1,781,849	902,166	11,826,927	
25 Dec	2013	11,041	45,516	2,208,829	95	7,173,267	1,820,546	918,217	12,177,511	

Assets of the Federal Reserve & Commercial System, 2009-2013 (millions USD)

1. See Appendix B for references.

Figure 23.3-6: Banking System Assets, 2009-2013

		At Federal Reserve Banks				At Commercial Banks				
Day	Year	Currency Outside Banks [1]	Treasury Cash [1]	Treasury Demand Deposits [1]	Foreign Demand Deposits	Demand Deposits	Treasury Demand Deposits [3]	Time Deposits [4]	Capital [2]	Total Liabilities	Error (%)
25 Mar	2009	899,798	310	56,198	1,587	7,295,645	293,700		862,183	9,409,421	2.48
24 Jun	2009	907,596	318	78,847	2,212	7,432,145	325,200		753,085	9,499,403	3.54
30 Sep	2009	912,652	287	50,907	2,371	7,542,337	213,600		669,952	9,392,106	2.70
30 Dec	2009	930,122	232	149,819	2,269	7,747,050	128,800		665,869	9,624,161	0.25
31 Mar	2010	933,542	224	50,104	2,420	7,736,879	157,500		641,108	9,521,777	3.32
30 Jun	2010	940,432	229	46,350	2,324	7,668,261	241,300		712,065	9,610,961	1.37
29 Sep	2010	954,794	237	57,829	2,411	7,756,707	268,600		799,645	9,840,223	0.21
29 Dec	2010	984,980	177	88,905	3,670	7,946,041	291,600		705,864	10,021,237	0.69
30 Mar	2011	1,005,313	209	59,201	131	8,030,748	78,200		689,535	9,863,337	4.07
29 Jun	2011	1,027,497	147	105,582	126	8,193,253	124,300		705,648	10,156,553	3.87
28 Sep	2011	1,038,076	124	44,942	225	8,359,353	66,700		763,374	10,272,794	4.33
28 Dec	2011	1,076,340	128	91,418	378	8,535,644	105,400		757,697	10,567,005	3.17
28 Mar	2012	1,098,319	150	68,452	127	8,619,520	90,000		734,764	10,611,332	3.53
27 Jun	2012	1,110,227	117	117,923	1,178	8,685,470	134,700		753,831	10,803,446	2.66
26 Sep	2012	1,128,192	122	65,665	5,560	8,893,033	76,300		767,361	10,936,233	2.35
26 Dec	2012	1,167,122	150	55,679	6,163	9,388,749	61,500		752,779	11,432,142	-0.01
27 Mar	2013	1,177,679	231	53,218	9,107	9,401,742	74,000		709,518	11,425,495	0.52
26 Jun	2013	1,193,377	121	94,271	10,014	9,340,450	103,700		676,897	11,418,830	2.29
25 Sep	2013	1,205,955	167	46,017	8,877	9,558,164	49,300		637,930	11,506,410	2.71
25 Dec	2013	1,238,524	234	93,893	7,980	9,916,861	107,800		646,344	12,011,636	1.36

Liabilities of the Federal Reserve and Commercial System, 2009-2013 (millions USD)

1. Some of these figures are one week prior to the listed date.
2. Used "other liabilities" from H.8 for Mar 1994 ff.
2. Treasury Demand Deposits not shown after Dec 1993 in FRB's; used US government total cash balance at commercial banks (series GDTCBW, H.6).
4. Time deposits included in demand deposits per H.8 after Dec 2003.

Figure 23.3-7: Banking System Liabilities, 2009-2013

Assets of the Federal Reserve & Commercial System, 2014-2018 (millions USD)										
				Federal Reserve Loans & Investments		Commercial Bank Loans and Investments				
Day	Year	Gold Stock	Treasury Currency Outstanding	U. S. Government Securities	Discounts & Advances	Loans	U. S. Government Securities	Other	Total Assets	Note
26 Mar	2014	11,041	45,661	2,311,539	23	7,211,102	1,871,625	913,628	12,364,619	
25 Jun	2014	11,041	45,926	2,396,972	224	7,362,015	1,898,557	904,580	12,619,315	
24 Sep	2014	11,041	46,131	2,448,625	299	7,475,210	1,981,847	889,713	12,852,866	
31 Dec	2014	11,041	46,339	2,461,420	119	7,700,925	2,060,835	900,325	13,181,004	
25 Mar	2015	11,041	46,469	2,459,666	15	7,764,969	2,114,242	894,743	13,291,145	
24 Jun	2015	11,041	46,839	2,460,911	207	7,936,208	2,146,631	895,546	13,497,383	
30 Sep	2015	11,041	47,107	2,461,946	283	8,097,403	2,161,075	885,281	13,664,136	
30 Dec	2015	11,041	47,567	2,461,554	634	8,316,512	2,238,676	883,896	13,959,880	
30 Mar	2016	11,041	47,728	2,461,326	32	8,418,061	2,248,202	891,539	14,077,929	
29 Jun	2016	11,041	47,927	2,462,303	156	8,632,590	2,294,280	907,124	14,355,421	
28 Sep	2016	11,041	48,211	2,463,460	242	8,700,321	2,376,779	915,805	14,515,859	
28 Dec	2016	11,041	48,538	2,463,601	47	8,829,612	2,426,264	898,344	14,677,447	
29 Mar	2017	11,041	48,726	2,464,335	11	8,782,764	2,436,853	913,138	14,656,868	
28 Jun	2017	11,041	48,949	2,465,046	192	8,917,308	2,435,484	906,977	14,784,997	
27 Sep	2017	11,041	49,162	2,465,427	233	9,005,747	2,472,415	901,931	14,905,956	
27 Dec	2017	11,041	49,360	2,454,219	141	9,195,996	2,538,697	910,931	15,160,385	
28 Mar	2018	11,041	49,549	2,424,883	16	9,176,234	2,495,659	880,578	15,037,960	
27 Jun	2018	11,041	49,685	2,378,250	181	9,372,101	2,548,122	862,086	15,221,466	
26 Sep	2018	11,041	49,785	2,313,208	359	9,421,290	2,553,765	854,680	15,204,128	
26 Dec	2018	11,041	49,859	2,240,717	77	9,680,189	2,689,664	828,108	15,499,655	

1. See Appendix B for references.

Figure 23.3-8: Banking System Assets, 2014-2018

Liabilities of the Federal Reserve and Commercial System, 2014-2018 (millions USD)											
				At Federal Reserve Banks			At Commercial Banks				
Day	Year	Currency Outside Banks [1]	Treasury Cash [1]	Treasury Demand Deposits [1]	Foreign Demand Deposits	Demand Deposits	Treasury Demand Deposits [3]	Time Deposits [4]	Capital [2]	Total Liabilities	Error (%)
26 Mar	2014	1,268,244	279	89,067	7,028	10,009,422	110,600		610,064	12,094,704	2.18
25 Jun	2014	1,280,096	146	108,064	5,952	10,086,575	118,500		577,520	12,176,853	3.51
24 Sep	2014	1,289,158	159	118,905	5,243	10,278,506	116,900		618,651	12,427,522	3.31
31 Dec	2014	1,338,522	197	177,911	5,209	10,597,225	185,200		662,783	12,967,047	1.62
25 Mar	2015	1,357,352	196	71,325	5,225	10,678,882	92,100		674,048	12,879,128	3.10
24 Jun	2015	1,365,349	102	240,762	5,243	10,658,235	243,100		619,048	13,131,839	2.71
30 Sep	2015	1,384,890	157	164,941	5,256	10,849,793	145,900		630,735	13,181,672	3.53
30 Dec	2015	1,426,176	266	324,846	5,231	10,991,280	277,900		588,478	13,614,177	2.48
30 Mar	2016	1,443,285	213	291,912	5,172	11,177,652	285,900		619,203	13,823,337	1.81
29 Jun	2016	1,462,755	71	346,642	5,194	11,237,908	336,000		660,760	14,049,330	2.13
28 Sep	2016	1,470,071	141	339,619	5,165	11,304,802	357,900		615,288	14,092,986	2.91
28 Dec	2016	1,509,076	166	372,825	5,165	11,593,245	385,000		570,058	14,435,535	1.65
29 Mar	2017	1,536,334	267	63,101	5,164	11,693,065	66,900		552,006	13,916,837	5.05
28 Jun	2017	1,559,134	187	197,597	5,165	11,674,214	216,000		559,326	14,211,623	3.88
27 Sep	2017	1,580,243	197	155,159	5,370	11,831,081	164,800		562,909	14,299,759	4.07
27 Dec	2017	1,616,323	214	186,486	5,254	12,081,382	186,900		546,250	14,622,809	3.55
28 Mar	2018	1,636,934	319	300,355	254	12,112,248	321,600		574,978	14,946,688	0.61
27 Jun	2018	1,665,308	198	362,175	5,256	12,131,155	381,300		567,910	15,113,302	0.71
26 Sep	2018	1,686,023	214	367,243	5,255	12,230,704	381,800		597,748	15,268,987	-0.43
26 Dec	2018	1,716,129	214	368,236	6,191	12,575,250	384,800		562,416	15,613,236	-0.73

1. Some of these figures are one week prior to the listed date.
2. Used "other liabilities" from H.8 for Mar 1994 ff.
2. Treasury Demand Deposits not shown after Dec 1993 in FRB's; used US government total cash balance at commercial banks (series GDTCBW, H.6).
4. Time deposits included in demand deposits per H.8 after Dec 2003.

Figure 23.3-9: Banking System Liabilities, 2014-2018

Assets of the Federal Reserve & Commercial System, 2019, 2020 (millions USD)										
				Federal Reserve Loans & Investments		Commercial Bank Loans and Investments				
Day	Year	Gold Stock	Treasury Currency Outstanding	U. S. Government Securities	Discounts & Advances	Loans	U. S. Government Securities	Other	Total Assets	Note
27 Mar	2019	11,041	49,895	2,175,596	27	9,676,568	2,743,801	826,065	15,482,993	
26 Jun	2019	11,041	50,009	2,110,256	184	9,845,449	2,826,884	828,284	15,672,107	
25 Sep	2019	11,041	50,067	2,212,683	96	9,914,903	2,971,904	819,197	15,979,891	
25 Dec	2019	11,041	50,124	2,563,831	13	10,112,965	2,998,682	828,753	16,565,409	
25 Mar	2020	11,041	50,239	3,330,727	50,768	10,600,459	3,171,382	845,212	18,059,828	
24 Jun	2020	11,041	50,387	4,267,605	6,251	10,670,577	3,311,454	871,055	19,188,370	
30 Sep	2020	11,041	50,397	4,431,523	3,400	10,483,256	3,531,851	912,085	19,423,553	
30 Dec	2020	11,041	50,521	4,689,916	1,735	10,461,491	3,761,486	943,932	19,920,122	
1. See Appendix B for references.										

Figure 23.3-10: Banking System Assets, 2019-2020

Liabilities of the Federal Reserve and Commercial System, 2019, 2020 (millions USD)										
		At Federal Reserve Banks				At Commercial Banks				
Day	Year	Currency Outside Banks [1]	Treasury Cash [1]	Treasury Demand Deposits [1]	Foreign Demand Deposits	Demand Deposits	Treasury Demand Deposits [3]	Time Deposits [4]	Capital [2]	Total Liabilities	Error (%)
27 Mar	2019	1,723,754	166	295,523	5,243	12,658,732	321,000		594,132	15,598,550	-0.75
26 Jun	2019	1,742,150	184	240,909	5,249	12,755,663	257,300		617,736	15,619,191	0.34
25 Sep	2019	1,762,927	180	305,810	5,187	12,916,057	316,800		646,374	15,953,335	0.17
25 Dec	2019	1,802,362	171	351,934	5,182	13,347,310	382,300		645,216	16,534,475	0.19
25 Mar	2020	1,872,242	328	384,890	16,261	14,165,886	399,500		907,861	17,746,968	1.73
24 Jun	2020	1,963,978	66	1,586,573	16,222	15,472,602	1,622,800		798,499	21,460,740	-11.84
30 Sep	2020	2,029,101	40	1,661,732	18,871	15,672,674	1,670,100		735,150	21,787,668	-12.17
30 Dec	2020	2,086,909	28	1,613,514	21,831	16,317,936	1,592,300		786,883	22,419,401	-12.55
1. Some of these figures are one week prior to the listed date.										
2. Used "other liabilities" from H.8 for Mar 1994 ff.										
2. Treasury Demand Deposits not shown after Dec 1993 in FRB's; used US government total cash balance at commercial banks (series GDTCBW, H.6).										
4. Time deposits included in demand deposits per H.8 after Dec 2003.										

Figure 23.3-11: Banking System Liabilities, 2019-2020

Figure 23.3-12 shows the total money supply for this period.

U. S. Money Supply per Federal Reserve H.6 Data, 2004-2020 (millions USD)					
1	2	3	4	5	6
Month, Year (~30 Jun except 2020)	Currency Outside Banks	Adjusted Commercial Demand Deposits	M1 [1]	M2 [2]	M3 [3, 4]
2004	678,000	333,800	1,347,700	6,272,500	9,281,400
2005	708,500	346,800	1,384,300	6,511,500	9,734,300
2006	741,300	318,800	1,379,000	6,851,600	
2007	756,600	306,400	1,370,800	7,283,900	
2008	768,900	316,900	1,407,300	7,730,600	
2009	852,800	449,000	1,661,700	8,441,800	
2010	884,000	465,100	1,732,300	8,607,100	
2011	964,600	584,400	1,954,100	9,114,200	
2012	1,048,100	802,100	2,271,000	9,962,600	
2013	1,125,000	945,900	2,523,500	10,644,000	
2014	1,213,400	1,127,400	2,824,800	11,337,600	
2015	1,296,000	1,216,700	3,020,700	11,963,500	
2016	1,383,700	1,333,400	3,247,000	12,791,100	
2017	1,479,900	1,476,000	3,527,700	13,529,200	
2018	1,584,500	1,461,300	3,656,900	14,095,500	
2019	1,660,000	1,522,400	3,830,500	14,757,500	
Jan 2020	1,714,000	1,586,200	3,982,300	15,419,800	
Feb 2020	1,718,200	1,557,600	3,940,300	15,405,700	
Mar 2020	1,747,400	1,826,700	4,288,000	16,079,100	
Apr 2020	1,784,300	2,047,400	4,849,400	17,126,600	
May 2020	1,824,300	2,125,700	16,184,400	17,791,700	
Jun 2020	1,857,100	2,216,500	16,562,200	18,130,900	
Jul 2020	1,884,200	2,261,000	16,765,200	18,280,400	
Aug 2020	1,908,800	2,274,100	16,888,000	18,349,400	
Sep 2020	1,929,200	2,387,400	17,156,300	18,572,900	
Oct 2020	1,944,100	2,427,400	17,341,400	18,720,300	
Nov 2020	1,957,900	2,753,000	17,663,200	19,011,300	
Dec 2020	1,973,800	3,356,400	17,972,200	19,281,100	

1. M1 (new definition, cf. 1979): Currency outside banks, demand deposits excluding those due to foreign commercial banks and U. S. government, plus other checkable depoits, (NOW, ATS, credit union share balances, and demand deposits at thrift institutions).

2. M2 (new definition, cf. 1979): M1 plus overnight repurchase agreements and overnight Eurodollars held by non-bank U. S. residents, plus money market mutual fund shares, and savings and small denomination time deposits at all institutions (formerly was commercial banks only).

3. M3 (new definition, cf. 1979): M2 plus large denomination time deposits at all depositary institutions including negotiable CD's, plus term repurchase agreements issued by commercial banks and savings and loan institutions.

4. M3 was discontinued in 2005.

Figure 23.3-12: Total Money Supply, 2004-2020

Figure 23.3-13 shows the CPI, total money supply, and per-capita money supply during this period.

Year	CPI [1] (1913 = 100)	Total Money Supply M2 [2] (USD)	Population [3]	Per Capita Money Supply (USD)	Annual Rate of Change in CPI (%)	Annual Rate of Change in Per-Capita Money Supply (%)
2004	1,908.081	6,272,500,000,000	292,351,359	21,455.35	2.628	3.631
2005	1,972.727	6,511,500,000,000	295,083,722	22,066.62	3.332	2.809
2006	2,036.364	6,851,600,000,000	297,816,085	23,006.14	3.175	4.170
2007	2,093.939	7,283,900,000,000	300,548,448	24,235.36	2.788	5.205
2008	2,174.747	7,730,600,000,000	303,280,812	25,489.91	3.787	5.047
2009	2,166.667	8,441,800,000,000	306,013,175	27,586.39	-0.372	7.904
2010	2,202.020	8,607,100,000,000	308,745,538	27,877.65	1.619	1.050
2011	2,271.717	9,114,200,000,000	310,819,397	29,323.14	3.116	5.055
2012	2,319.192	9,962,600,000,000	312,893,255	31,840.25	2.068	8.235
2013	2,353.535	10,644,000,000,000	314,967,114	33,794.00	1.470	5.955
2014	2,390.909	11,337,600,000,000	317,040,972	35,760.68	1.576	5.657
2015	2,393.939	11,963,500,000,000	319,114,831	37,489.64	0.127	4.722
2016	2,424.242	12,791,100,000,000	321,188,689	39,824.25	1.258	6.041
2017	2,475.758	13,529,200,000,000	323,262,548	41,852.05	2.103	4.966
2018	2,536.364	14,095,500,000,000	325,336,406	43,325.92	2.418	3.461
2019	2,581.818	14,757,500,000,000	327,410,265	45,073.42	1.776	3.954
2020	2,629.091	18,130,900,000,000	329,484,123	55,028.14	1.814	19.955

1. CPI data from Bureau of Labor Statistics, series CUUR0000AA0R (urban, all commodities, not seasonally adjusted), referenced to 1913
2. See notes in money supply data for sources.
3. Population is linearly interpolated from Census results.
4. Money supply for 2020 is from June to be consistent with other years.

Figure 23.3-13: Money Supply and CPI, 2004-2020

Figure 23.3-14 shows a summary of the CPI and per-capita money supply. Two distinct intervals are evident, between 2004 and 2019: 2004 to 2009 and 2009 to 2019. The average annual change in CPI and money supply for 2004 to 2009 are 2.5% and 5.0% respectively, and for 2009 to 2019 are 1.7% and 4.9% respectively. Figures 23.2-12 and 23.3-13 show the growth between 2019 and 2020, when an enormous amount of money was injected into the system due to unemployment benefits and loans arising from the lockdowns imposed by State Governors during the Wuhan virus. The U. S. should expect a large inflationary trend in 2021 to 2023 as a result of this depreciation of the dollar. But the government has continued in 2021 through 2023 to spend more money the taxpayers don't have in order to buy more votes and depreciate the currency even more.

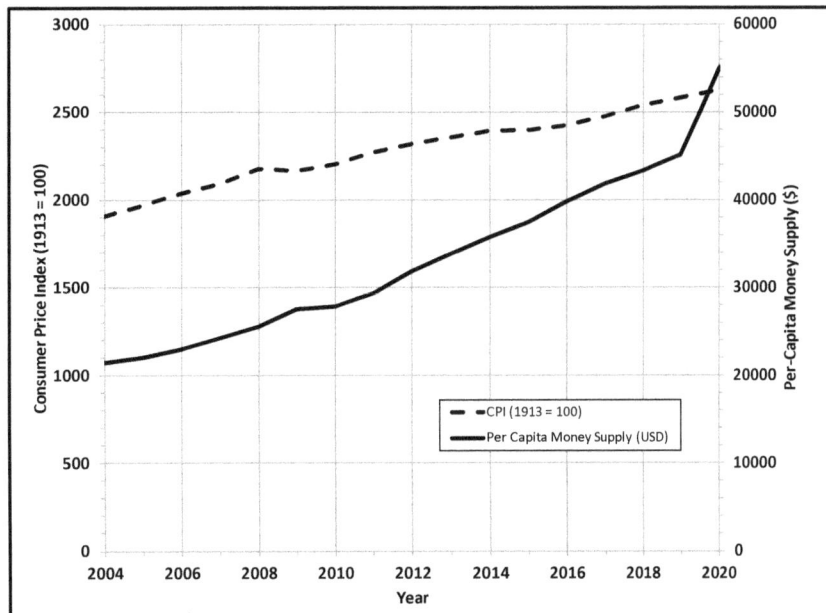

Figure 23.3-14: CPI and Per-Capita Summary, 2004-2020

Figure 23.3-15 shows the approximate median income index, consumer price index, and standard of living index for this period. See the Introduction to Part 2 for cautions regarding these curves.

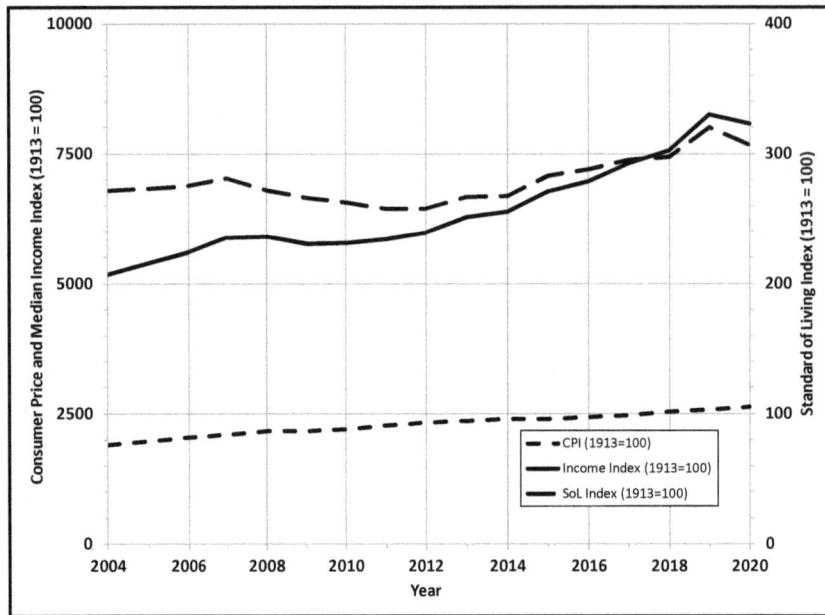

Figure 23.3-15: Median Income, Consumer Price, and Standard of Living Indices, 2004-2020

Figure 23.3-16 shows the changes in legal reserves on demand and time deposits at commercial banks during this period.

		Demand Deposits				Savings & Time Deposits
Day	Year	Lower Threshold ($ M)	Upper Threshold ($ M)	Between Thresholds (%)	Above Upper Threshold	
23 Dec	2004	7.0	47.6	3.0	10.0	0.0
22 Dec	2005	7.8	48.3	3.0	10.0	0.0
21 Dec	2006	8.5	45.8	3.0	10.0	0.0
20 Dec	2007	9.3	43.9	3.0	10.0	0.0
1 Jan	2009	10.3	44.4	3.0	10.0	0.0
31 Dec	2009	10.7	55.2	3.0	10.0	0.0
30 Dec	2010	10.7	58.8	3.0	10.0	0.0
29 Dec	2011	11.5	71.0	3.0	10.0	0.0
27 Dec	2012	12.4	79.5	3.0	10.0	0.0
23 Jan	2014	13.3	89.0	3.0	10.0	0.0
22 Jan	2015	14.5	103.6	3.0	10.0	0.0
21 Jan	2016	15.2	110.2	3.0	10.0	0.0
19 Jan	2017	15.5	115.1	3.0	10.0	0.0
18 Jan	2018	16.0	122.3	3.0	10.0	0.0
17 Jan	2019	16.3	124.2	3.0	10.0	0.0
16 Jan	2020	16.9	127.5	3.0	10.0	0.0
26 Mar	2020	None	None	0	0	0.0

Legal Reserve Ratio Changes, 2004-2020

1: Joshua N. Feinman, Reserve Requirements: History, Current Practice, and Potential Reform, Federal Reserve Bulletin, June 1993, p. 569-589
2. Federal Reserve Board, https://www.federalreserve.gov/monetarypolicy/reservereq.htm

Figure 23.3-16: Legal Reserve Ratios, 2004-2020

Figures 23.3-17 through 23.3-20 show some miscellaneous statistics of the banking systems, including overall reserve ratio, and the ratios of total deposits to reserves and total deposits to currency.

Miscellaneous Statistics of the Federal Reserve and Commercial System, 2004-2008 (millions USD)							
		Federal Reserve	At Commercial Banks				
Day	Year	Member Bank Reserves [1]	Total Deposits [2]	Reserve Ratio, Total Deposits	Currency Outside Banks	Ratio, Total Deposits to Reserves	Ratio, Total Deposits to Currency
31 Mar	2004	45,394	4,833,596	0.009	714,914	106.481	6.761
30 Jun	2004	45,722	4,964,822	0.009	727,776	108.587	6.822
29 Sep	2004	49,197	5,004,322	0.010	738,856	101.720	6.773
29 Dec	2004	49,237	5,175,511	0.010	758,397	105.114	6.824
30 Mar	2005	48,461	5,275,282	0.009	755,241	108.856	6.985
29 Jun	2005	47,333	5,348,084	0.009	763,437	112.988	7.005
28 Sep	2005	50,166	5,461,905	0.009	768,115	108.877	7.111
28 Dec	2005	48,126	5,644,245	0.009	794,900	117.281	7.101
29 Mar	2006	45,208	5,720,719	0.008	788,785	126.542	7.253
28 Jun	2006	46,621	5,791,045	0.008	795,479	124.215	7.280
27 Sep	2006	45,986	5,857,625	0.008	792,276	127.378	7.393
27 Dec	2006	46,911	6,136,138	0.008	819,930	130.804	7.484
28 Mar	2007	41,892	6,211,271	0.007	807,386	148.269	7.693
27 Jun	2007	46,236	6,248,045	0.007	812,339	135.134	7.691
26 Sep	2007	45,354	6,396,948	0.007	812,059	141.045	7.877
26 Dec	2007	47,441	6,718,067	0.007	829,913	141.609	8.095
26 Mar	2008	45,490	6,811,865	0.007	817,761	149.744	8.330
25 Jun	2008	48,815	6,792,636	0.007	825,203	139.151	8.231
24 Sep	2008	111,305	7,042,687	0.016	836,437	63.274	8.420
31 Dec	2008	855,566	7,330,679	0.117	886,651	8.568	8.268
1. Member bank reserves is reserve deposits at Federal Reserve Banks plus applied vault cash per H.3.							
2. Time deposits not shown separately in H.8 from Dec 2003ff.							

Figure 23.3-17: Miscellaneous Statistics of the Banking System, 2004-2008

Miscellaneous Statistics of the Federal Reserve and Commercial System, 2009-2013 (millions USD)							
		Federal Reserve	At Commercial Banks				
Day	Year	Member Bank Reserves [1]	Total Deposits [2]	Reserve Ratio, Total Deposits	Currency Outside Banks	Ratio, Total Deposits to Reserves	Ratio, Total Deposits to Currency
25 Mar	2009	823,749	7,295,645	0.113	899,798	8.857	8.108
24 Jun	2009	749,283	7,432,145	0.101	907,596	9.919	8.189
30 Sep	2009	980,925	7,542,337	0.130	912,652	7.689	8.264
30 Dec	2009	1,128,563	7,747,050	0.146	930,122	6.865	8.329
31 Mar	2010	1,158,668	7,736,879	0.150	933,542	6.677	8.288
30 Jun	2010	1,094,224	7,668,261	0.143	940,432	7.008	8.154
29 Sep	2010	1,032,552	7,756,707	0.133	954,794	7.512	8.124
29 Dec	2010	1,065,155	7,946,041	0.134	984,980	7.460	8.067
30 Mar	2011	1,505,680	8,030,748	0.187	1,005,313	5.334	7.988
29 Jun	2011	1,649,118	8,193,253	0.201	1,027,497	4.968	7.974
28 Sep	2011	1,637,938	8,359,353	0.196	1,038,076	5.104	8.053
28 Dec	2011	1,572,682	8,535,644	0.184	1,076,340	5.427	7.930
28 Mar	2012	1,587,654	8,619,520	0.184	1,098,319	5.429	7.848
27 Jun	2012	1,528,211	8,685,470	0.176	1,110,227	5.683	7.823
26 Sep	2012	1,486,680	8,893,033	0.167	1,128,192	5.982	7.883
26 Dec	2012	1,564,765	9,388,749	0.167	1,167,122	6.000	8.044
27 Mar	2013	1,840,906	9,401,742	0.196	1,177,679	5.107	7.983
26 Jun	2013	2,041,849	9,340,450	0.219	1,193,377	4.575	7.827
25 Sep	2013	2,349,673	9,558,164	0.246	1,205,955	4.068	7.926
25 Dec	2013	2,553,462	9,916,861	0.257	1,238,524	3.884	8.007
1. Member bank reserves is reserve deposits at Federal Reserve Banks plus applied vault cash per H.3.							
2. Time deposits not shown separately in H.8 from Dec 2003ff.							

Figure 23.3-18: Miscellaneous Statistics of the Banking System, 2009-2013

| Miscellaneous Statistics of the Federal Reserve and Commercial System, 2014-2018 (millions USD) | | | | | | | |
| | | Federal Reserve | At Commercial Banks | | | | |
Day	Year	Member Bank Reserves [1]	Total Deposits [2]	Reserve Ratio, Total Deposits	Currency Outside Banks	Ratio, Total Deposits to Reserves	Ratio, Total Deposits to Currency
26 Mar	2014	2,652,866	10,009,422	0.265	1,268,244	3.773	7.892
25 Jun	2014	2,726,747	10,086,575	0.270	1,280,096	3.699	7.880
24 Sep	2014	2,776,162	10,278,506	0.270	1,289,158	3.702	7.973
31 Dec	2014	2,648,363	10,597,225	0.250	1,338,522	4.001	7.917
25 Mar	2015	2,747,099	10,678,882	0.257	1,357,352	3.887	7.867
24 Jun	2015	2,634,489	10,658,235	0.247	1,365,349	4.046	7.806
30 Sep	2015	2,627,340	10,849,793	0.242	1,384,890	4.130	7.834
30 Dec	2015	2,277,374	10,991,280	0.207	1,426,176	4.826	7.707
30 Mar	2016	2,477,372	11,177,652	0.222	1,443,285	4.512	7.745
29 Jun	2016	2,317,644	11,237,908	0.206	1,462,755	4.849	7.683
28 Sep	2016	2,249,393	11,304,802	0.199	1,470,071	5.026	7.690
28 Dec	2016	1,965,470	11,593,245	0.170	1,509,076	5.898	7.682
29 Mar	2017	2,373,235	11,693,065	0.203	1,536,334	4.927	7.611
28 Jun	2017	2,185,002	11,674,214	0.187	1,559,134	5.343	7.488
27 Sep	2017	2,316,412	11,831,081	0.196	1,580,243	5.108	7.487
27 Dec	2017	2,191,599	12,081,382	0.181	1,616,323	5.513	7.475
28 Mar	2018	2,184,214	12,112,248	0.180	1,636,934	5.545	7.399
27 Jun	2018	1,996,693	12,131,155	0.165	1,665,308	6.076	7.285
26 Sep	2018	1,921,197	12,230,704	0.157	1,686,023	6.366	7.254
26 Dec	2018	1,712,756	12,575,250	0.136	1,716,129	7.342	7.328
1. Member bank reserves is reserve deposits at Federal Reserve Banks plus applied vault cash per H.3.							
2. Time deposits not shown separately in H.8 from Dec 2003ff.							

Figure 23.3-19: Miscellaneous Statistics of the Banking System, 2014-2018

| Miscellaneous Statistics of the Federal Reserve and Commercial System, 2019, 2020 (millions USD) | | | | | | | |
| | | Federal Reserve | At Commercial Banks | | | | |
Day	Year	Member Bank Reserves [1, 3]	Total Deposits [2]	Reserve Ratio, Total Deposits	Currency Outside Banks	Ratio, Total Deposits to Reserves	Ratio, Total Deposits to Currency
27 Mar	2019	1,692,266	12,658,732	0.134	1,723,754	7.480	7.344
26 Jun	2019	1,549,087	12,755,663	0.121	1,742,150	8.234	7.322
25 Sep	2019	1,462,392	12,916,057	0.113	1,762,927	8.832	7.326
25 Dec	2019	1,704,395	13,347,310	0.128	1,802,362	7.831	7.405
25 Mar	2020	2,108,932	14,165,886	0.149	1,872,242	6.717	7.566
24 Jun	2020	2,901,788	15,472,602	0.188	1,963,978	5.332	7.878
30 Sep	2020	2,854,690	15,672,674	0.182	2,029,101	5.490	7.724
30 Dec	2020		16,317,936		2,086,909		7.819
1. Member bank reserves is reserve deposits at Federal Reserve Banks plus applied vault cash per H.3.							
2. Time deposits not shown separately in H.8 from Dec 2003ff.							
3. The reserves shown for Sep 2020 are actually 9 Sep 2020, the last time reserves were reported in H. 3							

Figure 23.3-20: Miscellaneous Statistics of the Banking System, 2019, 2020

Figures 23.3-21 and 23.3-22 show the approximate monthly commercial bank prime interest rates and the Federal Funds Rates.

Approximate Monthly Average Bank Prime Rate (%) [1, 2]											
Year	Jan	Feb	Mar	Apr	May	Jun	Jul	Aug	Sep	Oct	Nov	Dec
2004	4.00	4.00	4.00	4.00	4.00	4.01	4.25	4.43	4.58	4.75	4.93	5.15
2005	5.25	5.49	5.58	5.75	5.98	6.01	6.25	6.44	6.59	6.75	7.00	7.15
2006	7.26	7.50	7.53	7.75	7.93	8.02	8.25	8.25	8.25	8.25	8.25	8.25
2007	8.25	8.25	8.25	8.25	8.25	8.25	8.25	8.25	8.03	7.74	7.50	7.33
2008	6.98	6.00	5.66	5.24	5.00	5.00	5.00	5.00	5.00	4.56	4.00	3.61
2009	3.25	3.25	3.25	3.25	3.25	3.25	3.25	3.25	3.25	3.25	3.25	3.25
2010	3.25	3.25	3.25	3.25	3.25	3.25	3.25	3.25	3.25	3.25	3.25	3.25
2011	3.25	3.25	3.25	3.25	3.25	3.25	3.25	3.25	3.25	3.25	3.25	3.25
2012	3.25	3.25	3.25	3.25	3.25	3.25	3.25	3.25	3.25	3.25	3.25	3.25
2013	3.25	3.25	3.25	3.25	3.25	3.25	3.25	3.25	3.25	3.25	3.25	3.25
2014	3.25	3.25	3.25	3.25	3.25	3.25	3.25	3.25	3.25	3.25	3.25	3.25
2015	3.25	3.25	3.25	3.25	3.25	3.25	3.25	3.25	3.25	3.25	3.25	3.37
2016	3.50	3.50	3.50	3.50	3.50	3.50	3.50	3.50	3.50	3.50	3.50	3.64
2017	3.75	3.75	3.88	4.00	4.00	4.13	4.25	4.25	4.25	4.25	4.25	4.40
2018	4.50	4.50	4.58	4.75	4.75	4.89	5.00	5.00	5.03	5.25	5.25	5.35
2019	5.50	5.50	5.50	5.50	5.50	5.50	5.50	5.25	5.15	4.99	4.75	4.75
2020	4.75	4.75	3.78	3.25	3.25	3.25	3.25	3.25	3.25	3.25	3.25	3.25

1. Source: Board of Governors of the Federal Reserve System, Bank Prime Loan Rate [MPRIME], Federal Reserve Bank of St. Louis; series MPRIME (https://fred.stlouisfed.org/series/MPRIME). These are averages of daily figures, not seasonally adjusted. The data is listed as "observation dates" on the first of the month; it is assumed they apply for the entire month, since the Federal Reserve cites them as monthly averages.

Figure 23.3-21: Monthly Average Bank Prime Rates, 2004-2020

Approximate Monthly Average Federal Funds Rate (%) [1]											
Year	Jan	Feb	Mar	Apr	May	Jun	Jul	Aug	Sep	Oct	Nov	Dec
2004	1.00	1.01	1.00	1.00	1.00	1.03	1.26	1.43	1.61	1.76	1.93	2.16
2005	2.28	2.50	2.63	2.79	3.00	3.04	3.26	3.50	3.62	3.78	4.00	4.16
2006	4.29	4.99	4.59	4.79	4.94	4.99	5.24	5.25	5.25	5.25	5.25	5.24
2007	5.25	5.26	5.26	5.25	5.25	5.25	5.26	5.02	4.94	4.76	4.49	4.24
2008	3.94	2.98	2.61	2.28	1.98	2.00	2.01	2.00	1.81	0.97	0.39	0.16
2009	0.15	0.22	0.18	0.15	0.18	0.21	0.16	0.16	0.15	0.12	0.12	0.12
2010	0.11	0.13	0.16	0.20	0.20	0.18	0.18	0.19	0.19	0.19	0.19	0.18
2011	0.17	0.16	0.14	0.10	0.09	0.09	0.07	0.10	0.08	0.07	0.08	0.07
2012	0.08	0.10	0.13	0.14	0.16	0.16	0.16	0.13	0.14	0.16	0.16	0.16
2013	0.14	0.15	0.14	0.15	0.11	0.09	0.09	0.08	0.08	0.09	0.08	0.09
2014	0.07	0.07	0.08	0.09	0.09	0.10	0.09	0.09	0.09	0.09	0.09	0.12
2015	0.11	0.11	0.11	0.12	0.12	0.13	0.13	0.14	0.14	0.12	0.12	0.24
2016	0.34	0.38	0.36	0.37	0.37	0.38	0.39	0.40	0.40	0.40	0.41	0.54
2017	0.65	0.66	0.79	0.90	0.91	1.04	1.15	1.16	1.15	1.15	1.16	1.30
2018	1.41	1.42	1.51	1.69	1.70	1.82	1.91	1.91	1.95	2.19	2.20	2.27
2019	2.40	2.40	2.41	2.42	2.39	2.38	2.40	2.13	2.04	1.83	1.55	1.55
2020	1.55	1.58	0.65	0.05	0.05	0.08	0.09	0.10	0.09	0.09	0.09	0.09

1. Source: Board of Governors of the Federal Reserve System, Federal Funds Effective Rate, Federal Reserve Bank of St. Louis, series = FEDFUNDS; https://fred.stlouisfed.org/series/FEDFUNDS. They are cited as "observed dates" always on the first of the month; it is assumed they apply as averages to the entire month, since the Federal Reserve cites them as "averages of daily figures".

Figure 23.3-22: Monthly Average Federal Funds Rates, 2004-2020

23.4 Summary, 2004-2020

Most of the failed bankers got bailouts during the collapse of the housing market, and there were considerable losses of employment in the financial sector. But easily forgotten are all the people who were hurt indirectly. There were a great many hidden costs of the housing collapse and bailout, not just in the real-estate and financial services industries. The banks became risk-averse, minimizing loans in order to preserve their positions, which hurt many small businesses that needed operating capital. That in turn, led to many layoffs among people not associated with the financial sector of the economy. The stock market incurred heavy losses due mostly to uncertainty; this affected many people's ability to retire, and introduced ambiguity as to the utility of their savings and investment plans.

The national debt continued to increase over this period as shown on Figure 23.3-3, culminating in a per-capita debt level of about $81,700 in 2020. Figure 23.4-1 illustrates the growth of the per-capita debt compared to median family income. The years were selected based on the highest debt level prevailing after major events. Even after World War II, the ratio of per-capita debt to median family annual income was 61%; it is 97% in 2020. It's official, ladies and gentlemen: the national debt has reached truly pathological levels. Notice that the events cited in Figure 23.4-1 are war debts, the bailouts of the banking system, and the Wuhan virus. But the growth of the debt is not due to these alone: keep in mind that the federal government began to expand spending in the 1930's in response to the Great Depression, which accelerated in the 1960's under the Great Society programs. These are in addition to the general growth of the administrative state along with benefits and subsidies paid to large corporations, all of which are now firmly embedded in the federal budget.

Event	Year	Approx. Median Weekly Family Income ($)	Approx. Median Family Annual Income ($)	Per-Capita National Debt ($)	Ratio (%) [1]	Income Reference [2]	National Debt Reference Figure No.
Revolutionary War Debt	1790	7.84	407	19.21	4.71	Figure 12-7	9.3-3
War of 1812 Debt	1815	10.53	548	15.09	2.76	Figure 12-7	11.3-3
Mexican War Debt	1850	8.69	452	2.74	0.61	Figure 12-7	13.3-3
Civil War Debt	1866	14.07	732	77.17	10.55	Figure 12-7	15.3-3
Spanish-American War Debt	1900	15.56	809	16.58	2.05	Figure 12-8	16.3-3
World War I Debt	1919	34.64	1,801	243.54	13.52	Figure 12-8	18.3-3
World War II Debt	1946	59.06	3,071	1,875.39	61.06	Figure 12-8	19.3-3
Korean War Debt	1954	80.13	4,167	1,660.35	39.85	Figure 12-9	20.3-3
Vietnam War Debt	1975	263.83	13,719	2,481.35	18.09	Figure 12-9	21.3-3
Savings & Loan Bailout	1987	595.58	30,970	9,709.45	31.35	Figure 12-9	22.3-3
Housing Collapse	2010	1,158.38	60,236	43,924.92	72.92	Figure 12-9	23.3-3
Iraq and Afghanistan War Debt	2012	1,196.94	62,241	51,347.36	82.50	Figure 12-9	23.3-3
Wuhan Virus	2020	1,615.54	84,008	81,780.55	97.35	Figure 12-9	23.3-3

1. This is the ratio of per-capita national debt to annual median family income. The median family size in the U. S. is about 3.
2. The income figure for 1790 is assumed to be the same as for 1800.

Figure 23.4-1: Ratio of Per-Capita Debt to Median Family Income for Selected Dates

Once the housing excesses were liquidated or compensated, the economy remained stable until China released the Wuhan virus in late 2019. Since then the economy has been in a recession, owing partly to an over-reaction by the Governors of many States.

Even as of 1 Jun 2021, some State Governors kept their residents under restrictions, partly as an over-reaction, and partly because they have become addicted to assuming arbitrary power: Alaska, California, Colorado, Delaware, Hawaii, Kentucky, Maine, Maryland, Massachusetts, Michigan, Minnesota, Nevada, New Hampshire, New Mexico, Oregon, Rhode Island, Tennessee, Utah, Washington State, Washington DC, and Wisconsin. The "COVID-19 Emergency" was finally formally ended 11 May 2023.

It is not necessary to carry the data any further than 2020 because the bad monetary and financial trends exhibited since the 1960's have accelerated under the Biden administration. First is the continued growth of government spending under the false pretense that the Wuhan virus requires it. Secondly, the government has continued the growth of social welfare "entitlements". Third, the increase in spending has led to higher debt which has continued the expansion of the money supply which in turn increased the inflation rate to levels not observed since the 1970's and 1980's. Fourth, the administration and Congress have continued to grant policy decisions to Executive branch departments in which the bureaucracy can formulate regulations with the force of law without Congressional concurrence. Those policy decisions have only served to increase business costs. Fifth, the administration has attempted to transfer the private student loan debt to a public debt. Sixth, the administration has promoted the importation of an unknown number of illegal immigrants; most of them must be supported by social spending. Seventh, the administration has attempted to destroy the domestic energy industry in favor of technologies that the U. S. will have to procure from China. The resulting increase in energy costs has contributed to increasing prices in addition to the monetary inflation. It is even worse than that: the increase in oil costs due to decreased production helped finance Russia's invasion of Ukraine, and the U. S. then proceeded to aid Ukraine. Thus the U. S. is indirectly financing both sides of the war.

References

[23.1-1]   Ben S. Bernanke, "Monetary Aggregates and Monetary Policy at the Federal Reserve: A Historical Perspective", Paper given at the Fourth Central Banking Conference, Frankfurt, Germany,, 10 Nov 2006. The quote is from his footnote #6.

[23.2-1]   Jelena McWilliams, *Federal Deposit Insurance Corporation 2020 Annual Report*, 18 Feb 2021, p. 145
[23.2-2]   op. cit., McWilliams, p. 145
[23.2-3]   Text of "An Act to provide for reconciliation pursuant to section 202(a) of the concurrent resolution on the budget for fiscal year 2006 (H. Con. Res. 95)", a.k.a. the Federal Deposit Insurance Reform Act of 2005, 109th Congress, Public Law 109-171, 8 Feb 2006
[23.2-4]   Text of "An Act to provide regulatory relief and improve productivity for insured depository institutions and for other purposes", a.k.a. the Financial Services Regulatory Relief Act of 2006, 109th Congress, Public Law 109-351, 13 Oct 2006
[23.2-5]   Text of "An Act to reauthorize the Export-Import Bank of the United States", 109th Congress, Public Law 109-438, 20 Dec 2006
[23.2-6]   op. cit., McWilliams, p. 145
[23.2-7]   Board of Governors of the Federal Reserve System, "Central Bank Liquidity Swap Lines", https://www.federalreserve.gov/regreform/reform-swaplines.htm
[23.2-8]   National Bureau of Economic Research (NBER), Cambridge, MA, (see website below)
[23.2-9]   Board of Governors of the Federal Reserve System, "Term Auction Facility", https://www.federalreserve.gov/regreform/reform-taf.htm
[23.2-10] Caroline Banton, *Term Auction Facility (TAF)*, 24 Nov 2020 https://www.investopedia.com/terms/t/term-auction-facility.asp
[23.2-11] Board of Governors of the Federal Reserve System, "Term Auction Facility", https://www.federalreserve.gov/regreform/reform-taf.htm
[23.2-12] op. cit., McWilliams, p. 145
[23.2-13] Text of "An Act to provide economic stimulus through recovery rebates to individuals,, incentives for business investment, and an increase in conforming and FHA loan limits", a.k.a. "The Economic Stimulus Act of 2008", 110th Congress, Public Law 110-185, 13 Feb 2008
[23.2-14] Financial Crisis Inquiry Commission (Phil Angelides, Chairman), *The Financial Crisis Inquiry Report*, NY: Public Affairs, 2011, p. 290
[23.2-15] Board of Governors of the Federal Reserve System, "Bear Stearns, JPMorgan Chase, and Maiden Lane LLC", https://www.federalreserve.gov/regreform/reform-bearstearns.htm
[23.2-16] Text of "An Act to provide needed housing reform and for other purposes", a.k.a. "Housing and Economic Recovery Act of 2008", 110th Congress, Public Law 110-289, 30 Jul 2008
[23.2-17] op. cit., Financial Crisis Inquiry Commission, pp. 309, 425, 444
[23.2-18] op. cit., Financial Crisis Inquiry Commission, pp. 323-327, 435
[23.2-19] op. cit., Financial Crisis Inquiry Commission, p. 435
[23.2-20] op. cit., Financial Crisis Inquiry Commission, pp. 432, 435
[23.2-21] Board of Governors of the Federal Reserve, "American International Group (AIG), Maiden Lane II and III", https://www.federalreserve.gov/regreform/reform-aig.htm
[23.2-22] op. cit., Financial Crisis Inquiry Commission, p. 436
[23.2-23] op. cit., Financial Crisis Inquiry Commission, p. 365
[23.2-24] Text of "An Act to provide authority for the Federal Government to purchase an insure certain types of troubled assets for the purpose of providing stability to and preventing disruption in the economy and financial system and protecting taxpayers, to amend the Internal Revenue Service Code of 1896 to provide incentives for energy production and conservation, to extend expiring provisions, to provide income tax relief, and for other purposes", a.k.a. the Emergency Economic Stabilization Act of 2008, 110th Congress, Public Law 110-343, 3 Oct 2008
[23.2-25] Board of Governors of the Federal Reserve System, Press Release 6 Oct 2008, "Board announces that it will begin to pay interest on depository institutions' required and excess reserve balances",

https://www.federalreserve.gov/newsevents/pressreleases/monetary20081006a.htm

[23.2-26]   Board of Governors of the Federal Reserve, "American International Group (AIG), Maiden Lane II and III", https://www.federalreserve.gov/regreform/reform-aig.htm

[23.2-27]   Board of Governors of the Federal Reserve System, "Commercial Paper Funding Facility (CPFF), https://www.federalreserve.gov/regreform/reform-cpff.htm

[23.2-28]   Board of Governors of the Federal Reserve, "American International Group (AIG), Maiden Lane II and III", https://www.federalreserve.gov/regreform/reform-aig.htm

[23.2-29]   op. cit., Financial Crisis Inquiry Commission, p. 381

[23.2-30]   Board of Governors of the Federal Reserve, Press Release, 25 Nov 2008, https://www.federalreserve.gov/monetarypolicy/20081125a.htm

[23.2-31]   Board of Governors of the Federal Reserve, "American International Group (AIG), Maiden Lane II and III", https://www.federalreserve.gov/regreform/reform-aig.htm

[23.2-32]   Board of Governors of the Federal Reserve, "American International Group (AIG), Maiden Lane II and III", https://www.federalreserve.gov/regreform/reform-aig.htm

[23.2-33]   op. cit., McWilliams, p. 145

[23.2-34]   op. cit., Financial Crisis Inquiry Commission, pp. 382-385

[23.2-35]   op. cit., Financial Crisis Inquiry Commission, pp. 385, 386

[23.2-36]   Board of Governors of the Federal Reserve, "Other lending facilities", https://www.federalreserve.gov/monetarypolicy/bst_lendingother.htm

[23.2-37]   Text of "An Act making supplemental appropriations for job preservation, and creation, infrastructure investment, energy efficiency and science, assistance to the unemployed, and State and fiscal stabilization, for the fiscal year ending September 30, 2009, and for other purposes", a.k.a. American Recovery and Reinvestment Act of 2009, 111th Congress, Public Law 111-5, 17 Feb 2009

[23.2-38]   Board of Governors of the Federal Reserve, "Other lending facilities", https://www.federalreserve.gov/monetarypolicy/bst_lendingother.htm

[23.2-39]   National Bureau of Economic Research, Cambridge, MA, https://www.nber.org/research/data/us-business-cycle-expansions-and-contractions

[23.2-40]   Board of Governors of the Federal Reserve, "American International Group (AIG), Maiden Lane II and III", https://www.federalreserve.gov/regreform/reform-aig.htm

[23.2-41]   op. cit., McWilliams, *Federal Deposit Insurance Corporation 2020 Annual Report*, 18 Feb 2021, p. 145

[23.2-42]   Board of Governors of the Federal Reserve System, "Central Bank Liquidity Swap Lines", https://www.federalreserve.gov/regreform/reform-swaplines.htm

[23.2-43]   op. cit., Banton, *Term Auction Facility (TAF)* https://www.investopedia.com/terms/t/term-auction-facility.asp

[23.2-44]   Text of "An Act to promote the financial stability of the United States by improving accountability and transparency in the financial system, to end "too big to fail", to protect the American taxpayer by ending bailouts, to protect consumers from abusive financial services practices, and for other purposes", a.k.a. the Wall Street Reform and Consumer Protection Act, a.k.a. the Dodd-Frank Act, 111th Congress, Public Law 111-203, 21 Jul 2010

[23.2-45]   Text of "An Act to amend the Internal Revenue Code of 1986 to extend certain expiring provisions and for other purposes", a.k.a. the "Unemployment Compensation Extension Act of 2010", 111th Congress, Public Law 111-205, 22 Jul 2010

[23.2-46]   Text of An Act to amend the Internal Revenue Code of 1986 to extend the funding and expenditure authority of the Airport and Airway trust Fund, to amend Title 49, United States Code, to extend authorizations for the airport improvement program and for other purposes", a.k.a., Tax Relief, Unemployment Insurance Reauthorization, and Job Creation Act of 2010", 111th Congress, Public Law 111-312, 17 Dec 2010.

[23.2-47]   op. cit., McWilliams, p. 145

[23.2-48]   Federal Register, Volume 76, No. 137, 18 Jul 2011, p. 42015

[23.2-49]   op. cit., McWilliams, p. 145

[23.2-50]   Text of "An Act to instruct the Inspector General of the Federal Deposit Insurance Corporation to study the impact of insured depository institution failures, and for other purposes", 112th Congress, Public Law 112-88, 3 Jan 2012

[23.2-51]   Text of "An Act to provide incentives for the creation of jobs, and for other purposes", a.k.a. "The Middle Class Tax Relief and Job Creation Act of 2012", 112th Congress, Public Law 112-96, 22 Feb 2012

[23.2-52] Text of "An Act to reauthorize the Export-Import Bank of the United States", 112th Congress, Public Law 112-122, 30 May 2012

[23.2-53] Board of Governors of the Federal Reserve System, Press release, 13 Dec 2012, "Federal Reserve and other central banks announce an extension of the existing temporary U. S. dollar liquidity swap arrangements through February 1, 2014", https://www.federalreserve.gov/newsevents/pressreleases/monetary20121213a.htm

[23.2-54] op. cit., McWilliams, p. 145

[23.2-55] Text of "An Act entitled the 'American Taxpayer Relief Act of 2012'", 112th Congress, Public Law 112-240, 2 Jan 2013

[23.2-56] op. cit., McWilliams, p. 145

[23.2-57] Text of "Joint Resolution making continuing appropriations for fiscal year 2015, and for other purposes", 113th Congress, Public Law 113-164, 19 Sep 2014

[23.2-58] op. cit., McWilliams, p. 145

[23.2-59] Text of "An Act to authorize funds for Federal-aid highways, highway safety programs, and transit programs, and for other purposes", a.k.a. the Fixing America's Surface Transportation Act (FAST Act), 114th Congress, Public Law 114-94, 4 Dec 2015

[23.2-60] op. cit., McWilliams, p. 145

[23.2-61] op. cit., McWilliams, p. 145

[23.2-62] op. cit., McWilliams, p. 145

[23.2-63] Text of "An Act to promote economic growth, provide tailored regulatory relief, and enhance consumer protections, and for other purposes", a.k.a. the Economic Growth, Regulatory Relief, and Consumer Protection Act, 115th Congress, Public Law 115-174, 24 May 2018

[23.2-64] op. cit., McWilliams, p. 145

[23.2-65] Text of "An Act making further consolidated appropriations for the fiscal year ending September 30, 2020, and for other purposes", 116th Congress, Public Law 116-94, 20 Dec 2019

[23.2-66] op. cit., McWilliams, p. 145

[23.2-67] Text of "An Act to implement the agreement between the United States of America, the United Mexican States, and Canada attached as an Annex to the Protocol Replacing the North American Free Trade Agreement", 116th Congress, Public Law 116-113, 29 Jan 2020

[23.2-68] Board of Governors of the Federal Reserve System, Press Release, 17 Mar 2020, "Primary Dealer Credit Facility", https://www.federalreserve.gov/monetarypolicy/pdcf.htm

[23.2-69] Board of Governors of the Federal Reserve System, Press Release 17 Mar 2020, "Commercial Paper Funding Facility", https://www.federalreserve.gov/monetarypolicy/cpff.htm

[23.2-70] Text of "An Act making emergency appropriations for the fiscal year ending September 30, 2020, and for other purposes", a.k.a. the "Families First Coronavirus Response Act", 116th Congress, Public Law 116-127, 18 Mar 2020

[23.2-71] Board of Governors of the Federal Reserve System, Press Release 18 Mar 2020, "Money Market Mutual Fund Liquidity Facility", https://www.federalreserve.gov/monetarypolicy/mmlf.htm

[23.2-72] New York Ste Executive Order 202-10, 23 Mar 2020, available at: https://www.governor.ny.gov/sites/default/files/atoms/files/EO_202.10.pdf

[23.2-73] Board of Governors of the Federal Reserve System, 15 Mar 2020 announcement, https://www.federalreserve.gov/monetarypolicy/reservereq.htm

[23.2-74] Text of "An Act to amend the Internal Revenue Code of 1986 to repeal the excise tax on high cost employer-sponsored health coverage", a.k.a. the Coronavirus Aid, Relief, and Economic Security Act, or CARES Act, 116th Congress, Public Law 116-136, 27 Mar 2020

[23.2-75] Board of Governors of the Federal Reserve System, Press release, 9 Apr 2020, "Paycheck Protection Program", https://www.federalreserve.gov/newsevents/pressreleases/files/monetary20200409a6.pdf

[23.2-76] Board of Governors of the Federal Reserve System, "Main Street Lending Program", https://www.federalreserve.gov/monetarypolicy/mainstreetlending.htm

[23.2-77] KPMG LLP, *Financial Statement: TALF II LLC*, 17 Mar 2021, p. 7, https://www.federalreserve.gov/aboutthefed/files/talfllcfinstmt2020.pdf

[23.2-78] KPMG LLP, Financial Statements: Corporate Credit Facilities LLC, 17 Mar 2021, p. 7, https://www.federalreserve.gov/aboutthefed/files/ccfllcfinstmt2020.pdf

[23.2-79] Text of "An Act making appropriations for the Department of the Interior, environment, and related agencies for the fiscal year ending September 30, 2019, and for other purposes", a.k.a. the Paycheck

Protection Program and Health Care Enhancement Act, 116th Congress, Public Law 116-139, 24 Apr 2020

[23.2-80] Board of Governors of the Federal Reserve System, "Municipal Liquidity Facility", https://www.federalreserve.gov/newsevents/pressreleases/files/monetary20200427a1.pdf

[23.2-81] Text of "An Act to amend the Small Business Act and the CARES Act to modify certain provisions related to the forgiveness of loans under the paycheck protection program, to allow recipients of loan forgiveness under the paycheck protection program to defer payroll taxes, and for other purposes", a.k.a. the "Paycheck Protection Program Flexibility Act of 2020", 116th Congress, Public Law 116-142, 5 Jun 2020

[23.2-82] Text of "An Act to extend the authority for commitments for the paycheck protection program and separate the amounts authorized for other loans under section 7(a) of the Small Business Act, and for other purposes", 116th Congress, Public Law 116-147, 4 Jul 2020

[23.2-83] Text of "An Act making consolidated appropriations for the fiscal year ending September 30, 2021, providing Coronavirus emergency response and relief, and for other purposes", 116th Congress, Public Law 116-260, 27 Dec 2020, (sections M and N, a.k.a. the Coronavirus Response and Relief Supplemental Appropriations Act)

[23.2-84] op. cit., McWilliams, p. 145

NBER website: https://www.nber.org/research/data/us-business-cycle-expansions-and-contractions

24

The Current Situation

24.1 The Current Failures of the Federal Reserve

The past few chapters have described the overall operation of the U. S. banking system under the Federal Reserve. The history of the U. S. prior to 1862 showed that without some sort of restraint, local bankers tended to issue more bank notes than they could redeem. The national bank system worked fairly well from 1862 to 1914, except there a few "financial panics" that disturbed the economy. Congress was led to believe in 1913 that with suitable regulation and control, the money supply could be tailored to the correct amount to meet the needs of the public, and with adequate supervision, would lead to greater stability in the banking industry and the economy in general. Congress therefore created the Federal Reserve and delegated to it Congress' power under the Constitution to "regulate the value" of money. It is instructive to read what the Federal Reserve said about itself on its 50th anniversary [24.1-1]:

> "On December 23, 1913, President Woodrow Wilson signed the Federal Reserve Act establishing the Federal Reserve System. Its original purposes, as expressed by its founders, were to give the country an elastic currency, to provide facilities for discounting commercial paper, and to improve the supervision of banking.
>
> From the outset, there was recognition that these original purposes were in fact parts of broader objectives, namely, to help counteract inflationary and deflationary movements, and to share in creating conditions favorable to a sustained, high level of employment, a stable dollar, growth of the country, and a rising level of consumption. Acceptance of the broader objectives has widened over the years.
>
> Over the years too, the public has come to recognize that these domestic objectives are related to the country's ability to keep its flow of payments with foreign countries in reasonable balance over time. Today it is generally understood that the primary purpose of the System is to foster growth at high levels of employment, with a stable dollar in the domestic economy, and with over-all balance in our international payments.
>
> How is the Federal Reserve related to production, employment, the standard of living, and our international payments position? The answer is that the Federal Reserve, through its influence on credit and money, affects indirectly every phase of American enterprise and commerce and every person in the United States."

We have the elastic currency as claimed, and the capacity to discount commercial paper. The regulatory part has worked well enough to suppress outright fraud, but it has not worked so well in restraining undue risks taken by the banking system. The two most recent examples of large-scale failure to control risk was the collapse of the Savings and Loan system in the 1980's and the real estate crash of 2008. There were other less severe problems as well: the tech crash of 2000, and the "junk bond" collapse of the 1980's.

The U. S. has experienced growth, a higher level of consumption, and higher standard of living since 1913. It would be a mistake however to attribute that entirely to the Federal Reserve, since the standard of living had been increasing steadily since the 1870's. It is easy to see that the Federal Reserve certainly has not provided a stable dollar or restrained inflationary trends, nor does the U. S. have sustained high levels of employment. The U. S. has not maintained a long-term balance of trade with foreign nations. All of the objectives cited are desirable, but what the authors forgot to mention is that the Federal Reserve has generally failed to achieve them. However, it would be unfair to blame any banking system for failure on all these fronts: given the intricacies of the economy and the banking business that supports it, achieving these "broader objectives" is a tall order indeed. In fact, basic economics shows that several of them are mutually exclusive. How the Federal Reserve could hope to accomplish all of these was wishful thinking from the very beginning. Worse than that, the Federal Reserve has succeeded at the one thing all central banks specialize in: a guarantee of long-term depreciation of the currency and the growth of the national debt [24.1-2], which the author above also neglected to mention.

The U. S. Federal Reserve is at present (2023) the undisputed leader of the international banking cartel. It holds this position only because the U. S. dollar is recognized as a de facto reserve currency for many other nations. As a reserve currency, the U. S. dollar can be exported to other nations to be held by them as reserves against their own fiat currencies. That implies, in turn, that those funds will never be returned to the U. S. as part of the domestic money supply, since it is either held in the foreign bank vaults, or is held as foreign demand deposits in U. S. banks, or circulates as currency in those nations. Those foreign deposits are considered government-owned, and are not counted against the U. S. domestic money supply. In other words, the U. S. can export excess dollars, thus reducing the amount of depreciation domestically. It can do so because the U. S. holds the position as banking industry leader, same as the Bank of England did before WW I, as the Bank of France did before the French Revolution, as the banks of Spain, Portugal, and Italy did before that. Consequences of WWI caused the Bank of England to lose its position because it became necessary to constantly devalue the pound sterling (against gold) as the national debt increased. Those nations that held the British pound sterling lost confidence in it, and turned instead to the U. S. dollar as a more stable currency. Currencies are all now fiat, but they are depreciating, which amounts to nearly the same thing as a devaluation against gold. History may not repeat, but it does rhyme: the U. S. Federal Reserve will lose its position eventually as well, probably to be replaced by a more reliable currency or a mixture of currencies. It will happen to the Federal Reserve because the U. S. Congress has forced it into managing an inherently unstable financial system. The Federal Reserve is not (as some believe) foreign-owned or involved in any overt crime or covert conspiracy. The Federal Reserve is an honest institution operating within a corrupt system; i.e., based on debt and wishful thinking. It performed the monetary magic in 2008 and 2020 because it had to do so for political reasons.

We can only hope that if the Federal Reserve as manager of the de facto reserve currency is displaced, that it not be replaced by the Bank of China managing the renminbi. The difference between the Bank of France, the Bank of England, and the U. S. Federal Reserve as against the Bank of China is that the three former institutions were not out to steal everything that came into their hands. The Bank of China, in its communistic greed and grasping for power, will attempt to confiscate everything.

Federal Reserve Notes are political money because the reserves that support them consist of U. S. government debt, which is political. The Federal Reserve Notes are then subject to the political axiom that 'perception is reality'. If the public believes (correctly or not) that they are declining in value or are worthless, then they are for practical purposes. If that notion becomes widespread, the public will do what is necessary to get rid of them. But, they will not cash in their stocks for notes, or cash their demand deposit accounts for the notes; they will instead demand the stock certificates and trade those for money they believe is stable in value, possibly to gold and silver. If there ever is a demand for stock certificates, and not just statements of account, consider it evidence that the ruling elite knows something about the Federal Reserve that you don't.

Many prominent economists inform us that the national debt doesn't matter too much so long as the economy can continue to grow. The explanation goes like this. The existence of the national debt means that interest has to be paid on it, even if the debt itself is not paid. The interest payments must come from current taxation. So long as the economy is growing, those interest payments are affordable, and so long as the rate of growth exceeds the additional interest due on the debt, the debt could (in theory) rise to any arbitrary level. In other words, if the debt increases in a given year requiring additional outlays for the interest payments, but the economy grows faster than the growth of the interest due, the national debt is not a problem. The reason is: the debt itself is constantly being rolled over by issuing Treasury bills that replace the ones that mature (i.e., not actually being paid), and it is only the interest that needs to be paid. If the economy grows fast enough, all is well, and the debt itself doesn't matter. This philosophy is sometimes called "growing our way out of debt". It means that so long as the depreciation causes GDP to increase, the ratio of debt to GDP will either remain constant or decline. If so, then the interest payments are affordable, and there is no problem with a constantly increasing debt. But there are two problems with this viewpoint. First, the additional debt has to be sold to someone, either individuals or the banking system. But history shows that there is a practical limit to how much debt will be purchased, and that is based on the public's sense of uncertainty as to whether buying the debt instruments are safe investments. No one knows what this tolerance level is; it is a matter of opinion, and such public opinion can change at a whim.

The second problem is more subtle. The economic experts recognize that, to a first approximation, the GDP is the product of the velocity of money (V) and the general price level (P). So we have:

$$GDP = V x P$$

The velocity of money is known to be fairly constant over long time periods (say 20 years or so); if that is the case, then GDP is a linear function of the price level. Federal Reserve data [24.1-3] shows that the velocity of the M2 money supply from 1959 to 2020 (62 years) has a mean value of 1.792 with a standard deviation of 0.203. That means that the velocity of money ranged between 1.589 and 1.995 in 39 of the 62 years, and ranged between 1.386 and 2.198 during 58 of the 62 years. An increase in the price level is partly due to the depreciation of the currency, which in turn is caused by the insertion of new money into the system, which in turn occurs because of the additional debt. Therefore, the theory arrives at the conclusion that so long as the money can be depreciated quickly enough to increase the GDP beyond the additional interest on the debt, then neither the depreciation rate nor the debt-to-GDP ratio matters. But depreciation does matter: prices increase faster than wages, and while the theory is correct on paper, there is a practical limit to how much depreciation can be tolerated (since it also causes disruptions in the economy). The poor and middle class end up paying indirectly via depreciation, same as always.

So those economists are really saying that the national debt is limited by the ability to make the interest payments, given that there is no need to pay the principal. We will thus have revolving debt as short-term Treasury bills mature and are renewed, and the debt can continue to accumulate so long as interest is paid and the buyers have confidence they will be paid. The system will collapse when the public cannot pay the taxes necessary to make the interest payments, or when buyers lose confidence (correctly or not) that they will be able to sell any bonds they hold, but there is no predictable threshold at which either of those can occur. In other words, the current fiat system will work until it doesn't. Interest rates were low until late 2022 in order to restrain the growth of the interest payments on the national debt. It was the same policy as in the 1930's and 1940's, when the U. S. Treasury pressured the Federal Reserve to support a price ceiling on U. S. bonds (i.e., keep the interest rate low) for the same reason. The increase in the Federal Funds Rate in late 2022 was done only as an attempt to counteract the inflation the government and Federal Reserve had created in 2021. Both the Federal Reserve and the Treasury are now further captives of Congress' inability to balance its budget.

Now you can see the issue -- if the debt becomes too large, the public won't be able to afford the taxes necessary to pay the interest (or, more likely, since no tax revolt is possible), a decline in the standard of living. Then Congress has to start cutting spending, which they don't want to do. Their idea is that we should continue to spend and increase the debt so long as the "investments" result in greater efficiency and higher growth. There is of course no guarantee that the additional spending will actually lead to higher "growth"; the "investment multiplier" is a fiction. If such "growth" is accompanied by depreciation, then there is the tax squeeze and revenue squeeze together, the very thing the government spending was intended to avoid.

The system may be at risk due to foreign opinion. If foreign nations begin to have doubts about the U. S. dollar, correctly or not, they will begin to make transactions, and hold their reserves, in currencies other than the U. S. dollar. OPEC will do so when it comes to believe, correctly or not, that the U. S. is not the reliable guarantor of security that the U. S. promised to be, or has sided with the enemies of the ruling families of the OPEC nations. If so, the OPEC cartel may decide to price oil in some other currency, or a mixture of currencies. When that happens, the U. S. will not be able to export either its dollars or the depreciation thereof; that means that the inflation returns home to the U. S., and prices rise. The Federal Reserve then has a problem: it cannot inject more money into the system since that will cause further depreciation. At the same time, Congress, unable to issue more debt, will have unpleasant choices: a) reduce spending; or b) reduce social insurance payments to individuals at a time when they are most needed; or c) increase taxes at a time when they are least affordable. At that point, the dollar will lose its place as a reserve currency, no new debt can be issued, and the U. S. economy will go into a near-permanent depression. That is when Congress has two choices: it can either steal everything from your 401K, IRA, and savings, or it can let the economics work itself out. If it chooses the latter, the result will be that all the superfluous expenditures will have to be eliminated, the bad investments liquidated, and the public goes back to work. The luxuries of minimum wages, unemployment insurance, welfare, etc. will go by the wayside, the very things Congress has always claimed to be essential for economic stability.

The Federal Reserve has power over the volume of money, but it cannot mandate the purchasing power of a dollar. It could do so only if it had the power to fix wages and prices. Does the Federal Reserve desire such a power? History shows that every federal agency wants more power. Are there any circumstances in which the Federal Reserve would assume such powers unilaterally? Yes, but only if doing so would benefit the banking industry and preserve the Federal Reserve's place as leader of the international banking cartel. Would Congress or the President assume such a power, or grant such a power to the Federal Reserve? We have already seen that wage and price controls do not work. But they would come back in style again, if re-implementing them benefitted the political and economic ruling elite, their families, and/or their cronies among the international corporations or the foreign nations that support them. You, the taxpaying chump, are not part of the equation.

24.2 The Real Problems

I once worked for a smart guy named Jerry Looper. One of his maxims was, "it is great fun to beat up on suppliers, but it's too late". In the engineering business, there are usually three reasons why it is too late: a) choosing a supplier that was not able to perform the job, either because it lacked access to the required technical expertise, or did not have the necessary experience, or did not have proper financing; b) the supplier either made mistakes in his proposal or made misrepresentations, and those were not caught during the evaluation; or c) the supplier was given either incorrect or incomplete specifications. In other words, problems with suppliers are often symptoms of a larger (self-induced) problem. We have the same situation now regarding the Federal Reserve: it is great fun to point out its failures and deficiencies, but it is too late. The Federal Reserve is not the core problem.

The Federal Reserve is the fall guy for four real problems. The first is that Congress cannot control its spending impulses, nor will it raise taxes to pay for what it spends, and therefore debt increases and the depreciation of the dollar continues. The debt and depreciation can only be reduced if Congress cuts spending and generates surpluses to pay off the existing debt. Here is a small example of this problem. The National Endowment for the Arts is a federal agency that partly finances artists and performers and promotes various entertainments. Every year, Congress allocates more money for the Endowment (its budget for 2020 was $162.5 M). Admittedly, that is not even pocket change when considering the total federal budget. That said, if Congress cannot cut small things, it cannot cut the large ones. Consider the following thought experiment. Suppose all 535 members of Congress were lined up, put under oath, and asked under penalty of perjury if they would go so far as to reduce the rate of increase in the funding of the Endowment. About 5% would go further: they would abolish it altogether. Another 5% would agree to abolish it over a period of ten years. Another 5% would agree to fix the funding at the current dollar level. But the other 85% would poop their lace dainties and assert their Fifth Amendment rights. Congress is a now a political prisoner of its own largesse (actually the taxpayer's largesse) and cannot cut funding for anything. Its favorite option is to raise hidden taxes on the middle class without cutting spending, which will eventually drive the middle class into poverty.

Why can't Congress cut spending? There are two reasons: first, it is the easy path to buying votes, and secondly, they'll be long gone when the bill comes due. Typically the members of Congress find it easy to go along to get along. Faction A supports faction B's spending priorities in return for faction B supporting faction A's spending priorities, and all of them get most of what they need to buy the votes necessary to get re-elected. Remember that it is perfectly legal for one member of Congress to bribe another member of Congress with your money; it is only illegal when you try to bribe a member of Congress with your money. See the difference/trick? This is how irresponsibility of Congress has caused the U. S. to degenerate into a fiat monetary system based on debt.

The second core problem is that the Federal Reserve has been tasked (by Congress) with achieving three mutually exclusive objectives: full employment, price stability, and economic growth. It can pretend to achieve economic growth by depreciating the currency, which will cause the GDP to increase given a fairly constant money velocity; but it is only on paper. But that same false tactic negates the possibility of price stability. When a politician brags about the increasing GDP, but in the next sentence whimpers about price increases due to inflation, he proves he is either a liar or a moron because they are in fact the same thing. Employment will fluctuate: it will increase at first as money is added, but will decline when wages catch up to prices. That is why the Federal Reserve, utilizing depreciation as its main tactic, is able to give the illusion of increased economic growth while failing to ensure price stability or employment.

Once again, it is easy to blame the Federal Reserve for our other economic problems that are out of its control. The third core problem is the policies of the government that have contributed greatly to the decline in wages: importation of a large number of illegal immigrants that expands the labor supply, and the exportation of the industrial base. Immigrants often work at jobs that Americans find too inconvenient, which occurs because the federal government pays welfare benefits to Americans who could be working. So the U. S. winds up with a double-edged problem. First, able-bodied Americans are collecting welfare thus increasing the federal expenditures. Secondly, illegal immigrants are performing the work, but at the same time are increasing the federal expenditures because they do not pay taxes, but do collect other benefits, namely health care and public schooling. Exportation of the industrial base is the natural outcome of the policies advocated by the utopian dreamers: first driving up taxes and labor costs such that U. S. companies relocated to Mexico and Asia, encouraged also by incoherent trade deals that put the U. S. companies at a disadvantage. The big reward came in 2001 when China joined the WTO and American companies got access to an infinite pool of slave labor.

The economic failures have led to issues within the U. S. culture. It was the Ivy League geniuses who came up with NAFTA that forced the traditional Mexican farmer off his land (causing illegal immigration). It was the same people that encouraged the trade deals that ultimately allowed the communists in China to offer up their slave labor and caused the U. S. industrial base to be exported. The lack of work affects the culture: idle hands being the devil's workshop, has led many people to become professional criminals since there is no other work to be had. The criminal underground also benefits because it has at its disposal a great number of under-educated people, since the Ivy League has also ruined the public schools with their half-baked ideology and failed teaching methods. It was the Ivy League who came up with the policy of destroying the families of the poor with welfare, and has led to great instability among low-income families. All this has now converged into widespread class warfare in the U. S., but the Ivy League graduates will escape all responsibility for imposing and promoting the policies that caused it. When their policies fail, they attribute it to the three all-purpose excuses of 'systemic racism', 'white supremacy', and 'man-made climate change'.

The fourth core problem is that the American people continue to elect people to Congress and the Presidency that are either ignorant, or don't care, or are not serious about addressing the economic and financial position. A significant fraction of voters now believe the fairy tale that somehow the social welfare benefits are all being paid for out of someone else's pocket, and vote for those who maintain the myth. The current situation, bad as it is, will continue until the public starts to recognize the problem, and take steps to elect people who are willing to deal with it before the system collapses.

It is possible that the Federal Reserve Notes (FRN) will become so depreciated that the government will intervene to give the illusion that they are dealing with the monetary problem. It is likely that the U. S. Treasury will issue a new currency, probably some new form of Treasury Notes and redeem the Federal Reserve Notes at 50 to one. All contracts, rents, prices, and social benefit payments will be re-priced in Treasury Notes. The national debt will be re-priced from $30 trillion down to $600 billion, and the politicians will brag about the great job they did nearly eliminating the national debt. Except of course, they did no such thing. If the Federal Reserve Notes are replaced by Treasury Notes at 50 to one, so are your wages. If you were making $20.00 per hour in Federal Reserve Notes, you now will be making four-tenths of a Treasury Note per hour. (The politicians won't mention that, and you'll be called a terrorist if you do.) If your share of the national debt came to 4,500 hours of your work, your share will still be 4,500 hours of your work, it will simply be tabulated in different units. It will be the same trick as when the French Directory redeemed the assignats for mandats at 30 to one; it did not solve the underlying problem; it just reduced the amount of paper and ink expended on issuing fiat money. The only real difference is that the Treasury Notes will be direct liabilities of the Treasury as opposed to liabilities of the Federal Reserve. But that does not matter because they are both actually liabilities of you, the taxpayer.

Treasury Secretary Fessenden gave a prudent warning about governments issuing money. This was written in 1864, just after the U. S. government began issuing legal tender non-redeemable United States Notes (greenbacks) [24.2-1]:

"The banking interest in the United States is an important one; it has grown with the business of the country, and has been largely instrumental in developing the national resources and in increasing the national wealth. Banks of issue, badly and dishonestly as many of them have been managed, and disastrous as have been the failures which bad management and dishonesty have produced, have still been of unquestionable advantage to the people. The capital of the country has been largely, and in good faith, invested in them and thousands of stockholders depend upon the dividends upon their bank stock for support. It is an interest which has stood by the government in its struggles with a gigantic rebellion; and now, when it is indispensable that the government should control the issues of paper money, there has been created a national banking system, not to destroy the State banks but to absorb them, and that, too, without prejudice to their stockholders.

Governments should not be bankers. None has existed which could be safely trusted with the privilege of permanently issuing its own notes as money. Circulating notes have been issued under peculiar circumstances by other governments, as it is now being done by that of the United States, but the judgment of the world is against it as a permanent policy, and nothing but an overpowering public exigency will at any time justify it. Under popular institutions like ours no more dangerous, no more corrupting power could be lodged in the hands of the party in possession of the government; none more perilous to official probity, and free elections. Give to a party dominant in the legislative and executive branches of the government the authority of issuing paper money for the purpose of furnishing the country with its currency, subject as it would be to no restraint but its own pleasure, and what guaranty would there be that this authority would be honestly and judiciously used? If there were no risk in the preparation of the notes, and checks were provided to make fraudulent issues an impossibility, the power of issuing government promises as a circulating medium is too dangerous a one to be conferred upon any party, except under extraordinary circumstances.

The present issue of United States notes as lawful money, and the decisions of the courts sustaining the constitutionality of the issue, have been justified by the consideration that under a great public necessity, when the nation's life is in peril, policies must be framed and laws must be interpreted with a view to the preservation of the government. This is the paramount consideration to which all others must bend. Whatever opinions may have been, in times past, entertained in regard to the propriety of the issue of United States notes, and the expediency as well as the constitutionality of the law making them a legal tender, there are now, I apprehend, very few intelligent persons who are not persuaded that without these notes, and the character of lawful money given to them by Congress and confirmed by the courts, the credit of the nation would have given way at the very outbreak of the rebellion. When the war has been concluded, and the exigency which made the issue of government notes a necessity has ceased to exist, there will be very few to advocate the continued use of them on the ground of economy.

If, however, there were no objections of the kind alluded to, there are other objections to the permanent issue of circulating notes by the government, which must be apparent to all who have considered the object and uses of a paper currency. Paper money has been found to be useful, or rather an absolute necessity in all commercial countries for the convenient transaction of business, and as a circulating representative of values too large to be represented by coin. Although the fruitful cause of great evils, by reason of its unregulated use, and of its uncertain and frequently deceptive character, the general utility of it can hardly be questioned. Now, what is needed in a paper circulating medium, is, that it should be convertible into coin; that it should be sufficient in amount to answer the purposes of legitimate business; that it should not, on the one hand, by being over-issued, encourage extravagance and speculation and give an artificial and unreliable value to property; nor, on the other hand, by being reduced below the proper standard, interrupt business and unsettle values. It should be supplied to just the extent of the demands of a healthy trade. It should be increased as the regular business of the country may require its increase, and be diminished as the proper demand for it is diminished. It is not pretended that banks of issue have furnished this kind of circulation. Bank notes, with few exceptions, have been convertible into coin when there was no demand for coin, and inconvertible when there was. They have, too generally, been issued for the exclusive benefit of the bankers, and not for the convenience of the public, and they have encouraged speculation, when their true mission was to facilitate trade. It has been the bane of a bank note circulation, that it has been expanded by the avarice of the bankers, and contracted by the distrust that over-issues have created.

Now, this objection to a bank note circulation applies with much greater force to government issues. There is always inducement enough for banks to keep up a full circulation, and against excessive issues there are the restrictions of law and the liability to redeem. Government notes, in the issue thereof, would be regulated only by the necessities of the government or the interests of the party in power. At one time they might be increased altogether beyond the needs of commerce and trade, thereby enhancing prices and inducing speculation; at another, they might be so reduced as to embarrass business and precipitate financial disasters. They would be incomparably worse in this respect than a bank note currency, because the power that should control circulation would be the power that furnishes it. Supplied by an authority not in sympathy with trade, they would not be accommodated to the requirements of trade. They might be the fullest in volume when there was the least demand for a full circulation, and the most contracted when there was a healthy demand for an increase. They would eventually become an undesirable circulation, because there would be no way in which the redemption of them could be enforced: they would be a dangerous circulation, because they would be under the control of political parties; an unreliable circulation, because, having no connection with trade and commerce, they would not be regulated by their necessities."

His main argument was that the United States Notes constituted political money, necessary to meet the needs of the Civil War, but afterwards could become dangerous political money controlled by political factions. That is what U. S. money has become under the Federal Reserve.

If the U. S. government cannot find voluntary customers for its new debt, it may decide to find involuntary ones. The method of honest repayment was mentioned in section 1.12; here are seven possible options that come to mind that avoid the inconvenience.

Option 1: Use the same tactic Adolf Hitler used in the 1930's as a way to "pay off" the debt Germany incurred and reparations that were demanded by the Allies at the end of World War I [24.2-2]. The scheme was simple: default on the bonds held by private investors and buy them back for pennies on the dollar, while continuing to make payments on the bonds held by the institutional investors. Obviously this won't do much if the holders of the bonds are mostly institutions such as pension funds (especially those of the large unions). It will be necessary beforehand to designate the bonds held by certain politically-important institutions such as the unions or Wall Street institutions as a unique "series" or category so that the default can be "suitably selective". This approach would require the "important institutional investors" to be warned ahead of time, and ensure that all the bonds to be defaulted upon end up in individual 401k's, IRA's, and Roth IRAs. Then it is the chosen individuals (mostly middle class, mostly non-union) who will take the losses.

Option 2: This method emulates the same means used to "redeem" the Continentals after the American Revolution: liquidate all the bonds and pay them off at a few cents on the dollar. The Continentals were redeemed at 2.5 cents on the dollar. Once again this method will require some careful maneuvering to make sure that the ruling elite, the politically connected, the wealthy who fund the political parties, and the major organized voting blocs are minimally affected: this is politically feasible only if the unaffiliated individual members of the middle class mostly take the losses. It simply means that a lot of secret agreements must be made beforehand.

Option 3: This method amounts to "asset swapping" from individual retirement accounts (401k's and IRA's). The idea is that viable earning assets such as stocks in profitable businesses would be seized and handed over to holders of government bonds and the bonds would then be cancelled. The government is then out of debt. The value of the seized earning assets would be replaced by a new type of government debt, not one payable at interest, but scrip redeemable only in special government stores, but having twice the face value of the earning assets. The only items sold in those stores are things that the government already has available or can be obtained fairly cheaply. The scrip will of course have an expiration date and gradually become worthless (after say ten years). Here's an example of how this would work. Suppose your 401k totals $100,000 and consists of $40,000 in U. S. Treasury bonds and $60,000 stocks. First, $40,000 of stocks will seized and will replace the $40,000 in U. S. Treasury bonds, and the $40,000 bonds will be cancelled. The remaining $20,000 in stocks will be seized to be used to pay other bonds held by other people. At this point, you now have $40,000 in stocks (that replaced the initial $40,000 in U. S. bonds). How will you be compensated for the other $20,000 in stocks that was taken and the initial $40,000 in bonds that were cancelled, which totals $60,000? It will be replaced by scrip having a face value of 50% greater than the total amount owed, i.e., $90,000. Your 401k then is worth the $40,000 plus $90,000 = $130,000. On paper, you will earn money, and that is how the program will be sold to the public. Those who own only stocks will of course be compensated by scrip at the ratio of 1.5 for 1. Those who own only Treasury bonds will be "rewarded" as it were since the bonds will be exchanged dollar for dollar by earning assets in the form of stocks confiscated from other people. As you can see, there is a fundamental "fairness" issue here as to how the ratios will be arbitrated. Who cares? The entire scheme is unfair. Meanwhile, the scrip will be transferable, extractable from the 401k without penalty, and redeemable at the special stores, but will no longer be an interest-earning liability of the government (i.e., the taxpayers). If the value of the earning assets available for asset swapping exceeds the amount of bonds in existence, the ratio of scrip face value and earning asset value can be adjusted so as to make the plan appear equitable. So how does the government actually escape paying, if the scrip has a face value of some multiple of the stocks confiscated? Simple: since the scrip can only be ultimately redeemed at government stores, the government has a pricing monopoly. Will the recipients shop there? Of course: what choice do they have, if the scrip expires in ten years? They will get what they can for it while they can. This plan is nothing more than Congress using its ultimate power of taxation while giving a veneer of compensation to the holders of actual earning assets.

Option 4: The government debt could be converted directly into currency; in other words, print Federal Reserve Notes or issue demand deposits up to the face value of the Treasury bonds, issue them to the holders thereof, and cancel the bonds. It is not a new idea. President Franklin Roosevelt, in a meeting 12 Mar 1933 to discuss how to reopen the banks, proposed to do so according to Meltzer, quoting George Harrison, Chairman of the Open Market Investment Committee [24.2-3]. The government bonds at that time amounted to $21 billion, and Meltzer states that converting them to currency on demand would have "doubled the money stock, currency, and demand deposits". The plan was never adopted; instead the stronger banks were allowed to reopen with government guarantees. Recall that the lower and middle classes would have been injured the most, since wages rise slower than prices during a sudden depreciation of the money. The government would have then been faced with balancing the federal budget, since it will have ruined its credit rating. This policy trades inflation and loss of confidence in return for a cancellation of the debt.

Option 5: The government could simply refuse to pay both interest and principal, which amounts to declaring bankruptcy. It happened once before (cf. Chapter 7, 17 Aug 1784), but that was before the current Constitution was established. Unfortunately, nations do not get to declare bankruptcy per se; it means that the government has decided to abandon all pretense of paying its obligations, and those holding the government bonds will take the full loss. Of course, the ruling classes will know about it well in advance so as to divest themselves of their holdings. The consequences are that the national budget will have to be balanced, since no credit will be available, and there will be large layoffs of government workers. Secondly, the politicians will be forced to admit they have failed the nation. For that reason alone, I suspect this is an unlikely option.

Option 6: A sixth option is to arrange a sale of all the outstanding debt to some consortium of foreign nations willing to pay off the notes (probably at a discount) in return for future services by the U. S. This amounts to a conversion of debt to equity. In return, the U. S. will become a tributary colony to that consortium of foreign nations: the U. S. will export large amounts of commodities at no charge, will permit unlimited imports of those nations' merchandise (possibly paying bounties on the imports), grant those nations either ownership or control of all ports of entry, and allocate the U. S. armed forces as proxies to fight the wars the foreign nations find too inconvenient. This is tantamount to being conquered because our politicians cannot control themselves; but no matter: the ruling class will not be inconvenienced because they will be appointed to high offices to run the U. S. as viceroys, implementing the orders of the foreign consortium.

Option 7: Pay the foreign holders of debt in commodities (convert debt to equity), and default on paying the domestic holders. Here is how this would work. Foreign individuals and corporations who hold U. S. debt will be paid by their governments in their currency; their government in turn will be compensated by the U. S. government, not in money, but in commodities that the foreign nation needs. For example, if Japanese individuals or institutions own a trillion dollars worth of U. S. debt, they will be paid in yen over a period of years by the Japanese government; the U. S. will ship to Japan a trillion dollars worth of oil, wheat, corn, soybeans, beef, and timber over a period of years. Any U. S. debt held by a foreign government will be cancelled in the same way, by shipping commodities. Individual U. S. citizens who hold U. S. debt in their IRAs or 401k's will receive a few cents on the dollar, but institutions holding U. S. bonds on behalf of pension funds will be paid in full. This will amount to a partial domestic bankruptcy in the course of a partial redemption of the debt. But for it to work, the U. S. government would have to impose strict controls on prices and wages in the industries whose products are to be exported in lieu of the debt, because only the difference between costs and wholesale prices can contribute to paying down the debt.

The single most important of these seven options is that the planning must be done in absolute secrecy except for those who need to take action in order to become exempt. None of these has to be used exclusively. There are no doubt a great many more sophisticated plans that could be devised should the need arise.

24.3 A Partial Remedy

Has the Federal Reserve as an institution failed to live up to its intentions? Yes. Are there sufficient grounds to abolish it? Yes. Would abolishing it solve our financial and economic problems? No. Former Congressman Dr. Ron Paul has long advocated for abolishing the Federal Reserve [24.3-1]. He is the one person in Congress who was consistent in arguing that it is necessary to restore a sound monetary system in the U. S. But I must disagree with him on abolishing the Federal Reserve on the grounds that it is politically impossible. Abolishing the Federal Reserve means that some other central bank will have to replace it because Congress needs some institution to act as a fiscal agent for the government. It seems to me that a better alternative exists so long as it meets two fundamental requirements. First, history shows that the best monetary system, even in advanced economies, is one based on paper money that is redeemable on demand in either gold or silver. The reason is: it restrains both Congress and the banking system because the money is backed by the labor of the past, not debt, which is labor of the future. At the same time, paper money or demand deposits based on metal would preserve the legitimate commercial credit system. Credit would be extended based on savings instead of government debt. I am proposing a return to a bimetal system, but with one caveat: the value ratio between the two metals would not be fixed by a "mint ratio"; they would be allowed to float per their market value. The money would have to be denominated in units of weight of metal instead of "dollars". It is not a new idea [24.3-2]. The unit of weight printed on the note, whether it is gold or silver, would be its actual redemption value in the designated metal. This does introduce one additional complication, namely, that products would have two prices, one for gold, and one for silver (or whatever other metal was used); and there would have to be some means of making small change in each, and some way to calculate combination prices if a customer chose to pay partly in one and partly in another. But that is just arithmetic; surely we can figure it out. The second requirement is that the Federal Reserve, structurally intact in its present form, would be subject to revisions of Sections 10, 10A, 10B, 13, 14, and 16 of the Federal Reserve Act: it would be prohibited from engaging in any transactions involving U. S. debt securities, including holding them as reserves for commercial banks, and be limited to the amount of credit it could extent to the U. S. government. It is not a new idea. The charter for the second Bank of the United States (cf. Chapter 11, 10 Apr 1816) contained the following provisions in section 11 [24.3-3]:

> "The said corporation [Bank of the United States] shall not, directly or indirectly, deal or trade in anything except bills of exchange, gold or silver bullion, or in the sale of goods really and truly pledged for money lent and not redeemed in due time, or goods which shall be the proceeds of its lands. It shall not be at liberty to purchase any public debt whatsoever, nor shall it take more than at the rate of six per centum per annum for or upon its loans or discounts.
>
> No loan shall be made by the said corporation, for the use or on account of the government of the United States, to an account exceeding five hundred thousand dollars, or of any particular State, to an amount exceeding fifty thousand dollars, or of any foreign prince or state, unless previously authorized by a law of the United States."

Adjusting the rules of the Federal Reserve is only a partial solution in that it would partly restrain Congress from increasing the debt; but it will still be necessary for Congress to get serious about its spending priorities and develop a method to pay down the debt that has already accumulated.

References

[24.1-1]   Board of Governors of the Federal Reserve System, *The Federal Reserve System: Purposes and Functions*, Washington, DC: U. S. Government Printing Office, 1963, pp. 1, 2

[24.1-2]   Murray N. Rothbard, *The Mystery of Banking,* Auburn, AL: Ludwig von Mises Institute, 2008, pp. 172-176, 239-242 (originally published 1983)

[24.1-3]   Federal Reserve M2 money supply velocity data, cf. https://fred.stlouisfed.org/series/M2V

[24.2-1]   W. P. Fessenden, *Report of the Secretary of the Treasury on the State of the Finances for the Year 1864*, 6 Dec 1864, Washington, DC: Government Printing Office, 1864, pp. 50, 51

[24.2-2]   L. Albert Hahn, *The Economics of Illusion*, Burlington VT: Fraser Publishing Company, 1949, pp. 28-36. The passage in question was first published as the essay "Capital is Made At Home", in the journal *Social Research*, May 1944

[24.2-3]   Allan H. Meltzer, *A History of the Federal Reserve*, Chicago, IL: University of Chicago Press, 2003, Vol. 1, p. 422

[24.3-1]   Ron Paul, *End the Fed*, New York: Grand central Publishing, Hachette Book Group, 2009

[24.3-2]   Condy Raguet, *A Treatise on Currency and Banking*, Philadelphia, PA: Grigg & Elliot, 1840, pp. 211-214 (Reprinted by Forgotten Books, FB&c Ltd., London)

[24.3-3]   Text of "An Act to incorporate the subscribers to the Bank of the United States", 14th Congress, Session 1, Chapter 44, 10 Apr 1816

A

Notes on the Banking System Condition Data Under the Federal Reserve

A.1 General Notes

The following general notes apply to the condition statements of the banking system from 1915 to 2020.

a. The Federal Reserve Bulletins reached their peak of consistency and readability in the 1950's, 1960's, and early 1970's. Afterward, the data started becoming available later, and not as much data was provided in each Bulletin. By the late 1980's, the Bulletins seemed to be designed to hide something. The last one was published in 2003, and replaced by the "statistical data" on the Federal Reserve website. The datasets of interest here are H.4.1, H. 6, and H.8, as noted.

b. All data in the Figures are for last-Wednesday of the month unless otherwise noted; early years are sometimes a mixture of data types due to lack of record-keeping by the Federal Reserve.

c. "The "error" in the Liabilities figures is defined as (Total Assets-Total Liabilities)/Total Assets, in percent. This is what the Federal Reserve refers to as "statistical discrepancy" or "residual", expressed as a percentage.

A.2 Setup of the Federal Reserve-Commercial Banking System Condition Statements

Figure A.2-1 shows the overall assets and liabilities of the banking system under the Federal Reserve, and Figure A.2-2 shows a reduced version [A.2-1].

As indicated in the notes to Figure A.2-1, some of the assets and liabilities between the Treasury and Federal Reserve Banks and between the Federal Reserve Banks and the commercial banks cancel out. All the non-monetary liabilities (Treasury cash, Treasury deposits at the Federal Reserve, Treasury demand deposits at commercial banks, and foreign Deposits), end up as overall liabilities of the banking system in general. Time deposits at commercial banks are included as direct liabilities, although technically are non-monetary liabilities, because the notice of withdrawal is never enforced. The tables shown chapters 18 through 23 include an error estimate in percent; it is calculated as 100*(Assets-Liabilities)/Assets.

Assets and Liabilities of the Treasury, Federal Reserve and Commercial Banking System				
	Assets	**Liabilities**	**Non-Monetary Liabilities**	**Net Worth**
U. S. Treasury	Gold Stock Silver [3]	Gold Certificates [1] Treasury Currency [2]	Treasury Cash	
Federal Reserve Banks	Gold Certificates [1] Treasury Currency [2] Loans [5] Investments [6]	Federal Reserve Notes [7] Commercial Bank Reserve Deposits [4]	Treasury Deposits Foreign Deposits	Capital
Commercial Banks	Treasury Currency [2, 3] Federal Reserve Notes Reserve Deposits [4] Loans Investments [9]	Demand Deposits Time Deposits [8]	Treasury Demand Deposits	Capital
1. Gold certificates as liabilities of Treasury and assets of Federal Reserve cancel.				
2. The portion of Treasury Currency as liabilities of the Treasury and assets of the Federal Reserve partially cancel.				
3. Silver is included as part of the Tresury Currency not cancelled per note 2; included as a general asset under "Treasury Currency Outstanding".				
4. The reserve deposits as assets of commercial banks and liabilities of the Federal Reserve cancel.				
5. Loans of Federal Reserve listed as "Discounts and Advances".				
6. Investments at Federal Reserve are in U. S. securities.				
7. Only the portion outside the Federal Reserve and commercial banks are liabilities, cited as "Currency Outside Banks".				
8. The tables include time deposits as liabilities of the commercial banks, since notification of withdrawal is not enforced.				
9. Investments in commercial banks include U. S. securities plus others.				

Figure A.2-1: Complete Assets and Liabilities of the Banking System

Figure A2-2 is a tabular version of Figure 17.4-3. The approximate relation between the items in Figure A.2-2 and the Federal Reserve H.6 statistics (money supply values M0, M1, M2):

a. M0 = currency outside banks (part of which is Treasury Currency in the form of minor coin and part is Federal Reserve Notes)

b. M1 = M0 plus demand deposits and time deposits at commercial banks

c. M2 = M1 plus large time deposits including negotiable CD's.

Reduced Approximate Assets and Liabilities of the Federal Reserve and Commercial Banking System		
	Assets	**Liabilities**
General	Gold Stock Treasury Currency Outstanding	Currency Outside Banks Treasury Cash
Federal Reserve Banks	Discounts and Advances U. S. Government Securities	Treasury Deposits Foreign Deposits
Commercial Banks	Loans Investments in U. S. securities Other investments	Demand Deposits Time Deposits Treasury Demand Deposits Capital [1]
1. The tables show only the capital of commercial banks, which greatly exceed the Federal Reserve capital accounts.		

Figure A.2-2: Approximate Summary Assets and Liabilities of the Banking System

Notice that the reserves of the commercial banks held in the Federal Reserve Banks cancel out using the method shown above. The reserves are shown separately in the miscellaneous statistics following the condition statements of the overall system.

A.3 Assets:

The assets of the banking system under the Federal Reserve were tabulated under the following guidelines:

a. "Treasury Currency Outstanding" excludes Federal Reserve Notes, since they are liabilities of the Federal Reserve.

b. "U. S. Government Securities" includes certificates of indebtedness, but excludes municipal warrants (applies only to data prior to 1933).

c. Federal Reserve "Discounts and Advances" includes those guaranteed by the U. S. Government.

d. Federal Reserve "Discounts and Advances" include Bills Bought and Bills Discounted, but excludes "Other" sometimes cited in the Federal Reserve Bulletins (cf. Jun 1930).

e. Federal Reserve "Discounts and Advances" excludes Acceptances and "Other Federal Reserve Assets" (cf. Federal Reserve Bulletin, Jan 1972, pdf p. 72, note 2).

f. Federal Reserve "Discounts and Advances" are referred to as Loans beginning with the Jan 1972 Federal Reserve Bulletin.

g. Data is Not Seasonally Adjusted, is either end-of-month or Last-Wednesday except as noted.

h. Loan data excludes interbank and items in collection.

i. The Commercial Bank data is for all commercial institutions, including branches of foreign banks (cf. Feb 1981, pdf p. 107, note 1).

j. Federal Reserve "U. S. Securities" includes owned outright plus those under repurchase agreements.

k. "Trading account assets" were shown separately, when applicable, under "Other Securities" in the Commercial Bank data until Apr 1994. Beginning in May 1994, the Federal Reserve Bulletins added "Other" and "Trading assets"; this made it necessary to use H.8 data for "Other" investment figures starting Mar 1994, since the "trading assets" are excluded in H.8.

l. "Discounts and Advances" are sometimes referred to as "Loans to Depository Institutions" in Federal Reserve Bulletins starting in 1987.

m. Federal Reserve statistical data H.4.1 (Gold Stock, Treasury Currency Outstanding, Federal Reserve U. S. Securities, and Discounts & Advances) is available only since 2002. The data from the Federal Reserve Bulletins is used for 1915 to 2002.

n. Federal Reserve statistical data H.8 (Commercial Bank Loans, U. S. Government Securities investments, and "Other" investments) is available back to 1973, but Federal Reserve Bulletin data is used until Sep 2003 to be consistent with the liabilities data.

o. The assets absorbed by the Treasury and Federal Reserve after the 2008 housing and mortgage financing collapse of 2008 were never included in the Federal Reserve balance sheet, and are not included here. This includes the Troubled Asset Relief Program, tabulated as Maiden Lane LLC and Commercial Paper (Mar 2009 ff), Term Auction Credit (Mar 2009 ff), mortgage-based securities (Jun 2009 ff), central bank liquidity swaps (Sep 2009 ff), the unamortized premium and discounts on securities held outright (Sep 2013 ff), Primary Dealer Credit facility, Mutual Fund Liquidity Facility, Commercial Paper Funding, Corporate Credit Facilities, and the Municipal Liquidity Facility.

p. The Paycheck Protection Liquidity Facility, Term Asset-Backed Securities Facility and Central Bank liquidity swaps (during the 2020 Wuhan virus pandemic) were not included as assets on the Federal Reserve balance sheet, and are not included here.

A.4 Liabilities

The liabilities of the banking system under the Federal Reserve were tabulated under the following guidelines:

a. Data is Not Seasonally Adjusted, is either end-of-month or Last-Wednesday except as noted.

b. Loan data excludes interbank and items in collections.

c. "Treasury Demand Deposits" at Commercial banks is shown in the Federal Reserve Bulletins under "non-deposit funds of commercial banks", starting in Mar 1979, and by U. S. Government total cash balance starting in Mar 1994.

d. Time deposits at commercial banks are listed as "savings and time" in the Federal Reserve Bulletins starting in Mar 1979.

e. Commercial bank capital accounts were no longer called out specifically in the Federal Reserve Bulletins starting in 1979. I have used the data for "other liabilities", which seems to correspond closely with H.8 data in later years.

f. "Currency Outside Banks" was no longer reported separately from 1979 to 2003; I have used the non-seasonally adjusted "Currency" at specific dates when provided from the money stock data. Averages of daily figures at specific dates were used otherwise. H.4.1 does show Currency Outside Banks as a separate category, and those values were used from Dec 2003 to Dec 2020.

g. "Demand Deposits" are referred to as "Transaction Deposits" in the Federal Reserve Bulletins beginning in 1985.

h. "Treasury Demand Deposits" at commercial banks were not shown separately starting in Mar 1993; presumably were combined with "Transaction Deposits". This seems to correspond to H.8 data from later years.

i. Beginning in Dec 2003, H.4.1 data shows all commercial bank deposits as a single category (combining Demand or Transaction, Treasury Demand, and Time). It shows "large time deposits" separately, but is a memo item under general deposits. Only the total is of interest here.

j. The "U. S. Treasury Supplementary Financing Act" figures from Sep 2008 to Jun 2011 were not included in the Federal Reserve balance sheet, and do not appear in these figures. The Supplementary Financing Act" was the bailout of the banking and mortgage finance system after the housing price and securities collapse in 2008.

k. "Treasury Demand Deposits" increased due to the bank and mortgage company bailout in 2009-2010, and "Paycheck Protection Program" in 2020.

A.5 Definitions of H.6 Statistics (M0, M1, M2)

The initial definitions of M0, M1, and M2 in Feb 1973 were [A.5-1]:

M1: "includes (1) demand deposits at all commercial banks other than those due to domestic commercial banks, and the U. S. government, less cash items in the process of collection, and the Federal Reserve float; (2) foreign demand balances at Federal Reserve Banks; and (3) currency outside the Treasury, Federal Reserve Banks, and vaults of all commercial banks".

M2: "includes, in addition to currency and demand deposits, savings deposits, time deposits open account, and time certificates of deposit (CD's) other than negotiable time CD's issued in denominations of $100,000 or more by large weekly reporting commercial banks. Excludes time deposits of the U. S. government, and of domestic commercial banks." In other words, M2 = M1 plus savings deposits, time deposits, and CD's greater than $100,000.

M3: "includes M2 plus the average of the beginning and end-of-month deposits of mutual savings banks and savings capital at savings and loan associations."

The revised definitions in Nov 1979 were [A.5-2]:

M1: Currency outside banks, demand deposits excluding those due to foreign commercial banks and U. S. government, plus other checkable deposits, (NOW, ATS, credit union share balances, and demand deposits at thrift institutions).

M2: M1 plus overnight repurchase agreements and overnight Eurodollars held by non-bank U. S. residents, plus money market mutual fund shares, and savings and small denomination time deposits at all institutions (formerly was commercial banks only).

M3: M2 plus large denomination time deposits at all depositary institutions including negotiable CD's, plus term repurchase agreements issued by commercial banks and savings and loan institutions.

Chairman of the Board of Governors Ben Bernanke commented in 2006 [A.5-3]:

"In 1971, M1 was currency and demand deposits at commercial banks. M2 was M1 plus commercial bank savings and small time deposits, and M3 was M2 plus deposits at mutual savings banks, savings and loans, and credit unions; data from the latter type of institution were available only monthly. M4 was M2 plus large time deposits, and M5 was M3 plus large time deposits. Changes in definitions make it difficult to track the historical development of the various monetary aggregates. Approximately, the 2006 definition of M1 is equivalent to this older definition, the 2006 definition of M2 is equivalent to the older definition of M3, and the definition of M3 at its date of last publication was equivalent to the older definition of M5. M4 and M5 were dropped in a 1980 redefinition of the monetary aggregates. See Board of Governors of the Federal Reserve System (1976), pp. 10-11 and Anderson and Kavajecz (1994)."

References

[A.2-1]   Clifton H. Kreps, Jr., *Money, Banking and Monetary Policy*, NY: The Ronald Press Co., 1962, pp. 34-44

[A.5-1]   Federal Reserve Board, *Federal Reserve Bulletin*, Feb 1973, p. 71
[A.5-2]   Federal Reserve Board, *Federal Reserve Bulletin*, Feb 1980, p. 98
[A.5-3]   Ben S. Bernanke, "Monetary Aggregates and Monetary Policy at the Federal Reserve: A Historical Perspective", Paper given at the Fourth Central Banking Conference, Frankfurt, Germany, 10 Nov 2006. The quote is from his footnote #6.

B

References for the Federal Reserve and Commercial Banking System Condition Statement Data

The tables in the later chapters indicate Federal Reserve statistical data called H.3, H.4.1, H.6, and H.8. They are defined as follows:

a. H.3 is the aggregate reserves of the depository institutions and the monetary base. It was published from 1967 to 2020.

b. H.4.1 is defined as "Factors affecting reserve balances of depository institutions and condition statement of Federal Reserve Banks". It contains data on the gold stock, Treasury currency outstanding, reserve deposits at Federal Reserve Banks, and currency in circulation. It has been published weekly since 1996.

c. H.6 shows the statistics of the money stock (M1, M2 and M3); it was first defined in 1973 and back-calculated to 1959. It is currently published monthly. Two other monetary measures, M4 and M5 are now obsolete.

d. H.8 data shows the assets and liabilities of the commercial banks, including capital, demand deposits and time deposits. It is published weekly.

It was necessary to resort to these overall metrics after the monthly Federal Reserve Bulletins began to report less data, and especially after they ceased publication in 2003.

The following tables indicate the source data for the banking condition statements given in chapters 18 through 23, correlated by date. Unless indicated otherwise as BMS1943 [1] or BMS 1976 [2], the references pertain to the *Federal Reserve Bulletins*. All page numbers in the *Federal Reserve Bulletin* references refer to the pdf page, not the *Federal Reserve Bulletin* page number. Example: "2/75, 63" means Feb 1975 Federal Reserve Bulletin, pdf page 63 (which is p. 114 in the document).

References

[1] BMS1943: The Board of Governors of the Federal Reserve, Banking and Monetary Statistics 1914-1941, Washington, DC, Publication Services, Division of Administrative Services, Board of Governors of the Federal Reserve System, Nov 1943

[2] BMS1976: The Board of Governors of the Federal Reserve, Banking and Monetary Statistics 1941-1970, Washington, DC, Publication Services, Division of Administrative Services, Board of Governors of the Federal Reserve System, Sep 1976

Chapter 18 (1915 to 1932)

		Assets		Liabilities			
Day	Year	Ref 1	Ref 2	Ref 1	Ref 2	Ref 3	Ref 4
31 Mar	1914						
30 Jun	1914						
30 Sep	1914						
31 Dec	1914			BMS1943, Table 9	BMS1943, Table 100	BMS1943, Table 93	BMS1943, Table 18
31 Mar	1915						
30 Jun	1915	BMS1943, Table 102	BMS1943, Table 3	BMS1943, Table 9	BMS1943, Table 100	BMS1943, Table 93	BMS1943, Table 18
30 Sep	1915	BMS1943, Table 102					
31 Dec	1915	BMS1943, Table 102					
31 Mar	1916	BMS1943, Table 102					
30 Jun	1916	BMS1943, Table 102	BMS1943, Table 3	BMS1943, Table 9	BMS1943, Table 100	BMS1943, Table 93	BMS1943, Table 18
30 Sep	1916	BMS1943, Table 102					
31 Dec	1916	BMS1943, Table 102					
31 Mar	1917	BMS1943, Table 102				BMS1943, Table 93	
30 Jun	1917	BMS1943, Table 102	BMS1943, Table 3	BMS1943, Table 9	BMS1943, Table 100	BMS1943, Table 93	BMS1943, Table 18
30 Sep	1917	BMS1943, Table 102				BMS1943, Table 93	
31 Dec	1917	BMS1943, Table 102				BMS1943, Table 93	
31 Mar	1918	BMS1943, Table 102				BMS1943, Table 93	
30 Jun	1918	BMS1943, Table 102	BMS1943, Table 3	BMS1943, Table 9	BMS1943, Table 100	BMS1943, Table 93	BMS1943, Table 18
30 Sep	1918	BMS1943, Table 102				BMS1943, Table 93	
31 Dec	1918	BMS1943, Table 102				BMS1943, Table 93	

Caption (table title): References for Federal Reserve & Commercial Banks Condition Statements, 1914-1918

1. BMS1943 is: Board of Governors of the Federal Reserve, Banking and Monetary Statistics, 1914-1941, Washington DC: Publication Services, Division of Administrative Services, Board of Governors of the Federal Reserve System, Nov 1943

		Assets		Liabilities			
Day	Year	Ref 1	Ref 2	Ref 1	Ref 2	Ref 3	Ref 4
31 Mar	1919	BMS1943, Table 102				BMS1943, Table 93	
30 Jun	1919	BMS1943, Table 102	BMS1943, Table 3	BMS1943, Table 9	BMS1943, Table 100	BMS1943, Table 93	BMS1943, Table 18
30 Sep	1919	BMS1943, Table 102				BMS1943, Table 93	
31 Dec	1919	BMS1943, Table 102				BMS1943, Table 93	
31 Mar	1920	BMS1943, Table 102				BMS1943, Table 93	
30 Jun	1920	BMS1943, Table 102	BMS1943, Table 3	BMS1943, Table 9	BMS1943, Table 100	BMS1943, Table 93	BMS1943, Table 18
30 Sep	1920	BMS1943, Table 102				BMS1943, Table 93	
31 Dec	1920	BMS1943, Table 102				BMS1943, Table 93	
31 Mar	1921	BMS1943, Table 102				BMS1943, Table 93	
30 Jun	1921	BMS1943, Table 102	BMS1943, Table 3	BMS1943, Table 9	BMS1943, Table 100	BMS1943, Table 93	BMS1943, Table 18
30 Sep	1921	BMS1943, Table 102				BMS1943, Table 93	
31 Dec	1921	BMS1943, Table 102				BMS1943, Table 93	
29 Mar	1922	BMS1943, Table 103				BMS1943, Table 93	
28 Jun	1922	BMS1943, Table 103	BMS1943, Table 3	BMS1943, Table 9	BMS1943, Table 100	BMS1943, Table 93	BMS1943, Table 18
27 Sep	1922	BMS1943, Table 103				BMS1943, Table 93	
27 Dec	1922	BMS1943, Table 103				BMS1943, Table 93	
28 Mar	1923	BMS1943, Table 103				BMS1943, Table 93	
27 Jun	1923	BMS1943, Table 103	BMS1943, Table 3	BMS1943, Table 9	BMS1943, Table 100	BMS1943, Table 93	BMS1943, Table 18
26 Sep	1923	BMS1943, Table 103				BMS1943, Table 93	
26 Dec	1923	BMS1943, Table 103	BMS1943, Table 3	BMS1943, Table 9	BMS1943, Table 100	BMS1943, Table 93	BMS1943, Table 18

Caption (table title): References for Federal Reserve & Commercial Banks Condition Statements, 1919-1923

1. BMS1943 is: Board of Governors of the Federal Reserve, Banking and Monetary Statistics, 1914-1941, Washington DC: Publication Services, Division of Administrative Services, Board of Governors of the Federal Reserve System, Nov 1943

References for Federal Reserve & Commercial Banks Condition Statements, 1924-1928							
		Assets		Liabilities			
Day	Year	Ref 1	Ref 2	Ref 1	Ref 2	Ref 3	Ref 4
26 Mar	1924	BMS1943, Table 103				BMS1943, Table 93	
25 Jun	1924	BMS1943, Table 103	BMS1943, Table 3	BMS1943, Table 9	BMS1943, Table 100	BMS1943, Table 93	BMS1943, Table 18
24 Sep	1924	BMS1943, Table 103				BMS1943, Table 93	
31 Dec	1924	BMS1943, Table 103	BMS1943, Table 3	BMS1943, Table 9	BMS1943, Table 100	BMS1943, Table 93	BMS1943, Table 18
25 Mar	1925	BMS1943, Table 103				BMS1943, Table 93	
24 Jun	1925	BMS1943, Table 103	BMS1943, Table 3	BMS1943, Table 9	BMS1943, Table 100	BMS1943, Table 93	BMS1943, Table 18
30 Sep	1925	BMS1943, Table 103				BMS1943, Table 93	
30 Dec	1925	BMS1943, Table 103	BMS1943, Table 3	BMS1943, Table 9	BMS1943, Table 100	BMS1943, Table 93	BMS1943, Table 18
31 Mar	1926	BMS1943, Table 103				BMS1943, Table 93	
30 Jun	1926	BMS1943, Table 103	BMS1943, Table 3	BMS1943, Table 9	BMS1943, Table 100	BMS1943, Table 93	BMS1943, Table 18
29 Sep	1926	BMS1943, Table 103				BMS1943, Table 93	
29 Dec	1926	BMS1943, Table 103	BMS1943, Table 3	BMS1943, Table 9	BMS1943, Table 100	BMS1943, Table 93	BMS1943, Table 18
30 Mar	1927	BMS1943, Table 103				BMS1943, Table 93	
29 Jun	1927	BMS1943, Table 103	BMS1943, Table 3	BMS1943, Table 9	BMS1943, Table 100	BMS1943, Table 93	BMS1943, Table 18
28 Sep	1927	BMS1943, Table 103				BMS1943, Table 93	
28 Dec	1927	BMS1943, Table 103	BMS1943, Table 3	BMS1943, Table 9	BMS1943, Table 100	BMS1943, Table 93	BMS1943, Table 18
28 Mar	1928	BMS1943, Table 103				BMS1943, Table 93	
27 Jun	1928	BMS1943, Table 103	BMS1943, Table 3	BMS1943, Table 9	BMS1943, Table 100	BMS1943, Table 93	BMS1943, Table 18
26 Sep	1928	BMS1943, Table 103				BMS1943, Table 93	
26 Dec	1928	BMS1943, Table 103	BMS1943, Table 3	BMS1943, Table 9	BMS1943, Table 100	BMS1943, Table 93	BMS1943, Table 18

1. BMS1943 is: Board of Governors of the Federal Reserve, Banking and Monetary Statistics, 1914-1941, Washington DC: Publication Services, Division of Administrative Services, Board of Governors of the Federal Reserve System, Nov 1943

References for Federal Reserve & Commercial Banks Condition Statements, 1929-1932							
		Assets		Liabilities			
Day	Year	Ref 1	Ref 2	Ref 1	Ref 2	Ref 3	Ref 4
27 Mar	1929	BMS1943, Table 103				BMS1943, Table 93	
26 Jun	1929	BMS1943, Table 103	BMS1943, Table 3	BMS1943, Table 9	BMS1943, Table 100	BMS1943, Table 93	BMS1943, Table 18
25 Sep	1929	BMS1943, Table 103				BMS1943, Table 93	
31 Dec	1929	BMS1943, Table 103	BMS1943, Table 3	BMS1943, Table 9	BMS1943, Table 100	BMS1943, Table 93	BMS1943, Table 18
26 Mar	1930	BMS1943, Table 103				BMS1943, Table 93	
25 Jun	1930	BMS1943, Table 103	BMS1943, Table 3	BMS1943, Table 9	BMS1943, Table 100	BMS1943, Table 93	BMS1943, Table 18
24 Sep	1930	BMS1943, Table 103				BMS1943, Table 93	
31 Dec	1930	BMS1943, Table 103	BMS1943, Table 3	BMS1943, Table 9	BMS1943, Table 100	BMS1943, Table 93	BMS1943, Table 18
25 Mar	1931	BMS1943, Table 103				BMS1943, Table 93	
24 Jun	1931	BMS1943, Table 103	BMS1943, Table 3	BMS1943, Table 9	BMS1943, Table 100	BMS1943, Table 93	BMS1943, Table 18
30 Sep	1931	BMS1943, Table 103				BMS1943, Table 93	
30 Dec	1931	BMS1943, Table 103	BMS1943, Table 3	BMS1943, Table 9	BMS1943, Table 100	BMS1943, Table 93	BMS1943, Table 18
30 Mar	1932	BMS1943, Table 103				BMS1943, Table 93	
29 Jun	1932	BMS1943, Table 103	BMS1943, Table 3	BMS1943, Table 9	BMS1943, Table 100	BMS1943, Table 93	BMS1943, Table 18
28 Sep	1932	BMS1943, Table 103				BMS1943, Table 93	
28 Dec	1932	BMS1943, Table 103	BMS1943, Table 3	BMS1943, Table 9	BMS1943, Table 100	BMS1943, Table 93	BMS1943, Table 18

1. BMS1943 is: Board of Governors of the Federal Reserve, Banking and Monetary Statistics, 1914-1941, Washington DC: Publication Services, Division of Administrative Services, Board of Governors of the Federal Reserve System, Nov 1943

Chapter 19 (1933 to 1950)

References for Federal Reserve & Commercial Banks Condition Statements, 1933-1937									
		Assets				Liabilities			
Day	Year	Ref 1	Ref 2	Ref 3	Ref 4	Ref 1	Ref 2	Ref 3	Ref 4
29 Mar	1933	BMS1943, Table 103					BMS1943, Table 93		
28 Jun	1933	BMS1943, Table 103	BMS1943, Table 3				BMS1943, Table 93	2/53, 49	
27 Sep	1933	BMS1943, Table 103					BMS1943, Table 93		
27 Dec	1933	BMS1943, Table 103	BMS1943, Table 3			BMS1943, Table 9	BMS1943, Table 93	9/34, 27	
28 Mar	1934	BMS1943, Table 103					BMS1943, Table 93		
27 Jun	1934	BMS1943, Table 103	BMS1943, Table 3			BMS1943, Table 9	BMS1943, Table 93	9/34, 27	
26 Sep	1934	BMS1943, Table 103					BMS1943, Table 93		
26 Dec	1934	BMS1943, Table 103	BMS1943, Table 3			BMS1943, Table 9	BMS1943, Table 93	9/35, 18	
27 Mar	1935	BMS1943, Table 103					BMS1943, Table 93		
26 Jun	1935	BMS1943, Table 103	BMS1943, Table 3			BMS1943, Table 9	BMS1943, Table 93	9/35,18	
25 Sep	1935	BMS1943, Table 103					BMS1943, Table 93		
31 Dec	1935	BMS1943, Table 103	BMS1943, Table 3			BMS1943, Table 9	BMS1943, Table 93	9/36, 31	
25 Mar	1936	BMS1943, Table 103					BMS1943, Table 93		
24 Jun	1936	BMS1943, Table 103	BMS1943, Table 3	2/37, 27		BMS1943, Table 9	BMS1943, Table 93	9/36, 31	
30 Sep	1936	BMS1943, Table 103		2/37, 27			BMS1943, Table 93		
30 Dec	1936	BMS1943, Table 103	BMS1943, Table 3	2/37, 27		9/37, 96	BMS1943, Table 93	1/48, 32, 33	
31 Mar	1937	BMS1943, Table 103		2/37, 27			BMS1943, Table 93		
30 Jun	1937	BMS1943, Table 103	BMS1943, Table 3	2/38, 58		9/37, 96	BMS1943, Table 93	1/48, 32, 33	
29 Sep	1937	BMS1943, Table 103		2/38, 58			BMS1943, Table 93		
29 Dec	1937	BMS1943, Table 103	BMS1943, Table 3	2/38, 58		9/38, 21	BMS1943, Table 93	1/48, 32, 33	

1. BMS1943 is: Board of Governors of the Federal Reserve, Banking and Monetary Statistics, 1914-1941, Washington DC: Publication Services, Division of Administrative Services, Board of Governors of the Federal Reserve System, Nov 1943

References for Federal Reserve & Commercial Banks Condition Statements, 1938-1942									
		Assets				Liabilities			
Day	Year	Ref 1	Ref 2	Ref 3	Ref 4	Ref 1	Ref 2	Ref 3	Ref 4
30 Mar	1938	BMS1943, Table 103		2/38, 58			BMS1943, Table 93		
29 Jun	1938	BMS1943, Table 103	BMS1943, Table 3	2/39, 26		9/38, 21	BMS1943, Table 93	1/48, 32, 33	
28 Sep	1938	BMS1943, Table 103		2/39, 26			BMS1943, Table 93		
28 Dec	1938	BMS1943, Table 103	BMS1943, Table 3	2/39, 26		9/39, 74	BMS1943, Table 93	1/48, 32, 33	
29 Mar	1939	BMS1943, Table 103		2/39, 26			BMS1943, Table 93		
28 Jun	1939	BMS1943, Table 103	BMS1943, Table 3	5/39, 47		9/39, 74	BMS1943, Table 93	1/48, 32, 33	
27 Sep	1939	BMS1943, Table 103		2/40, 44			BMS1943, Table 93		
27 Dec	1939	BMS1943, Table 103	BMS1943, Table 3	2/40, 44			BMS1943, Table 93	2/53, 27	
27 Mar	1940	BMS1943, Table 103		2/40, 44			BMS1943, Table 93		
26 Jun	1940	BMS1943, Table 103	BMS1943, Table 3	2/41, 44			BMS1943, Table 93	9/40, 53	
25 Sep	1940	BMS1943, Table 103		2/41, 44			BMS1943, Table 93		
31 Dec	1940	BMS1943, Table 103	BMS1943, Table 3	2/41, 44		3/41, 34	BMS1943, Table 93	1/48, 32,33	
26 Mar	1941	BMS1943, Table 103		2/41, 44			BMS1976, Table 10.1D		
25 Jun	1941	BMS1943, Table 103	BMS1943, Table 3	2/42, 38			BMS1976, Table 10.1D		
24 Sep	1941	BMS1943, Table 103		2/42, 38			BMS1976, Table 10.1D		
31 Dec	1941	BMS1943, Table 103	BMS1943, Table 3	2/42, 38		BMS1976, Table 1.3	BMS1976, Table 10.1D	2/53, 49	
25 Mar	1942	BMS1943, Table 103	2/43,36	2/42, 38	2/43, 36		BMS1976, Table 10.1D		
24 Jun	1942	BMS1943, Table 103	2/43,36	2/44, 46	2/43, 36	2/48, 67	BMS1976, Table 10.1D		
30 Sep	1942	BMS1943, Table 103	2/43,36		2/43, 36		BMS1976, Table 10.1D		
30 Dec	1942	BMS1943, Table 103	2/43,36	2/44, 46			BMS1976, Table 10.1D	1/48, 32, 33	

1. BMS1943 is: Board of Governors of the Federal Reserve, Banking and Monetary Statistics, 1914-1941, Washington DC: Publication Services, Division of Administrative Services, Board of Governors of the Federal Reserve System, Nov 1943
2. BMS1976 is: Board of Governors of the Federal Reserve, Banking and Monetary Statistics, 1941-1970, Washington DC: Publication Services, Division of Administrative Services, Board of Governors of the Federal Reserve System, Sep 1976

References for Federal Reserve & Commercial Banks Condition Statements, 1943-1947									
		Assets				Liabilities			
Day	Year	Ref 1	Ref 2	Ref 3	Ref 4	Ref 1	Ref 2	Ref 3	Ref 4
31 Mar	1943	2/44, 35				BMS1976, Table 10.1D		5/44, 51	9/44, 59
30 Jun	1943	2/44, 35	2/44, 46			BMS1976, Table 10.1D	BMS1976, Table 1.3	9/43, 57	9/44, 59
29 Sep	1943	2/44, 35				BMS1976, Table 10.1D		9/44, 59	
29 Dec	1943	2/44, 35	2/45, 52			BMS1976, Table 10.1D	BMS1976, Table 1.3	9/44, 59	
29 Mar	1944	2/45, 41				BMS1976, Table 10.1D		9/44, 59	
28 Jun	1944	2/45, 41	2/45, 52			BMS1976, Table 10.1D	BMS1976, Table 1.3	9/44, 59	
27 Sep	1944	2/45, 41				BMS1976, Table 10.1D		11/45, 35	
27 Dec	1944	2/45, 41	2/46, 51			BMS1976, Table 10.1D		11/45, 35	1/48, 32, 33
28 Mar	1945	2/46, 40				BMS1976, Table 10.1D		11/45, 35	
27 Jun	1945	2/46, 40	2/46, 51			BMS1976, Table 10.1D		11/45, 35	1/48, 32, 33
26 Sep	1945	2/46, 40				BMS1976, Table 10.1D		11/45, 35	
26 Dec	1945	2/46, 40	2/47, 59			BMS1976, Table 10.1D		11/46, 38	2/53, 49
27 Mar	1946	2/47, 48				BMS1976, Table 10.1D		11/46, 38	
26 Jun	1946	2/47, 48	2/47, 59			BMS1976, Table 10.1D		11/46, 38	1/48, 32, 33
25 Sep	1946	2/47, 48				BMS1976, Table 10.1D		11/46, 38	
31 Dec	1946	2/47, 48	2/48, 68			BMS1976, Table 10.1D		11/47, 49	2/53, 49
26 Mar	1947	2/48, 57				BMS1976, Table 10.1D		11/47, 49	
25 Jun	1947	2/48, 57	2/48, 68			BMS1976, Table 10.1D		11/47, 49	1/48, 32, 33
24 Sep	1947	2/48, 57				BMS1976, Table 10.1D		11/47, 49	
31 Dec	1947	2/48, 57	2/48, 68			BMS1976, Table 10.1D		11/48, 57	2/53, 49

1. BMS1976 is: Board of Governors of the Federal Reserve, Banking and Monetary Statistics, 1941-1970, Washington DC: Publication Services, Division of Administrative Services, Board of Governors of the Federal Reserve System, Sep 1976

References for Federal Reserve & Commercial Banks Condition Statements, 1948-1950									
		Assets				Liabilities			
Day	Year	Ref 1	Ref 2	Ref 3	Ref 4	Ref 1	Ref 2	Ref 3	Ref 4
31 Mar	1948	2/49, 30				BMS1976, Table 10.1D		11/48, 57	
30 Jun	1948	2/49, 30, 41				BMS1976, Table 10.1D	BMS1976, Table 1.3	11/48, 57	
29 Sep	1948	2/49, 30, 41				BMS1976, Table 10.1D		11/48, 57	
29 Dec	1948	2/49, 30, 41				BMS1976, Table 10.1D		11/49, 62	2/53, 49
30 Mar	1949	2/50, 56	10/49, 60			BMS1976, Table 10.1D		11/49, 62	
29 Jun	1949	2/50, 56, 68				BMS1976, Table 10.1D	BMS1976, Table 1.3	11/49, 62	
28 Sep	1949	2/50, 56, 68				BMS1976, Table 10.1D		11/49, 62	
28 Dec	1949	2/50, 56, 68				BMS1976, Table 10.1D		11/50, 68	2/53, 49
29 Mar	1950	2/51, 46	10/50, 85			BMS1976, Table 10.1D		11/50, 68	
28 Jun	1950	2/51, 46, 58				BMS1976, Table 10.1D		11/50, 68	2/53, 49
27 Sep	1950	2/51, 46, 58				BMS1976, Table 10.1D		11/50, 68	
27 Dec	1950	2/51, 46, 58				BMS1976, Table 10.1D		11/50, 68	2/53, 49

1. BMS1976 is: Board of Governors of the Federal Reserve, Banking and Monetary Statistics, 1941-1970, Washington DC: Publication Services, Division of Administrative Services, Board of Governors of the Federal Reserve System, Sep 1976

Chapter 20 (1951 to 1971)

References for Federal Reserve & Commercial Banks Condition Statements, 1951-1955						
		Assets		Liabilities		
Day	Year	Ref 1	Ref 2	Ref 1	Ref 2	Ref 3
28 Mar	1951	2/52, 41	10/51, 52	BMS1976, Table 10.1D	2/52, 51	
27 Jun	1951	2/52, 41, 51		BMS1976, Table 10.1D	2/52, 51	
26 Sep	1951	2/52, 41, 51		BMS1976, Table 10.1D	2/52, 51	
26 Dec	1951	2/52, 41, 51		BMS1976, Table 10.1D	2/53, 27	
26 Mar	1952	2/53, 40	8/52, 48	BMS1976, Table 10.1D	2/53, 27	
25 Jun	1952	2/53, 40, 50		BMS1976, Table 10.1D	2/53, 27	
24 Sep	1952	2/53, 40, 50		BMS1976, Table 10.1D	2/53, 27	
24 Dec	1952	2/53, 40, 50		BMS1976, Table 10.1D	2/54, 43	
25 Mar	1953	2/54, 34	8/53, 50	BMS1976, Table 10.1D	2/54, 43	
24 Jun	1953	2/54, 34, 44		BMS1976, Table 10.1D	2/54, 43	
30 Sep	1953	2/54, 34, 44		BMS1976, Table 10.1D	2/54, 43	
30 Dec	1953	2/54, 34, 44		BMS1976, Table 10.1D	2/55, 54	
31 Mar	1954	2/55, 45	8/54, 50	BMS1976, Table 10.1D	2/55, 54	
30 Jun	1954	2/55, 45, 55		BMS1976, Table 10.1D	2/55, 54	
29 Sep	1954	2/55, 45, 55		BMS1976, Table 10.1D	2/55, 54	
29 Dec	1954	2/55, 45, 55		BMS1976, Table 10.1D	2/56, 41	
30 Mar	1955	2/56, 32	8/55, 51	BMS1976, Table 10.1D	2/56, 41	
29 Jun	1955	2/56, 32, 42		BMS1976, Table 10.1D	2/56, 41	
28 Sep	1955	2/56, 32, 42		BMS1976, Table 10.1D	2/56, 41	
28 Dec	1955	2/56, 32, 42		BMS1976, Table 10.1D	2/57, 52	

1. BMS1976 is: Board of Governors of the Federal Reserve, Banking and Monetary Statistics, 1941-1970, Washington DC: Publication Services, Division of Administrative Services, Board of Governors of the Federal Reserve System, Sep 1976

References for Federal Reserve & Commercial Banks Condition Statements, 1956-1960						
		Assets		Liabilities		
Day	Year	Ref 1	Ref 2	Ref 1	Ref 2	Ref 3
28 Mar	1956	2/57, 43	8/56, 65	BMS1976, Table 10.1D	2/57, 52	
27 Jun	1956	2/57, 43, 53		BMS1976, Table 10.1D	2/57, 52	
26 Sep	1956	2/57, 43, 53		BMS1976, Table 10.1D	2/57, 52	
26 Dec	1956	2/57, 43, 53		BMS1976, Table 10.1D	2/58, 46	
27 Mar	1957	2/58, 37	8/57, 74	BMS1976, Table 10.1D	2/58, 46	
26 Jun	1957	2/58, 37, 47		BMS1976, Table 10.1D	2/58, 46	
25 Sep	1957	2/58, 37, 47		BMS1976, Table 10.1D	2/58, 46	
25 Dec	1957	2/58, 37, 47		BMS1976, Table 10.1D	2/59, 63	
26 Mar	1958	2/59, 54	8/58, 61	BMS1976, Table 10.1D	2/59, 63	
25 Jun	1958	2/59, 54, 64		BMS1976, Table 10.1D	2/59, 63	
24 Sep	1958	2/59, 54, 64		BMS1976, Table 10.1D	2/59, 63	
31 Dec	1958	2/59, 54, 64		BMS1976, Table 10.1D	2/60, 56	
25 Mar	1959	2/60, 46	8/59, 181	BMS1976, Table 10.1D	2/60, 56	
24 Jun	1959	2/60, 47, 57		BMS1976, Table 10.1D	2/60, 56	
30 Sep	1959	2/60, 47, 57		BMS1976, Table 10.1D	2/60, 56	
30 Dec	1959	2/60, 47, 57		BMS1976, Table 10.1D	2/61, 54	
30 Mar	1960	2/61, 45, 50	8/60, 46	BMS1976, Table 10.1D	2/61, 54	
29 Jun	1960	2/61, 45, 50, 54, 55		BMS1976, Table 10.1D	2/61, 54	
28 Sep	1960	2/61, 45, 50, 54, 55		BMS1976, Table 10.1D	2/61, 54	
28 Dec	1960	2/61, 45, 50, 54, 55		BMS1976, Table 10.1D	2/62, 58	

1. BMS1976 is: Board of Governors of the Federal Reserve, Banking and Monetary Statistics, 1941-1970, Washington DC: Publication Services, Division of Administrative Services, Board of Governors of the Federal Reserve System, Sep 1976

References for Federal Reserve & Commercial Banks Condition Statements, 1961-1965						
		Assets		Liabilities		
Day	Year	Ref 1	Ref 2	Ref 1	Ref 2	Ref 3
29 Mar	1961	2/62, 48	8/61, 51	BMS1976, Table 10.1D	2/62, 58	
28 Jun	1961	2/62, 49, 59		BMS1976, Table 10.1D	2/62, 58	
27 Sep	1961	2/62, 49, 59		BMS1976, Table 10.1D	2/62, 58	
27 Dec	1961	2/63, 94	2/62, 59	BMS1976, Table 10.1D	2/62, 58	
28 Mar	1962	2/63, 95	8/62, 84	BMS1976, Table 10.1D	2/63, 165	
27 Jun	1962	2/63, 95, 106		BMS1976, Table 10.1D	2/63, 165	
26 Sep	1962	2/63, 95, 106		BMS1976, Table 10.1D	2/63, 165	
26 Dec	1962	2/63, 95, 106		BMS1976, Table 10.1D	2/63, 165	
27 Mar	1963	2/64, 40	8/63, 62	BMS1976, Table 10.1D	2/64, 51	1/64, 61
26 Jun	1963	2/64, 41, 52		BMS1976, Table 10.1D	2/64, 51	
25 Sep	1963	2/64, 41, 52		BMS1976, Table 10.1D	2/64, 51	
25 Dec	1963	2/64, 41, 52		BMS1976, Table 10.1D	2/64, 51	
25 Mar	1964	2/65, 54	8/64, 102	BMS1976, Table 10.1D	1/65, 135	
24 Jun	1964	2/65, 55, 68		BMS1976, Table 10.1D	2/65, 67	
30 Sep	1964	2/65, 55, 68		BMS1976, Table 10.1D	2/65, 67	
30 Dec	1964	2/65, 55, 68		BMS1976, Table 10.1D	2/65, 67	
31 Mar	1965	2/66, 65, 79		BMS1976, Table 10.1D	2/66, 78	
30 Jun	1965	2/66, 66, 79		BMS1976, Table 10.1D	2/66, 78	
29 Sep	1965	2/66, 66, 79		BMS1976, Table 10.1D	2/66, 78	
29 Dec	1965	2/66, 66, 79		BMS1976, Table 10.1D	2/66, 78	
1. BMS1976 is: Board of Governors of the Federal Reserve, Banking and Monetary Statistics, 1941-1970, Washington DC: Publication Services, Division of Administrative Services, Board of Governors of the Federal Reserve System, Sep 1976						

References for Federal Reserve & Commercial Banks Condition Statements, 1966-1971						
		Assets		Liabilities		
Day	Year	Ref 1	Ref 2	Ref 1	Ref 2	Ref 3
30 Mar	1966	2/67, 62, 76		BMS1976, Table 10.1D	2/67, 75	
29 Jun	1966	2/67, 62, 76		BMS1976, Table 10.1D	2/67, 75	
28 Sep	1966	2/67, 63, 76		BMS1976, Table 10.1D	2/67, 75	
28 Dec	1966	2/67, 63, 76		BMS1976, Table 10.1D	2/67, 75	
29 Mar	1967	2/68, 150, 164		BMS1976, Table 10.1D	2/68, 163	
28 Jun	1967	2/68, 150, 164		BMS1976, Table 10.1D	2/68, 163	
27 Sep	1967	2/68, 151, 164		BMS1976, Table 10.1D	2/68, 163	
27 Dec	1967	2/68, 151, 164		BMS1976, Table 10.1D	2/68, 163	
27 Mar	1968	2/69, 93, 108		BMS1976, Table 10.1D	2/69, 107	
26 Jun	1968	2/69, 93, 108		BMS1976, Table 10.1D	2/69, 107	
25 Sep	1968	2/69, 94, 108		BMS1976, Table 10.1D	2/69, 107	
25 Dec	1968	2/69, 94, 108		BMS1976, Table 10.1D	2/69, 107	
26 Mar	1969	4/69, 117	2/70, 103	BMS1976, Table 10.1D	2/70, 102	
25 Jun	1969	7/69, 75	2/70, 103	BMS1976, Table 10.1D	2/70, 102	
24 Sep	1969	10/69, 50	2/70, 103	BMS1976, Table 10.1D	2/70, 102	
31 Dec	1969	3/70, 126	2/70, 103	BMS1976, Table 10.1D	2/70, 102	
25 Mar	1970	4/70, 89, 90	2/71, 107	BMS1976, Table 10.1D	2/71, 106	
24 Jun	1970	7/70, 60	2/71, 107	BMS1976, Table 10.1D	2/71, 106	
30 Sep	1970	11/70, 75	2/71, 92, 107	BMS1976, Table 10.1D	2/71, 106	
30 Dec	1970	1/71, 84	2/71, 92, 107	BMS1976, Table 10.1D	2/72, 112, 126	
31 Mar	1971	4/71, 103	2/72, 127	2/72, 112, 126	4/71, 104	
30 Jun	1971	7/71, 94	2/72, 127	2/72, 112, 126	7/71, 95	
29 Sep	1971	11/71, 90	2/72, 127	2/72, 112, 126	11/71, 91	
29 Dec	1971	1/72, 102	2/72, 127	2/73, 83, 97	1/72, 102	
1. BMS1976 is: Board of Governors of the Federal Reserve, Banking and Monetary Statistics, 1941-1970, Washington DC: Publication Services, Division of Administrative Services, Board of Governors of the Federal Reserve System, Sep 1976						

Chapter 21 (1972 to 1986)

		References for Federal Reserve & Commercial Banks Condition Statements, 1972-1976					
		Assets		Liabilities			
Day	Year	Ref 1	Ref 2	Ref 1	Ref 2	Ref 3	Ref 4
29 Mar	1972	4/72, 116	2/73, 98	BMS1976, Table 10.1D	2/73, 83, 97		4/72, 117
28 Jun	1972	7/72,89	2/73, 98	BMS1976, Table 10.1D	2/73, 83, 97		7/72, 90
27 Sep	1972	10/72, 98	2/73, 98	BMS1976, Table 10.1D	2/73, 83, 97		10/72, 99
27 Dec	1972	1/73, 55	2/73, 98	BMS1976, Table 10.1D	2/74, 110, 121, 123		1/73, 56
28 Mar	1973	4/73, 80	2/74, 123	BMS1976, Table 10.1D	2/74, 110, 121, 123		4/73, 81
27 Jun	1973	7/73,77	2/74, 123	BMS1976, Table 10.1D	2/74, 110, 121, 123		7/73, 78
26 Sep	1973	10/73, 73	2/74, 123	BMS1976, Table 10.1D	2/74, 110, 121, 123		10/73, 74
26 Dec	1973	1/74, 72, 80	2/74, 123	BMS1976, Table 10.1D	2/74, 110, 121, 123		1/74, 83
27 Mar	1974	5/74, 89	2/75, 85	2/75, 83, 85		4/74, 97	5/74, 90
26 Jun	1974	8/74, 85	2/75, 85	2/75, 83, 85		7/74, 65	8/74, 86
25 Sep	1974	11/74, 66	2/75, 85	2/75, 83, 85		10/74, 69	11/74, 67
25 Dec	1974	2/75, 73	2/75, 85	2/75, 83, 85		1/75, 61	2/75, 73
26 Mar	1975	5/75, 80	2/76, 134	2/76, 132, 134		4/75, 82	H.3
25 Jun	1975	8/75, 80	2/76, 134	2/76, 132, 134		7/75, 75	H.3
24 Sep	1975	11/75, 120	2/76, 134	2/76, 132, 134		10/75, 117	H.3
31 Dec	1975	2/76, 122	2/76, 134	2/76, 132, 134		1/76, 75	H.3
31 Mar	1976	5/76, 66, 74	12/76, 102	10/76, 83, 85		4/76, 121	H.3
30 Jun	1976	8/76, 86	12/76, 102	2/77, 104, 106		7/76, 99	H.3
29 Sep	1976	11/76, 98	12/76, 102	2/77, 104, 106		10/76, 74	H.3
29 Dec	1976	2/77, 94	2/77, 105	2/77, 104, 106		1/77, 104	H.3

1. BMS1976 is: Board of Governors of the Federal Reserve, Banking and Monetary Statistics, 1941-1970, Washington DC: Publication Services, Division of Administrative Services, Board of Governors of the Federal Reserve System, Sep 1976

		References for Federal Reserve & Commercial Banks Condition Statements, 1977-1981					
		Assets		Liabilities			
Day	Year	Ref 1	Ref 2	Ref 1	Ref 2	Ref 3	Ref 4
30 Mar	1977	5/77, 99	9/77, 120	10/77, 115		4/77, 131	H.3
29 Jun	1977	8/77, 68	12/77, 119	2/78, 104	10/77, 113	7/77, 98	H.3
28 Sep	1977	11/77, 79	2/78, 103	2/78, 102, 104		10/77, 103	H.3
28 Dec	1977	2/78, 92	2/78, 103	2/78, 102, 104		1/78, 72	H.3
29 Mar	1978	5/78, 95	9/78, 101	2/79, 104	10/78, 62	4/78, 98	H.3
28 Jun	1978	8/78, 95	9/78, 101	2/79, 104		7/78, 103	H.3
27 Sep	1978	11/78, 104	2/79, 104	2/79, 102, 104		10/78, 52	H.3
27 Dec	1978	2/79, 92	2/79, 104	2/79, 102, 104		1/79, 92	H.3
28 Mar	1979	5/79, 77	2/80, 110	2/80, 110	12/80, 78; 6/79, 86	4/79, 85	H.3
27 Jun	1979	8/79, 104	2/80, 110	2/80, 110, 118	8/79, 114	7/79, 66	H.3
26 Sep	1979	11/79, 73	2/80, 110	2/80, 110, 118		10/79, 101	H.3
26 Dec	1979	2/80, 98	2/80, 110	3/80, 120		1/80, 89	H.3
26 Mar	1980	5/80, 76	2/81, 107	6/80, 111, 114, 122		4/80, 86	H.3
25 Jun	1980	8/80, 76	2/81, 107	9/80, 146, 149, 157		7/80, 88	H.3
24 Sep	1980	11/80, 76	2/81, 107	12/80, 75, 78, 79		10/80, 58	H.3
31 Dec	1980	2/81, 94, 105		3/81, 88, 91, 92		1/81, 112	H.3
25 Mar	1981	5/81, 79, 90		6/81, 82, 85	7/81, 83	4/81, 126	H.3
24 Jun	1981	8/81, 58, 69		9/81, 117, 120	11/81, 82	7/81, 70	H.3
30 Sep	1981	11/81, 69, 80		12/81, 69, 72	1/82, 93	10/81, 69	H.3
30 Dec	1981	2/82, 55, 66		3/82, 96, 99, 100		1/82, 80	H.3

References for Federal Reserve & Commercial Banks Condition Statements, 1982-1986							
		Assets		Liabilities			
Day	Year	Ref 1	Ref 2	Ref 1	Ref 2	Ref 3	Ref 4
31 Mar	1982	5/82, 53, 64		6/82, 80, 83, 84		4/82, 78	H.3
30 Jun	1982	8/82, 90, 101		9/82, 51, 54, 55		7/82, 58	H.3
29 Sep	1982	11/82, 49, 61		12/82, 94, 97, 98		10/82, 121	H.3
29 Dec	1982	2/83, 71, 83		3/83, 139, 142, 143		1/83, 64	H.3
30 Mar	1983	5/83, 81, 94		6/83, 98, 101, 102		4/83, 75	H.3
29 Jun	1983	8/83, 89, 102		9/83, 99, 102, 103		7/83, 109	H.3
28 Sep	1983	11/83, 69, 80		12/83, 78, 81, 82		10/83, 82	H.3
28 Dec	1983	2/84, 115, 126		3/84, 107, 110, 111		1/84, 74	H.3
28 Mar	1984	5/84, 88	6/84, 80	3/85, 70	6/84, 69, 78, 81		H.3
27 Jun	1984	8/84, 75	6/85, 133	6/85, 133	8/84, 75, 84, 87		H.3
26 Sep	1984	12/84, 65	6/85, 133	6/85, 133	12/84, 65, 74, 78		H.3
26 Dec	1984	3/85, 56	6/85, 133	3/85, 56, 65, 69, 70			H.3
27 Mar	1985	6/85, 119	6/85, 133	6/85, 119, 128, 132, 133			H.3
26 Jun	1985	9/85, 78	6/86, 101	9/85, 78, 87, 91, 92			H.3
25 Sep	1985	12/85, 75	6/86, 101	12/85, 75, 84, 88	1/86, 105		H.3
25 Dec	1985	3/86, 56	6/86, 101	3/86, 56, 65, 69, 70	2/87, 116		H.3
26 Mar	1986	6/86, 87	6/86, 101	6/86, 87, 96, 100, 101			H.3
25 Jun	1986	9/86, 86	6/87, 132	9/86, 86, 95, 99, 100			H.3
24 Sep	1986	12/86, 44	6/87, 132	12/86, 44, 53, 57, 58			H.3
31 Dec	1986	3/87, 65	6/87, 132	3/87, 65, 74, 78, 79			H.3

Chapter 22: 1987 to 2003

References for Federal Reserve & Commercial Banks Condition Statements, 1987-1991					
		Assets		Liabilities	
Day	Year	Ref 1	Ref 2	Ref 1	Ref 2
25 Mar	1987	6/87, 118, 132		6/87, 118, 127, 131, 132	H.3
24 Jun	1987	9/87, 80	6/88, 61	8/87, 80, 89, 93, 94	H.3
30 Sep	1987	12/87, 63	6/88, 61	12/87, 63, 72, 76, 77	H.3
30 Dec	1987	3/88, 48	6/88, 61	3/88, 48, 61, 62	H.3
30 Mar	1988	6/88, 47	6/88, 61	6/88, 47, 56, 60, 61	H.3
29 Jun	1988	9/88, 45	6/89, 56	9/88, 45, 54, 58, 59	H.3
28 Sep	1988	12/88, 56	6/89, 56	12/88, 56, 65, 69, 70	H.3
28 Dec	1988	3/89, 126	6/89, 56	3/89, 126, 135, 139, 140	H.3
29 Mar	1989	6/89, 42	6/89, 56	6/89, 42, 51, 55, 56	H.3
28 Jun	1989	9/89, 74	6/90, 85	9/89, 74, 83, 87, 88	H.3
27 Sep	1989	12/89, 80	6/90, 85	12/89, 80, 89, 93, 94	H.3
27 Dec	1989	3/90, 87	6/90, 85	3/90, 87, 96, 100, 101	H.3
28 Mar	1990	6/90, 71	6/90, 85	6/90, 71, 80, 84, 85	H.3
27 Jun	1990	9/90, 97	6/91, 152	9/90, 97, 106, 110, 111	H.3
26 Sep	1990	12/90, 95	6/91, 152	12/90, 95, 104, 108, 109	H.3
26 Dec	1990	3/91, 61	6/91, 152	3/91, 61, 70, 74, 75	H.3
27 Mar	1991	6/91, 138	6/91, 152	6/91, 138, 147, 151, 152	H.3
26 Jun	1991	9/91, 91	6/92, 76	9/91, 91, 100, 104, 105	H.3
25 Sep	1991	12/91, 60	6/92, 76	12/91, 60, 69, 73, 74	H.3
25 Dec	1991	3/92, 60	6/92, 76	3/92, 60, 69, 73, 74	H.3

References for Federal Reserve & Commercial Banks Condition Statements, 1992-1996							
		Assets		Liabilities			
Day	Year	Ref 1	Ref 2	Ref 1	Ref 2	Ref 3	Ref 4
25 Mar	1992	6/92, 62	6/92, 76	6/92, 62, 71, 75, 76		H.3	
24 Jun	1992	9/92, 101, 115		9/92, 101, 110, 114, 115		H.3	
30 Sep	1992	12/92, 106, 120		12/92, 106, 115, 119, 120		H.3	
30 Dec	1992	3/93, 91, 105		3/93, 91, 100, 104, 105		H.3	
31 Mar	1993	6/93, 86, 100		6/93, 86, 95, 99, 100		H.3	
30 Jun	1993	9/93, 93, 108		9/93, 93, 102, 107, 108		H.3	
29 Sep	1993	12/93, 118, 133		12/93, 118, 127, 132, 133		H.3	
29 Dec	1993	3/94, 78, 93		3/94, 78, 87, 92, 93		H.3	
30 Mar	1994	6/94, 95, 108		6/94, 95, 104, 108	H.8	H.3	
29 Jun	1994	9/94, 98, 111		9/94, 98, 107, 111	H.8	H.3	H.6 GDTCBW
28 Sep	1994	12/94, 101, 114		12/94, 101, 110, 114	H.8	H.3	H.6 GDTCBW
28 Dec	1994	3/95, 111, 124		3/95, 111, 120, 124	H.8	H.3	H.6 GDTCBW
29 Mar	1995	6/95, 92, 105		6/95, 92, 101, 105	H.8	H.3	H.6 GDTCBW
28 Jun	1995	9/95, 107, 120		9/95, 107, 116, 120	H.8	H.3	H.6 GDTCBW
27 Sep	1995	12/95, 119, 132		12/95, 119, 128, 132	H.8	H.3	H.6 GDTCBW
27 Dec	1995	3/96, 93, 106		3/96, 93, 102, 106	H.8	H.3	H.6 GDTCBW
27 Mar	1996	6/96, 145, 157		6/96, 145, 153, 157	H.8	H.3	H.6 GDTCBW
26 Jun	1996	9/96, 99, 111		9/96, 99, 107, 111	H.8	H.3	H.6 GDTCBW
25 Sep	1996	12/96, 90, 102		12/96, 90, 98, 102	H.8	H.3	H.6 GDTCBW
25 Dec	1996	3/97, 61, 72		3/97, 61, 69, 72	H.8	H.3	H.6 GDTCBW

References for Federal Reserve & Commercial Banks Condition Statements, 1997-2001							
		Assets		Liabilities			
Day	Year	Ref 1	Ref 2	Ref 1	Ref 2	Ref 3	Ref. 4
26 Mar	1997	6/97, 86, 97		6/97, 86, 94, 97	H.8	H.3	H.6 GDTCBW
25 Jun	1997	9/97, 99, 109		9/97, 99, 106, 109	H.8	H.3	H.6 GDTCBW
24 Sep	1997	12/97, 101, 111		12/97, 101, 108, 111	H.8	H.3	H.6 GDTCBW
31 Dec	1997	3/98, 95, 105		3/98, 95, 103, 105	H.8	H.3	H.6 GDTCBW
25 Mar	1998	6/98, 134, 144		6/98, 134, 142, 144	H.8	H.3	H.6 GDTCBW
24 Jun	1998	9/98, 117, 127		9/98, 117, 125, 127	H.8	H.3	H.6 GDTCBW
30 Sep	1998	12/98, 117, 127		12/98, 117, 125, 127	H.8	H.3	H.6 GDTCBW
30 Dec	1998	3/99, 79, 89		3/99, 79, 87, 89	H.8	H.3	H.6 GDTCBW
31 Mar	1999	6/99, 98, 108		6/99, 98, 106, 108	H.8	H.3	H.6 GDTCBW
30 Jun	1999	9/99, 64, 74		9/99, 64, 72, 74	H.8	H.3	H.6 GDTCBW
29 Sep	1999	12/99, 63, 73		12/99, 63, 71, 73	H.8	H.3	H.6 GDTCBW
29 Dec	1999	3/00, 98, 108		3/00, 98, 106, 108	H.8	H.3	H.6 GDTCBW
29 Mar	2000	6/00, 83, 93		6/00, 83, 91, 93	H.8	H.3	H.6 GDTCBW
28 Jun	2000	9/00, 51, 61		9/00, 51, 59, 61	H.8	H.3	H.6 GDTCBW
27 Sep	2000	12/00, 71, 81		12/00, 71, 79, 81	H.8	H.3	H.6 GDTCBW
27 Dec	2000	3/01, 89, 99		3/01, 89, 97, 99	H.8	H.3	H.6 GDTCBW
28 Mar	2001	6/01, 71, 81		6/01, 71, 79, 81	H.8	H.3	H.6 GDTCBW
27 Jun	2001	9/01, 75, 86		9/01, 75, 83, 85	H.8	H.3	H.6 GDTCBW
26 Sep	2001	12/01, 45, 55		12/01, 45, 53, 55	H.8	H.3	H.6 GDTCBW
26 Dec	2001	3/02, 69, 79		3/02, 69, 77, 79	H.8	H.3	H.6 GDTCBW

References for Federal Reserve & Commercial Banks Condition Statements, 2002, 2003							
		Assets		Liabilities			
Day	Year	Ref 1	Ref 2	Ref 1	Ref 2	Ref 3	Ref. 4
27 Mar	2002	6/02, 61, 71		6/02, 61, 69, 71	H.8	H.3	H.6 GDTCBW
26 Jun	2002	9/02, 30, 40		9/02, 30, 38, 40	H.8	H.3	H.6 GDTCBW
25 Sep	2002	12/02, 51, 61		12/02, 51, 59, 61	H.8	H.3	H.6 GDTCBW
25 Dec	2002	3/03, 65, 75		3/03, 65, 73, 75	H.8	H.3	H.6 GDTCBW
26 Mar	2003	6/03, 72, 82		6/03, 72, 80, 82	H.8	H.3	H.6 GDTCBW
25 Jun	2003	9/03, 30, 40		9/03, 30, 38, 40	H.8	H.3	H.6 GDTCBW
24 Sep	2003	12/03, 48, 58		12/03, 48, 56, 58	H.8	H.3	H.6 GDTCBW
24 Dec	2003	H.4.1	H.8	H.4.1	H.8	H.3	H.6 GDTCBW

Chapter 23 (2004 to 2020)

References for Federal Reserve & Commercial Banks Condition Statements, 2004-2008							
		Assets		Liabilities			
Day	Year	Ref 1	Ref 2	Ref 1	Ref 2	Ref. 3	Ref. 4
31 Mar	2004	H.4.1	H.8	H.4.1	H.8	H. 3	H.6 GDTCBW
30 Jun	2004	H.4.1	H.8	H.4.1	H.8	H. 3	H.6 GDTCBW
29 Sep	2004	H.4.1	H.8	H.4.1	H.8	H. 3	H.6 GDTCBW
29 Dec	2004	H.4.1	H.8	H.4.1	H.8	H. 3	H.6 GDTCBW
30 Mar	2005	H.4.1	H.8	H.4.1	H.8	H. 3	H.6 GDTCBW
29 Jun	2005	H.4.1	H.8	H.4.1	H.8	H. 3	H.6 GDTCBW
28 Sep	2005	H.4.1	H.8	H.4.1	H.8	H. 3	H.6 GDTCBW
28 Dec	2005	H.4.1	H.8	H.4.1	H.8	H. 3	H.6 GDTCBW
29 Mar	2006	H.4.1	H.8	H.4.1	H.8	H. 3	H.6 GDTCBW
28 Jun	2006	H.4.1	H.8	H.4.1	H.8	H. 3	H.6 GDTCBW
27 Sep	2006	H.4.1	H.8	H.4.1	H.8	H. 3	H.6 GDTCBW
27 Dec	2006	H.4.1	H.8	H.4.1	H.8	H. 3	H.6 GDTCBW
28 Mar	2007	H.4.1	H.8	H.4.1	H.8	H. 3	H.6 GDTCBW
27 Jun	2007	H.4.1	H.8	H.4.1	H.8	H. 3	H.6 GDTCBW
26 Sep	2007	H.4.1	H.8	H.4.1	H.8	H. 3	H.6 GDTCBW
26 Dec	2007	H.4.1	H.8	H.4.1	H.8	H. 3	H.6 GDTCBW
26 Mar	2008	H.4.1	H.8	H.4.1	H.8	H. 3	H.6 GDTCBW
25 Jun	2008	H.4.1	H.8	H.4.1	H.8	H. 3	H.6 GDTCBW
24 Sep	2008	H.4.1	H.8	H.4.1	H.8	H. 3	H.6 GDTCBW
31 Dec	2008	H.4.1	H.8	H.4.1	H.8	H. 3	H.6 GDTCBW

References for Federal Reserve & Commercial Banks Condition Statements, 2009-2013							
		Assets		Liabilities			
Day	Year	Ref 1	Ref 2	Ref 1	Ref 2	Ref. 3	Ref. 4
25 Mar	2009	H.4.1	H.8	H.4.1	H.8	H. 3	H.6 GDTCBW
24 Jun	2009	H.4.1	H.8	H.4.1	H.8	H. 3	H.6 GDTCBW
30 Sep	2009	H.4.1	H.8	H.4.1	H.8	H. 3	H.6 GDTCBW
30 Dec	2009	H.4.1	H.8	H.4.1	H.8	H. 3	H.6 GDTCBW
31 Mar	2010	H.4.1	H.8	H.4.1	H.8	H. 3	H.6 GDTCBW
30 Jun	2010	H.4.1	H.8	H.4.1	H.8	H. 3	H.6 GDTCBW
29 Sep	2010	H.4.1	H.8	H.4.1	H.8	H. 3	H.6 GDTCBW
29 Dec	2010	H.4.1	H.8	H.4.1	H.8	H. 3	H.6 GDTCBW
30 Mar	2011	H.4.1	H.8	H.4.1	H.8	H. 3	H.6 GDTCBW
29 Jun	2011	H.4.1	H.8	H.4.1	H.8	H. 3	H.6 GDTCBW
28 Sep	2011	H.4.1	H.8	H.4.1	H.8	H. 3	H.6 GDTCBW
28 Dec	2011	H.4.1	H.8	H.4.1	H.8	H. 3	H.6 GDTCBW
28 Mar	2012	H.4.1	H.8	H.4.1	H.8	H. 3	H.6 GDTCBW
27 Jun	2012	H.4.1	H.8	H.4.1	H.8	H. 3	H.6 GDTCBW
26 Sep	2012	H.4.1	H.8	H.4.1	H.8	H. 3	H.6 GDTCBW
26 Dec	2012	H.4.1	H.8	H.4.1	H.8	H. 3	H.6 GDTCBW
27 Mar	2013	H.4.1	H.8	H.4.1	H.8	H. 3	H.6 GDTCBW
26 Jun	2013	H.4.1	H.8	H.4.1	H.8	H. 3	H.6 GDTCBW
25 Sep	2013	H.4.1	H.8	H.4.1	H.8	H. 3	H.6 GDTCBW
25 Dec	2013	H.4.1	H.8	H.4.1	H.8	H. 3	H.6 GDTCBW

References for Federal Reserve & Commercial Banks Condition Statements, 2014-2018							
		Assets		Liabilities			
Day	Year	Ref 1	Ref 2	Ref 1	Ref 2	Ref. 3	Ref. 4
26 Mar	2014	H.4.1	H.8	H.4.1	H.8	H. 3	H.6 GDTCBW
25 Jun	2014	H.4.1	H.8	H.4.1	H.8	H. 3	H.6 GDTCBW
24 Sep	2014	H.4.1	H.8	H.4.1	H.8	H. 3	H.6 GDTCBW
31 Dec	2014	H.4.1	H.8	H.4.1	H.8	H. 3	H.6 GDTCBW
25 Mar	2015	H.4.1	H.8	H.4.1	H.8	H. 3	H.6 GDTCBW
24 Jun	2015	H.4.1	H.8	H.4.1	H.8	H. 3	H.6 GDTCBW
30 Sep	2015	H.4.1	H.8	H.4.1	H.8	H. 3	H.6 GDTCBW
30 Dec	2015	H.4.1	H.8	H.4.1	H.8	H. 3	H.6 GDTCBW
30 Mar	2016	H.4.1	H.8	H.4.1	H.8	H. 3	H.6 GDTCBW
29 Jun	2016	H.4.1	H.8	H.4.1	H.8	H. 3	H.6 GDTCBW
28 Sep	2016	H.4.1	H.8	H.4.1	H.8	H. 3	H.6 GDTCBW
28 Dec	2016	H.4.1	H.8	H.4.1	H.8	H. 3	H.6 GDTCBW
29 Mar	2017	H.4.1	H.8	H.4.1	H.8	H. 3	H.6 GDTCBW
28 Jun	2017	H.4.1	H.8	H.4.1	H.8	H. 3	H.6 GDTCBW
27 Sep	2017	H.4.1	H.8	H.4.1	H.8	H. 3	H.6 GDTCBW
27 Dec	2017	H.4.1	H.8	H.4.1	H.8	H. 3	H.6 GDTCBW
28 Mar	2018	H.4.1	H.8	H.4.1	H.8	H. 3	H.6 GDTCBW
27 Jun	2018	H.4.1	H.8	H.4.1	H.8	H. 3	H.6 GDTCBW
26 Sep	2018	H.4.1	H.8	H.4.1	H.8	H. 3	H.6 GDTCBW
26 Dec	2018	H.4.1	H.8	H.4.1	H.8	H. 3	H.6 GDTCBW

References for Federal Reserve & Commercial Banks Condition Statements, 2019, 2020							
		Assets		Liabilities			
Day	Year	Ref 1	Ref 2	Ref 1	Ref 2	Ref. 3	Ref. 4
27 Mar	2019	H.4.1	H.8	H.4.1	H.8	H. 3	H.6 GDTCBW
26 Jun	2019	H.4.1	H.8	H.4.1	H.8	H. 3	H.6 GDTCBW
25 Sep	2019	H.4.1	H.8	H.4.1	H.8	H. 3	H.6 GDTCBW
25 Dec	2019	H.4.1	H.8	H.4.1	H.8	H. 3	H.6 GDTCBW
25 Mar	2020	H.4.1	H.8	H.4.1	H.8	H. 3	H.6 GDTCBW
24 Jun	2020	H.4.1	H.8	H.4.1	H.8	H. 3	H.6 GDTCBW
30 Sep	2020	H.4.1	H.8	H.4.1	H.8	H. 3	H.6 GDTCBW
30 Dec	2020	H.4.1	H.8	H.4.1	H.8	H. 3	H.6 GDTCBW

Index

Inflation, see Money, Depreciation
Interest rates, prime commercial
       1863-1914, 389, 390
       1915-1932, 438, 439
       1933-1950, 472
       1951-1971, 501
       1972-1986, 525
       1987-2003, 550
       2004-2020, 581
Jackson, Andrew, 265-270, 278, 279, 284, 341
Jefferson, Thomas, 190, 204, 206, 225
Jevons, W. Stanley, 29, 33, 81
Johnson, Lyndon B., 479, 480, 484

Kemmerer, Edwin Walter, 397
Kennedy, John F., 67, 480
Keynes, Lord John Maynard, 46, 60, 61, 81-83

Law, John, 56
Lawful money, 217, 294, 300, 313-324, 348, 355, 359, 360, 406, 419-421, 450, 451, 457, 592
Legal tender, 100-108, 131, 313, 319-326, 340, 341, 347, 349, 419
    Applies only to States, 213-216
    Continentals, 190-192, 197, 209
    Federal Reserve Notes, 448
    Foreign coins, 227, 230, 231, 251, 262, 264, 268, 275
    France, 139, 141
    Lawful money, 314, 406, 419
    Treasury Notes of 1812, not legal tender, 246
    Treasury Notes of 1862, not legal tender, 291
    Treasury Notes of 1862, are legal tender, 178, 294, 295, 317, 321, 322, 323, 351
    U. S. coins, 227, 269, 283, 284, 289, 290, 316, 319-323, 325, 348, 354, 485
    United States Notes (greenbacks), 304, 310, 313-315, 324-326, 340, 352, 592
        Constitutional, (Juilliard v. Greenman), 348
        Constitutional, (Knox v. Lee), 321, 323
        Unconstitutional, (Hepburn v. Griswold), 321
Lenin, Vladimir, 8, 23, 36, 515
Louis XIV, king of France, 35, 36, 77
Louis XVI, king of France
    American Revolution, 193, 201, 202
    French Revolution, 134-137, 139

Madison, James, 191, 204, 214, 215, 225, 249, 250
Malthus, Thomas, 52
Marivale, Charles, 7
Marx, Karl, 8, 9, 19, 36, 42, 68, 86, 167, 515
    Labor, 42
    Objective of, 85
Marxism, 9, 19, 42, 68, 86, 167, 515
    Progressive movement, 85
Median, definition, 187
Median Income Index
    Estimates, 1800 to 2020, 187
    1791 to 1811, 240
    1812 to 1816, 255
    1817 to 1836, 278
    1837 to 1862, 303

Silver certificates, 313, 348, 354, 355, 404-407, 419, 422, 451, 483-487
  Legal tender, 419
Socialism (see also Progressives)
  Characteristics of, 8, 84-87
  Code words, 87
  Collectivist, 8
  Democratic Party in U. S., 33
  Depreciation of money, 54
  Failures of, 9, 10, 34, 35, 65, 85
  France, 136, 142
  Nationalization, 9
  NAZI, 85, 86
  Objectives of, 9, 62, 85
  Opposition to freedom, 31, 40, 41, 62, 68, 84
  Requires force, 85
  Religion of, 9
  Tax policy of, 28, 29, 66
Smith, Adam, 52, 53
Soviet Union, 8, 9, 23, 32-34, 36, 507
Sprague, Oliver M. W., 313, 324, 341
Standard of Living Index
  Caution regarding its use, 187
  Defined, 187
  Two unusual periods, 187, 341, 390, 479
  1791 to 1811, 240
  1812 to 1816, 255
  1817 to 1836, 278
  1837 to 1862, 303
  1863 to 1878, 339
  1879 to 1914, 388
  1915 to 1932, 435
  1933 to 1950, 469
  1951 to 1971, 497
  1972 to 1986, 522
  1987 to 2003, 547
  2004 to 2020, 578
Stewart, Martha, 63
Strong, Benjamin, 397
Sumner, William Graham, 29, 106, 119, 262, 288

Taney, Roger B., 268
Taxation
  All paid by individuals, 28, 29
  Capital gains, 28
  Depreciation of money as a hidden tax, 112, 115, 118, 119, 126
  England, 75-77, 102, 103, 122
  Estate/Inheritance, 27
  Excise, 27, 117
  France, 56, 57
  General effects, 19, 25, 38-40, 59, 61, 62, 66-68, 74, 79, 80, 83, 87, 99, 104-108, 114
  Gift, 27
  Income, 27
  Mongol Empire, 7
  Ottoman Empire, 7
  Payroll, 14, 16-18, 26
  Profits, 27, 28, 117, 118